APPLIED X-RAYS

INTERNATIONAL SERIES IN PURE AND APPLIED PHYSICS

LEONARD I. SCHIFF, *Consulting Editor*

Allis and Herlin   Thermodynamics and Statistical Mechanics
Becker   Introduction to Theoretical Mechanics
Clark   Applied X-Rays
Collin   Field Theory of Guided Waves
Evans   The Atomic Nucleus
Finkelnburg   Atomic Physics
Ginzton   Microwave Measurements
Green   Nuclear Physics
Gurney   Introduction to Statistical Mechanics
Hall   Introduction to Electron Microscopy
Hardy and Perrin   The Principles of Optics
Harnwell   Electricity and Electromagnetism
Harnwell and Livingood   Experimental Atomic Physics
Harnwell and Stephens   Atomic Physics
Henley and Thirring   Elementary Quantum Field Theory
Houston   Principles of Mathematical Physics
Hund   High-frequency Measurements
Kennard   Kinetic Theory of Gases
Lane   Superfluid Physics
Leighton   Principles of Modern Physics
Lindsay   Mechanical Radiation
Livingston and Blewett   Particle Accelerators
Middleton   An Introduction to Statistical Communication Theory
Morse   Vibration and Sound
Morse and Feshbach   Methods of Theoretical Physics
Muskat   Physical Principles of Oil Production
Present   Kinetic Theory of Gases
Read   Dislocations in Crystals
Richtmyer, Kennard, and Lauritsen   Introduction to Modern Physics
Schiff   Quantum Mechanics
Seitz   The Modern Theory of Solids
Slater   Introduction to Chemical Physics
Slater   Quantum Theory of Atomic Structure, Vol. I
Slater   Quantum Theory of Atomic Structure, Vol. II
Slater   Quantum Theory of Matter
Slater and Frank   Electromagnetism
Slater and Frank   Introduction to Theoretical Physics
Slater and Frank   Mechanics
Smythe   Static and Dynamic Electricity
Stratton   Electromagnetic Theory
Thorndike   Mesons: A Summary of Experimental Facts
Townes and Schawlow   Microwave Spectroscopy
White   Introduction to Atomic Spectra

The late F. K. Richtmyer was Consulting Editor of the series from its inception in 1929 to his death in 1939. Lee A. DuBridge was Consulting Editor from 1939 to 1946; and G. P. Harnwell from 1947 to 1954.

APPLIED X-RAYS

GEORGE L. CLARK, Ph.D., D.Sc.

Research Professor of Analytical Chemistry
University of Illinois

FOURTH EDITION

McGRAW-HILL BOOK COMPANY, INC.

New York   Toronto   London

1955

APPLIED X-RAYS

III

11149

PREFACE

It has been nearly fifteen years since the third edition of this book appeared. The date of publication of the fourth edition will coincide with the sixtieth anniversary of the discovery of x-rays by Röntgen. It also will fall on the thirty-fourth anniversary of the dedication of the author's life to teaching and research in this chosen field, of which over twenty-seven have been happily spent at the University of Illinois.

The growth of x-ray science since 1940 is self-evident even to the layman, who has become familiar with the fearful and at the same time useful potentialities of high-energy radiation which is generated by nuclear fission in atomic bombs, but which is certainly akin to the rays discovered by Röntgen with his cathode-ray tube in 1895 and to one of the types of ray found by Becquerel in 1895 to be emitted spontaneously by uranium. Evidence of the growth of applied x-ray science is the progression in size of this book: first edition, 1927, 251 pages; second edition, 1932, 470 pages; third edition, 1940, 674 pages; fourth edition, 1955, 843 pages. It is fair to say, however, that the problem of condensation for this edition has been more acute than ever before. If the plan of making this text ever more self-sufficient in detail had been carried out, this might well have involved expansion into two volumes. But it is earnestly hoped that some measure of completeness has survived the requirements of sharply curtailed size.

In the preface to the third edition appear these statements: "For there is not so much need any longer for somewhat superficial missionary effort as for deepening interest to the point where the reader shall be eager to take for himself the steps toward the fundamental principles of interpretation of x-ray results. This is no small or easy task, but it has been attempted; and it is in this more rigorous and quantitative treatment that this new edition differs most markedly from the preceding one. And yet it is hoped that this effort to make the book more sufficient unto itself will not detract from the original intention, in 1926, of portraying x-rays as a great practical research tool in industry." Intensified, magnified, emphasized, and properly adapted to the 1955 status of the science, these statements apply to the fourth edition. The subject in its manifold phases has grown to such size and to such countless ramifications that it challenges the capacity of any one writer, however experienced, to

v

deal authoritatively with all the twenty-three chapters. The clinical approach—the joint effort of a whole group of experts in the various areas—seems to be the future solution to the problem of adequate coverage, much in the style of the valuable "Medical Physics" edited by Dr. Otto Glasser. But the author, in his abiding interest in every one of the directions of applications in physics, chemistry, biology, medicine, crystallography, and widely diversified industry, has done his best to keep abreast of the swiftly moving tides and currents and to present a unified and integrated account of progress.

An enumeration of the major changes since 1940 would run to considerable length, but it is well to note a few of these items as indicative of the task of bringing this book up to date. In equipment there have been notable new contributions, such as the betatron operating at 350 million volts to generate x-rays with wavelengths shorter than any known electromagnetic radiation, along with all the other electron accelerators which may produce energies up to 1 billion electron volts. At the other extreme are the portable, unbelievably lightweight x-ray units for industrial applications. Then there is a great resurgence of spectroscopy with the advent of Geiger counters, multiplier phototubes, and scintillation counters capable of detecting radiation of extremely low intensity, so that fine structure details of emission lines and bands and absorption edges, formerly almost a nuisance, are being intensively studied and related to electronic levels, especially in solids. For the same reason there is the coming of age of the long-known but little-used fluorescence-analysis methods and their adoption by industry to supplement or replace optical spectrographic analysis; the development of the photometer or absorptiometer for many types of chemical analysis; the upsurge of researches on chemical effects of x-rays and the development of the idea of free radical production in aqueous solutions; at least a fourfold increase in knowledge of biological effects arising from atomic-energy developments and intensified cancer research; the tremendous strides in techniques, interpretations, and results in the analysis of crystalline and molecular configurations, aided by ingenious mathematical, computational, optical, and electronic devices culminating in the solution of problems of the structure of penicillin, strychnine, and other increasingly complex molecules on up to the proteins; the formal establishment of the inclusive science of physics of the solid state, combining advanced theories of prevalent imperfections such as dislocations, of conduction bands and of deformation textures, with a vast store of supposedly unrelated experimental observations.

In this edition, the same general plan of organization is retained as in the third edition. A new chapter on Microradiography is introduced into Part I, but in Part II two chapters in the third edition are incorporated into one on The Texture of Metals. Chapters on biological effects, interpretation of diffraction patterns, textures of metals, and polymers especially have been expanded with a view to trying to include all essential information.

Almost all the new material has been derived directly from original papers. The journal *Acta Crystallographica* is of course a veritable mine of the newest information in the field of ultimate structures. It is the privilege of the author to cover for *Chemical Abstracts* all the medical radiological journals published in the world, and this has provided much of the new information included in the chapter on biological effects. Of course, many of the new books on specific topics have been consulted; Bunn's "Chemical Crystallography"; Barrett's "Structure of Metals," second edition; Wyckoff's three-volume compilation of "Crystal Structures"; the new edition of "International Tables for X-ray Crystallography" edited by Dr. Kathleen Lonsdale; "Physical Foundations of Radiology" by Glasser, Quimby, Taylor, and Weatherwax; and many others have been sources of great inspiration.

It is impossible to acknowledge adequately the help, the suggestions, and the guidance from many people, and the author's indebtedness to companies and publications which have generously supplied data and illustrations or granted permission for reproduction, for which acknowledgment is made, it is hoped fairly, in the figure legends. The real driving force behind the revision is the group of graduate students who over the past fifteen years have listened and learned and worked to extend the frontiers by their own efforts while at the university and subsequently in their positions in the academic and industrial worlds. It is hoped that they and many like them throughout the world with similar training, vocations, and devotion to x-ray science may keep on learning even as the author has had to do, most willingly, through more than three decades. Special thanks are due for skilled secretarial help to Miss Mary Murray over the whole period of revision, to Miss Jane Palmer, Mrs. Nancy Brewster and Mrs. Patricia Mason Bailey in the final stages of manuscript preparation and revision, and to two of the author's daughters, Mary Ann and Carolyn, for help in times of emergency.

To live patiently and helpfully through the trials of four editions, as a never-failing source of strength, has been the contribution of the author's wife, to whom this edition is dedicated.

GEORGE L. CLARK

CONTENTS

ix

PART I

GENERAL PHYSICS AND APPLICATIONS OF X-RADIATION

CHARACTERISTICS AND APPLICATIONS OF X-RADIATION

CHAPTER 1

BEFORE AND AFTER THE DISCOVERY BY RÖNTGEN

The Experiment of Röntgen. On Nov. 8, 1895, Wilhelm Conrad Röntgen, professor of physics at the University of Würzburg, Germany (Fig. 1), connected, as he had frequently done before, the terminals of a small induction coil with electrodes in an evacuated pear-shaped glass bulb. A similar apparatus might have been seen in laboratories of physics everywhere, for there was great interest in the phenomena of high-potential electrical discharges through vessels from which air had been pumped out as completely as possible. As far back as 1705 Hauksbee had observed flashes through evacuated spaces from electricity generated by friction. Abbé Nollet in 1753 had extended the observations with a series of bulbs. Morgan in 1785 had obtained a vacuum so high that no conduction occurred until a little gas was admitted to the tube. It is entirely possible that he produced x-rays. Faraday had discovered in 1825 a dark space in the luminous discharge between the electrodes if the residual gas pressure was low enough. In 1859 Plücker and in 1869 Hittorf

FIG. 1. Bust of Röntgen at Remscheid-Lennep, his birthplace.

had announced that in the process of electrical conduction through gases at very low pressures "cathode rays" move straight out from the negative electrode, since they cast sharp shadows of any object placed between the cathode and the glass which the rays caused to fluoresce. Then, in a series of experiments over 10 years, Sir William Crookes had greatly clarified the phenomena, particularly by his discovery that the rays were deflected by electric and magnetic fields and hence were probably negatively charged particles. In 1894 Lenard, the pupil of Hertz, succeeded in conducting cathode rays through a thin metallic-foil window into the outer air. Such in brief was the state of affairs when Röntgen, among many others, undertook by further experiments to elucidate the nature of these cathode rays and the effects produced by them. Interested especially in the fluorescence produced when the rays impinged upon the glass walls of the tube, he covered the apparatus with black paper. In the darkened room the eyes of the experimenter beheld a brilliantly glowing screen of barium platinocyanide, placed some distance away from the Crookes tube. It was correctly deduced that an invisible radiation passing through the air from the tube was exciting the fluorescence of the screen. After 6 weeks of intensive research the comparatively unknown scientist modestly announced at the December meeting of the Würzburg Physico-Medical Society the discovery of a new kind of radiation, which penetrated and photographed through various objects and were designated x-rays. In less than a month roentgen rays were being generated and studied in laboratories all over the world.[1,2]

The claim of envious critics, calculated to discredit the modest and reticent Röntgen, that the discovery of x-rays was purely accidental cannot be supported.[3] Actually it represented not only the scientific acumen of Professor Röntgen but also the culmination of more than two centuries of research by scores of great scientists, filling in the fundamental background of knowledge. Along various lines there had been developing independently experimental techniques and theories applied to high vacua, electricity and electromagnetic waves, discharges in vacuum, light and the science of optics, spectroscopy, ionization of gases, fluorescence of solids, photography, and other related physical and chemical phenomena. All these lines of development converged and made possible the rational plan and the successful result in the Röntgen experiment. It is certain that x-rays had been generated many times before the momentous day in 1895, particularly by Gassiot in 1859 and Hittorf in 1869. Sir William Crookes sought the cause of repeated and unaccountable fogging of his photographic plates stored near his cathode-ray tubes. In the prophetic words of Röntgen himself is a self-portrait:

---

[1] A dramatic account of the reception of the announcement and the amazingly rapid spread of the method, written in January, 1896, is given by H. J. W. Dam, *McClure's Mag.*, **6**, 403 (1896).

[2] An interesting account of a postwar visit to Würzburg by Lt. Col. L. E. Etter [*Am. J. Roentgenol. Radium Therapy*, **54**, 547 (1945)] describes the miraculous escape of the Physics Institute and Röntgen's laboratory and mementos though adjacent buildings and most of the city were destroyed by bombing.

[3] A particularly venomous attack by Lenard, who originally accepted Röntgen's discovery, probably was instigated by Hitler.

If some phenomenon which has been shrouded in obscurity suddenly emerges into the light of knowledge, if the key to a long-sought mechanical combination has been found, if the missing link of a chain of thought is fortuitously supplied, this then gives to the discoverer the exultant feeling that comes with a victory of the mind, which alone can compensate him for all the struggle and effort, and which lifts him to a higher plane of existence.[1]

Some of the milestones in radiology from 1600 to the present are listed in Table 1-1; these show the background of the Röntgen discovery and some of the consequences since 1895.

The Significance of the Discovery of Roentgen Rays. The importance of the discovery of x-rays, which has made the name of Röntgen immortal, cannot be estimated even after nearly 60 years. It came at a time when the greatest physicists honestly believed that the truths were all known and that the future of their science involved merely the addition of further decimal places in improved experimentation. Such complacency was completely shattered, for this gateway to the new physics opened the road directly to the discovery of radioactivity, natural and artificial, the foundation of nuclear physics and chemistry, the electron, the quantum theory, cosmic rays, radio, and all the electromagnetic spectrum, not to mention the direct services of x-ray science in medicine, biology, genetics, atomic physics, photochemistry, and structures of materials.

The Generation of X-rays. The investigation of the source and the mechanism of production of the mysterious new rays immediately engaged the attention of Röntgen. It was soon demonstrated that the fluorescence of the glass walls of the cathode-ray tube was an incidental phenomenon and that the generation of x-rays was associated directly with the stoppage of cathode rays. Though Crookes's experiments seemed to indicate that the rays consisted of negatively charged particles, it was not until 1897 that J. J. Thomson proved this to be the case and found in addition that each of the particles, or electrons, as they came to be known, had a mass about one eighteen-hundredth as great as that of the hydrogen atom.

[1] To Dr. Otto Glasser the world is indebted for his great biography "Wilhelm Conrad Röntgen" (English), published by Charles C Thomas, Publisher, Springfield, Ill., 1934 (German edition, 1931); see also The Life of Wilhelm Conrad Röntgen as Revealed in His Letters, *Sci. Monthly*, **45**, 193 (1937); "Dr. W. C. Röntgen," Charles C Thomas, Publisher, Springfield, Ill., 1945, commemorating the fiftieth anniversary of the discovery and the hundredth anniversary of the birth of the discoverer in 1845. These events were also commemorated in a symposium at Milwaukee on Nov. 9–10, 1945 [papers published in *Ind. Radiography*, **4** (3, 4)] and in a memorial issue of *Radiology*, **45** (November, 1945). The semicentennial had added significance in that the world was at peace for the first time since 1939. For in spite of immeasurably great contributions in war, these rays are an instrumentality for saving life. Dr. Glasser's most recent biographical contribution is Wilhelm Conrad Röntgen als Physiker, *Röntgen Blätt.*, **5**, 147 (1952).

TABLE 1-1. HISTORICAL MILESTONES IN ROENTGEN-RAY SCIENCE*

1600   Gilbert's (1540–1603) "De Magnete" created the foundation for the sciences of magnetism and electricity.

1643   Torricelli (1608–1647) constructed the barometer; produced the Torricelli vacuum.

1646   Guericke (1602–1686) invented an air vacuum pump and an electrostatic machine with a sulfur sphere.

1659   Boyle (1627–1691) constructed an improved vacuum pump, the *machina Boyleana.*

1675   Newton (1643–1727) built a more efficient electrostatic generator with a rotating glass sphere.

1705   Hauksbee (?–1713) observed glow discharges and many other new and curious phenomena *in vacuo.*

1729   Gray (1696–1736) distinguished conductors of electricity from nonconductors.

1733   Du Fay (1699–1739) discovered two different types of electricity, "vitreous" and "resinous" electricity.

1745   Kleist (1715–1759) constructed the Kleist jar, predecessor of the Leyden jar.

1746   Cuneaus and van Musschenbroek (1692–1761) constructed the Leyden jar.

1747   Watson (1715–1787) transmitted electricity over long conductors.

1749   Abbé Nollet (1700–1770) experimented with the "electrical egg" and made fundamental observations.

1750   Franklin (1706–1790) defined "positive" and "negative" electricity.

1760   Canton (1718–1772) built a pith electroscope to measure electric quantities.

1785   Morgan (?–1785) in vacuum experiments possibly produced x-rays.

1786   Galvani (1737–1798) discovered "animal electricity."

1800   Volta (1745–1827) constructed the first electric battery, the "voltaic pile."

1815   Prout (1785–1850) suggested that hydrogen is the fundamental building stone of matter.

1820   Oersted (1777–1851) discovered the link between electricity and magnetism.

1820   Ampère (1775–1836) formulated mathematically the discovery of Oersted.

1827   Ohm (1787–1854) formulated Ohm's law, stating the relationship between electric current, electromotive force, and resistance.

1831   Faraday (1791–1867) and Henry (1797–1878) discovered electromagnetic induction.

1836   Faraday conducted the first systematic experiments on discharge of electricity through gases at pressures of 0.4 mm Hg.

1836   Sturgeon and Page built the first induction coil (Neeff and Wagner improved it in 1853).

1843   Abria of Bordeaux discovered striations in gas discharge.

1845   (Mar. 27) Birth of Wilhelm Conrad Röntgen at Lennep, Germany.

1850   Plücker (1801–1868) observed green glass fluorescence opposite the negative electrode in a vacuum tube.

1851   Ruhmkorff of Paris made successful induction coils (demonstrated in London by Faraday in 1855).

1852   W. R. Grove rediscovered striations with an improved piston pump.

1858   Kohlrausch (1809–1858) and Lord Kelvin (1824–1907) improved electrometers.

1859   J. Gassiot undoubtedly produced cathode rays and magnetic deflection and must have produced x-rays.

* Adapted from Glasser, Quimby, Taylor, and Weatherwax, "Physical Foundations of Radiology," Paul B. Hoeber, Inc., New York, 1944.

TABLE 1-1. HISTORICAL MILESTONES IN ROENTGEN-RAY SCIENCE (*Continued*)

1860 Geissler (1815–1879) developed vacuum tubes containing various gases and found that some gases become luminous when high-voltage discharges are passed through the tube.

1869 Hittorf (1824–1914) observed numerous properties of cathode rays (must have produced penetrating x-rays).

1869 Röntgen received the Ph.D. degree at the University of Zurich.

1873 Maxwell (1831–1879) published his famous equations in the book "Treatise on Electricity and Magnetism."

1874 Stoney announced the idea of atomistic electricity and gave its name to the electron.

1879 Crookes (1832–1919) found that cathode rays can be deflected by a magnet and felt that he was dealing with "a fourth state of matter" (experiments same as Hittorf's in 1869).

1881 Riecke published a note on the path of an electrically charged particle of finite mass in a magnetic field.

1884 A. Schuster formulated the general theory of discharge of electricity in gases.

1885 Hertz (1857–1894) proved Maxwell's equations by experimental methods.

1886 Goldstein discovered positive canal rays in the vacuum tube.

1888 Röntgen proved that a magnetic field is set up in a dielectric moving between electrically charged condenser plates—the "roentgen current."

1890 Helmholtz (1821–1894) foretold theoretically certain properties of electromagnetic oscillations of high frequencies.

1892 H. Hertz demonstrated the passage of cathode rays through thin metal foils.

1892 Lenard built improved cathode-ray tubes and made important observations on the properties of cathode rays.

1893 J. J. Thomson published a supplementary volume to Maxwell's "Treatise," describing in detail the passage of electricity through gases.

1895 (November) W. C. Röntgen discovered x-rays with a Hittorf-Crookes vacuum tube.

1896 (January) O. T. Lindenthal made the first contrast x-ray picture of a hand into the veins of which Teichmann's mixture had been injected.

1896 (January) A. W. Wright made the first photographic paper roentgenogram.

1896 (February) J. Carbutt and A. W. Goodspeed worked on the first special x-ray photographic plate.

1896 (February) E. A. Woodward built the first metal x-ray tube.

1896 (March) M. I. Pupin discovered the intensifying screen method.

1896 (March) Röntgen, A. A. Campbell-Swinton, O. B. Shallenberger, H. Jackson, and others presented the first metal-target x-ray tubes.

1896 (March) J. Trowbridge built the first oil-immersed x-ray tube.

1896 (April) L. Fomm, E. Mach, and E. Thomson developed the use of stereoscopic methods in roentgenography.

1896 (April) W. König and W. J. Morton made the first dental radiographs.

1896 (May) The first roentgen-ray journal, *Archives of Clinical Skiagraphy*, was published in Great Britain.

1896 (May) First use of roentgen rays in war, Italian-Ethiopian campaign.

1896 (July) J. M. Bleyer, A. Battelli, and J. McIntyre were the first to use a "photofluoroscope."

1896 (November) J. Perrin measured by means of an air condenser the loss of electrical charge caused by the ionization produced by x-rays.

TABLE 1-1. HISTORICAL MILESTONES IN ROENTGEN-RAY SCIENCE (*Continued*)

1896 (November) A. H. Becquerel presented to the Paris Academy of Sciences the results of his discovery of radioactive radiations emitted by uranium compounds.

1897 J. J. Thomson discovered that cathode rays are made up of discrete particles of negative electricity or electrons, considerably smaller than atoms.

1897 Roentgen rays used in hospitals close to the front in the Greco-Turkish war, Tirah campaign, and Sudan and Boer wars, especially for locating bullets.

1897 Rutherford examined the radiations from uranium after Becquerel's discovery of radioactivity and found two types, which he called α- and β-rays. Later he found that α-particles consist of nuclei of helium and that β-particles consist of the electrons discovered by Thomson.

1898 Marie and Pierre Curie announced the discovery of polonium in July and of radium in December.

1898 Villard discovered γ-rays and found them to be the same type of ray as the x-ray.

1899 A. Wehnelt suggested the use of electrolytic interrupters for induction coils.

1900 (March) The Roentgen Society of the United States was founded in St. Louis, Mo.

1901 L. Benoist introduced an instrument to measure the penetration, or "quality," of roentgen rays, called the "penetrometer" or "radiochromometer."

1901 Dec. 10, Röntgen received the first Nobel prize in physics.

1902 G. Contremoulins introduced a fluoroscopic method to measure dosages in x-ray therapy.

1902 G. Holzknecht presented his first dosimeter for x-ray therapy, the "chromo-radiometer," consisting of a fused mixture of KCl and Na_2CO_3 which became discolored when exposed to roentgen rays.

1904 R. Sabouraud and H. Noiré proposed a "radiometer" based upon the degree of discoloration of small pastilles of compressed barium platinocyanide under the effects of x-rays.

1905 R. Kienböck used strips of silver bromide photographic paper to estimate dosages in radiation therapy.

1906 Work on the perfection of cellulose acetate "safety" x-ray film was begun.

1907 Interrupterless transformers became available, using either the crossarm or the disk type of rectification.

1908 P. Villard proposed a dosage unit based upon ionization of air by x-rays.

1909 Millikan measured the charge of the negative electron in his "oil-drop" experiment.

1912 W. Friedrich, P. Knipping, and M. von Laue discovered that roentgen rays can be diffracted.

1912 C. T. R. Wilson studied fog tracks, produced by highspeed particles, with the cloud chamber developed in 1897.

1913 Th. Christen expressed radiation quality in "half-value layers."

1913 Coolidge built a successful roentgen tube with a hot-tungsten filamentary cathode and a solid tungsten anode.

1914 W. H. Bragg and W. L. Bragg discovered that roentgen rays can be reflected; the Bragg law is $n\lambda = 2d \sin \Theta$.

1914 H. J. G. Moseley related atomic number with wavelength characteristic of targets.

1914 W. Duane presented an "E" unit of roentgen-ray intensity.

1914 B. Szilard constructed a dosimeter to measure ionization and calibrated it in "mega-mega-ions."

TABLE 1-1. HISTORICAL MILESTONES IN ROENTGEN-RAY SCIENCE (*Continued*)

1915   R. Fürstenau measured x-ray dosages by determining the changes of resistance in a selenium cell under the influence of roentgen rays.

1916   W. Friedrich defined the "e" unit of dosage.

1916   Hull in the United States and Debye and Scherrer in Switzerland independently discovered the powder diffraction method.

1917   Self-rectifying x-ray generators were presented.

1919   Rutherford concluded that all matter is made up of protons (hydrogen), concentrated in a dense nucleus, around which the electrons revolve like planets.

1919   H. F. Waite constructed oil-immersed shockproof high-voltage generators with enclosed Coolidge tubes.

1920   Bohr accepted Rutherford's conception of the atom model but assigned the electrons to orbits with certain levels of energy. The electrons can jump from orbit to orbit as they gain or lose energy. The Rutherford-Bohr atom model is based on the theory that the number of protons in the nucleus determines the number of electrons outside and therewith the place of the atom in the periodic table.

1921   Total reflection, refraction, and diffraction of rays by ruled gratings discovered by Compton and Doan.

1922   A. H. Compton discovered the "Compton effect."

1925   De Broglie suggested the possibility that each electron might be accompanied by a train of waves. Davisson and Germer discovered experimentally that sometimes the electron behaves not as a particle but as a wave (1927).

1925   H. Fricke and O. Glasser developed the thimble ionization chamber with "air wall."

1926   High-voltage transformers with valve-tube rectification came into general use.

1928   O. Glasser, V. B. Seitz, U. V. Portmann, and J. Victoreen constructed the condenser dosimeter.

1930   C. C. Lauritsen developed the supervoltage single-section x-ray tube.

1930   Erection of memorial to Röntgen in Remscheid-Lennep (his birthplace) and beginning of the Röntgen Museum.

1931   W. D. Coolidge built successful multisection "cascading" high-voltage tubes.

1931   Lawrence invented the cyclotron.

1932   Chadwick announced the discovery of the neutron.

1932   Heisenberg recognized that the nucleus of the atom consists of protons and neutrons.

1932   Cockroft and Walton disintegrated lithium with 700-kv protons and found that energy is released during the disintegration.

1932   D. H. Sloan constructed a r-f supervoltage x-ray generator.

1932   L. S. Taylor developed an American standard air ionization chamber to determine the value of the "roentgen."

1932   Urey discovered double-weight hydrogen, "heavy hydrogen," or deuterium.

1933   Anderson discovered the positron, the electrical opposite of the electron.

1933   Van de Graaff made great strides in improving the old-type electrostatic generator and obtained electric discharges of several million volts. In 1948, mobile 2-million-volt units were commercially produced for radiography and therapy.

1934   Joliot and Irène Joliot-Curie discovered artificial radioactivity. They first produced radio nitrogen, then radio magnesium and radio silicon. Many hundreds of radioactive isotopes of elements are now known, many identified by x-ray spectra, including neptunium (93), plutonium (94), americium (95), curium (96), berkelium (97), and californium (98).

TABLE 1-1. HISTORICAL MILESTONES IN ROENTGEN-RAY SCIENCE (*Continued*)

1935   Fermi shot deuterons into uranium and other atoms and observed the phenomena of artificial disintegration and fission, leading to atomic "piles" and bomb.

1937   The Fifth International Congress of Radiology accepted the international roentgen, first suggested in Stockholm, in 1928.

1937   Radiography and autoradiography by photoelectrons first mentioned by Seeman, later developed by Trillat and others.

1940   D. W. Kerst invented the betatron with which electrons were accelerated to 5 million volts by magnetic induction. Commercial 10- and 20-million-volt units have been developed, and in 1948 construction began on a 350-million-volt unit at the University of Illinois, completed in 1950.

1941   Very high intensity x-ray pulses of extremely short duration for flash radiography of rapidly moving objects made possible by Westinghouse Micronex surge generator.

1944   Two-million-volt x-ray tube commercially produced.

1945   (Mar. 27) Centennial of birth of Röntgen.

1945   (August) Atomic bomb used in Japan.

1945   (Nov. 8) Semicentennial of discovery of roentgen rays—Milwaukee symposium.

1945   The synchrotron was invented as a means of electron acceleration to very high energies to compete with the betatron.

1946   Molecular structure of penicillin uniquely determined from x-ray crystal-structure data, enabling synthesis of antibiotic, the best example of Fourier analysis of complex organic molecular structure now being carried out all over the world with the aid of electronic computers.

1946   New high-intensity tubes capable of delivering $5\frac{1}{2}$ million r/min make possible photochemical and biological studies, preparation of vaccines, and high-speed radiography heretofore impossible.

1947   Development of commercial instruments for x-ray photometry in chemical analysis, for example, of tetraethyllead in gasoline.

1947   X-ray microscope devised by Kirkpatrick with reflection of grazing beams from spherical and elliptical mirrors.

1948   First Congress of International Union of Crystallography, Harvard University.

1948   X-ray microanalyzer designed, operating on principle of electron microscope with x-rays liberating photoelectrons from specimen, which are then magnetically focused.

1949   Electronic amplification of fluoroscopic images and reproduction on kinescopes. Wireless transmission of radiographs.

1949   Successful microwave linear accelerator of traveling-wave type for 3- to 20-Mev x-rays.

1949   Mesons were produced from carbon by x-rays generated in a 335-Mev synchrotron at the University of California and in 1950 from the 350-Mev betatron at the University of Illinois.

1950   Increasing evidence of therapeutic value of 20-Mev x-rays.

1950   Successful mass chest radiography of whole populations in Minneapolis, Minn., Washington, D.C., and elsewhere.

1950   Discovery of chemical protection of tissues against ionizing radiations by injection of compounds to provide excess —SH (thiol) groups; renewed intensive effort to develop dosimeters, chemical, ionization, and biological.

1950   First use of cadmium sulfide crystals to detect x-rays by self-amplification 10^7-fold of photoconducting currents.

TABLE 1-1. HISTORICAL MILESTONES IN ROENTGEN-RAY SCIENCE (Continued)

1950 Successful use of SF_6 gas as insulating medium at atmospheric pressure in transformers, replacing oil, freon gas, etc., in portable medical diagnostic x-ray units on Korean War battle front.

1951 (December) Celebration of fiftieth anniversary of Nobel prize and issuance of German commemorative stamp.

Millikan subsequently by means of measurements with minute oil droplets determined the unit charge of the electron, which now has the generally accepted value of 4.80223×10^{-10} esu. Cathode rays, or streams of rapidly moving electrons, are always identical, regardless of the kind of gas or of the material of the cathode. This is but one of the evidences that electrons are a fundamental constituent of all matter and of atoms. They are spontaneously emitted by the radioactive disintegrations of some atoms and are called β-rays. They are liberated as photoelectrons under proper conditions when radiant energy—visible light, ultraviolet rays, x-rays, etc.—impinges upon matter. Glowing-hot wires produce thermionic emission of electrons; heated gases dissociate into electrons and residual ions; free electrons course through metallic conductors as a flow of electric current.

X-rays are emitted whenever matter is bombarded by cathode rays; in other words, the sudden stoppage of swiftly moving electrons by the atoms of matter is accompanied by the generation of x-rays. In addition to this process it will be shown that under certain conditions primary x-rays, upon being absorbed in matter, will themselves generate secondary x-rays. The essential parts of an x-ray-generating apparatus, therefore, are (1) a source of electrons proceeding from a cathode, (2) a target or anticathode or anode in the path of the cathode-ray stream, and (3) a means of applying a potential difference between the cathode and the target which will accelerate the electrons to the requisite velocity during passage across the intervening space. The β-rays emitted with characteristic energies from artificially produced radioisotopes (such as strontium 90) may also impinge upon targets to produce x-rays in "pocket-size" generating units.

X-rays, Light, and the Electromagnetic Spectrum. The investigations of the discoverer and of other early experimenters demonstrated that there were certain striking similarities between these new rays and ordinary light. Both x-radiation and light moved in straight lines, passed through space without apparent transference or intervention of matter, affected a photographic plate, excited fluorescence or phosphorescence in some substances, and ionized gases. Both were unaffected by electric or magnetic fields, indicating the absence of electric charges, and both exhibited polarization, or different properties in different directions at right angles to the line of propagation. Finally, convincing evidence was obtained, which has since been rigorously confirmed, that the velocities of the propagation of light and of x-rays were identical.

On the other hand, there were some respects in which x-rays and light seemed to differ. Röntgen and his contemporaries were unsuccessful in all their efforts to observe deflection of the new rays from mirrors, prisms, and lenses, to obtain diffraction by gratings, or to obtain double refraction and polarization in crystals. These phenomena in the case of light were, of course, well known. It is almost tragic that, aside from his discovery of x-rays, most of Röntgen's researches as reported in his 58 published papers were devoted to crystals; but it remained for others to bring x-rays and crystals together to prove the nature of the radiation. As a matter of fact, a quarter of a century passed before it was demonstrated that x-rays may be totally reflected at very small glancing angles from mirrors, refracted in prisms, and diffracted by finely ruled parallel lines on glass or speculum metal.

According to the classical theory, derived largely by Maxwell, light consists of waves of electromagnetic origin which are propagated in the ether. Maxwell conceived of an electric field whose intensity or direction might vary periodically so as to create waves. Since action at a distance between electric charges is not instantaneous, these waves can be produced by giving an electric charge a rapid oscillatory motion. Each of these electric waves must be accompanied by a magnetic wave propagated with the same velocity; the periodically variable electric and magnetic fields must be perpendicular to each other and to the direction of propagation—hence, transverse. But such a condition is actually found in light waves, which are, therefore, electromagnetic waves. As an experimental verification, Hertz, by using oscillating electric discharges, was able to produce waves similar to light in that they could be reflected, refracted, diffracted and polarized. Thus all radiation throughout the spectrum finds its origin in what may be termed the unrest of electric charges.

In 1912 Laue, reasoning from the electromagnetic-wave theory, predicted that x-rays would be diffracted by crystals, which serve as three-dimensional gratings, just as light is diffracted by the finely ruled lines of an ordinary optical grating, which is essentially two-dimensional. The complete experimental verification by Laue and his assistants Friedrich and Knipping[1] of this prediction established beyond question the identical nature of x-rays and light. They are distinguished only by the fact that x-rays have a wide range of wavelengths shorter than those of light. Table 1-2 shows that the known x-ray range lies between 0.006 A as generated in regular x-ray tubes operated at 2 million volts,

---

[1] These physicists were colleagues of Röntgen at Munich. The great scientist, who had discovered the rays 17 years earlier, studied carefully the method and the photographed crystal-diffraction patterns but found no apparent experimental error and also no certain proof in the results of the wave nature of the rays.

0.00012 A generated by the betatron at 100 million volts, 0.000035 A at 350 million volts (University of Illinois), or 0.00001 (1×10^{-5}) A at 1 billion volts, and 1,019 A, thus overlapping the ranges of both γ-rays and ultraviolet rays. In the laboratory for crystal analysis an average wavelength employed is 1 A, or a value about one six-thousandth the wavelength of yellow light in the visible region. Not only are light and x-rays thus closely related, but also included in the electromagnetic spectrum are the γ-rays from radioactive disintegrations; possibly rays associated with the cosmic rays; the ultraviolet rays, which are just shorter than visible light; the infrared, or heat, rays; the long range of radio, or Hertzian, waves; and finally the very long electric waves such as are associated with alternating currents. All these waves, seemingly so different in properties and produced by such vastly different methods, are actually identical in every respect except length. All have the same velocity of propagation, namely, 30 billion cm/sec.

The spectrum of electromagnetic waves is presented in Table 1-2. The ranges in octaves and in angstroms (one angstrom, A $= 10^{-8}$ cm, or one one-hundred-millionth centimeter),[1] and brief statements of the methods of generation and detection are included in this table.

The simple facts of the fundamental mutual similarity of electromagnetic waves and of the essential difference only in wavelength suggest immediately the general practical properties and the uses that may be made of x-radiation of average wavelength as compared with ordinary light. Since their wavelengths λ are so much shorter, or their frequencies ν greater ($\lambda = c/\nu$, where c is the velocity of light), x-rays may be expected to penetrate materials that are opaque to light and to be intimately related to a far finer subdivision of matter than is possible for light waves. Even under the ultramicroscope the examination of matter with the aid of visible light rays can reach only a definite limit of size that is still far removed from that of the ultimate constituents. The ultraviolet microscope, successfully developed by Lucas[2] and by Barnard,[3] has a sufficiently greater resolving power so that it may disclose a fine structure in specimens that appear perfectly homogeneous under visible light rays, but here again a limit is reached. The electron microscope has at present a limiting resolving power of about 20 A (2 mμ). Beyond this, x-rays are able to take the investigator on to the ultimate molecules and atoms, even on to the universe within the atom, if he but interprets his informa-

---

[1] Other units frequently used for x-rays are 1 X, also called the Siegbahn unit, approximately equal to 10^{-3} A or 10^{-11} cm, and 1 kX, approximately equal to 1 A. (Accurately, 1 A $= 1.00202$ kX.)

[2] An Introduction to Ultraviolet Metallography, *AIMME Pamphlet* 1576E (June, 1926), followed by several later publications.

[3] For the Beck-Barnard microscope and its use see Martin, *J. Roy. Soc. Arts*, **79**, 887 (1931); Wyckoff and Ter Louw, *J. Exptl. Med.*, **54**, 449 (1931).

TABLE 1-2. RANGE OF ELECTROMAGNETIC WAVES

Type	Octaves	Wavelength range, A (1 A = 10^{-8} cm)	Generation	Detection
γ-Rays............	..	0.001–1.4 0.06–0.5 used in radiology	Emitted when atomic nuclei disintegrate (radioactivity)	As for x-rays but more penetrating
X-rays............	14	0.006–1019 (0.0001 and less in betatron)	Emitted by sudden stoppage of fast moving electrons	a. Photography b. Phosphorescence c. Chemical action d. Ionization e. Photoelectric action f. Diffraction by crystals, etc.
Ultraviolet rays....	5	136–3,900	Radiated from very hot bodies and emitted by ionized gases	Same as x-rays a–e: reflected, refracted by finely ruled gratings
Visible rays........	1	3,900–7,700 Violet 3,900–4,220 Blue 4,220–4,920 Green 4,920–5,350 Yellow 5,350–5,860 Orange 5,860–6,470 Red 6,470–7,700	Radiated from hot bodies and emitted by ionized gases	Sensation of light; same as ultraviolet rays
Infrared rays.......	9	7,700–4 × 10^6	Heat radiations	Heating effects on thermocouples, bolometers, etc. Rise in temperature of receiving body. Photography (special plates). Reflected, refracted, diffracted by coarse gratings
Solar radiation......	..	Limiting wavelengths reaching earth 2,960–53,000		
Hertzian waves.....	28	1 × 10^6 to 3 × 10^{14}		
Short Hertzian.....	17	1 × 10^6 to 1 × 10^{11}	Spark-gap discharge oscillating triode valve, etc.	Coherer. Spark across minute gaps in resonant receiving circuit. Reflected, refracted, diffracted
Radio............	11	1 × 10^{11} to 3 × 10^{14}	Same	Coherer. Conversion to alternating current. Rectification with or without heterodyning and production of audible signals
Broadcasting band..	..	2 × 10^{12} to 5.5 × 10^{12}		
Electric waves......	..	3 × 10^{14} to 3.5 × 10^{16}	Coil rotating in magnetic field	Mechanical. Electrical. Magnetic. Thermal effects of alternating currents

tion properly, the reason lying in the fact that in solid crystalline matter the spacings of the ultimate particles of mass are of the same order of magnitude as the wavelength of the x-rays, namely, 10^{-8} cm.

In the consideration of radiation as continuous electromagnetic waves in the ether, the fact must not be dismissed that radiation also appears to be propagated in discontinuous bundles, or quanta, in accordance with the laws first enunciated by Planck at the beginning of this century. In diffraction, refraction, and polarization and in phenomena involving interference, x-rays, together with all other related radiations, appear to act as waves, and λ has a real significance; in other phenomena, such as the appearance of sharp spectral lines, a definite short wavelength limit of the continuous spectrum, the shift in the wavelength of x-rays scattered by electrons in atoms, and the photoelectric effect, the energy seems to be propagated and transferred in quanta defined by the values of $h\nu$, where h is the Planck action constant and ν the frequency of the rays. Such a corpuscle, or quantum, is called a *photon*.

Radiation, however, is not alone in displaying these dual properties. Electrons long considered to be definitely corpuscular were shown first by Davisson and Germer in 1927 and later by G. P. Thomson, Rupp, and others to possess definite wave properties in that they could be diffracted by crystals in very much the same way as x-rays. The electron-diffraction patterns for metal foils, for example, are formed of concentric rings just like the familiar Debye-Scherrer x-ray powder photographs, and diffraction by single crystals is observed just as it is for x-rays. From the positions of the diffraction interference maxima and the lattice spacing of the crystal it is possible to deduce the wavelength of the waves causing them; this is in agreement with the theoretical expression due to De Broglie, $\lambda = h/mv$, where h again is the Planck constant always associated with quanta, m the mass, and v the velocity of the electron. Hence, electrons behave as though guided by a train of waves. In 1930 Dempster proved that hydrogen atoms are diffracted by crystals, so that even the combination of a proton and electron constituting the corpuscular atoms acts as though guided by a train of waves. In 1948, neutrons were also diffracted by crystals in experiments at Oak Ridge by Shull and associates. The dual aspect of the ultimate building stones of the universe as waves and particles must, therefore, be fundamental, although it is obviously impossible to construct a satisfactory model of electrons, radiation, or atoms. The mathematics of the quantum and wave mechanics developed by De Broglie, Born, Heisenberg, Schrödinger, Dirac, and others is alone adequate to define the atom and the fundamental units of matter—the electron, the positron, the meson (heavy electron), the neutron, the proton, and some other particles considered probable on the basis of indirect evidence. The 1953 list of the elementary particles is given in Table 1-3.

The Properties of X-rays. Some of the properties of x-rays have been mentioned already. For the purpose of a general summary of these and as an introduction to other properties which will be discussed in detail in later chapters, the tabulation starting on page 17, essentially in the chronological order of discovery, will suffice.

TABLE 1-3. THE ELEMENTARY PARTICLES

Particle	Mass	Charge	Remarks
			The Nucleons Components of atomic nucleus
Proton.......	1,836.6	+	Number of protons in the nucleus of an atom ranges from 1 for hydrogen to 100 for most recently discovered element. Protons give the nucleus its positive charge. Discovered in 1919
Neutron.......	1,839.0	0	Neutrons and protons in combination make up the atomic nucleus. Uranium 238, for example, contains 92 protons and 146 neutrons. Discovered in 1932
			Electrons Basic units of electricity and matter
Electron.......	1	−	Electrons are distributed about the atomic nucleus as satellite planets around a central sun. Each atom contains an equal number of protons and electrons; thus U-238 has 92 protons and 92 electrons. Discovered in 1897
Positron.......	1	+	Discovered in 1932 in cosmic-ray phenomena. Collision of electrons and positrons causes annihilation of both with consequent production of photons (below)
			Mesons and V-particles Intermediate particles' function in nature obscure
Meson μ.......	210	+	Found in cosmic-ray phenomena 1937
Meson μ.......	210	−	Found in cosmic-ray phenomena 1937
Meson π.......	265	0	
Meson π.......	276	+	Found in cosmic-ray phenomena 1947 ⎫ produced by Mev x-rays, 1949
Meson π.......	276	−	Found in cosmic-ray phenomena 1947 ⎭
Meson.........	550	±	Existence doubtful
V-particle, V_2^0..	850	0	
Meson τ.......	975	±	
Meson κ.......	1,100	±	
Meson χ.......	1,400	±	
V-Particle, V_1^0..	2,190	0	
V-Particle, V^+..	2,200	+	Existence doubtful

TABLE 1-3. THE ELEMENTARY PARTICLES (*Continued*)

Massless Particles

Particle	Mass	Charge	Remarks
Photon	0	0	Basic unit of light, x-rays, γ-radiation, and all other forms of radiant energy. First postulated by Einstein in 1905
Neutrino	0	0	Carrier of kinetic energy and momentum. Generally accepted on grounds of indirect experimental evidence
Graviton	0	0	Corresponds to gravitational field; since only large masses produce observable effects, individual graviton may never be observed

Probable Particles

Antiproton	1,836.6	—	Existence believed possible. In theory a negatively charged proton could exist in nucleus of an "inverted atom," in conjunction with positrons. Such an atom would be unstable. Suggested in 1931. Indirect evidence in 1948–1949; direct evidence reported in June, 1954.
Antineutron	1,839.0	0	Existence believed possible in nucleus of postulated "inverted atom." Its magnetic moment would be opposite to that of ordinary neutron. Evidence in 1948–1949

X-rays, then, are:

1. Invisible, and pass through space without transference of matter.
2. Propagated in straight lines.
3. Unaffected by electric or magnetic fields—hence, nonelectrical in nature.
4. Reflected, diffracted, refracted, and polarized just as is light.
5. Propagated with a velocity of 30 billion cm/sec, as is light.
6. Transverse electromagnetic vibrations.
7. Characterized by a wide range of wavelengths (approximately 0.0001 to 1,000 A.)
8. Produced by the impact of cathode rays (and also positive ions) upon matter; probably generated on the interior of hot stars; produced during nuclear disintegrations by bombardment in the cyclotron, and in the atomic bombs.
9. Capable of blackening the photographic plate.
10. Capable of producing fluorescence and phosphorescence in some substances and of coloring some stones and minerals.
11. Able to ionize gases and to influence the electrical properties of liquids and solids.
12. Differentially absorbed by matter.
13. Able to liberate photoelectrons and recoil electrons to produce electron-positron pairs at energies above 1 Mev and mesons at still higher energies.
14. Capable of acting photochemically.
15. Able to damage or kill living cells and to produce genetic mutations.

16. Emitted in a continuous spectrum whose short wavelength limit is determined only by the voltage on the tube.

17. Emitted also with a line spectrum characteristic of the chemical elements in the anticathode.

18. Found to have absorption spectra characteristic of the chemical elements.

19. Diffracted by crystals acting as gratings in accordance with the fundamental equation $n\lambda = 2d \sin \Theta$, to which a correction for refraction must be applied for very accurate work.

20. Diffracted by optical gratings and totally reflected at very small glancing angles by mirrors to form enlarged images or x-ray microscopes.

21. Found to act in interference and related phenomena as waves but in other phenomena as discrete quanta of energy which may be scattered by single electrons.

X-rays Applied.   A radiation with as many distinctive characteristics obviously finds manifold applications in science, industry, and daily life. Some of these were immediately apparent to Röntgen.   Before his death in 1923 he saw roentgen rays being used throughout the world as an indispensable tool, but even then as compared with the science of today only the barest beginning had been made.   To mention only a few examples at random, he did not live to see rays generated at millions of volts today in contrast with the 20,000 volts at which the rays were generated in his original discovery.   Today he would find that radiograph of Frau Röntgen's hand showing bones and wedding ring, which required in 1896 an exposure of 30 min, could be made far more safely and efficiently in $\frac{1}{1000}$ sec.   He could observe the construction of giant dams and bridges guided by searching x-ray test; x-ray apparatus as an indispensable equipment of art galleries; industry calling upon x-ray methods to solve the most difficult problems; the high quality of commodities, assured by routine x-ray examination; a whole new science of the ultimate architectural plan of the solid state; new alloys, new textiles, and a host of other products derived from x-ray research; the analysis of the complex molecular structures of viruses, proteins, penicillin, amino acids, and a long list of substances formed in living processes.

Any attempt to classify completely all the ramifications of roentgen-ray science must fail.   But perhaps the principal applications may be summarized as shown in Table 1-4.

In the succeeding chapters of this book each of these items will be considered briefly as an integral part of the unified science of applied x-rays.

TABLE 1-4. BRANCHES OF ROENTGEN-RAY (X-RAY) SCIENCE

Subject	Purpose or method	Property involved
1. Engineering	Design and operation of tubes and power plants	
2. Microscopy	Enlarged images (70 × or more) and resolution of 70 A	Total reflection of grazing beams from cylindrical, spherical, and elliptical mirrors

TABLE 1-4. BRANCHES OF ROENTGEN-RAY (X-RAY) SCIENCE (*Continued*)

Subject	Purpose or method	Property involved
3. Spectrometry	Identification of chemical element; atomic number; energy levels in atoms and solids; quantum theory; atomic structure	Characteristic emission and absorption of rays; scattering
4. Fluorescence analysis	Nondestructive chemical analysis with permanent apparatus	Generation of fluorescent secondary characteristic rays in spectrum by intense primary rays
5. Absorption photometry (absorptiometry)	Chemical analysis, porosity and thickness gaging (often with automatic electronic equipment)	Quantitative measurement of general absorption in passing through specimen
6. Roentgenology (radiology) (medical):		
a. Radiography	Medical diagnosis (photographic)	Differential absorption (between bones and tissues, etc.)
b. Fluoroscopy	Diagnosis (visual fluorescence)	
7. Industrial and art radiography	Testing of gross structures for homogeneity, soundness (castings, welds, etc.); examination of old paintings	Differential absorption
8. Microradiography	Gross structure of small specimens, metallurgical, biological, enlarged up to 400 ×	Differential absorption of soft general or monochromatic radiation
9. Radiochemistry	Chemical effects (photographic, oxidation, reduction, activation of H_2O, etc.	Liberation of high-speed electrons, ionization, activation, free radical (H and OH) formation
10. Radiobiology	Identification of cells and tissues	Specific sensitiveness of cells and tissues to radiation
11. Radiogenetics	Production of mutations in sublethal doses	Effects on chromosomes and genes
12. Roentgen therapy	Treatment of cancer, etc.	Lethal effect upon abnormal cells
13. X-ray crystallography (diffractometry) and crystal chemistry	Fine structures and textures of materials	Diffraction of x-rays by crystals
14. Structural metallurgy, ceramics, mineralogy, etc.	Applications to specific materials	Diffraction

CHAPTER 2

X-RAY TUBES

There are two general types of x-ray tube that fulfill the requirements for generation outlined in the previous chapter. In the first type, the so-called gas, or ion, tubes, the residual gas plays an important part; in the second, or electron, type the tubes are exhausted of gas to such an extent that no discharge takes place when a large difference of potential is applied.

X-ray tubes are also classified according to the use to which they are put, which in turn depends upon the penetrating quality of the rays and the applied voltage.

TABLE 2-1. CLASSIFICATION OF X-RAY TUBES

Class	Type	Kilovolts
1. Supervoltage sources................................	Betatron	5,000–400,000
2. Special high-voltage tubes......................	Electron	800–3,000
3. Deep therapy.....................................	Electron	Average 160–400
4. Industrial radiography (conventional)............	Electron	100–400
5. Diagnostic......................................	Electron	Average 50–110
6. Diffraction......................................	{Electron / Ion	Average 25–50
7. Superficial therapy, or grenz, ray...............	Electron	Average 10

Gas Tubes. The gas tubes were the first to be developed for practical use. They still find application for purely scientific purposes, but the electron tubes now in operation undoubtedly far outnumber the older type. In the gas tube the gas molecules are split up into electrons and residual ions when the voltage is applied. These positive ions are then hurled against the cathode by the electric field, so that electrons are set free in the bombardment. The cathode-ray stream thus generated bombards the positive electrode, or anticathode, and the x-rays are produced.

The cathode-ray tube used by Röntgen in the discovery of x-rays is diagrammatically represented in Fig. 2. A flat disk served as cathode, and the cathode rays impinged upon the opposite glass wall with the production of strong fluorescence, while the new rays passed through the glass. It is not surprising that it was thought that the source of the new rays resided in the fluorescence until Becquerel proved that this was not the case. The result of Becquerel's study was the discovery of radioactivity in 1896, only two months after Röntgen's discovery. Röntgen very soon constructed a tube with a special anticathode screen. Other tubes had both an anode and an anticathode bound together, with the idea that greater stability and less pitting of the anticathode would be attained. Some of Röntgen's tubes which now are at the Röntgen Museum

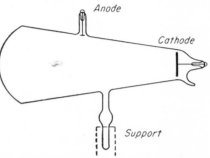

Fig. 2. Diagram of cathode-ray tube used by Röntgen in the discovery of x-rays.

in Remscheid-Lennep are illustrated in Fig. 3. With these are to be contrasted the group of modern tubes shown in Fig. 9.

Of necessity, medical diagnosis and superficial therapy depended upon ion tubes during the first 20 years of the development of medical radiology

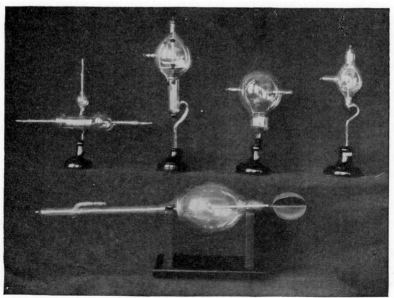

Fig. 3. Some of Röntgen's early tubes.

and in many cases for some years after the advent of the Coolidge-type tubes. The fact that gas pressure, voltage, and tube current could not be varied independently in ion tubes caused erratic performance and easily explains why these have been completely displaced by the hot-filament tubes pumped to a very high vacuum in which voltage and current may be controlled in terms of constant quality, or penetrating power, and quantity, or intensity, of the x-ray beam.

The older varieties of the ion tube were provided with a device with which it was possible to add small amounts of fresh gas. The "hardness" of the x-ray tube (by which is meant the penetrating quality of the x-rays produced) is determined by the amount of the residual gas, since the lower the gas pressure, the higher the voltage required for production of x-rays. During operation the hardness of the tube increases as the amount of the available gas diminishes owing to adsorption on the glass walls and metal parts. Consequently, in order to maintain constancy, gas must be admitted by diffusion through thin metal or by heating or passing a spark through a small cylinder of some substance in a side tube.

Several modifications of the old gas-type tube were made in Europe and America with such success that for many types of investigation of x-ray spectra and crystal structure these have competed favorably with the electron tubes. Seemann, Shearer, Hadding, Siegbahn, Müller, Wever, Becker, Wyckoff, Aminco-Ksanda, Baird, Hägg, and others have constructed tubes largely of metal, with interchangeable targets (iron, copper, and molybdenum usually), thin-foil windows, water cooling, and permanent connections with vacuum pumps by means of which the gas pressure could be readily regulated, thus eliminating special devices for controlling hardness. These tubes were very simple and rugged in construction, economical because of long use without necessity of replacement of parts, and often surprisingly efficient in producing x-ray beams of as high intensity as those from comparable hot-filament tubes.

Another advantage of great importance for precise spectroscopic and diffraction work is the purity of the spectrum, since it has been found easier to build a controllable gas tube than to prevent tungsten (from the hot-cathode filament) depositing on the target in one of the electron type.

Electron Tubes. *The Coolidge Tube.* In the electron-type tube it is necessary to have an independent source of electrons, since there is insufficient gas present to enable passage of the current. For an x-ray tube to operate with a pure electron discharge, it is necessary to evacuate to the highest attainable vacuum, usually 0.01 bar, or 0.0075 μ, of mercury. These electrons are supplied by application of the Edison effect, *i.e.*, emission from a hot-wire cathode. This principle was utilized successfully by Dr. W. D. Coolidge of the General Electric Company more than 40 years ago in the design and construction of the very familiar Coolidge tube, which has been manufactured ever since on a large scale for research, therapy, medical diagnosis, industrial radiography, and diffraction analysis. The original Coolidge tube consisted of a glass bulb into which were sealed a solid metal target and a spiral of tungsten wire backed by a focusing shield of molybdenum as cathode. The emitting wire was 0.216 mm in diameter, 33.4 mm long, and wound in a flat spiral of $5\frac{1}{2}$ turns with a diameter of 3.5 mm. The spiral is heated to incandescence by a current of 3 to 5 amp at 1.8 to 4.6 volts supplied in an independent circuit from storage batteries or stepdown transformers.

Under these conditions the wire has a temperature of 1890 to 2540°K. Electrons are liberated, and under a potential gradient between the terminals of the x-ray tube they are drawn across to the target. The ordinary commercial Coolidge tubes are usually supplied with massive tungsten targets. In the "universal" type the target is not cooled and becomes white-hot.

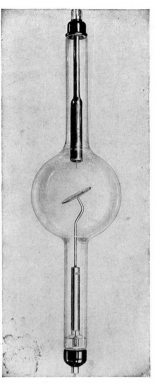

Thin plate targets enabling more rapid dissemination of heat are a more recent development (Fig. 4). These tubes are pumped to the proper vacuum at the factory by the very special technique involving pumping, baking, and operation under increasing voltages in order to remove the gas which is occluded in metal parts. Such tubes fail very often from development of gas during operation, and large currents begin to pass. Even if the operation is normal, however, there is a limit to the life. The glowing filament of the cathode vaporizes, and thus it becomes thinner and thinner until it is burned through. The time over which the resistance of the wire increases by 10 per cent may be designated the life, which on the average for the ordinary Coolidge tubes is about 2,000 hr. Danger

FIG. 4. Deep-therapy tube of conventional design with thin-plate target. (*Westinghouse.*)

of failure from puncturing these tubes at high voltages is lessened by immersing them in transformer oil.

One great advantage of the Coolidge tube is the independence of the current through the tube and the voltage. One may be altered without affecting the other, whereas in gas tubes it is obvious that the number of the electrons and, hence, the current will increase with the voltage. The current in the electron type depends upon the number of electrons N, and this in turn depends upon the temperature of the hot-wire filament, by the Richardson relationship $N = CT^2e^{-d/T}$, where C and d are constants depending upon the metal (1.86 × 10^{11} and 4.95 × 10^4, respectively, for tungsten) and T is the absolute temperature. On account of the building up of a space charge, since the tube current does not increase so rapidly as does the number of electrons when the temperature of the filament is increased but the voltage held constant, a maximum, or saturation, current is reached at a point expressed by the equation deduced by Langmuir

$$i_{max} = \frac{\sqrt{2}}{4\pi} \sqrt{\frac{e}{m}} \frac{V^{\frac{3}{2}}}{x^2}$$

where e and m are the charge and the mass of the electron, V is the voltage, and x is the distance between electrodes. This relationship has

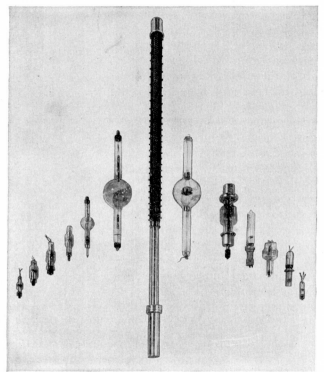

Fig. 5. A group of modern x-ray tubes. (*Machlett.*)   *Center*, 2-million-volt tube; *outside*, 5-in. tube for dental radiography.

enabled investigators to predict correct design for tubes. Figure 5 pictures a group of modern Coolidge-type tubes now produced by one of the American manufacturers (Machlett). These range from a 9-ft 2-million-volt tube in the center to small dental tubes about 5 in. long on the outside.

Problems in Tube Design. The steadily increasing demands for x-ray tubes to operate at higher and higher voltages in order to generate more penetrating radiation and at higher and higher currents in order to gain increased intensity call for the utmost care in the design of every detail.

The first of these requirements involves essentially proper insulation of the two electrodes; the second involves adequate protection of the target from destruction. Coordinate with these problems of tube protection are those of protection of the operator against shock and against exposure to x-radiation, which may be solved by integral constructional details of tube design. Depending on the tube classification in terms of use, these problems appear in greater or lesser degree and in varying combinations. The best methods of solution as a general case are summarized here.

1. *Insulation of Tube Electrodes and Electrical Stabilization.* Obviously, the body of an x-ray tube—a bulb or cylinder of glass or porcelain—usually must serve not only as a rigid support but also as the insulating medium between two oppositely charged electrodes at high voltage. It is not surprising, therefore, to find x-ray tubes varying in length from a few inches (dental radiographic tubes, oil-immersed) to 30 or 40 ft (for operation at 1 million volts or more, though these are now largely superseded by much smaller tubes operating in a gaseous or liquid insulating medium).

For a long time, serious difficulties were encountered in attempts to operate x-ray tubes of usual design at voltages very much higher than 220,000, not because power plants were not available, but because of electrical phenomena within the tubes that prevented a satisfactory "life." Today this problem has been solved to the point where tubes of conventional design are built to operate successfully over a satisfactory life at 400 kv. In the first place, it was discovered that the autoelectronic effect, or the release of electrons from metallic points or sharp edges in the electric field, produces a discharge in the tube operated above a critical voltage. Momentary currents of several amperes may pass, followed by high-frequency electric oscillations which may result in ruin of the transformer and of the x-ray tube, especially if the discharge strikes the glass walls. In less severe cases the natural distribution of potential along the tube is affected, and gas is liberated from the glass walls in certain areas. This difficulty was counteracted, so that higher potentials could be applied safely, by careful rounding of the cathode.

The second group of phenomena that was found to introduce difficulties is the back diffusion of electrons from the anode to the inner glass walls, which become negatively charged. Next the outer glass wall becomes charged almost to the potential of the cathode, so that a high difference of potential is set up between the glass and the anode. A stream of ions will travel from the anode, through the glass, then through the air to the metal anode cap. It has been demonstrated that gaseous electrolytic products are liberated as a result of the passage through the glass of the current, even though smaller than 10^{-5} amp. The result again may be destructive discharge, depending on the potential and also the current. In order to avoid these effects so that a tube might operate with safety, many devices were introduced by manufacturers, such as protecting rings of large diameter on terminal caps. Today nearly all high-potential tubes are oil- or gas-immersed both for purposes of insulation and electrical protection and for cooling. A typical example is the Machlett IR-250 tube for radiography and fluoroscopy in industrial applications up to 250 kv, shown in Fig. 5, second to the right from the center, and alone in Fig. 6.

Aside from proper design of the electrodes the most important development in electrical stabilization of tubes was the use of a metal discharge chamber, with glass serving only to insulate the electrodes. The entire middle part of the Philips Metalix tube, manufactured in Eindhoven, Netherlands, prior to the war, was a chrome iron cylinder, which was sealed vacuum-tight and mechanically rigid to the glass of the electrode end sleeves. This metal center was grounded, which prevents destruction by interior discharges and also serves both as a shockproof and a rayproof feature. A number of American tubes still retain this design.

A new development in 1949 was the successful introduction of an efficient "getter" in all types of medical tube which serves to clean up gas liberated during discharge and maintain the necessary high vacuum. The result is longer life and higher energies and smaller tube size for a given load. This Dunlee tube is illustrated in Fig. 7.

2. *Special Tubes for Very High Voltages.* There are many points of interest in operating x-ray tubes at increasingly higher voltages. Since the effective wavelength decreases as the voltage increases, the point might be reached where x-rays in the wavelength range of γ-rays might be generated with an output equivalent to thousands of grams of radium or with millions of times greater intensity than is observed for cosmic rays. The advantage in therapy and in biological action is obvious, even supposing that the *kind* of biological action might be anticipated as independent of wavelength. The intensity of radiation in the voltage range of modern deep therapy with usual filtration increases with a high power (at least V^3) of the voltage. The gain in intensity with mounting voltage and constant current makes possible material reductions in time of irradiation even with stronger filtration and increased distance from focal spot to patient, and a far higher percentage depth dose is attained. The physicist is also interested in the spectra of radiation excited at the highest attainable voltages and in the test of theories of atomic structure.

Throughout the world there are many, probably well above 100, x-ray installations in hospitals and research laboratories and testing laboratories in which the x-ray tube is operating at 1 million or 2 million volts and generating rays with wavelengths shorter than 0.01 A. These followed the pioneer tubes of Lauritsen[1] (600,000 volts, California Institute of

[1] *Phys. Rev.*, **32**, 850 (1928), **36**, 988, 1680 (1930).

Technology), Coolidge[1] (900,000 volts, Memorial Hospital of New York), Tuve and associates[2] (2 million volts, Carnegie Institution of Washington), and several others. Difficulties in elimination of cold-cathode discharges, proper insulation, screening off of back-diffusion electrons, and maintenance of high vacua have been overcome to such an extent that

| FIG. 6 | FIG. 7 | FIG. 8 |

FIG. 6. Machlett 250-kv tube, usually oil-immersed, for industrial applications.
FIG. 7. Double-focus diagnostic tube with "getter." (*Dunlee.*)
FIG. 8. One-million-volt tube. (*General Electric.*)

sealed-off tubes to operate at 2 million volts are commercially advertised and available. The newest tube for operation with the tuned resonance transformer, described in Chap. 3 and designed by General Electric, is illustrated in Fig. 8. This tube is built with 11 intermediate metal rings for control of the potential gradient, and with grounded anode, and operates at 1,000 kv and 3 ma. The Machlett 2-million-volt tube is shown in the center in Fig. 5 and diagrammatically in Fig. 9. It is less than 9 ft long in comparison with the 24-ft length of an older tube oper-

[1] *Am. J. Roentgenol., Radium Therapy,* **19,** 313 (1928); **24,** 605 (1930).
[2] *Phys. Rev.,* **35,** 66, 1406 (1930).

ating at 1,400,000 volts at the National Bureau of Standards. This sealed-off tube has 180 sections to provide uniform accelerating steps of 12,000 volts each. The greatest problem in construction was 300 ft of glass-to-metal seal in each tube, accomplished by a combination of gas flame and high-frequency induction heating. The tube operates with an electrostatic generator of the van de Graaff type. Coordinate in interest with the design and operation of these supertubes is the comparative biological and therapeutic effects of rays generated at 2 million and, say, 200,000 volts. The results of two decades of experience, especially in cancer therapy, are considered in Chap. 12 on The Biological Effects of X-radiation.

3. *The Betatron "Donut" Tube.* For potentials above 2 million volts the betatron, designed by Prof. D. W. Kerst of the University of Illinois, is employed instead of conventional transformers. The x-ray tube is the evacuated "donut," which serves also as the secondary of a high-voltage transformer. The donut used in the 100-Mev† General Electric betatron is illustrated in Fig. 10. Electrons are introduced from a filament and describe a circular path in the tube, which is placed between the poles of a magnet. With each circuit the electrons gain in velocity and kinetic energy up to the desired maximum, and then they are slightly deviated from the circular path to impinge on a target. The betatron as a high-potential power unit will be considered in the following chapter, and the properties of the x-rays generated at 5 million up to 400 million volts and the applications in medical therapy and industrial radiography will be noted under the appropriate topics. The donut, now generally constructed from a high grade of porcelain or glass, may be constructed from two or more sections assembled with vacuum-tight junctions and may have a beryllium-foil window for exit of the rays.

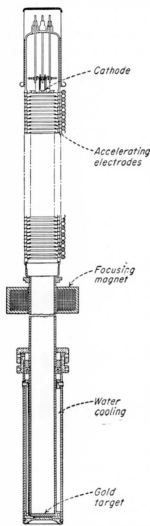

Fig. 9. Constructional details of Machlett 2-million-volt tube (Fig. 5), showing sections for applying potential gradient.

† Million electron volts: expresses energy of the electrons and the corresponding x-rays excited by them.

4. *Operation of Tubes at High Currents.* *a. The focal spot.* The desire in every branch of x-ray science is the production of the most intense beam of radiation possible. For example, from the medical roentgenographic standpoint, any motion of the patient or areas under observation results in blurred details with consequent failure to obtain that definition which is vital to the most accurate and complete interpretation. The history of the development of x-ray tubes and accessories for diagnosis has been one of an unremitting struggle to obviate the effects of such motion. The trend has been definitely toward shorter and shorter exposures, demanding the employment of greater and greater electrical energies.

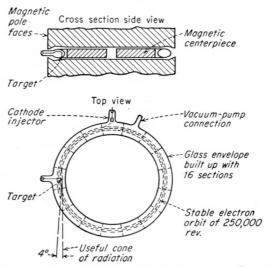

FIG. 10. Diagram of "donut" tube in 100-Mev betatron. (*General Electric.*)

In an x-ray tube of conventional type, the electron stream is directed against a fixed area on the target called the focal spot, which is usually defined as a pitted or etched area on the target face. The size of this spot is determined by the method of focusing of the electrons, which in turn is defined by the size and shape of a shield around the filament and the position of the filament within this shield. Thus, a fine-focus or a broad-focus tube represents, respectively, a small or a large focal spot in which the energy is concentrated. Since sharply defined diagnostic radiographs require the finest focus possible, the trend to shorter exposures and the need to retain fine focal spots have been in direct opposition to each other.

The rating of an x-ray tube is limited by the ability of the target or anode to dissipate the heat generated. The product of peak kilovolts (kv[1]), milliamperes (ma), and time or "heat units" must be such that no

[1] The abbreviation kv implies *peak* kilovolts when the electric power is generated in pulses as in a-c transformers.

portion of the area bombarded is brought too close to the melting point. The heat-storage capacity in units per minute must be specified for each type of tube. If exposures are to be continued after the heat-storage capacity of the tube has been utilized, cooling intervals between subsequent exposures must be allowed so that the average rate of heat input does not exceed the maximum cooling rate.

The necessity for cooling the target is explained by the following example: At 200 kv and 3 ma the kinetic energy of the electrons, which have a velocity of 220,000 km/sec as they strike the target, is transferred to the target at the rate of 150 cal/sec, or enough energy in 10 min to raise 1 liter of water from 10°C to boiling. Only about 2 per cent of this energy is transformed to x-radiation, and the remaining 98 per cent goes into heat.

b. Stationary-target cooling. The original Coolidge-tube design still retained in the "universal" type for operation at relatively small loads involved a massive "horse-hoof" target of tungsten, which could become white-hot because of the high melting point of the metal. Greater energy could be used by constructing the target as a large thin plate (Fig. 4) from which heat could be dissipated more readily. The next step was to add external air-cooling fins to the anode connection or a reservoir containing oil or water. Still more efficient cooling is effected by a continuous stream of water conducted into a hollow target past the inner face of the target. If the anode is grounded, it may be connected directly with the city water mains and a continuous stream of 1 or more liters per minute used, depending on the heat evolution. If the anode is at high potential, an insulated pumping and radiator-cooling system keeps the liquid in circulation. Or if the voltage is not too high, water from the mains may be circulated and the anode insulated from ground through a column of water in glass tubing 40 or 50 ft in length. Several protective devices to shut off the electric current in case of failure of the cooling supply have been described and are highly desirable. Tubes with cooled targets through which currents of 200 ma may be passed for 1 sec or longer, or 400 ma for 0.1 sec, are now fairly common. Complete immersion of the entire tube in oil, one of the best methods of shockproofing, has the added advantage of rapid heat transfer from the anode, heavier loads being thus permitted.

c. The line-focus filament. The desire to increase the load and intensity of x-radiation from such tubes in order to cut down exposure time to a minimum is opposed by the fact that greater energy input in a small focal spot results in melting and destruction of the target. Increase in size of the focal spot in all directions causes diagnostic photographs to lose sharpness. Hence it is necessary to change the focus so that the cross section through the x-ray bundle at the focal spot is as small as possible. The line-focus filament of Goetze employed first in the Philips tubes was a successful solution. A long cylindrical spiral of very small diameter produces a line focal spot on the target which by virtue of length can take up a very considerable amount of energy without damage to the target. The face of the target is inclined at an angle of 80 deg to the tube axis, so that the line-focus spot in the principal direction of emergence of the x-rays appears shortened to a small point. The focal spot is actually about 2 mm wide and 16 mm square (Fig. 11). Almost all x-ray tubes for all purposes now employ a line-focus filament.

d. The rotating target. The ultimate step in attaining a tube with minimum focal-spot area with maximum energy is obviously that of

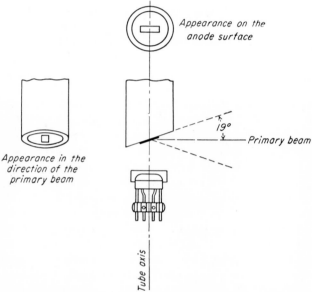

Appearance on the anode surface

19°

Primary beam

Appearance in the direction of the primary beam

Tube axis

Fig. 11. Diagram showing operation of a line-filament cathode.

rotating the target at high speed so that relatively cool metal is brought continuously before the electron stream. This principle is used in highly successful tubes constructed by Philips, General Electric, Machlett, and others. A typical design is shown in Fig. 12. The anode is a disk of metal (tungsten for medical radiography) fastened to the end of a short shaft on the proximal end of which is the rotor of an induction motor, the assembly being mounted on ball bearings. Outside the glass wall of the tube and surrounding the circumference of the rotor is the stator of the motor. When this is energized by 60-cycle current, electromagnetic induction causes the anode to rotate at about 3,000 rpm. The single- or double-filament cathode is arranged so that bombardment of the target takes place near the periphery. Thus, during operation the focal area becomes in effect a completely encircling ribbon with the effective, or projected, focal spot in the form of a small square, 1 or 2 mm on a side. Actually for the 2-mm spot the heat is distributed over an area $7\frac{1}{2}$ mm wide and 190 mm long.   The new, very heavy duty Superdynamax rotating-anode tube is illustrated in Fig. 13.   A maximum voltage rating of

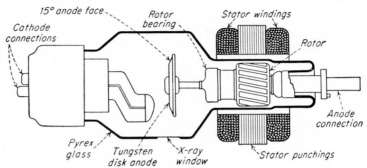

Fig. 12. Diagram of rotating-target x-ray tube.   (*General Electric.*)

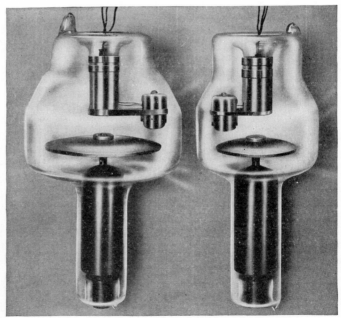

Fig. 13. Superdynamax rotating-target tube.   (*Machlett.*)

120 kv and current of 900 ma make possible applications to angiocardiography and cinematography.   A solid-tungsten anode structure of massiveness never before utilized provides heat-storage capacity and heat-dissipation rate far in excess of these characteristics in previous rotating-anode tubes.

The capabilities of this new type of rotating-anode tube are well portrayed by the condensed table (Table 2-2) of characteristics and ratings. The ratings are at least 6 times those of the best available stationary-target tubes; *i.e.*, at the same voltage and time, 6 times the milliamperage; or at the same voltage and milliamperage, 6 times the length of time for safe continuous operation; or at the same voltage, milliamperage, and time, only $\frac{1}{6}$ the size of focal spot for safe operation.

TABLE 2-2. SUPERDYNAMAX ROTATING-TARGET TUBE CHARACTERISTICS
AND RATINGS

Focal-spot sizes: 1.0 mm and 2.0 mm (double focus)
Anode heat-storage capacity: 135,000 heat units
Over-all heat-storage capacity: 1,250,000 heat units
Maximum cooling rate: 45,000 units per min
Maximum voltage rating: 120 kv
Typical exposure ratings:

Large focus:	120 kv. 400 ma,	$\frac{1}{10}$ sec
	120 kv, 200 ma,	3 sec
	100 kv, 500 ma,	$\frac{1}{20}$ sec
	100 kv, 100 ma,	12.0 sec
	50 kv, 900 ma,	$\frac{1}{5}$ sec
Small focus:	120 kv, 200 ma,	$\frac{1}{30}$ sec
	120 kv, 100 ma,	4 sec
	100 kv, 200 ma,	$\frac{3}{10}$ sec
	100 kv, 100 ma,	7 sec
	50 kv, 400 ma,	$\frac{1}{5}$ sec

One of the principal problems involved in the construction of rotating-target tubes is a permanent dry lubricant for the bearings. Pure silver was selected because of its resistance to high temperature and has been found so satisfactory that getters are not needed for maintaining high vacuum, nor massive copper anodes for protecting bearings, thus enabling an all-tungsten rotating anode to be used.

A matter of primary concern in the use of rotating-target tubes, as for all other types of tube and rectifying valve, is satisfactory life. Damage resulting in shortened life or complete destruction can be brought about by excessively high filament temperature for too long a period of time, overheating or overloading the anode, application of excess anode voltage, gas accumulation, or mechanical damage. Figure 14 indicates eloquently what happens to the life of the large filament of a rotating-anode tube as filament current is increased. On this graph 4.0 amp is equivalent to a current of approximately 50 ma through the x-ray tube, and at this temperature the filament will give approximately 27,000 hr of life. On the other hand 4.8 amp filament current, equivalent to 500 ma through the tube, will give only 350 hr of life, so that a tenfold increase in milliamperage reduces the life by 99 per cent.

Several rotating-target tubes have been constructed for research purposes and for very rapid examinations of structures of materials. Most of these involve mechanical rotations through suitable vacuum-tight joints. Mercury seals covered with a layer of apiezon oil to prevent access of mercury vapor are generally successful. A 50-kw water-cooled tube with rotating target and leather-packed vacuum stuffing boxes is in satisfactory use at the Davy-Faraday Laboratory of the Royal Institution[1] and an even more powerful tube at the University of Leeds.[2] An

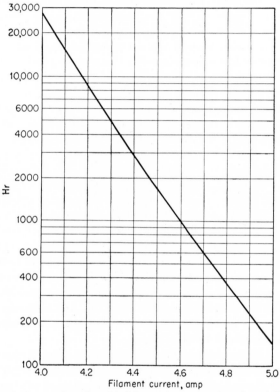

Fig. 14. Life of rotating-anode tube with 2.0-mm focus as a function of filament current. (*Machlett Laboratories.*)

account[3] of the proceedings of an entire conference on high-intensity x-ray beams, held in London in April, 1950, summarizes all recent developments in this field.

e. High-intensity radiation from beryllium-window tubes. The low atomic number and low density of beryllium (atomic number 4) give it the lowest absorption coefficient which might, by virtue of other suitable physical characteristics, be employed for windows in x-ray tubes. Until

[1] Müller and Clay, *J. IEE* (*London*), **84**, 261 (1939).
[2] MacArthur, *Electronic Eng.*, **17**, 277 (December, 1944), 317 (January, **1945**).
[3] *Brit. J. Appl. Phys.*, **1**, 305 (1950).

malleable beryllium was available such thin-foil vacuum-tight windows were not feasible, but in 1942 Claussen and Skehan[1] succeeded in making alloys of beryllium with less than 0.5 per cent titanium or zirconium which were easily hot-rolled into thin foils. This foil was first used in diffraction tubes, described in a subsequent section of this chapter, because of the desire to reduce to a minimum the loss of intensity due to absorption in the window of the characteristic radiation of the target material, which is of relatively long wavelength, particularly in the case of lower atomic number materials like cobalt, iron, and chromium. The extraordinary advantage of beryllium over glass or aluminum foil as windows is shown by the relative total intensities: beryllium 100, pyrex glass 7.9, aluminum 4.9. Furthermore the beryllium transmits longer waves, which are absorbed by the other two. For special radiographic purposes (see Chap. 9) and microradiography, photochemical and biological studies, tubes with beryllium windows were developed to produce a beam over a 40-deg solid focal angle. Because of heat resistance the window may be placed less than 2 cm from the target spot. At 50 kv and 50 ma an intensity of 2,330,000 r/min (the unit of dosage is defined in Chap. 4) is obtained from this Machlett AEG-50 tube.[2] The envelope of the tube consists of (1) a copper section containing the target as an integral part with ducts for water cooling and incorporating a beryllium window for x-ray exit; (2) a pyrex glass section to support and insulate the cathode. Type T has a focal-spot size 5 mm square in projection and will operate continuously at 50 ma at 50 kv; type A has a 1.5-mm focal spot and is rated to operate at 20 ma. A later development is the OEG-50 with identical specifications but is an oil-insulated (hermetically sealed) unit for heavy-duty industrial use, where the air-insulated shield is inadequate (such as for metal sheet gaging in the presence of splashing water). A cutaway illustration is shown in Fig. 15. Applications of this intense long-wavelength radiation will be illustrated in later chapters in therapy, sterilization, genetics, microradiography, historadiography, radiography of small animals and art objects, thickness gaging of rolled sheet and coated metals, examination of welds in thin and low-density materials, and chemical analyses by spectrometry as the intense primary source for exciting secondary fluorescent radiation. Such tubes have enabled new results heretofore impossible or requiring a prohibitive amount of time. With the commercial development of these AEG-50 tubes with tungsten, molybdenum, and copper targets, there are further steps in design which may be taken. First a cylindrical beryllium-foil window entirely around the body of the tube permits use of all the radiation around 360 deg tangential to a flat target perpendicular to the tube axis. This enables multiple exposures, or, for irradiation of chemical solutions and bacterial

---

[1] Claussen and Skehan, *Metals & Alloys*, **15**, 599 (1942).

[2] Rogers, T. H., *Radiology*, **48**, 594 (1947).

suspensions, the fluids may be circulated in a jacket around the window. Finally, the logical extension is to a beryllium-foil aome on one end of the tube as illustrated in Fig. 16a giving a beam over a 180-deg solid angle. The cathode, which conventionally is opposite the target and thus interferes with the forward components of the beam from the target, is an annular filament coaxial with the target. The filament and beryllium-foil dome, which is attached to the body of the tube by a metal bellows, are connected together at ground potential while the target is at high potential (thus requiring an insulated cooling system). In the electric field within the dome the electrons describe curved trajectories onto the target surface and are brought into focus by adjustment of the

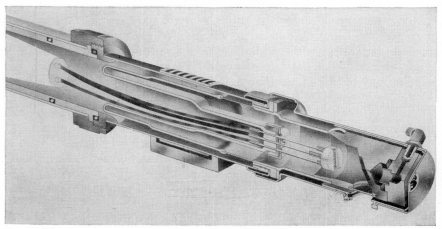

Fig. 15. Cutaway illustration of Machlett OEG-50 tube. (*T. H. Rogers, Cathode Press, Fall issue,* 1952, *p.* 10.)

bellows (Fig. 16b). Over the 25 cm² of this dome a beam is delivered with an intensity of 5,500,000 r/min, far in excess of the dosage recorded for any previous tube. The instantaneous and intense fluorescence and phosphorescence in minerals irradiated with this beam are rough indications of its intensity. This tube is still in the experimental stage, but a simplified commercial modification, with a flat beryllium window on one end of the tube and a ring filament, opposite the grounded target, through which the x-ray beam passes, recalls a similar gun-type model of some years ago which did not have the advantage of the low-absorbing beryllium window.

f. Tubes with conical targets producing beams convergent to a point. A new type of high-intensity tube which is at once simple in design and unique in operation was described in 1950.[1] The design, still in the experimental stage, is best indicated by reference to the diagram in Fig.

[1] C. H. Bachman and S. J. Silverman, *J. Appl. Phys.,* **21,** 615 (1950).

17a. A filament is arranged coaxially with a target in the shape of a truncated cone. All the electrons from the cathode are drawn out radially, to strike the inner face of this cone, so that the entire surface serves as the source of x-rays emitted in all directions. Much of the radiation is cut off by the shape of the tube, but through the end window appears the hollow cone of rays, which converge by overlapping at one point where intensity is a maximum. Better control is afforded by placing a collimating block on the window to remove all radiation except a hollow-cone sheath of radiation of controlled thickness which crosses

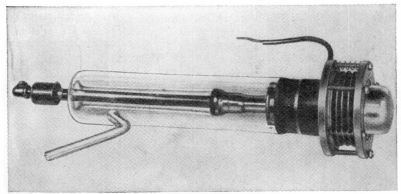

Fig. 16a. Photograph of experimental tube with domed window, permitting 180-deg solid-angle x-ray beam. (*Machlett.*)

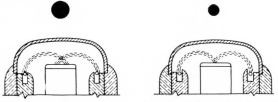

Fig. 16b. Diagrams of focusing obtained with domed-window tube at various positions of the bellows with respect to the anode.

out at a sharply defined point (photographed in Fig. 17b) and again diverges beyond.

In this tube no problem of electron focusing is involved since *all* electrons contribute regardless of where they hit the cone. The very large target area eliminates the cooling problem, so that very great energy may be utilized; the greater the axial length of the conical target, the greater the power rating and x-ray output. For a variety of purposes such as radiography and diffraction the very sharply defined beam at the crossover point may be used; or for other purposes a beam of larger annular cross section may be useful. An adaptation to a tube to generate secondary fluorescent x-rays is indicated in Chap. 7.

g. Condenser-discharge and field-emission tubes for very high intensities. Even with all the devices mentioned in foregoing sections a limit is reached in the nondestructive operation of tubes to attain maximum intensity. There remain only practically instantaneous discharges of relatively enormous energies.

The most practical approach to excitation of x-rays of very high intensity is the design of a tube operated by a surge generator in which controlled bursts of extremely high emission currents produce x-radiation of such intensity that radiographs may be made in 1/1,000,000 sec or less. This tube makes use of the very property which is usually so troublesome in high-potential hot-filament tubes, namely, cold field emission from

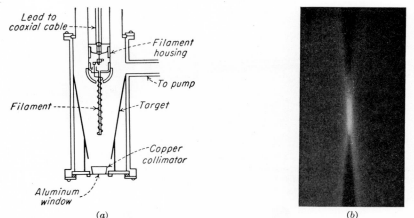

Lead to coaxial cable

Filament housing

To pump

Filament

Target

Copper collimator

Aluminum window

(a)   (b)

FIG. 17. (a) Construction of tube with conical target. (*Bachman-Silverman.*) (b) Photograph of crossover beam from this tube.

sharp points and corners, especially in the presence of occluded gas. In 1945 Slack, Ehrke, and Zavales[1] decided to make deliberate use of this sudden flow of very large currents of several thousand amperes. The electrodes in the resulting tube are pictured in Fig. 18. Here the cathode *B* is a small rectangular sharp-edged piece of molybdenum set in a slot in the trough-shaped auxiliary electrode *C*, which is connected with the anode through a high resistance and serves to concentrate a high field at the cathode and initiate a discharge which is forced by the voltage drop across the high resistance to transfer to the anode. As soon as the auxiliary electrode has started the discharge, it assumes a potential close to that of the cathode and by virtue of its cupped shape focuses the electrons on the anode. The target *A* is a rectangular slab of tungsten. The surge generator which supplies the enormous bursts of power to this tube is illustrated in the next chapter, and the applications to radiography

[1] Slack, Ehrke, and Zavales, *Westinghouse Engr.*, **5**, 98 (1945).

of moving objects in Chap. 9. In 1948 this high-speed unit was further improved so that x-ray exposures of 1/10,000,000 sec are combined with a shutterless camera capable of making moving pictures up to 2,000 frames per second.

h. Shock- and rayproofing. The majority of x-ray tubes are built today with construction features designed to protect patients and operators

FIG. 18. Anode and cathode of high-speed x-ray tube: *C*, field-emission cathode; *B*, focusing cap; *A*, anode or target. (*Westinghouse.*)

against the danger of shock from high tension or undue exposure to radiation. Protection against shock involves an outer casing around the tube at ground potential with similarly protected leads. Better still, the tube is entirely immersed in oil inside a shockproof casing. Best of all, the tube is enclosed in the same grounded case and oil or gas insulating medium as the high-tension transformer coils and the rectifying valves (Fig. 19). Such devices also provide rayproofing so that the desired beam of radiation is limited to certain openings. For example, the housing for a Superdynamax rotating-target tube has rayproofing equivalent to at least 2.0 mm of lead in the path of x-rays except the port.

Diffraction Tubes for Fine-structure Examination of Materials.   In this branch of x-ray science the diffraction of rays by a suitable grating is used as a means of discovering the ultimate fine structures of crystals and materials of all kinds.

Fig. 19. Shock- and rayproof unit with x-ray tube (*top, center*) enclosed in oil-filled case with transformer coils and rectifying-valve tubes.   (*General Electric.*)

Though it was found that for determination of the gross structure of materials the medical deep-therapy or diagnostic tubes could be used, special attributes are desirable in tubes for studies of fine structure:

Moderate voltages, 25 to 50 kv.
Largest possible tube currents so as to cut down exposure times.
Continuous operation, since diffraction photographs may require many hours or days.
Medium or fine focus.
Small dimensions so that distance from target to specimen may be a minimum.
Minimum absorption of beam in desired directions.
Target usually not tungsten, but molybdenum, copper, iron, etc., and preferably easily interchangeable.
Multiple beams from the same target for routine examination of numerous specimens; hence flat target at right angles to cathode-ray beam from which rays at grazing angles may be defined radially.

Numerous modifications of the hot-cathode tube have been made, largely aimed at adapting it for use in x-ray diffraction work with crystals, where interchangeable targets, small dimensions in order to approach as closely as possible to samples and spectroscopic apparatus, and general flexibility and ruggedness are required.

The best features of the diagnostic tubes in which requirements are similar have been embodied by various manufacturers in diffraction tubes of the electron type. The most important of these are as follows:

1. Line-focus filaments for great intensity and sharp focus. In such a tube a maximum of four diffraction photographs may be made simultaneously with opposite beams from the line focal spot, two from the length (strong), and two from the breadth (weak), on a target at right angles to the cathode rays. Generally only two beryllium windows for

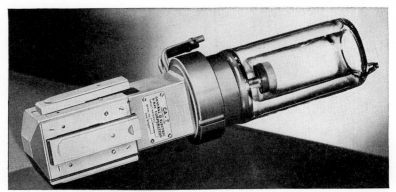

FIG. 20. CA-7 diffraction tube with three beryllium windows. (*General Electric.*)

the strong beams are provided; the new General Electric CA-7 tube has three $\frac{2}{3}$-in. windows (Fig. 20).

The Machlett diffraction tube of newest design with shock- and rayproof outer casing and replaceable inserts is illustrated in Fig. 21; a nonshockproof type is also manufactured. Two windows of beryllium, through which the beam passes with little absorption, thus permit the study of two specimens simultaneously. These tubes may be operated up to 50 kv and 30 ma continuously.

2. Demountable tubes. Besides the several varieties supplied by the manufacturers already pumped and permanently sealed off, demountable tubes are available. It is convenient to be able to interchange targets in the same tube for diffraction research and particularly for spectroscopic analysis in which the unknown substance must constitute the target and must be mounted or pasted on a suitable backing. This, of course, means that the tubes must be pumped during operation. To one skilled in high-vacuum technique this does not present great difficulty, since equipment combining a mechanical-backing pump, mercury- or oil-

diffusion pumps in one or more stages, and liquid-air traps is well standardized.

Several tubes made largely of metal have been commercially produced, and many others have been designed and built in various laboratories.

Of all the newer demountable tubes for crystal-analysis work the Hilger tube combines the most unusual features such as flexibility. One of these tubes in position on the Hilger HRX diffraction unit is shown in Fig. 223, Chap. 14. The x-ray tube has four beryllium-foil windows and four filaments, but a single anticathode of large area, water-cooled, mounted by a greased cone. The nose of the anticathode, beveled at 6 deg, pressed from high-conductivity sheet copper, and soft-soldered to

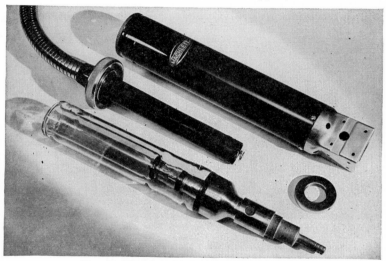

Fig. 21. Machlett shockproof diffraction tube.

the main target body, may have multiple electrodeposited targets of different metals, and therefore each of the four windows can, if need be, simultaneously emit a different type of x-radiation. Moreover this radiation may be changed at one or more of the windows without disturbance to that of the others, without breaking the vacuum. When one set of focal areas of the anticathode becomes pitted as a result of electron bombardment, a small rotation of the anticathode brings a new target area into the electron stream. The total output of this tube is 160 ma at 50,000 volts, half-wave rectification, continuously. This energy is divided equally between the four filaments, and in each case the load is applied to an effective focal area 1 mm square. These filaments are not separately controlled, but a pair is provided with a variable electrostatic focus. The tube provides an ingenious use of vacuum-tight washers, without resort to grease, wax, or sealing compounds, except for the greased target cone.

CHAPTER 3

HIGH-VOLTAGE EQUIPMENT

Of the various methods of producing the difference of potential across an x-ray tube, the a-c high-voltage transformer is now of greatest practical importance. Static induction machines and induction coils operating on direct current with interrupters were used widely for many years after the discovery of x-rays.

Singularly enough, the principle of the electrostatic generator, supposedly relegated to museums, has been resurrected in the Van de Graaff generator, which has already contributed great impetus to the installation of supervoltage x-ray units as well as to the popular and fertile field of nuclear physics. Besides the transformer and the electrostatic generator, the General Electric resonance transformer, the surge generator for very high speed radiography, and the various supervoltage devices including the betatron, synchrotron, and linear accelerators warrant consideration.

Transformers. Most of the x-ray power units on the market are designed for therapeutic and diagnostic use at voltages up to 400 kv. These commercial machines are all similar in general operation but differ in details of design. They usually include:

A 60-cycle 110- or 220-volt a-c closed-core oil-immersed high-voltage transformer.
A transformer for filament current up to 5 amp at about 12 volts in the x-ray tube and in the rectifying valve.
An autotransformer or resistances for controlling input and thus secondary voltage.
A device for stabilizing and controlling the tube current.
A device for rectifying the alternating high-voltage current, of either a mechanical or an electron-tube type.

The transformer comprises a magnetic core wound with primary and secondary windings. Alternating current supplied to the primary induces in the core a magnetic flux that cuts the secondary winding, thus generating in it an emf proportional to the number of turns. The fundamental equation involved for the induced emf (root mean square), on the assumption of sine-wave form, is $E = (2\pi f/\sqrt{2})\phi N \times 10^{-8}$ volt, where ϕ is the total magnetic-flux lines through the core, N is the number of turns in the winding, and f is the frequency in cycles per second. The core is built up in laminar form from thin sheets of an alloy, usually

43

silicon steel, with high magnetic permeability. Since a radial field between primary and secondary windings represents the most uniform electrical-stress distribution, circular coils are generally used in x-ray transformers. In practically all cases, core and windings are immersed in insulating oil. Recently, however, it has been discovered that the colorless, odorless, nontoxic gas SF_6 can be used very successfully at atmospheric pressure as insulation in therapeutic and diagnostic apparatus, with consequent great advantages over oil in reliability of operation, ease of installation and repair, cleanliness, and vastly decreased weight. The gas, 5.1 times heavier than air, may be poured into a transformer to displace air very simply, and the presence of residual air has little effect on the dielectric strength. Spark-overs do not produce electrically conducting products as they do in oil, freon (CCl_2F_2), and other gases where carbonization occurs. (SF_6 is employed in military diagnostic units operating at 100 kv, 100 ma, full-wave rectification.[1]) Portable units of this type have been in use in the Korean War. The chief disadvantage thus far for SF_6 is the high cost, of the order of $2 per pound, since it is made from elemental fluorine.

The great majority of units operate on single-phase current though three-phase systems are sometimes employed. Engineering problems include proper dimensions for desired loads, insulation within and between coils and of external terminals, cooling, tapping and grounding of the secondary, capacitance effects and screening, and combination with condensers for constant potential. Ordinarily the transformer is earthed at the center in the case that the x-ray tubes are operated with both ends at high potential, or at one end, especially when the anode of the tube is cooled by water from city mains. Complete details and specifications of transformer design are supplied by manufacturers or illustrated in suitable texts.[2]

Rectifiers. The x-ray tube is a device that can operate successfully only with a unidirectional electric current, *i.e.*, with the target serving as the anode and the filament as the cathode. However, an end of the secondary winding of the high-voltage transformer is oscillatory between $+V$ and $-V$, so that each electrode in the x-ray tube connected with this secondary will be at negative potential half of the time and at positive potential the other half. In order to ensure that electrons will flow only from negative filament to positive target, the current must be rectified in the x-ray tube itself or by auxiliary mechanical or electron-tube rectifiers. In half-wave rectification, current flows only during the half time when the filament is negative and the target positive, the inverse wave being suppressed. In full-wave rectification the total energy is

[1] M. J. Gross, *Am. J. Roentgenol. Radium Therapy,* **65,** 103 (1950).

[2] Sarsfield, "Electrical Engineering in Radiology," Instrument Publishing Company, 1936.

utilized, the terminals of the secondary being connected alternately to opposite ends of the x-ray tube in synchronism with the alternations of the current.

Mechanical Type. The mechanical full-wave rectifiers are crossarm arrangements revolving on the shaft of the a-c generator or driven by a synchronous motor. This rotating switch connects the terminals of the secondary alternately to opposite ends of the x-ray tube in synchronism with the alternations of the current. Only a portion of the top of these waves is applied to the x-ray tube, since the contacts are intermittent. The tube is therefore excited by pulses which are alike, as illustrated in Fig. 22. The mechanical rectifier has the advantage of ruggedness and adjustment so as to pick off any position of the voltage sine wave. It has the disadvantage of noise, moving parts, and electrical disturbances. Although some mechanically rectified units are still in operation and continue to give satisfactory service, further consideration need not be given them in view of the overwhelming preference for the electron-tube valve, especially since these have become far less fragile than the early models.

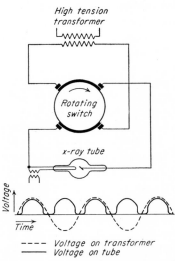

FIG. 22. High-voltage circuit and wave form with mechanical rectifier.

Valve-tube Type. This electron-tube rectifier is a vacuum tube operating on the same principle as the x-ray tube. In the original Coolidge Kenotron, shown in modern form in Fig. 23, a tungsten-wire filament is

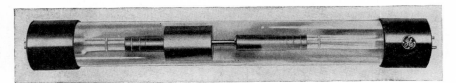

FIG. 23. Electron valve-tube rectifier (Kenotron). (*General Electric.*)

at the center of a coaxial cylinder of sheet molybdenum. The filament is heated by a current from step-down transformers. Current passes through the valve, of course, in one direction only, since the hot wire is the only source of electrons. During the time of flow of current from hot cathode to anode, a difference of potential of only a few hundred volts at the most is required to overcome the space charge that develops around the filament owing to the emission of electrons. During the other half period when the cathode is positively and the anode negatively charged, the entire difference of potential on the x-ray tube is impressed on the valve tube, so that it must be constructed to withstand this.

One of the chief dangers of the valve tube is the generation of x-rays when operated beyond the saturation point defined by the equation

$$V = AI^{\frac{2}{3}}\left(1 + \frac{BI}{I_s - I}\right)$$

where V is the voltage, I is the current, I_s is the saturation current, and A and B are constants for particular valve and filament temperature (about 1000°C). If the anode becomes hot, this is an indication that extensive power is being dissipated.

In another type the filament consists of three or more hairpin loops of wire, and the anode is a cup or disk. The filament heating current is 7.8 to 8.2 amp at 12 to 14 volts, and such a tube passes a current of 300 to 400 ma. In most installations today valve tubes are oil-immersed in the same tank as the transformer itself or in a separate tank. Thus tubes of small dimensions may be used because of cooling and electrical insulation in the oil. A value tube 22 in. long for operation in air and one 14 in. long, oil-immersed, may have the same ratings, as the typical data in Table 3-1 show.

TABLE 3-1. RATINGS OF 14-IN. OIL-IMMERSED VALVE TUBE

Filament volts	Approximate filament current, amp	Maximum peak voltage, inverse	Maximum d-c load, ma	Time
12.00	11.8	140,000	30	Continuous
13.00	12.4	120,000	100	Continuous
14.00	13.0	120,000	300	Discontinuous
15.00	13.5	120,000	500	Discontinuous
16.00	14.0	120,000	1000	Discontinuous

A still later development is the successful use of thoriated-tungsten filaments (tungsten wire covered with a monatomic layer of metallic thorium) in very small valve tubes.

Thoriated-tungsten filaments have been in widespread use for low-voltage tubes for many years. By the addition of the carbonization process, which produces tungsten carbide on the surface as the reducing agent for thorium dispersed throughout the wire, they are used successfully at several thousand volts. The generally accepted view as recently as 1941 was that 5,000 volts was the maximum voltage for a thoriated-tungsten filament. Today, it is well known that during World War II the demands of radar and other electronic equipment raised the ceiling for thoriated carbonized-tungsten filaments to 35,000 volts. This led in 1947 to the development of a very small tube primarily intended for the x-ray diagnostic application which would require a maximum of 110 kv and 250 ma from a full-wave bridge rectifier with four rectifier tubes. The valve tube developed has a 25-watt thoriated-tungsten filament in place of the 125 watts required by the pure-tungsten-filament valves now used in the x-ray industry.

With lower work function, an emitter of thorium on tungsten as provided by a thoriated-tungsten filament gives a much greater electron emission at a lower operating temperature range of 1800 to 2200°K as compared with the 2200 to 2600°K range for pure tungsten. Expressing the efficiency of emission in milliamperes per watt, 30 to 40 ma/watt can be obtained with a life of 2,000 hr from a thoriated-tungsten filament. In comparison, a pure-tungsten filament is limited to 10 ma/watt, even with as little as 250 hr life. At 5 ma/watt, the thoriated-tungsten filament has a life potential in excess of 50,000 hr.

For high-voltage testing and for developmental work in nucleonics, x-rays, and such industrial applications as food processing on an intermittent or continuous basis, cascade rectifiers are particularly suitable. The standard basic unit is rated 125 kv, 30 ma and consists of an oil-filled tank containing the rectifier and another containing the resistance voltage divider. Up to eight standard units can be stacked, one above the other, giving voltages up to 1,000 kv.

Another high-voltage rectifier, which has come into use especially in Great Britain and is distinguished by both ruggedness and absence of moving parts, employs copper oxide film rectifier units connected in series and immersed in oil.

Circuits. Numerous types of circuit involving transformers and valve-tube rectifiers with auxiliary equipment are employed for various x-ray purposes. Some of the more important may be listed as follows:

Self-rectifying Coolidge-type X-ray Tube. This circuit has half-wave rectification; it is for diffraction and other equipment up to 60 kv where loss in power is not so important as simplicity and economy (Fig. 24).

Single-valve Half-wave Rectification. This circuit with or without condensers gives impulses; it is for use with gas- or ion-type tubes up to 80 kv primarily (Fig. 25).

Full-wave Rectification. The Gratz Circuit. This circuit employs four valves, as shown in Fig. 26. When q, one end of the secondary winding, is negative and p is positive, electrons will flow from q through valve 2, the x-ray tube, and then through valve 1 to p; when p is negative, the electrons will flow through valve 4, the x-ray tube, through valve 3 and then to q.† Thus the continually changing transformer current reaches

---

† It should be remembered that in electrical engineering practice the current is opposite in direction to the flow of electrons; thus when p is positive, the current is described as flowing from p, through valve 1, the x-ray tube, and valve 2 to q.

the x-ray tube so as to flow in one direction. This circuit has the disadvantage that two valves always must sustain the full transformer voltage.

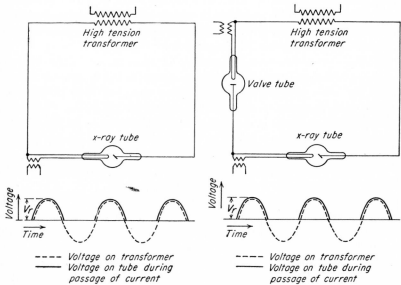

Fig. 24. Circuit and wave form for self-rectifying x-ray tube (half-wave).

Fig. 25. Circuit and wave form with one valve tube (half-wave).

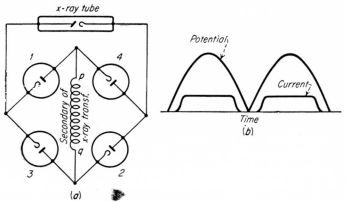

Fig. 26. (a) Gratz circuit for four-valve whole-wave rectification.   (b) Tube potential and current wave forms.

Other full-wave circuits are the potentiometer, in which the x-ray tube is excited at half the transformer voltage; and the Deman, which employs a valve, between one pole of the secondary and anode of the x-ray tube, and a condenser connected between the center of the transformer and the tube anode.

Voltage-multiplying Circuits. (1) In the Villard circuit (Fig. 27) the transformer secondary is connected to the x-ray tube through two condensers, one at each pole. Across the x-ray tube in opposition is one

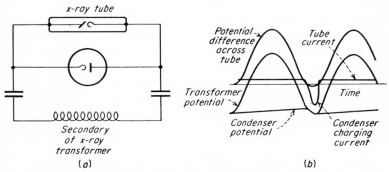

FIG. 27. Villard voltage-multiplying circuit (*a*), with wave forms (*b*).

valve. The sum of condenser voltages is alternately supplemented and reduced by transformer voltage so that the potential across the tube varies from $2V$ to 0. (2) The Witka circuit is similar except that it has two valves and two condensers so arranged as to treble the voltage. Each condenser is charged to the full voltage of the transformer during a half period. During the following half period, the valves are nonconducting, and the condensers are thrown in series with the transformer to make the potential across the x-ray tube three times that of the transformer. (3) The Greinacher constant-potential circuit is the best-known circuit that combines voltage multiplying with a constant potential (Fig. 28).

If two opposed valves are connected to the end of the transformer secondary whose potential is oscillating between $+V$ and $-V$, then the total difference of potential across the plates of the condenser and the terminals of the x-ray tube will be $+V - (-V) = 2V$. The rectifiers must be able to withstand this voltage.

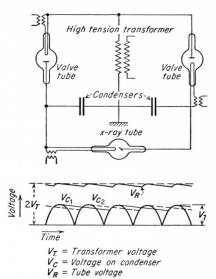

V_T = Transformer voltage
V_C = Voltage on condenser
V_R = Tube voltage

FIG. 28. Greinacher voltage-multiplying, constant-potential circuit with two valve tubes.

Cascade Circuits. The Greinacher circuit is especially well adapted to the plan of cascading a number of similar units so as to obtain any desired

supervoltage.   Various combinations with mid-point or one end earthed
have been described.   Figure 29 shows a 300-kv cascade circuit built up
from three 50-kv units.   Many American supervoltage installations up
to 1 million volts are of this type.

The Van de Graaff Generator.   As previously indicated, the old
principle of the electrostatic machine has reappeared in the newest supervoltage installations as the Van de Graaff generator, which has proved so
successful for therapy and for research in physics.   In the first unit constructed, a system of moving belts conveyed an electric charge to collecting spherical terminals, which were 15 ft in diameter.   The belt material
was electrical insulation paper, about 4 ft in width.   The charge as
sprayed on the belt from a system of corona wires was removed from the

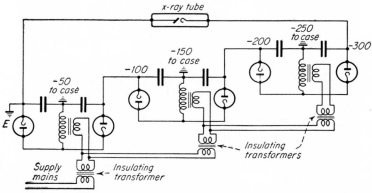

Fig. 29. 300-kv cascade circuit using three 50-kv transformers and three insulating transformers. (The figures indicate kilovoltages with respect to earth at various points.)

ascending belt inside the terminal by a collector connected to an insulated
upper frame.   As the voltage of this frame increased owing to collector
current, corona was produced at the upper spray wire and a charge of
opposite sign was deposited on the descending belt.   A difference of
potential between two generator terminals, one positive and one negative,
could therefore reach 5 to 6 Mv and provide a maximum current of 2 ma
for the x-ray tube or any other type of accelerating tube.

It should be noted that this generator produces constant-potential
direct current (requiring no rectifiers).

No high-voltage engineering development has been more useful, however, than the reduction in size of the early Van de Graaff 1-million-volt
generator requiring an entire hangarlike building to a 2-million-volt
generator in a mobile compact head which also contains the x-ray tube.
This new unit, developed under the direction of Prof. J. G. Trump of the
Massachusetts Institute of Technology by the High Voltage Engineering
Corporation of Cambridge, Mass., especially for deep therapy, is illustrated in Fig. 30.   The weight of the generator unit is less than 2,000 lb.

The secret of these small dimensions is the use of nitrogen at 27 atm (400 psi) as the gas insulation. The steady d-c high voltage is maintained by a natural balance between the controllable current brought to the high-voltage terminal by the rapidly moving insulating belt and the currents down the x-ray tube and generator column. This column is divided into a series of equipotential planes, and the terminal potential is distributed uniformly along this column and the tube, in which electrons from the cathode are accelerated smoothly in a uniform electric field. A

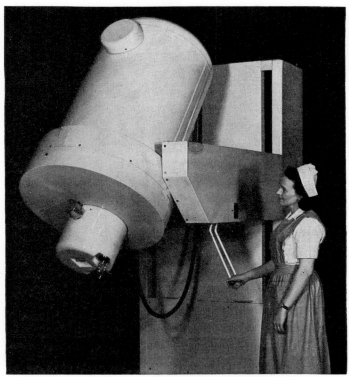

Fig. 30. 2,000-kv Van de Graaff generator for hospital use.

small transformer rectifier which supplies the belt charge by a corona-spray method is inside the pressure region. The generator voltage is brought to any equilibrium value by regulating the corona-spray voltage from a control panel. There are no resonance conditions or other difficult adjustments whatever in the operation of this unit. The current in the x-ray tube is normally 0.25 ma. Even with this apparently small value the x-ray intensity with a filtration equivalent to 9 mm of lead is 200 r/min (unit of dosage defined in Chap. 4) at 50 cm distance. The beam of x-rays transmitted through the water-cooled gold target at the end of the tube may be directed as desired by orientation of the whole generator on its suspending support.   A 10-million-volt unit of this type will soon be available for supervoltage x-ray and cathode-ray studies.   The properties of x-rays generated at these high voltages are discussed in connection with industrial radiography and deep therapy in Chaps. 9 and 12.

The General Electric Resonance Transformer.   This transformer utilizes a new principle and embodies a resonant system tuned to a frequency three times that of the supply; thus in the case of 60-cycle power

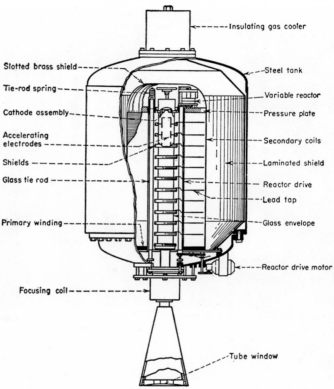

Fig. 31. Sectional drawing of 1,000-kv resonance transformer unit.   (*General   Electric.*) This may be used to operate a cathode-ray tube (shown in figure), or an x-ray tube with thin gold transmission target replacing tube window.

service the transformer will operate at 180 cycles, which frequency is obtained by means of a phase-reducing frequency-tripling transformer device connected to a three-phase power service.   The transformer does not have a core through the coils, and the space usually occupied by the core is occupied by the x-ray tube.   The only transformer iron used in the transformer is placed outside the coils and just inside the wall of the cylindrical steel tank.   Because of the absence of iron in the transformer and also because a gas is used for insulation instead of the usual transformer oil, the construction is exceptionally light in weight in comparison with its capacity. One hundred pounds of gas, usually freon (1,2-dichlorodifluoromethane, CCl_2F_2), at 60 psi performs the insulating function of 6 tons of oil. More recently SF_6 has proved to be an even more effective dielectric at similar pressures in high-voltage apparatus[1] and at atmospheric pressure in 100-kv or lower-voltage transformers as described on page 44. The 1,000-kv transformer, which is shown in a sectional drawing in Fig. 31, is housed within a cylindrical steel tank approximately

FIG. 32. 2,000-kv unit with resonance transformer. (*General Electric.*)

3 ft in diameter and 4 ft in length with the extension chamber of the x-ray tube projecting from the bottom. The 2,000-kv unit is larger but still is constructed so that it is mobile and thus permits adjustment of the x-ray tube in any direction (Fig. 32).

The x-ray tube is a multisection tube (Fig. 8) and operates with the anode at ground potential. The tube is located at the center of the tank, inside the secondary coils of the high-voltage transformer, and the anode end projects through the bottom as shown in Fig. 31. Many of these units are in operation in hospitals for cancer therapy and in industry for radiography of thick sections (see Chap. 9).

The Surge Generator. In the preceding chapter an x-ray tube was described which employed cold-cathode field emission and produced x-ray

[1] H. Camilla and J. J. Chapman, *Trans. AIEE*, **66**, 1463 (1947).

pulses of such intensity that radiographic exposures of the order of 1/1,000,000 sec were possible. Development of the high currents in the x-ray tube requires a large but brief rate of power flow. During the period of peak operation the amount of power flowing to the tube is of the order of 600,000 kw, of course for only microseconds. Such a requirement is fulfilled by a surge generator such as is commonly used for simulated-lightning studies. This unit as designed and built by Westinghouse is illustrated in Fig. 33. Without attempting to describe the circuit in detail it may be said that six 0.04-μf condensers are arranged in a Marx circuit. Each condenser can be charged to a potential of 50 kv,

FIG. 33. Surge generator (Marx circuit) for operation of high-intensity field-emission tube (Fig. 18). (*Westinghouse.*)

thereby resulting in an output potential of 300 kv across the x-ray tube (shown at the right of the figure, with stabilizing resistors). The condensers are arranged to be charged in parallel through 10,000 ohms resistance so that on discharge in series through sphere gaps no appreciable loss of energy in the resistor occurs. When the condensers have been fully charged, an impulse is sent from a timing unit through the primary of the triggering transformer. The pulse is supplied by a condenser which is caused to discharge by removing the negative bias on the grid of a thyratron. The triggering is done by either making or breaking a contact. The pulse delivered to the circuit by the secondary of the triggering transformer causes the gap between ground and another condenser to break down, which results in the breakdown of another condenser and the immediate discharge of all the condensers at a voltage on the x-ray tube equal to six times the charging voltage on the condensers. The x-ray tube then operates as explained in the previous chapter. The applications of high-speed radiography made possible by this unit, including those to the science of ballistics, are indicated in Chap. 9.

The Betatron. In the preceding chapter, a description was given of the betatron "donut," which serves as the x-ray tube for generating

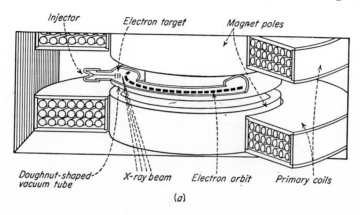

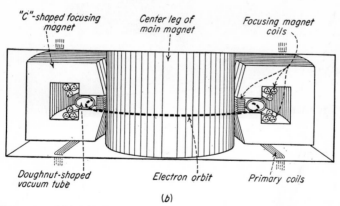

Fig. 34. Diagrams of (a) 24-million-volt and (b) 340-million-volt betatrons. (*University of Illinois.*)

x-rays from 5 million volts up to the 350-million-volt unit now in operation. It is here the purpose to consider briefly the generating unit of the betatron, which is diagrammatically represented for the 24-million- and 340-million-volt units in Fig. 34. Actually, the evacuated donut is the secondary of a high-voltage step-up transformer in the place of the usual coils of wire. This is inserted between the halves of a magnet constructed from silicon-steel sheets. Each coil develops about 6,600 volts in the 24-million-volt betatron. The core of each coil is a pole, shaped to produce the magnetic-field variation necessary to permit both accelerating the electrons and maintaining them in the same orbit in the vacuum-tube donut between these pole faces. The machine is powered by a frequency-tripling transformer (180 cps), and the commercial 24-million-volt unit operates at 30 kw. Electrons from a heated filament are injected into the donut tangentially with such an energy at 60,000 volts that the natural curvature of their trajectory keeps many of them within the donut, while focusing and amplitude-damping forces act to keep them confined to the neighborhood of the equilibrium orbit. These electrons

FIG. 35. Dr. D. W. Kerst with 2.5- and 24-million-volt betatrons.

are then accelerated, gaining about 70 volts/revolution and making 330,000 revolutions before a time is reached at which the equilibrium conditions are disturbed in such a way that the electrons circling the donut in pulses intercept the pinpoint target (0.005 by 0.010 in.), which defines the fine focal spot. Figure 35 depicts Prof. D. W. Kerst with the original 2.5-million-volt and the first 24-million-volt unit, the latter serving as the prototype of the commercial (Allis-Chalmers) betatron, used for research, radiography of thick metal specimens,[1] and cancer therapy. A new 10-million-volt unit produced by the General Electric Company, which may be mounted on a yoke and made mobile as in the case of the x-ray-generating units in Figs. 30 and 32, is illustrated in Fig. 36. Improvements in design resulting in much greater efficiency in

[1] G. D. Adams, Radiography with the Betatron, *Ind. Radiog.*, **14** (3), 23 (1946).

Fig. 36. Ten-million-volt industrial betatron with magnet and donut assembly lifted out of case with round x-ray beam port in side. (*General Electric.*)

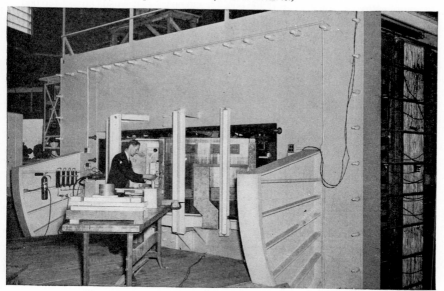

Fig. 37. University of Illinois 340-million-volt betatron.

use of power and reduction in dimensions were first introduced in 1948 in an 80-million-volt unit at the University of Illinois, built by Kerst and associates, as a model for the 340-million-volt unit pictured in Fig. 37, which was completed in 1950. The uncut center leg of the main magnet produces the electron acceleration, while separate C magnets, through the points of which the donut tube passes, produce a circular magnetic

TABLE 3-2. UNIVERSITY OF ILLINOIS BETATRONS

Year in operation	1940	1941	1948	1950
Energy, volts	$2\frac{1}{2}$ million	24 million	80 million	340 million
Uses	Research	Industry Medicine Research	Research	Research
Produces	X-rays	X-rays Electron beam	X-rays	X-rays
Main magnet:				
Length	19 in.	5 ft	5 ft	23 ft
Height	10 in.	3 ft	3 ft	13 ft
Thickness	8 in.	$1\frac{1}{2}$ ft	$1\frac{1}{3}$ ft	$6\frac{1}{4}$ ft
Weight	200 lb	4 tons	4 tons	400 tons
Diameter of vacuum tube	8 in.	19 in.	23 in.	9 ft
Cross section of tube	1×2 in.	$2\frac{1}{2} \times 3$ in.	$1 \times 2\frac{1}{4}$ in.	6×10 in.
Pulsations per second	600	180	1 in 3 sec	6
Speed of electrons, per cent of light speed	98	99.97	99.998	99.99986
Electron travel, miles	60	250	650	650
Interval of travel, sec	0.0004	0.001	0.004	0.004
Revolutions by electrons	200,000	330,000	650,000	140,000
Injector energy, volts	1,500	60,000	40,000	100,000
Average energy gain per turn, volts	25	90	200	3,000
Volts output per pole-face inch	250,000	1,250,000	3,300,000	3,000,000
Power consumption, kw	5	30	3	170

field which controls the orbit. In Table 3-2 are compared the characteristics of the 2.5-, 24-, 80-, and 340-million-volt betatrons at the University of Illinois. The unique features and medical and industrial applications of x-rays generated by the betatron are described in Chaps. 8 and 9. References to the publications on the theory, design, and operation of the betatron by Kerst and associates are given in the footnote.[1]

[1] D. W. Kerst et al., Phys. Rev., **60**, 47, 53, 58 (1941), **74**, 503 (1948); Rev. Sci. Instr., **13**, 387 (1942), **21**, 462 (1952), **18**, 681, 799 (1947); Radiology, **40**, 120 (1943); Natl. Nuclear Energy Ser. V, No. 3, Phys. and Chem. Techniques, p. 169 (1952). See also latest contributions from other laboratories: Fawcett and Crittenden, Rev. Sci. Instr., **21**, 935 (1950); Widerse, J. Appl. Phys., **22**, 362 (1951); Davis, Rev. Sci. Instr., **21**, 971 (1950). Many details of instruments and results remain unpublished as classified security information.

The Synchrotron. A more recent principle for an accelerator is that of the synchrotron (MacMillan, 1945; Veksler, 1945; Oliphant and associates, 1947).[1] Like the betatron it accelerates electrons in a circular orbit to which they are constrained by a guiding magnetic field at right angles to the plane in which they move. During each revolution the electron passes through a r-f field which has an electric component tangential to the orbit. The electrons passing through this field during the favorable part of the r-f cycle will receive a small increase in energy. To maintain the orbit radius constant, the guiding magnetic field must increase at the same rate as the particle energy. Thus in a synchrotron an annular chamber, or donut, is placed between the poles of an a-c magnet, and electrons are accelerated during a quarter of the a-c cycle. The essential

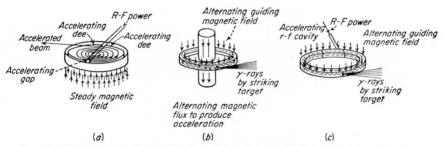

Fig. 38. Diagrams of cyclic accelerators: (a) cyclotron; (b) betatron; (c) synchrotron.

differences between the cyclotron, betatron, and synchrotron are illustrated in Fig. 38. For the betatron the guiding field is still required, and in addition an iron core is necessary to carry the flux providing the induction field acting on the electrons. The obvious advantage of the synchrotron is smaller size and weight, permitting greater flexibility in mounting as a clinical instrument. A number of units even up to 1 billion electron volts (Bev) have been or are being built, particularly in England and America, since the principle has been thoroughly tested.[2] A 335-Mev synchrotron[3] is in successful operation at Berkeley, Calif., and with x-rays from electrons of this energy the production of mesons was discovered.

The Microwave Linear Electron Accelerator. This device was first suggested in 1929 as a possible device in which an electron while traveling in a straight-line path may obtain an energy corresponding to many times x electron volts but without the use of a potential difference greater

[1] MacMillan, *Phys. Rev.*, **68**, 143 (1945); Veksler, *J. Phys. (USSR)*, **9**, 153 (1945); Oliphant, Gooden, and Hide, *Proc. Phys. Soc. (London)*, **59**, 666 (1947).

[2] D. W. Fry, The Synchrotron Accelerator—Its Potentialities as a Generator of X-rays and Electrons of 10–50 Mev Energies for Medical Use, *Brit. J. Radiol.*, **22**, 462 (1949).

[3] G. F. Chew and B. J. Moyer, *Am. J. Phys.*, **18**, 125 (1950).

than x volts. Essentially the electrons (or positive ions) pass through a series of cylindrical electrodes (gaps) connected to a source of high-frequency alternating voltage. The prohibitive length of the system was actually the motivating cause of the invention of the cyclotron by Lawrence. However, the wartime development of high-power pulsed magnetrons and other microwave techniques has led to successful construction of linear electron acceleration, especially as a source of x-rays in the range of 3 to 20 Mev which is compact and silent. There are three types, traveling-wave, standing-wave, and multiple-cavity, all dependent on either propagation or storage of electromagnetic energy in the form of high-power radio waves of wavelength about 10 cm. The electromagnetic field associated with this energy must have a component of electric field in the direction along which acceleration is required. Attention here will be limited to the traveling-wave accelerator, which is thus far the most promising and simple. It consists of a special wave guide, or cylindrical tube, through which are passed simultaneously a beam of electrons from a gun and a progressive electromagnetic wave having an axial electric field. The wave with this axial field is made by the wave guide to travel at the same velocity as the electrons, which will therefore gain energy from the wave as they travel together down the tube. The velocity of the electrons and hence of the wave will increase and approach the velocity of light. Only those electrons which are on or slightly in front of the crest of the wave will be accelerated all the way, after the fashion of a surf rider gaining energy from a sea wave. Rapid experimental progress is being made in the United States and in England toward the development of a satisfactory medical unit less than 8 m long which may be flexibly mounted. A successful unit is already in operation at Stanford University. An excellent account of the theory and design of linear accelerators is given by Newberry.[1] In the period 1950 to 1953 several papers have indicated experimental progress in France, Australia, Canada, and Germany as well as the United States and England.[2]

Compact X-Ray Sources Utilizing β-Ray Excitation. In Chap. 1 brief mention was made of the possibility of utilizing β-rays emitted by some of the radioisotopes produced artificially in cyclotrons and piles to excite x-rays by target bombardment, thus permitting an extremely compact or "pocket-size" combined x-ray tube and generator. Such a process is to be clearly distinguished from the emission of γ-rays in another radioactive mechanism. The x-rays so generated have some marked advantages over γ-rays in radiography, absorptiometry, and other applications.

In 1954, L. Reiffel of the Armour Research Foundation developed this method of producing a practically monoenergetic K-line x-radiation by β-ray bombardment of a suitable target such as lead. The β-ray emitter

[1] G. R. Newberry, *Brit. J. Radiol.*, **22**, 473 (1949).
[2] Listed in *Chemical Abstracts Indices* under Accelerators.

can be a radioisotope of long half-life (for example, strontium 90–yttrium 90, half-life 25 years with a rather energetic β-radiation of 2.2 Mev), or a number of emitters covering a range of half-lives and energies, and thus of characteristics of the x-ray beam. A small chamber (diameter 0.1 in.) constructed with thin lead walls acting as transmission target to contain 20 or more millicuries of strontium 90 may serve as the source of radiation, 75 per cent of which is lead K-radiation. The characteristic x-rays may be "turned off" by replacing the heavy metal with plastic or metal of low atomic number, leaving only a very weak and easily absorbed "bremsstrahlung" or general radiation (see Chap. 6). Radiographs of very satisfactory density and contrast have been photographed in 75 sec with a 20-millicurie source containing 49 mg of carrier-free strontium 90. Another possible application is spectroscopic identification of elements (see Chap. 7) by excitation of characteristic x-ray lines, directly by the β-rays or as secondary fluorescent rays by the primary x-rays generated in one of these compact units.

Electrical Measurements. Tube current is, of course, measured by the milliammeter, a moving-coil galvanometer with a permanent magnetic field. Since dosage is often based on its reading, it is essential that it be a good instrument and well protected. It may be placed, properly screened against corona, in the high-voltage circuit in any position except between the filament transformer and the tube, or it may be placed in the earthed part of the tube circuit and thus mounted in the control board.

The various methods of determining the peak or effective voltages applied to the x-ray tube are as follows:

1. Voltmeter reading of the transformer primary with known transformation ratio, a method accurate only with constant-potential apparatus.

2. Sphere gap, the method most commonly used and the simplest, but giving only very approximate readings.

3. Electrostatic voltmeter. One type consists of large balls charged with high voltage and small balls on a bifilar suspension turning in the electrostatic field. This instrument requires calibration and is then very satisfactory, as a measure not only of the voltage but also of the constancy of the potential.

4. Measurement by ammeter of the current through a very high known resistance, 10 million ohms, for example.

5. Spectrometric method. This consists in determining the shortest wavelength in the spectrum of a beam of x-rays reflected from a crystal of known planar spacing, and substitution of this value in the very accurate quantum equation $V = hc/e\lambda$, where V is the voltage (peak), e, h, and c are constants (respectively, the charge of the electron, the Planck action constant, and the velocity of light, so that $hc/e = 12,400$), and λ is the short-wavelength limit of the spectrum. This method is extremely accurate but, of course, requires special equipment and skilled technique.

6. Generating voltmeter, consisting of a simple armature rotating in an electrostatic field and a galvanometer for measuring the generated current.

7. Tapped condenser and oscillograph. The oscillograph strip is energized by currents in the plate circuit of a valve, the grid of which is connected to an appropriate tap from a capacitive voltage divider.

8. Condenser charging current. A condenser in series with a valve and ballistic milliammeter is connected across the x-ray tube whose voltage e is to be measured from $e = it/c$, where i is milliamperes, t is seconds, and c is microfarads, the known capacity of the condenser.

9. Tapped resistance method. Voltage is directly measured by a voltmeter connected across a tap in a high resistance.

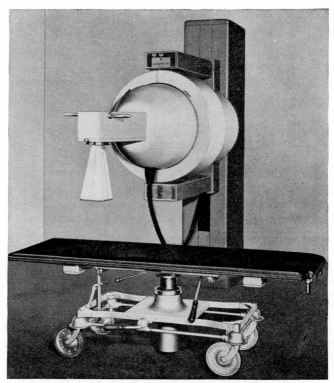

FIG. 39. Maxitron 250 therapy unit. (*General Electric.*)

10. Secondary tapping, a direct voltage measurement by means of a tapping taken from a part of the transformer secondary winding near to earth, the number of turns being in a simple ratio to the total number.

Electrical Precautions. Proper installation of x-ray equipment involves adequate protection for the operator both from the high-voltage electrical power plant and leads and from the x-rays themselves. The following are recommended electrical precautions:

1. Wooden, cork, or rubber floors or coverings.
2. High-voltage leads concealed in an assembled unit with outside grounded; for exterior leads, preferably metal tubes or rods or tightly stretched insulated wire, suspended at a proper distance from floor and ceiling and screened from operator and patient.
3. Efficient earthing of all metal parts.

4. Safety switches, warning lights or signals, and fuses no heavier than absolutely necessary.

5. Magnetic circuit breakers to break contact with any unexpected surges.

6. Shockproof equipment. One of the best modern developments in commercial medical x-ray equipment has been a shockproof equipment. The x-ray tube is enclosed in the transformer itself with outer grounded and lead-covered cases. The therapy unit, the Maxitron 250, manufactured by the General Electric X-ray Corporation, is pictured in Fig. 39. The resonance transformer already described is enclosed in the rotatable cylinder, from which the end of the x-ray tube with attached treatment cone extends. A mobile adjustable table for the patient undergoing treatment is in position.

Suitable equipment for industrial radiography, including new light-weight portable x-ray machines, is illustrated in Chap. 9. Protective measures to be used against x-rays are considered in Chap. 8.

CHAPTER 4

THE MEASUREMENT OF INTENSITY (DOSAGE)

A beam of x-rays is characterized by two factors, quantity (dosage or intensity) and quality (spectral-energy distribution). The quantity terms dose (exposure) and intensity, though often loosely used interchangeably and expressed in the same unit, the roentgen, are not synonymous. Strictly speaking, the intensity of radiation is the energy carried by the radiation in a unit of time through a small surface perpendicular to the direction of the radiation divided by the area of the surface. In other words, it is the energy flux in the beam and thus applies to the output of generators. It can be expressed in ergs per square centimeter per second or watts per square centimeter. The dose (exposure), which usually refers especially to radiotherapeutics, involves the intensity of x-rays *and* the duration of application. It refers to the energy absorbed in any particular region of a specimen and can be expressed in ergs per gram or joules per gram. Thus the intensity is a dose rate. Since there is often confusion concerning the significance of these terms, it should be clearly understood that both dose and intensity are properties of the radiation only. The number of units of quantity (this unit is defined on page 74) is a partial description of the x-rays at the place where it is measured or calculated. It tells nothing about what happens to the radiation or about what effects it produces. It tells nothing about the material it penetrates.[1] Certain physical, chemical, or biological effects of x-rays may be utilized for measurement of these defining factors. The measurement of intensity and dosage to be considered in this chapter can be accomplished by evaluating such x-ray properties as ionizing air and other gases, reducing silver bromide in a photographic emulsion to silver, exciting various chemical compounds to luminescence, and several other methods.

Heat Methods. If a small beam of x-rays be allowed to impinge upon a metal block of such size that practically complete absorption of the beam occurs (97 per cent or more), the net effect of the absorption will be an increase in the heat content of the block. That is, essentially all secondary rays, photoelectrons, etc., are absorbed in the block, and their

---

[1] O. Glasser, E. H. Quimby, L. S. Taylor, and J. L. Weatherwax, "Physical Foundations of Radiology," 2d ed., Chap. XI, p. 179, Paul B. Hoeber, Inc., New York, 1952.

energy is converted into heat. This fact is the basis of possible methods of determining accurately the total energy content of an x-ray beam. Such methods have been used to study the distribution of energy in the x-ray spectrum, the dependence of intensity upon the potential on the x-ray tube and upon the current through the tube, the relation between the energy input to the tube and the x-ray energy produced, the relation between energy, wavelength, and ionization, and the relation between energy and photographic darkening.

The instruments employed generally consist of two elements, one heated by x-rays and one by electricity, which are balanced, by several different methods, against each other; the electric-energy input is measured directly and, since the heat effects in the two elements are the same, is equal, after the instrumental corrections have been applied, to the x-ray-energy input.

Many years ago Terrill used the method to determine the total energy of x-rays from a tungsten-target tube excited by constant-potential direct current at 30 to 100 kv. The total output of the tube was thus found to be 0.00025 to 0.00192 times the input. Plotted against the square of the voltage, these values give a straight line to 69.3 kv, where a change of slope occurs, probably due to the selective absorption of the target itself.

All these heat-measuring devices require the most careful construction and manipulation, the chances of experimental error being very great as the measured effects are usually very small; hence they are not available for routine intensity measurements.

A highly quantitative calorimetric evaluation of the unit of intensity, the roentgen, for 400-kv and 22.5-Mev x-rays has been recently made at the University of Illinois College of Medicine.[1] With greatly improved equipment, including thermistors (ceramic semiconductors) for sensitive temperature measurements, absorbing cylinders in the calorimeter, and special amplifier circuits to register unbalance in a d-c bridge, the extremely difficult problem involved in the inadequacies of ionization measurements for high-energy radiation was successfully solved. Moreover, this absolute method of energy measurement has been indispensable in the supervoltage (20-Mev) range of radiation, where other methods, primarily designed for evaluating intensities of radiation excited at much lower energies, fail.

Ionization. When the x-rays pass through the gas, they liberate photoelectrons; they excite those characteristic radiations of the gas whose critical absorption frequencies are less than the frequency of the incident x-ray beam; they produce scattered radiation of the frequency of the incident beam; and they may produce recoil electrons and the accompanying secondary radiation (Compton effect).

[1] J. S. Laughlin, J. W. Beattie, W. J. Henderson, and R. A. Harvey, *Am. J. Roentgenol. Radium Therapy Nuclear Med.*, **70**, 294 (1953).

Mechanism of Ionization. The mechanism of ionization is now agreed to be as follows: The high-speed photoelectrons released by the x-ray beam have too much kinetic energy to be at once absorbed by adjacent molecules, and they consequently break down the molecules with which they come in contact into pairs of ions. The energy necessary for the production of one pair of ions in air, expressed as the number of volts necessary to impart to a single electron a kinetic energy equal to the energy in question, is 33 volts. Thus they progressively dissipate their kinetic energy until it becomes so small that the electron is absorbed either by a molecule to form a negative ion or by a positive ion to cause neutralization. All this was excellently shown by the experiments of

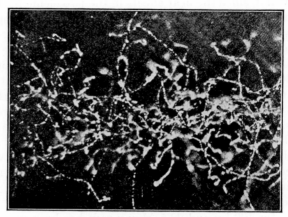

Fig. 40. Tracks of β-rays liberated in gas by x-rays.

C. T. R. Wilson, who, by condensing water on the ions at the moment of formation and simultaneously photographing them, was able to obtain actual photographic records of the paths of the photoelectrons. One of Wilson's photographs is reproduced in Fig. 40. Recoil, or Compton, electrons in addition to photoelectrons are excited by rays of shorter wavelength; these electrons, though having little ionizing power, absorb much of the energy in the x-ray beam.

Ionization in Different Gases. Table 4-1, which lists values of relative ionization produced in various gases, shows that those which contain a heavy atom are most effective in producing large and easily measured ionization currents.

Measurement of Ionization. Ionization experiments are usually conducted so that the ionization is measured by the electric current passing through the ionized gas, under a definite potential difference. The gas is held in an ionization chamber between two electrodes which are connected to the source of electric potential. It is essential that this voltage should be high enough to produce a saturation current, *i.e.*, to draw all

TABLE 4-1. RELATIVE IONIZATION PRODUCED IN VARIOUS GASES BY
HETEROGENEOUS X-RAYS

Gas or vapor	Density relative to air = 1	Ionization relative to air = 1	
		Soft x-rays	Hard x-rays
Hydrogen, H_2	0.07	0.01	0.18
Carbon dioxide, CO_2	1.53	1.57	1.49
Ethyl chloride, C_2H_5Cl	2.24	18.0	17.3
Carbon tetrachloride, CCl_4	5.35	67	71
Nickel carbonyl, $Ni(CO)_4$	5.90	89	97
Ethyl bromide, C_2H_5Br	3.78	72	118
Methyl iodide, CH_3I	4.96	145	125
Mercury methyl, $Hg(CH_3)_2$	7.93	425	

ions produced by the x-rays across to the electrodes. The condition of saturation is recognized by the fact that further increase of the voltage applied to the chamber electrodes causes no further increase in the ionization current. It is also essential that the primary rays whose intensity is being measured shall not be permitted to strike directly on the walls or electrodes of the chamber, since otherwise secondary electrons with their own ionizing effect will be liberated.

Ionization Chambers. Several types of ionization chambers have been designed for the determination of intensities. The pioneer Duane ionization chamber, or iontoquantimeter, was one of especial merit. It consisted simply of a series of aluminum sheets about 5 cm long and 2 cm broad, held parallel to each other and 5 mm apart by hard-rubber frames. Alternate sheets were connected, thus forming a small condenser with layers of air between the sheets. The condenser was joined in a simple electric circuit with a battery and sensitive galvanometer which was calibrated by means of a Weston standard cell and resistance. By comparison of the deflection produced by the known current with the deflection produced by the current from the ionization of air by the x-ray beam in the chamber of known volume, the intensity of the beam in roentgens could be calculated. Glasser at the Cleveland Clinic, Taylor at the National Bureau of Standards, and others have designed large air-ionization chambers for standardization purposes.[1]

Friedrich introduced the use of an ionization chamber made of horn, the chemical elements in which are those found in the body, and containing only 1 cc. This has the advantage that intensities in absolute units may be read on a scale of the deflecting electroscope. Dauvillier devised a spherical gas chamber containing xenon as the absorbing gas. Several

[1] Glasser, Quimby, Taylor, and Weatherwax, *op. cit.*, p. 189.

other similar devices of bakelite, graphite, etc., are manufactured by equipment builders.

An unusually simple and efficient portable instrument is the Victoreen roentgen meter (r-meter) (Fig. 41), consisting of a small ionization chamber with condenser tube which may be connected with a string electrometer, the scale of which is calibrated in international units. The chamber is exposed for 1 min to the rays and again inserted into the socket of the electrometer, and the scale read, the figure being in roentgens per minute. A red plastic thimble chamber is used for ordinary purposes on a 25-r scale, and a black nylon chamber, with a wall thickness of 0.005 in., or

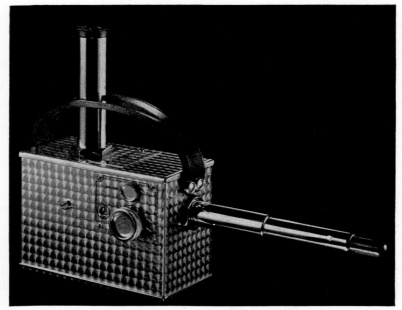

FIG. 41. The Victoreen r-meter for measurement of intensity or dosage.

one-fifth as great, is used particularly for soft x-rays generated at low voltages on a 250-r scale. This instrument also serves readily in all kinds of absorption measurements, including the determination of effective wavelength. Still another instrument, the Iometer, is a constancy meter, the function of which is to indicate continuously any variation from a previously established rate of roentgens per minute. The Integron is a dosimeter of the integrating type designed to measure total treatment dose, for example, at skin surface, and to terminate automatically the treatment by shutting off the power to the x-ray machine. The Proteximeter is a small condenser with integral electrometer designed especially for measurement of very weak radiation as a means of protection of the worker against stray radiation.

Alternatively, by using a properly designed ionization chamber and by recording simply the ionization-chamber current as the index of intensity, the method becomes very valuable for many kinds of work, particularly in analysis of crystal structure by the ionization spectrometer (Chaps. 5 and 14), where only a relative measure of intensity is needed. The ionization chamber should be large enough to absorb the rays completely or nearly completely; the electrodes must not be exposed to the incident rays; a gas of quite heavy molecular weight is most satisfactory, methyl iodide or ethyl bromide being often used.

There are several accepted ways of measuring the current through the ionization chamber. Early experimenters used an electroscope and timed the fall of the leaf. Others used a quadrant or string or vibrating-reed electrometer. Today it is a simple matter with vacuum-tube circuits and electron-multiplier tubes to amplify the current to such a magnitude that it may be measured by a microammeter or other devices. With the advent of the atomic bomb and the development of the atomic-energy program in the United States, there has been a parallel intensive investigation of all types of radiation detector and dosimeter. These have included ionization instruments of decreasing size down to pocket types of fountain-pen dimensions. Representative of several of these is the Tracerlab SV-8 self-reading dosimeter for measurements in the range of 0 to 100 mr, designed to specifications of the Argonne National Laboratory. The wearer may determine exposure at any time simply by looking into the instrument. A simple charging device returns the scale fiber to zero. The SV-8 is less than 30 per cent energy-dependent between 70 kv and 1 Mev and is linear on a voltage basis within 10 per cent. The accuracy is 5 per cent, and the leakage less than 2 mr (milliroentgens)/day.

Ion Chambers, Proportional Counters, and Geiger Counters.[1] Three distinctly different types of counting may be performed with the simple gas-filled tube, comprising a cylindrical cathode and an axially mounted wire anode. If the tube is included in a circuit with a battery to supply the electric field between the electrodes and a resistor to complete the circuit, it behaves as an ionization chamber at relatively low voltages, a proportional counter at intermediate voltages, and a Geiger counter at higher voltages. When the gas is ionized by the passage of x-rays, the charge collected by the electrodes is equal to the original ionization if the tube is operated in the low-voltage ionization-chamber region. In the intermediate-voltage, or proportional-counter, region, the original number of ions may be multiplied 10,000 times by the mechanism of gas amplification. In the Geiger-counter region this amplification factor may

---

[1] From a paper by H. Friedman, *Ind. Radiography Non-Destructive Testing*, **6**, 1 (1947).

reach 10 billion. The three operating regions are illustrated by Fig. 42.

Gas Amplification. At low voltages, the electric field is small, and an electron never acquires sufficient velocity to knock another electron loose from a neutral molecule upon impact. At higher voltages, an electron may be accelerated in the stronger field until it has sufficient velocity to ionize a neutral atom. The newly detached electron is then accelerated, together with the original electron, until they collide with neutral atoms and repeat the ionization process. The secondary electrons join the initial ones in the path of further acceleration, and the process can repeat

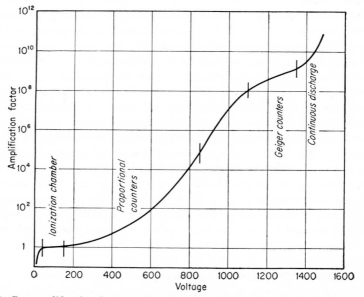

FIG. 42. Gas-amplification factor as function of applied voltage for ionization chamber, proportional and Geiger counters.

itself a thousandfold in the proportional-counting range. This avalanche of cumulative ionization is known as a Townsend avalanche. The electric-field conditions between the wire and cylinder are such that the major part of the multiplication process takes place within a distance of a few wire diameters.

Wherever an electron is formed, there remains a positively charged ion. The positive ions are attracted to the negatively charged cylinder, but since their mass is thousands of times that of an electron, they never attain comparable speeds. In fact, most of the electrons reach the wire in a time of the order of 1/1,000,000 sec, while the positive ions remain virtually stationary in the vicinity of the wire. The positive ions then move slowly out toward the cylinder, where they arrive about 10^{-4} to

10^{-3} sec after the avalanche process has been completed.   If the circuit were not completed by the resistor R, the potential difference across the electrodes would reach its maximum change when the positive ions reached the cylinder.   The resistance R, however, carries away and neutralizes the electrical charges at a rate determined by the rate of arrival of ions, the capacity of the wire system, and the magnitude of the resistance.   The potential difference between the wire and the cylinder finally returns to its initial value in the same manner as a small condenser being charged to the voltage of a battery through a series resistance.

The sequence of events just described is the elementary discharge process.   Two initial electrons would trigger a discharge of twice as many avalanche electrons as one initial electron.   In the proportional-counting region this proportionality between initial ionization and the total discharge current holds true up to amplifications of the order of 10^7 for a few initial ion pairs such as are produced by a low-energy β-ray or photoelectron or 10^4 for the thousands of initial ion pairs produced by an α-particle.

The shape of the amplification vs. voltage curve depends on the type of gas filling.   If hydrogen, helium, neon, argon, or similar gases are employed, the amplification curve becomes extremely steep in the proportional region and requires highly stabilized voltage for reliable operation. Hydrocarbon vapors such as methane, alcohol, and ether exhibit amplification curves with much more gradual slopes, and the voltage-stabilization requirements for operation in the proportional region are much less severe.

The Geiger Counter.   If the voltage across the tube is increased beyond the proportional region, a new multiplication mechanism appears in addition to the elementary avalanche process and the amplification factor can be increased to as to much as 10 billion.

At the higher voltage the electric field in the neighborhood of the wire is not only sufficiently strong to produce ionization impacts between electrons and atoms or molecules but can also accelerate electrons to velocities that enable them to excite light radiation by the gas molecules.   The light quanta have wavelengths in the far-ultraviolet or soft x-ray region and can readily release photoelectrons from the electrodes and from the gas.   The newly released photoelectrons trigger additional Townsend avalanches, which regenerate light quanta and further avalanches in cascade fashion.   The light quanta thereby spread the discharge over the entire length of the tube.

The above multiplication process could go on indefinitely were it not for the accumulation of a large positive-ion space charge, since the slowly moving positive ions barely move at all in the short time it takes the electrons to travel to the wire.   The sheath of space charge about the wire effectively nullifies the original strong electric field close to the wire so that further ionization by electron impact cannot take place.   The discharge then terminates, and the positive ions move to the cylinder, giving rise to a voltage pulse in the same manner as illustrated for the proportional counter.

The slowly moving positive ions limit the pulse-frequency response of the Geiger counter. The de-ionization time in an average tube is about 10^{-3} to 10^{-4} sec, during which time the entire counter tube is insensitive. Maximum rates are generally limited to a few thousand counts per second.

In the proportional-counting region, the discharges are localized, and the space-charge desensitizes the counter only in the neighborhood of the single avalanche. The remainder of the tube remains sensitive, with the result that linearity of response is obtainable at pulse rates 1,000 times greater than the Geiger-counter limit.

The Geiger counter did not come into use for intensity measurements of x-rays until 1940. As a result of the wartime development of the atomic bomb and its attendant intense radioactivity as measured in Japan, the Bikini tests, etc., the Geiger counter has become one of the most familiar of all scientific instruments, even to the layman. Prospectors all over the world are using it to locate new deposits of the all-important element uranium. The Geiger counter is used not only for direct dosage measurements but also for strip-metal gaging, measurement of thin coatings, determination of wall thickness of curved sections from one side, liquid-quantity gaging, and quantitative chemical analysis by absorption (Chap. 8) and as an integral part of the newest x-ray spectrometers for fluorescence chemical analysis (Chap. 7) and diffraction analysis of crystal structure (Chap. 14). In all these applications low intensities require high sensitivity, and wavelengths are such that the rays are more or less completely absorbed.

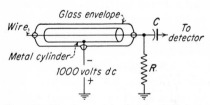

FIG. 43. Fundamental circuit of Geiger counter.

Sullivan[1] and Eisenstein and Gingrich[2] described early designs and uses.

In its simplest form a Geiger counter consists of a coaxial wire and cylinder arrangement as shown in Fig. 43. The electrodes are usually enclosed in a glass envelope containing a suitable gas mixture at a small fraction of atmospheric pressure. The passage of ionizing radiation triggers a momentary discharge and develops a voltage pulse at capacitor C. Following the discharge, the counter recovers quickly to its original condition and is ready to detect the next ionization.

[1] Rev. Sci. Instr., 11, 356 (1940).
[2] Rev. Sci. Instr., 12, 582 (1941).

The characteristic curve of a Geiger counter, in Fig. 44, indicates the number of discharges or counts per second as a function of applied voltage. Up to a minimum voltage, the threshold, no counts are detected.   Above this threshold, the counting rate increases only slightly over a range of 100 volts or more. This region is called the plateau. The upper limit to the plateau is set by the inception of self-sustained discharges. The various curves of Fig. 44 correspond to different intensities of radiation.

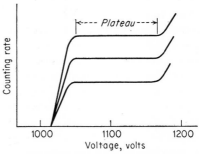

FIG. 44. Geiger-counter plateau curves for various intensities of radiation.

The counter tube employed most commonly is designed for almost complete absorption of the x-ray beam in the gaseous volume.   This is accomplished by filling the counter tube with a high pressure of gas, usually argon or krypton, whose absorption coefficient is large for the x-ray wavelength employed.

The counter tubes are designed to permit passage of the x-rays through a gas path 10 cm in length without striking the electrodes.   A photograph of a late model with a mica window and a cathode cylinder of chrome iron sealed directly to soft glass is shown in Fig. 45.

The addition of a small amount of organic vapor, such as ethyl alcohol, to the rare-gas filling, makes these tubes self-quenching. The discharges are extinguished internally by a space-charge mechanism, and a large external series resistance is not essential to the counting action. Maximum counting rates of the order of 5,000 per second are obtainable with conventional detecting circuits.

Two types of intensity measurement are employed, a counting-rate meter for rapid scanning and a scale-of-64 vacuum-tube counting circuit with timed counting intervals of 15,

FIG. 45. Photograph of one type of Geiger tube.   (*Norelco*.)

30 or 60 sec.   Details of these circuits are supplied by manufacturers of Geiger counters.

The Unit of Dose and Intensity.   For the correlation of the dose of any ionizing radiation with its biological or related effects the International Commission on Radiological Units (London, 1950) recommends that the dose be expressed in terms of the quantity of energy adsorbed per unit mass (ergs per gram) of irradiated material at the place of energy.   As already explained, calorimetric methods are not practicable so that ionization methods are generally employed.   For this purpose the quantity which must be measured is the ionization produced in a gas by the same flow of corpuscular radiation as exists in the material under consideration.   The energy, E_m, imparted to unit mass of the material is then related to the ionization per unit mass of gas, I_m, by the equation $E_m = WSI_m$, where W is the average energy expended by the ionizing particles per ion pair formed in the gas and S is the ratio of the mass stopping power of the material to that of the gas; thus tables of data on W and S must be compiled and revised.   However, this commission favors the continued recognition of a very simple unit of dosage which has had an established usefulness since 1928.

The aim of practical dosage measurement, particularly for therapy, must consist in the selection of a radiation effect which can be measured and which changes with wavelength in the same way as a given biological reaction, $e.g.$, skin erythema.   Repeated experimentation has proved convincingly that a complete parallelism between skin erythema and air ionization exists independent of the quality of the radiation.   Since the absorption coefficient depends not only on wavelength but also on the density and on the atomic number of the elements constituting a material, it is to be expected that air consisting of the light elements oxygen and nitrogen should possess the same absorption properties as tissues consisting of organic compounds of carbon, nitrogen, and oxygen, or water.   At the second International Congress of Radiology in 1928, therefore, the measurement of air ionization was accepted as the basis of international dosage measurement, and a definition was given of the unit of dosage, designated the roentgen and written as "r."

The amended definition accepted since 1937 is as follows: "The roentgen shall be the quantity of X- or γ-radiation such that the associated corpuscular emission per 0.001293 grams of air produces, in air, ions carrying 1 e.s.u. of quantity of electricity of either sign."

The effective intensity, or dose rate, of rays is expressed in roentgens per minute or roentgens per second.   It becomes increasingly difficult to measure the dose in roentgens as the quantum energy of x-radiation approaches very high values.   The unit may, however, be used for most practical purposes for quantum energies up to 3 Mev.

The range of a 50,000-volt electron in air is 4.5 cm, but the 500,000-volt electron has a range of 100 cm.   The difficulty in collecting all ions produced by the absorption of x-rays above 400 kv in an ion chamber of reasonable dimensions is apparent.   As the energy of the radiation is increased, the measurement of the true roentgen becomes more difficult and its interpretation more ambiguous.   Similarly the output of 50-kv beryllium-window generators (such as AEG-50 Machlett tubes or diffraction tubes) is so high that ion recombination makes ionization measurements unreliable.   These considerations led Laughlin, Beattie, Henderson, and Harvey[1] to measure the roentgen calorimetrically with these results:

400 kv (3 mm copper half-value layer), 2,880 ergs/cm²/r.
22.5 Mev (3.5 g/cm² carbon filter), 5,700 ergs/cm²/r.

For the lower energies equilibrium between primary and secondary photons, as well as between primary photons and secondary electrons, is attained fairly near the surface, and measurements with a suitable thimble chamber still give values meaningful in terms of roentgens. . But as the primary radiation increases in energy, secondary electrons become more energetic, so that equilibrium is difficult to attain.   The absorption coefficient for x-rays ceases to decrease with increasing energy and finally increases; in this region the roentgen cannot be realized.   As a result there is much discussion of alternative principles of dosimetry[2] involving supervoltage x-rays, γ-rays, α- and β-rays, and neutrons. Since measurement of x-rays in roentgens consists of two parts, (1) conversion of a portion of photon energy into energy of secondary corpuscular radiation under controlled conditions and (2) the measurement of the ionization produced by this corpuscular radiation, it is the first step which is impracticable at high energies and must be eliminated, leading to dosage measurement on actual ionization-energy absorption in the medium.   However, to permit accurate reporting of observations obtained from ionization measurements made under conditions in which reductions to ergs per gram is hindered by inadequate knowledge of necessary constants, Fano and Taylor recommend that ionization measurements should be made under conditions referred to as infinitesimal cavity conditions such that the ionization in the gas is produced by the same flow of corpuscular radiation as is present in the material under consideration.   Results are expressed in terms of the quantity of charge of either sign separated per unit mass of gas in the ionization chamber.

The question of a biological dose unit as a means of correlating radiation dosage and expected biological effect is still unsolved since experience has shown that equal ionizations by two different types of radiation do not necessarily lead to the same biological effect.   The inequality will not be changed by measurement in energy units or any other physical

---

[1] *Loc. cit.*
[2] E. H. Quimby, W. Fano, and L. S. Taylor, *Brit. J. Radiol.*, **24**, 2 (1951); *Radiology*, **55**, 743 (1950); **63**, 629 (1954.)

terms. However, the dose for these different high-energy radiations or particles has been concurrently expressed as the "rep" (roentgen-equivalent-physical). It represents the energy absorption of approximately 93 ergs per gram of tissue. For calculations of dose, for example, a β-ray dose of 1 rep is said to be physically equivalent to an x-ray dose of 1 r at a given point. The absorbed dose unit, 100 ergs per gram, is now the *rad*.

Effect of Wavelength. Except for heat methods involving complete absorption, the actual extent of various other effects of x-rays including ionization depends on radiation intensity and also on wavelength, and on

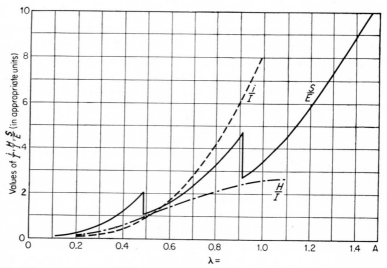

Fig. 46. Effects of x-rays of different wavelengths on gas ionization, fluorescent screen brightness, and photographic blackening.

$$\frac{i}{I} = \frac{\text{ionization}}{\text{incident-ray intensity}}$$

$$\frac{H}{I} = \frac{\text{fluorescent-screen brightness}}{\text{incident-ray intensity}}$$

$$\frac{S}{E} = \frac{\text{photographic blackening}}{\text{incident-ray energy}}$$

this account a different fraction of the initial radiation with varying intensity for different wavelengths is transformed in the irradiated medium into other energy forms. The action is independent of wavelength only when the beam of given initial intensity, inclusive of secondary rays arising therefrom, is completely absorbed in the irradiated material. Hence the ionization current is a measure of the absorbed, not the incident, radiation intensity. The difference in the dependence of the sensitiveness of different methods of measurement upon the wavelength is demonstrated in Fig. 46. If different homogeneous rays fall simultaneously with equal intensity upon an air-ionization chamber, a fluorescent screen, and a photographic plate, the brightness of the screen changes much less with wavelength than the ionization current; the photographic sensitiveness changes with sudden jumps at 0.49 and 0.91 A. Since these wavelengths coincide with the discontinuities in absorption coefficients of silver and bromine, the two effective constituents of the photographic emulsion, the photographic action is closely connected with absorption. Hence the action of the rays changes with wavelength in the same way as the intensity of the absorbed portion of the incident rays changes; exceptions occur in the rays of very short wave x-rays when the Compton effect (see Chap. 8) is appreciable and in the case of the excitation of characteristic fluorescent rays of the irradiated material. The general rule holds for each known physical and chemical effect: The effect changes with wavelength in the same way as the fraction of the incident-radiation energy transformed into the energy of photoelectrons and Compton electrons. The values may be calculated for certain chemical compositions of a material from physical data (absorption coefficient, recoil coefficient, etc.), and Glocker has found excellent agreement between theory and experiment for ionization.

The Effect of X-rays on the Electrical Conductivity of Solids and Liquids. Although there have been few experiments directly aimed at studying ionization in solids and liquids, it is certain that the increase in electrical conductivity of certain solid dielectrics such as sulfur, paraffin, hard rubber, and amber when exposed to x-radiation is exactly the same phenomenon as ionization of gases.

An effect somewhat similar is the well-known change in the electrical resistance of selenium crystals when illuminated with ordinary light, ultraviolet rays, or x-rays. This phenomenon of resistance decrease, which must find its explanation ultimately in the peculiarities of the structure of the selenium crystal, has been explained on the basis of several hypotheses, one of the most promising being that of resonance. By this theory the electrons in the crystal that have radiation frequencies in approximate correspondence with the frequency of the exciting radiation are temporarily loosened from their atomic bonds and become available for the transfer of electricity. In a practical way this phenomenon has found some application in estimating x-ray intensity. The method is only qualitative, and the cells must be checked frequently against a standard, since they change characteristics during usage.

The conductivity C of insulating liquids exposed to x-rays has been investigated a few times. A few typical results are as follows for $C = 10^{-4}$ mho/cm: carbon tetrachloride 8, carbon disulfide 20, amylene 14, benzene 4, liquid air 1.3, petroleum ether 15, vaseline oil 1.6.[1]

The Crystal Detector and Amplifier. In 1946 Frerichs[2] found that synthetic cadmium sulfide crystals show a relatively large photoconduc-

[1] L. S. Taylor, *J. chim. phys.*, **48**, 168 (1951).
[2] R. Frerichs, *Naturwissenschaften*, **33**, 281 (1946); *Phys. Rev.*, **72**, 594 (1947), **76**, 1869 (1949); *J. Appl. Phys.*, **21**, 312 (1950).

tivity (of the order of 30×10^{-6} amp measurable on a microammeter) under irradiation with x-rays and thus could be used as a detector and amplifier with a sensitivity equal to that of the combination of a crystal phosphor and a photomultiplier tube (page 80) introduced in 1941 by Hodges and Morgan.[1] The primary process is the raising of a number of slow electrons into the conduction band, followed by amplification on the order of 10^4 of the electron current in the crystal itself. There is a linear relation between photocurrent and intensity of x-rays at relatively low levels, while at high intensities saturation effects occur. Extremely low intensities on the order of 150 quanta per second can be registered with a current employing a trigger electron tube with an efficiency of 4.2×10^5 electrons per x-ray quantum. The response of CdS crystals is rapid enough to detect at least 60 x-ray pulses per second (as generated in transformers with half-wave rectification). One disadvantage is that the photocurrent reaches a final value only after long irradiation, but on the other hand the CdS crystals have the advantages of no fatigue effects, observed with multiplier tubes, and simplicity in that the crystal size defines the sensitive volume and in that they require no treatment other than mounting on a polystyrene strip with Aquadag (colloidally suspended graphite) electrodes. No other crystals thus far discovered compare with CdS in this property. The diamond as a crystal detector is discussed in Chap. 15.

The Excitation of Luminescence in Irradiated Substances. The excitation of luminescence in many substances when irradiated by x-rays is a property that has played an important role in the history of the science. As a matter of fact, the fluorescence of neighboring objects led to Röntgen's discovery of the radiation. The phenomenon depends upon the ability of substances to absorb the rays and transform the energy into radiation of longer wavelengths in the ultraviolet or visible regions.

TABLE 4-2. WAVELENGTHS OF FLUORESCENT LIGHT EXCITED BY X-RAYS

	Region, A	Position of maximum, A
Fluorspar	3,640–2,400	2,840
Fluorspar and iron spar	3,900–2,310	2,800
Scheelite (Ca tungstate)	4,800–3,750	4,330
Zinc sulfide	5,090–4,120	4,500
Potassium platinocyanide	4,900–4,120	4,500
Barium platinocyanide	5,090–4,420	4,800
Calcium platinocyanide	5,090–4,550	4,800
Uranium NH_4 fluoride	4,400–3,800	4,100
X-ray tube glass	5,090–3,000	3,750

[1] *Am. J. Roentgenol. Radium Therapy,* **47,** 777 (1942).

Schuhknecht was the first to study the fluorescence of materials under x-rays, with the quartz spectrograph. Because of the excellence of his work, the results are presented in Table 4-2, showing the spectral regions and the wavelengths of the intensity maxima, in angstroms. Schuhknecht observed that the spectral distribution of the luminescence was profoundly influenced by minute amounts of impurities, as is well known for fluorescence under visible light.

Nichols and Merritt[1] found that the intensity distribution in a fluorescent band was independent of the exciting radiation, x-rays, ultraviolet light, or cathode rays. Wick[2] studied the fluorescence of uranium salts, and Newcomer[3] that of about 500 chemical compounds (mostly organic). The latter found sodium bromide very strongly fluorescent in the ultraviolet and benzoic acid and naphthalene and their derivatives in the yellow-green.

Twenty years later the interest in phosphors suddenly increased with the advent of multiplier phototubes and the possibility of evaluating dosage, culminating in the appearance of the scintillation counter, the most sensitive method yet devised. The investigation of solids, inorganic and organic, and solutions has continued intensively. These techniques are considered in a later section, but attention is here directed to the surveys of all crystalline solids suitable for scintillation counters by Hofstadter[4] and of liquids by Kallman and Furst.[5]

All workers with x-rays are probably familiar with the fact that when the radiation strikes the eyes there ensues a sensation of luminescence which may continue for several seconds after the exciting source is removed. This latter phenomenon is an example of *phosphorescence;* with x-rays, phosphorescence, in general, is usually more pronounced than with light because of the deeper penetration of the former and hence of a greater volume effect. Gases and many solids are phosphorescent. Even powdered rock salt is easily visible in a darkened room for a half hour or more after its exposure to x-rays. Extraordinarily brilliant luminescence results from irradiation of many solids with beams of very high intensity, as described in Chap. 2.

There are several practical uses of fluorescence under x-rays. The property may be used to differentiate between chemical substances, *e.g.,* diamond and a glass substitute. It may serve as the basis of developing invisible inks and identification marks.

For measuring intensity of x-rays by fluorescence methods, until recently the fluorescence of a screen was compared with the fluorescence

[1] *Phys. Rev.,* [1]**21,** 247 (1905), **28,** 349 (1909).
[2] *Phys. Rev.,* [2]**5,** 418 (1915).
[3] *J. Am. Chem. Soc.,* **42,** 1997 (1920).
[4] R. Hofstadter, *Nucleonics,* **6** (5), 70 (1950).
[5] H. Kallman and M. Furst, *Nucleonics,* **8** (3), 32 (1951); *Phys. Rev.,* **79,** 857 (1950).

produced by a standard radiation. This is obviously a comparative method and is open to the objections that the fluorescing salt becomes "tired" under the action of the rays and that the screen may not be of uniform fluorescing power. The objections to using fluorescence methods to determine absolute intensity are that the relation between fluorescence and the x-ray intensity is unknown and that certain rays will excite a characteristic fluorescence. But now the combination of x-ray fluorescent screen and multiplier phototube, originally introduced for automatic exposure timing in medical diagnostic radiography, has such excellent sensitivity and stability that it is widely accepted for continuous quantitative x-ray-intensity measurement.

The fluorescence of screens impregnated with such materials as zinc silicate or zinc sulfide–cadmium sulfide is the basis of the very important application of visual radiography, or fluoroscopy, which will be described in Chap. 9, together with the newest developments in the electronic amplification of fluoroscopic images.

X-ray Phosphor and Multiplier-phototube Detector. The fluorescent screen, or x-ray phosphor, also plays an essential role in a much more sensitive and quantitative method for measuring intensities than visual estimation of the brilliance of the light emitted by calcium tungstate or other crystals when x-rays are absorbed. Nearly twenty years ago it was suggested that a photoelectric cell be used with the phosphor to measure the light intensity and hence the x-ray energy. But a much greater improvement came with the development of the electron-multiplier phototube (often less accurately called photomultiplier tubes).

When a beam of electrons in a vacuum tube strikes a metal plate, secondary electrons are emitted. The number of secondary-emission electrons leaving the bombarded surface is proportional to the number of primary electrons striking it. The ratio of secondaries to primaries varies with the nature of the emitting surface and the kinetic energy of the primary electrons. With silver-oxygen-cesium surfaces, of the type commonly used in photocells, the secondary-emission ratio is 4 when the primary electrons are accelerated by a potential difference of 100 volts.

The multiplier phototube consists of a primary source of electrons, the photoelectric surface on which the light from the phosphor falls, and a series of secondary-emission electrodes, or dynodes, each about 100 volts positive with respect to the preceding surface (Fig. 47). If the secondary-emission ratio is 4, then the primary photoelectrons are amplified fourfold when they are swept to the first dynode by the 100-volt potential difference. The amplified current is similarly amplified once again at the second electrode. If the process is repeated at n secondary-emission surfaces, the final current is 4^n. In a nine-stage multiplier such as the 931 A, the amplification factor at 100 volts per stage is about 200,000.

Other tubes with the electrodes arranged like the slats in venetian blinds are even more sensitive.

Because the secondary-emission process is virtually instantaneous, the frequency response of the multiplier tube is almost constant up to many megacycles. In combination with x-ray phosphors, especially organic crystals such as anthracene having very rapid decay characteristics, it has been used to measure x-ray pulses as short as less than 0.1 μsec. For maximum sensitivity the x-ray phosphor is chosen to match the spectral-sensitivity curve of the photosurface.

The absorption of x-rays in the $CaWO_4$ fluorescent screen leads to a process in which the high-energy electron ejected by an x-ray photon releases a large number of slow electrons, which eventually are responsible

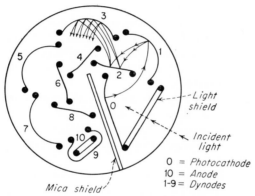

Light shield

Incident light

0 = *Photocathode*
10 = *Anode*
1-9 = *Dynodes*

Mica shield

FIG. 47. Multiplier phototube.

for the excitation of many blue light quanta. These light quanta may release a number of photoelectrons when they strike the photocathode of the multiplier tube. The ratio of the number of bursts of photoelectrons to the number of x-ray quanta incident on the fluorescent screen may be called the fundamental efficiency of the multiplier-phototube x-ray detector. Presumably, with sufficient secondary-electron amplification and external-amplifier sensitivity, these photoelectron bursts could be counted in the same manner as the discharge pulses of a Geiger counter.

Fundamental efficiencies, calculated on this basis, vary from 3 per cent at 30 kv to 12 per cent at 10 kv. The efficiency falls steadily with increasing primary-photon energy except for a discontinuity at the *K* absorption limit of tungsten. At energies in the γ-ray region, the efficiency becomes steadily smaller and does not rise again as in the Geiger-counter case. It is reasonable to conclude that the fundamental efficiency of the multiplier x-ray detector is about an order of magnitude less than that of a well-designed Geiger counter for photon energies under

70 kv. In the γ-ray region, from 1 to 10 Mev, its efficiency may fall below that of the Geiger counter by a factor of 100.

There are three possible techniques which employ a combination of a phosphor and a multiplier phototube. These are (1) the counting method, which measures the number of quanta absorbed per second but not the total amount of energy absorbed; (2) the integrated intensity method, which measures the total light energy emitted by fluorescent substances when energized (the phosphor–multiplier-phototube combination under discussion in this section); and (3) the storage method, in which energy stored in the phosphor during an exposure over a period of time can be released by irradiation with infrared rays and the total energy measured. The first two measure dose rate, or intensity; the third, of course, measures the total dose. These methods differ in the requirements of the fluorescent materials and to a lesser extent in those of the sensitivity and response of the multiplier phototube. Any adequate discussion of details in this book is impossible, but a fairly extensive bibliography selected from a much larger number of important papers is listed at the end of this chapter to give some idea of the active research and rapid progress in this whole field.

Scintillation Counters. It follows from the foregoing description of the combination of a phosphor and a multiplier tube that the scintillations in the phosphor produced by the individual x-ray quanta may be counted on a scaler or integrated by a ratemeter, exactly as in the case of the Geiger counter.

The scintillation counter obviously has the most rigorous requirements as regards energy response (or peak heights or intensities of the individual flashes of light upon impact of photons, electrons, or particles), speed, the decay time of each flash, and general flexibility. It is not surprising that searching investigations have been made and still are in progress on various inorganic- and organic-crystal systems and on solutions principally of organic compounds in organic solvents. Table 4-3 summarizes some of the data on intensities from the work of Kallmann, Furst, and Sidran. In general, inorganic phosphors such as the alkali halides containing impurities such as 0.5 per cent thallium show linear response, the highest peaks, and decay times greater than 0.1 μsec; organic crystals, of which anthracene is still the best, are nonlinear in response and have a lower peak height but decay times of less than 0.1 μsec; solutions such as 0.5 per cent terphenyl in toluene or xylene are less efficient in all respects but have the advantages of ease of preparation, in comparison with laborious crystallizations, and the simple production of large areas, especially useful in cosmic-ray measurements. In general, emitted light from the various phosphors is in the range of 3,300 to 4,800 A, largely independent of the kind of exciting radiation or particles.

The mechanism of fluorescence has stimulated much theoretical and experimental work.   Probably the best understood is the process in such a crystal as NaCl(Tl), a designation of the presence of Tl ions as an impurity in the salt crystal.   Such a crystal has a so-called defect lattice, a subject which is discussed in some detail in Chap. 17, along with the band theory of solids.   Briefly, there are present F-centers, due to the absence of negative ions, which serve as traps for electrons.   The presence at random of Tl^+ ions produces centers with perturbed potential; electrons are raised to the conduction band by irradiation of the crystal, and energy travels through the crystal to the points of perturbation and near the Tl^+ ions is converted into radiation.   The increased fluorescence has a wavelength characteristic of the impurity.

Of greatest difficulty is the explanation of solutions as scintillation counters.   The emission is characteristic of the solutes, even when the ratio of these molecules to solvent molecules is as low as 1 in 100,000; but the quantity of energy is characteristic of the solvent.   Hence the radiation energy must have been absorbed by the solvent and transferred to the solution by a quantum-mechanical process in a time on the order of 3×10^{-11} sec.

Several types of scintillation counters involving various phosphors, multiplier tubes, and electronic circuits have been described in papers listed in the Bibliography.   A new General Electric portable radiation probe is supplied with interchangeable phosphor caps, with zinc sulfide for α-particle counting, anthracene for β-particle counting, sodium iodide or anthracene for γ-photon counting, and a new phosphor for thermal neutrons.   Here is another example of the resurrection of an old method and adaptation to new quantitative instrumentation; for scintillations in thin layers of fluorescent materials were the earliest indicator of radio-active minerals as used by Becquerel and by the Curies and contemporaries, following the discovery of roentgen rays by the fluorescence of a sheet of barium platinocyanide paper under the invisible rays from a cathode-ray tube on Nov. 8, 1895.   Two or three scintillation counters can be combined in a "coincidence" circuit which will produce a pulse of its own only when there are simultaneous pulses in the two or three counters.   In this way complex events particularly in nuclear research, such as the scattering of π-mesons by protons, can be separated and evaluated.   By this means in October, 1953, the first real experimental evidence of the neutrino (Table 1-2) produced in the decay of neutrons into protons and electrons was obtained at Los Alamos Scientific Laboratory.   The reverse reaction of the capture of a neutrino by a proton to yield a neutron and positron was detected by successive flashes in a 10-ft^3 scintillation counter.

The Storage-phosphor Dosimeter.   The storage method of total dosage measurement is still largely in the experimental state, but it has very great potential applications.   NaCl (1 per cent AgCl) crystals are

TABLE 4-3. COMPARISON OF PHOSPHORS AS SCINTILLATION COUNTERS (γ-RAYS
OR HIGH-VOLTAGE X-RAYS)—PEAK INTENSITIES RELATED TO
ANTHRACENE 100*

	Solids	Solutions in xylene
Anthracene	100	6
Anthranilic acid	15	15
Carbazole	33	12
Chrysene	35	0
1,4-Diphenylbutadiene	67	12
Diphenyl hexatriene	4	21
Durene	54	12
Fluoranthrene	31	8
Naphthalene	15	3
α-Naphthylamine	5	17
β-Naphthyl ethyl ether	56	14
Phenanthrene	46	0
Phenyl α-naphthylamine	27	27
Pyrene	52	9
Quaterphenyl	85	20
Stilbene	73	4
m-Terphenyl	25	20
p-Terphenyl	55	48
CsBr (0.5Tl)	210	
CsI (Tl)	145	
KI (Tl)	83	
NaCl (AgCl)	115	
NaI (Tl)	200	
ZnS (type D)	200	

*H. Kallmann, M. Furst, and M. Sidran, *Nucleonics*, **10** (9), 15 (1952).

known to store energy over the range from 10 mr to 10,000 r.   As already indicated, the stored energy is released as visible light by irradiation of the storing phosphor with infrared rays.   A direct application to radiography and microradiography (Chaps. 9 and 10) is immediately apparent. The specimen is placed in contact with the storage phosphor, just as if it were the photographic film, and irradiated.   The potential radiographic image is stored, and at a later convenient time the phosphor is placed in contact with the photographic emulsion and irradiated with infrared rays. The released energy registers the "shadowgraph" on the emulsion.

Fluorescent Intensifying Screens.   A very practical use of the property of fluorescence is the intensifying screen, used with photographic films in x-ray-radiographic and crystal-diffraction applications in order to cut down the time of exposure, sometimes to one-twentieth of the usual value.   For these screens, calcium or cadmium tungstate has been preferred until recently because of intense blue-violet fluorescence.   The screens are usually placed as a pair with a thin screen in front and a thick screen behind the photographic plate or film, and the fluorescent portions add their action on the sensitive emulsion to the direct x-ray effects. Unless care is used, difficulties with the screens may arise, as follows:

1. If the calcium tungstate is not pure, the screen may have an appreciable hangover, or phosphorescence. Several years ago some of the best commercial screens produced a distinct effect on a photographic plate for as long as three months after their exposure to x-rays. Hence this extraneous action of previously used screens may lead to misinterpretation of newly obtained x-ray photographs.

2. Unless the screen is very carefully prepared for uniform particle size and is placed in the closest proximity to the sensitive emulsion, it may reduce the definition of the photograph by broadening the image. This effect is observed easily, even when only the thickness of the glass of a photographic plate separates the emulsion and the luminescent image.

3. The intensity of fluorescence depends upon the wavelengths; although quantitative data on this point are lacking, De Broglie showed that a screen had no intensifying effect upon rays with wavelengths of 1.25 A but displayed a gradual increase in effectiveness up to the critical absorption wavelength of tungsten at about 0.179 A, at which point, corresponding to greater absorption, a sharp increase occurred for the shorter wavelengths. For this reason fluorescence cannot serve satisfactorily as a means of measuring x-ray intensities.

An interesting comparison is given in Fig. 48 of the spectral ranges of sensitivity of the eye, the fluoroscope screen (containing as the most

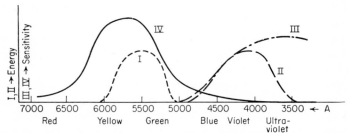

Fig. 48. Curves showing spectral ranges of maximum sensitivity of the eye and photographic plate, to which should correspond, respectively, the fluorescent screen and the intensifying screen. I, fluorescent screen; II, calcium tungstate intensifying screen; III, silver bromide of photographic emulsion; IV, human eye.

important constituent zinc silicate), the silver bromide emulsion, and the calcium tungstate photographic intensifying screen. Very properly the first two and the last two show sensitivities over the same spectral range.

Hi-Speed. The latest development in increasing the speed and sensitivity of intensifying screens is the use of lead barium sulfate (Hi-Speed). At 70 kv an exposure of 100 ma-sec with Hi-Speed can be made to give the same photographic effect as 150 ma-sec with Par-Speed (calcium tungstate) screens. Furthermore the fluorescence of lead barium sulfate shows a maximum response at 3,800 A, or 500 A farther into the ultraviolet, than the tungstate, with consequent greater photographic effect.

On this account the new screens appear less bright to the eye than the tungstate screens when energized by x-rays in a darkroom.

The Photographic Effect. In their action on the photographic plate, x-rays seem similar to ordinary light, for there are no known plates sensitive to x-rays that are not also sensitive to the visible radiation. Examination of microscopic sections through the sensitive layer of exposed plates has shown, however, that x-rays, unlike light, produce an equal distribution of grains of reduced silver throughout the whole thickness of the layer. Consequently a greater blackening of the plate, when exposed to x-rays, can be obtained by increasing the thickness of the sensitive layer. Here, indeed, is found the chief difference between ordinary photographic films or plates and those manufactured for x-ray use; the latter are provided with a thicker sensitive layer and are usually "duplitized," or coated on both sides with the sensitive silver bromide emulsion.

The laws of the blackening of photographic plates are more complex than might be expected. The frequency and intensity of the incident rays and the time of exposure are important factors. Rays of differing frequencies do not have an equal quantitative effect. Kulenkampff made calculations, based on intensity and ionization measurements, which appeared to show that equal blackening will result from equal energy absorption regardless of wavelength. Furthermore, rays of frequencies higher than the critical absorption frequencies of bromine and silver are very highly absorbed and produce a large photographic effect, whereas rays of slightly lower frequency produce a relatively lower effect, though the incident intensities may be the same.

The portions of a developed plate or film that have been exposed to x-rays are darkened by the deposit of silver grains. This darkening is quantitatively described as the blackening S, where $S = \log (L_0/L)$, where in turn L_0 is the initial intensity of a beam of light, as in a view box used to observe the film, and L is the intensity after the light has passed through the silver deposit; or sometimes as the density D, where $D = \log (1/T)$, where T is the transparency. The logarithmic definition is in accord with the tendency of the eye to judge relative intensities of light in proportion rather to the logarithm of the intensity than to the intensity itself. Thus a film density of 1.0 means that the blackening is such that only one-tenth of the incident light passes through; for $D = 2.0$, one one-hundredth is transmitted; etc. Actually S and D are identical since L_0/L may be defined as $1/T$. For the quantitative evaluation of the intensity of an x-ray beam the relation between intensities and densities must be established. This is best shown by plotting, as in Fig. 49, D (or S) against $\log E$, where E, the exposure, is x-ray intensity multiplied by time, or $I \times t$, since $D = \log E - \log k$ with k as a proportionality constant. In the case of constant intensity the logarithmic time of exposure may be plotted horizontally. At low intensities the sensitometric, or H and D, curve rises very slowly, then more steeply as a

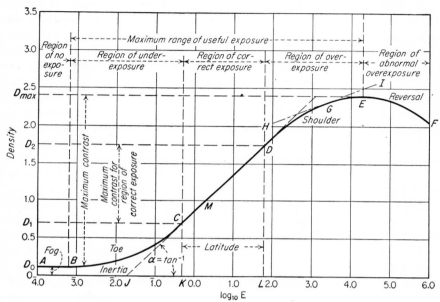

FIG. 49. Photographic blackening curve. (*Photo Technique.*)

straight line, until it reaches a point of inflection where the slope decreases again. The straight-line steep portion of the curve defines the working region of the film, over which the x-ray image is faithfully rendered in terms of density, usually lying between 0.4 and 1.5 or an average of 0.7. The smallest difference in blackening of two adjacent areas that may be safely detected visually under the best conditions is 0.02. It is evident that small intensity variations cannot be detected at the lower or upper ends of the curve. At the lower end, D or S is linearly related to intensity or time directly rather than to the logarithm.

Film emulsions are distinguished by speed, contrast, and latitude. Speed is a function of the length of the range of inertia at the left of the curve. Fig-ure 50 shows how the use of double intensifying screens modifies the characteristic speed. The contrast is measured by the slope

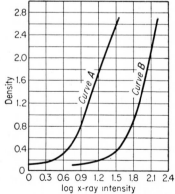

FIG. 50. Characteristic curves for x-ray film. Curve A is taken with double intensifying screens and curve B without screens.

of the characteristic working curve ($\gamma = \tan \alpha$). Thus a great contrast means a very steep slope, or a great difference in blackening for very slight differences in intensity of x-rays, and the working range of 0.4 to 1.5 is easily exceeded. This is sometimes a disadvantage, especially in radiography, where an object of varying thickness is involved, and thus contrast must be sacrificed for a lower slope or latitude for a single exposure; or high contrast and detection of very small differences or defects may be obtained by subjecting portions of different thicknesses to different exposure times. In general, x-ray films at present are less likely to have any considerable linear range in their curves. The slope at a single point is the gradient. For some films the gradient may increase steadily, since the curve may not have a linear portion, up to the highest densities that can be utilized with high-intensity illuminators. Such a film gives the highest magnification of subject contrast and therefore best differentiation of detail in higher densities. A gradient of 3, for example, increases a 2 per cent x-ray-intensity difference to a 6 per cent difference in transmitted light. Most x-ray films utilize gradients higher than 1.0. Figure 51 reproduces the characteristic curves for Eastman films[1] from which the proper radiographic technique may be selected, as described in Chap. 9.

The assumption is usually made that over the working range equal densities result from equal products of time × intensity (Bunsen's reciprocity law). However, this assumption must be used with the greatest care, since intensifying screens and other factors introduce complications. The blackening curve of the visible light excited in intensifying screens is quite different from that of the direct action of the x-rays. Background corrections present one of the most serious and complex factors for very accurate quantitative measurement of intensity for dosage, spectroscopic, and diffraction analysis. The expression

$$\frac{I_1}{I_2} = \frac{S_1 - S_0}{S_2 - S_0}$$

where S_0 is the background fogging, can be considered only as a working approximation simply because of the varying sensitivity of different silver halide grains in the same emulsion. The photographic effect as a means of intensity measurement and as a photochemical reaction will be considered in specific applications in subsequent chapters.

Increase by Electric Discharge of Photographic Sensitivity. The newest method of increasing photographic sensitivity[2] involves combination of an emulsion with an electric discharge, similar to the one in a propor-

---

[1] The best account of the entire subject of the sensitometric characteristics of x-ray film (especially industrial) is to be found in the monograph "Radiography in Modern Industry," published by the Eastman Kodak Company, Rochester, N.Y.

[2] K. S. Lion, *J. Appl. Phys.*, **24**, 367 (1953).

tional or Geiger counter which is triggered off by incident radiation and which acts on the emulsion. A vessel with magnesium plates serving as electrodes, upon one of which the photographic film or paper is cemented, is filled with an air-ether mixture and 1,100 volts applied. When exposed

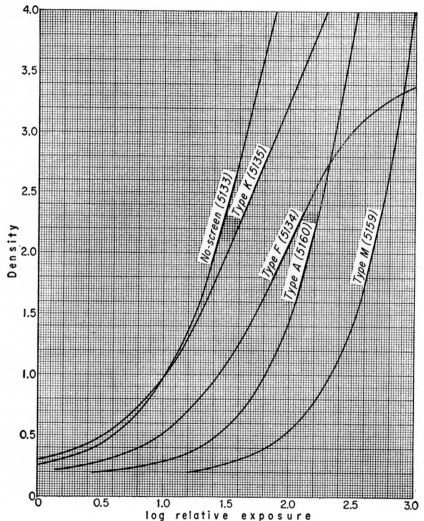

FIG. 51. Characteristic curves of Kodak films used in industrial radiography. (*Eastman Kodak Company.*)

to x-rays an increase in photographic density of the order of 100 may be obtained as a result of highly localized discharge pulses. The number of individual discharge pulses produced is proportional to the number of incident quanta, and the photographic density increases with the number of discharges at any picture point. A radiograph or microradiograph can be made in 2 min with an x-ray intensity of only 1 r/hr. Fluorescent or phosphorescent effects may also be similarly augmented.

The Microphotometer. The microphotometer is an instrument that has become practically indispensable for any kind of x-ray photographic work. The general principle of its operation is as follows: A light of constant intensity passes through the film, which is moved slowly and at constant speed. The light of varying intensity, depending upon the density of the photographic layer, then falls upon a delicate thermocouple

Fig. 52. Leeds and Northrup microphotometer, used with Micromax recorder (not shown).

(thermopile, photoelectric cell, etc.) which is connected with a galvanometer. The deflections of the mirror, which are a function of the thermoelectric current, the light intensity, and the photographic density, are then indicated by causing a reflected beam of light to register on sensitized paper on a slowly moving drum.

Spectral lines on the film are thus converted into peaks, and the completed curve gives a method of quantitative measurement.

The excellent Leeds and Northrup instrument with Micromax recorder is illustrated in Fig. 52. The microphotometer is useful in the following types of investigation:

1. In accurate measurement of wavelength and of relative intensities of spectral lines; in indication of resolution of doublets; etc. The photometric curves measure position, fine structure, intensity from height of peak, and inherent breadth of lines.

2. As an indispensable aid in quantitative chemical analysis, for which line intensities or height of absorption edges must be accurately compared with standards; indications of very faint foreign lines; etc.

3. In quantitative representation of radiographs.

4. In determining position and intensities of lines in diffraction photographs.

5. As an indispensable aid in measurement of colloidal-particle size from widths of diffraction lines.

The most recent developments in densitometry are the use of a television camera-amplifier-clipper system as a continuously acting sensitometer with electronic enhancement of x-ray-film contrast. Such a system is described in Chap. 9.

Xerography. A completely dry photographic process, invented by C. F. Carlson in 1938, developed by Battelle Memorial Institute and commercialized by the Haloid Company, since 1947, has been so successfully utilized in radiography and other x-ray applications that a brief description is warranted.[1] Basically, xerography depends on: (1) the formation of an electrostatic image on an insulated photoconductive surface (usually a layer of vitreous selenium on glass, paper, or plastic) by exposure to radiation; (2) the development of this latent image by a finely divided, electrically charged powder; (3) the transfer of this powder image to a permanent support such as a sheet of paper; and (4) fixing the image to the sheet by moderate heating. Selenium films have high electrical resistance in the dark, and low resistance when exposed to light or x-rays. Xerographic plates are sensitized by charging the surface to several hundred volts by spraying them with ions formed by a corona discharge from very fine wires. Upon exposure the uniform charge on the surface leaks through the photoconductive selenium film in the illuminated areas. The dark areas of the image, the unexposed areas of the plate, retain their charge, thereby producing a latent electrostatic image. This is developed by a finely divided powder which has an opposite electrostatic charge produced by mixing the powder with a granular carrier so chosen that triboelectric effects leave the proper electric charge on the powder when the two are separated. The powder particle size is in the range 0.1 to 20 μ, and that of carrier granules 300 μ. An interesting triboelectric series has been discovered from which choices of powder and carrier are made; for example, micronized tartaric acid powder and corn meal carrier develop positively charged images, while pigmented lycopodium powder and sand carrier develop negatively charged images.

The resulting powder image on the plate is next transferred to a sheet of paper for the permanent record by subjecting the paper to a corona discharge to produce a charge of opposite sign to the charge on the powder. The image is then made permanent by heating the powder,

[1] R. M. Schaffert and C. D. Oughton, *J. Opt. Soc. Amer.* **38**, 991 (1948); W. T. Reid, *Battelle Tech Rev.*, November, 1953.

which is usually a resin with low fusing temperature. This process may be repeated as often as desired for multiple copy reproduction. The original plate may be cleaned for reuse by cascading coarse salt grains over the surface to remove residual powder. Xeroradiography, a special application of xerography in the x-ray field, is now an established and increasingly important technique.

Chemical Dosimeters. Certain photochemical reactions can be used as measures of x-ray intensity, for cases where a measurable change such as a precipitation or gas evolution is directly related to dosage and has been calibrated in terms of roentgens. One of the best examples is the reaction between mercuric chloride and ammonium oxalate to precipitate calomel, Hg_2Cl_2 (0.58 mg as mercury per 840 r), and evolve carbon dioxide gas. The decoloration of methylene blue, the reduction of 2,3,5-triphenyl tetrazolium chloride (colorless solution) to formazan (red precipitate), the polymerization and precipitation of acrylonitrile, the formation of hydrochloric acid from chloroform, and other reactions enumerated in Chap. 11 are used specifically as dosimeters. These chemical effects of high-energy radiation, employed as dosimeters, have great importance potentially, for they may be analogous or related to chemical changes in irradiated biological objects such as living tissues; and because of simplicity and economy they might best serve as detectors and dosimeters of atomic-bomb radiation for an entire population in the event of war attack. For these reasons intensive research under government auspices is being directed to the discovery of chemical systems sufficiently sensitive to visual change and linear in response to radiation dosage.

Biological Dosimeters. The method of estimating dosage from skin reddening, or erythema, is familiar to all x-ray workers. This can never serve as an accurate method because of the widely varying sensitivity of the skin of different individuals to radiation. Glasser and Portmann[1] compiled data from 40 clinics on the number of roentgens for average erythema reaction in deep therapy. These varied from 500 to 1,250 r, or an average of 930. The threshold value of erythema is commonly taken to be 840 r.

A much more accurate "biological ionization chamber," as designated by Wood[2] are *Drosophila* (fruit fly) eggs. Invariably 50 per cent of the eggs are killed by 180 r and 90 per cent by 500 r. The points for the effect of radium fall directly on the curve experimentally determined for the percentage of eggs hatching as a function of roentgens (see Chap. 11).

Specifications of the Conditions of Roentgen Treatment. It will be shown convincingly in Chap. 12 on The Biological Effects of X-radiation that the effective use of x-rays in therapy such as the treatment of cancer

[1] *Radiology,* **14,** 346 (1931).
[2] *Radiology,* **12,** 461 (1929).

depends upon very carefully controlled and measured dose. It is not surprising, therefore, that the International Commission on Radiological Units should set up very definite specifications for treatment conditions, which, in 1950, were recommended as follows:

1. *Quantity.*   The quantity of radiation (expressed in roentgens) estimated to have been received by the lesion.

2. *Quality.*   a. The spectral-energy distribution of roentgen radiation (see next chapter) shall be designated by some suitable index, called quality.   For most medical purposes it is sufficient to express the quality of the roentgen radiation by the half-value layer (HVL, or the thickness of material required to cut the beam intensity in half) in a suitable material: up to 20 kv, cellophane or cellone; 20 to 120 kv, aluminum; 120 to 400 kv, copper; 400 kv, tin.   The complete absorption curve in the same material is preferable.

b. Material and thickness of filters, including tube walls.

c. Target material.

3. *Technique.*   a. Total quantity of radiation per field (incident and emergent) received in an entire course of treatment.

b. Quantity of radiation per field measured at the surface (D_0) at each individual irradiation.

c. The dosage rate expressed in roentgens per minute during each individual irradiation.

d. The total time over which a course of treatments is spread.

e. The time interval between successive doses.

f. The target-skin distance.

g. The number, dimensions, and locations of the ports of entry (as in "cross-firing" beams to converge in a deep-seated tumor).

BIBLIOGRAPHY

Multiplier Phototubes

Pierce, J. R.: *Bell Labs. Record*, **16**, 305 (1938).

Allen, J. S.: *Phys. Rev.*, **55**, 966 (1939).

Zworyken, V. K., and J. A. Rajchman: *Proc. IRE*, **27**, 558 (1939).

Rajchman, J. A., and R. L. Snyder: *Electronics*, December, 1940.

Bay, Z.: *Rev. Sci. Instr.*, **12**, 127 (1941).

Allen, J. S.: *Rev. Sci. Instr.*, **12**, 484 (1941).

Marshall, F. H., J. H. Coltman, and L. P. Hunter: *Rev. Sci. Instr.*, **18**, 504 (1947).

Engstrom, R. W.: *Rev. Sci. Instr.*, **18**, 587 (1947).

Allen, J. S.: *Rev. Sci. Instr.*, **18**, 739 (1947).

Coltman, J. W., and F. H. Marshall: *Nucleonics*, **1** (3), 53 (1947).

Marshall, F. H., J. W. Coltman, and A. I. Bennett: *Rev. Sci. Instr.*, **19**, 744 (1948).

Morton, G. A., and J. A. Mitchell: *RCA Rev.*, **9**, 632 (1948).

Allen, J. S.: *Nucleonics*, **3** (1), 34 (1948).

Sommer, A., and W. E. Turk: *J. Sci. Instr.*, **27**, 113 (1950).

Dunkelman, L., and C. Lock: *J. Opt. Soc. Amer.*, **41**, 802 (1951).

Clancy, E. P.: *J. Opt. Soc. Amer.*, **42**, 357 (1950).

Turk, W. E.: *Photoelec. Spect. Group Bull.*, **5**, 100 (1952).

Engstrom, R. W., R. G. Stouderheimer, and A. M. Glover: *Nucleonics*, **10** (4), 58, (1952).

Post, R. F.: *Nucleonics*, **10** (5), 46 (1952).

Mueller, D. W., G. Best, and J. Jackson: *Nucleonics*, **10** (6), 53 (1953).

Scintillation Counters

Jordan, W. H., and P. R. Bell: *Nucleonics*, **5** (4), 40 (1949).

Morton, G. A.: *RCA Rev.*, **10**, 525 (1949).

Coltman, J. W.: *Proc. IRE*, **37**, 671 (1949).

Hofstadter, R.: *Nucleonics*, **6** (5), 70 (1950).

Kallmann, H., and M. Furst: *Phys. Rev.*, **79**, 857 (1950); *Nucleonics*, **8** (3), 32 (1951).

Post, R. F.: *Phys. Rev.*, **80**, 1113 (1950).

Allen, J. S., and T. C. Engelder: *Rev. Sci. Instr.*, **22**, 401 (1951).

Ter-Pogossian, M., and W. B. Ittner: *Rev. Sci. Instr.*, **22**, 646 (1951).

Latest Developments in Scintillation Counting (Conference Proceedings), *Nucleonics*, **10** (3), 32 (1952).

Harrison, F. B.: *Nucleonics*, **10** (6), 40 (1952).

Garwin, R. L.: *Rev. Sci. Instr.*, **23**, 755 (1952).

Post, R. F.: *Nucleonics*, **10** (6), 56 (1952).

Kloepper, R. M., and M. L. Wiedenbeck: *Rev. Sci. Instr.*, **23**, 446 (1952).

Reynolds, G. F.: *Nucleonics*, **10** (7), 46 (1951).

Greenblatt, M. H., M. W. Green, P. W. Davison, and G. A. Morton: *Nucleonics*, **10** (8), 45 (1952).

Herbert, R. I. T.: *Nucleonics*, **10** (8), 37 (1952).

Kallmann, H., M. Furst, and M. Sidran: *Nucleonics*, **10** (9), 15 (1952).

Birks, J. B.: "Scintillation Counters," McGraw-Hill Book Company, Inc., New York, 1953.

An excellent semipopular account of scintillation counters is given by G. B. Collins in *Sci. American*, **189** (5), 36 (November, 1953).

CHAPTER 5

THE MEASUREMENT OF QUALITY (WAVELENGTH): X-RAY OPTICS

By x-ray quality is meant spectral-energy distribution, or the constitution of the beam with regard to wavelength. Ordinary white light is proved to be a mixture of many rays of visible light of different wavelengths and corresponding to pure colors, for the beam is spread into a spectrum from violet to red by refraction in a prism or by diffraction by the finely ruled lines of a grating. In analogous fashion the spectrum of a beam of x-rays whose constitution previous to analysis is unknown identifies the quality.

The following methods of measuring quality, "hardness," or wavelengths of an x-ray beam are classified according to the properties which are the same (refraction, diffraction) as those of the optical ranges of the electromagnetic spectrum and also according to the properties which are different (power to penetrate matter opaque to light):

1. Diffraction by ruled gratings.
2. Diffraction by crystals.
3. Refraction in prisms.
4. Measurement of absorption by known materials.

By observations on absorption in screens of various elements of beams of x-rays generated at tube targets of known elements, many important facts of quality were discovered before wavelengths were actually evaluated: increasing absorbability of rays, the lower the voltage on the tube; the discovery by Barkla of the characteristic emission series for each element, K (most penetrating), L, M, etc.; increasing absorbability of the x-rays, the lower the atomic number of the target; the evaluation of hardness of a heterogeneous beam, in terms of "effective wavelength," or the wavelength of the monochromatic ray that is absorbed to the same extent as the beam of mixed rays of many wavelengths. However, though absorption coefficients do define penetrating power, they do not of themselves resolve and evaluate all the wavelengths in a beam in the sense that spectroscopy implies. Furthermore, Chap. 8 is concerned with absorption and scattering of x-rays, so that the subject can be dismissed from further immediate consideration.

X-ray Diffraction by Crystals. Glass prisms or diffraction gratings consisting of finely ruled parallel lines on glass or metal can be used only under very special conditions for the spectra of x-rays, because these have wavelengths many times shorter than light. Crystals, however, are natural gratings in which parallel planes of regularly marshaled atoms are spaced from each other at distances that are of the same order of magnitude as x-ray wavelengths.

The analysis for quality is best made, therefore, with the crystal spectrometer originally designed by the Braggs. It is a device upon which crystals of known interplanar spacings are mounted and rotated; the quantities measured are the angles at which the various components of the beam are reflected by the crystal planes. Upon the photographic plate or plotted from ionization-current readings is the spectrum of the beam. The analysis is complete because the whole process is governed by a simple law $n\lambda = 2d \sin \Theta$, where λ is a wavelength, n is the order of the reflection, d is the known distance between the parallel planes in the crystal, and Θ is the spectrometrically measured angle of incidence of the ray upon these planes (or 2Θ, the angle of diffraction or reflection).

If crystals are built up of atoms and molecules marshaled in definite rows and in parallel planes with their mutual forces restraining them to relatively fixed positions in the rigid solid and if x-rays are scattered by atoms, then these crystals are potential three-dimensional diffraction gratings for x-rays. Such was the prediction in 1912 of Laue, after he had accepted the work of Schoenfliess and Federov leading to the conception of space groups and had calculated from the density, molecular weight, and weight of the hydrogen atom that the distances between regularly disposed particles of mass in crystals must be of the same order as the wavelength of x-rays (10^{-8} cm). Friedrich and Knipping verified the prediction, using a crystal of zinc blende. The original analysis by Laue was of considerable mathematical complexity, but the Braggs were able to reduce the interaction between x-rays and crystals to terms of great simplicity by considering primary x-rays to be reflected by the face of a crystal. As a matter of fact, the mechanism is far more complicated, since planes and atoms far below the "reflecting" surface are concerned and since the emergent "secondary" x-rays have been emitted as a consequence of electronic changes in the atoms across which the primary beam passes. Experiments have shown that the whole phenomenon appears to be simple reflection of the primary beam in accordance with the simple equation $n\lambda = 2d \sin \Theta$.

The Bragg Law. The simple relations among λ, d, and Θ are at once seen from Fig. 53, which shows the incident beam I reflected at O_1 and O_2. The line ab is perpendicular to the reflected rays $O_1 1$ and $O_2 2$. The length of path $O_1 O_2 b$ is greater than the length of the path $O_1 a$ by the length of the line $cO_2 b$, the line Oc being perpendicular to $O_1 O_2$. The length of the line cO_2b is, obviously, $2d \sin \Theta$. The condition that there should be a reflected beam is therefore that the reflected train O_22 shall be exactly one wavelength or an integer multiple of wavelengths n behind the train O_11 or that

$$n\lambda = 2d \sin \Theta$$

This is the fundamental equation of x-ray spectroscopy and of the analysis of structure of crystalline materials. For ordinary purposes it may be considered as rigorous; slight departures from it, observed particularly at higher orders of reflection, are due entirely to refraction, for

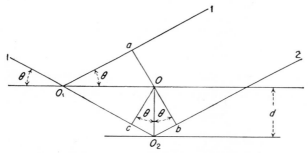

FIG. 53. Derivation of Bragg law: $n\lambda = 2d \sin \Theta$.

δ, in the expression for refractive index $\mu = 1 - \delta$, is not zero but of the order of 10^{-6}.

The application of the Bragg law may be illustrated by the following examples:

At what angles may a ray of the wavelength 0.440 A be reflected from the cube face of a rock salt crystal ($d = 2.8197$ A)?

$$\sin \Theta_1 = \frac{n\lambda}{2d} = \frac{1 \times 0.440}{5.6394} = 0.0782 \qquad \Theta_1 = 4°29.2'$$

$$\sin \Theta_2 = 2 \times 0.0782 \qquad \Theta_2 = 8°59.75'$$
$$\sin \Theta_3 = 3 \times 0.0782 \qquad \Theta_3 = 13°34'$$
$$\sin \Theta_4 = 4 \times 0.0782 \qquad \Theta_4 = 18°13.5'$$
$$\sin \Theta_5 = 5 \times 0.0782 \qquad \Theta_5 = 23°0.6', \text{ etc.}$$

What wavelengths in a beam containing the range 0.2 to 1.0 A will be reflected when incident at 9 deg upon the cube face of a rock salt crystal?

$$1\lambda_1 = 5.639 \sin 9° = 0.8804$$
$$2\lambda_2 = 5.639 \sin 9° = 0.8804 \qquad \lambda_2 = 0.440$$
$$3\lambda_3 = 5.639 \sin 9° = 0.8804 \qquad \lambda_3 = 0.293$$
$$4\lambda_4 = 5.639 \sin 9° = 0.8804 \qquad \lambda_4 = 0.220$$

Hence the reflected beam contains four wavelengths, 0.880, 0.440, 0.293, and 0.220, which are related as $1 : \frac{1}{2} : \frac{1}{3} : \frac{1}{4}$.

Standard Crystal Gratings. It is at once evident that the values of d for spectrometer crystal gratings and hence of all values of wavelength λ had to be based in the beginning on a calculated standard crystal interplanar spacing. Thus the Braggs calculated both the d_{100} or cube-face interplanar spacing for rock salt and that of the planes parallel to the cleavage face of calcite, using the best available values for the physical constants involved. The rock salt value was calculated as follows on the basis that in the crystal Na^+ and Cl^- ions occupy alternate positions at the corners of elementary cubes:

Atomic weight of sodium.. 23.00
Atomic weight of chlorine... 35.46
Molecular weight of NaCl, M... 58.46
Avogadro's number (involving value of electronic charge), N_0......... 6.064×10^{23}
No. of atoms in 58.46 g NaCl... $2N_0$
Density of rock salt (pycnometer), ρ.............................. 2.163

No. of atoms in 1-cm cube......................... $n = 2 \times 6.064 \times 10^{23} \times \dfrac{\rho}{58.46}$

Distance between centers of two atoms and along cube edge.................. d

No. of atoms in a row 1 cm long.. $\dfrac{1}{d}$

No. of atoms in 1-cm cube.. $n = \dfrac{1}{d^3}$

Solving two equations of n,

$$\frac{1}{d^3} = 2 \times 6.064 \times 10^{23} \times \frac{2.163}{58.46}$$
$$d = 2.81400 \times 10^{-8} \text{ cm}$$

Thus this value is dependent upon M, N_0, and ρ, and certainly the last two could not be known to be better than 0.1 per cent. But the *entire series of d and λ values* in tables used throughout the world, whose precision measurement is due largely to Siegbahn, are based on this value of the grating constant for rock salt. It followed from the Bragg law that any other crystal-grating spacing d_c would be evaluated from

$$n\lambda = 2d_{\text{NaCl}} \sin \Theta_{\text{NaCl}} = 2d_c \sin \Theta_c$$

The calcite cleavage spacing thus came out 3.02945×10^{-8} cm, and this crystal was adopted for practical use. Siegbahn proposed a more convenient unit called the X unit, *approximately* 1×10^{-11} cm, while of course the angstrom was *exactly* 1×10^{-8} cm. Thus, recognizing the uncertainty in the values of N_0 and ρ, the d value of rock salt was arbitrarily set as

$$2,814.00 \text{ X}$$

or

$$2.81400 \text{ kX}$$

and for calcite

$$3.02945 \text{ kX}$$

It was soon discovered that wavelengths measured with ruled gratings (see pages 104 and 105) involving no assumptions as to the structure of a crystal or the value of N_0 were always about 0.2 per cent higher than those measured on the basis of the above crystal values.   Thus in 1935 Bearden determined the value of λ with a ruled grating and with it calculated the corresponding d value for calcite as 3.03560×10^{-8} cm instead of the value generally used.   For many years there was no adequate explanation of the discrepancy until an error was found in the value of the electronic charge e, which in turn affected the value of N_0. The international values[1] accepted in 1952 are

$$e = 4.802 \times 10^{-10} \text{ esu}$$
$$= 1.601864 \times 10^{-20} \text{ emu}$$
$$N_0 = 6.02380 \times 10^{23}$$

Recalculated, the corrected values of d values of crystals used in spectrometry are listed in Table 5-1.

TABLE 5-1. CRYSTAL-GRATING CONSTANTS

Crystal	Grating spacing d at 18°		Change in d per deg C, kX or 10^{-8} cm
	Siegbahn kX	Corrected $\times 10^{-8}$ cm	
Rock salt, NaCl	2.81400	2.81971	0.11
Calcite, $CaCO_3$	3.02945	3.03560	0.03
Quartz, SiO_2	4.24602	4.25465	0.04
Gypsum, $CaSO_4.2H_2O$	7.56470	7.6001	0.29
Mica	9.94272	9.9629	0.15

All Siegbahn wavelengths universally used in tables are now to be corrected by multiplying by an internationally accepted factor 1.00202, or

$$1.00202 \text{ kX} = 1 \text{ A or } 1 \times 10^{-8} \text{ cm}$$

Siegbahn and his associates in the measurement of long wavelengths introduced the use of crystalline lauric acid ($d = 27.268$ kX), palmitic acid ($d = 35.49$ kX), and stearic acid ($d = 38.7$ kX) and lead melissate ($d = 87.5$ kX).   In recent years, however, the use of such organic crystals has been practically discarded in favor of ruled gratings.

The Ionization Spectrometer.   Immediately following the discovery in 1912 of diffraction of x-rays by crystals, the ionization spectrometer was designed by the Braggs and used by them in the early measurements of wavelengths, as well as by Moseley, Duane, Richtmyer, Siegbahn (who usually photographed spectra), and others who firmly established the

[1] Rossini, Gucker, Johnston, Pauling, and Vinal, *J. Am. Chem. Soc.*, **74**, 2699 (1952): see also Bearden and Watts, *Phys. Rev.*, **81**, 73 (1951).

science of x-ray spectrometry both as a means of analysis of elements and as a means to derivation of atomic structures. Thus the ionization spectrometer is historically significant. It is still a valuable instrument used in many older laboratories, though largely replaced by Geiger-counter spectrometers of greater sensitivity and resolving power, with automatic registration of results with modern electronic circuits. It remains, however, the basic unit behind all modern improved designs.

The ionization spectrometer consists essentially of a crystal table, which rotates about the axis of the spectrometer with reference to a fixed scale graduated in degrees and minutes; readings to seconds of arc may be made by means of a vernier or with microscopes with micrometer eye-pieces. A separate movable arm carries the ionization chamber, whose angular position can be read on a second concentric scale. Two or more slits define the x-ray beam impinging on the crystal, and another slit is adjusted in front of the ionization chamber.

The ionization chamber is simply a container for a gas or vapor and two electrodes; reflected x-rays passing into the gas ionize it; with a sufficient difference of potential between the electrodes, a current results, which is measured by the speed of discharge of a gold-leaf electroscope or the deflection per second of a quadrant electrometer. In an experiment the ionization chamber is adjusted so as to receive the reflection from the crystal face. Then the crystal and ionization chamber are moved step by step (the latter at twice the rate of the former), and the ionization current is measured for each step. When the ionization current is plotted against the angle Θ, or angular scale reading, a curve is obtained showing the characteristic peaks, which appear as spectral lines if a photographic plate is substituted for the ionization chamber.

The theory of ionization and the practical utilization of air ionization as a measure of x-ray dosage in tissues were considered in the preceding chapter.

The photograph of a precision spectrometer, now nearly 30 years old, in the author's laboratory is reproduced in Fig. 54 simply to show the type of apparatus with which the foundations of x-ray spectrometry were originally laid. Upon the spectrometer, built (by the Société Genèvoise d'instruments de physique) with circular scales which may be read to 0.2 second of arc, is mounted an ionization chamber of the original Duane design, consisting of a long glass tube, containing a cylindrical electrode connected with a battery and a central insulated-rod electrode running along the axis of the tube and connected with a pair of quadrants in an electrometer.

Numerous attempts have been made to displace the quadrant electrometer, string electrometer, and gold-lead electroscope as measuring devices for ionization currents. Fonda and Collins[1] first described an amplifying

[1] *J. Am. Chem. Soc.*, **73**, 113 (1931).

system for ionization currents employing a four-element vacuum tube characterized by a very high input resistance.   Many amplifying circuits with automatic recording of spectra have since been described.   The Geiger counter described in the preceding chapter has largely replaced ionization chambers on x-ray spectrometers.

FIG. 54. Ionization spectrometer with quadrant electrometer.

Many modifications of the Bragg spectrometric method have been made; chief among these are the precise instruments of Siegbahn, who has preferred the photographic method originally developed by De Broglie. Depending upon the range of wavelengths to be used, somewhat different types of spectrometer were devised by this experimenter; the vacuum type for the spectroscopy of very soft x-rays, which are easily absorbed in air, is perhaps of the greatest interest and importance.   These spectrographs are fully described in Siegbahn's book. A curved sheet of mica is often used as a focusing crystal grating on spectrometers, illustrating another type of variation. The curved crystal for focusing and collecting x-ray beams for the purpose of assuring maximum intensity of spectral lines and for producing monochromatic rays for diffraction analyses has become standard practice. The curved-crystal spectrometer has had its best development in the researches of Mlle Cauchois (Chap. 6). Focusing monochromators, especially for powder-diffraction patterns, are illustrated and discussed in Chaps. 6 and 14.

The finest Bragg spectrometer in the world is the automatic instrument in the Crystallography Laboratory of the University of Cambridge, designed and built by Wooster and associates.[1] In six hours with this instrument, accurate intensity data are registered on photographic paper for 50 sets of planes in a crystal.

The Double Spectrometer. A very useful modification of the spectrometer is that which employs two crystals, the first serving to select a ray of given wavelength from the primary beam, by its setting at a given angle, and the second serving to analyze in detail this reflected beam for precision measurements of absolute glancing angles and for evidences of fine structure, width, etc. Or, of course, the second crystal may have an unknown structure for analysis by the strictly monochromatic beam from the first crystal. There are two arrangements for these crystals: type I, in which the rays incident on crystal A and leaving from crystal B are on the same side of the ray between crystals, antiparallel, designated by the symbol 1, 1; type II, in which the rays incident on crystal A and leaving from crystal B are on opposite sides of the ray between the crystals, designated by the symbol 1, −1. These are illustrated in Fig. 55. The theory, design, and use of the double spectrometer are fully treated by Compton and Allison.[2]

FIG. 55. Arrangement of crystals in double spectrometer: *left*, 1, −1; *right*, 1, 1. Dotted lines represent crystal faces; heavy lines below, planes parallel to the first crystals above.

A logical extension of this principle is a multicrystal spectrometer with still greater resolving power. Several of this type have been designed for special research purposes.

[1] Wooster and Martin, *Proc. Roy. Soc.* (*London*), **155**, 150 (1936).

[2] "X-rays in Theory and Experiment," p. 709, D. Van Nostrand Company, Inc., New York, 1935.

Refraction and Total Reflection of X-rays.   It will be remembered that Röntgen and his contemporaries in investigations of the nature of x-rays failed to find any experimental evidence of refraction because of the extremely small magnitude of the effect.   The subsequent discovery of refraction and the measurement of indices of refraction represent the great improvement in experimental technique.   Refraction is indicated and measured by three different effects:

1. *Departures from the Bragg Law.*   In 1921 it was discovered that wavelengths of a given line calculated from higher orders of reflection ($n = 2, 4, 5$) from a crystal face were smaller by several tenths of a per cent.   Thus the Bragg law in its simple form is only an approximation, and the discrepancies are to be ascribed to an index of refraction a little *less* than unity.   Actually $n\lambda' = 2d \sin \Theta'$, where λ' and Θ' are, respectively, wavelength and angle of incidence *in the crystal*, is accurate; but, for the wavelength *in air* λ and the angle of incidence on the crystal face Θ, the formula must be slightly corrected for refraction,

$$n\lambda = 2d \sin \Theta \left(1 - \frac{1 - \mu}{\sin^2 \Theta} \right)$$

where μ is the index of refraction of x-rays in the crystal.   In general, μ differs from 1 by a quantity only of the magnitude of 10^{-6}, *i.e.*,

$$\delta = 1 - \mu = \frac{ne^2\lambda^2}{2\pi mc^2} = 10^{-6}$$

where n is the number of electrons per unit volume.

2. *Measurement by a Prism.*   By the use of a double spectrometer a monochromatic beam of rays from the first crystal K_1 falls on a second crystal K_2, so that when this is exactly parallel to K_1 the beam is reflected into an ionization chamber.   If a prism is now placed between K_1 and K_2, the x-ray beam is deflected (in the opposite direction from that for light), so that K_2 must be moved to a new position in order to reflect the beam. The angular displacement Δ in position of the given line as reflected from K_1 onto K_2 is measured, and the value introduced into the equation $\mu = 1 + \sin (\Delta/2) \cot (\Theta/2)$.

3. *Measurement by Total Reflection.*   Since the index of refraction of materials for x-rays is less than 1, a beam of x-rays incident upon a polished surface at very small grazing angles should be totally reflected. From optics, $\cos \Theta_R = \mu = 1 - \delta$; $\sin \Theta_R = \Theta_R = \sqrt{2\delta}$.   Some values for the limiting grazing angle are as follows: glass 6 min 10 sec ($\lambda = 0.7078$), calcite 14 min 25 sec ($\lambda = 1.537$ A).   A. H. Compton first measured the values of δ by this method in 1922, by slowly turning a mirror through a small angle, over which the beam at grazing angle may be totally reflected.

Measurement of Wavelengths by a Ruled Grating. The discovery of total reflection of x-rays immediately opened the way for the use of a ruled grating to measure wavelengths, exactly as in the optical range, provided that the glancing angle of incidence of the beam on the grating is less than the critical angle of total reflection Θ_R. Compton and Doan

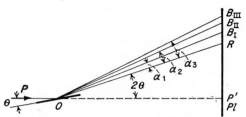

Fig. 56. Diagram of grating spectrum. P, primary beam; O, ruled diffraction grating; Pl, photographic plate; R, totally reflected beam; B, diffracted rays.

in 1925 were the first to obtain such a spectrum with a grating of speculum metal with 50 lines per millimeter. Other gratings with 200 lines per millimeter have given results of great precision. The general experimental arrangement is shown in Fig. 56. On the photographic plate, besides the primary intensity maximum and the totally reflected beam R, are lines for the diffracted ray in various orders B_I, B_{II}, B_{III}, on both sides of R. The negative orders (below R) are so weak in intensity as to

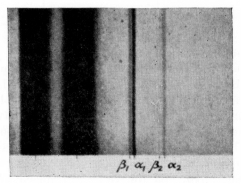

Fig. 57. X-ray spectrum from ruled grating: K series of copper. (*Thibaud.*)

be negligible, and only the positive orders are shown. Then the wavelength is calculated from

$$n\lambda = d[\cos \Theta - \cos (\Theta + \alpha_n)]$$

where d is the grating constant and n the order. On a photographic plate appear a central maximum for the primary beam, another for the total reflection, the distance between these being 2Θ; finally there is observed a diffraction spectrum of beam. In Fig. 57 is shown probably the first such result for x-rays from a copper target. By means of such gratings

Thibaud bridged the gap between the x-ray and ultraviolet regions and obtained in many cases the same wavelength for a chemical element from the spectrum of a beam from an x-ray tube and from an ultraviolet-spark spectrum. This region of long waves that are easily absorbed can be studied with the crystal spectrometer only in vacuum and with the greatest difficulty. The discrepancies between crystal- and ruled-grating data and the corrections in the former which make them conform with the absolute values from ruled gratings have already been noted.

THE FORMATION OF OPTICAL IMAGES BY X-RAYS AND THE X-RAY MICROSCOPE

Since Röntgen's first unsuccessful experiments in attempting to concentrate x-rays by lenses and mirrors, many similar efforts have been made and the failures recorded in the literature. It has been evident always that a successful x-ray microscopy would open up fields of investigation closed to optical microscopy because of limited resolution and to electron microscopy because of the very limited penetration of electrons, thus necessitating extremely thin specimens. All such attempts until the one announced in September, 1948, were unsuccessful, so that focusing and a microscope were generally considered to be impossible. Accepting the known fact of total reflection of x-rays from mirrors at extremely small grazing angles of incidence, Prof. Paul Kirkpatrick of Stanford University has taken a great step forward toward a successful solution of a seemingly impossible problem.[1] A concave spherical mirror receiving x-rays at grazing incidence images a point into a line in accordance with a focal length $f = Ri/2$, where R is the radius of curvature and i the grazing angle. The image is subject to an aberration such that a ray reflected at the periphery of the mirror misses the focal point of central rays by a distance given by $S = 1.5Mr^2/R$, where M is the magnification of the

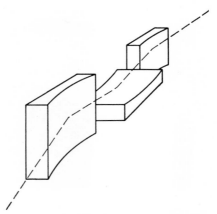

FIG. 58. Arrangement of mirrors in x-ray microscope. (*Kirkpatrick.*)

image and r is the radius of the mirror face. The possible resolving power is such as to resolve points separated by 70 A, independent of wavelength. Point images of points and, therefore, extended images of extended objects may be produced by causing the x-rays to reflect from

[1] *J. Opt. Soc. Amer.*, **38,** 766 (September, 1948); also a manual prepared by A. V. Baez.

two concave mirrors in series, particularly when crossed at right angles to each other. Figure 58 gives a schematic idea of the arrangement of the mirrors of the apparatus, Fig. 59 a photograph of the Kirkpatrick micro-

FIG. 59. Photograph of Kirkpatrick microscope with x-ray tube removed.

scope, and Fig. 60 a reproduction of the photographed enlarged images from a 350-mesh screen. This figure shows, besides the full image from both mirrors (upper left), partial images from each mirror separately

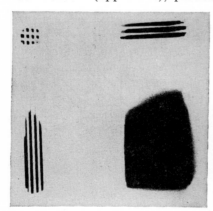

FIG. 60. Enlarged images of 350-mesh screen in x-ray microscope. (*Kirkpatrick.*) *Upper left*, full image from two mirrors; *upper right*, partial image from horizontal mirror; *lower left*, partial image from vertical mirror; *lower right*, direct radiation.

(*H*, upper right, *V*, lower left, and the large spot, lower right, caused by direct radiation). While this development is still in its early stages both in theory and in practice, it is evident that there is every prospect of a successful x-ray microscope. Elliptical surfaces already have been found to be superior to spherical or cylindrical ones in tests with mirrors made by coating a spherical mirror with a continuously variable amount of gold. Magnifications of 70 diameters already obtained are bound to be exceeded. The optical system is also suitable for focusing of very soft x-rays with wavelengths up to 45 A used for diffraction analysis of structures of materials with very large *d* spacings; and for focusing of neutrons.

Actually x-ray optics is a far better developed science than might be suspected. Any process involving focusing, collimating, or image formation may be classed as optics even when crystals are employed instead of reflecting mirrors.   Thus Mlle Cauchois[1] has constructed a microscope with a curved crystal of mica.   The x-ray beam undergoes regular Bragg reflections from crystal planes, but these serve the same purpose as curved mirrors, and an image of a specimen, itself serving as the source of x-rays or bathed by a beam of rays, may be formed as indicated in Fig. 61 and enlarged in accordance with the same principles and equations as apply to light optics.   Guoy, von Hamos, and others mentioned in Mlle Cauchois's paper anticipated the development of optics with plane

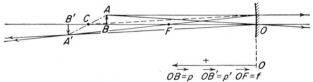

Fig. 61. The production of optical images from a bent crystal. O, bent crystal; AB, specimen; $A'B'$, image.   (*Cauchois.*)

and bent crystals; the focusing effect of bent crystals used in spectrometers as diffraction gratings has been mentioned in a previous section of this chapter.

MICRORADIOGRAPHY AND SHADOW MICROSCOPY

The technique of microradiography, considered in detail in Chap. 10, is another aspect of x-ray microscopy.   In the first type the shadow of a small specimen in direct contact with a fine-grained photographic emulsion is recorded from the penetration of relatively soft x-rays, and the 1:1 image is then photographically enlarged several hundredfold to the point of interference by the emulsion graininess.   Even more intimately related to microscopy is the new shadow-projection technique developed at the Cavendish Laboratory of the University of Cambridge.[2]   A point source of x-rays is produced by a two-lens electron optical system that reduces the electron source to a fine beam 0.5 μ in diameter.   The electron spot strikes a 1-μ tungsten-foil target that also forms the vacuum wall of the x-ray tube.   A specimen placed close to this target (less than 0.1 mm to avoid Fresnel diffraction) casts an enlarged shadow image on a distant photographic plate with a resolution in the image equal to the x-ray-spot size.   All the specimen is in focus at once, and stereoscopic examination reveals the three-dimensional form of the specimen.   Highly successful application to living and frozen-dried insects and other very small biological specimens is reported.

[1] Y. Cauchois, Sur la formation d'images des rayons X, *Rev. opt.*, **29**, 151 (1950).

[2] Reported at the November, 1952, meeting of the Electron Microscope Society of America, Cleveland, Ohio.

COLLIMATION OPTICS

As x-ray spectrography and crystal-diffraction analysis have developed since 1912, there has been a continuing experimental effort to improve collimation of x-ray beams into finer pencils while retaining the maximum intensity of the radiation. Pinhole systems to a large extent allow passage of only a small fraction of the incident energy. However, reflection from walls under grazing-angle conditions is a method of collimation which may retain high intensities. Thus calcite-faced line slits, lead-glass fine capillary tubes, converging polished walls, bent optical flats, and similar devices have been used for optical collimation to produce beams as small as 1 μ in width with 200 times the intensity of a slit system having the same definition at the same working distance.[1] Conversely the total reflection of x-rays may be used to investigate the structure of optical surfaces from the widening of images; these polished surfaces seem to consist of irregular hills and valleys of about 10 A height and 1 mm width. Reflecting-wall collimators also yield some degree of monochromatization of beams since the harder components are not reflected into the convergent beam. Monochromators are considered in Chap. 6, and in later chapters reference will be made to the applications of very intense collimated x-ray beams.

---

[1] Summarized proceedings of conference on high-intensity x-ray beams, London, April, 1950. *Brit. J. Appl. Phys.*, **1**, 305 (1950). Lely and Russel, *Acta Cryst.*, **2**, 337 (1949). Ehrenberg, *J. Opt. Soc. Amer.*, **39**, 746 (1949).

CHAPTER 6

X-RAY SPECTRA AND ATOMIC STRUCTURE

The Continuous Spectrum. Two kinds of x-radiation are known: (1) the general, "white," or continuous-spectrum x-radiation; (2) the characteristic x-radiation, which is composed of several monochromatic rays grouped in series, with wavelengths depending upon the atomic number of the emitting element. The continuous spectrum may be generated in a tube at sufficiently low potentials over certain ranges of wavelengths without characteristic lines under certain conditions, but the characteristic spectrum is always superimposed upon a background of the general radiation. The outstanding property of the general radiation is that the smooth curve obtained by plotting intensity against wavelength or spectrometer reading has a sharp, short wavelength limit (zero intensity), which does not depend upon the material of the target of the tube but upon the voltage applied to the tube, according to the fundamental Planck-Einstein quantum equation $Ve = h\nu_0 = hc/\lambda_0$, where V is the constant potential, e is the charge on the electron, h the Planck action constant,[1] c the velocity of light, ν_0 the maximum frequency, and λ_0 the minimum wavelength occurring in the spectrum. This law was first applied to x-rays by Duane and Hunt in 1914, and it has been proved

---

[1] h has the dimensions $L^2 m T^{-1}$ of a moment of momentum: action = energy × time.

	(I)	(II)
N (Avogadro's number)	Chemistry 6.02402 ± 0.00017 × 10^{23} Physics 6.02566 ± 0.00016	6.02380 ± 0.00016 × 10^{23}
h	6.62363 ± 0.00016 × 10^{-27} erg-sec	6.62377 ± 0.00027 × 10^{-27} erg-sec
e	4.80217 ± 0.00006 × 10^{-10} esu 1.601844 ± 0.000021 × 10^{-20} emu	4.80223 × 10^{-10} esu 1.601864 × 10^{-20} emu
c	299,790 ± 0.7 km/sec	299,790.2 ± 0.000013 km/sec

The latest values for h, e, c, etc., are taken from Fundamental Atomic Constants by J. A. Bearden and H. M. Watts, *Phys. Rev.*, **81**, 73 (1951) (column I), and Status of the Values of the Fundamental Constants for Physical Chemistry as of July 1, 1951, by F. D. Rossini, F. T. Gucker, Jr., H. L. Johnson, L. Pauling, and G. W. Vinal, *J. Am. Chem. Soc.*, **74**, 2699 (1952) (column II).

subsequently to be rigorously true, far more so than the other famous equation, $n\lambda = 2d \sin \Theta$.

According to this equation, Ve is the work required to carry an electron from anode to cathode, or the gain in energy in passing from cathode to anode in an electrostatic field. This can be expressed in *ergs* or *electron volts* (ev);

$$1 \text{ ev} = \frac{e(\text{esu})}{300} = \frac{4.80217 \times 10^{-10}}{300} = 1.6018 \times 10^{-12} \text{ erg}$$

At a potential difference of 150,000 volts, the energy Ve is 150,000 ev, or $500 \times 4.80217 \times 10^{-10} = 24.011 \times 10^{-8}$ erg. According to this equation

$$\lambda_0 \text{ (cm)} = \frac{h \text{ (erg-sec)} c \text{ (cm)}}{V \text{ (esu)} e \text{ (esu)}}$$

$$\lambda_0 \text{ (A)} = \frac{hc}{Ve \times 10^{-8}}$$

1 esu of potential $V = 300$ volts

Hence

$$\lambda_0 \text{ (A)} = \frac{hc}{\dfrac{V \text{ (volts)}}{300} e \text{ (esu)} \times 10^{-8}} = \frac{6.62363 \times 10^{-27} \times 2.9979 \times 10^{10}}{\dfrac{V}{300} \times 4.80217 \times 10^{-10} \times 10^{-8}}$$

$$= \frac{6.62363 \times 10^{-27} \times 2.9979 \times 10^{10}}{1.601844 \times 10^{-20} \times V \text{ (volts)}} =$$

$$\frac{12,403.246}{V}, \text{ or approximately } \frac{12,400}{V}$$

Thus, at 300,000 volts, often employed in deep therapy, the minimum wavelength is 0.04 A; a tube at 2.6 million volts must generate rays with a minimum wavelength of 0.005 A, in the extreme γ-ray region of the electromagnetic spectrum; and the new 350-million-volt betatron, a beam with $\lambda_0 = 0.000035$ A. A comparison of the continuous spectra generated by 3-, 2-, 1-, and 0.5-million-volt electrons with the γ-ray line spectrum emitted by radium in equilibrium with its products is shown in Fig. 62.

It is obvious that precision researches on the general radiation spectrum should provide a very exact method for evaluating the constant h; λ_0 can be spectrometrically evaluated from $n\lambda_0 = 2d \sin \Theta$; V can be measured accurately, by reading the current after passage through carefully calibrated high resistances; and e has the accepted value already noted. The present internationally accepted value is $6.62363 \pm 0.00016 \times 10^{-27}$ erg-sec.

Furthermore, the law of Duane and Hunt leads to the most accurate evaluation of peak voltage, which is directly calculated from the sharp limit of a crystal spectrum,

$$V_0 = \frac{hc}{e\lambda_0} = \frac{12,400}{(2d/n)\,\sin\Theta_0}$$

where $2\Theta_0$ is the experimentally measured angle of the limit.

While the short wavelength of the spectrum is entirely independent of the target element, the integrated intensity at a given voltage and tube current is a function of the atomic number of the target element and with a given target and tube current is proportional to the square of the

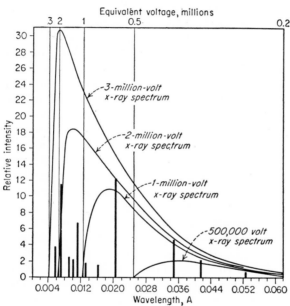

FIG. 62. Comparison of continuous x-ray spectrum produced by 3-million-, 1-million-, and 500,000-volt electrons with the γ-ray line spectrum emitted by radium in equilibrium with its products.

voltage of the atomic number of the target element. The relationships are, however, quite complicated and remain still in doubt. The curves rise sharply to an intensity maximum, defined roughly by $\lambda = 1.5\lambda_0$, and then fall away more gradually.

The question of the mechanism of the production of the general radiation is one of the most difficult in x-ray science, and a completely satisfactory answer has not been given, although modern quantum-mechanical treatment has been far more successful than the classical wave theory. The spectrum is emitted as a consequence of the deflection of cathode electrons by the strong fields surrounding the nuclei of atoms of the target. If cathode rays are accelerated in an x-ray tube by the voltage

V, the kinetic energy E_k will be $Ve = E_k$. If the electrons are stopped instantaneously at the target, the kinetic energy is transformed into the maximum possible radiation energy, or $E_k = V_0e = h\nu_0 = hc/\lambda_0$.

In addition to the maximum frequency ν_0 there may be a whole spectrum of lower frequencies emitted by electrons which lose only a part of their energy in a single encounter with a nucleus in the form of a smaller quantum $h\nu$. It is evident that predominantly an electron will experience many collisions with target atoms before being brought to rest and that in each collision some of the initial energy Ve is dissipated. It would be predicted that for very thin targets more of the general radiation energy would lie near the Ve limit than for thick targets. This is experimentally found to be true. For a thick target only 0.01 to 0.1 per cent of the energy of the cathode electrons is converted into x-ray energy.

The general radiation is of practical importance since it is employed in the Laue method of crystal analysis. In all applications at high voltages including therapy, radiography, etc., it comes quite prominently into play. The spectrum can be profoundly modified by filtration, inasmuch as rays of short wavelengths are absorbed far less than are those of the long wavelength. The effect of filtration in the absence of characteristic effects is, then, to sharpen the curve and to shift the maximum to the shorter wavelengths, without in any way affecting the value of λ_0. Filtration and the measurement of effective wavelength of general radiation will be considered in Chap. 8.

Characteristic Emission Spectra. In addition to the continuous x-radiation, rays that have wavelengths characteristic of the anticathode elements are recognized. If the potential on the x-ray tube is sufficiently high, the spectrum of the emitted beam will show sharp lines (or peaks if the ionization current measured with an ionization spectrometer is plotted) superposed upon the continuous background. These same characteristic x-rays are emitted as fluorescent rays if a beam of primary x-rays with sufficiently short wavelengths falls upon an absorption screen containing the same element as the tube target. The characteristic emission lines appear in groups designated as the K, L, M, N, O, etc., series (beginning with the most penetrating or shortest wavelength group), following the nomenclature of Barkla, who discovered the characteristic emission in the course of his absorption measurements.

Each of the series of *emission lines* contains several definite lines of different wavelengths. Probably the most remarkable characteristic of the x-ray range of the electromagnetic spectrum is the uniform simplicity of these spectra. The K series of all the elements except the lightest consists of four principal lines, the γ (also designated β_2 and actually a very close doublet), β (really a close doublet β_1 and β_3), and the doublet α_1 and α_2, in the order of increasing wavelengths. The typical appearance of this spectrum as it was plotted from measurements with an ionization spectrometer of relatively low resolving power is shown in Fig. 63. Practically, this is the most important series, since it is now used almost exclusively in crystal analysis. The more numerous L-series lines, illustrated in Fig. 64, are in three groups γ, β, and α, corresponding to the three L absorption discontinuities. About 30 have been identified. Because of the long wavelengths, measurements of the M and N series have been largely confined to the heaviest elements.

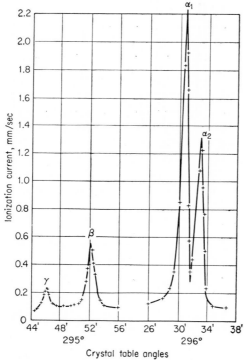

FIG. 63. *K*-series emission spectrum.

Characteristic Absorption Spectra. There are also absorption discontinuities observed in x-ray spectra whenever a beam of x-rays undergoing spectroscopic analysis passes through absorbing material; the wavelengths corresponding to these discontinuities, or edges, are also characteristic of each of the chemical elements. All rays with wavelengths shorter than that of a given discontinuity, or edge, will be absorbed by the element to a markedly greater extent than rays with wavelengths longer than this critical value. In other words, an absorbing screen that is relatively "opaque" to x-rays of a range of wavelengths up to a characteristic value is "transparent" to longer rays. Similarly, if a beam of x-rays is absorbed by a gas in which the ionization current is being measured, sharp discontinuities occur which correspond to wave-

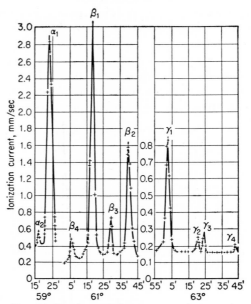

FIG. 64. *L*-series emission spectrum (tungsten).

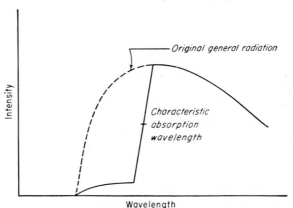

FIG. 65. Characteristic *K* absorption edge plotted from ionization spectrometer data.

lengths characteristic of the elements in the gas. A single absorption discontinuity[1] is associated with the *K* series (Fig. 65), three with the *L*, five with the *M*, probably seven with the *N*, and five with the *O*. Absorption edges which are observed on all photographs correspond to the *K* discontinuities of silver and bromine; the intensities as compared with the ionization curves are, of course, reversed because the absorbed energy blackens the emulsion to the greatest extent.

[1] Figure 65 is plotted with wavelengths on the horizontal axis increasing from left to right. In present work on fine structure it is preferred to plot increasing frequency or energy in electron volts from left to right, so that this figure would be reversed.

The Relationship between Characteristic Emission and Absorption Discontinuities. It is a singular fact that all the lines in the K-series emission spectrum are excited simultaneously when the energy conditions permit. Thus the α doublet of the K series with definitely longer wavelengths cannot be made to appear without the γ and β lines, by adjusting the value of the voltage in the equation $Ve = hc/\lambda_{K\alpha}$. It is true that the spectrum obtained under such conditions will show the presence of rays with the same wavelengths as the $K\alpha$ lines, but this spectrum is due only to general radiation and is not characteristic of the chemical element on the target. Nor will the K-series lines appear when $\lambda_{K\gamma}$, corresponding to the emission line of shortest wavelength, is substituted in the energy equation. An examination of the value of the wavelength corresponding to the K absorption discontinuity for a given element serving as an absorber discloses the fact that this value is slightly shorter than the wavelength of the characteristic $K\gamma$ line emitted by this same element serving as a target. When the voltage on the x-ray tube is adjusted so that $Ve = hc/\lambda_{K\,abs}$, then the entire emission series appears. It follows, also, that fluorescent x-rays can be emitted only when the primary x-ray beam contains rays with these critical wavelengths numerically the same as those which correspond to the absorption discontinuities or shorter (*i.e.*, rays generated by a definite minimum voltage or higher). The energy represented by hc/λ_{abs} must be vitally related, therefore, to definite processes that are occurring in atoms when electrons in the cathode-ray stream strike them or x-rays pass over them. The L series can be generated in three groups, since there are three quantum wavelengths, or absorption discontinuities. Similarly there are $5M$, $7N$, $5O$, and $3P$ absorption edges (or energy levels) possible.

The effect of voltage on characteristic spectra differs markedly from that on the continuous spectrum. The latter is produced at any voltage, but the short-wavelength limit moves to smaller values as the voltage is increased. An emission series appears only at a critical voltage, and the only effect of a further increase of voltage is to increase the intensity of all the lines without altering them in position or in relative intensities.

THE EXPERIMENTAL RESULTS OF THE MEASUREMENT OF WAVELENGTHS[1]

Characteristic Absorption. The wavelengths of the K absorption limits have been measured for the elements with few exceptions from

[1] For the "International Tables for X-ray Crystallography" now in preparation, the wavelengths adopted are those given in "Tables de constantes et données numériques; longueurs d'onde des émissions X et des discontinuités d'absorption X," by Y. Cauchois and H. Hubukei (Hermann & Cie, Paris, 1947). These values are in X units and so must be multiplied by the factor 1.00202 to give angstroms. These agree well with the values of W. L. Bragg [*J. Sci. Inst.*, **24**, 27 (1947)] and new experimental values by J. A. Bearden.

magnesium (12) to uranium (92); of the three L limits for those from rubidium (37) to uranium (92); of the five M limits for tungsten (74) to uranium (92). In each case scattered data have been reported for elements of lower atomic number than those just mentioned. The characteristic absorption discontinuities were observed by Barkla in his absorption measurements with screens before the discovery of the use of crystals as diffraction gratings. De Broglie in his first spectral photographs discovered the sudden changes in the blackening of the photographic plate

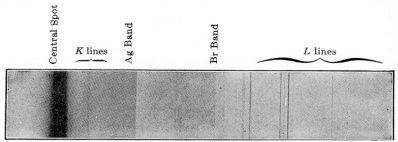

Fɪɢ. 66. Spectrum from tungsten-target x-ray tube, showing the absorption edges of silver and bromine in photographic emulsion. (*De Broglie.*)

due to the characteristic absorptions of silver and bromine in the photographic emulsion (Fig. 66); in both cases the plate was blacker on the side nearer the zero direct-beam line, a phenomenon which accords with the definition of critical-absorption wavelength as the one such that the absorbing element absorbs x-rays of wavelengths shorter than the discontinuity to a greater extent than x-rays of longer wavelengths.

The values in angstroms (kX units or Siegbahn values multiplied by 1.00202 to convert to angstroms) of the K absorption limits for a few of

TABLE 6-1. CRITICAL ABSORPTION WAVELENGTHS, K SERIES

Element		Wavelength	Element		Wavelength
12	Mg	9.5304	35	Br	0.9101
13	Al	7.9470	40	Zr	0.6888
17	Cl	4.4027	42	Mo	0.6198
22	Ti	2.4973	45	Rh	0.5338
23	V	2.2690	46	Pd	0.5092
24	Cr	2.0701	47	Ag	0.4858
25	Mn	1.8964	53	I	0.3746
26	Fe	1.7433	56	Ba	0.3315
27	Co	1.6081	74	W	0.17837
28	Ni	1.4880	78	Pt	0.15849
29	Cu	1.3804	79	Au	0.15375
30	Zn	1.2833	82	Pb	0.1413
31	Ga	1.1957	92	U	0.1075
32	Ge	1.1165			

TABLE 6-2. CRITICAL ABSORPTION WAVELENGTHS, L SERIES

Element	L_{I} (L_{11})	L_{II} (L_{21})	L_{III} (L_{22})
47 Ag	3.2540	3.5138	3.6983
53 I	2.3887	2.5526	2.7194
56 Ba	2.0662	2.2037	2.3616
74 W	1.0226	1.0735	1.2140
78 Pt	0.8939	0.9340	1.0731
82 Pb	0.7822	0.8152	0.9519
92 U	0.5698	0.5932	0.7231

the more commonly used elements are as shown in Table 6-1. Some values of the L absorption limits are given in Table 6-2. M absorption limits for tungsten, bismuth, thorium, and uranium are given in Table 6-3.

TABLE 6-3. CRITICAL ABSORPTION WAVELENGTHS, M SERIES

Element	M_{I}	M_{II}	M_{III}	M_{IV}	M_{V}
74 W	4.39	4.84	5.46	6.63	6.86
83 Bi	3.106	3.349	3.897	4.583	4.773
90 Th	2.393	2.576	3.064	3.559	3.729
92 U	2.233	2.390	2.879	3.333	3.498

Emission Spectra. *The K Series.* In the wavelength region above 0.1 A there have been experimentally measured four groups of emission lines, the K, L, M, and N series. For the heaviest atoms, O- and P-series lines are theoretically possible though these would lie in the ultraviolet range. Each group in general retains the same appearance from one element to the next, with a given line simply displaced to a shorter wavelength in passing from one element to a heavier. The K series, as first photographed by Moseley in 1914, seemed to consist of two lines, β and α, but these were later resolved into four lines γ (β_2 in the "International Critical Tables"), β, α_1, and α_2. The γ and β lines in experiments of great precision are further resolved into doublets. The wavelength difference between α_1 and α_2 varies from 0.0044 A for tin to 0.00484 A for hafnium and the remaining heavy elements. The separation of the β doublet is about 0.00076 A although there is a considerable variation; the numerical difference $\lambda_\beta - \lambda_\gamma$ varies from 0.00955 A for tin to 0.0048 A for the elements above tungsten.

The relative intensities of the K lines have been the subject of several investigations. Duane and Stenström more than a third of a century ago found the following relative values for the K lines of tungsten:

α_3	α_2	α_1	β_1	γ
4	50	100	35	15

The ratio $\alpha_1/\alpha_2 = 2/1$ seems to be generally true for practically all the elements. Allison and Armstrong obtained precision measurements for the following ratios: Mo $K\beta$/Mo $K\alpha = 1/7.7$; Mo $K\beta_1$/Mo $K\beta_3 = 2/1$ (the resolved doublet); Cu $K\beta$/ Cu $K\gamma = 42/1$; Cu $K\alpha$/Cu $K\alpha_3\alpha_4 = 100/1$. The appearance of lines and the relative intensities are, of course, of the utmost importance in their bearing upon the structure of atoms and the levels of energy within them.

The K emission wavelengths are now known with considerable accuracy for most of the elements between carbon (6) (λ for unresolved $K\alpha$ 44.79 A) and uranium (92) and even for the transuranium elements (93 to 98). In Table 6-4 are the most probable values for the elements most commonly employed as targets in x-ray tubes.

For the lightest elements as many as 12 or more lines may appear in the K series instead of the usual 4 or 5. Wentzel first claimed that these lines are due to multiple ionization of the relatively simply constructed atoms and, therefore, are related to the ordinary lines (γ, β, α_1, α_2) as the spark lines are to the arc lines in optical spectra. Thus an $\alpha_3\alpha_4$ line or doublet and other "nondiagram" lines appear in all elements below zinc, in addition to the regular $\alpha_1\alpha_2$ doublet. In the past 20 years progress has been made on the interpretation of "satellite" or nondiagram lines by Richtmyer, Langer, and others as due to two-electron jumps in an atom.[1] Data on satellite lines and interpretations are considered in later sections.

Under some conditions *band* spectra are observed for the light elements. For solid metallic sodium, magnesium, or aluminum diffuse bands appear as part of the emission spectra, whereas the same element in vapor form produces only the usual sharp lines. Cauchois and associates[2] have recently made many experimental studies of this phenomenon. The effect on the emission bands of Al or Mg of alloying is an interesting phenomenon; $K\beta$ of Al in Cu_9Al appears as a doublet instead of the unique band of pure Al; $K\beta$ of Mg in alloys with Al is a simple broad band like that of the pure metal but with a completely changed intensity distribution.

It will be observed from the foregoing data that the wavelength of the $K\gamma$ emission line is only a fraction of a per cent longer than that of the K absorption limit. It is a point of great interest whether or not there

---

[1] A complete account is found in Siegbahn, "Spektrographie der Röntgenstrahlen," pp. 370–378.

[2] Y. Cauchois, *J. chim. phys.* **46**, 21 (1949); *Compt. rend.*, **231**, 574 (1950); *Acta Cryst.*, **6**, 352 (1953).

TABLE 6-4. K EMISSION LINES, IN ANGSTROMS

Element		$\gamma(\beta_2)$	β_1	β_3	α_1	α_2
22	Ti	. . . .	2.51381	2.522	2.74841*	2.75207
23	V	. . . .	2.28434	2.2924	2.50347*	2.50729
24	Cr	. . . .	2.08480	2.0899	2.28962*	2.29351
25	Mn	. . . .	1.91015	1.9144	2.10175*	2.10569
26	Fe	. . . .	1.75653	1.76001	1.93596*	1.93991
27	Co	. . . .	1.62075	1.62338	1.78891*	1.79278
28	Ni	1.48861	1.50010	1.50213	1.65785*	1.66169
29	Cu	1.38102	1.39217	. . . .	1.54051*	1.54433
30	Zn	1.28366	1.29522	. . . .	1.43511*	1.43894
31	Ga	1.1962	1.20784	. . . .	1.34003*	1.34394
32	Ge	1.11684	1.12890	. . . .	1.25401*	1.25797
42	Mo	0.62095	0.63225	0.632819	0.70922*	0.71354
44	Ru	0.58164	0.54559	0.57309	0.61323*	0.61761
46	Pd	0.57021	0.52052	0.52114	0.58541*	0.58980
47	Ag	0.48701	0.49701	0.497650	0.55938*	0.56378
74	W	0.17935	0.184363	0.185143	0.208992	0.213813
78	Pt	0.15920	0.163664	. . . .	0.185504	0.190372
79	Au	0.15457	0.158971	. . . .	0.180185	0.185064

* Considered by Bearden to be the wavelength standards.

are any additional lines between $K\gamma$ and the limit. Larsson measured a $K\beta_4$ line for molybdenum at 0.61825 A. Duane in 1931 examined K-series x-rays by means of a Bragg spectrometer, the Moseley photographic method being employed. The incident ray and that reflected by the crystal to the photographic plate through distances of 4,725 mm passed through long metal tubes, exhausted of air in order to reduce the absorption. The $K\beta$ doublet lines of molybdenum ($\Delta\lambda = 0.00056$ A), examined by photometric curves, were separated 0.88 mm. No third line lay in the immediate neighborhood of the β doublet. Between the γ line and the short-wavelength limit of the series appeared a marked blackening that represented several lines close together. The new lines may be due to O electrons falling into the K level; but a better explanation is, perhaps, that the lines are produced by falls into the K level of conductivity electrons which may from time to time lie in outer atomic-energy levels. Several photographs produced by long exposures showed a fainter single line, roughly halfway between the β and the γ lines. It did not correspond to a known x-ray line of any chemical element reflected in the first or second order. Ross[1] also found this line, which he calls β_4, with an intensity of one one-thousandth that of $K\alpha$, another β_5, and two groups of still fainter lines near γ and β lines.

The L Series. The complexity of the L series, which has already been referred to, prevents its extensive use for practical purposes. It is

[1] *Phys. Rev.*, **39**, 536, 748 (1932).

interesting to note, however, that the new elements hafnium (72), rhenium (75), and illinium (now called promethium) (61) were all dis- covered by means of analysis of their L emission lines.   More than 20 lines in the α, β, and γ groups have been identified for uranium; this number decreases with decreasing atomic number, as is to be expected upon the basis of atomic models in which outer shells of electrons dis- appear.   Measurements of the tungsten L series give the values in Table 6-5.

TABLE 6-5. WAVELENGTHS, TUNGSTEN L SERIES

γ_4	L_{11}–O_{22}	1.02854
γ_9	L_{11}–N_{33}	1.04601
γ_3	L_{11}–N_{22}	1.06179
γ_2	L_{11}–N_{21}	1.06799
γ_6	L_{21}–O_{32}	1.0742
γ_8	L_{21}–O_{11}	1.0812
γ_1	L_{21}–O_{32}	1.09774
γ_5	L_{21}–N_{11}	1.1315
β_9	. . . .	1.2045
β_8	L_{11}–M_{32}	1.2058
β_{10}	. . . .	1.2118
β_5	L_{22}–$O_{32,33}$	1.2149
β_7	L_{22}–$N_{43,44}$	1.2233
$\beta_{11,12}$	. . . .	1.2379
β_2	L_{22}–$N_{32,33}$	1.24442
β_3	L_{11}–M_{22}	1.26255
β_1	L_{21}–M_{32}	1.28175
β_6	L_{22}–N_{11}	1.2897
β_4	L_{11}–M_{21}	1.30136
β_{11}	L_{11}–M_{11}	1.3371
η	L_{21}–M_{11}	1.4207
α_1	L_{22}–M_{33}	1.47646
α_2	L_{22}–M_{32}	1.48752
1	L_{22}–M_{11}	1.67843

The relative intensities of the lines $L\alpha_1/L\alpha_2$ are $10/1$; the γ lines are in the order $\gamma_1:\gamma_2:\gamma_3:\gamma_4:\gamma_5:\gamma_6 = 100:14.0:22.3:7.0:3.0:2.3$; for the β lines $\beta_1:\beta_2:\beta_3:\beta_4:\beta_5:\beta_6:\beta_7:\beta_9:\beta_{10} = 100:49.3:15.0:7.7:0.47:2.0:0.4:0.68:0.60$.

The L-series wavelengths are known more or less completely for all the elements from vanadium (23) to uranium (92).

By using, as diffraction gratings in their vacuum spectrograph, crystals of palmitic and stearic acid, Siegbahn and Thoraeus made measurements upon the very long wavelength α and β lines in the L-series spectra of zinc, copper, nickel, cobalt, and iron, the values ranging from 11.99 to 17.66 A. The longest L line recognized by the "International Critical Tables" is the $\alpha_{1,2}$ line of vanadium at 24.200 A.   Practically all measurements are now being made with ruled gratings rather than with organic crystals.   How- ever, it has been possible lately to construct a focusing crystal grating by depositing 300 layers of barium stearate on a cylindrical backing by the Blodgett-Langmann technique (see Chap. 20). For measuring wavelengths greater than 20 A, this stratified molecular film with a d spacing of 50.47 A is highly successful.[1]

The M and N Series. The M series was discovered by Siegbahn in 1916, and later measurements with crystal gratings were made for the elements from uranium (92) to barium (56). In 1931 Lindberg, using

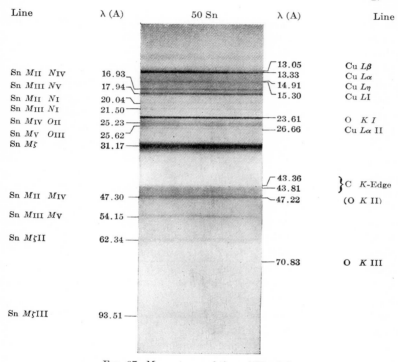

Line	λ (A)	50 Sn	λ (A)	Line
Sn M_{II} N_{IV}	16.93		13.05	Cu $L\beta$
Sn M_{III} N_V	17.94		13.33	Cu $L\alpha$
Sn M_{II} N_I	20.04		14.91	Cu $L\eta$
Sn M_{III} N_I	21.50		15.30	Cu LI
Sn M_{IV} O_{II}	25.23		23.61	O KI
Sn M_V O_{III}	25.62		26.66	Cu $L\alpha$ II
Sn $M\zeta$	31.17			
			43.36	} C K-Edge
			43.81	
Sn M_{II} M_{IV}	47.30		47.22	(O K II)
Sn M_{III} M_V	54.15			
Sn $M\zeta$II	62.34			
			70.83	O K III
Sn $M\zeta$III	93.51			

FIG. 67. M spectrum of tin. (*Kiessig.*)

ruled gratings, determined with great completeness and accuracy the wavelength of the M-series lines for elements from uranium (92) to cerium (58), with values ranging from 2.440 A for the $M_{II}O_{IV}$ line of uranium to 14.030 for the $M_V N_{VI}$ or α_I line of cerium. For tungsten the wavelengths of the strongest M emission lines are 6.076 (γ or $M_{III}N_V$), 6.743 (β or $M_{IV}N_{VI, VII}$), and 6.969 A (α or $M_V N_{VII}$). Siegbahn and Magnusson[2] in 1934 extended the measurements down to bromine (35) with the ruled grating. Especially careful measurements were made by Kiessig.[3] Figure 67 shows his grating spectrum for tin with 11 M lines together

[1] A. Lemasson, *Acta Cryst.*, **6**, 97 (1953).
[2] *Z. Physik*, **88**, 559 (1934).
[3] *Z. Physik*, **109**, 671 (1938), **95**, 555 (1935).

with L lines from copper in the backing of the target, K lines of oxygen, and the K absorption edge of carbon.

Hjalmar first photographed lines belonging to the N series of uranium, thorium, and bismuth. The line at 13.805 A for thorium was the longest wavelength spectroscopically measured prior to the studies of Siegbahn and Thoraeus using stearic acid crystals as gratings. Several other studies of the N series and some O lines have been reported in recent years.

The Measurement of Long Wavelengths by Methods Other than X-ray Spectroscopy. Many investigators have attempted to measure wavelengths of the soft x-rays, particularly for the very lightest elements, by locating the discontinuities in the slope of the curves representing the photoelectric current as a function of the exciting voltage. Essentially the method consists in allowing radiation from the target of a highly evacuated x-ray tube to fall on a plate within the tube, which is connected to an electrometer. The current is kept constant and the voltage varied in steps. The various potentials corresponding to discontinuities in the curve are considered to be the limiting voltages for the K and L series. Important values in kX units so obtained are H K 912, He K 493, C K 42.6 to 45.4, N K 33.0 to 35.1, O K 23.8 to 25.8, Na L 35.3, Al L 100, Al M 326, etc.

In the range of very long wavelengths the same lines are obtained from an x-ray tube and from an ultraviolet vacuum spark. Grating results are as follows: O $K\alpha$ 23.8, N $K\alpha$ 31.8, C $K\alpha$ 44.9, B $K\alpha$ 68.0, Fe $L\alpha$ 17.7, Fe $L\eta$ 19.6, Fe Ll 20.1, Mo M 65.0, 54.9, Ta N 58.3, 61.4, W N 56.0, 59.0, Pt N 48.0, 51.0, Au N 46.8, 49.4. These values have been a powerful aid in the establishment of energy levels.

The Effect of Valence and the Fine Structure of X-ray Spectral Lines and Absorption Edges. Up to this point the principal features of x-ray spectra such as are observed with ordinary spectrometers have been discussed. As spectrometers have been improved in design and increased in sensitivity and resolving power with enlarged dimensions, curved crystals, double spectrometers, improved focusing and collimation, Geiger counters, and intensified primary or secondary fluorescent radiation, it has been possible to detect additional features of spectra such as very faint satellite lines, a fine structure for absorption edges and emission bands (for light elements) or lines which previously appeared to be singly resolved, variations in wavelengths with mode of combination of elements or their valences, small but distinct differences between results for free atoms (in gases or liquids) and for these atoms bound in crystals, spectral distinctions between solid conductors and insulators, and a variety of other second- or higher-order phenomena. Until about 10 years ago, many were not adequately explained or applied to the solution of problems of energy levels, the solid state, or mechanisms of excitation.

With the rapid rise of a new quantum-mechanical science of the solid state, it was realized that these details of fine structure were an important experimental method of testing theories. Suddenly spectrometry of highest precision became a revivified science, and intensive investigations were undertaken and still continue in laboratories all over the world, conducted especially by Mott at Bristol, Cauchois at Paris, Kiestra at Groningen, Sandström at Uppsala, Slater at Massachusetts Institute of Technology, Parratt at Cornell, Beeman at Wisconsin, and many others. The subject is one of considerable complexity and beyond the scope of this book, except for some simple typical examples, cited later in this chapter. But for a good cross section of the topic, reference may be made to the report published by the U.S. Department of Commerce, Office of Technical Services (Navexos, p. 1033), of the Conference on the Applications of X-ray Spectroscopy to Solid State Problems held at the University of Wisconsin in October, 1950.[1]

Since characteristic x-ray absorption and emission are processes in which the innermost electrons in the atom are concerned, it is reasonable to suppose that the external, or valence, electrons have little or no effect upon the wavelengths. For many years it was generally agreed that the characteristic wavelengths were entirely independent of the state of chemical combination of the element; thus sulfur or manganese as elements, or exhibiting various valences in compounds, were thought to give always the same critical absorption or emission wavelength values. Precision researches, largely in the Siegbahn laboratory, demonstrated that for lighter elements there are small but distinct variations in these values depending upon the state of the element in the absorbing screen or target of the x-ray tube.

TABLE 6-6. EFFECT OF CHEMICAL COMBINATION ON K ABSORPTION EDGES
OF IRON*

Valence state	Absorber	$\Delta\lambda$, X units, compared with pure iron
II	$FeCO_3$	1.4
	$FeSO_4.(NH_4)_2SO_4.6H_2O$	1.9
II and III	Fe_3O_4	1.9
	$FeSO_4.(NH_4)_2SO_4.6H_2O + FeCl_3.6H_2O$	1.8
III	$FeCl_3.6H_2O$	2.5
	Fe_2O_3	2.5

* Lindsey and Voorhees, *Phil. Mag.*, **6**, 910 (1928).

[1] In the paper contributed to this conference by Mlle Y. Cauchois, there is a bibliography of 122 papers between 1932 and 1951.

TABLE 6-7. PRINCIPAL AND SECONDARY ABSORPTION EDGES FOR CL AND S[†]

Absorber	K_1	K_2	Absorber	K_1	K_2
Cl_2...........	4.3938	4.3816	S monoclinic...	5.0090	4.9946
HCl...........	4.3853	.....	S rhombic.....	5.0086	4.9938
Chlorides‡.....	4.3829	4.3600	S crystal......	5.0088	4.9941
Chlorates......	4.3769	4.3574	Sulfides.......	5.0093	Depends on metal ion
Perchlorates....	4.3698	4.3478	Sulfites.......	4.9960	4.9881
			SO_2..........	5.0040	4.9964
			Sulfates......	4.9879	Depends on metal ion
			S^{2+} (organic)..	5.0068	
			S^{4+} (organic)..	5.0019	
			S^{6+} (organic)..	4.9939	

† SOURCE: Lindh.

‡ The different edges for chloride, chlorate, and perchlorate enable an analysis for purity of any salt.

As a single example, the values of the K absorption limit for iron compounds may be cited from the work of Lindsey and Voorhees as shown in Table 6-6.

Among several others reports Cairns and Ott[1] used such measurements to prove the existence of trivalent metal compounds. Furthermore, a fine structure is found for the lines and absorption limits of certain elements. Lindh investigated both the emission lines and the absorption edges of chlorine, sulfur, phosphorus, and other elements. Results on wavelengths of the absorption edges of chlorine and sulfur are listed in Table 6-7 (K_1 and K_2 principal and secondary edges, respectively). These values have been verified and extended by Stelling and others. Since 1945 Mlle Cauchois in Paris has made a major contribution in this field[2] with bent-crystal spectrometers of high resolution and precision.

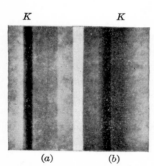

K K

(a)   (b)

FIG. 68. K absorption spectra showing (a) simple edge, (b) edge with secondary absorption. (*Hanawalt.*)

Monatomic vapors exhibit no secondary structure in absorption edges, whereas polyatomic vapors may, although there is usually additional structure observed for the same material in the solid state. This is shown in Fig. 68. The two crystalline forms of calcium carbonate, calcite and aragonite, have markedly different absorption patterns, a fact showing that the crystalline structure must have a primary influence in

[1] *J. Am. Chem. Soc.*, **56**, 1094 (1934).

[2] *Compt. rend.* **227**, 65 (1948), **228**, 1003, 1720 (1949); **231**, 574 (1950); *J. chim. phys.*, **46**, 21 (1949).

giving to the absorption edge a complex fine structure. The fine structure of absorption edges for practically free atoms as in gases cannot extend over more than 10 ev from the main edge. In crystalline matter, however, the fine structure may extend over 300 ev or more from the edge. White lines may appear, representing maximum absorption in this fine structure. As an example of the Cauchois work may be quoted measurements for anhydrous $NiCl_2$: the K absorption discontinuity 1.48313, white ray (Cauchois RB) 1.48237; complex α band–black ray 1.4813, minimum 1.47973, maximum 1.4775; A (region of strong absorption) 1.4732; β band 1.4676; B (region of strong absorption) 1.4616; γ band 1.4502. These represent in order the following differences in energy (Δ ev) from the K

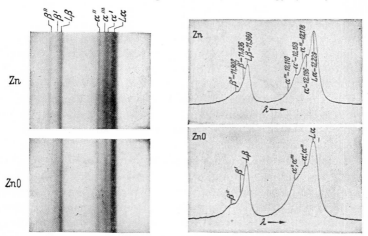

FIG. 69. $L\beta$ and $L\alpha$ emission lines of zinc and zinc oxide, showing satellites. (*Gwinner.*)

discontinuity: 0, 5.1, 13.5, 21.7, 31.2, 57, 88, 123, 190. These values vary for various nickel salts in solid anhydrous or hydrated form and in solution. Elements showing a white ray near the K discontinuity are Zn, Ga, Ge, As, Se, while Cd, In, Sn, Sb, Te do not; nor do Hg, Tl, Pb, and Br at the L_I edge; oxides and salts of Zr, Nb, and Mo have a white ray, and those of Hf, Ta, and W do not. Oxygen seems to be favorable for the maximum absorption line, for ZrO_2, $ZrSiO_4$, $ZrOCl_2$ solid or in solution show the white line, and $ZrCl_4$ does not.

The "satellites" associated with emission lines have been mentioned. An example showing the fine structure of the $L\beta$ and $L\alpha$ lines of zinc and zinc oxide from the work of Gwinner is given in Fig. 69.

As a very recent example illustrative of many studies of satellite lines may be cited the work of Jossem and Parratt[1] on the $K\beta$ lines of K and Cl in solid KCl. For the former, there are in addition to the strongest β line

[1] "Conference on Applications of X-ray Spectroscopy to Solid State Problems, 1950," p. 47, U.S. Department of Commerce, Office of Technical Services, Washington.

the following lines on the high-frequency or short-wavelength side with the corresponding energy positions from β, in electron volts: β_i (2.2), β_{II} (3.7), β_V (8.0), and β_5 (11.7). For Cl, there are β_x (2.4), β_i (3.0), and β_5 (4.7). Previously 9 β lines for K and 13 for Cl have been reported. Reliable information on component-line slopes, widths, and relative intensities offers significant new bases for interpreting the observed x-ray spectra, for making rational electron-transition assignments, and for understanding the outer-energy-level scheme in solids.

Theories of the origin of these fine-structure features and, conversely, the use of these experimental data in deriving adequate atomic mechanisms are considered in a later paragraph in this chapter.

Methods of Obtaining Homogeneous Monochromatic X-rays. The beam of x-rays produced by an ordinary x-ray tube is obviously heterogeneous and contains many wavelengths. The general radiation is a continuous band, and upon this is superposed above certain voltages the characteristic spectral series. In many applications of x-rays it is highly desirable to have a homogeneous beam of known wavelength. This is particularly true for the analysis of the fine structure of materials. Even at very high voltages for deep therapy, the effort is made to homogenize the beam by filtration through sheets of metal so that dosage can be reproduced.

There is only one method of assuring a monochromatic ray, and this is the use of the double spectrometer. At a given angular setting Θ of a crystal grating with constant d, only those rays with a certain wavelength λ can be reflected at the definite angle 2Θ from the primary undeviated beam. Consequently the second spectrometer or other apparatus can be adjusted to receive the purely monochromatic beam.[1] Davis, Compton, Allison, and others have made excellent use of the double spectrometer to measure wavelengths accurately, to study the natural widths of spectral lines, etc. For practical purposes the method has the disadvantage that a loss in energy occurs in every reflection or diffraction process, and the intensity of the radiation is thus diminished. However, the monochromator with crystals of quartz, pentaerythritol (Table 6-8), etc., is an essential part of good diffraction equipment, particularly for patterns of glass and other noncrystalline materials. Recently there has been renewed interest in preparing crystal monochromators which will provide much higher reflected intensities. Some of the most promising are bent aluminum crystals,[2] bent plane-parallel quartz slabs,[3] and calcite and LiF crystals ground off at an angle to Bragg planes to form "cutoff" concentrating monochromators.[4]

[1] *Cf.* Compton, *Rev. Sci. Instr.*, **2**, 365 (1931). Allison, *Phys. Rev.*, **41**, 1 (1932).

[2] Y. Cauchois, T. J. Tiedema, and W. G. Burgers, *Acta Cryst.*, **3**, 372 (1950).

[3] P. M. de Wolff, *Acta Cryst.*, **1**, 207 (1948).

[4] R. C. Evans, P. B. Hirsch, and J. N. Kellar, *Acta Cryst.*, **1**, 124 (1948).

TABLE 6-8. SOME CRYSTALS FOR USE AS MONOCHROMATORS WITH BRAGG ANGLES FOR VARIOUS $K\alpha$-RADIATIONS

Crystal	Reflection	Radiation, $K\alpha$						
		Mo	Cu	Ni	Co	Fe	Mn	Cr
α-alumina............	00.2	1.8°	3.9°	4.2°	4.6°	4.9°	5.4°	5.8°
Gypsum.............	020	2.7	5.8	6.3	6.8	7.3	8.0	8.7
β-alumina...........	00.4	3.6	7.9	8.5	9.1	9.9	10.8	11.8
Pentaerythritol......	002	4.7	10.1	10.9	11.8	12.8	13.9	15.2
Quartz..............	10.0	6.1	13.3	14.4	15.6	16.9	18.4	20.1
Fluorite.............	111	6.5	14.1	15.2	16.5	17.9	19.5	21.3
Urea nitrate.........	002	6.5	14.2	15.3	16.6	18.0	19.6	21.4
Calcite..............	200	6.7	14.7	15.8	17.1	18.6	20.3	22.2
Rock salt............	200	7.2	15.9	17.1	18.5	20.1	21.9	24.0
Diamond............	111	9.9	22.0	23.8	25.8	28.1	30.8	33.9

The second method of rendering a beam homogeneous is by the use of the characteristic absorption edges. Suppose that a molybdenum-target tube is excited at 30 kv: the spectrum shows the K-series lines superposed on the smooth general radiation curve. If, however, the first part of this band and the $K\gamma$ and $K\beta$ lines could be suppressed and the $K\alpha$ doublet left in essentially undiminished intensity, a useful "dichromatic" (since the doublet cannot be separated satisfactorily) beam would result. It is necessary only to discover an element whose K absorption-edge wavelength lies between the $K\beta$ and $K\alpha$ wavelengths of molybdenum (*i.e.*, between 0.631 and 0.708 A), and use this for a filtering screen. Table 6-1 shows that zirconium has a K critical absorption wavelength of 0.6888 A; a thin screen interposed in the molybdenum-target beam will cut out practically completely radiation with wavelengths shorter than this value but will be nearly transparent to the most intense α doublet.

Table 6-9 presents some representative examples of selective absorption for obtaining homogeneous rays.

TABLE 6-9. FILTERS FOR OBTAINING NEARLY MONOCHROMATIC X-RAYS

Target	Lowest approximate voltage for K series, kv	λ for $K\alpha$ doublet	Filter	Thickness, mm	G/cm²
Chromium.......	6	2.287	Vanadium	0.0084	0.0048
Iron............	7	1.935	Manganese	0.0075	0.0055
Copper..........	9	1.539	Nickel	0.0085	0.0076
Molybdenum....	20	0.710	Zirconium	0.037	0.024
Silver...........	25	0.560	Palladium	0.03	0.036

The third method of generating a nearly monochromatic ray is largely of theoretical interest only. Reasoning from the probable mechanism of the excitation of the continuous spectrum, Duane conceived the idea of bombarding a very thin stream of mercury vapor and liquid with cathode rays so that there would be little chance for stepwise slowing up of the electrons. Under ideal conditions a single line for the short-wavelength limit, instead of a continuous band, would be obtained. This ideal was very nearly realized by Duane in obtaining a very narrow sharp peak with a maximum only slightly longer than the λ, defined by $Ve = hc/\lambda_o$.

GENERALIZATIONS FROM X-RAY SPECTROSCOPIC DATA

The Moseley Law. The brilliant young Englishman Moseley, who was called from his researches to lose his life in the Dardanelles in 1915,

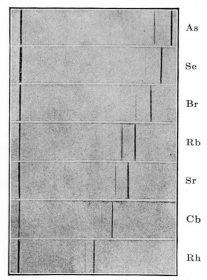

was the first to recognize the essential simplicity of the K emission series. He showed that the wavelengths of a given spectral line varied *continuously* step by step in proceeding from one atomic number to the next, and not *periodically* as is the case with so many atomic properties. Even in optical line spectra there are definite relationships for chemically similar elements—doublets for the alkali metals, singlets and triplets for the alkaline earths—and spectra of increasing complexity in passing from left to right in the periodic table. The periodic properties such as these optical spectra, atomic volumes, etc., must find their origin in the outermost parts of the atoms; the nonperiodic properties such as the x-ray spectra must be ascribed to the interior. The original Moseley K-series

Fig. 70. K-series spectral lines as photographed by Moseley for several neighboring elements, illustrating the continuous wavelength progression and the Moseley law.

spectra for several neighboring elements beginning with arsenic (33) are reproduced in Fig. 70.

Moseley went further and showed that, if the square root of the reciprocal of the wavelength (or of the frequency or of the wave number,[1] or

[1] There is considerable confusion in symbols; in spectroscopic work it is preferred to use wave numbers instead of frequencies. The frequency ν = number of vibrations per second, or ν sec^{-1}; wave number $\bar{\nu}$ = number of vibrations per centimeter, or $\bar{\nu}$ cm^{-1}; $\nu = \bar{\nu}c$, $\nu = c/\lambda$, $\bar{\nu} = 1/\lambda$, where c = velocity of light. The Rydberg constant is a fundamental wave number, $\bar{\nu}$ cm^{-1}, equal to 109,737.323 cm^{-1}.

the wave number divided by a fundamental constant R, the Rydberg constant) of a given x-ray line $K\beta$, $K\alpha$, $L\alpha$, etc., were plotted against atomic number, a practically straight line resulted. Precision researches have demonstrated that the curves are very slightly concave upward. For a K line the curve is characterized by the equation

$$\sqrt{\frac{\tilde{\nu}}{R}} = \sqrt{\frac{3}{4}}\,(Z - 1)$$

where Z is the atomic number, or

$$\tilde{\nu} = R(Z - 1)^2\left(\frac{1}{1^2} - \frac{1}{2^2}\right)$$

a form which is of great significance in its analogy to that expressing the frequencies of the ultraviolet Lyman spectral series of hydrogen. Similarly an L-series line frequency is given approximately by

$$\tilde{\nu} = R(Z - 7.4)^2\left(\frac{1}{2^2} - \frac{1}{3^2}\right)$$

which is analogous to the expression for the Balmer series for hydrogen.

An extension of the Moseley law was made in the region of optical spectra by Millikan and Bowen in their experiments with stripped atoms. Working with elements in the second horizontal row in the periodic table, they compared the spectra of sodium, magnesium$^+$ (one electron removed), aluminum^{2+}, silicon^{3+}, phosphorus^{4+}, sulfur^{5+}, and chlorine^{6+}, all of which, therefore, have exactly the same number of electrons and differ only in the mass and charge of the nucleus. The spectra are identical in appearance, and the square roots of the frequencies of a given line are a linear function of atomic number. Richtmyer demonstrated also that Moseley relationships hold true for nondiagram or satellite lines. A Moseley diagram for M-series lines is illustrated in Fig. 71.

Applications of the Moseley Law. The simplicity of the relationship between spectral-line frequency and atomic number, which according to present conceptions represents the net positive charge on the nucleus, and also the number of non-nuclear electrons, suggests several valuable applications.

1. The law proves that a fundamental relationship exists among all elements from hydrogen to element 100; that all are constructed of the same building units in definitely progressing complexity; and that if x-ray spectral lines are to be ascribed to the innermost electrons in atoms, as is indicated by the high frequencies and consequently large energy changes, these inner electrons must be essentially the same in number and disposition in all atoms, regardless of the number of electrons in the outer portions or of the state of chemical combination of the element.

2. The law has been the fundamental basis upon which the discovery and identification of the recently discovered new elements have depended. Interpolation of the $\sqrt{\nu}$–atomic-number curves, or calculation, gives the wavelength that should be expected for a given K or L or M line in the spectrum of an unknown element. In every case the process of discovery

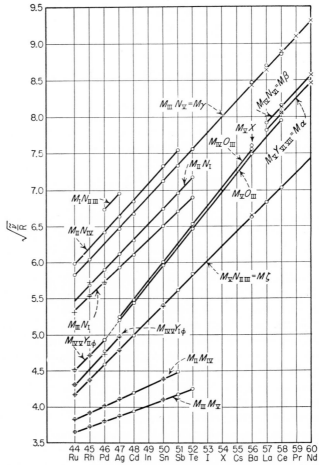

Fig. 71. Moseley diagram for the M series of elements 44 (ruthenium) to 60 (neodymium).

has been the matching of experimental lines from the material used as the target of an x-ray tube with the theoretical values. In this way Coster discovered hafnium (72), Tacke and Noddack discovered masurium (43) and rhenium (75), and Hopkins and his students in 1926 identified the rare earth illinium (61) now called promethium for the artificially produced isotope. In this last case the measured wavelengths of strong lines were 2.2781 and 2.0770 A, corresponding to the predicted values for the $L\alpha_1$ and $L\beta_1$ lines of the element 61, respectively, of 2.2777 and 2.0730 A. Elements formed by nuclear bombardment in the cyclotron and by artificial radioactive transformations are now being identified from the characteristic x-rays that are frequently emitted in these processes. Neptunium (93), plutonium (94), americium (95), curium (96), berkelium (97), and californium (98) are well established. Technetium (43), promethium (61), astatine (85), and francium (87) have been claimed by nuclear chemists and were accepted by the International Union of Chemistry in September, 1949.

3. Qualitative and even quantitative analysis of any unknown substance are, of course, directly possible by analysis in similar fashion of the emission lines. Analytical applications of x-rays will be considered in Chap. 7.

The Combination Principle. Though the Moseley law gives the relationship among elements of varying atomic number from the standpoint of any given x-ray spectral line, another principle observed from experimental data gives important information concerning the relationship between lines and absorption discontinuities in different series for the same element. Thus the frequency ν (or $\tilde{\nu}$ or $\tilde{\nu}/R$) of the $K\beta$ line equals the sum of the ν, $\tilde{\nu}$, or $\tilde{\nu}/R$ values, respectively, of the $K\alpha$ and $L\alpha$ lines. The differences between the K critical absorption frequency and two of the L critical absorption frequencies equal, respectively, the frequencies of the $K\alpha$ emission lines; and the difference between the K absorption frequency and one of the M critical absorption frequencies is equal to the frequency of the $K\beta$ emission line; thus the differences between values of $\tilde{\nu}/R$ of the absorption discontinuities of tungsten are equal to $\tilde{\nu}/R$ values for emission lines, as follows:

$$K - L_{III} = 4.367 \rightarrow K\alpha_1 = 4.3682$$
$$K - L_{II} = 4.268 \rightarrow K\alpha_2 = 4.2693$$

In the same way the frequencies of L and M absorption discontinuities give the frequencies of certain L emission lines. Thus the combination principle, long known in optical spectra, applies simply to x-ray spectra. In addition, Sommerfeld, Siegbahn, and others have noted important relationships between doublets in x-ray spectra. As an example may be cited the following pairs of values of the wave numbers $(\tilde{\nu}/R)$ for tungsten:

$L\eta$	642.78	$L\beta_1$	712.39	$L\gamma_5$	831.81
L_l	544.03	$L\alpha_2$	613.85	$L\beta_6$	733.76
	98.75		98.54		98.05
$L\gamma_6$		850.07	$K\alpha_1$		4,368.5
$L\beta_5$		751.56	$K\alpha_2$		4,270.0
		98.51			98.5

Here are at least six doublets with the same difference, which is simply that between two L absorption limits L_{II} 849.59 $-$ L_{III} 750.88 $=$ 98.71.

The wavelength differences corresponding to these values for each of these doublets (regular or relativity) remain practically constant for all the elements. Another type of doublet (irregular or screening) is that observed by Hertz, where the difference in $\sqrt{\bar{\nu}/R}$ values for pairs of critical absorption values (L_{II} and L_I) is constant from one element to the next. These two types of doublet occur alternately in the structure; thus L_{III} and L_{II} are relativity, L_{II} and L_I are screening, M_V and M_{IV} relativity, M_{IV} and M_{III} screening, and so on. Such facts as these indicate at once the possibility of definite levels of energy in atoms, the differences corresponding to the frequencies of emitted or absorbed radiation and doublets to a doubling of energy levels.

The Facts of X-ray Spectra to Be Explained by a Theory of Atomic Structure. Any comprehensive theory of atomic structure must be able to account for the following facts of x-ray spectroscopy:

1. Characteristic absorption wavelengths.
2. Sharp characteristic emission lines.
3. Grouping of spectral lines in series.
4. Critical excitation potentials for groups of lines.
5. Emission satellites and fine structure of absorption edges.
6. The Moseley law, continuous, nonperiodic progression in wavelengths.
7. The combination principle, regular and irregular doublets, and the relation between emission and absorption.

The Bohr Theory of Atomic Structure. Before outlining very briefly the Bohr theory of atomic structure, by means of which a very useful mechanical model could be constructed and processes related to radiation clearly pictured, it must be frankly stated that the model is deficient and unable to meet the demands of the newest experimental physics. However, new quantum- or wave-mechanics theory, in which the mechanical model of the atom is replaced by mathematical vector equations, has not advanced as yet to the stage where any very satisfactory geometrical model can be visualized in terms of the facts of x-ray spectra. Hence the Bohr theory of the planetary atom still is worthy of presentation and use as a qualitative tool, particularly as it utilizes fundamental quantum laws. Sir William Bragg advises that science must not be criticized for dropping one theory in favor of another, as a carpenter is not scolded for dropping his saw to use his chisel. In a word, science cannot believe wholly in the Bohr atom, nor can it do without it.

In addition to some of the experimental facts of x-ray spectroscopy, there were in 1916 four other great factors, which were largely unrelated and even discrepant, to be taken into consideration by any theory. These were the classical electromagnetic (wave) theory of radiation, the Planck quantum theory of radiation, the Rutherford nuclear atom, and the empirical (optical) spectroscopy of Balmer, Ritz, and Rydberg. The last factor refers to the relationships such as the following for the optical series of hydrogen:

Lyman series: $\quad \tilde{\nu}_1 = \tilde{\nu}_0 \left(\dfrac{1}{1^2} - \dfrac{1}{n_1^2} \right) \qquad n_1 = 2, 3, 4, \ldots$

Balmer series: $\quad \tilde{\nu}_2 = \tilde{\nu}_0 \left(\dfrac{1}{2^2} - \dfrac{1}{n_2^2} \right) \qquad n_2 = 3, 4, 5, \ldots$

Paschen series: $\quad \tilde{\nu}_2 = \tilde{\nu}_0 \left(\dfrac{1}{3^2} - \dfrac{1}{n_3^2} \right) \qquad n_3 = 4, 5, 6, \ldots$

Brackett series: $\quad \tilde{\nu}_4 = \tilde{\nu}_0 \left(\dfrac{1}{4^2} - \dfrac{1}{n_4^2} \right) \qquad n_4 = 5, 6, 7, \ldots$

Pfund series: $\quad \tilde{\nu}_5 = \tilde{\nu}_0 \left(\dfrac{1}{5^2} - \dfrac{1}{n_5^2} \right) \qquad n_5 = 6, 7, 8, \ldots$

or in general $\quad \tilde{\nu} = \tilde{\nu}_0 \left(\dfrac{1}{m^2} - \dfrac{1}{n^2} \right) \qquad n = m + 1, m + 2, m + 3, \ldots$

These relations of course indicate that there are various energy levels or states in an atom of hydrogen. These energies may be expressed in ergs, in electron volts, or in wave-number units. The last is convenient since the difference of two energies then gives at once the wave number of the corresponding spectral line. If W_e is energy in ergs, then the value in wave-number units $W_{\tilde{\nu}}$ is

$$W_{\tilde{\nu}} = \frac{W_e}{ch}$$

In spectroscopy it is customary to use not the energy, which is negative, but the positive numerical value. These values are called term values or terms. The wave number of the spectral line is obtained by subtracting the term value of the initial state from that of the final state. In the above expressions for the spectral series

Lyman series: $\quad \tilde{\nu} = \tilde{\nu}_0 \left(\dfrac{1}{1^2} - \dfrac{1}{n_1^2} \right)$; as n_1 becomes ∞, $\tilde{\nu} = \tilde{\nu}_0 \left(\dfrac{1}{1^2} \right) = \tilde{\nu}_0$

the convergence wave number or limit of the series. From this value is subtracted the appropriate term to obtain the wave number of each spectral line; thus, $\tilde{\nu}$ of the first line is

$$\tilde{\nu}_1 = 109{,}737 \left(\frac{1}{1^2} - \frac{1}{2^2} \right) = 109{,}737 - 27{,}434 = 82{,}303 \qquad \text{or}$$

$$\lambda_1 = 1{,}215.0 \text{ A}$$

The second line would have the value

$$\tilde{\nu}_2 = 109{,}737 \left(\frac{1}{1^2} - \frac{1}{3^2} \right) = 109{,}737 - 12{,}193 = 97{,}544 \qquad \text{or}$$

$$\lambda_2 = 1{,}025.8 \text{ A}$$

For the first line in

Balmer series: $\bar{\nu}_1 = 109{,}737 \left(\dfrac{1}{2^2} - \dfrac{1}{3^2} \right) = 27{,}434 - 12{,}143 = 15{,}241$

$$\lambda_1 = 6{,}562.8 \text{ A}$$

Paschen series: $\bar{\nu}_1 = 109{,}737 \left(\dfrac{1}{3^2} - \dfrac{1}{4^2} \right) = 12{,}193 - 6{,}858 = 5{,}335$

$$\lambda_1 = 18{,}756 \text{ A}$$

Brackett series: $\bar{\nu}_1 = 109{,}737 \left(\dfrac{1}{4^2} - \dfrac{1}{5^2} \right) = 6{,}858 - 4{,}389 = 2{,}469$

$$\lambda_1 = 4.05\mu, \text{ etc.}$$

Thus the integer in the first or final-state term fundamentally defines the series as a quantum number—Lyman 1, Balmer 2, Paschen 3, Brackett 4, Pfund 5.

The fundamental assumptions of the original Bohr theory are as follows:

1. The atom consists of a positively charged, extremely minute nucleus, which accounts for practically all the mass, and of negative electrons as satellites. The number of these electrons is equal to the net number of positive charges on the nucleus, and this number is the atomic number. The table of elements is constructed by the addition of one net positive charge and one non-nuclear electron for each element, beginning with hydrogen with one positive charge on the nucleus and one electron.

2. The atom is a dynamic system, for the electrons are in rapid orbital motion.

3. Three laws govern this atom:

a. An acceleration law. In a simple atom like hydrogen, with the assumption that the mass of the nucleus M is infinitely great in comparison with the electron so that the nucleus remains in fixed position, the Coulomb force of attraction between positive and negative charges is opposed by the centrifugal force required to keep the electrons revolving in a circle; in other words, $e^2/a^2 = mv^2/a$, where e is the electric charge ($+$ or $-$), a the distance between two charges, m the mass of the electron, and v its velocity.

b. A momentum law. The angular momentum is governed by the equation $mva = nh/2\pi$, where n is an integer and h is a constant. In other words, the motion of the electron is very definitely restricted to orbits whose angular moment multiplied by 2π is equal to nh. The possible configurations under this quantum condition are called stationary states because no radiation is emitted while the atom remains in such a state.

c. A frequency law. While an electron is revolving in any definite orbit of definite energy W_1, it is conceived to be nonradiating, for otherwise energy would be lost and the electron would be pulled gradually into the nucleus. Another orbit W_2 would correspond to a different energy level. It is only in the process of transition of an electron from one orbit to another that radiation may be emitted or absorbed; in other words, the energy difference $W_1 - W_2 = h\nu$, where ν is the frequency of the radiation and h the Planck action constant. Ordinarily an atom exists in the stationary state of lowest energy, but by absorption of radiation or some kinds of collision it may be "excited" to a higher energy state. Radiation is emitted during the transition from a higher to lower state of energy.

A combination of these simple laws gives the equation

$$\nu = \frac{2\pi^2 e^4 m}{h^3} \left(\frac{1}{n_1^2} - \frac{1}{n_2^2} \right) \quad \text{or} \quad \bar{\nu} = \frac{2\pi^2 e^4 m}{h^3 c} \left(\frac{1}{n_1^2} - \frac{1}{n_2^2} \right) \quad \text{or} \quad \bar{\nu} = \bar{\nu}_0 \left(\frac{1}{n_1^2} - \frac{1}{n_2^2} \right)$$

where $\bar{\nu}_0$ is a fundamental constant wave number, the Rydberg constant already mentioned, and n_1 and n_2 whole numbers; the equation expresses the wave numbers or frequencies of the spectral lines of hydrogen. There is thus immediate explanation for the empirical spectroscopic formulas of Balmer, Ritz, and Rydberg.

After the simple Bohr theory of hydrogen was announced, many corrections and additions were made. Briefly enumerated these were as follows:

1. Allowance for the mass of the nucleus by introducing Z^2, the square of the atomic number in the Bohr equation. Thus singly ionized helium will give a hydrogen spectrum with values 4 times as great; doubly ionized lithium, 9 times; trebly ionized boron, 16 times; etc.

2. Allowance for the revolution of the nucleus around the common center of gravity, by substituting the "reduced" mass of the atom for the mass of the electron m in $mM/(m + M)$, where M is the mass of the nucleus.

3. A relativity correction, taking into account the variation in mass with the velocity of electrons.

4. The introduction of elliptical orbits, in addition to Bohr's circular ones, to account for the fine structure of spectral lines. These orbits, in order to have energies which differ from those of the circular ones and thus to account for the complexity of apparently single lines, must undergo precession around the nucleus.

5. The most striking characteristic of the Bohr quantum theory of atomic structure was the frequent occurrence of integers and half integers; it was essentially a theory of numbers that are combined in all possible ways, and to this day this feature has been retained in the newer vector models of the atom. The types of elliptical orbit, upon which the electrons in the complicated atoms revolve, were characterized by quantum numbers n, k, j. The number n is related to the size of the orbit, k (the azimuthal quantum number) to its shape, and j to its position in the atoms relative to other electronic orbits. For convenience a particular orbit was referred to as n_{kj}. The larger the value of n, the more loosely is the electron bound to the atom. Thus the innermost electron "shell" consists of a single circular orbit 1_{11}, the second of two ellipses, 2_{11} (most eccentric) and 2_{21}, and a circle 2_{22}, and so on.

6. By combination of x-ray, spectroscopic, and chemical information the complete arrangement of electrons in various shells or orbits was derived for all the elements from hydrogen to uranium. As an example may be cited the structure for the rare gases of the atmosphere, which, except helium, always have eight outside electrons:

2. He $1_{11}(2)$

10. Ne $1_{11}(2)$; $2_{11}(2)$; $2_{21}(2)$; $2_{22}(4)$

18. A $1_{11}(2)$; $2_{11}(2)$; $2_{21}(2)$; $2_{22}(4)$; $3_{11}(2)$; $3_{21}(2)$; $3_{22}(4)$

36. Kr $1_{11}(2)$; $2_{11}(2)$; $2_{21}(2)$; $2_{22}(4)$; $3_{11}(2)$; $3_{21}(2)$; $3_{22}(4)$; $3_{32}(4)$; $3_{33}(6)$; $4_{11}(3)$; $4_{21}(2)$; 4_{22} (4)

54. Xe, same as Kr and in addition $4_{32}(4)$; $4_{33}(6)$; $5_{11}(2)$; $5_{21}(2)$; $5_{22}(4)$

86. Rn, same as Xe and in addition $5_{32}(4)$; $5_{33}(6)$; $6_{11}(2)$; $6_{21}(2)$; $6_{22}(4)$

This system explains many chemical and spectroscopic facts, the similarity in such homologous elements as Li, Na, K, Rb, and Cs, the chemical similarity of the triads Fe, Co, Ni; Ru, Rh, Pd; and Os, Ir, Pt; and the place of the 14 rare earths (57 to 71). Here the successive electrons are added in the 4_{43} and 4_{44} orbits, previously unoccupied, though electrons are being added in the fifth shell beginning with rubidium, atomic number 37.

LIMITATIONS OF THE BOHR THEORY AND THE DEVELOPMENT OF NEW ATOM MODELS

The Bohr theory, even with its additions, corrections, and empirical analogies, was not directly applicable to atoms containing more than one electron revolving around the nucleus, since there was no way to calculate the very appreciable effect of the presence of other electrons on the energy W corresponding to a particular orbit, or state. Furthermore, physicists became aware of the fact that they were not justified in their literal assignment to an imagined atomic architecture of the concepts of electrons revolving in privileged orbits, "jumps" from one orbit to another, and other geometrical pictures.

Language is incapable of describing processes occurring within atoms, for it was invented to express the experiences of daily life, which consist of processes involving exceedingly large numbers of atoms. Furthermore, it is almost impossible to modify language so as to describe these atomic processes, since words can describe only things of which we can form mental pictures, and this ability is a result of daily experience. Mathematics is not subject to this limitation.

Contradictions between theory (Bohr) and experiment led to the necessity of demanding that no concept which has not been experimentally verified should be involved in scientific formulations. For example, it was clear from both experiment and quantum mechanics that the azimuthal number k could be equal to 0; on the basis of the elliptical-orbit model this would mean that the path of the electron with designation n_0 would be a straight line passing through the nucleus, and at the end of the path the electron would have to stop and reverse—an obvious absurdity.

The principle of uncertainty was introduced to show among other things that the position and velocity of an electron (say, in an orbit) cannot be known simultaneously. Determinism is dropped out of the latest formulations of theoretical physics.

And yet these mechanical models or pictures with which the Bohr theory was associated are not easily discarded, for they help us to keep in mind the various states of the atoms. The picture may be defective and artificial, but the *energy associated with the various stationary states* is real. We speak of "orbit" and "energy corresponding to a given state" as synonymous terms, but only the latter has real physical significance. An energy-level diagram arising out of the Bohr solar system of orbits is an expression today of atomic "structure" and origin of spectral lines, free from artificial concepts of atomic architecture.

The new atom model departs from the older in the concept that the total angular momentum of the atom is the vector sum of the several components of momentum arising from the spin of the nucleus, the spin of the several electrons, and the orbital motion of the electrons around the nucleus (without any attempt to predict where they are or how they might look, for the recognition of the dual wave and particle behaviors of electrons as well as radiation precludes this). In the words of Richtmyer the vector model of the atom is built up out of these component parts, to each of which is assigned a quantum number; the numerical value of the latter may be conveniently thought of as the length of the vector, which represents the angular momentum of that component part. The axes of the several angular momenta may point in various directions, subject to rules of quantization. Thus with each quantum state there are associated the following quantum numbers $nljm$:

1. Total quantum number n, identical with the Bohr integers to designate the orbits $K = 1$, $L = 2$, $M = 3$, $N = 4$, $O = 5$, $P = 6$, and now referring to energy levels within the atom.

2. Orbital quantum number l, related to k, the Bohr azimuthal quantum number for designation of a subshell, by $l = k - 1$, and having values from 0 to $n - 1$. In spectroscopic nomenclature an electron for which $l = 0$ $(k = 1)$ is an s electron; $l = 1$, p electron; $l = 2$, d electron; $l = 3$, f electron; etc. Thus neon, for example, with a completed L shell of eight electrons has the electron configuration

$$1s^2 2s^2 2p_x^2 2p_y^2 2p_z^2 \qquad \text{or} \qquad 1s^2 2s^2 2p^6$$

the numerical prefixes 1 and 2 being the principal quantum number n, and the superscripts showing the number of electrons occupying the orbitals. This last word is used to refer to the wave function associated with the orbital motion of an electron. Uranium (92) has the designation

$$\underset{1s^2}{K} \underset{2s^2 2p^6}{L} \underset{3s^2 3p^6 3d^{10}}{M} \underset{4s^2 4p^6 4d^{10} 4f^{14}}{N} \underset{5s^2 5p^6 5d^{10}}{O} \underset{6s^2 6p^6 6d^4}{P} \underset{7s^2}{Q}$$

3. Spin quantum number $s = \pm\frac{1}{2}$ always, expressing angular momentum due to spin of electron around its own axis. Thus the completed K shell consists of two electrons with opposed spin occupying the stable $1s$ orbital.

4. Total angular quantum number j, the vector sum of the orbital and spin momenta. For some states $j = 1 + s = 1 + \frac{1}{2}$, and for others $j = 1 - s = j - \frac{1}{2}$, except that, if $l = 0$, $j = \frac{1}{2}$.

5. A quantum number m, corresponding to a j vector drawn at such an angle to some chosen axis that the projection on this axis is of length m; m may have any one of $2j + 1$ integrally spaced values from $m = j$ to $m = -j$. In a subshell full of electrons the total angular momentum, the spin momenta, and the sums will be zero. But if an electron is removed, the subshell is left in a state characterized by certain values of $nljm$. The energy should not vary with m; so for practical purposes it may be neglected, and only nlj considered.

These several vectors combine to make up the total angular momentum of the atom; thus **S** is a resultant vector representing the total spin moment; **L** the total orbital momentum; and **J**, from the combination of **S** and **L**, the total angular momentum. Since **S**, **L**, and **J** depend on the configuration of the electrons, they are characteristic of the energy states of the atom.

The Explanation of the Facts of X-ray Spectroscopy by the Atom Model. It is now certain that the fundamental energy level (or orbit) of the x-ray

K series is a one-quantum orbit ($n = 1$), that of the L series a two-quantum orbit ($n = 2$).

The existence of individual, widely separated spectral series leads directly to the fundamental conception that a number of electron groups are present in the atom which differ considerably from each other with respect to orbital energy and the distance between the electrons and the nucleus. Therefore, the K series arises from the transition of an electron from one of the outer groups (*e.g.*, the L, M, or N group) to the inner K group if by ionization a vacancy occurs. The fine structure of the individual lines is due to the energy differences within a definite group; *e.g.*, the $K\alpha_1$ and $K\alpha_2$ lines are to be explained by transitions from two somewhat different L levels to the single K level. For the production of $K\alpha_1$ the initial state of the atom is the K-ionized state (one electron from the innermost completed shell expelled), and the final state is an L_{III}-ionized state (one L_{III} electron missing by transition into the K shell). The atom itself undergoes the transition from the state K to the state L_{III}, in producing $K\alpha_1$.

The energies of the various orbits or shells or levels are designated by the $h\nu$ values of the experimentally measured critical limits, $1K$, $3L$, and $5M$, and presumably $7N$, $5O$, and $3P$. As a matter of fact, these are the energies required to lift an electron in its particular orbit out of the atom. For this reason, the various levels may be designated by reference to the letters K, L_I, M_I, etc., corresponding to a state of the atom in which an electron is missing from the corresponding subgroup. With the aid of Pauli's exclusion principle, which states that no two electrons can have all quantum numbers the same, it has been possible to distribute the electrons in subshells and thus to build up the configuration of electrons in all the chemical elements. In the K shell the two electrons ($n = 1$, $l = 0$) differ only in that the spin axes are oppositely directed ($m_j = +\frac{1}{2}$ and $-\frac{1}{2}$). In the L shell the eight electrons are distributed as follows in three levels (m_j is the projection of the vector j in the direction of the magnetic field):

n	l	j	m_j	Subgroup
2	0	$\frac{1}{2}$	$-\frac{1}{2}$ } orbital	
2	0	$\frac{1}{2}$	$+\frac{1}{2}$ } $2s$	L_I
2	1	$\frac{1}{2}$	$-\frac{1}{2}$ } orbital	
2	1	$\frac{1}{2}$	$+\frac{1}{2}$ } $2p_x$	L_{II}
2	1	$\frac{3}{2}$	$-\frac{3}{2}$ } orbital	
2	1	$\frac{3}{2}$	$-\frac{1}{2}$ } $2p_y$	L_{III}
2	1	$\frac{3}{2}$	$+\frac{1}{2}$ } orbital	
2	1	$\frac{3}{2}$	$+\frac{3}{2}$ } $2p_z$	

The theory, therefore, explains the facts of x-ray spectra as follows:

1. *Characteristic Absorption Limits.* These are defined by the energy required in primary radiation photons, or in cathode rays colliding with an atom, to lift electrons from a given energy level out of this atom. The number of limits, $1K$, $3L$, $5M$, $7N$, etc., is defined by nlj values of the energy levels.

2. *Sharp Emission Lines in Series.* When a K electron is removed, raising the whole atom to the K state, L electrons may fall into the vacancy, producing $K\alpha_1$ and $K\alpha_2$ from two of the three L levels. The $K\beta$ doublet results from the transition of electrons from two of the five M levels, and $K\gamma$, an ordinarily unresolved doublet, from transition from two N levels. Thus the totality of such transfers in a large number of atoms gives rise to the entire K series. The relative intensities of the lines are governed by the relative probabilities of transfer from the various shells to the K shell. These probabilities depend partly on the number of electrons in each level. Thus the chance that an electron will drop from the L_{III} shell with four electrons should be twice that from the L_{II} shell with two electrons. Experimentally $K\alpha_1$ is twice as intense as $K\alpha_2$. If electrons in the L level are removed, the L series results by the transition from the higher M, N, etc., levels to the L level. With three L and five M levels, there are thus possible 15 lines from this one type. However, not all the lines so predicted appear. The spectra are governed by a *rule of selection* which states that the quantum number n must change, that l must change by one unit, and that j may change by one unit or remain unchanged, or $\Delta l = \pm 1$, $\Delta j = \pm 1$ or 0. Thus there is no $K\alpha_3$ line representing a transition from the K state to the L_I state (or electron jump from L_I to K) since $l = 0$ for both K and L_I, whereas $l = 1$ for L_{II} and L_{III} to account for the $K\alpha_1\alpha_2$ doublet experimentally observed. Recently a number of "forbidden" lines have been discovered, but they are very faint; for example, $L_{III} \rightarrow N_{II}$ and $L_{III} \rightarrow N_{III}$, for each of which $\Delta l = 0$. These are called quadripole lines, subject to a different set of selection rules from the common dipole lines. Lines of very long wavelength whose origins are transitions *within* the N shell ($\Delta n = 0$) have been reported. Energy-level diagrams have been constructed for all the atoms to show how spectral lines in x-ray and optical regions are related to these transitions. Optical spectral lines are produced, of course, by electronic changes between the orbits farthest removed from the center. The complete energy-level diagram is given in Fig. 72; each horizontal line represents a level characterized by an n_{lj} value, and the lines joining these levels represent electron transitions resulting in spectral lines. The diagram is a remarkably terse and complete expression of the origin of radiation and its relationship to atomic structure. It is independent of conceptions of orbits and the mechanism of electron jumps.

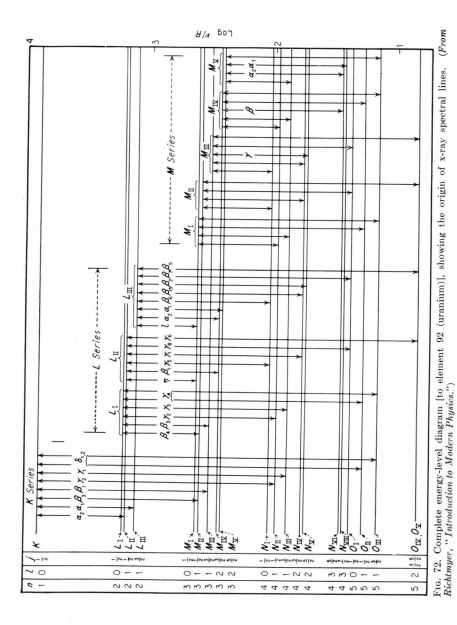

Fig. 72. Complete energy-level diagram [to element 92 (uranium)], showing the origin of x-ray spectral lines. (*From Richtmyer, "Introduction to Modern Physics."*)

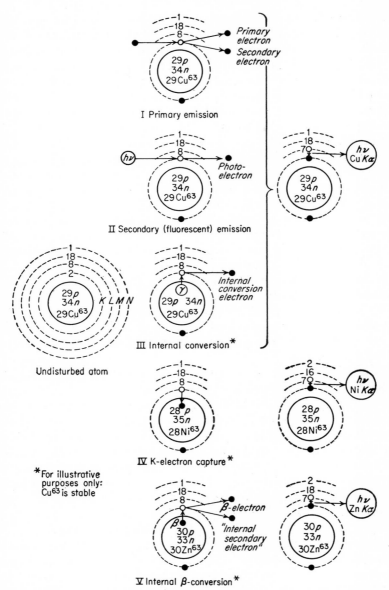

I Primary emission

II Secondary (fluorescent) emission

III Internal conversion*

Undisturbed atom

IV K-electron capture*

V Internal β-conversion*

*For illustrative purposes only: Cu^{63} is stable

FIG. 73. Possible atomic mechanisms involved in emission (simplified and idealized diagrams).

3. *Critical Excitation Potentials.* The K-series lines are not excited separately but appear together only when the kinetic energy of the bombarding electron stream in the x-ray tube is equal to or greater than the value given by the equation $E_k = Ve = h\nu_{K_{abs}}$. Only under these conditions is it possible to impart sufficient energy to the K electron to remove it entirely from the atom (not to the L or M levels, for example, which may be full, with the result that no absorption line corresponding to an emission line is ever found). The vacancy is supplied then by an L, M, or N electron; the new vacancy is filled from a still more distant shell. The atom returns to a neutral state by a process which, in general, takes place as a series of steps; but jumping over several steps and even the direct return of an outer electron to the K level are not unusual.

Again it is emphasized that though we speak of electron "jumps" the energy of each state or level involved in a transition belongs to the atom as a whole, and it is incorrect to assign this energy to a single electron. Actually the excitation of a $K\alpha_1$ line means the transition K (ionized state) $\rightarrow L_{III}$ state.

All the possible mechanisms involved in characteristic emission are illustrated in the idealized diagram in Fig. 73. These are primary emission by bombardment with an electron; secondary fluorescent emission by bombardment with a primary x-ray photon; internal conversion in the case of γ-rays from nuclear radioactivity; K-electron capture; and internal β conversion.

4. *Soft X-ray Emission-band Spectra.* As previously mentioned, emission spectra of elements of low atomic number, such as solid metallic sodium, magnesium, or aluminum, are characterized by diffuse bands, whereas the same element in vapor form produces only the usual sharp spectral lines. This can only mean that in the solid metal, in which the atoms are packed in a crystal lattice, the valence electrons must have energies extending over a band or range of energies, with the result that there will no longer be a constant difference in energies between a valence electron and an electron in a lower shell. The equation $h\nu = E_1 - E_2$ is still perfectly correct and is borne out by the experiment. The origin of emission bands and lines is illustrated in the diagram in Fig. 74a. Thus these soft x-ray spectra afford a method of exploring the energy characteristics of electrons in solids, just as the earlier spectroscopy investigated the energy of electrons in free atoms. The widths of these bands is on the order of 1 to 10 ev. In sodium, for example, the $3s$ and $3p$ orbitals are broadened so much as a result of squeezing atoms together in a body-centered lattice that they overlap and form a continuous band. Thus the valence electrons under these conditions occupy *hybridized orbitals*, described by the superposition of two wave functions. A further test of these relationships can be made by experiments at very low temperatures. Contrary to earlier beliefs, R. W. B. Skinner and others have

proved that the valence-electron energies at absolute zero are still spread over a range, which, however, has a sharper termination at a limiting value, termed E_{max}, the lower the temperature.   Photometric curves of the soft x-ray emission bands prove that the band edge is more nearly vertical, *i.e.*, sharper, the lower the temperature.   The curve of intensity distribution across an emission band is roughly the same as the plot of $n(E)$ against E, where $n(E)\, dE$ is the number of electrons per unit volume of a metal with energies between E and $E + dE$; or of $N(E)\, dE$, the number of electronic states each of which contains two electrons with opposite spins.   Each type of crystal structure gives rise to a character-istic $N(E)$ curve; hence from a knowledge of such a curve the stability

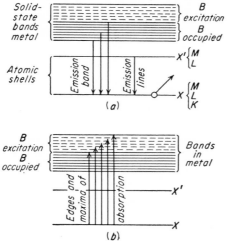

Fig. 74. (*a*) Origin of soft x-ray emission bands and lines.   (*b*) Origin of secondary structure in absorption edges.

may be predicted, as will be shown for alloys in Chap. 19.   According to the simple band theory of solids, there should be full coincidence between the position of an emission edge, such as K, and the corresponding absorption edge of an element when present in a conducting material; but there should be a gap between the emission edge and the absorption edge of the same element present in a nonconducting material.   From the spectra Cauchois deduced that NiAs, NiO, and NiS were nonconducting and CuS conducting, but many results are apparently uncertain and complex.   It is from such spectra as the L absorption spectrum for pure copper, in Fig. 75, that extended interpretations of electron distribution, bound levels of the exciton type in metal conductors, and effects of alloying have been made.   The dispersion shape of lines is a measure of the shape or width of the various levels or bands.

The ideas of hybridized orbitals and electron-distribution curves are of great significance in the understanding of bonds, especially in solid metals, and the structures of metals, alloys, and complex coordination compounds. In Chap. 19, further consideration will be given to electrons in crystals and the so-called zone theory of solids.

5. *Emission Satellites and Fine Structure of Absorption Edges.* No entirely adequate explanations of these effects have been given. The very weak satellite emission lines on the short-wavelength side of the principal lines, described in a preceding paragraph, do not correspond to lines forbidden by the selection rules or to any others. In general, elements Na 11 to Zn 30 show K satellites but no L or M satellites; Cu 29 to Sn 50 show L but no K or M satellites; Tb 65 to U 92 show M but no K or L satellites. Thus the K satellites are connected with a growing L shell, the L satellites with a growing M shell. Wentzel in 1921 presented the first theory for satellites as arising from single electron jumps in multiply ionized atoms. Thus $K\alpha_4$ corresponds to an initial state KK

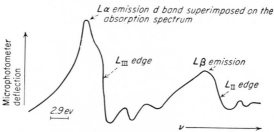

FIG. 75. Copper L absorption spectrum. (*Cauchois.*)

(two electrons missing in the K shell) and final state KL. Serious objections led to a modification in 1927 to the effect that multiple ionizations do not occur in the same level; thus $K\beta \sim K \rightarrow M$, $K\beta''' = KL \rightarrow LM$. The origin and mechanism of doubly ionized atoms form a major objection to these theories. In 1929 Richtmyer proposed a theory of a two-electron jump between multiply ionized states with but one emitted quantum of radiation; thus $h\nu_{sat} = h\nu_i + h\nu_0$, with $h\nu_i$ the energy liberated when an electron drops into an inner shell, and $h\nu_0$ the energy liberated when a valence electron drops into an outer shell. In 1935 Coster and Kronig modified earlier theories with an Auger, or internal photoelectric, effect. For example, an atom originally in an L_I state will be left in a doubly ionized $L_{III}M$ state because a radiationless $L_I \rightarrow L_{III}$ transition takes place, the energy being used to eject an M electron. The doubly ionized atom is then in a state to emit satellites, by the Wentzel theory. These radiationless transitions seem to be generally accepted, especially because the Auger effect is well established from measurements of β-ray spectra (Chap. 8).

For the satellites for K and Cl in solid KCl as observed by Jossem and Parratt and mentioned on page 125, it is probable that the transitions in states responsible for various lines for potassium are $K\beta_1$, $K^{2+}1s \rightarrow$

$K^{2+}3p$ (the double positive charge indicates another inner vacancy); β_i, a narrow line from higher ionization levels than β_1; β_{II}, a wide line representing transition from $1s$ to the solid-state $3p$ band; β_V and β_5, which are cross transitions $K1s \rightarrow Cl3p$ and $K1s \rightarrow Cl3s$.

To explain the fine structure of absorption edges, the most comprehensive theory has been proposed by Kronig in 1931, based on wave mechanics. The absorbing crystal was considered as a periodic array of potential walls corresponding to the ions in the lattice. The ejected electron, resulting from the ionization of the K level, can enter only into certain energy bands resulting from the crystal-lattice structure. The transition of an electron from a K level of an atom to the lowest of these energy bands accounts for the absorption edge. Absorption lines in the secondary structure of the edge correspond to energies an electron may possess after being ejected from the K shell. The mechanism is suggested by the diagram in Fig. 74b. The values of these energies are given by $W_r = n^2h^2/8ma^2$. Kronig suggested that the separation in the secondary structure should be inversely proportional to the square of the lattice constant of the crystal used as absorber.

While there has been some disagreement, the preponderance of evidence in 1953 is favorable to the Kronig theory.[1] The general conclusion is that if the energy of the ejected electron is increased, the region of the crystal that plays a part in determining the fine structure is extended more and more. (a) In a region close to the edge, the behavior of the absorption coefficient is mainly a property of the atom in question. (b) In the following region, the fine structure is determined by the immediate surroundings of the atom. (c) In the region of highest energy, the fine structure depends on the whole crystal lattice. For the transition metals and their compounds, (a) comprises the region up to 40 ev from the edge, (b) the region between 40 and 150 ev, (c) the region above 150 ev.

6. *The Moseley Law.* This is a consequence of the fact that the innermost levels in atoms, which take part in the production of x-rays, are all similarly constituted as regards number and disposition of the electrons. The stepwise change in wavelength is simply a consequence of the increasing effect of the net positive charge of the nucleus on the inner electron shells in passing from one atomic number to the next higher. The mechanism of the production of spectral lines suggests the explanation of the factor $Z - 1$ instead of Z in the Moseley equation for K lines. When one K electron is removed from the atom by bombardment, the other K electron is still left near the nucleus to "screen" it and make the effective nuclear charge one unit less.

[1] S. Kieston, "Conference on Applications of X-ray Spectroscopy to Solid State Problems, 1950," p. 26, U.S. Department of Commerce, Office of Technical Services, Washington (Navexos, p. 1033).

7. *The Combination Principle.* This is a direct consequence of different energy levels with definite values. The same wave-number difference may be obtained by several combinations of the wave numbers of critical absorption limits and emission lines, when these are pictured as distinct jumps from lower to higher levels, or vice versa. The principle thus affords several checks for numerical evaluation of the energy levels.

8. *The Chemical Bond and Molecular and Crystalline Structure.* The significance of the vector model of the atom, orbitals, spins, and quantum numbers is by no means limited to purely theoretical characterization of individual atoms. For they determine the nature of the chemical bond between atoms which form molecules and crystals and thus the summation of physical and chemical properties of all matter. Electrostatic attraction between positively and negatively charged ions accounts for the bonds in salts. The covalent bond of elements, such as diamond, all organic compounds, and many inorganic compounds, is an electron pair with opposed spins. The formation of complexes such as $Co(NH_3)_6^{3+}$ involves orbitals not only of the valence shell but also of the next underlying shell. Hybridized orbitals seem to be involved in the metallic bond. Resonance between covalent and ionic bonds and between single and double bonds is the consequence of electronic configuration which is assigned to atoms upon the basis of experimental x-ray data. These fundamental new principles in chemistry are considered in some detail in Chap. 17, Crystal Chemistry.

CHAPTER 7

CHEMICAL ANALYSIS FROM X-RAY SPECTRA

Since definite x-ray wavelengths, both emission and absorption, are characteristic of the chemical elements, it follows that x-ray spectroscopy may find practical application in qualitative and quantitative analysis. The Moseley law, of course, is of splendid assistance, more particularly in the qualitative discovery of new elements in complex mixtures, since the wavelengths for these elements may be accurately predicted.

The five general procedures employed in analysis are as follows:

1. Measurement of primary spectral-emission lines (K or L or M series) in which the unknown substance undergoing analysis is made the target of an x-ray tube. The bombarding electrons may be cathode rays from a heated filament or β-rays from a radioisotope.

2. Measurement of secondary fluorescent-emission lines in which the unknown is so placed on some device *inside* the x-ray tube that it is screened from the cathode rays but directly irradiated by the primary x-ray beam.

3. The same, except that the unknown is irradiated *outside* the x-ray tube; on this account the intensities with usual equipment are greatly decreased, and the time required for photographic registration of the spectrum is increased, but with new high-intensity tubes for primary rays and Geiger-counter registration of spectrum lines these objections are largely eliminated.

4. Measurement of wavelengths of characteristic absorption edges in which the unknown serves as an absorbing screen.

5. Use of a cathode-ray tube with thin windows for passage of rays, with bombardment of unknown outside and spectrographic analysis of x-rays generated.

6. The use of a magnetic spectrometer to analyze the photoelectrons with characteristic energies, emitted by irradiation with primary x-rays. This technique is described in the next chapter. Geiger counters have made this method practicable, whereas photographic registration required excessively long times for any determination.

Apparatus. The essential apparatus for analysis comprises the x-ray tube and power plant and a crystal spectrograph. Special demountable tubes are required for methods 1 and 2. In the first case the sample must be pasted or fused on a cooled metal surface serving as anode. The tube so prepared is then pumped continuously. Any of the demountable electron or ion tubes described in Chap. 2 are used. For method 2 either a second target or some other special holder is required inside the tube, which must then be pumped.

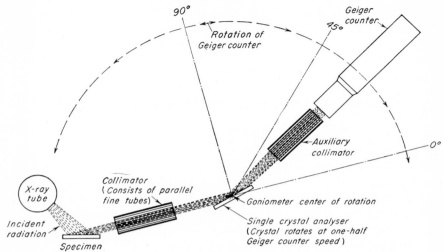

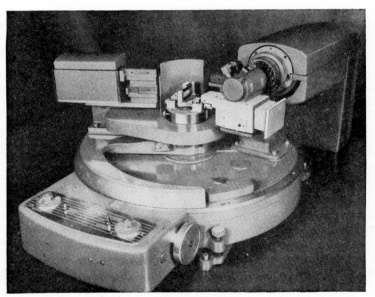

FIG. 76. Diagram of basic geometry of fluorescence-analysis method.

FIG. 77. General Electric Geiger spectrometer for fluorescence analysis.

With the advent of the new high-intensity tubes such as that illustrated in Fig. 15 (Chap. 2) and the Geiger counter (Chap. 4), method 3 has largely superseded both 1 and 2. A diagram of the experimental arrangement is shown in Fig. 76. A commercial unit designed especially for fluorescence analysis is illustrated in Fig. 77. A high-intensity tungsten-target tube produces primary rays which fall upon a specimen and excite secondary K-rays, which are then analyzed by the spectrometer crystal and detected at the appropriate angles by the Geiger tube. Pulses received by the counter are transmitted to a scaling unit and totalized on a register over a suitable, accurately controlled period of time.   This unit

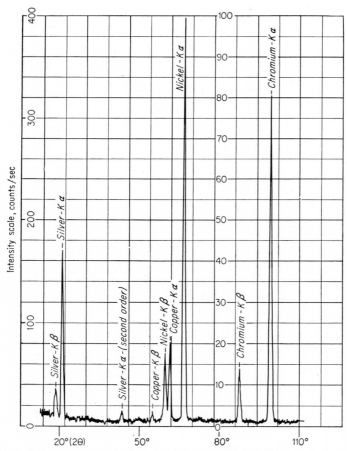

Fig. 78. Typical fluorescence-analysis chart of chrome-nickel plating on silver-copper base. (*North American Philips Company.*)

is limited to the analysis of elements between titanium (22) and tin (50). A typical fluorescent-spectrum curve automatically registered on a Geiger spectrometer is illustrated in Fig. 78.   A new fluorescent-spectrometry unit was announced by Applied Research Laboratories, of Glendale, California, in March, 1953, as a companion to the well-known optical spectrometer, which automatically registers intensity ratios on a quantometer.   The x-ray unit is designed to be attached to the quantometer interchangeably with the spectrograph.   Both dispersive (utilizing a crystal) and nondispersive (utilizing the principle of a filter photometer) analyzers, combined with multichannel recording, have been successfully developed in 1954.

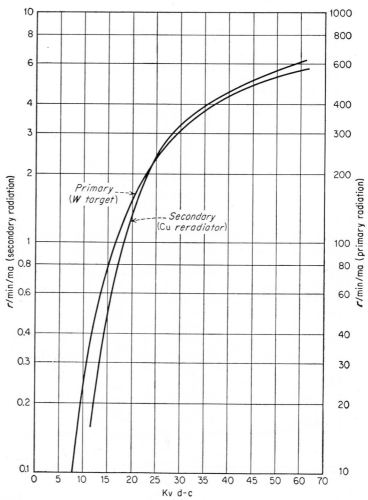

FIG. 79. Intensities of primary tungsten rays (measured at 20 cm) and secondary copper fluorescent rays (measured at 5 cm) as functions of voltage on x-ray tube.

With increasing demands at present for very intense monochromatic x-ray beams for microradiography, diffraction analysis of crystals, and other special purposes, attention is being directed to the design of tubes which will generate essentially monochromatic rays by fluorescence. A simple and promising design is one in which an intense flux of primary x-rays produced by bombardment of the surrounding cylindrical or conical anticathode falls upon a needle of the metal from which fluorescent rays are desired, inside of, and at the same potential as, the filament.   On the other hand, Rogers[1] has demonstrated very recently that fluorescent rays of useful intensity and high degree of monochromaticity for micro-radiography (Chap. 10) may be generated with commercial high-intensity tubes with beryllium windows as primary source and external radiators. Figure 79 shows that under these conditions the intensity of fluorescent Cu radiation as a function of the voltage on a W tube supplying primary rays is about 0.01 that of the W rays, measured respectively at 5 cm from the radiator and 20 cm from the target.

ADVANTAGES OF X-RAY ANALYSIS

1. Over chemical methods.
   a. Analysis of extremely minute amounts, even 0.2 μg—triumph of discovery of elements 72, 43, 75, 61, 85, 87, 93, 94, 95, 96, 97, 98; adaptable to micro- and histochemical analysis, and to point-by-point analysis of areas as small as 1μ square on heterogeneous specimens.
   b. Analysis of rare earths, platinum metals, etc., where separations are difficult or impossible.
   c. Material used in any available form without special preparation, independent of chemical combination, and without loss; hence valuable for rare metals, gems, etc.   Fluorescent methods completely nondestructive.
   d. Greater safety, since no separation of elements is involved; hence much less work and great saving of time.
   e. Permanent record on plates or Geiger-spectrometer curves, largely independent of personal equation.
2. Over optical spectroscopy.
   a. The great simplicity of x-ray spectra, particularly the K-series emission, as compared with the great complexity of optical spectra (notably iron).
   b. Absolute independence of x-ray spectra (number of lines and relative intensities) from excitation conditions; optical spectra are affected by differences in arc and spark spectra, changes in capacity and induction of the current for ultraviolet causing disappearance or strengthening of lines, etc.
   c. Independence of x-ray spectra from chemical combination or valence, since only atoms and not molecules are involved; optical spectra are affected by kind of chemical combination, band spectra of molecules, presence of foreign substances, etc.

DISADVANTAGES

1. Cannot be used for analysis of lightest elements, since characteristic wavelengths are too long for measurement by usual crystal gratings; the practical limit is calcium $(Z = 20)$.

2. Somewhat expensive and special equipment, although diffraction apparatus may be adapted.

3. Special technique, including selection of proper voltage, etc., for accurate quantitative analysis.

4. Somewhat limited accuracy for quantitative work involving comparison of line intensities with standards.   The line intensities are not proportional strictly to the weight proportions of elements in the preparation, for several reasons noted below.

[1] T. H. Rogers, *J. Appl. Phys.*, **23**, 881 (1952).

Intensities also depend on the particle size of the substance undergoing analysis, and minimum size is essential for true values.

5. Selective volatilization of constituents of mixture from focal spot of target for primary-emission method, with erroneous results; this difficulty is partly alleviated by rotating the anode in order to present fresh surface or by using the fluorescent-spectra methods.

6. Great decrease in intensities and prolongation of time for fluorescent-spectra methods, now largely offset by high-intensity primary rays and Geiger-counter registration.

7. Serious difficulty for quantitative analysis in the effect of absorption edges on emission lines; if in a mixture one element has one characteristic absorption edge of longer wavelength than the emission lines of other constituents of the mixture, these lines will be selectively absorbed. Such difficulties are avoided, when standardizing substances are used, by not mixing but by using a rotating target with the samples contiguous and excited to emission separately but, of course, registering on the same photographic plate. The effect of the absorption edges of silver and bromine in the plate must be taken into account also.

8. Line coincidence, which may occur and cause difficulties; avoided only by greater resolution of spectra and use of higher orders of reflection.

9. Appearance of foreign lines, such as mercury from diffusion pump, tungsten from metal sputtered in target from hot cathode, fluorescent metal lines from slits, traces of material from previous experiments on surface of anode, etc.; these can be checked with blank runs of apparatus. A claim of the discovery of a new element some years ago was shown to be based on spectrum artifacts from a defective calcite crystal.

10. In certain mixtures characteristic rays of one element can be excited by the characteristic rays of another element and thus produce a strengthening of intensity of lines for the first. Günther, Stransky, and Wilcke observed that a mixture of chromium and copper in the ratio of 46:54 appeared to have the 60:40 on account of characteristic rays of chromium excited by copper rays. Dilution with ground quartz produced true results.

11. Varying sensitivity of the photographic emulsion to different wavelengths; long-wave lines are blacker in proportion to intensity than shorter.

Qualitative Analysis. For the case of qualitative analysis of materials most of the foregoing disadvantages of the x-ray method are unimportant, and the method is straightforward for the analysis, particularly of rare earths and alloys of every kind. As already indicated, the fluorescent method, which has been hampered by low intensities and long exposure times, is coming into almost universal use with the advent of high-power tubes, producing very intense radiation, and Geiger counters.

Quantitative Chemical Analysis. *a. Primary Emission Spectra.* Methods of quantitative analysis using the primary emission spectrum have been described by Coster, Stintzing, Günther and Wilcke, Hevesy, Glocker, Goldschmidt, and others. In general these methods depend upon the comparison of the intensities of corresponding spectral lines of two neighboring elements in the periodic table, the assumption being made that the intensities of, say, the K lines of two such elements would be the same because of the similar electronic configurations, provided that the elements were present in the same amounts on the anticathode and provided also that the excess of the potential on the tube over the potential required to excite these lines was great compared with the difference between the characteristic excitation potentials of the two lines. (In the first approximation the intensity of a spectral line is proportional to the second power of the difference between the potential used and the characteristic potential.)

The actual procedure in all these methods consists in determining the emission spectrum of a mixture containing an unknown amount of the element for which the determination is being made and a known amount of the reference element. The intensities of the two corresponding lines of these two elements which have been chosen for comparison are then measured, and the elements are then, on the previous assumptions, present in amounts proportional to the intensities of their respective lines; or the amount of the reference material may be changed until the two intensities are equal, when their atomic amounts are also equal.

The differences in the methods mentioned are mainly differences in the technique of measuring the line intensities. Coster used a Siegbahn spectrograph and measured the relative line intensities with a Moll microphotometer. Günther and Wilcke used spectrograms made with very small times of exposure, the lines being hardly visible to the eye. By using a microscope of $800\times$ magnification, they then directly counted the reduced silver grains in the film. The choice of the time of exposure is very delicate with this procedure, for too long a time causes agglomeration of the grains, which makes counting inaccurate and difficult. Stintzing proposed the use of several superimposed photographic plates to record the spectrogram, the intensities of the several lines being indicated by the number of films they penetrate. Today intensities are almost universally measured with Geiger and scintillation counters.

Coster and Nishina, indeed, found the assumption of equal intensity of the lines for equal atomic concentration to be valid only under certain conditions. For instance, in analyzing zirconium ores for hafnium, tantalum was added as the reference element, and correct results were obtained if the tantalum was used as the dioxide. If, however, the pentoxide was used, the tantalum lines were $2\frac{1}{2}$ times as weak as the assumption would predict. Furthermore, the presence of only a small amount of lutecium oxide caused the dioxide to give results similar to those obtained with the pentoxide. These differences led Coster and Nishina to the adoption of an entirely empirical method in which any two lines near each other in the photographic plate may be used. Thus Hevesy and Jantzen used the Lu $L\beta_1$ line and the Hf $L\beta_2$ lines, which are 0.004 A apart, in analyzing for hafnium. The method of Coster and Nishina has been used for the analysis of a large number of zirconium ores for their hafnium content. The determinations are said to have been made to 0.1 per cent with an accuracy of 10 per cent.

b. Secondary Fluorescent Spectra. Hevesy[1] performed a very careful study of the factors that determine the results by analysis with fluorescent secondary rays. Characteristic primary rays ordinarily give six or seven times more intense secondary rays than rays with a continuous spectrum. For greatest intensity a metal must be chosen for target whose characteristic rays are 0.15 to 0.20 A shorter than the absorption bands of the elements undergoing analysis.

Especial attention also has been paid to the distorting effects upon emission-line intensity of absorption edges of a foreign element between comparison lines or lines of a foreign substance between the edges of the elements being compared, etc. The general conclusion is that the comparison element should be chosen so that the lines and absorption edges are as near as possible to those of the element being determined. Table 7-1 gives examples of correct choice.

TABLE 7-1. COMPARISON ELEMENTS FOR QUANTITATIVE ANALYSIS

Element analyzed	Line λ, A	Edge λ	Comparison element	Line λ	Edge λ
Pt	$L\alpha_1$ 1.310	1.070	Ta	$L\beta_3$ 1.303	1.058
In	$L\alpha_1$ 3.764	3.313	Cd	$L\beta_1$ 3.730	3.322
Cd	$L\alpha_1$ 3.948	3.496	Ag	$L\beta_1$ 3.927	3.505
Mo	$L\alpha_1$ 5.394	4.914	Cb	$L\beta_1$ 5.480	5.012
Rb	$L\alpha_1$ 7.303	6.841	Si	$K\alpha_1$ 7.109	6.731
Ge	$K\beta_1$ 1.126	1.115	Ta	$L\alpha_1$ 1.135	1.112
Zn	$K\beta_1$ 1.293	1.281	Hf	$L\beta_2$ 1.324	1.293
Ni	$K\beta_1$ 1.497	1.489	Er	$L\beta_2$ 1.511	1.480
Ti	$K\beta_1$ 2.509	2.494	Cs	$L\beta_2$ 2.506	2.466
S	$K\beta_1$ 5.021	5.012	Mo	$L\beta_2$ 4.909	4.909
Al	$K\alpha_1$ 8.319	7.947	Br	$L\alpha_1$ 8.108	8.357
Mg	$K\beta_1$ 9.535	9.511	As	$L\beta_1$ 9.394	9.300

Fortunately the distorting effect is appreciable only when there is a considerable amount of a foreign element present; in ordinary cases it may be neglected without seriously affecting the quantitative analysis. An important application of secondary-ray analysis is that of complex minerals down to 0.1 per cent of a constituent or even 0.001 mg of any element.

As already indicated, the development of high-intensity x-ray tubes and of Geiger counters has made entirely practicable quantitative chemical analysis from fluorescent spectra. Clark and Wagner[2] critically studied analysis of rubidium from a ratio of Geiger counts of the Rb $K\alpha_1$ line to those of the As $K\alpha$ line as an internal standard, as an approach to

---

[1] "Chemical Analysis by X-rays and Its Applications," McGraw-Hill Book Company, Inc., New York, 1932.

[2] Unpublished work for Office of Naval Research.

the difficult chemical problem of separating K, Rb, and Cs. When a working curve of the percentage of rubidium against the ratio Rb $K\alpha_1$ count/As $K\alpha_1$ count was determined, remarkably accurate analysis of any sample was possible. Then the same technique was extended to one of the most challenging of all problems—the analysis of the rare earths in monazite sand. One-gram samples of four monazite sands containing 0.1000 g of pure As_2O_3 were analyzed for thorium, first by a comparison of the Th $L\alpha_1$ count with the As $K\alpha_1$ count. From a smooth, experimental working curve for samples with 4.0, 5.6, 6.1, and 10.1 per cent ThO_2, further analyses have been rapid and reliable. The same has been true for Yb_2O_3, Nd_2O_3, etc., so that analyses of rare-earth samples are reduced to a routine. Possibly the simplest and most rapid of all analytical methods, chemical or instrumental, for samples of this complexity and difficulty of separation is secondary fluorescent spectrography.

A very practicable application lately announced has been the fluorescence-spectrum analysis of tetraethyllead and bromine in gasoline[1] by the U.S. Naval Research Laboratory presented in a symposium of the petroleum industry on this topic. Chemical methods, polarography, and x-ray absorption photometry, described in Chap. 8, are alternative methods. The $L\alpha$ line of lead at 1.17 A and the $K\alpha$ line of bromine (which is present in ethyl fluid as ethylene dibromide) were used; Geiger-spectrometer counts of only 1 min on the peak of the lead line gave a probable error of ±0.06 ml/gal in a content of 4 ml of tetraethyllead per gallon of gasoline, and for bromine ±0.16 ml/gal in 1.8 ml. of ethylene dibromide per gallon of gasoline. The accuracy is increased in proportion to the square root of the length of the counting period and is easily comparable with that of other methods, while having the advantage that variation in the gasoline base stock or presence of additives such as chlorine has negligible effects. Typical results are shown by the curves in Fig. 80.

Several practical metallurgical applications of x-ray fluorescence analysis in the research laboratories of one of the great steel companies have resulted from improved techniques of quantitative analysis from characteristic spectrum-line intensities for elements from titanium (22) on up.[2] A bent mica crystal is used with a Geiger spectrometer; for fluorescent rays of long wavelength a thin mica crystal diffracts more efficiently, while for shorter wavelengths a thicker crystal does better. K- and L-radiations are weaker at the extreme ends of lower and higher atomic numbers. Thus for general and routine analyses empirical plots are made of measured intensity of the Fe $K\alpha$-radiation of an alloy relative to 100 per cent Fe vs. the weight per cent of Fe in Fe-Al, Fe-Ni, Fe-Ag, and Fe-Cr alloys. Such calibration curves must be made for any com-

[1] Birks, Brooks, Friedman, and Roe, *Anal. Chem.*, **22**, 1208 (1950).

[2] Koh and Caugherty, *J. Appl. Phys.*, **23**, 427 (1952).

mercial complex alloys whose compositions are to be controlled.   In view
of the fact that the minimum effective thickness of a metallic element to
produce maximum fluorescent yield is very low, the analysis is an excellent means for observing chemical change on or near the surface, thus
supplementing the electron-diffraction method.   This has been applied
to the study of oxide films formed on alloys at elevated temperatures.
Thus in Fe-Cr alloys there is an impoverished Cr content in layers next to
the oxide-film boundary, then a Cr-rich layer next to the unoxidized
metal.   For substitutional solid solutions, diffraction patterns alone may
be insufficient for identification since crystal spacings may not be changed;
the fluorescence analysis, of course, will detect all elements present.   For

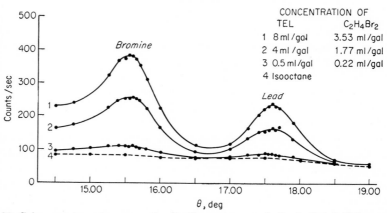

FIG. 80. Geiger-spectrometer curves for the fluorescence analysis of ethyl fluid in gasoline.

example, a bromine extract from type 347 stainless steel gives a diffraction
pattern for CbC (face-centered cubic, $a_0 = 4.44$ A); the fluorescent
spectrum shows Cr, Fe, Ni, W, and Br, besides Cb.
     Another application has been the use of fluorescence analysis by one of
the oil companies to detect the poisoning by arsenic of platinum re-form-
ing catalysts in the refining of gasoline and the effective elimination of the
difficulty; thus the x-ray equipment paid for itself in short order.
     In the analysis of the hazardous dusts in steel foundries which may
result in the lung conditions known as silicosis (from crystalline quartz)
and siderosis (from iron), the same Geiger-counter x-ray unit may be used
for the quantitative determination of quartz by diffraction and of iron by
fluorescence spectroscopy down to trace amounts, utilizing in both cases
powdered nickel as the internal standard.[1]   These analytical results are
then directly correlated with the diagnostic radiographs of the lungs of

     [1] Clark, Loranger, Bodnar, Terford, and Holly, *Anal. Chem.*, **26,** in press (1954)
(three papers in series).

the foundrymen—an example of three separate x-ray techniques brought to bear on one important problem.[1] References to many other recent examples of fluorescent x-ray spectroscopy (now coming to be designated simply emission spectroscopy or spectrography) are listed in the footnote.[2]

c. *Micro- and Histochemical Analyses by Emission Spectra.* Exceptionally promising is the microanalysis of thin sections of biological tissue by the fluorescence technique.[3] Here the intensity of the excited secondary radiation from a given area of the thin sample is proportional to the quantity of the element in question per unit of surface. By means of comparison between the intensity of a certain spectral line from the

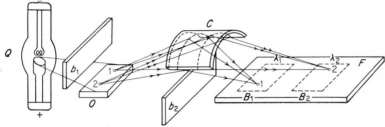

Fig. 81. The x-ray image spectrograph for microanalysis by fluorescent rays.   (*von Hamos.*)
Q, x-ray tube; O, sample to be analyzed; F, photographic film; b_1, b_2, diaphragms; C, bent crystal; B_1, B_2, spectral images of specimen from focused monochromatic rays.

specimen and the intensity of the same line from a similar specimen excited under the same external conditions, but with a known quantity of the element per unit of surface, the quantity in the unknown specimen can be estimated. Figure 81 shows the x-ray image spectrograph devised by von Hamos, employing a curved crystal which focuses secondary radiation to true monochromatic images of the specimen in accordance with the equation

$$2X = 2R \sqrt{\left(\frac{2d}{n\lambda}\right)^2 - 1}$$

where $2X$ is the distance between corresponding points in the sample to the image in the film, R is the radius of the bent-crystal surface, and n, λ, and d are the usual values in the Bragg equation. The intensity of the image, which is a distribution of the elements whose secondary

[1] Clark, Loranger, Bodnar, Terford, and Holly, *Anal. Chem.*, **26**, 1413–1421 (1954) (three papers in series).

[2] "Symposium on Fluorescent X-ray Spectrographic Analysis," *ASTM Special Tech. Publ.* **157** (1954). L. S. Birks, E. J. Brooks, and H. Friedman, Fluorescent X-ray Spectroscopy (in symposium on "X-rays as an Analytical Chemical Tool"), *Anal. Chem.*, **25**, 692 (1953). H. A. Liebhafsky, X-ray Absorption and Emission (review for 1953), *Anal. Chem.*, **26**, 26 (1954). W. J. Campbell and H. F. Carl, Quantitative Analysis of Niobium and Tantalum in Ores by Fluorescent X-ray Spectroscopy, *Anal. Chem.*, **26**, 800 (1954).

[3] L. von Hamos and A. Engström, Microanalysis by Secondary Röntgen Spectrography, *Acta Radiol.*, **25**, 325 (1944).

characteristic rays are registered, is measured with a microphotometer. Distinct zinc peaks are produced for only 0.2γ of zinc in the area of the thin microtome section of pancreas 200 μ thick, exposed to copper radiation; and a similar amount of iron in a spleen section 80 μ thick exposed to chromium radiation.

TABLE 7-2. LIMITS OF SENSITIVITY FOR CHEMICAL ANALYSES BY
X-RAY PROCEDURES

Author	Excitation method	Name of specimen	Spectrograph	Sensitivity, per cent
Hevesy (1932)...	Primary	Alloy, determination of 22 Ti in 26 Fe	Plane crystal, Siegbahn	0.001
Eddy and Laby (1930); Laby (1930)	Primary	Impurities in alloy, e.g., 30 Zn	Plane crystal	0.0001
Faessler (1934)...	Primary Secondary	Metal alloy Powder mixture	Plane crystal Plane crystal	0.001 0.005
Jesse (1935).....	Primary outside the roentgen tube	Powder mixture	Plane crystal, Seeman	0.006–0.05
von Hamos and Engström (1944)	Secondary	Biological tissue, determination of 26 Fe and 30 Zn	Curved crystal, radius 10 mm	0.01–0.001

That x-ray emission spectrography (which today generally connotes x-ray fluorescence) can be used for rapid and direct analysis of trace quantities, with techniques of sample preparation resembling the familiar spot tests on filter paper, has been clearly demonstrated. For example, Pfeiffer and Zemany[1] have found a linear relationship when micrograms of zinc (0 to 16) are plotted against Geiger counts (above background) per second, for the $K\alpha$ line.

In Table 7-2 are given the limits of sensitivity for the different analysis procedures, according to the investigations of certain authors published in the literature. It emerges from the table that it is possible to determine elements with atomic numbers above 20 occurring in powder mixtures in a concentration of at least 0.005 per cent. When the element analyzed has a lower atomic number than 20, the method does not afford such great sensitivity, both because of absorption of such soft rays and also because of the minor lower output of characteristic radiation from elements of low atomic number. The sensitivity may be estimated approximately at 0.1 to 0.05 per cent for the range 15 P to 19 K in the case of secondary-emission analysis.

[1] General Electric Research Laboratory, private communication prior to publication.

The best technique of microanalysis by primary-emission spectra is probably that of Guinier and Castaing.[1]   An electron beam less than 1 μ in cross section is defined by electron-microscope lenses and impinges on surface areas of a specimen on the order of 1 μ^2.   The emitted x-rays are analyzed with a sensitive Geiger spectrometer and thus permit a point-by-point analysis of composition of individual grains in a metal or alloy, for example, as well as of textures.

Micro- and histochemical analyses by absorption techniques are considered in Chaps. 8 and 10.

Because of the inherent difficulties of the emission-spectrum method, Glocker and Frohnmayer developed a method which depends upon the relative intensities of the general radiation on each side of a characteristic absorption discontinuity of the element for which the analysis is being made.   An ordinary Coolidge tube may be used; the sample may be in a number of different forms and may even be used without change if necessary.   A photographic absorption spectrum is obtained in the usual way, and the relative intensities are determined by a microphotometer; or an absorption spectrum may be determined by using an ionization chamber or Geiger counter.   The relation between the intensities and the amount of the element in the sample is given in general by the equation

$$\frac{i_1}{i_2} = e^{-cp}$$

where i_1 is the intensity of the radiation leaving the absorption screen on the short-wavelength side of the discontinuity and i_2 is the intensity of the long-wave side, c is a coefficient that must be experimentally determined, being actually a function of the mass absorption coefficient (see next chapter), and p is the amount of element present.

TABLE 7-3. MINIMUM MASS OF ELEMENTS REQUIRED FOR ABSORPTION EDGE

Element		c K edge	c L_1 edge	m K edge	m L_1 edge
42	Mo	69	. .	0.7	
47	Ag	45	. .	1.1	
50	Sn	34	. .	1.5	
51	Sb	31	. .	1.6	
56	Ba	24	. .	2.1	
58	Ce	22.5	. .	2.2	
74	W	8	. .	6.0	
82	Pb	5.7	. .	9.0	
90	Th	3.2	50	16.0	.0
92	U	. . . .	45	. . . .	1.1

[1] *Anal. Chem.*, **25**, 724 (1953).

The data in Table 7-3 include values of c and of the smallest mass m, in milligrams per square centimeter for the production of a true absorption edge (5 per cent intensity difference in two sides).

This method was used by Glocker and Frohnmayer in the successful analysis of barium in glass, antimony in a silicate, salt mixtures of antimony, barium, and lanthenum, bismuth in alloys, etc. It cannot be used to advantage for elements below molybdenum, largely because of the unfavorable intensity conditions for the continuous x-ray spectrum at wavelengths longer than about 1 A. Thus it is not adapted for analysis of biological specimens. However, a modification of this simple absorption spectrography does permit analysis even for nitrogen (7) and oxygen (8). This consists in measuring the absorption of *two different x-ray beams* with wavelengths on each side of the characteristic absorption edge for the element in question (for example, Ni $K\alpha$ 1.656 A, and Co $K\alpha$ 1.756 A on the two sides of the Fe $K\alpha$ absorption edge, 1.740 A). Since the calculations involve the mass-absorption coefficients at the two wavelengths, this technique, which is remarkably well adapted for micro- and histochemical analysis, will be considered in the next chapter, following the presentation of the definition and evaluation of these coefficients.

CHAPTER 8

THE ABSORPTION AND SCATTERING OF X-RAYS

The fact that x-rays are absorbed in matter in accordance with definite laws is, of course, of very great practical importance. Differential absorption by heterogeneous matter of varying density is the fundamental basis of the entire science of radiography, both medical and industrial, microradiography, gaging, and photometric analysis. The laws of absorption determine the protection that x-ray workers require against the harmful effects of the x-rays. Similarly, absorption must precede any effects of x-rays upon chemical action or biological functions.

X-ray science owes much to absorption measurements, since properly interpreted, they give valuable information upon atomic structure. They were the sole method of investigating the quality of x-rays from the time of Röntgen's discovery down to 1913, when Laue and the Braggs introduced crystal analysis. By absorption measurements with screens of various materials Barkla discovered the absorption and emission of x-rays with wavelengths that are characteristic for each chemical element.

The Absorption Coefficients. In traversing matter of all kinds, x-rays are absorbed in accordance with the usual exponential equation $I_x = I_0 e^{-\mu x}$, or $\log I_0/I_x = \mu x$, where I_x is the intensity after passage through homogeneous matter of thickness x, I_0 is the initial intensity, e is the natural base of logarithms, and μ is the absorption coefficient. One of the most useful applications of this formula is the expression of absorption properties in terms of the "half-value layer" (HVL), or that thickness of an absorbing screen which diminishes the intensity of a parallel bundle of rays to one-half the initial value; thus $\frac{1}{2} = e^{-\mu \mathrm{HVL}}$, HVL $= \log 2/\mu = 0.69/\mu$. When the intensity of a monochromatic beam of x-rays is plotted against the thickness of absorbing material (presupposing no characteristic absorption effects), a curve of the form illustrated in Fig. 82a is obtained. If values of $\log I$ are plotted against x, a linear relationship holds, as shown in Fig. 82b, always provided that the beam is strictly homogeneous. The slope of the line is an indication of quality, or wavelength: the steeper the slope, the softer the ray.

If the beam of radiation has a cross section of 1 cm², then μ represents the fraction of energy absorbed per cubic centimeter of the absorber traversed. Because of a more frequent interest in absorption per gram, the absorption formula appears as $I_x = I_0 e^{-(\mu/\rho) \cdot \rho x}$ where ρ is the density and μ/ρ, the mass-absorption coefficient, denotes the absorption by a screen of such thickness that it contains unit mass per square centimeter. Only in this way is it possible to compare rationally the absorption coefficients of different substances and the properties of the atoms themselves. This μ/ρ is a simple function of atomic number, whereas μ is not. The mass coefficient is independent of physical state, state of aggregation, and temperature and for chemical compounds is in the first approximation additive from the mass coefficients of the constituent elements. Thus, in an example cited by Sproull[1] x-rays passing from ceiling to the

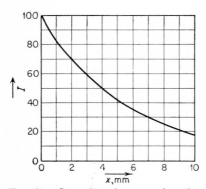

FIG. 82a. Intensity of x-rays plotted as a function of thickness (x) of an absorbing screen.

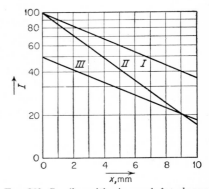

FIG. 82b. Semilogarithmic graph for absorption of x-rays; I and III represent beams with the same wavelength but different initial intensities, while II has the same initial intensity as I but a longer wavelength.

floor of a room containing hydrogen and oxygen may be 90 per cent absorbed through the total height of gas so that on the floor the intensity is 10 per cent of the initial value. A spark is passed to cause combination to steam. The floor intensity is still 10 per cent as it also is if the steam is condensed to water or ice.

By dividing μ/ρ by the number of atoms per gram, given by N_0/A, where N_0 is the Avogadro number, 6.024×10^{23} atoms/g atom, and A the atomic weight, or multiplying μ/ρ by the absolute mass of an atom, A/N_0, the atomic-absorption coefficient is obtained. Since this refers to a screen that contains 1 atom/cm^2, it leads to some interesting information concerning atomic structure. The variations of ratios of μ/ρ of lead, bromine, and sulfur to μ/ρ for carbon over a range of wavelengths from 0.1 to 10.0 A are shown in Fig. 83;[2] for lead, μ/ρ increases rapidly up to $\lambda = 0.1405$ and $\mu/\rho = 8$, then drops at this K absorption limit,

[1] "X-rays in Practice," p. 72, McGraw-Hill Book Company, Inc., New York, 1946.
[2] The ratios make possible analyses of gasoline containing ethyl fluid.

absorption having been accompanied by ejection of the K electrons; again μ/ρ increases, but with drops at $\lambda = 0.780, 0.813$, and 0.950 A, corresponding to L_I, L_{II}, and L_{III} absorption limits. Mass-absorption values of wavelength values from 0.010 to 2.0 A for air, water, plastics, and a number of important chemical elements are listed in Table 8-1.

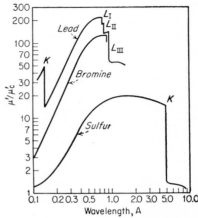

It is now definitely established that μ/ρ is really the sum of two coefficients τ/ρ, the true, or fluorescent-ray, mass-absorption coefficient, and σ/ρ, the mass-absorption coefficient due to scattering. The latter is usually much smaller in value than the coefficient for the absorption due to fluorescence. For light elements σ/ρ has a practically constant value of 0.17 independent of the wavelength for intermediate ranges. For heavier elements its experimental value changes in a complicated fashion.

FIG. 83. Ratios of mass-absorption coefficients of lead, bromine, and sulfur to that of carbon, showing basis of analysis by absorptiometry of gasoline containing ethyl fluid.

Barkla obtained the approximately constant value of 0.2 for σ/ρ in his pioneer experiments. When this value is equated with the J. J. Thomson theoretical value of scattering by electrons in accordance with the classical wave theory, ($\sigma = \frac{8}{3}\pi n e^4/m e \rho c^4$, where n is the number of electrons per cubic centimeter, ρ is the density, e and m the electronic charge and mass, and c the velocity of light), the result comes out that the number of electrons per atom is half the atomic weight. Subsequent developments have proved that this deduction is only approximate, for the Thomson formula indicates that σ is independent of wavelength, which is not true. The experimental facts are accurately expressed by the Klein-Nishina formula, useful especially for very hard x-rays and γ-rays:

$$\sigma = \frac{2\pi n e^4}{m^2 c^4 \rho} \left\{ \frac{1+\alpha}{\alpha^2} \left[\frac{2(1+\alpha)}{1+2\alpha} - \frac{1}{\alpha} \log_e (1+2\alpha) \right] + \frac{1}{2\alpha} \log_e (1+2\alpha) - \frac{1+3\alpha}{(1+2\alpha)^2} \right\}$$

where $\alpha = h\nu/mc^2$.

The true, or fluorescent, coefficient may be written as a function of the cube of the wavelength, that is, $K\lambda^3$. The atomic-fluorescent coefficient of absorption refers to a process of actual transformation of x-rays in the absorbing screen. It is a function of both the atomic number Z and the

TABLE 8-1. MASS-ABSORPTION COEFFICIENTS μ/ρ FOR CHEMICAL ELEMENTS, AIR, WATER, AND PLASTICS, $\lambda = 0.010$ TO 20.0A†

		0.010	0.050	0.100	0.5	1.0	5.0	10.0	20.0
1	H	0.1134	0.2252	0.2794	0.3660	0.3939	1.984	13.09	101.6
2	He	0.0571	0.1134	0.1407	0.1899	0.2433	6.570	50.80	398.9
3	Li	0.0494	0.0981	0.1219	0.1773	0.3156	18.61	145.2	1,120
4	Be	0.0506	0.1006	0.1252	0.2083	0.5330	44.43	343.5	2,576
5	B	0.0528	0.1048	0.1307	0.2455	0.7819	73.47	563.9	4,149
6	C	0.0571	0.1135	0.1419	0.3357	1.402	144.3	1,082	7,522
7	N	0.0571	0.1136	0.1428	0.4376	2.208	236.4	1,731	11,320
8	O	0.0571	0.1138	0.1440	0.5769	3.305	356.5	2,524	14,957
9	F	0.0541	0.1080	0.1378	0.7192	4.485	479.6	3,251	
10	Ne	0.0566	0.1132	0.1460	0.9807	6.476	678.1	4,330	
11	Na	0.0546	0.1096	0.1432	1.218	8.353	849.5	5,075	
12	Mg	0.0563	0.1134	0.1505	1.594	11.21	1,097		
13	Al	0.0551	0.1112	0.1502	1.950	13.95	1,304		
14	Si	0.0570	0.1155	0.1588	2.420	17.51	1,591		
15	P	0.0553	0.1127	0.1567	2.891	21.08	1,803		
16	S	0.0570	0.1168	0.1690	3.622	26.52	2,107		
17	Cl	0.0548	0.1130	0.1683	4.181	30.65			
18	A	0.0515	0.1070	0.1646	4.673	34.21			
19	K	0.0555	0.1164	0.1852	5.932	43.30			
20	Ca	0.0570	0.1206	0.1990	7.107	51.64			
22	Ti	0.0525	0.1134	0.2024	8.617	62.37			
24	Cr	0.0528	0.1169	0.2266	11.29	79.59			
26	Fe	0.05333	0.1215	0.2567	14.38	99.10			
28	Ni	0.0546	0.1288	0.2958	18.23	122.1			
29	Cu	0.0523	0.1255	0.3018	19.25	126.9			
30	Zn	0.0526	0.1287	0.3230	21.28	138.0			
32	Ge	0.0506	0.1290	0.3517	24.41	152.1			
34	Se	0.0494	0.1319	0.3896	28.05				
35	Br	0.0503	0.1375	0.4219	30.78				
36	Kr	0.0494	0.1385	0.4410	32.51				
37	Rb	0.0498	0.1431	0.4722	35.05				
38	Sr	0.0499	0.1473	0.5037	37.54				
42	Mo	0.0505	0.1669	0.6461	47.96				
46	Pd	0.0500	0.1863	0.8010	57.09				
47	Ag	0.0505	0.1945	0.8558					

		0.010	0.050	0.100	0.200	0.400
50	Sn	0.0490	0.2078	0.9733	6.324	38.46
52	Te	0.0475	0.2152	1.045	6.764	
53	I	0.0488	0.2282	1.127	7.292	
54	Xe	0.0481	0.2327	1.167	7.544	
56	Ba	0.0478	0.2473	1.277	8.221	
58	Ce	0.0486	0.2507	1.293	8.177	
60	Nd	0.0490	0.2694	1.415	8.884	
65	Tb	0.0485	0.3142	1.734	10.64	
73	Ta	0.0488	0.4082	2.357		
74	W	0.0488	0.4210	2.439		
78	Pt	0.0490	0.4781	2.794		
79	Au	0.0493	0.4955	2.899		
80	Hg	0.0493	0.5100	2.986		
82	Pb	0.0492	0.5403	3.163		
83	Bi	0.0496	0.5605	3.279		
90	Th	0.0488	0.5747	3.236		
92	U	0.0490	0.6124	3.426		

	0.010	0.050	0.100	0.50	1.0	5.0	10.0
Air..............	0.0570	0.1136	0.1433	0.5250	2.879		
H₂O............	0.0634	0.1263	0.1591	0.5533	2.979	316.9	2,243
Nylon...........	0.0624	0.1242	0.1554	0.3845	1.667	171.3	1,258
Polyethylene.....	0.0651	0.1295	0.1617	0.3406	1.257	123.9	928.8
Polystyrene......	0.0614	0.1221	0.1526	0.3380	1.324	133.3	999.5

† Victoreen, "Medical Physics," Vol. II, p. 891, Year Book Publishers, Inc., Chicago, 1950.

wavelength; thus $(\tau/\rho)(A/N_0) = CZ^4\lambda^3$ (law of Bragg and Peirce). C for each element is constant only over certain ranges and then changes abruptly at wavelengths that are characteristic of each element; the same is true of K in

$$\frac{\mu}{\rho} = \frac{\tau}{\rho} + \frac{\sigma}{\rho} = K\lambda^3 + \frac{\sigma}{\rho}$$

The accepted values of the constants for six metals in the equations for the mass-absorption coefficients above, K_K, and below, K_L, the first discontinuity (the characteristic K absorption) are given in Table 8-2.

TABLE 8-2. VALUES OF CONSTANTS IN ABSORPTION EQUATION

	Mo(42)	Ag(47)	Sn(50)	W(74)	Au(79)	Pb(82)
K_K	375	545	595	1,870	2,230	2,570
K_L	50	70	90	330	395	476
K_K/K_L	7.5	7.8	6.6	5.65	5.65	5.40
$\tau_A \times 10^{-21}$	13.3	11.0	8.90	3.19	2.57	2.37

The formulas in Table 8-3 for total mass-absorption values (μ/ρ) for several elements are useful.

TABLE 8-3. TYPICAL FORMULAS FOR μ/ρ

Absorber	λ	μ/ρ
Al	0.1–0.4	$14.45\lambda^3 + 0.15$
Al	0.4–0.7	$14.30\lambda^3 + 0.16$
Fe	0.1–0.3	$110\lambda^3 + 0.18$
Co	0.1–0.3	$124\lambda^3 + 0.18$
Ni	0.1–0.3	$145\lambda^3 + 0.20$
Cu	0.1–0.6	$147\lambda^3 + 0.5$
Mo	0.1–0.35	$450\lambda^3 + 0.4$
Mn	$>\lambda_{K_{abs}}$	$51.5\lambda^3 + 1.0$
Ag	0.1–0.4	$603\lambda^3 + 0.7$
Ag	$>\lambda_{K_{abs}}$	$86\lambda^3 + 0.6$
Pb	$>\lambda_{K_{abs}}$	$510\lambda^3 + 0.75$

Much credit is due Prof. S. J. M. Allen for almost single-handed efforts to collect absorption data and to derive these generalized expressions for calculation.

In the attempt better to correlate data on absorption, Victoreen[1] has presented a semiempirical method of calculating any mass-absorption coefficient, which has an accuracy on the order of 1 per cent in comparison

[1] *J. Appl. Phys.*, **19**, 855 (1948), **20**, 1141 (1949).

with the most reliable experimental values. The equation has the simplified form

$$\left(\frac{\mu}{\rho}\right)_z = C\lambda^3 - D\lambda^4 + \sigma_e N_0 \frac{Z}{A}$$

where C and D are constants tabulated in the paper, σ_e is the scattering coefficient per electron (Klein-Nishina formula), and the other symbols have their usual significance.

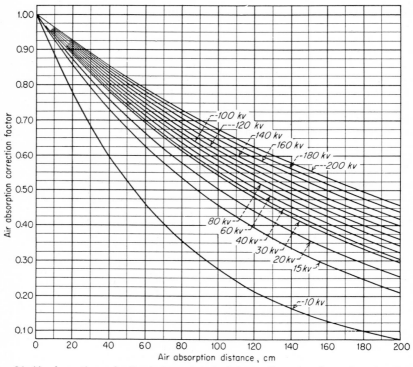

FIG. 84. Air-absorption reduction in intensity of minimum-filter x-ray beam from beryllium-window tube with inherent filtration by 1.5 mm Be. (*National Bureau of Standards.*)

Absorption in air is of great significance in all applications. Figure 84 represents the latest National Bureau of Standards values,[1] for beams generated at 10 to 200 kv of the correction factor $C = I_x/I_0$, where I_0 is the initial intensity and I_x that after passage through x cm of air. The intensity of an x-ray beam is measured at a single point with an r-meter (air ionization), the intensity to be expected at a more distant point calculated by the inverse-square law, and this value multiplied by the correction factor to determine the true intensity.

[1] Day and Taylor, *J. Research Natl. Bur. Standards,* **40,** 393 (1950).

Mechanism of Absorption. When a beam of x-rays impinges upon matter, the radiation energy is partly transformed, as already indicated, and partly scattered. Figure 85a indicates the principal phenomena that have been identified, though others have some experimental proof.

Fluorescent Characteristic X-rays. The energy of these secondary rays is accounted for in the term τ/ρ in the mass-absorption equation $\mu/\rho = (\tau/\rho) + (\sigma/\rho)$. Upon analysis with a spectrometer the rays are shown to be identical with those which would be emitted if the absorber element were used as an x-ray-tube target, in that the line spectra in the

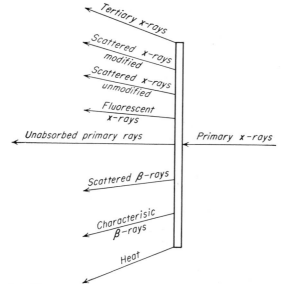

FIG. 85a. Phenomena occurring when x-rays impinge upon matter.

K, L, M, etc., series are obtained with the same wavelengths. This presupposes that if the K-series spectrum appears, the exciting primary beam must contain rays with a frequency equal to or greater than that which is characteristic of the K critical absorption limit of the absorber element. Fluorescent x-rays are unpolarized.

Primary x-ray quanta with an energy equal to or greater than $h\nu_{\text{absorber } K \text{ limit}}$ remove electrons from characteristic levels in the atom just as effectively as the cathode rays in an x-ray tube.

Scattered X-rays Unmodified. These rays have the same wavelengths as the primary beam; for instance, if the primary beam contains the tungsten characteristic rays, then the spectrum of the scattered x-rays will show the tungsten lines; thus reflection from crystals is essentially a special case of scattering. If the primary x-rays are transferred in energy quanta, the scattering is produced by atoms or groups of atoms that are too massive to be sensibly affected by the radiation quantum. These rays are polarized, usually completely; thus no reflection from a crystal occurs, when the primary rays are linearly polarized, if the direction of the reflected ray coincides with the electric vector of the incident ray.

Scattered X-rays Modified by the Compton Effect. One of the great contributions in physics was the discovery by Compton and by Debye that the spectra of scattered rays, characteristic of the primary rays and not of the secondary radiators, show not only lines with the same wavelength as those in the primary beam but also, on the long-wavelength side of these lines, other lines which indicate that in the process of scattering a distinct change has occurred. These modified lines were shown to be quantitatively explained on the basis of a purely quantum phenomenon. A primary quantum of x-radiation energy $h\nu_0$ strikes an electron and imparts to it a certain amount of kinetic energy, resulting in recoil. The radiation quantum is changed in its direction and proceeds with an energy $h\nu$, smaller by the amount involved in the recoil of the electron. Consequently the wavelength will be longer.

From the law of conservation of energy

$$h\nu_0 = h\nu + mc^2 \left(\frac{1}{\sqrt{1 - \beta^2}} - 1 \right) \tag{1}$$

where the last term is the kinetic energy of the recoil electron with relativity correction ($\beta = v/c$, or ratio of velocity to that of light).

From the law of conservation of momentum

$$X \text{ component:} \quad \frac{h\nu_0}{c} = \frac{h\nu}{c} \cos \phi + \frac{m\beta c}{\sqrt{1 - \beta^2}} \cos \Theta \tag{2}$$

$$Y \text{ component:} \quad 0 = \frac{h\nu}{c} \sin \phi + \frac{m\beta c}{\sqrt{1 - \beta^2}} \sin \Theta \tag{3}$$

where ϕ is the angle between the incident and scattered rays and Θ is that between the incident ray and the direction of recoil of the electron. Combining the three equations above and converting frequency ν to wavelength λ,

$$\lambda = \lambda_0 + \frac{h}{mc} (1 - \cos \phi)$$

or

$$\delta\lambda = \lambda - \lambda_0 = \frac{h}{mc} (1 - \cos \phi) = \gamma \text{ vers } \phi$$

Thus, at $\phi = 0$ deg (direction of primary ray), $\delta\lambda = 0$; at 90 deg, $\delta\lambda = 0.0242$ A (the numerical value of γ).

It is at once apparent that the Compton effect is independent of the atomic number of both the target and the scattering element and depends only upon the direction of the scattered beam with reference to the primary beam.

The Compton effect is well illustrated in the diagram in Fig. 85b. Here $h\nu_0$ is the primary quantum scattered by the electron e. The length of the arrow $h\nu_0$ measures the energy magnitude. According to classical, or unmodified, scattering, the scattered quanta will always have the same $h\nu_0$ value independent of the direction. This can be represented by the dotted semicircle with radii $h\nu_0$. Actually there is a wavelength change, and this is represented for five directions 1, 2, 3, 4, 5, as full lines, the lengths $h\nu$ being smaller the greater the scattering angle, and the energy changes being the vector difference between the dotted and full portions of each radius. This energy change is ac-

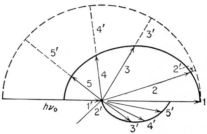

FIG. 85b. Diagram showing Compton effect as a function of the angle between primary and scattered x-ray beams.

counted for in the kinetic energy of the recoil electrons represented by the arrows in the smaller curve; $1'$ is 0 because for the scattering angle 0 deg no energy is available; $2'$, which is too small to show, corresponds to 2, $3'$ to 3, etc.

The ratio of the intensities of modified and unmodified rays in the Compton effect, however, varies with the atomic number of the radiator element, from ∞ for lithium (all energy modified) to 5.48 for carbon, 1.91 for sulfur, 0.51 for iron, 0.21 for copper, and decreasing values for heavier elements to practically zero for lead. No such change in wavelength has been observed in the reflection of x-rays by crystals or in the scattering of rays of light. As independent proof the tracks of the recoil electrons have been photographed by C. T. R. Wilson's cloud-expansion method.

The energy distribution

$$E_{\text{kinetic}} = h\nu_0 \frac{\alpha \text{ vers } \phi}{1 + \alpha \text{ vers } \phi} = h\nu_0 \frac{2\alpha \cos^2 \Theta}{(1 + \alpha)^2 - \alpha^2 \cos^2 \Theta}$$

$$\cot \tfrac{1}{2}\phi = -(1 + \alpha) \tan \Theta$$

where $\alpha = \gamma/\lambda$, is verified experimentally.

It is interesting to calculate how much energy is involved in the recoil electrons for a practical case of irradiation of the human body from a tube at 200 kv (average wavelength 0.04 A):

$$E_{\text{kinetic}} = h(\nu_0 - \nu)$$

If the average increase in wavelength ($\phi = 90$ deg) is 0.024 A,

$$E_k = h\left(\frac{c}{\lambda_0} - \frac{c}{\lambda_0 + 0.024}\right)$$

Expressing E in volts, the recoil electrons have a velocity of about 50 kv. Thus $\frac{50}{200}$, or 25 per cent, of each quantum in the human body goes into the energy of recoil electrons. For rays generated at 200 kv, 2.5 per cent of the x-ray energy in each part of a tissue is transformed into the energy of photoelectrons. Of the fraction of primary energy that is scattered (12 per cent), 3 per cent (25 per cent of 12 per cent) goes into recoil-electron energy.

Scattered and Characteristic β-rays. X-rays that are impinging upon the surface of a secondary radiator eject photoelectrons. If the radiation is monochromatic (frequency ν_0), then the kinetic energy of some of the liberated (scattered) electrons will be $E_k = h\nu_0$ independent of the secondary radiator. The electrons are those so loosely bound in the atoms that the work required for their removal is negligible. In addition, however, other photoelectrons are ejected with kinetic energies that depend upon the particular kind of atom from which they are liberated; hence, their removal has involved a certain amount of work W. If a beam of these electrons is analyzed by causing them to bend in a magnetic field, then all electrons with the same value of $E_k = h\nu_0 - W$ will register a sharp spectral line on a suitably disposed photographic plate. By means of these characteristic β-ray spectra, De Broglie showed that the energy necessary to eject an electron from an inner atomic shell, which is involved in the correction term W, is simply the quantity of energy representing the energy levels K, L, M, N, etc., which is in turn measured by the frequency values of the critical absorption limits. These β-ray spectra therefore constitute another important method of measuring energy levels. In one photograph for photoelectrons ejected from a silver plate irradiated by the K-radiation of tungsten (and of course producing the secondary fluorescent silver K-radiation), De Broglie obtained six lines, corresponding to six different kinetic energies. He showed that these were:

(1) $h\nu_{\text{Ag } K\alpha} - L_{\text{Ag}}$ (where L_{Ag} is the energy required to remove an L electron from the silver atoms, or $h\nu_{\text{AgLabs}}$)

(2) $h\nu_{\text{Ag } K\alpha} - M_{\text{Ag}}$ (4) $h\nu_{\text{W } K\alpha_2} - K_{\text{Ag}}$

     $h\nu_{\text{Ag } K\beta} - L_{\text{Ag}}$ (5) $h\nu_{\text{W } K\alpha_1} - K_{\text{Ag}}$

(3) $h\nu_{\text{Ag } K\beta} - M_{\text{Ag}}$ (6) $h\nu_{\text{W } K\beta} - K_{\text{Ag}}$

More recently Robinson and his associates have made notable contributions to the field of magnetic spectra of secondary electrons. By means of greatly improved experimental methods the values of energy levels have been determined for many of the chemical elements, including measurement of absorption limits in the range of long wavelengths in which the crystal-grating method is not practicable.[1] This work has also included measurement of energy levels in multiply ionized atoms. Not only do the magnetic spectra yield energy values of secondary electrons that are ejected from inner levels by action of the primary x-rays; the secondary fluorescent x-rays generated in the radiator are also effective in liberating electrons. The process may be pictured as follows: a K electron is ejected through the agency of the primary x-rays, followed by the transition of an L electron, for example, to fill the vacancy. Normally a $K\alpha$-ray is emitted as a consequence of liberation of energy. However, this energy so released can be transformed in the atom into forms other than the quantum of radiation (the Auger effect). For example, the transition $L \rightarrow K$ (i.e., from the state K with one electron missing, to the state L) may lead to the ejection of an M electron with a kinetic energy represented by the difference between the first energy $(L \rightarrow K)$ and the work required to remove this M electron from the atom. This work is greater than that which normally corresponds to the M level, for an electron is missing from an inner level with the result that there is diminished screening of the positive nucleus. Therefore the work of separating an outer electron is equal to that required normally for the element of next higher atomic number. Such processes have been experimentally verified in Robinson's work.

Chemical Analysis by the Photoelectron Spectrometer. Only recently has the photoelectron spectrometer come into use for chemical analysis with the perfection of ultra-thin-windowed Geiger counters for detection. An instrument for this purpose, together with typical photoelectron spectra for copper, zinc, silver, gold, and binary alloys, is described by Steinhardt and Serfass.[2] From the spectrum of an 80 atomic per cent Ag–20 atomic per cent Au shown in Fig. 86, these authors have obtained a fairly good quantitative analysis. The equation used is $T = h\nu_0 - h\nu - \omega_0$, where ν_0 = frequency of primary, or exciting, radiation, ν = frequency of fluorescent radiation (instead of characteristic absorption), and ω_0 = work function of irradiated sample. Thus the major Ag peak is identified as Mo $K\alpha$–Ag $L\beta$, and others as Mo $K\alpha$–Ag $L\beta$ and Mo $K\alpha$–Au M.

The Characteristics of Super-voltage Radiation. With the increasing significance in physics, medical therapy, and industrial radiography of x-rays generated at 1-million to 20-million volts and higher, special con-

---

[1] For further detailed information see "International Critical Tables," Vol. VI, p. 2, McGraw-Hill Book Company, Inc., New York, 1926–1930. The data of Robinson, together with all references, are given in Siegbahn, "Spektroskopie der Röntgenstrahlen," 2d. ed., pp. 413–428.

[2] R. G. Steinhardt and E. J. Serfass, *Anal. Chem.*, **23**, 1585 (1951), **25**, 697 (1953).

sideration must be given to the characteristics of these rays, especially with respect to absorption.

a. Efficiency of Production.   As the voltage applied to an x-ray tube is raised, the efficiency of production of x-rays rapidly increases.   In fact, if the amount of radiation is measured in terms of energy, for the same electric power passing through the tube, the x-ray emission is very nearly

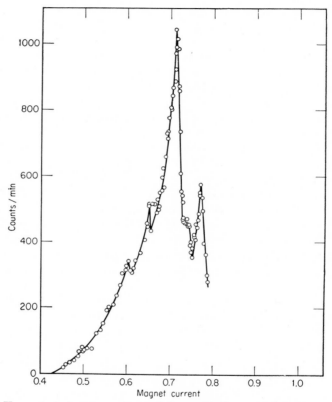

FIG. 86. X-ray photoelectron spectrum of silver-gold alloy.   (*Steinhardt and Serfass.*)

proportional to the voltage.   For a tungsten-target tube operated at different potentials, the amount of x-rays per kilowatt of energy passing through the tube is approximately as listed in Table 8-4.   The feature of this table that is of greatest interest is the variation of the roentgens of x-ray dosage with the tube potential.   It will be seen that the usual therapeutic range, of between 100 and 200 kv, is at just the minimum of efficiency.   The physical reason for this is that for softer x-rays a greater fraction of the energy is spent in producing the recoil electrons which are responsible for the ionization of air.   It is because of this change in the

TABLE 8-4. X-RAY PRODUCTION*
(Quantity of x-rays emitted by a tungsten-target tube per kilowatt of energy in cathode-ray beam)

Operating potential, kv	Power in total x-rays from focal spot, watts	"Effective" wavelength (unfiltered), A	R/sec at 1 m from target (unfiltered)
50	2.5	0.56	1.2
70	3.5	0.40	0.62
100	5	0.28	0.34
200	10	0.14	0.39
500	25	0.056	1.1
1,000	48	0.028	2.1
2,000	95	0.014	4.0

* Compiled by A. H. Compton; "effective" wavelength is defined on page 179.

absorption process that the emission as expressed in roentgens does not follow that expressed in watts of power.

Efficiency of production of x-rays at 2 Mev has been experimentally measured by Beuchner[1] et al. Intensity distribution from thick targets is integrated over the entire solid angle surrounding the target to give the dependence of total x-ray flux emitted as a function of voltage and atomic number of the target. For a given voltage the total flux is linear with atomic number in agreement with the theory of Bethe and Hertler. Thus 7.4 per cent of the incident electron energy is converted into x-radiation for a gold target at 6.25 Mev.

b. Spatial Intensity Distribution above the Target. Of great significance in the study of absorption and scattering of rays generated at 1 million volts or more is the spatial intensity distribution around a target as a function of the voltage of the impinging electrons. Careful meas-

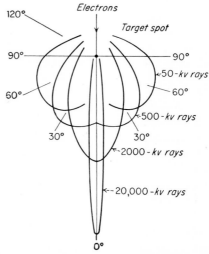

FIG. 87. Spatial intensity distribution of x-rays about the target as a function of the voltage of the impinging electrons.

urements have led to the graphical representation in Fig. 87 of these radiation envelopes for 50-, 500-, 2,000-, and 20,000-kv rays. It is at once evident that the higher the voltage and the greater the energy of the

[1] *ASTM Special Tech. Publ.*, **96**, 75 (1946).

electrons, the smaller is the sidewise scattering until the beam from the 20-million-volt betatron is a very narrow pencil straight forward, the angle from maximum intensity to half intensity being less than 4.5 deg. The shape of these beams therefore plays a prominent part in the absorption and scattering in passing through matter. For secondary and scattered rays must also be largely constrained to move forward in such constricted volumes of the primary rays. This conditions the technique to be employed in therapy and radiography and the over-all results to be obtained.

c. Absorption of High-voltage Radiation. For the x-rays produced at less than 70 kv the greater part of the energy absorbed in air or in body tissue is spent in producing photoelectrons. These particles in turn spend themselves in producing the ionization by which the rays are measured and which is responsible for the biological effects of the radiation. As the tube potential increases, the photoelectron production rapidly diminishes to a negligible value, and scattering of the x-rays becomes the most prominent phenomenon. This scattering process may best be thought of as a diffusion of the x-ray photons as they traverse the cloud of electrons of which the matter is composed. Most of the scattered energy reappears as x-rays going in every direction; an important part, however, appears as the energy of motion of the electrons with which the photons collide. These recoiling electrons take 10 to 40 per cent of the energy spent in the scattering process, for the range of wavelengths under consideration, and use their energy in ionization. The scattered photons form diffused x-rays of increased wavelength which will probably escape from the region before they are again scattered or absorbed.

When the applied potential exceeds 1 million volts, some of the highest energy x-rays may spend themselves in a new type of process, similar to the photoelectric effect, known as *pair production.* This process consists in the creation, by using the energy of an absorbed photon, of a positive electron (positron) and a negative electron. A part of the energy thus spent reappears as ionization by the resulting positive and negative electrons; the greater part, however, is used in forming another photon (or two photons), when the positive electron reunites with a negative electron. The photon thus produced is a very hard x-ray which will probably escape from the region before it is absorbed. Such a process may be viewed as the excitation of a kind of fluorescence.

To illustrate the contributions to the total absorption coefficient of the photoelectric effect, the Compton effect, and pair production, Fig. 88 displays the variation of μ with energy (voltage) when the absorber is iron. Curves *A*, *B*, and *C* are, respectively, the partial absorption coefficients for the three fundamental processes just enumerated, which may contribute to the total absorption coefficient, which is curve *D*.

The total absorption coefficient is seen to have a minimum in the neighborhood of 7 Mev (for iron). For lead, the minimum is near 4 Mev, whereas for aluminum it is near 16 Mev. The old rule of thumb relating increased penetration to increased kilovoltage can hold only when the bulk of the intensity in the x-ray spectrum being considered is below this minimum. These facts, together with the negligible scattering, are of greatest significance in radiography (Chap. 9) and therapy (treatment of deep-seated cancer) (Chap. 12).

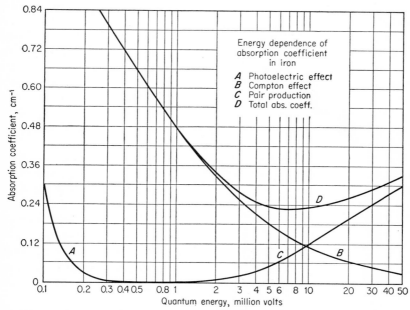

FIG. 88. Energy dependence of absorption coefficient for x-rays in iron. [G. D. Adams, Ind. Radiog., **4**, 3, 23 (1946).]

Two conclusions may be drawn from the fact that the absorption coefficient is practically constant over the bulk of the x-ray spectrum: (1) hardening of the spectrum by filtering should be negligible and (2) in detecting flaws, an absolute sensitivity should be found. The second observation means that, for a given technique, the least detectable flaw is independent of the total thickness of the absorber: small scattering and fine focal spot allow this fact to be realized. At still higher energies other phenomena may be expected. Thus with the 335-Mev synchrotron at the University of California, *mesons* (see Chap. 1) have been produced in a carbon source by the x-ray beam resulting from the impact of electrons of this energy on a platinum target. Mesons were recorded on plates with densities as high as 100 per square centimeter in a 100-μ emulsion.[1]

[1] E. M. McMillan, J. M. Peterson, and R. S. White, *Science*, **110**, 579 (1949).

d. The Depth Dose. The actual quantity and quality of x-radiation which will be delivered at a particular point below the surface of an irradiated object, in other words, the depth dose, are of primary concern in the field of deep radiation therapy of the human body. Since the laws of absorption and scattering are of vital importance in devising the proper technique and the proper dosage in the treatment of a deep-seated cancer, brief preliminary consideration is given here as an introduction to the principles of therapy in Chap. 12. A vast number of the experimental measurements required have been made by means of "phantoms," built of materials simulating the human body in absorbing power and so designed that thimble ionization chambers can be located at any given depth below the surface for dosage measurement which integrates the linear absorption in the given thickness and the attendant effects of scatter. The phantom may be a tank of water, or a container full of rice, or layers of cellulose or wood such as Presdwood. With soft x-rays generated at low voltages it is evident that the dosage measured in air, on the skin, and at a depth may be greatly different because of absorption and scattering.

There are obvious advantages in supervoltage rays. An isodose chart, or depth dose, for 2-million-volt rays is reproduced in Fig. 89a. The penetration of the very hard rays equivalent to γ-rays from radium permits a larger dosage to deep tumors. Thus at a depth of 10 cm in the human body the depth dose is 55 per cent in comparison with 35 per cent for 200-kv rays. Another method of comparison of relative depth doses for radiation with energies between 200 kv and 20 Mev is indicated in Fig. 89b. Since all soft rays easily absorbed by the skin, whose tolerance therefore is the limiting factor in ordinary therapy, are easily filtered out (9 mm lead equivalent), skin damage can be minimized in deep cancer therapy even when a single partial treatment is used. Because of its lack of scattering and the sharpness of its definition, the

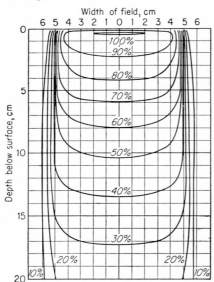

Fig. 89a. Isodose chart for 2-million-volt x-rays (100 cm distance, 10- by 10-cm field, 9 mm Pb equivalent filtration).

beam may be directed at the tumor without damage to adjacent tissue, especially with cross firing, *i.e.,* irradiating from several angles so that the beams cross at the desired point in the tumor to give the desired dose while keeping at a minimum the effect on adjacent healthy but radiosensitive tissue.

Filtration. The x-ray beams directly from a tube target are not of greatest usefulness as generated. The rays contain a large proportion of very soft components which are absorbed in the uppermost layers of any absorbing substance. For medical diagnosis and deep therapy they are

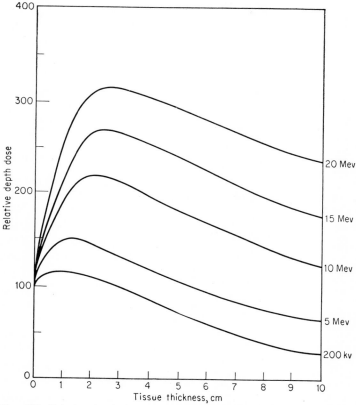

Fig. 89b. Relative depth doses in tissue of x-rays from 200 kv to 20 Mev.

obviously useless, particularly as they may cause harmful skin reactions because the absorption per unit volume for the soft rays is relatively so great. The necessity presents itself in medical and other uses of working with the most nearly homogeneous rays possible, namely, those for which the relative ratios of components of various wavelengths do not change during penetration of the irradiated object. The effect of filtration is illustrated by the following example. A mixture of rays consisting of three parts, soft, hard, and very hard constituents, with equal intensity, is filtered through 5 mm of aluminum. For the very hard ray, $\mu = 0.405$,

80 per cent penetrates through; for the hard ray, $\mu = 1.08$, 60 per cent; and for the soft, $\mu = 6.75$, only 4 per cent. Thus, out of a continuous heterogeneous mixture actually generated, a beam less and less heterogeneous and with greater and greater average hardness (shorter wave-

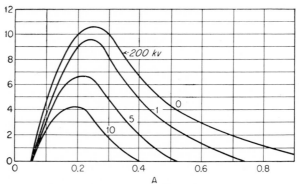

Fig. 90. Curves showing effect of filtration of heterogeneous x-ray beam through 1, 5, and 10 mm of aluminum.

length) results from greater filtration. Actual experimental results showing the effect of passage through 1, 5, and 10 mm of aluminum are illustrated in Fig. 90. When the absorption results are plotted logarithmically as in Fig. 91, it is seen that the slope of the curve for small

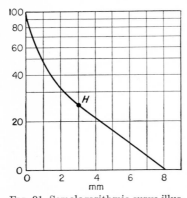

Fig. 91. Semologarithmic curve illustrating the homogenizing effect of filtering a beam of x-rays through copper foil. Compare with Fig. 82b for monochromatic rays.

thicknesses changes continuously instead of being constant as is true for monochromatic rays (Fig. 82b), showing that the quality of the beam is changing. Finally a point is reached where the curve approaches linearity and below this homogeneity point negligible changes in quality occur. This does not mean that the beam is monochromatic or even homogeneous when filtered through other materials. A beam generated at 200 kv and filtered through 1 mm of copper behaves as though it were homogeneous when passed next through water or the human body, for the curve is linear; but the same filtered beam passed through more copper is by no means homogeneous. These different behaviors are, of course, determined by the relation between values of μ and σ. Hence filtration for the purposes of homogenizing is easily accomplished with a substance of higher atomic number than that of the object or body in which the rays are to remain homogeneous.   In general medical practice copper, tin, and lead are most frequently used as the homogenizing filters.

Measurement of Quality by Absorption Methods.   Since absorption depends so definitely upon the nature of the absorber or filter and upon the wavelength of the ray, a practical measurement of the quality or hardness of an x-ray may be based upon it; for example, by comparing the absorption power of layers of aluminum to that of fixed thicknesses of silver, as judged by the fluorescent or photographic power of the emergent ray, a scale may be constructed and used without reference to wavelengths.   Röntgen himself used such a device, and the Benoist penetrometer, consisting of a thin silver disk 0.11 mm thick, surrounded by 12 numbered aluminum sectors from 1 to 12 mm thick, was used for many years, particularly in the measurement of dosage in x-ray therapy.

In many cases an x-ray beam with a variety of wavelengths may be used, and the simple absorption equations cannot be used directly. Duane suggested more than 30 years ago the determination of the "effective" wavelength, or the wavelength of a monochromatic ray that has the same absorption under given conditions as the whole polychromatic beam.   An experimental curve was constructed, based upon the fact that the thickness of aluminum which has the same absorbing power as a given thickness of copper depends upon the wavelength of the radiation; for soft or long-wavelength x-rays the thickness of aluminum must be large, and for hard x-rays small.   Experimentally, the percentage of the beam absorbed in 1 mm of copper was first measured by the ionization produced in a gas or by the effect on a fluorescent screen or photographic plate; then the absorption in increasing thicknesses of aluminum was measured until it had the same value as for the copper.   The wavelength as a function of this equivalent thickness was read from a graph such as is shown in Fig. 92.   Another method consisted in the successive measurements of absorption in 1 mm of copper and 4 mm of aluminum. The wavelength was then read from the curves in Fig. 92.   The description of quality by the "effective" wavelength is mentioned for historical interest since it is no longer used.   The standard curve at present is based upon absorption in 0.25 mm of copper.   Actually each test metal gives effective wavelengths which differ from those obtained with the same radiations but different metals.   The fact remains that the half-value layer (HVL) method, defined at the beginning of this chapter, for describing quality, is most generally accepted throughout the world.[1]

Protection from X-rays.[2]   The definite laws that govern the absorption of x-rays also permit an exact determination of the thickness of protecting

[1] Glasser, Quimby, Taylor, and Weatherwax, "Physical Foundations of Radiology," 2d Ed., Chap. XII, Paul B. Hoeber, Inc., New York, 1952.
[2] See L. S. Taylor, "Medical Physics," Vol. I, p. 1382, Year Book Publishers, Inc., Chicago, 1944.

material that must be employed in all work with these rays in order to prevent dangerous physiological effects such as burns and anemia. Of the more readily available materials, lead is the best for protective purposes.

Adequate protection is a factor of vital importance that must be considered in the installation of x-ray equipment. Undue exposure to the radiation may lead to a lowering of the white-blood-corpuscle count (leukopenia), to low blood pressure and anemia, as well as to the skin

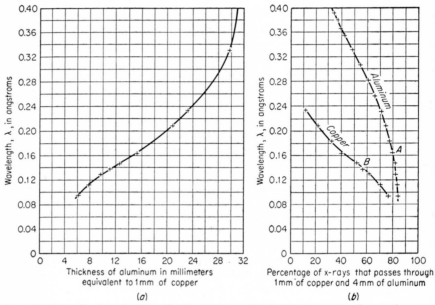

FIG. 92. Methods of evaluating effective wavelength of a heterogeneous beam of x-rays. (a) Curve showing the thickness of aluminum having the same absorption as 1 mm of copper for a heterogeneous beam of x-rays; (b) curves showing the percentage absorption in 1 mm of copper and in 4 mm of aluminum as a function of wavelength. (*Duane.*)

burns that were so fatal to the early workers. For those engaged in x-ray researches a frequent check on stray radiation with Geiger counters or pocket dosimeters is essential. A "tolerance dose" which the human body may withstand without ill effects was for many years considered to be 1×10^{-5} r/sec[†] for 200 working hours per month.[1] Geneticists, however, claim that only a dosage rate one-tenth as great, or 1×10^{-6} r/sec, can be considered safe against obscure biological effects. This problem has had renewed interest in view of radiations from atomic bombs.

An International Commission on Radiological Protection under the auspices of the International Congress of Radiology has functioned since

[†] The r unit of dosage is defined on page 74.
[1] Mutscheller, *Am. J. Roentgenol. Radium Therapy,* **13,** 65 (1925).

1931 in standardizing requirements for adequate x-ray protection. As higher and higher voltages are being used in therapy, such standards become increasingly important. The 1950 recommendations are that a maximum permissible dose received by the whole body surface shall be 0.5 r for any one week or 0.3 r measured in free air. For exposure to hands and forearms alone the dose may be 1.5 r per week. The maximum dose for neutrons and β-rays is in terms of energy absorption per gram of tissue; for neutrons there can be only one-tenth that permitted for high-energy quantum radiation. A new advisory committee formed in the United States has prepared a unified and detailed set of safety recommendations (x-ray and high-voltage protection, storage of inflammable film, etc.).[1]

The transmission values through lead of x-rays generated at 60 to 2,000 kv are listed in Table 8-5.

TABLE 8-5. TRANSMISSION TABLE FOR LEAD

Kv (peak)	Half- value layer	Per cent transmission				
		10 mm Pb	5 mm Pb	1 mm Pb	0.5 mm Pb	0.1 mm Pb
60	0.50 mm Al	0.05	0.07	0.15	0.21	0.42
84	0.75 mm Al	0.07	0.12	0.32	0.46	0.71
100	1.00 mm Al	0.09	0.16	0.45	0.68	1.17
120	1.50 mm Al	0.14	0.25	0.60	0.80	1.40
140	1.70 mm Al	0.16	0.27	0.64	0.86	1.50
140	0.15 mm Cu	0.31	0.48	0.97	1.22	1.82
140	0.50 mm Cu	0.48	0.70	1.26	1.52	2.17
200	1.00 mm Cu	0.65	0.93	1.65	1.97	2.77
250	2.00 mm Cu	1.00	1.37	2.31	2.77	3.90
250	3.00 mm Cu	1.22	1.68	2.87	3.45	4.8
400	4.00 mm Cu	1.60	2.30	4.10	4.90	6.9
400	5.00 mm Cu	2.45	3.50	6.20	7.40	10.3
1,000	3.20 mm Pb	14.0	20.5	38.0	46.0	65.0
2,000	6.00 mm Pb	31.5	43.0	71.5	84.0	114.0

Some Practical Applications of Absorption Measurements. Aside from the value of characteristic absorption edges in qualitative and quantitative analysis (Chap. 7) the simple exponential law $I = I_0 e^{-\mu x}$ is the basis from which valuable information may be obtained. Filtration, for the purpose of homogenizing beams for therapy, and the determination of quality and effective wavelength have been considered already.

Other possibilities that have found interesting practical use are as follows:

[1] Medical X-ray Protection Up to Two Million Volts, *Natl. Bur. Standards Handbook* XX, p. 41 (1950).

1. *Thickness Gaging and Porosity Measurement.* The exponential law indicates that absorption of a given x-ray beam of given intensity must vary with x, the thickness of the homogeneous material. This suggests the simplest application of an absorption technique, namely, the evaluation of gage and its constancy. Many materials occur in such shapes that micrometer thickness measurements are difficult or impossible. With an x-ray beam such determinations can be made without in any way touching the sample. It is necessary only to measure the diminution in initial intensity I_0 in passage through a layer. This may be done with a fluoroscopic screen or a photographic film, although only roughly since under the best conditions a difference in thickness of about 2 per cent is required for visual differentiation of the blackening of the photographic emulsion. Still better is an ionization chamber or r-meter or Geiger counter which can be made extremely sensitive so that a difference certainly of the order of 0.1 per cent is detectable. The logical practical equipment is a combination of a phosphor and an electron-multiplier photoelectric tube (Fig. 47) first used for intensity measurement in 1942 by Morgan,[1] for preliminary chemical analysis by Liebhafsky and Winslow[2] in 1945, and for rapid examination of fuses by Smith[3] in 1945. Operation with amplifiers and automatic continuous operation have followed. During World War II it became necessary to roll thin metal sheet of constant gage, free from defects, for various types of precision equipment. At a constant voltage and current x-rays could be passed through the sheet on the rolling mill traveling at 800 fpm, as illustrated in Fig. 93. The unabsorbed radiation passes into an electron-multiplier tube, the current in which is amplified to be read on an ammeter or otherwise arranged to signal when there is variation in gage of the sheet. Variations in primary-x-ray intensity are compensated by a null method since a beam from the opposite side of the target passes through a stationary sample of standard required gage and then into another multiplier tube and the circuit linked with that registering absorption in the moving sheet. Unbalance actuates a servomechanism which automatically tightens or loosens the mill rolls to yield the desired gage. This technique of gaging is now established practice for a wide variety of rolled metal sheets. Plated strips or sheets and tubing may also be checked for uniformity of thickness. Friedman and Birks[4] devised a method for determining the thickness of thin coatings with the x-ray source and Geiger counter both on the same side. X-rays pass through the coating and are reflected at a Bragg diffraction angle from the base back to the counter, the intensity being reduced by absorption due to double trans-

[1] R. H. Morgan, *Am. J. Roentgenol. Radium Therapy,* **48,** 88 (1942).

[2] H. A. Liebhafsky and E. H. Winslow, *Gen. Elec. Rev.,* **48,** 36 (1945).

[3] H. M. Smith, *Gen. Elec. Rev.,* **48**(3), 13 (1945).

[4] *Rev. Sci. Instr.,* **17,** 99 (1946).

mission through the coating. Continuous testing of deviations from concentricity of wire cores in insulation of high-voltage cables is now established practice. X-ray gage methods are particularly useful on compressible materials such as leather, cellophane, cloth textiles, rubber blankets, plastic films, paper, etc. It follows that *porosity*, as well as gage, can be accurately determined, for x-rays measure only the true thickness X_t of solid matter through which they pass without reference to free spaces and pores, whereas only the apparent thickness X_a is measurable by mechanical means such as micrometers. The porosity of the negative metallic lead plates in storage batteries as a function of temperature of formation and charging down to low temperatures is a large

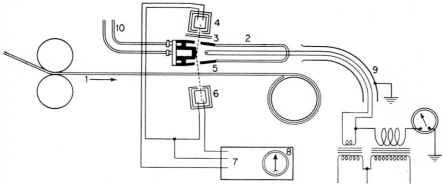

FIG. 93. X-ray gaging of sheet metal.

1. Flow direction of material being gaged.
2. Shockproof, rayproof x-ray tube.
3. Standard-gage specimen for comparison.
4. Electronic cell for standard value.
5. Material being gaged.
6. Electronic cell for material value.
7. Power pack and amplifier.
8. Indicating meter or recorder.
9. Grounded high-voltage cable.
10. Water cooling for x-ray tube.

factor in determining plate capacity, which depends on the penetration of sulfuric acid into the interior of the active mass. No possible mechanical measurement of the apparent thicknesses of the spongy mass could be made; but, by placing a plate exactly perpendicular to a photographic film and directing an x-ray beam parallel to the plate, a shadowgraph of the specimen edge on may be measured for apparent cross section. Then the true thickness is evaluated from measurement of absorption of x-rays through sections of the plate of the same area and same mass of active material. Thus the ratio of X_t/X_a and the known values of the linear absorption coefficient μ for lead give the variations in thickness and porosity, the latter decreasing nonlinearly with formation and charging temperatures of the negative plates and also with capacity.

2. *Chemical Analysis from Relative Absorptions (X-ray Photometry).* It is at once apparent that rapid chemical analysis can be made to depend upon differences in absorption of x-rays, for the concentration of one

chemical element in the presence of others determines the difference in absorption between a sample and a reference.   In 1929 Aborn and Brown[1] used x-ray apparatus with an ionization chamber in the laboratory established by the author at the Massachusetts Institute of Technology to analyze gasoline for tetraethyllead content, utilizing the large difference in mass-absorption coefficients of carbon and hydrogen in gasoline and the lead.   It was possible to achieve an accuracy of 1 part in 14,000.

In 1946 Sullivan and Friedman of the Maryland Naval Research Laboratory[2] successfully utilized a Geiger counter for x-ray absorption measurements for this same analysis of tetraethyllead in gasoline.   As shown in the formula already presented the mass-absorption coefficient increases as the cube of the wavelength.   In a single-component system it is logical to employ the longest wavelength transmitted by the sample, thus obtaining a maximum change in intensity for a given change in sample thickness.   However, leaded gasoline is a two-component system in which the μ/ρ values change at different rates as the wavelength is varied.   Hence an optimum wavelength generated at 17 kv was used with an absorption cell length of 15 to 25 cm.   A counter tube filled with krypton was designed so that 80 per cent of the x-ray beam so generated is absorbed; or 80 out of 100 quanta entering the counter produce counts.   At comparable sensitivity of the photomultiplier tube, the counter registered over 1,000 counts per second.   Standard deviation was 0.05 ml of $Pb(C_2H_5)_4$/gal of gasoline, or 1 per cent.   Similarly a precision of 1 per cent was obtained with samples containing a maximum of 0.46 ml/gal corresponding to the detection of 0.005 ml of $Pb(C_2H_5)_4$ per gallon, or 0.0002 per cent lead.   The analysis could be made in one-tenth the time of any of the far less satisfactory chemical methods.

In spite of the success of this analysis and the fact that many others have been suggested to be applied to mixtures of gases, liquids, and solids, no suitable equipment was placed on the market until late in 1946. The General Electric x-ray photometer is now in routine as well as research use for a wide variety of analytical problems.[3]   The general arrangement is illustrated in Fig. 94.   A tungsten-target x-ray tube with beryllium window is operated at 15 to 45 kv and 1 to 20 ma with an enclosed power unit.   Above the x-ray unit is a synchronous motor-driven chopper which alternately interrupts one half of the x-ray beam after the other.   A variable-thickness aluminum attenuator is placed beyond the chopper in one beam.   Duplicate sample tubes are placed in the two beams, beyond the attenuator in one case.   Sample cells up to 25 in. long can be used; those for liquids and gases provide for continuous

[1] *Ind. Eng. Chem., Anal. Ed.,* **1,** 26 (1929).

[2] M. V. Sullivan and H. Friedman, *Ind. Eng. Chem., Anal. Ed.,* **18,** 304 (1946).

[3] T. A. Rich and P. C. Michel, *Gen. Elec. Rev.,* **50,** 45 (1947).

flow of the sample. Both halves of the beam fall on a common fluorescent screen protected from visible light by a thin metallic filter. An electron-multiplier phototube with associated power supply and amplifier determines when the beams are of equal intensity. In operation a reference sample is placed in the cell beyond the attenuator and the unknown in the other sample tube. The attenuator is adjusted until the balance indicator shows that the two beams are of equal intensity; this position indicates a certain thickness of aluminum in mils, which is equal in absorption to the difference between the reference sample and the unknown. Prior calibration enables an immediate determination in

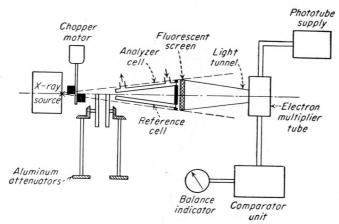

FIG. 94. X-ray absorption photometer (absorptiometer).

terms of the amount of impurity or solute in the unknown. The instrument may operate automatically to indicate or record this result directly. Best results in quantitative analysis are obtained from a comparative method in which there is rapid commutation in the x-ray beam from the unknown to a suitable standard, which may be aluminum.

The exploratory work leading to the development of the successful commercial absorption photometer was done by Liebhafsky and associates[1] for solids, liquids, and gases under simplest conditions. The relation between x-ray absorption and two masses (m_1 and m_2) of sample is

$$\log \frac{I_1}{I_2} : \log \frac{i_1}{i_2} = k(m_2 - m_1)$$

where I_1 and I_2 are the intensities of the x-ray beams transmitted, i_1 and i_2 are the corresponding average output currents (from the phototube), and k is a proportionality factor. With a monochromatic beam

[1] Liebhafsky and Winslow, *op. cit.*, p. 35; H. A. Liebhafsky, J. M. Smith, H. E. Tanis, and E. H. Winslow, *Anal. Chem.*, **19**, 861, 866 (1947); P. D. Zemany, E. H. Winslow, E. S. Poellmitz, and H. A. Liebhafsky., *Anal. Chem.*, **21**, 493 (1949).

$\log (I_0/I) = \log (i_0/i) = k_m$, where I_0 and i_0 refer to the empty cell. With the commonly used polychromatic beam from a tungsten-target tube, k varies inversely with m. It is defined by $\mu/\rho = 2.303ak$, where a is the cross-sectional area of a cell containing m g of sample; as already indicated, μ/ρ varies with λ^3, and the value of $\lambda_{\text{effective}}$ changes by absorption of the longer wavelengths. For quantitative analysis the effective wavelength must be determined for various thicknesses in order to determine μ/ρ in turn.

The analysis of gases is particularly interesting and significant. The equation used is $2.303 \log (i_0/i) = \mu_m \rho l$ where μ_m is the mass-absorption coefficient, ρ is the gas density, and l is the cell length in centimeters. Excellent precision on methyl chloride is demonstrated, graphically for various vapor pressures, again representing various concentrations. Long wavelengths make possible a ratio of 6,000:1 between output for hydrogen and chlorine.

The following examples of actual analyses for which the photometer is employed are typical of an almost endless list of possibilities. A paper published in December, 1949, describes routine control testing of many problems in the petroleum industry[1] by x-ray absorption.

1. Characterization of plastics (for use in cell windows, all lying between beryllium and aluminum).

2. Sulfur content of crude and refined oil. The latest and most quantitative study leading to routine commercial analyses is that of Levine and Okamoto.[2] The equation $\ln (I_{\text{CHS}}/I_{\text{CH}}) = -(\mu'_S - \mu'_{\text{CH}})\rho_{\text{CHS}}XF_S$, where I is the intensity of the x-ray beam after passing, respectively, through the S-containing petroleum hydrocarbon (CHS) and a pure hydrocarbon (CH, represented by calibrated polystyrene rods), μ' is the mass-absorption coefficient (for S and CH), ρ_{CHS} is the petroleum density, X is the length of the absorber, and F_S is the mass fraction of S in the C—H base (to be determined). Accuracy of analysis is ± 0.02 per cent S; one operator can analyze 30 samples per day, much faster and more economically than by chemical means and with comparable accuracy, together with nondestruction of samples.

3. Tetraethyllead content of gasoline. Since the appearance of the photometer other critical investigations have been made of the x-ray absorption method of analysis for tetraethyllead and reported in a symposium devoted entirely to the subject. Calingaert, Lamb, Miller, and Noakes[3] improved accuracy by reducing primary-voltage fluctuation on the x-ray tube to ± 0.10 volt and further reduced sensitivity of the measurements of such fluctuations by a factor of 10 by introducing a polystyrene block in the reference beam. These authors found the method sensitive to 0.01 ml of tetraethyl/gal and the precision ± 0.01 ml for known gasoline-base stocks. The varying percentage of sulfur in gasoline was the chief obstacle to more accurate determination. Hughes and Hochgesang[4] found further advantage in using monochromatic radiation (preferably thorium lines near a lead absorption discontinuity, but for practical routine purpose the molybdenum $K\alpha$ doublet). The tetraethyllead

[1] R. C. Vollmar, E. E. Patterson, and P. A. Petruzzelli, *Anal. Chem.*, **21**, 1491 (1949).
[2] *Anal. Chem.*, **23**, 699 (1951).
[3] *Anal. Chem.*, **22**, 1238 (1950).
[4] *Anal. Chem.*, **22**, 1248 (1950).

fluid actually added to automotive gasoline consists of 61.48% $PbEt_4$, 17.86% $C_2H_2Br_2$, 18.81% $C_2H_2Cl_2$, 1.7% kerosene, and 0.124% dye, corresponding to 4.8% H, 26.7% C, 13.8% Cl, 15.4% Br, and 39.4% Pb; aviation mixture differs only in having 35.68% ethylene dibromide and no dichloride. A straight-line working curve derived from the usual mass absorption equation with Mo $K\alpha$-radiation is obtained by plotting $\log (P/P_0)$ or $\log (t/t_0)$ against $\rho(0.587 + 9.31f_s) + 0.0478C_T$, where P is the radiant power of the x-ray beam of initial power P_0 after passing through the sample in an 8-ml absorption cell ($4\frac{1}{8}$ in. long) or t and t_0 are the corresponding times for a fixed Geiger count of 10,000, ρ is the density, f_s the weight of fraction of sulfur, and C_T the concentration of tetraethyllead in milliliters per gallon. When the sulfur content is known, an exact correction is made; otherwise an average value accepted by the ASTM of 0.064 per cent gives a satisfactory result.

It is interesting to compare accepted methods of tetraethyllead analysis in Table 8-6. The saving in personnel time of the x-ray over the chemical method pays the

TABLE 8-6. COMPARISON OF METHODS OF ANALYSIS FOR TETRAETHYLLEAD IN GASOLINE

| | Speed | | | Accuracy, ml/gal | Relative cost | |
	Relative elapsed time	Operator time, min	Samples per day		Equipment	Operator time
Chemical.........	24	40	12	0.04–0.06	1	57
Polarographic......	1–4	30	16	0.05	10	4.3
X-ray absorption...	0.12	7	60	0.10	15	1.0

equipment cost every 6 months or in comparison with polarographic analysis every 8 months. Another x-ray method of analysis, by utilization of the intensity of the characteristic fluorescence spectrum for determination of lead and bromine, has been described on page 155. A Geiger count of only 1 min at the peak of the $L\alpha$ line of lead gave a probable error of ± 0.06 ml/gal of gasoline and for the Br $K\alpha$ line of ± 0.16 ml/gal. Chlorine, sulfur, and other elements have negligible effect. Thus accuracy and speed are comparable with those of the x-ray absorption technique.

4. Control of constancy of metal composition of metallo-organic compounds.

5. Additives in heavy-duty lubricating oils.

6. Ash content and quality of coal.

7. Heavy-metal content of glass.

8. Chlorine or fluorine content of polymers and plastics. Here values of μ/ρ are H = 0.435 (independent of wavelength), C = 0.567, Cl = 12.0, etc.

9. Bromine content in gaseous brominated derivatives.

10. Determination of formula of organic compound (C, H, O). Typical results are as follows:

	μ/ρ (measured)	μ/ρ (calculated)	Formula (experimental)	Formula (true)
Methyl alcohol..............	0.869	0.867	$CH_3O_{1.01}H$	CH_3OH
Acetone..................	0.734	0.728	$(CH_3)_2CO_{1.06}$	$(CH_3)_2CO$
Sucrose (solution)..........	0.869	0.884	$C_{12}H_{22}O_{10.8}$	$C_{12}H_{22}O_{11}$

11. Concentration of fillers and impregnants in wood, paper, cloth, and rubber.

12. Mineral content and efficiency of softening of water.

13. Soil composition (qualitatively on account of complexity).

14. Adsorbed contents of charcoals and silica gels.

15. Concentration of reagent solutions containing metallic ions. The latest example is the determination of uranium in solution,[1] a matter of the greatest importance in contemporary atomic-energy research. In the absence of contaminating elements the precision is ± 0.05 g/liter between limits of 0.1 to 10 g/liter. The presence of Na^+, NH_4^+, F^-, and other light ions had no effect, but heavier ions require separations. These solutions may also be analyzed as in the case of tetraethyllead by fluorescence-spectrum analysis (see page 154),[2] which has the advantage of no interference by contaminating elements.

16. Alloy analysis especially when one alloying element is appreciably heavier than the base metal.

It is self-evident that this method has the general advantage of being completely nondestructive to any specimen, besides being rapid, accurate to within 1 per cent, and continuous in all cases where it may be applied.

17. Density measurements in supersonic flow. This striking application was developed by the U.S. Naval Ordnance Laboratory[3] and is well suited for nozzle calibration. The amount of absorption can be adjusted to the density range by proper selection of wavelength.

3. *Radiography.* Finally, the examination of all materials for gross interior structure, the discovering particularly of inhomogeneities and imperfections, depends upon the differential absorption of x-rays. This constitutes the familiar and extremely important and practical science of radiography, to which the next chapter is devoted.

[1] T. W. Bartlett, *Anal. Chem.*, **23**, 705 (1951).

[2] L. S. Birks and E. J. Brooks, *Anal. Chem.*, **23**, 707 (1951).

[3] Eva M. Winkler, *J. Appl. Phys.* **22**, 201 (1951).

CHAPTER 9

RADIOGRAPHY (ROENTGENOGRAPHY)

Although x-rays because of their short wavelengths are able to penetrate matter, still they are differently absorbed by different substances; that is to say, all materials are not equally transparent to x-rays. These facts are the basis of the science of radiography, or, more specifically, roentgenography. Broadly defined, the experimental technique consists

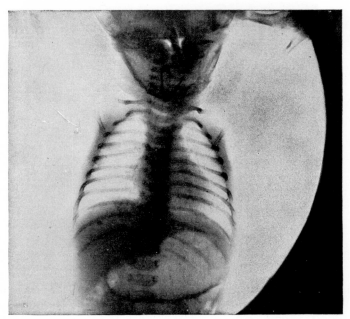

Fig. 95. Typical medical diagnostic radiograph for location of foreign bodies.

in passing a beam of x-rays through the object to be examined and, by means of a fluorescent screen or photographic plate, recording the varying intensities of the emergent beam and thus obtaining a shadow picture of the interior of the object. Probably the first practical uses of x-rays were of a radiographic nature, and radiography today is a most useful tool to the medical and industrial diagnosticians.

189

MEDICAL DIAGNOSIS

In the discovery and location of internal defects of the human body, radiography has become indispensable. The use of x-rays to examine fractured bones preparatory to setting, to study conditions of the teeth as an index to subsequent treatment, and to locate bullets, swallowed pins (Fig. 95), etc., has become so much a matter of routine that everyone is acquainted with it. Not so obvious, perhaps, are the uses of x-rays in the diagnosis of tumors (Fig. 96), of incipient tuberculosis of the lungs

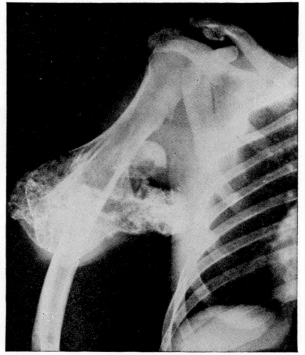

FIG. 96. Radiograph showing bone tumor. (*Eastman Kodak Co.*)

and joints, of diseases of the alimentary tract, of stones in the kidney and the gall bladder, of diseases of the liver and the pelvic organs, and of pregnancy (Fig. 97).

Radiography in World War II at the battle fronts reached the very peak of effectiveness in the skilled hands of the Army Medical Corps. Lives were saved and bodies shattered by bullets, shells, or land mines rehabilitated. Typical radiographs made in a United States Army hospital are reproduced in Figs. 98 and 99, respectively, for a left arm with humerus shattered by a rifle bullet, before and after repair, and for an injured skull in which a tantalum plate was applied.

In the examination of the alimentary tract the use of barium sulfate or bismuth salts or emulsions and other similar agents, mixed with the food to produce opacity in the part to be examined, has become a science in itself. Similarly, sodium tetraiodophenolphthalein in the gall bladder, iodized poppy-seed oil (Lipiodol) in the bronchi, sodium iodide in the kidneys, colloidal thorium dioxide for uterus, sinuses, liver, arteries, veins, etc., and other "opaques" such as Telepaque and Urokon injected into affected parts enable these to be thrown into relief for diagnosis from

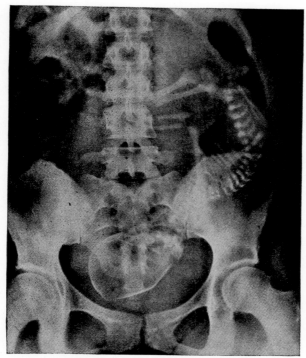

Fig. 97. Radiographic diagnosis of pregnancy. (*Eastman Kodak Co.*)

radiographs. The use of opaques is indicated by the specific techniques of myelography (for the spinal cord), angiography (for the blood and lymph vessels), angiocardiography (for the heart and blood vessels), pyelography (for the kidneys), etc. Figure 100 is an example of angiography showing an aneurysm in a brain artery. The bursting of such a sac caused by weakened walls results in hemorrhage. This was probably the cause of the deaths of President F. D. Roosevelt and of Joseph Stalin.

The application of such schemes is continually extending the field of x-rays in medical diagnosis, and wider and wider applications are certain to be found.

An exceedingly interesting outgrowth of medical diagnosis has been the x-ray photography of mummies taken through wrappings.   Some very interesting anatomical comparisons of ancient Egyptians with modern man have been made possible and the same evidences of disease and malnutrition in bone structures obtained as are common today.

Still other applications are the identification of skeletons by radiographs of the skull, which is as highly individualistic as fingerprints;

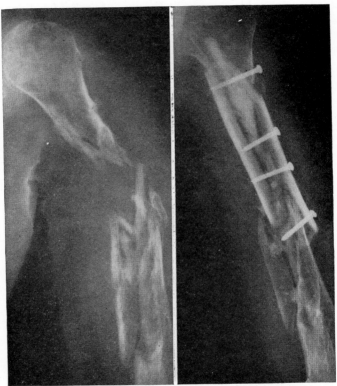

Fig. 98. United States Army radiograph of shattered humerus.

scientific studies of the diet as it affects bone and tooth structures of rats and test animals or produces rickets; and identification of the cause of diseases in fish such as the knot-head carp in the Illinois River radiographed in the author's laboratory.

A new study[1] shows the effect on bones in children of poisoning due to excess vitamin A.   Figure 101 clearly demonstrates the marked deposit (cortical hyperostosis) on the ulna of a two-year-old child as the result of overenthusiastic dosage of a vitamin A and D concentrate by parents. The damage from excessive dosage far exceeds that of vitamin deficiency.

[1] J. Caffey, *Am. J. Roentgenol. Radium Therapy,* **65,** 12 (1951).

It is obvious that a quantitative measurement of blackening of radiographic films by means of the microphotometer (page 90), or densitometer, may have important diagnostic and research significance. Densitometers and techniques have been described for the following determinations: degree of mineralization of bone as a function of nutrition;[1]

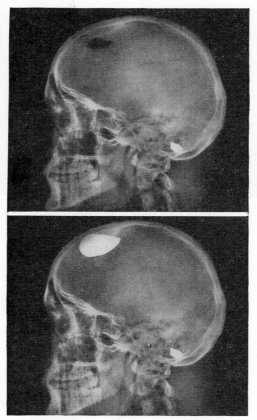

FIG. 99. United States Army radiograph of skull with tantalum plate.

tuberculous calcifications;[2] densities of bone and of muscle and other tissues in studies of child growth;[3] reduction of calcium salts in bones of patients with chronic polyarthritis[4] (the normal value being 0.4 mg/mm³ on the average). Bone density is evaluated usually by comparison with an ivory or aluminum step wedge radiograph on the same film. The Bone Density Research and Evaluation Center of Pennsylvania State College

[1] Mack, *Science*, **89**, 467 (1938). Mack, Brown and Trapp, *Am. J. Roentgenol. Radium Therapy*, **61**, 808 (1949).

[2] Block *et al.*, *Am. J. Roentgenol. Radium Therapy*, **41**, 642 (1939).

[3] Webber, *Science*, **90**, 115 (1939).

[4] Engstrom and Welin, *Acta Radiol.*, **31**, 483 (1949).

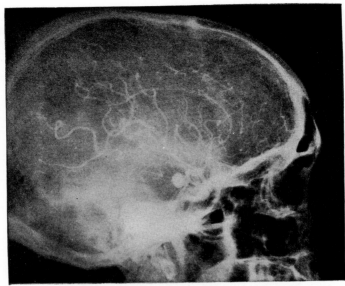

Fig. 100. Head radiograph with opacified blood vessels (angiography) showing aneurysm (ballooning) in brain artery. (*Courtesy of Dr. Joseph Gast, Houston, Tex.*)

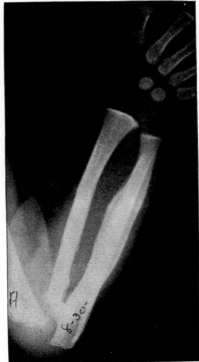

Fig. 101. Deposition on ulna of two-year-old child as a result of overdose of vitamin A. (*Courtesy of Dr. J. Caffey.*)

supplies a standardized aluminum-alloy wedge and detailed instructions for this important diagnostic measurement. In the extended experience of the Center, it has been possible to divide "normal" human adults into 10 classes of bone mineralization.[1] An enlarged microradiograph (see Chap. 10) can be similarly employed to investigate such a problem as inflammatory destruction of the mastoid bone. It is interesting to note that rickets may be detected in x-ray diffraction analysis of ultimate bone structure.

Diagnostic technique has gradually improved, particularly in the use of the finest possible focal spots for sharp radiographic definition, consistent with the highest possible intensities, so that times of photographic exposure may be reduced to the minimum as a safeguard against motion of the patient. The best modern technique, therefore, involves the use of the rotating-target tube described on page 31. The examples in Table 9-1 serve to indicate present routine procedures, the voltages representing average values. Complete details of techniques for diagnostic radiography of every part of the body are to be found in such books as Files's "Medical Radiographic Technic."[2] The "Year Book of Radiography"[3] summarizes yearly the newest advances in techniques, interpretations, and applications to pathological conditions.

TABLE 9-1. MODERN DIAGNOSTIC TECHNIQUE

Part of the body	Kv	Ma	Sec	Distance, in.
Chest:				
Posterior-anterior..........	88	500		72
Lateral..................	94	400		60
Gastrointestinal tract:				
Stomach.................	75	300	$\frac{1}{4}$	30 (Bucky)
Colon...................	75	300	$\frac{1}{2}$	30 (Bucky)
Gall bladder...............	75	300	$\frac{1}{4}$	30 (Bucky)
Spine.....................	80	100	2	40
Head.....................	70	100	2	25 (Bucky)
Extremities...............	40–50	200	$\frac{1}{3}$	40

The Bucky diaphragm is described in a later paragraph.

SPECIAL MEDICAL DIAGNOSTIC TECHNIQUES

In the field of medical diagnosis a number of special radiographic techniques have been devised, some of which are applicable also to industrial radiography. Some of these are as follows:

[1] Brown and Birtley, *Rev. Sci. Instr.*, **22**, 67 (1951); W. McFarland, *Science*, **119**, 810 (1954).

[2] Charles C Thomas, Publisher, Springfield, Ill., 1946.

[3] Published each year by Year Book Publishers, Inc., Chicago.

1. Stereoscopy. For most purposes an ordinary radiograph representative of two dimensions is adequate, but in some cases, for the exact location of an object such as a tumor, the third dimension is desirable. This is accomplished by making two exposures with the x-ray tube in two positions separated by a distance corresponding to the interpupillary distance, on the average $2\frac{9}{16}$ in. The two films are then viewed in a stereoscope which operates on the principle shown in Fig. 102 so that the third dimension appears.

2. Laminography (Stratigraphy, Planigraphy, Tomography). Here usually the tube and film are moved parallel to each other and in opposite directions so that there is registered as a sharp image one plane in the

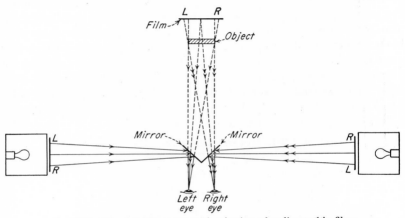

Fig. 102. Principle of stereoscopic viewing of radiographic films.

body. A series of such photographs in various planes enables a three-dimensional exploration called serioscopy. Sometimes a spiral motion is employed for tube and film. In Fig. 103 such a photograph is shown for an amplitude of 20 cm, four turns (1 per second), and a planar depth of 2.5 cm. A convincing application to diagnosis of osteomyelitis and to recognition of some types of bone fracture has been made recently in Switzerland.[1]

3. Kymography. This technique records the motions of internal organs such as the heart and lungs. Between the patient and film is placed a lead diaphragm with a 1-mm slit. The film is moved during exposure at a speed corresponding with the normal chest exposure for 1 slit width until the motion corresponds to 20 to 40 or more slit widths. Thus the heart shadow in the slit will increase or decrease in length as the heart beats and the recorded saw-tooth image is a time record of the

[1] Theilkas, *Acta Radiol.*, **31**, 398 (1949).

heartbeat. For the slower motions of stomach, lungs, and other organs the film speed is proportionately decreased.

4. Roentgen Cinematography. It is possible either to take motion pictures of fluoroscopic images (indirect) or to make successive direct exposures on x-ray film. Some success has been achieved in special cases of motion study, though very intense beams are required. Some attempts with rotating-target tubes at maximum capacity have been made at slow speeds, but the first really successful unit for making 100 pictures on a

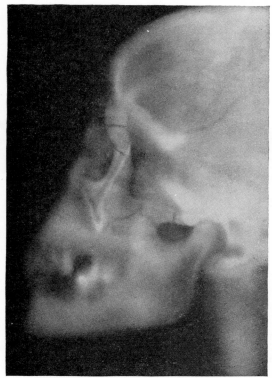

FIG. 103. Skull radiograph made by technique of laminography.

continuously moving film with an exposure of 10 μsec for each was developed in 1949, particularly for the study of burning of fuels in rockets. It is described on page 216 of this chapter.

5. Photofluoroscopy (Indirect Radiography)—Mass Radiography of the Chest. For the usual radiograph of a chest a 12- by 17-in. film is ordinarily required. The expense, on the order of 90 cents each, precludes any widespread examination, even though many years ago it became evident that incipient tuberculosis and other pathological conditions could thus be detected. It has long been desirable to have such a test of school children, industrial workers, and indeed of all the people. It was inevitable, therefore, that apparatus should be developed such that chest fluoroscopic images could be photographed on 35- or 70-mm photographic film at a cost of a very few cents, which then could be enlarged by projection on a screen for diagnostic study. A modern unit for this purpose is illustrated in Fig. 104.

Institutions, school systems, counties, public-health districts, the armed forces, and industries have installed such equipment, in many

FIG. 104. Modern unit for mass chest radiography: *left*, x-ray tube; *right*, fluoroscopic screen and 70-mm camera.

cases in trucks, and a true mass radiography has resulted, with untold value to the health of individuals, groups, and whole communities. The tubes used produce quite intense radiation at 50 to 60 kv and 500 to 600 ma so that exposures of the order of 0.2 sec are possible, thus enabling radiography of one person per minute at a cost of less than 10 cents each. Periodic examinations assure protection of masses of people against exposure to disease. Plans had been made in Germany prior to World War II to examine in this way the entire population. An authoritative book on mass radiography, written by Hilleboe and Morgan, provides a full account of equipment, technique, and interpretation.[1]

In 1948 over 440,000 persons in Washington, D.C.,[2] were given chest surveys with 70-mm film, with the following results:

	Number	Per cent
Total 70-mm films interpreted..........	440,491	100.0
Negative.............................	423,577	96.2
Abnormal findings....................	16,403	3.8
Definite tuberculosis................	4,405	1.0
Suspected tuberculosis...............	6,166	1.4
Cardiac cases.......................	2,537	0.6
Other pathology.....................	3,806	0.8

Individuals with abnormal chest indications on the small films were then directly radiographed with standard 14 by 17 films, with the following results:

	Number	Per cent
Total 14 by 17 films....................	16,206	3.8
Negative.............................	5,996	1.4
Tuberculosis........	6,401	1.5
Cardiac cases.........................	1,540	
Other pathology......................	2,269	

Also in 1948 in Minneapolis, Minn.,[3] 306,020 chest examinations were made with the 70-mm film. Of these 96.6 per cent were negative and 3.4 per cent required further study with 14 by 17 film. Of these 28 per cent were negative, 46.2 per cent indicated tuberculosis, and 25.8 per cent other thoracic diseases. More than 80 new and entirely unsuspected cases of pulmonary tuberculosis were uncovered in the mass survey.

Special interest is centered in diagnosis of pneumoconiosis, a general term used to describe all forms of pulmonary reaction to dust lodging in the lungs (hence to occupational hazards). Silicosis (caused by α-quartz), asbestosis, siderosis (from iron and its ores and compounds), and symptoms in workers with barium and vanadium ores, tin dioxide, and graphite are fairly frequently encountered with or without respiratory symptoms, fibrosis, and development of tuberculosis as more or less dense nodules. Figure 105 shows lung radiographs diagnosed as silicotic

---

[1] H. E. Hilleboe and K. H. Morgan, "Mass Radiography of the Chest," Year Book Publishers, Inc., Chicago, 1945.

[2] A. C. Christie, *Am. J. Roentgenol. Radium Therapy*, **61**, 141 (1949).

[3] *Public Health Repts. (U.S.)*, **63**, 1285 (Oct. 1, 1948).

(nodules) and siderotic[1] in steel foundrymen.   Far more dangerous and insidious are the pulmonary changes in beryllium workers, only recently fully realized and significant because of the widespread use of beryllium compounds in fluorescent lamps.   Severe pneumonitis may develop as long as six years after exposure has ceased, and the general result is chronic pulmonary granulomatosis.   This may simulate silicosis in radiographic appearance.

A recent very valuable summary has been given of the possibilities and limitations of roentgen diagnosis of the thorax.[2]   Pulmonary edema can

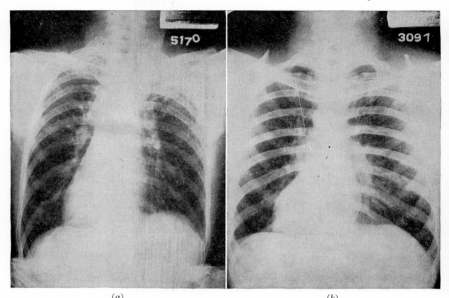

(a)   (b)

Fig. 105. Lung radiographs for foundrymen diagnosed as (a) silicotic (nodules from inhalation of quartz), (b) siderotic (dense areas from inhalation of iron dusts).

be detected very early if intra-alveolar but not if interstitial; bacterial pneumonias only poorly after 24 to 48 hr; pulmonary tuberculosis is evident on roentgenograms in 10 to 20 weeks after first exposure, while miliary tuberculosis gives other symptoms long before roentgen evidence; some carcinomas give roentgen evidence before and some after respiratory symptoms.

6. Monochromatic Radiography.   All the laws of absorption considered in the preceding chapter are based on single values of the wavelength λ, in other words, on monochromatic beams.   But normally radiography, both medical and industrial, is conducted with the poly-

[1] From a study of the effects of foundry dusts by G. I. Clark, W. F. Loranger, and L. E. Holly, Symposium on Air Pollution, Los Angeles meeting of American Chemical Society, March, 1953.   For the dust analyses by x-ray diffraction, see Chap. 18.

[2] L. G. Rigler, *Am. J. Roentgenol. Radium Therapy,* **61,** 743 (1949).

chromatic radiation from a tungsten target, a mixture of general plus characteristic radiation depending on the voltage.   It would immediately appear that sharper images and clearer and finer detail might be disclosed if beams of essentially a single wavelength could be employed.   Experience with microradiography discussed in the next chapter, in which small images are photographically enlarged, proved that for beams of moderate hardness the monochromatic x-rays were essential for best resolution. Thus it was logical to extend this to the parent 1:1 radiography.   Essentially monochromatic beams predominantly of $K\alpha$-rays are produced by molybdenum, copper, iron, cobalt, and chromium targets, in tubes

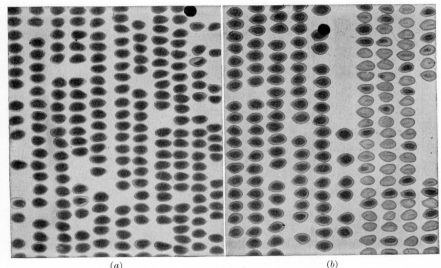

(a)   (b)

Fig. 106. Radiographs of seeds, illustrating sharper definition with monochromatic rays. (a) Polychromatic tungsten radiation; (b) monochromatic (molybdenum $K\alpha$) radiation.

ordinarily designed for diffraction analysis of crystals, and properly filtered.   The author[1] has demonstrated in radiography with such rays at 30 to 50 kv the predicted increase in fine detail.   The difference in ordinary polychromatic and monochromatic techniques is illustrated for such small objects as fine seeds in Fig. 106 and for a 48-hr-old chick, in which sex could be determined only by sharpest definition, in Fig. 107. Extraordinary detail is observed for bone structure, thus permitting diagnosis of incipient pathological conditions.   Clinical use on special diagnostic problems requiring ultimate refinement in detail has confirmed the predictions and test experiments.   For example, in December, 1948, it was demonstrated that such radiographs of the bones of the hand, the most convenient of all examinations, may be used to detect abnormal

[1] G. L. Clark, Medical, Biological and Industrial Applications of Monochromatic Radiography and Microradiography, *Radiology*, **49**, 483 (1947).

thyroid activity, nutritional disorders such as scurvy and rickets, gout, cancer of the chest (which shows up as new bone laid down around normal bone), and arthritis.

7. Electronic Amplification of the Fluoroscopic Image.[1]

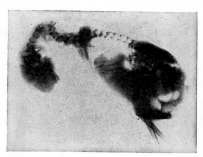

FIG. 107. Monochromatic radiograph of 48-hr-old chick, for purpose of identifying sex.

Fluoroscopy offers many advantages in diagnosis because it is faster, cheaper, and more complete in replacing thousands of radiographs and enabling step-by-step following of medical procedures; but it suffers the serious limitation of inherent dimness. The brightness of the radiographic image as observed on an illuminator during the reading of films is controllable and is selected to have an average value on the order of 30 millilamberts.† While fluoroscopic screens have been greatly improved, their brightness is far below this value, as shown by the following data:[2]

Type of examination	Brightness, Patterson B2 screen, millilamberts	Increase needed to equal film reading of 30 millilamberts
Chest, 22 cm	0.019	1,580
Abdomen, 15 cm	0.0052	5,770
Abdomen, 20 cm	0.0017	17,800
Abdomen, 25 cm	0.00065	46,200
Abdomen, 30 cm	0.0003	100,000

On the other hand a wide range of brightness useful to the human eye is indicated by Table 9-2 compiled by W. Edward Chamberlain; at fluoroscopic levels the acuity of the eye is low, however, but if the brightness can be increased to approach the levels of film reading, there is a great improvement in acuity. Electronic devices are making possible

---

[1] The whole subject of screen-intensification systems and their limitations is discussed in papers by Sturm and Morgan, Morgan and Roach, and Moon, *Am. J. Roentgenol. Radium Therapy,* **62,** 617–640 (1949). See also E. P. Bertin, Visual Presentation of X-ray Diffraction Patterns by Electronic Means, *Anal. Chem.,* **25,** 708 (1953).

† The lambert is the cgs unit of brightness and is equal to the brightness of a surface which is radiating or reflecting 1 lumen per square centimeter (the unit of luminous power, or the light emitted in a unit solid angle by a uniform point source of 1 international candle).

[2] From an exhibit by Westinghouse Research Laboratories.

TABLE 9-2. RANGE OF BRIGHTNESS USEFUL TO THE HUMAN EYE*

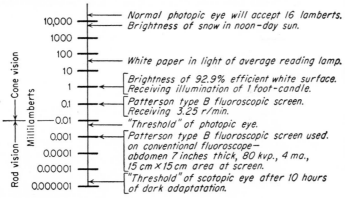

* From W. Edward Chamberlain.

this increase in the brightness of fluoroscopic images; of these the two most promising at present will be briefly described.

One of the most brilliant recent developments is that of Moon[1] in 1948 in designing a roentgenological unit which would operate on a much smaller dose rate for the patient than is used at present in fluoroscopy and which at the same time would yield an even more brilliant image than is usually obtained—and one which might even be transmitted by radio. The essential scheme illustrated in Fig. 108 has been successfully realized.[2] A scanning x-ray tube generates a scanning beam (in other words, the spot where the cathode particles strike the target moves back and forth across the target in a series of paths one below the other to the bottom, just as a spot scans the face of a picture tube in a television receiver); the beam is defined by a minute pinhole and after passage through the patient falls on a clear, dense crystalline fluorescent screen, preferably a mosaic of calcium tungstate crystals. Here the rays produce light quanta, and these create photoelectric current which is amplified and subsequently used to modulate the magnitude of an electron-beam current in a kinescope. Since the electron beam in the x-ray tube and that in the kinescope are both driven by the same sweep circuits, an x-ray shadow image is reconstructed on the kinescope screen. Besides the great advantage of minimum exposure and danger to the patient in comparison with those usually entailed, the observer may examine the picture on the kinescope without *any* exposure to x-rays.

Another scheme of fluoroscopic-image brightening by electronic means is that of Coltman[3], of the Westinghouse Research Laboratories, illus-

[1] R. J. Moon, *Am. J. Roentgenol. Radium Therapy,* **59,** 886 (1948).
[2] *Ibid.,* **62,** 637 (1949).
[3] J. W. Coltman, *Radiology,* **51,** 359 (1948); *Proc. IRE,* **37,** 671 (1949).

trated in Fig. 109. X-rays fall on a fluorescent screen mounted in contact with a transparent photoelectric surface (such as cerium-antimony) from which electrons are emitted. They are accelerated by an electrical

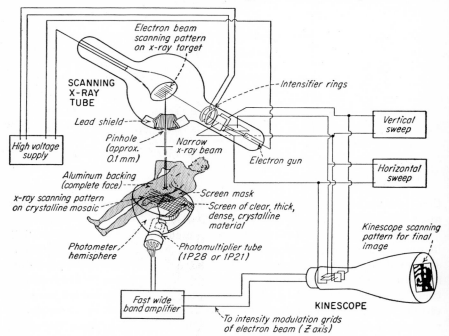

FIG. 108. Moon scheme for the intensification of the fluoroscopic image.

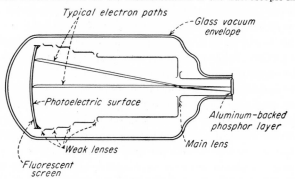

FIG. 109. The Fluoricon, for electronic intensification of the fluoroscopic image. (*Westinghouse-Coltman.*)

potential imposed across the tube and strike an aluminum-backed phosphor (zinc–cadmium sulfide) layer, where a brighter identical image is formed. The electron acceleration is combined with a system of electrostatic cylinder lenses which reduce image size and thereby increase brightness inversely as the square of the reduction. The small image can be optically magnified to the original dimensions without changing the amplified brightness. A 500-fold increase in brightness therefore is easily possible with this device, called the Fluoricon.

The ultimate achievement, of course, is direct visual presentation of radiographs, microradiographs (Chap. 10), and even diffraction patterns (Chap. 14) on a television screen. This has been accomplished in the RCA Laboratories[1] by development of a television-pickup-tube arrangement using a vidicon for direct recording of x-ray images, depending upon the photoconductivity of evaporated layers of amorphous selenium and of antimony trisulfide. The transmitted x-ray picture shows noise characteristics that are clearly those of the absorbed x-ray photons, with an internal conversion gain of 500 by a simple electron-multiplier mechanism for the noise current in the photoconductive selenium target. The appearance of x-ray noise means that all the information contained in the absorbed fraction of the x-ray beam is being transmitted. Thirty pictures per second are transmitted when irradiating the vidicon with a 5-ma, 100-kv x-ray beam at a distance of 2 ft. Radiographic images of transistors with wires of 1 mil diameter are clearly observable. The same thing has been accomplished in the Philips Laboratories of Eindhoven, Netherlands.[2] More recently, in the RCA Laboratories, the Westinghouse-Coltman Fluoricon image intensifier has been combined in a single envelope with the image orthicon pickup tube; the increase in sensitivity has permitted visual observation on a television picture tube of Laue diffraction patterns of germanium crystals.

8. Electronic Enhancement of X-ray-film Contrast. It is logical that television principles may also be employed as a continuously acting densitometer for diagnostic films in order to resolve small but distinct differences in density. A unique feature of the television-camera amplifier unit is the "clipping" off of the darkest and lightest portions of the film by adjustment of the vacuum tube so that it is insensitive below and above certain voltages. A suitable high-gain video amplifier with adjustable cutoffs for both black and white ends of the signal can expand any portion of the gray to the fullest contrast.[3]

9. Radio Transmission of Radiographs. Hospitals in rural communities are usually equipped to make satisfactory diagnostic radiographs but lack the services of experienced radiologists. This has led to the development and installation of equipment adapted from newspaper services for rapid long-distance transmission of picture facsimiles by radio or telephone wires. The diagnostic film is wrapped on a glass cylinder which rotates at a speed of 180 rpm, while a small beam of light is focused on an elemental area of $\frac{1}{50}$ in.^{2}; the light passing through the

[1] A. D. Cope and A. Rose, *J. Appl. Physics,* **25,** 240 (1954).
[2] J. Heijne, P. Schagen, and H. Bruning, *Nature,* **173,** 220 (1954).
[3] J. S. Garvin and C. W. Goodwin, *Science,* **110,** 481 (1949).

film is picked up by a photocell connected with a preamplifier for building up the picture signal before it is passed on to the output amplifier connected to the telephone line or radio transmitter. Over a modern voice-frequency circuit 2,700 elemental areas can be transmitted per second, or an entire 14- by 17-in. film in $4\frac{1}{2}$ min. At the receiving end in a large city hospital the transmitted radiograph is re-recorded on film wrapped on a cylinder rotating at the same rate from light coming from a "crater lamp" as square elements $\frac{1}{100}$ in. on a side which can be noticed only on enlargement. This process has been named *Telognosis* by its originators,[1] who put the system into successful operation between West Chester and Philadelphia, Pa., in 1948.

INDUSTRIAL DIAGNOSIS

Just as the inside of the opaque human body may be observed on the photographic film or fluorescent screen by virtue of the differential absorption of penetrating x-rays, and without damage, so also may any object be radiographed for the purpose of determining the gross structure and the presence of inhomogeneity or defect. The immeasurable importance of this information is evident in terms of the satisfactory behavior or failure of metal or other objects of practical utility and of the safety of human life that is so frequently involved.

General Principles and Techniques of Radiography Applied to Industrial Materials.[2] 1. *General Equipment.* The technique for preparing radiographic pictures is comparatively simple. A tungsten-target x-ray tube of the hot-filament type is ordinarily employed. The filament is heated to incandescence by a separate circuit, and this constitutes the cathode in the high-voltage circuit, with the target as the anode. The targets may be oil- or water-cooled by an insulated circulating system, thus enabling the passage of large currents through the tubes. Since radiographic exposures are usually of short duration, x-ray tubes of the universal type, in which the targets become hot, may be employed. A closed-core oil-immersed high-voltage single or cascaded transformer which may produce up to 500 kv is the most common modern equipment. The alternating high-voltage current is rectified by vacuum-tube valves. With increasing demand for penetration of thicker and thicker metal sections, however, the special resonance transformers, van de Graaff generators, and betatrons described in Chap. 3 have produced in commercial units potential ranges from 1 million to 20 million volts applied to the supervoltage tubes described in Chap. 2. Some of these are further illustrated in the next section on Industrial Radiographic Equipment.

---

[1] J. Gershon-Cohen and A. G. Cooley, *Radiology,* **55,** 582 (1950).

[2] For the latest treatise see H. R. Clauser, "Practical Radiography for Industry," Reinhold Publishing Corporation, New York, 1952.

2. *Distances and Inverse-square Law.* The object that is to be radiographed is placed at some distance from the tube (30 in. is a standard) so that the rays proceeding from the focal spot on the target are essentially from a point source (Fig. 112). Radiographs are merely shadow pictures produced by radiation traveling in straight lines from a point source. Of course, intensity of the beam is governed by the inverse-square law, which holds approximately for fairly hard rays. It is illustrated by the following example: If an exposure of 100 ma-sec will produce a given density at 30-in. target-film distance, an exposure of 400 ma-sec will be required for the same density at a 60-in. distance.

3. *Registration.* Registration of the radiograph is either photographic or visually observed on the fluorescent screen (of calcium tungstate, usually, or zinc silicate, cadmium tungstate, etc.). The general arrangements for the two methods are shown in Fig. 110 for the photographic method and in Fig. 111 for visual observation. In the latter case a mirror is arranged so that the observer will not be in the direct path of the x-rays. For practical use of fluorescent observation an x-ray dose of at least 5×10^{-3} r/sec must fall on the screen. However, electronic amplification of the brilliance of

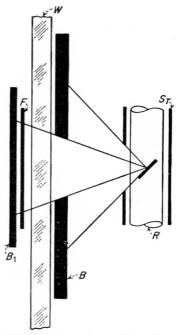

FIG. 110. General arrangement for photographic radiography. *R*, x-ray tube; S_T, protecting cylinder; *B*, diaphragm; *W*, specimen; *F*, photographic film; B_1, lead screen.

images may be employed as in the case of medical diagnosis.

4. *Voltages.* For each material and each thickness there is a certain optimum voltage for excitation of the x-ray tube: *e.g.*, 80 kv for 4-cm Al, 110 kv for 10-cm Al, 200 kv for 6-cm Fe, 230 kv for 6-cm brass, and on up to 1,000 to 20,000 kv for steel 10 to 20 cm thick.

5. *Scattered Rays.* Secondary and scattered radiation plays a large part in the results obtained and, for the certain identification of small imperfections in an object on the plate, must be eliminated. The absorption equation on page 161 indicates that the difference in intensities of two homogeneous beams through sound material and through a section containing a defect should depend only on the thickness *D* of the defect and not on its position or on object thickness. Actually the thicker the object and the farther the defect from the film, the less sharp or the more "fuzzy" will be the image owing to rays scattered in all directions from

the path of the primary beam with longer wavelength on account of the
Compton effect.   One solution is the use of 1,000-kv rays even for 2-in.
specimens since scattering from such short wavelengths is mainly in the
direction of the primary rays.   Another solution to the problem of
obtaining a sharp image with x-rays up to 300 kv is the use of a device to
allow only the direct primary rays through the specimen to reach the
film.   A grid such as a Bucky diaphragm, consisting of narrow strips of

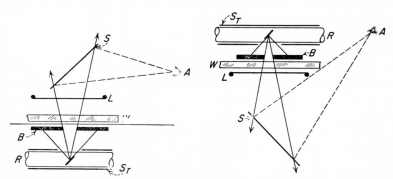

FIG. 111. Two arrangements for x-ray fluoroscopy: *R*, x-ray tube; *S*$_T$, protecting cylinder;
B, diaphragm; *W*. specimen; *L*, fluorescent screen; *S*, mirror for observation of fluorescent
image without direct exposure to x-rays; *A*, eye.

lead or other metal edgewise with free space between the strips, is often
placed between the object and the plate.   The primary rays pass straight
through the gaps between these strips, while the secondary rays at various
oblique angles from the specimen are entirely cut off.   Such diaphragms
must be moved slowly across the plate.   The improvement in sharpness
with a Bucky is best for light metals.   The following comparative data
are typical:

Metal	Thickness, in.	Kv	Per cent detectable variation in thickness	
			With Bucky	Without Bucky
Al	4	125	0.3	1.2
Al	8	200	2.0	6.0
Fe	2.5	230	0.25	1.0

Secondary rays also arise from the walls of the room and other objects,
so that the film must be thoroughly protected by covering the back and
edges with sheet lead.   As a matter of fact a simple metal-foil screen such
as lead between the specimen and film may very effectively increase
sharpness since the scattered rays, softer by virtue of the Compton effect,
emerge at a greater angle than the primary beam and hence have a
longer path through the absorbing metal.

Of course, a lead screen reduces intensity also of the primary rays, but since intensity increases as the square of the voltage, this may be increased. A single example will illustrate the time advantage of 1,000-kv rays. A 2-in. weld radiographed at 400 kv with a Bucky requires $7\frac{1}{2}$ hr exposure; at 1,000 kv with a 0.030-in. lead screen, 8 min.

6. *Effects of Focal-spot Size and Location.* Tubes with the sharpest possible focal spots are necessary for sharp definition and contrast on photographs at the boundaries of portions indicating different densities.

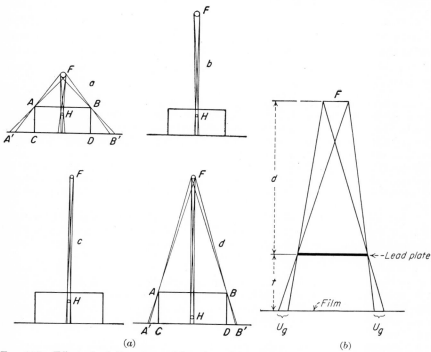

Fig. 112a. Effect of relative size and location of focal spot on definition in a radiograph: *ABCD*, specimen; *F*, focal spot; *H*, cavity in specimen.

Fig. 112b. The geometry of radiographic image formation: *F*, focal spot; *d*, distance from focal spot to specimen; *t*, distance from specimen to film; U_g, penumbral unsharpness of image.

This is seen very readily from the diagrams in Fig. 112. The relationship between size F and distance of the focal spot to the lead plate (or specimen defect) and of the distance of a defect to the film is best shown in Fig. 112b. Here d is the distance from focal spot to defect, t that of the defect to the film, and Ug the additional width of the penumbral shadow. Then $Ug/F = t/d$, or $Ug = Ft/d$. The haziness of the image Ug is proportional to t and inversely proportional to d; it is fixed if d/t is fixed. It is clear that if t is very small, as for a spot weld in thin sheet metal, or if the defect is very close to the film, the size of the focal spot may be large and

d small without undue effect upon sharpness. However, the ASTM Boiler Code specifies a minimum d/t ratio of $7:1$, but for fine cracks this may well be $15:1$.

7. *Photographic Technique.* Careful photographic technique must be employed in order to ensure distinction between the smallest differences in blackening of the plate. Experiment has indicated that the optimum blackening is $S = 0.7$ to 0.9 [$S = \log (L_0/L)$, the photometrically measured light intensities before and after passage through the photographic layer]. The normal eye can detect with certainty a minimum blackening difference between adjacent areas of 0.02. The principles of photographic blackening are presented in Chap. 4. It should be remembered that each object under radiographic examination must be subjected to a controlled technique and properly selected film in terms of contrast, latitude, and sensitivity.

1. Contrast is the difference in density in a radiograph produced by a change in thickness x. It is always true that the shorter the wavelength, or the more penetrating the beam, and hence the higher the voltage, the smaller is the contrast. Also, filtration of the beam causes a decrease in contrast since the softer rays in the heterogeneous beam are removed. High-contrast film should not be used for great differences in thicknesses since the thinner sections will be overexposed. Hence for uniformly thick specimens the lowest voltage that will give a radiograph in a reasonable length of time should be chosen, but for variable thicknesses the highest possible voltage.

2. Latitude is the extent of object thickness that can be reproduced in the working range of densities. This is the opposite of high contrast, but both high contrast and high latitude may be achieved by exposing thick and thin sections to different intensities, by screening off thin sections after an optimum time of exposure.

3. Sensitivity is difficult to define since it is a combination of contrast and definition; but roughly it is the smallest fractional increase in thickness detectable, or that which will produce an S difference of 0.02. Actually greater sensitivity is obtained today with high densities of 2 to 2.5, though these may be difficult to use visually and require a microphotometer. Slower, fine-grained films permit better sensitivity than fast, coarse-grained films.

4. Definition is the rate of change at which a density increase manifests itself, or the fidelity with which the radiograph delineates a discontinuity in the shape or radiographic opacity of a specimen (sometimes erroneously called sharpness); hence it is a factor in sensitivity.

5. Speed is a film characteristic as regards the initial period of inertia in exposure before the blackness curve turns upward; it is controlled by intensifying screens.

8. *Exposure Charts.* The amount of exposure is usually defined by the product of the milliamperage through the x-ray tube and the time of exposure in seconds. This is derived from the usual absorption equation $I = I_0 e^{-\mu x}$. For a fixed voltage and distance from target to film, I_0 will vary with tube current i and time t, or $I_0 = k(it)$. I is fixed at a chosen film density D, say 1.0, hence is a constant C; or $C = k(it)e^{-\mu x}$, $\ln it = (C/k)\mu x$. For a given material μ is fixed; so $\ln it = kx$, which means that a plot of it (milliampere-seconds) on a logarithmic scale

against the thickness x on a linear scale will produce a straight line. A series of these at different values of voltage (kilovolts) results in an exposure chart. Extensive data in the form of charts are now available for iron, aluminum, copper, brass, and other metals and alloys. The chart for iron in thicknesses up to 80 mm is reproduced in Fig. 113, for voltages from 120 to 200 kv, and for both small field (less than 3 cm²) and large field (50 to 100 cm²), focal distance 50 cm, two intensifying screens

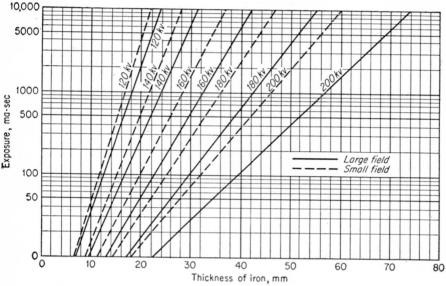

FIG. 113. Exposure chart for radiography of iron or steel specimens.

with Agfa films, absolute blackening 0.7. An exposure chart for 200- to 1,000-kv x-rays and radium is shown in Fig. 114.

The practical limits of penetration and satisfactory radiographic examination of aluminum, iron, and copper are listed in Table 9-3 for the following conditions: 200 kv 15 ma, 50 cm focal distance, two intensifying screens, Agfa film, blackening $S = 0.7$, without screens for eliminating scattered radiation.

TABLE 9-3. LIMITS OF THICKNESS IN MILLIMETERS FOR
RADIOGRAPHIC EXAMINATION

Element	Photographic, small field		Photographic, large field		Fluorescent screen, small field	Fluorescent screen, large field
	10 min	60 min	10 min	60 min		
Aluminum.........	240	280	355	415	120	175
Iron..............	59	70	73	86	30	40
Copper...........	39	46	46	56	20	25

9. *Limits of Recognition of Failures.* The limit of recognition of inhomogeneities in a material of certain thickness is practically measured by the smallest sharply defined difference in thickness of this same material that can be recognized. Blowholes and gas pockets have little or no absorbing power, so that this definition accurately holds for such cases.

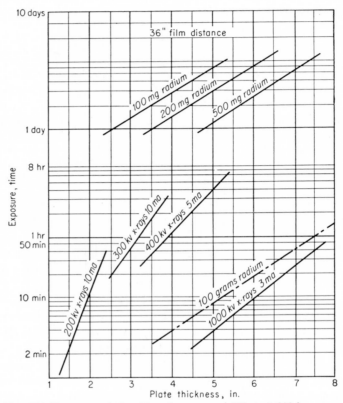

FIG. 114. Exposure relationships of γ-rays and 200- to 1,000-kv x-rays.

This limiting difference in blackening of a film is on the order of 2.4 per cent. Thus

$I_A = I_0 e^{-\mu x}$ for the sound specimen

$I_B = I_0 e^{-\mu(x-D)}$ for a specimen containing an air pocket of thickness D

Then, assuming negligible absorption for the defective area,

$$I_B = I_A e^{\mu D}$$

By means of such absorption calculations, taking into account scattering, which serves to obscure the sharpness of delineation of defective areas, it is possible to calculate the limits of failure recognition and experimentally verify these data, such as are shown in Table 9-4.

TABLE 9-4. REQUIREMENTS FOR RECOGNITION OF FAILURE RADIOGRAPHICALLY

Kv	Material thickness, mm			Smallest thickness difference, mm			Per cent of irradiated material		
	Al	Fe	Cu	Al	Fe	Cu	Al	Fe	Cu
80	72	..	....	0.42	....	.....	0.6		
120	173	23	12.7	2.7	0.11	0.058	1.6	0.48	0.46
160	247	41	25	12	0.30	0.14	4.9	0.73	0.56
180	290	54	34	30	0.55	0.25	10	1.0	0.73
200	355	73	46	.....	1.20	0.49	....	1.6	1.05

Conditions: Milliampere-seconds 9,000 (10 min at 15 ma), field < 100 cm², 50-cm focal distance, constant potential, blackening 0.7, no scattered-ray screen, film with two intensifying screens.

For observation of inhomogeneities on the fluorescent screen, a difference in brightness of two adjacent areas of the shadow must be 15 per cent, and a blowhole or gas pocket in aluminum, iron, or copper must be 5 to 7 per cent of the total thickness of sound metal for certain conclusions.

10. *Penetrameters.* While the variables of technique for the production of a satisfactory radiograph of metals may be deduced theoretically, it is advisable for practical work to have a method of checking technique, particularly for evaluation of the minimum size of a defect which can be revealed. Such a part is played by the penetrameter, a standardized superimposed defect placed on the object and its shadow registered on the radiograph. So important is this device that its specifications are rigidly established by the ASME Boiler Code and the Air Force, Army Ordnance, Bureau of Ships, and other inspection groups. The registry of any defect is a function of the thickness of the defect in the direction of the beam and of the distance of the defect from the film. An acceptable technique will reveal a defect whose thickness is 2 per cent of the section thickness (2 per cent sensitivity); hence a penetrameter of the same metal as the object to be examined has a thickness not greater than 2 per cent of the object thickness. Penetrameters are made in sets of metal strips of progressive thicknesses to correspond with 2 per cent of specimen thicknesses and also contain three holes with diameters usually two, three, and four times the thickness, to reveal the clarity with which a defect may be revealed. Step penetrameters serve the purpose of a whole series of single plates. Details of construction and use are to be found in specifications issued by the various agencies mentioned above.

11. *Equalizing of Irregular Shapes.* Special technique is required for specimens of irregular shape in order that parts of the radiograph will not

be over- or underexposed. Cylindrical bars or other specimens with circular parts should be placed in suitable holders of the same material so that the x-ray beam will pass through a constant thickness. Immersion in liquids, such as methylene iodide, lead acetate (for steel), carbon tetrachloride (for aluminum alloys), etc., having nearly the same opacity to x-rays as the piece to be examined removes this difficulty. Otherwise, sheet lead of varying thickness, lead shot, lead oxide paste, barium sulfate paste, and other absorbing materials can be used with irregularly shaped pieces and for the prevention of the undue fogging of the film by scattered radiation or halation from direct rays at the edges of the specimen.

Because of absolute sensitivity radiographs made with the betatron require no such provisions for irregular shapes, since thin and thick sections are simultaneously properly exposed, as shown in a later section of this chapter.

12. *Intensification.* Intensifying screens, usually one on each side of the film, have played a most important part in bringing this branch of radiography to its present high state. The ordinary calcium tungstate screens are usually employed, but the more efficient new lead barium sulfate screens described on page 85 are also coming into use. It may be mentioned here that a metal screen may also be used, lead foil being sometimes employed. The intensifying factor of such screens is lower than that of calcium tungstate screens; this is due not to luminescence but to the release of photoelectrons, which also affect the photographic emulsion. These lead screens have some advantages over the tungstate screen. As described on page 208, they absorb some of the secondary radiation from the underside of the piece being examined and hence reduce the fogging of the film; they produce finer grained and hence more sharply defined images and are therefore especially useful for the examination for fine cracks in the metal. For thick pieces, where a higher intensifying factor than a lead screen provides is necessary (*i.e.*, above 2 in.), the two kinds of screen may be used together, with the lead one next to the film. Metal screens may find an increasing usefulness as higher powered tubes come to be used for thicker sections, because of their ability to reduce fogging. A combination of tin and lead is especially good since the tin will absorb the K-rays of lead and the characteristic rays of tin will be absorbed by the aluminum-foil cover of the film *cassette*.

A new method of intensification of radiographs by electric discharge such as occurs in Geiger tubes is described on page 88.

13. *Thickness Determination Radiographically.* From a single exposure the thickness of a metal plate may be calculated as shown in Fig. 115. A lead sheet with a hole of diameter a is placed on the upper surface. The large image b is measured on the film after passage through thickness x. If h is the distance of the focal spot to the plate, then

$$\frac{h}{h + x} = \frac{a}{b} \qquad \text{or} \qquad x = \frac{db}{a} - d$$

14. *Locating a Defect.* Stereoscopic radiography for industrial diagnosis is often as valuable as it is in medical diagnosis. The depth and angular disposition of an inhomogeneity in any material may be ascertained with greater certainty than is possible with the ordinary tech-

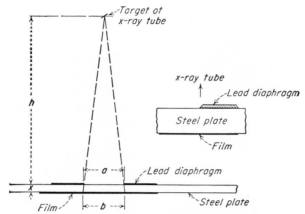

FIG. 115. Thickness determination radiographically.

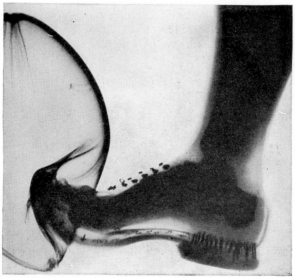

FIG. 116. High-speed radiograph made in 1/1,000,000 sec, showing football at impact of kicker's foot. (*Westinghouse.*)

nique. Two radiographs are made, in each of which the tube has been shifted about 1.25 in. on either side of the center of the object. The two films are then viewed in the stereoscope which fuses the two pictures into one with the appearance of three dimensions. Position of a defect may also be calculated from the shift in position of its image on one film when the tube is in two positions.

15. *Instantaneous- and Cineradiography.* The Westinghouse Marx-circuit Micronex surge generator described on page 53 was developed largely for the purpose of making industrial radiographs of objects in rapid motion in 1/1,000,000 sec, especially for ballistics research. The familiar example of the football at the impact of the kicker's foot is shown in Fig. 116, and bullets in flight and piercing wood in Fig. 117.

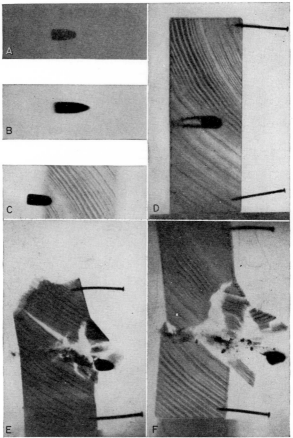

Fig. 117. High-speed radiography of bullets in flight.   (*Westinghouse.*)

Studies of the bursting of bombs, passage of shells in gun barrels, and penetration of armor plate added immeasurably to the science of ballistics in World War II. But in many cases there was an urgent desire to be able to radiograph a succession of events. A series of Micronex units side by side could be fired in sequence, but this was uneconomical and limited in scope. Thus there was developed for the Navy especially for the study of burning of solid rocket fuels a very high intensity x-ray source to take 100 radiographs at an exposure time of 10 μsec for each.[1] For this purpose a hot-filament cathode can be employed with a temperature so high that the filament life is only 15 min.   However, the tube operates at 150 kv and 60 amp in pulses for each photograph, since the focal spot and electrode spacing are adjusted so that enough tungsten from the target is vaporized to dissipate the space charge and permit such a current to pass.

A radar-type circuit produces these pulses.   Since 10 μsec is so short an exposure time, continuously moving film can be used without blurring to record either a fluoroscopic image or, much better, the x-rays directly. Any individual frame identified by a timing-scale interval from the instant of firing of the rocket may be examined or the whole series projected in a standard motion-picture projector.

Already this method of cineradiography has been extended to welding research, flow of materials in pipes and agitators, motion of enclosed machine parts, and medical radiography (see page 197).   In the last case previous efforts without great success had been limited to the use of maximum intensities of x-ray beams from rotating-target tubes.

16. *Radiography with the Betatron.*   In the preceding chapter are discussed the characteristics, particularly with respect to absorption, of supervoltage x-rays generated at 1 million volts or higher.   Since commercial betatrons to operate at 10 million and 20 million volts are on the market for industrial radiography (as well as medical therapy), it is of interest to summarize here the phenomena which are inherent in this technique and which differ from common experience with lower voltage machines.

a. Relative freedom from scattered radiation.   Since scattered rays retain the direction of the narrow beam of primary rays, there is no necessity for Bucky diaphragms, blocking around irregular objects or behind *cassettes.*

b. Increased penetration of radiation.   This follows from the dependence of minimum wavelength on voltage.   Rate of absorption is very high for long waves and decreases with decreasing wavelength until a minimum absorption is passed and then rises again.   If radiation from an x-ray machine includes the wavelength of minimum absorption, the penetration of that radiation cannot be exceeded.   With a 20-million-volt betatron, the minimum absorption in iron is at 7 Mev, whereas the maximum energy of the x-ray spectrum is 20 Mev.   The energy dependence of the absorption coefficient in steel is given in Fig. 88.   Through 20 in. of steel an exposure time of 18 min is required with the 20-million-volt unit.

c. Absolute sensitivity.   The very slow change of absorption with wavelength over the range of 3 to 20 Mev from the minimum of 7 Mev for iron means that there is no filtering and hence absolute sensitivity in radio-

[1] C. M. Slack, L. F. Ehrke, D. C. Dickason, and T. C. Zavales, *Non-Destructive Testing,* **7** (4), 7 (1949).

graphs, so that the size of a minimum detectable flaw does not depend on the total thickness of the specimen; in other words, both thin and thick sections of a specimen appear properly exposed at the same time, as shown for the automatic revolver in Fig. 118.

d. *Extremely fine focal spot.* This inherent characteristic plus absence of scattering meets the requirements of radiographs so sharply defined that they may be enlarged without loss of detail.

e. *Latitude and contrast.* Great penetration implies great latitude and hence small contrast. Sharpness of edges such as is realized by small scattering and a minute focal spot produces a radiograph with details clearly visible even with low contrast. Thus whole assemblies may be radiographed with equal visibility at any point in the specimen.

Fig. 118. Radiograph of automatic pistol made with 10-Mev betatron radiation. (*General Electric.*)

17. *Electronic Radiography.* Two new techniques of radiography employing secondary electrons instead of x-rays as a means of registration of images on the photographic emulsion were announced by Trillat[1] in 1948.

In the first, or reflection, technique, hard x-rays (180 kv) pass through a Lippmann fine-grained film and strike the surface of an object in close contact with the film, which is unaffected by the x-ray beam. The photoelectrons liberated from the specimen surface affect the photographic emulsion. Since their number depends upon the atomic number of the absorber, an image of the surface is produced and metals, alloys, and ores are distinguished. A photographic negative can thus be reproduced as an exact copy as a result of emission of photoelectrons from the silver of the image. In the second, or transmission, technique, hard

[1] J. J. Trillat, *J. Appl. Phys.*, **19**, 844 (1948).

x-rays pass through a thin sheet of lead from which photoelectrons are generated; these in turn pass through the very thin specimen and register on the film. In a sense this is a type of microradiography discussed in the next chapter, since the specimens are restricted to very small thickness, and the images on the fine-grained film may be enlarged.

18. *Monochromatic Radiography.* The use of X-ray beams of essentially a single wavelength in medical diagnosis is pointed out in an earlier section of this chapter. The same principles apply to industrial materials where extremely fine detail is required.[1] Monochromatic beams were found to be essential for microradiography; hence they could be successfully used in cases of very small hairline defects such as cold shuts in aluminum-alloy airplane-motor castings, as illustrated in Fig. 119. Both usual diffraction and high-intensity tubes with molybdenum targets are successfully used with filters to isolate the $K\alpha$ doublet. Hence the technique is limited to thin sections and light elements, though isolation

Fig. 119. Monochromatic radiograph of hairline defects in aluminum-alloy airplane-motor casting.

by crystals of monochromatic rays of much shorter wavelengths from the general radiation spectrum is a distinct possibility.

INDUSTRIAL RADIOGRAPHIC EQUIPMENT

With the rapid development of industrial radiography manufacturers found that 200- to 400-kv medical equipment could be adapted readily for examination of the internal gross structure of materials ranging from steel 6 in. thick down to small fabricated objects, food, fabrics, etc.

In Fig. 120 is illustrated a typical installation for radiographic examination of welded pressure vessels. The x-ray tube and valve tubes are enclosed in the transformer case (see Fig. 28). Figure 121 shows a 150-kv mobile unit which may be used for a variety of purposes. Trucks and railway cars fully equipped with x-ray equipment are to be found in increasing numbers.

An engineering achievement in x-ray equipment is the Triplett and Barton lightweight portable 260-kv unit developed for the United States Navy. The self-contained high-voltage transformer and tube-head

---

[1] G. L. Clark and R. W. Eyler, Development of a Monochromatic Radiographic Method for Locating Small Defects in Aluminum Alloy Castings, *Ind. Radiography,* **3** (1), 13 (1944).

FIG. 120. 400-kv oil-immersed industrial radiographic unit. (*General Electric.*)

FIG. 121. 150-kv mobile Picker unit for industrial radiography.

assembly is pictured in Fig. 122. The diameter is 15 in., the over-all length with tube 38 in., and the weight 110 lb., thus making it possible for one man to carry the unit. The transformer is of the resonance type, 1,200-cycle, and gas-insulated. The anode-grounded tube mounted at the end of the housing at the top is of the side-emission type, permitting closest access to the x-ray beam; all electrical and water connections are in a recessed portion of the housing at the opposite end. The power and cooling assembly and the master control can easily be transported by a jeep. Ease of positioning and economy in original cost and in labor time have been so well demonstrated that this machine has become indispensable in shipyards for radiographic inspection of welding and many other types of construction.

The Andrex, another lightweight portable industrial unit, originally developed in Denmark, is illustrated in Fig. 123, for three models: 120 kv (dimensions 20 by 12 by 8 in., weight 130 lb); 175 kv (32 by 14 by 8 in., 180 lb); 250 kv (37 by 15 by 9 in., 275 lb). The control unit, with dimensions 21 by 16 by 9 in. and weight 90 lb, is also shown.

Figure 124 shows fluoroscopic testing of large cables for bridge suspension. Figure 125 shows a unit in operation inside one of the giant welded penstocks at Norris Dam during construction several years ago. Three such units were in constant operation

FIG. 122. Triplett and Barton 260-kv lightweight portable industrial x-ray unit, developed for the United States Navy.

in testing every inch of 75 miles of welds at Hoover Dam, and similarly at other dams. Figure 126 shows a 2-million-volt unit of the type described on page 52 for the radiographic testing of huge forgings and castings. Figure 36 illustrates the 10-million-volt betatron for radiography of steel up to 15 in. in thickness. This whole unit is adjustable, since the dimensions of the magnet assembly are only 15 by 45 by 47 in.

FIG. 123. Andrex portable industrial x-ray units: *left*, 120 kv; *center*, 175 kv; *right*, 250 kv (*Holger Andreasen, San Francisco.*)

FIG. 124. Fluoroscopic examination of cable for suspension bridge. (*Courtesy of W. W. Offner.*)

FIG. 125. Radiographic unit inside welded penstock at Hoover Dam.   (*General Electric.*)

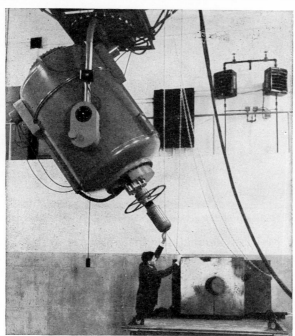

FIG. 126. Two-million-volt radiographic unit with resonance transformer.   (*General Electric.*)

PRACTICAL APPLICATIONS OF RADIOGRAPHY

1. Metal Castings. This is the most important application of x-ray radiographic diagnosis simply because of the wide use of castings and because of the uncertainty of gross structure with empirically developed foundry practice. The following defects may be radiographically detected on the interior of castings without in any way destroying or marring the specimens, although the diagnosis may be confirmed by "post-mortem" incisions:

Gas cavities.
    Due to gases liberated from the hot metal.
    Due to gases from the mold.
Sand inclusions.
Slag inclusions.
Pipe or shrinkage cavities.
Porosity.
    Due to small gas cavities.
    Due to small shrinkage cavities.
Cracks.
Metal segregations.

Figure 127 shows the interior gross structure of a steel casting 1.25 in. thick which is characterized by every type of defect noted above, par-

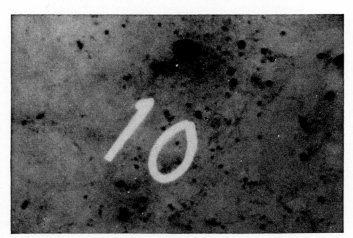

Fig. 127. Radiograph of steel casting, showing all types of internal defect.

ticularly gas cavities, nonmetallic inclusions, and shrinkage cavities. The photographic reproduction is a negative, and the spots of smaller absorbing power show up darker than the surrounding metal. Figure 128 demonstrates with remarkable clearness the presence of internal cracks entirely unsuspected in cast steel 1.5 in. thick. New radiographs of much thicker sections made with the 10-million-volt betatron (Fig. 36) are reproduced in Figs. 129 and 132, respectively, for a 9.25-in.-thick steel ingot with 1 per cent sensitivity gage showing (type A film, 0.040-in. lead filter in contact with film) and a heavy crankshaft outwardly sound. The use of the radiographic technique in discovering defects in an

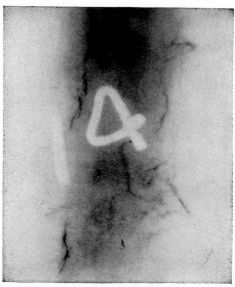

Fig. 128. Radiograph of steel casting, showing internal cracks.

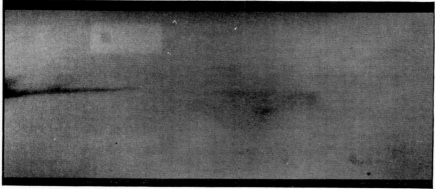

Fig. 129. Radiograph with 10-million-volt betatron of flaw in 9.25-in. steel ingot (1 per cent sensitivity gage shown). (*General Electric.*)

aluminum-alloy sand casting, verified by sectioning the specimen, is illustrated in Fig. 130.

The value of the x-ray method of inspection of castings to ensure soundness and safety in operation is readily apparent. The method may seem too expensive to utilize in the examination of every piece, but it may be employed to tremendous advantage in the derivation of a proper foundry technique and changes in the design of core and mold or in the process of gating.   Many progressive foundries have adopted this practice, although in spite of wartime specifications many still cling to the old empirical methods with the attendant uncertainty whether a casting will survive or fail.   On the other hand, it is the part of wise economy often to radiograph every unit of cast metal in an installation required to withstand high stresses or every piece that is intended for expensive machining operations.   An outstanding early example in which extensive radiographic tests were used as specification for acceptance of parts is that of

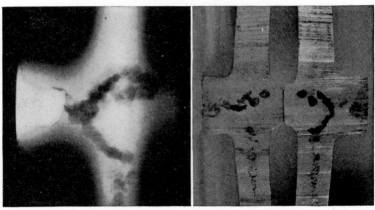

Fig. 130. Defects in aluminum-alloy sand casting discovered by radiograph and verified in sectioned specimen.   (*General Electric*.)

the high-pressure steam installation in the Edgar power plant of the Boston Edison Company at Weymouth, Mass.   The pipe and fittings for the 1,200-lb steam line and the cast shell of a 3,000-kw steam turbine were all examined, and many rejections were made upon the basis of the radiographs before acceptance.   The justification lies in the fact that not a single failure or break of any kind has occurred since installation, even though the conditions represented are extreme.   Examples of this type are being multiplied rapidly at the present time, and radiography must be considered an indispensable and thoroughly scientific testing and control method in the foundry industry.

Similarly, the United States Army, Navy, and Air Force have been foremost in the world in the application of radiography as an indispensable test for soundness of materials.

The American Society for Testing Materials continues to have an active committee at work on radiographic specifications for foundry practice as the most generally practical method of nondestructive testing.[1]

[1] Lester, *Bull. ASTM*, October, 1938, p. 5, January, 1939, p. 13; "Symposium on Radiography and X-ray Diffraction Methods," p. 53, 1936.

2. Welds. Closely allied to the problem of testing metal castings for soundness is that of welds. Here again there is no positive assurance by the usual methods that a weld has been made perfectly. With the agency of x-rays the smallest defects, such as lack of fusion, incomplete penetration, porosity from entrapped gas, undercutting, entrapped slag and crater, and filler and hairline cracks, are indicated directly, with the result that a vast improvement in the technique of welding has taken place in the space of a very few years. Welds are now made with certainty of safety where they would never have been attempted previously. In 1930 the United States Navy accepted welded steam boilers manufactured under radiographic control. In 1931 the American Society of Mechanical Engineers recognized in its boiler code radiographically tested welds for unfired pressure vessels. Numerous installations in this country are now in use for this purpose. Figure 131 shows the actual condition of a typical weld that appeared perfect on the outside. The radiography of welds in locomotive parts subjected to vibrations and stress is widely used.

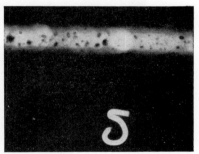

FIG. 131. Radiograph of a defective weld.

Taxpayers may well be proud that every inch of welds in great public-works projects such as Hoover Dam and Norris Dam has been radiographically tested (Fig. 125) and approved in the interest of enduring safety.

Spot welds for thin sheets of aluminum and aluminum alloys became a common procedure in the production of aircraft wing covering during the war, and radiographic inspection was essential for dependable attachment. Soft x-rays are required for sufficient contrast, and these are generated in high-intensity copper-target tubes with beryllium windows of the type illustrated in Fig. 15. Often the images on fine-grained film, which will be discussed in the following chapter, require enlargement, and thus the technique becomes microradiography.

3. Automotive and Aircraft Parts. It may be truthfully stated that the remarkable dependability of automobile and aircraft motors in races and endurance flights may be ascribed primarily to the assurance of soundness promoted by radiographic testing. This is particularly true for propellers, in which soundness is absolutely necessary. Not only internal defects but also *surface* cracks that have escaped attention are immediately detected. Pistons have been surprisingly prone to disclose serious though unsuspected defects. All parts of an airplane may be inspected with x-rays, from the cast cylinders to the spark plugs, the wing covering, and the framework.

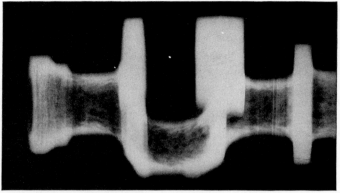

FIG. 132. Radiograph of a defective Ford crankshaft, made with 10-million-volt betatron (*General Electric.*)

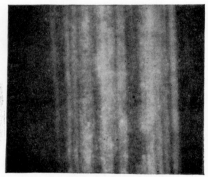

FIG. 133*a*. Radiograph of rolled sheet steel containing slag inclusions.

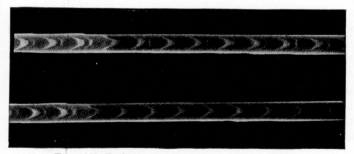

FIG. 133*b*. Radiograph of overdrawn aluminum rod.

The development of a monochromatic radiography for detection of extremely fine cold shuts (lack of fusion of two streams of molten metal flowing in a mold around cores in a casting because the fronts are oxidized or too cold) was described in the preceding section. Such a defect in an aluminum-alloy motor-head casting is illustrated in Fig. 119. The inspection of crankshafts is shown in Fig. 132.

Where the safety of life is so utterly dependent upon sound mechanism and faithful performance, it would seem little short of criminal not to use this positive method of specification and selection.

4. Rolled and Drawn Metal. Figure 133*a* is the radiograph of a rolled sheet of steel containing slag inclusions which have been fibered with the metal in the rolling process. The very poor quality of such a sheet is clearly demonstrated by entire failure in forming operations. Figure 133*b* shows how an aluminum rod is affected by extreme cold-drawing. The structure is such as to render the specimen worthless.

5. Miscellaneous Applications of Metal Radiography. Among many applications may be mentioned the inspection of insulated wires and cables and coated metals for breaks, of metal tubes and capillaries for clogging, of intricate assembled objects for proper adjustment of parts, of projectiles for proper location such as the two ends of an important vacuum tube, the image orthicon, in Fig. 134, of projectiles for proper location of caps and fuses as well as for complete filling by explosive (a routine government procedure during the war with the 1-million- and 2-million-volt units), of gun barrels for rifling and defects, of molten metals inside furnaces for melting point and surface tension (Fig. 135), of ball bearings for soundness, of electric insulators for the presence of metallic particles, of metal radio-transmission tubes for proper position of grid and filament, of all sorts of sheets suspected of corrosion, and of steel Dewar flasks used for liquid air or oxygen, where corrosion may result in great decrease in wall thickness.

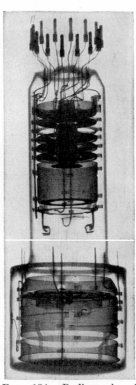

Fig. 134. Radiograph of image orthicon (central portion omitted).

5. Miscellaneous Practical Applications. Besides those for innumerable metal products, numerous other practical applications of radiography have been made, and some of these are briefly enumerated:

Arc electrodes for soundness.

Coal for classification as to foreign mineral content (Fig. 136*a*) and for control of cleaning by flotation (Fig. 136*b*).

Rubber tires for imperfect bonding to cords, presence of nails, or internal breaks.

Reclaimed rubber for nails and other foreign bodies.

Golf balls for centering of core.

Complicated glass, hard rubber, and plastic pieces of various kinds with internal seals, etc., for improper fabrication.

Wood for cracks, wormholes, rot, knots, embedded nails, etc., as employed in aircraft
frames, special lumber, telephone poles, etc.   By this means the aged wooden roof
of the great cathedral at York, England, was found to be dangerously weakened
by living larvae of the deathwatch beetle in a honeycomb of tunnels.

Railway ties for compression or erosion under the plates (after soaking in mercuric
chloride solution to increase x-ray absorption).

Shells and cartridges for improper filling.

Porcelain insulators, thermocouple tubes, spark plugs, etc., for internal cracks, and
mica for metal inclusions.

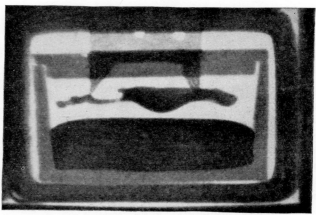

Fig. 135. Radiograph through furnace, showing solid and liquid copper in equilibrium at
the melting point.

Location of pipes and wires in building walls.

Trunks with false bottoms for contraband goods, and suspicious packages for bombs,
etc.

Routine fluoroscopic examination of food products of all kinds, tobacco, etc., in
trays, packages, and cans and in bulk for the presence of foreign bodies (utilized
especially by large candy manufacturers as an indispensable factor of safety).

Inspections of grains (corn, barley, rice) used in brewing and flour milling, for worms,
insects, etc.   One of the largest breweries in the United States was recently
indicted for using infected grain.   With a commercial automatic unit (Hayes's
grain inspector), radiographs are made of several hundred kernels at a time after
insertion of a tray into the instrument.   Typical results for corn and barley are
illustrated in Fig. 137.   These radiographs are somewhat enlarged and hence
constitute an example of "semimicro" radiography, as a transition to the next
chapter on microradiography.   These types of inspection may also be done
fluoroscopically.

Oranges for quality (juicy or pithy), fluoroscopically examined on belt conveyer and
differentiated as shown in Fig. 138.

Counting of packaged materials such as cigarettes.

Identification of glass (used by National Physical Laboratory of England in testing
clinical thermometers).

Measurement of plasticity of opaque materials such as tooth paste from the position
of a steel ball sinking through the specimen.

Fabrics, cardboard, paper, and leather for texture, identification of fibers, and presence
of fillers.

FIG. 136a. Radiographs of coal lumps, showing nearly pure coal (lower right) contrasted with lumps containing mineral inclusions.

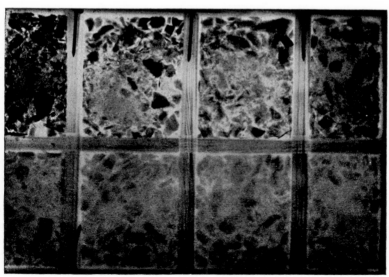

FIG. 136b. Radiograph showing steps in cleaning of coal by flotation: *upper left*, maximum content of impurities; *lower right*, nearly pure coal

6. Art and Museum Radiography.   One of the most striking applications of x-rays has been their use in the field of art.   A well-established branch of radiography is now that of the examination of old paintings and art objects for evidences of retouching, work of more than one

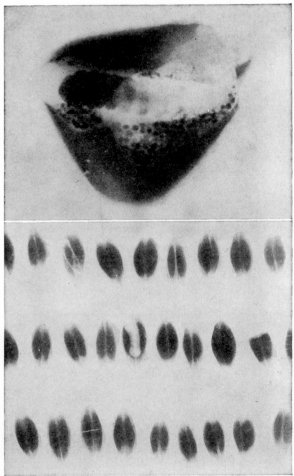

Fig. 137. Radiographs (enlarged) of worm-infected corn (above) and barley (below).

artist, and original paintings covered over with others, as well as to distinguish true masterpieces from copies.   Important court cases have been decided upon the base of x-ray evidence.   The old paint pigments consisted of inorganic substances, which are heavily absorbing to x-rays as compared with modern organic dyes.   Excellent x-ray laboratories are now to be found at the Fogg Art Museum of Harvard University, the

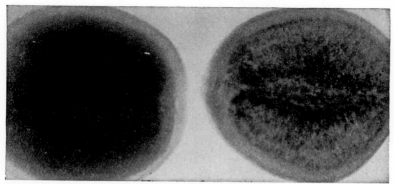

FIG. 138. Radiographic classification of quality of oranges: *left*, juicy; *right*, crystallized or pithy. (*General Electric.*)

FIG. 139. Typical result of application of radiography to old paintings. Detail from "Mars and Venus" by Veronese. The head at the right had been painted out and was disclosed only by x-rays. (*Burroughs.*)

Metropolitan Museum in New York, and the museums in Chicago, Philadelphia, Minneapolis, and elsewhere.

An example is reproduced in Fig. 139 from the paper by Dr. Alan Burroughs,[1] an outstanding authority on this subject. The x-ray photograph represents a portion of the painting "Mars and Venus" by Veronese. The painting shows the head of Venus upright, whereas the x-ray

[1] *Smithsonian Repts.* 529 (1927).

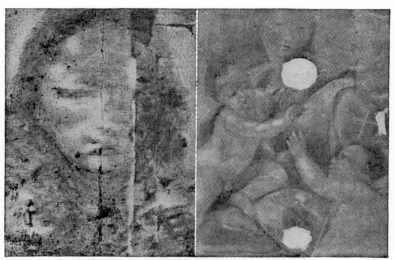

FIG. 140. Radiographic identification of masterpieces from characteristic techniques of painters. *Left*, "Madonna of the Tower," ascribed to Raphael; *right*, "Garvagh Madonna," known to have been painted by Raphael. (*National Art Gallery, London.*)

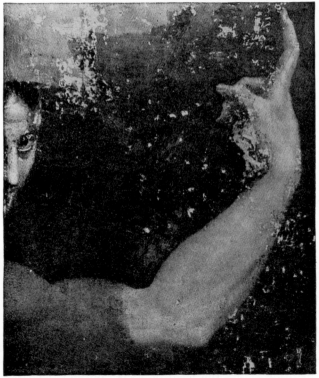

FIG. 141. Photograph of detail of St. John's arm in "Vision of St. Jerome" by Parmigiano, half cleaned after disclosure of masterly detail in radiograph. (*National Art Gallery, London.*)

photograph shows two heads, the one more inclined to the right having been painted out, very probably by the master himself.   Figure 140 shows a comparison of two Raphael madonnas.   Experts at the National Gallery in London suspected that the "Madonna of the Tower," though pleasing and of good composition, did not compare in technique with the "Garvagh Madonna."   The x-ray negatives fully confirmed this and led to the conclusion that, although the composition of the "Madonna of the Tower" may have been that of Raphael, the painting was probably done

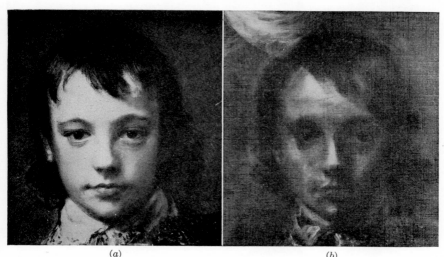

(a)   (b)

FIG. 142. Gainsborough's "Blue Boy": (a) photograph of head; (b) radiograph showing underlying painting.   (*Courtesy of Burlington Magazine.*)

by students.   Finally the decision to clean paintings by removal of layers of varnish often depends on details revealed by the radiograph.   A good example from the National Art Gallery in London is illustrated in Fig. 141.

Even the most beloved and valuable painting in the United States, Gainsborough's "Blue Boy," at the Huntington Art Museum in California, discloses an astonishing hidden detail.   Not long ago a faint pentimento (reappearance of a design previously covered over by layers of paint) became evident on critical inspection over the head to the left. The painting was radiographed with the result shown in Figs. 142a and 142b, which reproduce for the area of the painting including the Blue Boy's head a photograph and a radiograph side by side.   The pentimento becoming increasingly visible was the white stock around the neck of an old man, on top of whose portrait Gainsborough painted his masterpiece. Several of Rembrandt's paintings also were made on canvases used previously.   Figure 143 shows the Healy portrait of the first American

Cardinal and the radiograph which reveals that one head and a medallion at the neck had been painted out.

Closely allied with the examination of paintings is the use of x-rays in paleontology museums for delineation of fossils[1] in rocks (Fig. 144) where

FIG. 143. Photograph and radiograph of portrait of Cardinal McCloskey by Healy. (*National Gallery of Art.*)

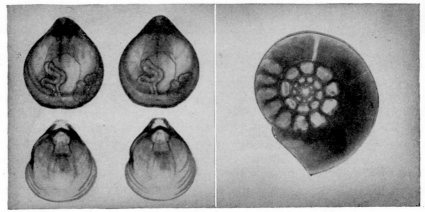

FIG. 144. Radiographs of fossils. (*Ruth A. M. Schmidt, U.S. Geological Survey.*)

nondestructive separation is impossible. Closed vessels, figures, idols, and other items discovered as evidence of prehistoric peoples have often disclosed strange objects sealed within. Actually art and museum radiography had its beginning in the attempt to radiograph a mummy inside its case. On the film appeared the image of the beautifully designed decorations painted on the inside surface of the case.

[1] Ruth A. M. Schmidt, *Am. J. Sci.*, **246**, 615 (1948).

RADIOGRAPHY BY THE USE OF γ-RAYS

The presentation of this subject would be incomplete without mention of the pioneer radiographic results obtained by Mehl and his associates with the γ-rays from radium emanation and the successful subsequent practical development of the technique, at present largely with radioactive isotopes, such as cobalt.[60] Since the wavelengths of γ-rays are shorter than those of x-rays as generated under practical conditions, it follows that they should penetrate thicker sections. Successful photographs have been made through 10 in. or more of steel; only a small bulb of radium emanation or other artificial radioactive source at a certain distance from the specimen and a photographic film are utilized. Exposures of hours or days may be required in comparison with only minutes for 1-million-volt x-ray units; but, of course, this is often not a serious handicap, since no attention is required. The method is useful, because of the extreme simplicity and absence of all machinery, for the examination of structures in position and for hollow pieces in which the radium capsule can be suspended by a fishing line. Since 100 mg of radium can be rented for a fee as low as $10 per day, γ-radiography is economical for occasional tests. Cobalt[60] is, of course, less expensive on direct purchase from Oak Ridge. As an example of present tests of radioactive isotopes formed in nuclear reactors, it was announced in April, 1953, that radioactive thulium, a rare element for which no practical use has been found, emits soft γ-rays useful for radiography of small objects. Iridium[192] is another useful isotope for industrial radiography.

CHAPTER 10

MICRORADIOGRAPHY

History. Attempts to produce enlarged radiographs of small heterogeneous specimens date back to 1913,[1] and the names of Goby, Dauvillier, and Lamarque appear in several publications on biological materials especially. It was recognized that an enlarged radiographic image could be obtained in two ways, (1) increasing the distance from specimen to plate and (2) photographic enlargement of an image registered on fine-grained emulsion. By consideration of absorption indices these authors also limited their efforts to very low voltages on the order of 4,000 to 8,000, at which potentials, of course, only soft general radiation was generated. These efforts were not generally successful as medical and biological techniques. Increasing distance from specimen to plate to gain enlargement served only to decrease sharpness and definition, even though smaller and smaller focal spots were tried. Suitable tubes for such soft radiation were not generally available, and at best photographs had to be made in vacuum. Nor were suitable fine-grained photographic emulsions available to enable magnifications to a useful range of 100 diameters or above. Some improvements were made in France and Russia; but in 1938 microradiography was still in a largely unsatisfactory and unused state. In that year the author obtained in Belgium some Gevaert Lippmann emulsion, in which the silver halide grains are on the order of 1/10,000 as large as in ordinary roentgen film. With this, experiments were made with monochromatic radiation from molybdenum, copper, cobalt, iron, and chromium targets, generated at 20,000 to 30,000 volts in commercially available diffraction equipment, thus eliminating the necessity for vacuum techniques. Granting that the differential between linear-absorption coefficients for two constituents is less favorable even for the chromium $K\alpha$ radiation than for a single ray generated at 4,000 volts, yet the advantages in ease, speed, contrast detail, and sharpness of the monochromatic ray have usually outweighed the greater differential absorption of the polychromatic beam at 4,000 volts. The result has been a successful development beyond all expectations.

Theory. The ordinary absorption law discussed on page 162 holds

---

[1] Haycock and Neville in 1898 were the first to use radiography, at unit magnification, to show the phase structure of a gold-sodium alloy.

for microradiography and may be expressed as

$$I = I_0^{-(\mu/\rho)\rho x}$$

where μ/ρ is the mass-absorption coefficient, x is the thickness of the sample in centimeters, and ρ is the density of the particular sample used. The ratio of intensities for x-ray beams passing through two adjacent sections, 1 and 2, of a given sample (of the same thickness) may be written

$$\frac{I_1}{I_2} = e^{-\left(\frac{\mu_1}{\rho_1}\rho_1 - \frac{\mu_2}{\rho_2}\rho_2\right)x}$$

This expression may be simplified for two cases, (a) that in which density differentiation is important, most common with biological materials where the absorption coefficient is often essentially constant throughout the specimen, and (b) that in which a variation in chemical composition and therefore of absorption coefficient appears, as, for example, in metal alloys, bone, or specimens in which some impregnating agent is used for "absorption staining":

(a)
$$\frac{I_2 - I_1}{I_2} = \frac{\mu}{\rho} x(d_2 - d_1)$$

(b)
$$\frac{I_2 - I_1}{I_2} = x(\mu_2 - \mu_1)$$

where the μ values are linear-absorption coefficients.

The first formula (a) requires that the sensitivity of the differentiation on the radiograph be proportional to the differences in density; the second equation (b) that the sensitivity be proportional to the differences in the linear-absorption coefficients.

The first successful application was to complex alloy systems in which detection of phases as well as submicroscopic cracks, flaws, porosity, etc., presented a major problem. In this connection arose the use of multiple radiations for bringing out, one step at a time, complex structures of five or more components. Taking the simple case of two components (Fig. 145), the $\mu_2 - \mu_1$ values are plotted as a function of wavelength from known tabulated data (for example, a copper-aluminum alloy). At some wavelength will appear a peak representing maximum difference between μ_2 for copper and μ_1 for aluminum; at another wavelength the curve may cross a zero axis and at still another a large negative value when $\mu_1 > \mu_2$. Obviously a monochromatic ray can be chosen, usually the $K\alpha$-ray, which will fit into these peaks and thus produce the maximum differentiation in blackening, and in detail on the plate. For a second pair of components another wavelength is the optimum selection. One phase may appear black with one radiation and white with another, along with all gradations of grays.

Table 10-1 lists the linear-absorption coefficients of some of the common elements for copper, iron, and molybdenum characteristic radiation values.

Selective monochromatic microradiography or historadiography would, of course, be greatly aided by the generation of fluorescent secondary rays

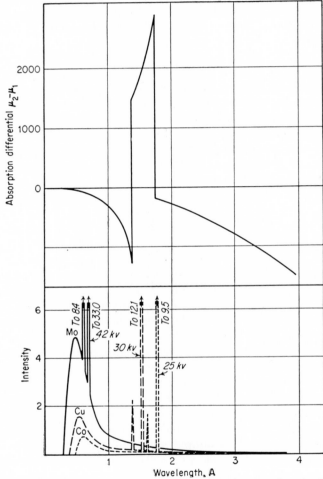

FIG. 145. Plot of binary absorption differential $\mu_2 - \mu_1$ against wavelength of x-ray beam.

from a variety of elements with a single high-intensity source of primary rays, such as the AEG-50 tungsten-target tube previously described. That fluorescent rays of useful intensity and a much higher degree of monochromaticity than obtainable by direct bombardment can be generated has been demonstrated by Rogers.[1]   With W, Mo, Cu, Fe, and Cr

[1] T. H. Rogers, *J. Appl. Phys.*, **23**, 881 (1952).

primary radiations titanium (22) gave on the average the most intense
secondary rays, and the linearity of the absorption curves proved that the
beam was nearly monochromatic.   In Fig. 146 are plotted typical curves
for the relative intensity from various elements as a function of voltage

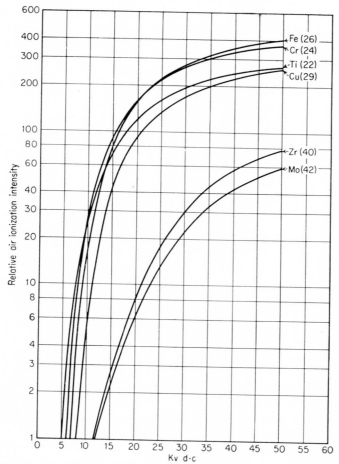

FIG. 146. Relative intensity of secondary radiation from various elements as a function of
the voltage applied to tungsten-target tube as a primary-radiation source.   (*Rogers.*)

applied to a tungsten-target x-ray tube as primary-radiation source.
Fluorescent rays have been applied successfully to metallurgical microradiography.   Exposure times are not prohibitive, and there is a large
gain in homogeneity.[1]   The technique is diagrammatically shown in
Fig. 148.

[1] H. R. Splettstosser and H. E. Seemann, *J. Appl. Phys.*, **23**, 1217 (1952).

Table 10-1 may, therefore, be used to ascertain whether these particular characteristic radiations are suitable for the examination of any particular binary system of metals. Thus, nickel and cobalt may be easily differentiated with characteristic copper radiation although a rather thin sample would probably be required; however, iron or molybdenum radiation would not be suitable. Beryllium and magnesium are well differentiated by iron radiation, and even better by the characteristic chromium radiation. Lead and iron could not be distinguished by copper

TABLE 10-1. LINEAR-ABSORPTION COEFFICIENTS FOR CU, FE, AND MO RADIATIONS

Copper radiation		Iron radiation		Molybdenum radiation	
Be	2.96	Be	5.64	Be	0.58
Mg	71.4	Mg	135	Mg	7.53
Al	132	Al	252	Al	14.1
Si	144	Si	266	Si	15.2
S	182	S	346	S	19.8
Ag	228	Fe	560	Ti	109
Zn	418	Zn	785	Mo	203
Ni	427	Ni	797	Cr	221
Cu	454	Cu	868	Sn	248
Ti	958	Ti	1,777	Ag	289
Cr	1,659	V	2,612	Fe	303
Sn	1,798	Sn	3,422	Co	383
Mn	2,124	Cr	2,460	Zn	421
Pb	2,609	Ag	4,253	Ni	427
Fe	2,578	Pb	4,854	Cu	455
Co	3,186	W	5,790	Pb	1,537
W	3,397			W	2,007

radiation, but molybdenum radiation would furnish an exceedingly sensitive method of detecting lead in iron. Such examples could be multiplied at length on the simple principle that the sensitivity for differentiation is greater, the greater the difference in linear absorption.

With biological tissues there are usually involved varying densities or thicknesses of very similar materials composed of carbon, hydrogen, oxygen, nitrogen, etc., rather than phases of markedly differing absorbing power. But here again the far greater sensitivity of the monochromatic ray in contrast and definition makes it possible to delineate the finer structure of tissues. Then there is always available the "staining" technique with differentially absorbing materials such as thorotrast, lead and mercury salts, iodized oils, gases, and other agents already familiar in macroradiography.

Experimental Technique. The principal features of the practical microradiographic technique which has been developed and tested are:

1. Preparation of the sample in the form of a small piece with a thickness of 0.1 mm or less for metals or other dense materials, or considerably greater if necessary for biological specimens.

2. Registration of the radiograph by a very simple technique involving a special photographic emulsion.

3. Enlargement of the radiograph to a suitable size.

The two chief essentials are (1) a photographic emulsion of sufficiently small grain size to stand enlargements of 100 to 300 diameters without loss of definition from graininess and (2) the selection of x-radiation of suitable wavelength and intensity.

Photographic Emulsions. Tests on microradiographs and electron-microscope photographs at 60,000 diameters magnification have demonstrated that the Lippmann photographic emulsion is sufficiently fine-grained so that it has a resolving power of more than 1,000 lines per mm, and thus enlargements may be made of the radiograph up to 300 diameters without serious loss in definition. To physicists this transparent emulsion is generally familiar. It has been rather widely used in aerial photography when great enlargement is desired.

The first work on microradiography by the author in 1938 was carried out with Gevaert Lippmann film. When this supply was cut off by the war, Eastman type 548-0 and 649 spectrographic plates became available and have proved entirely satisfactory.

Table 10-2 gives a comparison of fine-grained emulsions used for microradiography with other types used in radiography. As expected,

TABLE 10-2. COMPARISON OF PHOTOGRAPHIC EMULSIONS FOR MICRORADIOGRAPHY*

Film emulsion	Relative sensitivity	Resolving power lines/mm
Eastman No-screen.................	1	10
Agfa Printon.....................	$\frac{1}{4}$	50
Ilforo High Resolution.............	....	75
Eastman Spectroscopic 548-0........	1/10,000	500
Eastman Spectroscopic 649..........	1/5,000	1000
Lippmann......................	1/10,000	1000

* A. Engström and E. Lindström, *Acta Radiol.*, **35**, 33 (1951).

the Lippmann emulsion is very slow in comparison with the usual type of x-ray films. As a matter of fact, it may be developed in any light safe for ordinary chloride photographic papers. However, added to the advantage of the highest resolving power is the straight-line relationship between density and incident energy up to a relatively high density. This fact can be used for quantitative purposes, as the ratio of two densities also is the ratio of the corresponding incident-x-ray energies on the film.

Preparation of the Sample. The thickness of the sample is dependent upon the intensity of the available radiation and upon the linear-absorption coefficient of the material being investigated. Using commercial diffraction x-ray tubes as radiation source, it has been found advisable for best results to take steel samples down to about 0.075 mm (0.003 in.) in

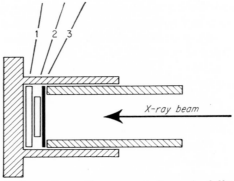

Fig. 147a. Diagram of microradiographic camera: 1, fine-grained film; 2, sample; 3, black paper.

Fig. 147b. Microradiographic cameras mounted on diffraction unit.

thickness; copper alloys are usually suitable up to 0.124 mm (0.005 in.) in thickness, magnesium up to 0.25 mm (0.010 in.). When the sample is too thick, the microradiograph will show ordinarily only diffuse resolution of detail rather than well-defined structural effects. The metal sample may be cut to approximate size by any method, and the only finishing necessary is a final treatment with 2(0) emery paper, moistened with oil to remove pits and tool marks. It is evident that such preparation is considerably simpler and less critical than that required for photomicrography

of polished surfaces.   For biological objects the whole specimen if sufficiently thin (100 μ or below) or a microtomed section such as is used in
histological examination is placed in close contact with the film.

Radiographic Technique.   Cameras may easily be made for holding
the sample and film, or the assembly can be improved by binding the
sample against the fine-grained film or plate with a piece of black paper
and simply exposing it to the x-ray beam.

In the laboratory, it has been convenient to make small cylindrical
cameras (Fig. 147a) which will fit in the collimating-tube system of the
regular x-ray-diffraction equipments as pictured in Fig. 147b.   The

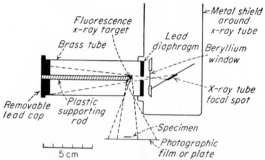

FIG. 148. Diagram of method of microradiography employing fluorescent x-rays.

method employing fluorescent rays is diagrammatically shown in Fig. 148.
In special cases it may be well to use a *cassette* such as is described by
Sherman[1] which may be evacuated to assure closest contact between
specimen and film.

The period of exposure required is dependent upon the nature of the
sample, its thickness, and the intensity of the x-ray beam as expressed in
the formula

$$\text{Time of exposure} = Ke^{\mu x}$$

where x is the thickness of the sample in centimeters, μ is the linear-
absorption coefficient for the material predominant in the sample, e is the
base of natural logarithms, and K is a constant for any given source of
x-radiation. K varies inversely as the intensity of the x-ray beam.

Microradiography of Metals.   From the foregoing account of the scope
and technique of microradiography it is obvious that there are innumerable applications in the metallurgical field, ranging from the detection of
flaws in small specimens requiring only a few diameters' magnification to
the analysis of phase structures in multicomponent alloys.   Microradiography supplements the long-established metallographic microscope, which is so powerful and indispensable in the hands of the skilled
metallographer.   In some respects information from the two techniques

[1] H. F. Sherman, *Rev. Sci. Instr.*, **18**, 80 (1947).

overlaps, and in other respects each is unique in aiding interpretation. The advantages and disadvantages of each may be summarized in the following comparison:

Microradiography	*Photomicrography*
Specimen need not be highly polished	High polish required
Requires preparation of two surfaces	One surface required
Shows entire thickness, three-dimensional	Only surface effects observable
Limited by grain size of photographic emulsion	No direct limitation
Differential absorption necessary	Etching reagents, etc., required
Detects interior cracks; shows variation in density	Requires heterogeneous phase and boundary structures
Superposed images	Single image
Interpretation simple—dependent only on absorption	Interpretation complicated by large variety of reactions required

From among hundreds of photographs the following are selected as examples which best illustrate technique, comparisons, interpretations,

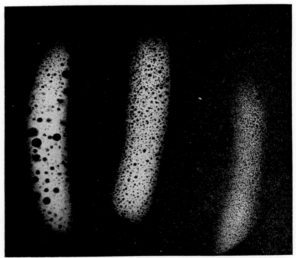

Fig. 149. Gas porosity in bronze casting (2×) with increasing bubble size by coalescence the nearer the cope surface.

and applications. In all cases the photographs correspond directly to the original unmagnified negatives so that heavily absorbing areas for high-atomic-number elements appear light and low-absorbing areas dark. Figure 149 at a magnification of only 2× shows the gas porosity in three slices of a bronze casting with increasing bubble size by coalescence the nearer to the cope surface. Figure 150 illustrates three steps in the study of a magnesium casting: (a) slices of the specimen mounted on black-paper covering film; (b) the macroradiograph (1×) of one of the slices;

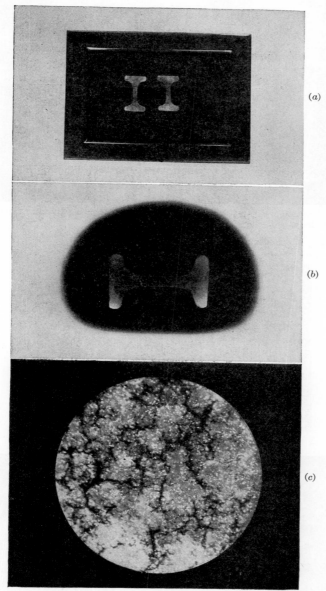

FIG. 150. Testing the soundness of a small magnesium casting: (*a*) film holder with 2 slices of casting; (*b*) macroradiograph (1×) of slice; (*c*) microradiograph (50×) showing shrinkage cavities, black; matrix, gray; Mn segregation, white dots.

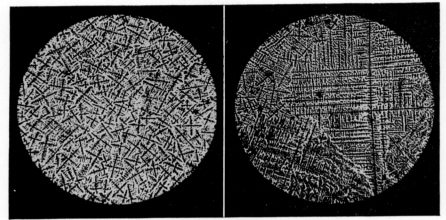

Fig. 151. Microradiograph (100×) of 70-30 copper-lead bearing lining: copper-rich dendrites, black; lead, white.

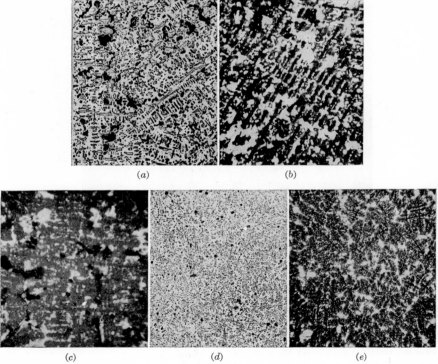

Fig. 152. 80-10-10 bronze (80% Cu, 10% Sn, 10% Pb), sand- and centrifugally cast: (a) photomicrograph of sand casting; (b) microradiograph (100×) with Cu $K\alpha$-rays; (c) same with W general radiation: (d) photomicrograph of centrifugal casting; (e) microradiograph (100×) with Cu $K\alpha$-rays.

(c) the microradiograph (50 ×) of one small area, showing as a dark network the grain-boundary shrinkage cavities, the gray metal matrix, and the white dots corresponding to a heavy metal segregation (manganese).

Figure 151 reproduces two microradiographs (100 ×) of a copper-lead bearing lining with copper-rich dendrites black and lead white. Great variability is observed for the phase structure of this alloy, and since photomicrographs are unsatisfactory because of softness of the lead, production was controlled by the x-ray method.

Figure 152 gives an interesting comparison of techniques both of delineating phase structure and of casting of a so-called 80-10-10 bronze

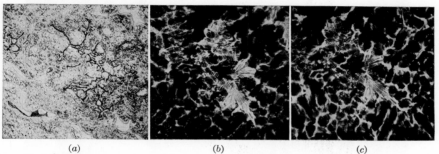

(a)   (b)   (c)

Fig. 153. J-metal ingot; chemical composition Cu 9.40%, Si 0.73%, Fe 0.65%, Mn 0.030%, Mg 0.12%, Ni 0.10%, Zn 0.07%, Al remainder.

(a) Photomicrograph (250×), Keller's etch: black constituent, α(Al, Fe, Mn, Si) present as "Chinese script"; white constituent, $CuAl_2$.

(b) Microradiograph (100×), Cu rays: dark gray, primary Al dendrites; black, porosity; light, $CuAl_2$ (interdendritic); white and most prominent, Chinese-script phase.

(c) Microradiograph (100×), Co rays; $CuAl_2$ more pronounced and Chinese-script phase less than in (b).

(80% copper, 10% tin, and 10% lead) with other impurities: (a) is a photomicrograph at 75× in which both lead constituents and porosity appear black and cannot be distinguished; (b) the microradiograph (100×) with copper $K\alpha$-rays in which lead is white, porosity black, and copper-rich dendrites gray; (c) is the microradiograph made with tungsten general radiation, showing far less contrast and detail than (b); (d) is the photomicrograph for a centrifugally cast specimen of this alloy from which it cannot be determined whether lead or porosity causes the black spots; (e) is the corresponding microradiograph showing no porosity and the greatly refined structure in comparison with the sand casting.

Figure 153 presents the very interesting case of an aluminum alloy, J metal, with the characteristic α(Al, Fe, Mn, Si) phase designated "Chinese script" most prominent on the microradiographs. Copper and cobalt radiation are compared as an example of the selective technique. This is a case of comparatively small difference, but the script is more prominent with the former, the $CuAl_2$ network with the latter.

A considerably larger difference in effect of different wavelengths is

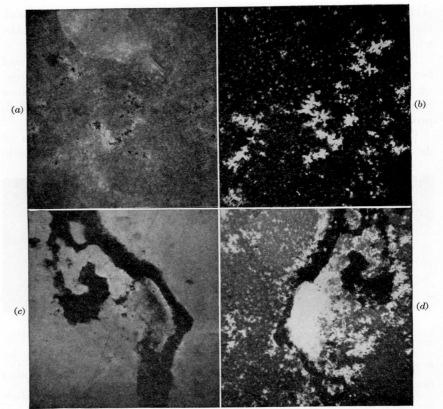

Fig. 154. Mn bronze (Hi-Tensil brass), sand-cast; chemical composition Cu 59.45%, Al 3.30%, Fe 2.18%, Mn 3.34%, Zn remainder.

(a) Microradiograph (100×), Co rays.

(b) Same, Cu rays. Small cross-shaped white constituents are Fe compounds; larger star-shaped white constituents either pure Fe or a different Fe-rich compound, appearing black in (a) and white in (b), which are mirror images of same area.

(c) Microradiograph (100×), Co rays.

(d) Same (mirror image), Cu rays, taken in vicinity of large shrinkage cavity (black), showing large segregation of Fe or Fe-rich compound.

indicated in Fig. 154 for a manganese bronze (Hi-Tensil brass). Here iron or an iron compound separates as star-shaped crystals which appear as black with cobalt radiation and intensely white with copper radiation.

Some Other Chemical and Industrial Applications. Besides the metallographic applications there have been many uses of microradiography in the study of materials, including the following:

1. Storage battery plates and grids for porosity and bonding.
2. Electroplates for porosity, inclusions, bonding.
3. Ceramic materials for uniformity, porosity, inclusions, incipient cracks, bonding of enamels, devitrification; foreign particles and incipient failures in insulators.
4. Ores and minerals, especially those too opaque for examination with a polarizing microscope, such as zinc blende, ZnS, containing inclusions of galena, PbS, in a

gangue of quartz; cassiterite with quartz and muscovite; pyrite or calcite with quartz; pyrolusite, MnO_2 with diallagite, $MnCO_3$.[†]

5. Crystallization phenomena. Figure 155 illustrates the earliest stages of crystallization of silver chromate and cesium bismuth iodide.

6. Rubber for sulfur, carbon black, and filler distribution and particle size for following the mechanism of vulcanization; for behavior on stretching as in incipient ruptures or strong adhesion between solid particles and rubber matrix;

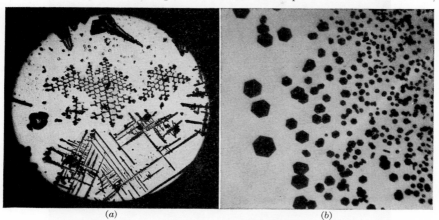

(a)   (b)

FIG. 155. Microradiographs of first stages of crystallization of (a) silver chromate; (b) cesium bismuth iodide.

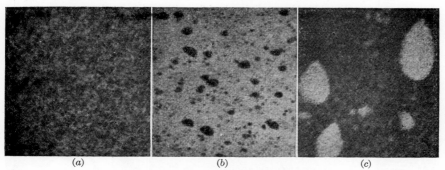

(a)   (b)   (c)

FIG. 156. Microradiographs of gum rubber with 32 per cent sulfur before and after heating at 143° for 15 min. (a) After milling (16×), positive print; (b) after heating (16×), positive print; (c) same (100×), negative print.

for uniformity of blending of natural and synthetic rubber since absorption coefficient differs. In Fig. 156 microradiographs by Trillat[1] illustrate (a) gum rubber with 32 per cent of sulfur milled in; (b, c) the same after heating at 143°C for 15 min.; (a) and (b) are positive prints (sulfur dark) at 16× magnification and (c) a negative print (sulfur white) at 100×. The large elliptical aggregates disappear completely after 6 hr of heating.

7. Plastic impregnation of paper, laminated wood, etc., for complete penetration and bonding;[2] sodium silicate bonds in corrugated fiberboard.[3]

[†] J. J. Trillat and P. Urbain, *Compt. rend.*, **216**, 534 (1943).
[1] J. J. Trillat, *Rev. gén. caoutchouc*, **22**, 63 (1945).
[2] G. L. Clark and J. A. Howsmon, *Ind. Eng. Chem.*, **38**, 1257 (1946).
[3] O. E. Schupp and E. R. Boller, *Ind. Eng. Chem.*, **30**, 603 (1938).

Biological Applications (Historadiography).   As already indicated the early experimenters, Goby, Dauvillier, Lamarque, and others, attempted microradiography, or as Lamarque terms it, historadiography, of biological objects in the certain knowledge that to the zoologist, physiologist,

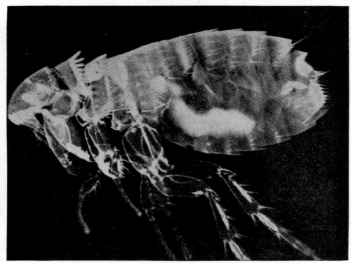

FIG. 157. Microradiograph of flea with barium meal.

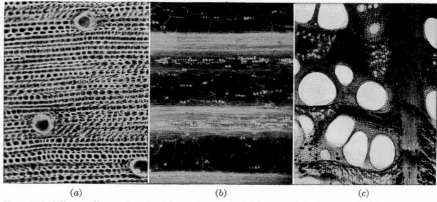

(a)   (b)   (c)

FIG. 158. Microradiographs of white oak wood, (a) tangential, (b) radial, (c) transverse (100×).

pathologist, entomologist, and medical diagnostician there were great potentialities.

Ordinary film may often be used with small biological specimens when an enlargement of 5 to 10 is sufficient.   Figure 157 shows a highly magnified radiograph of a flea with a barium meal, made with grenz rays (x-rays generated at 4,000 volts with long wavelengths).   A logical extension, of course, is to motion pictures, to show, for example, the peristaltic wave in the intestines of insects.[1]

Figure 158 demonstrates the striking photographs of three sections of white oak wood, respectively tangential to the tree trunk, radial with white calcium oxalate crystals in rows, and transverse with the clearly defined channel openings. The microradiograph of wood is as characteristic of each species as a fingerprint, and it is easily possible to identify a piece of wood or sawdust by comparison of a microradiograph with standards for known materials. Such an experiment is assigned to the laboratory class taught under the direction of the author. In Fig. 159 a microradiograph of cigarette paper at the remarkable magnification of 800 diameters shows the transparent lumen in the center of each fibril. X-rays were generated at only 2 kv, 100 ma/3 min exposure.

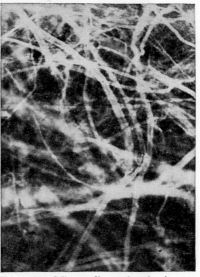

Figure 160 illustrates four types of biological specimen: (A) the body of a small sweat bee with pollen caught on fine hairs appearing as white spots; (B) detail of a very small bone from a frog's foot; (C) thorotrast-impregnated kidney; (D) liquid nutrient circulation in an embryonic

FIG. 159. Microradiograph of cigarette paper (800×). (*Lamarque.*)

bean, utilizing lead acetate in solution as a "stain" to gain contrast. Similarly, the passage of mineral substances up the stems of plants and the distribution in leaves may be easily followed.[2]

Figure 161 depicts microradiographs of parts of the common housefly: (A) mouth; (B) wing; (C) antenna; (D) eye showing multiple facets.

The obvious extension is to the utilization by the pathologist, particularly for diagnosis and study of cancerous tissue. Lamarque in France and Bohatyrtschuk have done notable preliminary work on the tissues and blood vessels, but only the barest beginnings have been made. The former has used specimens without injection of absorbing stains to discover relative densities within the cell or tissue. Thyroid follicles are opaque because of colloidally dispersed iodine, which upon extraction with acid, sodium nitrite, and chloroform leaves the tissue quite transparent (Fig. 162). Figure 163 reproduces for a transverse section of a

[1] Sherwood, *J. Biol. Phot. Assoc.*, **5**, 138 (1937); *J. Soc. Motion Picture Engrs.*, **28**, 614 (1937).

[2] Barclay and Leatherdale, *Brit. J. Radiol.*, **21**, 544 (1948).

rectal cancer a negative microradiograph. Bohatyrtschuk[1] has introduced opaque media such as thorotrast into the vascular system to show the disturbances caused by metastasis of carcinoma in his "microvasorontgenograms." More and more microradiography is coming into clinical use to supplement older diagnostic techniques. This is splendidly

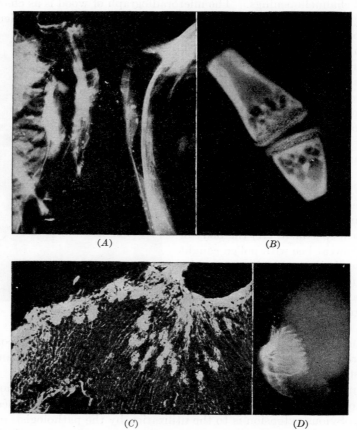

(A)   (B)

(C)   (D)

FIG. 160. Microradiographs of biological specimens: (A) sweat bee; (B) bone of frog; (C) thorotrast-impregnated kidney; (D) bean injected with mercury salt solution.

shown in the work from the Caylor-Nickel Clinic of Bluffton, Ind.[2] Normal organs from rabbits have been injected with 10 per cent silver iodide in 3 per cent acacia. Examples for heart and kidney are reproduced in Figs. 164 and 165. This technique of blood-vessel injection is called microangiography by Bellman and Engström.[3] It is used for

[1] Am. J. Roentgenol. Radium Therapy Nuclear Med., **70**, 119 (1953).

[2] W. S. Tirman, E. C. Caylor, H. W. Banker, and T. E. Caylor, Radiology, **57**, 70 (1951).

[3] S. Bellman and A. Engström, Acta Radiol., **38**, 98 (1952).

incipient bone pathology,[1] lead poisoning, psoriasis, inflammatory destruction of the mastoid bone,[2] deposition of iron in cell nuclei in hematite miners,[3] etc.

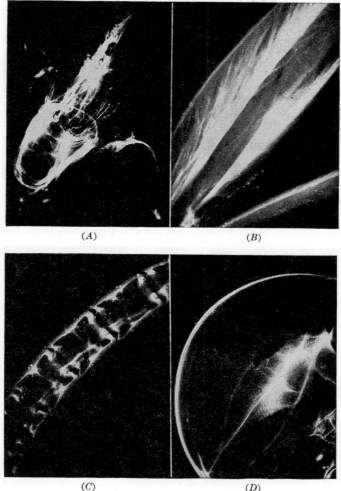

(A) (B)

(C) (D)

FIG. 161. Parts of common housefly: (A) mouth, (B) wing, (C) leg, (D) eye.

Special Techniques and Applications. 1. *Stereoscopy.* Just as in the case of macroradiography two microradiographs may be made of a specimen in properly shifted position and then viewed in a stereoscope to gain a third-dimensional impression for locating depth below the surface of any

[1] H. A. Sissons, *Brit. J. Radiol.*, **23**, 2 (1950).
[2] R. Engström, C. A. Hamberger, and S. Welin, *Brit. J. Radiol.*, **22**, 309 (1949).
[3] A. E. Barclay, *Brit. J. Radiol.*, **22**, 268 (1949).

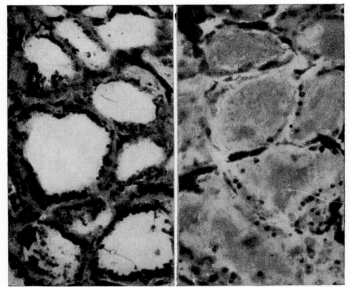

FIG. 162. Thyroid follicle before (*left*) and after (*right*) extracting iodine.

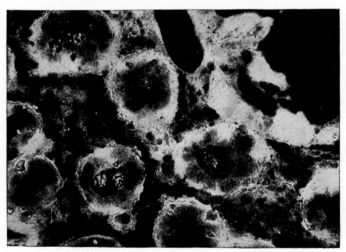

FIG. 163. Rectal cancer, transverse section.   (*Lamarque.*)

detail.   Clark and Eyler[1] have described in detail a stereoscopic camera which has proved of great value in particular investigations.

2. *Fluoroscopy.*   It is possible to examine an image of the object on a fluorescent screen directly with a microscope at a magnification of 50 diameters.   This permits a qualitative microchemical analysis in many cases such as an inclusion in an alloy.   The voltage on the x-ray tube is

[1] G. L. Clark and R. W. Eyler, *Rev. Sci. Instr.*, **14**, 277 (1943).

adjusted so that the wavelength of the beam is on the long-wave side of the K absorption edge of the sought-for element. Then the voltage is increased so that the radiation is on the short-wave side. The area where the element sought is localized will then appear darker and the rest of the preparation lighter.[1]

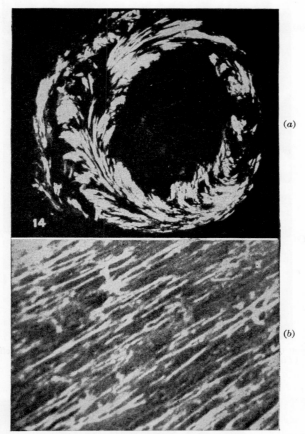

FIG. 164. Cross section of heart of rabbit [(a) 3× and (b) 150×], showing blood vessels injected with AgI in agar. (*Tirman, Caylor, et al.*)

3. *Electronic Microradiography.* In the preceding chapter was discussed the production of radiographic images by reflected photoelectrons liberated from specimens irradiated with hard x-rays, which first pass through the photographic emulsion, or by photoelectrons liberated from a lead screen and transmitted through the specimen. In a sense electronic radiography as developed by Trillat and associates is always really a special type of microradiography even when the image is not photograph-

[1] A. Engström, *Experientia*, **3**, 208 (1947).

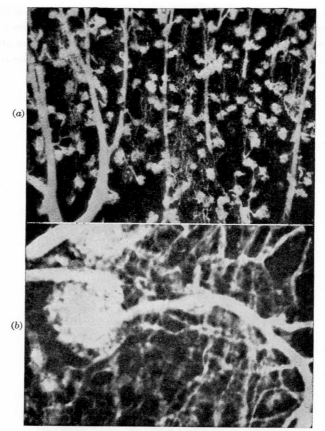

FIG. 165. Section of kidney [(a) 25× and (b) 250×], showing afferent and efferent vessels to glomeruli. (*Tirman, Caylor, et al.*)

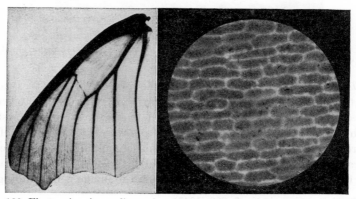

FIG. 166. Electronic microradiographs of butterfly wing and onionskin. (*Trillat.*)

ically enlarged, because of the necessary limitation to very thin specimens. It follows, of course, that any such images on fine-grained films can be enlarged exactly as in the case of images directly produced by x-rays, with noteworthy results. Figure 166 for an insect wing and for a single layer of onionskin illustrates the method. Another example is the examination of postage stamps for collectors, to detect repairs or establish genuineness and to identify watermarks in the paper, even on covers, inks, and cancellations. Three techniques actually are used, very low voltage primary x-rays, electrons liberated from a lead sheet over the specimen, and electrons liberated from metallic elements in inks.[1]

4. *Microradiography of Distorted Crystals.* Monochromatic x-rays transmitted through a polycrystalline foil of pure metal would be expected to produce uniform blackening of the film and no evidence of grain detail. Smoluchkowski and associates[2] have observed, however, that sometimes one or more grains appear well defined and lighter on the photographic plate, because they are oriented so that a set of crystallographic planes satisfies the Bragg law. Thus some of the rays which would be transmitted through the specimen are reflected and form an adjacent dark area on the plate. Any strain in the grain will of course produce non-parallelism of crystal planes, and the distribution of light and dark on the microradiograph will indicate the existence and distribution of this strain. Tilting of the specimen brings other grains into proper position and changes the appearance of the image very sensitively. This technique supplements strain determination by Barrett's method of diffraction microscopy by surface reflection (Chap. 22).

5. *Quantitative Microradiography.* Engström in Sweden has contributed largely to the use of microradiographs and of absorption phenomena in general for quantitative mass and chemical analysis (see Chap. 8). For determining the mass of very thin biological objects, a microradiograph of the specimen and one of a collodion wedge are made on the same film. Absorption in single-cell structures can be compared with absorption in the collodion foils, and the relative distribution of the amount of dry substance in the sample can be computed by photometric measurements on the enlarged image. Knowing the chemical composition and the weight per unit area of the foils, the absolute values of weight in the sample can be calculated. Thus the myelin sheath of a single nerve fiber has the mass 0.3×10^{-12} g/μ^3 and the central axon only one-third to one-eighth as much; half the myelin-sheath mass is lost with lipid solvents. The course of solvent extraction, enzyme removal, and reactions of protein with phosphotungstic acid, glycogen with iodine, nucleic acids with lanthanum, etc., are similarly followed. The mass of gastric mucosa cells has been accurately measured by Engström and Glick with

[1] H. C. Pollack and C. F. Bridgman, *Stamps*, **85** (2), 50 (1953).

[2] R. Smoluchkowski, C. M. Lucht, and M. Mann, *Phys. Rev.*, **70**, 318 (1946).

x-rays generated at 3,000 to 4,000 volts and filtered through an aluminum foil 9 μ thick to give a beam with maximum intensity at 8 to 12 A. Each microradiograph included a simultaneous exposure of a reference system consisting of two strips of thin nitrocellulose film (0.350 mg/cm^2). By photometric measurements of small areas in the enlarged images, the x-ray absorption in the cells was compared with that in the reference system, and the mass per unit volume was calculated. Mucus- and enzyme-secreting cells have a greater mass (0.1 $\times$ 10^{-12} g/μ^3) than acid-secreting. In contrast with this method, which may employ soft general radiation, a second method permits elementary chemical analysis by microradiography with monochromatic x-rays. As previously mentioned the absorption of two rays on either side of the K edge of the element in question is measured to estimate the size of this absorption jump, which in turn is proportional to the amount of the element. Thus two microradiographs are made with the two radiations (which may be generated as secondary fluorescent rays) and the densities determined photometrically. The amount of element is given by

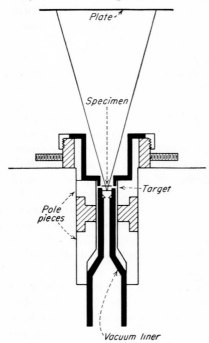

FIG. 167a. Diagram of Cosslett-Nixon shadow microscope: objective lens, target, specimen, plate portion.

$$X = \frac{\ln\,(i_2/I_2)(\lambda_1/\lambda_2)^p - \ln\,(i_1/I_1)\,Y}{(\mu_1/\rho) - (\mu_2/\rho)(\lambda_1/\lambda_2)^p}$$

where I and i are incident and transmitted intensities, the subscripts corresponding to the two wavelengths with mass-absorption coefficients μ_1/ρ and μ_2/ρ; p is an exponent, a function of $Z \cdot \lambda$ (values 3 to 2.3); and Y is the area (square centimeters) being examined. Thus one element may be determined in the presence of others, and also its minimum detectable amount. The quantitative distribution of calcium and phosphorus in the teeth and sulfur in the skin (greatest in the stratum corneum) and the decrease of the calcium content of the mastoid bone in inflammatory processes have been measured by Engström.

Extending these techniques, Brattgard and Hyden[1] in October, 1952, announced results on the mass, lipids (by chloroform extraction), pentose

[1] S. O. Brattgard and H. Hyden, *Acta Radiol.*, Supplement 94, 48 pp. (1952); **39**, 494 (1953).

nucleoproteins (after digestion by crystalline ribonuclease), and residual cell proteins for various nerve cells—Deiters' cells and spinal-ganglion and Purkinje cells, all of which are distinctively different in composition. This contribution to medical chemistry opens the way for many others by microradiography.

6. *X-ray Shadow Microscope.* Microradiography, as indicated on page 107, is one aspect of optics, especially when the shadow is projected to an

Fig. 167b. Historadiograph by shadow microscope of freeze-dried *Drosophila melanogaster* (95×).

enlarged image instead of the usual technique of photographic enlargement of the 1:1 image on fine-grained emulsion. Image sharpness requires x-rays from a point source, which is achieved by a two-lens electron optical system that reduces the electron source to a fine beam 0.5 μ in diameter. This electron spot strikes a tungsten-foil target 1 μ thick that forms the vacuum wall of the x-ray tube. A specimen placed close to this target casts an enlarged shadow image on a distant photographic plate with a resolution in the image equal to the x-ray spot size. Excellent results have been obtained especially with frozen-dried insects at the

Cavendish Laboratory at Cambridge, England.[1] A diagram of the objective lens, target, specimen, and plate illustrate the technique in Fig. 167a; and a typical photograph of a freeze-dried *Drosophila melanogaster* (fruit fly) at a magnification of $95 \times$ is reproduced in Fig. 167b.

BIBLIOGRAPHY

The following list includes most of the available references on the more general phases of microradiography.

Ball, L. W.: *Ind. Radiography*, **4**(1), 29 (1945).   Foundry control.

Bohatyrtschuk, F.: *Fortschr. Gebiete Röntgenstrahlen*, **35**, 253 (1942), **68**, 4 (1943); *Virchow's Arch. pathol. Anat. u. Physiol.*, **313**, 216 (1944); *Acta Radiol.*, **25**, 351 (1944); *Am. J. Roentgenol. Radium Therapy and Nuclear Med.*, **70**, 119 (1953). Blood vessels, tumors.

Clark, G. L., and associates: *Photo Tech.*, **1**(12) (1939); *Trans. Am. Soc. Metals*, **13**, 732 (1941); *Ind. Eng. Chem., Anal. Ed.*, **14**, 676 (1942); *Ind. Radiography*, **1**(2), 21 (1942); *Iron Age*, **152** (4), 44 (1943); "Colloid Chemistry" (edited by J. Alexander), Vol. 5, Reinhold Publishing Corporation, New York, 1944; *Radiology*, **49**, 483 (1947). Monochromatic rays, technique, general applications.

Dauvillier, A.: *Compt. rend.*, **190**, 1287 (1930).   Cells.

Engström, A., and associates: *Acta Radiol.*, **25**, 328 (1944); Supplement 63 (1946), **31**, 503 (1949), **35**, 33 (1951); *Instruments and Measurements Conf., Stockholm Trans.* (1949); *Rev. Sci. Instr.*, **18**, 681 (1947); *Nature*, **161**, 168 (1948); *Experientia*, **3**, 10, 191 (1947), **163**, 563 (1949); *Brit. J. Radiol.*, **22**, 309 (1949); *Science*, **111**, 379 (1950); *Acta Radiol.*, **38**, 98 (1952). Quantitative biological analysis, microangiography.

Goby, P.: *Compt. rend.*, **156**, 686 (1913).

Lamarque, P.: *Compt. rend.*, **202**, 684 (1936); *J. radiol. Électrol.*, **20**, 325 (1936); *Presse méd.*, **44**, 478 (1936); *Bull. histol. appl. physiol. et pathol. et tech. microscop*, **14**, 1 (1937); *J. belge radiol.*, **27**, 169 (1938); later papers with J. Turchine, *Schweiz. Z. Pathol. u. Bakteriol.*, **5**, 10 (1942).   Biological—cancer.

Maddigan, S. E., *J. Appl. Phys.*, **15**, 43 (1944); *Metals Technol.*, February, 1944; *Ind. Radiography*, **4** (4) (1946).

Mitchell, G. A. G.: *Brit. J. Radiol.*, **24**, 110 (1951).

Popisil, R.: *Non-Destructive Testing*, **7** (4), 16 (1949).   Electronic microradiography, metallurgical, petrographic.

Trillat, J.: *J. Appl. Phys.*, **19**, 844 (1948).   Giving all prior references.   Electronic microradiography.

Woods, R. C. and V. C. Cerone: *Metals & Alloys*, **18**, 1320 (1943).

[1] V. E. Cosslett and W. C. Nixon, *Proc. Roy. Soc. (London)*, **B140**, 422 (1952).

CHAPTER 11

THE CHEMICAL EFFECTS OF X-RAYS

Threefold interest is attached to the subject of the chemical effects of x-rays, in regard to:

1. Pure radiation chemistry, the mechanism and rate of reactions, the stability of chemical bonds, etc.
2. Light thrown on biological and therapeutic effects by the study of chemical changes.
3. Discovery of reactions that could be used as suitable dosimeters for quantity or intensity of radiation.

The casual observer might well believe that x-rays by virtue of their penetration and energy would have innumerable profound chemical effects, but as a matter of fact the examples of considerable chemical change are extraordinarily few in number. Many systems that undergo change in ultraviolet light are apparently unaffected. The photographic effect, a few oxidation-reduction reactions, and some condensations and decompositions of organic compounds are almost unique among the large number of experiments already empirically tried. However, the hope remains that other chemical effects may be discovered which may serve the purpose even of a convenient dosimeter. Interest in the subject has been greatly intensified since the first atomic bombs were exploded in Japan in 1945. Detection and measurement of the radiation emitted and its biological effects are of immediate concern to every living person today. It is a major project of the United States government to provide every man, woman, and child with a sensitive, simple chemical dosimeter, and intensive research is being directed to that end.

The Mechanism of Chemical Action. First a distinction should be made between photochemistry (and "photobiology") and radiation chemistry (and biology), though the terms are often used interchangeably; the first connotes light, the latter high-energy rays, such as x-rays, γ-rays, β-rays, neutrons, etc. In both cases radiation, usually from an external source, impinges upon an aggregate of molecules in stable states. Absorption of radiation energy must precede any physical, chemical, or biological effects which may be observed, and the process raises some of the molecules to the excited state, thus permitting chemical interactions which could not proceed with normal molecules. The primary processes of high-energy radiation are much more complex because the energies of the photons or liberated particles (high-speed electrons, conveniently though perhaps inaccurately called photoelectrons) are very much greater than the energies of transitions of a molecule, which are usually less than 15 ev, whereas the energy units of true photochemical processes, commonly those of photons of visible or ultraviolet light at 2 to 10 ev, lie in the range of the most likely transitions of molecular electronic systems.   In photo-effects the quanta are absorbed in single events, while in high-energy radiation effects the energy loss occurs gradually in hundreds or thousands of steps.   Monochromatic light ensures a unique excited state; high-energy radiation, even though monoenergetic, produces a wide variety of excited and ionized molecules, and most of the products are formed not by the incident radiation but indirectly by secondary, tertiary, etc., rays. The transfer of energy from the x-ray photons to a K electron is usually several times the K ionization energy, especially for lighter elements which are especially concerned in biological systems (284 ev for carbon, 400 ev for nitrogen, and 531 ev for oxygen).   But in case of K ionizations an energy transfer of many hundreds of electron volts to the molecule containing the atom has occurred.   If the molecule is large, it will actually retain this energy.   For heavier atoms creation of a K-shell vacancy is followed by emission of an x-ray photon as an electron drops into the K vacancy; thus the potential energy of the ionized atoms becomes the energy of secondary characteristic rays.   As already indicated, the ionized atom even during its short life can enter into chemical reactions. But for the light atoms there is a radiationless transition, known as the Auger effect (see page 144), in which an L electron drops into the K vacancy and then instead of an emitted photon another L electron is ejected, resulting in a doubly ionized atom.   Before emitting a photon of x-radiation an atom persists in its ionized state for $10^{-8}Z^{-4}$ (Z = atomic number) sec; this is so much longer than the time for the radiationless transfer (10^{-15} sec) that the latter occurs first in at least 99 per cent of such events, and thus radiation from C, N, and O atoms will be emitted to an extent of only 1 per cent.   Several Auger transitions might follow a single K ionization since very much more than sufficient energy is available to carry several valence electrons at or near the site of the original vacancy.

It is evident that, whenever a K ionization occurs, a relatively great amount of energy may be communicated to a single molecule or portion of a large molecule.   The primary process at the site of the original atom affected by the primary photon is then K ionization, the Auger electron, and multiple ionization.   This energy will be converted to molecular potential energy by electronic rearrangements and may then shatter the molecule by a complex but relatively slow polyatomic dissociation.   Stress has been placed upon the foregoing probable processes in the light atoms because of their significance in understanding the effects of x-rays upon biological systems. The most authentic summary of available information on these complex phenomena is to be found in the recently published (1952) "Symposium on Radiobiology," sponsored by the National Research Council, Atomic Energy Commission, and Office of Naval Research.

Our knowledge of the distribution of ions formed in matter by electrons (from β-, γ-, and x-radiation) is based on observations in air by use of the Wilson cloud chamber. By means of this instrument a supersaturated condition is produced in moist air just prior to the passage of the ionizing particle through the chamber. Water vapor in the form of a single droplet around each ion then condenses, and these droplets may be photographed to obtain a permanent record of positions and numbers of ions. Unfortunately no corresponding procedure has been found to record ion positions in liquids or solids, but it has been demonstrated experimentally that the ratio of rate of loss in energy of the ionizing electrons in a liquid or solid medium to that in a gas is the ratio of densities of the two media. In the absence of quantitative data it is assumed that the number of ions formed in a given length of path is in the same ratio. Most photographs show clusters of ion pairs, with on the average three pairs per cluster.

A comparison of cloud-chamber photographs for 1 Mev and 22 kv (silver $K\alpha$-rays) electrons, from corresponding primary x-rays, shows ions far closer together for the latter case; and indeed as the electron slows down, there are no longer resolved clusters. It is a general rule that the slower the particle the closer together the clusters and the greater the specific ionization or linear ion density. Lea,[1] Gray, and others have established a correlation between speed and linear ion density. In Fig. 168 x-ray-tube kilovoltage is plotted against ionization per micron of an organic solid such as tissue.

As the kilovoltage applied to the x-ray tube is increased, the average energy of the secondary electrons generated in the irradiated tissue increases and the average ion density decreases. But a hump appears on the curve because the less energetic Compton recoil electrons increase in number, while the more energetic photoelectrons become less numerous, so that over a range of 25 to 180 kv the ion density remains the same within 10 per cent (100 ions per micron). At higher potentials it begins again to decrease to 15 ions per micron at 1 Mev and 6 at 2 Mev.

Table 11-1 presents a summary of all present information on ion densities produced by different ionizing particles. The symbol LET (linear energy transfer) is coming into accepted usage to indicate rate of energy dissipation along the tracks, expressed as in this table in ion pairs per micron, or in $Mev/(g/cm^2)$, which expresses track lengths independent of

[1] D. E. Lea, "Actions of Radiations on Living Cells," Cambridge University Press, New York, 1946.

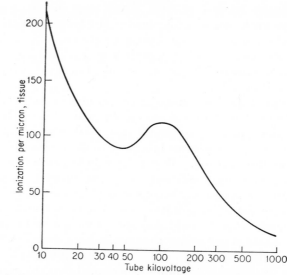

Fig. 168. Graph showing correlation between speed of ionizing particle in terms of x-ray-tube kilovoltage and linear ion density (ionization per micron) in tissue.

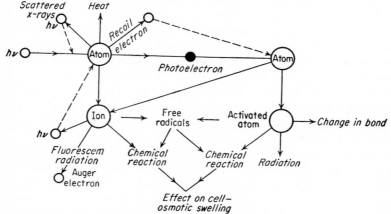

Fig. 169. Simplified representation of mechanisms of chemical and biological effects of x-rays.

the density of the material traversed. A complete statement of dosimetry must include dose (energy dissipation per unit mass), and LET.[1]

The complex theory of chemical action, illustrated in simplified form in Fig. 169, has been subjected by many workers to experimental test. Glocker and Risse[2] studied the decomposition of hydrogen peroxide and

[1] U. Fano, *Radiation Research*, **1**, 3 (1954); R. E. Zirkle, "Biological Effects of External X and Gamma Radiation," McGraw-Hill Book Company, Inc., New York, 1954.

[2] *Z. Physik*, **48**, 845 (1928); *Z. physik. Chem.*, **A140**, 133 (1929).

potassium persulfate in very dilute solutions. The amounts decomposed corresponded to the energy of the secondary electrons liberated in the system during passage of x-rays; 70,000 cal (electrons in motion) is required to decompose 1 mole of H_2O_2 in 0.06 normal solution, and 2.45 times as much for potassium persulfate. The dependence of chemical effect upon x-ray wavelength is a question entirely of how much energy during passage of an x-ray beam of certain wavelength through matter of

TABLE 11-1. ION DENSITIES FOR VARIOUS IONIZING PARTICLES[*]

Radiation	Generation	Mean linear ion density, ions/μ	Ionizing particle
Very high energy β and γ	Theoretical minimum ion density, any particle	6.3	
	—20 to 30-million-volt betatron	8.5	
	Natural and artifical radioelements	8.5	Electron
γ	—Ra, screened by 0.5-mm Pt	11	
	—Supervoltage 1,000 kv	15	
	—Deep therapy 200 kv	80	
	—30 to 180 kv	100	
X-rays	—Cu Kα-rays (8 kv)	145	
	—Cyclotron 12 million volts	290	
	—Ag L (3 kv)	300	
	—Cyclotron 8 million volts	380	
	—Al K (1.4 kv)	460	
	—900-kv deuterium ions bombarding Li	840	Proton
	—400-kv deuterium ions bombarding D	1,100	
α-particles	Natural radon disintegration	3,700	
	Natural polonium disintegration	4,500	α-particle
	Artificial bombardment of B or Li by slow neutrons	9,000	Atomic
Atomic	Uranium fission	130,000	

[*] L. H. Gray, *Brit. J. Radiol.*, Supplement 1, p. 13, 1947.

certain composition is transformed into the energy of secondary electrons. Taking into account the complications of scattered and fluorescent rays that may form secondary electrons, Glocker and Risse in 1928 obtained verification of the theory, and further substantiation has been obtained by other workers for other systems.

In general, the exact mechanism and kinetics of chemical reactions, though due to activation by electron impact, have been explained in only a very few instances. The photographic action is unusually simple, in that the silver and bromine ions are converted endothermically into neutral atoms through the energy of the secondary electrons. The evolution of hydrogen chloride from chloroform is an example of a reaction where far greater change is observed than can be accounted for by electron impact. It is, therefore, a chain reaction: a residual chloroform molecule disturbed by electron impact can react with an unchanged chloroform molecule, the product of this reaction with another unchanged chloroform molecule, and so on.

The principle of activation is the most important discovery in the elucidation of the photochemical results, especially in water solutions. In passing through water the photoelectron may come so close to an electron in a molecule that the repulsive force becomes sufficiently large to cause

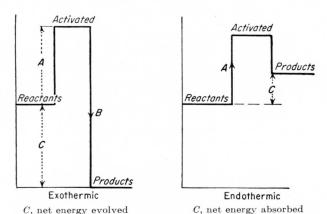

Exothermic   Endothermic

C, net energy evolved C, net energy absorbed

Fig. 170. Activated states in exothermic and endothermic chemical reactions.

the orbital of this electron to become unstable. As a result the electron moves into an orbital, or energy level, different from that in the normal molecule. The characteristics of an activated molecule are instability and a high degree of chemical reactivity. It is generally accepted that a molecule, in order to pass from one state to another, must pass through an intermediate activated state for two cases, as shown in Fig. 170.

The energy of activation may include: (1) chemical change of the molecule involving the initial activated bond; (2) emission as a quantum of light; (3) transmission of energy to another part of the molecule, activating another bond; (4) collision of the activated molecule with another molecule to which energy is transmitted.

Reactions of Water. The pioneer work of Fricke and associates first indicated the importance of the reactions of water and of very dilute aqueous solutions. A dosage of 1,000 r produces 2.8×10^{-6} g-ion pair in 1,000 g of water. With this are to be compared the numbers of activated water molecules,

(1) $H_2O \rightarrow (H_2O)'_{act}$; 0.55 micromole/1,000 cc/1,000 r.

(2) $H_2O \rightarrow (H_2O)''_{act}$; 2.2 micromoles/1,000 cc/1,000 r.

(3) H_2O, pure, gas-free—unchanged.

(4) For water with dissolved oxygen: $(H_2O)'_{act} + \frac{1}{2}O_2 = H_2O_2$; 1.1 micromoles/1,000 cc/1,000 r or 0.55 micromole of oxygen molecules activated, independent of oxygen pressure but dependent on hydrogen-ion concentration.

(5) $(H_2O)'_{act} + H_2O$ (presence of iodide ion, acid pH) $= H_2 + H_2O_2$; 0.55 micromole H_2/1,000 cc/1,000 r.

(6) $(H_2O)'_{act} + H_2O$ (I^-, alkaline pH) $= H_2 + \frac{1}{2}O_2 + H_2O$.

Examples of chemical transformation by irradiation of substances present in the water in such high dilution that their direct activation by the rays is negligible are as follows:

(1) $NO_2^- + (H_2O)'_{act} \rightarrow NO_3^- + H_2$; 0.55 micromole/1,000 cc/1,000 r.

(2) $AsO_3^{3-} + (H_2O)'_{act} \rightarrow AsO_4^{3-} + H_2$; 0.55 micromole/1,000 cc/1,000 r.

(3) $SeO_3^{3-} + (H_2O)'_{act} \rightarrow SeO_4^{3-} + H_2$; 0.55 micromole/1,000 cc/1,000 r.

(4a) $2FeSO_4 + H_2SO_4 + (H_2O)'_{act} = Fe_2(SO_4)_3 + H_2 + H_2O$ (gas-free) depends on H^+ concentration. In the presence of oxygen, the same reaction occurs, except that hydrogen is oxidized to water in a secondary reaction, and in addition a reaction independent of pH is observed:

(4b) $(H_2O)''_{act} + O_2 \rightarrow H_2O + O_{2,act}$.
$4FeSO_4 + 2H_2SO_4 + O_{2,act} \rightarrow 2Fe(SO_4)_3 + 2H_2O$; 8.8 microequivalents/1,000 cc/1,000 r.

(5) $CO + H_2O(+h\nu) \rightarrow CO_2 + H_2$; part of this hydrogen reacts $CO + H_2 \rightarrow CH_2O$. This is a method of successful treatment of CO poisoning.

Reactions Involving Hydrogen Peroxide. It has been shown that hydrogen peroxide is formed when water containing dissolved oxygen is irradiated with x-rays or by decomposition of water in the presence of iodide ion as catalyst at an acid pH. It is interesting to note that α-particles produce H_2O_2 in oxygen-free water. It is very important to determine whether or not reactions and radiation effects on living cells may be explained by the primary formation of hydrogen peroxide in solution, so that the net result is the same as though reagent H_2O_2 were added. X-rays not only cause its formation but also its decomposition: $H_2O_2 \rightleftharpoons H_2O + \frac{1}{2}O_2$. In contrast with most other reactions the amount decomposed per unit of dosage varies inversely as the square root of the x-ray intensity and increases with the square root of the H_2O_2 concentration. Only in some cases is it found that irradiation induces reactions that can be obtained also with H_2O_2, if sufficient time is allowed for it to react. Thus solutions of $K_2Cr_2O_7$ at pH < 1 are reduced exactly the same as if the acid solution is irradiated and added to the dichromate. Solutions at pH 3 to 4 are unchanged; also, H_2O_2 added to a solution in this pH range has no effect, since H_2O_2 is decomposed by the dichromate whether formed by irradiation or added.

Since 1941 considerable work[1] has been done in France on the radiochemistry of H_2O_2. It is detected colorimetrically for the reaction with

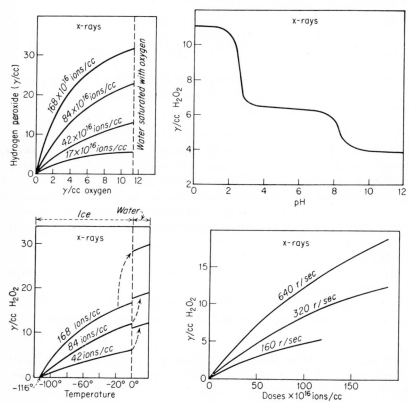

FIG. 171. Production of H_2O_2 in water and dilute aqueous solutions irradiated with x-rays as functions of dosage, oxygen concentration, pH, temperature, and dosage rate. (*Bonet-Maury and Frilley.*)

titanium sulfate (10^{-7} g H_2O_2/ml) or by a precipitate of silver ferrocyanide when ferricyanide is added to an H_2O_2 solution. The yields shown in Fig. 171 from the work of Bonet-Maury and Frilley[2] are independent of wavelength but depend on the amount of dissolved oxygen, the pH, the temperature, and the rate of irradiation. The yield initially is 0.54 molecule of H_2O_2/ion pair (1 r = 1.6×10^{12} ion pairs/cc). It increases with increase in pH and becomes negligible as oxygen in solution

[1] Reviewed in a paper by M. Frilley, *Brit. J. Radiol.*, Supplement 1, p. 50, 1947.

[2] *Compt. rend.*, **218**, 400 (1944); *Brit. J. Radiol.*, **24**, 422 (1951).

is removed; it increases in the presence of reducing agents such as hydroquinone, cysteine, ascorbic acid, and aldehydes but decreases in the presence of organic acids. The mechanism postulated by the French workers was

$$2(OH^-) + O_2 \rightarrow H_2O_2 + \begin{matrix} O- \\ | \\ O- \end{matrix}$$

which accounts for the reduction in pH. The oxygen molecular ion can react with any oxidizable substance in solution or with hydrogen ions.

$$\begin{matrix} O- \\ | \\ O- \end{matrix} + 2H^+ \rightarrow H_2O_2$$

An equally effective mechanism involves H and OH radicals, as explained later.

Other reactions taking place in the presence of dissolved oxygen in water are hydroquinone $\rightarrow$ quinone; $H_2S \rightarrow$ precipitated sulfur; oxidation of tyrosine, dioxyphenylalanine, pyrogallol, etc.

Quantitative Measurements of Reduction. Table 11-2 shows a comparison of energy relations of the reduction of ceric sulfate, potassium permanganate, and iodate and the formation of H_2O_2, as found by Clark and Coe.[1] Hydrogen peroxide is formed by the following mechanism:

$$\begin{aligned} H_2O_{act} + O_2 &= H_2O_2 + O & \Delta H &= -105,000 \text{ cal} \\ \underline{H_2O + O = H_2O_2} & & \underline{\Delta H} &= \underline{58,000 \text{ cal}} \\ \text{Total } 2H_2O + O_2 &= 2H_2O_2 & \Delta H &= -47,000 \text{ cal} \end{aligned}$$

Though H_2O_2 reduces ceric sulfate according to

$$2Ce^{4+} + H_2O_2 = 2Ce^{3+} + 2H^+ + O_2$$

the actual reduction can be accounted for only in part by this mechanism and the remainder by the reaction

$$2Ce^{4+} + H_2O''_{act} = 2Ce^{3+} + 2H^+ + \tfrac{1}{2}O_2$$

Potassium iodate, reduced by x-rays, is completely unaffected by H_2O_2, either added or formed by irradiation.

Ceric Ions Reduced per Roentgen. Values are obtained for amount of reduction of 0.0002 M and 0.0004 M ceric sulfate in 0.1 N H_2SO_4 by tungsten radiation (effective $\lambda = 0.60$) for varying periods of exposure. From these results it was found that 41 min was necessary for the reduction of 1.0 microequivalent weight, or 6.06×10^{17} ceric ions. Since the incident intensity was 590 r/min/cm²,

$590 \times 11.94 = 7,050$ r/min incident radiation on the total surface

[1] *J. Chem. Phys.*, **5**, 97 (1937).

Of this amount 47.5 per cent was absorbed by 0.1 N H_2SO_4; the absorption due to the small amount of $Ce(SO_4)_2$ present is negligible. From this it is calculated that 137,000 r was absorbed in 41 min. Therefore, 6.06×10^{17} ions/137,000 r or 4.42×10^{12} ions/r absorbed was reduced; 1.37×10^{11} r was necessary for complete reduction of 1 mole of ceric ions.

TABLE 11-2

Experimental and calculated quantities	$Ce(SO_4)_2$ reduced (0.1 N H_2SO_4)	$KMnO_4$ reduced (1.0 N H_2SO_4)	KIO_3 reduced (0.1 N H_2SO_4)	H_2O_2 formed (0.1 N H_2SO_4)
"Equivalions" converted per roentgen absorbed...........	4.42×10^{12}	7.45×10^{12}	1.27×10^{12}	2.30×10^{12}
Roentgens absorbed per equivalent converted..............	1.37×10^{11}	0.81×10^{11}	4.78×10^{11}	2.63×10^{11}
Ions converted per ion pair.....	2.0	3.7	0.62	1.1
Calories of absorbed energy per equivalent reduced*........	379,500	205,135	1,224,193	690,000
Calories electronic energy for conversion of 1 equivalent†...	344,000	204,000	1,095,000	602,000

NOTE: "Equivalions" equal gram equivalents times 6.06×10^{23}.

* Calculated from ions per ion pair, electron volts per ion pair, and heat equivalence of electron volts.

† Calculated from total heat equivalence of the roentgen and total heat dissipated as electronic energy.

By definition 1 roentgen corresponds to an ionization such that a current of 1 electrostatic unit flows in 1.0 cc of air under saturation potential. The number of ion pairs in air is therefore

$$\frac{\text{Total energy}}{\text{Charge on electron}} = \frac{1}{4.770 \times 10^{-10}} = 2.1 \times 10^9 \text{ ion pairs/cc in air}$$

and

$$2.1 \times 10^9 \times 795† = 1.7 \times 10^{12} \text{ ion pairs/cc/r incident radiation on water surface}$$

These calculations are based on the assumption of a very thin layer of fluid so that the incident intensity is the same on all portions. Since this was not the case for the experimental conditions used, it is necessary to calculate the average incident intensity compared with that at the surface. Using the absorption equation $I = I_0 e^{-\mu x}$ and allowing I_0 to be 100 per cent, the area under the curve of intensity against depth of solution can be found as $\int_{0.84}^{0} 100 e^{-\mu x}\, dx$. Dividing this value by 0.84 gives an average

† The best value correlating the number of ion pairs in water and in air in terms of density difference.

for all portions of the solution of 73.3 per cent of the intensity incident upon the surface. There were, then,

590 r/min $\times$ 0.733 $\times$ 1.7 $\times$ 10^{12} = 7.35 $\times$ 10^{14} ion pairs/cc/min in the
solution under the conditions used

But 1 microequivalent (6.06 $\times$ 10^{17} ions) of ceric ions was reduced for a 41 min exposure in 10 cc; this gives

$$\frac{6.06 \times 10^{17}}{7.35 \times 10^{14} \times 10 \times 41} = 2.01 \text{ ions reduced per ion pair}$$

At the present time the yield, which is a measure of the chemical change per unit energy input, is expressed by the symbol G. Thus G_{Ce4+} is the number of ceric ions reduced per 100 ev absorbed in the solution.

Energy of Reduction in Calories per Equivalent of Ceric Ions. This calculation comes out directly from the ions reduced per ion pair (2.01), the energy in electron volts to produce an ion pair (33 volts), and the heat equivalence per mole of the electron volt (23,000). The result is 379,000 cal/mole of ceric sulfate. By an entirely independent method based on the best data available on total heat equivalence of the roentgen (148 ergs/r at the given wavelength) and the proportion of total heat dissipated as electronic energy (0.71), the value 344,000 cal is obtained as a very satisfactory check.

Decomposition of Organic Compounds. The results of irradiating solutions of organic materials is of the greatest significance. In all cases, hydrogen is produced and, for certain highly oxidized molecules, CO_2.† The amounts decomposed increase with concentration, a fact indicating secondary reactions, but the attachment of the oxygen molecule of the activated water molecule to the organic molecule is the primary reaction. Particularly interesting is formic acid.

(1) $HCOOH = H_2 + CO_2$ (pH 2 to 3) or $(HCOOH)_{act} + (HCOOH) = 2H_2 + 2CO_2$(3.2 $\times$ 10^{-6} M/1,000 cc/1,000 r of each).
(2) $HCOOH = \frac{1}{2}(COOH)_2 + \frac{1}{2}H_2$ (pH 6).
(3) $2HCOOH = HCHO + CO_2 + H_2O$ at high concentrations.
(4) $(COOH)_2$ (oxalic acid) $= 2CO_2 + H_2$.
(5) $2CH_3COOH$ (acetic acid) $= (CH_2COOH)_2$ (succinic acid) $+ H_2$.
(6) Higher acids, no CO_2, two-thirds as much H_2.

In the presence of oxygen, no hydrogen is liberated, but there is an increase in hydrogen peroxide produced, as tested by reduction of dichromate.

(7) Alcohols, aldehydes, urea, glycine, dextrose, and creatine give hydrogen.

† Fricke, Hart, and Smith, *J. Chem. Phys.*, **6**, 229 (1938).

The Preparation of Very Pure Water. The decomposition with evolution of gases of organic compounds when present in the minutest traces suggests a method of testing and preparing the purest water. Fricke has found that when gas-free water from an ordinary tin still is irradiated there is generated as much as 10 or 20 micromoles of hydrogen and carbon dioxide/1,000 cc, from organic impurities. After further purification by prolonged heating with acid dichromate, then basic permanganate, followed by distillation through a quartz tube at 900°C, the water still yields 2 micromoles of H_2 and CO_2. It is only by *prolonged irradiation with x-rays* that finally a product essentially free from organic impurities is obtained. The measurement of properties, such as conductivity, of water of this highest degree of purity should yield interesting data.

The Free-radical Theory of Photochemical Action. Fricke's discovery that in dilute aqueous solution there is a linear relationship between the number of molecules reacting and the ion pairs produced in the solution has been verified by Dale[1] for inactivation of enzymes in dilute solution, and by Leichti, Minder, and Wegmüller.[2] Thus the initial process in radiochemical reactions must be activation of the solvent water molecules, followed by transfer of energy to the solute by inelastic collision. This is the "indirect-action theory" of the effects of radiations. What, then, is the nature of "activated" water originally postulated by Fricke and the mechanism of its indirect action? Kinetic studies indicate that the primary process is the sum of two reactions, a "forward reaction" (F) and a "radical reaction" (R). The first, corresponding to Fricke's $H_2O'_{act}$, is

$$2H_2O \rightarrow H_2 + H_2O_2 \qquad (F)$$

For the second, corresponding to Fricke's $H_2O''_{act}$, in 1944 J. Weiss[3] proposed that the intermediary formed as a result of ionization of water by irradiation is simply free hydrogen and hydroxyl radicals

$$H_2O + h\nu \rightarrow H^+OH^- \xrightarrow[\text{transfer}]{\text{electron}} H + OH \qquad (R)$$

The theoretical and experimental support of this simple theory in the subsequent years has been convincing to such an extent that there is now general acceptance. Modifications have been concerned solely with a mechanism which will permit H and OH radicals to be sufficiently separated so that they will not instantly recombine before secondary reactions with solute molecules can occur. In 1936 Lea in his book proposed the following:

[1] W. M. Dale, *Brit. J. Radiol.*, Supplement 1, p. 46, 1946.
[2] A. Liechti, W. Minder, and F. Wegmüller, *Radiol. Chem.*, **14**, 167 (1945).
[3] *Nature*, **153**, 748 (1944).

$$H_2O + h\nu \rightarrow (H_2O)^+ + e^- \quad [(H_2O)^+ \text{ identified in mass spectrograph}]$$
$$(H_2O)^+ \rightarrow H^+ + OH$$

At a distance

$$e^- + H_2O \rightarrow H + OH^-$$

In 1947 Burton suggested another variation,

$$H_2O + h\nu \rightarrow (H_2O)^+ + e^-$$
$$(H_2O)^+ + H_2O \rightarrow (H_3O)^+ + OH$$

At a distance

$$H_2O + Aq + e^- \rightarrow H + (OH)^-Aq$$
$$(H_3O)^+ + e^- \rightarrow H + H_2O$$

Free radicals and atoms have an established place in the mechanism of many chemical reactions; the quantum theory has given an understanding of the fact that atoms and radicals are more reactive than molecules. In other words, the height of the barrier A, or energy of activation, in Fig. 170 is very much lower. A free radical has preferential affinity for the most chemically active part of a large molecule. The possible reactions are

(1) Recombination: $\quad A + A'(+m, \text{ third body}) \rightarrow AA'(+m)$
(2) Addition: $\qquad\qquad A + BC(+m) \rightarrow ABC(+m)$
(3) Exchange: $\qquad\qquad A + R_1R_2 \rightarrow AR_1 + R_2$

On this free-radical theory some of the reactions studied by Fricke above may be restated:

1. *Recombinations.*

$$(1) \quad H + H = H_2 \ (+103 \text{ cal})$$
$$(2) \ OH + OH = H_2O_2 \ (+54 \text{ to } 64 \text{ cal})$$
$$(3) \ OH + OH = H_2O + O \ (+18 \text{ cal})$$
$$(4) \quad H + OH = H_2O \ (+118 \text{ cal})$$

Of these, on the basis of energies, (1) and (4) will be the principal reactions, but since the reversal $H_2 + OH \rightarrow H_2O + H$ will occur, there remains essentially $H + OH = H_2O$, or no decomposition of pure water.

2. *Formation of* H_2O_2.

$$H + O_2(+m) = HO_2(+m) \quad \text{(the powerful free hydroperoxyl radical)}$$
$$2HO_2 = H_2O_2 + O_2$$

or

$$HO_2 + H = H_2O_2$$

Reactions of hydroperoxides in irradiated fats are discussed in the following chapter.

3. *Decomposition of* H_2O_2.

$$H_2O_2 + H = H_2O + OH$$
$$H_2O_2 + OH = H_2O + HO_2 \; (HO_2 \rightleftharpoons H^+ + O_2^-)$$
$$H_2O_2 + HO_2 = O_2 + H_2O + OH$$
$$OH + HO_2 \rightarrow H_2O + O_2$$

4. *Formation of* I_2 *from* I^-.

$$I^- + OH = I + OH^-$$
$$2I = I_2$$

5. *Oxidation of* Fe^{2+}.

$$Fe^{2+} + OH = Fe^{3+} + OH^-$$

6. *Reduction of* Ce^{4+}.

$$Ce^{4+} + H = Ce^{3+} + H^+$$

7. *Reductions of* Hg^{2+} *in the Presence of* H_2 (far greater yield than in presence of O_2).[1]

$$H_2 + OH \rightarrow H_2O + H$$
$$Hg^{2+} + H \rightarrow Hg^+ + H^+$$
Without H_2: $Hg^+ + OH \rightarrow Hg^{2+} + OH^-$
With O_2: $H + O_2 \rightarrow HO_2$ (prevents reduction)

8. *Dehydrogenations.*

$$RH + H = \overset{.}{R} + H_2$$
$$RH + OH = \overset{.}{R} + H_2O \qquad \overset{.}{R} = \text{free radical}$$

9. *Reactions of Biologically Active Substances Such as Enzymes.* It was formerly supposed that redox reactions of enzymes such as peroxidase, catalase, and myoglobin were due to peroxide production and not to free radicals. In new work,[2] however, intermediate compounds are identified, and 1-equivalent reduction steps necessitate the production of free radicals.

Accelerators and Inhibitors. Further weight is given to the free-radical hypothesis by its successful explanations of the effects of additives in the aqueous solutions. Since 1934 it has been known that radiation-induced reactions in dilute aqueous solutions may be accelerated or inhibited (the protection effect) by the presence of small concentrations of inorganic ions or of organic compounds. Harker[3] found that small quantities of the latter accelerate the γ-ray oxidation of $FeSO_4$. In the 1937 work of Clark and Coe[4] referred to on page 271, it was observed that silver ion has a marked inhibiting and mercuric ion an accelerating effect

[1] G. Stein, R. Watt, and J. Weiss, *Trans. Faraday Soc.*, **48**, 1030 (1952).

[2] P. George and D. H. Irvine, *Trans. Faraday Soc.*, **49**, 323 (1953).

[3] *Nature*, **133**, 3–78 (1934).

[4] *Loc. cit.*

upon ceric salt reductions. The explanation given at that time, before the free-radical mechanism was evolved, was that Ag^+ absorbs the activation energy from H_2O before it is effective in producing a reaction, and Hg^{2+} acts as an acceptor by intermediate reduction to mercurous ion Hg^+ and reoxidation by Ce^{4+} ion. It was also found that the organic compound, acetic acid, had an accelerating effect on the reduction, 33 per cent greater than that of mercuric ion in 0.1 M concentration. Fricke and Brownscombe[1] had found a similar effect of organic compounds on the reduction of the dichromate solutions by x-rays. This accelerating effect has been recently reexamined in the light of the free-radical (H and OH) mechanism by Dewhurst,[2] for the effect of aliphatic alcohols on the oxidation of aerated aqueous $FeSO_4$. The value of $G_{Fe^{2+}}$ varies with concentrations of ferrous ion and alcohol. The efficiency of an alcohol (octyl alcohol was found to be best) is markedly dependent on its structure, and for a concentration of 5×10^{-4} M the initial yield increased linearly with the number of carbon atoms in the chain. The enhancing action is suppressed by NaCl, although in the absence of alcohol the salt has a negligible effect upon the yield of ferric ions from the x-ray oxidation of $FeSO_4$. These results closely parallel those of Kolthoff and Medalia[3] on the $Fe^{2+} + H_2O_2$ reaction in aerated aqueous solution containing organic compounds. The mechanism is probably as follows:

$$H_2O \xrightarrow{x\text{-ray}} H + OH \tag{1}$$

$$H + O_2 \longrightarrow HO_2 \quad \text{(aerated solutions)} \tag{2}$$

$$Fe^{2+} + HO \longrightarrow Fe^{3+} + OH^- \tag{3}$$

$$\underset{\text{Organic compound}}{RCH_2OH} + OH \rightarrow \underset{\text{Free radical}}{R\overset{\cdot}{C}HOH} + H_2O \tag{4}$$

$$R\overset{\cdot}{C}HOH + O_2 \rightarrow \underset{|}{RCHOH} \quad \text{(organic peroxides)} \tag{5}$$
$$O_2$$

$$Fe^{2+} + \underset{|}{RCHOH} + H^+ \rightarrow Fe^{3+} + \underset{|}{RCHOH} \tag{6}$$
$$O_2 \qquad\qquad O_2H$$

$$Fe^{2+} + \underset{|}{RCHOH} \rightarrow Fe^{3+} + \underset{|}{RCHOH} + OH^- \tag{7}$$
$$O_2H \qquad\qquad O$$

$$Fe^{2+} + \underset{|}{RCHOH} + H^+ \rightarrow Fe^{3+} + RCHO + H_2O \tag{8}$$
$$\overset{\cdot}{O}$$

$$\underset{|}{RCHOH} + RCH_2OH \rightarrow RCHO + R\overset{\cdot}{C}HOH + H_2O \tag{9}$$
$$\overset{\cdot}{O}$$

$$Fe^{2+} + HO_2 \rightarrow Fe^{3+} + HO_2^-(H_2O_2) \tag{10}$$

$$Fe^{2+} + H_2O_2 \rightarrow Fe^{3+} + OH^- + OH \tag{11}$$

[1] J. Am. Chem. Soc., **55**, 2358 (1933).

[2] H. A. Dewhurst, Trans. Faraday Soc., **48**, 905 (1952).

[3] J. Am. Chem. Soc., **71**, 3784 (1949).

Chloride ion (from NaCl) is known to be a powerful inhibitor of free radical reactions involving OH† by the reaction

$$Cl^- + OH + H^+ \rightarrow Cl + H_2O \qquad (12)$$

which predominates over reactions (3) and (4); no organic peroxides are formed, and the initial yield is restored to the value observed in the absence of alcohol.

Of great significance both chemically and biologically is the protection effect when two solutes, each of which alone is radiosensitive, are irradiated together in aqueous solution: one is preferentially destroyed and protects the other. The substances with highest relative protective power are those most likely to react with hydroxyl radicals. This is of the greatest importance in biological materials and has best been shown for deactivation of enzymes and viruses by Dale.[1] On carboxypeptidase solutions the following compounds have characteristic protective power per microgram: thiourea 1,120, formate 320, viruses 20 to 30, albumins 20, alanine 34, glucose 34, alloxan 13, oxalate 1.5, urea 0.5.

Since OH and H both oxidize (or dehydrogenate) and H can hydrogenate and break C bonds, the end result is a catalyzed recombination of H atoms to H_2, leaving an irreversible breakage of carbon bonds. The very important desoxyribosenucleic acid, a nuclear constituent, is completely depolymerized in aqueous solution when irradiated, as measured by structural viscosity, streaming birefringence, and sedimentation, and also by chemically generated free radicals. Thiourea, cyanide, cystinamine, cysteinamine, and other agents which have a marked protective effect on irradiated animals, as described in the following chapter, inhibit the depolymerization completely when present during irradiation but not when added afterward.[2] That the mechanism is indirect, through H and OH from the water, is proved by the inability of the rays to depolymerize the nucleic acid in the dry state, in ethylene glycol, or in frozen aqueous solutions. The degradation of aqueous solutions of high-molecular-weight polymethacrylic (PMA) acid brought about by HO_2 radicals formed during irradiation (there is no effect in the absence of oxygen and, therefore, by H and OH) is also inhibited by the protective —SH compounds, amines, alcohols, cyanides, etc.[3]

Intensive researches on the chemical protection of organisms and tissues against radiation are described in the following chapter. Besides compounds containing —SH groups, cyanides, and others, lipids (fats) have been found to exercise a protective action. A recent study has

† Taube and Bray, *J. Am. Chem. Soc.*, **62**, 3357 (1940).
[1] Dale, *loc. cit.*
[2] B. E. Cornway and J. A. V. Butler, *Trans. Faraday Soc.*, **49**, 327 (1953).
[3] P. Alexander, M. Fox, and S. F. Hitch, *Trans. Faraday Soc.*, **49**, 330 (1953); *Brit. J. Radiol.*, **26**, 413 (1953).

been made of the effect of one of the constituents of lipids, the trihydric alcohol glycerol, on aqueous solutions of dyes such as methylene blue, Nile blue, etc., which are decolorized by reduction upon irradiation with x-rays.[1] The results, evaluated spectrophotometrically, prove that the presence or absence of oxygen is a determining factor, as in the case of the reduction of mercuric salt solutions, but there is a marked effect of glycerol on reversibility of the systems upon reexposure to oxygen.

In work on chemical dosimeters it has been repeatedly found that in a wide variety of systems, both aqueous and nonaqueous, the presence of impurities or additives has profound effects on sensitivity to radiation, dependence of chemical change on dosage rate, and total dosage and stability in visible light. Eventually adequate explanations will be found so that such effects can be predicted. Certainly in aqueous solutions the reactions of H and OH have accounted for all observed facts thus far.[2]

Nonaqueous Solutions. That free radicals also play an essential role in reactions to x-rays of nonaqueous solutions is proved in new work by Clark and Bierstedt[3] on solutions of dithizone and other indicators in chloroform, carbon tetrachloride, absolute ethanol, and mixed solvents. Color changes result from formation of free Cl and from HCl where H is available. Radiation-insensitive solutions of 2-hydroxy-4-nitrophenyl-azo-β-naphthol and of resazurin in alcohol are so greatly sensitized by the addition of CCl_4 and $CHCl_3$ that very satisfactory dosimeters of high-energy radiation can be based on the marked color changes upon irradiation. Especially valuable are solutions containing both of the above-mentioned compounds in the ratio of 1:4 and sensitized by various proportions of CCl_4.

Additional Important Reactions. Besides the reactions of water, oxidation-reduction reactions, and decompositions of organic molecules already mentioned, some of the more important further reactions, some of which have possibilities as chemical dosimeters, are summarized in Table 11-3.

Effects on Colloidal Suspensions. X-rays and radium produce aggregation in positively charged suspensoids (precipitation of lyophobic and gelation of lyophilic), probably as the result of the discharge of charged particles by electrons freed in the ionization of the solvent; they disperse

[1] C. Piffault, J. Duhamel, and D. Longuet, *Acta Radiol.*, **39**, 64 (1953).

[2] For the latest contributions to this subject see E. J. Hart, Molecular Product and Free Radical Yields of Ionizing Radiations in Aqueous Solutions, *Radiation Research*. **1**, 53 (1954); H. A. Dewhurst, A. H. Samuel, and J. L. Magee, A Theoretical Survey of the Radiation Chemistry of Water and Aqueous Solutions, *ibid.*, p. 62; A. D. Allen, The Yields of Free H and OH in the Irradiation of Water, *ibid.*, p. 85; E. S. G. Barron, The Role of Free Radicals and Oxygen in Reactions Produced by Ionizing Radiations, *ibid.*, p. 109.

[3] G. L. Clark and P. E. Bierstedt, *Radiation Research*, **2**, 199, 295 (1955).

TABLE 11-3. PARTIAL ADDITIONAL LIST OF THE CHEMICAL EFFECTS OF X-RAYS

System	Reaction	Energy relations	Reference
		Inorganic	
1. Ferrous sulfate..........	Oxidized to ferric sulfate	0.0027 mg $FeSO_4$/cc 1,000 r. Independent of wavelength between 0.204 and 0.765 A	Fricke and Morse, *Phil. Mag.*, **7**, 129 (1929)
2. Mercuric chloride and potassium oxalate	$2HgCl_2 + C_2O_4^= \rightarrow Hg_2Cl_2 + 2Cl^- + 2CO_2$	6×10^5 mole/ion pair	Roseveare, *J. Am. Chem. Soc.*, **52**, 2612 (1930)
3. Mercuric chloride + ammonium oxalate (Eder's solution)	Hg_2Cl_2 precipitated, CO_2 evolved	0.58 mg Hg/840 r	Wyckoff and Baker, *Am. J. Roentgenol. Radium Therapy*, **22**, 551 (1929) Quimby and Downes, *Radiology*, **14**, 468 (1930)
4. Potassium dichromate..........	Reduced in 0.8 N H_2SO_4	3.31×10^{-6} equivalent/1,000 cc/ 1,000 r independent of concentration and temperature; due to formation of activated H_2O_2; very sensitive to organic impurities	Fricke and Brownscombe, *J. Am. Chem. Soc.*, **55**, 2358 (1933)
5. Potassium iodide..........	Iodine liberated	Amount decomposed linear with dosage in absence of oxygen; larger unit in presence of oxygen	Clark, Pickett, and Johnson, *Radiology*, **15**, 245 (1930)
6. Potassium nitrate..........	Reduced to KNO_2	Proportional to dosage 5.58×10^{11} molecules/r, **0.2** molecule/ ion pair	Clark, Pickett, and Johnson, *loc. cit.*
7. Catalysts..........	Activated in the presence of moisture (contact Pt for SO_2 oxidation)	Activity decays with time, H_2O_2 formation	Clark, McGrath, and Johnson, *Proc. Natl. Acad. Sci.*, **11**, 646 (1925)
8. Minerals, glass, etc..........	Colored by formation of colloidal aggregates	Positive ions neutralized by photo-electrons	Bayley, *Phys. Rev.*, **24**, 495 (1924)

9. Quartz oscillator plates	Depth of smokiness to control frequency adjustment	....	Dauvillier, *Compt. rend.,* **171,** 627 (1922)
10. Metastable solid states	Converted to stable forms (SO_3 crystals)	Measured by x-ray patterns, vapor pressures, and melting points	C. Frondel, privately printed pamphlet, 1944
			Smits and Schoenmaker, *J. Chem. Soc.,* 1926, pp. 1120, 1603

Organic

11. Oxyhemoglobin	Methemoglobin	Independent of wavelength 50 per cent transformed by 56,000 r	Fricke and Peterson, *Am. J. Roentgenol. Radium Therapy* **17,** 611 (1927)
12. Sucrose	Solution inverted, crystals turned reddish brown	6.5 per cent change in 2 per cent solution in 40 hr	Reinhart and Tucker, *Radiology,* **12,** 151 (1929)
13. Amino acids	Cystine unchanged, tyrosine changed in phenol group	Proportional to dosage	Stenstrom and Lohmann, *J. Biol. Chem.,* **79,** 673 (1928)
	Deaminated, except for S-containing amino acids (cysteine) and peptides (glutathione) from which H_2S is split preferentially	Ionic yield 4.2 (moles per ion pair) in 5% solution of serine	Dale, Davies, and Gilbert, *Biochem. J.,* **45,** 543 (1949), **48,** 129 (1951); *Brit. J. Radiol.,* **24,** 433 (1951)
14. α-Acetoxymercuri-β-methoxy-hydrocinnamic ethyl ester	Mercury liberated	0.293 mg **Hg** precipitated by 28,500 r	Clark, Pickett, and Johnson, *loc. cit.*
15a. Chloroform	Liberates HCl, which may be extracted into water layer and detected by pH color indicator, conductance, etc.	Very sensitive 9% bromocresol purple → 200 r 20% → 400 r 30% → 600 r	Taplin and Douglas, *Radiology,* **56,** 577 (1951)
15b. Other halogenated compounds, C_6H_5Cl, $C_6H_4Cl_2$, DDT, $CHBr_3$, etc.	Liberate HCl, HBr, etc. See preceding discussion on nonaqueous solutions	In solution yield independent of concentration to critical value; decrease to $37\%(= 1/e)$ highly characteristic and gives "reacting volumes"	W. Minder, *Brit. J. Radiol.,* **24,** 435 (1951)

TABLE 11-3. PARTIAL ADDITIONAL LIST OF THE CHEMICAL EFFECTS OF X-RAYS (*Continued*)

System	Reaction	Energy relations	Reference
16. Aldehydes..................	Condense with ketones	Markedly catalyzed by x-rays	Clark, Pickett, and Johnson, *loc. cit.*
17. Methylene blue..........	Decolorized; change measured spectrophotometrically; best concentration 0.0016 mg/cc; acetone, etc., inhibits change. Solutions protected by presence of glycerol (component of lipids)	Change not proportional to dosage	Stenstrom and Lohmann, *Radiology*, **16**, 332 (1931) Clark, Pickett, and Johnson, *loc. cit.* Clark and Fitch, *Radiology*, **17**, 285 (1931) Piffault, Duhamel, and Longuet, *Acta Radiol.*, **39**, 64 (1953)
18. Aromatic colors..........	127 examples studied; tetraphenyl methane, alazarine, anthracine, indigo types promising	....	Clark and Fitch, *loc. cit.*
19. Thioglucose, etc........	In presence of acceptor such as silver on a developed photographic paper easily reduced, forming Ag_2S; no reaction without x-rays	Very efficient; new light on biological effects	Unpublished
20. Oil drops on water......	Greatly increase diameter and spreading; oxidation and unsaturation	Increase with dosage, independent of wavelength; greatest effect from oil first irradiated in test tube	Stenstrom and Vigners, *J. Chem. Phys.*, **5**, 298 (1937); *Am. J. Roentgenol. Radium Therapy*, **40**, 427 (1938)
21. Desoxyribosenucleic acid......	Depolymerized in aqueous solution; but not in dry state, or in ethylene glycol, or in frozen solution	Reaction inhibited by thiourea	Limperos and Mosher, *Am. J. Roentgenol. Radium Therapy*, **63**, 681 (1950)
22. *d*-Amino acid oxidase........	Deactivated	Ionic yield 0.14 (mole per ion pair)	Dale, *Biochem. J.*, **36**, 80 (1942)

23. Ribonuclease..........	Deactivated	Ionic yield 0.03	Lea and Holmes (unpublished)
24. Tobacco mosaic virus.........	Deactivated	Ionic yield 0.0001	Lea, Smith, Holmes, and Markham, *Parasitology*, **36**, 110 (1944)
25. Ferric orthophenanthroline complex (blue)	Reduced to ferrous complex (red)	Ionic yield 2.0	Clark (unpublished)
26. Sulfanilamide 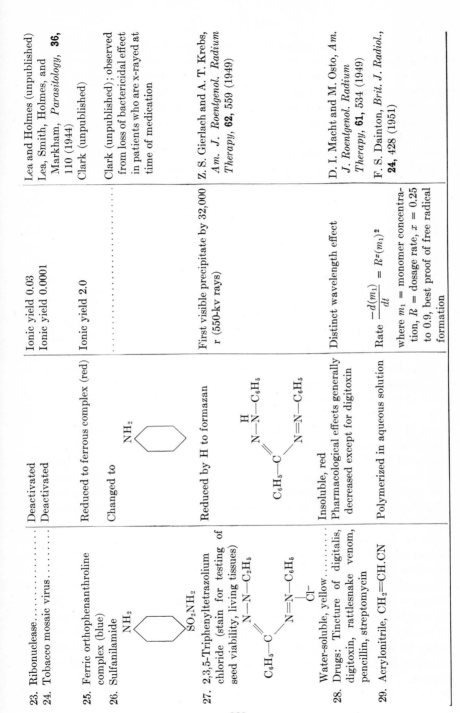	Changed to	....	Clark (unpublished); observed from loss of bactericidal effect in patients who are x-rayed at time of medication
27. 2,3,5-Triphenyltetrazolium chloride (stain for testing of seed viability, living tissues)	Reduced by H to formazan	First visible precipitate by 32,000 r (550-kv rays)	Z. S. Gierlach and A. T. Krebs, *Am. J. Roentgenol. Radium Therapy*, **62**, 559 (1949)
28. Water-soluble, yellow.......... Drugs: Tincture of digitalis, digitoxin, rattlesnake venom, penicillin, streptomycin	Insoluble, red Pharmacological effects generally decreased except for digitoxin	Distinct wavelength effect	D. I. Macht and M. Osto, *Am. J. Roentgenol. Radium Therapy*, **61**, 534 (1949)
29. Acrylonitrile, $CH_2=CH.CN$	Polymerized in aqueous solution	Rate $\dfrac{-d(m_1)}{dt} = R^x(m_1)^2$ where m_1 = monomer concentration, R = dosage rate, $x = 0.25$ to 0.9, best proof of free radical formation	F. S. Dainton, *Brit. J. Radiol.*, **24**, 428 (1951)

negatively charged suspensoids, making them more stable. Emulsoid colloids such as proteins are denatured whether they are positively or negatively charged, but only after prolonged irradiation. After denaturation, proteins flocculate if brought to the isoelectric point and are more easily precipitated by salts, alcohol, or heat. The decrease in solubility is most marked in albumins. Denaturation is accompanied or followed by an increase in viscosity and decrease in surface tension, most marked in globulins. The first step seems to be due to the ionization of water, followed possibly by formation of hydrogen peroxide, which sometimes has similar effects on colloids. Crowther with his coworkers has been an outstanding leader in this field of investigation, which is fraught with great difficulty because of the extreme sensitiveness to impurities and other eccentricities of these colloids. It has also been demonstrated that a steadily increasing exposure to x-radiation produces alternate increases and decreases in the electrokinetic potential of certain colloid particles. The decrease in potential at the minima of the curve is sufficient to bring the colloid to its flocculation point. Gold sols were completely coagulated when exposed to doses of 4.9 to 5.5 r, partially at 5.8, and not at all from 6 up to about 13 r, when a new period of coagulation began. Similar observations on proteins have been made in the author's laboratory. Clark and Pickett found that the flocculation of clay slips as measured by viscosity changes is a direct function of the amount of organic protein matter present.

The irreversible denaturation and coagulation of cell proteins are obviously two of the most important factors in the lethal and other biological effects of radiation, with which the following chapter is concerned.

High-intensity Irradiation. Attention is called again to the great usefulness of the new high-intensity x-ray tubes, described in Chap. 2. With dosages of 2 million to 5 million r/min it is possible to produce in a brief time chemical changes such as the coloration of gems and minerals, which formerly required as much as hundreds of hours. A particularly practical use indicated in Table 11-3 was developed during the war. By virtue of the piezoelectric properties of quartz innumerable plates were cut and used to control oscillation frequencies in radio, radar, etc. Frequently such plates had too great frequencies. These could be lowered and regulated exactly to a stated value by irradiation with x-rays to produce a smoky color, even while the plate was oscillating, while the frequency change was followed usually on a meter. The quartz plates lose the smoky color and regain the original oscillation frequency reversibly simply by heating the irradiated plates at 175°C. Use of high-intensity radiation in producing serums and vaccines is considered in the next chapter.

CHAPTER 12

THE BIOLOGICAL EFFECTS OF X-RADIATION

The value of x-rays as a research tool to the biologist in the field of genetics has been convincingly demonstrated by the work of a very considerable number of investigators. Much less well known are the great possibilities of cell studies depending upon an increasingly quantitative evaluation of characteristic radiosensitiveness, which may well become the most powerful method of pathologic diagnosis. Uncertainty remains as to fundamental differences between normal and pathological tissues and the mechanism involved in radiobiology and therapy of cancer cells. It has seemed desirable, therefore, to summarize briefly our present knowledge of the biological effects of x-radiation, under the following heads:

I. Bactericidal and general lethal effects.
II. Antigenicity of bacteria killed by x-rays and production of immunizing sera.
III. Viruses as models of biological actions.
IV. "Biological" dosimeters.
V. Effects on the hereditary material (chromosomes and genes).
VI. Effects on embryos.
VII. Effects on normal cells.
VIII. The radiosensitiveness of cells.
IX. Recovery and the time factor.
X. Effects on human tissues.
XI. The indirect reaction to radiations.
XII. The stimulating effects.
XIII. Photochemical effects bearing on biological action.
XIV. Chemical protection of tissues against radiation.
XV. Mechanism of biological actions.
XVI. The maximum permissible exposure.
XVII. Radiopathology.
XVIII. Cancer.
XIX. Supervoltage therapy.
XX. A third x-ray application in medicine.

I. Bactericidal and General Lethal Effects of X-rays. This is considered first since the first suggested possible biological application of the new rays, following announcement of their discovery by Röntgen in November, 1895, was directed to bactericidal properties. The rays were considered to be present in sunlight. Since the sun's rays were known to have bactericidal properties and were beneficial in treatment of diseases, especially tuberculosis, it was natural to turn to these rays as possibly possessing even more powerful physiological effects. On Jan. 29, 1896, T. Glover Lyon made definite suggestions in a letter to the London *Lancet*. But on Feb. 17, 1896, in another letter, he announced negative results on tuberculosis and diphtheria bacteria. This was the beginning of experiments on every type of organism in laboratories throughout the world, an account of which would occupy an entire volume. Some of the experiments were highly favorable, but the great majority were negative; positive bactericidal effects in one laboratory were entirely disproved in another. Thus began the great science of x-ray therapy under these highly unfavorable conditions. Though it became nearly universally agreed that bacterial cultures were nearly inert except to relatively enormous doses of radiation, the tremendous effect of rays on living tissue also became apparent. In 1902, Pusey and Caldwell stated in their book the following:

The fact that organisms in living tissues can be destroyed by exposure to x-rays, while the same organisms in inert cultures are uninfluenced by x-ray exposure, proves positively that it is not the influence of the x-ray *per se* that causes destruction, but that the tissues themselves doubtless under the conditions of activity excited by the x-rays play the important role in the germicidal process.

It would be profitless to enumerate the long series of experiments on bacterial cultures. The reputable results agree in showing logarithmic death rates for very large dosages, as exemplified in the results by the author on *Bacillus coli* and *Erythrobacillus prodigiosus*.

The irradiation was effected with a tungsten-target tube, using a potential of 65 kv and a current of 4 ma. At certain time intervals, test tubes were removed and dilutions plated out to determine the total counts.

The following conclusions may be derived from these data:

1. X-rays act like sterilizing agents upon cultures of *B. coli* and *E. prodigiosus*, in that the curves are characteristic sterilization or death-rate curves, a fact showing that the total counts decrease logarithmically with time.
2. In this experiment *B. coli* did not show variation or mutation when it was treated with x-rays.
3. With increasing irradiation, *E. prodigiosus* showed a tendency toward lack of ability to produce its characteristic red pigment. By allowing the organism to grow on the plate for a period of 5 days, the greater portion of the colonies produced their pigment. If a transfer of a white colony is made to an agar slant, the characteristic pigment is produced in 12 hr.

Of course, the final absolutely general effect of x-rays on living organisms is a lethal one.

The present information concerning the radiation variables which are concerned in the biologic lethal effect may be briefly summarized as follows: (1) The effects of a wide range of whole-body exposures to x-rays on survival time are graphically illustrated in Fig. 172 from the compilation of data by Evans,[1] primarily on mice. (2) For data on the influence of quantity of radiation on affected populations the dose-survival curve is sigmoid in character, showing that in even carefully selected populations a few individuals are especially sensitive, a few unusually resistant, but most have a sensitivity approaching the mean value. The LD_{50} (lethal dose for 50 per cent of a population) is lower for whole-body radiation than for local or superficial exposures. (3) As the intensity in roentgens per minute is reduced, the lethal action for the same dose becomes less pronounced. Thus protraction decreases the effect, but as will be shown later, this is not true for rates of mutation, depending on

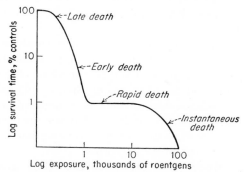

Fig. 172. Effect of exposure to x-rays on survival time for mice. Late death—survive until few weeks before controls. Early death—survive 1 month. Rapid death—2 to 5 days after irradiation. Instantaneous death—during or a few minutes after irradiation. (*Evans.*)

effects on genes. (4) Fractionation of a certain dose produces less effect than if it is delivered at one time, indicating that some recovery may take place between different exposures. Animals receiving smaller daily exposures lived longer, but the total accumulated exposure at the time of death was less than that of mice exposed to heavier treatments. This indicates that the over-all effect is one of aging, according to Henshaw; and if radiation acts to hasten the process of aging, normal aging would be expected to exert a relatively greater effect in those animals which lived longest. In contrast, fractionated exposures are more effective on reproductive cells; all of these are not equally sensitive at one time, and hence fractionation is more likely to expose every cell at least once in division. (5) Low-energy radiation is more effective in producing changes in tissues than extremely high energy x-rays or γ-rays because of a much higher density of ion pairs per unit length of path of ionizing particles. X-rays preferentially injure cells either beginning division or preparing for

[1] T. C. Evans, "Symposium on Radiobiology, 1952," p. 393, John Wiley & Sons, Inc., New York.

mitosis, whereas neutrons damage both inactive and dividing cells; but the final injury is the same.

II. Antigenicity of Bacteria Killed by X-rays, and Production of Immunizing Sera. The new high-intensity x-ray tubes (page 34) provide a possible method of preparing easily and quickly antigens from bacteria killed by irradiation. Sera and vaccines can then be prepared from blood of animals immunized by injections of the antigen. Previously the time required for administering bactericidal dosage with irradiation from conventional tubes was too long for practical purposes, and the antigenicity was poor in comparison with heat-killed bacteria. In the author's laboratory the first studies were made on *Eberthella typhosa* irradiated with a Machlett tube delivering 2,500,000 r/min at the window. Slightly more than 5 min was sufficient, in comparison with 1 hr heating at 60°C.

Immunity was induced by inoculating rabbits with small amounts of the antigen every third day. Two to four days after the last injection the animals were bled by cardial puncture, the blood clotted, and the sera centrifuged and preserved by additions of phenol. Titration of the sera with homologous antigens showed two plus agglutination at dilutions below 1:1,024. There is every evidence that the antigens in the irradiated cells are as effective in producing immunity against typhoid infection as the antigens of the heat-killed bacterins.

III. Viruses as Models for Study of Biological Action of X-rays. Probably the most intensive and successful researches in the past few years on biological effects of irradiations are those on viruses. These comprise a large group of obligate pathogens which appear to have affinities on the one hand with what are recognized as true organisms and on the other with protein molecules. They are not cells and perhaps are not any more truly living entities than enzymes. They multiply only through the agency of the host; some of them have been crystallized and their molecular weights evaluated just as if they were purified proteins, in the work of Wendell Stanley, Nobel prize laureate, and others. And yet the study of their inactivation by x-rays, γ-rays, electrons, α-rays, and neutrons has given the most quantitative biological answers, and so in this respect they are regarded provisionally as living.[1]

Interest in viruses arises from their extremely small sizes, which, however, range over a "spectrum" from the comparatively large and complex vaccinia virus to the foot-and-mouth virus, which is no larger than a hemoglobin molecule; their diversified effects upon animals, plants, and bacteria (the phages); an increasing fund of information on their sizes and shapes from electron microscopy, most of them being beyond the resolving power of optical microscopes; the comparative ease of "titration" of virulence effects on dilutions (similar to the mortality-log dose

[1] Roy Markham, *Brit. J. Radiol.*, Supplement 1, p. 16, **1947**.

curves for drugs) before and after irradiation. Such semilogarithmic virulence curves are also rectilinear, so that inactivation of viruses has dosimetric possibilities.

There are two fundamentally important applications of virus-irradiation experiments: one is the evaluation of the size of the virus, and the other is a test of the mechanism of the biological effects of ionizing radiations. Great credit is due especially to D. E. Lea and associates for leadership and for the authoritative book "Action of Radiations on Living Cells" (1946). Since inactivation curves for viruses are rectilinear, it follows that this result is due to one hit, i.e., the passage of an ionizing particle through the virus. As an example of formulas and graphical methods for evaluating the cross section d may be cited the following:

$$d = \frac{9.8 \times 10^4 \text{ m}\mu}{\sqrt{D_{10}}}$$

where D_{10} is the dosage in ion pairs per cubic micron (ipm) which reduces the activity of the virus to one-tenth. Many authors prefer D_{37}, where the dosage reduces activity to 37 per cent (or e^{-1}).

The results of comparative sizes of the important viruses, vaccinia ($D_{10} = 13.5 \times 10^{-4}$ ipm for α-rays and 132 for x-rays), phage ϕ–x–174 ($D_{10} = 1.9 \times 10^{-4}$ ipm for α-rays and 190 for x-rays), and foot-and-mouth ($D_{10} = 600 \times 10^{-4}$ ipm for α-rays and 100 for x-rays) are given in Table 12-1 from the work of Bonet-Maury.

TABLE 12-1. VIRUS-SIZE MEASUREMENTS*

Method	Vaccinia, mμ	Foot-and-mouth, mμ	Ratio	Phage ϕ–x–174, mμ
Filtration...............	150	12	125	10
Centrifugation...........	240	17–30	10	16
Ultraviolet microscopy....	275	40–300		
Electron microscopy......	245	25	10	18
Irradiation (α-rays).......	255	30	8	18
Irradiation (x-rays).......	22	25	0.9	17

* Brit. J. Radiol., Supplement 1, p. 25, 1947.

There is reasonably good agreement (especially between electron-microscopy and α-particle irradiation results, which are the most reliable) except for the vaccinia size with irradiation by x-rays. The explanation of this discrepancy is highly significant. The irradiation method gives the *radiosensitive volume* of the virulent particle in the volume of the virus. If this diameter differs from that of the whole virus given by other methods of direct observation, the difference represents a "coefficient of organization" and indicates a biological structure of the virus. For the foot-and-mouth virus and the phage the sensitive volume is the same as the total volume, and hence these must be single blocks of homogeneous unorganized material (they have been called "naked genes"), whereas the vaccinia virus has a sensitive volume of about the same size from x-ray data, but only a fraction of the total virus volume. It is not clear why α-rays give a sensitive volume the same as the total, but evidently there is an agglomeration of the small virulent units, and with the much greater density of ion pairs from α-rays there must be a migration of energy which inactivates the whole corpuscle. Salaman presents further evidence that there appears to be a large number of small units with small volume but large cross-sectional area. Changes in germ cells result from a single ionization in the genetic material, or genes. Vaccinia virus is analogous in that a single hit on the sensitive "genetic" material produces loss of infectivity.

Finally, distinction is to be made between direct and indirect action of ionizing rays on viruses. In the preceding chapter it was shown that photochemical change may result from direct hits on molecules or, in dilute solutions, indirectly by the ionization of water and formation of free H and OH. In virus inactivation precisely the same thing is true. In direct action the ionizing radiation passes through the virus particle and dissipates energy within it; in indirect action virus particles are inactivated without any ionizing particle having passed through the virus. Direct action is found in irradiation of dry virus preparations, while in aqueous suspensions the indirect action becomes more and more predominant the lower the virus concentration. If to the dilute solution other materials such as proteins are added which will react with free radicals and so compete with the virus, the indirect effect on the virus at a given concentration and dosage is reduced. It is the total concentration of protein in a virus preparation which determines whether action is predominantly direct or indirect. Actually the ionic yield for the indirect effect is less than one-thousandth that for the direct effect. These phenomena have been quantitatively demonstrated by Lea, and they serve as powerful proofs of the "protection phenomena" discussed for chemical systems and of the validity of the free-radical theory of indirect chemical and biological action of ionizing radiations.

IV. **"Biological" Dosimeters.** The quantity of radiation required for death is so definite for each particular type of cell that a lethal count serves as a quantitative dosimeter of the radiation. A few years ago, Wood showed that for *Drosophila* eggs 50 per cent are killed by 180 r and 90 per cent by 500 r.

The extended work by Packard has confirmed these values, and also the fact that these eggs give probably the best results of any biological material when used with a definite technique, such that generally average ages of the eggs are involved. For the radiosensitivity increases rapidly during early stages of nuclear division, attaining a maximum when the embryo shows the first sign of differentiation and falling abruptly thereafter. The 50 per cent survival dose for eggs 90 min old is 163 r; for those 330 min old, it is 1,044 r. Equal doses of x-rays generated at potentials from 12 to 700 kv kill equal proportions of the eggs. This biological-test object is also suitable for γ-ray dosage; Packard has found that the number of equivalent or biological roentgens per millicurie-hour is 5.00 r/millicurie-hr at 1 cm distance and with a 0.5-mm platinum filter.

The explanation of the fact that just half of a given number of eggs are killed by 180 r or that the survival curve in general is S-shaped either lies in the fact that eggs collected over a 2-hr period have a distribution of ages and sensitiveness, giving on the average with a fixed routine this constant effect, or depends on the assumption of a differential portion in each cell, more sensitive than the rest, the destruction of which by one or more x-ray quanta will cause death. Therefore, the survival curve is determined by the size of the sensitive spot and the number of quanta required to kill it. This hypothesis requires that this spot shall be equally sensitive at all times, whereas the sensitiveness is known to change rapidly during mitosis. This method involves incubating the irradiated eggs and counting the survivors. Direct and immediate observation upon lethal effects of x-rays can be made on the hearts of the transparent *Daphnia magna*, which stop beating upon death. Other biological systems that have been suggested are the familiar erythema reaction, the growth of seedlings and root tips, the hatching of *Ascaris*, grasshopper, and hen's eggs, colony development of bacteria, and, as indicated in the preceding section, inactivation of viruses.

V. Effect of X-rays on Hereditary Material. The experiments with bacteria have shown that the only observable biological effect is death, whereas in yeast it is indicated that reproductive processes may be greatly affected by irradiation energies far smaller than required for the death of the organism. This brings us to a brief discussion of x-rays in the science of genetics, already recognized by all biologists. In 1903, Albers-Schönberg discovered the sterilizing effect of x-rays. From that day to this, interest has centered in the question as to what effect may have been suffered by those germ cells irradiated but not sterilized, or in which only temporary sterility is induced, and therefore whether or not sterilization of human beings by x-rays is safe.

The latest information on radiation effects on reproductive activity in man and in animals is summarized in Table 12-2.

C. R. Bardeen, in 1906, first found that the ova of a toad fertilized by spermatozoa exposed to x-rays developed abnormally, and he concluded that the action of the rays must be on those unknown substances in the nucleus or the protoplasm most intimately associated with the nucleus which control the morphogenetic activities of the cell. Thus Bardeen was lacking only the concept of the chromosome. Now we know that each cell of the body of an animal or higher plant contains a nucleus in which are threadlike structures, the chromosomes, fixed in number for a given individual and kind of organism.

TABLE 12-2. RADIATION EFFECTS ON REPRODUCTIVE ACTIVITY*

	X-ray dose, r	
	Male	Female
Permanent sterility		
Man....................	500–600	300–320
Mouse and rat..........	1,600–3,000	800–1,500
Drosophila..............	12,000	5,000
Temporary sterility		
Man....................	250(12)†	170(12–36)
Mouse.................	800(4)	
Rabbit.................	....	1,500–2,000(24)

* A. Glücksman, *Brit. J. Radiology*, Supplement 1, p. 103, 1947.
† Duration in months in parentheses.

In the human species there are 24 chromosomes in the mature male germ cell (male gamete), or sperm, and 24 chromosomes in the mature female germ cell (female gamete), or egg. The fertilized egg (zygote) formed by the union of such a pair of gametes therefore contains 24 pairs of chromosomes. In the subsequent repeated process of cell division each body cell of the new individual receives 48 chromosomes, half of which are duplicates of the 24 chromosomes supplied by the individual's mother and the other half duplicates supplied by the individual's father. Thus each body (somatic) cell carries within it an inheritance pattern derived equally from the two parents.

The chromosomes are composed of protein and are largely, if not wholly, constituted of genes, the hereditary particles which control the characters developed by the organism. It is not known how many genes per set of chromosomes there are in man, but in *Drosophila melanogaster*, which has only four pairs of chromosomes, there are some 1,000 genes per chromosome (Fig. 173). The chromosomes in a body cell pass through a cycle of division called mitosis whereby two nuclei, each an exact reproduction of the parent nucleus, are produced. In preparation for mitosis each gene reproduces itself by somehow synthesizing a new gene like itself from the material of the surrounding medium. When the adult produces new germ cells, a special process of cell division called meiosis takes place such that the resulting gametes have only 24 chromosomes each. Each of these has an equal chance of having been derived from the individual's father or mother.

Most of the work between 1905 and 1925 has limited value largely because a great preponderance of new gene mutations probably escaped attention, since almost without exception these are recessive and cannot be detected until the third generation. Starting with the work of Koeneke, in 1905, on lilies, visible alterations on chromosomes of irradiated cells were recorded. Mohr, in 1919, reported that irradiation of locusts often caused a chromosome to enter the wrong cell (nondisjunction). It has remained for the work of Muller and associates, especially

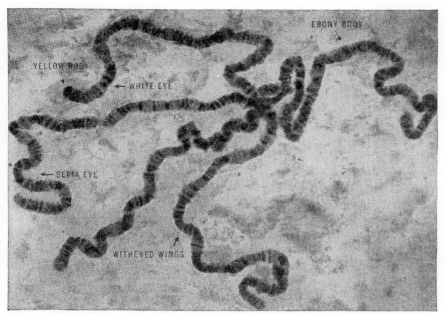

FIG. 173. Chromosomes and genes of *Drosophila* (salivary-gland cell).

on *Drosophila*, to found a technique and an entire science of radiogenetics. Briefly outlined, some of these facts are as follows:

1. Radiations affect cells in different ways depending upon the stage: lengthening of the nuclear-division cycle; sticking or clumping together of chromosomes on cells already in division, as the result of the radiation effect on the nucleic acid coating; recovery by nuclei irradiated at resting, though delayed in division.

2. There are two kinds of alteration in the hereditary material: (a) intrachromosomal, or structural, change in linear arrangement of genes within the chromonema, which forms the basis of the chromosome, by simple break and loss, simple translocation, mutual translocation, inversion, deletion, and complex combinations of these; (b) a change in the

composition of the genes themselves. Simple breaks increase in linear proportion with dose, independently of rate of dosage, and hence are the result of the passage of an ionizing particle; if an exchange between two breaks occurs, the two breaks are produced by two ionizing particles (Lea) and the frequency of translocations requiring two or more breaks is proportionate to the square of the number of hits, whereas a neutron can produce both breaks.

Changes of both kinds can be produced in abundance in *Drosophila*, 150 or more times as abundant as in the controls. Over half of the sperm remaining capable of taking part in fertilization and development are genetically affected. Mutated genes and changed chromosomes are inherited in accordance with usual Mendelian and chromosomal properties. For a variety of organisms the probability of a spontaneous gene mutation is on the order of 10^{-5} to 10^{-6} per gene per generation, independent of life span. Mutations induced by radiation are entirely similar to those which occur spontaneously.

3. Visible mutations extend to bodily form and size, colorations, conformation of individual organs, fertility, reaction to light and gravity, and heat tolerance. In plants like corn, barley, and rice the ray-produced changes may result in albino plants lacking in chlorophyll and therefore unable to nourish themselves or in plants with stalks that cannot support their own weight. Morphologic changes are often obscure and secondary to physiological ones; at least 80 per cent are lethal and most of the rest detrimental.

According to Muller, *Drosophila* spermatozoa given a moderate dose of only 150 r will respond so that 85 per cent of the offspring will receive no gene mutation demonstrable by present methods; 10 per cent will carry detrimental mutations, mainly recessive in action, which cause no externally visible change even when they finally "show" owing to having been received from both parents alike; much smaller percentages will have recessive lethals (which kill all individuals when like mutant genes from both parents are brought together); still smaller percentages, dominant lethals (which kill with certainty when received from only one parent); still smaller percentages, recessive visibles (small eyes) appearing rarely in the first generation; and finally for 1 in 1,000 offspring there will be a dominant visible change, seen in the first generation. This dose of 150 r has been given intentionally to the ovaries of women to induce ovulation or to men for producing temporary sterility; it is the amount received by the skin in the course of two or three fluoroscopic examinations, or that received in 10 years by a weekly permissible dose of 0.3 r.

Changes are distinctly random; hence a very few may happen to be beneficial. For example, experiments by the General Electric Company on irradiation of bulbs of the lily *Lilium reginum* have led to a species that will not shed pollen; hence, discoloration of the flower and early wilting are prevented.   Here a distinctly unfavorable mutation from the standpoint of propagation is very favorable commercially to the florist. Penicillin is today produced from a mutant of the fungus *Penicillium* resulting from irradiation, at double the rate of the parent fungus.

The chromosome changes usually are more detrimental than gene mutations.   Nonviable changes account for dominant lethals, *i.e.*, for failure of zygotes to develop to maturity when sperm or egg is irradiated before fertilization.   Viable changes lead to hereditary partial sterility, for example, in mice.

4. The mutations and changes are produced by x-rays in germ cells of all types, spermatozoa, whether irradiated in the testis or after reception by the female, spermatogonia, mature eggs, oöcytes, and oögonia.   Once produced a mutation remains permanently, *i.e.*, there is no recovery from it since reverse mutations are far rarer.

A great variety of plants and animals show results confirming those on *Drosophila*, including wasps and other insects, barley, tobacco, Jimson weed, maize, wheat, cotton, primroses, snapdragons, petunias, mice, frogs, etc.   Snell, in 1933, demonstrated that a quarter of the functional sperm of mice, after irradiation with only 400 r, carries chromosomal translocations to be detected through inheritable infertility in the first and later generations; also, that over 50 per cent of embryos die *in utero* when one parent comes from an affected line and that morphologic changes occur, such as misshaped spleens and dwarfism. Abnormal embryos produced by irradiation of grasshopper eggs are illustrated in Fig. 174; and Fig. 175 demonstrates the fatal mark upon future generations of irradiation of the reproductive cells of the first male parent mouse and the abnormality of one of the grandchildren of the x-rayed mouse.

5. The mutation rate is independent of wavelength of radiation up to 2.6 A from the usual tungsten target, but, with strictly monochromatic rays at the same dosage, mutation rates in *Drosophila* are appreciably greater.[1]   The rate is linearly proportional to dosage (except in very small doses) and is also independent of the time occupied by irradiation, *i.e.*, of ordinary intensities down to 0.001 r/min, but this independence does not extend to beams from new high-intensity tubes on the order of 5 million r/min; it is independent of whether the dose is fractionated or a single exposure (note that this is not true for the lethal effect, Sec. I); it is independent of temperature and of the natural mutation rate of the particular race employed.   Hence induced mutations must be due to single ionizations in a sensitive volume—the gene itself.   Ionization adds energy to the affected gene, and the excited molecules rendered temporarily unstable must create the properties of the gene which are disclosed as a mutation.

[1] G. L. Clark, unpublished work, 1949.

Experimentally it has been demonstrated many times that mutations and dosage are linearly related, in agreement with the "target" theory. When, however, the straight line is extrapolated to zero dose, the frequency of mutation is greater than is observed to occur spontaneously. Consequently it must be assumed that the relation between mutation rate and dose is curvilinear.[1] This can be explained on the basis that the effect of radiation has two components. One starts from the spontaneous

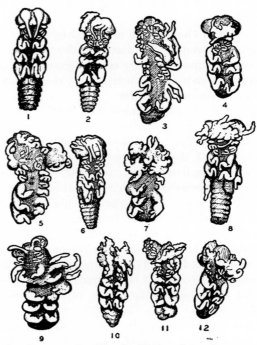

FIG. 174. Abnormal embryos produced by irradiation of grasshopper eggs, compared with normal type (No. 1). (*T. C. Evans.*)

frequency and increases linearly, whereas the other rapidly increases from zero to a constant maximum value which it reaches at a fairly low dosage level. The first meets the requirements of the target theory, the second of an indirect force. The latter has been shown to occur in *Drosophila* in the production of gynandromorphs (animals with one part of the body having female chromosomal equipment and another male chromosomal equipment). Irradiated females may produce in progeny gynandromorphs owing to elimination of the paternal (untreated) chromosome at a higher rate than in controls owing to an indirect effect via the egg cytoplasm.

6. Other mutagenic agents are: ultraviolet light at 2,600 A, the effi-

[1] G. Bonnier, *Brit. J. Radiol.*, **25**, 180 (1952).

ciency following the absorption curve of thymonucleic acid; mustard gas and allyl isothiocyanate;[1] and antisera (at least to Neurospora).

7. Calculations on the basis of the quantum theory were made before 1940 to derive the effective volume of a single gene upon which x-rays must produce their effect. For *Drosophila* the sex-chromosome volume

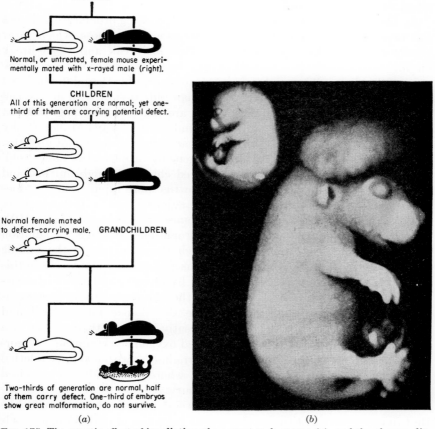

PARENTS

Normal, or untreated, female mouse experimentally mated with x-rayed male (right).

CHILDREN
All of this generation are normal; yet one-third of them are carrying potential defect.

Normal female mated to defect-carrying male.   **GRANDCHILDREN**

Two-thirds of generation are normal, half of them carry defect. One-third of embryos show great malformation, do not survive.

(a)   (b)

Fig. 175. The genetic effect of irradiation of a parent male mouse (a), and the abnormality of the embryo of one of the grandchildren compared with normal embryo above at left (b).

has 0.00829 of its volume composed of vital dominant genes. Since there are 1,280 of these, the size of one of them would be 1.1×10^{-18} cc. In the cell there are 2,000 to 15,000 of these volumes. Catcheside in 1949 revised the gene size, on new data, assuming the target theory, to $3 - 24 \times 10^{-20}$ cc.

8. In the cells of the body, somatic cells, mutations of genes are pro-

[1] Similarities and differences between chemical and ionizing agents are discussed on page 269.

duced by radiation just as in germ cells and with the same frequency for a given dose. Mutations can seldom be detected, but occasionally a cell will be given the property of more extensive growth, to the point of overgrowth into a malignant tumor or leukemia for white cells. In mice a dose of only 25 to 50 r will induce ovarian tumors in 70 per cent of the individuals. Cancers induced by overexposure may not be evident till 10 to 20 years after irradiation.

9. The law of Lacassagne states that faster growing proliferating tissues are more detrimentally affected by radiation than those which grow slowly or not at all; in other words, multiple-break and single-break chromosome aberration is formed by having many cells in mitosis, or the state of dividing. Thus embryos are more susceptible than differentiated organisms; young, growing organisms than old; tissues with active cell division than bone or new cells which are inactive (see page 306 on specific sensitivity). "We can further understand," says Muller, "why the radiation in addition to 'blowing hot' and causing malignant growths, quite possibly through the induction of gene mutations, also 'blows cold' by means of chromosome damage induced chiefly through mitosis, and thereby tends to destroy those same growths more rapidly than it does the normal, slow-growing tissues that adjoin them." Inflammation, ulcers, radiation sickness, lowered resistance to disease (see page 310), etc., are all long-term evidences of chromosome damage. Radiation damage is increased by colchicine, which stops mitosis in the middle phase at the most sensitive period and thus accumulates many cells in this condition. Damage is markedly altered by physical and chemical measures which change the metabolic level of the test organisms: low temperatures and anoxemic conditions increase the chance for survival and enhance tissue resistance. Thyroxine greatly increases the lethality of a given dose by the accompanying increased oxygen consumption. Vigorous exercise has the same effect. After irradiation with 600 r, a sublethal dose, 50 per cent of exercised rats died, whereas unirradiated exercised and irradiated nonexercised animals all survived.[1]

10. There are three reasons why genetic damage is more serious than that to other cell constituents: (a) a gene mutation or chromosome loss is virtually irreparable; (b) a gene or chromosome change is reproduced and handed down to cells or individuals; (c) a cell and its descendants needs its normal system of thousands of genes to avoid disturbances since its functioning is a chain of thousands of links, a break in any one of which may snap the chain and wreck it permanently. The individual gene or chromosome is not necessarily more sensitive to radiation, but the sensitivity must be multiplied by their vast number in order to measure true vulnerability.

---

[1] D. J. Kimeldorft, D. C. Jones, and M. C. Fishler, *Science*, **112**, 175 (Aug. 11, 1950).

11. Damage may occur from genetic changes even at the lowest intensities. In other words, there is no threshold dose. In the light of present knowledge it seems impossible for the spontaneous mutations to be due to unavoidable radiation. Table 12-3 lists the estimates of "natural" radiation by various authorities.

TABLE 12-3. UNAVOIDABLE DAILY RADIATION

Source	Dose per day, r	Observer
Cosmic rays, sea level.....................	0.0001	Sievert
Cosmic rays + local γ.....................	0.0003	Evans
Naturally occurring radioelements...........	0.001	Sievert
Cosmic rays + ground radiation............	0.002	Lea
Radioelements in the body................	0.0001	Brues
$\quad$ C^{14}, 3×10^{-6}		
$\quad$ K^{40}, 1×10^{-4}		
$\quad$ Ra, 4×10^{-6}		
Probable maximum........................	0.0021 = 2.1 mr	

Experiments with animals indicate that continued exposure to 0.1 r per working day or a total of 30 r each year might shorten life possibly by 3 years on the average in a population (a dose of 30 r will also double the number of mutations over the spontaneous rate). The more concentrated these small doses, the greater the chance of proportionality of loss of pieces of chromosome to a power higher than 1 of the dosage, and hence the greater the chance of permanent damage in comparison with the same total dose distributed over a long period. As already indicated, gene changes are probably independent of dosage rate since only single hits are required.

It is clear that the greatest care is required in regard to the dosage received by reproductive organs in fluoroscopy, skin therapy, and other treatments. Exposure of patients by successive radiologists without inquiry as to prior use of radiation, and general apathy are obstacles to be confronted in a campaign of education. Those opposing restrictions and scoffing at danger point out that evolution has come about as a result of mutations; therefore, they claim, the increase in mutation frequency will only cause a speeding up of this progressive process. But Muller points out the subtle error. Each species has a spontaneous mutation frequency which has been regulated in the past by natural selection so as to be not much too high or too low. Natural selection has worked by choosing genes which have appropriate effects, plus or minus, on the spontaneous mutation frequency. Hence any increase in this frequency by artificial means would not speed up evolution in such a species but must hasten degeneration by producing mutations faster than they can advantageously be utilized.[1]　Actually it is fortunate that there is some somatic damage to the exposed generation; for if the individual himself realizes his *own* risk, better protection will be provided and thus the interests of future generations will be protected as well.　The recent work at Oak Ridge on radiation hazards to the embryo and fetus, described in the following section, is evidence of the necessity for extreme precautions.

These are some of the reasons why the world is now so radiation-conscious and looks with such concern upon the new generations at Hiroshima and Nagasaki, where survivors of atomic bombs were subjected to intense ionizing radiations.

VI. Effects on Embryos.　Closely related to the effects on chromosomes and genes are those on the developing embryo.　Here some of the most amazing evidence of the power of x-radiation is displayed.　From a growing fund of experimental observations two examples are cited.　T. C. Evans in his great work on all phases of the effects of x-radiation on grasshopper eggs[2] found that the frequency of appearance of abnormal embryos such as are illustrated in Fig. 174 is highest in the sixth and seventh days of development, which is a period of expansion and fundamental differentiation, with an optimum dosage of 200 to 400 r.　This period corresponds to the gastrulation stage in many other organisms which has been found most susceptible to radiation.　The anomalies are the result of injurious selective action of x-rays on more active cells, causing removal of inhibitory control over the development of cells of the head regions which have retained the potentiality of forming whole embryos.　It is evident that embryonal rapidly dividing cells are extremely sensitive to radiations.

In a study of the effects of x-rays on the developing chick,[3] dosages of 40 to 600 r and at egg ages ranging from 19 to 243 hr were given.　The following interesting results were noted:

1. In 45 per cent, there was no further development after irradiation.
2. In 24 per cent, chicks died in the shell at full development.
3. In 11.9 per cent, chicks died after developing 15 ± days.
4. In 9 per cent, the legs of the chicks were paralyzed.
5. In 6 per cent, the legs and feet were deformed, ranging from distortion of toes to a total absence of one or both feet.
6. In 1.4 per cent, there was a hydrocephalic head deformity.
7. In 1 per cent, there were miscellaneous deformities (brain, wing, beak, etc.)

In recent work[4] x-rays have been found to exert both an acute and a delayed toxic effect on the chick embryo.　The acute effect results in

---

[1] H. J. Muller, Radiation Damage to Genetic Material, *Am. Scientist*, **38**, 33, 399 (1950).

[2] *Physiol. Zoöl.*, **10**, 58 (1937).

[3] Essenberg, *Radiology*, **25**, 739 (1935).

[4] D. A. Karnofsky, P. A. Patterson, and L. P. Ridgeway, *Am. J. Roentgenol. Radium Therapy*, **64**, 280 (1950).

death of the embryo within 20 hr after irradiation.   In embryos 8 days and older the acute toxic effect is dependent on a dose rate above 5 to 10 r/min and is relatively independent of the total dose above 800 r.   The delayed effects of x-rays are cumulative, and the LD_{50} for chick embryos of 2 to 12 days of age is in the range of 1,000 to 1,500 r at dose rates varying from 1 to 43.4 r.   The effects are still cumulative to produce delayed deaths at a dose rate of 0.55 r/min.   The embryos succumbing to the delayed lethal effect of radiation may show vascular injury and hemorrhage, generalized edema, consisting of either a watery or a gelatinous fluid, necrosis of the liver, and stunting in growth.   Developmental abnormalities are common and are chiefly evident in the beak, limbs, head, and eyes.   These toxic and pathological effects may be observed even in irradiated hatched chicks.   Acute deaths are produced in young chicks at dose rates above 10 r/min and total doses of 1,000 r.   The delayed LD_{50}, in those chicks surviving the acute effects of high dose rates, is about 800 r and at low dose rates is 1,100 to 1,200 r.   Adult chickens of both sexes may die at total doses of 1,250 to 3,000 r, but they have often survived a dose of 5,000 r for several days.

The most comprehensive and provocative of all studies on radiation hazards to embryo and fetus is the recent work from Oak Ridge.[1]   The malformations induced by radiation in a variety of animals are illustrated in Fig. 175 for mice.   There is no reason to doubt that the significant findings apply to human embryos.   There are well-defined critical periods in the development of most characters; gross abnormalities in mice occur at a time which, in man, corresponds to the second to sixth week of gestation, during which pregnancy may still be unsuspected. Irradiation at more advanced stages produces less obvious and delayed effects, which in human beings may be as harmful as gross monstrosities. It seems evident that the malformations are due to direct radiation effect on the embryo rather than indirect action following maternal injury. Doses as low as 25 r applied at the critical time certainly produce particular changes, and it is possible that lower doses within the range used in diagnostic fluoroscopy may cause in human beings important developmental alterations.   A time schedule of radiation effects on malformations in embryos based upon recent careful experimental work with rats is diagrammatically shown in Fig. 176.   All these results point to the necessity of avoiding even diagnostic irradiation during pregnancy.

VII. The Effects of X-rays on Normal Cells.   The very first step in a long series of events attendant upon irradiation of cells is a purely physical one—the collision of radiation quanta with electrons in the atoms and molecules of the chemical substances of a cell, and the release of these photoelectrons, leaving ionized atoms, or the raising of electrons to higher energy levels, leaving an activated atom or molecule.   The ionized

[1] L. B. Russell and W. L. Russell, *Radiology*, **58**, 369 (1952).

or activated atoms have properties no longer to be associated with the original unirradiated atom.   The protoplasm and the protein molecules are of necessity changed and are usually broken down to other substances ordinarily simpler.   These degradation products or molecular fragments must be as foreign to the cell in its normal structure and functions as though we had introduced materials from the outside by some micro-inoculation.   Under these circumstances the morphology and physiology of the cell must change in such a way that at least the gross features can be recognized by the histologist and physiologist.

1. All changes follow a latent period after irradiation, which may be very short if our methods of detection are sufficiently sensitive for minute structural, chemical, and biological changes but may be very

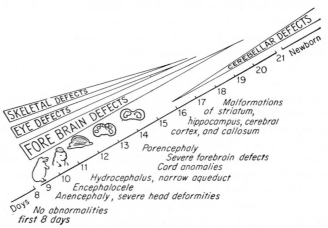

Fig. 176. Timetable of radiation malformations.   [*S. P. Hicks, Am. J. Roentgenol. Radium Therapy Nuclear Med.*, **69**, 272 (1953).]

long if we judge only by death or a gross phenomenon such as skin erythema.   This latency is not yet explained, except that the radiation induces in the nucleus of the cell certain chemical changes which only gradually run their course and only at their completion set free irritative or destructive action.   An entire symposium of 16 papers on the after-effects of radiation has been recently published.[1]   Especially delayed are the effects on fats, chromosome breakage, inactivation of the enzymes, pepsin and trypsin, and of bacteriophage, etc.   Many of these effects are markedly dependent on temperature.   However, very rapid acute toxic effects are also observed in the case of chick embryos mentioned in the preceding section.

2. It has long been known that exposure of young organisms to suffi-ciently large doses of short-wavelength radiation inhibits subsequent growth and development.   That there is a marked effect upon normal

[1] *Trans. Faraday Soc.*, **49**, 323 (1953).

cells is unquestioned. But the *possible seat of attack of the radiation* (and the high-speed photoelectrons liberated by it) is a far more difficult problem. Much research in the past years has attempted to find the mechanism, but the answer is as yet incomplete. In studies with plants such as wheat and oat seedlings, Skoog and others proposed, in 1934, that inhibition of growth is attributable to the destruction of a growth-promoting substance, or plant hormone, auxin, which is produced in twice as great amount in light-grown seedlings as compared with dark-grown. Chesley has found this hypothesis supported experimentally in some but not in all respects. Considerably less is known about x-ray effects on growth-promoting hormones in animal or human tissues.

3. Translucent protoplasm first becomes turbid and then granular, indicating that the state of aggregation of protein molecules completely changes, because of disturbance in distribution of electric charges making for coagulation. The same effect may be produced in vitro by chemical effects and unfavorable mediums. Obviously, since irradiated cells are known to return to normal unless subjected to unbearable dosages, the process can be reversible. One theory due to Dessauer, and held by a number of radiologists, was coagulation by minute points of radiation heat generated in the tissue from the conversion of kinetic energy of the photoelectrons.

4. Many workers have demonstrated the stickiness, shrinking, and clumping of chromosomes, moving irregularly to daughter cells, some lagging behind and some entering the wrong cell. Many of these chromosome aberrations may be classed as temporary. In more advanced stages the chromatin falls to pieces, and the pieces swell up and fill the cell body. After very heavy x-ray dosage the protoplasm is vacuolized and the mitochondria are fragmented; of course, death follows.

The number of chromosome fragments in cells varies with the dose; one or two may be seen after 25 r and five or more after 300 r. The number of cells with fragments also increases. As already indicated, cells with short development and resting stages, or those which have frequent mitoses, are more sensitive to radiation and suffer a greater amount of damage than cells with a longer life cycle. It is now clear that desoxynucleic acid, an essential constituent of nuclei, is directly involved in chromosome breakage through its depolymerization by irradiation, along with chemical changes in other constituents.

5. The rate of cell division is changed. It is a universal finding that cells which are in mitosis at the time of exposure to x-rays complete the division even with inordinately high dosages up to nearly 100,000 r, while other cells are prevented from undergoing mitosis. They lose motility and then may literally explode. After a while they may regain apparent normal behavior but occasionally after a few further divisions may die suddenly. In work in the author's laboratory on salamander larvae, the

depressing effect of x-rays on mitotic division was clearly demonstrated. A study of the neural tube of the larvae, given sublethal dosages of 400 and 800 r, reveals as the initial effect a disappearance of mitotic figures from the germinal cells of the ependymal layer; a period of pseudo recovery, lasting 4 or 5 hr, during which mitotic activity reappears; a period of severe degenerative changes, occurring mainly among cells in the resting stage; and a period of remarkable regeneration which leads to evident recovery. Irradiation causes mitochondria to enspherulate at a dosage of 1,200 r given at a single exposure. The Golgi substance gives no specific reaction and is regarded most resistant. From this work the cell components in the order of their sensitiveness to irradiation are found to be as follows: nucleus, mitochondria, and Golgi substance.

The dose required to induce chromosome disturbance, leading to death of the cell through breakdown of mitosis, may be only 50 to 100 r, while a much higher dose is needed to kill a cell irrespective of mitosis. Here again desoxyribosenucleic acid is involved. As it is synthesized by the cell from various fragments, a level of concentration is reached which results in cell division. If this synthesis is interfered with, as by irradiation, possible through inactivation of an essential enzyme, the mitotic process is stopped. For ribonucleotides accumulate in the cytoplasm owing to the inability of the irradiated cell to reduce ribonucleotide to desoxyribonucleotides in the nucleus. That oxidation plays an important role in this effect upon mitosis, as well as in many other biological effects of radiation, is proved by the experiments in which the presence of oxygen greatly accelerates these changes in comparison with the results of the same irradiation in the absence or reduced concentrations of this element.

6. Often the marked swelling of irradiated nuclei and the ballooning of the cytoplasm are easily observed and must be interpreted as an increased capacity of these structures to absorb water through an altered cell membrane. Although this system is too complex for complete understanding and explanation, it is logical to believe that intracellular changes produce new electrolytes by decomposition of salts, proteins, and fats and that water is drawn in by simple osmosis.

7. The viscosity of protoplasm is increased following irradiation, although the first effect may be liquefaction.

8. The hydrogen-ion concentration is increased for the protoplasm. This effect may last for only a very short time in the case of the skin up to hours and days, for example, in lymphoid tissue. The importance of this in therapy will become readily apparent when it is considered that in cancer the blood becomes decidedly more alkaline.

9. Cell respiration is decreased, according to a number of workers (Gottschalk and Nonnenbruch, Evans, Noller, Crabtree). On the other hand, Chesley irradiated wheat seedlings and marine eggs with x- and γ-rays in such doses as markedly to impede growth as measured 24 hr

after treatment and found that oxygen consumption per gram of growing tissue is not affected. In other words, growth is inhibited before respiratory rate changes. Developmental anomalies in the marine eggs appear before the respiratory rate is altered and do not depend upon respiratory impairment.

10. Some processes are accelerated, such as the keratinization of epidermal cells.

11. Curtis, in work on such invertebrates as coelenterates, planarians, and annelids, Sheremetjava and Brunst, with axolotls, and Butler, with the vertebrate *Amblystoma*, have shown that the normal ability of these species to regenerate lost parts is completely destroyed when subjected to x-radiation. Hence, x-rays afford a method of studying experimentally the differentiation process in regeneration as compared with differentiation in normal embryonic development.

12. Several effects of x-rays on the blood and blood supply of tissues have been newly studied.[1] There is evidence that the perfusion rate of blood through the liver may be decreased after acute irradiation. Mice showed a 30 per cent reduction in rate of uptake of colloidal chromic phosphate by the liver, divided between a reduction in phagocytic efficiency and decreased perfusion rate. There are disturbances in the coagulability of blood, and the development of opalescence of blood serum, due to lipids in dispersed particles much larger than normal. In rabbits this effect, developed during the first 24 hr after irradiation, is prognostic of subsequent death. The uptake of iron by bone marrow in red-cell formation decreases by 50 per cent for a dose of 150 r.

13. Cytological analysis has proved that radiation-induced damage in normal cells of any human tissue is the same as that observed in experimental material and also in *tumor cells*. Because the division rate in normal tissues is lower than in tumors, fewer normal cells are killed through the damage induced in their chromosome mechanism than tumor cells. This is the reason why healthy, normal tissue cells which surround the tumor can tolerate a greater quantity of radiation energy than the malignant cells. This makes the treatment of tumors by radiation possible.[2]

14. The very earliest stages of radiation damage are strikingly shown by a new technique developed by the United States Army Medical Research Laboratory at Fort Knox, employing staining of living protoplasm by fluorochromes, especially acridine orange.[3] *Allium cepa* epi-

[1] H. B. Jones, Some Physiological Factors Related to the Effects of Radiation in Mammals, "Symposium on Radiobiology, 1952," p. 414, John Wiley & Sons, Inc., New York.

[2] P. C. Koller, *Brit. J. Radiol.*, Supplement 1, p. 84, 1947.

[3] S. P. Strugger, A. T. Krebs, and Z. S. Gierlach, *Am. J. Roentgenol. Radium Therapy Nuclear Med.*, **70**, 365 (1953).

dermis (onionskin) irradiated with adequate x-ray doses to produce damage, then immediately stained, showed the initial effects in the form of "spots" along the cell walls, due to partial destruction of cytoplasmic areas. Irradiated sections, stained at different time intervals after irradiation, showed a spreading of damage as a result of delayed effects. Damage in prestained sections can be observed in a minute after irradiation begins.

15. Since it is believed that the whole action of radiation is due to the liberation of high-speed electrons whose energy, upon being stopped, produces destruction, the effects on cells are generally independent of wavelength of x-rays (except that monochromatic rays seem to be more effective than polychromatic, as previously noted). But the biological effects in the bulk of *tissue* as a whole vary enormously with the wavelength as a result of back scatter, damage or closing of the blood vessels, vasometer changes, poisonous effects from decomposition products set free from dying or dead cells or by formation of hydrogen peroxide in water, etc. Indirect effects which are indicated by the fact that normal tissue surrounding a tumor greatly increases the efficiency of radiation action on the tumor itself are discussed on page 312.

16. In the very intensive work carried on under the Plutonium Project[1] on the effects of irradiation on cells and tissue, usually by whole-body treatment of animals, prior results are verified that irradiation does not cause specific effects, for these are strikingly like those produced, for example, with mustard gas in blood-forming organs and the intestinal tract.[2] Furthermore, with a single exception there are no qualitative differences in reactions of animals to comparably effective doses of x-rays, γ-rays, fast and slow neutrons, and, for the skin, external β-rays. These agents at $LD_{50}/30$ (lethal dose for 50 per cent of a population after 30 days) cannot be differentiated in the same animal species on the basis of histological effects. The single exception is a greater effectiveness of x-rays on bone marrow of the metaphysis. A dose of 1 n of fast neutrons is ordinarily four to five times as effective as 1 r of x-rays.

VIII. The Radiosensitiveness of Cells. This is the basis of one of the most important applications of radiation in biology, of identification of cells, of medical diagnosis, and of x-ray therapy.

---

[1] "Histopathology of Irradiation from External and Internal Sources" (National Nuclear Energy Series); edited by William Bloom, McGraw-Hill Book Company, Inc., New York, 1948.

[2] That there are striking differences, however, in the mechanisms and effects between the so-called radiomimetic chemicals and ionizing radiations is demonstrated by L. H. Gray, *Radiation Research*, **1**, 189 (1954). The arguments for an identity of primary causes, and thus for the overthrow of the concept of tracks (the essence of radiobiological theory) which can have no place in a theory of chemical mutagenesis, cannot be supported.

For many years cells were classified, according to their radiosensitiveness, in the order listed in Table 12-4.

TABLE 12-4. RELATIVE SENSITIVITY OF A NORMAL TISSUE TO RADIATION OF MEDIUM HARDNESS (SKIN = 1.0)

Leukocytes:
  2.5 Lymphocytes
  2.4 Polynuclear
Epithelial cells of salivary glands
Germinal cells:
  2.3 Ovarian
  2.2 Testicular
Blood-forming organs:
  2.1 Spleen
  2.0 Lymphatic tissue
  1.9 Bone marrow
Endocrine glands:
  1.8 Thymus
  1.7 Thyroid
  1.6 Adrenal
Blood vessels:
  1.5 Endothelium (intima)

Dermal structures:
  1.4 Hair papillae
  1.3 Sweat glands
  1.2 Sebaceous glands
  1.1 Mucous membrane
  1.0 Skin
  0.9 Serous membrane
Viscera:
  0.8 Intestine
  0.7 Liver, pancreas
  0.6 Uterus, kidney
Connective tissue:
  0.5 Fibrous tissue
  0.4 Muscle, fibrocartilage
  0.3 Bone
  0.2 Nerve tissue
  0.1 Fat

Since 1944 many radiologists have classified tissues and tumors as follows:

Radiosensitive—those severely damaged by less than 2,000 r in divided therapeutic doses.
Radioresponsive—affected by 2,500 to 5,000 r.
Radioresistant—unaffected by less than 5,000 r.

In the Plutonium Project already referred to the subject of radiosensitivity has been critically examined. Differences are grouped among: (1) species; (2) individuals within species; (3) organs; (4) cells. The differences between species is markedly shown by the $LD_{50}/30$ of x-rays for guinea pigs, 175 r; rats, 600 r; rabbits, 800 r. There is no essential difference histologically between individuals though some survive a given dose and some do not. Young animals are more sensitive than old. Radiation accelerates aging processes such as sealing off of bone growth in the metaphysis and age involution in the thymus. Repeatedly it has been proved that in organs lymphatic tissue, testis, ovary, etc., are very sensitive. The sensitivity of cells cannot be uniquely rated, according to this late work, since the environment is a determining factor. The same cells may be resistant in vitro and sensitive in vivo. In lymph nodes lymphocytes of various sizes are equally sensitive, while in the spleen the medium-sized cell is more sensitive than either large or small lymphocytes.

The relative sensitiveness of blood cells in 1-day-old chicks has been determined by Roberts, Card, and Clark,[1] with doses of 360 and 720 r,

[1] *Biodynamica*, **6**, 165 (1948).

given over periods of 120, 30, and 6 minutes. Typical data for the smaller dosage of blood counts (average number per cubic millimeter), made 48 hr after treatment, are given in Table 12-5. This table shows that the lymphocytes are most sensitive and that the number is significantly lower in chicks irradiated for 120 min than in those given the same dosage in 30 min. The mean number of basophils is also reduced, as are leukocytes, but the remaining types are not significantly affected. The reduction in the number of lymphocytes by x-rays caused an immediate decrease in the resistance of baby chicks to pullorum disease.

TABLE 12-5. BLOOD COUNTS OF 1-DAY-OLD CHICKS

Treatment.................	None	360 r, 120 min	360 r, 30 min
Number of chicks............	177	176	177
Erythrocytes.................	1,794,230	1,778,570	1,807,580
Leukocytes..................	10,508	7,511	7,537
Heterophils.................	4,385	4,944	4,377
Lymphocytes................	5,476	2,373	2,986
Monocytes..................	78.3	56.1	55.9
Eosinophils.................	103.3	82.4	74.8
Basophils...................	130.7	55.2	37.3

To summarize: Primitive cells are more damaged by irradiation than adjacent, more differentiated cells, though this is true in many locations but not in all. Radioresistance is a regular function not so much of primitiveness of the cell as of its condition at the time of irradiation. Cells in mitosis or about to enter mitosis are most affected, and thus in resistant tissues like brain and muscle mitoses are rare—this is true in almost all cases. The different sensitivity of normal and malignant cells to radiation can be attributed primarily to the different life cycle of these cells. Cells of normal tissues which undergo frequent mitosis (bone-marrow, testis, embryonic tissue) and which have a short development are just as sensitive as cells of the tumor, or more so. Herein lies the danger in cancer therapy, and the requirement for expert diagnosis and treatment.

Although the difference in susceptibility between the most sensitive and the least sensitive varieties of cells is considerable, none of the cells is wholly invulnerable to radiation; all cells, whatever their variety, may be destroyed or injured if exposed to a sufficiently large dose of rays, especially if doses within the therapeutic range are disregarded.

IX. Recovery and the Time Factor. Closely connected with sensitiveness is the power of recovery, obviously a phenomenon of enormous importance in therapy. The protozoan paramecium can recover after x-ray dosages as high as 60,000 r. Numerous experiments have demonstrated that the best recovery is associated with the *low* reproductive and metabolic rate of the cells. Hence, susceptibility and recuperative powers are inversely proportional. It is not surprising that the intensity of the x-ray beam has a determining effect on the biological change. Weak dosages over a long time are decidedly less effective than intense radiation delivered in a short time. Holthusen found that, with intensities varying from 500 to 0.5 r/min, erythema resulted with a total of 500 r for the maximum intensity; with a total of 1,200 r for a beam of 5 r/min for 240 min; and with a total of 2,000 r for an intensity of 0.5 r/min. Thus a much larger total amount of radiation may actually be given underlying tissues by the fractional weak doses, without fear of skin injury or scarring, than with a single exposure to intense radiation. An injury slowly effected may be offset by definite repair processes. Packard calls attention to the analogy of a burning house. The most inflammable objects go first and then those which are more resistant. But when the house becomes a furnace of flame, everything is consumed equally, regardless of whether some materials are slightly more resistant than others. So with intense doses, all tissues are injured, whereas with prolonged weak irradiation even small differences in susceptibility are revealed.

Recovery from damage by ionizing radiation is a sensitive function of temperature and nutrition, as shown by experiments on bacteria.[1] *Escherichia coli* survives an otherwise lethal dose of x-rays if it is incubated at suboptimal temperatures (12 to 30°) after exposure. Also some bacteria may be restored by postirradiation treatment with catalase, which seems to divert long-lived organic peroxides from the lethal pathway by means of coupled oxidations.[2] However, the most important experimental observation is that on the effect of regionally fractionated irradiation. Greatly lowered mortality results from 875-r x-radiation of the entire body in mice if the abdomen is exposed 90 min prior to or following exposure of the remainder of the body. Shielding the exteriorized spleens of mice during total body exposure to 900 r brings about appreciable reduction in radiation mortality even though the spleens alone have been irradiated with the same dose prior to exposure of the body. These results indicate the existence of a factor (or factors) emanating from the body region *shielded* during the first irradiation and acting to protect or promote recovery in the region or organ *exposed* in that irradiation.[3]

X. X-ray Effects on Human Tissues. *Action on the Skin.* According to the dose applied, it is customary to recognize four degrees of skin reaction.

[1] A. Hollaender, G. E. Stapleton, and D. Billen (Oak Ridge), *Trans. Faraday Soc.,* **49**, 331 (1953).

[2] R. Latarjet, *Trans. Faraday Soc.,* **49**, 334 (1953).

[3] M. N. Swift, S. T. Taketa, and V. P. Bond, *Radiation Research,* **1**, 241 (1954)

First degree. No visible inflammation, but epilation followed by tanning; lasts 2 to 4 weeks and is followed by complete recovery.

Second degree. Moderate erythema with definite vascular dilation (hyperemia) and a sensation of increased temperature in the treated area; epilation and pigmentation; duration 6 to 12 weeks, with eventual recovery and disappearance of tanning.

Third degree. Erythema of reddish-blue color with vesiculation; epilation; loss of papillae and of sweat and sebaceous glands; pain; duration 8 to 15 weeks; heals with epilated thin scar and often develops telangiectasis in an atrophic scar; danger of late reaction years after the injury.

Fourth degree. Deep reddish-blue erythema with vesiculation and necrosis of cutis, developing into an ulcer; extremely painful; prognosis as to complete recovery doubtful. In most cases, wide excision is the only remedy.

It is obvious, of course, that between these four degrees there are all types of variation possible.

Numerous histological studies of the irradiated skin have been undertaken; they lead to the conclusion that the acute x-ray reaction of the skin is essentially a degeneration of the epithelium (germinative layer), combined with inflammatory processes (interstitial edema and leukocyte infiltration). There are also changes in the capillaries, namely, dilatation and later thickening of the walls. This picture is most characteristic in the base of a typical ulcer resulting from an x-ray burn.

Entirely different from this acute reaction in the skin are the findings of radiologists following the cumulative effect of numerous small doses or x-rays. Marked blood-vessel changes are absent. There are hyperemia, changes in the blood distribution, and hypertrophy of the epithelium (hyperkeratosis). Hair papillae and sweat and sebaceous glands have almost disappeared. Usually, there is edema in the corium accompanied by atrophy of the elastic elements. Microscopically, an acute ulcer can present the same changes, and that, undoubtedly, explains the tendency of both to terminate in malignant degeneration (roentgen carcinoma).

Other Tissues. The effects on other organs and tissues are those to be predicted from the general radiosensitiveness of the constituent cells, summarized as follows:

Circulating blood—resistant; but coagulability is decreased, owing to reduction in prothrombin following liver damage or in thromboplastin following bone-marrow damage or the production of an anticoagulant.[1]

Bone-marrow-stem cells from which red cells arise—very sensitive.

Genital glands—very sensitive; 30 per cent of an erythema dose (600 r) effective in the testicle will produce temporary sterility; 50 per cent will produce permanent sterility; 28 and 34 per cent, respectively, effective in the ovaries will produce temporary and permanent sterilization; irradiation causes marked atrophy, especially of ovarian follicles.

[1] Silverman, *Am. J. Roentgenol. Radium Therapy*, **62**, 541 (1949).

Liver—resistant.

Lung—production of fibrosis.

Kidney—interstitial nephrosis with heavy doses.

Thyroid gland and goiter—resistant.

Thymus gland—very sensitive.

Pituitary and adrenal glands—fairly susceptible.

Intestinal mucosa—destroyed by large doses.

Nervous systems (spinal cord, brain)—large doses without symptoms.

Eye—insensitive except lens.

Bone—with not too intense doses, resistant, except marrow and epiphyseal junctures, where permanent shortening of limbs of young people may result from checking of growth by two or three doses of 540 r.

General Systemic Effect. Following the application of a sufficiently high dose of x-rays to the human body, the organism responds, in a certain percentage of patients, with a syndrome of symptoms usually embraced under the term "x-ray sickness." The clinical picture nearest to it is that of the well-known seasickness. Numerous investigations have been undertaken to find the cause of this systemic reaction, and several theories have been advanced to explain that x-ray sickness is, in all probability, due to the flooding of the organism with the products of cell destruction following the irradiation. This involves seepage of blood from the vessels, an effect which may be connected with lowered clotting power. This in turn may be caused by prior destruction of the multiplying cells that form the blood platelets which help to control the clotting.

Other theories list as causes the lowering of sodium chloride content in blood serum (in many cases injection of 5 per cent salt solution has been effective); decrease in cholesterol content; increase in calcium and decrease in potassium; nitrogen increase in blood; formation of H_2O_2 in water and H_2S from sulfur-containing amino acids, etc., acting as poisons; liberation of histaminelike substances (though there is only a slight effect from the new antihistamine drugs or atropine);[1] changes in protein; changes in blood sugar; increase in blood coagulability; change in sedimentation rate of red-blood corpuscles; release of H substance from injured cells, etc. Injection of 1 cc of liver extract is effective in eliminating this effect. However, Wood points out that nausea occurs only when the abdomen is irradiated and that the sympathetic ganglia and adrenal glands must be responsible.

XI. The Indirect Reaction to Radiation. One of the oldest problems connected with an analysis of the effects of irradiation upon protoplasm is whether or not irradiation releases substances capable of adversely affecting other parts of the body. The existence of such toxic substances is suggested by the marked generalized symptoms (radiation sickness) produced in patients as a result of exposure to localized irradiation. This is the reason for the interest in the reactions of hydrogen peroxide or H,

[1] Larkin, *Am. J. Roentgenol. Radium Therapy*, **62**, 547 (1949).

OH, and HO_2 free radicals discussed in the previous chapter—the so-called poisoning, or indirect, action.   It is safe to say that the effects of irradiation in a radiosensitive organ are more pronounced at a given level of whole-body irradiation than at a higher level of localized irradiation. Hydrogen peroxide which destroys catalase, the vitally important enzyme in vitro, also destroys it when injected into intact mice; x-radiation of whole mice also brings about a sharp reduction in catalase activity of the liver.[1]   That poisons in the blood stream are responsible for generalized symptoms is proved in a recent experiment.   Irradiated dogs were transfused with blood from nonirradiated dogs.   Of control irradiated dogs a much larger per cent died than of irradiated transfused animals.

It is certain that tumors are greatly affected by irradiation of surrounding normal tissue; some in the body may be eliminated by as small a dose as 3,200 r,† whereas 20,000 or more is required to destroy isolated tumor tissue in vitro.   Those cells which lie on the periphery of the infiltrating tumor edge have a high division rate, and they are also the ones in contact with connective tissue and thus in the most favorable location to the food supply derived from or through this tissue.   A disturbance in histological organization of connective tissue then results in the tumor cells being deprived of food supply and thus leads to suppression of mitosis and destruction.   Thus differences in response of tumors to radiation are often due to differences in the relationship of tumor and tumor bed and in radiation-induced stroma reaction.   Fibrosarcomas resist treatment because the connective tissue itself is malignant and only the direct action of radiation is effective, whereas in other cases such as tuberculous glands doses of radiation too small for direct damage may effect cure by indirect action.

The suppression of mitosis suggests that radiation alters nucleic-acid and protein-forming systems of the cell, which underlies cell division as previously described.   Thus Mitchell,[2] using an ultraviolet absorption method of analysis, showed that irradiation prevented the conversion of ribose into desoxyribosenucleic acid, which is needed for chromosome synthesis and mitosis.   Ross and Ely[3] found upon irradiation a marked reduction in the amounts of nucleic acid and of tyrosine, tryptophan, arginine, and nitrogen and thus of total protein in the cells of the rat intestine.   The synthesis of thymo- and ribonucleic acids in living tissue, especially cancerous, is greatly reduced by x-radiation both directly and indirectly, i.e., from irradiation of another part of the body from the screened-off tumor.

[1] Feinstein, Butler, and Hendley, Science, 111, 149 (1950).

† Koller and Smithers, Brit. J. Radiol., 19, 89 (1946).

[2] J. L. Mitchell, Brit. J. Radiol., 16, 339 (1943).

[3] M. H. Ross and J. O. Ely, Am. J. Roentgenol. Radium Therapy, 62, 718 (1949).

Most of the investigations concerned with effects of ionizing radiation on living cells have been concerned with the nucleus. There is very little information on possible disturbances of cytoplasmatic functions, although the complicated chemical picture of radiation sickness suggests that these must be abundant. It has now been found that there is a disturbance of energy supply provided by oxidative phosphorylation which is centered in the mitochondria of the cytoplasm. A 50 per cent decrease in phosphorylative activity and a decrease in oxygen consumption were found in mitochondria isolated from spleen cells of rats after whole-body irradiation with 1,100 r.†

XII. Stimulating Effect of Irradiation. For years the legend that x-rays or radium, under certain conditions of dosage, may increase the growth and metabolism of cells has gained wide circulation. This notion has arisen from the attempt to apply to these agents the so-called Arndt-Schultz law, according to which small doses stimulate and large doses depress cellular metabolism. Based on pharmacologic grounds, this doctrine has not been generally accepted, even by pharmacologists. The attempt to apply it to the action of x-rays is unwarranted, for the experimental evidence on which it is based is extremely meager and apparently invalid. A measure of acceleration is a transient phase of reaction and is invariably followed by more or less pronounced inhibition of function and cellular degeneration. Another factor in the propagation of this notion of a stimulating action of the rays has been the regression of pathological lesions after exposure to small doses of x-rays. Such regression is best explained by the exceptional radiosensitiveness of certain varieties of cells. As the result of primary degeneration of certain cells a secondary and indirect stimulation may sometimes be observed. Such is the increase in connective-tissue cells in certain tissues and organs after repeated irradiation; the connective tissue is laid down to replace other cells that the rays have caused to undergo degeneration. Any primary, or direct, acceleration of cellular metabolism must be regarded as an effort of the cell to counteract or compensate for the noxious influence of the rays; in other words, it is purely a defense reaction. Continued acceleration of metabolism cannot be induced by x-rays or radium, which always cause degenerative changes or have no effect whatever. Irradiation of certain tissues, such as the skin, repeated over a long period of time may cause hyperplasia of the epithelium, and this in turn may lead to malignant transformation. This is not stimulation in the sense here employed, but the alteration of a normal to an aberrant function due to chronic irritation.

In the extensive Plutonium Project experiments there were no evi-

† D. W. van Bekkum, H. J. Jongepier, H. T. M. Nieuwerkerk, and J. A. Cohen, *Trans. Faraday Soc.*, **49**, 329 (1953).

dences whatever of stimulation in any zone of tissue at any distance from the point of irradiation. However, some experiments seemed to indicate that some degree of radioresistance may develop, especially with radioactive isotopes, but not for the most sensitive types of cells.

A stimulating effect with decidedly abnormal results is illustrated in Fig. 177, from United States Navy experiments. A rat, given a heavy dose of x-rays, grew an extra pair of lower front teeth with abnormal, weakened dentine and enamel. At the same time the upper teeth were stunted. The conclusion is that teeth of patients, particularly children, must be protected during x-ray treatment for any disease of the face.

New experiments by Pape and others in 1953 (see page 315 on protective action) indicating that a preliminary dose of as little as $\frac{1}{4}$ r may have a powerful protective effect against subsequent massive doses (600 r) delivered to germinal epithelium of rat testicle again open the question of the stimulating effect of x-rays in small doses ($\frac{1}{4}$ to 20 r).

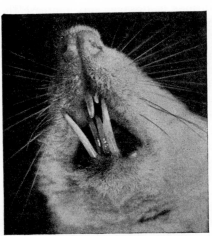

FIG. 177. Production of extra pair of lower teeth and deterioration of upper teeth of irradiated rat. (*U.S. Navy, previously published in Life*, 1953.)

XIII. Photochemical Experiments with a Possible Bearing on Biological Effects. As indicated in the preceding chapter, a considerable number of experiments on the photochemical effects of x-rays on simple systems have been attempted in the effort to throw some light on observed biological effects. However, there are very few chemical reactions in which the measurable change on irradiation is comparable with changes in the normal or abnormal cell. Of direct significance biologically are the following:

1. Formation of hydrogen peroxide when water containing dissolved oxygen is irradiated.
2. Decomposition of water (comprising 70 per cent of cells) only in the presence of a catalyst such as iodide ion; formation of H, OH, and HO_2 free radicals.
3. Precipitation of proteins produced by irradiation of serum or albumin in vitro; denaturation.
4. Change of phenol group of tyrosine in aqueous solution; also tryptophan, etc.
5. Deactivation of solutions of various ferments, especially destruction of catalase, which rapidly destroys H_2O_2.
6. Oxidation of oxyhemoglobin to methemoglobin.
7. Depolymerization of desoxyribosenucleic acid, and prevention of its synthesis in cell nuclei as a requirement for mitosis.

8. Disappearance of sulfhydryl (—SH) groups in irradiated proteins,[†] these being necessary for mitosis, by oxidation of four equivalents per ion pair,

$$2 —SH + 2OH = —S—S— + 2H_2O$$
$$2 —SH + 2HO_2 = —S—S + 2H_2O_2$$
$$2 —SH + H_2O_2 = —S—S— + 2H_2O$$

9. Formation of unstable organic peroxides in irradiated amino acids, which when fed to bacteria induce mutations. The importance of unsaturated peroxide formation is proved by new experiments on irradiated mice (950 r of 250-kv x-rays). In butanol extracts of the mice by means of analysis with $SnCl_2$ a significant increase of unsaturated peroxide is measured, on the order of 2.27×10^{-7} mole/g, which is an ionic yield of 84.[‡]

Peroxide formation is certainly involved in irradiated fats, as proved by experiments with butterfat.[1] Two distinct reactions occur over a period of days following irradiations. The first is an increased susceptibility to autoxidation due to destruction of antioxidants (tocopherols), which stabilize unirradiated fat; after an induction period a typical chain reaction occurs which leads to hydroperoxide formation and breakdown of the fat. The second reaction is a true aftereffect, with the products still unknown although they react with standard reagents[2] for fat peroxide and with a reagent for high-molecular-weight aldehydes.[3]

10. Decomposition of very dilute solutions of organic compounds in the absence of oxygen, as measured by hydrogen, carbon dioxide, and oxygen evolution, must be the result of reaction with activated water molecules rather than a direct effect of the radiation or the formation of hydrogen peroxide. The primary reaction is evidently the attachment of the oxygen of the activated water molecule to the organic molecule, with liberation of hydrogen.

The conclusion is that biological changes produced by x-rays may result from the partial transformation of a great number of different substances present in the cell and very difficult to ascertain. However, the whole change observed in a mixture of substances, each of which would change if irradiated separately, may be in only one substance even in very low concentration. When a complex molecule is irradiated, the change may be in one sensitive bond only. When such a molecule with a physiological function is irradiated, the very first change in the molecule may and often does destroy its potency.[4]

11. Much has been made of the possibilities of secondary radiation from heavy-metal atoms in biological systems, without conclusive results.

XIV. Chemical Protection of Tissues against Radiation.

Over many years attention has been directed almost exclusively to the positive effects of and damage to cells and tissues by ionizing radiations, and in the preceding section some of the possible chemical reactions have been listed which may occur in living matter along with direct genetic damage. It is

[†] E. S. G. Barron, "Symposium on Radiobiology, 1952," p. 216, John Wiley & Sons, Inc., New York.

[‡] V. J. Horgan and J. Philpot, *Trans. Faraday Soc.*, **49**, 324 (1953).

[1] R. S. Hannan and H. J. Shepherd, *Trans. Faraday Soc.*, **49**, 326 (1953).

[2] Lea, *J. Soc. Chem. Ind.* (*London*), **65**, 286 (1946). Loftus, Hills, and Thiel, *J. Dairy Research*, **14**, 340 (1946).

[3] Shibsted, *Ind. Eng. Chem., Anal. Ed.*, **4**, 204 (1932).

[4] This and many other problems are critically examined by L. H. Gray, Some Characteristics of Biological Damage Induced by Ionizing Radiations, *Radiation Research*, **1**, 189 (1954) (71 references).

the destruction of cancer cells which has held the limelight. But the reverse process of protecting individuals or the whole population against radiation gained overwhelming importance when the first atomic bomb exploded at Hiroshima, Japan, in 1945. Intensive research investigations have continued as an important item in defense preparations. The progress already made was termed at the International Congress of Radiology, meeting in London in 1950, as the most important in radiation biochemistry since 1937; and only a beginning has been made. Some of the discoveries about chemical protection have been accidental in a sense, but all have been the result of logical ideas. For example, since sulfhydryl groups are destroyed in irradiated tissue,[1] it would seem to be logical to inject an excess of a compound containing —SH groups, preferably cysteine, to supply the deficiency. This is what Patt and associates[2] did, with enormously improved survival of rats irradiated with 800 r, whereas cystine with —S—S— groups was entirely ineffective. This has been verified by Forssberg[3] with bacteria and with guinea pigs. Cysteine injected into the skin prevents epilation, which would otherwise result. Other compounds containing —SH groups are similarly effective. Limperos and Mosher[4] found that thiourea protected desoxyribosenucleic acid against x-ray depolymerization in aqueous solution and in vivo. Injections of thiourea or use in drinking water before irradiation markedly lowered the mortality of mice, by protecting such vital cell constituents as nucleic acid and other easily oxidized constituents. The protective effect of thiourea is greatly diminished by simultaneous injection of folic acid or administering it in drinking water after irradiation. Barron and associates[5] reported that enzymes containing —SH groups are inactivated by x-rays because of oxidation of these groups, but were reactivated by addition of glutathione. Ephrati[6] found inactivation of tetanus toxin and staphylococcus hemolysis was inhibited by reducing agents such as ascorbic acid and glutathione. Obviously all these oxidizing reactions to destroy —SH groups may be connected with the production of H_2O_2, which repeatedly has been shown to be a poison as an oxidizing agent or "thioloprive" substance. Also there is a striking similarity in the protective role of cysteine, thiourea, glutathione, etc., and that of anaerobiosis (page 298). Aberrations from chromosome breakage are reduced threefold upon irradiation of cells in the absence of oxygen; hence oxygen concentration in the medium surrounding chromosomes profoundly influences their susceptibility to damage by x-rays. On the other hand anaerobiosis

[1] J. Frederic, Arch. Biol., **60**, 39 (1949).

[2] H. M. Patt et al., Science, **110**, 213 (1949).

[3] A. Forssberg, Acta Radiol., **33**, 296 (1950).

[4] G. Limperos and W. A. Mosher, Science, **112**, 86 (1950); Am. J. Roentgenol. Radium Therapy Nuclear Med., **67**, 810 (1952).

[5] E. S. G. Barron et al., J. Gen. Physiol., **32**, 537 (1949).

[6] E. Ephrati, Biochem. J., **42**, 383 (1948).

has no effect on damage influenced by α-rays, which shows that the influence of oxygen is closely linked with the type of ionizing radiation acting on the chromosome. Similar differences between x-rays and α-rays are found in H_2O_2 production in water; for the former, ionic yields depend on pH, temperature, dose rate, and concentration of dissolved oxygen, while for the latter there is no such dependence upon various factors.

Noteworthy is the recent proof in Belgium of protection against x-rays by cyanide, azide (NaN_3), malononitrile, and nitrite.[1] Mice receiving an injection of 0.1 mg of NaCN before irradiation with 600 r showed 80 per cent survival against 0 per cent survival for noninjected irradiated animals; injection after irradiation only delayed mortality. Cyanide is rapidly detoxicated into —SCN by a liver enzyme, but NaSCN has no effect, and the cyanide ion must be responsible. It is known to reduce —S—S— bonds to —SH, but in small concentration it is more likely that it inhibits some heavy-metal catalyst or enzyme responsible for H_2O_2 disposal and thus decreases the rate of reaction of the peroxide with a reducing substance. Cyanide also reduces metabolic activity and thereby, as previously indicated, the radiosensitivity of tissues. Nitrites have about the same effect. Other chemical substances such as flavonides possessing vitamin P action[2] and semicarbazone of adenochrome[3] have been reported to have protective effects. Vitamin P factors seem to have a specific affinity for the intercellular cement of the capillary wall by strengthening it and giving it protection against whole-body near-lethal doses of ionizing radiations. Blood and spleen cultures on mice subjected to a single exposure of 450- to 600-r total-body radiation showed that bacteremia rose and fell parallel with the daily death rate. This suggested that infections may be a significant factor in death from radiation injury. Injection of antibiotics, especially streptomycin, has given good protection (16 per cent died against 81 per cent controls).[4]

With intensive work continuing in the United States, England, France, and Belgium, it is certain that further great progress will be made toward practical chemical protection and in consequence better understanding of the biological effects of x-rays. A rapid physicochemical method of testing protective action of chemical compounds against lethal effects of ionizing radiations is the depolymerization of polymethacrylic acid (measured by viscosity change), as discussed in the preceding chapter.

There is now convincing evidence that fats (lipids) exert a protective

---

[1] Z. M. Bacq, A. Herve, J. Lecomte, and P. Fischer, *Science*, **111**, 356 (1950); *Brit. J. Radiol.*, **24**, 617 (1951); *Acta Radiol.*, **38**, 489 (1952); *Bull. acad. roy. méd. Belg.*, **17**, 13 (1952); *Experientia*, **7**, 11 (1951).

[2] J. B. Field and P. E. Rekers, *Am. J. Med. Sci.*, **218**, 1 (1949).

[3] A. Herve and J. Lecomte, *Arch. intern. Pharmacodynamic*, **79**, 109 (1949).

[4] C. P. Miller, C. W. Hammond, and M. Tompkins, *Science*, **111**, 719 (1950).

effect against radiation, although the mechanism is still uncertain. Hydroperoxide formation in irradiated fats alone is discussed on page 315. When cottonseed oil, methyl linolate, and other lipids are introduced into the diet of rats, there is a, decided increase in survival of animals after irradiation doses of 300 r/week in comparison with controls.[1] Nutrition of the epidermis is probably involved; also a modification of the supra-renal emission of lipids plays a role in the protection against irradiation. These experiments suggested the study of possible protective action of glycerol, the trihydric alcohol in fats which were glyceryl esters, on radiation-sensitive chemical systems in aqueous solution discussed in the preceding chapter.

In 1953 experiments by Pape verified in other laboratories indicated that a preliminary irradiation of a biological system by as little as $\frac{1}{4}$ r gives a marked protective effect on specimens subjected to subsequent irradiations with doses on the order of 600 r. It is not certain what the mechanism of this effect is, but it bears again on the problem of a possible stimulating effect of doses of 1 to 20 r.†

XV. Mechanism of Biological Action of Radiation. The complex mechanisms of the chemical effects of x-rays have been outlined in the preceding chapter, and some of the reactions pertinent to effects on cells and tissues have just been enumerated. It remains to consider the effects characteristic of a cell structure, the most important of which is the swelling. From a consideration of colloidal systems it is evident that swelling is caused by a difference in ion concentrations across a semipermeable cell boundary. Dilution of cell cytoplasms may easily result in damage and then death. Failla[2] presented the first comprehensive theory based upon known experimental observations for the swelling process. The x-ray photon liberates in the irradiated area photoelectrons and Compton electrons, which in their passage produce "radio ions," atoms, molecules, or aggregates which have gained or lost electrons. Ordinarily there are rapid recombination and disappearance of the effect in contrast with the constant equilibrium between electrolytic ions and undissociated molecules. However, in proteins the *radio* ionization may easily induce chemical changes which produce new molecules by rearrangement or fragmentation. These in turn may be capable of *electrolytic* ionization. Some of these new ions and molecules may not be able to pass through a cell wall, with the result that ionic concentration within the cell increases persistently. This would be sufficient to set up an osmotic system in which water must pass from the environment through the wall and thus cause dilution and swelling. But the tendency

---

[1] A. L. S. Cheng *et al.*, *J. Nutrition*, **48**, 161 (1952); *Science*, **117**, 254 (1953).

† Pape, *Strahlentherapie*, **81**, 331 (1950), **84**, 245, 449 (1951), **91**, 108 (1953). Trautman, Frey, and Schaaf, *Strahlentherapie*, **91**, 602 (1953). Schoen and Magnus, *Strahlentherapie*, **90**, 559 (1953).

[2] "The Cancer Problem," p. 202, Science Press, 1937.

is still further aided by the removal of ions outside the cell by the constant renewal of streaming fluid which conveys nutrition to the cell and waste products away from it.   A still further assisting factor is the possibility of weakening of the cell membrane by the superposed bombardment of electrons in localized areas.   Once swelling and dilution have been initiated as a result of excessive ion concentration within the cell, this may continue because of interference with normal biological processes. Furthermore, as already indicated, new chemical substances within the cells may be as incompatible to normal existence as though toxins were introduced by microinjections; or coagulated colloidal particles would induce fluid intake by the cell in the attempt to dissolve them.   Such effects are enhanced in the smaller, more sensitive, nucleus, which normally is protected by the outer parts of the cell but to which the radiation penetrates easily.   Upon the basis of the theory a distinctly cellular tissue should be, and in general is, more radiosensitive than connective and similar tissues.   Time is required for uniform diffusion of ionized substances throughout the cell from the initially concentrated tubular areas along the electron tracks.   A biologically active cell, such as one in the process of dividing, will aid this diffusion, thus accelerating the establishment of a differential ionic concentration and swelling, and therefore is more radiosensitive.   Recovery is explained by the fact that some of the electrolytic ions produced within the cell by radiation are small enough to diffuse out of the membranes, thus decreasing the deleterious effect.   In cells that divide rapidly the excess in ion concentration is halved at each division and soon becomes harmless.   According to this theory it should be expected that tissues into which *excess water* has been injected should show a greater response to irradiation by osmotic swelling than ordinary untreated controls.   This was verified experimentally and clinically in 1939 by Failla and associates.

At the present time considerably more stress is placed on the chemical changes resulting from indirect radiation effects as described in the preceding sections; these are not incompatible with the physicochemical and colloidal mechanisms just described.   Even the apparent contradiction in the "target" and the indirect-action theories may be eliminated by a "diffusion" model, which assumes the formation of intermediates by the ions of the primary radiation.   These may migrate in the cell and chemically interact with genic and extragenic components.   In this modified theory the size of the target loses significance.   Individual sensitive "sites" may exist in the cell, which are important because of their biological role, not because they form targets.   With this model Tobias[1] has accounted for variation in radiation sensitivity with substrates, state of cell division, water content, externally applied cell poisons, etc.

[1] C. A. Tobias, "Symposium on Radiobiology, 1952," p. 357, John Wiley & Sons, Inc., New York.

XVI. The Maximum Permissible Exposure. In all the foregoing sections of this chapter the chief concern has been with the damage which may occur by exposure of living matter to ionizing radiations. The effects have been listed by the International Commission on Radiological Protection as follows:

1. Superficial injuries (skin changes may be caused by as little as 0.08 r/day and may appear as long as 25 years after exposure).

2. General effects on the body, particularly the blood and blood-forming organs, such as production of anemia and leukemia (some changes may result from weekly exposures of 1.0 r).

3. Induction of malignant tumors (produced in rats and mice, and probably in humans, but at larger doses than some other changes).

4. Other deleterious effects, including cataract, obesity, impaired fertility and reduction of life span (not at dose levels below skin and blood effects). Cataract, for example, produced by ionizing radiations is due to oxidation of the —SH groups of the lens protein to produce —S—S— bridge formation with consequent polymerization, thickening of the protein molecules, and resultant opacity.

5. Genetic effects.

Present efforts, therefore, are directed to the measurement of the maximum exposure to radiation, especially of human beings without causing detectable effects. Special interest is attached to records of detected changes from very low dosages, which are assembled in Table 12-6, taken from the summary of this subject by Stone.[1]

TABLE 12-6. EFFECTS OF SMALL SINGLE DOSES OF RADIATION

Dose, r	Effect	Observer
0.001	Natural radiation + cosmic rays	Sievert
0.001	Change in growth rate of single cell of *Phycomyces blakesleeanus*	Forssberg
0.005	Change in time of life cycle of *Drosophila melanogaster*	Sievert
0.1–1.0	Inactivation of catalase enzyme	Forssberg
1.0	Decreased liberation of phosphorus-myosin in aged	Barron
5.0	Inhibition of mitotic activity in skin	Knowlton, Hemplemann
5.0	Threshold for mitotic effect in grasshopper neuroblast	Hollaender
25.0	Threshold for recognizable reduction of lymphocytes in animals	Jacobson
50.0	Minimum dose showing injury to lymph nodes	Bloom

The concept of a maximum permissible exposure now rests on a fairly large number of experiments and observations which have led to the recommendation by the International Commission on Radiological

---

[1] R. S. Stone, The Concept of a Maximum Permissible Exposure, *Radiology*, **58,** 639 (1952); 95 references.

Protection already mentioned on page 180, namely, 0.3 r/week measured in free air (0.5 r on body surface or 1.5 r/week on the hands and forearms). But the Commission states:

While the values proposed for maximum permissible exposures are such as to involve a risk that is small compared to the other hazards of life, nevertheless in view of the unsatisfactory nature of much of the evidence on which our judgments must be based, coupled with the knowledge that certain radiation effects are irreversible and cumulative, it is strongly recommended that every effort be made to reduce exposures to all types of ionizing radiations to the lowest possible level.

XVII. Radiopathology. X-ray therapy is indicated when it is desirable to produce the following effects:

1. *Inhibition of the growth or function of glands and cells.* Differentiated cells such as those composing glands and hair follicles, physiologically active cells, young cells, cells about to divide, lymphoid tissue, and tissue of embryonic type are all markedly radiosensitive. Skin diseases characterized by hyperactivity of the glands, hyperthyroidism, diseases that may be cured by checking ovulation, leukemia, and many other conditions are succesfully treated by irradiation.

2. *Solution of hyperplastic connective tissue* such as uterine fibroid (microscopic examination reveals atrophy of myomatous cells) and hyaline sclerosis of the connective tissue with dilatation of blood vessels.

3. *Reduction of lichenification,* by inhibition of overgrowth of epidermal cells, and destruction of fungi.

4. *Anodyne effect.* The relief of itching has been very frequently accomplished. The relief of pain, except when due to a lesion that can be cured by irradiation, is less certain, though many writers have reported an analgesic effect upon neuralgic pain.

5. *Reduction of inflammation.* There is a favorable experience in the treatment of carbuncles, pneumonia in certain stages, erysipelas, etc. The rate and mode of reaction of inflammatory lesions indicate that the rays act chiefly by destroying the infiltrating lymphocytes, the exceptional sensitiveness of which has already been pointed out. Evidently these cells contain protective substances that enable them to neutralize bacterial or other toxic products, which give rise to the inflammation. When the cells are destroyed by irradiation, these protective substances are liberated and become immediately available for defensive purposes.

6. *Gas gangrene infections.* Unquestionably x-ray treatments are a definite aid to recovery, either because hydrogen peroxide, fatal to anaerobic organisms, is formed in body fluids or because, as previously indicated, a substance resistant to toxins is released.

7. *Miscellaneous pathological conditions.* At one time or another x-rays have been used in the treatment of almost every conceivable ailment—tuberculous meningitis, arthritis, poliomyelitis, whooping cough, hay fever, angina, pituitary and adrenal disturbances, vasomotor disturbances, hyperinsulinism, hyperthyroidism, goiter, leukemia, etc., in addition to tumors of all varieties. A recent report on end results in 40,000 x-ray treatments on 96 pathological conditions ranging from excellent to none is typical of the growing statistical data.[1]

8. *Destruction of benign and malignant tumors.*

XVIII. Cancer. There is no greater challenge, and no greater achievement, in x-ray science than the treatment and cure, in a great number of cases, of cancer, or, specifically, carcinomas and sarcomas.

[1] R. R. Ruff, *Mississippi Valley Med. J.,* **71,** 178 (1949).

1. *Statistics of the Cancer Problem.*   During the present year 200,000 people, the great majority above 50 years of age, will die of cancer in the United States, a mortality second only to that caused by heart diseases. For the age group 35 to 44 the cancer death rate remains about 60 per 100,000; for 45 to 54, 170; for 75 and above, 1,200.   Women will be in the majority for ages under 55, and men for ages over 55.   Of cancers in men, 57 per cent will be in the digestive tract, 7 per cent in the mouth, and 3 per cent on the skin; 40 per cent of the women will die of cancers of the digestive tract, 30 per cent of cancers of the genital organs, and 15 per cent of cancers of the breast.   Cancer of the stomach is silent, or produces no symptoms, in 25 per cent of autopsies performed on persons who have died of the disease.   Other interesting data on cancer are as follows: new cases in 1952, about 300,000; cases cured 30 per cent, not cured 70 per cent; number of persons in 1952 with cancer or history of cancer, about 900,000; cases surviving 5 years, 240,000; ratio of deaths to living cases, 1 in 5; delay in diagnosis and treatment, 70 per cent of all cases; amount contributed to cancer control, 1938 to 1949, $141,262,213 by the National Cancer Institute, American Cancer Society, Atomic Energy Commission Cancer Fund, Damon Runyon Memorial Fund, and Babe Ruth Cancer Fund, but amounts have greatly increased since 1949—an indication of the growing awareness of the challenge of cancer and the necessity for all-out research.

On the other side of this extraordinarily dark picture is the fact that tens of thousands of cancer patients will be cured by x-rays, γ-rays, surgery, or a combination; others diagnosed too late will have their pain and suffering alleviated and their lives prolonged by the agency of radiation—in spite of the fact that cancer remains one of the great enigmas of medical science.

2. *What Is Cancer?*   The general term "cancer," originally assigned in ancient times from an imagined resemblance to the claws of a crab, is applied to an abnormally organized tissue which usually grows at a greater rate and to a much greater extent than the normal tissue from which it develops.   More specifically, carcinoma refers to a malignant epithelial tumor, and sarcoma to such a growth derived from a non-epithelial tissue of mesodermal embryonic origin (connective lymphoid, cartilage, bone tissue, etc.).   C. C. Little advocated instead of the word cancer the phrase "hypernomic histoplasia," meaning "tissue formation outside the law" of orderly ontogenetic processes or of growth control. Cancerous growth is initiated whenever other types of growth (normal, regenerative, or inflammatory) are intensified and continued over relatively long periods of time.   In abnormal growth, cells undergoing proliferation never exceed a certain intensity and are always under control. Some types of abnormal growth are self-limiting or are terminated by eliminating stimuli such as bacteria.   But in cancerous growths there is

an increase in normal proliferative energy that is continuous and unending without regard for the physiological needs of the tissue in which they have arisen or for its physiological boundaries.

Cancer cells never again assume the behavior and reactions of normal cells; they easily invade neighboring tissues and lymph or blood vessels, because of failure of the normal mutual interactions of adjoining cells, causing metastases, or new tumors of exactly the same kind of cells. They may remain structurally immature since there is no time for full differentiation and hence may usually be distinguished microscopically from corresponding normal cells by distinctive features of anaplasia, loss of specific form and polarity, variation in size, multiform nuclei, atypical mitosis, and increased chromatin (which proves increased power of growth); they may be transplanted easily and made to grow in successive generations indefinitely, thus making possible researches on cancer, especially in mice and fowls. Cancer cells possess an unusual capacity for establishing connection with a regional blood supply. By interfering with various organ functions, by their degeneration products, by causing hemorrhage, and by undergoing secondary infection the cancerous growths cause anemia, emaciation, loss of strength, and finally death.

3. *Chemical Behavior of Cancer Cells.* Besides the morphological differences just noted, it has been demonstrated that a marked similarity exists in chemical properties (composition, enzyme and metabolic pattern) of malignant tissue regardless of species or of histogenetic origin of tumor tissue. If this were strictly true, all malignant tumors should respond to uniform therapy, whereas each type may demand a separate therapy since the malignant process may be conditioned or controlled by several factors which vary with the etiology and the tissue from which the tumor arises. On the other hand, there is a generally abrupt change in the chemistry and metabolic pattern from a normal or "irritated" tissue to a malignant one.[1]

The cancer cell is distinguished from the normal cell in many respects, the following being only a partial list:

1. In tumor tissue, for every 13 sugar molecules attacked, 12 are split into lactic acid and 1 is oxidized, whereas in normal tissue the ratio is 1:1. Hence nutrition of the cancer cell is derived from a fermentation process.

2. In cancer, blood plasma pH is 7.47, or 8.7 per cent more alkaline than normal.

3. Blood glucose is high.

4. Calcium is low.

5. Potassium is high.

6. The glycolysis activator in cancer tissue is known to be pyruvic acid.

7. Carrel showed that malignant types of cell digest fibrin and feed upon substances or tissues that are not utilized to the same extent by normal cells.

8. Cancer tissue does not utilize hexose phosphates or glycogen added to the suspending medium, whereas most types of normal tissue do.

[1] A. C. Ivy, *Science,* **106,** 455 (1949).

9. Blood serum reduces methylene blue to leuko base, while normal serum does not.

10. Total protein and nitrogen are less than normal.

11. The globulin fraction of protein is increased relative to albumin from 30 to 80 per cent.

12. Fibrinogen is increased.

13. Incoagulable proteins such as histones and protamines with low molecular weights are increased.

14. Amino acids, lysine, cystine, and tryptophan, are increased.

15. Lipoids change with increase in cholesterol and lecithin (decrease in surface tension from cholesterol causing flocculation is the basis of many blood-cancer tests).

16. The most striking early effect of cancer on the biochemistry of the host is in the reduction of renal and hepatic catalase and the increase of protein digestive enzyme.

17. All cancer tissue has an enhanced content of the "spreading factor" hyaluronidase.

18. In 1939 Kögel and Erxleben[1] of Utrecht showed that the proteins of malignant tissues are partially racemized. Normal tissues yield on short acid hydrolysis l-glutamic acid with normal optical rotation, while the products isolated from tumors have as high as 50 per cent of the d-glutamic acid.

4. *The Cause of Cancer.* The fundamental cause of cancer is an intracellular change that becomes self-perpetuating.

The cancerous change may be initiated according to Morton by any irritating or stimulating agent of the following three main groups and by combinations of 1, 2, and 3.

1. Physical.
    a. Traumatic (injury).
    b. Thermic.
    c. Actinic—ultraviolet, x-rays, radium.
2. Chemical.
    a. Stasis (arrest of blood current in capillaries).
    b. Carcinogenic chemicals. In 1915 it was found by Japanese workers that malignant growths of typically cancerous nature could be induced by applying coal tar to the skin or to rabbit ears. The attempts to isolate and synthesize specific carcinogenic hydrocarbons began and continues to this day in the laboratories of Fieser at Harvard, Riegel at Northwestern, Buu Hoi of the Radium Institute in Paris, and others. The hydrocarbon first shown (1930) to have carcinogenic activity was 1,2,5,6-benzanthracene, in which ABC or CDE are phenanthrene nuclei:

[1] *Nature,* **144,** 71 (1939).

In 1933 there was isolated from coal tar a much more active carcinogen, 3,4-benzopyrene, in which *ABD* or *BDE* are phenanthrene nuclei:

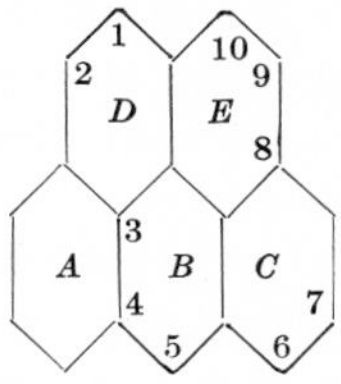

Introduction of a substituent group such as a single OH group, for example, may destroy completely the activity.   Perhaps the most active of all compounds is methylcholanthrene, closely related to cholic acid, one of the bile acids:

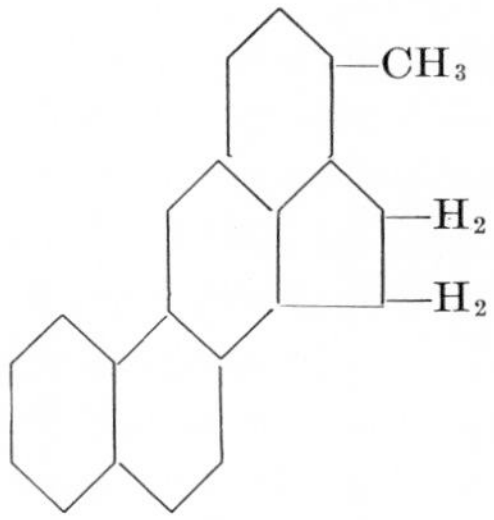

Recently 6,10-dimethyl-1,2-benzacridine (I) with the configuration was found to have intense activity, while 3,10-dimethyl-5,6-benzacridine (II) does not.

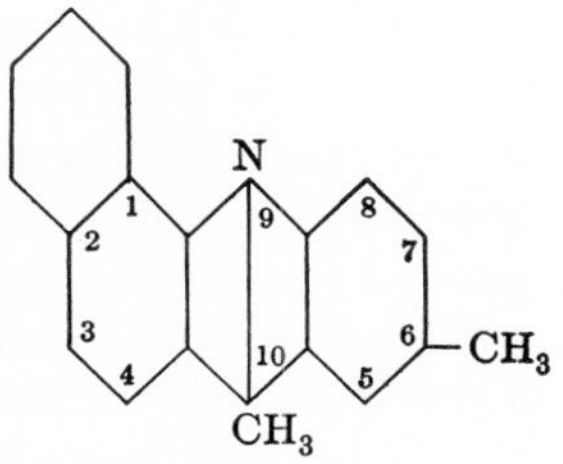

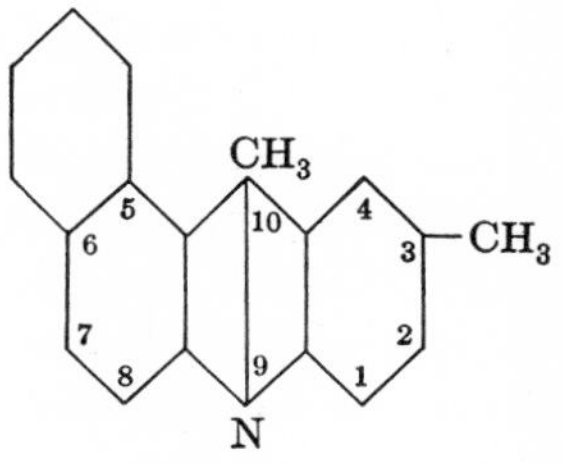

Here the 3,4 positions in the carcinogenic isomer seem to be the center in terms of electron density and formation of some kind of van der Waals complex with cell constituents, resulting in the carcinogenic change.   Most of these active agents are closely related chemically to bile acids, sterols, and hormones.   Vitamin B_{12} itself was found in 1951 by Buu Hoi to have carcinogenic activity.

   c. Coal tars.

   d. Heated fats and cholesterol.

   e. Internal secretions—estrogens, hormones.

3. Biological.

   a. Bacteria.

   b. Viruses.

   c. Helminths (intestinal worms).

Every potentially growing cell can be made to undergo neoplastic change by long-continued and unremitting action of the inciting agent (except viruses). After a certain summation of action on the cell, the change proceeds inexorably regardless of whether or not the inciting factor is withdrawn. Next to the chemical stimulants, greatest interest is developing in the effects of hormones.

Experimentally, development of breast carcinoma in mice can be prevented by ovariotomy, which eliminates the hormone oestrin. That the latter is responsible for such cancers is proved by injecting it into normal animals, whereupon it acts by inducing rhythmic growth process in the mammary tissue. Similarly, for mammary cancers, which are often responsible for bone metastases, there is marked palliation by treatment with testosterone (male hormone).[1]

The question of the factor of heredity in cancer has been one of the most bitterly controversial because of its obvious incalculable importance. It is certain that some factor is transmitted from generation to generation in certain families and strains of mice. Breast cancer never occurs in certain strains, whereas in others every female mouse becomes cancerous if it reaches a certain age. A single recessive gene cannot be responsible for the hereditary transmission since the hereditary tendency of the mother to acquire cancer is more important in determining its development in the offspring than the hereditary constitution of the father. Thus cancer is due to cooperation of various kinds of stimulating factors and certain specific substances acting together with hereditary constitutional factors. In mice these factors have been variable and known but in man unknown. The greatest difficulty in the search for stimuli and agents responsible for cancer in man is due to the conditioning influence of susceptibility and resistance, which must be multiple factors in inheritance. Cancer as such is not handed down in heredity. It is the result of interplay between constitution and environment. Inherited susceptibility to cancer may never appear if the individual is protected from adverse environmental stimulating factors; inherited resistance can be broken down by repeated application of strongly inciting factors, such as x-rays or occupational hazards.

A possible complication is the fact that in certain tumors of fowls it is possible to separate from the tumor a substance free from living cells which on injection into another individual of the same or related species gives rise to a new tumor. Furthermore Peyton Rous has shown that the virus which causes skin papilloma in cottontail rabbits transmits the disease. Hence viruses may act as growth stimulators, which may be present in the tissues in a nonpathogenic condition and become pathogenic for the cells when these have been sufficiently altered by the action of a carcinogenic agent (such as oestrin in breast cancer in mice).

[1] Andersen, *Acta. Radiol.*, **32**, 159 (1949).

Very little is known about the effect of diet on cancer and its control. Hepatoma in rats is known to have specific nutritional requirements, and since the metabolic pattern of malignant tissue is specific, dietary control may be an important factor in inhibition of tumor induction and control.

No one has demonstrated antibodies to cancer tissue in the serum of the host or immunity in a host to a graft of its own cancer.

That there are precancerous states seems now well established. Lesions of different types, tissues, and origin after long latent periods, at the age when senescence of tissues is marked, undergo malignant changes. Senile keratosis is the manifestation in the elderly of the effects of actinic rays, leukoplasia a deficiency disease, Bilharzia lesions an example of so-called chronic irritation, polyposis of the colon an inherited, transmissible disease, goiter a degenerative process, chondroma a true benign tumor—all these conditions, so varied in origin and present for long periods, acquire malignant characteristics at a time when endocrine activities begin to fail, the precipitating factor being senescence. By themselves precancerous states seem to indicate that malignancy is due to more than one factor, the one causative, the other precipitating or catalyzing. The varieties of precancerous conditions indicate a lack of specificity and suggest that, as in the laboratory, so within the living body, carcinogens are innumerable in number and variety and by themselves are controlled possibly by anticarcinogens, which as age advances are less potent or are altogether lost.[1]

5. *Cancer Therapy.* All sorts of procedure have been suggested for treating cancer other than surgery, x-rays, radium, or neutrons, but as yet no chemical (including snake venom), hormonal, biological, or dietetic method has proved of the least value in the control of this disease.

In the problem of x-ray cure of cancer, two important phases must be recognized: (1) destruction of the localized growth, together with detoxication and elimination of cell debris; (2) repair at the site of the destroyed neoplasm by normal tissue and compensation for the damage created in the organism by the tumor, its toxins, and x-rays. Ewing upon the basis of long experience lists four factors in the process of cure: (1) destruction of tumor cells; (2) destruction of normal epithelium; (3) regeneration of normal epithelium; (4) adaptation by epithelium. Normal epithelium acquires a resistance to the rays by a process of adaptation and is able to regenerate under a dosage that originally destroyed the preexisting epithelium. The tumor cells, subjected to the same dosage, do not exhibit this power of adaptation and regeneration but perish.

Modern therapeutic technique involves not only the radiosensitiveness of tumors but also the relationship of the normal matrix. Tumors proceeding from radioresistant matrix tissues are likewise radioresistant in a

[1] Cade, *Brit. J. Radiol.*, **22**, 331 (1949).

state of complete differentiation. Osteosarcomas, fibrosarcomas, and adenocarcinomas showing little sensitiveness imitate the structure of the matrix tissue and in all such cases, even including growths in relatively atypical manner, have the same radiobiological quality as their matrix tissue. What in practice divides radiosensitive from radioresistant tumors is not the amount of radiation required for destruction of the tumor but whether or not this amount is permissible from the standpoint of its effects on other tissues that are necessarily included in the irradiation. The radiosensitiveness of malignant tumors is not in all cases greater than that of their matrices; otherwise there would be no malignant tumor that could not be made to disappear under irradiation, and cancer would be a completely curable disease. Complete disappearance of the tumor can be achieved with certainty only when the matrix tissue can be destroyed. However, some tumors have an entirely different structure from their matrices, such as round-cell sarcomas. These are composed of cells not found in mature connective tissue and possess a radiosensitiveness that makes possible their disappearance. Spindle-cell sarcoma, on the other hand, does not differ in sensitiveness from its matrix, but in most cases therapy must involve an injury to the irradiated matrix, the reaction of which is a criterion of the reaction of tumor tissue.

This gives us a new principle of dosage, based not on the destruction of the tumor, but on disappearance of normal tissue of the matrix; the radiobiology of the normal tissue becomes the basis of radiotherapy of malignant tumors.

One question repeatedly raised for 50 years is whether x-rays possess the power to induce increased differentiation in malignant tumors and whether the curative effect may be partly or wholly due to increased differentiation, which is lacking in malignant cells. Such changes should be histologically observed. In extended research, Andersen[1] has demonstrated that irradiation does not produce increased differentiation; histologically demonstrable changes in irradiated tumors are signs of nonspecific degeneration.

Questions naturally arising in connection with x-ray therapeutic technique are concerned with the dosage required to kill tumor cells: whether the irradiation should be massive, *i.e.*, given at one time, or fractionally divided; whether the effect is a function of wavelength; and whether 1-million-volt x-rays have great advantages over 200,000-volt x-rays and radium. The answers upon the basis of present available knowledge are as follows:

a. The dosage required to kill tumor cells varies with different tumors but averages, with back scatter eliminated, 2,500 to 3,500 r (five to seven times the erythema dose) (Wood).

b. For the great majority of cases the fractional method of treatment usually identi-

[1] S. R. Andersen, *Acta Radiol.*, **33**, 57 (1950).

fied as the Coutard method seems greatly to be preferred by the majority of roentgenologists. This involves frequent doses of relatively small proportions (50 to 250 r/day), well below an erythemal effect, and protraction until a large total dose has been administered. Certainly this type of treatment is best for palliation of advanced malignant disease. However, many prominent authorities still believe that the single massive dose is essential to prevent the recuperative powers of the cancer cell from repairing the destructive effects of x-rays, in spite of possible irreparable damage to normal tissue. The skin effect with the massive dose is avoided by irradiation through multiple ports instead of restriction to one area.

c. The lethal point for cancer cells is independent of wavelength for the same number of roentgens administered.

d. Many experiments have indicated that both soft and hard (supervoltage) x-rays produce the same biological result as concerns mortality in animals, occurrence of necrosis, and various effects such as failure of tail regeneration in a test animal like triton. Another long series of papers presents the opposite opinion, namely, that different results are obtained with soft and hard rays. In most cases, however, these differences can be ascribed to the gradual decrease in dosage corresponding to depth for soft rays, while hard rays are homogeneous throughout a thick specimen. Brunst and Sheremetieva found that tails of tritons regenerate perfectly symmetrically for high-voltage rays but unsymmetrically for soft rays since one side of the animal receives a dosage different from the other.

XIX. Supervoltage Therapy. There are now several 1-million- and 2-million-volt x-ray installations in cancer hospitals, and there is available the accumulating experience of nearly 25 years. In addition a few 20-million-volt betatron units are now being used for therapy on an experimental basis. The design and construction of supervoltage equipment, and the properties of rays so generated, have been described in Chaps. 3 and 8. Advantages of the million-volt technique are deeper penetration and less damage to the skin because of less absorption and back scatter, together with less radiation sickness. But the popular conception that higher voltage means better treatment is not generally correct. The results do not as yet show that this form of therapy can replace the procedure with the usual 200-kv unit, and they are not more startling. However, in a small group of deep-seated tumors, as those of the bladder and esophagus, formerly almost hopeless, unquestionably favorable results are being obtained with supervoltage therapy, particularly at the University of Illinois Research Hospital in Chicago.

At the University of Illinois careful researches during 1948–1952 and still in progress have sought to set up proper therapeutic techniques for the 20-million-volt betatron and to evaluate the physical, chemical, and biological effects. The studies have been on acute roentgen death in mice, decoloration of hair in mice, recessive sex-linked lethals in *Drosophila melanogaster*, and efficiency measured by the lethal effect of divided doses in mice. First of all, measurement and evaluation of dosage presents new problems which are absent for dosage measurement of 200-kv rays with r-meters. Readings with a 25-r chamber of a Victoreen dosimeter embedded in a phantom are calibrated with regard to 200-kv rays by means of quantitative tests. In the above mentioned cases (lethal, decoloration, mutagenic) 1 r so measured has the biological effect of 0.75 r of 200-kv rays. At a dosage level which causes death in mice after 1 week of daily treatments, high-energy radiation is about as effective as in a massive-dose test; but at a dosage level which causes death in 3 weeks of daily treatments, the efficiency is significantly lowered. This is in contrast with increasing efficiency of neutron beams and is explained by differences in specific ionization.[1]

To summarize the advantages of the betatron radiation in cancer therapy over conventional 200-kv radiation:

1. Deep penetration leads to very efficient depth-dose distributions, measured by the ratio to highest local dose.

2. Ratio is independent of tumor depth; hence entrance fields may be used which would be uneconomical at conventional energies.

3. Field size may be made as small as desired without changing dose distribution; hence the number of efficient beams available for cross-firing deep-seated cancers is much higher, and it is possible to irradiate any tumor region without delivering high doses outside this region. This means nearly perfect geometric selectivity, which in itself should yield clinical gains in respecting tolerance limits of healthy structures.

The answer to the question as to whether better results may be obtained at energies still higher than 20 Mev is that too high an energy is possible, for the following reasons:

1. Secondary rays become more penetrating than the primary beam, and lateral scattering increases.

2. The beam becomes more sharply peaked along the central ray, and drastic compensating filters are required.

3. The ionization peak is deeper than desired.

4. Annihilation radiation is increasingly more intense.

5. The number of atomic nuclei activated increases rapidly so that positrons could contribute to dose and activated nuclei could be transported in the blood stream.

XX. A Third X-ray Application in Medicine. Thus far two great fields of x-ray contributions to medical science—diagnosis by radiography and microradiography, and therapy—have been considered. The great value of optical and electron microscopes in diagnosis is self-apparent. And yet it is clear that many problems of cell structure and behavior are beyond the power of any microscope to solve. For this reason other methods such as specific radiosensitiveness have been welcomed. A few years ago the x-ray diffraction method of structure research was extended to the actual structure of normal and pathological tissues, which can now be studied exactly as crystals of metals, or cellulose, or fibrous proteins

---

[1] G. D. Adams *et al.*, Techniques for Application of the Betatron to Medical Therapy, *Am. J. Roentgenol. Radium Therapy*, **60**, 153 (1948), **61**, 591 (1949). H. Quastler *et al.*, Biological Evaluation of 20-million Volt Röntgen Rays, *Am. J. Roentgenol. Radium Therapy*, **54**, 723 (1945), **57**, 359 (1947), **62**, 555 (1949), **63**, 566 (1950).

can be studied. With this "supermicroscopic" penetration down to molecules of the complex substances of cells, a fundamental molecular change from normal to abnormal was demonstrated with comparable specimens. Hence, though only the slightest beginning has been made, another great application of x-rays has been opened to biology and medicine. It is singular that x-rays will produce subtle changes in tissues and that we can use x-rays, now in a different sense, to find out what change has been wrought by the original irradiation. Beyond a doubt, in some great clinic with every intellectual and experimental facility, this method of fine-structure analysis can be made to answer many of the unanswered questions of radiobiology and by improved diagnosis lessen the scourge of cancer on the earth.

PART II

THE X-RAY ANALYSIS OF THE ULTIMATE STRUCTURE OF MATERIALS

CHAPTER 13

CRYSTALLOGRAPHY AND X-RAY DIFFRACTION

The Solid State of Matter. Knowledge of the crystalline state of matter was decidedly limited prior to the discovery by Laue and the Braggs that x-rays could be applied to the analysis of the internal structure of crystals. The great and relatively aged science of crystallography had been built up to the conclusion, from careful observations with microscopes and optical goniometers, that apparently almost all true solids were really crystals, either single entities with pairs of parallel bounding surfaces disposed in definite geometric fashion at angles which could be measured, or aggregates of these single crystals. Though regularity of exterior appearance indicated some kind of regular internal arrangement of unit building material, whatever that might be, yet, without experimental methods of investigation and without adequate conceptions of atomic and molecular structure and the forces holding atoms and molecules together, physicists and chemists were unable to find points of useful contact with the essentially applied geometric science of crystallography. Concerning the gaseous and liquid states of matter, much more was known in the sense that their behavior could be explained by simple hypotheses. They are characterized by disordered arrangement of atoms or molecules which are relatively free to move, even in liquids. Since all directions are alike, it is possible to calculate with considerable accuracy the behavior of gases and liquids in very practical phenomena. Chemists have worked very largely with gases and liquids because the freedom of motion of the molecules has permitted reactions more readily. But in solids great complications arise because the atoms and molecules are bound together tightly by their mutual forces. It is evident that the exercise of these forces should tend to produce regularity of arrangement. X-ray analysis has shown that such a regularity does exist in practically every solid substance.

The great practical importance of scientific knowledge of the ultimate structure of solids, which are crystals in the natural state, is self-evident when consideration is given to the definition of desired physical and chemical properties. The strength of steel girders, the corrosion of aluminum alloys, the wearing properties of casehardened steel, the plasticity of lime, the dielectric capacity of materials, the lubricating properties of long-chain paraffins or of graphite, the stretching of rubber, the covering power of pigments, and innumerable other practical phenomena of every-day life—all depend upon ultimate crystalline structure. Bragg has shown clearly that as a matter of fact the only properties of solid bodies which are not directly and obviously related to crystal structure are those, few in number, which depend upon atomic characteristics alone, such as weight. With few exceptions every aspect of the behavior of a solid substance depends on the *mode of arrangement* of its atoms and molecules.

A clear distinction must be made relative to the ultimate crystalline structure of materials. Sir William Bragg spoke in the following inimitably clear fashion of the three types of assemblage:

The simplest is that of the single atom as in helium in the gaseous state, in which the behavior of every atom is on the whole the same as the behavior of any other. The next is that of the molecules, the smallest portion of a liquid or a gas which has all the properties of the whole; and lastly, the crystal unit, the smallest portion of a crystal (really the simplest form of a solid substance) which has all the properties of the crystal. There are atoms of silicon and oxygen; there is a molecule of silicon dioxide, and a crystal unit of quartz containing three molecules of silicon dioxide. The separate atoms of silicon and oxygen are not silicon dioxide, of course, in the same way the molecule of silicon dioxide is not quartz; the crystal unit consisting of three molecules arranged in a particular way *is* quartz.

The new chemistry of the solid state derived from direct structural analysis is decidedly unconventional and almost shocking to some chemists. The conception of the molecule has come to play far too great a part in chemistry, for, though the molecule is a very real entity in the gaseous state, this is by no means necessarily so in the solids. Here it is the exception rather than the rule for the molecule to have a discrete existence. In its turn this picture of the sanctity of the molecule has created a quite false impression of the importance of the classical laws of chemistry. The laws of constancy of composition and of simple proportions now appear as trivial and insignificant consequences of geometrical requirements rather than as profound and fundamental expressions of the laws of nature. The conception of valence, too, so successful in organic chemistry, has been widely and sometimes blindly applied in fields altogether outside its scope, until, on chemical grounds alone, it has become clear that certain classes of compounds refuse resolutely to conform to accepted chemical principles. This is notably the case with intermetallic systems, but we shall find that it is also true of other types of compounds, including many that have been revealed and could only have been revealed by x-ray methods. Therefore, this new chemistry presents a challenge of remarkable interest which we shall try to indicate in briefest and simplest fashion in this and succeeding chapters.

The first aim of the x-ray analysis of crystals is to determine the arrangement of the atoms in the crystal unit and to account for the properties of the crystal in terms of that arrangement.   The interference of x-rays in gases and liquids has made possible more recently fine-structure determination even for these states.   The simple Bragg law $n\lambda = 2d \sin \Theta$, derived on page 96, governs the process of analysis of ultimate fine structure of materials.

Fundamentals of Crystallography.   In Chaps. 1 to 12 attention has been given primarily to the fundamental properties of x-rays, which are to be used subsequently simply as a tool in the analysis of fine structure of matter.   The crystal grating of known constant by which it is possible to analyze x-radiation and measure wavelengths has been taken more or less for granted.   It is now appropriate to take the radiation for granted and to inquire into the reasons for the satisfactory action of crystals as gratings and for the fact that the analysis of x-ray spectra from each crystal leads directly to the interpretation of how a particular crystal is built from ultimate atomic units.

Entirely apart from x-ray data a systematic science of crystallography has been developed which serves as the basis for rational interpretation of x-ray data.   The steps in the development of this information may be summarized briefly as follows:

1. *The Indices of Crystal Faces and Planes.*   The important properties of a crystal visible to the eye are the planar bounding faces and the symmetry.   The first logical step is to measure the *angles* between faces with the goniometer.   In order to express then the positions in space of these planes relative to each other, it is essential to derive a system of coordinates.   The planes may then be indexed in terms of their intercepts upon the axes of a system of coordinates; upon each axis a unit distance is chosen, and then the distances from the origin of the given plane along the three axes is measured; the reciprocals of these intercepts are then the indices of the plane.   Thus a plane intersecting the X axis at unit distance from the origin and parallel to the Y and Z axes has the intercepts 1, ∞, ∞ and the indices 1, 0, 0, usually written (100) (Fig. 178).   Other cubic faces have the indices (010) and (001), and the planes that bisect diagonally the cube faces are (110), (101), and (011).   Also there are the similar planes with negative indices where the intercepts are in other octants such as $\bar{1}10$, $1\bar{1}0$, $\bar{1}10$, etc.   A single specific plane or crystal face is usually designated with parenthesis, thus (100), as well as the whole family of planes parallel to the face: if the faces of a crystal are completely developed, then the form is designated {100} to include the six cubic faces, etc.   A crystal in the cubic system may have the form {100}, cubic shape, or {111}, an octahedron.   In Fig. 178 are shown six of the various sets of planes into which a cube may be imagined to be sliced up.   Planes in general are designated by the indices *hkl*.

Expressed in another way, more generally we may think of three unit axial values $\vec{a}$, $\vec{b}$, and $\vec{c}$ (along X, Y, and Z), where both directions and length are indicated by the arrows; thus these are vectors and represent the primitive triplet. The plane is named in terms of intercepts $\dfrac{\vec{a}}{h}$, $\dfrac{\vec{b}}{k}$, $\dfrac{\vec{c}}{l}$, and thus the plane is (hkl), which also designates the whole set of parallel planes whose uniform spacing d_{hkl} is that given by the Bragg law $n\lambda = 2d_{hkl}\sin\Theta$ and expressed in terms of a, b, c, h, k, l, and the angles α, β, γ between the axes $\vec{a}$, $\vec{b}$, $\vec{c}$, (see page 339).

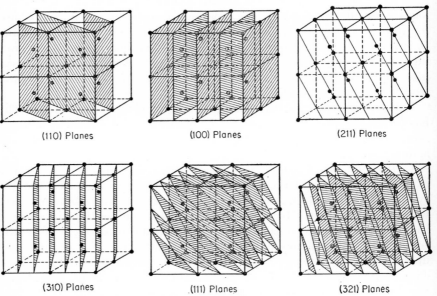

(110) Planes   (100) Planes   (211) Planes

(310) Planes   (111) Planes   (321) Planes

FIG. 178. Typical sets of parallel planes in a cubic lattice.

Designation of *direction* in a crystal is also important. Moving a point from the origin 000 in a given direction by motions parallel to the X, Y, and Z axes can be represented by u times the unit distance a along X, v times b along Y, and w times c along Z. The direction then is $[uvw]$, written with square brackets, to indicate a row of points 000, uvw, $2u2v2w$. The X axis has the indices [100], the Y axis [010] and the Z axis [001], and the body diagonal [111]; and negative signs again indicate the translations in the negative directions of the axes. It is apparent in Fig. 179 that in the cubic system the [100] direction is perpendicular to the (100) planes like a string along which square sheets of paper are strung at even intervals, and the same is true of other directions. But in other systems in which there are not equal lengths along X, Y, and Z axes and in which these axes may not be at 90 deg, the direction is not necessarily normal to a set of planes. The direction indices are not derived on the same reciprocal basis as the planar indices. The plane with indices (hkl) contains the direction $[uvw]$ if $hu + kv + lw = 0$. Two planes $h_1k_1l_1$ and $h_2k_2l_2$ both contain $[uvw]$ as a common direction if $h_1u + k_1v + l_1w = h_2u + k_2v + l_2w = 0$, or $u = k_1l_2 - l_1k_2$, $v = l_1h_2 - h_1l_2$, $w = h_1k_2 - k_1h_2$. This value of $[uvw]$ then defines the *zone* axis, which is an important relationship for the outer faces of crystals. The aggregation of all faces or planes that intersect with parallel edges is the zone and the common edge direction the zone axis. Planes (111) and (123) intersect in a line $u = 1$, $v = -2$, $w = 1$, or $[1\bar{2}1]$, and any other planes with the same zone axis must satisfy the condition $h - 2k + l = 0$. The importance of the concept will become shortly apparent since, in the most powerful x-ray diffraction methods for single crystals, these are rotated in an x-ray beam around a zone axis, and interpretation of the x-ray results necessarily must

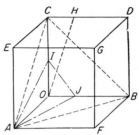

Fig. 179. Directions and planes in cubic lattice; direction OA, [100]; direction OD, [011]; direction OG, [111]; direction OH, [013]; plane $AEGF$, (100); plane $ABDE$, (110); plane ABC, (111); plane AIJ, (132).

depend on the ability to establish the identity of this axis.

2. *Crystal Systems.* Now an immense amount of experimentation has proved that all angle measurements and indexing of plane faces are accounted for by seven systems of coordinates (Fig. 180). In other

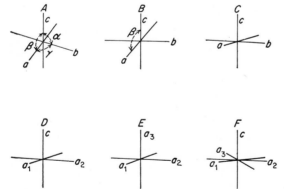

Fig. 180. The coordinate axes of crystal systems: a, b, c, unit lengths, respectively, along X, Y, Z axes; angles $\alpha = Y \wedge Z$, $\beta = Z \wedge X$, $\gamma = X \wedge Y$. (A) Triclinic, $a \neq b \neq c$, $\alpha \neq \beta \neq \gamma \neq 90°$. (B) Monoclinic, $a \neq b \neq c$, $\alpha = \gamma = 90° \neq \beta$. (C) Orthorhombic, $a \neq b \neq c$, $\alpha = \beta = \gamma = 90°$. (D) Tetragonal, $a = b \neq c$, $\alpha = \beta = \gamma = 90°$. (E) Cubic, $a = b = c$, $\alpha = \beta = \gamma = 90°$. (F) Hexagonal, $a_1 = a_2$ (or b) $= a_3 \neq c$, $\alpha = \beta = 90°$, $\gamma = 120°$. (G, not shown) Rhombohedral, $a = b = c$, $\alpha \neq \beta \neq \gamma \neq 90°$.

words, there are seven crystal systems: triclinic, monoclinic, orthorhombic, tetragonal, hexagonal, rhombohedral or trigonal, and cubic. As an example of these relationships whereby a crystal is characterized, the case of tetragonal tin (Schiebold) is represented in Fig. 181. The outer form of a single crystal is represented on tetragonal axes, a, a, c, $\alpha = \beta = \gamma = 90$ deg. The most characteristic faces are designated p, the indices being (111), (1$\bar{1}$1), ($\bar{1}\bar{1}$1), ($\bar{1}$11), (11$\bar{1}$), (1$\bar{1}\bar{1}$), ($\bar{1}\bar{1}\bar{1}$), ($\bar{1}$1$\bar{1}$), or

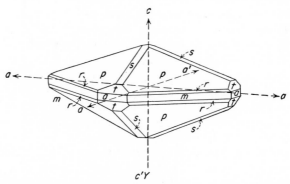

Fɪɢ. 181. Diagram of faces of a single crystal of white tin. (*After Schiebold.*) See text for method of indexing face planes.

the form {111}. The other faces can also be symbolically represented, so that the crystal habit is completely described as follows:

$$p = \{a,a,c\} = \{111\} \qquad r = \left\{ \frac{a}{3}, \frac{a}{3}, c \right\} = \{331\}$$

$$m = \{a:a: \;\infty\; c\} = \{110\}$$

$$s = \{a, \;\infty\, a, \; c\} = \{101\} \qquad t = \left\{ \frac{a}{3}, \;\infty\, a, \; c \right\} = \{301\}$$

$$a = \{a: \infty\, a: \infty\, c\} = \{100\}$$

From the angle between the faces $s:a = 68°54'$, the axial ratio can be calculated to be $a:c = 1:0.3857$.

Another important property is illustrated by this figure, namely, that several faces intersect in parallel edges—*stats, prmrp*, etc. The aggregation of all faces or planes that intersect with parallel edges is called a *zone* and the common edge direction a *zone axis*. It follows that every possible crystal face must belong to at least two crystallographic zones.

3. *Hexagonal Indices.* Since hexagonal crystals are characterized by four axes (Fig. 180*F*), three coplanar equal axes at 120 deg, perpendicular to a fourth, c, which is not equal to a, special consideration must be given to indexing of the planes. The reciprocal intercepts of a plane on all four axes will be $hkil$. Reference to Fig. 182, which shows some of the planes indicated, will show that always $i = -(h + k)$. Thus i may be indicated by a dot $hk.l$, but often even this is eliminated. However, it is always preferable to indicate all four indices since the relationship between equivalent planes is much more clearly seen. Prism

planes of type I, $(1\bar{1}00)$, $(10\bar{1}0)$, $(0\bar{1}10)$, $(\bar{1}100)$, $(\bar{1}010)$, and $(01\bar{1}0)$, are equivalent on this basis but do not appear to be on the three-index system $[(1\bar{1}0)$, (100), etc.$]$.   Directions similarly have four indices such that the third is the negative of the sum of the first two.

It has sometimes been customary to include hexagonal and rhombohedral systems under the same classification.   It is a fairly simple matter to transform indices of one into the other.   Thus if the $(10\bar{1}1)$ plane in the hexagonal system (H) is made the (100) plane of the rhombohedral (R), then any plane $hkil$ (H) will be $h'k'l'$(R) if:

$$
\begin{aligned}
h' &= 2h + k + l & h &= \tfrac{1}{3}(h' - k') \\
k' &= k - h + l & k &= \tfrac{1}{3}(k' - l') \\
l' &= -2k - h + l & i &= -(h + k) \\
& & l &= \tfrac{1}{3}(h' + k' + l')
\end{aligned}
$$

The whole matter of transformations of indices in general is comprehensively treated in Buerger's "X-Ray Crystallography."

4. *Space-lattices.*   As a further result of the experience of 200 years it is now definitely assured that the indices of all the plane faces of crystals are always small whole numbers (*i.e.*, 100, 321, 568, etc.)—the law of rational indices.   The crystallographer is guided by the external form of the crystal in selecting three nonparallel faces of the crystal whose intersections give the directions of crystal axes OA, OB, OC.   A fourth plane may be chosen as standard and called (111) since it intercepts all three axes at distances proportional to a, b, c.

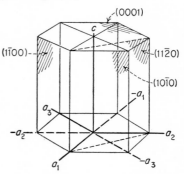

Fig. 182. Planar indices in the hexagonal system.

Then faces of the crystal are parallel to planes making intercepts a/h, b/k, c/l on the axes where h, k, l are small integers.   Thus we think of the axes OA, OB, OC divided up into h, k, and l equal parts, respectively, the indices of the set of planes being (hkl).   The crystallographer measures simply the ratio $a:b:c$, with b usually given the value unity, whereas x-ray methods measure the actual lengths of the unit translations.   In most cases these are proportional to the axial ratios of the goniometer measurement.   If this is true, then only a definite *lattice* in three dimensions formed by the intersection of three sets of parallel planes can explain the rational intersections on axes.   These so-called Bravais lattices are, of course, considered to be built on the above-mentioned systems of coordinates, and there are 14 of these spatial patterns geometrically possible (Fig. 183).

There is only one true space-lattice for each crystal pattern, but the choice of axes, the ways of drawing row lines and net standard planes, or

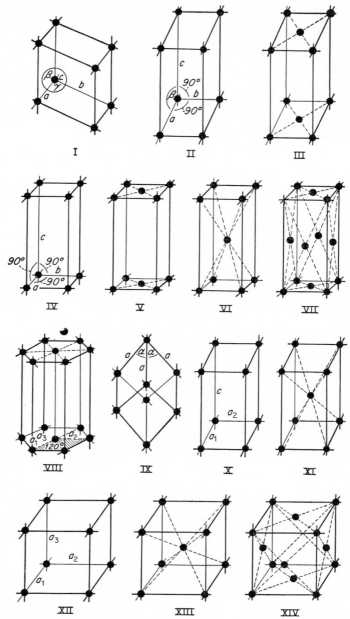

FIG. 183. Space lattices: I, triclinic; II, simple monoclinic; III, end face-centered mono-clinic; IV, simple orthorhombic; V, end face-centered orthorhombic; VI, body-centered orthorhombic; VII, face-centered orthorhombic; VIII, hexagonal; IX, rhombohedral; X, simple tetragonal; XI, body-centered tetragonal; XII, simple cubic; XIII, body-centered cubic; XIV, face-centered cubic.

unit cells formed by joining points in the lattice so that space is divided into a series of parallel-sided equal volumes, is arbitrary. The best guide is that the indices of the commonest faces shall be as simple as possible and that the largest number of points (atoms) shall lie in them. The lower the indices of a set of lattice planes, the more thickly populated are they with points and the greater is the interplaner spacing ($d_{100} > d_{110} > d_{321}$ etc.). Similarly along any line or *direction* the lower the indices, the larger the number of points through which it passes and the shorter the identity period.

5. *The Unit Cell.* The unit cell as defined by the vectors $\vec{a}$, $\vec{b}$, $\vec{c}$, is the smallest possible subdivision which has the properties of the visible macrocrystal and which, by the repetition or translation of itself in all directions, builds the crystal. There are many ways in which a cell can be drawn in a unique space-lattice; but usually the edges, a, b, c or unit translations are parallel with the respective crystallographic axes, and the smallest of the several possibilities is chosen.

The necessity of a unit cell such as that defined above arises from observations made upon the geometrical regularity of crystals. A "primitive cell" postulated long before the discovery of x-rays contained the essentials of the foregoing definition.

Since the unit cell builds the crystal through repetition, it is necessary that every possible interplanar spacing of the crystal can be described in terms of one unit cell. This is true since each interplanar spacing must be repeated along a given direction in the crystal if it is to be detected by x-ray methods, and the only manner in which such a condition may be satisfied is that the interplanar spacing represent a rational fraction of the repeating unit in the direction considered. For if the interplanar spacing represented some irrational fraction of the unit-cell dimension and was repeated throughout the crystal, the arrangement of atomic planes in the adjacent unit cell could not be exactly the same as that in the first, and we have a contradiction of the given definitions. The geometric unit cell itself is pictured such that by starting from any point in the structure, by going a distance equal and parallel to any cell edge, or by any combinations of such movements we arrive at a point where the whole surrounding structure has the same form and orientation as at the point from which we started. But the spacings between planes with which x-rays are concerned need not refer only to the perpendicular distance between opposite faces, edges, or corners of the unit cell.

Thus, every effective interplanar spacing must represent some fraction of the effective dimension of the unit cell in the direction considered, *i.e.*, if the effective, or repeating, dimension of the unit cell in one direction may be designated d, possible x-ray interferences may occur only for those positions with an interplanar spacing d/n, where n is an integer.

The expression d/n suggests the use of analogous fractions already mentioned which indicate the intercepts of the plane, a_0/h, b_0/k, and c_0/l, where a_0, b_0, and c_0 are the edge lengths of the unit cell and h, k, and l are integers, representing the number of parts into which each edge is divided.

By doubling the values of h, k, and l we double the number of equal divisions along each edge of the unit cell; thus we halve a given interplanar spacing of interest, and the condition is exactly the same as though we had considered the second order, or $n = 2$, in $n\lambda = 2d_{hkl} \sin \Theta$ of x-ray reflections from the original planes. This permits us to simplify our x-ray investigations by completely disregarding n, the quantity for order in the Bragg formula, and using suitable hkl values to designate all reflections (the hkl corresponds to a plane that would produce a given reflection on a pattern whether such a plane actually exists in the physical sense or not). Thus an x-ray interference may be identified as related to (200) planes as if these had real existence, whereas actually the reflection is the second order from the (100) planes.

6. *Macrosymmetry Operations and Point Groups.* To the systematic classification into seven crystal systems, the experimentally founded law of rational indices, and the consequent hypothesis of space-lattices may be added other types of information affording an approach to the subject of symmetry. Some of these are velocity of solution of different crystal faces, etch figures, birefringence, optical activity, piezo- and pyroelectric properties. In general, it might be expected that two crystals which gave identical measurements of angles between faces indicating identical disposition of planes should also have identical properties. It soon becomes evident, however, that the formal classification of crystals thus made has not been extended far enough. Mark[1] points out that angle measurements class both barium antimonyl tartrate and calcium molybdate as tetragonal, but this in no sense explains why one has optical activity and the other has not. Account, therefore, must be taken of different symmetries.

The symmetry of an object is an expression of the fact that the object has equal properties in different directions. Two positions of a crystal, in which the equivalent directions may be brought into coincidence, say, by a simple rotation around an axis, are not distinguishable by any physical-chemical means. Now the following symmetry operations, which are classed *macro* because they are observable from the outer form of crystals by optical examination, may be performed to bring equivalent points in space into coincidence:

a. Axes of symmetry (cyclic operation). Points in crystals may have one-, two-, three-, four-, or sixfold axes, by which is meant coincidence of

[1] *Z. Metallkunde*, **20**, 342 (1938).

equivalent points by rotation of 360 (every point has this identity operation), 180, 120, 90, or 60 deg.

In Fig. 184 is shown first a prism with an axis vertical, the axis being designated below. Below this graphical definition is shown the symmetry of the axis in a plane normal to the axis. In this case the plane is the plane of the paper, and we are looking down the axis of symmetry.

With the pure rotation axis, the equivalent points are all included in a common plane, which stands normal to the rotation axis.

The fact that there is no five- or seven- or eightfold axis is further indication of a space-lattice structure, since the unit of pattern possessing a given symmetry must be capable of repetition in space without leaving gaps. Thus hexagons fit together as in a honeycomb, but octagons leave square gaps. The claim that nature provides an instance of fivefold

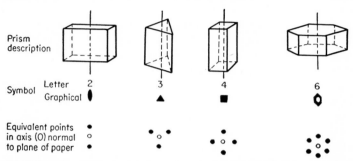

FIG. 184. Prism description, symbols, and equivalent points defining rotation axes.

axial asymmetry in the starfish has long since been disproved by reference to the existence of an alimentary canal inlet and outlet. The symbols for the rotation axes are 1, 2, 3, 4, 6.

b. Plane of symmetry (mirror operation). Here points on one side of a plane are mirror images of points on the other. The symbol is *m*.

c. Combined rotation-inversion. Here a point is rotated around a one-, two-, three-, four-, or sixfold axis (*i.e.*, through 360, 180, 120, 90, or 60 deg) and then inverted through the origin to an equal distance beyond. The corresponding symbols are $\bar{1}$, $\bar{2}$, $\bar{3}$, $\bar{4}$, $\bar{6}$. Thus $\bar{1}$ is the symbol for a *center of symmetry*, since a rotation of 360 deg plus inversion through the origin brings two positions into coincidence by passing through such a center. The symbol $\bar{2} = m$, since it is clear that rotation of 180 deg and inversion back through the origin bring a position below an imaginary plane which is the mirror image of the original point position.

These symmetry elements are well illustrated by the ornamental figures selected by Schiebold, shown in Fig. 185. The symmetry planes, axes, and center for the highest form of cubic symmetry are illustrated in Fig. 186. These elements are:

1. Fourfold axis [100].
2. Threefold axes [111].
3. Twofold axes [110].
4. Reflection planes [100].
5. Reflection planes [110].
6. Center of inversion, $\bar{1}$, and also rotation-inversion axes $\bar{4}$.

When now these symmetry operations are combined in every possible way, using the seven systems of coordinates, it develops that there are 32 point groups which define 32 crystal classes in terms of symmetry.

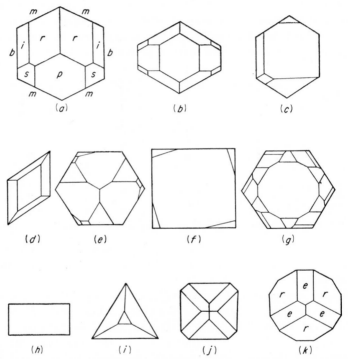

FIG. 185. Ornamental figures illustrating crystal symmetry: (a) plane of symmetry, hornblende; (b) two planes of symmetry, aragonite; (c) ornament without a plane of symmetry; (d) twofold axis of symmetry, gypsum; (e) threefold axis of symmetry, quartz; (f) fourfold axis of symmetry, wulfenite; (g) sixfold axis of symmetry, apatite; (h) ornament with mirror and rhythmic symmetry; (i) planes of symmetry and threefold axis, tourmaline; (j) planes of symmetry and fourfold axis, tinstone; (k) planes of symmetry and threefold rhythmic symmetry, calcite. (After Schiebold.)

By all odds the simplest method of representing and correlating the 32 point groups is graphically by means of a simplified stereographic projection, as is done in Fig. 187. The principle of the stereographic projection, long used by crystallographers to depict crystal habit in the two dimensions, is shown in Fig. 188. Here the crystal is considered to be the center of a sphere, and normals are drawn from each face to the surface of the sphere.   All the points on the surface of the northern hemisphere are then connected to the south pole, and vice versa.   The intersections of these connecting lines with the equatorial plane of the sphere, which is the plane of projection, produce the stereographic projection, which in turn is an instant graphical indication of the symmetry elements of the crystal.

In the first row of Fig. 187 are classes in the triclinic, monoclinic, rhombohedral, tetragonal, hexagonal, and cubic systems which have only principal rotation axes normal to the plane of the paper.   In the second row are those classes with inversion axes; in the third, a plane of symmetry perpendicular to the principal rotation axis, indicated by $\dfrac{X}{m}$ or X/m, and in the fourth row parallel to it Xm; in the fifth, a plane of symmetry parallel to an inversion axis $\bar{X}m$; in the sixth a secondary two-fold axis is added to the principal rotation axis $X2$; and in the last row highest general symmetry is achieved by adding planes of symmetry both perpendicular and parallel to the principal rotation axis $\dfrac{X}{m}\,m$ or X/mm.   Com-

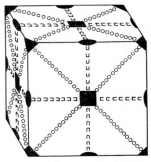

FIG. 186. Symmetry elements in a cubic crystal: squares, fourfold axes; triangles, three-fold; ellipses, twofold.

bination of two symmetry elements often automatically introduces further elements, but in standard usage the point-group symbols are kept as simple as possible in most cases.   It is evident that because of the high symmetry the cubic classes in this tabulation seem to depart from the otherwise straightforward relationships.   The cubic point groups are distinguished by four threefold axes lying along cube diagonals which are secondary, while the primary axes are twofold or fourfold and are expressed first in the symbols followed by the symbol of one secondary axis.

In crystallography usually the interest resides in three-dimensional lattice structures, and therefore in the 32 three-dimensional point groups. However, in graphite and other layer structures where there may be random stacking of two-dimensional sheets of atoms there may be direct concern with two-dimensional point groups.   The symmetry operations used in these are one-, two-, three-, four- and sixfold rotations (designated as before by the numbers) and mirror reflection across a line (symbol m). The various combinations of these give rise to 10 different two-dimensional point groups with the symbols 1, 2, $1m$ or m, $2mm$ or mm, 4, $4mm$ or $4m$, 3, $3m$, 6, $6mm$ or $6m$.

Points in a set which come into coincidence by the operation of symmetry elements are called *equivalent points*.   Barrett cites an excellent

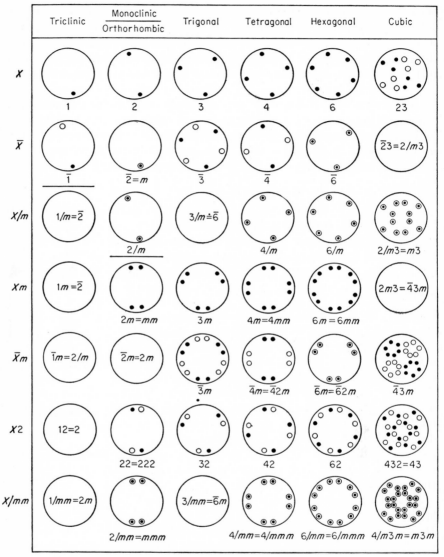

Fig. 187. The 32 point groups illustrated as stereographic projections.

example in the $4/m$ point group (a fourfold axis perpendicular to a mirror plane) which is represented in Fig. 189. Starting with a general point with coordinates xyz (distance $+x$ along the X axis, $+y$ along the Y axis, and $+z$ along the Z axis) at the upper right, there is an equivalent point at $xy\bar{z}$ below the XY plane; moving counterclockwise, there is another equivalent point at distance y along the negative X axis, or $\bar{y}$, $+x$ along the Y axis, and $+z$ along the Z axis, or $\bar{y}xz$. Similarly the other six equivalent points in this tetragonal point group are derived to give the total list of eight: xyz, $xy\bar{z}$, $\bar{y}xz$, $\bar{y}x\bar{z}$, $\overline{xyz}$, $\overline{xyz}$, $y\bar{x}z$, $y\bar{x}z$. In this way the equivalent points of all the 32 point groups may be derived by consideration of the symmetry operations.

A combination of goniometric and physical measurements makes it possible to classify crystals as to system and as to the finer subdivision of class or point group. But it is to be observed that this is still a macroclassification, and the idea of the lattice, except as an explanatory hypothesis, or of the ultimate units from which crystals

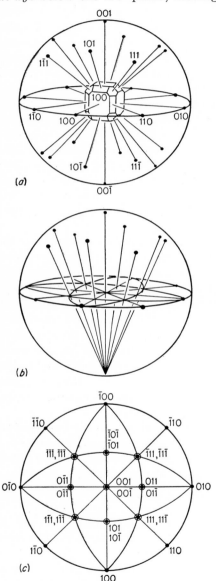

(a)

(b)

(c)

FIG. 188. The stereographic projection of crystal faces.

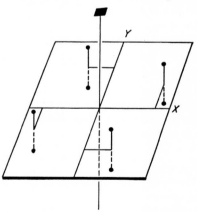

FIG. 189. Equivalent points in point group $4/m$. (C. S. Barrett, "Structure of Metals," 2d ed., p. 18, McGraw-Hill Book Company, Inc., New York 1952.)

are built does not enter in. For by definition all the symmetry elements of each point group are associated with a single unmoved central point and translation is impossible.

7. *Microsymmetry Operations and Space Groups.* The final step in the further refining of classification of crystals was taken as a result of the work of Schoenfliess in 1890, with the three-dimensional-lattice theory and the idea of atoms at the points of the lattice as a basis. In other words, by combining the 32 classes of symmetry around a point with translation in three directions to other equivalent points, arranged according to a definite spatial pattern (the lattice), at a distance on the order of 10^{-8} cm or atomic dimensions apart, other symmetry operations involving this translation become evident, namely, two-, three-, four-, and sixfold *screw* axes of symmetry, involving rotations about and translations along an axis, and glide planes of symmetry in which a figure is brought into coincidence by reflection in a plane combined with translation of a definite length and direction in the plane. These were called by Schoenfliess "microscopic symmetry elements." When these are included in the process of placing each of the 32 point groups at the points of the appropriate 14 lattices, the result is a total of 230 combinations, or space groups.

It must be remembered that if the space group has a screw axis the point group has a corresponding rotation axis. The *macroscopic* properties of the crystal, optically observable, cannot distinguish between screw or rotation; but x-ray diffraction analysis of ultimate structure *does* distinguish between them. Similarly reflection and glide planes both correspond to the reflection planes of the point group. The translation that accompanies the rotation or reflection is immaterial to the symmetry of the crystal considered as a single unit; but it has vital importance in the location of atoms and molecules from which a crystal is built, and in the way in which x-rays are diffracted by such an array. Rotation axes, mirror planes, and rotation-inversion axes are *optical* macroelements; screw axes and glide planes are *x-ray* microelements.

a. Screw axes. The screw axis is designated p_q; p denotes a p-fold axis of rotation associated with a translation in such a manner that for each rotation of $2\pi/p$ there is a displacement of q/p of the shortest translation parallel to the axis. The following screw axes exist:

$$2_1, \ 3_1, \ 3_2, \ 4_1, \ 4_2, \ 4_3, \ 6_1, \ 6_2, \ 6_3, \ 6_4, \ 6_5$$

These are illustrated in Fig. 190. In those figures where the axis is designated by (O), it stands normal to the plane of the paper, and fractions indicate the distance of the point above the paper.

Two axes having the same principal number and the sum of whose indices is equal to the principal number stand to each other in an enantiomorphic relation. Only the axes 2_1, 4_2, and 6_3 are enantiomorphic with themselves, and fundamentally they represent a rotation of 180, 90, and 60 deg, respectively, combined with a displacement of half the shortest translation parallel to the axis. The axis 4_2 is a twofold axis, the axis 6_3 is a threefold axis, as pure rotation axes; the screw character of these axes can be recognized only when the full multiplicity is examined.

   b. Glide planes. When a glide plane of symmetry is present, every corner, edge, and face has a corresponding corner, edge, or face which

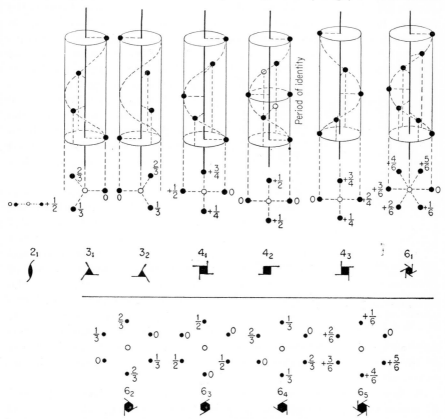

Fig. 190. Description, symbols, and equivalent points for screw axes.

can be brought into coincidence with the former by a mirror operation combined with a definite translation in the plane of the mirror. Various symbols are assigned, depending upon the direction and length of this glide or translation, as follows:

a, b, or *c*—a glide reflection plane with a glide of $\frac{1}{2}a$, $\frac{1}{2}b$, or $\frac{1}{2}c$ is simply given the corresponding symbol.

n—a glide plane with a glide of $\frac{1}{2}(b + c)$, $\frac{1}{2}(a + b)$, etc., is called *n* because by connecting a point to all its equivalent neighbors (into which it is transformed by this operation) a net is formed.

d—glide reflection planes with a glide of $\frac{1}{4}(b + c)$, etc. Called *d* because of the diagonally arranged construction leading in this case to diagonally arranged chains, just as in the case of *a*, *b*, or *c* it leads to chains running parallel to the direction of the axis. A *d* plane involves equivalence of the mid-point and corner of the parallelogram built up of the two elementary translations parallel to the reflection plane; *d* planes can, therefore, exist only parallel to centered faces.

Thus a space group is an extended network of reflection planes, glide planes, rotation axes, screw axes, axes of rotation-inversion and symmetry centers, based on a space-lattice. Its operations are self-consistent in that each operation or translation brings all the others into self-coincidence. Copper and diamond both have the same holohedral cubic point group; but they represent 2 of 10 entirely different space groups. Whereas copper has the symmetry elements for the cube in Fig. 186, diamond has fourfold *screw* axes and *glide* planes, as illustrated in Fig. 191.

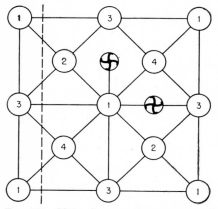

Fig. 191. Glide planes and screw axes of the diamond structure. Atoms marked (1) are on the lower face of the cubic unit cell and repeat again in the upper face. If the cubic edge is denoted by *a*, atoms marked (2), (3), and (4) are at heights *a*/4, *a*/2, 3*a*/4, respectively.

It is obvious that the classification of a crystal by its space group is unique. X-ray diffraction analysis alone has made possible this last refinement in classification and has verified the geometrical theory of space groups. Conversely the theory of space groups is an indispensable tool to the x-ray analyst.

For each space group is distinguished by certain definite x-ray diffraction criteria, which are discovered in the course of interpretation of patterns, as will be illustrated in the next chapter.

8. *Space-group Notation.* The 230 space groups have been designated for many years by the symbols proposed by Schoenfliess. A symbol was assigned to each point group, such as C_{2h} for monoclinic holohedral, O_h for cubic holohedral, etc. The space groups in each class are designated by indices, such as C_{2h}^1, C_{2h}^2, etc. Subsequently, Wyckoff proposed an improved notation. A far more rational system was suggested by Hermann and Mauguin, and this has been adopted internationally now by all x-ray workers and is employed in the standard "International Tables for X-ray Crystallography" (1952). The symbolism of the Hermann-Mauguin method is built upon two principles: (1) a symbol for the translation group (which involves such translations of a fundamental group as are necessary to build the crystal lattice) and (2) one to three symbols

for the elements of symmetry that lie along special directions in the crystal system of interest.

a. Translation groups. The translation group furnishes a picture of the method in which groups are distributed throughout space to give the three-dimensional lattice necessary for the description of the crystal. Such translations simply consist in taking some point in the unit cell (identified by its symmetry) and arranging like points throughout space to give the crystal. Such arrangements of points may be considered to designate a number of unit cells.

These translation groups are represented by capital letters; each precedes the section used to describe it.

P—the simply primitive translation group, *i.e.*, such a group as can be represented with the aid of a cell that is as nearly rectangular as possible. A *P* cell has the property that all elements of symmetry of the same kind belonging to one axial direction have gliding components equal to each other.

C—*c*-face-centered cell. The point $\frac{1}{2}\frac{1}{2}0$ is equivalent to the corner point of the cell, $0\,0\,0$. This symbol serves to denote the hexagonal translation group also, since the group can be referred to a rectangular cell with its base face-centered, and the axial ratio $a{:}b = 1{:}(3)^{\frac{1}{2}}$ (orthohexagonal cell).

A—*a*-face-centered cell, analogous to *C*.

B—*b*-face-centered cell, analogous to *C*.

H—hexagonal cell similar to *C*, but having the inverse axial ratio. (This symbol is no longer used in the 1952 "International Tables for X-ray Crystallography.")

I—body-centered cell. The mid-point $\frac{1}{2}\frac{1}{2}\frac{1}{2}$ is equivalent to the corner $0\,0\,0$.

F—lattice with all faces face-centered (the smallest rectangular cell is already quadruply primitive). Here $0\frac{1}{2}\frac{1}{2}$, $\frac{1}{2}0\frac{1}{2}$, and $\frac{1}{2}\frac{1}{2}0$ are equivalent to $0\,0\,0$.

R—The rhombohedral cell, which can be based upon a rectangular one only by using the axial ratio given above. In this case $\frac{1}{2}\frac{1}{2}0$, $0\frac{1}{3}\frac{1}{3}$, $0\frac{2}{3}\frac{2}{3}$, $\frac{1}{2}\frac{5}{6}\frac{1}{3}$, $\frac{1}{2}\frac{1}{6}\frac{2}{3}$ are equivalent to $0\,0\,0$. This cell is a sextuply primitive one.

After the lattice has been described by the first symbol of the symmetry expression, one to three other symbols are given for the elements of symmetry which lie along special directions in the crystal system. The special directions are:

Monoclinic system. The orthoaxis (*b* direction).

Orthorhombic system. The directions of the three mutually perpendicular axes.

Tetragonal system. The "principal axis" (*c* direction), the secondary axis (*a* direction) perpendicular to this, and the tertiary axis, which is also perpendicular to the principal axis and cuts the secondary axis at 45 deg.

Trigonal and hexagonal systems. The principal axis (*c*) and secondary and tertiary axes as above, which here form an angle of 30 deg.

Cubic system. The principal axis [100], the secondary axis [111], and the tertiary axis [110].

The symbols for the elements of symmetry, as already described, are as follows:

Rotation axes: 1 (the identity operation signifying no symmetry), 2, 3, 4, 6.

Rotation-inversion axes: $\bar{1}$ (center of symmetry), $\bar{2}$ ($= m$), $\bar{3}$, $\bar{4}$, $\bar{6}$.

Screw axes: 2_1, 3_1, 3_2, 4_1, 4_2, 4_3, 6_1, 6_2, 6_3, 6_4, 6_5.

Mirror (reflection) plane: *m.*
Glide planes: *a, b, c, n, d.*

The symbols for all 230 space groups are listed in the Appendix; and Figs. 192*a* and 192*b* graphically illustrate some examples (all triclinic and monoclinic are included).

The crystal class isomorphous with any space group is obtained by omitting the translation symbol and replacing all screw axes by the corresponding rotation axes and all glide reflection planes by *m* planes.

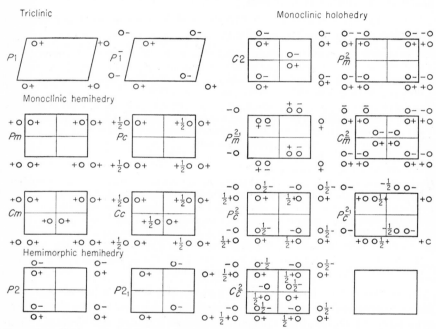

FIG. 192*a*. Projections illustrating symmetry characteristics of triclinic and monoclinic space groups.

9. *Coordinates of Equivalent Points.* Since a space group is an array of symmetry elements in three dimensions on a space-lattice, it follows that these elements operating on a point in a unit cell will produce a set of equivalent points in the cell. In an actual crystal, then, identical atoms or groups of atoms should be found at each of the equivalent points. The coordinates of equivalent points for each space group are listed in the "International Tables for X-ray Crystallography," following the lead of Wyckoff with his original book on the analytical expression of the theory of space groups. The number of equivalent points belonging to each set, and therefore the number of equivalent atoms or groups, is called the multiplicity. If these points lie on no symmetry elements, there is a *general* set; if they lie, say, on rotation axes, the effect is to reduce the

multiplicity for the *special* positions.   Thus coordinates are listed for the general and all special cases.   For example, a commonly found space group among more complex crystals is the orthorhombic $P2_12_12_1$, which is defined in terms of coordinates of equivalent points in the unit cell as follows:

Multiplicity	*Set*
2 (special)	$00z,\ \frac{1}{2}\,\frac{1}{2}\,\bar{z}$
	$0\,\frac{1}{2}\,z,\ \frac{1}{2}\,0\,z$
4 (general)	$xyz;\ \overline{xyz};\ \frac{1}{2}+x,\ \frac{1}{2}-y,\ \bar{z};\ \frac{1}{2}-x;\ \frac{1}{2}+y,\ z$

It is obvious that one of the important steps in crystal structure analysis is to determine the number of atoms or molecules, or generally speaking the multiplicity, per unit cell from the measured density of the crystal.

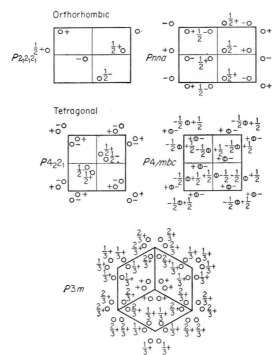

FIG. 192*b*. Selected examples of orthorhombic, tetragonal, and hexagonal space groups.

Steps in the X-ray Analysis of Crystal Structures.
Regardless of the experimental method of analysis (considered in the next chapter), the information vouchsafed by interference patterns of crystals is essentially the same.   This is the determination of a series of values of d for different sets of planes by use of the Bragg equation.   Now, if a crystal is really a lattice, it follows that planes of three sets in the principal directions will enclose a small unit cell—the smallest possible subdivision which has the

properties of the visible macrocrystal and which by repetition or translation of itself in all directions actually builds the crystal. It is the size of this fundamental architectural unit that may be determined directly from the experimental values of d_1, d_2, and d_3—the respective edge lengths of the small parallelepiped. This presupposes some previous information about the crystallographic system, whether the axes are at right angles or not or are of equal length or not. As previously indicated, this may easily be obtained by goniometer measurements of angles between faces. But if optical data are not available, the angles between the axes and axial ratios may be measured by reflection of x-rays from a crystal mounted on a goniometer head just as readily as by the optical method. Assuming this to be the process employed, the steps in analysis are as follows:

1. Goniometric determination of crystallographic system.

2. Determination of dimensions and volume of unit cell. The scheme of repetition regardless of the detail of the figure or "motif" (molecule) which is being repeated or translated according to a three-dimensional spacial pattern.

3. Determination of the number of atoms or molecules in each unit cell. This involves a measurement of the density of the crystal and the use of the volume of the unit cell in the following formula:

$$n = \frac{\rho A V}{M}$$

where n is the number of atoms (of an element) or molecules per unit cell; ρ is the density; V is the volume of the unit cell (d^3 for a cubic crystal, or, in general,

$$V = abc \sqrt{\sin^2 \alpha + \sin^2 \beta + \sin^2 \gamma - 2(1 - \cos \alpha \cos \beta \cos \gamma)}$$

where a, b, and c are edge lengths, and α, β, and γ the angles enclosed by the edges); M is the atomic or molecular weight; and A is Avogadro's number (see page 99) From the value of n the multiplicity of equivalent points in a cell is indicated, i.e., whether atoms or molecules lie in general or special positions. The contribution of the symmetry of molecules to crystal symmetry can often be deduced.

4. Identification of interference maxima with the indices of planes.

5. Application of the theory of space groups. Each of these space groups is characterized by certain diffraction criteria, to be considered in Chap. 15, such as the apparent halving of spacings due to nonappearance of odd-order ($n = 1, 3, 5$, etc.) interferences. Screw axes and glide planes can be detected.

6. Up to this point the geometrical information from diffraction data has been used to discover the scheme of repetition in three dimensions, analogous with the observation of how some figure or motif repeats itself on wallpaper by some characteristic transition. An analysis of the structure factor from intensity measurements, defining the positions within the unit cell of the diffracting centers, and even of the symmetry and positions of atoms in molecules if these are the lattice units, leads to the configuration of the motif (the molecule in organic crystals, for example) itself. This is the most difficult, least direct, and yet the most interesting stage in crystal analysis. Briefly put, the process consists in assuming certain values for parameters and upon the basis of known laws of scattering and interference in calculating from these the theoretical intensity of reflections from a set of planes. These results are compared with observed intensities, and the process of trial and error is continued

until there is an agreement. Bernal has likened the process to the solution of a cross-word puzzle. The cell and space group provide the square and pattern, the atoms the letters, and the intensities the clues. A more elegant method is the use of Fourier equations for the calculation of the distribution of electrons and thus unique atomic positions in unit cells.

7. A coordination and test of the completed structure with other known physical and chemical properties, such as atomic or ionic radii, optical activity, and polarization.

Types of Information Obtainable from X-ray Diffraction Data. From the foregoing development of the subject it might be concluded that the lattice type, unit-cell dimensions, space group, and ultimately the motif configuration of crystals, together with the consequent explanation of certain properties, are the only facts to be gained from x-ray diffraction data. Suppose that we know that a whole series of samples of metal has exactly the same crystal structure, characteristic of iron or copper, etc. Is there any further differentiation possible upon the basis of x-ray diffraction patterns?

The dependence of x-ray interferences upon the condition or texture of a specimen as well as the characteristic crystal geometry makes it possible to detect very minute changes in atomic position or in lattice constituents as well as effects of grain size, deformation, and strain. Consequently a fund of purely scientific and technological information is obtained from this fine-structure method, which is almost universal in its scope.

Following is a listing of the principal types of information, each of which will receive discussion:

1. Crystalline or noncrystalline, percentage of crystalline and amorphous phases.
2. Crystallographic system, unit-cell dimensions, space group, parameters of atoms or molecules.
3. Deduction of crystal unit (atom, ion, molecule), of size of unit, of type of binding, and of general properties of solid to be expected.
4. Atomic and molecular weights, defect lattices and those with extra interstitial atoms.
5. Chemical identity, chemical and crystallographic changes and stability.
6. Allotropic modifications.
7. Type and mechanism of chemical combination, solid solutions, and alloy formation.
8. Single crystal or aggregate.
9. Crystallographic orientation of single crystal or of grains in aggregate.
10. Random or fibered aggregate and relative degree of preferred orientation in intermediate stages.
11. Grain size in an aggregate (particularly in the colloidal range).
12. Internal strain or distortion, below and above the elastic limit.
13. Extent of deformation and mechanism of fabrication in rolling, drawing, etc.
14. Analysis of effect of heat-treatment, grain growth, control and mechanism of recrystallization.
15. Differentiation between surface and interior structure, and film structure.
16. Atomic distribution in liquids and glasses and in mesomorphic or subcrystalline states.
17. The nature of substances with very high molecular weights.

CHAPTER 14

THE EXPERIMENTAL X-RAY METHODS
OF CRYSTAL ANALYSIS

The several methods of analysis of crystal structure from x-ray diffraction patterns have in common first of all the determination of the angle Θ in the Bragg law. The methods and cameras differ, primarily, depending upon the type of specimen, whether a single crystal or aggregate or powder; the radiation, whether monochromatic or polychromatic; the method of registration of diffracted beams, whether photographically or by ionization chamber, Geiger counter, etc.; and diffraction by a single set of parallel planes, a few sets, or many simultaneously. A description of each technique and the relationship between methods is best shown by listing all the possible variables, as in Table 14-1, and then defining each method in terms of these variables, as in Table 14-2.

Special Notes on Apparatus. 1. *The Laue Method.* The experimental equipment here is relatively so simple, as shown in Fig. 193, that little additional explanation is required. Typical Laue patterns are illustrated in Figs. 194a and 194b. The design and construction of the pinhole for

TABLE 14-1. VARIABLES OF DIFFRACTION TECHNIQUES

I. Radiation
    1. Polychromatic (unfiltered)
    2. Monochromatic (filtered or reflected by monochromator crystal) (Chap. 6)
II. Beam definition (collimation)
    3. Pinholes; totally reflecting lead-glass capillary tubes
    4. Slits, single and multiple (Soller)
    5. Single orifice—widely divergent beam
III. Specimen type
    6. Single crystal
    7. Oriented film on flat or curved surface
    8. Fiber
    9. Powder (in capillary, button, wedge, compressed wire)
    10. Solid aggregate
    11. Glass or liquid
IV. Specimen motion
    12. Stationary
    13. Oscillated
    14. Translated
    15. Rotated
    16. Precession of axis normal to reciprocal lattice plane

358

TABLE 14-1. VARIABLES OF DIFFRACTION TECHNIQUES (*Continued*)

V. Origin of reflections
    17. From single set of planes
    18. From limited number of planes
    19. From large number of planes simultaneously
VI. Registration
    20. Ionization chamber
    21. Geiger, proportional, or scintillation counter
    22. Film
VII. Film arrangement
    23. Flat film
    24. Curved film
VIII. Film motion
    26. Stationary film
    26. Moving film
        a. Translation
        b. Rotation
        c. Precession
IX. Direction of diffracted rays registered on patterns
    27. Transmission forward
    28. Reflection forward from surface
    29. Back reflection
    30. Interferences around 360°
X. Typical pattern
    31. Spots (on elliptical loci)
    32. Sharp line or peak in several orders
    33. Interferences on layer lines
    34. Interferences fanned out
    35. Symmetrical lattice of points
    36. White lines on gray background
    37. Random peppering of spots
    38. Continuous rings, spotted, smooth, sharp, or diffuse
    39. Array of curved lines (powder spectrum)
    40. Peaks on automatic recorder chart
    41. Discontinuous rings (symmetrical intensity maxima)
    42. Halos
XI. Selection of method
    43. Uses:
        a. Symmetry
        b. Orientation
        c. Unit-cell dimensions
        d. Indexing
        e. Extinctions
        f. Intensities
        g. Identification
        h. Texture
XII. Special features
    44. *a.* High and low temperatures
        b. Vacuum or special atmospheres
        c. Extremely high precision
        d. High speed
        e. Calibration, etc.

TABLE 14-2. DESCRIPTION IN TERMS OF VARIABLES OF TABLE 14-1
OF PRINCIPAL EXPERIMENTAL DIFFRACTION METHODS

1. Laue 1, 3, 6, 12, 19, 22, 23, 25, 27, 31, 43a, b, d, e
2. Bragg (spectrometer) 2, 3, 6, 13 (15), 17, 20 (21, 22), 24, 25, 28, 32, 43c, e
3. Rotation (Schiebold-Polanyi) 2, 3, 6, 15, 18, 22, 24 (23), 25, 27, 33, 43c, d, e, f
4. Oscillation 2, 3, 6, 13, 18, 22, 24 (23), 25, 27, 33, 43c, d, e, f
5. Moving-film (goniometer) methods
    a. Weissenberg 2, 3, 6, 15, 18, 22, 24, 26a, 30, 34, 43d, e, f
    b. Sauter 2, 3, 6, 15, 18, 22, 23, 26b (perpendicular to crystal rotation axis), **27, 34,** 43d, e, f
    c. DeJong-Bouman (Clark-Gross) 2, 3, 6, 15, 18, 22, 23, 26b (parallel to crystal rotation axis) 27, 35, 43d, e, f
    d. Buerger precession 2, 3, 6, 12, 18, 22, 23, 26c, 27, 35, 43d, e, f
6. Lonsdale divergent beam 2, 3, 6, 12, 18, 22, 23, 25, 27 (absorption lines) 36, 43a, b, c
7. Powder (Hull-Debye-Scherrer) 2, 3, 9 (10), 12, 19, 22 (21), 24 (23), 25, 27 (30), 39 (38, 40) 43g, 44
8. Powder (Straumanis) 2, 3, 9 (10), 12, 19, 22, 24, 25, 27, 29 (30), 39, 43g, 44c
9. Fiber (monochromatic pinhole) 2, 3, 8 (7, 11), 12, 18, 22, 23, 25, 27, 41 (42), 43b, g, h
10. Back reflection 2, 3, 10 (9, 6), 12, 18, 22, 23, 25, 29, 38 (37), 43h, 44c

defining the beam are most important. With a single orifice, of course, a pinhole image of the target is obtained by the pinhole camera effect. The longer the collimator, which is simply a pinhole in a solid block or two apertures in metal plates separated by a fixed distance, the more nearly parallel is the x-ray beam. The diameter of the pinhole is of

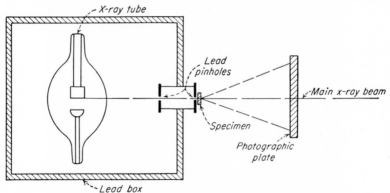

FIG. 193. Diagram of the Laue and monochromatic pinhole x-ray methods.

importance from the standpoint of detail in the diffraction pattern. The interferences become sharper the smaller the diameter.

On the other hand, the time of exposure increases with increase in length or decrease in diameter. For average purposes a size of 0.025 in. is satisfactory, although a range from 0.005 to 0.060 in. may be employed for various specimens.

As Table 14-1 indicates, the Laue method is the only one now in use which employs general, or "white," radiation, usually from a tungsten

FIG. 194a. Symmetrical Laue pattern of an iron crystal.

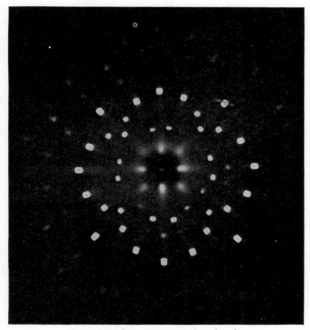

FIG. 194b. Laue pattern of rock salt.

target below 60,000 volts. Since the direction of the x-ray beam is fixed and the crystal is stationary, the angles made by the incident beam with every possible set of reflecting planes are fixed and the only variables in the Bragg equation $n\lambda = 2d \sin \Theta$ are n and λ. If λ were fixed and since n must be an integer, it follows that very few sets of planes would be in a favorable position to meet the requirements of the Bragg equation and reflections would of course be rare. But since there is a whole range of wavelengths in the continuous spectrum, there will be discrete values of λ which satisfy the Bragg condition no matter what may be the orientation of the lattice planes. In other words, each set of planes picks out from the heterogeneous beam bathing it the one particular wavelength which can be reflected in accordance with the Bragg law.

The voltage on the tube of course determines the short-wavelength limit in the spectrum; obviously the wavelengths for all Laue spots must lie above this limit. Laue spots from planes with a common zone axis lie on ellipses; for if the x-ray beam is at an angle Θ to a zone axis, the reflected rays must also be at the angle Θ to each plane and therefore to the zone axis, thus lying on the surface of a cone of semivertical angle Θ. The trace of this cone on the photographic film is an ellipse with one end of its major axis lying on the center spot of the pattern. Since a crystal plane can be parallel to two zone axes, each Laue spot then must be common to two reflection ellipses and lie at their point of intersection. This fact permits a simple approach to the identification of spots in terms of planar indices, as will be explained in the next chapter on interpretation. Since each spot is made up of several overlapping orders of different wavelengths, it is at once apparent that the correct use of intensity data is difficult.

The average length of exposure with ordinary equipment for a Laue photograph of a single crystal without heavily absorbing elements is 30 min to 1 hr. The new high-powered tubes described on page 34 allow a reduction of time to a matter of seconds or minutes. A flat *cassette*, or film holder, is shown in Fig. 195.

2. *The Bragg Method (Spectrometry)*. Since the Bragg method of crystal analysis involves direct angular measurements of Θ, the use of monochromatic radiation, and reflection from a single set of planes, usually parallel to a face, the significance of the results is readily understood in terms of the preceding development. By successive resettings of the crystal so that the planar distances for various sets of planes that have a common zone axis are ascertained, it is usually possible to arrive at something like a complete structure; the difficulty arises in the tedious repetition of measurements and the accurate orientation of the crystal specimen on the spectrometer. This method is described in some detail in Chap. 5.

3. *The Rotation Method*. The most powerful method of crystal analysis is undoubtedly the rotation method, which is known in several modifica-

tions. Ordinarily the single crystal is mounted and rotated around a principal axis. Three such photographs around the principal axes make possible almost complete information. In the usual method a stationary film is used, either flat at a fixed distance from the crystal or preferably bent on the circumference of a circle with the crystal at the center. The high-precision Unicam (Cambridge Instrument Company) rotation camera, useful also with a flat film, is pictured in Fig. 196.

Frequently it is desirable to mount the crystals on a goniometer head by means of which the angles between axes may be measured. If, for

FIG. 195. Flat *cassette* for Laue patterns, for use on Hayes multiple diffraction unit.

example, a rational layer-line pattern for the rotation method is obtained for one orientation of an orthorhombic crystal, another will be obtained when the crystal is shifted 90 deg and again rotated and still another after it is shifted 90 deg in the third direction. In all cases a complete spectral diagram for all possible reflections from a given crystalline zone (the rotation axis) is obtained, such as appears in Fig. 197.

It is apparent from these patterns made on cylindrical films and then laid out flat that the reflections are distributed along horizontal parallel lines called *layer* lines (all but the equatorial line are hyperbolas if a flat film is used) and also along vertical curved *row* lines.

A complete diagram for rotation around 360 deg is, of course, the summation of a series of diagrams which may be prepared by oscillating the

FIG. 196. Unicam camera for rotation patterns.   (*Cambridge Instrument Company.*)

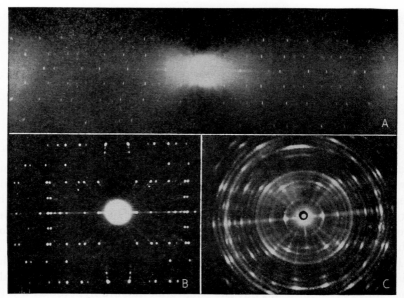

FIG. 197. Typical rotation patterns: (*A*) $CsNO_3$; (*B*) $Na_3PO_4.12H_2O$; (*C*) $Na_3PO_4.16H_2O$ after losing water.

crystal over fixed angles, 1 to 20 deg, 20 to 40 deg, etc., by means of a heart-shaped cam.   This interpretation of a complex rotation pattern is often greatly simplified by such oscillation diagrams, as will be demonstrated in the next chapter.

Aside from the arrangement of the photographic film and the method of mechanically rotating or oscillating the crystal, the principal variable in the simple method is the method of beam definition.   Here as in the Bragg spectrometer the most common equipment is a pair of slits for rendering the rays parallel.   These are made of lead, lead alloy, gold, or even brass for softer rays.   For only very small crystals the slits may be so short as actually to be pinholes.   The smaller the slit width or pinhole diameter, the sharper are the interferences.

4. *Moving-film Methods.*   In many rotation patterns the individual interferences may be so numerous and close together on a layer line as to overlap.

For increasing accuracy and sensitiveness special modifications of the rotation method are employed as follows:[1]

1. Displacement of the film parallel to the direction of the axis of rotation of the crystal (Weissenberg goniometer).
2. Displacement of the plate or film parallel to the X axis (Dausar).
3. Displacement of the film parallel to the direction of the primary beams (Kratky).
4. Rotation of the photographic film around the Z axis (parallel with crystal axis) (DeJong-Bouman, Clark-Gross).
5. Rotation of the film around the Y axis (primary beam) (Schiebold-Sauter goniometer).
6. Displacement of two photographic plates in directions parallel and perpendicular to the axis of rotation.
7. Precession motions of crystal and film.

Of these the Weissenberg and the Buerger precession methods are most generally employed, largely because of the simplicity of interpretation and because of the availability of excellent commercial instruments. The purpose of all moving-film methods is to resolve or sweep out a single layer line in a rotation pattern consisting often of many very close or overlapping interference spots.

5. *The Weissenberg Camera.*   Figure 198a shows a Weissenberg goniometer as designed by Bohm and built by Supper to Buerger's design. The cylindrical film, coaxial with the rotating crystal fragment, is gradually displaced during the exposure in the direction parallel to the axis. The principle of the apparatus is shown diagrammatically in Fig. 198b, and in Fig. 199 is reproduced a Weissenberg pattern for zinc salicylate, for the zero layer line (equator) of the ordinary rotation pattern (above) around the C axis of this monoclinic crystal.

[1] The moving-film methods and goniometers are described, together with full references, in M. J. Buerger, "X-ray Crystallography," John Wiley & Sons, Inc., New York, 1942.

FIG. 198*a*. Buerger-Supper Weissenberg goniometer.

In the Weissenberg diagram the spectra of the various surfaces of the zone of rotation are not superimposed but are arranged in hyperbolas which allow relatively simple assignment of indices. When several lattice planes are equivalent, such as (110), (1$\bar{1}$0), ($\bar{1}$10), ($\bar{1}\bar{1}$0) in a rhombic crystal, and have the same lattice spacing d and the same diffraction angle 2Θ, they will all register on a stationary film the same interference point, whereas in this modification with moving film each set of planes will register its own interference lying on a vertical line.

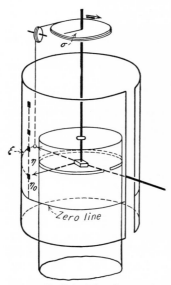

FIG. 198*b*. Principle of operation of the Weissenberg goniometer.

6. *The Schiebold-Sauter Camera.* The Schiebold-Sauter camera such as is pictured in Fig. 200 consists essentially of a rotating crystal, arranged with a shield so that only the interferences from one layer line may be recorded on a flat circular film, which is rotated at the same rate as is the crystal. With this arrangement, the angular distance separating two interferences of the same interplanar spacing is equal to the angular distance through which the crystal must be turned in order to pass from the position for reflecting the first set of planes to the position for reflecting the second set. This makes the camera suitable for the study of layer lines higher than the equatorial layer line. The equatorial layer

line is ordinarily employed, since this will furnish the data necessary for determination of the unit-cell dimensions and shape.   Since reflection occurs from a crystal face when the crystal is tilted at Θ deg to the incident x-ray beam, the interferences are recorded when the crystal is turned

Fig. 199. Weissenberg pattern (*below*) for zero layer of rotation pattern (*above*) of zinc salicylate (monoclinic) rotated around *c* axis.

Θ deg beyond the point at which the set of reflecting planes are normal to the x-ray beam.   For calculations it is necessary that we consider the angular distances separating the *normals* of the different sets of planes, so that in most cases it is necessary to subtract (or add, as the case may be) Θ deg from the angular position of each interference on the film.   If this is done, the curved lines formed by interferences of various orders from the same set of planes will be straightened and the interpretation will be greatly simplified.

7. *DeJong-Bouman Camera.* By bending the film, or by proper selection of the angle of the rotating film with respect to the primary x-ray beam and the axis of crystal rotation (DeJong-Bouman method, independently developed by Clark and Gross and first described in the third edition of this book), the corrections may be made directly on the film, so that the patterns obtained, such as those in Fig. 201, are characterized

Fig. 200. Schiebold-Sauter goniometer. (*General Electric X-Ray Corporation.*) *Left,* defining pinholes; *center,* goniometer head and rotating mechanism; *right,* holder for circular flat film, rotated around horizontal axis.

by linear arrangements of interferences which are easily interpreted. The general scheme of this method, one of the two for photographing the so-called reciprocal lattice (see the following chapter), is shown in Fig. 202.

8. *Precession Camera.* The newest and perhaps most powerful method of spreading out the interferences in a single layer line of a rotation pattern into an undistorted two-dimensional array is the Buerger precession technique.[1] A photograph of the Buerger-Supper camera is shown in Fig. 203. Accurate description of the precession motion of the rotating crystal and of the synchronously moving film is difficult: it requires the

[1] M. J. Buerger, The Photography of the Reciprocal Lattice, *ASXRED Mon.* 1 (1944); "X-ray Crystallography," John Wiley & Sons, Inc., New York, 1942.

concept of the reciprocal lattice, which is described in detail and utilized in the next chapter. Briefly, this imaginary lattice of points is constructed from the direct lattice by drawing vectors as normals to each set of planes for a length inversely proportional to the interplanar spacing. Since on an x-ray pattern a single interference *spot* represents diffraction by a set of *planes,* the reciprocal lattice is much closer to the appearance

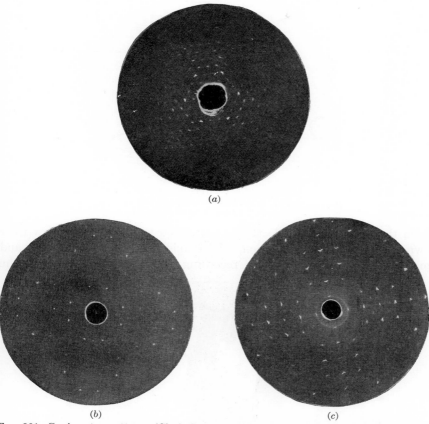

FIG. 201. Goniometer patterns (Clark-Gross modification of Schiebold-Sauter method): (a) orthophenanthroline (equator); (b) Pb$_3$O$_4$ (equator); (c) Pb$_3$O$_4$ (first layer line).

of the pattern. If by some device the points of the pattern could be made to register on an undistorted network, this would be a "photograph" of the reciprocal lattice, easily interpreted in terms of the direct lattice.

If the direct axis of a crystal be made to follow the surface of a cone of opening angle μ whose apex is at the origin of the reciprocal lattice normal to that axis, circular central sections of the various recordable levels of the reciprocal lattice will be rolled in and out of the surface of the sphere of reflection. Points of the reciprocal lattice record at each contact with the surface of the sphere.   Now, if a film be parallel to the lattice at all times during this precessing motion, the reciprocal lattice will be recorded with no distortion; *i.e.*, the recorded points will be at vector distances

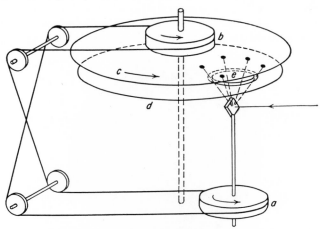

Fig. 202. General scheme of DeJong-Bouman goniometer.   *a*, drum rotating crystal about a vertical axis; *b*, drum of same size as *a*, rotating flat camera *c* in synchronism with *a*; *c*, flat camera rotating about vertical axis displaced sideways relative to axis of *a*; *d*, stationary screen with slot *e*; *e*, slot in screen *d* to isolate one layer line.

from the origin.   The reflected beams of the various levels follow their own unique cone of diffraction, whose axis is the precessing axis, and may be selected for individual recording by a suitable aperture.   The

Fig. 203. Buerger-Supper precession goniometer.

mechanism of the precession technique is best shown in Fig. 204; and a typical pattern for sodium chloride, rotated around the cube axis, in Fig. 205.

A mechanism to effect this type of recording was described by Buerger in 1944.[1]   This instrument precesses crystal and film in unison by means of a follower mechanism.   The setting of the precession angle $\bar{\mu}$ determines the area of the reciprocal lattice to be explored.   An independent

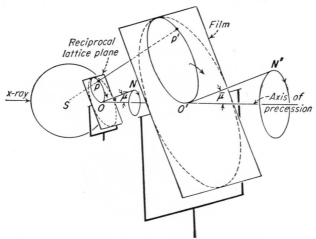

FIG. 204. Diagram illustrating mechanism of precession goniometer.   (*Buerger, ASXRED Mon. 1.*)

setting F, the distance of the center of the film to the crystal, determines the magnification of the lattice.   A holder for a set of circular apertures for layer-cone selection is rigidly fixed to the crystal holder in such a way that its center is on and normal to the precessing axis.   The setting of the circular aperture is determined by $\bar{\mu}$ and the translation distance along the crystallographic axis. The crystal is adjusted relative to the x-ray beam by a large dial on the instrument and the two small arcs of the goniometer head.   Orientation of the crystal is achieved conveniently on the instrument by a combination of optical and x-ray methods.

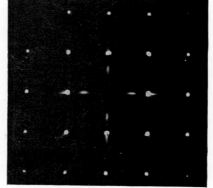

FIG. 205. Typical precession pattern: sodium chloride rotated around cube axis.

The unique advantage of the precession camera is that it produces a nondistorted, highly magnified image of the reciprocal lattice, from which symmetry and extinctions may be determined by inspection.   This feature makes it particularly convenient in working with very large unit

[1] *ASXRED Mon.* 1 (1944).

cells, which on the Weissenberg patterns are exceedingly tedious to index. As only a small section of the lattice is swept out by the beam, exposure times are very short compared with the various rotating-crystal methods. A less perfect crystal is required, which simplifies the investigation of plastic crystals and twins. The disadvantages of the method are that the central portion of n layers is missing and that entire levels are not recorded. The latter is not serious in the case of most organic compounds, as the temperature factor quite often reduces the intensities of the higher-order reflections to an undetectable level.

Experience in the author's laboratory has produced a very high regard for the precession camera. A Weissenberg-precession combination makes it possible to use one crystal to provide information from all principal

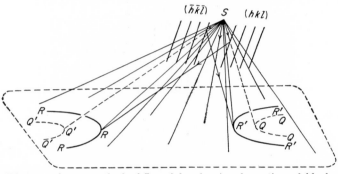

Fig. 206. Divergent-beam method of Lonsdale, showing formation of black and white conics.

RR, reflection conic $\Big\}$ planes hkl;
QQ, deficiency conic

$R'R'$, reflection conic $\Big\}$ planes $\bar{h}\bar{k}\bar{l}$.
$Q'Q'$, deficiency conic

axes of a crystal: two axes may be investigated by the precession camera and the third by the Weissenberg camera.

In view of the authoritative and exhaustive treatise by M. J. Buerger "X-Ray Crystallography,"[1] especially on the moving-film methods, no attempt is made here to present in detail the theory, apparatus, and applications of these techniques. The reader is referred to this work.

9. *Divergent-beam Method.* Lonsdale[2] has developed an ingenious method which employs a divergent beam of x-rays instead of a collimated beam of parallel rays, which is essential in all other methods. A point source (single orifice) of divergent rays is placed close to a stationary crystal. On the photographic plate may appear, after a few seconds' exposure, a pattern distinctly different from the usual black spots or rings. It consists of white lines on a gray background, which are

[1] John Wiley & Sons, Inc., New York, 1942.
[2] *Phil. Trans. Roy. Soc.*, **240**, 222 (1947).

sections of cones. The experimental arrangement and the principle involved are illustrated in Fig. 206, and a typical pattern is reproduced in Fig. 207. The diagram shows that the lines represent increased absorption of x-rays in directions corresponding to the Bragg reflection. The curvature of the absorption lines gives the Bragg angle and the spacing, and the symmetry and orientation of the crystal may be seen by inspection. The method is best adapted to an analysis of texture, particularly crystal perfection; for a perfect crystal gives no visible lines, while an imperfect or mosaic crystal does. By this means it is possible to classify diamonds, for example.

Powder Diffraction Cameras. Thus far the consideration of the reflection or diffraction of x-rays by crystals has been on the assumption of essentially single crystals. On account of the fact that so many interest-

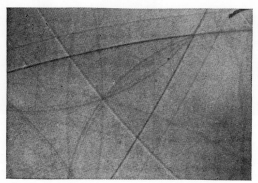

FIG. 207. Divergent-beam pattern of a diamond, type II, which gave no extra Laue spots but is mosaic. (*Lonsdale.*)

ing chemical substances, including practically all metals, cannot be obtained in the form of sufficiently large single crystals, one of the great contributions to x-ray science has been the discovery, independently by Debye and Scherrer in Europe and by Hull in America, that fine powders, or crystalline aggregates of all kinds, may be analyzed for ultimate crystalline structure in a most satisfactory way. The diffraction depends upon the fact that in a fine powder the grains are arranged in an entirely chaotic manner. There should be enough particles in this array, turned at just the right angle to the incident primary beam of monochromatic x-rays, to allow strong reflection from one set of parallel planes; other particles turned at another angle will produce reflection from another set of planes (the same set in many particles cooperating). Thus a beam passing through a powder specimen will fall upon a perpendicular flat photographic film as a series of concentric rings (Fig. 208), each uniformly intense throughout and corresponding to one set of planes of spacing d. A horizontal section cut through this diagram has, therefore, the appearance of a line spectrum (Fig. 209). This same result may be obtained by bending a narrow film in a *cassette* on the circumference of a circle, at the center of which is the specimen. In the so-called Debye-Scherrer camera the film is bent around 360 deg, and the beam, defined by pinholes, passes through a hole in the film; in other modifications where larger dispersion is desired, the film may occupy only a quadrant or semicircle.

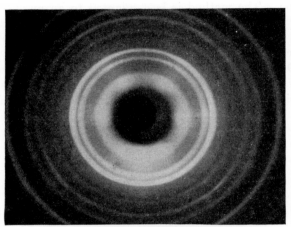

Fig. 208. Monochromatic pinhole diagram of steel ribbon, showing continuous rings.

The sample may have one of various forms, the essential point being random orientation of grains; powders of 200 mesh or smaller size may be placed in fine capillary tubes of glass or cellulose acetate,[1] pasted by collodion on ribbons or threads, pressed into slabs, or extruded after mixing with a binder from small orifices. Metals may be used in the form of fine wires or as small beveled plates with the beam grazing the blunt knife-edge at a small angle and passing through a sharp edge. Wedge-shaped samples even of powders formed in small cradle holders are often

Fig. 209. Powder diffraction pattern for metallic lead made with cylindrical camera.

used in the author's laboratory. A camera designed for precise analysis of penicillin samples in the author's laboratory is illustrated in Fig. 210. Two high-intensity high-resolution linear-background powder cameras

[1] The best capillary tubes are made by coating fine wires with cellulose acetate dissolved in chloroform and alcohol, drying, and stretching the wire to detach the thin cylinder; details are given by Fricke, Lohrmann, and Schröder, *Z. Elektrochem.*, **47**, 374 (1941).

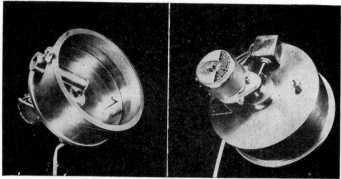

FIG. 210. Precision powder camera used at the University of Illinois.

FIG. 211. Two Norelco high-intensity high-resolution linear-background powder cameras in position at x-ray-tube windows.

(Norelco) mounted in position at the x-ray tube windows are shown in Fig. 211.

A critical discussion of the design of powder cameras by Buerger serves as the guide for construction of cameras with desirable features.[1]

[1] M. J. Buerger, *J. Appl. Phys.*, **16**, 501 (1945).

For powders of heavily absorbing substances such as lead it is desirable to use a noncrystalline diluent such as gum tragacanth or powdered starch. A complete table of proper proportions has been worked out by Davey. The volume of the diluting material with 1 volume of a chemical element varies from 1 for elements 10 to 26, 3 for 18 to 28, 5 for 29 to 44, 6 for 36 to 46, 7 for 47 to 53, 8 for 54 to 57, and 9 to 10 for up to 92.

It is advantageous at times, especially when the diffraction lines may appear spotty from too large powder grains, to rotate the specimen in its capillary tube, so that many cameras are equipped with small motors. The effect is to smooth out the lines. Such provision is made for the cameras in Figs. 210 and 211.

Because of the complexity of the spectrum it is desirable that the beam of x-rays should be as nearly monochromatic as possible. With molybdenum rays the zirconium filter eliminates all but the $K\alpha$ doublet, and a nickel filter serves for copper, etc. Still better is the use of crystal monochromators, discussed in some detail on page 126, especially when combined with focusing by bent crystals in the interest of the highest possible intensity.[1]

The accurate measurement of the crystal-powder spectrum lines is, of course, of great importance in analyses of unknown mixtures. Where semicircular *cassettes* or cylindrical cameras are used, the undeflected beam strikes the center of the film and diffraction lines are registered on both sides of this zero position. Uncertainties as to this are eliminated by measuring from one line to the corresponding line on the opposite end of the film. If, however, the zero position is at one end of the film as in the case of quadrant *cassettes*, greater resolution is possible but it is often necessary to run a calibrating spectrum for known pure crystal powders such as sodium chloride on the same film, either mixed with the unknown or placed in half of the small capillary tube. Since the spacings for each of these lines are accurately known and, hence, the necessary displacement on the film, the zero position may be accurately determined as well as all evidences of film shrinkage and inaccurate alignment of the specimen.

By its very nature the powder method requires more energy to produce a suitable photograph than is necessary for single crystals; consequently a greater time of exposure is required, and this may well run into many hours for some substances on usual apparatus. High-intensity x-ray tubes, of course, can be used to advantage. The Seemann-Bohlin camera employs a divergent beam of x-rays and a focusing principle. Here the focal spot of an x-ray tube, the specimen in the form of a ribbon

[1] A few significant references from among many are R. M. Bozorth and F. E. Haworth, *Phys. Rev.*, **53**, 538 (1938); A. Guinier, *Ann. phys.*, **12**, 161 (1944); J. D. H. Donnay, *Rev. Sci. Instr.*, **15**, 128 (1944); R. C. Evans, P. B. Hirsch, and J. N. Keller, *Acta Cryst.*, **1**, 124 (1948).

or flat surface, and the photographic film are on the circumference of the same circle.   Better still, the beam monochromatized by a bent crystal is focused on the same circumference with the film and specimen, as shown in Fig. 212.[1]

Spectra are registered very rapidly, and the method has proved of greatest value in technical examination of materials such as alloys. Scores of cameras have been described in the literature for use with vacuum, at low temperatures, at high temperatures, for double exposures, microspecimens, etc.   The design of a very successful mount for as little as 0.001 mg of sample by Frevel and Anderson[2] is shown in Fig. 213.

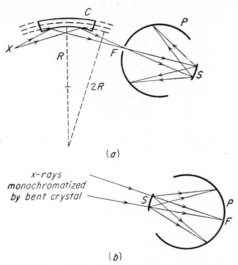

(a)

(b)

Fig. 212a. Diagrammatic representation of arrangements for use of focusing cameras with radiation monochromatized by a bent crystal. X, x-ray source; S, specimen; C, bent crystal; P, photographic film; F, focus of incident monochromatic x-ray beam.

For diffraction analysis of the highest precision, leading even to atomic or molecular-weight measurements and determination of the Avogadro number, lattice perfection, and coefficients of expansion, the Straumanis technique has been most successful.   The camera does not involve any new principles but provides simultaneous registration on the same film of forward and back reflections.   Because of this it is called the asymmetric powder method since the film is not symmetrically arranged on a circle with respect to the axis of the primary beam.   A hole is cut near one end of the film, through which the beam passes, and around which the back-reflection interferences are registered.   The film is bent around one side

[1] A focusing monochromator and powder camera designed by A. Guinier and commercially produced by Compagnie Générale de Radiologie, Paris, is illustrated in Fig. 212b.

[2] L. K. Frevel and H. C. Anderson, Acta Cryst., 4, 186 (1951).

of the camera so that the primary beam impinges near the opposite end of the film and provides the zero position from which the forward reflections are measured (see Fig. 219). The great precision in measurements

Fig. 212b. Guinier focusing monochromator, second scheme in Fig. 212a. A, entrance slit; B, bent crystal monochromator; C, exit slit; D, rotatable specimen; E, powder camera 76 mm in diameter.

by Straumanis, which are described in Chap. 15, lies in extraordinarily precise machine work on the cameras, thermostatic control, calibration, allowance for film variability, careful preparation and alignment of

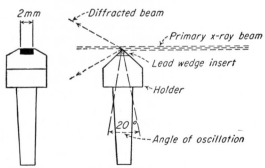

Fig. 213. Specimen mount in powder diffraction camera for microquantities (0.001 mg). (*Frevel and Anderson.*)

powder specimens on glass hairs, and extremely careful statistical line measurements.[1] The achievements of Professor Straumanis constitute a challenge to all x-ray diffraction workers.

[1] Detailed description of apparatus and technique in *J. Appl. Phys.*, **20**, 726 (1949).

The Geiger Diffractometer.   One of the great steps forward in recent years in practical developments of x-ray diffraction has been the design and construction of diffractometers[1] with Geiger counters primarily for powder analysis.   By means of automatic recorders integrating the Geiger counts at continuously varying angles, the powder pattern appears as a series of peaks on a continuous background, each corresponding in position to a line on a photographed crystal spectrum, and each providing a direct measure of intensity from peak height (Fig. 214).   The same graph may be obtained, of course, from a film run through a

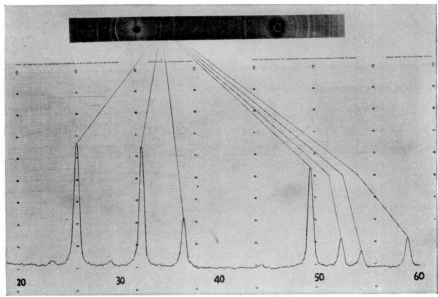

Fig. 214. Straumanis asymmetric powder pattern and Geiger-counter diffractometer patterns corresponding to one portion.   (*North American Philips.*)

microphotometer; but the Geiger unit eliminates the film entirely.   By virtue of the great sensitivity of the Geiger tube, which is discussed in detail on page 71, the analysis is completed in a few minutes since cumulative photographic registration is not required.   Generally the powder sample is arranged as a flat surface upon which the primary x-rays impinge at a glancing angle.   The beam is collimated by Soller slits (a series of parallel slits made from thin lead foil with spacers, to permit maximum use of energy); or it may be monochromatized and focused with bent crystals.   The diffracted rays enter the Geiger tube, which moves automatically on an arc either horizontal or vertical around the

[1] This name is recommended by the International Union of Crystallography in preference to the commonly used spectrometer which connotes an instrument for measurement of x-ray spectra (Chaps. 5 to 7).

center at a controlled rate of speed which determines the scale of magnification and resolution. Registration is on ruled paper in a Brown recorder; or Geiger counts can be made in fixed angular positions for highly quantitative evaluation of intensities. In Fig. 214 is shown a typical Geiger diffractometer curve compared with the photographically recorded patterns by the Straumanis camera. The first successful commercial Geiger spectrometer, the Norelco (North American Philips), in

Fig. 215. Norelco Geiger-counter diffractometer. Geiger tube (*upper right*) moves on vertical arc. X-ray tube, transformer, mounting, and recorder not shown.

its latest form is pictured in Fig. 215 and the General Electric instrument, which is also adapted for fluorescence analysis and photographic methods, in Fig. 216. Various circuits for amplifying and integrating the Geiger pulses are mentioned in Chap. 4 and are supplied and serviced by the manufacturers.

Back-reflection Methods. In practically all cases, x-ray diffraction patterns are made by transmission through the specimens. But in industrial practice it is frequently desired to know the ultimate crystalline condition of a finished product or of a large specimen that cannot be cut up. For example, in steel rails, in aluminum-alloy airplane propellers,

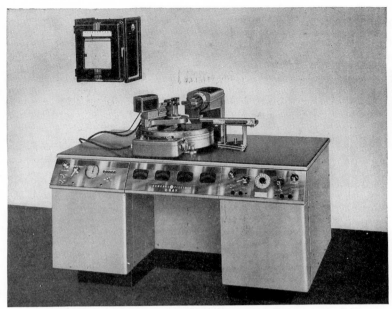

FIG. 216. General Electric Geiger-counter diffractometer.   Geiger tube (*left*) moves on horizontal arc.   (Complete unit.)

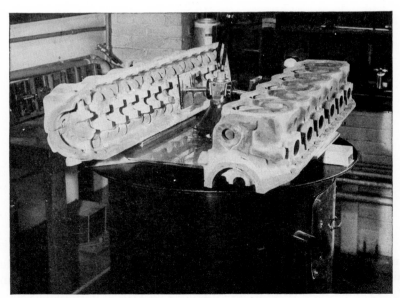

FIG. 217. Back-reflection method for testing airplane-motor cylinder-head castings. *Center*, Machlett x-ray tube with film holders attached.

and in very large steel structures such as oil stills where sound structure and freedom from strain are so essential for safety at high temperatures and pressures, such an examination of a finished unit before installation would be invaluable.

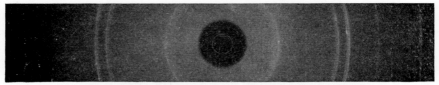

FIG. 218. Back-reflection pattern from a specimen of metallic lead.

One method would, of course, consist in making hollow borings, with subsequent welding of the holes. However, nearly 30 years ago it seemed advisable to develop a method in which the x-ray beam might be reflected

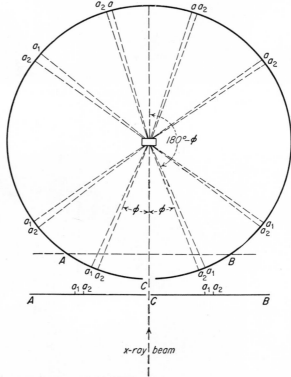

FIG. 219. Diagram explaining diffraction interferences on film at ABC in back reflection.

from the surface. With the usual equipment, it is necessary to reflect straight back from the surface of very large specimens such as airplane-motor cylinder-head castings (see Chap. 22 for typical patterns) as shown in Fig. 217. In this case, therefore, the photographic film is mounted

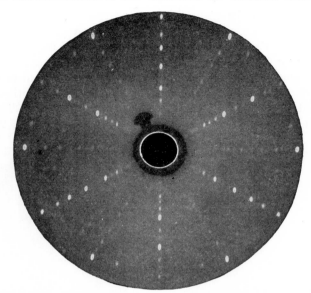

FIG. 220. Back-reflection Laue pattern for quartz plate used in radio-transmission circuit (normal to 0001).

FIG. 221. Back-reflection camera for measurements of high precision; a sectored screen in front of the film makes it possible to photograph patterns of two specimens on the same film and thus to compare line positions.

around the pinhole and registers the patterns of rays diffracted directly back from the surface. A typical pattern from a specimen of metallic lead is shown in Fig. 218. The concentric pairs of rings seem at first sight to be very familiar until it is noticed that the less intense line is inside the stronger line of each pair. If these pairs represent resolution of the $K\alpha$ doublet of copper, then in ordinary powder diffraction films, of course, the stronger $K\alpha_1$ line comes inside the weaker $K\alpha_2$. This apparent reversal is readily explained by a consideration of Fig. 219. The

Fig. 222. Norelco multiple diffraction unit showing Geiger-counter diffractometer unit and powder camera in position.

photographic plate is at ACB. If a cylindrical film, as in the Debye-Scherrer method, were placed coaxial with the specimen, the primary beam passing through the specimen would strike the film at the top of the circle and the diffraction lines would appear as shown. The pattern in Fig. 218 is therefore to be read from the *outside in* toward the center, rather than from the center, as would be the case if the film were placed on the opposite side of the circle. These diffraction circles correspond, therefore, to lines appearing at the very end of the usual spectra and hence to planes of relatively high indices.

The method has the disadvantage that long exposure is required to develop sufficient intensity for these diffraction effects from sparsely populated but closely spaced planes.   Because of the large resolutions of the $K\alpha$ doublet the method is useful for evaluating spacings very accurately, as in the Straumanis technique, and for following small changes due to solid solution and to deformations as in fatigue (see Chap. 22).   The grinding and orientation of quartz-plate oscillators used in radio-transmission circuits may be tested with great accuracy from back-reflection Laue patterns (Fig. 220).   A back-reflection camera of high precision is illustrated in Fig. 221.

Multiple Apparatus.   The most useful apparatus for industrial and chemical applications is the multiple diffraction unit.   This consists of a

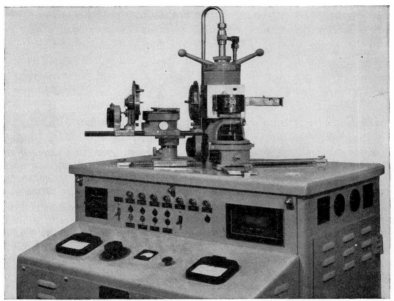

Fig. 223. Hilger multiple diffraction unit showing back reflection (*left*) and powder camera (*center*) around demountable tube (discussed in Chap. 2).

transformer operating usually at 30,000 to 50,000 volts with an enclosed filament transformer, an operating switchboard with filament current stabilizer, a water-cooled self-rectifying tube (or rectified by a single-valve tube), a pinhole system which permits two, three, or four simultaneous exposures radially around the vertical tube at a grazing angle upon the target, and the various cameras or Geiger-counter units mounted in fixed positions on slides or suspended directly from the x-ray tubehead.   The Norelco multiple diffraction unit with Geiger-counter diffractometer and powder camera mounted around the tube is shown in Fig. 222; the Hilger with cylindrical powder and back-reflection cameras in Fig. 223; and the General Electric interchangeable Geiger-counter spectrometer and photographic diffractometer, with these units replaceable by powder, rotation, and Weissenberg cameras, in Fig. 216.

CHAPTER 15

THE INTERPRETATION OF DIFFRACTION PATTERNS IN TERMS OF ULTIMATE STRUCTURE

Steps in the Derivation of Structure from the Diffraction Pattern. Having photographed the diffraction patterns of a crystal under structural investigation by one or more of the methods outlined in Chap. 14, the experimenter is confronted with the problem of measuring and extracting every possible bit of information from the patterns that may lead to the final proof of structure. The steps in the analysis have been enumerated in Chap. 13. It is now necessary to examine in detail the available tools that the analyst has at hand as he begins the interpretation of the pattern of lines or spots registered on the film before him as the result of the diffraction of x-rays by the ordered array of atoms or molecules or ions in the crystal.

1. First of all, he has made use of observations of the outer form of his crystal, recognizing that single crystal data will almost invariably be required for a complete analysis, in order to orient the specimen properly in his x-ray camera or goniometer. Optical examination has classified the crystal as triclinic, monoclinic, hexagonal, rhombohedral, orthorhombic, tetragonal, or cubic, and the crystallographic axes have been located so that symmetrical Laue patterns and rational clear-cut rotation patterns are registered. Or by trial and failure he has changed his crystal orientation until such patterns are obtained.

2. He may know from symmetry observations deduced from crystal habit, angles, etc., to which class or point group the crystal belongs. He has available certain auxiliary diagnostic tests for symmetry, such as pyro- and piezoelectric effects, which may be useful as preliminary information leading to proper space-group identification or which may be introduced in cases of uncertainty.

3. He has Bragg's law, $n\lambda = 2d \sin \Theta$, by means of which he may proceed to calculate the interplanar spacings d_{hkl} for each interference on his pattern. On a flat film perpendicular to the primary x-ray beam he measures the distance from the center of the undiffracted beam to the diffraction interference. This distance a, divided by the known fixed distance from specimen to film, b, gives the tangent of the diffraction angle 2Θ, from which Θ, $\sin \Theta$, and d are readily determined On a film exposed in a cylindrical camera $a = R$ arc 2Θ, where R is the radius of the camera, or Θ in degrees $= \frac{1}{2}a(360/2\pi R) = 90a/\pi R$, with a and R measured in millimeters.

4. The dimensions of the unit cell are deduced fairly easily, especially if the analyst has a rotation pattern around each of the three axes (two for tetragonal, one for cubic, etc.). For, independent of other data, a measurement of the layer-line displacement gives these fundamental spacings. The analyst also knows that the boundary planes

of the unit cell almost certainly have very low indices and maximum spacings and produce maximum diffraction intensities because these planes are most thickly populated with atoms.

5. The analyst knows that he can test his preliminary decision on the size of the unit cell from the pycnometrically measured density of the crystal. For the number of atoms or molecules per unit cell is necessarily a whole number, in order to preserve the identity of the cell and of the chemical formula. This does not mean that the value of n must come out, for example, exactly 4.0, for a value such as 3.94 is evidence of this. The x-ray density is an ideal limiting value, which does not take into account cracks and imperfections that influence the pycnometer value. This true limiting density can be calculated by substituting the integral value of n back in the formula $\rho = nMm/V$.

6. There are available the formulas for calculating all planar spacings in all directions through the unit cell; for example,

$$d_{hkl} = \frac{a_0}{\sqrt{h^2 + k^2 + l^2}}$$

in the cubic system. These formulas give the values for all planes and hence of the maximum possible number of diffraction interferences that may ever be expected. They are not concerned with interferences that may be missing. In any case, however, all the observed interferences for a given crystal system must be interrelated by means of the appropriate equation.

7. The analyst before applying the theory of space groups must identify each interference with the corresponding planar indices. In simple cases the method of the preceding section is adequate, i.e., by trial and failure bringing a whole series of values of d_{hkl} into correspondence. In most complex cases the experimenter has at his command various methods of projection of interferences on networks—stereographic and gnomonic for Laue patterns, nets for rotation and goniometric methods. He has available the very fruitful concept of the reciprocal lattice, in which points represent ordinary lattice planes and which thus simplifies difficult calculations. In fact, he may find it possible to produce an *actual pattern that is itself a direct representation of the reciprocal lattice* and hence immediately interpreted.

8. Now the theory of space groups may be applied, for all the interferences have been listed in terms of the planar indices. By inspection the experimenter notes certain regularities in the interferences that are and are not present, and hence the *extinctions* are noted, as the clues to the selection of the proper space group that uniquely defines the crystal. These criteria are conveniently listed in tables by Astbury and Yardley, Wyckoff, and in the "International Tables for X-ray Crystallography." The well-trained experimenter could calculate for himself these criteria, of course, from the principles of interference that determine intensities. Whether the atomic units occupy general positions in the unit cell (maximum number without affecting symmetry) or special positions may be deduced from the available data, and hence the coordinates of scattering points will be useful in further intensity calculations.

9. The analyst begins the last stage of his interpretation with the fundamental formulas relating intensities of interferences with structure factors. Tables of atomic-structure factors that lead to the crystal-structure factor now are available. He knows how to calculate intensities from a logical assumed structure, which are to be compared with experimental values. Better still he uses these experimental F values as coefficients in a Fourier series to calculate electron densities throughout the unit cell and thus to find the unique parameters that define the position of every atom even in a molecule. He recognizes that his enormous task is greatly simplified if the

crystal has a center of symmetry. He uses the mathematical aids—calculating machines, printed strips of numbers, etc.—to shorten the task of summation. From this analysis come the size, shape, and disposition of molecules, the length of bonds, the existence of hydrogen bonds, and all the information that finally explains just why the crystal and its component atoms and molecules act as they do in physical and chemical phenomena.

10. Finally, with this rigorous analysis completed correctly, all auxiliary tests— packing radii, physical and chemical properties—are found to be in accord with an architectural plan in which atoms and molecules in spatial arrangement have inscribed their own signatures which have been deciphered.

It is obvious that an exhaustive treatment of the details of the extended process of complete interpretation just outlined would run far beyond the bounds of this book. In the paragraphs that follow, the attempt is made to explain as simply as possible some of the aids to interpretation.

Interplanar-spacing Formulas. With the concept of the planes already developed it is not difficult to develop general formulas for the interplanar spacings in a given unit cell. At this point we shall discuss only the cubic, tetragonal, and orthorhombic cells, i.e., those with their coordinate axes at right angles.

If line d is normal to a plane and the reference plane is assumed to pass through the origin, length d represents the interplanar spacing. Since d is normal to the plane, we may write

$$d = a_0 \frac{\cos \alpha}{h} = b_0 \frac{\cos \beta}{k} = c_0 \frac{\cos \gamma}{l}$$

But if α, β, and γ are the direction cosines of the normal to the plane, we may write

$$\cos^2 \alpha + \cos^2 \beta + \cos^2 \gamma = 1$$

Substituting, we find

$$d^2 \left(\frac{h^2}{a_0^2} + \frac{k^2}{b_0^2} + \frac{l^2}{c_0^2} \right) = 1$$

or

$$d = \frac{1}{[(h^2/a_0^2) + (k^2/b_0^2) + (l^2/c_0^2)]^{\frac{1}{2}}}$$

This formula may be written in a form more generally useful as

$$\sin \Theta = \frac{\lambda}{2} \left(\frac{h^2}{a_0^2} + \frac{k^2}{b_0^2} + \frac{l^2}{c_0^2} \right)^{\frac{1}{2}}$$

Of course, in the tetragonal system, $a_0 = b_0$; in the cubic system

$$a_0 = b_0 = c_0.$$

Thus for a cubic crystal

$$n\lambda = \frac{2a_0}{\sqrt{h^2 + k^2 + l^2}} \sin \Theta$$

where a_0 is the lattice constant or length of the unit-cube edge and h, k, l are the indices of any planes. Hence

$$d_{hkl} = \frac{a_0}{\sqrt{h^2 + k^2 + l^2}}$$

If an unknown crystal is cubic, all the diffraction interferences must be related in this way; the usual method is therefore to correlate calculations with experimental values. In the same way equations may be derived for all other simple lattices. In general

$$n\lambda = 2d_{hkl} \sin \Theta_n = \frac{2a_0}{\sqrt{F(hkl;abc;\alpha\beta\gamma)}} \sin \Theta_n$$

where abc are unit lengths in three dimensions and $\alpha\beta\gamma$ are axial angles. Table 15-1 lists the formulas for d_{hkl} in convenient form.

From the mathematical expressions, $n\lambda$ may be calculated by substituting the values of d_{hkl} in $n\lambda = 2d \sin \Theta$. For the cubic system therefore

$$n\lambda = \frac{2a_0}{\sqrt{h^2 + k^2 + l^2}} \sin \Theta_n$$

Squaring,

$$n^2\lambda^2 = \frac{4a_0^2}{h^2 + k^2 + l^2} \sin^2 \Theta_n$$

$$\sin^2 \Theta_n = \left(\frac{n^2\lambda^2}{4a_0^2}\right)(h^2 + k^2 + l^2)$$

All the possible values of $\sin^2 \Theta_n$ may then be calculated when the cube-edge length a_0 and the wavelength are known, assigning all values of hkl. These values are then compared with the experimental $\sin^2 \Theta$ values for the interferences appearing on the pattern, and the crystallographic system is thus established. The interferences may be those on different photographs for different zones or all on the same film as in the powder method.

It is clear that with decreasing symmetry the number of possible interference maxima increases. The derivation of the quadratic form from the x-ray data therefore becomes difficult except in the cases of highest symmetry. In a cubic lattice it is possible to have 48 planes of the same form $\{hkl\}$ where h, k, and l are all different, with the same spacing, and hence cooperating to produce only a single interference maximum, whereas in the triclinic lattice there are 24 different spacings and hence 24 reflection lines or spots corresponding to these hkl planes. Theoretically possible maxima may overlap and thus render derivation of the quadratic form and the crystal system practically impossible.

TABLE 15-1. CALCULATION OF INTERPLANAR SPACINGS, d_{hkl}

System	$a:b:c$	$\alpha,\ \beta,\ \gamma$	d_{hkl}
Cubic	1:1:1	$\alpha = \beta = \gamma = 90$ deg.	$\dfrac{a_0}{\sqrt{h^2 + k^2 + l^2}}$
Tetragonal	1:1:c	$\alpha = \beta = \gamma = 90°$	$\dfrac{a_0}{\sqrt{h^2 + k^2 + (l/c)^2}}$
Orthorhombic	a:1:c	$\alpha = \beta = \gamma = 90°$	$\dfrac{b_0}{\sqrt{(h/a)^2 + k^2 + (l/c)^2}}$
Hexagonal	1:1:c	$\alpha = \beta = 90°,\ \gamma = 120°$	$\dfrac{a_0}{\sqrt{\frac{4}{3}(h^2 + hk + k^2) + (l/c)^2}}$
Rhombohedral	1:1:1	$\alpha = \beta = \gamma \neq 90°$	$\dfrac{a_0\sqrt{1 + 2\cos^3\alpha - 3\cos^2\alpha}}{\sqrt{(h^2 + k^2 + l^2)\sin^2\alpha + 2(hk + hl + kl)(\cos^2\alpha - \cos\alpha)}}$
Monoclinic	a:1:c	$\alpha = \gamma = 90°,\ \beta \neq 90°$	$\dfrac{b_0}{\sqrt{\dfrac{(h/a)^2 + (l/c)^2 - \dfrac{2hl}{ac}\cos\beta}{\sin^2\beta} + k^2}}$
Triclinic	a:1:c	$\alpha \neq \beta \neq \gamma \neq 90°$	$\dfrac{b_0}{\sqrt{h/a\begin{vmatrix} h/a & \cos\gamma & \cos\beta \\ k & 1 & \cos\alpha \\ l/c & \cos\alpha & 1 \end{vmatrix} + k\begin{vmatrix} 1 & h/a & \cos\beta \\ \cos\gamma & k & \cos\alpha \\ \cos\beta & l/c & 1 \end{vmatrix} + l/c\begin{vmatrix} 1 & \cos\gamma & h/a \\ \cos\gamma & 1 & k \\ \cos\beta & \cos\alpha & l/c \end{vmatrix} \Big/ \begin{vmatrix} 1 & \cos\gamma & \cos\beta \\ \cos\gamma & 1 & \cos\alpha \\ \cos\beta & \cos\alpha & 1 \end{vmatrix}}}$

DETERMINATION OF SPACE GROUP FROM X-RAY EXTINCTIONS

I. Translation groups or space-lattices.

   P—no regular extinctions associated with the primitive lattice.

   A, B, C—with the face-centered lattices of this type:

       A face-centered: $k + l = 2n$ for every reflection hkl.

       B face-centered: $h + l = 2n$ for every reflection hkl.

       C face-centered: $h + k = 2n$ for every reflection hkl.

   F—face-centered lattices; hkl all odd or all even.

   $$\left. \begin{array}{l} h + k = 2n \\ h + l = 2n \\ k + l = 2n \end{array} \right\} \text{ if reflection } hkl \text{ is to occur.}$$

   I—body-centered lattice.

       $h + k + l = 2n$ for reflection hkl to occur.

II. Microsymmetry elements.

   1. Screw axis: screw axis p_q in x direction; $h00$ may appear only when $h = pn/q$(integer). Similarly in direction y and direction z in case the screw axis lies parallel to one of their directions.

   2. Glide planes.

      a. Glide plane normal to x axis with glide b. $0kl$ can appear only when $k = 2n$.

      (Index of normal to glide plane must be 0; direction of gliding has spacings halved.)

      b. The n glide plane. Assume the n glide plane takes place normal to direction x [glide $= \frac{1}{2}(b + c)$].

      $0kl$ appears only when $k + l = 2n$.

      (Index of normal to glide plane 0.)

      c. The d glide plane. Assume a d glide plane normal to the a direction [glide $= \frac{1}{4}(b + c)$].

      $0kl$ appears only when $k + l = 4n$.

The lattice restrictions may tend to cover up those due to symmetry elements, i.e., with A lattice $k + l = 2n$, whether the interference is hkl or $0kl$; but an n glide plane normal to direction x requires the $0kl$ to reflect only when $k + l = 2n$—therefore, in this case the existence of the glide plane cannot be demonstrated.

Example. BaCl$_2$.2H$_2$O is monoclinic; $\beta = 91°5'$; $a_0 = 6.69$ A, $b_0 = 10.86$ A, $c_0 = 7.15$ A; and $n = 4$. Some of the observed interferences are listed below:[1]

$h00$	$h0l$	$0k0$	$hk0$	$0kl$	$00l$	hkl
200	101	020	110	011	002	111
400	202	040	120	021	004	211
600	103	060	210	012	006	131
...	301	080	130	031	...	122
...	402	...	220	022	...	221
...	105	...	140	032	...	113
...	...	...	310	041	...	311
...	...	...	150	013	...	321

[1] Naray-Szabo and Sasvari, Z. Krist., **97**, 235 (1937).

I. *The Space-lattice.* In the monoclinic system only C and P are possible, and since cases may be observed in which $h + l =$ odd integer ($k \neq 0$), the lattice may be described as primitive.

II. *The symmetry elements.* Only four regularities may be found, $h00$ (h even), $0k0$ (k even), $00l$ (l even), and $h0l$ ($h + l$ even). Since the last regularity includes the first two, we may write

$$h0l \text{ appears when } h + l = \text{even integer}$$
$$0k0 \text{ appears when } \qquad k = \text{even integer}$$

This requires that the crystal class have both an axis and a plane of symmetry; that is, 2_1 is necessary for the second restriction, and the first can be described only with an n glide plane normal to the twofold axis.

Therefore, we may designate the space group

$$P2_1/n$$

The equivalent points may be expressed analytically as

$$xyz;\ \bar{z}\bar{y}\bar{x};\ \tfrac{1}{2} + x,\ \tfrac{1}{2} - y,\ \tfrac{1}{2} + z;\ \tfrac{1}{2} - x,\ \tfrac{1}{2} + y;\ \tfrac{1}{2} - z$$

Since four molecules of $BaCl_2.2H_2O$ are present per cell, no special positions can be occupied. Since the intensity contribution of Ba may be considered as predominant, its position may be roughly fixed by a consideration of the following intensities:

Interference	Intensity observed		
200	10	020	12
400	0.5	040	0.5
600	0.5	060	8
002	8	080	0.5
004	6	0,10,0	3
006	4	0,12,0	2

Other important intensities are 202(10), 012(10), 170(12), 103(10), 131(10).

The Interpretation of Laue Photographs. The usefulness of this historically first method for obtaining information, even as to the probable space-group characteristics of a crystal, makes desirable some further comment upon interpretation, although detailed discussion is to be found in the several technical treatises on crystal analysis. A single Laue photograph taken alone yields only a limited amount of information. It appears as a series of spots (Figs. 194a, b) whose loci are symmetrically disposed ellipses, passing through the central direct-beam image if the primary beam has passed through the crystal parallel to a principal axis. The galaxy of spots is an indication of the ability of the many families of planes, each at a certain angle Θ with respect to the primary x-ray beam, to pick out, from the assortment of rays of different wavelengths, the particular one for reflection according to $n\lambda = 2d \sin \Theta$. The symmetry is a proof of the orderly arrangement within the crystal, suggested by the external crystalline form. Thus, if the beam passes parallel to a cubic axis, with fourfold symmetry, the pattern has a fourfold symmetry.

The 32 point groups may be divided into 11 groups by the symmetries displayed by Laue patterns. These patterns are such that all crystals seem to have a center of symmetry, and for this reason unique identification cannot be made. In Table 15-2 the point-group symbols are those listed in Fig. 187.

TABLE 15-2. SYMMETRY OF LAUE PATTERNS

Crystallographic classes	System	Symmetry of Laue diffraction effects
1, $\bar{1}$	Triclinic	$\bar{1}$
2, m, $2/m$	Monoclinic	$2/m$
mm, 222, mmm	Orthorhombic	mmm
3, $\bar{3}$	Trigonal	$\bar{3}$
$3m$, 32, $\bar{3}m$	Trigonal	$\bar{3}m$
4, $\bar{4}$, $4/m$	Tetragonal	$4/m$
42, $4mm$, $\bar{4}2m$, $4/mmm$	Tetragonal	$4/mmm$
6, $\bar{6}$, $6/m$	Hexagonal	$6/m$
62, $6mm$, $\bar{6}2m$, $6/mmm$	Hexagonal	$6/mmm$
23, $m3$	Cubic	$m3$
43, $\bar{4}3m$, $m3m$	Cubic	$m3m$

The spots on any ellipse correspond to reflections taking place at a number of faces that have a common zone axis (*i.e.*, a row of atoms through which various planes pass). If the incident rays are inclined at an angle Θ to the zone axis, the reflected rays will also make an angle Θ with this axis, so that all the rays lie on a circular cone whose axis is that of the zone. The direction of the incident rays also lies on this cone; consequently the loci of the reflected spots are situated on the ellipse formed by the intersection of the cone with the photographic plate. Important zones of the crystal structure correspond to those ellipses which are densely packed with spots in the Laue diagram. The symbol of the zone that corresponds to each ellipse can be found and, since each spot may be considered as lying at the intersection of two ellipses, the plane that reflects it can be identified by cross multiplication of the zone symbols.

It is much more convenient, however, to use a system of projection in the assignment of indices to spots. The stereographic method converts the ellipses into circles. In Fig. 224 a crystal is at the center of a sphere that touches the photographic plate at the point N, where the direct beam SN is intercepted by the plate. The cone of reflected rays about any zone axis will cut the sphere in a circle that can be projected on the plate. A reflected spot appears on the plate at R. A line from S through Q, where the ray cuts the sphere, meets the plate at R', the projection of R. This spot will be on a circle with the projections of the other spots originating from planes with a common zone axis.

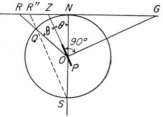

FIG. 224. Method of stereographic projection of Laue patterns.

A stereographic projection of potassium chloride is shown in Fig. 225. The Laue projection of this simple cubic crystal is characterized by spots with perfectly regular distribution of intensities, at every intersection of circles. The Laue pattern for sodium chloride, on the other hand, differs in that the spots which for potassium chloride have odd and even indices (*e.g.*, 341) are absent. Thus the face-centered cubic lattice for which the structure factor predicts this very fact may be assigned as the underlying arrangement of the heavier chlorine atoms in rock salt.

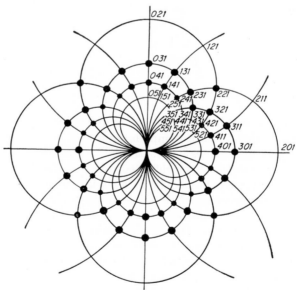

FIG. 225. Stereographic projection of Laue pattern of KCl.

The gnomonic projection is even more valuable for the complicated types of Laue patterns. The essential process involved is shown in Fig. 226; R is the Laue spot and OQ the zone axis of the plane which is perpendicular to the plane of the paper. The perpendicular to this plane strikes the plane of projection, and

$$P'S = P'O \cot \Theta \qquad \text{and} \qquad PR = PO \tan 2\Theta$$

where $P'S$ is the distance of the gnomonic projection from the center, $P'O$ is the radius of projection, PR is the distance of the Laue spot from the center, and PO is the radius of the Laue film (*i.e.*, distance from specimen to film). $P'O$ and PO may be different, but usually both are made 5 cm. Thus any Laue spot and its projection lie on a straight line passing through the common center. On this account the plotting of the gnomonic projection is most simply and rapidly accomplished with a suitable ruler. The left side is divided in millimeters for measurement of the distance of the Laue spot PR, and the right side is graduated in accordance with the expressions $P'S = 5 \cot \Theta$ and $PR = 5 \tan 2\Theta$ to measure corresponding projected lengths $P'S$. This method has been widely used with success by Wyckoff and by Schiebold. It is evident that, the closer the reflected Laue spot, the farther from the center is the projection. Planes parallel to a zone axis lie on a straight line, which is the intersection of the plate and a plane through O parallel to the zone axis. It results that the gnomonic projection of a cubic crystal is based on a network of squares whose sides are equal to the distance from the

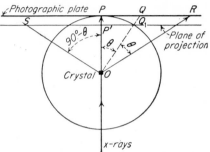

FIG. 226. Method of gnomonic projection of Laue patterns.

crystal to the plane of projection (usually 5 cm); for an orthorhombic crystal the network will be rectangles, the lengths of whose sides are in the same ratio as the axial ratios; for a rhombohedral or hexagonal close-packed lattice, it will be parallelograms with an angle of 120 deg between sides; etc. The indexing of the planes corresponding to each spot is usually not difficult, particularly when the axis of a crystal is normal to the plane of projection, say, the Z or l index. This will then always be l, and X and Y (or h, k) can be read directly from the coordinates on the network. Thus for a cubic crystal in which the Z axis is perpendicular to the plane of projection, or paper, a spot two squares to the right of the center and one square up would have the indices 211; a spot two to the right and one-half down is $4\bar{1}2[2 \times (2, \frac{\bar{1}}{2}, 1)]$; etc.

Wyckoff has used, with great success, unsymmetrical Laue photographs, obtained by inclining one of the crystal axes to the beam. In Fig. 227 is shown the gnomonic projection for such a photograph of a potassium iodide crystal.

Laue patterns sometimes display abnormal effects which may have a highly significant bearing upon the condition or texture of the crystal.

These are "asterism" streaks on bending or distorting the specimen (Chap. 22), first observed in 1913, by Friedrich; and faint diffuse extra spots which become increasingly intense as the temperature is raised. These spots were found by Clark and Duane for crystals of potassium iodide, etc., in 1922. They are evident in the Laue pattern of pentaerythritol (Fig. 228). In 1914 Debye had made a theoretical study of the x-ray interference effects due to heat motions of atoms, which would

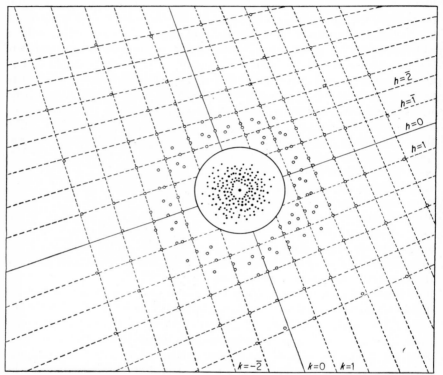

FIG. 227. Gnomonic projection of an unsymmetrical Laue pattern of KI.

be independent of crystal orientation, and some experimental observations during 1922 and 1938 seemed to confirm this. The Faxén-Waller theory in 1925 differed from the Debye theory in predicting that the heat movements of the atoms would give intensity maxima, weak and diffuse by comparison with Bragg reflections but dependent upon crystal orientation. This theory was confirmed by Laval in 1938 in work which remained obscure for many years.[1]

[1] The whole matter of crystal dynamics and the production of diffuse interferences is ably covered by Kathleen Lonsdale in *Proc. Phys. Soc. (London)*, **54**, 314 (1942); *Proc. Roy. Soc. (London)*, **179**, 8 (1941); *Repts. Progr. Phys.*, **9**, 256 (1942); and several subsequent publications.

In 1939 Preston in the study of age-hardening of Cu-Al alloys found extra weak spots and streaks which were greatly intensified by heating to 500°C. He ascribed this effect as due to thermal vibrations of the lattice which break the crystal up into groups, consisting, for a face-centered cubic lattice, of an atom and its twelve neighbors (dodecahedral coordination) so that each group is slightly out of phase with neighboring groups during x-ray scattering.

In 1940 Raman in his comprehensive study of diamonds proposed a theory that incident x-rays excite a characteristic vibration of the crystal in all unit cells but varying in phase from one to the next, resulting in a coherent reflection of x-rays of changed frequency by the phase waves in the crystal.

FIG. 228. Laue pattern of pentaerythritol, showing extraneous "Preston" spots (four strong and four weak diffuse spots) from effect of temperature on lattice.

Subsequently Lonsdale and others have given a solid theoretical background for the appearance of diffuse reflections. Debye and Waller originally developed the equation relating temperature, atomic vibrations, and intensity of x-ray reflections after observing that intensities of these Bragg reflections decreased with increasing temperatures. The Debye-Waller correction therefore must be made in evaluations of intensities, as indicated later in this chapter. There is ample evidence that the atoms in crystals are vibrating. The elastic constants of crystals may be calculated from compressibility, Young's modulus, shear modulus, and other physical measurements. If these constants are large, then large forces are required to distort or deform a crystal, the bonds are strong and the thermal vibrations around a fixed lattice point small, as for example in diamond or tungsten, whereas small constants mean small forces and larger vibrations as in the alkali metals, lead, organic crystals, etc. Although the intensity of Bragg reflections diminishes with increasing atomic vibration, the total amount of scattered energy must be the same, so that the residual energy must appear somewhere. Lonsdale has shown that the concept of the reciprocal lattice provides this explanation. For in reciprocal space the reduction in scattering power at the reciprocal lattice points is compensated for by spreading around the point, with the result that a diffuse instead of sharp interference appears. The same phenomenon occurs, as will be shown in Chap 21, when crystals are of colloidal dimensions or when there is some kind of lattice irregularity but the causes can be distinguished. The thermal-vibration diffusions of course must decrease as temperatures are lowered, while this is not ordinarily the case for the particle-size effect. Furthermore the intensity and shape of scattering will be different for different reciprocal lattice points, in other words, for different sets of planes in the crystal, whereas diffusions caused by small particle size will be the same for all points. From the shape of the diffuse reflection it is possible to determine the shape of the "cloud" around the reciprocal lattice point. Reflection occurs when any bit of this cloud intersects the sphere of diffraction. This cloud may be so curious in shape by virtue of thermal oscillations that there is a continuous bridge from one point to another, particularly well shown for benzil[1] (Fig. 229, above) and for that most remarkable of all crystalline substances, ice[2] (Fig. 229, below).

These diffuse reflections are not only interesting in themselves but often give valuable clues to structure. In long-chain compounds vibrations occur not parallel to the chain axis, which would mean elongation and contraction, but laterally. The occurrence and shapes of diffuse reflections as thin disks parallel on the chain can then give immediate indication of the orientation of the chains. For layer structures the vibrations are normal to the planes, and an ellipsoidal spot results. In cases where elastic constants are known, as for alkali halides, it is possible to plot surfaces of isodiffusion around reciprocal lattice points from a formula derived by Jahn and to compare with actual Laue patterns. Illustrations for potassium chloride, sodium, and other crystals are given in papers by Lonsdale,[3] who also has listed the vibration amplitudes of atoms in cubic crystals.[4] Several recent papers have been concerned with diffuse reflections for $NaClO_3$.[†] Of great importance is the use of the anomalous reflections as an aid in the classification of diamonds, especially since the discovery that some diamonds have excellent properties for radiation counting. To this subject Raman, Lonsdale, Grenville-Wells, and others have contributed several papers, in which there is a considerable difference of opinion. In general diamonds have come to be classified as follows:[5]

Radiation counting	Nil	Strong
Infrared absorption	8, 13 μ	Absent
Anomalous x-ray effects	Strong	Absent
Crystal texture	Perfect	Mosaic

[1] K. Lonsdale and H. Smith, *Proc. Roy. Soc. (London)*, **179**, 8 (1941).

[2] P. G. Owston, *Acta Cryst.* **2**, 222 (1944). Owston and Lonsdale, *J. Glaciol.*, **1**, 118 (1948).

[3] *Proc. Roy. Soc. (London)*, **54**, 314 (1942); "Crystals and X-rays," pp. 150–161, D. Van Nostrand Company, Inc., New York, 1949.

[4] *Acta Cryst.*, **1**, 142 (1948).

[†] G. Garrido, *Acta Cryst.*, **1**, 3 (1948).

[5] H. J. Grenville-Wells, *Atomic Scientists' News*, **1**, 86 (1952).

However, recent work has proved that there are exceptions of several kinds to this classification. In the words of Grenville-Wells, the diamond problem continues to baffle scientists.

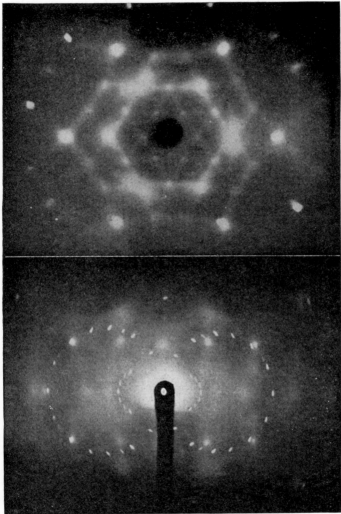

Fig. 229. Above, Laue pattern of benzil showing bridges between spots. (*Lonsdale.*) Below, Laue pattern for ice, showing diffuse and sharp spots. (*Owston and Lonsdale.*)

The dimensions of the unit cell may sometimes be estimated from Laue data, and, of course, for cubic crystals the value of $n\lambda$ for each spot is given by $\sin \Theta$ and a_0 and hkl from the equation

$$n\lambda = \left(\frac{2a_0}{\sqrt{h^2 + k^2 + l^2}} \right) \sin \Theta_n$$

The fact that general radiation is employed, however, is always a complication. At moderate voltages, 50,000 kv, the maximum intensity in the spectrum is at 0.48 A, the characteristic absorption wavelength of the silver in the photographic emulsion. If the voltage is known, λ_{min} is, of course, at once established and this immediately limits the possibilities of interpretation of Laue spots and eliminates some of the alternative possible unit crystal cells.

Intensity data from Laue patterns are not accurately determined but are simply classed relatively by visual comparison on the photographic negative. Numerous complications are involved, as explained earlier, and in addition there is absorption in the crystal. However, the Laue data even though only approximate are sometimes very important, since

FIG. 230. Rotation pattern of a crystal of orthophenanthroline.

by this method alone are reflections from planes of high indices and complicated structure registered. The greatest usefulness of the method therefore lies in conjunction with other methods with which quantitative information can be easily obtained.

The Interpretation of Rotation Patterns. When a single crystal is rotated around one of its principal crystallographic axes in the path of an x-ray beam defined by pinholes or slits, a very characteristic pattern is registered on the photographic film. It is called a layer-line diagram because the interference maxima all lie on horizontal layers or lines. If a flat film is used, these lines are hyperbolas above and below a straight equatorial line. On a cylindrical film bent on the circumference of a circle at the center of which is the crystal the layer lines are straight lines parallel to the equator. Representative photographs are shown in Figs. 197 and 230. It follows that all the interference maxima lying on these layer lines are produced by planes with the same zone axis, namely, the common crystallographic and rotation axis. The spectrum is therefore "complete." The familiar Bragg spectra are, of course, produced by only one set of planes, the experimental arrangement of slits and crystal being such that other planes cannot register.   The lines or spots lying on the equator of the oscillation or rotation pattern therefore are really the "Bragg principal spectrum."

As explained in the preceding chapter, the angles between principal axes may be determined in many cases by reorienting the crystal on its goniometer head until sharp layer-line diagrams are obtained.   With three such rotation patterns corresponding to the three principal axes, the dimensions of the unit crystal cell may be directly deduced.   These patterns have the great advantage that one lattice spacing, namely, that for the atomic planes along the rotation axis, may be measured independently of any assumption as to crystal system or planar indices.   It is

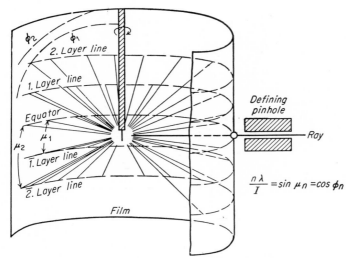

$$\frac{n\lambda}{I} = \sin \mu_n = \cos \phi_n$$

Fig. 231. Diagram of the rotation method.

necessary only to measure the distances e_1, e_2, . . . , e_n of the vertices of the hyperbolas on the tangent film (or the straight layer lines on a film that has been bent on a cylinder coaxial with the specimen) from the central zero point of the main beam.   The distance from specimen to film, a, being known, the diffraction angles μ_1, μ_2, . . . , μ_n (Fig. 231) may be calculated, since $\tan \mu_n = e_n/a$ (or $\tan \phi_n = a/e_n$).   The identity period or spacing along the rotation axis is then simply calculated from

$$I = \frac{n\lambda}{\sin \mu_n} = \frac{n\lambda}{\cos \phi}$$

where ϕ is the complement of the diffraction angle μ and where n is the number of the layer line (1, 2, 3, . . . , -1, -2, -3, . . .).   Then identically the same value is obtained from all the layer lines.   Three such values of I for each of the principal axes give the size of the unit cell.

The process of assigning indices to the interference maxima lying on the layer line is usually straightforward.   Thus again, assuming the *c* axis as the rotation axis on the equatorial line, the index *l* in *hkl* is zero; in other words, all indices must be *hk0*; *l* must be 1 on the first horizontal layer line, 2 on the second, etc.   These maxima lie not only on horizontal layer lines but also on vertical loci which are zone curves or row lines (Fig. 232).   Schiebold calculated these two types of layer line (*Schicht-linien*) of the I and II kind.   Thus if the first maximum on the equator is due to 100 planes, then the spot on the first layer line lying on the common vertical zone curve is 101; if the second spot on the equator is 110, the spot above or below it on the first layer line and the second zone

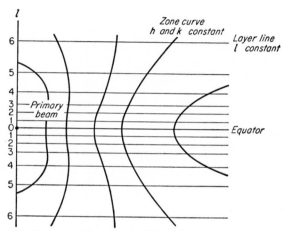

FIG. 232. Diagram of two types of layer lines on rotation patterns

curve is 111.   It is at once evident that oscillation photographs taken over a fixed angle are much simpler to interpret than a composite pattern made for a complete rotation around 360 deg.

Besides giving direct information concerning the crystallographic system and the dimensions and shape of the unit cell together with the number of atoms or molecules per unit cell, these spectrum photographs permit space-group assignment.   When the interference maxima have been identified with the planar indices, the presence or absence of possible reflections can at once be noted and the criteria for a specific space group set up.

The matter of interpretation may become very complex for the monoclinic and triclinic systems unless a more powerful aid is sought.   This is found in the concept of the reciprocal lattice introduced by Ewald, in 1921.

The Reciprocal Lattice.   The idea of reciprocal space and a reciprocal lattice seems at first entirely fanciful and remote, even granted that the direct space-lattice itself is only an imaginary framework.   And yet the space-lattice and atomic models are decidedly convenient concepts. Similarly the reciprocal lattice is a most useful aid in interpreting diffraction patterns, for it enables the study of periodic distribution of reflecting power by a crystal.   As a background we may consider the prevalence of reciprocal relationships, the earlier efforts and methods to represent the slopes of planes, and the relation of the x-ray diffraction picture to the crystal which produces it.   Lonsdale[1] reminds us of many instances of reciprocity: Bragg's law itself, since the larger the value of d, the smaller the value of Θ, at constant λ; the smaller the crystal, the broader the reflections on a diffraction pattern, thus permitting evaluation of colloidal-particle size (Chap. 21); long unit cells for long-chain compounds perpendicular to the thinnest dimensions of crystal flakes, and shortest unit-cell distances parallel to the length of needle crystals; octahedral habit as the reciprocal of a cube, since the distance from center to surface of one is the reciprocal of that of the other.

Crystallographers have long struggled with the problem of representing adequately crystallographic planes of several slopes.   The slope is fixed by the geometry of the plane or by the geometry of the normal to the plane, which has the added advantage that the normal has one less dimension than the plane.   Recourse has been had therefore to various ways of projecting the normals onto a surface or plane of projection as in spherical, stereographic, and gnomonic projections.   But in the matter of x-ray diffraction by crystals these projections do not provide for an additional essential variable.

Finally the nature of the x-ray pattern itself is the clue to a useful approach.   A single *spot* on a single crystal pattern is the signature, as it were, of a whole set of parallel *planes*, for it is the registration of a diffracted beam in a definite characteristic direction, and the manifestation of the scattering power of atoms or molecules lying on those planes. Thus the whole pattern itself on a two-dimensional film is in a sense a simplified representation of many sets of planes at different slopes and with different scattering powers.   By two ingenious diffraction methods (DeJong-Bouman and Buerger precession) it is even possible to make these spots lie on a perfectly undistorted network and thus have the diffraction pattern constitute a photograph of a lattice.   If then we might devise a scheme by which we could represent planes by points at the end of normals with characteristic direction to indicate the slope and with length to correspond to interplanar spacings d_{hkl}, we should have a lattice of points and a close analogy with the pattern itself.   This is precisely what is done in the reciprocal lattice.   It is built from the direct crystal lattice by constructing a normal to each plane, with a length which is the reciprocal of the interplanar spacing (so that, the larger d_{hkl}

is, the shorter the line) and then placing a point at the end of the normal. The collection of such points immediately represents (1) a collection of the slopes of the direct lattice planes indicated by the slopes of the normals and (2) a collection of interplanar spacings of the direct lattice in terms of reciprocal spacings. Man has not yet devised a scale with which he can measure directly the dimensions of 10^{-8} cm involved in interatomic spacings. However, if the reciprocal of a very small dimension is used, then this distance can be measured directly by the scales now available.

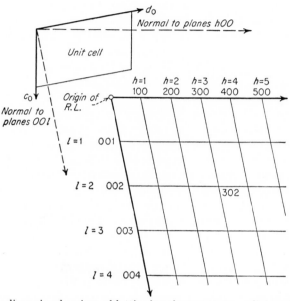

FIG. 233. Two-dimensional reciprocal lattice in reference to monoclinic unit crystal cell.

To show the relationship more clearly, a two-dimensional reciprocal lattice plane for a monoclinic crystal is shown in Fig. 233, with its position in respect to one of the monoclinic unit cells. There is a point in the reciprocal lattice for every possible reflection. The line connecting the origin and the reciprocal lattice point is a vector and can be considered by the usual methods applicable to vectors. As can be noted from the diagram of the monoclinic lattice, the indices of the reciprocal lattice point are exactly the same as the Miller indices defining the original interplanar distances, and this is, of course, due to the fact that the Miller indices are reciprocal quantities.

It is clear from Fig. 233 that any plane network of points in the reciprocal lattice corresponds to a zone of planes in the crystal. As the crystal is rotated around a zone axis, the reciprocal lattice is also being rotated around the perpendicular to the network of points. This network of

nh, nk, nl points in reciprocal space suitably weighted with the nth-order reflection from the corresponding set of (hkl) planes represents the potential x-ray pattern. Assuming crystal perfection and freedom from various disturbing effects, the diffracted beams will be confined to these sharp points of the reciprocal lattice.

Thus a rotation photograph around the c axis as in Fig. 234 is strongly similar to the pattern obtained by rotating the reciprocal lattice around the c axis of the crystal and marking the positions where the reciprocal-lattice points pass through a plane through the c axis. It is evident that the resemblance between the x-ray pattern and the reciprocal-lattice rotation pattern is closest near the center of the photograph, while further out the usual x-ray pattern is a distorted version of a perfect reciprocal lattice.

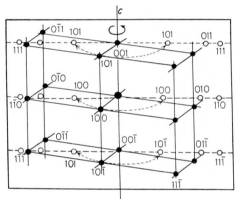

FIG. 234. Formation of reciprocal-lattice rotation diagram. (*Bunn.*)

The importance of this concept may be shown by considering a set of planes undergoing the Bragg reflection. If an arbitrary distance K is selected along the incident beam and transferred to the reflected beam, we may construct an isosceles triangle with a height ρ' (see Fig. 235) along the normal to the planes. An analysis of the figure shows that

$$\rho' = K \sin \Theta \qquad (1)$$

where K or $O'Q$ is the distance selected along the incident beam and Θ is one-half of the diffraction angle. If we use the Bragg relation to eliminate the $\sin \Theta$, the following equation, which serves to define the reciprocal lattice, is obtained:

$$\rho'd = K \frac{\lambda}{2} = K' \qquad \text{for a given } \lambda \qquad (2)$$

It is convenient to let the arbitrary constant equal $2/\lambda$, whence $\rho'd = 1$. Equation (2) shows that ρ' varies inversely as d (the wavelength being considered constant), so that ρ' can be considered as the distance from a point in the reciprocal lattice to its origin. (Since ρ' was constructed normal to the planes diffracting and passes through the origin, it fulfills the conditions for the reciprocal lattice.)

Thus diffraction can occur, for any interplanar spacing, when the reciprocal-lattice point P' intersects the locus of all such possible points, i.e., upon our diagram a small circle or in three-dimensional space a sphere. Such a sphere is usually termed the "sphere of diffraction." The dimension of the sphere of diffraction is, of course, dependent upon the constant chosen in converting the unit cell to a reciprocal lattice, or conversely we may say that the constant employed in converting the reciprocal lattice to a unit cell is determined by the size of the sphere of diffraction employed.

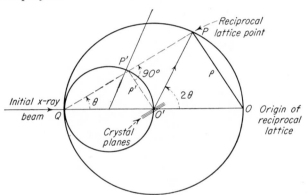

Fig. 235. Construction of the reciprocal lattice and sphere of diffraction.

The reciprocal-lattice intersections with the sphere, however, furnish, when projected from the pole of the sphere to a cylindrical or spherical surface, a pattern which although distorted is still similar to the original reciprocal lattice. Calculations are simplified with this method since all that is necessary is to correct the distortion from the x-ray pattern made and determine directly the reciprocal-lattice dimensions (this, of course, also determines the h, k, and l for each interference). After the reciprocal lattice is known, the unit vectors may be converted readily with the formulas given below, to give the dimensions (and, in some cases, the angles) of the unit cell.

The unit vectors along the coordinate axes of the reciprocal lattice are, of course, related to the (100), (010), and (001) *interplanar spacings* by formulas of the type

$$b_r^* d_{010} = K' \tag{3}$$

The equations necessary to transform *any* unit cell into the reciprocal lattice involve vectors (since a lattice point represents not only a magnitude $K \sin \Theta$ but also a direction). It should be noted that operation of the equations carried out on a reciprocal-lattice unit will rederive the unit cell, since these quantities are reciprocal. The most general case is, of course, the triclinic crystal. The volume of a triclinic solid, bounded by parallel planes, is given by

$$V = abc(1 + 2 \cos \alpha \cos \beta \cos \gamma - \cos^2 \alpha - \cos^2 \beta - \cos^2 \gamma)^{\frac{1}{2}}$$

The distance between parallel planes making up a triclinic figure may be expressed

$$d_a = \frac{V}{bc \sin \alpha} \qquad d_b = \frac{V}{ac \sin \beta} \qquad d_c = \frac{V}{ab \sin \lambda}$$

where d_a is the normal distance between the set of planes separated in the figure by the edge designated a_0. Angular transformation to or from the reciprocal lattice is

$$\cos \alpha_r^* = \frac{\cos \beta \cos \gamma - \cos \alpha}{\sin \beta \sin \gamma}$$

$$\cos \beta_r^* = \frac{\cos \alpha \cos \gamma - \cos \beta}{\sin \alpha \sin \gamma}$$

$$\cos \gamma_r^* = \frac{\cos \alpha \cos \beta - \cos \gamma}{\sin \alpha \sin \beta}$$

If all angles in the unit cell are 90 deg, the corresponding angles in the reciprocal lattice cell will be 90 deg and in the monoclinic system the relations give 90 deg angles for all but one, where $\cos \beta_r^* = - \cos \beta$.

Transformation formulas for reciprocal lattices or unit cells are as follows:

If $K\lambda/2 = K' = \rho'd$,

$$a_r^* = \frac{K'bc \sin \alpha}{V}$$

$$b_r^* = \frac{K'ac \sin \beta}{V}$$

$$c_r^* = \frac{K'ab \sin \gamma}{V}$$

The reciprocal lattice is especially well adapted for analysis of the patterns made from rotating crystals. Although its importance with the ordinary rotation pattern cannot be neglected, its most effective use is with patterns made upon x-ray goniometers. For this purpose, it is somewhat more convenient to reconstruct the geometrical figure in Fig. 235 by incorporating it in the sphere of diffraction itself. Consideration of the diagram will show that, if the sphere of diffraction is drawn with the diffraction planes as the center and the reciprocal lattice (magnified by a value of 2) rotated about one end of a diameter of the sphere of reflection, the direction of the diffracted radiation is determined by the reciprocal-lattice point without additional geometrical construction.

In this diagram ρ is the basis of the new reciprocal lattice and R is taken as the *radius* of the sphere of diffraction. We may note briefly the following relations:

$$\rho' = R \sin \Theta \qquad \rho = 2R \sin \Theta \qquad \rho d = R\lambda$$

If we imagine a spherical film, with a diffracting crystal at the center, each point at which a reciprocal-lattice point cuts the sphere will represent a possible interference recorded on the film. A line drawn from the center of the sphere (the sample) through such a point must represent the direction of the diffracted x-ray beam.

For circular cameras the picture must be modified a trifle, since in this case the film does not coincide with the sphere except as the circumference of a circle. The sphere may be used, however, to indicate the direction of the diffracted x-ray beams for purposes of construction.

The Reciprocal Lattice in the Interpretation of Laue Patterns. Even the Laue method can be subjected to reciprocal-lattice treatment, as Lonsdale has shown.[1] The range of wavelengths in the incident polychromatic beam corresponds to an infinite series of spheres, all touching each other at the point O on the incident beam, and the centers along a common direction as shown in Fig. 236. The sphere of maximum radius corresponds to the minimum wavelength and that of minimum radius to the longest effective wavelength. So all reciprocal-lattice points between the maximum and minimum reflect simultaneously, with especially intense spots corresponding to the most intense range of the general radiation spectrum or any superposed characteristic rays. If the direction lies on a symmetry element such as a fourfold axis, the spheres will be symmetrically arranged relative to reciprocal-lattice points and so the pattern will be symmetrical.

The Reciprocal Lattice in the Interpretation of Rotation Patterns. It has been shown that a single crystal may be regarded as a reciprocal lattice in space. When we study rotating crystals, we can simply con-

o Reflecting points
● Strong reflection
• Non-reflecting points
◎ Origin of reciprocal lattice

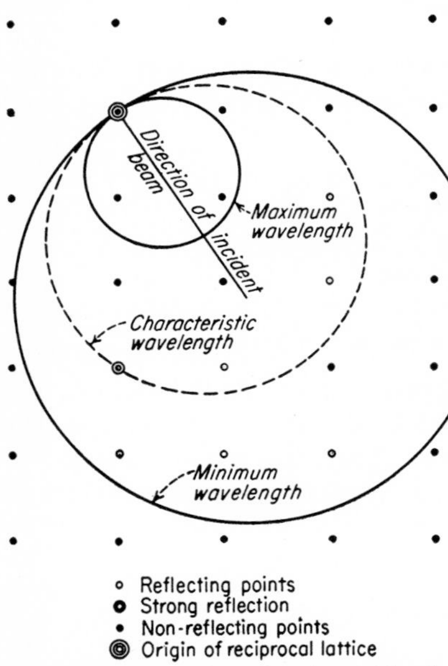

Fig. 236. Application of reciprocal lattice to Laue method. (*Lonsdale.*)

[1] K. Lonsdale, *Proc. Phys. Soc.* (*London*), **54**, 314 (1942).

sider the reciprocal lattice as rotating and we have a quasi-geometrical picture, then, of the reflecting process as it occurs. This picture is the basis of all single-crystal techniques employed at the present time.

Layer Lines. If the reciprocal lattice is rotated in such a manner that a set of planes is rotated about a common normal, we find layers of reciprocal-lattice points intercepting the rotating axis at equal intervals. As the crystal (or lattice) rotates, these planes of points will remain at a constant height above the equatorial plane and so must intersect the sphere of reflection at a certain height. The circle formed by this intersection will contain all possible positions in which the points lying in the specific reciprocal-lattice plane considered may intersect the sphere.

From the preceding section it is obvious that all interferences would fall upon the circle defined by the intersection of the plane and the sphere as designated above if a spherical film were used to record the pattern. Spherical films, however, are not feasible, so that it is necessary to consider the commonly used circular camera. The direction of the interferences for any specific layer of the lattice can be defined by two angles, one corresponding to elevation and the other to a rotation from the direction of the incident beam. The elevation remains constant for any given lattice plane, and therefore a circular film will exhibit all interferences from a given plane of the reciprocal lattice on an imaginary straight horizontal line, at a fixed distance above the equator of the pattern. (The equator is that straight line which contains the undiffracted-x-ray beam effects in its center.) The height of this set of interferences above the equatorial layer line must evidently fix the identity unit (or distance) between the layers of the reciprocal lattice along the axis that was used for rotation. The height of a layer line may, of course, be measured from any interference occurring on the layer line of interest, and usually the measurement is made to the symmetrical interference in the layer line on the opposite side of the equator, for greater accuracy.

For a specific case let us assume a crystal rotating in such a manner that the planes rotating about their normal are the $00l$ planes; *i.e.*, the normal (in case the crystal is orthogonal) corresponds to the direction [001]; and the identity period along this axis will be in the reciprocal lattice c_r^*. Let μ_n be the angle measured from the equator to the nth layer line, and, of course, the normal distance separating the planes will then be nc_r^*. From the reciprocal-lattice sphere-of-reflection diagram we can see that

$$nc_r^* = R \sin \mu_n$$

Of course, c_r^* corresponds to the reciprocal-lattice distance describing the 001 dimension of the unit cell (d_{001}) so that since

$$\rho d = R\lambda$$
$$c_r^* d_{001} = R\lambda$$

then

$$d_{001} = \frac{nR\lambda}{R \sin \mu_n}$$

$$d_{001} = \text{(orthogonal)} \; c_0 = \frac{n\lambda}{\sin \mu_n}$$

Of course, any set of planes may be used, not only those normal to [001]. Each of the three principal dimensions of the unit cell may be determined and such other interplanar spacings as are of importance.

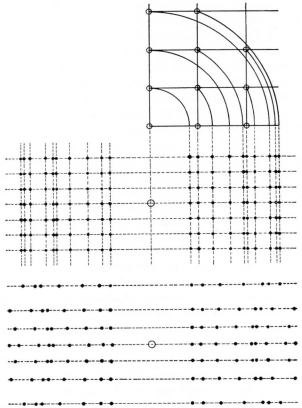

FIG. 237. The rotation pattern (*below*) in relation to the construction of the reciprocal lattice.

Analysis of Rotation Patterns. The preceding section has indicated the use of the reciprocal lattice in permitting the visualization of many data at the same time. The results of such a procedure are quite correct in terms of the Bragg law.

To visualize the pattern better, though, let us approximate our general geometrical picture. We shall assume that the sphere of diffraction has infinite radius and thus becomes, rather than a sphere, a plane of diffraction.

If the reciprocal lattice is now rotated in this plane, each point of the lattice as it passes through the plane may be considered to leave a mark; the plane with its marks would then correspond to a rotation pattern as already shown in Fig. 234. If the reciprocal lattice is orthorhombic, with rotation about c, we shall find a definite regularity in this arrangement of marks. Our pattern will tend to resemble Fig. 237. To express this in words, we shall have lines of spots formed vertically as well as those formed horizontally. A horizontal line of spots, as we know, contains interferences in which l has the same value; these vertical lines (which are somewhat distorted on the actual pattern, the more so the further from the center of the x-ray pattern) are "row lines" or "secondary layer lines," and all spots on such a line will have the same hk values. That is, $hk1$ must be directly above the $hk0$ in the reciprocal lattice (with the orientation we are considering).

Bernal Charts.[1] However, to relate spots on a film lying on layer lines which are produced by networks of the reciprocal lattice perpendicular to the rotation axis and row lines from rows of points on reciprocal space parallel to the rotation axis to points in the reciprocal lattice, cylindrical coordinates of the lattice points are used as illustrated in Fig. 238. Here ξ is the perpendicular distance from the axis

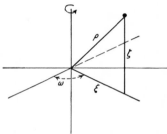

FIG. 238. Cylindrical coordinates of lattice point.

of rotation to a lattice point, ζ is the distance parallel to the axis from the origin to the point, and ω is the angular position with respect to a reference line, which is not determined since it acquires all values in a complete rotation. The coordinates ξ and ζ can be computed for each lattice point by measurements of the position of the spot on the film; but it is more convenient to use the Bernal chart ruled with ξ (0 to 1.6) and ζ (0 to 0.9) values. The film is superposed on the chart, which is the size appropriate to the camera dimensions and the reciprocal-lattice coordinates of the spots read off.

Limitations of the Rotation Method. In the rotation method not all planes can reflect because the number of reciprocal-lattice points which may intersect the surface of the sphere of reflection is limited. Rotation of the crystal with respect to the beam can be represented by rotating the sphere of reflection and keeping the lattice fixed; the sphere of reflection will sweep out a tore. Each point within the tore will pass through the surface of the sphere twice in a rotation to produce symmetrical reflec-

[1] See M. J. Buerger, "X-ray Crystallography," John Wiley & Sons, Inc., New York, 1942.

tions on the right and left side of the rotation pattern. Only those planes can reflect which correspond to the reciprocal-lattice points within the tore. It is further true that some of the planar reflections which would appear on a spherical film may not be recorded depending on the cylindrical or flat-film arrangement.

Powerful though the crystal-rotation method is in providing information on each pattern of the reflection from a zone of planes, with the exceptions mentioned above, the very richness of the patterns often constitutes a limiting factor. Many of the reflections may overlap on the layer lines, with consequent confusion in assigning indices and evaluating intensities. Recourse must then be had to other experimental devices, either to cut down the number of reflections on one pattern or to spread them apart or add another parameter to the coordinates of each reflection.

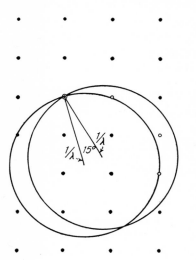

° Points reflecting during oscillation of 15°
• Points not reflecting during oscillation

Fig. 239. Reciprocal-lattice points reflecting in oscillation of 15°. (*Lonsdale.*)

The Oscillation Method. The first alternative for simplifying rotation patterns is accomplished by the oscillation method. Instead of rotating the crystal through 360 deg, it is oscillated in the same camera through 10 to 15 deg usually and a succession of photographs made over one such range after another. The reciprocal-lattice diagram in Fig. 239 clearly shows that only those reflections will appear which are located on the lattice between the circles representing extreme positions of the 15-deg oscillation around the crystal axis perpendicular to the plane of the paper. In this figure the reciprocal lattice is represented as standing still while the beam and circle of contact rotate. For the zero layer the circle of contact has the same radius as the sphere of reflection, but for higher layers this circle of contact will have a smaller radius defined by $\sqrt{1 - (n/c)^2}$, where n is the nth layer and c is the identity period along the c axis. A Bernal chart can also be used to select graphically the circles of contact for various reciprocal-lattice levels. The oscillation method has had excellent use in the hands of Bernal, Bunn, Lonsdale, and others since 1926.[1]

[1] Bunn, "Chemical Crystallography," p. 158, Oxford University Press, New York, 1945.

The Tilted-crystal Method.   A second method, requiring no additional diffraction equipment, for resolving rotation patterns is the tilted-crystal method, developed principally by Bunn.[1]   Crystals rotated around a direction inclined a few degrees to a principal axis will give patterns on which the individual reflections are displaced from the layer lines by different characteristic amounts.   By means of charts and calculations it is possible to relate the displaced spots to the reciprocal-lattice point; for example $X = \zeta \csc \phi$, where X is the distance of a point from the line of intersection of the equatorial plane and the tilted reciprocal-lattice plane, ζ is the vertical distance of any point from the equatorial level, and ϕ is the angle of tilt, experimentally found by means of a goniometer head.   It is essential that it be known to which level the scattered spots belong, so that crystals with a short d spacing, or large layer-line separation, should be used, such as many needle-shaped crystals of aromatic compounds in which the shortest spacing of the unit cell is parallel to the needle axis.

In the attempt to resolve rotation patterns the moving-film goniometers, now to be discussed, are used more frequently than oscillation and tilted-crystal techniques.

X-ray Goniometer Patterns.   Diffraction patterns of rotating crystals, made so that the angle of the crystal at the moment of diffraction is recorded on a moving film, furnish valuable information in the determination of unit-cell dimensions and space groups, especially in dealing with the oblique systems.   Since the added coordinate of a spot on the film is related to the position of the crystal when the reflection takes place, it follows that the position of the reciprocal-lattice points can be derived directly from the reflection coordinates.   Such instruments may be generally termed "x-ray goniometers."

1. *The Weissenberg Goniometer Pattern.*   Perhaps the most widely known is the Weissenberg goniometer, in which the film is moved behind a shield as the crystal rotates, in such a manner as to add a new coordinate to the recorded diffraction spots.   The coordinate system obtained with this instrument is rather complex, but with many available aids to interpretation little difficulty usually is encountered.

The Weissenberg goniometer is described in the preceding chapter and pictured in Fig. 198, and typical patterns are illustrated in Figs. 199 (zinc salicylate) and 240 (n-methyldodecyl ammonium chloride).   These show an array of spots lying on straight diagonal lines or on a family of curves. Again it should be emphasized that all the spots on a pattern are from a single layer in a rotation pattern, since a slotted screen around the crystal in front of the cylindrical film allows only one cone of diffracted rays to register; hence one index in hkl must be common; for example, $hk0$ for the zero layer of a crystal rotated around the c axis.   The Weissenberg photo-

[1] *Loc. cit.*

graph is a two-dimensional projection of one of the reciprocal lattice layers, but by its very nature the rows of points of the reciprocal lattice appear distorted. Interpretation consists then in recognizing visually or

FIG. 240. Weissenberg pattern of 9-n-methyldodecyl ammonium chloride rotated around b axis, first layer line.

identifying the curved loci of these rows by appropriate charts or by measuring on the film two coordinates for the spots which lie on straight

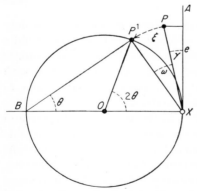

FIG. 241. Determination of reciprocal-lattice coordinates for spots on equatorial layer.

lines (any row of points passing through the origin gives a straight line representing the various orders of reflection from one set of planes) or on curves.

Referring again to Fig. 238, which illustrates cylindrical coordinates ξ, ζ and ω (not measured) for reciprocal-lattice points on a rotation diagram, we now measure for Weissenberg patterns the coordinates ξ and ω, ζ being fixed by choice of the particular layer line. In Fig. 241 is graphically represented a figure defining reciprocal-lattice coordinates for spots on a zero or equatorial layer. Here XA perpendicular to the beam and XB along the beam are axes of reference of the reciprocal lattice. P is a reciprocal-lattice point whose position is defined by $\xi(PX)$ in polar coordinates and the angle ω.   When the crystal rotates counterclockwise, P moves to P^1 on the sphere of reflection and the reflected ray has the direction OP^1; the reciprocal lattice has rotated through the angle ω while the film has moved synchronously through a distance d, related to the total length of travel D by $d/D = \omega/180$ deg.   On the Weissenberg film the coordinate ξ of the reciprocal-lattice point is measured by measuring the distance X of the spot from the center line of the film (which is the same as the distance along the equator of a rotation pattern with

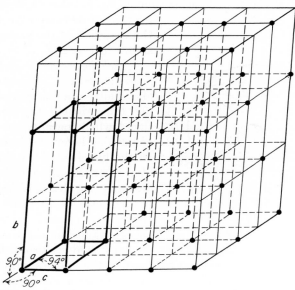

Fig. 242. Three-dimensional reciprocal lattice for zinc salicylate, showing reciprocal unit cell chosen from extinction data.

fixed film).   If the radius of the film in the cylindrical holder is r, then $X/\pi r = 2\Theta/180$ deg (where Θ is the Bragg angle), and $\xi = 2\sin\Theta$. Since $\omega + \gamma = \Theta$, the angle γ is given by

$$\gamma = \Theta - \omega = \Theta - (d/D) \times 180 \text{ deg}$$

Thus the layer of the reciprocal lattice can be plotted in terms of ξ and γ, or in cartesian coordinates $e = \xi \cos \gamma$ and $f = \xi \sin \gamma$.   A graphical chart may be constructed, therefore, for reading off the reciprocal-lattice coordinates of spots of a Weissenberg pattern placed over it so that the base line of the chart lies on the middle of the band running the length of the photograph, or the line which would be traced on the film by the undeviated x-ray beam.   These coordinates are plotted to give an undistorted network.   Figure 242 is a complete three-dimensional plot which is the reciprocal lattice of zinc salicylate and the unit reciprocal cell chosen from extinction data.[1] Indexing of the spots on a two-dimensional plot can be done when it is decided which is the X^* and which is the Y^* axis, for example, if rotation is around Z^*.

There are two variations of the Weissenberg technique: the normal beam type in which the x-ray beam is perpendicular always to the rotation axis; and the equi-inclination method of Buerger, in which the incident and diffracted beams make equal angles with the axis of rotation.   The latter method is especially useful for the layer lines higher than the zero, since the same chart of coordinates may be used for all layers.   The angle of inclination defined by $\cos \Theta = l\lambda/2c$ so that the lth cone of reflected rays will include the direction of the primary beam is shown in Fig. 243.

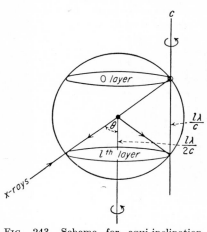

FIG. 243. Scheme for equi-inclination method; when $\cos \Theta = l\lambda/2c$, the lth cone includes the direction of the primary beam.

2. *Schiebold-Sauter Pattern.*   The Schiebold-Sauter camera consists essentially of a rotating pillar (bearing the oriented crystal) before a shield which permits the reflections of but one layer line to be recorded on the film behind the shield.   This film is arranged to rotate perpendicularly to the undiffracted x-ray beam at exactly the same rate as the crystal is rotated.   The interferences obtained lie at the intersections of a distorted reciprocal lattice, and usually the indices may be determined by examination.

The usual arrangement of reflections is on double spirals which cut the central primary-beam spot.   Each curve is the geometrical locus of the reflections of different orders from the same lattice planes.   The distance r of a reflection from the central spot is $r = A \tan 2\Theta$, where A is the distance of the crystal axes of rotation to the center of the rotating films.   The azimuthal angle ϕ of the diagram in polar coordinates is equal to the rotation angle of the crystal.   The angles ϕ_1, ϕ_2, etc., of interferences are proportional to Θ_1, Θ_2, and the radial distances V_1, V_2, etc., are proportional to $\tan 2\Theta_1$, etc.   In Fig. 244a is shown a pattern of urea rotated around the c axis, and in Fig. 244b the indexed network, representing a distorted reciprocal lattice made directly from the pattern.   The shaded area represents the unit cell.   The interference D_1 is, therefore, 220, D_1', $2\bar{2}0$, etc.   Thus the edge lengths of the elementary cell for the a and b directions are directly evaluated, and the c dimension is derived from

[1] Clark and Kao, *J. Am. Chem. Soc.*, **70**, 2151 (1948). $a = 30.80$; $b = 10.72$; $c = 9.18$; $\beta = 93.8$ deg; number of molecules per unit cell = 8; space group $C2/m$.

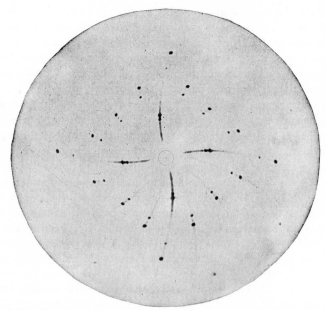

FIG. 244a. Schiebold-Sauter goniometer pattern for urea crystal, rotated around c axis. (*Glocker.*)

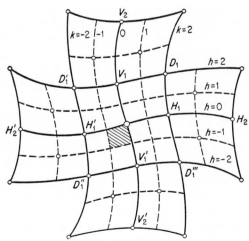

FIG. 244b. Projection and indexing of pattern in Fig. 244a, showing distorted reciprocal lattice.

the layer-line displacements on the ordinary rotation pattern. The angle that the two edges of the cell make with each other is equal to the angle of intersection of the two curves $n00$ and $0n0$ in the primary spot; for urea that is a right angle. The principal value of the Schiebold-Sauter diagram consists in the immediate disclosure of which planes are reflecting and which are not.

3. *DeJong-Bouman Method.* The most recent development gives the undistorted reciprocal-lattice image itself. Essentially the method consists in placing the film in the exact position of a plane of points (normal to the axis of rotation) in the reciprocal lattice, as shown in Fig. 202 in the preceding chapter. The film and lattice are then rotated together through a sphere of diffraction. If the interferences of other layer lines are screened off, the only x-ray beams striking the film pass at the same time through a reciprocal-lattice intersection in the plane of the film. Effectively, this transfers the position of the lattice intersection defining the specific interference to the film, and the final result is a scale diagram of the intersections of the reciprocal-lattice net that correspond to the permitted hkl values.

The dimensions of the equipment fix the constants, so that the dimensions on the film are related to those of the unit cell by

$$\rho'd = K = K' \text{ (equipment)}$$

If the x-ray beam is perpendicular to the rotating crystal, then a specific K' value may be used for all layer lines. However, if the x-ray beam is placed at an angle to the rotating crystal, for the purpose of obtaining the reciprocal-lattice diagram of the equatorial or low layer line, this constant will change. The constant will also be different if a different wavelength radiation is employed. The patterns shown in Fig. 201 were made in this manner at the angle of 30 deg so that each is a completely undistorted representation of a reciprocal-lattice plane.

4. *The Buerger Precession Method.* The newest and in many respects the most interesting method of producing a single crystal diffraction pattern which is a perfect undistorted representation of the reciprocal-lattice layer is the special Buerger-Supper goniometer, which together with a typical pattern is illustrated in Figs. 203 to 205 in the preceding chapter. A particularly beautiful precession pattern of dodecyl ammonium chloride, b-axis precession, made by Dr. C. R. Hudgens in the author's laboratory, is shown in Fig. 245. On such photographs the principal directions are generally easy to find; they will contain the highest point density (unless modified by systematic extinctions) and usually the strongest reflections. The zero layer is compared with one or more n layers and indexed accordingly. Actually this procedure is usually superfluous, for one may inspect the photographs and evaluate systematic extinctions in the terms set forth by the "International

Tables for X-ray Crystallography." From the precession photographs the unit cell is found to have the dimensions $a = 5.658$ A, $b = 7.176$ A, $c = 17.73$ A, $\beta = 92°30'$, with two molecules per unit cell. For this compound a mirror plane in the c axis and a twofold screw axis on the b axis indicated by Laue patterns are confirmed by precession patterns, indicating the monoclinic system. Reflections of $0k0$ appear only when $k = 2n$, giving $P2_1$ and $P2_1/m$ as possible space groups. Since one end of a dodecyl ammonium chloride molecule differs from the other, there cannot be a mirror plan perpendicular to a twofold screw axis in a unit cell containing only two molecules; so $P2_1$ must be the space group.

To recapitulate, the precession method has the following advantages, especially over the Weissenberg method: indexing by inspection instead

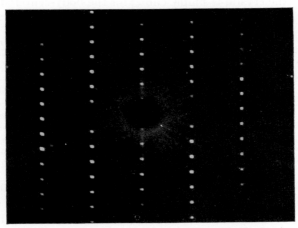

Fig. 245. Precession pattern for dodceyl ammonium chloride, b-axis precession.

of tedious projection of distorted patterns; symmetry easier to detect; invaluable for large unit cells; very short exposures; time for space-group and unit-cell determination only a fraction of that necessary with the Weissenberg; successful patterns with quite imperfect and twinned crystals, which give no satisfactory Laue, rotation, or Weissenberg patterns.[1]

But there are also disadvantages: high-angle reflections not recorded and the centers of n-layer records missing; as an intensity-measuring device limited largely to zero layer lines and to crystals which yield diffuse reflections by other techniques. Any complete analysis must be effected with the aid of the Weissenberg, for only the equi-inclination Weissenberg method records all possible reflections. Therefore, the combination of Weissenberg and precession methods presents the most powerful techniques of single crystal analysis now available.[2] For further details of

[1] Clark and Chu, *Acta Cryst.*, **4**, 470 (1951).
[2] Clark and Kao, *loc. cit.*

the precession technique the reader is referred to Buerger's *ASXRED Mon.* 1.

The Interpretation of Powder Spectra. In this method there is simultaneous registration of all sets of planes due to the random distribution of fine grains. If the crystal system and unit-cell dimensions are known from independent measurements with single crystals, the assignment of indices is not difficult, since $d_{hkl} = a_0/\sqrt{F(hkl;\ abc;\ \alpha\beta\gamma)}$, or for the cubic system $d_{hkl} = a_0/\sqrt{h^2 + k^2 + l^2}$. Under the discussion of determination of space groups from the absence or extinction of certain reflections, a differentiation was found for simple, body-centered, and face-centered cubic lattices depending upon nonappearance of reflections for certain planes. The structure factor clearly indicates that if all possible values of hkl appear the crystal is simple cubic; for the body-centered lattice the

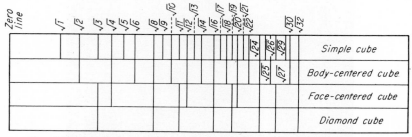

Fig. 246. The relations between powder spectra for various cubic crystals.

sum of hkl indices must be even, and 110, 200, 211, 220, 310, 222, 321, 400, etc., will appear; and for the face-centered cubic lattice the indices must be all odd or all even as in 111, 200, 311, 222, 400, etc. The powder spectra are illustrated in a diagram in Fig. 246. It will be noticed that even for the cubic system lines related to $\sqrt{7}$, $\sqrt{15}$, $\sqrt{23}$, $\sqrt{28}$, $\sqrt{31}$, etc., are absent, since in $\sqrt{h^2 + k^2 + l^2}$ no sum of squares of integers will give these numbers. If values of a_0, etc., are unknown, trial-and-failure methods may be successfully used. Thus for a cubic crystal

$$d_{hkl} = \frac{a_0}{\sqrt{h^2 + k^2 + l^2}} = \frac{n\lambda}{2 \sin \Theta_n}$$

$$\frac{4a_0^2 \sin^2 \Theta_n}{\lambda^2} = (h^2 + k^2 + l^2)n^2$$

Any two powder-spectra lines must have $\sin^2 \Theta_n$ values which will be in the ratio of whole numbers, since $(h^2 + k^2 + l^2)n^2$ is always an integer and a_0 and λ are constant. Thus a slide rule by virtue of its principle of construction can be used to demonstrate cubic structure. For other systems the ratio will not be that of whole numbers. In Table 15-3 are given typical calculations for cubic, tetragonal, and hexagonal lattices.

TABLE 15-3. POSITIONS OF POWDER DIFFRACTION INTERFERENCES FOR CUBIC, TETRAGONAL, AND HEXAGONAL CRYSTALS

Cubic — I. Cubic lattice $\quad a = 4.0\,A$
$$\sin^2\theta = \frac{\lambda^2}{4a^2}(h^2+k^2+l^2)$$

Tetragonal — II. Tetragonal lattice $a = 4.0\,A \quad \dfrac{c}{a} = 0.67_4$
$$\sin^2\theta = \frac{\lambda^2}{4a^2}\left(h^2+k^2+l^2\frac{a^2}{c^2}\right)$$

Hexagonal — III. Hexagonal lattice $a = 4.0\,A \quad \dfrac{c}{a} = 1.633$
$$\sin^2\theta = \frac{\lambda_0}{4a^2}\left[\frac{4}{3}(h^2+k^2+kh)+l^2\frac{a^2}{c^2}\right]$$

$$\lambda = 1.529\,A$$
$$\frac{\lambda^2}{4a^2} = 0.037$$

I

$h\ k\ l$	$h^2 + k^2 + l^2$	$\sin^2\theta$
0 0 1	1	0.037
0 1 1	2	0.074
1 1 1	3	0.111
0 0 2	4	0.148
0 1 2	5	0.185
1 1 2	6	0.222
0 2 2	8	0.296
{ 0 0 3, 1 2 2 }	9	0.333
0 1 3	10	0.370
1 1 3	11	0.407
2 2 2	12	0.444
0 2 3	13	0.481
1 2 3	14	0.518
0 0 4	16	0.592
{ 0 1 4, 2 2 3 }	17	0.629
{ 1 1 4, 0 3 3 }	18	0.666
1 3 3	19	0.703
0 2 4	20	0.740
1 2 4	21	0.777
2 3 3	22	0.814
2 2 4	24	0.888
0 0 5	25	0.925
{ 0 3 4, 3 4 0 }	25	0.925
{ 0 1 5, 3 1 5 }	26	0.962
{ 0 3 3, 3 3 5, 1 1 5 }	27	0.999

II

$h\ k\ l$	$h^2 + k^2 + l^2\frac{a^2}{c^2}$	$\sin^2\theta$
1 0 0	1	0.037
1 1 0	2	0.074
0 0 1	2.2	0.081
1 0 1	3.2	0.118
2 0 0	4	0.148
1 1 1	4.2	0.155
2 1 0	5	0.185
2 1 1	6	0.222
2 0 1	6.2	0.229
2 2 0	8	0.296
0 0 2	8.8	0.325
3 0 0	9	0.333
1 3 0	9.8	0.363
2 2 1	10.2	0.370
3 0 1	10.8	0.377
1 3 1	11.2	0.400
2 0 2	12.2	0.415
2 1 2	12.8	0.451
3 2 0	13	0.474
2 1 2	13.8	0.481
etc.		0.511
		etc.

III

$h\ k\ l$	$\frac{4}{3}(h^2 + k^2 + hk)$	$l^2\frac{a^2}{c^2}$	$\frac{4}{3}(h^2 + k^2 + hk) + l^2\frac{a^2}{c^2}$	$\sin^2\theta$
0 0 1	0	0.37₅	0.37₅	0.014
1 0 0	1.33	0	1.33	0.049
0 0 2	0	1.5	1.5	0.055
1 0 1	1.33	0.37	1.7	0.063
1 0 2	1.33	1.5	2.83	0.104
0 0 3	0	3.37	3.37	0.125
1 1 0	4	0	4	0.148
1 1 1	4	0.37	4.37	0.162
1 0 3	1.33	3.37	4.70	0.174
2 0 0	5.33	0	5.33	0.198
1 1 2	4	1.5	5.5	0.204
2 0 1	5.33	0.37	5.7	0.211
0 0 4	0	6	6	0.222
2 0 2	5.33	1.5	6.83	0.253
1 0 4	1.33	6	7.33	0.272
1 1 3	4	3.37	7.37	0.273
2 0 3	5.33	3.37	8.70	0.322
2 1 0	9.33	0	9.33	0.345
0 0 5	0	9.37	9.37	0.346
2 1 1	9.33	0.37	9.7	0.359
1 0 5	1.33	9.37	10.70	0.370
2 1 2	9.33	1.5	10.83	0.396
2 0 4	5.33	6.0	11.33	0.401
3 0 0	12.00	0	12.00	0.419
etc.			etc.	0.444
				etc.

In systems of symmetry lower than cubic (in which only the cube edge length need be known) the calculations from quadratic equations listed in Table 15-2 may become increasingly difficult, particularly when the crystal system is unknown. Numerous criteria have been set forth, but most useful probably is the graphic method of Hull and Davey for the hexagonal, rhombohedral, and tetragonal and (partially) the orthorhombic systems. For each system the logarithms of the spacing d calculated for each set of planes are plotted against axial ratios. The experimental data are plotted to the same logarithmic scale and then moved over the graph until a match is found, system and axial ratios as well as planar indices for each interference being thus identified. A great many other techniques of indexing powder patterns are to be found in the literature.[1]

The measurements taken from an x-ray pattern may be expressed in one of two useful forms: (1) as the sin Θ values and (2) as the interplanar spacing (d) values. We shall consider the sin Θ values. Generally for an orthorhombic crystal

$$\sin \Theta = \frac{\lambda}{2} \left(\frac{h^2}{a_0^2} + \frac{k^2}{b_0^2} + \frac{l^2}{c_0^2} \right)^{\frac{1}{2}}$$

For simplification we shall designate $a_r^* = 1/a_0$, $b_r^* = 1/b_0$, and $c_r^* = 1/c_0$. Let $1/R = \lambda/2$. Then we may write the equation above in a form reminiscent of the reciprocal lattice,

$$R \sin \Theta = [(ha_r^*)^2 + (kb_r^*)^2 + (lc_r^*)^2]^{\frac{1}{2}}$$

Let us first consider all those reflections which may be described by the indices $hk0$. For this simplified case, we may write

$$R^2 \sin^2 \Theta = (ha_r^*)^2 + (kb_r^*)^2$$

This is simply the description of the hypotenuse of a right triangle equal to $R \sin \Theta$ with the sides equal to ha_r^* and kb_r^*.

If we draw two sets of parallel lines (see Fig. 247) perpendicular to one another, with all the lines in one set separated by the distance a_r^* and all those of the other separated by b_r^*, we may choose one intersection as origin. A line drawn from this origin to any other intersection must correspond to the hypotenuse of such a right triangle, and such a line can be drawn for every possible hk combination. So circles of radius $R \sin \Theta$ may be drawn to correspond to the observed pattern, and in the two-

[1] As a few examples: L. K. Frevel, *J. Appl. Phys.*, **8**, 553 (1937) (from shift in lines of patterns taken at two temperatures), *ibid.* **13**, 109 (1942) (use of isomorphous substances); R. Hesse, *Acta Cryst.*, **1**, 200 (1948) (numerical method for tetragonal, hexagonal, and orthorhombic crystals); M. E. Straumanis, *Am. Mineralogist*, **37**, 48 (1952) (graphical, reciprocal lattice); N. F. M. Henry, H. Lipson, and W. A. Wooster, "The Interpretation of X-ray Diffraction Photographs," Chap. XII, p. 177, D. Van Nostrand Company, Inc., New York, 1951.

dimensional case every circle must pass through some intersection that fixes an h and a k value of the Miller indices.

In the general case we are dealing with a three-dimensional network rather than a two-dimensional one. One three-dimensional graph could be used exactly in the manner indicated by the treatment of the special case; but since we cannot easily treat with a three-dimensional figure, we find it more convenient to replace the three-dimensional graph by two graphs of two dimensions. One of these graphs may be considered as the special case above.

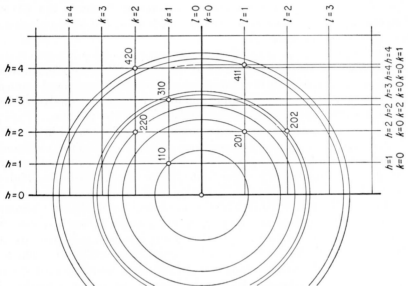

FIG. 247. Reciprocal-lattice construction of powder pattern of Pb_3O_4.

We can construct a second graph with one set of parallel lines spaced at lc_r^*, the other set spaced at distances designated by the sin Θ values as determined from the first graph, that is, h and k values of 10, 11, 01, 20, 21, etc. In Fig. 247 the two graphs, for convenience, are chosen in such a manner that they have the same origin. Consider some intersection on graph 2 due to the line 1 and that designated hk (sin Θ determined by hk). The line from the origin to the intersection in question may be designated ρ. From the theorem of Pythagoras we may write

$$\rho^2 = (lc_r^*)^2 + (R \sin \Theta_{hk0})^2;$$

but from the conditions of the first graph

$$(R \sin \Theta_{hk0})^2 = (ha_r^*)^2 + (kb_r^*)^2,$$

so that

$$\rho = [(lc_r^*)^2 + (ha_r^*)^2 + (kb_r^*)^2]^{\frac{1}{2}}$$
$$= R \sin \Theta_{hkl}.$$

This provides a picture of the sin Θ values for cases in which h,k,l all have integral values other than zero; and, of course, reflections such as $h0l$, $0kl$, etc., may also be described since we have in our composite set of parallel lines those described by $h = 0$, $k = k$, and by $h = h$, $k = 0$.

With assumed unit cells, synthetic patterns may be determined rapidly by this method. The reverse process, however, is not so clear. It is, in brief, to construct the various sets of parallel lines so that intersections are provided to account for every interference observed on the patterns in question.

The Practical Use of the Powder Diffraction Pattern; the Crystal "Fingerprint." The following facts are obvious in the interpretation of these line crystal spectra:

1. Only definite lines in a definite pattern correspond to a pure crystalline substance in the same sense as a "fingerprint." The identification of any pattern with that of a known pure chemical compound immediately constitutes a usually unique qualitative chemical analysis of an unknown crystalline substance that has produced the pattern. Typical patterns for a number of pure lead compounds are illustrated in Fig. 248.

2. Foreign lines indicate the presence of other crystalline substances as impurities; each entity produces its own spectrum if present in sufficient quantity (above 0.2 to 1 per cent usually, but sometimes as high as 5 per cent).

3. In 1938 Hanawalt, Rinn, and Frevel of the Dow Chemical Company devised a logical system of cataloguing[1] the powder diffraction data for about 1,000 pure substances. This beginning has been enlarged into the ASTM card index for several thousand crystalline substances, which is being kept up to date with supplements and by a punched-card system employing IBM machines. Each substance is catalogued according to the values of d for the first, second, and third strongest lines. Each substance has three cards, one for each of these spacings. On each card appear also relative intensity values and, on the one for the strongest line, crystallographic data and a list of all the lines in the powder pattern. If a compound is contained in the index, it may be identified readily in an unknown specimen by measuring d for the strongest line and comparing with the same value in the index, with the additional two lines for further aid.

Since the data in the ASTM index are collected from a wide variety of sources with widely different and sometimes undependable techniques, it is not surprising that more than 300 substances are represented by more than one pattern each, many of the patterns differing materially from each other. Upon recommendation of a Joint Committee on Chemical Analysis by X-Ray Diffraction Methods, representing the American Crystallographic Association, the American Society for Test-

[1] *Ind. Eng. Chem., Anal. Ed.*, **10**, 457 (1938).

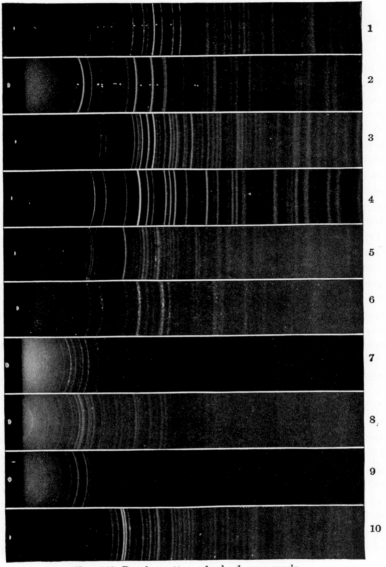

FIG. 248. Powder patterns for lead compounds.

1. PbO (orthorhombic)
2. PbO (tetragonal)
3. Pb_3O_4
4. PbO_2
5. Pb_2O_3

6. Pb_5O_8
7. $4PbO.PbSO_4$
8. $3PbO.PbSO_4$
9. $2PbO.PbSO_4$
10. $PbSO_4$

ing Materials, and the Institute of Physics (England), the National Bureau of Standards has undertaken a critical experimental reexamination by carefully devised standard techniques of diffraction and measurement of repeated patterns in the file. In 3 volumes of NBS Circular 539 already published through June 1954,[1] data for 118 elements and inorganic compounds have been published, of which 110 are recommended to replace 354 cards in the file. This service is giving added value to the index, which has become an indispensable part of the equipment of any x-ray laboratory concerned with chemical analysis from powder diffraction patterns.

There are a few cases in which there may be ambiguity in patterns, especially where solid solutions in alloys and minerals may occur without changing very much d spacings and intensities; similarly LiF and Al are amazingly similar. Frevel[2] has published a list of some of these possible ambiguities. Other cases are Si, β-ZnS, CuCl; CoO, Cu_2O, FeO; CdO, Ag_2O; α-Ce, LiCl; ThO_2, Ca, AgCl. It is on this account that independent optical and chemical tests may be advisable. Also, when the number of compounds increases until there is crowding of spacing intervals Frevel suggests that all compounds containing, Al, Al plus Fe, etc., be grouped together, thus requiring a preliminary qualitative spectroscopic analysis. In instances where patterns sought for an unknown are not found in the index, the matching method can be augmented by trying to establish isomorphism between unknowns and one of the standard structures. Frevel has published tabulated diffraction data for cubic (705) and tetragonal (329) isomorphs[3] which are very useful even for mixtures and solid solutions.

4. Microanalysis is possible with powder diffraction patterns. As indicated in the preceding chapter, this is largely a matter of handling of extremely minute amounts of sample, and one mount for this purpose was described (Fig. 213). Rooksby has described the many problems of microanalysis which confront the Research Laboratories of the General Electric Company, Ltd., Wembley, England,[4] such as deposits in vacuum devices, extremely thin films or discolorations on cathodes or heated foils, interfacial films at glass-metal seals, etc., together with the techniques employed. In the author's laboratory alkaloid opiates have been identified in amounts as small as 0.7γ (0.0007 mg) by mounting in perforated metal disks.[5]

5. Solid solution is indicated by no change in the pattern of lines of a

[1] U.S. Government Printing Office, Division of Public Documents, Washington 25, D.C. Authors are Howard E. Swanson, Eleanor Tatge, Ruth K. Fuyat, and G. M. Ugrinic.

[2] L. K. Frevel, *Ind. Eng. Chem., Anal. Ed.*, **16**, 209 (1944).

[3] *Ind. Eng. Chem., Anal. Ed.*, **14**, 687 (1942), **18**, 83 (1946).

[4] *Analyst*, **73**, 326 (1948).

[5] S. T. Gross and F. W. Oberst, *J. Lab. Clin. Med.*, **32**, 94 (1947).

pure constituent, but by a shift in position of the lines, toward smaller angles (nearer the zero main beam) if the lattice is expanded by the addition of foreign atoms or to larger angles if contracted. In many cases the lattice spacing is linearly related to atomic percentage of constituents of a solid-solution alloy, as will be illustrated later.

6. The powder method may be made very accurate, indeed the most accurate of any diffraction technique, in evaluating the unit-cell dimensions of a pure substance and from this the ideal density of the material. The value for tungsten so obtained has been of the utmost value in vacuum-tube applications where tungsten filaments are employed.

There are a number of reasons for attempting to achieve highest accuracy in evaluation of unit-cell dimensions: (1) certain identification of a crystalline substance, especially when there may be several compounds with closely similar spacings (single crystal patterns may often be necessary when powder reflections overlap); (2) determination of composition in a solid-solution series from the positions of shifted lines, where there is an established relationship between composition in a two- (or more) component system and unit-cell dimensions; (3) the determination of atomic and molecular weights and of lattice defects, best achieved by the Straumanis technique discussed in the next section; (4) the determination of shapes of molecules and their orientation in the unit cell, often possible without the further more laborious recourse to intensity calculations.

The chief sources of error in the very accurate measurement of lines on a powder pattern are as follows: (1) uncertainty as to zero position of undeviated primary beam from which linear displacement of lines is measured; (2) variable radius of cylindrical camera, and film or specimen not at center of camera; (3) shrinkage of film; (4) effects of absorption in fairly thick or heavily absorbing specimens such that diffraction occurs in the outer layer instead of center of the specimen, thereby causing corresponding arcs on each side of the pattern to be too far apart. Many devices have been suggested for correction of errors. For case 1 lines or arcs are measured from one side of the center to the corresponding lines on the other, thus giving a linear distance related to a total diffraction angle of 4θ. For cases 2, 3, and 4, a fiduciary mark is printed on the film which represents a very accurately measured true angle, from which measurements may be made; or more generally for correcting for all errors a standard substance whose spacings are very accurately known is added to the unknown and the superposed patterns registered, with the result that all along the film unknown lines may be measured with respect to the standard line whose exact diffraction angle is known. For this purpose quartz, sodium chloride, or sodium fluoride are frequently used. With the Geiger spectrometer a standard quartz specimen is always used to calibrate and check angular positions and intensities. As indicated in the preceding chapter, the Straumanis technique of asymmetric patterns with high-precision cameras carefully thermostatted has led to the most accurate measurements depending upon the *positions* of diffraction lines, especially those produced by back reflection. Straumanis in his several papers[1] has given detailed directions for obtaining and measuring powder patterns for precision determination of lattice parameters, expansion coefficients, and atomic and molecular weights by the equation

$$A_x = \frac{N_0 V \rho}{n}$$

where N_0 is Avogadro's number, V is the volume of the unit cell in cubic angstroms, ρ is the density in grams per cubic centimeter, and n is the number of atoms (or molecules) per unit cell. Some examples of his measurements are as follows: lattice parameter of diamond at 20°C, 3.55960 ± 0.000016 kX or 3.56679 A; coefficient of expansion,

$$\alpha = 1.38 \times 10^{-6}$$

Avogadro's number, 6.02403×10^{23} per mole; atomic weights, as follows:[2]

	Chemical	X-ray
Ag	107.88	107.86
Cu	63.54	63.540
Fe	55.85	55.858
Pb	207.21	207.17
Te	127.61	127.62
F ($M_{LiF}-A_{Li}$)	19.00	18.999
C	12.010	12.0096
Si	28.09	28.083
Ge	72.60	72.593

Other x-ray workers also have striven to attain highest precision in lattice-parameter measurements, among whom are Taylor and Sinclair, who have critically examined types of systematic error and extrapolation methods,[3] Klug and Alexander,[4] who have measured a_0 for Pb as 4.9408 ± 0.0001 kX, and Lonsdale and Hume-Rothery, who have made the difficult measurements of lattice spacings for Li and Rb between −183 and 19°C† (Chap. 16) and thereby determined the coefficients of expansion. One of the earliest precise determinations of coefficient of expansion (α) was

[1] Summarized at the X-ray Symposium, Atlantic City meeting of the American Chemical Society, September, 1952; *Anal. Chem.*, **25**, 4 (May, 1953).

[2] *J. Am. Chem. Soc.*, **72**, 5643 (1951); *J. Appl. Phys.*, **23**, 330 (1952); *Acta Cryst.*, **2**, 82 (1949); *Z. Physik*, **126**, 49 (1949).

[3] A. Taylor and H. Sinclair, *Proc. Phys. Soc. (London)*, **57**, 126 (1945).

[4] *J. Am. Chem. Soc.*, **62**, 1492 (1940), **68**, 1493 (1946).

† *Phil. Mag.*, **7**, 36, 799, 842 (1945).

for Mg, with the values 27.7×10^{-6} perpendicular and 29.3×10^{-6} parallel to the c axis.† Other recent measurements of high precision are on CsI‡ ($a = 4.5667$ A); KCl ($a = 6.29294$ A, $\alpha = 3.37 \times 10^{-5}$ per deg C); KI ($a = 7.06555$ A, $\alpha = 4.06 \times 10^{-5}$); TlCl ($a = 3.94270$ A, $\alpha = 5.35 \times 10^{-5}$).§

7. Quantitative analysis of powder mixtures results from the accurate measurement of *intensities* of powder diffraction lines (in contrast with evaluation of lattice parameters from *positions* of lines in the preceding section). A large number of researches has been concerned with various techniques for measuring intensities on films with the aid of micro-photometers and directly with Geiger spectrometers, in the effort to discover whether peak intensities or integrated peak areas best represent true values; what corrections must be made for absorption and other variables; what are the necessary requisites of the sample; and what kind of calibration with standards is required. The pioneer work in this field was done by Brentano[1] beginning in 1925, Compton[2] in 1927, and Brindley and Spiers[3] in 1934. The present status of this and all other phases of powder diffraction analysis is exhaustively covered in a new book by Klug and Alexander.[4]

Methods of quantitative analysis may be exemplified by considering four typical procedures.[5]

a. If an unknown mixture consists of two components, say $X + Y$, and if pure samples X and Y are available, then a series of standard mixtures $X_n + Y_{100-n}$ may be made up (where n is percentage). From the relative intensities of suitable lines in the $X_n + Y_{100-n}$ patterns a graph may be drawn of relative intensity plotted against percentage n of the X constituent. From the measured relative intensity in the $X + Y$ pattern, the percentage of X and therefore also of Y may be read off from the graph.

This method was used by Redmond[6] to determine the percentage of tungsten carbide in mixtures containing molybdenum carbide and

† J. D. Hanawalt and L. K. Frevel, *Z. Krist.*, **98**, 84 (1937).

‡ T. B. Rymer and P. G. Hambling, *Acta Cryst.*, **4**, 565 (1951).

§ P. G. Hambling, *Acta Cryst.*, **6**, 98 (1953).

[1] J. C. M. Brentano, *Proc. Phys. Soc. (London)*, **37**, 184 (1925), **47**, 932 (1932), **50**, 237 (1938).

[2] A. H. Compton, "X-Rays and Electrons," D. Van Nostrand Company, Inc., New York, 1923.

[3] G. E. Brindley and F. W. Spiers, *Proc. Phys. Soc. (London)*, **46**, 841 (1934), **50**, 17 (1938).

[4] Harold P. Klug and LeRoy E. Alexander (Mellon Institute), "X-Ray Diffraction Procedures for Polycrystalline and Amorphous Materials," John Wiley & Sons, Inc., New York, 1954.

[5] From an excellent summary by J. Shearer, *J. Roy. Soc. W. Australia*, **35**, 9 (1948–1949).

[6] J. C. Redmond, *Ind. Eng. Chem., Anal. Ed.*, **19**, 773 (1947).

titanium carbide, respectively. The method may be exemplified as follows:

$$\text{Sample} \qquad X + Y$$
$$\text{Standard} \qquad X_n + Y_{100-n}$$

b. Consider the case of a mixture $X + Y+$, where X is the component to be determined quantitatively and $Y+$ is any number of unknown components. As before, it is necessary that a pure sample of X be available. A suitable diluent D is mixed with X in order to simulate the mixture $X + Y+$. A number of these standard mixtures are made up, $X_n + D_{100-n}$, where n is the percentage. To the same quantity of each standard mixture and of the "unknown" mixture, a given quantity S of a suitable internal standard is added. From the diffraction pattern of each of the standard mixtures a graph may be drawn of the relative amounts of S and X plotted against the relative intensity of two convenient lines, one in the S pattern and one in the X pattern. From this graph and the relative intensity of the same two lines in the pattern of the "unknown" mixture the percentage of X in $X + Y+$ may be deduced. The method may be exemplified as follows:

$$\text{Sample} \qquad X + S + Y+$$
$$\text{Standard} \qquad X_n + S + D_{100-n}$$

This method has been used by Clark and Reynolds[1] to determine the amount of quartz in mine dust. Calcite was chosen for D and fluorite for S. The method applies whether components $Y+$ are crystalline or amorphous (*i.e.*, give no patterns by which they may be identified). From the percentage of X, the percentage of $Y+$ immediately follows. This may be very valuable information if $Y+$ is wholly or partially amorphous. If, in the sample $X + Y$ analyzed by the first method, any amorphous material is also present, that method will yield the relative proportions of X and Y (which may be all that one is interested in) and not their percentages. The amount of amorphous material present would be obtained only if the second (internal-standard) method were used to determine separately the percentage of X and the percentage of Y. No diluent in that case may be necessary in that Y would serve as a diluent of X, and vice versa. Applied in this way, the second method may be exemplified:

$$\text{Sample} \qquad X + Y + Z + S+$$
$$\text{Standard} \qquad X_n + Y_{100-n} + S$$

Both methods *a* and *b* have the advantage that it is not necessary to reproduce an exposure. The lines whose intensities are compared occur

---

[1] G. L. Clark and D. H. Reynolds, *Ind. Eng. Chem., Anal. Ed.*, **8**, 36 (1936).

in one and the same diffraction pattern. This is not the case in the following methods.

c. Gross and Martin[1] working in the author's laboratory developed a method for determining the amount of a constituent X in a composite sample which employed no synthetic mixtures except the addition of an internal standard S to the sample to be analyzed in percentage (C_s) comparable with the percentage (C_x) of X. Provided that an empirical constant k can be determined, the percentage of X is given by

$$C_x = \frac{C_s I_x I_0 k}{I_s}$$

where I_x is the intensity of an X line in the diffraction pattern of the sample (containing the internal standard), I_s is the intensity of an S line (very close to the previous) in the diffraction pattern of the same sample, I_0 is the intensity of the same S line in the pattern given by a sample consisting of 100 per cent of S with an x-ray beam of the same intensity as was used in irradiating the sample with internal standard, and k is a constant involving all the factors (crystal structure and geometrical and absorption factors) upon which the absolute intensity of a line in a powder diffraction pattern depends. The last is constant for any given diffraction line in a pattern of a particular crystalline material and will vary from line to line, i.e., from direction to direction of diffracted beam. This is the reason why the selected line in the pattern of the internal standard must lie very close to (theoretically must be superposed upon) the selected line in the X pattern.

This method may be exemplified as

Sample $X + S + Y +$
Standard S

Any number of constituents could be determined quantitatively in this way, and by difference the quantity of amorphous residue (if present) could be determined.

d. Methods of quantitative analysis have been developed which dispense entirely with synthetic mixtures or internal standards. The methods require, however, that a powdered sample can be prepared consisting of 100 per cent of the constituent whose percentage in the "unknown" mixture is required. Arising out of the theory given by Gross and Martin and deduced independently by Hellman and Jackson,[2] the following simple relationship holds provided that the mass irradiated in each case is the same and that the densities and x-ray absorptions are the same,

[1] S. T. Gross and Dorothy E. Martin, *Ind. Eng. Chem., Anal. Ed.*, **16**, 95 (1944).

[2] N. N. Hellman and M. L. Jackson, *Proc. Soil Sc. Soc. Amer.*, **8**, 135 (1944).

$$\frac{C_x}{C_0} = \frac{I}{I_0}$$

where C_x is the required percentage, C_0 is the percentage in the standard sample (100 per cent or any known concentration), and I and I_0 are the intensities of any line in the pattern of the "unknown" and standard.

Hellman and Jackson applied this method to the analysis of clay mixtures. In the case of such material the conditions required are approximately fulfilled.

Any number of constituents could be determined quantitatively in this way, and by difference the quantity of amorphous residue (if present) could be determined.

Hellman and Jackson used the photographic technique and a wedge-shaped specimen mounted so as to expose a constant mass to the x-ray beam. Wilchinsky[1] employed a similar quantitative method, using the Geiger-tube technique, as already described. When the flat powder sample is of thickness sufficient to absorb completely the x-ray beam traversing the powder at a grazing angle equal to the Bragg angle for the particular line under observation, the percentage concentration of X in the unknown sample is given by

$$C_x = \frac{100 I_x \mu}{I_0 \mu_0}$$

where I_x is the intensity of the particular line under observation in the pattern of the unknown, I_0 is the intensity of the same line in the pattern of the pure sample of X, and μ and μ_0 are the mass-absorption coefficients of the unknown sample and the pure sample, respectively. These absorption coefficients, being coefficients for the powder, require to be known (or measured). If they are substantially the same, the formula reduces to the same form as in the previous case of Hellman and Jackson. In each case we have

Sample $X + Y +$
Standard X

It is obvious that if the powder diffraction method could be adapted to quantitative analysis without the use of internal standards, it would be more practicable and rapid, especially for routine industrial practice. In 1948 Alexander and Klug[2] devised such a method, involving measurements of intensities of diffraction lines and x-ray absorption in the sample. The fundamental equation derived was

$$I_1 = \frac{K_1 x_1}{\rho_1 [x_1 (\mu_1^* - \mu_m^*) + \mu_m^*]} \tag{1}$$

[1] Z. W. Wilchinsky, *J. Appl. Phys.*, **18**, 429 (1947).

[2] L. Alexander and H. P. Klug, Basic Aspects of X-ray Absorption in Quantitative Diffraction Analysis of Powder Mixtures, *Anal. Chem.*, **20**, 886 (1948).

where K_1 is a constant defined by $K_1 = \frac{1}{2}(I_1)_0 A$, where $(I_1)_0$ is the intensity diffracted by unit volume of pure component 1 and A is the cross-sectional area of the x-ray beam impinging on the sample at angle Θ; x_1 is the weight fraction of component 1; ρ_1 is the density; $\mu_1^* = \mu_1/\rho_1$, the mass-absorption coefficient of component 1; and μ_m^* is the mass-absorption coefficient of the matrix or all other constituents combined.

There were three important cases for analysis: (1) Where

$$\mu_1^* = \mu_m^* \quad I_1 = kx_1 \tag{2}$$

which shows that the diffracted intensity is directly proportional to concentration, allowing direct linear analysis. An example would be the analysis of quartz in the presence of cristobalite, both polymorphs of SiO_2. (2) When $\mu_1^* = \mu_2^*$ in a two-component system, then

$$\frac{I_1}{(I_1)_0} = \frac{x_1\mu_1^*}{x_1(\mu_1^* - \mu_2^*) + \mu_2^*} \tag{3}$$

The intensity-concentration curve is not linear but is easily calculated and plotted for such cases as quartz-BeO, or quartz-KCl. (3) When $\mu_1^* \neq \mu_m^*$ and the latter value is unknown, analysis requires the addition of an internal standard. When this is added in a constant proportion, x_1, the concentration of the unknown component, is proportional to the intensity ratio I_1/I_s, again a linear relationship for such cases as quartz mixtures with fluorite, CaF_2, as an internal standard.

Upon the basis of the Alexander-Klug equation, a further development was made in the Canadian Occupational Health Laboratory[1] for the purpose of complete elimination of internal standards. The following equation was derived:

$$x_1 = \left(\frac{I_1}{(I_1)_0}\right)\left(\frac{\mu_s^*}{\mu_1^*}\right) \tag{4}$$

where μ_s^* is the mass-absorption coefficient for the sample. The ratio of absorption coefficients is evaluated from

$$\frac{\mu_s^*}{\mu_1^*} = \frac{\rho_1 \log (T_s/T_0)}{\rho_s \log (T_1/T_0)} \tag{5}$$

where T_s is the intensity transmitted per unit area by the sample placed normal to the x-ray beam of the same wavelength as used in the diffraction pattern, T_0 is the intensity of the incident beam per unit area, T_1 is the intensity transmitted by a sample of pure component 1 of the same thickness, and ρ_s and ρ_1 are the densities corresponding.

This method, then, requires measuring diffraction-intensity ratios and mass-absorption ratios. Upon experimental test with quartz in various

[1] J. Leroux, D. H. Lennox, and K. Kay, *Anal. Chem.*, **25** (May, 1953).

mixtures, it was discovered that there was a deviation in slope of the curves from the theoretical slope of -1. Consequently Eq. (4) was modified to

$$x_1 = \left(\frac{I_1}{(I_1)_0}\right)\left(\frac{\mu_s^*}{\mu_1^*}\right)^{-c} \tag{6}$$

C has the value -0.78 for quartz. This discrepancy lies in the diffraction-intensity ratios rather than the absorption measurements; thus the analysis depends upon evaluations of C for each kind of material, the instrument, wavelength, and method of sample preparation. The method has proved to be especially suitable, not only for dust analyses, but for routine analysis in such industries as ceramics, refractories, paint, and cement.

All the methods for quantitative analysis require not too dissimilar particle size and random particle orientation in the sample under test and the standard. If integrated peak areas, instead of peak heights, are measured (assuming microphotometer records), considerable difference in particle size may be permissible; but (unless the same degree of preferred orientation is reproducible) preferred orientation must be absent. This is difficult (or even impossible) to achieve with platy materials like clay minerals. Perhaps it can be completely achieved only with crystals showing conchoidal fracture.

Even when preferred orientation is absent, statistical factors affect the degree of randomness in the powder, arising from the fact that a finite number (as distinct from an infinite number) of crystal particles are irradiated. These statistical factors affecting the intensity of diffracted x-rays have been studied theoretically and experimentally by Klug and associates at Mellon Institute with special reference to the Geiger-tube diffractometer.[1]

In considering the part played by absorption in the specimen it is easily demonstrated that it is not involved in the first three methods and the part played in (d) has been explained.

Other important contributions have been made by Taylor,[2] Hägg and

---

[1] H. P. Klug, L. Alexander, and K. Kummer, Quantitative Analysis with the X-ray Spectrometer, *Anal. Chem.*, **20**, 607 (1948). Alexander, Klug, and Kummer, Statistical Factors Affecting the Intensity of X-rays Diffracted by Crystalline Powders, *J. Appl. Phys.*, **8**, 742 (1948); Alexander and Klug, Basic Aspects of X-Ray Absorption in Quantitative Diffraction Analysis of Powder Mixtures, *Anal. Chem.*, **20**, 886 (1948); Klug, Quantitative Analysis of Powder Mixtures with the Geiger-Counter Spectrometer, *ibid.*, **25**, 704 (1953).

[2] A. Taylor, The Influence of Crystal Size on the Absorption Factor as Applied to Debye-Scherrer Diffraction Patterns, *Phil. Mag.*, **35**(7), 215 (1944); On the Optimum Thickness of Powder Specimens in X-ray Diffraction Work, *ibid.*, p. 632; The Influence of Absorption on the Shapes and Positions of Lines in Debye-Scherrer Powder Photographs, *Proc. Phys. Soc.* (*London*), **57**, 108 (1945).

Regnström[1] on intensity measurements with focusing cameras of the Seemann-Bohlin type, and Rooksby,[2] who shows how it is possible to analyze MgO for as little as 0.1 per cent CaO and 0.2 per cent ZnO in ZnS.

As previously mentioned, the quantitative analysis of industrial and mine dusts has been one of the most important of all applications, and the method originally suggested by Clark and Reynolds has general acceptance by hygiene experts.   Silicosis of the lungs is caused by α-quartz, as proved in the subsequent work by Sweany, Klaas, and Clark[3] on clinical specimens.   Hence it is essential to make an analysis *in the solid state*, since quartz would disappear as such in the chemical method.

In 1952 Clark and Loranger[4] made a complete dust analysis of every part of a very large steel foundry with a Geiger spectrometer in order to correlate quartz concentration (varying from 0 to 80 per cent of the dust) with lung radiographs of all workers in each area, to determine the effectiveness of aluminum therapy (inhaling of powdered aluminum, which protects or isolates lesions due to quartz), and to determine the effect of iron in causing benign siderosis, which is indicated by lung shadows where quartz concentration is negligible. Similarly pathological lung conditions for workers with graphite, asbestos, beryllium compounds, etc., may be correlated with dust analysis.

Fig. 249. Pinhole pattern illustrating effect of large grain size (black diamond of carbonado used in mining drills).

8. The widths of the diffraction lines serve as a means of determining grain size in the specimen as will be demonstrated in Chap. 21.

9. Any departure of the powder or aggregate from purely random arrangement that results in continuous diffraction circles or lines of uniform intensity is manifested by the patterns.   Thus if the grains are too large to permit the probability of random arrangement, the lines become spotted and dashed owing to reflection from individual grains (Fig. 249). In general, the grain diameter must be smaller than 10^{-3} cm to prevent this.   Most metals with grains that will pass through a 200-mesh sieve will give uniform lines.   Rotation or rocking the specimens assists in smoothing out the spotty lines by bringing more grains into effective

[1] *Arkiv Kemi Mineral Geol.*, **18A**(5), 1 (1944).

[2] H. P. Rooksby, *Analyst*, **70**, 166 (1945).

[3] H. C. Sweany, R. Klaas, and G. L. Clark, *Radiology*, **31**, 299 (1938).

[4] G. L. Clark and W. F. Loranger, presented at the Los Angeles meeting of the American Chemical Society, March, 1953.   *Anal. Chem.*, **26**, 1413 (1954)

participation in diffraction. Again, if the grains are sufficiently small but are oriented in some preferred direction, as by some deforming force, some lines may become weakened or may disappear or be intensified by localized intensity maxima in comparison with intensities on normal powder patterns. These are indications of fiber structure which will receive frequent mention in later sections.

10. Chemical and industrial applications. Papers on powder diffraction techniques, interpretations, and applications now run into the hundreds; anything like an adequate summary is obviously impossible. A classification of actual applications by the general fields[1] and a few examples follow.

a. Mineralogical and geological.
Determination of crystallographic properties of minerals.
Identification of minerals in ore and prospect samples, for example, quantitative analysis of bauxite exploration samples.[2] A list of powder diffraction lines and

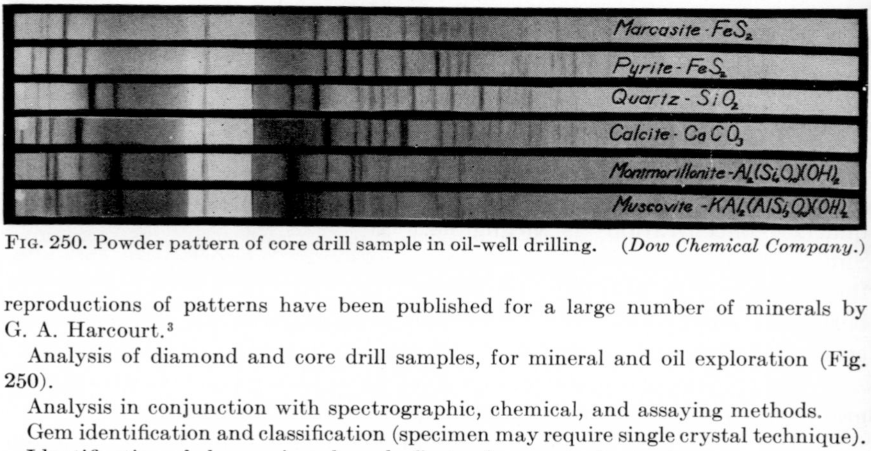

FIG. 250. Powder pattern of core drill sample in oil-well drilling. (Dow Chemical Company.)

reproductions of patterns have been published for a large number of minerals by G. A. Harcourt.[3]

Analysis of diamond and core drill samples, for mineral and oil exploration (Fig. 250).

Analysis in conjunction with spectrographic, chemical, and assaying methods.
Gem identification and classification (specimen may require single crystal technique).
Identification of clays, minerals and effects of reagents, heat, etc.
b. Petroleum exploration and production.
Analysis and identification of ore samples.
Control analysis of ore dressing, classification, and flotation processes.
Control of sintering and roasting.
Analysis of tailings and waste products.
c. Petroleum refining.
Identification of asphalts and waxes.
Control of production and operation of cracking and hydroforming catalysts. X-ray patterns have contributed greatly to the nature of the SiO_2-Al_2O_3 cracking catalysts. The isomorphous replacement of Si^{4+} by Al^{3+} coordinated tetrahedrally

---

[1] Based in part on J. L. Abbott, "Industrial Control with X-ray Diffraction," Anglo-Am. Ind. Newsletter, May, 1947.
[2] R. H. Black, Anal. Chem., **25**, 743 (1954).
[3] Am. Mineralogist, **27**, 63 (1942).

ith four oxygen ions results in a surplus negative charge and acidic properties neces-
ary for the formation of carbonium ions serving as intermediates in hydrocarbon
racking.[1]

d. *Water purification for power-plant boilers and turbine deposits.*

Analysis of boiler scales, condenser-tube deposits, sludges, corrosion products, etc.
Masterly work in solving boiler-water treatment problems was carried out a decade
go by Imhoff and Burkardt.[2] No less than 17 compounds were found for the first
ime in such material as boiler scales and sludges and turbine-blade, superheater-tube,
nd corrosion deposits, including the positive identification of acmite, burkcite, can-
rinite, forsterite, whitlockite, sodalite, pectolite, etc., in addition to the more familiar
ilica (crystalline and amorphous), silicates of a wide variety, oxides, hydroxides,
ulfates, sulfides, phosphates, carbonates, metals, sodium chloride, etc.

Inevitably with the knowledge gained of the nature of these power-plant deposits,
vhich could not be identified in any other way, great strides have been made in boiler-
vater treatment and boiler design, construction and materials used in boilers, turbines,
uperheaters, etc. This whole problem is well illustrated by studies made in the

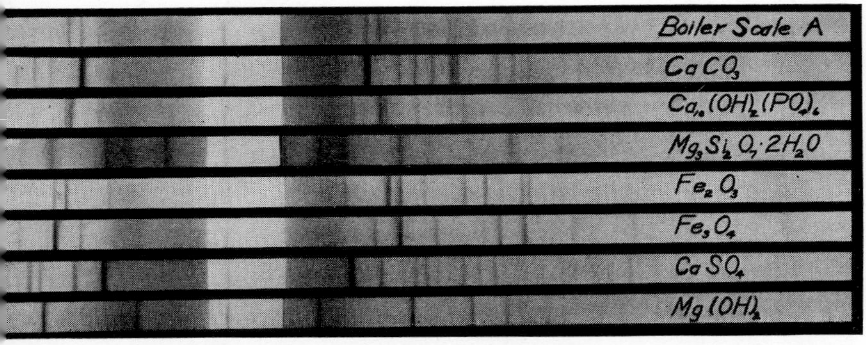

FIG. 251. Identification of a boiler scale. (*Dow Chemical Company.*)

x-ray laboratory of the Dow Chemical Company. Figure 251 gives the pattern of a
boiler scale along with patterns of some of the materials found in it, resulting in a
direct analysis of 40% $CaCO_3$, 40% $Ca_{10}(OH)_2(PO_4)_6$, 10% $Mg_3Si_2O_7.2H_2O$, and 10%
Fe_2O_3. To solve the problem of the cause of rupture of tubes in a new 1,250-lb high
pressure boiler (Fig. 252), the x-ray patterns disclosed the nature of layers of hard
scale containing analcite, $Na_2Al_2Si_4O_{12}.2H_2O$, sodalite, $Na_8Al_6Si_6O_{24}.Cl_2$, and noselite,
$Na_8Al_6Si_6O_{24}.SO_4$, with softer layers comprised of hydroxyapatite, Fe_3O_4, and an
unidentified phase. The hard scale was on the hotter side of the tubes so that it was
concluded that this scale lowered heat transfer, causing excessive temperature, metal
oxidation, and thinning and bulging; and it was proved that the source of the scale was
in the feed-water system, which was condensate returns from 400-lb boilers, given an
oil-removal treatment which introduced alumina and silica. The hydroxyapatite
deposit, easily washed out, came from the reaction between calcium compounds in the
water and Na_3PO_4 added to remove them.

[1] A. G. Oblad, T. H. Milliken, and G. A. Mills, "Advances in Catalysis," Vol. III,
p. 199, Academic Press, Inc., New York, 1951.

[2] C. E. Imhoff and G. A. Burkardt, *ASTM, Standards*, **43**, 1276 (1943); *Ind. Eng.
Chem.*, **35**, 873 (1943), **39**, 1427 (1947). L. M. Clark and C. W. Bunn, *J. Soc. Chem.
Ind.*, **59**, 155 (1940).

e. Rubber manufacturing.

Study and identification of pigments, filler, plasticizers, carbon blacks, acceleratio◦ activators,[1] reinforcing agents, etc.

Development and control of synthetic rubbers.

Research and control of copolymerization.

Butadiene production control analysis.

f. Storage-battery manufacture.

Analysis and control of PbO† production; mixing, drying, aging, and forming ◦ plates (development of basic sulfates); mechanisms of self-discharge; presence ◦ amorphous materials.

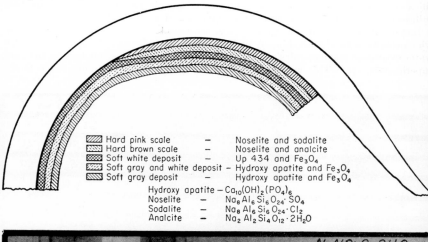

		Hard pink scale	—	Noselite and sodalite
		Hard brown scale	—	Noselite and analcite
		Soft white deposit	—	Up 434 and Fe_3O_4
		Soft gray and white deposit	—	Hydroxy apatite and Fe_3O_4
		Soft gray deposit	—	Hydroxy apatite and Fe_3O_4

Hydroxy apatite — $Ca_{10}(OH)_2(PO_4)_6$
Noselite — $Na_8 Al_6 Si_6 O_{24} \cdot SO_4$
Sodalite — $Na_8 Al_6 Si_6 O_{24} \cdot Cl_2$
Analcite — $Na_2 Al_2 Si_4 O_{12} \cdot 2H_2O$

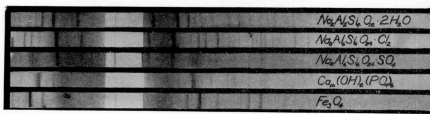

Fig. 252. Identification of hard scale which caused rupture of boiler tube. (*Dow Chemica◦ Company.*)

g. Paint manufacturing.

Analysis and identification of the various phases and forms of lead, chromium◦ cadmium, zinc, and other pigment compounds; iron oxide pigments.[2]

Analysis of carbonates—whiting (identifies forms such as calcite, vaterite, an◦ aragonite).

Identification of the structural form of titanium dioxide (identifies rutile an◦ anatase) and thus correlates structure with pigment-covering power in paints an◦ enamels.

[1] G. L. Clark, R. L. LeTourneau, and J. M. Ball, X-ray Study of Reactions Involv◦ ing Accelerators, *Ind. Eng. Chem.*, **35**, 198 (1943).

† G. L. Clark *et al.*, *J. Am. Chem. Soc.*, **59**, 2305 (1937), **61**, 58 (1939), **63**, 1299◦ (1941), 1302, 1305, **64**, 1637 (1942).

[2] C. W. Bunn, *J. Sci. Instr.*, **18**, 70 (1941).

Analysis and study of vehicles and driers.

h. Cement manufacture.

Analysis and identification of kiln products.

Identification of various phases and structural forms of raw minerals, and progress of the structural changes resulting during the sintering.

Identification and analysis of accelerators, retarders, etc.

i. Commercial-fertilizer manufacture.

Identification and analysis of fertilizer ingredients including potash, phosphate, nitrate, sulfate, etc. Quantitative analysis by comparison with standards. Control of lime during calcining process.[1] Development of a suitable composition of phosphate slags with suitable P_2O_5 content and availability (only α-tricalcium, $3CaO.P_2O_5$, and tetracalcium, $4CaO.P_2O_5$, phosphates are soluble in 2 per cent citric acid, a test for availability as fertilizer).

j. Metallurgical applications.

Determination of phase and structural changes occurring during heat-treating processes.

Control and inspection of heat-treated alloys.

Aging and phase changes resulting during service life of high-temperature-resistant alloys.

Analysis and identification of carbides in tool steels, sintered carbides, and tools made from them.

Study of alloys, determination of phases, lattice parameters, degree of alloying, and structural changes resulting from various alloying agents.

Determination of phases and distribution in bearing materials.

Determination of the degree of alloying and phase changes resulting during the sintering of powder metallurgy products.

Aging and precipitation determinations in nonferrous alloys.

Particle-size estimation and distribution in powdered metals.

Slag analysis and control in steel manufacture and melting practice.

Analysis of corrosion products and corrosion-resistant films and coatings; and mechanical wear products.

k. Phosphors and electronic parts.

Analysis and control of thermionic cathode coatings (solid solution of BaO-SrO), better than either oxide or mixture; and behavior on operating cathode;[2] control of temperature in making cathodes in high-pressure mercury lamps.

Fundamental research on phosphors [$3Cd_3(PO_4)_2.CdCl_2$, a very successful phosphor developed entirely from x-ray work]; specifications for useful phosphor composition (such as $3ZnO.B_2O_3$ and $ZnO.B_2O_3$).

Distinction between polymorphic forms of same compound (2 ZnS, 2 Zn orthosilicates, 4 Mg tungstates, etc. Patent claims for phosphors based solely on x-ray patterns[3]).

Analysis of the role of activating impurities (Mn substitutes for atoms of matrix lattice with expansion, Be with contraction); the correlation of fluorescence color with structure; discovery and control of new phosphors for x-ray fluoroscopy and intensifying screens (solid solution of $BaSO_4$ and $PbSO_4$, page 85).

l. Organic and biological chemistry.

Identification of crystalline organic compounds, for example anilides of fatty acids,[4]

[1] G. L. Clark, W. F. Bradley, and V. J. Azbe, *Ind. Eng. Chem.*, **32**, 972 (1940).

[2] H. P. Rooksley, *J. Sci. Instr.*, **18**, 84 (1941).

[3] H. P. Rooksley, *Trans. Faraday Soc.*, **37**, 242 (1941).

[4] F. W. Matthews and J. H. Michell, *Ind. Eng. Chem.*, *Anal. Ed.*, **18**, 662 (1941).

penicillins[1] (Fig. 253), alkylated phenols, phenyl isocyanate derivatives,[2] commercial soaps (seven phases),[3] 2,4-dinitrophenyl hydrazones of aldehydes and ketones,[4] composition of "glutose" and various sugars.[5]

Estimation of product purity.

Order and disorder studies in aliphatic acid series.

Atomic positions in isomeric substances.

Molecular-weight determinations, especially on large-molecule substances such as the proteins and high polymers.

Research studies on proteins, viruses, sterols, etc.

Production control and analysis of biological and pharmaceutical compounds, such as the penicillins (Fig. 253), streptomycin, cholesterols, the various hormones, and their intermediate products.

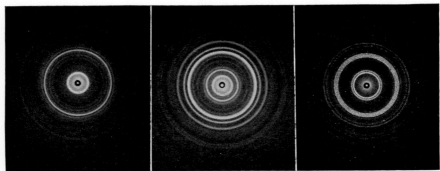

FIG. 253. Patterns for three varieties of sodium pentenyl penicillin made during wartime researches on penicillin structure.

Dye analysis and identification.[6]

Research and study of plastic materials.

m. Medical and pharmaceutical research.

Study of bone,[7] tooth, and muscle tissues. Particularly valuable is the new micro-camera technique; urinary calculi are found to contain calcium acetate monohydrate (whewellite), calcium oxalate dihydrate (weddelite), magnesium ammonium phosphate hexahydrate (Struvite), carbonate-apatite and hydroxyl-apatite, calcium hydrogen phosphate dihydrate (brushite), uric acid, cystine, and sodium acid urate.[8]

[1] G. L. Clark, W. I. Kaye, K. J. Pipenberg, and N. C. Schieltz, "The Chemistry of Penicillin," Chap. XII, p. 367, Princeton University Press, Princeton, N.J., 1949.

[2] J. B. McKinley, J. E. Nickels, and S. S. Sidhu, *Ind. Eng. Chem., Anal. Ed.* **16**, 304 (1944).

[3] M. J. Buerger, L. B. Smith, F. V. Ryder, and J. E. Spike, *Proc. Natl. Acad. Sci.,* **31**, 226 (1945).

[4] G. L. Clark, W. I. Kaye, and T. D. Parks, *Ind. Eng. Chem., Anal. Ed.,* **18**, 310 (1946).

[5] G. L. Clark, Hung Kao, L. Sattler, and F. W. Zerban, *Ind. Eng. Chem.,* **41**, 530 (1949).

[6] G. Susich (for Quartermaster Corps), *Ind. Eng. Chem., Anal. Ed.,* **18**, 662 (1946).

[7] G. L. Clark and J. N. Mrgudich, Effects of Rickets, *Am. J. Physiol.,* **108**, 74 (1934), C. I. Reed *et al., Am. J. Physiol.* **138**, 27, 34 (1942).

[8] E. L. Prien and C. Frondel, *J. Urology,* **57**, 949 (1947).

Drug analysis[1] and manufacturing-process control.[2]

Cosmetic analysis and manufacturing control.

n. Analytical chemistry.[3]

Analysis of crystallinity, identification and purity of analytical precipitates (solid solution, coprecipitation, etc.), for example, proof of solid solution (line shifts) of Fe^{3+}, NO_3^-, and Cl^- in $BaSO_4$ precipitates.[4]

Determination of proper temperatures for drying precipitates, for example, with 8-hydroxy quinoline, anhydrous iron and aluminum oxinates are obtained at 98°, while the dihydrates of the zinc and magnesium are dehydrated only at 160°C.†

Control of separations as functions of pH.

Grain size and perfection (Chap. 22) of precipitates, and combination with electron micrography.

o. Ceramics and refractories.

Calcining and hydration of limes.[5]

Identification and analysis of clays, etc.

Study and identification of sintered products.

Differentiation between various forms of the common clay minerals, such as kaolinite, fuller's earth, dickite, and montmorillonite; three forms of mullite.

Identification of impurities and adulterants.

Estimation of firing temperatures.

p. Welding.

Welding-rod-coating analysis. Identification of coating constituents, such as feldspar, ferromanganese, silica, magnetite, titanium dioxide, etc.

Welding control. Study of alloying and structural changes during the welding process.

Determination of grain-size changes through the welded zone.

q. Electroplating.

Measurement of plating thickness.

Analysis of plated deposits, alloy deposition, selective plating, and diffusion zones, etc.

Analysis and control of plating solutions.

r. Corrosion-resistant coatings.

Study of galvanizing and tinning operations, and measurement of coating thickness.

Analysis and study of rust-resistant and decorative coatings such as the phosphate coatings,[6] etc.

s. Internal-combustion-engine engineering.

Analysis of combustion-chamber deposits.[7]

Analysis of lubricating-oil sludges and deposits.

Investigation of bearing and bushing materials.

[1] Gross and Oberst, Opiates (by Micro-technique), *loc. cit.*

[2] S. F. Kern, X-Ray Testing and Research on Pharmaceuticals, *Anal. Chem.*, **25**, 731 (1953).

[3] See Symposium on "X-Rays as an Analytical Tool," *Anal. Chem.*, **25**, 688–748 (1953); combined reprint on sale by American Chemical Society.

[4] C. A. Streuli, H. A. Scheraga, and M. L. Nichols, *Anal. Chem.*, **25**, 306 (1953).

† R. C. Chirnside, C. F. Pritchard, and H. P. Rooksby, *Analyst*, **66**, 399 (1941).

[5] G. L. Clark and R. S. Sprague, *Anal. Chem.*, **24**, 688 (1952).

[6] G. L. Clark and A. P. Tai, Phosphate Coating of Aluminum and Polymorphism of Chromic Phosphate, *Science*, **107**, 505 (1948).

[7] Examples of compounds formed from ethyl fluid: $PbO.PbBr_2(2)$, $PbO.PbCl_2$, $PbO.PbCl.Br(2)$, $2PbO.PbBr_2$, $2PbO.PbCl_2$, $2PbO.PbCl.Br$, $PbO.PbSO_4$, $4PbO.PbSO_4$. F. W. Lamb and L. M. Niebylski, *Anal. Chem.*, **25**, 740 (1953).

Investigation and analysis of high-temperature-resistant and corrosion-resistant alloys.

Control of manufacturing processes including heat-treating, machining, and grinding.

t. Public health.

Identification of silica, silicotic lung nodules, and industrial dusts.[1]

Studies of contaminants and adulterants.

u. Miscellaneous.

Agriculture—soil, fertilizer, and plant-ash analysis.

Determination of casein changes in cheese ripening[2] and manufacture of processed cheese. Determination of rancidity of butter occurring during storage; control of lactose crystallization.

Chemical processes—study and identification of bleaching agents, decolorizers, catalysts, etc.

Asbestos products—classification and selection of various types of asbestos fibers.

Dry-cell manufacture—identification and selection of suitable manganese dioxide ores.

Paper manufacturing—study and identification of cellulose products; study of paraffin crystallization in manufacture of wax papers.

Wood products—study of cellulose structures.

Textiles—classification of textile fibers, and study of synthetic fibers such as rayon, nylon, etc.

Plastics—study of structural changes, polymerization, and properties of plastic products; control and selection of photographic film.

Catalysts—investigation and control of structural changes in catalytic agents during their manufacture and during operation.

The Fiber Pattern. Figure 254 taken by the monochromatic pinhole method is reproduced as an example of the structure of a natural fiber, asbestos. This mineral is not a single crystal, since otherwise it would give a Laue pattern of symmetrical spots. But neither is it constituted of grains in random arrangement, since this would mean a pattern of concentric uniformly intense rings. It may be seen, however, that circles may still be drawn through the diffraction maxima, although the more prominent loci are hyperbolas. These would be parallel straight horizontal lines (as in Fig. 230) if a cylindrical film had been used instead of a flat one. In this mineral, therefore, the grains are oriented in a common direction with respect to the fiber axis. The pattern is typical of a fibered aggregate. Similarly many natural materials—cotton, stretched rubber, silk, hair, tendon, etc.—and many synthetic polymer fibers such as nylon produce fiber patterns. It should be noted that the pattern obtained by rotating a crystal around a principal axis is a layer-line diagram exactly like that produced by a fiber without rotation. With a fiber, of course, only one such result is obtainable, whereas with a single crystal three patterns corresponding to rotations around the three principal axes are possible. Now a fine-grained aggregate may be made

---

[1] Clark and Reynolds, *loc. cit.* G. L. Clark, W. F. Loranger, and S. J. Bodnar, *Anal. Chem.*, **26**, 1413 (September, 1954). Sweany, Klaas, and Clark, *loc. cit.*

[2] G. L. Clark, S. L. Tuckey, and H. A. Ruehe, *J. Dairy Sci.*, **21**, 767, 777 (1938).

fibered by rolling or drawing in one direction, as shown by Fig. 255 for cold-drawn aluminum wire. The desirability of a pattern 360 deg in azimuth is at once apparent if the degree of fibering is to be estimated and if the actual location of the symmetrically placed maxima is to be used in the determination of the mechanism of deformation by mechanical work, as explained in Chap. 22. A fiber diagram has a great advantage over an ordinary powder pattern, and this is that a measurement of a lattice spacing, namely, the atomic plane periodicities along the fiber axis, may be made independently of any assumption as to crystal system or planar indices. It is necessary only to measure the distances e_1, e_2, e_3, . . . , e_n of the vertices of the hyperbolas (or of the straight layer lines on a film

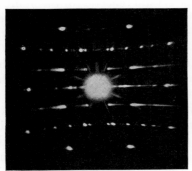

FIG. 254. Monochromatic pinhole diagram of crysotile (asbestos), showing almost perfect fiber structure. The smearing of spots along the layer lines is a significant indication of distortion.

FIG. 255. Fiber diffraction pattern for cold-drawn aluminum wire.

that has been bent on a cylinder coaxial with the specimen) from the central zero point of the main beam. If we know the distance from specimen to film, a, the diffraction angle μ_1, μ_2, . . . , μ_n may be calculated, since the tangents are e_n/a. The identity period, or spacing along the fiber axis, is then simply calculated from $I = n\lambda/\sin \mu_n$, where n is the number of the layer line (1, 2, 3, etc.). Thus identically the same value is obtained from all the layer lines. For the other lattice spacings it is necessary, of course, to interpret the pattern exactly as in the powder method since the Debye-Scherrer circles may still be evident. The degree of perfection of preferred orientation is, of course, indicated at once by the patterns, since there may be a continuous transition between the concentric circles for a random aggregate and the sharp horizontal layer lines for perfect fibering. The interpretation of fiber patterns in terms of the preferred orientation of planes and the texture of materials is considered in Chap. 22.

The Laws That Determine the Intensities of X-ray Interferences.
On page 391 there were listed certain effects in the geometrical arrangement of crystallographic planes that result in the nonappearance of expected x-ray interferences, *i.e.*, interferences that have zero intensity. Other factors in the structure may contribute to a maximum intensity from cooperating planes or for a whole range of possible values between a maximum and zero. A proper measurement and interpretation of intensities thus lead to the final and most powerful step in complete analysis of the structure. The intensity of a given interference from a given set of parallel planes depends upon a number of factors which will be briefly enumerated: (1) the intensity of the primary beam; (2) the wavelength of the x-rays used; (3) the size, perfection, and absorbing power of the crystal; (4) the angle at which selective reflection from a set of planes takes place; (5) the time during which the crystal reflects; (6) the number of planes which cooperate in a given reflection; (7) the degree of polarization of the incident and reflected beams; (8) the geometry of the experimental apparatus; (9) the scattering power of a single electron; (10) the total number of electrons in the atomic shells or orbitals; (11) the existence and the amplitude of the thermal vibration of atoms in the lattice; (12) the electron density distribution in the unit-cell structure.

1. *The Atomic-structure Factor* f_0. First of all, scattering and intensity must basically depend on the kind of atom or the number of electrons in it. The atomic-structure factor is defined as the ratio of the amplitude of waves scattered by the atom to that of a free classically scattering electron. If the atom were essentially a point, then $f_0 = Z$, the atomic number, or number of external electrons. However, the atom has a diameter comparable in size with the wavelengths. Hence the secondary waves from the different electrons in space have phase differences so that in certain directions there is strengthening and in others weakening of radiation. It is found that f_0 is a function of $\sin \Theta/\lambda$, or, completely expressed,

$$f_0 = \int_0^\infty \frac{U(r) \sin [4\pi r \sin (\Theta/\lambda)]}{4\pi r \sin (\Theta/\lambda)} \, dr \tag{1}$$

where $U(r)$ is the density of electrons between r and $r + dr$. For small values of Θ

$$f_0 = \int_0^\infty U(r) \, dr = Z \tag{2}$$

Values of f_0 are now known with considerable accuracy from the work of Hartree, Pauling-Sherman, and Thomas-Fermi and are listed in the "International Tables for X-ray Crystallography." Particularly important are the values for cesium (55) inasmuch as f_0 for elements of higher atomic number can be calculated by multiplying f_0 for cesium by $Z/55$. In Table 15-4 values are listed for cesium, diamond, and graphite (important for organic compounds) and for a number of elements involved in structure analysis of silicates.

TABLE 15-4. ATOMIC-STRUCTURE FACTORS

sin Θ/λ	0.0	0.1	0.2	0.3	0.4	0.5	0.6	0.7	0.8	0.9	1.0	1.1	1.2	1.3
Cesium.............	55	50.7	43.8	37.6	32.4	28.7	25.8	23.2	20.8	18.8	17.0			
Diamond............	6	5.35	4.25	2.85	2.1	1.75	1.6							
Graphite............	6	5.2	3.0	1.95	1.3	0.8	0.5							
Oxygen.............	8	8.0	5.8	3.7	2.5	1.7	1.1	0.7	0.5	0.4	0.3			
Fluorine............	9	8.6	6.6	4.8	3.3	2.4	1.7	1.2	0.9	0.6	0.5	0.4		
Sodium.............	11	9.5	8.0	6.4	4.8	3.6	2.6	2.0	1.5	1.2	0.9	0.7	0.6	
Magnesium..........	12	10.4	8.5	7.0	5.5	4.2	3.2	2.5	1.9	1.5	1.2	1.0	0.8	
Aluminum...........	13	10.6	9.0	7.5	6.1	4.9	3.9	3.0	2.4	1.9	1.5	1.2	1.1	1.0
Silicon.............	14	11.2	9.6	8.0	6.6	5.5	4.4	3.6	2.9	2.4	1.9	1.6	1.4	1.3
Chlorine............	17	15.2	11.6	9.2	7.6	6.4	5.3	4.4	3.7	3.0	2.5	2.1	1.7	1.5
Potassium..........	19	16.9	13.0	10.5	8.6	7.2	6.0	5.1	4.3	3.7	3.1	2.6	2.2	2.0
Calcium............	20	17.6	13.8	11.1	9.1	7.6	6.4	5.5	4.6	4.0	3.4	2.9	2.6	2.3
Iron...............	26	22.6	18.0	14.9	12.5	10.7	9.3	8.2	7.2	6.3	5.6	4.9	4.3	3.7

All these values correspond to atoms at rest at absolute zero; hence for ordinary temperatures at which intensities are appreciably weakened, a correction deduced by Debye and Waller must be used, namely,

$$f = f_0 e^{-M} = f_0 e^{-B\left(\frac{\sin\theta}{\lambda}\right)^2} \tag{3}$$

where $M = \dfrac{6h^2}{mk\Theta}\left(\dfrac{\sin\Theta}{\lambda}\right)^2\left(\dfrac{\phi(X)}{X} + \dfrac{1}{4}\right)$, where k is the Boltzmann constant, Θ is the characteristic temperature (Debye) calculated from specific heat, $X = \Theta/T$, $\phi(X)/X = \pi^2 T^2/6\Theta^2$ and B is a constant.

2. *The Crystal-structure Factor F.* The scattering intensity of a lattice unit cell, which contains only a single atom, is expressed by $f_0^2 e^{-2M}$. If more atoms are present in the cell, as is the actual case, then the phase differences of scattered waves from different atoms must be taken into consideration. The crystal-structure factor, F, a pure number representing a number of electrons, involves the coordinates of atoms in the unit cell. Thus for a cell containing N atoms and with f_n as the scattering factor of the nth atom

$$F = \sum_{n=1}^{N} f_n e^{2\pi i\left(\frac{hx}{a} + \frac{ky}{b} + \frac{lz}{c}\right)} = \sum_{n=1}^{N} f_n \exp 2\pi i(hx_n + ky_n + lz_n) \tag{4}$$

where i is an imaginary unit, or $\sqrt{-1}$, and the coordinates of a given point xyz are expressed as fractional parts of the axial lengths a, b, c. F is a complex quantity, so that the absolute value $|F|^2$ to which intensity is proportional is expressed, as follows, (remembering that

$$e^{iy} = \cos y + i \sin y$$

and $e^{-iy} = \cos y - i \sin y$):

$$|F(hkl)|^2 = \left[\sum\sum f_n \cos 2\pi\left(\frac{hx}{a} + \frac{ky}{b} + \frac{lz}{c}\right)\right]^2$$

$$+ \left[\sum\sum f_n \sin 2\pi\left(\frac{hx}{a} + \frac{ky}{b} + \frac{lz}{c}\right)\right]^2 \quad (5)$$

$$|F(hkl)| = \sqrt{(\Sigma f_n A)^2 + (\Sigma f_n B^2)} = \sqrt{A'^2 + B'^2} \quad (6)$$

Thus $|F(hkl)| = A' + iB'$.

$$A = \sum \cos 2\pi\left(\frac{hx}{a} + \frac{ky}{b} + \frac{lz}{c}\right) \quad \text{and} \quad B = \sum \sin 2\pi\left(\frac{hx}{a} + \frac{ky}{b} + \frac{lz}{c}\right)$$

are characteristic of each space group, since they depend entirely on the equivalent points in the unit cell. Values of A and B have been calculated for each space group by Lonsdale in the "Structure Factor Tables." For crystals with a center of symmetry the B, or sine, term becomes zero, and calculations are greatly simplified.

3. *Simple Examples of Structure-factor Calculation (Debye-Waller Temperature Correction Included).* a. *Body-centered cubic element (tungsten)* Fig. 261.

Equivalent point coordinates: 000, $\frac{1}{2}\frac{1}{2}\frac{1}{2}$.

$$F = (e^{2\pi ni0} + e^{\frac{2\pi ni(h+k+l)}{2}})f = (1 + e^{\pi ni(h+k+l)})f$$
$$F = (1 + 1)f = 2f \qquad h + k + l \text{ even}$$
$$F = 1 - 1 = 0 \qquad h + k + l \text{ odd}$$

b. *Body-centered cubic compound* (NH_4Cl) (Fig. 267a). The above equation refers of course to a metallic element such as α-iron, with a unit cell containing two identical atoms. The diffraction pattern then has lines only for those planes for which $h + k + l$ is an even number, and in the succession of all possible planes in a cubic crystal (Table 15-3) (100), (110), (111), (200), (210), (211), (220), (221), (300), (310), (311), (222), etc., and associated planes only those underlined will produce reflections because of destructive interference from interleaving planes of exactly the same scattering power in all other cases. Consider now the case of NH_4Cl, also a body-centered cubic crystal, with NH_4^+ ion at the center and Cl^- ions at the corners, or one molecule of NH_4Cl per unit cell. NH_4^+ ions have 10 electrons, Cl^- 18 ions, and hence, disregarding other factors, Cl^- ions should have $\frac{18}{10}$ greater diffracting power. While α-iron has no 100 line on its pattern whatever, there will appear a fairly weak 100 line (to which 001 and 010 also contribute) for NH_4Cl. The 100 reflection is produced when x-rays from one plane of chlorine ions are exactly one wavelength behind those from the next plane of chlorine ions; but waves from NH_4^+ ions lying at the center of the unit cell and thus on an interleaving plane will be one-half wavelength behind and thus opposite in phase. But since the diffracting power is only $\frac{10}{18}$ of the Cl^- ion, there will not be complete interference and the amplitude of the resultant wave for 100 will not be zero but $f_{Cl} - f_{NH_4}$, or less than half from chlorine ions alone, and the *intensity* less than one-fourth (since $I \propto F^2$). The second 101 reflection on the pattern for NH_4Cl is very strong because both NH_4^+ and Cl^- ions lie on the planes, with the result that the intensity is about 8 times as great as for 100. The third line represents 111 (not present for α-iron), also weak for the same reason as 100, namely, that NH_4^+ planes interleave Cl^- planes. The fourth line 200 is strong, for here the waves from one Cl^- plane are two wavelengths behind those from the next Cl^- plane, while the waves from interleaving NH_4^+ planes are *one* wavelength behind; hence all are in phase. Thus

$$F = f_{Cl^-} + f_{NH_4} \qquad h + k + l \text{ even}$$
$$F = f_{Cl^-} - f_{NH_4} \qquad h + k + l \text{ odd}$$

There is no simple relationship between intensities, as there would be if there were exactly the same number of planes contributing to each reflection. This complication arises in the multiplicity factor (or the number of equivalent reflections superposed in each line). Thus 211 is stronger than 002 because there are only 3 planes of type 002 (200, 020, 002) or 6 orientations including $\overline{2}00$, $0\overline{2}0$, $00\overline{2}$, while there are 12 of type 211, or 24 reflections. In general for these cubic systems there are the following number of superposed reflections: 6 $h00$, 12 $hh0$, 24 $hk0$, 8 hhh, 24 hhl, 48 hkl.

c. *Face-centered cubic element (copper)* (Figs. 262a, 263b).
Equivalent point coordinates: 000, $\frac{1}{2}\frac{1}{2}0$, $\frac{1}{2}0\frac{1}{2}$, $0\frac{1}{2}\frac{1}{2}$.

$$F = (1 + e^{\pi n i(h+k)} + e^{\pi n i(h+l)} + e^{\pi n i(k+l)})f$$
$$F = 4f \qquad h, k, l, \text{ all odd or all even}$$
$$F = 0 \qquad h, k, l \text{ mixed}$$

d. *Face-centered cubic compound* (NaCl). Again the above F values refer to a crystal of an element with four identical atoms per unit cell such as Al. Consider now the case of NaCl, which crystallizes with Cl^- ions on a face-centered cubic lattice and Na^+ ions on another face-centered lattice interpenetrating with the Cl^- position so that the actual occupied points in the lattice appear to form a simple cubic lattice, only one-eighth the size of the true face-centered lattice. Thus

Equivalent point coordinates: Na^+ 000, $\frac{1}{2}\frac{1}{2}0$, $\frac{1}{2}0\frac{1}{2}$, $0\frac{1}{2}\frac{1}{2}$.
$$Cl^- \;\frac{1}{2}\frac{1}{2}\frac{1}{2}, 0\,0\,\frac{1}{2}, 0\frac{1}{2}0, \frac{1}{2}0\,0.$$

$$F = f_{Na^+}(1 + e^{\pi n i(h+k)} + e^{\pi n i(h+l)} + e^{\pi n i(k+l)})$$
$$+ f_{Cl^-}(e + {}^{\pi n i(h+k+l)} + e^{\pi n i l} + e^{\pi n i k} + e^{\pi n i h})$$

Then for 100 and 110 (planes containing both Na^+ and Cl^-) ions there will be interference,

$$F_{100} = 0$$
$$F_{110} = 0$$

But $F_{111} = 4(f_{Cl^-} - f_{Na^+})$ means that a weak line will appear since Cl^- has $\frac{18}{10}$ as great reflecting power as Na^+.

Similarly

$$F_{200} = 4(f_{Cl^-} + f_{Na^+})$$
$$F_{220} = 4(f_{Cl^+} + f_{Na^+})$$

All evidence seems to point to an identical structure for KCl, but curiously enough there is not a trace of a 111 reflection, for example, while NaCl does have one. Actually the structures are the same, but it must be noted that Cl^- and K^+ both have identically the same number of extranuclear electrons, $18(Cl^-, 17 + 1; K^+, 19 - 1)$ and thus x-rays cannot distinguish between (111) planes with all Cl^- ions and all K^+ ions, so that the 111 reflection cannot appear: $F_{111} = 4(f_{Cl^-} - f_{K^+}) = 0$. For the same reason patterns of NaF, RbBr, and CsI will be distinguished from those of the salts with other halogens.

e. Hexagonal close-packed element (Zinc) (Figs. 262b, 263c).

Equivalent point coordinates: 000, $\frac{1}{3} \frac{2}{3} \frac{1}{2}$.

$$F = (1 + e^{(\pi i/3)(2h+4k+3l)})f = [1 + e^{\pi i l}e^{(\pi i/3)(2h+4k)}]f$$

$$F = 0 \qquad l \text{ uneven}$$
$$h + 2k = 3n$$

$$F = \sqrt{3}f \qquad l \text{ uneven}$$
$$h + 2k = 3n + 1 \text{ or } 3n + 2$$

$$F = 2f \qquad l \text{ even}$$
$$h + 2k = 3n$$

$$F = f \qquad l \text{ even}$$
$$h + 2k = 3n + 1 \text{ or } 3n + 2$$

f. ZnS (Fig. 267b).

Coordinates: Zn 000, $0 \frac{1}{2} \frac{1}{2}$, $\frac{1}{2} 0 \frac{1}{2}$, $\frac{1}{2} \frac{1}{2} 0$.

S $\frac{1}{4} \frac{1}{4} \frac{1}{4}$, $\frac{1}{4} \frac{3}{4} \frac{3}{4}$, $\frac{3}{4} \frac{1}{4} \frac{3}{4}$, $\frac{3}{4} \frac{3}{4} \frac{1}{4}$.

$$F = f_{Zn}(1 + e^{\pi i(h+k)} + e^{\pi_i (k+l)} + e^{\pi i(h+l)}) + f_S(e^{(\pi i/2)(h+k+l)}$$
$$+ e^{(\pi i/2)(h+3k+3l)} + e^{(\pi i/2)(3h+k+3l)} + e^{(\pi i/2)(3h+3k+l)}$$

$$= (f_{Zn} + f_S e^{(\pi i/2)(h+k+l)})(1 + e^{\pi i(h+k)} + e^{\pi i(k+l)} + e^{\pi i(h+l)})$$

$$F = 0 \qquad\qquad hkl \text{ mixed}$$

$$F = 4(f_{Zn} - f_S) \qquad hkl \text{ unmixed}$$
$$h + k + l = 4n + 2$$

$$F = 4(f_{Zn} + f_S) \qquad hkl \text{ unmixed}$$
$$h + k + l = 4n$$

$$F = 4(f_{Zn} + if_S) \text{ or } 4\sqrt{f_{Zn}^2 + f_S^2} \qquad hkl \text{ unmixed}$$
$$h + k + l = 4n + 1$$

g. *Monoclinic Space Group* $P2_1/c$.

Symmetry elements: Dyad axes parallel to b axis.

Glide planes $a/2$ parallel to 010.

Coordinates: xyz; $\bar{x}\bar{y}\bar{z}$; $x, \frac{1}{2} - y, \frac{1}{2} + z$; $\bar{x}, \frac{1}{2} + y, \frac{1}{2} - z$.

$$A = 4 \cos 2\pi \left(hx + lz + \frac{k+l}{4} \right) \cos 2\pi \left(ky - \frac{k+l}{4} \right)$$

$B = 0$

$h00$	$A = 4 \cos 2\pi hx$	h even or odd
$0k0$	$A = 4 \cos 2\pi ky$	k even
	$A = 0$	k odd
$00l$	$A = 4 \cos 2\pi lz$	l even
	$A = 0$	l odd
$0kl$	$A = 4 \cos 2\pi ky \cos 2\pi lz$	$k + l$ even
	$A = -4 \sin 2\pi ky \sin 2\pi lz$	$k + l$ odd
$h0l$	$A = 4 \cos 2\pi(hx + lz)$	l even
	$A = 0$	
$hk0$	$A = 4 \cos 2\pi hx \cos 2\pi ky$	k even
	$A = -4 \sin 2\pi hx \sin 2\pi ky$	k odd

4. *Intensity and the Structure Factor.* This relation is one of considerable complexity as indicated by the list of 12 variables on page 444. The theory was originally developed by Darwin and Ewald.

The x-ray reflection from a crystal does not occur sharply but takes place over a small angular range on either side of Θ defined by the Bragg law. The integrated intensity is experimentally measured by $E\omega/I_0$, where E is the total energy received by the photographic film or ionization chamber, while the crystal is turned through the reflecting position with angular velocity ω, and I_0 is the incident-beam energy per second per square centimeter at the crystal. For a crystal of volume V for time τ,

$$\frac{E\omega}{I_0} = \frac{\tau}{4\pi} \left[N \frac{e^2}{mc^2} F(hkl) \right]^2 \lambda^3 PV \frac{1 + \cos^2 2\Theta}{2 \sin 2\Theta} \frac{\cos \Theta}{\sqrt{(\cos^2 \phi - \sin^2 \Theta)}} A$$

where N is the number of unit cells per unit volume, or the reciprocal of the volume V of the unit cell; e^2/mc^2 comes from $\bar{A} = Ae^2/mc^2$, the classical electromagnetic equation for amplitude $\bar{A}$ of rays, primary amplitude A, scattered by an electron; P is the number of hkl planes giving coincident reflections; $1 + \cos^2 2\Theta/2$ is the polarization factor for unpolarized rays; $1/(\sin 2\Theta)$ is the Lorentz factor, which is a measure of time for a reciprocal lattice point of finite size to pass through the surface of reflection; ϕ is the angle between reflecting plane and axis of rotation; and A is the absorption factor depending on x-ray beam, composition, size, and texture of the crystal and on Bragg angle. This equation applies only to ideally imperfect crystals with mosaic structure or to powders. For perfect crystals with reflection over a very small angle

$$\frac{E\omega}{I} = \frac{8}{3\pi} N \frac{e^2}{mc^2} F(hkl)\lambda^2 \frac{1 + |\cos 2\Theta|}{2 \sin 2\Theta}$$

with F only in the first power.

Nearly all crystals lie somewhere between the perfect and the ideal mosaic structure, but nearer to the latter. A number of formulas have been deduced taking into account the type of specimen and absorption of radiation and are listed in the "International Tables for X-ray Crystallography." For example, to a powder pattern taken with a cylindrical film is assigned the formula

$$\frac{I_l}{I_0} = \frac{l}{8\pi r} \left(\frac{Ne^2}{mc^2} F(hkl)\right)^2 \lambda^3 HV \frac{1 + \cos^2 2\Theta}{2 \sin 2\Theta} \cdot \cos \Theta \cdot A$$

where l is the height of a section of a Debye-Scherrer ring of radius r as it intercepts the cylindrical film, H is the number of planes $\{hkl\}$ producing interferences that coincide [48 cubic, 16 tetragonal, 8 orthorhombic for (hkl)], V is the volume irradiated, and $(\cos \Theta/\sin 2\Theta)$ includes the number of crystallites in proper reflecting position defined by the circle $2\pi R \cos \Theta$, and the effect of blackening of the photographic film of the size of the circle of intersection (the smaller the blacker) defined by $1/(2R \sin 2\Theta)$. Except for $F(hkl)$ all these factors may be measured or eliminated; H and the Θ correction terms may be read from the tables. In all these cases, F includes the Debye-Waller temperature corrections.

The principal corrections to be made for actual crystals are for two kinds of extinction. The formula for the mosaic crystals implies the condition that the number of planes in a mosaic block m_p multiplied by the relative amplitude of reflection from a single plane must be very small: for NaCl, m_p must be less than 500, or a size of 1,400 A for the 200 reflection. Actual crystals have mosaic blocks that are too coarse to satisfy the condition. In other words, they approach to an ideal perfect crystal. This is serious only for strong reflections, where F is large and $\sin (\Theta/\lambda)$ small. Nothing can be done to correct for this primary extinction because there is no way to measure mosaic-block size. Secondary extinction occurs even in good mosaic specimens, so that upper planes in each block shield the lower part from the radiation with the result that the effective absorption coefficient of the crystal is increased when set at the reflecting angle. Corrections can be made in the intensity formula, but the extinction is largely avoided by working with fine powders. Experience has shown that in the exceedingly important complete structure determinations of organic crystals the uncorrected formulas above can be used safely with small single crystals which have small absorbing power and ordinarily produce no very strong reflections because of unsymmetrically arranged atoms. An exhaustive modern treatment of extinction has been given by Lonsdale.[1] In recognition of the fact that $I \propto TLpF^2$ (where T is time, L is the Lorentz factor, and p the polarization factor) numerous papers have appeared recently which deal intensively with the correction factors for F_{hkl} values, especially the Lorentz-polarization factor. Obviously as methods of crystal-structure analyses have become more refined, it is all the more necessary to have accurate experimental values of F's from intensity measurements for use as coefficients in Fourier syntheses. Buerger and Klein have published complete tables for correcting intensities for Lorentz and polarization factors[2] and for the reverse problem of computing expected x-ray diffraction intensities from a set of diffracted amplitudes, F. Graphical charts have also been presented[3] for corrections on Weissenberg rotation and oscillation patterns, with the factors expressed in terms of the reciprocal lattice.

Such corrections of course presuppose the best possible evaluation of the integrated intensities of individual reflections. Series of papers have described various types of photometer and multiple-film technique for this purpose. A critical comparison of measurements of integrated intensities by photography, ionization, and Geiger-counter spectrometers leads to the conclusion that for long exposures the photographic spectrometer is as sensitive as the counter spectrometer used for a few minutes and more sensitive than the ionization spectrometer. For speed and convenience the Geiger counter is superior.[4] The fact remains, however, that most single-crystal workers have measured intensities by eye comparisons of a standard intensity scale against the series of unknown spots, usually with an accuracy better than 10 per cent.

5. *The Procedure in Crystal-structure Analysis*.[5] The usual procedure in analysis is to determine experimentally the values of $F(hkl)$ from intensity measurements for as many planes as possible especially for planes in the principal zones. The kinds and numbers of atoms or ions in the unit cell being known, all the peculiarities of intensity distribution are next used in order to decide approximately the most probable distribution of scattering material in the cell, *i.e.*, the most probable values of xyz for each kind of atom or ion. At this stage it may be necessary to use other available crystallographic, physical, or chemical information about the substance (for example, optical and magnetic properties, cleavage planes, presence or absence of pyro- or piezoelectric effects, presence of long-chain

[1] K. Lonsdale, *Mineralog. Mag.*, **28**, 14 (1947).

[2] *J. Appl. Phys.*, **16**, 408 (1945).

[3] E. G. Cox and W. F. B. Shaw, *Proc. Roy. Soc. (London)*, **127**, 71 (1930). W. Cochran, *J. Sci. Instr.*, **25**, 253 (1948). B. E. Warren and I. Fankuchen, *Rev. Sci. Instr.*, **12**, 90 (1941). Chia-Si Lu, *Rev. Sci. Instr.*, **14**, 531 (1943). G. Kaan and W. F. Cole, *Acta Cryst.*, **2**, 38 (1949).

[4] W. A. Wooster, F. N. Ramachandran, and A. Lang, *J. Sci. Instr.*, **25**, 12 (1948).

[5] As described by Lonsdale, "Structure Factor Tables," George Bell & Sons, Ltd., London, 1938.

or ring-shaped molecules, etc.); or in particularly favorable cases it may be possible to ignore all such outside information in the first place and to use it only as a final check on the structure obtained from x-ray results alone. The approximate values of xyz so obtained when substituted in Eq. (6) should give values of $F(hkl)$ not far from the observed values for all the observed reflections. Experimental observation alone cannot determine the phase angle $\alpha(hkl)$; but if this can be estimated with sufficient accuracy from the approximate structure, then a Fourier analysis in two or three dimensions can be carried out (note that this is a step of refinement rather than a primary operation) and the distribution of electron density in the unit cell can be determined accurately and uniquely. If on comparison of the Fourier analysis it is found that the approximate structure was not sufficiently exact, it may be necessary to repeat the analysis, using as an approximate structure the result of the previous analysis and thus arriving at the true structure by a series of successive approximations.

6. *Evaluation of Atomic Parameters and Structure Amplitudes—Trial Methods.* In order to calculate $F(hkl)$ values for comparison with experimental values derived from intensities, it is necessary to determine atomic parameters, or the xyz coordinates, from any available information. The details of this procedure go beyond the bounds of this book, and reference is made to other treatises, one of the best brief accounts appearing in Bunn's "Chemical Crystallography" pages 248 to 334. In Lipson and Cochran's "The Determination of Crystal Structures"[1] an exhaustive and up-to-date account is given from the stage at which a set of structure amplitudes has been obtained to the final accurate positioning of the atoms. Some of the steps may be outlined briefly.

a. First of all every bit of information possible is derived from the properties of the assigned space group—molecular or ionic symmetry, molecular dimensions, especially when there is one molecule per unit cell, and the location of atoms in relation to symmetry elements (equivalent positions and their multiplicities). In the last case if an atom is placed in a space group including the symbol 6, this means it is multiplied by 6 unless it lies *on* the sixfold axis. Furthermore an atom cannot be closer to a rotation axis, if in a general position, than the atomic radius, and the same is true for the plane or center of symmetry. This simple procedure actually led to the determination of the original silicate structures.

b. Since the contribution of each atom in any crystal plane hkl with coordinates xyz to the structure amplitude is $f \cos 2\pi(hx + ky + lz)$ and $f \sin 2\pi(hx + ky + lz)$, the cosine terms for a whole group of atoms related to each other by symmetry elements may be combined into a single expression for A, and the sine terms for B; then $F^2 = A^2 + B^2$. For example, in $P2_12_12_1$ a commonly occurring orthorhombic space group

[1] Vol. III of "The Crystalline State," edited by Sir Lawrence Bragg, George Bell & Sons, Ltd., London, 1953.

$$A = +4f \cos 2\pi \left(hx - \frac{h-k}{4} \right) \cos 2\pi \left(ky - \frac{k-1}{4} \right) \cos 2\pi \left(lz - \frac{1-h}{4} \right)$$

$$B = -4f \sin 2\pi \left(hx - \frac{h-k}{4} \right) \sin 2\pi \left(ky - \frac{k-1}{4} \right) \sin 2\pi \left(lz - \frac{1-h}{4} \right)$$

This is the method for deriving the A and B equations for all space groups in the "International Tables for X-ray Crystallography."

c. Whenever a parameter can be isolated for a crystal, its determination may be fairly simple; for example, in NH_4HF_2, $h00$ reflections depend only on the value of x along the a axis, and $0k0$ is the value of y.

d. The determination of space groups has depended upon zero intensities for reflections; for atomic parameters first attention is given to reflections of maximum intensity as indicative of the largest concentration of atoms. If all atoms lie on certain planes, the structure amplitudes of all orders of reflection must be equal and the intensities must decrease regularly from one order to the next. If this decrease is not regular, the atoms must be dispersed from this given set of planes. The great intensity of the $20\bar{1}$ reflection for benzoquinone, but the very greatly diminished intensity of $40\bar{2}$ and $60\bar{3}$, led Robertson to place the flat molecules *nearly* on the $20\bar{1}$ planes. If two or three reflections in a principal zone are more intense than all others, the atoms must be along lines parallel to the zone axis. This has been a useful observation for many polymer fibers. Very strong reflections at larger angles may often be clues to positions [0, 3, 17 for chrysene (Ibalt); 10, 0, 0 for rubber (Bunn); 340, $4\bar{7}0$, and $\bar{7}30$ for hexamethylbenzene(Lonsdale).

e. In isomorphous crystals in which different atoms with different f values are in corresponding positions, the difference in intensities and of F values will locate the atoms. If two atoms are quite similar in scattering power a greater chance of distinguishing them is gained by using an x-ray wavelength lying between the absorption edges.

f. Graphical methods. When by ingenious use of the foregoing steps some rough agreement between observed and calculated $F(hkl)$ values has been obtained, it is next necessary to change more or less the assigned atomic positions, obeying all symmetry requirements, until there is unquestionable correspondence. Which atoms to move, how far, and in what direction is a complex problem for which graphical shortcut methods are indicated. Bragg and Lipson in 1936 constructed such graphs for principal zones ($hk0$, $h0l$, $0kl$) in which only two coordinates of atoms are involved in structure amplitudes; so charts of functions such as $\cos 2\pi(hx + ky)$ are drawn and the contribution of groups of atoms read off, as well as the proper movements to increase or decrease intensity of any reflection. Since these are two-dimensional projections, this scheme utilizes the idea of plane groups, the most important of which are illustrated by Bunn in his "Chemical Crystallography" (page 264). While the construction of these charts is laborious, the procedure is of course a great aid in comparison with direct calculations of $F(hkl)$ values.

7. *Instrumental Aids to Computation.* It is logical that machines should be constructed to shorten these computations. Evans and Peiser in 1942 made a machine from Meccano parts which evaluates $f \cos$ (or $\sin$) $2\pi(hx + ky)$. Cox devised probably the first electronic device, consisting of a condenser whose capacity is proportional to f, charged by a voltage proportional to the cosine or sine of the phase angle Θ, so that the resulting charge is proportional to $f \cos \Theta$.

8. *The "Fly's Eye" Camera.*   In 1939 Sir Lawrence Bragg[1] proposed an optical method to avoid completely calculations of F; the method has since had great success in the early stages of analysis of molecular structures of compounds such as penicillin, whose structure is discussed in Chap. 20.

A reasonable arrangement of atoms in a unit cell is projected on a single plane; the atoms are represented by holes in a screen illuminated by a source of light.   A multiple photograph of the one unit cell is produced by means of a multiple pinhole camera.   This is made by drawing a large number of black dots on a white card and then making a greatly reduced photograph of this so that there are 600 to 700 pinholes (clear dots on the

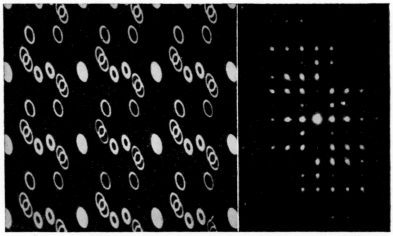

FIG. 256. Grating for fly's-eye-camera method of reproducing pattern of diopside and optical diffraction pattern.   (*De Vos.*)

developed negative film) in an area 5 mm square.   In 1946 Stokes improved the "fly's eye" by making a regular array of tiny Perspex lenses embossed on a Perspex sheet.   Black disks for the atoms were mounted on an illuminated background and the whole multiple picture made at one exposure.   This picture now consists of transparent apertures on an opaque background.   Monochromatic light from a point source is passed through this repeating pattern representing the crystal structure, and the optical diffraction pattern so produced as observed through a telescope or by means of a microscopic objective lens corresponds to the x-ray pattern produced by the real crystal; for the relative intensities of the optical images should correspond to $hk0$ reflections for a c projection.   The first highly successful use of this optical method was with phthalocyanine.   Figure 256 from the work of De Vos shows the prepared grating form and the resulting optical diffraction pattern.

Again it should be emphasized that all these approaches are trial

[1] *Nature,* **143,** 678 (1939), **149,** 470 (1942).

methods in which crystal structures are determined by attempting to define atomic positions which will account for the observed intensities of diffracted x-ray beams.   Success then depends upon how closely a true structure may be approximated.   The opposite, or direct, method would be to measure diffraction patterns and combine the results mathematically or instrumentally to a direct picture of crystal structure.   This possibility, even granting great obstacles such as unknown phase angles, has led to the Fourier synthesis.

9. *Expression of Electron Density by Fourier Series.*[1]   It is clear that though the process is a difficult one the magnitude of the structure factor $F(hkl)$ can usually be determined from the experimental measurements of intensity.   The relation between $F(hkl)$ and the density of the scattering medium $\rho(xyz)$ is written

$$F(hkl) = \frac{V}{abc} \int_0^a \int_0^b \int_0^c \rho(xyz) e^{2\pi i\left(\frac{hx}{a} + \frac{ky}{b} + \frac{lz}{c}\right)} \, dx \, dy \, dz$$

It is important to note that $F(hkl)$ for any given plane is a complex quantity, characterized by an amplitude and a phase constant.   It is obvious that the experimental measurements of intensity, though defining the amplitude of the structure factors $F(hkl)$, can give no information regarding these relative phase relationships.   The different reflections are measured at different times with the crystal in different positions, so that information regarding phase relationships is necessarily lost in making the experiment.   This ambiguity represents the fundamental difficulty in x-ray analysis.   Although we assume no symmetry in the density distribution, the nature of the crystal requires the structure to be essentially periodic over a range defined by a, b, c of the unit cell.   Hence $\rho(xyz)$, the electron density at any point, can be represented by a Fourier series

$$\rho(xyz) = \sum_{-\infty}^{+\infty} \sum_{-\infty}^{+\infty} \sum_{-\infty}^{+\infty} \frac{F(hkl)}{V} e^{-2\pi i\left(\frac{hx}{a} + \frac{ky}{b} + \frac{lz}{c}\right)}$$

where $F(hkl)/V$ values are the coefficients of the terms.   The zero term $F(000) = \frac{V}{abc} \int_0^a \int_0^b \int_0^c \rho(xyz) \, dx \, dy \, dz = Z$, the total number of electrons in the unit cell.

In accordance with Friedel's law, $|F(hkl)| = |F(\bar{h}\bar{k}\bar{l})|$; then

$$\rho(xyz) = \sum \sum \sum \left| \frac{F(hkl)}{V} \right| \cos\left[2\pi\frac{hx}{a} + 2\pi\frac{ky}{b} + 2\pi\frac{lz}{c} - \alpha(hkl) \right]$$

---

[1] An able popular account of the most advanced phases of crystal-structure analysis leading to molecular configurations is given in a staff report, Crystal Gazing with X-rays, *Chem. Eng. News*, **30**, 4356 (Oct. 20, 1952).   Perhaps the clearest short technical account has been given by J. M. Robertson, "Organic Crystals and Molecules," Chap. V, p. 81, Cornell University Press, Ithaca, N.Y., 1953.

where $\alpha(hkl)$ is the phase constant and is the angle $\tan^{-1}(B/A)$, where B and A are the quantities defined on page 446.

Therefore, if the electron-density distribution in a crystal lattice is analyzed into a series of harmonic terms corresponding to various possible crystal planes, then the coefficients of these terms are given by the absolute values of the structure factors for the corresponding plane divided by the volume of the unit cell. The resultant wave scattered by the unit cell is compounded from the contributions of all the electrons in the cell. There is an infinite series of such resultant waves corresponding to all possible crystal planes, and these waves can themselves be compounded by means of a Fourier series to give an expression of the electron distribution in the unit cell.

The method is most readily applied to those structures which contain a center of symmetry, an element that fortunately occurs quite frequently in crystals. When this symmetry is present in the unit cell as a whole, it must apply to each of the component waves that define the structure. Hence, if we had the origin of coordinates (xyz) at the center of symmetry, then either a peak or a trough of each of these components must coincide with the origin. The phase angle $\alpha(hkl)$, which measures the displacement of the peak of the wave from the origin, must in this case be limited to the value 0 or π, and these two cases can be covered by making the signs of the coefficients $F(hkl)/V$ either positive or negative. For a center of symmetry

$$\rho(xyz) = \sum \sum \sum \pm \frac{F(hkl)}{V} \cos 2\pi \left(\frac{hx}{a} + \frac{ky}{b} + \frac{lz}{c} \right)$$

The determination of the configuration of penicillin salt molecules by three-dimensional Fourier analysis represents the crowning achievement to date, as is discussed in Chap. 20 on Organic Compounds.

Most frequently the two-dimensional series for all reflections $(hk0)$ from one zone in the crystal is used, and the density per unit area A in any projection of the structure is given by the series

$$\rho(xy) = \sum \sum \pm \frac{F(hk0)}{A} \cos 2\pi \left(\frac{hx}{a} + \frac{ky}{b} \right)$$

The electron-density contour map of molecular structure which will be illustrated for organic molecules in Chap. 20 is the result of such an analysis. The simple one-dimensional series gives the density per unit length d arranged in sheets parallel to any given plane, and the successive orders of reflections from that plane $(h00)$ give the coefficients in the series

$$\rho(x) = \sum \pm \frac{F(h00)}{d} \cos 2\pi \frac{hx}{a}$$

Aids to computation. Within the range of experimental limitations the larger the number of terms included in the Fourier series, the more perfect will the representation become. Such a process may become extremely laborious. Robertson cites the case of two projections of the double series for phthalocyanine. A total of 281 different terms were used in the series, which had to be evaluated at 1,800 different points over half the molecule in each case. Thus the total number of terms necessary to evaluate and add for these two projections is well over 500,000. Devices for shortening calculations are obviously called for.

The double-series equation may be written

$$\rho(xy) = \Sigma(\Sigma K \cos h\Theta_1) \cos k\Theta_2 - \Sigma(\Sigma K \sin h\Theta_1) \sin k\Theta_2$$

where K is the coefficient and $\Theta_1 = 2\pi x/a$, $\Theta_2 = 2\pi y/b$. The summations in parentheses are carried out first and become the coefficients for the final summation $\rho(xy) = \Sigma P \cos k\Theta_2 - \Sigma Q \sin k\Theta_2$. The method of Beevers and Lipson, which is the most familiar, involves 4,000 strips of cardboard upon which are printed all two-figure F coefficients, positive and negative, for sines and cosines of angles at intervals of 6 deg and all values of the index h from 0 to 20. The synthesis reduces to selecting sets of cards and adding up successive columns of figures. The expression $\cos 2\pi(hx + ky)$ is converted to $\cos 2\pi hx \cos 2\pi ky - \sin 2\pi hx \sin 2\pi ky$. Each strip gives $F \cos 2\pi hx$ (or the sine term) for given values of F and h and a range of values for the coordinate x (in steps of one-sixtieth of the cell edge up to one-fourth the edge). All reflections, for example with $h = 3$, are grouped together into $\cos 2\pi 3x(F_{310} \cos 2\pi y + F_{320} \cos 2\pi 2y + F_{330} \cos 2\pi 3y + \cdots)$. Terms within the parentheses for y values are added up from the appropriate strips, to give a new coefficient F^1 for each value of y: thus $F^1 \cos 2\pi x(h = 1)$, $F^1 \cos 2\pi 2x(h = 2)$, and as above $F^1 \cos 2\pi 3x(h = 3)$, and so on. Numbers on these strips are added up to give electron densities over the range of x values. The strip principle now has been applied to punched cards so that summations may be carried out with IBM accounting machines.

It is obvious that such computations in mathematical synthesis have been immeasurably aided by the development within the past few years of the computing machines ranging from IBM office machines for summations to the most complex of electronic instruments such as X-Rac (Fig. 257) developed by Pepinsky at the Pennsylvania State College.[1] This synthesizer sums the two-dimensional Fourier series representing planar centrosymmetric projections of electron densities in a crystal unit cell, and the projection is presented by a television scan on the screen of a cathode-ray oscilloscope (Fig. 258). The specific advantage of this device is the immediate observability of effects on the projection of alterations in signs of one or any number of Fourier coefficients. A large

[1] R. Pepinsky, *J. Appl. Phys.*, **18**, 601 (1942).

number of papers within 2 years in *Acta Crystallographica* and elsewhere present details of these machines.

Optical synthesis. In summing up a Fourier series in the calculation of an image of a crystal structure from an x-ray diffraction pattern we have

Fig. 257. View of X-Rac with presentation and photographic oscilloscopes.

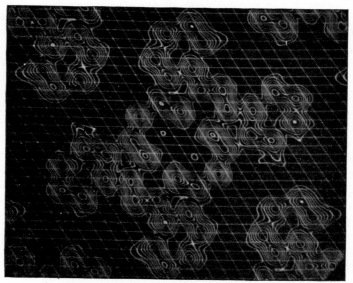

Fig. 258. X-Rac diagram of phthalocyanine molecules.

the same process as the superposition of many sets of interference fringes in a microscopic image. Hence optics has provided a method of Fourier synthesis in place of mathematical calculations. This method proposed by Sir Lawrence Bragg, diagrammatically represented in Fig. 259, is

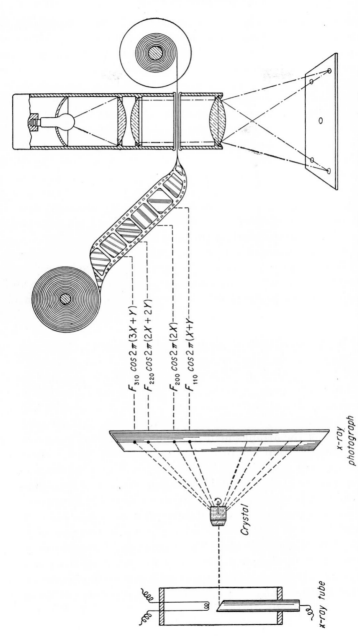

$F_{310} \cos 2\pi (3X + Y)$
$F_{220} \cos 2\pi (2X + 2Y)$
$F_{200} \cos 2\pi (2X)$
$F_{110} \cos 2\pi (X + Y)$

x-ray
photograph

Crystal

x-ray tube

(*Chemical and Engineering News.*)

Fig. 259. Bragg-Huggins photographic-analogue (optical-fringe) method.

described in detail in "The Crystalline State," Vol. 1, pages 231 to 240. Imitation interference fringes are printed on photographic plates in sets. For each pair of reflections $hk0$ and $kk0$ a set of light and dark bands is printed so that the photographic density of the films in a direction perpendicular to the bands follows a modified sine law. Each of these films is characterized by the unique features (1) that the perpendicular distance between parallel bands is proportional to d_{hk0}, the interplanar spacing corresponding to a diffraction spot, and (2) that the direction of the parallel bands corresponds to the direction that an $hk0$ family of planes cuts the xy face of the unit cell. The time of exposure is proportional to the structure amplitude, as these bands are registered in superposition on a photographic plate. The final developed image represents a somewhat rough photograph corresponding to an electron-density contour map which might be accurately plotted. The Eastman Kodak Company provides a film roll of these various band patterns, as devised by Huggins.

Another Bragg method utilizes real optical-interference effects. As described briefly by Bunn,[1] beams of light, one for each x-ray reflection in a chosen zone, are arranged so as to produce by interference an image of the projected crystal structure. The apparatus consists of two lenses, each of about 6 ft focal length, placed a few inches apart. At the principal focus of one lens is a pinhole source of monochromatic light; between the lenses is placed an opaque plate drilled with a pattern of holes so that multiple images of the point source are formed at the principal focus of the second lens. This is a diffraction pattern of the original pattern of holes optically produced. If the holes are arranged like the points in the reciprocal lattice of the crystal zone and the area of each hole is proportional to the structure amplitude, the diffraction pattern appears as a representation of the arrangement of atoms in a crystal as seen along the zone axis, provided that the phases of all x-ray reflections concerned are the same. A very small image is photographed by a microscope.

Another machine uses sand in building models of two-dimensional Fourier projections instead of photographic film in the Bragg summation method.[2] From the x-ray data the three quantities d_{hk0}, ψ_{hk0} (directional angle), and F_{hk0} are transformed into adjustable features of the sand machine. A photograph is made by illuminating the grid, on which the sand is poured at an oblique angle, and photographing from above.

The ultimate extension of the optical-analogue method is the two-wavelength microscope. Since x-rays cannot be focused as visible light, it is possible only to collect a diffraction pattern. But W. L. Bragg also conceived the idea that, if visible light could be made to continue in the paths of the x-ray diffracted beams, it could be focused to give an image

[1] C. W. Bunn, "Chemical Crystallography," p. 348, Oxford University Press, New York, 1945.

[2] Dan McLachlan and E. F. Champaygne, *J. Appl. Phys.*, **17**, 1006 (1946).

of the crystal.   Such a two-wavelength microscope (Fig. 260a) has been successfully constructed by Buerger[1] at MIT, starting with a diffraction pattern photographed in his precession camera (an undistorted reciprocal-lattice photograph) which is equivalent to the interference pattern that would be formed by visible light and photographed by a lens.

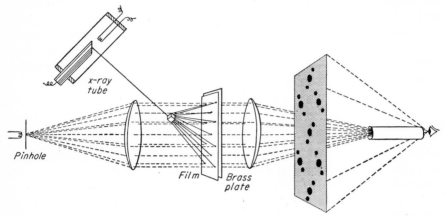

Fig. 260a. Scheme of Buerger two-wavelength microscope.   (*Chemical and Engineering News.*)

A replica of the x-ray pattern is made by boring holes in a brass plate and is placed in an optical system that produces an interference pattern which is the image of the original crystal.   The most complex part of the apparatus involves the use of mica plates behind the holes in the brass plate capable of being tilted to produce phase shifts by varying the length of optical path.   Individual rows of holes produce optical patterns as

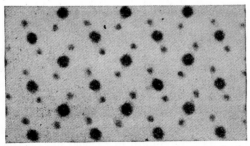

Fig. 260b. Two-wavelength microscope image of atoms in FeS_2 (marcasite) magnified 2.6×10^7 diameters.   (*Buerger.*)

lines at right angles to the rows similar to the Bragg-Huggins fringes. The total effect is optical summation of all patterns to give the structure pattern.   The result for marcasite, FeS_2, is shown in Fig. 260b.

Thus the good features of x-rays, with wavelengths short enough to be

[1] M. J. Buerger, *J. Appl. Phys.*, **21**, 909 (1950).

compatible with atomic dimensions, are combined with the scaling up by substitution of visible light of the whole optical image-forming process, so that the image is magnified by a factor of the quotient of the wavelength of visible light to that of x-rays, or 10^7 diameters.

Patterson-Harker Fourier Synthesis.[1]   The uncertainties involved in the phase angle for the usual Fourier analysis led Patterson[2] to develop a new direct method of analysis which has proved invaluable in the field of organic structures. This involves deducing interatomic vectors, or the lengths and directions of lines joining atomic centers, but not directly the positions of atoms. The quantity $P(u)$ represents the weighted average distribution of density about a point X, or

$$P(u) = \frac{1}{a} \int_0^a \rho(x)\rho(x + u)dx$$

where $\rho(x + u)$ is the distribution about x as a function of the parameter u, weighted by the amount of scattering matter between x and $x + dx$. Expanded by a Fourier series

$$P(u) = \frac{1}{d^2} \sum F^2(h00)e^{2\pi i(hu/a)}$$

for the one-dimensional case.   Thus $P(u)$ depends upon F^2 instead of F and is independent of signs or phase constants.   In three dimensions

$$P(uvw) = \frac{1}{V} \int_0^a \int_0^b \int_0^c \rho(xyz)\rho(x + u, y + v, z + w) \, dx \, dy \, dz$$

$$= \frac{1}{V} \sum\sum\sum |F(hkl)|^2 \cos 2\pi \left(\frac{hu}{a} + \frac{kv}{b} + \frac{lw}{c} \right)$$

$P(uvw)$ will be large only when there are high values in $\rho(xyz)$ both at xyz and $x + u, y + v, z + w$.   A peak in the function $P(uvw)$ at u, v, w corresponds to an *interatomic distance* in the crystal.   The only difficulty involved sometimes is an ambiguity as to which pairs of atoms are involved.   Harker's[3] extensions have included simplifications by including symmetry properties of the crystal.   For example, for a crystal with a plane of symmetry and equivalent atoms at xyz and $x\bar{y}z$ the vector components are $0 \, 2y \, 0$.   The maximum in $P(uvw)$ lies on the b axis, and the series becomes only one-dimensional with the far simpler calculations

[1] For the most complete account of this, as well as all other advanced phases of crystal structure determination, see H. Lipson and W. Cochran, The Determination of Crystal Structures, Vol. III of "The Crystalline State," George Bell & Sons, Ltd., London, 1953.

[2] *Z. Krist.*, **90**, 517 (1935).

[3] *J. Chem. Phys.*, **4**, 381 (1936).

$$P(0v0) = \sum_{k=-\infty}^{\infty} \left[\sum_{k=-\infty}^{\infty} \sum_{l=-\infty}^{\infty} |F(hkl)|^2 \right] \cos 2\pi \frac{kv}{b}$$

The F^2 synthesis has the inherent limitation that vectors are all erected from a single point, and interpretation in terms of atomic coordinates may be quite obscure. In the words of Buerger, "If one views the crystal structure from a fixed point, he sees a true image of the crystal structure, but if one occupies each of n atoms of the structure in turn, viewing the crystal structure from each one, and then superposes all n parallel images, the composite image is the Patterson synthesis." The Patterson method is most useful for unit cells containing heavy atoms which will give very prominent Patterson peaks. The projection then gives direction and magnitude of vectors joining the heavy atoms; this placing of heavy atoms in the structure usually may decide the signs of enough F terms to make possible a preliminary Fourier synthesis.

Buerger has also made valuable additions to the Patterson-Harker synthesis, particularly the *implication* diagram. This results from transformation for a Harker synthesis of polar coordinates, depending on the number of operations in the cyclical group of axial symmetry for which the Harker synthesis is prepared. The implication diagram actually is a map of the location of atoms in the crystal structure, plus additional *ambiguities* which would give rise to the same Harker synthesis, plus satellite locations (which are easily identified). Space groups which yield an implication map with ambiguities and no satellites and those with neither are analyzed.[1]

Fourier Transforms. Since 1940 several authors[2] have advocated the use of the concept of transforms in the determination of crystalline and molecular structures. Basically this is concerned with the structure factor of a *pattern* of atoms. In the case of a single atom referred to its center as origin, the structure factor is the atomic-scattering factor, f. Reciprocal space may be visualized mapped with the spherically symmetric function. Inserting the reciprocal lattice of a *particular* crystal into this map, we sample the map at those points and obtain the contribution to the structure factor of the crystal of this atom placed at the origin in the unit cell. Similarly a set of atoms with a chosen origin may be represented by its structure factor as a mapping of reciprocal space with this function and again this map of the reciprocal lattice of any crystal

[1] M. J. Buerger, Interpretation of Harker Synthesis, *J. Appl. Phys.*, **17**, 579 (1942); Phase Determination with the Aid of Implication Theory, *Phys. Rev.*, **73**, 927 (1948); Some Relations between F's and F^2's of X-ray Diffraction, *Proc. Natl. Acad.*, **34**, 277 (1948).

[2] G. Knott, *Proc. Phys. Soc. (London)*, **52**, 229 (1940). D. Wrinch, *USXRED Mono.* II, Murray, Cambridge, Mass., 1946. A. Klug, Structure of Triphenylene, *Acta Cryst.*, **3**, 165, 176 (1950).

is sampled.   The structure factor for any constellation of atoms could
be mapped throughout reciprocal space and then used in evaluating the
structure factor of any crystal in which this constellation occurs, such as
points (or atoms in a molecule) at the corners of an octahedron, at the
vertices of a tetrahedron, at the corners of a plane or crumpled hexagon,
triangle, etc.   Many of these simple sets of points are relevant to atomic
groupings which occur in crystals.   But the term structure factor, as
already indicated, refers generally to any electron-density distributions.
Thus the Fourier transform may be defined by an equation similar in
form to that expressing regular electron-density distribution, $\rho(xyz)$.   It
follows that the structure factor for a distribution at any point is the
transform of the distribution of that point multiplied by VW, where V is
the volume of the unit cell and W is the "weight," or number of electrons.

Attempts to Determine Phase.   As already indicated an infinite number of different electron distributions may be derived from the measured
structure amplitudes in a given crystal by assigning various arbitrary
values to the unknown phase constant and then summing the resulting
Fourier series.   Obviously there is no unique mathematical solution to
the general problem unless conditions are attached to the electron density
function.   The abiding question, as Robertson has pointed out, is whether
there is a unique *physical* solution.   Several methods have been designed
to reduce the laborious and time-consuming trial-and-failure method of
determining phases of Fourier synthesis, particularly the signs of coefficients for crystals with centers of symmetry.   This whole subject is most
ably and comprehensively presented in its very latest aspects in the book
edited by Ray Pepinsky, "Computing Methods and the Phase Problem,"
published by Pennsylvania State College in 1952.   Only a brief listing of
some of the possible methods of arriving at satisfactory Fourier syntheses
can be given here.[1]

   a. The *Patterson-Harker* synthesis in two and three dimensions may provide sufficient evidence of positions of molecules to determine phases approximately, from which
state the structure is refined by Fourier methods.   The complexity increases with the
number of atoms in the cell to a point where deductions are not sufficient to permit
refinement.
   b. *Implication diagrams* of Buerger[2] are an extension of the usefulness of the Patterson-Harker synthesis, but these, too, may reach a point of limiting difficulty.
   c. *Vector sets.*   Arising out of the Patterson vector map, the formation and interpretation of the sets of vectors derived from isolated arrays of atoms, with extensions to
periodic distributions in crystals, present attractive possibilities for direct analysis
of structures.   Forming the vector array from a given distribution amounts to
"squaring" the distribution.   This is not difficult but the converse problem of extracting the square root, or finding the original array of points from a vector set, is the

---

   [1] Most of the papers have been published in *Acta Cryst.*, vols. 1–6 (1948–1953).
The best summary is given by Robertson, *loc. cit.*, Chap. VI, p. 119.
   [2] *J. App. Physics*, **17**, 579 (1946); *Phys. Rev.*, **73**, 927 (1948); *Acta Cryst.*, **1**, 259
(1948).

fundamental problem in x-ray analysis. The vector set consists of N superposed images of the original set of N points. Wrinch,[1] Buerger,[2] and others have developed systematic algebraic procedures for extracting fundamental sets from any given two-dimensional vector set and then attempting to solve the Patterson map even with unresolved vector peaks by forming image-seeking functions.

d. The *fly's-eye camera* and similar devices are designed to greatly speed up trial projections.

e. X-Rac, the electronic synthesizer or analogue computer of Pepinsky, is the supreme achievement to this moment of aids to structural analysis; for into this machine are fed available data on structure factors and on phases from information based on sound chemical intuition, and on a cathode-ray screen appears immediately the electron-density contour map for the crystal in question. Instantly the effect of changing the sign of any term on the electron density can be observed; the computations normally requiring weeks or months become a matter of minutes and hours. This instrument is described in detail in Dr. Pepinsky's book mentioned at the beginning of this section. In Fig. 257 is pictured a portion of X-Rac with the coefficient panels and presentation and photographic oscilloscopes; in Fig. 258, the electron-density map of phthalocyanine photographed from the image on the oscilloscope screen (see also Chap. 20 for the structure of this compound).

f. Harker and Kasper inequalities[3] are a direct application of purely mathematical Schwartz and Cauchy inequalities to observed values in order to yield limitations on some of the phases due to crystal symmetry. Many electron distributions obtained by varying the unmeasured phase constants will display regions of negative density, which can be eliminated as having no physical reality. This condition and the fact that some of the inequalities are more powerful than others help to limit the possible values of the phase constant. If $F(hkl)$ is defined as $F(hkl)/f(hkl)$ where $f(hkl)$ is a suitable mean atomic-scattering factor normalized to make $F(000) = 1$, then for a crystal with a center of symmetry

$$F^2(hkl) \leqq \tfrac{1}{2} + \tfrac{1}{2}F(2h,2k,2l)$$

Hence, if $F^2(hkl) > \tfrac{1}{2}$, $F(2h,2k,2l)$ must be positive; or if $F^2(hkl) > \tfrac{1}{4}$ and

$$|F(2h,2k,2l)| = \tfrac{1}{2}$$

then $F(2h,2k,2l)$ is again positive. Gillis used this approach to determine the signs of 40 most important terms in $F(h0l)$ data for oxalic acid dihydrate. Hughes has further extended this method and defined its limitations.

g. The *steepest descents* of A. D. Booth[4] is a device for minimizing systematically by means of an electronic computer a function of observed and calculated structure factors: $R = \sum_{hkl} ||F_{obs}| - |F_{calc}||$ or $R_2 = \sum_{hkl} (F_{obs}^2 - F_{calc}^2)^2$ or $R_3 = \sum_{hkl} (\log I_{obs} - \log I_{calc})^2$.

R is a constant represented as a set of surfaces in $3N$-dimensional space, where N is the number of crystallographically different atoms present. R is minimized by proceeding in the direction of the normal to the initial surface until the function no longer decreases. Having arrived at a new R surface, the procedure is repeated until the minimum is reached. The method is adaptable in cases where atomic positions are approximately known, or the configuration of the molecule is known but not its position or orientation in the cell, or the molecular shape is only vaguely known as for compounds with giant molecules.

[1] D. M. Wrinch, *Phil. Mag.*, **27**, 98 (1939).

[2] M. J. Buerger, *Acta Cryst.*, **3**, 87 (1950).

[3] *Acta Cryst.*, **1**, 70 (1948).

[4] *Nature*, **160**, 196 (1947); **161**, 765 (1948); *Proc. Roy. Soc.*, **197**, 336 (1949).

h. Least-squares methods. Hughes's method[1] minimizes $\Sigma w(F_{obs} - F_{calc})^2$, where w is the weight given an observation. Cochran shows that Fourier refinement which minimizes $\Sigma 1/f(F_{obs} - F_{calc})^2$ is a special case. Thus the Fourier method may be modified by weighing observations and minimizing $\Sigma w(F_{obs} - F_{calc})^2$.

i. Statistical handling of errors. Sources of errors in atomic coordinates derived from Fourier synthesis may be due to (1) experimental errors in observed factors; (2) termination of Fourier series at a finite Θ value while coefficients are still appreciables; and (3) rounding off errors in computation. Booth, Cruickshank, and others have developed procedures for correcting systematic errors and estimating standard deviations; this approach is of significance in determining with accuracy bond lengths. The Beevers-Lipson method of summation, rounding off F and $F \cos 2\pi hx$ to the nearest integer, is sufficiently accurate unless F's are measured to an accuracy such that standard deviation is less than 2. Rounding off to 0.1 with new Fourier steps is always adequate.

j. Artificial temperature factors applied to Fourier coefficients while still appreciable in order to terminate the series are a device studied by several authorities; this leads to a smearing out of detail and errors in atomic positions.

k. Statistical relations between structure factors. Recently Hauptman and Karle[2] have claimed the direct mathematical solution of the phase problem with a probability distribution function related to the Patterson synthesis. However, Vand and Pepinsky[3] strongly maintain that these claims are unfounded, though perhaps some advantage may be taken of statistical procedures in simplifying the interpretation of interatomic vector maps.

l. Phase determination with heavy-atom derivatives and/or isomorphous crystals. In spite of all the intensive mathematical efforts to solve even partially the phase problem, there remain only two direct approaches to the determination of the phase constant, by means of which it is possible to apply the Fourier series method directly at its full power, or at least to proceed by stages of successive approximation to the true structure. These are (1) the effect of one or more heavy atoms with dominant scattering power situated at known or easily determined points in the crystal structure; and (2) the isomorphous replacement of these special atoms by others of different scattering power, without disturbing to any great extent the over-all lattice structure. These two cases may be illustrated by the simplest examples. (1) If the heavy atom is situated at the center of symmetry (space group P and others), it makes a positive contribution, F_A, to all the reflections. The amplitude for the combined effect of all the light atoms, F_O, may be positive or negative at the symmetry center. By addition the total resultant amplitude, F_{AO}, will be positive if F_A is greater than F_O. Such a condition is realized, for example, with platinum phthalocyanine; in less ideal cases it is still possible with the available information to make successive Fourier approximations. (2) Isomorphous replacement, or successive substitution of two different heavy atoms in a molecule without disturbing the crystalline arrangement, is a still more powerful phase-determining method, since the phase relationships can be determined from a difference effect, $F_{A_1O} - F_{A_2O} = F_{A_1} - F_{A_2} = \Delta F$, the contribution of O being constant. Hence the signs of the F terms in the Fourier synthesis are unequivocally assigned. The phthalocyanine series (without and with a whole series

[1] *J. Am. Chem. Soc.*, **63**, 7137 (1941).

[2] H. Hauptman and J. Karle, Solution of the Phase Problem. I. The Centro-Symmetric Crystal, Monograph 3, American Crystallographic Association, The Letter Press, Wilmington, Del., 1953.

[3] V. Vand and R. Pepinsky, "The Statistical Approach to X-Ray Structure Analysis," X-Ray and Crystal Analysis Laboratory, Pennsylvania State University, State College, Pa., 1954.

of replaceable metal atoms at the center of the molecule), camphor and sucrose derivatives, isomorphous bromides and chlorides, selenates and sulfates (enabling analysis of the complex structure of strychnine, Chap. 20), and pairs of salts (K-Rb, Pb-Sr) are examples of successful application of isomorphous replacement.[1]

Results of Fourier-synthesis Improvements.   Only a few structures of organic compounds have been determined with full accuracy, potentially available in the foregoing methods.   But it is already certain that the influence of hydrogen atoms on structure factors can be and are being demonstrated; and that deductions may be made from regions where density is less than $\frac{1}{2}$ electron/A^3.   Peaks in electron-density maps have been found in positions consistent with known lengths of bonds to hydrogen (naphthalene,[2] decaborane,[3] aminopyrimidines,[4] and others).

The necessary conditions for maximum accuracy are: (1) intensities of all reflection to $\Theta = 90$ deg for copper radiation must be measured and corrected accurately; (2) three-dimensional methods are applied to refinement of coordinates; (3) corrections are made for systematic errors and estimates for random errors.   The published structures of dibenzyl, thiophthene, and 2,6-dichloro-4-aminopyrimidine prior to 1950 and an increasing number since 1950 meet these criteria.   The successive steps in the determination of the central-bond length in dibenzyl[5] are instructive:

1. From two-dimensional Fourier projections $\sim$1.58A.
2. From three-dimensional Fourier section and line synthesis 1.48.
3. From three-dimensional differential Fourier synthesis 1.501.
4. After correction for finite-series error (standard deviation 0.015A) 1.510.

[1] J. M. Robertson, *loc. cit.*, p. 148.

[2] Abrahams, Robertson, and White, *Acta Cryst.*, **2**, 233, 238 (1949).

[3] Harker, Kasper, and Lucht, *J. Am. Chem. Soc.*, **70**, 881 (1948).

[4] Clews and Cochran, *Acta Cryst.*, **2**, 46 (1949).

[5] Cruickshank, *Acta Cryst.*, **1**, 92 (1948).   Jeffrey, *Proc. Roy. Soc. (London)*, **A188**, 222 (1947).

CHAPTER 16

THE RESULTS OF CRYSTAL ANALYSIS: ELEMENTS
AND INORGANIC COMPOUNDS

The Chemical Elements. By the methods of x-ray analysis outlined in the preceding chapter about 85 of the known chemical elements have been assigned definite crystalline structures in the solid state. More than 20 of these crystallize in two or more different polymorphic modifications. At least 26 types of structure have been definitely established, designated A1 to A26 by Ewald and Hermann in the "Strukturbericht"; a few others (X_1 to X_{12}) have been only partially analyzed. These types are listed and defined in Tables 16-1 and 16-2; Table 16-3 presents in detail the most recent and reliable data for the elements alphabetically arranged.

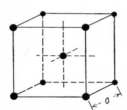

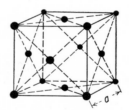

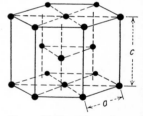

FIG. 261. Body-centered cubic lattice (tungsten type).

FIG. 262a. The close-packed crystal structures, face-centered cubic (copper type).

FIG. 262b. The close-packed crystal structures, hexagonal close-packed (zinc type).

Pure metals are, of course, chemical elements. Every metal except a few of the rarest in nature may be classified now according to the pattern by which its atoms form crystals and according to the numerical values which define the unit crystal cell.

Fortunately for practical purposes most of the metals are grouped in only three structures, face-centered cubic (A1) (Fig. 262a), hexagonal close-packed (A3) (Fig. 262b), and body-centered cubic (A2) (Fig. 261). The first two represent the alternative methods of packing spheres in closest array. A layer is formed such that each atom is in contact with six neighbors at the corners of a regular hexagon. The next layer is placed on this so that each sphere is in contact with three spheres in the layer below. The difference between A1 and A3 is to be found in the placing of the third layer. For A3 the third layer is exactly over the

468

TABLE 16-1. CRYSTAL-STRUCTURE TYPES OF THE ELEMENTS

Type symbol (Ewald-Hermann)	Type element	Space-lattice	Space group	$Z=$ atoms per unit cell	Elements and modifications	Distinctive feature
A1	Copper	Face-centered cubic (fcc)	$Fm3m$	4	Ag, Al, A, Au, α-Ca, β-Ce, β-Co, Cu, γ-Fe, Ir, Kr, β-La, Ne, β-Ni, Pb, Pd, Pt, β-Pr, β-Rh, Sc, α-Sr, Th, Xe, Yb	CN 12
A2	Tungsten (α)	Body-centered cubic (bcc)	$Im3m$	2	Ba, γ-Ca, Cb(Nb), Cr, Cs, Eu, α, β, δ-Fe, K, Li, Mo, Na, γ-Np, Rb, γ-Sr, Ta, β-Ti, β-Tl, γ-U, V, α-W, β-Zr	CN 8
A3	Magnesium	Hexagonal close-packed (hcp)	$C6/mmc$	2	α-Be, β-Ca, Cd, α-Ce, α-Co, Cp, α-Ni, β-Cr, Dy, α-Er, Gd, Hf, He, Ho, α-La, Mg, α-Nd, Os, α-Pr, Re, α-Ru, Sc, β-Sr, Tb, α-Ti, α-Tl, Tn, Y, Zn, α-Zr	CN 12
A4	Diamond (carbon)	Two interpenetrating fcc	$Fd3m$	8	C (diamond), Ge, Si, α-Sn (gray)	CN 4
A5	β-Tin (white)	Double bc tetragonal	$I4/amd$	4	β-Sn (white)	Flattened A4
A6	Indium	Fc tetragonal	$I4/mmm$	2	Indium, γ-Mn	
A7	Arsenic	Bc rhombohedral	$R\bar{3}m$	2	As, Bi, Sb, β-Graphite	Deformed simple cubic
A8	γ-Selenium hexagonal)	Hexagonal (deformed simple cubic)	$C3_12$	3	Se, Te	
A9	Graphite (carbon)	Hexagonal	$C6/mmc$	4	Graphite, C	Planar rings of 6C
A10	Mercury	Rhombohedral	$R\bar{3}m$	4	Hg	CN 6
A11	Gallium	Orthorhombic	$Cmca$	8	Ga	6 (5 in one layer)
A12	α-Manganese	Bcc complex	$I\bar{4}3m$	58	α-Mn, γ-Cr	Mg₃Al₂ isomorphous
A13	β-Manganese	Cubic	Pr_13	20	β-Mn	
A14	Iodine	Orthorhombic	$Coma$	8	I₂, Br₂	Molecular lattice
A15?	β-Tungsten	Cubic	$Pm3n$	8	....	Actually W₃O with 6W and 2O at random over 8 positions. Hägg and Schönberg, 1954
A16	α-Sulfur	Orthorhombic	$Fddd$	128	α-S	Puckered S₈ rings
A17	Phosphorus	Fc orthorhombic	$Bmab$	8	P(black)	Double layers

TABLE 16-1. CRYSTAL-STRUCTURE TYPES OF THE ELEMENTS (*Continued*)

Type symbol (Ewald-Hermann)	Type element	Space-lattice	Space group	$Z =$ atoms per unit cell	Elements and modifications	Distinctive feature
A18	Chlorine	Orthorhombic	*Cmca*	4	Cl_2	Molecular lattice of Cl_2
A19	Polonium	Monoclinic	C_2	12	Po	Distorted A_{10}
A20	α-Uranium	Orthorhombic	*Cmcm*	4	α-U	Distorted A_3, CN 4, 8
A21	β-Uranium	Tetragonal	*P4nm*	30	....	Puckered layers with atoms between
A22	α-Selenium	Monoclinic	*P2/1n*	32	....	Puckered 8-membered rings similar to A16
A23	β-Selenium	Monoclinic	*P2/1a*	32	....	8-membered chain like ring with broken bond, terminal atom double bonded (Burbank); puckered true ring [Marsh, Pauling, and McCullough, *Acta Cryst.*, **6**, 71 (1953)]
A24	α-Neptunium	Orthorhombic	*Pmcn*	8	....	Zachariasen, *Acta Cryst.*, **5**, 660 (1952); heavily deformed bcc, reducing CN from 8 to 4
A25	β-Neptunium	Tetragonal	....	4	....	Four short bonds
A26	Protactinium	Bc tetragonal	....	2	....	Zachariasen, *Acta Cryst.*, **5**, 19 (1952); CN 10, 8 at 3.212 and 2 at 3.238
A27	Samarium	Rhombohedral	*R3̄m*	3	....	Repeating period 9 times that of close-packed layers in sequence [ABABCBC-AC], Ellinger and Zachariasen, *J. Am. Chem. Soc.*, **75**, 5650 (1954)

TABLE 16-2

Type symbol	Type element	Space-lattice
X_1	β-Beryllium	Hexagonal
X_2	Boron† (2 forms)	Tetragonal, orthorhombic, pseudotetragonal
X_3	Hydrogen (para-), β-nitrogen	Hexagonal
X_4	α-Nitrogen, γ-oxygen ($8O_2$)	Cubic
X_5	α-Oxygen ($2O_2$)	Bc rhombic
X_6	β-Oxygen ($6O_2$)	Rhombohedral
X_7	Phosphorus (white) ($4P_4$)	Cubic
X_8	α-Rhodium	Cubic
X_9	S(fibers)	Monoclinic (112 atoms per unit cell)
X_{10}	γ-Sulfur	Monoclinic (48 atoms per unit cell)
X_{11}	δ-Sulfur	Rhombohedral (18 atoms per unit cell)

† "Crystallized" boron always contains some Al and may be the intermetallic compound AlB_{12} rather than a solid solution approximating pure B. A "diamond-like" and two "graphitelike" modifications have been analyzed [Noray-Szabo, *Z. Krist.*, **94**, 367 (1937); Halla and Weil, *Z. Krist.*, **101**, 435 (1939)].

first layer so that the sequence of all layers is 1 2 1 2 1 2; for cubic A1, the third layer differs from 1 or 2, thus producing the sequence 1 2 3 1 2 3 . . . as illustrated in Fig. 263a. But in both A1 and A3, each atom has 12 equidistant neighbors; in other words, a coordination number (CN) of 12. For both the volume of space occupied by each sphere is

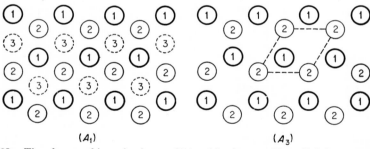

(A_1) (A_3)

FIG. 263a. The close packing of spheres: (A_1) cubic close packing; (A_3) hexagonal close packing. In (A_3) the hexagonal unit cell is outlined. The numbers correspond to the successive layers of the structures. In both arrangements each sphere is surrounded by 12 equidistant neighbors.

5.66a, where a is the radius. The axial ratio c/a for hexagonal close packing of spheres must be $2\sqrt{2}/\sqrt{3} = 1.633$; of 27 elements crystallizing in this manner, all but 2 or 3 have this value within 4 per cent. But there is an important difference which is clearly reflected in the properties of metals belonging to each type of structure. In A3, there is only one direction normal to which atoms are arrayed in individually close-packed sheets, whereas, in A1, such sheets are disposed in four directions normal

TABLE 16-3. UNIT-CELL CONSTANTS FOR ELEMENTS, 1953

Element	Symbol	Atomic number	Lattice type	Edge length a; a, c; a, b, c	Density (x-ray)
Aluminum	Al	13	A1	4.0414	2.694
Antimony	Sb	51	A7	4.4976, $\omega = 57°6.5'$	6.686
Argon	A	18	A1	5.42	1.654
Arsenic	As	33	A7	4.123, $\omega = 54°10'$	5.71
Barium	Ba	56	A2	5.009	3.590
Beryllium	Be	4	αA3 to 630°	2.286, 3.588	1.857
			βX$_1$ 630° to mp	6.93, 11.35	1.89
Bismuth	Bi	83	A7	4.7364, $\omega = 57°16'$	9.785
Boron	B	5	αX$_1$	8.93	
			X$_2$	17.86, 8.93, 10.13	
Bromine	Br	35	A14	6.67, 8.72, 4.48	
Cadmium	Cd	48	A3	2.9731, 5.607	8.634
Calcium	Ca	20	αA1 to 450°	5.56	1.537
			γA3 450 to 610°	3.98, 5.52	1.52
			βA2 610° to mp		
Carbon	C	6	Diamond A4	3.5547	3.408
			α-Graphite A9	2.46, 6.78	2.227
			β-Graphite A7	3.635, 39°30'	
Cerium	Ce	58	αA3 to mp	3.65, 5.96	5.775
			βA1, room temperature	5.140	6.792
Cesium	Cs	55	A2	6.05	1.977
Chlorine	Cl	17	A18	6.29, 4.50, 8.21	
Chromium	Cr	24	αA2 to mp	2.8796	7.188
			βA3 (electrolytic)	2.717, 4.418	6.07
			γA12, room temperature	8.717	7.507
Cobalt	Co	27	αA3 to 420°	2.514, 4.105	8.766
			βA1 420° to mp	3.554	8.72
Columbium	Cb	41	A2	3.294	8.567
Copper	Cu	29	A1	3.6077	8.923
Cysprosium	Dy	66	A3	3.578, 5.648	
Erbium	Er	68	A3	3.53, 5.589	7.49
Europium	Eu	63	A2	4.573	
Fluorine	F	9			
Gadolium	Gd	64	A3	3.622, 5.748	
Gallium	Ga	31	A11	4.410, 4.416, 7.645	5.925
Germanium	Ge	32	A4	5.62	5.316
Gold	Au	79	A1	4.0704	19.28
Hafnium	Hf	72	αA3	3.1952, 5.05769	
			βA2 (1310°)	3.50	
Helium	He	2	A3 (-271°C)	3.57, 5.83	
Holmoim	Ho	67	A3	3.557, 5.620	
Hydrogen (para)	H	1	X$_3$	3.75, 6.12	0.089
Indium	In	49	A6	3.244, 4.938 pseudocubic	7.28

TABLE 16-3. UNIT-CELL CONSTANTS FOR ELEMENTS, 1953 (*Continued*)

Element	Symbol	Atomic number	Lattice type	Edge length a; a, c; a, b, c	Density (x-ray)
Iodine............	I	53	A14	4.797, 7.25, 9.7718	4.933
Iridium..........	Ir	77	A1	3.8312	22.64
Iron..............	Fe	26	αA2 to 909°	2.86075	7.861
			γA1, 909 to 1403°	3.63	8.13
Krypton..........	Kr	36	A1	5.684 (82°K)	3.005
Lanthanum.......	La	57	αA3 to mp	3.754, 6.063	6.188
			βA1, room temperature	5.294	6.165
Lead.............	Pb	82	A1	4.9396	11.341
Lithium..........	Li	3	A2	3.5023 (20°) 3.4762 (−183°C)	0.53
Lutecium.........	Lu	71	....	3.509, 3.559	
Magnesium.......	Mg	12	A3	3.2028, 5.1998	1.7365
Manganese.......	Mn	25	αA12 to 742°	8.894	7.464
			βA13 742 to 1191°	6.300	7.24
			γA6 1191° to mp (electrolytic)	3.774, 3.533	7.21
Mercury..........	Hg	80	A10	2.999, 70°31.7′	14.24
Molybdenum.....	Mo	42	A2	3.140	10.22
Neodymium......	Nd	60	A3	3.657, 5.8890	6.984
Neon.............	Ne	10	A1	4.52 (5°K)	1.44
Neptunium.......	Np	93	αA24 to 278°	4.723, 4.887, 6.603	20.45
			βA25 278 to 540°	4.897, 3.388	
			γA2 540 to 640° (mp)	3.52	19.36
Nickel............	Ni	28	αA1 to mp	2.65, 4.32	8.8
			βA3 (electrolytic)	3.5168	8.895
Nitrogen..........	N	7	αX₄	5.66	1.02
			βX₃	4.039, 6.670	0.995
Osmium..........	Os	76	A3	2.730, 4.310	22.69
Oxygen...........	O	8	αX₅	5.50, 3.82, 3.44 (21°K)	1.46
			βX₆	6.19; ω = 99.1° (35°K)	1.394
			γX₄	6.83 (48°K)	1.32
Palladium........	Pd	46	A1	3.8823	12.028
Phosphorus.......	P	15	White X₇	7.17	2.22
			Black A17	3.31, 4.38, 10.50	3.686
			Red, violet, unknown		
Platinum.........	Pt	78	A1	3.9158	21.438
Polonium.........	Po	84	A19	7.42, 4.29, 14.10	
Potassium........	K	19	A2	5.333	0.850
Praseodymium....	Pr	59	A3	3.662, 5.908	6.77
			A1	5.151	
Protoactinium....	Pa	91	A26	3.925, 3.238	15.37

TABLE 16-3. UNIT-CELL CONSTANTS FOR ELEMENTS, 1953 (*Continued*)

Element	Symbol	Atomic number	Lattice type	Edge length a; a, e; a, b, c	Density (x-ray)
Radium...........	Ra	88			
Radon............	Rn	86			
Rhenium.........	Re	75	A3	2.7553, 4.4493	20.996
Rhodium.........	Rh	45	αX_8 (electrolytic)	9.21	10.42
			$\beta A1$ to mp	3.7956	12.418
Rubidium........	Rb	37	A2	5.624 ($-183°C$)	1.587
				5.698 (19°)	
Ruthenium.......	Ru	44	$\alpha A3$	2.699, 4.274	12.436
			β, γ, δ reported		
Samarium........	Sm	62	A27	8.982, $\alpha = 23.31°$	
Scandium.........	Sc	21	$\alpha A1$	4.532	
			$\beta A3$	3.302, 5.245	
Selenium.........	Se	34	γ hexagonal A8	4.355, 4.949	4.845
			α monoclinic A22	9.05, 9.07, 11.61, $\beta = 90°46'$	4.48
			β monoclinic A23	12.85, 8.07, 9.31, $\beta = 93°4'$	4.40
Silicon...........	Si	14	A4	5.4198	2.326
Silver............	Ag	47	A1	4.0778	10.489
Sodium...........	Na	11	A2	4.282	0.954
Strontium........	Sr	38	$\alpha A1$	6.0726 (25°)	2.577
			$\beta A3$	4.31, 7.05 (248°)	
			$\gamma A2$	4.84 (614°)	
Sulfur............	S	16	$\alpha A16$	10.48, 12.92, 24.55	2.04
			βX_9	26.4, 9.26, 13.3, $\beta = 79°15'$	2.00
			δX_{10}	10.96, 11.02, $\beta = 83°16'$	
Tantalum.........	Ta	73	A2	3.296	16.79
Technetium.......	Tc	43	A3	2.735, 4.388	
Tellurium........	Te	52	A8	4.447, 5.915	6.23
Terbium..........	Tb	65	A3	3.585, 5.662	
Thallium.........	Ti	81	$\alpha A3$ to 231°	3.450, 5.520	11.842
			$\beta A2$ 231° to mp	3.874	11.878
Thorium..........	Th	90	A1	5.04	11.695
Thulium..........	Tm	69	A3	3.523, 5.564	
Tin..............	Sn	50	Gray $\alpha A4$ to 18°	6.46	5.806
			White $\beta A5$ 18 to 161°	15.8197, 3.1749	7.278
			$\gamma A3$ 161° to mp		
Titanium.........	Ti	22	$\alpha A3$	2.92, 4.67	4.42
			$\beta A2$	3.32	
Tungsten.........	W	74	$\alpha A2$ to mp	3.1583	19.255
			$\beta A15$ (electrolytic), actually W_3O	5.038	18.97

TABLE 16-3. UNIT-CELL CONSTANTS FOR ELEMENTS, 1953 (*Continued*)

Element	Symbol	Atomic number	Lattice type	Edge length a; a, c; a, b, c	Density (x-ray)
Uranium.........	U	92	αA20 to 640°	2.85, 5.865, 4.945	18.97
			βA21 640 to 760°	10.759, 5.656	18.11
			γA2 760° to mp	3.418	
Vanadium........	V	23	A2	3.034	6.015
Xenon...........	Xe	54	A1	6.24 (88°K)	3.56
Ytterbium........	Yb	70	A1	5.468	
Yttrium..........	Y	39	A3	3.629, 5.750	4.34
Zinc..............	Zn	30	A3	2.6595, 4.9368	7.128
Zirconium........	Zr	40	αA3 to 862°	3.223, 5.123	6.525
			βA2 862° to mp	3.61	6.39

to four cube diagonals. This relationship is shown by the models constructed from a Paul Bon Hop set in Figs. 263*b* and *c*. Several metals crystallize in both ways as polymorphic forms stable over different temperature ranges. Occasionally diffraction patterns for cobalt show lines for both A1 and A3, with some of the lines for the hexagonal form broadened. This is caused by occasional faults in the stacking of layers, from

(*b*)   (*c*)

FIG. 263*b*, *c*. Models for cubic and hexagonal close-packed crystals.

ABABAB . . . to BCBCBC . . . to ABCABC, etc. The type A2 body-centered cubic is characterized by a coordination number of 8 and a less tightly packed structure. The simple cubic lattice representing still looser packing is not represented by any element but requires ions of opposite charge for its stabilization.

Among the true metals there are only a few departures from these simple structures. Some cases of complex structures are actually not anomalous; β-manganese with 20 atoms per unit cell has a structure intermediate between body-centered and face-centered structures. Similarly one of the supposed modifications of tungsten (A15) has two kinds of atom, one with 12 neighbors at 2.816 and the other with 2 neighbors at 2.519, 4 at 2.816, and 8 at 3.025 A, again a transition between face-centered cubic and body-centered cubic. However, in 1954, Hägg and Schönberg proved this alleged electrolytic form to be W_3O, with 6W and 2O atoms distributed at random over 8 positions in the unit cell.

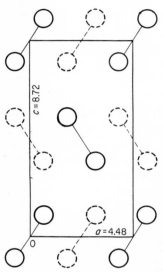

Fig. 264. Structure of crystalline bromine projected upon the 010 plane. Full circles represent atoms in the plane of the paper; broken circles represent atoms above and below the plane of the paper by $b/2$. The Br_2 molecules are indicated by the connecting lines. (*Vonnegut and Warren.*)

The B subgroup metals Zn, Cd, Hg, Al, Ga, In, Tl, Si, Ge, Sn, Pb, As, Sb, Bi, Se, Te as a class are far more complicated. Al, Tl, and Pb actually are close-packed but still possess some properties of both true and B subgroup metals.

There is a veritable mine of information in the assembled data of crystal structures of the elements. Only a few of the generalizations can be considered here: for example, the crystallized rare gases of the atmosphere in Group 0 are face-centered cubic except helium, which is hexagonal close-packed very probably; the alkali metals and barium are body-centered cubic; Group II metals are hexagonal close-packed except strontium and barium with a transition at calcium, which is dimorphic, and mercury; Group V and VI metals are body-centered cubic; Group VIII triad metals, copper, silver, and gold, are close-packed as face-centered cubic or hexagonal. The periodic table might be divided into four classes of element. The nonmetallic elements in classes I and II present a number of interesting problems. The crystals of the rare gases exist only at very low temperatures, and hence the forces holding the atoms in ordered array in a three-dimensional lattice must be exceedingly weak. An examination of the models for crystalline iodine, bromine, and chlorine shows that the molecules I_2, Br_2, and Cl_2 retain a very definite identity in the lattice (Fig. 264). Thus each atom has one close twin neighbor as written electronically : $\overset{..}{I} : \overset{..}{I} :$; or a completed electron shell 8 minus 7, the number of electrons in the outer shells of these halogen atoms equals 1, the number of neighbors, or the coordination number. This suggests an $8 - n$ rule, which may be tested now for other elements. Selenium crystallizes as a series of endless spiral chains (Fig. 265) by actual analysis; here $8 - 6 = 2$ neighbors or a chain—:Se:Se:Se:Se:—with each selenium atom showing an electron pair on either side with other atoms.

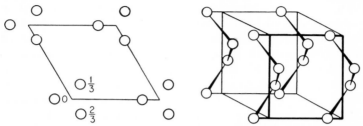

FIG. 265. Plan and perspective diagram of the hexagonal unit cell of the structure of selenium and tellurium. The spiral chains extend indefinitely through the crystal in the vertical direction.

Arsenic, for which $8 - 5 = 3$, would be expected to crystallize in sheets, with each atom having 3 neighbors; and so it does. Carbon $(8 - 4 = 4)$ should have each atom tetrahedrally surrounded by 4 other carbon atoms. This is precisely the structure of diamond (Fig. 266).

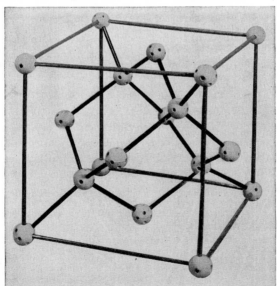

FIG. 266. The unit crystal cell of diamond (type A4).

So far the $8 - n$ rule has not failed, for these cases of homopolar combinations. But when we try to apply the principle to a Group II element such as calcium or zinc, we should expect a coordination number $8 - 2 = 6$, whereas actually it is 12 for face-centered cubic or hexagonal close-packed. This discrepancy in the fact that there are not enough electrons to account for the large number of equidistant lattice neighbors seems to reside, therefore, in what may be termed the property of being a metal, one of the states that will be considered later. Zinc and cadmium, though metallic in nature, still seem to retain some of the character of Group IV, V, and VI elements. These are hexagonal but with an axial ratio $c/a = 1.856$ and 1.886, respectively, instead of 1.633 for the closest packing of spheres in the hexagonal close-packed arrangement. Thus of the 12 neighbors of each atom, 6 are closer than the remaining 6 (2.660 and 2.907 A for zinc, 2.973 and 3.287 A for cadmium); the closest 6, therefore, represent an example of the $8 - n$ rule (homopolar bonds), and the other 6 are linked by metallic bonds. Mercury has a similar coordination in its rhombohedral lattice of 6 at 2.999 and 6 at 3.463 A.

It is obvious that very precise measurements of unit-cell dimensions of elements or compounds at different temperatures will permit an evaluation of the linear coefficients of expansion and a comparison of lattice expansion with expansion data for massive specimens. In many cases the x-ray data have been of great practical value. Typical data are:

Rubidium	$+19$ to $-97.5°$	6.6×10^{-5}[†]
Lithium	$+20$ to $-183°$	16×10^{-5}[‡]
Magnesium	$+50$ to $+250°$	27.7×10^{-6} perpendicular to c[§]
		29.3×10^{-6} parallel to c
Uranium	$+20$ to $720°$	23×10^{-6} along a axis[¶]
		4.6×10^{-6} along c axis

[†] K. Lonsdale and W. Hume-Rothery, *Phil. Mag.* (7), **36**, 799 (1945).
[‡] *Ibid.*, p. 842.
[§] J. D. Hanawalt and L. K. Frevel, *Z. Krist.*, **98**, 84 (1937).
[¶] J. Thewlis, *Acta Cryst.*, **5**, 790 (1952).

Questions naturally arise as to why an element crystallizes as it does, what are the relationships between structure and properties, and what can be done about predicting the structures of other elements or the behavior in alloys and compounds. The answers to these and many more questions are the province of the young and incomplete science of

TABLE 16-4. TYPES AND CLASSES OF CRYSTAL STRUCTURE*

Type	Formula	Classes
B	RX	41
C	R_2X, RX_2	61
D	R_mX_n	52
E	$R(MX_2)_n$	17
F	$R_n(MX_3)_p$	25
G	$R_n(MX_4)_p$	48
H	$R_x(MX_m)_y$	36
I	Hydrates and ammoniates	58

* Wyckoff, "Crystal Structures."

crystal chemistry, which has grown directly from experimental x-ray determinations.

Inorganic Compounds. Several hundred inorganic compounds have now been subjected to crystal-structure examination and more or less complete analysis by x-rays. These data are readily available for reference in Wyckoff's "Crystal Structures" (three volumes published in loose-leaf form), in the monumental "Strukturbericht" (seven volumes for data through 1939) of Ewald and Hermann, which appeared serially in the *Zeitschrift für Krystallographie* and is now being brought up to date through the sponsorship of the International Union of Crystallography, and in current periodicals such as *Acta Crystallographica*. Hence only the general types and relationships need be considered here. The Wyckoff classification logically based on the earlier Ewald-Hermann system is indicated in Table 16-4, which shows the number of classes under each type of general inorganic formula. The list does not include hundreds of compounds which have been subjected to crystal analysis but for which results are still incomplete owing to extreme structure complexity, such as some of the natural silicates, or to very complex or poorly defined chemical formulas.

A general impression to be gained from a tabulation of x-ray crystal analyses is that the field of inorganic chemistry is a hopelessly complex one from the structural standpoint. Thus for the various classes of compound there are the definitely classified types shown in Table 16-4, to which must be added numerous highly characteristic

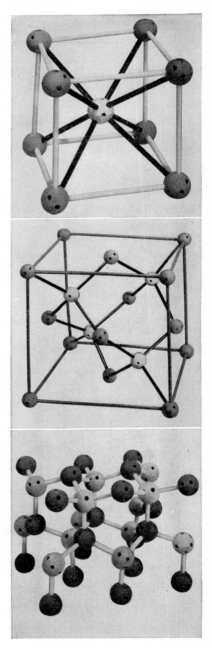

FIG. 267. Models of (*a*, above) cesium chloride; (*b*, center) zinc blende, ZnS; (*c*, below) wurtzite, ZnS.

TABLE 16-5. RÉSUMÉ OF CRYSTAL STRUCTURES OF INORGANIC COMPOUNDS
(Binary compounds RX)

Type	Typical compound	Lattice	Space-group	Number of mols, Z	Cell dimensions	Remarks; other examples
B1	NaCl	Simple cubic (pseudo)	$Fm3m$	4	5.628	(Li, Na, K, Rb) (F, Cl, Br, I); CsF, β-CsCl; NH$_4$ (Cl, Br, I); Ag (F, Cl, Br); (Mg, Ca, Sr, Ba, Cd, Mn, Fe, Co, Ni, Sm) O; (Mg, Ca, Sr, Eu, Ba, Pb, Mn) S; β (Na, K, Rb) (SH, SeH) (Mg, Ca, Sr, Ba, Yb, Eu, Pb, Mn) Se; (Ca, Sr, Ba, Eu, Yb, Sb, Pb) Te; (Sc, Ti, Zr, V, Cb) N; (Ti, Zr, V, Cb, Ta) C; LiH; LiD; (Na, K) CN at 25°, (La, Ce, Pr, Nd) (N, P, As, Sb, Br)
B2	CsCl (Fig. 267a)	Bcc	$Pm3m$	1	4.110	(α-Rb, Cs, NH$_4$, Tl) (Cl, Br, I); CsSH; CsCN; TlCN; TlSb, TlBi, Li (Ag, Hg, Tl); Cu (Zn, Pd); Ag (Mg, Zn, Cd, La, Ce); Au (Mg, Zn, Cd); Be (Co, Cu, Pd); Mg (Hg, La, Ce, Pr, Tl, Sr); CaTl, SrTl, Zn (La, Ce, Pr); Cd (La, Ce, Pr) ; Al (Ni, Nd)
B3	ZnS (zinc blende) (Fig. 267b)	Diamond cubic	$F\bar{4}3m$	4	5.42	Cu (F, Cl, Br, I); AgI, (Be, Zn, Cd, Hg) (S, Se, Te); AlP, GaP, AlAs, GaAs, AlSb, GaSb, InSb, SnSb, β-CSi— 30 or more compounds
B4	ZnS (wurtzite) (Fig. 267c)	Hexagonal	$C6mc$	2	$a = 3.84$ $c = 6.28$	NH$_4$F, BeO, ZnO, ZnS, CdS, MgTe, CdSe, AlN, AgI, GaN, InN, CuH
B5	Carborundum III	Hexagonal	$C6mc$	4	$a = 3.095$ $c = 10.09$	Also other rhombohedral types, all regularly repeated mixed sequences of hexagonal and cubic closed-packed ions or tetrahedra.
B6	Carborundum II	Hexagonal	$C6mc$	6	$a = 3.095$ $c = 15.17$	
B7	Carborundum I	Hexagonal	$R3m$	15	$a = 3.095$ $c = 37.95$	
B8	Nickel arsenide, NiAs	Hexagonal	$C6/mmc$	2	$a = 3.61$ $c = 5.03$	(Fe, Co, Ni, V, Cr) S; (Fe, Co, Ni) Se; (Co, Ni) Te; NiAs (Cr, Mn, Fe, Co, Ni) Sb; (Ni, Cn, Pt, Au) Sn. (Complicated by superlattices and variable composition FeS$_{1+x}$, Fe$_{1.5}$Sb, etc.)
B9	Cinnabar, HgS	Hexagonal	$C3_12$	6	$a = 4.14$ $c = 9.49$	Layer, but deformed B1
B10	PH$_4$I	Tetragonal	$P4/nmm$	2	$a = 6.34$ $c = 4.62$	NH$_4$SH; β-NH$_4$ (Br, I); N (CH$_3$)$_4$ (Cl, Br, I, ClO$_4$, MnO$_4$) distorted B2 (Pb, Sn, Pd) O, LiOH
B11	PbO (red)	Tetragonal	$P4/nmm$	2	$a = 3.98$ $c = 5.01$	
B12	BN	Hexagonal	$C6/mmc$	4	$a = 2.51$ $c = 6.69$	Same as A9
B13	Millerite, NiS	Rhombohedral	$R3m$	3	5.65	Chains—changes to B8

TABLE 16-5. RÉSUMÉ OF CRYSTAL STRUCTURES OF INORGANIC
COMPOUNDS (*Continued*)

Type	Typical compound	Lattice	Space-group	Number of mols, Z	Cell dimensions	Remarks; other examples
B14	FeAs	Orthorhombic	$Pmcn$	4	$a = 3.67$ $b = 6.02$ $c = 5.43$	Similar to B8
B15	FeB	Orthorhombic	$Pbnm$	4	$a = 4.053$ $b = 5.495$	B in three-sided prism in zig-zag chains parallel to c
B16	GeS	Rhombic	$Pbnm$	4	$a = 4.29$ $b = 10.42$ $c = 3.64$	
B17	PtS, cooper-ite	Tetragonal	$P4/mmc$	2	$a = 3.47$ $c = 6.10$	Similar to B3 NH_4CN, nearly B2 with CN vibrating along c Pt, fc. S in tetrahedral holes
B18	CuS, covel-line	Hexagonal	$C6/mmc$	6	$a = 3.80$ $c = 16.4$	Cu and S each in 2 groups
B19	AuCd	Orthorhombic	$Pmcm$	2	$a = 3.144$ $b = 4.851$ $c = 4.745$	Transition between B2 and A3 CN 14
B20	FeSi	Cubic	$P2_13$	4	4.467	7-coordination
B21	CO	Cubic	$P2_13$	4	5.63	CO molecules
B22	KSH	Rhombohedral	$R\bar{3}m$	1	4.374	α(Na, K, Rb) (SH, SeH); pseudo cell like B1
B23	α-AgI	Cubic		2	5.034	Ag^+ ions at random; disorder
B24	TlF	Rhombic	$Fmmm$	4	$a = 5.180$ $b = 5.495$ $c = 6.080$	Deformed B1, layer
B25	γ-NH_4Br	Tetragonal	$P4/nmm$	2	$a = 6.007$ $c = 4.035$	Rotating NH_4^+
B26	CuO (tenor-ite)	Monoclinic	$C2/c$	4	$a = 4.653$ $b = 3.410$ $c = 5.108$ $\beta = 99°24'$	CN 4
B27	FeB	Orthorhombic	$Pbnm$	. . . . . .	. . . .	Fe resonating between 2 va-lences (Pauling)
B28	FeSi	Cubic	$P2_13$	4	4.438	Cf. B20 (Fe, Co, Mn, Cr, Ni) Si
B29	SnS	Rhombic	$Pmcn$	4	$a = 3.98$ $b = 4.33$ $c = 11.18$	Deformed B1, CN 6; also $PbSnS_2$
B30	MgZn	Hexagonal	$C6/mmc$	48	$a = 10.66$ $c = 17.16$	Like C14 ($MgZn_2$) Layers—Mg-Zn-Mg
B31	MnP	Rhombic	$Pbnm$	4	$a = 5.905$ $b = 5.249$ $c = 3.167$	Closely similar to B8 P in zigzag chains
B32	NaTl	Cubic	. . . .	8	7.742	Na and Tl both A4 interpene-trating $\frac{1}{2} \frac{1}{2} \frac{1}{2}$. Also, LiZn, LiCd, LiGa, LiIn, NaIn, LiAl
B33	TlI	Rhombic	$Amma$	4	$a = 5.24$ $b = 4.57$ $c = 12.92$	Layer
B34	PdS	Tetragonal	$P4_2/m$	8	$a = 6.43$ $c = 6.53$	Similar to B17
B35	CoSn	Hexagonal	$C6/mmm$	3	$a = 5.268$ $c = 4.249$	PtTl, FeSn

TABLE 16-5. RÉSUMÉ OF CRYSTAL STRUCTURES OF INORGANIC
COMPOUNDS (Continued)

Type	Typical compound	Lattice	Space-group	Number of mols, Z	Cell dimensions	Remarks; other examples
B36	LiOH.6H$_2$O	Monoclinic	$C2/m$	4	$a = 7.37$ $b = 8.26$ $c = 3.19$ $\beta = 110°18'$	
B37	TlSe	Tetragonal	$I4/mcm$	8	$a = 8.02$ $c = 7.00$	
B38	(Na, K) CN low temperature	Orthorhombic	Imm	2	$a = 3.74$ $b = 4.71$ $c = 6.16$	
B39	Hg$_2$Cl$_2$	Tetragonal	$I4/mmm$	2	$a = 4.47$ $c = 10.89$	Hg$_2$(F$_2$, Cl$_2$, Br$_2$, I$_2$)
B40	PbO (yellow)	Orthorhombic	Pba	4	$a = 5.48$ $b = 4.74$ $c = 5.88$	Sheets of lead atoms along c axis with every second interspace containing puckered sheet of oxygen
B41	AsS (realgar)	....	$P2_1/n$	16	$a = 9.27$ $b = 13.50$ $c = 6.56$ $\beta = 106°37'$	4 As$_4$S$_4$ groups; related to A$_2$S$_3$ (orpiment) structure

structures for individual compounds reported since 1940 by workers throughout the world.

Thus almost 350 crystal types, not counting organic compounds, have been established in the Ewald-Hermann classification, with the possibility of many more as further crystal analyses are reported. In Table 16-5 are listed the data for the 41 types of simple binary RX compounds as classified in the "Strukturbericht," with some additions to illustrate the general method. At first sight the fact alone that there are at least 41 ways in which compounds whose molecules consist of only two atoms may crystallize is discouraging evidence of the extraordinary complexity in nature's building plans. But there is difficulty only so long as strict adherence to traditional concepts of chemistry incorrectly applied to the solid state is maintained. The new and still incomplete science of crystal chemistry has arisen as one of the most fascinating fields in science directly from experimental x-ray diffraction determinations of structure. It has demanded a profound reorientation of accepted principles of chemistry. Instead of chaos a remarkable orderliness is indicated as crystal-structure plans are laid down in obedience to geometric laws far more fundamental even than the concepts of chemical valences and rigid stoichiometric proportions. And the 41 types of RX compounds are accounted for, not as a complication, but as a simplification. Details of all other types and classes of crystal structure listed in Table 16-4 are presented in Wyckoff's "Crystal Structures." Several succeeding chapters deal with the crystal chemistry of elements and inorganic compounds, minerals and silicates, alloys, organic compounds, and natural materials.

Very little was known prior to World War II about the compounds and their crystal structures of such an element as uranium. Coincidental with the development of atomic energy from the fission of uranium atom nuclei, a great advance was made on uranium and the other so-called $5f$ elements (referring to atomic structure), especially by W. H. Zachariasen of the University of Chicago. The structures of more than 30 compounds of uranium, plutonium, and thorium, published in a series of papers in *Acta Crystallographica*, have contributed greatly to an understanding of the chemical properties and valences of these elements.

A considerable number of inorganic compounds have been completely analyzed by Fourier methods during 1948–1953. Here interest has been in accurate measurement of bond length (compared with sum of atomic radii), angles, peculiarities of packing, resonance and transformations, and defects and explanation of physical and chemical properties, along with crystalline identification and space groups.

CHAPTER 17

CRYSTAL CHEMISTRY

The complexities that confront the crystal analyst when he attempts to generalize on the modes of crystal construction have been amply demonstrated by the data of the preceding chapter. In spite of the immensity of the field, however, a brilliant chapter in science is being written. From this work it is possible to advance a theory of why crystals are built as they are, which not only explains at least the simpler types of structure already known semiquantitatively but allows even the prediction of new structures and properties. The concepts of the new wave mechanics have assisted materially in these developments, and great further progress may be expected. The fundamental unit to be considered in these structural inquiries is, of course, the atom, which may be now pictured roughly (see Chap. 6) as a nucleus surrounded by shells of diffuse negative electricity, which is denser the nearer the nucleus. On the older theory each shell is thought of as composed of a set of Bohr orbits. Thus the atom has a size, and since it certainly is not rigid, it must have a certain degree of compressibility and deformability. It has been amply demonstrated many times that the chemical and crystallographic properties of atoms depend on the size and particularly on the condition of the outer shells of electrons, including what is now termed the hybridization of atomic orbitals. Each ion or atom in a compound must be considered as forming a lattice of its own, the interpenetration of the various lattices resulting in the structure of the compound. Or it may be that a whole molecule may be placed at the points in a lattice. In the past 10 years the scope of crystal chemistry has greatly expanded, but only a few of the simpler and most fundamental generalizations need be considered here.

Types of Crystal in Terms of Bonding Forces. A careful survey of all crystal-structure data leads to the conclusion that all crystalline substances may be classed under four principal types according to the types of combination of atoms into molecules and solid crystals: ionic, or heteropolar; homopolar, or covalent (sharing of electron pairs); molecular; metallic. A structure characterized by a single kind of principal bond is called *homodesmic*, and one with mixed types is called *heterodesmic*, in which case the weakest binding force determines the crystalline character.

This does not mean that the division lines are clear-cut, for many substances may be thought of as in the transition zone between two or more types. Bernal therefore added three of the most important intermediate classes, silicates, layer lattices, and metalloids. The fundamental classification and properties assembled by Bernal[1] years ago as shown in Table 17-1 is still basically sound, although mixed types of bond are now more readily understood.

Ionic, or Heteropolar, Combination. There remains little doubt that in a large number of crystals the atoms are really ions in the familiar chemical sense and that they are held together in space with requisite rigidity by electrostatic forces of attraction between positively and negatively charged particles, inversely as the square of the distance. When the outer electron shells of positive and negative ions are in close proximity, however, a repulsion sets in inversely at about the ninth power of the distance between them. There are no valence bonds, no flexibility of electronic structure, and no electronic conductivity. Thus in a crystal like rock salt a condition is easily reached like

$$Na^+Cl^- \rightarrow \begin{matrix} Na^+Cl^- \\ Cl^-Na^+ \end{matrix} \rightarrow \begin{matrix} Cl^-Na^+Cl^- \\ Na^+Cl^-Na^+ \\ Cl^-Na^+Cl^- \end{matrix} \rightarrow$$

and so on, till the whole single crystal is thus constructed. Thus sodium chloride diffracts x-rays in a way that leads to the assignment of a structure in which each sodium ion is not bound to a single chlorine ion as in the simple chemical molecule (vapor state) but exerts its attraction on six equidistant chlorine neighbors, and each chlorine ion is surrounded by six sodium ions. Stated otherwise, each ion has a *coordination number* of 6. Thus each ion tends to surround itself with as many oppositely charged ions as possible. In the electrically neutral crystal there are no pairs of sodium and chlorine atoms or ions, but simply an equal number of oppositely charged ions. In a sense, the chemical molecule seems to be lost sight of, and proper formulas would seem to be Na_6Cl and $NaCl_6$. However, an analogy cited by Sir William Bragg serves to clarify the situation. Several couples of men and women go in to dinner and are seated at a circular table. Each man now has a lady on either side (or coordination number 2), and the identity of the original couple is obscured though by no means destroyed on account of the seating arrangement.

It follows that the structure of an ionic crystal is determined very largely by the purely geometric concept that each ion is surrounded by the largest possible number of oppositely charged neighbors, consistent with the requirement that electrical neutrality be maintained for the

[1] Encyclopaedia Britannica, 14th ed., Vol. 23, p. 857.

TABLE 17-1. CLASSIFICATION OF CRYSTALS

Crystal type	Crystal units	Type of binding	Characteristic properties				Typical crystals
			Optical	Electrical	Thermal	Mechanical	
Ionic..........	Simple and complex ions	Electrical attraction between ions of opposite signs (e/r^2) balanced by repulsion of negative outer shells $\left(\dfrac{-e}{r^9}\right)$	Transparent; absorption invisible color if present is due to atoms	Moderate insulators in high fields; conduct by transfer of ions	Fairly high melting point; ionization occurs in liquid and vapor	Hardness increasing with higher ionization. Tendency to fracture by cleavage	NaCl, CaF₂, CaCO₃, K₂SO₄, (NH₄)₂PtCl₆
Silicate.........	O²⁻ or F⁻ ions Sc⁴⁺ or Be²⁺ or Al³⁺ and other positive ions	Weak to moderate polarization	In short infrared due to complex ions. In long infrared Refractivity due to crystal lattice due to positive ions	When polarization is slight they dissolve with ionization in ionizing solvents (water); when stronger are insoluble	Very high melting points, glasses formed on cooling of melt	Very hard with tendency to cleave or fracture conchoidally	Olivine, Mg₂SiO₄; Cyanite, Al₂SiO₅; Garnet, R^II₃R^III₂Si₃O₁₂; Spinel, Al₂MgO₄; Corundum, Al₂O₃
Homopolar (covalent)	Atoms of the fourth group and groups on either side of it	Homopolar bonds throughout or strongly polarized ionic binding	Transparent with high refractivity or opaque metalloidal	Diamond is a perfect insulator. The others conduct metalloidally. Very insoluble	Very high melting points with tendency to vaporize except in more metalloidal	Very hard. Hardness less for metalloidal types	Diamond, C; Zinc Blende, ZnS; Wurtzite, ZnS; Carborundum, CSi

Type	Constituents	Binding	Optical	Electrical	Melting point	Hardness	Examples
Molecular van der Waals	Inert gas atoms. Non-polar and polar molecules	Van der Waals forces or residual electric fields between molecular poles	Transparent optical properties due to molecules and similar to gas and liquid phases	Insulators except when very polar; soluble in non-ionizing (molecular) solvents except when polar	Melting point very low with neutral atoms, rises with heavier molecules and polar molecules	Very soft, hardness increasing with polarity of molecules. Deformation plastic	Argon, A; CO_2; Ice H_2O; Paraffins, C_nH_{2m+2}; Calomel, Hg_2Cl_2
Layer	Strongly polarizing and easily polarized ions	In layers. Homopolar or polarized ionic. Between layers molecular	As homopolar	Various, similar to both molecular and homopolar	Various, similar to both molecular and homopolar	Cleaving readily in layers which are soft and flexible	Graphite, C; CdI_2
Metallic	Positive ions and electron gas	Electrical attraction between positive ions and electron gas	Opaque (due to free electrons) with selective reflection in infrared	Conductors, conductivity inversely proportional to number of free electrons. Soluble in acids where H^+ ions absorb free electrons	Moderate to very high melting points. Long liquid interval	Moderate hardness increased by alloying. Elastic but yield by glide plane slipping when overstressed	Copper, iron; Iron, sodium; Zinc
Metalloidal	Metal atoms and atoms of the sulfur and arsenic type	Mixture of homopolar ionic and metallic binding	Opaque metallic or transparent with high refractivity and color	Medium to bad conductors. Soluble only with decomposition	Tendency to vaporize or decompose at high temperatures	Moderately hard to soft. Properties a mixture of those of other types	Nickel arsenide, NiAs; Fahlertz, $R^{II}_2SbS_2$; Pyrites, FeS_2

crystal as a whole. Sodium chloride and cesium chloride are closely related and would be expected to crystallize alike. However, they crystallize differently, simply because the question of geometric size enters. Six chlorine ions are octahedrally arranged around each sodium ion; but eight chlorine ions are cubically arranged around each cesium ion because there is room for them.

Application of Ionic-crystal Chemistry Laws to Prediction of Properties. Goldschmidt has shown that the hardness and related cohesive properties of ionic crystals depend directly upon the electrostatic forces between ions. The hardness of crystals increases with decreasing distance between the ion centers, the charge being kept constant; and the hardness increases with increasing ionic charge when the distance is kept constant; for example:

Property	BeO	MgO	CaO	SrO	BaO	NaF	MgO	ScN	TiC
Distance R–X....	1.65	2.10	2.40	2.57	2.77	2.13	2.10	2.23	2.23
Hardness.........	9.0	6.5	4.5	3.5	3.3	3.2	6.5	7–8	8–9

Partial correlations have been made between ionic structure and optical properties,[1] elastic constants, cohesion, melting point, and solubility.

Thus in a series of related salts the melting point decreases, and the coefficient of expansion increases with increasing interatomic distance:

Property	NaF	NaCl	NaBr	NaI	NaF	KF	RbF	CsF
Distance...............	2.31	2.79	2.94	3.18	2.31	2.66	2.82	2.98
Melting point..........	988	801	740	660	988	846	775	684
Coefficient of expansion, $\alpha \times 10^6$.............	39	40	43	48				

Covalent, or Homopolar, Combination. In terms of modern theories of valence this means that atoms are held together by sharing electrons, usually in pairs called covalences. The stable diatomic molecules such as H_2, O_2, N_2, etc., and H_2O, CO_2 are built up in this fashion in order to complete the various quantum electron shells. In aliphatic organic molecules the carbon atoms form long chains by homopolar bonds. The best example is in diamond, where each carbon atom is sharing electron pairs with four others, so that this linking is extended indefinitely in all directions to the limits of the crystal itself, which thus may be considered a single solid molecule. The word "adamantine" has been ascribed to this class by Bernal.

[1] See, for example, Wooster, Relation between Double Refraction and Crystal Structure, Z. Krist., **80**, 495 (1931).

The covalent bond is distinguished from the ionic bond in many ways. The latter is essentially undirected, hence spherically distributed, since it is distributed by coordination over as many neighbors of opposite charge as can be packed around a central ion, whereas the number of homopolar bonds by which a given atom can be linked to others is limited.

Saturation of valence is a familiar aspect—the way in which, when an atom has made a number of bonds with its neighbors equal to its valence, it cannot make additional bonds to other atoms. If the valences are saturated, the electronic structure is in a sense frozen in position, not capable of easy change, whereas if it has unsaturated valences, it is easy for other bonds to form and there is a certain flexibility in structure. It follows that, if an atom in a crystal finds itself near just enough neighbors to saturate its valences, the approach of an additional atom will have quite different results from what it would have had if there had been fewer neighbors. These facts have important implications in mechanical properties and deformation of crystals.

This type of bond is the essence of the $8 - n$ rule, discussed in Chap. 16. Homopolar compounds differ also from ionic in that they are nonconductors in the molten state. They are insoluble in water, but so also are many ionic compounds. The optical properties differ because the character of the binding is such that electrons are linked, not in atomic orbitals of individual ions, but in diatomic orbitals embracing two neighboring atoms, though varying widely in tightness in such a series as diamond to tin. On this account, the optical absorption of solutions of ionic compounds is essentially the same as that of the solid, whereas in the homopolar compounds a great change results from disappearance of the diatomic orbitals.

It is now generally recognized that, given two electrons with opposed spins, an atom can form an electron pair or covalent bond for each stable orbital (the wave function associated with the orbital motion of an electron). Hydrogen with only one stable orbital can form only one covalent bond; carbon with four electrons in the L shell can and does form four covalent bonds. A molecule is the more stable the greater the number of electron-pair bonds; thus $:N:::N:$ is more stable than $:\overset{\cdot}{N}:\overset{\cdot}{N}:$, and the former is probably the predominating structure of the nitrogen molecule. The energy of a covalent bond has been shown to be largely the energy of resonance of two electrons between two atoms. Such bonds may be directed in space where the p orbitals (s is spherical) are involved, since it was found by Slater that these tend to be at right angles to each other. Hence the measurement of *bond angles* has been one of the important contributions of crystal analysis. For a large number of substances these have been found to be between 90 and 110 deg (water, H—O—H 105 deg, H—S—H 92 deg, etc.), the discrepancy being accounted **for** either by steric effects or by a partial ionic character of the bond.   Quantum-mechanical treatment of orbitals and related magnetic measurements have accounted remarkably well for double and triple bonds; tetrahedral bonds; octahedral bonds in $[Co(NH_3)_6]^{3+}$, $(PdCl_6)^{2-}$, etc.; square bonds as in $[Ni(CN)]_4^{2-}$, $(PdCl_4)^{2-}$, and $PdCl_2$, which polymerizes into a chain of nearly perfect square configuration

and the configuration of such polyhalide ions as $(ICl_4)^-$, which actually has two unshared electron pairs of the iodine atoms octahedrally arranged above and below the plane of the square.

It is perhaps strange that the homopolar bond is characteristic of the ZnS structure (also AgI, AlP, etc.), which is like that of diamond except that adjacent atoms are of opposite kind (four sulfur atoms around each zinc atom, and vice versa).   It is sufficient that the total number of valence electrons is just four times the total number of atoms, and it is for this reason that the homopolar bond is practically invariably associated with tetrahedral coordination.

Diamond C, silicon, and germanium all crystallize with the same diamond structure, each atom having four well-defined valence bonds to four adjacent neighbors.   It would be expected that these elements would all be electrical insulators like diamond, but silicon and germanium are actually two of the best-known semiconductors.   Another explanation besides the simple atomic picture must be introduced, and this is the so-called band theory, explained in a later section.

The single- and triple-electron homopolar bonds are predicted by quantum theory, as is also their rarity.   These bonds can exist between atoms A and B, respectively, if $A \cdot + B$, and $A + \cdot B$, and $A : + \cdot B$, and $A \cdot + :B$ have essentially the same energy.   The compound B_2H_6 has two single-electron bonds between B and H, resonating over the six hydrogen atoms and increasing thereby the stability of the molecule. Magnetic measurements on crystals as a valuable aid in crystal-structure analysis are of especial significance for the homopolar bond.   Paired electrons with opposing spins contribute nothing to the magnetic moment of a molecule or complex ion, so that observed moments determine at once the number of unpaired electrons present.

Polarization and Ionic-Covalent Bonds.   Many inorganic compounds display properties that are characteristic of both ionic and covalent bonds.   Modern quantum mechanics provides for resonance of a system between structures I and II, for example, so that over a period of time a bond may represent a mixture of two types. Polarization is really another way of expressing this possibility. For example, if a small, highly charged positive ion is combined with a larger diffuse negative ion like S^{2-}, this would be not only activated but actually distorted, since the negative shell would be pulled toward the cation and the nucleus repelled. For a series of ions with the same charge, the smaller the ionic radius, the greater the polarizing effect of the ion and the higher the ionization potential. Of the alkali metals Li^+ has the greatest polarizing effect and the greatest tendency to form a covalent bond. For two ions of the same size, one with 18 electrons in the outer shell exhibits a greater polarizing effect and has a higher ionization potential than an ion with an 8-electron shell. For example, Ca^{2+} (radius 0.98 A) and Cd^{2+} (0.99 A) have the same ionic radii, but Ca^{2+} has an 8- and Cd^{2+} an 18-electron shell. The latter is more strongly polarizing, is more likely to form a covalent bond, and, as a matter of fact, gives rise to layer lattices. The larger the negative ion, the more easily may it be polarized and the lower is its electron affinity. Thus, of the halogens, the iodide ion is most easily polarized and most likely to form a covalent bond. In Table 17-2 are correlated polarizabilities,

TABLE 17-2

O^{2-}	F^-	Ne	Na^+	Mg^{2+}	Al^{3+}
S^{2-}	Cl^-	A	K^+	Ca^{2+}	Sc^{3+}
Se^{2-}	Br^-	Xe	Rb^+	Sr^{2+}	Y^{3+}
Te^{2-}	I^-	Kr	Cs^+	Ba^{2+}	La^{3+}

Decreasing polarizability
Increasing polarizing power
Decreasing radius

(vertical axis, upward) Decreasing polarizability / Increasing polarizing power / Decreasing radius

(horizontal axis, rightward) Decreasing polarizability / Increasing polarizing power / Decreasing radius

polarizing power, and sizes of a number of ions. The importance of this whole matter lies in the fact that compounds with purely ionic bonds may be expected to obey a series of generalizations and have essentially constant radii and properties in agreement with predictions, while discrepancies are to be ascribed to this admixture of bond types. Thus the distance between the nuclei of two atoms R and X joined by a covalent bond will generally be smaller than the distance between the nuclei of the ions of the same elements. In fact, X atoms may be drawn in so closely around R that the coordination number may be decreased. The compounds CaO, CaS, CaSe, and CaTe all crystallize like NaCl (coordination number 6); but CdS, CdSe, and CdTe crystallize like ZnS (coordination number 4) though Ca^{2+} and Cd^{2+} have the same size. ZnS is a typical case of mixed ionic and covalent bond. Pauling calculates that the salts of alkali and alkaline-earth metals are more than 50 per cent ionic except Li—I, Li—C, Li—S; Be—F 79%, Be—O 63%, Be—Cl 44%; Be—Br 35%; Be—I 22%; B—F 63%, B—O 44%, B—Cl 22%; C—F 44% (highest ionic); Si—F 70%, Si—Cl 30%, Si—O (silicates) 50%; Ag—F 70%, Ag—Cl 30%, Ag—Br 23%, Ag—I 11%.

Resonance and Covalent Mixed Single and Double Bonds.   Attention already has been directed to one type of mixed bond, the covalent-ionic, representing resonance between the two types of structure.   Another type of resonance is involved in some covalent single bonds that seem to possess some double-bond character.   This is of special significance in C—C linkages, making possible the exact equivalence of the six carbon atoms in the benzene ring; these cases will be discussed in Chap. 20. Attention here may be directed to fluorides and chlorides of silicon, phosphorus, sulfur, germanium, arsenic, tin, and antimony, for the interatomic distances such as Si—Cl are all shorter (2.00 A) than the sum of the covalent radii in a single covalent bond (2.16 A).   It has been demonstrated amply that the bond resonates between the two bond types Si—Cl and Si$=$Cl (the dash representing covalent bonds with partial ionic character).   The same is true of the tetrahedral ions SiO_4^{4-}, PO_4^{3-}, SO_4^{2-}, and ClO_4^-† and of a variety of other acid ions.

	Si—O	P—O	S—O	Cl—O
Observed............	1.60	1.55	1.51	1.48
Radius sum..........	1.83	1.76	1.70	1.65

Finally some of the difficult questions that arise in connection with covalent complexes of the transition elements, *e.g.*, cobaltammines, $[Fe(CN)_6]_4^-$, $Ni(CO)_4$, are explained by the fact that these atoms can form multiple covalent bonds with electron-accepting groups by making use of electrons and orbitals of the *shell within the valence shell.*

The Metallic Bond.   Metallic combination, which is considered in detail in Chap. 19, occurs when atoms tend to lose electrons easily. Typical metal structures have been described in the preceding chapter. The best simple picture of metallic structure is that of a lattice of positive ions held together by an electron gas in which no particular electron belongs exclusively to a particular metal atom.

This arrangement confers neither spatial nor numerical limitations on the metallic bond; hence, as expected, high coordination numbers are the general rule.   The metallic bond resembles the ionic in this respect but differs in that it is exerted not between two entirely different ions of opposite charge but between identical atoms in metallic elements or chemically similar atoms in alloys, without being called upon to satisfy

† Pauling, "The Nature of the Chemical Bond," 2d ed., p. 222, Cornell University Press, Ithaca, N.Y., 1939.

electrical neutrality. In this respect, there is a much closer resemblance to the covalent bond, with added freedom of motion, giving a flexibility that alone is adequate to explain why laws of constant composition and simple proportions arising for ionic compounds through the demands of electrical neutrality need not and do not apply to alloy systems. In a sequence, diamond, carborundum, CSi, silicon, germanium, gray tin, all are tetrahedral, and the typical metallic properties first appearing in carborundum increase rapidly toward tin. Here is a case where identical structures in which each atom is bonded to four neighbors cannot account for the fact that diamond is an insulator and the others semiconductors. The ease of deformation of metals (malleability and ductility) is a structural characteristic arising from the undirected nature of metallic bonds, as a result of which the crystal may glide on atomic planes, in contrast with the generally brittle character of ionic and homopolar combinations. A further consequence is that a metal can form bonds after deformation of an original structure with considerable ease and thus "heal" itself.

The Hydrogen Bond. One of the most important modern concepts in chemistry is the hydrogen bond, or bridge, between two atoms. It plays an important role in an ever-increasing list of known compounds from water up to the most complex proteins. First mentioned in 1912, its importance was first pointed out by Latimer and Rodebush in 1920. It is characterized as a link between two electronegative atoms only, the strength of the bond increasing with the electronegativity of the two bonded atoms in the order chlorine, nitrogen, oxygen, and, strongest, fluorine. The hydrogen bond will be illustrated for organic compounds in Chap. 20, but note may be taken here of direct crystal structure evidence in NH_4F, which differs from all other ammonium halides in that each nitrogen atom is surrounded tetrahedrally by four fluorine atoms with which it forms hydrogen bonds. The striking physical properties, melting point, boiling point, dielectric constant, etc., of H_2O, HF, and NH_3 in solid, liquid, and even gas (polymerized HF molecules) are now explained by this bonding. In NH_4HF_2 around each nitrogen ion are four fluorine ions at a distance 3.07 A, and four are drawn in to 2.76 A by N—H, . . . , F bonds. The same is true of NH_4N_3. Boric acid contains layers of $B(OH)_3$ molecules held together by hydrogen bonds. Each oxygen forms two hydrogen bonds coplanar with and holding together the BO_3 groups. A classical example is KH_2PO_4 which has received much attention because the O—H, . . . , O distance of 2.54 A is the shortest known. This crystal is built from H^+ ions, PO_4 groups, and irregular KO_8 groups, so that each O^{2-} ion belongs to one PO_4 and two KO_8 groups, with a bond strength of $\frac{5}{4} + 2 \times \frac{1}{8} = \frac{3}{2}$. Since two positive charges are required to saturate each O^{2-}, it is satisfied by a bond of strength $\frac{1}{2}$ to H^+. An excellent recent example of a complete analysis by both double Fourier series and least-squares methods (Chap. 15) is that performed on H_2O_2.[†] Here the point of interest is that each oxygen atom has two close approach distances of 2.78 A and two longer ones of 2.90 A.   Figure 268 shows the structure and the disposition of hydrogen bonds along the short distance to form infinite helices around the fourfold screw axes.   Finally several minerals, notably diaspore, AlO(OH), and lepidocrocite, FeO(OH), have their unique crystalline structures determined by O—H, . . . O bonds.   The concept, so well proved from crystal structures even though the actual positions of hydrogen atoms cannot be ascertained from x-ray data[1] because of negligible scattering power, has the great support of the infrared absorption spectrum.

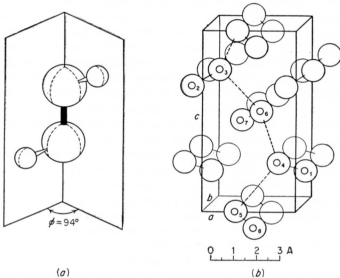

FIG. 268. Structure of H_2O_2 molecule (a), and unit cell showing hydrogen bonds, (b). (*Abrahams, Collin, and Lipscomb.*)

Van der Waals Bond, or Molecular Combination.   Organic compounds form the great class of crystals whose pattern units are the whole molecules in which, in turn, the atoms are linked together by pairs of electrons held in common.   While in the ionic lattice the identity of the single molecule of potassium chloride, for example, is somewhat obscured (though by no means destroyed) by the division of the bonding forces of one atom among six neighbors, in the molecular lattices the molecule of the chemists' formula and of the gaseous phase is built essentially unchanged into the solid structure.   The van der Waals bond is quite

† S. C. Abrahams, R. L. Collin, and W. N. Lipscomb, *Acta Cryst.*, **4**, 15 (1951); at −89°C the structure is tetragonal, space group $P4_12_1$, $a = 4.06$ A, $c = 8.00$ A.

[1] In the latest work of highest precision on inorganic compounds the electron-density contour maps in some cases show evidence of hydrogen atoms.   Neutron diffraction is able to show hydrogen atoms without question.

similar in some respects to the metallic bond in that it may link an indefinite number of neighbors and is spatially undirected. By virtue of the residual stray fields of the electrically neutral molecules, it is possible for one molecule to lie up against another and form the regularly built-up solid. Thus there are two molecules of naphthalene in the unit crystal cell. Because the stray forces holding the molecules in their fixed position cannot compare in intensity with the strong polar or nonpolar bondings between atoms, the substance easily melts or throws off single whole molecules in the process of sublimation. This type of combination will be considered in detail in Chap. 20 on the structure of organic crystals. In the case of electrically neutral inert-gas atoms, the residual attraction is effective only at very close distances, and consequently except at lowest temperature the substance remains a gas. Molecular structures are also to be found among inorganic compounds, notably solid HCl, SnI_4,[†] and the cubic forms[1] of arsenious and antimonious oxides.

The Band Theory of Solids—Insulators, Semiconductors, and Conductors. The simplest picture of solid-state structure is an atomic one based on the various types of bond. Thus in a homopolar, or "valence," compound, the bonds between the atoms of molecules are saturated usually, the electronic structure is rigid, and electrons cannot flow. The molecules are held to each other by the weak van der Waals forces, so that as a whole such materials are insulators. An ionic crystal is made up of ions forming closed electronic shells, held together by electrostatic attraction, kept from collapsing by electronic repulsions, and having no valence bonds and no electronic flexibility or conductivity. Only in the molten state can the ionic character be demonstrated in conductivity. In metals the valences bonding one atom to another are unsaturated, no molecules form, and electrons move from one bond to another or from one part of the crystal to another, so that there are electronic flexibility and conductivity. Almost all properties, mechanical, electrical, and magnetic, can be accounted for by these bonds. It is in a series of crystals like carbon (diamond), silicon, germanium, and gray tin, all crystallizing alike in the diamond structure with four valence bonds for each atom, that complications such as electrical conductivity arise. All would be expected to be insulators; but the last three are well known semiconductors. This and other facts led to the development of the band theory. The simplest and clearest description in words has been given by Slater:[2]

An electronic energy level in an isolated atom is very sharp, meaning that the electron in such a level always has just the same energy. If two atoms are brought into contact, this level is displaced, the displacement depending on the interatomic dis-

† Dickinson, *J. Am. Chem. Soc.*, **45**, 958 (1923).
1 Bozorth, *J. Am. Chem. Soc.*, **45**, 1621–1629 (1923).
2 J. C. Slater, *J. Appl. Phys.*, **22**, 237 (1951).

tance. If the two atoms were identical so that each had an identical energy level, the interaction of the atoms would result not only in a displacement of this level, but in a splitting into two levels, the separation between them increasing as the atoms approached. If many atoms are brought together to form a crystal a similar effect occurs in a much greater scale. All the originally identical levels of the identical atoms will split up, so that there will be as many levels as there are identical atoms in the crystal; but the total splitting will be about the same that it was for two atoms. Thus with many atoms in the crystal, the group of levels will be practically continuously filled, and we call the result an energy band. Each of the original atomic energy levels will split into a band, and since these bands become broader as the atoms get closer together, it may well be that they will overlap into a continuation of levels; on the other hand if the splitting is less, there may be gaps left between the bands.

We can now compare the number of levels in each band and the number of electrons actually present in the crystal. We find that with valence (homopolar) and ionic compounds, as a rule there are just enough electrons to fill certain lower lying bands and leave high bands empty. On the other hand, with a metal, certain bands are only partly filled and there are empty levels immediately above them. It now proves to be the case that in an electric field, if the material conducts electricity, the field will accelerate the electrons, increasing their energy by very slight amounts. Thus, we can get only conductivity, as in a metal, when there are empty levels for the electrons to go into immediately above the occupied bands; in the valence crystals and ionic compounds, where there is a gap above the valence levels, we get no conductivity. All this is as in the atomic picture, but now an additional feature comes in which allows us to handle such cases as Si and Ge. In diamond, the gap between the valence level and the next occupied level is quite wide, and the material is a good insulator; but in Si and Ge, the gap is small at high temperatures, electrons from the occupied valence band can be excited by thermal agitation, to the upper, conduction, band, and then the material becomes a conductor; this is called intrinsic conductivity, and such conductivity increases rapidly with temperature (the opposite is true for metal conductors). But there is another mechanism for conductivity, which is now important. If there are impurity atoms in the crystal, their energy levels will not be incorporated into the main bands, for these bands come only from the interaction of the energy levels of identical atoms. Some of these impurity levels may be within the gap between the valence and conduction bands . . . . In some cases a moderate temperature will excite an electron from one of these impurity levels to the upper, unfilled conduction band, thereby allowing conductivity; such an impurity atom is called a donor atom, and the resulting conductivity is called n-type, since the carriers are negative electrons knocked into the upper level. The other case is one in which an impurity level is normally unoccupied, and a moderate temperature will excite an electron from the lower valence band to this level, which is then an acceptor level. The resulting conductivity is called p-type, since the carriers are holes in the valence band, which can then be shown to have the characteristics of positive charges.

The phenomena just considered are involved in the use of germanium in transistors which perform the functions of vacuum-tube rectifiers, amplifiers, etc. The existence of bands has been proved by the band emission spectra considered in Chap. 6. The band theory is applied more specifically to metals and alloys in Chap. 19.

Coordination and Radius Ratios. The various types of structure enumerated in Chap. 16 for inorganic compounds are distinguishable by their coordination numbers as originally defined chemically by Werner, *i.e.*, the number of neighbors possessed by each ion; thus the following simple coordination types for the compounds RX and RX$_2$ may be recognized:

RX. 1: single molecules and molecular lattices.
    2: double molecules, molecular chains.
    3: BN type.
    4: diamond-type lattices of zinc blende and zinc oxide.
    6: NaCl and NiAs types.
    8: CsCl type.

RX$_2$. 2 and 1: single molecules and molecular lattices.
    4 and 2: α- and β-quartz, cristobalite, tridymite, cuprite.
    6 and 3: anatase, rutile, brookite, layer lattice CdI$_2$.
    8 and 4: fluorite.

Each of these types is characterized by a definite energy stability, which may be deduced theoretically and the constants evaluated from the compressibility and related data.

Goldschmidt has shown from simple geometry that, in order to arrange a number of spheres X so that they will touch around a central sphere R, the following ratios must hold:

Number spheres X	Arrangement	Limiting r_R/r_X
2	Opposite	
3	Equilateral triangle	0.15
4	Tetrahedral corners	0.22
4	Square corners	0.41
6	Octahedral corners	0.41
8	Cube corners	0.73

Such simple relationships, which determine possible arrangements in space for given ratios of radii, hold true in remarkable fashion for the packing of ions in crystals.

The way in which atomic diameter influences structure can be seen from the simplest purely ionic structure of the type RX, with equal numbers of ions of opposite signs. The simplest of these is the structure of rock salt, where sodium and chlorine ions occupy alternate corners of a cubic lattice. The coordination number is 6:6; *i.e.*, each sodium ion has six chlorine neighbors, and vice versa. Actually, the chlorine ions are enough larger compared to the sodium so that they form an octahedron which encloses it almost completely. Simple geometry of spheres shows that this can be the case only if r_R (radius of positive ion)/r_X (radius of negative ion) ≤ 0.73. This structure holds for all halides of the alkaline metals with the exception of the chloride, bromide, and iodide of cesium, where the ratios r_R/r_X are 0.91, 0.84, and 0.75, respectively. Now these last three are the only alkaline halides that belong not to the sodium chloride type but to the cesium chloride type. Here the coordination number is 8:8, and there is, so to speak, more room for the larger cesium ion inside the cube of chlorine ions. On the other hand, some of the alkali halides with the sodium chloride type of structure seem to be anomalous since $r_R/r_X > 0.73$, for example, KF 1.00, RbF 0.89, RbCl 0.82, CsF 0.80, and RbBr 0.76. The geometrical relationship in these cases is affected by polarization or deformability of a large ion such as Cs^+ by a small ion such as F^-. Similarly LiBr with r_R/r_X 0.40 and LiI 0.35 retain the NaCl structure below the critical value of 0.41 because of polarization of large Br^- and I^-.

All these exceptions represent cases where **ionic** bonds have some covalent character.

An example of a compound with radius ratio close to a critical value is NiO. At low temperatures the normal cubic close packing of ions is distorted into a rhombohedral symmetry with an axial angle of 60°12′. The transition takes place smoothly, as shown by the following data:

$$-183° \text{ rhombohedral:} \quad a = 2.946$$
$$\alpha = 60°12′$$
$$18° \text{ rhombohedral:} \quad a = 2.9518$$
$$\alpha = 60°4.2′$$
$$275° \text{ fcc:} \quad a = 4.1946$$
$$(\text{Rhombohedral cell:} \quad a = 2.9660, \ \alpha = 60°)[1]$$

Where r_R/r_X is very small, the factor of extreme polarization comes in and the structure ceases to be ionic and becomes covalent or molecular.

Types of structures for RX compounds, therefore, may be represented by the following:

Compound	Bond type	r_R/r_X	CN
CsCl	Ionic	>0.73	8
NaCl	Ionic	0.41–0.73	6
NiAs	Covalent metallic	0.41–0.73	6
ZnS—ZnO	Covalent	0.22–0.41	4
BN	Covalent (layer)	0.15–0.22	3
HCl	Molecular	<0.22	
Etc.			

If we pass to the next series RX_2, a similar situation occurs. Where r_R/r_X is greater than 0.73, the structure is of the fluorite type (see Fig. 269a). Here the coordination number is 8:4, the calcium ions being surrounded by a cube of eight fluorine ions just as the cesium is by the chlorines. A number of compounds belong to this type, which includes

[1] H. P. Rooksby, *Acta Cryst.*, **1**, 226 (1948).

the fluorides of the alkaline earths and the dioxides of zirconium, thorium, praseodymium, cerium, and uranium. If r_R/r_X lies between 0.73 and 0.41, a structure is formed analogous to rock salt. This is the rutile structure (see Fig. 269b). Here the coordination number 6:3 cannot be satisfied in the cubic system, and the octahedron of oxygen ions is placed on its side in a tetragonal structure. The two other forms of TiO_2,

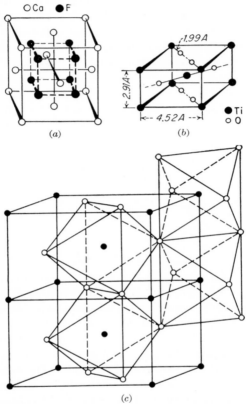

FIG. 269. (a) Crystal unit cell for fluorite, CaF_2. (b) Crystal unit cell for rutile, TiO_2. (c) The structure of PbO_2, showing the coordinating octahedra of O^{2-} around Pb^{4+}.

anatase and brookite, are also built with the same coordination but with the octahedra distorted and differently placed. A large number of substances belong to the rutile structure: the fluorides of Mg, Mn, Co, Fe, Ni, Zn and the dioxides of Mn, V, Ti, Ru, Ir, Os, Mo, W, Cb, Sn, Pb, and Te. The coordination structure of PbO_2 is drawn in Fig. 269c.

When r_R/r_X lies between 0.41 and 0.22, the coordination number is 4:2, which is approaching a homopolar structure. This is the case for the different forms of silica, SiO_2, cristobalite, tridymite, and quartz. Though apparently different, these structures have the essential point in common that they are built from silicon ions completely surrounded by four oxygens in a tetrahedron. Each oxygen is shared between two tetrahedra, and the different forms of structure are due merely to different arrangements of these tetrahedra. Thus the polymorphism of silica is not due to any change in the molecule. The tetrahedral coordination does not determine whether the bonds are ionic or covalent. An ionic structure would allow the oxygen bonds to assume any angles, while covalent bonds should be limited to 90 or 109.5 deg.; β-tridymite with an angle of 180 deg is ionic, and α-quartz probably covalent.

Table 17-3 shows the influences of radius ratio and polarization (increasing homopolar character) in determining the structures in RX_2 compounds.

TABLE 17-3

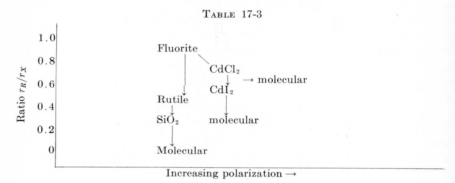

Increasing polarization →

Layer Lattices. The most important influence, next to the size of the ions, in determining how a compound shall crystallize is the phenomenon of polarization, which includes all alterations that particles show under the influence of electric forces. Polarization resolves itself into resonance between ionic and covalent bonds. The simplest case is the formation of a dipole under the influence of an electric field. The negative iodide ion is a typical polarizable ion. Cadmium iodide, by analogy with related compounds and the transition $CdF_2 \rightarrow CdI_2$ and by consideration of the ratio of ionic radii $r_{Cd^{2+}}/r_{I^-}$, would be expected to have a rutile structure, but instead it forms a distinctive type of its own. The coordination arrangement is such that any cadmium ion is surrounded symmetrically by six iodine ions rhombohedrally, but each iodine ion is in contact with three cadmium ions *on one side*, an ideal condition for polarization. The structure is built up in layers, with the sequence iodide ion–cadmium ion–iodide ion layers being repeated. In each layer there is really a giant ionic molecule as large as the extension of the layer, whereas the layers are held together by secondary forces, which accounts for the very prominent cleavage. Of course, graphite is a prominent example among the elements. The transitions $TiO_2 \rightarrow TiS_2$ and $SnO_2 \rightarrow SnS_2$ also result in changes to layer lattices. Layer lattices in minerals are illustrated in the next chapter.

The Sizes of Atoms and Ions. One of the earliest deductions from atomic separations in crystal-structure data was the concept of "radii" characteristic of each atom which upon addition could express interatomic distances in other crystals. Obviously such data on packing sizes could be of the greatest value to crystal analysts in predicting crystalline spacings or in testing interpretations. It soon became apparent that no simple additivity principle could be expected to hold, since many factors influence atomic separations in crystals. There has been a great stimulus as a result to improve, on the one hand, experimental measurements of interatomic distances and to develop, on the other hand, adequate theories for the calculation of radii. The distance between a pair of atoms depends on coordination, deformability, and the nature of the bonding forces. Hence several systems of radii have been introduced. It is still highly debatable what physical meaning should be attached to radii other than as devices for expressing relative sizes. But a sound experimental approach to the question is afforded by accurate plots of electron densities based on Fourier summations.

In Table 17-4 are listed the latest values for (1) the elemental radii, which require no special calculations and are merely half the minimal atomic separations in the crystals of the pure elements, independent of the type of bond (these same values appear in the columns for metallic, covalent, or van der Waals bonds, depending on the nature of the element itself); (2) the radii of atoms in covalent compounds for single, double, and triple bonds and for the special cases of tetrahedral and octahedral coordination; (3) metallic radii calculated from the crystal structures of the metallic elements for coordination members of both 12 (closest packing, face-centered cubic, or hexagonal close-packed) and 8 (body-centered cubic), these being similar to but not identical with covalent radii; (4) ionic radii for valence states corresponding to periodic table positions; and (5) van der Waals, or nonbonded, radii, or the radial distance of nearest approach of adjacent molecules in a lattice held by van der Waals forces.

Covalent Radii. Since the values of equilibrium distance between atoms A and B connected by a single covalent bond are very nearly the same whether determined from x-ray data on crystals, band spectra, or electron diffraction by gas molecules, bond length or the radii r_A, r_B can be deduced fairly readily; these radii then provide a useful basis for predictions of structures of molecules and crystals. In diamond the C—C distance is 1.54 A, and in a great variety of organic compounds the same value is obtained; hence the radius 0.77 A may be assigned to carbon. In compounds with the linkage C—O the value is 1.43 A, so that 0.66 is obtained for the covalent radius of oxygen by simple subtraction of 0.77

Table 17-4. Radii of Atoms and Ions, in Angstroms

Element	Elemental	Covalent* Single	Covalent* Double	Covalent* Triple	Metallic (atomic) CN 12	Metallic (atomic) CN 8	Ionic	van der Waals
1. Hydrogen	.....	$0.37^\dagger$	.....	.....	.....	.....	2.08^-	1.25 CH_3 $2.0\ \frac{1}{2}$ aromatic 1.85
2. Helium	.....						.....	
3. Lithium	1.51	1.34	.....	.....	1.58	1.52	0.68^+	
4. Beryllium	1.13	1.06^t	.....	.....	1.12	1.07	0.30^{2+}	
5. Boron	.....	0.88	0.76	0.68	.....	.....	0.16^{3+}	
6. Carbon	0.77	0.77	0.67	0.60	.....	.....	$0.15^{4+}\ 2.60^{4-}$	1.44
7. Nitrogen	0.53	0.74	0.60	0.55	.....	.....	$0.11^{5+}\ 1.71^{3-}$	1.5
8. Oxygen	.....	0.74	0.55	.....	.....	.....	$0.09^{6+}\ 1.46^{2-}$	1.4
9. Fluorine	.....	0.72	0.55	0.51	.....	.....	$0.07^{7+}\ 1.33^-$	1.35
10. Neon	1.59	.....	.....	.....	.....	.....	.....	1.60
11. Sodium	1.85	1.54	.....	.....	1.92	1.86	0.98^+	
12. Magnesium	1.60	1.40	.....	.....	1.60	1.55	0.65^{2+}	
13. Aluminum	1.43	1.26^t	.....	.....	1.43	1.39	0.45^{3-}	
14. Silicon	1.17	1.16	1.07	1.00	.....	.....	$0.38^{4+}\ 2.71^{4-}$	
15. Phosphorus	1.09	1.10	1.00	0.93	.....	.....	$0.34^{5+}\ 2.12^{3-}$	1.9
16. Sulfur	1.05	1.04	0.94	0.88	.....	.....	$0.29^{6+}\ 1.90^{2-}$	1.85
17. Chlorine	0.91	0.99	0.89	.....	.....	.....	$0.26^{7+}\ 1.81^-$	1.80
18. Argon	1.91	.....	.....	.....	.....	.....	.....	1.91
19. Potassium	2.25	1.96	.....	.....	2.38	2.31	1.33^+	
20. Calcium	1.96	.....	.....	.....	1.97	1.91	0.94^{2+}	
21. Scandium	1.63	.....	.....	.....	1.66	1.60	0.68^{3+}	
22. Titanium	1.45	1.36^o	.....	.....	1.47	1.42	$0.60^{4+}\ 0.69^{3+}$	
23. Vanadium	1.31	.....	.....	.....	1.36	1.31	$0.59^{5+}\ 0.66^{3+}$	
24. Chromium	1.35 1.25	.....	.....	.....	1.30	1.26	$0.52^{6+}\ 0.64^{3+}$	
25. Manganese	1.12 1.50	1.56 (MnS$_2$)	.....	.....	1.27	1.24	$0.46^{7+}\ 0.80^{2+}$ 0.62^{3+}	

Table 17-4. Radii of Atoms and Ions, in Angstroms (*Continued*)

Element	Elemental	Covalent* Single	Covalent* Double	Covalent* Triple	Metallic (atomic) CN 12	Metallic (atomic) CN 8	Ionic	van der Waals
26. Iron	1.24	1.23^o II	1.20 IV	.....	1.26	1.23	0.75^{2+} 0.60^{3+}	
27. Cobalt	1.25	1.22^o III	1.32 II	.....	1.25	1.22	0.72^{2+}	
28. Nickel	1.32 1.24	1.21^o IV	1.30 III	1.39 II	1.25	1.22	0.70^{2+}	
29. Copper	1.27	1.35^t	.....	.....	1.28	1.24	0.96^{+}	
30. Zinc	1.32 1.47	1.31^t	.....	.....	1.37	1.32	0.74^{2+}	
31. Gallium	1.22 1.38	1.26^t	.....	.....	1.53	1.48	0.62^{3+}	
32. Germanium	1.22	1.22	1.12	.....			0.53^{4+} 2.72^{4+}	
33. Arsenic	1.25	1.21	1.11	1.18			0.47^{5+} 2.22^{3-}	2.0
34. Selenium	1.16	1.17	1.08	1.14^t			0.42^{6+} 2.02^{2-}	1.73
	1.13			1.40^o				
35. Bromine	1.13	1.14	1.05	1.11^t			0.39^{7+} 1.96^{-}	
				1.52^o				
36. Krypton	2.01							
37. Rubidium	2.44	2.11			2.53	2.43	1.48^{+}	
38. Strontium	2.13				2.15	2.07	1.10^{2+}	
39. Yttrium	1.79				1.82	1.76	0.88^{3+}	
40. Zirconium	1.60	1.48^o			1.60	1.54	0.77^{4+}	
41. Niobium	1.42				1.47	1.43	0.67^{5+}	
42. Molybdenum	1.36				1.39	1.36	0.62^{6+}	
43. Technetium	.....				1.35	1.32		
44. Ruthenium	1.33	1.33^o			1.34	1.31		
45. Rhodium	1.34	1.32^o			1.34	1.31		
46. Palladium	1.37	1.31^o			1.37	1.34		
47. Silver	1.44	1.53^t			1.44	1.40	1.26^{+}	
48. Cadmium	1.48 1.65	1.48^t			1.54	1.49	0.97^{2+}	

TABLE 17-4. RADII OF ATOMS AND IONS, IN ANGSTROMS (*Continued*)

Element	Elemental	Covalent* Single	Covalent* Double	Covalent* Triple	Metallic (atomic) CN 12	Metallic (atomic) CN 8	Ionic	van der Waals
49. Indium	1.62 1.68	1.44^t	1.30	1.45^o	1.67	1.62	0.81^{3+} 2.94^{4-}	
50. Tin	1.40	1.40	1.31	1.36			0.71^{4+} 2.45^{3-}	2.2
51. Antimony	1.43	1.41	1.28	1.32^t			0.62^{5+} 2.22^{2-}	1.57
52. Tellurium	1.43	1.37	1.24	1.28^t			0.56^{6+} 2.19^{1-}	1.77
53. Iodine	1.35	1.33					0.50^{7+}	
54. Xenon	2.20							
55. Cesium	2.62	2.25			2.72	2.62	1.67$^+$	
56. Barium	2.17				2.24	2.17	1.29^{2+}	
57. Lanthanum	1.56				1.86	1.80	1.04^{3+}	
58. Cerium	1.82				1.86	1.80	0.92^{4+}	
59–71. Rare earths	1.74–1.98				1.86	1.80		
72. Hafnium	1.66				1.62	1.57		
73. Tantalum	1.63				1.49	1.44		
74. Tungsten	1.36				1.41	1.37		
75. Rhenium	1.37				1.37	1.33		
76. Osmium	1.35	1.33^o			1.35	1.31		
77. Iridium	1.35	1.32^o			1.36	1.32		
78. Platinum	1.38	1.31^o			1.39	1.35		
79. Gold	1.44	1.50^t	1.40^o		1.46	1.42	1.37$^+$	
80. Mercury	1.50 1.73	1.48^t			1.57	1.52	1.10^{2+}	
81. Thallium	1.67 1.70	1.47^t			1.71	1.66	0.95^{3+}	
82. Lead	1.74	1.46^t	1.50^o				0.84^{4+}	
83. Bismuth	1.55	1.46^t					0.74^{5+} 1.37	
84. Polonium							2.30^{2-}	
85. Astatine							2.27^{1-}	
86. Radon								

TABLE 17-4. RADII OF ATOMS AND IONS, IN ANGSTROMS (*Continued*)

Element	Elemental	Covalent*			Metallic (atomic)		Ionic	van der Waals
		Single	Double	Triple	CN 12	CN 8		
87. Francium	....	....	....	....	2.80	....	1.75^{1+}	
88. Radium	....	....	....	....	2.35	....	1.37^{2+}	
89. Actinium	....	....	....	....	2.03	....		
90. Thorium	....	....	....	....	1.79	1.54	1.08^{3+} 0.99^{4+}	
91. Protactinium	....	....	....	....	1.63	....	1.05^{3+} 0.96^{4+} 0.90^{5+}	
92. Uranium	....	....	....	....	1.54	....	1.03^{3+} 0.93^{4+} 0.89^{5+} 0.83^{6+}	
93. Neptunium	....	....	....	....	1.50	....	1.01^{3+} 0.92^{4+} 0.88^{5+} 0.82^{6+}	
94. Plutonium	....	....	....	....	....	....	1.00^{3+} 0.90^{4+} 0.87^{5+} 0.81^{6+}	
95. Americium	....	....	....	....	....	....	0.99^{3+} 0.89^{4+} 0.86^{5+} 0.80^{6+}	
96. Curium	....	....						
97. Berkelium	....	....						
98. Californium	....	....						
99. _____	....	....						
100. _____	....	....						

* Numbers followed by superscript symbols refer not to single, double, or triple bonds, but to octahedral covalent radii, *o*, or tetrahedral covalent radii, *t*, at valence states represented by Roman numerals. Radii without superscripts generally represent values for molecules in which atoms form covalent bonds to a number determined by position in the periodic table.

† The radius of the hydrogen atom is more variable than any other if the additivity rule for bond lengths is accepted. Thus in HF with an interatomic distance of 0.92 and the older value of 0.64 for F, H would have the value 0.28. With the new value of 0.72 for F, this would mean 0.20 for H. But with demonstrated nonadditivity because of partial ionic character the average value of 0.37 (formerly 0.30) may be generally used.

from 1.43. If the valence configuration is not the normal single covalent one, other covalent radii are used for double and triple bonds or for tetrahedral, octahedral, or square configurations often found in crystals.

The additivity relation $r_{AB} = r_A + r_B$ was used by Pauling and Huggins[1] to derive the values for the covalent radii, generally accepted as the standard values for many years. Recently, however, increase in precision in measurement of interatomic distances by all three methods mentioned above, especially on fluorine, hydrogen peroxide, and hydrazine, has led to the necessity of upward revisions of the covalent single-bond radius for fluorine (from 0.64 to 0.72), oxygen (from 0.66 to 0.74), and nitrogen (from 0.70 to 0.74) and lately for other elements. The result is that the bond lengths r_{AB} are observed to be significantly less than the sum $r_A + r_B$. Schomaker and Stevensen[2] in revising the Pauling-Huggins values showed that the deviation from additivity was to be ascribed to extra *ionic* character of the bond A—B, since Pauling already had demonstrated the presence of ionic character of the normal covalent bond between like atoms.[3] The additive equation is therefore to be corrected as follows:

$$r_{AB} = r_A + r_B - \beta|X_A - X_B|$$

where the constant $\beta = 0.09$ and $|X_A - X_B|$ is the absolute value of the difference of the Pauling electronegativities, derived from bond energies and listed in Chap. 2 of "The Nature of the Chemical Bond." The interest in the effect of ionic character on the length of an essentially covalent bond has very greatly increased. The effort in the past few years has been to increase accuracy in Fourier analysis of organic molecules to the point of dependable values of bond lengths. As will be shown in Chap. 20, there have come to light unexpected variations in bond lengths, even between different carbon atoms in the same molecule.

In the table of radii are listed the revised values for covalent radii of hydrogen, nitrogen, oxygen, and fluorine and the new values for the alkali elements, all other radii being the Pauling-Huggins values.

Atomic Radii. The atomic radii present no particular difficulty in calculation but show the following interesting features:

1. A small and systematic decrease in radius with decreasing coordination, as follows:

CN	Radius
12	1.00
8	0.97
6	0.96
4	0.88

[1] *Z. Krist.*, **87**, 205 (1934).
[2] *J. Am. Chem. Soc.*, **63**, 37 (1941).
[3] *Op. cit.*, 2d ed.

2. A metal atom very often has a different state of coordination in an alloy from that which it has in the pure element. Thus the radius of germanium with 12-fold coordination may be deduced from the hexagonal close-packed copper-germanium alloy, whereas no such coordination may be found for the element.

3. There is no wide variation in values of radii, since the expected increase in size of the electron shells in heavier atoms is compensated by greater nuclear charge. In each period the alkali metal has by far the largest radius.

4. A noticeable decrease in radius occurs for the elements immediately following lanthanum so that the radii of the elements of the third long period are about the same as those of the second long-period elements. This has been called the *lanthanide contraction* and leads to the close similarity between zirconium and hafnium and between columbium and tantalum.

Ionic Radii. Numerous methods have been employed to calculate the radii of ions, but the most widely accepted values today are those of Goldschmidt, empirically determined from crystal-structure data such as Lande's suggestion that in LiI the I^- ions are so large in comparison with Li^+ that they are essentially in contact and from Wasastjerna's values (optical) $F^- = 1.33$ and $O^{2-} = 1.32$ A; and those of Pauling, calculated from quantum-mechanics considerations starting from experimental interionic distances in NaF, KCl, RbBr, CsI, and Li_2O. Here oppositely charged ions contain an equal number of electrons and have related ionic sizes determined by nuclear charges diminished by the screening effects of the outer electrons; or $r = C^n/(Z - s)$, where C^n is a constant for ions with the same configuration of outside electrons (4.52 for Na^+ and F^-) and s is the screening constant calculated from theory and mole refractions. For multiply charged ions (in $Mg^{2+}O^{2-}$) further corrections must be made. Zachariasen made calculations similar to those of Goldschmidt but corrected the radii for the effects of coordination. He assumed that the interionic distance D can be represented by

$$D_N = R_C + R_A + \Delta_N - K$$

where N is the coordination number for the cation, R_C and R_A are standard radii of the cation and anion, corresponding to r_R and r_X used earlier in this chapter, and Δ_N is a correction for the coordination number. The correction term K is zero if the binding is predominantly ionic.

The correction Δ_N as given by lattice theory is:

N	Δ_N, A	N	Δ_N, A	N	Δ_N, A
1	-0.50	5	-0.05	9	0.11
2	-0.31	6	0	10	0.14
3	-0.19	7	0.04	11	0.17
4	-0.11	8	0.08	12	0.19

The agreement in values is remarkably good. The Pauling values are listed in the table, except for the 1950 revisions by Zachariasen for ions with inert-gas configurations and for the $5f$ ions Ac, Th, Pa, U, Np, Pu, and Am.

It may be seen at once that the positive ion of an element is always smaller and the negative ion always larger than the neutral atom of the same element and that the size of the positive ions in the same periodic group increases with atomic number, whereas it decreases in the same periodic series with increasing charge which tends to tighten the structure. In negative ions the increased size due to repulsion of the extra electrons is balanced by the greater electric field, so that doubly charged negative ions are no larger, and are sometimes smaller, than singly charged ions. The tightening effect of increased charges is shown by comparing K^+Cl^- and $Ca^{2+}S^{2-}$; although all four ions have 18 electrons, the interatomic spacing for KCl is 3.14 A and for CaS 2.84 A. In general, the factors that affect the size of an atom or ion are: (1) type of bond; (2) coordination number; (3) valence of coordinated ions; (4) radius ratio of central ion and coordinated ions. The influence of coordination on distance in ionic crystals is illustrated in the following table:

Transition in lattice type	Change in CN	Decrease in distance, per cent
CsCl → NaCl	8 → 6	3
NaCl → ZnS	6 → 4	5.8
CaF₂ → TiO₂, rutile	8, 4 → 6, 3	3
Metal → metal	12 → 8	3

Thus, the fewer the neighbors around an ion, the shorter the interionic distance. Similarly the radius of a cation is larger when its neighbors are univalent than when they are divalent.

Correction tables for these effects have been published by Zachariasen and Pauling.[1] Departures from additivity for many types of crystal are pointed out by Wyckoff.[2]

Van der Waals Radii. The van der Waals, or nonbonded, radius is illustrated by the distance 2–3 between adjacent chlorine molecules in the crystal

$$1 \quad 2 \qquad 3 \quad 4$$
$$:\overset{..}{\underset{..}{Cl}}:\overset{..}{\underset{..}{Cl}}: \qquad :\overset{..}{\underset{..}{Cl}}:\overset{..}{\underset{..}{Cl}}:$$

This radius should be larger than the covalent bond between atoms 1 and 2 because there are two electron pairs between atoms instead of one; it

[1] Zachariasen, *Z. Krist.*, **80**, 137 (1931); spring, 1950, meeting of the American Crystallographic Association; *Acta Cryst.*, **5**, 660 (1952). Pauling, *J. Am. Chem. Soc.*, **50**, 1036 (1928).

[2] Wyckoff, "Crystal Structures," Vol. III, pp. 6*ff.*

should be about the same as ionic chlorine since the bonded atom presents the same outer appearance away from the bond as the ion. The two values are, respectively, 1.80 and 1.81 A. Pauling suggested that the van der Waals radius may be calculated by adding 0.80 A to the corresponding covalent radius. Improved measurements have shown that this additive term varies from 0.4 to 0.9. Rees[1] has shown that better agreement in calculating packing radii from covalent radii is given by the equation $r_p^2 = r_c^2 + 1.22$.

Isomorphism, Morphotropism, Polymorphism. Goldschmidt's great contributions before 1940 were the result of his experimental method of substituting one ion for another in compounds and observing what change in structure occurred. It is clear that comparability in size of ions of analogous formulas and polarizabilities is the most important attribute contributing to isomorphism. This accounts for unsuspected cases of ismorphism such as lead and strontium, and magnesium and cobalt or nickel salts, and $NaNO_3$ and $CaCO_3$, and for lack of isomorphism among salts far more nearly related chemically, such as salts of magnesium and calcium and even of sodium and potassium. In general, one atom or ion may be replaced by another or solid solution may occur without destroying the crystalline arrangement when the ionic distances do not differ by more than 10 per cent.[2] This is also the degree of disarrangement thermally possible before a crystalline arrangement of planes is destroyed by melting; thus the isomorphic and thermal tolerances are the same. When by chemical substitution the limit of homogeneous deformation is surpassed, a new atomic arrangement in space takes place; such a process Goldschmidt calls morphotropism. This occurs in the series of dioxides when the ratio r_R/r_X reaches 0.7 and in numerous other series of compounds in which stepwise substitutions are made to points where sudden changes in properties occur. Polymorphism, the phenomenon in which the same substance under different thermodynamic conditions may have different crystal structures, is simply a case of morphotropism brought about not by substitution but by thermodynamic alteration (temperature, pressure, directed force, etc.) so that the substance is no longer isomorphous with itself. These are but a few simple examples of the rational explanations of crystal chemistry based on x-ray crystal-structure data.

Goldschmidt has gone even further and used a model principally employing substitution of ions of the same size and shown that TiO_2 is like MgF_2, ThO_2 like CaF_2, $SrTiO_3$ like $KMgF_3$, $BaSO_4$ like $RbBF_4$, Zn_2SiO_4 like Li_2BaF_4. Thus the properties of a very difficultly prepared

---

[1] *J. Chem. Phys.*, **16**, 995 (1948).

[2] However, ability to form solid solutions or mixed crystals is not always a safe criterion of isomorphism; AgBr (NaCl structure) and AgI (ZnS structure) form mixed crystals, as do CaF_2 and YF_3.

salt may be anticipated by the study of a substituted model more easily available.

Mixed Oxides. Growing importance is being attached to the structures of ionic compounds such as aluminates, gallates, titanates, zirconates, stannates, antimonates, niobates, ferrites, etc., which appear to be salts of hypothetical or nonexistent oxyacids but are really double oxides. By far the most important are the compounds $A_mB_nO_x$, in which oxygen ions are coordinated with two cations, particularly in the type compounds perovskite (ilmenite), ABO_3, and spinel, AB_2O_4.

a. Perovskite Type. Figure 270 shows the unit perovskite cell in which the larger A cations are at the corners, coordinated with 12 oxygen ions, and a B ion is at the center of the octahedra, coordinated with 6 oxygen ions. Thus each oxygen ion is linked to four A and two B cations. The following compounds have this structure: $NaNbO_3$, $KNbO_3$, KIO_3,[†] $RbIO_3$, $CaTiO_3$ (perovskite), $SrTiO_3$, $EuTiO_3$,[‡]

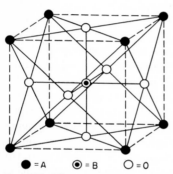

● = A   ◉ = B   ○ = O

FIG. 270. The structure of perovskite, ABO_3.

$[La_1^{3+}(Li_1^+Na_1^+K_1^+Rb^+)](TiO_3)_2$,[‡] $CaZrO_3$, $CuSnO_3$, $YAlO_3$, $LaAlO_3$, $LaGaO_3$, $(KMgF_3$, $KZnF_3)$. Such a family of closely related structures has been given the name "sister structures" by Naray-Szabo. It is evident that the valences of the cations A and B are of no significance so long as they have a combined valence of $+6$ (or $+3$ in the fluorides) to impart electrical neutrality; so there are combinations above of $1 + 5$, $2 + 4$, and $3 + 3$ in the oxides. It is especially significant that in KIO_3 and $RbIO_3$, the iodate ion with I^{5+} does not exist as an entity as is true in chlorates. $Re^{6+}O_3$ has a very closely related structure and thus properly belongs in this series.

b. Alkali Tungsten Bronzes. Sodium tungsten bronze, $NaWO_3$, which is neither an alloy nor an intermetallic compound but has a metallic luster, high electric conductivity, and density 7 to 8, also has the perovskite structure, which it retains even though the composition varies to a deficiency in sodium atoms $Na_{1-x}WO_3$, the range being $Na_{0.93}WO_3$ to $Na_{0.32}WO_3$. A tetragonal form exists in the range below this to

[†] Actually the K, NH_4, Rb, and Cs iodates are monoclinic hemihedral and the Na salt orthorhombic with deformed perovskite structure, while $LiIO_3$ is hexagonal, with IO_6 and LiO_6 octahedra sharing faces. The tendency, then, to form IO_3 discrete groups is clearly found in α-HIO_3, where IO_3 is pyramidal, and IO_6 groups are distorted with three strong and three weak bonds and two hydrogen bonds forming a bifurcated bond, which displaces oxygen from the line joining I atoms. M. T. Rogers and L. Helmholz, *J. Am. Chem. Soc.*, **63**, 278 (1941).

[‡] J. Brous, I. Fankuchen, and E. Banks, *Acta Cryst.*, **6**, 67 (1953).

$Na_{0.28}WO_3$. In this case there must be *vacancies* in the lattice, and one W^{5+} must change to a W^{6+} for every missing Na^+, these being distributed absolutely at random in order to retain the cubic crystal. The potassium bronze has a distorted perovskite tetragonal structure (on account of the size of the K^+ ion) with unoccupied sites over a range from $K_{0.57}WO_3$ to $K_{0.475}WO_3$.

The corresponding lithium bronze, $LiWO_3$, does not exist but $Li_{0.56}WO_3$, representing an excess of WO_3, does; this limiting compound may absorb WO_3 on up to 68 per cent, retaining the perovskite structure, beyond which a new tetragonal phase appears. Na-W bronze will dissolve the Li-W bronze up to 65 per cent by weight with lattice contraction. The structural units then are Na^+, Li^+, vacant sites, WO_3^- and WO_3.[†] These are the first examples of a fascinating field of lattice defects and disorder in the solid state which will be further considered.

c. Barium Titanate and Ferroelectrics. This compound, $BaTiO_3$, which normally belongs to the perovskite group, has unusual properties and has been intensively studied recently. In the first place it is polymorphic; at room temperature, it is tetragonal ($P4nm$) and nearly all crystals are twinned. At 120°C it changes to a cubic structure ($Pm3m$), in a transition in which there is no structural breakdown and the atomic parameters are unaltered. The change is simply in axial lengths, which vary continuously with temperature, though not linearly. X-ray patterns of these crystals oscillated about any cubic axis show only layer lines for a repeat distance of about 4.0 A. Since $a = 3.9932$ and $c = 4.0341$ A, this indicates that all component twins lie with c axis parallel to one of the cubic axes of the macrocrystals. Discontinuous crystal changes occur at -4.1 and $-89°C$, while at temperatures below $-183°C$ the structure becomes again cubic from present indications. The room-temperature structures can be explained only by the existence of directed bonds (partial covalent character) which break at the 120° temperature, while the low-temperature form has a more complete set of bonds, as an octahedral complex. In the second place $BaTiO_3$ belongs to the class of substances known as *ferroelectrics*, by analogy with ferromagnetism. In ferroelectricity and ferromagnetism the substance consists of regions, or domains, containing electric dipoles in one case and magnetic dipoles in the other. The application of external electric and magnetic fields, respectively, modifies the domains; they may be reoriented or changed in shape, or some may grow at the expense of others. Curves of the dielectric displacement, or induced electrical polarization plotted against applied voltage, show a typical hysteresis loop—saturation at high field strengths, hysteresis lag in addition to normal dielectric loss (power

[†] M. E. Straumanis and G. F. Doctor, *J. Am. Chem. Soc.*, **73**, 3492 (1951); *Z. anorg. allgem. Chem.*, **265**, 209 (1951). A. Magneli *et al.*, *Acta Chem. Scand.*, **5**, 372, 670 (1951).

factor), and remanent polarization. Permittivity (specific inductive capacity in farads) is a maximum at 120°, when the tetragonal structure having ferroelectric behavior changes to the cubic perovskite structure without ferroelectric behavior. Thus below 120° a Ti^{4+} ion moves toward one of the six surrounding O^{2-} ions, creating a dipole moment. This dipole in a domain makes it a ferroelectric. When an external electric field is applied, the system of domains lines up by reorientation of a proportion of dipoles coupled with the growth of some preferred domains at the expense of others. Thus $BaTiO_3$ becomes important as an insulator or capacitor; a single small unit replaces 20 $MgTiO_3$ units as a r-f by-pass capacitor. It also has piezoelectric properties and can act as an electromechanical transducer for phonograph pickups, microphones, ultrasonic generators, and vibration and pressure detectors. Finally by careful reduction $BaTiO_3$ becomes deficient in oxygen ions (indicated on x-ray patterns), and the insulator becomes a semiconductor. Since the conduction has a temperature coefficient, tiny threads of the ceramic may serve for temperature and pressure measurements (as for blood temperatures in arteries).[1]

d. *Ilmenite Type.* A second ABO_3 group includes ilmenite, $FeTiO_3$; corundum, $\alpha\text{-}Al_2O_3$; hematite, $\alpha\text{-}Fe_2O_3$; $MgTiO_3$; $NaSbO_3$; etc. Here the metal atoms occupy octahedral holes in a hexagonal close-packed oxygen lattice.

e. *Spinel Type.* Spinels, AB_2O_4, show similar interesting phenomena. The unit cell with 8 molecules has 32 oxygen ions, 4 tetrahedrally coordinated with each A and 6 octahedrally with each B. Usually A is divalent (Mn^{2+}, Fe^{2+}, Co^{2+}, Ni^{2+}, Zn^{2+}, Mg^{2+}, etc.) and B trivalent (Al^{3+}, Cr^{3+}, Fe^{3+}, Ga^{3+}, etc.); but all that is essential is that the valences of A + 2B shall be 8. Thus Fe_3O_4, Fe_2TiO_4, Zn_2SnO_4, and others are also members of the spinel group.

The following curious facts have been established: (1) Besides the normal type of spinel above described, there is another described as "variate atom equipoint." In $MgGa_2O_4$, half the Ga^{3+} ions occupy the fourfold coordinated positions, and the other half plus the Mg^{2+} ions are distributed at random over the sixfold positions—in other words, $B(AB)O_4$. (2) In $ZnAl_2O_4$, etc., the smaller ion, Al^{3+} has the higher coordination. Another example of an "inverse" spinel is $NiFe_2O_4$, whereas $ZnFe_2O_4$ is normal. (3) $LiAl_5O_8$ has a spinel structure, derived from $Mg_2Al_4O_8$ by replacing $2Mg^{2+}$ with $Li^+ + Al^{3+}$. (4) S_4, F_4, and $(CN)_4$ may replace O_4 in several compounds; the valence sums of A + B are 4 instead of 8 for the F^- and CN^- [$BeLi_2F_4$, $ZnK_2(CN)_4$]. (5) Fe_2O_3 and Al_2O_3 form unlimited solid solutions with spinels for the reason that their structures are closely compatible, as shown more clearly when the

[1] Helen Megaw, *Proc. Roy. Soc. (London)*, **A189,** 261 (1947). L. A. Thomas, "*The Times*" *Rev. Ind.*, July, 1949. H. F. Kay, *Acta Cryst.*, **1,** 229 (1948).

formulas of a typical spinel, $MgAl_2O_4$, the oxide Al_2O_3, and the homogeneous solid solution phase are expressed, respectively, as $Mg_3Al_6O_{12}$, $Al_2Al_6O_{12}$, and $(Mg_3,Al_2)Al_6O_{12}$. In this case the unit cell contains 32 oxygen atoms, and $21\frac{1}{3}$ *cations distributed over* 24 positions, leaving $2\frac{2}{3}$ cation positions vacant per unit cell.

In $MgFe_2O_4$ the tetrahedrally coordinated A sites are occupied by $Mg_{0.1}Fe_{0.9}$ and the octahedral B sites by $Mg_{0.9}Fe_{1.1}$ in contrast with Fe, MgFe, which would be expected in A, B, respectively, for a fully inverted spinel structure, and with Mg, 2Fe in A, B, for a normal structure. In solid solutions of $MgFe_2O_4$ and $MgAl_2O_4$ all the Al^{3+} ions go into B sites, causing reversion of Mg^{2+} into A sites and in transformation from the largely inverse $MgFe_2O_4$ structure to normal arrangement in $MgAl_2O_4$. X-ray data indications have been fully substantiated by measurements of saturation magnetization[†] and by neutron diffraction[‡] in which Mg^{2+} and Al^{3+} are clearly distinguished.

f. Other Mixed Oxides. Other mixed oxide series are $LiFeO_2$ and Li_2TiO_3 (cubic with random distribution of metal atoms); $KFeO_2$, $KAlO_2$, etc., have a structure like SiO_2 (cristobalite); the manganese minerals,[1] hollandite, cryptomelene, coronadite, and also α-MnO_2 form an isostructural (tetragonal series) of the general form $A_{2-y}B_{8-z}X_{16}$, where A is Pb^{2+} (coronadite), Ba^{2+} (hollandite), K^+, and Na^+; B is Mn^{4+} with replacement by $Fe^{3+}Mn^{3+}$ and $Mn^{2+}Zn^{2+}$; and X is O^{2-} or OH^-. This means that α-MnO_2 must contain large A cations.

g. Other "Sister" Structures. A number of fluorides belong to the cryolite (Na_3AlF_6) family, such as $(NH_4)_3FeF_6$, $(NH_4)_3AlF_6$, K_2NaAlF_6 (elpasolite), etc. Most of these display polymorphic transitions such as the change in cryolite from monoclinic to cubic at $550°$.[§]

Solid Phases with Variable Composition ("Berthollides"); Disorder in the Solid State; Defect Structures. The observations on perovskite- and spinel-structure types have introduced a revolutionary and fascinating new concept in the chemistry of the solid state—that of variable composition, disorder, or defect in solid crystalline structures, first proposed by Strock in 1936. The following types are possible.

1. *Complete Lattice.* Two or more chemically different atoms occupy crystallographically equivalent sites, a phenomenon, called by Hassel "internal mixed crystal." Examples are variate equipoint spinel; intermetallic systems (see Chap. 19); $(NH_4)_3MoO_3F_3$ (Pauling), in which O^{2-} and F^- occupy one set of equivalent positions; $Li_2Fe_2O_4$ and Li_2TiO_3, with cubic rock salt structure, in which Li and Fe or Ti are just as randomly distributed as Cl^- and Br^- in a solid solution of $KCl + KBr$ and form solid

† G. O. Jones and F. F. Roberts, *Proc. Phys. Soc.*, *(London)*, **B65**, 310 (1952).

‡ G. E. Bacon and F. F. Roberts, *Acta Cryst.*, **6**, 57 (1953).

[1] A. Byström and A. M. Byström, *Acta Cryst.*, **3**, 146 (1952).

§ E. G. Steward and H. P. Rooksby, *Acta Cryst.*, **6**, 49 (1953).

solutions with each other and with MgO because of the close similarity of radii of Li^+, Mg^{2+}, Fe^{3+}, Ti^{4+}; solid solutions of CaF_2 and YF_3 $(Ca, YF)F_2$ with interstitial addition of F^- for each Y^{3+} which substitutes for Ca^{2+}; solid solutions of $LiFeO_2$ and Li_2TiO_3, in which the mechanism of cation substitution is shown by the formulation $(Fe_3, LiTi_2)Li_3O_6$. For all cases of variable composition the term "berthollides" is given in contrast with the term "daltonides" for phases with constant composition.[1] Numerous cases of random distributions and variable composition are to be found in the silicates, discussed in the next chapter. Here random isomorphous replacement of Si^{4+} by Al^{3+} requires addition of monovalent cations or replacement of M^+ by M^{2+}, etc.

2. *Incomplete Lattice.* One or more sets of crystallographically equivalent positions are only partially occupied, leaving vacant spaces in the lattice. Examples are sodium bronze, $Na_{1-x}WO_3$ (missing Na^+); γ-Al_2O_3 $(2\frac{2}{3}$ missing $Al^{3+})$; pyrrhotite, or $Fe_{1-x}S$ (and also $Fe_{1-x}O$, $Cu_{2-x}O$, $Fe_{1+x}Sb$, $Mo_{2+x}C$, etc.) (missing Fe^{2+}); α-AgI stable above $146°$, body-centered cubic iodine lattice stable up to $555°$, with silver atoms *at random* wandering as fluid through structure, whereas in β- and γ-AgI silver atoms are fixed. Ce_2S_3 with the same structure as Ce_3S_4 has $\frac{16}{3}$ molecules per unit cell, or every ninth site vacant; Th_7S_{12} is another example of disorder in having a homogeneity range. γ-MnO_2 is an example of very considerable disorder in its lattice structure, probably owing to random changes of manganese ions in polymorphic transitions from ransdellite to pyrolusite (β-MnO_2). Plaster of paris, $CaSO_4.\frac{1}{2}H_2O$, is unique in that the same structure is found for the range of compositions from 0 (soluble anhydrite) to $\frac{2}{3}H_2O$. Lead peroxide in the positive plate of the storage battery always has a deficiency in oxygen, usually about $PbO_{1.8}$, but retains its structure down to $PbO_{1.66}$. Metallic germanium may be used as a rectifier since atoms may be moved, leaving positive holes. Other examples are the solid solution of γ-Al_2O_3 in spinel, mentioned in the discussion of mixed oxides, and Ag_2HgI_4 (Ketelaar) with ZnS structure, in which $2Ag^+$ and Hg^{2+} ions are distributed at random over four positions (Fig. 271). It is obvious that densities should be criteria for structural vacancies or interstitial additions compared with normal perfect lattice structure. With the highest precision techniques molecular weights may be calculated from x-ray data (Straumanis) and then $M_x - M = -\Delta M$ represents the number of vacant sites and $M_x - M = \Delta M$ the number of interstitial atoms (see page 428).

3. *Stacking Disorder.* Several cases are known in which layer-type structures may show remarkable variations in the manner of stacking of layers even though the single-crystal form may be retained. $CdBr_2$ is a mixture of CdI_2 and $CdCl_2$ types of stacking, but like CdI_2 the arrangement may be random. CdI_2 itself, which is typical of layer structures

[1] See G. Hägg, *Acta Chem. Scand.*, **4**, 88 (1950).

(type C27), may have a completely random lattice when crystallized rapidly from solution, condensed from vapor, or ground; at intermediate rates of crystallization there are disordered structures lying between the random layer lattice and the ordered stacking.[1] In the system, $CdBr_2$ (C19 structure) will dissolve 43 mole per cent CdI_2, and CdI_2 (C27) will dissolve 44 mole per cent $CdBr_2$ with one intermediate phase CdBrI (rhombohedral), but in all cases random layer lattices result on grinding or rapid crystallization. Metallic cobalt, as mentioned on page 475, may display mixed cubic and hexagonal close packing. Graphite may show rhombohedral as well as hexagonal *layer* stacking of carbon layers so that the succession of ABABAB . . . layers may be interrupted by ABCABC; in other words, every fourth instead of every third layer duplicates a plane chosen as base. Minerals and clays often show stacking disorder, detectable on x-ray diffraction patterns. Molecular complexes of organic compounds such as 4,4'-dinitrodiphenyl with 4-chlorodiphenyl, in which interplanar spacings are not uniform,[2] are found in increasing number. Disorder is present in high-polymer natural materials such as collagen (Chap. 23). VO_2F_2[†] is a good example of stacking disorder increasing with heat by lateral displacement, since weak O—O and O—F bonds hold layers together.

Electrical Conductivity of Solids and Defect Structure. In many solid ionic compounds electrical conductivity is caused by the movement of ions. Disorder in AgCl is represented by Frenkel as follows:

In such a case only the cations are in disorder; some Ag^+ ions are at interstitial positions, having left their original places in the lattice, and conductivity is the result of movement of the cations. This has been confirmed by Wagner (Darmstadt), who showed that $CdCl_2$ will go into solid solution in AgCl up to 10 per cent, greatly increasing the electrical conductivity. For in $CdCl_2$ the ratio of cations to anions is 1:2 instead

---

[1] G. Hägg and E. Hermansson, *Arkiv Kemi. Mineral. Geol.*, **16B**, 1 (1942), **17B**, 1 (1943).

[2] R. W. James and D. H. Saunder, *Acta Cryst.*, **1**, 81 (1948).

[†] W. Zachariasen, *Phys. Rev.*, **71**, 715 (1947); *Acta Cryst.*, **1**, 277 (1948).

of 2:2 for AgCl, so that there is one cation too few for every Cd^{2+} ion and a vacant position when $CdCl_2$ substitutes for AgCl:

$$
\begin{array}{cccccc}
Ag^+ & Cl^- & Ag^+ & Cl^- & Cd^{++} & Cl^- \\
Cl^- & \square & Cl^- & Ag^+ & Cl^- & Ag^+
\end{array}
$$

Koch and Wagner have determined for AgCl at 350° the following values: an electrical conductivity of 7.57×10^{-3} mho/cm, a mobility of the vacant positions in the Ag^+ lattice having a velocity (in centimeters per second) for 1 volt/cm of 6.6×10^{-4}; and the fraction of Ag^+ ions in interstitial positions equal to the vacant positions in the Ag^+ lattice 1.5×10^{-3}. α-AgI represents extreme disorder of Ag^+ ions in an iodine lattice so that the ionic conductivity of solid and molten AgI are nearly the same (1 mho/cm). Schottky disorder is exemplified by KCl, in which both anions and cations contribute to electrical conductivity.

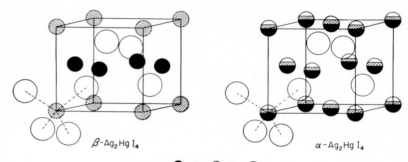

$\bullet = Ag$ $\oslash = Hg$ $\bigcirc = I$

Fig. 271. Crystal structures of β- and α-Ag_2HgI_4.

In NaCl there are perhaps 10^{14} vacant lattice points of either sign per cubic centimeter.

In most oxides and sulfides electrical conductivity is caused by *deviations from strict stoichiometric* composition. ZnO conducts at 600° because oxygen has been lost, an excess of metal atoms being left as cations and free electrons. Conductivity at this temperature decreases with increasing oxygen pressure because the excess of zinc ions and electrons is reduced. Exactly the opposite is true of Cu_2O, for excess oxygen tends to remove electrons from Cu^+ to form Cu^{2+}, with increase in conductivity by electron exchange between Cu^+ and Cu^{2+}.

$$
\begin{array}{cccccc}
Cu^{++} & Cu^+ & \square & Cu^+ & Cu^+ & Cu^+ \\
 & O^{2-} & & O^{2-} & O^{2-} & O^{2-} & O^{2-} \\
Cu^+ & Cu^{++} & Cu^+ & Cu^+ & \square & Cu^+
\end{array}
$$

Empty cation spaces in FeO, FeS, FeSe, VO, NbO, etc., have been proved by x-ray analysis (Jette and Foote, Hägg).

The remarkable case of α-Ag_2HgI_4 has been mentioned. Figure 271 shows the unit cells of the β form, in which silver and mercury atoms are in fixed positions, and the α form, where silver and mercury ions statistically fill three out of four equivalent positions. Between 40 and 50° a transformation (β to α) sets in with relatively enormous increase in conductivity as a result of disorder in which Hg^{2+} ions transfer 6 per cent and Ag^+ ions 94 per cent of the current.

These disorder phenomena are extended to the explanation of chemical reactions of solids.

Wagner and associates have shown that oxidation or rusting of metal surfaces proceeds as a result of varying ratio of metal to oxygen and by actual diffusion of cations and electrons from the *metallic phase toward the oxygen phase*. At an iron surface the ratio of $Fe : O = 1 : 1$, whereas at the oxide-gas boundary there may be as high as a 10 per cent deficit of iron, with the result that iron tarnishes more rapidly than other metals.

Physics of the Solid State. The foregoing discussion of defect lattice structures gives a glimpse of a relatively new and rapidly growing science, which is concerned with every possible correlation between structure and texture of solids, primarily crystals, and measurable physical and mechanical properties. Crystal chemistry is primarily concerned with the relationship between structure and chemical properties, but it is clear that there is considerable overlapping. It is rare that the concept of a perfect, or ideal, crystal can explain the observed properties of deformation, strain, electrical conductance, optical properties, diffusion phenomena, and a variety of other attributes of *real* crystals. The explanation of discrepancies between calculations and experimental observations, therefore, must be found in imperfections in nearly perfect crystals; the theories of the types of imperfections and their operation in real solids form a large part of the physics of the solid state. Although x-ray diffraction techniques have contributed indispensably to the discovery of facts and to the test of theories, it is beyond the scope of this book on applied x-rays to cover these theories in any adequate sense. The recent book " Imperfections in Nearly Perfect Crystals"[1] by 20 eminent authorities on solid-state physics presents the subject in its latest aspects. Seitz, in the first chapter, summarizes the primary imperfections which may account for properties of real solids operating singly or together, as follows: (1) Phonons (imperfections or "particles" associated with unit quantum excitation of one of the modes of elastic vibration of an ideal crystal); (2) free electrons and holes (the band theory of conductors, insulators, semiconductors, etc.) (3) excitons (produced when an insulator is raised to the first, nonconducting excited state of its electronic system); (4) vacant lattice sites and interstitial atoms; (5) foreign atoms in either interstitial or substitutional positions; (6) dislocations. The first three, based on the band theory of solids with its solid theoretical background from wave mechan-

[1] Edited by W. Shockley, J. H. Hollomon, R. Maurer, and F. Seitz, John Wiley & Sons, Inc., New York, 1952.

ics, are aspects of this band theory, considered in this chapter, in Chap. 6, and in Chap. 19. The fourth type is described in the preceding section of this chapter; the fifth in Chaps. 19 and 22; and the sixth in some detail in Chap. 22. As a matter of fact all of Chap. 22 can be considered to be within the province of physics of the solid state.

Anion Radicals in Solids. Whenever a positively charged ion usually of relatively high charge and small size is coordinated with negative ions with bond strength $z/n > 1$, for example, N^{5+} with $3O^{2-}$ for $\frac{5}{3}$ bond strength, a discrete complex group or radical exists in the crystal which is bound together by forces so much stronger than those binding it to the rest of the structure that it may persist even in solution. The shape and size of this radical are the determining factors, though details of structures may vary depending on the relative dispositions of the cations with respect to anion radicals.

The structures of some of the common complex anions are classified in Table 17-5. As a recent example of a more complex anion,[1] the paramolybdate ion $(Mo_7O_{24})^{6-}$ is pictured as an assembly of seven MoO_6 octahedra stacked in two layers with shared edges.

TABLE 17-5. ANION SHAPES

Type	Arrangement	Examples
XY	Linear	CN^-, O_2^-, O_2^{2-}, N_2^-
XYZ	Linear	N_3^-, CNO^-, CNS^-, Cl_3^-, $ClICl^-$
	Bent	ClO_2^-, NO_2^- (132°)
BX_3	Plane equilateral triangle	CO_3^{2-}, NO_3^-
	Regular trigonal pyramid	PO_3^{3-}, SO_3^{2-}, ClO_3^-
BX_4	Regular tetrahedron	PO_4^{3-}, SO_4^{2-}, ClO_4^-, CrO_4^{2-}, MnO_4^-, SeO_4^{2-}, BF_4^{2-}
	Distorted tetrahedron	MoO_4^{2-}, WO_4^{2-}, ReO_4^{2-}, IO_4^-
	Plane square	$Ni(CN)_4^{2-}$, $PdCl_4^{2-}$, $PtCl_4^{2-}$
BX_6	Regular octahedron	SiF_6^{2-}, $TiCl_6^{2-}$, $SiCl_6^{2-}$, $ZrCl_6^{2-}$, $SnCl_6^{2-}$, $PtCl_6^{2-}$, $PbCl_6^{2-}$

Special Notes on Inorganic Structures. 1. *Peroxides and Dioxides.* BaO_2 and SrO_2 are easily distinguished from MnO_2, PbO_2, etc., with two separate O^{2-} ions, by the existence of the O_2^{2-} ion, consisting of two O atoms strongly bound by a single homopolar bond $(O—O)^{2-}$. The normal valence of Ba^{2+} and Sr^{2+} is maintained. In KO_2 the ion O_2^- represents resonance between the neutral oxygen molecule $(O=O)°$ and the ion $(O—O)^{2-}$.

2. *Calcite and Aragonite.* Rhombohedral calcite is derived from a cubic NaCl structure, Ca^{2+} for Na^+ and CO_3^{2-} for Cl^-, by compression along a triad axis. The CO_3^{2-} groups are planes parallel to each other and normal to the triad axis. The ions show the following coordinations: each Ca^{2+} by irregular octahedron of six O^{2-}; each O^{2-} by two Ca^{2+} and

[1] I. Lindquist, *Acta Cryst.*, **3**, 159 (1950).

C^{4+}. This is the structure for all carbonates and nitrates with radius of cation less than 1.1. $CaCO_3$ is dimorphous because the Ca^{2+} radius of about 1 A approaches the critical value. Orthorhombic aragonite is derived from NiAs structure, with CO_3 groups still planar and parallel. Coordination is as follows: each Ca^{2+} by nine O^{2-}; each O^{2-} by three Ca^{2+} and C^{4+}. For radii above 1.45 A the structures of nitrates and carbonates change to the $RbNO_3$ or $NH_4NO_3(I)$ type (cubic).

Here again the chemical molecule is completely obscured. A structural formula for $CaCO_3$ such as

$$Ca \diagdown O \diagup \diagdown O \diagup C=O$$

has no meaning and furthermore is erroneous since it distinguishes one oxygen atom from the other, whereas all three are structurally equivalent and linked both to calcium and carbon ions. The following formula alone is possible, though it fails to represent correct geometrical disposition of the bonds:

Similarly

bear no relation whatever to the crystal structures of potassium sulfate, nitrate, and chlorate.

3. *Polynuclear Anions—the Sulfur Acids.* Zachariasen has shown some remarkable relationships in the series of $S_mO_n^{2-}$ groups that explain chemical behavior: SO_4^{2-} is tetrahedral; $S_2O_6^{2-}$, dithionate, is formed by removing one oxygen atom from each of two sulfate tetrahedra and joining the two sulfurs as in Fig. 272b; $S_2O_5^{2-}$, pyrosulfite, is formed by removing one oxygen from $S_2O_6^{2-}$, the structure

usually accepted being thus eliminated. $S_2O_2^{2-}$, $S_2O_3^{2-}$, and $S_2O_4^{2-}$ are formed from the same basic structure; SO_3^{2-} is represented by one of the single pyramids in Fig. 272a; SO_2^{2-}, by the top of Fig. 272d; and S_2 of pyrites, by stripping the dithionate ion (Fig. 272a) of all oxygen atoms, $S_2O_8^{2-}$; persulfate, shown in Fig. 272c, is made from two SO_4 tetrahedra joined by an O—O bond; and $S_3O_6^{2-}$, trithionate, consists of two tetrahedra sharing a common third sulfur atom, which has replaced a shared oxygen in a S_2O_7 group.

4. *Rotation in the Solid State.* It would be expected that highly symmetrical groups such as tetrahedral BX_4 and octahedral BX_6 should act

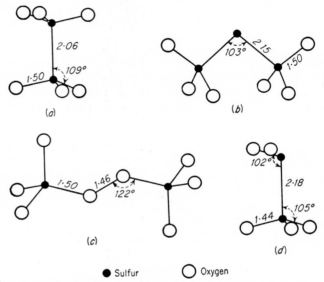

(a)

(b)

(c)

(d)

● Sulfur   ○ Oxygen

Fig. 272. Structures of polynuclear complex sulfur acid ions. (a) Dithionate ion, $S_2O_6^{2-}$; (b) trithionate ion, $S_3O_6^{2-}$; (c) persulfate ion, $S_2O_8^{2-}$; (d) pyrosulfite ion, $S_2O_5^{2-}$.

like spheres and result in comparatively simple structures. Such is indeed the case. It is very difficult to account for the simplicity of some structures with nonsymmetrical anions such as CN^- (NaCN is like NaCl), C_2^{2-}, O_2^{2-}, CO_3^{2-}, NO_3^-, ClO_3^-, and ClO_4^-. In 1930 Pauling proposed the concept of free rotation in the solid state to account for anomalous entropy of solid hydrogen, and this has now been widely applied to many other cases of apparently inconsistent crystal structures. Free rotation is most common with symmetrically shaped molecules of small moment of inertia, in loosely bound structures, at high temperatures. The transition to the state of free rotation extends over a finite temperature range. Unsymmetrical molecules may have rotations around different axes excited successively at different temperatures, accompanied by structural change and anomalies in physical properties. Alkyl ammonium halides, at first thought to have linear carbon chains with C—C spacing of 1.25 A, entirely contrary to the usual tetrahedral zigzag chain with C—C spacings 1.54, now are believed to have the carbon chains rotating around their lengths so that the 1.25 spacing is simply the projection on the axis of the chain of the inclined 1.54-A bonds. In the most recent work complete analyses with electron-density maps have been made on two modifications of *n*-propyl ammonium chloride.[1] The room-temperature forms of the chloride, bromide, and iodide have the space group $P4/nmm$ with two molecules of $C_3H_7NH_3X$ per unit cell. The structure is that of tetragonal PbO, with the $C_3H_7NH_3$ replacing Pb^{2+}. The cations extend along the fourfold axis and hence *must* either rotate or have orientational disorder. The analysis convincingly proves that free rotation of the cation fits the x-ray data better. At low temperatures this form goes over into the monoclinic $C2/m$ with a fixed position of the cations.

The NH_4^+ ion rotates in its cubic halides but not in NH_4F (wurtzite structure). The most remarkable case is NH_4NO_3, in which both ions may or may not rotate, six modifications being the result. In the cubic form only, stable above 125° (Hendricks, Posnjak, and Kracek), both ions are rotating and behave as spheres (NH_4^+, 1.46 A and NO_3^-, 2.35 A). In the other forms with more complex crystal structures, some or all of the rotational degrees of freedom of one or both ions are inhibited.

5. *Unusual Structures among Relatively Simple Inorganic Compounds.* An examination of crystal-structure data (see Wyckoff's "Crystal Structures") will disclose many truly fascinating types of structure, some entirely unsuspected from the chemistry involved. And yet the complete analyses often have explained anomalies in formation, reactions, and properties.

a. In 1940 simultaneously in laboratories at Illinois, Cambridge, and Oxford it was found that solid PCl_5 is built up from $(PCl_4)^+$ tetrahedra and $(PCl_6)^-$ octahedra, arranged in a slightly distorted body-centered cubic Cs^+Cl^- structure, with tetrahedral groups replacing Cs^+ and octahedral groups Cl^-. On the other hand, PBr_5 is entirely differently built into an orthorhombic crystal from $(PBr_4)^+$ tetrahedra and Br^- ions.

b. In 1950 simultaneously at MIT and at Amsterdam the crystal structure of N_2O_5 was proved to be true nitronium nitrate, $(NO_2)^+(NO_3)^-$. The hexagonal space group is $C6/mmc$ with unit-cell dimensions $a = 5.41$ A and $c = 6.57$ A. The structure is composed of layers of NO_3^- ions perpendicular to the c axis and spaced $c/2$ apart. The $(NO_2)^+$ ions are normal to these layers and pierce them in such a manner that the nitrogen in $(NO_2)^+$ is at the center of an equilateral triangle formed by three surrounding NO_3^- ions.

c. The classical work at Uppsala, Sweden, on the oxides of molybdenum and tungsten have disclosed exceptional formulas of some of the phases

[1] M. V. King and W. N. Lipscomb, *Acta Cryst.*, **3**, 222, 227 (1950).

(α-MoO_3, β-Mo_8O_{23}, β'-Mo_9O_{26}, γ-Mo_4O_{11}, δ-MoO_2, ϵ) and the tungsten oxides closely analogous ($W_{18}O_{49}$, $W_{20}O_{58}$, WO_3, etc.). But in this seeming complexity all Mo and W oxides are characterized by regular octahedral configurations of oxygen atoms around the metal atoms. There is a common appearance of a 3.8-A spacing (the diagonal distance between two oxygen in the octahedra). Evidently the coupling of the octahedra must be very intricate. This general plan is maintained in $MoWO_6$.†

6. *Hydrate and Ammoniate Structures.* Neutral molecules of H_2O and NH_3 may be bound in ionic structures, quite contrary to usual rules, because of their small size and electric polarity.

The large dipole moment of water is due to a tetrahedral distribution of charge over the surface of the spherical molecule (Bernal, Fowler), with two corners positive and two corners negative regions. Thus water must be packed into crystals so that the charged areas are directed toward ions of opposite sign, or two molecules of water are linked to each other by having opposite charges turned together. This requirement limits and complicates hydration of solid salts, as well as the structure of ice. This has the same structure as the silicon ions in β-tridymite, SiO_2, with each molecule coordinated by four neighbors at the corners of a tetrahedron, so disposed that regions of opposite charge are adjacent (see diagrams in discussion of zedites, next chapter).

The structures of water and ice are further considered in Chap. 21. Coordination of NH_3 molecules around the cation as in $Co(NH_3)_6Cl_3$ is very similar usually to that of H_2O molecules in hydrates, in that the cation is enlarged so that it may coordinate a larger number of anions and produce actually simpler lattice structures than anhydrous compounds. Thus $Co(NH_3)_6I_2$ crystallizes like cubic CaF_2, while CoI_2 has a layer lattice because of the polarizing effect of Co^{2+} ions on I^-. Sometimes H_2O and NH_3 molecules are interchangeable as in isomorphous $Co(NH_3)_4$-$(H_2O_2)_2Co(CN)_6$, $Co(NH_3)_5(H_2O)Co(CN)_6$, and $Co(NH_3)_6Co(CN)_6$; in other cases such as $Al(H_2O)_6Cl_3$ and $Al(NH_3)_6Cl_3$ there is a marked difference in structures. Wyckoff's "Crystal Structures," Volume II, lists 58 classes of hydrates and ammoniate structures.

Types of Hydrate. 1. *Coordinated Water.* This functions to surround cations with neutral shell, increase radius, and thus coordinate larger number of anions [Al^{3+} 0.75, $Al(H_2O)_6^{3+}$ 3.3 A]; x-ray patterns are entirely different from those of anhydrous salt, for water molecules play an essential part in determining the stability of the lattice as a whole and cannot be removed without complete breakdown of the structure.

The complete structure analyses of hydrates such as $NiSO_4.7H_2O$, $CuSO_4.5H_2O$, etc. (Beevers and associates), represent an outstanding

† The preparation and identification by powder diffraction patterns of these oxides are described by A. Magneli, G. Andersson, B. Blomberg, and L. Kihlborg, *Anal. Chem.*, **24**, 1998 (1952).

achievement, since they involve the correct bonding of H_2O molecules with their tetrahedral disposition of charges. The bond structure of the familiar blue vitriol, $CuSO_4.5H_2O$, is shown in Fig. 273. Each Cu^{2+} ion is coordinated with four H_2O molecules and two O^{2-} ions from the SO_4 groups. The fifth H_2O molecule, long known on chemical grounds to be different from the other four, is coordinated only by other H_2O molecules and O^{2-} ions.

Many compounds $A^{2+}B^{4+}X_6^-$ (such as $NiSnCl_6.6H_2O$) are isomorphous and have comparatively simple structures of octahedra of $A(H_2O)_6^{2+}$ and BX_6^{2-}.

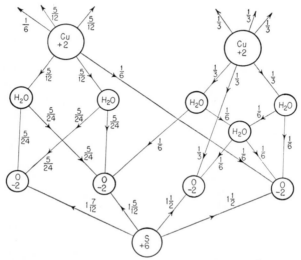

FIG. 273. The electrostatic valence bond structure of copper sulfate pentahydrate, $CuSO_4.-5H_2O$.

Jansen in his book on crystalline salt hydrates (Copenhagen, 1948) laid down the rule that in these structures each water molecule must touch one or two positive neighbors on one side and two negative neighbors on the opposite side. However, Lindquist[1] has shown that salt monohydrates such as $(NH_4)_2FeCl_5H_2O$ are built from NH_4^+ ions and octahedral (distorted) $(FeCl_5H_2O)^{2-}$ ions, and similarly the isomorphous compounds $Cs_2(TlCl_5H_2O)$ and $(NH_4)_2InCl_5H_2O).†$ These cannot possibly obey the Jansen rule for stable hydrate configuration.

2. *Hydrates of Mixed Type.* In alums $A^+B^{3+}(SO_4)_2.12H_2O$, Lipson and Beevers showed that each cation is surrounded by six H_2O but quite differently in detail. In $KAl(SO_4)_2.12H_2O$, each of the six H_2O is closely bound to Al^{3+} and has two external contacts. Each of the six around K^+ contacts two O^{2-} ions of SO_4 groups and one H_2O of the

---

[1] *Acta Chem. Scand.*, **2**, 531 (1948).

† Klug, Kummer, and Alexander, *J. Am. Chem. Soc.*, **70**, 3064 (1948).

$Al(H_2O)_6$ group, this outer contact being more important than the high coordination expected for K^+. X-ray analysis alone has revealed that there are three different cubic structures among alums, depending on the arrangement of the groups: $A(H_2O)_6^+$, $B(H_2O)_6^{3+}$, and SO_4^{2-}.

3. *Structural Water.* H_2O molecules occupy interstices in the lattice; in many cases they may be expelled from the lattice without breakdown of structure; the x-ray pattern is the same or very similar to that of anhydrous salt.

The role of water in zeolites (water softeners) and various silicate minerals will be noted in the next chapter. In some of these, the three-dimensional crystal framework of SiO_4 is so rigid that water may be bound or expelled, all in accordance with the dipole properties without affecting the crystal structure. In other minerals the H_2O plays a more important role in holding layers together. A similar case is found in gypsum, $CaSO_4.2H_2O$, analyzed by Wooster. This is a layer lattice in which sheets of Ca^{2+} and SO_4^{2-} ions are arranged so that each cation is surrounded by six O^{2-} ions and two H_2O molecules. Each H_2O molecule is linked to one Ca^{2+} ion, to one O^{2-} ion in its own sheet, and to one O^{2-} ion in a neighboring sheet, this last bond holding the sheets together and yet accounting for the perfect cleavage and high thermal expansion across this weak bond.

Plaster of paris is perhaps the simplest known example of a substance with a constant lattice but a variable composition. While it is generally accepted to be $CaSO_4.\frac{1}{2}H_2O$, it has only recently been shown that the water content may vary from 0 to $\frac{2}{3}$, with the same structure and the same patterns with very slight shifts in lines, which can be used to identify the exact composition. The edge lengths of the pseudohexagonal cell change from $a_0 = 6.915$, $c_0 = 6.35$ A for the anhydrous compound, which is "soluble anhydrite," entirely different in structure from true anhydrite.[1] Thus the structure consists of a framework of Ca^{2+} and SO_4^{2-} ions with channels through which water molecules may pass in or out without disturbing the framework.

4. *Colloidal Hydrous Oxides, Oxide Hydrates, and Hydroxides.* A subject of considerable difficulty, which has commanded attention for more than a century in analytical chemistry and in industry as in the manufacture of paint pigments, is the composition and structure of the gelatinous precipitates, thrown down from salt solutions above some critical pH value and generally termed "hydrous oxides" and exemplified by gels of ferric, aluminum, chromic, titanium, zirconium, and silicon oxides. The implication of the term is that gel water is held by the oxide by means of absorption and capillary forces. Sometimes water is chemically bound in stoichiometric ratio, and the result is a hydrous hydrate or hydroxide.

---

[1] C. W. Bunn, *J. Sci. Instr.*, **18**, 70 (1941).

The latter indicates indubitable evidence of the presence of OH^- ions, but the two terms are used interchangeably.

In years past very complex polymerized structures have been postulated for these hydrous systems. But careful phase-rule structures, and especially the method of x-ray diffraction analysis, have greatly clarified the whole field and revealed comparative simplicity of constitution. Typical x-ray results are illustrated in Fig. 274 for aluminum and iron oxides, hydroxides, and silicates from the recent work by Tamura and Jackson.[1] These relationships are particularly important in showing the origin of soil constituents (see Chap. 18, The Silicates) arising from the hydroxides or hydrous oxides. There are marked similarities in the two

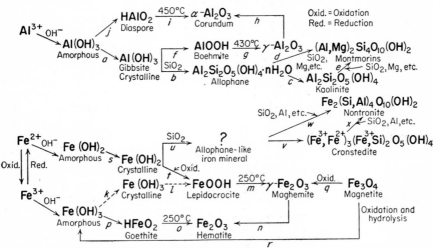

FIG. 274. Structural and energy relationships of Fe and Al oxides, hydroxides, and silicates. (*Tamura and Jackson.*)

series, the chief difference residing in the two valence states of iron as compared with only one for aluminum.

Figure 275 reproduces the standard patterns for the hydrated and anhydrous aluminas made by Rooksby.[2] These are of especial interest because of the petroleum "fluid" cracking catalysts containing alumina.

The gel of gallia is hydrous Ga_2O_3, which goes over into hydrous $Ga_2O_3 \cdot H_2O$. The trihydrate is known, also.

The gel of scandia is hydrous $Sc_2O_3 \cdot H_2O$ only, disproving many complex formulas in the literature.

All precipitated stannic oxides, including so-called ortho- and meta-stannic acids, give identical patterns among themselves and with anhy-

[1] T. Tamura and M. L. Jackson, *Science*, **117**, 381 (1953).

[2] H. P. Rooksby, *X-Ray Diffraction Techniques in the Industrial Laboratory, Repts. Progr. Phys.*, **10**, 83 (1946).

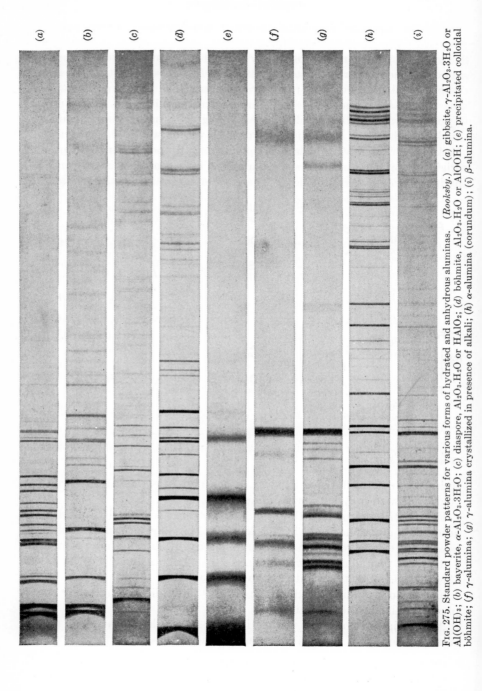

FIG. 275. Standard powder patterns for various forms of hydrated and anhydrous aluminas. (*Rooksby*.)   (*a*) gibbsite, γ-Al_2O_3.3H_2O or Al(OH)$_3$; (*b*) bayerite, α-Al_2O_3.3H_2O; (*c*) diaspore, Al_2O_3.H_2O or HAlO$_2$; (*d*) böhmite, Al_2O_3.H_2O or AlOOH; (*e*) precipitated colloidal böhmite; (*f*) γ-alumina; (*g*) γ-alumina crystallized in presence of alkali; (*h*) α-alumina (corundum); (*i*) β-alumina.

526

drous SnO_2 (allowing, of course, for much broader lines for the colloidal preparations). The gel precipitates from stannous salts as hydrous $SnO.0.5H_2O$, which dehydrates spontaneously at room temperature to α-SnO.

There is a single hydrous oxide of TiO_2, ZrO_2, and ThO_2, and α and β modifications do not exist, as in the case of SnO_2. TiO_2 gels are interesting in that one formed from hydrolysis of titanium chloride or nitrate has the rutile structure, whereas one from the sulfate corresponds to anatase.

The constitution and identification of the important iron oxide pigments (paints, ceramics, etc.) furnish a case where the microscope can give no help, because of the extremely small particle size of the precipitated material, but where the powder diffraction pattern is indispensable. The yellow pigment is α-FeO(OH), goethite; the orange, β-FeO(OH); the brown, γ-FeO(OH), lepidicrocite; the black, Fe_3O_4; the red, rhombohedral Fe_2O_3, formed by heating the others to 500°C; the purple-brown, cubic Fe_2O_3 with lattice vacancies. Thus color is dependent on structure, but how and why is still one of the unsolved problems.

Finally the hydrous oxide sols produce x-ray patterns of water and simple oxide or oxide hydrate as above noted for the gels. Basic salts containing chloride have no real existence, for in these sols the chloride is merely adsorbed in amounts depending on the size and physical character of the primary particles.

Clathrate compounds; rare-gas hydrates. Clathrate compound formation involves the complete enclosure of a molecule of one component by one or more molecules of another component in such a way that the first molecule cannot escape from its position unless the strong forces holding its surrounding "cage" together are overcome. This type of compound formation provides a means of uniting different substances which may have little attractive interaction. Thus, in effect, we find the molecules of one component caught within a cage formed by the other component. Hence, the name "clathrate," from *clathri*, meaning lattice, hence enclosed or protected by the crossbars of a grating, was suggested by Powell in 1948.[1]

In order to become enclosed within the cage, it is essential that the molecules to be enclosed are present during the formation of the cage, *i.e.*, during crystallization of the enclosing species. For, after the cage is formed, a molecule can no more get into the cage than get out of it.

Only two cage-forming substances have been investigated extensively to date, quinol and water. In forming the clathrate structure, quinol molecules link through hydrogen bonds to form infinitely extended three-dimensional cageworks. Owing to the size of the covalently bound group of atoms connecting the two points of hydrogen-bond attachment of each molecule, the resulting structure is an extremely open one. In fact, the

[1] D. E. Palin and H. M. Powell, *J. Chem. Soc.*, 1947, p. 208.

available space is so great and the holes of entry are so large that a second identical cagework is formed which completely interpenetrates the first. This gives an association of two giant molecules which have no direct linkages but which are inseparable without the breaking of hydrogen bonds. This arrangement of interpenetrating quinol frameworks leaves unoccupied cavities or voids which are able to contain small molecules M such that, if every cavity were filled, the formula would be $3C_6H_4(OH)_2.M$, where $M = SO_2$, CO_2, C_2H_2, H_2S, HCN, HCl, HBr, HCOOH, CH_3OH, or CH_3CN. These compounds are very stable under ordinary conditions of storage and have no odor of the volatile substance but are decomposed into their components when heated to their melting points or dissolved in water, alcohol, or ether.

Although the idea that the quinol molecules are somehow able to lock the volatile component into position dates back to 1886,[1] it was only in 1947 that Palin and Powell determined by three-dimensional Fourier methods that $3C_6H_4(OH)_2.SO_2$ is a clathrate compound. A year later they showed by another detailed crystal-structure determination that the so-called "β-quinol" (quinol crystallized from CH_3OH) is also a clathrate compound, $3C_6H_4(OH)_2.CH_3OH$, rather than a polymorphic form of quinol as had been previously supposed.

It is evident that the only restrictions on the type of molecule capable of being enclosed in a cage structure are size restrictions. That is, the molecule can be neither larger than the cavity into which it must fit nor smaller than the exit holes in the lattice which forms the cavity. Thus HCN is just large enough to be unable to escape from the quinol cage, while CO (which is not much smaller than HCN) is just small enough to escape through the exit holes. In spite of this fact, CO can be held within a quinol cavity provided that adjacent cavities are occupied by larger molecules such as HCOOH.

Recently Powell has prepared quinol clathrate compounds of the type $3C_6H_6(OH)_2.M$, where M = argon, krypton, or xenon, by crystallization of quinol from aqueous solutions which were subjected to high pressures of the inert gas in question. In the case of xenon, for example, a pressure of 14 atm was used, and the resulting product had a composition represented by $3C_6H_4(OH)_3.O.88Xe$. It is interesting to note that this quantity of xenon in the form of a gas occupying the same volume at 15°C would have a pressure of 80 atm.

When water acts as the cage-forming medium, the structure is highly complex. In fact two structures have been proposed,[2] one for enclosing small molecules and the other for enclosing larger ones. In these structures, the water molecules are linked to each other by hydrogen bonds, but, rather than forming the usual ice structure, the water molecules form

[1] F. Mylius, *Ber. deut. Chem. Ges.*, **19**, 999 (1886).
[2] W. F. Claussen, *J. Chem. Phys.*, **19**, 259, 262, 1425 (1951).

a cavity-containing structure which is stabilized by the presence of gas molecules which fill the cavities.

In structure I, the unit cell contains 136 water molecules which are arranged so that they form 16 pentagonal dodecahedra (small cavities) and 8 hexakaidecahedra (large cavities). Thus if structure I is formed, the formula for large molecules would be $8M.136H_2O = M.17H_2O$; for small molecules, $(16 + 8)M.136H_2O = M.5\frac{2}{3}H_2O$. In structure II, the unit cell contains 46 water molecules which are arranged so that they form 2 pentagonal dodecahedra (small cavities) and 6 tetrakaidecahedra (medium-sized cavities). Thus if structure II is formed, the formula for medium-sized molecules would be $6M.46H_2O = M.7\frac{2}{3}H_2O$; for small molecules, $(6 + 2)M.46H_2O = M.5\frac{3}{4}H_2O$.

Preliminary x-ray investigations by von Stackelberg and Müller,[1] confirmed by Rodebush and Cole,[2] support the existence of both structures. Since both structures are cubic (cell constant; 17 A and 12 A, respectively), x-ray powder diffraction data are all that should be needed to determine which of the two structures has been formed.

As would be expected, when large molecules (e.g., $CHCl_3$, CH_2Cl_2, CH_3I, C_2H_5Cl, C_3H_8) hydrate, a cubic structure with cell constant = 17 A, space group $Fd3m$ (diamond type), and formula corresponding approximately to that of structure I (namely, $M.17H_2O$) is formed. Similarly, smaller molecules (e.g., H_2S, SO_2, CO_2N_2, CH_4, CH_3Cl, Cl_2, and Br_2) hydrate to form a cubic structure with cell constant = 12 A, space group $Pm3n$ (modified body-centered cubic), and formula corresponding approximately to that of structure II. A crowning achievement in this latest investigation is the proof of this same structure for xenon hydrate.

A related type of cagelike structure, found for the complex of urea with aliphatic straight-chain hydrocarbons which enables separation of these from branched-chain, or aromatic, hydrocarbons, is discussed in Chap. 20.

[1] M. von Stackelberg, *Naturwissenschaften*, **36**, 327, 359 (1949). M. von Stackelberg and H. R. Müller, *J. Chem. Phys.*, **19**, 1319 (1951).

[2] Ph.D. thesis, University of Illinois, 1952.

CHAPTER 18

THE SILICATES

It is perhaps not surprising that chemistry in the past has avoided, whenever possible, consideration of the natural silicate minerals (as it also tried to overlook most alloys) because of the very complex formulas, apparently often in entire disagreement with the traditional principles of chemical valence and, because of variability of composition, with laws of definite proportion. There were no clarifying principles of classification beyond those of the optical mineralogist; chemical analysis merely confused the issue. It is to the credit of x-ray crystal-structure analysts that they brought their methods to bear upon this chaos fearlessly and without prejudice. It was necessary to drop the traditional principles of chemistry and to violate the rigorous concept of the chemical molecules in the solid state. Out of these efforts to interpret structures came principles so simple and straightforward that silicates even of the most complex type are now as well known and completely classified as any group of crystals. Nature takes the same simple building blocks and puts them together in a variety of ways, corner to corner, edge to edge, face to face, to form all the silicate minerals. Thus their chemical formulas, if they mean anything, are the logical consequence of architectural geometry, rather than a violation of laws of chemical valence. This chemical analysis vs. the architectural plan may be illustrated as follows:

A sample of hornblende on analysis gave the following number of atoms present per 24 oxygen atoms:

$$\left.\begin{array}{l} \text{Si } 5.98 \\ \text{Al } 2.32 \end{array}\right\}8.30 \qquad \left.\begin{array}{l} \text{Ti}^{4+}\ 0.13 \\ \text{Fe}^{3+}\ 0.90 \\ \text{Mg}^{2+}\ 0.46 \\ \text{Fe}^{2+}\ 3.16 \\ \text{Mn}^{2+}\ 0.10 \end{array}\right\}4.75 \qquad \left.\begin{array}{l} \text{Na}^{+}\ 0.37 \\ \text{K}^{+}\ 0.66 \\ \text{Ca}^{2+}\ 1.84 \end{array}\right\}2.87$$

Now this apparently hopelessly complex mineral has exactly the structure of an idealized $(OH)_2Ca_2Mg_2(Si_4O_{11})_2$; 2.02 Al atoms substitute for Si, and 0.30 are in octahedral coordination along with ions of closely similar size in the second group; most of the Mg in the ideal compound has been replaced by iron. The true formula is thus derived:

$$(OH)_2(Ca,\ Na,\ K)_2(Mg^{2+},\ Al^{3+},\ Ti^{4+},\ Fe^{3+},\ Fe^{2+},\ Mn^{2+})_2[(Si,\ Al)_4O_{11}]_2$$

Examples without end thus could be cited to show how these structural equivalent points can be occupied by a variety of atoms as long as they will fit in the available space and thus rationally explain heretofore meaningless empirical formulas. Silicates are classed then, not by formula, but according to the way in which SiO_4 tetrahedra are linked together, as will now be described.

An authoritative work, "The Atomic Structure of Minerals," by Sir Lawrence Bragg, gave more than two decades ago the classification and detailed structures of minerals, including the silicates. Bragg gave the first clue to these complex structures earlier through the idea of close packing of oxygen ions as the largest units present. Since that time the principles of coordination of anions at the corners of polyhedra around cations, discussed in the preceding chapter, have developed into a comprehensive representation of structures.

The Pauling Rules. In 1929 Pauling formulated five rules of coordination applicable to all ionic crystal structures but particularly helpful in the interpretation of the complex silicates. These rules remain essentially unchallenged to this day.

1. A coordinated polyhedron of anions is formed around each cation, the cation-anion distance being determined by the radius sum and the coordination number of the cation by the radius ratio (the first law of crystal chemistry, Goldschmidt, 1926). In silicates the fundamental unit is the tetrahedral arrangement of $4O^{2-}$ around each Si^{4+}.

2. In a stable coordination structure the total strength of the valence bonds that reach an anion from all the neighboring cations is equal to the charge of the anion (electrostatic valence principle). In perovskite, $CaTiO_3$, previously considered, each Ca^{2+} is coordinated by 12 O^{2-} and each Ti^{4+} by 6 O^{2-}, so that the electrostatic-valence strengths of Ca—O and Ti—O are $\frac{2}{12} = \frac{1}{6}$ and $\frac{4}{6} = \frac{2}{3}$; each O^{2-} ion is bound to 4 Ca^{2+} and 2 Ti^{4+}, since $\frac{4}{6} + \frac{4}{3} = 2$, which satisfies the valence of oxygen.

3. The existence of edges, and particularly of faces, common to two anion polyhedra in a coordinated structure decreases its stability; this effect is large for cations with high valence and small coordination number and is especially large when the radius ratio approaches the lower limit of stability of the polyhedron. Thus SiO_4 tetrahedra almost invariably share only corners, TiO_6 octahedra may have common edges, and AlO_6 octahedra common faces.

4. In a crystal containing different cations those of high valence and small coordination number tend not to share polyhedron elements with each other.

5. The number of essentially different kinds of constituent in a crystal tends to be small (principle of parsimony).

Additional Complications in Silicates. Besides the foregoing rules the following features of silicate structure account for some of the apparent complexities:

1. Isomorphous replacement of cations by others of same charge but similar size, or of several cations by others of different valence but same aggregate charge (already noted for mixed oxides, perovskite, and spinel types, page 510).

2. Isomorphous substitutions of anions O^{2-}, OH^-, F^-, wholly or statistically.

3. Stable mixed structures, with parts of crystal of one type and remainder of another.

4. The peculiar role of Al^{3+}, arising from the fact that the Al:O radius ratio 0.43 is nearly the critical value 0.414 for transition from sixfold to fourfold coordination: thus Al may appear in the same structure in both capacities or, when fourfold-coordinated, may substitute for Si^{4+}, necessitating a corresponding substitution of Ca^{2+} for Na^+, Al^{3+} for Mg^{2+}, Fe^{3+} for Fe^{2+}, etc., to maintain neutrality.

5. The appearance of O^{2-} and OH^- as water of hydration or uncoordinated with Si^{4+}, giving false indication of composition and structure; thus cyanite, Al_2SiO_5, has one O^{2-} uncoordinated with Si^{4+}, and the formula is OAl_2SiO_4, an orthosilicate.

6. In addition to the schemes of sharing and the substitution, particularly, of Al for Si, x-ray analysis has further shown the peculiar structures formed by fitting together of layers of entirely different compounds. The best example is the series of Mg_2SiO_4 and $Mg(OH)_2$ lamellar structures. If layers of the latter are designated by X and of the former by Y, the following minerals may be defined by the repeat schemes:

Brucite	$Mg(OH)_2$	XXX
Olivine	$(Mg, Fe)_2SiO_4$	YYY
Norbergite	$Mg_2SiO_4.Mg(OH)_2$	XXY
Chondrodite	$2Mg_2SiO_4.Mg(OH)_2$	XY, XXY
Humite	$3Mg_2SiO_4.Mg(OH)_2$	XY, XY, XXY
Clinohumite	$4Mg_2SiO_4.Mg(OH)_2$	XY, XY, XY, XXY

Classification of Silicates. The SiO_4 tetrahedra and the sharing of corners determine the general composition and classification of silicates, which are tabulated in Table 18-1.

Zeolites and Ultramarines. The zeolite minerals call for special attention on account of their unique constitution, structure, properties, and uses, for example, in permutite water softening. Essential facts established by x-ray analysis may be summarized as follows:

1. They have an open-framework structure with large open channels, consisting of $(Si, Al)_nO_{2n}$.

2. They contain water, which in many cases may be driven off by heat without destroying structure (see preceding chapter, on hydrates) and reversibly replaced. While water molecules are situated in channels through which they and positive ions can diffuse, they have definite neighbors owing to requirements of the tetrahedral charge distribution as follows:

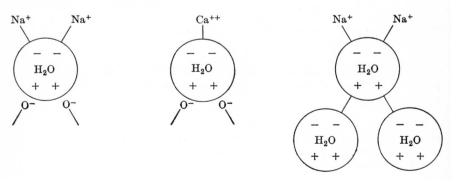

3. Water may be substituted by NH_3, alcohol, Hg, I_2, etc.

4. Cations may be substituted reversibly without affecting structure.

a. Two by two others of similar sizes and same total charge, such as $K^+ + Si^{4+} \rightleftharpoons Ba^{2+} + Al^{3+}$; $Na^+ + Si^{4+} \rightleftharpoons Ca^{2+} + Al^{3+}$.

b. Change in number of cations, such as $Ba^{2+} \rightleftharpoons 2K^+$, $Ca^{2+} \rightleftharpoons 2Na^+$, $Na^+ + 2Ca^{2+} \rightleftharpoons 3Na^+ + Ca^{2+}$, as in permutite water softeners, in which Ca^{2+} is removed from hard water by replacing Na^+ and the zeolite regenerated by NaCl.

5. Defect structures are characteristic; in analcite, $NaAlSi_2O_6.H_2O$, 16 Na^+ ions in the unit cell occupy 24 equivalent positions, hence are in a decidedly "fluid" condition; this is proved in x-ray patterns by substituting Ag ions for Na^+.

6. The structures may display fibrous or lamellar properties, though still retaining the ratio O: (Si, Al) 2:1. Natrolite, $Na_2(Al_2Si_3O_{10}).2H_2O$, is fibrous, made up of chains with regular repetition of a unit of five tetrahedra, as the formula indicates, and heulandite, $Ca(Al_2Si_7O_{18}).6H_2O$, lamellar.

7. Closely related are framework structures that do not contain water, including ultramarine, the first framework silicate to be established, by Jaeger, in 1927. Two representative minerals are sodalite, $Na_8(Al_6Si_6O_{24}).Cl_2$, and noselite, $Na_8(Al_6Si_6O_{24}).SO_4$, which may be converted one into the other by heating in fused Na_2SO_4 or NaCl, respectively. The natural compound that gives its blue color to lapis lazuli and artificial ultramarines is the result of replacement of Cl and SO_4 in the above compounds by sulfur, which in varying amounts is responsible for a wide range of colors. Industrial ultramarines are classified according to the ratios of Al:Si, 1:1 and 1:1.5. Base exchange is possible, but it is likely that the ions tend to remain more nearly in fixed positions than in analcite.

The Forms of Silica. Silica, SiO_2, exists in six different crystalline forms, although all are frameworks of tetrahedra, each sharing all four oxygen atoms. The modifications are:

$$\text{Quartz} \underset{\beta}{\overset{\alpha}{\downarrow}} 573° \qquad \text{Tridymite} \underset{\beta}{\overset{\alpha}{\downarrow}} 120\text{–}160° \qquad \text{Cristobalite} \underset{\beta}{\overset{\alpha}{\downarrow}} 200\text{–}275°$$

$$\xrightarrow{\quad\quad\quad} 870° \xleftarrow{\quad\quad\quad\quad} 1479° \xleftarrow{\quad\quad\quad\quad} 1710°$$
$$\text{(melting point)}$$

In each case the low- to high-temperature transformation takes place quickly and reversibly, while the transformations quartz to tridymite to cristobalite are so sluggish that tridymite and cristobalite are found in minerals and remain indefinitely in their metastable states; their α to β inversions are studied actually at temperatures where they are metastable forms.

The structure of β-cristobalite proposed by Wyckoff is the only case of a linear arrangement of —Si—O—Si— consistent with a purely ionic bond; for all other forms the angle of the bond is less than 180 deg so that there is a tendency toward the spatially directed bonds of homopolar type. Barth assigned a lower symmetry, however, to β-cristobalite, and it is possible that in it also the bonds are inclined while cubic symmetry is attained through rotation of the oxygen atom.

The complexity of this system is a never-ending source of speculation, and it is not surprising that detailed structures of all six forms are not yet

TABLE 18-1. THE SILICATES

Structural arrangement	Oxygen-silicon ratio	Examples
1. Independent SiO_4 tetrahedra bound in structure by cations	4:1 $(SiO_4)^{4-}$	Orthosilicates—olivine, Mg_2SiO_4; or better $9Mg_2SiO_4 \cdot Fe_2SiO_4$, cyanite, sillimanite, andalusite, Al_2SiO_5 really OAl_2SiO_4; (half of Al 6-coordinated and half in 6, 4, and 5, respectively); closely related staurolite, $Fe(OH)_2 \cdot 2Al_2SiO_5$; topaz, $(F, OH)_2Al_2SiO_4$; euclase, (OH)-$BeAlSiO_4$; chondrodite (mixed lattice), $Mg(F, OH)_2 \cdot n\text{-}Mg_2SiO_4$; phenacite, Be_2SiO_4, complex rhombohedral because both Be and Si tetrahedrally coordinated
2. Pair of tetrahedra sharing one O atom	7:2 $(Si_2O_7)^{6-}$	Thorveitite, $Sc_2Si_2O_7$; hemimorphite, $(OH)_2Zn_4 \cdot Si_2O_7 \cdot H_2O$ (formerly H_2Zn_2-SiO_5); vesuvianite (both SiO_4 and Si_2O_7), $(OH)_4Ca_{10}Al_4(Mg, Fe)_2[(Si_2O_7)_2 \cdot (SiO_4)_5]$
3. Closed rings of tetrahedra, each sharing two O atoms	3:1 $(SiO_3)_n^{2n-}$	Three-membered ring, benitoite, $BaTiSi_3O_9$; six-membered, beryl (emerald), $Be_3Al_2Si_6O_{18}$ (Fig. 276), with marked open-channel structure
4. Infinite chains of tetrahedra, each sharing two O atoms	3:1 $(SiO_3)_n^{2n-}$	Pyroxenes—diopside, $CaMg(SiO_3)_2$ (Fig. 277), spodumene, $LiAl(SiO_3)_2$, etc.
5. Infinite double chains of tetrahedra sharing alternately two and three O atoms	11:4 $(Si_4O_{11})_n^{6n-}$	Amphiboles—tremolite, $(OH, F)_2Ca_2Mg_5$-Si_8O_{22} (formerly $Ca_2Mg_6Si_8O_{24}$); chrysotile (asbestos), $(OH)_6Mg_6Si_4O_{11} \cdot H_2O$, chains held by weak attraction of OH instead of by metal ions as in pyroxenes and amphiboles, fibrous, cleavage parallel to chains (Fig. 277) characterized by extensive isomorphous substitutions, including Al^{3+} for Si^{4+}; general formula $(O, OH, F)_2$-$(Ca, Na)_{2-1}(Na, K)_{0-1}(Mg, Fe^{2+}, Fe^{2+}; Al, Fe^{3+})_4[(Al, Si)_2Si_6O_{22}]$
6. Infinite sheets of tetrahedra, each sharing three O atoms	5:2 $(Si_2O_5)_n^{2n-}$	1. Talc, $(OH)_3Mg_3Si_4O_{10}$ 2. Micas—muscovite, $(OH)_2KAl_2(Si_3Al)$-O_{10} 3. Margarite, $CaAl_2(Si_2Al_2)O_{10}$ [note K in (2) and Ca in (3), made possible by substitution of one Al^{3+} for one Si^{4+} and two Al^{3+} for two Si^{4+}] 4. Phlogopite, $(OH)_2KMg_3(Si_3Al)O_{10}$
7. Infinite framework of tetrahedra each sharing all four O atoms	2:1 SiO_2 $[(Si, Al)O_2]^-$	In the case of $[(Si, Al)O_2]^-$, in which aluminum replaces silicon, the framework is negatively charged, and positive ions may just be accommodated in the holes. The replacement is illustrated by the following formulas of familiar minerals: Si:Al Ratio SiO_2 (silicas)............................ ∞ Orthoclase, $K[AlSi_3O_8]$ (feldspars).... 3:1 Analcite, $Na[AlSi_2O_6] \cdot H_2O$........... 2:1 Natrolite, $Na_2[Al_2Si_3O_{10}] \cdot 2H_2O$....... 3:2 Anorthite, $Ca[Al_2Si_2O_8]$.............. 1:1

completely known.   Present data are listed in Table 18-2.   For example, in typically precise measurements by Buerger α-tridymite from California

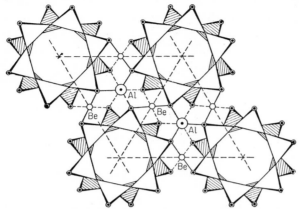

FIG. 276. The structure of beryl, $Be_3Al_2Si_6O_{18}$.

was found to have the following dimensions for the face-centered orthorhombic cell:

$$a_0 = 9.91 \text{ A} \qquad b_0 = 17.18 \text{ A} \qquad c_0 = 81.57 \text{ A}$$

Another specimen from Mexico had the same a_0 and b_0 values but a c_0 axis only half as long.   The presence of impurities is believed to be the cause of the doubled c axis. The California crystal inverted from low form to high form at 127°C, while the Mexican showed two inversions, low to middle at 121°C and middle to high at 135°.

It is certain, however, that the three main forms of SiO_2 are all built up of that most fundamental and common of all building brick, the SiO_4 tetrahedra, linked together so that every oxygen atom is common to two tetrahedra (in accordance with the composition SiO_2) but the arrangement of the linked tetrahedra is quite different.   The same difference exists between tridymite and cristobalite as that between α and β

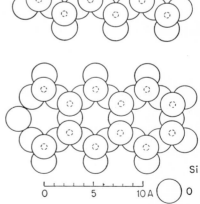

FIG. 277. Silicon-oxygen chains in pyroxene (diopside) (*above*), and double chains in amphibole (*below*).   Mica is built from a further extension of these chains into a sheet.

forms of each variety, which differ only in slight detail, the β always having a higher symmetry (Fig. 278).   There are involved only slight rotations of tetrahedra relative to one another, a rapid and reversible process in which, for example, levorotatory quartz remains levorotatory, whereas the change from quartz to tridymite involves the breaking of Si—O—Si bonds and relinking of the tetrahedra in a different way, a sluggish

TABLE 18-2. CRYSTAL STRUCTURES OF SiO₂

Form	Structure	Space group	Z	Cell dimensions
α-Quartz..............	Trigonal	$C3_12$	3	$\begin{cases} a = 4.903 \\ c = 5.393 \end{cases}$
β-Quartz..............	Hexagonal	$C6_22$	3	$\begin{cases} a = 5.01 \\ c = 5.446 \end{cases}$
α-Tridymite...........	Rhombic	? (complex)	64	$\begin{cases} a = 9.88 \\ b = 17.1 \\ c = 16.3 \end{cases}$
β-Tridymite...........	Hexagonal	$C6/mmc$	4	$\begin{cases} a = 5.03 \\ c = 8.22 \end{cases}$
α-Cristobalite..........	Tetragonal	$D4_32_1$	4	$\begin{cases} a = 4.96 \\ c = 6.92 \end{cases}$
β-Cristobalite..........	Cubic	$Fd3m$	8	7.16

process and one in which the optically active quartz becomes optically inactive tridymite. The right- and left-handed spirals of linked tetrahedra in quartz are clearly indicated in the crystal-structure interpretations from x-ray data.

The identification of these various modifications forms one of the principal applications of diffraction analysis to ceramic materials, gems, industrial dusts, soils, devitrified glass, etc.

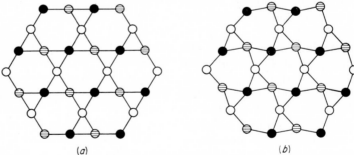

(a)   (b)

FIG. 278. The relation between (a) β-quartz and (b) α-quartz. Silicon atoms only are shown.

Industrial Dusts and the Diagnosis of Silicosis. The identification and quantitative determination of the crystalline constituents of mine and industrial dusts and the correlation of these with the appearance of silicosis in the lungs are among the useful and unique applications of x-ray diffraction analysis. The mineralogical composition, or state of chemical combination, of a dust has vastly greater pathological significance than the elementary composition deduced by chemical or spectroscopic analysis. The failure of the usual and generally dependable petrographic immersion microscope to distinguish between free quartz and some silicate minerals in the dusts of some Canadian gold mines led to the development by Clark and Reynolds[1] of a quantitative x-ray diffraction procedure, utilizing the familiar "internal-standard" technique. A pure crystalline powder, known not to be present in the dust being examined, was added to the unknown in a definite ratio and the diffraction pattern registered. The ratio of the density of a line sought to that of a nearby line of the added standard was determined photometrically. The ratio thus obtained was proportional to the line intensity of the substance sought, which in turn was proportional to the amount of the substance in the mixture. By reference to a curve that was prepared empirically from

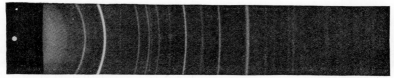

Fig. 279. Powder diffraction pattern for quartz as standard for dust analysis.

mixtures of known composition, the percentage of the constituent sought was obtainable at once. Figure 279 shows the pattern for a typical dust sample compared with a standard pattern for ordinary quartz. This method, of course, is applicable to the determination of any selected mineral constituent. The next step was to attempt to identify the particular variety of silica or silicate responsible for silicosis. Through cooperation with the Municipal Tuberculosis Sanitarium of Chicago, it was possible to make an x-ray analysis of lung tissue from 31 cases of known or suspected silicosis (among miners, stonecutters, cement workers, etc.) with the usually attendant tuberculosis.[2] In all definite cases of silicosis, crystalline quartz was identified, varying in amount from a threshold value of 0.2 per cent (about 0.09 per cent silica can be found in an infant's lungs) up to nearly 2.5 per cent. The lungs of some persons showed high contents of silicon by chemical analysis; but wherever the crystal lines corresponded to a compound other than quartz, there was no silicotic condition. This analysis must be made after death, but the method can be made to apply to body fluids, particularly sputum, for diagnosis. Best of all is the protection of workers against industrial dusts shown to contain crystalline quartz. Powdered aluminum in

[1] *Univ. Toronto Studies, Geol. Ser.*, **38**, 13 (1935); *Ind. Eng. Chem., Anal. Ed.*, **8**, 36 (1936).

[2] Sweany, Klaas, and Clark, *Radiology*, **31**, 399 (1938).

amounts of only 1 per cent is the most effective combative agent against quartz. X-ray and electron diffraction analyses have proved that an extremely thin film (less than 250 A) of a hydrous alumina hydrate gel forms on the surface of silica particles, which prevents them from dissolving in the lung tissues and thus prevents toxic effects. The hydrous material dries to α-Al_2O_3.H_2O, böhmite.[1] As indicated on page 429 in the discussion of quantitative analysis by powder diffraction, the Geiger-counter diffractometer is extremely useful for dust analysis. The details of proper techniques were established at the Mellon Institute[2] and at the Canadian Department of National Health and Welfare.[3] In 1952 Clark and Loranger made a detailed dust analysis on a large steel foundry, utilizing the Geiger-counter diffractometer, with the results indicated in Table 18-3 (see also page 435).

TABLE 18-3. ANALYSIS OF FOUNDRY DUSTS

Areas	Per cent quartz	G dust/hr	G quartz/ hr
1. Electric furnace....................	19.3	0.2271	0.0438
2. Sand mills........................	22.5	0.0678	0.0305
3. Casting...........................	37.7	0.0480	0.0181
4. Double shakeout...................	24.8	0.3750	0.3720
5. Cove sand mill....................	27.2	0.0684	0.0372
6. Large core room...................	28.0 ⎫ ventilated	0.0375	0.0105
7. Core room........................	7.1 ⎭	0.0375	0.0027
8. Sand slinger......................	54.8	0.2375	0.1301
9. Between (8) and big floor shakeout....	81.0	0.0902	0.0744
10. Big floor shakeout.................	16.5	0.1762	0.0290
11. Near 10..........................	18.0	0.0536	0.0096
12. Chipping and cleaning.............	5.5	0.0456	0.0025
13. Swing grinding....................	36.0	0.0700	0.0251
14. Small-casting cleaning.............	0	0.1987	0
15. Cleaning, heat-treating, and welding...	0	0.0431	0
16. Cleaning, heat-treating, and welding...	0	0.0990	0

Since to an unusual extent most of the foundry workers had worked in the same areas for many years, it was possible to establish correlation with lung radiographs for active, arrested, or absent silicosis, the effectiveness of aluminum therapy, and the effects of high iron concentrations in producing indications of siderosis (page 200, Chap. 9).

Clay and Soil Minerals.[4] The classification and constitution of the clay minerals present a problem, at once of the greatest importance and of

[1] Germer and Storks, *Ind. Eng. Chem., Anal. Ed.,* **11**, 583 (1939).

[2] H. P. Klug, L. Alexander, and E. Kummer, *J. Ind. Hyg. Toxicol.,* **30**, 166 (1948); *Anal. Chem.,* **20**, 886 (1948).

[3] K. Kay, *Am. Ind. Hyg. Assoc. Quart.,* **11**, 185 (1950).

[4] This subject is comprehensively treated in the book "X-ray Identification and Structures of Clay Minerals," edited by G. W. Brindley, Mineralogical Society, London, 1951.

great difficulty, upon which only a beginning has been made.[1] It is certain that the essential structure must be a layer silicate; that base exchange must be possible; that water and nutrient solutions must be held in unique fashion; that individual crystals are extremely small ordinarily, which in itself limits the x-ray method largely to the powder method and renders almost impossible the derivation of complete structures depending upon single crystals. However, the tendency of wet clay particles to orient with their cleavage faces parallel to a surface

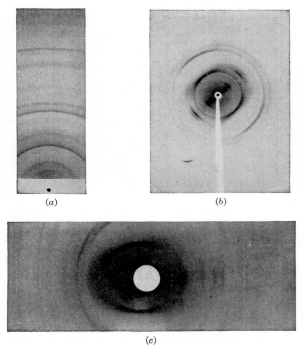

(a)　　　　(b)

(c)

FIG. 280. Patterns for clay: (a) powder; (b) flake formed on surface of evaporated suspension; (c) oscillation (Bragg) pattern of flake.

makes it possible to employ oriented flakes for obtaining a fiber pattern. This is the basis of the development of the commercial sheet material from clay called Alsifilm (E. A. Hauser). In Fig. 280 are shown the powder pattern and the fiber pattern of a flake of clay composed of kaolinite and mica. Here the short arcs represent successive orders of basal reflections (001) which are most significant in the identification of clay minerals. Oscillation Bragg patterns record many more orders. These clay minerals therefore are micaceous in structure, consisting of thin hexagonal flakes with perfect cleavage, built up from the linked tetrahedral SiO_4 groups referred to in Table 18-1.

[1] The formation of some of the silicate minerals from Al and Fe hydroxides is illustrated in Fig. 274 in the preceding chapter.

The clay minerals are classified as follows:

1. Kaolin type. Kaolinite, nacrite, dickite, with a formula formerly written $2H_2O.Al_2O_3.2SiO_2$ but structurally $Al_2(OH)_4Si_2O_5$; single sheets, polar with one side consisting of bases of SiO_4 tetrahedra, the other of OH^- and metal (Al^{3+}) ions in six-coordination, with the polar OH^- groups in contact with the basal oxygen atoms of tetrahedra of the next sheet as shown in a simplified structural diagram in Fig. 281; in other words, composition rather exact; crystals very small and perfect.

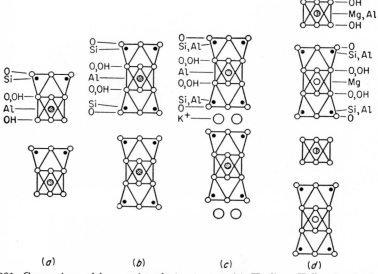

FIG. 281. Comparison of layer mineral structures. (a) Kaolin. Halloysite (hydrated) similar, with water layer between layers. (b) Pyrophyllite (double layer). Talc same, except Mg^{2+} for Al^{3+}. (c) Muscovite mica; when Al^{2+} replaces Si^{4+} in second layer, negative charge is balanced by K^+ ions between layers. Phlogopite same, except Mg^{2+} in center layer instead of Al^{3+}. (d) Chlorite; negatively charged double layer (when Al^{3+} replaces Si^{4+}) balanced by layers of brucite, $Mg(OH)_2$, in which Mg^{2+} is replaced by Al^{3+} to give net positive charge.

2. Montmorillonite (beidellite)[1] type (bentonite, fuller's earth), $(OH)_2(3Mg.2Fe.2Al)Si_4O_{10}.nH_2O$. This is built when the kaolin layer in Fig. 281 is doubled symmetrically by using the OH groups on both sides of Al ions and thus SiO_4 tetrahedra at the two layer surfaces, as diagrammatically represented in Fig. 282 in comparison with mica and pyrophyllite.

Bradley, Grim, and Clark[2] have demonstrated that 0, 1, 2, 3, or 4 layers of H_2O molecules may be introduced in swelling to form discrete

[1] These two names are used interchangeably since the same patterns are obtained for both minerals. However, "beidellite" refers to the limiting aluminum mineral, "nontronite" to the limiting ferric composition, and "montmorillonite" to the magnesium-bearing mineral.

[2] *Z. Krist.*, **97**, 216 (1937).

hydrates (possibly 0, 4, 8, 12, 16 H_2O molecules) with periodicity values along the c axis of 9.6, 12.4, 15.4, 18.4, and 21.4 A. As d_{001} increases with hydration, it becomes difficult to understand what forces hold the layers together at all. Above the highest hydrate it may be assumed that layers are comparatively free, and it is under this condition that exchange bases have access to the mineral and assume the role of binding it together as water content decreases. Gieseking[1] has shown for bentonite that large substituted ammonium ions, NH_3R^+, NH_2R^+, NHR_3^+, NR_4^+, and

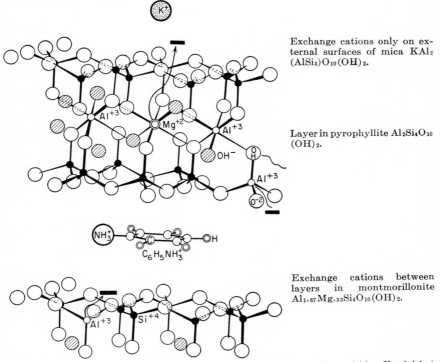

Exchange cations only on external surfaces of mica KAl_2 $(AlSi_3)O_{10}(OH)_2$.

Layer in pyrophyllite $Al_2Si_4O_{10}$ $(OH)_2$.

Exchange cations between layers in montmorillonite $Al_{1.67}Mg_{.33}Si_4O_{10}(OH)_2$.

FIG. 282. Relationships of montmorillonite with mica and pyrophyllite. (*After Hendricks.*)

methylene blue replace H^+, Na^+, or Ca^{2+} with great increase in the 001 or c spacing and hence that cation substitution takes place in this variable spacing rather than within a layer by breaking of bonds. Montmorillonite must be defective in metal cations (usually Mg^{2+}), giving a net negative charge on the oxygens; in the water layers are found the compensating H^+, Na^+, or Ca^{2+} ions. Bradley[2] has made x-ray studies of the stable complexes with glycol, polyglycol, and amines. He has used the

[1] *Soil Sci.*, **47**, 1 (1939).

[2] W. F. Bradley, *J. Am. Chem. Soc.*, **67**, 975 (1945); *Am. Mineralogist*, **30**, 704 (1945); *J. Phys. Chem.*, **52**, 1404 (1948); *Trans. Intern. Congr. Soil Sci.*, **1**, 421 (1950); *Am. Mineralogist*, **35**, 590 (1950).

complexes with ethylene glycol as diagnostic criteria for the clay minerals. Individual layers of montmorillonite interleaved with double layers of glycol molecules comprise a periodicity of 17 A; kaolinite, no reaction; endellite (hydrated halloysite), 10.8 A changed from 10.2 A; illite, no reaction; mixed-layer minerals, characteristic changes.   Random intergrowth of montmorillonite-illite systems is proved by comparison of patterns with theoretical scattering-distribution curves for 10 and 12.5, 10 and 15, and 10 and 17 A.   The *fixed* alternating-layer sequence in the mineral rectorite deduced from x-ray patterns is represented as follows:

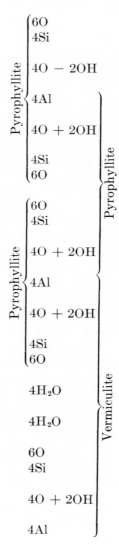

X-ray diffraction by structures with random interstratifications and by randomly displaced layer lattice minerals is considered in detail in the recent book "X-ray Identification and Structures of Clay Minerals."[1]

All these clay minerals, including the micas, resemble each other in the definiteness of hexagonal network structure of linked SiO_4 tetrahedra in the plane of the sheets ($a = 5.1$ to 5.3, $b = 9.0$ to 9.3 A) and in the variation of the ways in which sheets are piled on each other and of the spacing along the c axis; all are pseudohexagonal but actually monoclinic, with β nearly 90 deg.

In x-ray analysis of clays it is common practice to distinguish the montmorillonite group from the hydrous mica group by the $c(001)$ spacing, respectively, usually 15 to 16 and 10 to 13 A. In view of the variations in c with type of base used for saturation and the medium from which the clay is dried, confusion may result. Jackson and Heller[2] found the most reliable treatment, which includes drying from benzene suspensions at 35°. Best results are obtained by saturating the fine clay particles with calcium, suspended in a benzene-water-ethanol mixture, hydrated to 50 per cent of the weight of the clay by expulsion of water through addition of benzene, freed of excess liquid, dried at 30°C and 65 per cent relative humidity, and x-rayed while exposed to a relative humidity of 92 per cent. This results in a 16-A line of very high intensity for montmorillonite and 13 A for hydrous mica. The relative intensities of these two lines is the basis for quantitative analysis for the two constituents in clays. The expanding-lattice minerals disperse on suspension into free, single crystal plates. On drying, the free plates reorient, with the possibility that hydrous mica and montmorillonite plates may pair up and hydrate at 92 per cent relative humidity like paired montmorillonite plates.

Results on 45 fine clays from soils and bentonites showed montmorillonite to be the dominant constituent. A very complete analysis of sediments from the Pacific Ocean also showed the wide prevalence of montmorillonite and the possibility of far-reaching geological interpretations.[3]

One important commercial utilization of montmorillonite is in the preparation of drilling muds. X-ray patterns illustrate the contrasting properties of suspensions of montmorillonite compared with those of a conventional clay mineral, kaolinite, whose crystalline particles disperse as entities; the diffraction effects are observed upon irradiation of a flowing stream of suspension as discharged through a capillary nozzle. The diagram of the kaolinite suspension includes *all* the lines normally observed in solid specimens superposed over the characteristic water halos. The diagrams of the Wyoming bentonite suspension and of the

[1] *Op. cit.*

[2] *Soil Sci. Soc. Amer.*, **6**, 133 (1941), **7**, 194 (1942).

[3] Grim, Dietz, and Bradley, *Bull. Geol. Soc. Amer.*, **50**, 785 (1940).

montmorillonite base shale include the normal diagrams for the non-clay mineral accessories in each case and the normal diffraction effects related to the prism zone—*i.e.*, to the lateral extension of the individual silicate sheets. No normal reflections or higher orders of reflection related to any basal spacing are observed. Except for the water halos, there is observed only a remarkably prominent low-angle scattering feature, which arises from the dissemination of solid particles in the liquid medium (Chap. 21).

3. Micas. Muscovite, a typical mica, has the composition $(OH)_2KAl_2$-$(Si_3Al)O_{10}$. Like montmorillonite it has sheets of SiO_4 tetrahedra arranged in pairs, with their vertices and bases alternately together (Fig. 283). These vertices are strongly cross-linked by Al^{3+}, each of which is

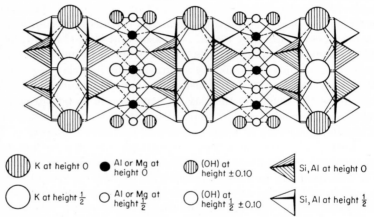

FIG. 283. The structure of muscovite mica $(OH)_2KAl_2(Si_3Al)O_{10}$. The sheets are seen edge on.

octahedrally coordinated by 4 O^{2-} belonging to the sheets and 2 OH. The bases of the tetrahedra are linked through K^+ ions coordinated by 12 O^{2-} neighbors, but only in so far as Si^{4+} is replaced by Al^{3+} are these O^{2-} ions actively bound by electrostatic valences. As Si^{4+} increases relative to Al^{3+}, K^+ ions, which serve to "tack" layers together, decrease. Many Middle Western clays have constituents of this type, down to the limiting case of talc, $(OH)_2Mg_3(Si_4O_{10})$, or pyrophyllite $(OH)_2Al_2$-(Si_4O_{10}), with no K^+ ions and with layers held solely by the van der Waals forces. Thus there are the following related compounds:

$$Mg_3(OH)_4Si_2O_5\text{-}Al_2(OH)_4Si_2O_5$$
$$\text{Unknown} \qquad\qquad \text{Kaolin}$$

$$Mg_3(OH)_2Si_4O_{10}\text{-}Al_2(OH)_2Si_4O_{10}$$
$$\text{Talc} \qquad\qquad \text{Pyrophyllite}$$

$$KMg_3(OH)_2Si_3AlO_{10}\text{-}KAl_2(OH)_2Si_3AlO_{10}$$
$$\text{Phlogopite} \qquad\qquad \text{Muscovite}$$

$$CaAl_2(OH)_2Si_2Al_2O_{10}$$
$$\text{Margarite (brittle mica)}$$

These structural relationships between kaolin, halloysite, pyrophyllite, muscovite, and phlogopite micas and chlorite are illustrated in Fig. 281. Chlorites have intermediate Mg-Al hydroxide layers, with a change resulting from substituting Al^{3+} for Mg^{2+} in brucite, $Mg(OH)_2$, layer structure, or $[Mg_2Al(OH)_6]^+$, while the micalike layers range from $[Mg_3(AlSi_3O_{10})(OH)_2]$ to $[Mg_2Al(Al_2Si_2O_{10})(OH)_2]$; and vermiculites have intermediate H_2O layers. Other constituents in shales are only imperfectly known. Apophyllite $KF.Ca_4Si_8O_{20}(8H_2O)$, has, instead of rings of six SiO_4 tetrahedra with vertices all pointing to one side as in micas, rings of four and eight members with vertices in opposite directions alternately.

Analysis of Soil Profiles. An example of soil analysis is afforded by studies of fractions of genetic soil profiles, especially 1- to 2-μ particles.[1] Quartz, mica, calcite, beidellite, kaolinite, montmorillonite, muscovite, etc., can all be identified by characteristic spacings, although many spacings are common to several of the sheet minerals. These results lead to definite conclusions as to origin of soils at different profile levels, and these to valuable contributions to geology and agronomy. It has been established recently in soils that, as weathering of true micas proceeds through illite, intermediates, vermiculite, and montmorillonite, a given K^+ interlayer is rapidly depleted of K^+ along a preferential weathering plane, leading to some expansions. Concurrent hydroxylation by K^+ additions to the octahedral layer, together with dealumination, accounts for loss of some of the mica-layer charges. Increasing proportions of such weathered planes leads to various combinations of x-amorphous and x-crystalline zones typical of illite, vermiculite, and montmorillonite found in soils, accounting for diffraction properties, internal surface, K^+, H_2O, and OH^- contents, and exchange properties.[2]

Cement.[3] The characteristic feature of cement compounds is ability to react with water and harden. The compounds are formed at high temperatures and seem to involve the active and unstable coordination by Ca^{2+} of oxygens already claimed by SiO_4 coordination in close-packed structure. These anhydrous compounds undergo polymorphic transformations on account of instability or split hydrolytically on contact with water and are changed into stable lime silicate, lime aluminate, or hydrates with "inactive" calcium ions.

[1] Clark, Riecken, and Reynolds, *Z. Krist.*, **96**, 273 (1937). Whiteside, Loess Deposits in Illinois, *Proc. Soil Sci. Soc. Amer.*, **12**, 415 (1947).

[2] M. L. Jackson, Y. Hseung, R. B. Cosey, E. J. Evans, and R. C. Van der Heuvel, *Proc. Soil Sci. Amer.*, **16**, 3 (1952).

[3] For the most comprehensive account, see "Symposium on the Chemistry of Cements," Stockholm, 1938. Not much research work has been done since this date. Perhaps the most critical is that of Guinier and Brocard, published by Centre d'études et de recherches de l'industrie des liants hydrauliques, *Tech. Pub.* 1, Paris, 1948. In this monograph detailed data are given for powder diffraction lines of the most important identified compounds.

Commercial cements are ordinarily manufactured from blast-furnace slag, clinker, etc., and so are very complex in composition. Identification of the constituents depends largely on phase-rule studies as on the $CaO-Al_2O_3-SiO_2$ ternary systems and synthesis of various possible compounds, which may then be characterized by powder diffraction patterns, aided by microscopy, differential etching by reagents, and any other available techniques. There is still some disagreement as to the precise stoichiometric formulas of some of the crystalline phases. The following cement compounds have been identified almost solely by x-ray methods in spite of great difficulties in obtaining crystals:

(1) $CaO.Al_2O_3$.

(2) $3CaO.Al_2O_3$. Cubic, $a_0 = 15.22$, 24 moles per unit cell, related to perovskite, network of AlO_4, AlO_0, and CaO_6 groups (Ca^{2+} in an open basket of O^{2-} ions) with embedded "inactive" Ca^{2+}; reactivity due to CaO_6 and large holes.

(3) $8CaO.Na_2O.3Al_2O_3$. Obtained by substituting Na_2O for CaO in compound above, with resulting distortion.

(4) $12CaO.7Al_2O_3$ (or $5CaO.3Al_2O_3$) constituents of hydraulic cements.
(5) $CaO.2Al_2O_3$ (or $3CaO.5Al_2O_3$)

(6) $2CaO.Al_2O_3.SiO_2$ (gehlenite). Does not react with water; SiO_4, AlO_4 tetrahedra held together in eight-coordination by inactive Ca^{2+} ion.

(7) $4CaO.Al_2O_3.Fe_2O_3$. Reactive because of FeO_4 tetrahedra and CaO_6 "baskets" open toward cavities.

(8) $3CaO.SiO_2$ (most important cement compound). Since $Si:O = 1:5$, some oxygen ions are coordinated with Ca^{2+} alone, which is active as a coordination center of six O^{2-}.

(9) $2CaO.SiO_2$. Exists in four forms, α, α', and β (active, (γ) (inactive), because of complete difference in Ca^{2+} coordination. α, rhombohedral, high temperature; α', orthorhombic, medium temperature (β-K_2SO_4 type); γ, like room-temperature stable olivine; β, monoclinic, $P2_1n$, room temperature metastable, sets to hard mass with water.[1]

The recognized hydrates after reaction and setting with water, upon which x-ray work is still fragmentary, are:

(1) $Ca(OH)_2$.

(2) $Al_2O_3.3H_2O$. Probably $Al(OH)_6$ octahedra.

(3) $AlOOH$. Diaspore. Formed at 15° from hydration of $CaO.Al_2O_3 = 2CaO.-Al_2O_5.7H_2O$ hexagonal.

(4) $3CaO.Al_2O_3.6H_2O$. Cubic, $a_0 = 15.56$. $3CaO.Al_2O_3.12H_2O$ hexagonal.

(5) $4CaO.Al_2O_3.12H_2O$. Hexagonal.

(6) $3CaO.Al_2O_3.6H_2O$ cubic, and possibly seven or eight other hydrates, all resembling each other. According to Brandenberger, formed from mixed layers of $Ca(OH)_2$ and hydrous alumina with water.

(7) $CaO.SiO_2.4H_2O$. The principal cement "glue."

(8) $CaO.SiO_2.2.5H_2O$.

[1] $\alpha\alpha'$, M. A. Bredig, *J. Am. Chem. Soc.*, **33**, 188 (1950). γ, H. O'Daniel and L. Tscherschwili, *Z. Krist.*, **104**, 124 (1942). β, C. M. Midgley, *Acta. Cryst.*, **5**, 307 (1952).

[2] For the most recent account, see "Symposium on the Chemistry of Cements," Stockholm, 1938.

(9) $2CaO.SiO_2.H_2O$. Four different hydrates of this composition have been described. The α-hydrate has been intensively studied by Heller.[1] It has the orthorhombic unit-cell dimensions $a = 9.34$, $b = 7.22$, $c = 10.61$ A, $Z = 8$, space group $P2_12_12_1$. It contains discrete $(SiO_3.OH)^{3-}$ tetrahedra, and its formula must be $Ca_2(SiO_3OH)$ OH.

(10) $3CaO.2SiO_2.3H_2O$ (afwillite), which is actually $Ca_3(SiO_3OH)_2.2H_2O$; was analyzed by three-dimensional Fourier methods, the most complete attempt for any of these compounds.[2] The most important crystalline hardening agent in portland cement. Probably the same as (7).

(11) $2CaO.Al_2O_3.SiO_2.xH_2O$. Lime water plus dehydrated kaolin, or tricalcium silicate and tricalcium aluminate precipitated in water.

(12) $3CaO.Fe_2O_3.6H_2O$. Corresponds to (4) above.

(13) $3CaO.Al_2O_3.CaSO_4.12H_2O$. Precipitated when gypsum is added as a retarder to setting; as a film, protects grains of compounds from hydration.

Thus, upon the basis of x-ray research, normal set may be represented by

$$3CaO.Al_2O_3 \ + \ CaSO_4.2H_2O \ + \ 10H_2O \ \rightarrow \ 3CaO.Al_2O_2.CaSO_4.12H_2O$$
$$\text{(crystals as protective film)}$$
$$3CaO.SiO_2 + 5H_2O \rightarrow 2CaO.SiO_2.4H_2O \text{ (microcrystalline)}$$

Quick set is represented by

$$3CaO.Al_2O_3 + Aq \rightarrow Ca \text{ aluminate solution}$$
$$3CaO.SiO_2 + Aq \rightarrow Ca \text{ silicate solution}$$
$$\text{Silicate solution} + \text{aluminate solution} \rightarrow (SiO_2.xH_2O).(Al_2O_3.yH_2O).zH_2O$$
$$\text{coagulate}$$

The low strength at quick set is due to the mechanical properties of this gel.

Thus a retarder is a compound that decreases solubility of aluminates and forms a semipermeable membrane around cement grains.

An accelerator like $CaCl_2$ hastens solution of the silicates by decreasing pH and increasing Ca^{2+} concentration, without dissolving aluminates. Complexes with $CaCl_2$ have been identified by x-rays.

A destroyer is a compound that dissolves aluminates (sugar, borax, humus) and causes quick set or that precipitates insoluble and impermeable film around grains (phosphates, fluorides).

Basic blast-furnace slag reacts like portland cement if the solubility of aluminates is reduced by a retarder and the reaction of silicates quickened by an accelerator.

Electron microscopy has made a notable contribution to the mechanism of set in cements.

Ceramic Materials. The x-ray diffraction unit has become as indispensable in ceramic laboratories as the microscope, and a large number of

[1] Heller, *Acta Cryst.*, **5**, 724 (1952).
[2] H. Megaw, *Acta Cryst.*, **5**, 477 (1952).

papers has been published on identification of crystalline materials from raw materials, such as kaolinite and other clay minerals, to the finished product, including the reactions during firing. A general summary is given by the author in the 1946 Orton Lecture before the American Ceramic Society, entitled "Röntgen Ceramics, Past, Present and Future."[1]

To select only a few of the ceramic applications, quoted largely from this reference, the following are typical:

(A) Detection and quantitative analysis of one or more of the six polymorphic forms of SiO_2, three of calcium carbonate and three of $FeO(OH)$.

(B) Calcination of calcite and dolomite to high calcium and dolomitic limes, and their hydration and recarbonation in plasters.

The claim has been made that all dolomitic plasters fail because MgO in the lime undergoes, with volume change, hydration on the wall. This theory was based on water, determined by chemical analyses of limes treated in an autoclave at high temperatures and pressures, and arbitrary assignment of this water to $Mg(OH)_2$, formed in the autoclave. The x-ray patterns made in extensive work in the author's laboratory disprove this completely by showing unchanged MgO lines in both sound and failed plasters, independently confirmed by thermal analyses. These thermal curves prove that water is adsorbed; hence, plaster failure is mechanical rather than due to hydration of MgO. Converting MgO to $Mg(OH)_2$ in an autoclave certainly is not a duplication of reactions on walls. Plasters from dolomitic limes which are 400 years old still show MgO lines.

(C) *Silica Refractories.* Silica refractories have been studied with great success, both in the sense of identifying phases and in providing suitable texture. The raw material, quartz, is first identified. The suitability for brick manufacture is determined by heating to 1450°C and examining the x-ray powder pattern. The degree of conversion is determined from the relative amounts of residual quartz and newly formed cristobalite and tridymite. Silica brick are fired in order to promote a condition more stable than that of quartz; they may have a routine x-ray test to determine consistency of supply in respect to conversion; the cause of premature softening; and research on the life of silica brick in furnace roofs. The hard-fired brick may have a composition, such as 5 per cent quartz, 40 to 50 per cent cristobalite, and 40 to 50 per cent tridymite. After several weeks' use in an open-hearth furnace, a distinct zonal structure is revealed, first analyzed by Clark and Anderson[2] in 1929. The hot zone is primarily cristobalite (equilibrium phase above 1470°C) and minor phases, principally magnetite. The second zone is tridymite (870 to 1470°C) with increasing development of crystals toward the hot zone. The third approximates the original structure and texture. In an arc furnace roof, however, the face is tridymite instead of cristobalite, and the temperature therefore must never have exceeded 1470°C. It is controlled by the fluidity of the SiO_2-FeO solid-liquid phase region.

(D) *Fire Clay.* Fire clay offers a fascinating field of identification and has been thoroughly studied by Jay[3] with some of the following results: Quartz in siliceous clay begins to be converted to cristobalite at 1100°C and is no longer found after a 1300°C

---

[1] *J. Am. Ceram. Soc.*, **29**, 177 (1946).

[2] G. L. Clark and H. V. Anderson, X-ray Study of Zonal Structure of Silica Brick from Roof of Basic Open-hearth Furnace, *Ind. Eng. Chem.*, **21**, 781–785 (1929).

[3] A. H. Jay, X-ray Analysis in Industry. Applications of X-ray Analysis Methods to Steel-works' Problems, *J. Sci. Instr.*, **18** (5), 81–84 (1941); *Ceram. Abstr.*, **20** (10), 250 (1941).

firing; γ-alumina is present at 900 to 1100°C and no higher; cristobalite is first obtained at 1100° from "free" silica from dissociated clay rather than from quartz; cristobalite disappears at 1400°C with formation of a glass; mullite is first observed at 1100° and does not increase in amount at higher temperatures but produces sharper and sharper patterns with complete resolution of $K\alpha$ doublets after a 1500° heat-treatment. All of these observations have been correlated with service behavior and with variation in raw materials.

(E) *Kaolin.* The heat-treatment of kaolin has received considerable attention from x-ray workers. The china clay breaks down at 400 to 500°C into a noncrystalline complex of silica and alumina, retaining the original hexagonal flake form in electron micrographs, though there has been confusion from the invariable presence of mica, which on heat-treatment gives $Al_2O_3.2SiO_2$. At higher temperatures, γ-alumina and mullite, $3Al_2O_3.2SiO_2$, are observed; and, as observed previously, the sharpness of this mullite pattern is a certain indication of the temperature. This is used to determine the efficacy of firing glass tank blocks and also the correlation with porosity and resistance to corrosion.

(F) *Mullite.* Mullite presents a perennial and fascinating problem. The powder patterns of mullites from different sources reveal small but significant differences. α mullite is prepared synthetically from alumina and silica in the theoretical proportions $3Al_2O_3.2SiO_2$; β-mullite occurs naturally in North America and the Isle of Mull with the composition $2Al_2O_3.1SiO_2$, but with extremely small changes in the crystal pattern in spite of increase in Al_2O_3 content; γ-mullite exists generally in aluminumsilicate refractories from clays, kyanite, etc., and corresponds to the α composition but with 1 per cent or less of TiO_2 and/or ferric oxide in solid solution. These are all mullite, but they may be distinguished by the differences in detail of the patterns.

(G) *Boiler-scale Analysis.* Boiler-scale analysis, as already discussed on page 437, is of interest from the ceramic viewpoint and also has great industrial significance, particularly to the end of utilizing the information for boiler-water treatment. The Allis-Chalmers and Dow Companies have completely justified installation of x-ray diffraction equipment in this matter alone. Most calcium silicates belong to the same species as the mineral xonotlites, $5CaO.5SiO_2.H_2O$, with minor variations; the sodium–calcium silicate scale is essentially pectolite, $Na_2O.4CaO.6SiO_2.H_2O$; the sodium aluminosilicates belong to the sodalite group, $Na_4Al_3Si_3O_{12}Cl$, where the chloride may be replaced isomorphously by sulfate; another group corresponds to analcite, $NaAl(SiO_3)_2.H_2O$. Phosphate scales are apatite, $3Ca_3(PO_4)_2.CaX_2$, where X_2 may be Cl_2, $(OH)_2$, CO_3, or combinations. These are examples of the remarkable behavior of so many silicates—the persistence of a framework structure through amazingly wide and apparently nonstoichiometric variations in composition by random isomorphous replacement of atoms or ions or groups by others. The proof of this phenomenon is at once a great triumph of the x-ray pattern and at the same time a limitation on unique identification of a given pattern with a definite stoichiometric composition. . . .

(J) *Oxide Opacifiers and Pigments.* These analyses are not limited to silica or silicates but to the wide range of oxides used as opacifiers in enamels or as pigments or stains; the distinction between two forms of TiO_2, rutile and anatase, is frequently necessary. The constitution of iron oxide pigments is another typical example where the microscope can give no help because of the extremely small particle size of the precipitated materials. The yellow pigment is α-$FeO(OH)$(goethite), the orange β-$FeO(OH)$, the brown γ-$FeO(OH)$(lepidicrocite), the black Fe_3O_4, the red Fe_2O_3 (rhombohedral) formed by heating the others to 500°C, and the purple-brown cubic Fe_2O_3 with a structure like Fe_3O_4 but with iron atoms missing. Thus color is dependent on structure, but how and why is not yet known. One excellent application has been to the analysis of the unusual pigments in ancient ceramic ware. This can be done nondestructively by back-reflection techniques; thus, along with the radiographic examination of paintings, the diffraction unit becomes a valuable adjunct of the art museum. The brilliant azure pigment, "Egyptian blue," is identified from the patterns from many sources as $CuAl_2O_4$. Various red and pink colors are due to calcium stannate ($CaO + SnO_2$) in which a colloidal dispersion of fine-grained Cr_2O_3 is stabilized.

(*K*) *Fluorescent Silicates.* The fluorescent silicates are a good example of x-ray detection of solid solution. Manganese is an impurity frequently used as an activator, and it promotes strong green fluorescence in zinc orthosilicate whose lattice is expanded by measurable amounts from shifted lines detectable to as little as 0.5 per cent manganese. It acts similarly in other oxides and silicates so that its importance as activator is due not only to characteristic electronic structure but also to readiness with which it substitutes for zinc or cadmium.

Ore Mineralogical and Geological Applications. It would be a formidable task to evaluate the contributions of x-ray diffraction to these sciences. The discussion of the clay minerals is an indication of the value of identification from powder patterns of the various constituents, their relationships, and the geological processes which have produced these. Base exchange in soils has been more clearly understood from structural studies. Many of the most interesting ones from a crystallographic point of view have been subjected to single-crystal analysis—notably Buerger's work on chalcocite, Cu_2S[†]; digenite, Cu_9S_5[‡]; cubanite, $CuFe_2S_3$[§], a ferromagnetic crystal with paired iron atoms; orpiment, As_2S_3[||]; pyrrhotite, $Fe_{0.48}S_{0.52}$[¶]; and a great many others.

Ito at the University of Tokyo has made a series of noteworthy contributions to single-crystal Fourier analysis of various minerals. In the course of this work, especially from observations of polymorphism, he has introduced the concept of twinned space groups, obtained by superimposing a group of operations called a twinning group onto one of the usual Schoenfliess space groups. One result is that every other unit cell, instead of every one, is in parallel and superposable position. At the boundary planes continuity of the lattice is destroyed by the twinning operations, but the homogeneity of the crystal as a whole is maintained. By this means Ito accounts for many peculiarities of x-ray data for minerals.[1] An example of complete structural analysis is tourmaline, $(Na, Ca)(Li, Al)_3Al_6(OH)_4(BO_3)_3Si_6O_{18}$, which crystallizes in space group $R3m$ with unit-cell dimensions of $a = 16.0$, $c = 7.17$ A and three molecules per cell. The Fourier projection of electron density on 0001 and the structure derived from it for part of a unit cell are reproduced in Fig. 284

† N. W. Buerger, *Econ. Geol.*, **36**, 19 (1941). N. W. Buerger and M. J. Buerger, *Am. Mineralogist*, **29**, 55 (1944).

‡ N. W. Buerger, *Am. Mineralogist*, **27**, 712 (1942).

§ M. J. Buerger, *Am. Mineralogist*, **32**, 415 (1947).

|| M. J. Buerger, *Am. Mineralogist*, **32**, 411 (1947).

¶ M. J. Buerger, *Am. Mineralogist*, **27**, 301 (1942).

[1] T. Ito, "X-ray Studies on Polymorphism," p. 134, Tokyo, 1950; *Acta Cryst.*, **4**, 385 (1951).

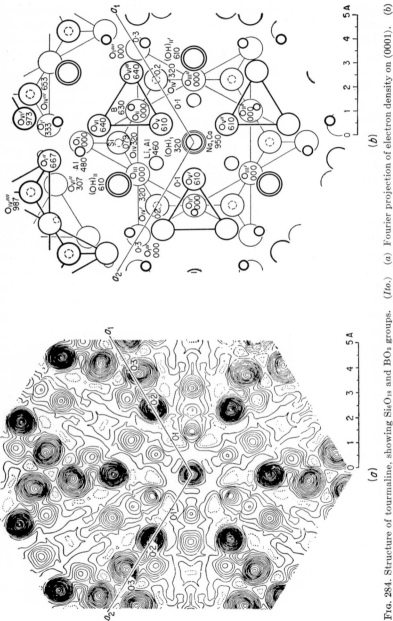

FIG. 284. Structure of tourmaline, showing Si_6O_{18} and BO_3 groups. (*Ito.*) (*a*) Fourier projection of electron density on (0001). (*b*) Structure projected on (0001). Numbers give height of each atom as a permillage of the c translation (7.17 A).

to show the discrete Si_6O_{18} held together by (LiAl) or $Mg_3(Na, Ca)Al$ and OH and BO_3 groups. Parallel and independent investigation was made by G. Donnay and Buerger on a magnesium tourmaline, with essentially identical results except for details in the Si_6O_{18} configuration.[1] Other very recent Fourier analyses by Ito and associates are on axinite,[2] $H(Fe, Mn)Ca_2Al_2BSi_4O_{16}$ (triclinic), composed of separate Si_4O_{12} and BO_3 groups bound together by Fe, Al, and Ca atoms; milarite,[3] $K_2Ca_4Be_4$-$Al_2Si_{24}O_{00}H_2O$ (hexagonal), a three-dimensional network of linked Be, Al, Si-O, and Be, Si-O tetrahedra reinforced by K and Ca atoms; datolite,[4] $HCaBSiO_5$; gadolinite,[5] $FeY_2Be_2Si_2O_{10}$; and the lamellar structure of microcline and anorthoclase feldspars,[6] including the exceptionally complex structure of moonstone, which is composed of two monoclinic and three triclinic feldspars, the latter twinned. One monoclinic constituent is potash-rich, the others being soda-rich.[7]

A useful service was performed in 1942 by G. Alan Harcourt in preparing tables of powder diffraction data, similar to the Dow-Hanawalt tables and the ASTM card index for pure compounds, and in providing actual copies of the patterns. The minerals were classed as follows: those bearing antimony (30), arsenic (27), bismuth (23), cobalt (8), copper (29), germanium (2), gold (6), iron (31), lead (26), manganese (9), mercury (6), molybdenum (1), nickel (21), platinum (1), selenium (3), tellurium (13), silver (21), thallium (1), tin (4), titanium (1), and tungsten (3). Of these 162 were positively identified and analyzed ore minerals.[8]

Glasses. Glasses form one of the most important groups in silicate chemistry, not only because they are a major industrial product, but also because they are present frequently in minerals and cements. Since a glass is a state of solid matter, rather than a chemical composition, and since it is not crystalline but still may be studied by x-ray diffraction methods, with suitably modified methods of structural interpretation, the subject will receive special consideration in conjunction with liquids in Chap. 21.

[1] G. Donnay and M. J. Buerger, *Acta Cryst.*, **3**, 379 (1950).
[2] *Acta Cryst.*, **5**, 202 (1952).
[3] *Ibid.*, **5**, 209 (1952).
[4] *Ibid.*, **6**, 24 (1953).
[5] *Ibid.*, **6**, 130 (1953).
[6] *Ibid.*, **6**, 441 (1953).
[7] "X-ray Identification and Structures of Clay Minerals," *op. cit.*, p. 122.
[8] *Am. Mineralogist*, **27**, 63 (1942).

CHAPTER 19

ALLOYS

The Metallic State. In Chap. 16 the crystalline structures of pure metals have been summarized; and in Chap. 17 have been considered the characteristic features of the metallic bond that give to some chemical elements those peculiar properties of opacity, conductivity, etc., which distinguish the metallic state. Again reviewed, these features are as follows:

1. All theories are variations on the theory of a structure of a lattice of positive ions in an electron gas, or of electrons free to conduct electric current through the lattice.

2. The bond is associated with high coordination number (up to 12 in metals and 16 in alloys) and is spatially undirected, in some respects resembling features of both ionic and covalent bonds.

3. The metallic state may be attained at sufficiently high temperatures and pressures, as in the interior of stars, so that all elements and compounds may become metals in the sense of conduction by electron transport.

4. The average concentration of valence electrons is far more important than atomic number or atomic weight.

5. The bond is equally efficacious in the liquid state.

6. Its force varies inversely as some high power of internuclear distance, as shown by extreme weakness in the alkali metals with low melting points and large atomic volumes, in contrast with the opposite properties of the platinum-group metals; in equilibrium with this force of attraction is a force of repulsion that is an atomic property as shown by the constancy of atomic volume in alloy formation.

7. Characteristic mechanical properties arise from the ease with which a metal is deformed by gliding and the bond is reestablished or healed, particularly for simple structures.

8. One of the chief difficulties of dealing with the metallic state is the fact that there are so many degrees of what may be termed metallic properties. It is impossible to find, for example, where metallic combination leaves off and homopolar begins. This difficulty leads to the classification of metals on the basis of crystal structures into true metals (alkali and alkaline earth, Be, Mg, Cu, Ag, Au, and transition elements) and B subgroup metals (Zn, Cd, Hg, Al, Ga, In, Tl, Si, Ge, Sn, Pb, As, Sb, Bi, Se, Te). In general the latter are distinguished by: (1) more complex structures and lack of closest packing; (2) obedience to the $8 - n$ rule; (3) hard and brittle properties and anisotropic thermal expansion and compressibility; (4) possession of structural diamagnetism, thus revealing partially homopolar binding, which disappears on melting; (5) anomalous positions of Al, Tl, and Pb which confer on them properties of both true and B subgroup (or half) metals; (6) greatly different behavior in alloy formation.

Electrons in Metals—Pauling Hypothesis. The early theories of Drude and Lorentz in which the electrons were treated as particles of a gas obeying the classical laws were inadequate to explain the fact that observed specific heats of metals could not be reconciled with a number of electrons of the same order as atoms, as required by electrical and optical properties. In 1928 Sommerfeld tried to meet the impasse by treating electrons as particles of gas obeying Fermi-Dirac statistics; but even this was too simple and led to the application by Block, Brillouin, Mott, and Jones of wave mechanics to the motion of electrons in a three-dimensional periodic field, whose periodicity is the crystal lattice. The wave-mechanical theory of metals was briefly described in connection with the classification of bonds in Chap. 17 and is further considered in the next section.

Electrons in the Periodic Field of a Metallic Crystal—Brillouin Zones.[1] If the periodicity of the field in a crystal lattice is perfectly regular, the wavelike characteristics of the electron enable it to move unimpeded through the lattice and the long free paths indicated by electrical con-

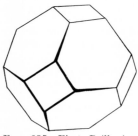

FIG. 285. First Brillouin zone for face-centered cubic structures.

ductivities are understood. The state of an electron in a crystal lattice can be expressed by $2\pi/\lambda = k$, the wave number, which is a vector. For electrons whose states lie in any one direction of k there will be certain values of k for which λ of the electron satisfies conditions for Bragg reflection by atomic planes. Thus these cannot move freely through the crystal; so for each direction of k there are ranges of forbidden energies which separate the bonds or zones of permitted electron energies. In other words, as the wave number is increased, there is a sudden increase in energy at each of the critical wave numbers, which lie in planes in k space; the planes bound the Brillouin zones, and k space is divided into a number of polyhedral zones whose shape depends on the crystal structure inside of which the energy increases continuously with wave number while there is an abrupt increase in energy at the surface or in passing from the state within a zone to one just outside. Figure 285 illustrates the first Brillouin zone of a face-centered cubic structure; here the octahedral faces indicate the wave numbers which satisfy the condition for reflection for the (111) octahedral planes, the first strong line on an x-ray pattern, and the cube faces refer to 200 reflections on diffraction patterns. Other zones outside this one refer to other planes and interferences (hkl all odd or all even). If the energy gap at the zone surface is large, then with an increasing number of electrons all the states of the first zone will be occupied before any electrons enter the second zone. If the energy gap is small, then the lowest states of the second zone may have lower energy

[1] One of the best general references is W. Hume-Rothery, "Electrons, Atoms, Metals and Alloys," Iliffe and Sons, London, 1948.

than the highest states of the first zone and there will be overlapping of the curves representing the number of electronic states, $N(E)$, against energy. Metals have such overlapping curves.

It has been shown on page 142 that these curves may be derived from x-ray data such as soft emission bands and that they lead to predictions of structure and stability.

This quantum-mechanical zone theory not only has explained insulators, semiconductors, and normal conductors but permits quantitative calculation of physical constants of crystals such as lattice spacings, binding energies, and compressibilities of lithium, sodium, and beryllium and, with some complications, of copper, aluminum, iron, tungsten, etc.; and the properties of some alloys. The theory fails only to explain superconductivity or lend itself to the calculation of mechanical effects dependent upon mosaics, dislocations, lattice defects, and other secondary structure beyond the elastic limit.

The Pauling Hypothesis of Metallic Bonds. To meet some of the above difficulties and in order to explain the firmness of atomic binding in metallic crystals in Groups VI and VII of the periodic table (as evaluated from atomic diameters, melting points, and compressibilities), Pauling made the first of a notable series of contributions in 1938. The band theory represents each electron as a wave function extending over the whole crystal, and the emphasis is on the crystal assembly as a whole. Pauling considered the behavior of electrons in the immediate vicinity of each atom, and particularly the number of electrons involved in binding an atom to its neighbors, and reached the conclusion that the metallic bond is closely related to the ordinary covalent bond. In the alkali metals the atomic binding involves four orbitals of each atom—one s and three p—and the metallic bond results from the resonance between all possible arrangements of available electrons in one or two electron bonds between 14 close neighbors of each atom. In the transition elements (Group VIII) this bonding involves also five d orbitals. Thus in passing from potassium to vanadium the numbers of bonding electrons increase in unit steps from 1 to 5 per atom with a regular increase in covalent bonds and consequently with a steady increase in cohesion. Since the covalent bonds involve paired electrons of opposite spin, there is adequate explanation for the fact that the metals are not strongly paramagnetic or ferromagnetic in spite of an incomplete d shell. To explain almost constant diameters following Group VI, Pauling assumed that some of the d orbitals are not available for bond formation; and from saturation moments of the ferromagnetic metals iron, nickel, and cobalt he determined that of five $3d$ orbitals 2.56 are involved in bond formations and 2.44 are not. The revolutionary idea of nonintegral valences or orbitals represents a condition such that at a given instant some atoms are in one state and some in another, the fractional number being a time average.

Assuming that in chromium 0.22 electron per atom enters the atomic orbitals, the following scheme results:

	Atomic d orbital		Saturation moment		Bonding $3d$ electrons	Total number
	+	−	Assumed	Observed		
Cr	0.22	....	0.22	....	5.78	6
Mn	1.22	....	1.22	....	5.78	7
Fe	2.22	....	2.22	2.22	5.78	8
	3.22 ⏜					
Co	2.44	0.78	1.66	1.61	5.78	9
	4.22					
Ni	2.44 ⏜	1.78	0.66	0.01	5.78	10

In cobalt the number of electrons to be distributed among d orbitals (3.22 per atom) is greater than the number of orbitals (2.44); so some $3d$ electrons will be paired, with a resulting saturation moment $2.44 - 0.78 = 1.66$.

Extending this theory to copper, silver, and gold and succeeding elements, the outermost d electrons are still involved in metallic bonding, so that the bonding electrons are in hybridized $3d$, $4s$, $4p$ orbitals (as indicated also in coordination compounds). So the valences of IB, IIB, IIIB, and IVB elements are 5.44, 4.44, 3.44, and 2.44, respectively (for example, copper, zinc, gallium, and tin).

Upon the basis of these considerations Pauling has derived the equation expressing the relation between apparent atomic radius and (fractional) bond number (or number of shared electron pairs). From the data on iron, titanium, zirconium, and thallium a curve is constructed from which the radius for coordination number 12 can be deduced from

$$R_1 - R_{12} = C \log n$$

Some of these data are included in the atomic-radii tables in Chap. 17.

Pauling's theory of the metallic bond has been fruitful and is widely accepted. However, Hume-Rothery[1] has severely criticized certain phases on account of the empirical, or *ad hoc*, features and the multiplication of assumptions. The extension to alloy structures will be considered in the section on intermetallic compounds.

The Classification of Binary Intermetallic Systems. We begin the discussion of the crystal chemistry of alloys with a summary in Table 19-1 of general structure types that have been deduced from the x-ray diffraction analyses of hundreds of binary intermetallic systems. Specimens are

[1] *Ann. Repts. Prog. Chem. (Chem. Soc. London),* **46**, 42 (1949).

prepared from melts of the metals; or alloys are made by electrodeposition under suitable conditions from solution. The determination of equilibrium diagrams by x-ray methods requires the most careful and judicious technique with annealed powders, often combined with use of the metallographic microscope. The precautions and limitations as well as the great contributions have been critically considered by Owen, Hume-Rothery, Bradley, and Gayler, all eminent authorities.[1] Limitations are failure to determine liquidus and solidus of a system, some microstructures, extra phases and errors from nonequilibrium or delayed transitions.

TABLE 19-1. CLASSIFICATION OF ALLOYS†

True metals			B subgroup metals	
			B1 Groups II, III, IV	B2 Groups IV, V, VI
True metals	Transition metals, Cu, Ag, Au **T**	1. Wide range of solid solution Superlattices	2. Electron compounds	4. NiAs, FeS$_2$, MoS$_2$, and CdI$_2$ structures
	A group metals (alkali, alkaline-earth metals, Be, Mg) **A**		3. CsCl and NaTl • structures	5. Ionic, NaCl, and CaF$_2$ structures
B subgroup metals	B1 Groups II, III, IV	2, 3	6. Solid solution if chemically similar and of comparable size	7. Zinc blende and wurtzite (homopolar) structures
	B2 Groups IV, V, VI	4, 5	7	8. NaCl structure

† SOURCE: Evans.

Perhaps the most useful contributions of x-rays have been the following: (1) high-temperature cameras have given important information about structures which could not be retained by quenching; (2) superlattice structures are much more easily detected (though these are not true phases); (3) the powders required for x-ray patterns attain equilibrium more rapidly than the lumps required for microscopic examination; (4) cold work and (5) recrystallization are much more easily detected; (6) solubility limits and (7) identification of precipitates in early stages of age-hardening are most readily determinable by x-rays.

1. *Alloys Formed by a Continuous Series of Solid Solutions* (*Substitutional*). In such alloys the atoms of one kind of metal that is being

[1] *J. Inst. Metals*, **69**, 1 (1943).

alloyed with another replace at random, or more likely with short-range order, the atoms of the latter at the lattice points.

Microscopic evidence: Only one kind of crystal appears in any specimen ranging from one pure component to the other.

Thermal evidence: Smooth continuous curve in phase diagram between pure components.

X-ray evidence: Only one type of diffraction pattern throughout, the only variation being a change in the lattice parameter. Figure 286 shows how the diffraction lines for a pure metal are shifted for a solid solution. It is generally true that the lines remain sharp in spite of some localized distortion around solute atoms.

Requirements: Only two metals that have the same lattice structure (*i.e.*, both face-centered cubic, for example) can form a continuous series of solid solutions. All pairs of metals with common lattice structure do not form continuous series (*e.g.*, aluminum-gold). Two metals may be miscible in all proportions if the atoms are small, highly charged, and of

Fig. 286. Powder diffraction patterns illustrating solid solution; *upper*, α-brass, 80 per cent copper, 20 per cent zinc; *lower*, pure copper.

similar electronic configuration and differing in size by not more than 10 or 15 per cent. Some complications arise with respect to estimating size from elemental radii. Indium, white tin, thallium, and lead dissolve in some metals as if in fully ionized state with atomic diameters effectively about 0.3 A smaller than those calculated from crystals of these metals. In Ga and α-Mn there are two interatomic distances; the shortest distance between atoms in Ga is 2.44 A, but in solid solutions the value is 2.6 A. On the other hand, the 15 per cent rule explains many facts. The atomic diameter of Cu is 2.54 A and 15 per cent or ±0.38 A for a favorable sized zone; for Ag the values are 2.88 ± 0.48 A. On this basis Be is outside the zone for Ag, inside for Cu; it has very limited solubility in Ag, but 18 per cent in Cu. The situation is reversed for magnesium, and there is low solubility in Cu, 30 at. per cent in Ag. Zn has a favorable size factor for both.

Additivity relations: Vegard's law of additivity states that in a binary system forming a continuous series of solid solutions the lattice parameters are linearly related to atomic percentage of one of the components. In other words, upon a straight line joining the numerical values of the edge lengths of the unit crystal cells of the two pure metals lie all the lattice values for all possible solid solutions of the two metals.

General properties: The electrical and mechanical properties of these solid-solution alloys vary more or less as expected with the lattice constant. All compositions retain metallic properties; the solid solution is usually harder than the pure solvent metal; the conductivity decreases as one metal is dissolved in another but is less dependent upon temperature than that of a pure metal (constantan, an alloy of copper and nickel containing small amounts of iron and manganese, is especially valuable for resistance measurements on this account). Quite characteristic also are the differential vaporization of one metal from the other, the lattice constant changing in the purely solid phase with change in composition, and the behavior in corrosive media. For example, Graf and Glocker[1] in an x-ray study analyzed gold-copper crystals after etching with oxidizing agents. The resulting specimens produced the interferences for pure gold in a surface layer oriented exactly like the original alloy layer. Thus with the removal of the less noble copper atoms from the mixed crystal lattice the remaining gold atoms had sufficient mobility to group themselves together into a pure-gold crystal layer with entirely different lattice spacing from the underlying unattacked alloy. In some cases a small fraction of copper atoms completely surrounded and protected by gold atoms remains in the layers, as is readily ascertained from the diffraction patterns.

Examples investigated by x-rays are: gold-copper, gold-silver, gold-palladium, nickel-copper, cobalt-nickel, nickel-palladium, platinum-palladium, potassium-rubidium, strontium-calcium, etc. All such primary solid solutions show no long-range order and are usually described as random or disordered. There is growing evidence that actually short-range order exists in the sense that solute atoms tend to avoid being closest neighbors to an extent greater than that which would result from a purely random arrangement. The relative intensities of diffraction lines and background have given this evidence, and a great deal of theoretical work is in progress by Warren and others.

2. *Substitutional Solid Solution over Limited Ranges.* It follows, of course, that other systems which do not form a continuous series of solid solutions will show substitutional mixed crystals over limited ranges of B in A and A in B. In cases where atomic sizes differ by more than 15 per cent, two metals may be immiscible. But in cases where the size factor may be favorable, another determining influence may be the case where one metal is strongly electropositive to the others with the resultant tendency to form stable intermediate phases or intermetallic compounds. Thus it is very unusual for the alkali metals to form solid solutions with an element of another group (lithium, the least electropositive, may be an exception). In the series Cu-Zn, Cu-Ga, Cu-Ge, Cu-As, and Ag-Cd,

---

[1] *Metallwirtschaft*, **11**, 77 (1932).

Ag-In, Ag-Sn, Ag-Sb increasing valence results in steeper falls in liquidus and solidus curves and regular decrease in the extent of solid solution. These facts mean that with increasing valence for a given atomic percentage of solute an increasing number of electrons is being added to the lattice with consequent effects on the equilibrium between phases. It is generally true with the alloys of Cu, Ag, and Au with metals of higher valences that the solubility of Cu, Ag, and Au in the latter is smaller than in the reverse case (32 per cent Zn in Cu, about 4 per cent Cu in Zn).

3. *Superlattice Structures.* The solid solutions involving random substitution just considered are typical ordinarily of specimens at high temperatures or quenched. A good example is the copper-gold system. When, however, such a specimen is very carefully annealed, a new phenomenon enters: the two kinds of atom tend to occupy definite geometrical positions, instead of a random distribution. At a composition corresponding exactly to AuCu, the segregation is complete, as shown

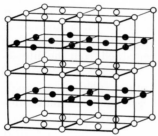

FIG. 287. The structure of the ordered phase, CuAu.

in Fig. 287. There are now gold atoms at the corners of each cell and in the top and bottom face centers and copper at the centers of the side faces, or vice versa; and the layers and difference in radii of the two atoms result in a departure from cubic symmetry (tetragonal $c/a = 0.932$). Again as more copper is added to this, statistical distribution begins; but, at the composition $AuCu_3$, again there is regular arrangement with gold atoms at the corner and copper at the face centers. Further addition of copper atoms replaces gold atoms one at a time until the face-centered lattice of pure copper remains. Structures for AuCu and $AuCu_3$ in the ordered state, in which the pattern of all positions is that of the initial random solution but over which the two kinds of atom are distributed in a regular way, are *superlattices*. Such a condition was predicted in 1919 by Tammann from corrosion experiments. It is recognized on diffraction patterns through the appearance of new lines, a redistribution of intensities, splitting of single lines (cubic to tetragonal), etc. The list of examples is surprisingly large, not only for alloy systems of true metals, but for more complex cases such as Fe-Al, where the two metals have different initial structures. In the alloy Fe_3Al, quenched from very high temperatures, the structure is random, with some kind of short-range order developing the lower the temperature; quenched from 700°C, long-range order is found in the sense that some sites on the body-centered cubic lattice (corners) are occupied by iron atoms only and others (cube centers) contain either Fe or Al. Finally, when annealed at low temperatures, the Al atoms take fixed positions as far as possible from one another.   FeAl takes up the CsCl structure analogous to the behavior of β-brass.

These cases of order-disorder transformations were the first to be recognized and led to the extended general application of defect structures considered in Chap. 17.   W. L. Bragg in 1933 showed that the development of superlattices was the natural consequence of the tendency of solute atoms to be as widely separated as possible.   The presence of a foreign atom in a lattice of solvent atoms must introduce local strains, and the most stable structure, obtained under the equilibrium conditions of annealing, will have these strains as widely distributed as possible.   This will be the ordered structure, since in disorder two solute atoms may statistically come into juxtaposition.   It is clear that at low concentrations the probability of such a condition will be small, and hence the structure remains disordered; or if solute and solvent atoms are very nearly alike in size as in silver-gold, the strain will be inconsequential and the disordered solid solutions will prevail over all ranges.   Thus superlattices will usually be found in systems where size factors are neither too favorable (Ag-Au) nor too unfavorable, in which case the atoms will not fit together to form a solid solution.

It is also true that every possible condition may be found between the limits of order and complete disorder, each as a function of an exact temperature of heat-treatment.   The Bragg-Williams theory considers a state of thermal equilibrium in which the atoms seek to assume the ordered structure of lowest potential energy, whereas thermal agitation seeks to promote a state of disorder.   Thus the actual degree of order (estimated from intensities of new "forbidden" x-ray lines) will be determined by temperature and by a parameter of the system representing the difference in energy between ordered and disordered states.   Also there is a critical temperature above which every trace of order disappears and at which it is expected properties, such as specific heat, should display sharp changes.   The theory involves also the rate of attainment of equilibrium, which may be very slow—and, indeed, a metastable disordered state preserved by quenching.   The actual behavior of any system, therefore, is determined by the relation of the critical temperature T_c to an annealing temperature T_a and a quenching temperature T_q.   There has been much debate as to whether superlattice changes should be classed as phase changes or not.   They are now usually called phase changes of the second order to distinguish them from ordinary phase changes of the solid-liquid type covered by the phase rule.

4. *Alloys*, T-B₁; *Hume-Rothery Electron Compounds*.[1]   These may be represented by the familiar system Cu-Zn, or brass (Fig. 288); starting with pure copper and adding zinc in increasing amounts up to pure zinc, the following phases are identified:

[1] 'The Metallic State," Oxford University Press, New York, 1931.

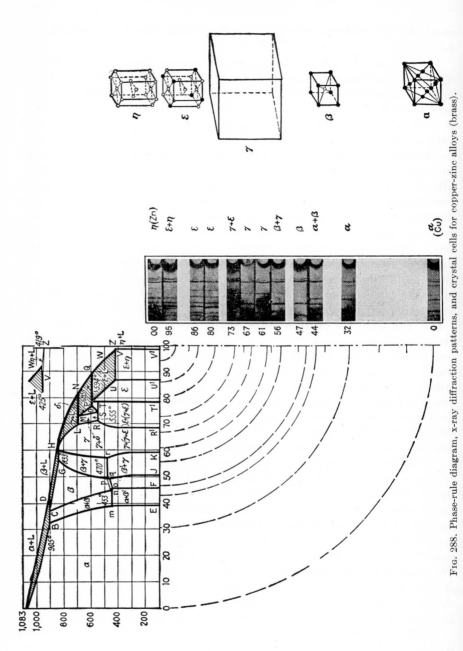

Fig. 288. Phase-rule diagram, x-ray diffraction patterns, and crystal cells for copper-zinc alloys (brass).

α—pure copper, face-centered copper ($a_0 = 3.61$ A), and solid solution of zinc in this lattice; 38% Zn, $a = 3.68$ A.

β, (β')—CuZn, body-centered cubic; 46 to 48% Zn, $a = 2.945$ A; disordered, high temperatures; ordered, low temperatures.

γ—Cu$_5$Zn$_8$, cubic, 52 atoms per unit cell; 61% Zn, $a = 8.85$ A.

ϵ—CuZn$_3$, hexagonal; 80% Zn, $a = 2.745$, $c = 4.294$; 86% Zn, $a = 2.761$, $c = 4.286$.

η—solid solution of copper in zinc to pure Zn, hexagonal; 96% Zn, $a = 2.67$, $c = 4.92$; 100% Zn, $a = 2.66$, $c = 4.94$.

The beginning and end phases of binary systems naturally depend upon the particular metals involved; but more important are the remarkable generalizations that apply to the intermediate β, γ, and ϵ phases. Mechanical and electrical properties of brasses are graphically shown in Fig. 289 as functions of the phase compositions. Thus tensile strength

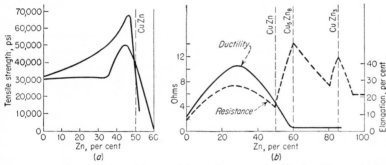

Fig. 289. Physical properties of brass: (a) tensile strength; (b) ductility and electrical resistance. (*Stillwell, "Crystal Chemistry."*)

reaches a maximum at β, then falls off greatly for γ and ϵ; electrical resistance reaches maxima at γ and ϵ, showing the presence of homopolar as contrasted with metallic bonds; ductility has minima at γ and ϵ.

a. β, β' phase. In 1926 W. Hume-Rothery suggested that the β phases of the systems Cu-Zn, Cu-Al, and Cu-Sn are analogous in structure. As their compositions correspond approximately to the formulas CuZn, Cu$_3$Al, and Cu$_5$Sn, he also put forward the hypothesis that their structural similarities might be due to the fact that in each case the ratio of valence electrons to atoms is 3:2. X-ray investigations have confirmed the assumption that these phases have the same type of structure. In each case the atoms occupy the points of a body-centered cubic lattice. In the β copper-tin phase the copper and tin atoms seem to be distributed at random over the lattice points; but in the β' copper-zinc and β' copper-aluminum phases the different kinds of atom are oriented in networks of their own, thus forming ordered structures. Phases of this structure have been found in several binary alloys of the transition-group metals copper, silver, and gold, with other metals of the B subgroups in the second and third vertical rows of the periodic table; and, in fact, they all occur at concentrations making the ratio of valence electrons to atoms $3:2$. Examples are CuBe, AgMg, CuZn, AgZn, AuZn, $MnZn_3$, CuCd, AgCd, AuCd, Cu_3Al, Cu_5Sn, MnAl, FeAl, CoAl, NiAl, LiHg, and Cu_3Ga. The number of valence electrons assigned to each metal is as follows: Cu, Ag, Au $= 1$; Be, Mg, Zn, Cd $= 2$; Al, Ga $= 3$; Sn $= 4$; Mn, Fe, Co, Ni $= 0$ (see under γ phase below).

There are, however, a number of notable exceptions to the $3:2$ ratio for β alloys, probably owing to the very simple structure and the important effect of relative sizes of the atoms. These are LiAg (1.0), LiTl (2.0), BeCo (1.0), BePd (1.0), MgHg (2.0), MgTl (2.5), CaTl (2.5), SrTl (2.5), AlNd (3.0), PdCu (0.5), TlSb (4.0), TiBi (4.0).

b. μ phase. In some cases when in an alloy the ratio of valence electrons to atoms is $3:2$ and a phase having body-centered cubic lattice might thus have been expected, the atoms are found to be grouped instead in the same way as in β-manganese. Just as this material differs from its neighboring elements in respect to crystal structure and actually seems to act like an alloy of itself, these intermetallic phases for some reason form exceptions to the general rule. A phase of this kind designated μ (formerly β' which now symbolizes an ordered β phase) is found in the silver-aluminum system (Fig. 290). Its range of homogeneity is so narrow that it may be denoted by a mere line in the equilibrium diagram. Its composition corresponds to Ag_3Al, from which it is evident that the ratio of valence electrons to atoms is $3:2$. In β-manganese there are two groups of equivalent positions with 12 and 8 atoms, respectively. In Ag_3Al, also, with 20 atoms per unit cell the 15 silver atoms are more than adequate for the 12 equivalent positions so that some must occupy positions equivalent to aluminum. In other words, the silver and aluminum atoms are distributed at random and approximately uniformly over the two groups of structurally equivalent positions. Other good examples are Au_3Al, Cu_5Si, and $CoZn_3$.

c. ζ, ζ' phase. In a few other cases on increasing the valence of solute a hexagonal close-packed structure, both disordered and ordered, has been found for the $3:2$ ratio. Thus Cu_3Ga has a β phase at high temperatures and ζ at low; Cu_5Ge only the ζ phase.

d. γ phase. In many cases a γ phase of complicated cubic structure has been found in alloy systems of the T and B_1 metals, having usually 52, but in some cases $8 \times 52 = 416$, atoms, in its unit cell. Thus when copper, for example, is combined with zinc, the homogeneity range of this phase corresponds to a formula Cu_5Zn_8; for copper and aluminum, it corresponds to Cu_9Al_4; and for copper and tin, to $Cu_{31}Sn_8$. In all these cases the ratio of valence electrons to number of atoms is $21:13$. Other examples are Cu_5Cd_8, Cu_5Hg_8, Cu_9Ga_4, Cu_9In_4, $Cu_{31}Si_8$, $Na_{31}Pb_8$, $Ag_{31}Sn_8$, Ag_5Zn_8, Ag_5Cd_8, Ag_5Hg_8, Ag_9Al_4, Au_5Zn_8, Au_5Hg_8. Phases of the systems Mn-Zn, Fe-Zn, Co-Zn, Ni-An, Rh-Zn, Pd-Zn, Ni-Cd, etc., all give the same diffraction pattern as γ-brass and with common formulas, typified by Fe_5Zn_{21}, again corresponding to a ratio 21:13, if zero valence is assigned to manganese and the transition (Group VIII) elements. This seems to indicate that only loosely bound electrons in valence shells

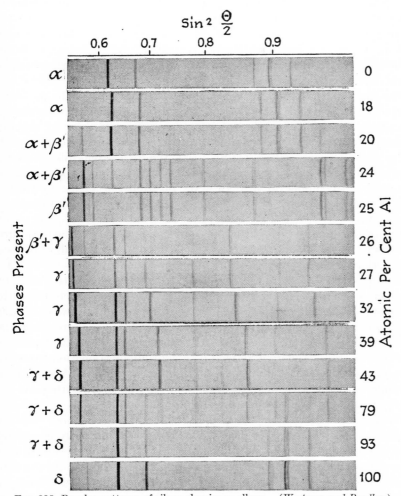

FIG. 290. Powder patterns of silver-aluminum alloys. (*Westgren and Bradley.*)

are involved in the formation of these compounds. Magnetic measurements have proved that no electron contribution is made by these particular metals. It is probably true that some of the 4s valence electrons of iron, for example, are contributing to the structure, but the fact that iron atoms have incomplete 3d shells means that they tend to take up electrons from the relatively electropositive zinc; the two processes tend to cancel each other, and so iron behaves as though it had 0 valence depending on electronegativities. One ternary alloy, $Cu_7Zn_4Al_2$, thus far investigated, obeys the rule for γ alloys. Exceptions are $Li_{10}Pb_3(22:13)$ and $Li_{10}Ag_3(13:13)$.

e. The close-packed hexagonal ϵ phase. An atomic grouping which is connected with a ratio of valence electrons to number of atoms 7:4 is also commonly present in these systems. Examples are $CuBe_3$, $CuZn_3$, $CuCd_3$, Cu_3Si, Cu_3Sn, Cu_3Ge, $AgZn_3$, $AgCd_3$, Ag_5Al_3, Ag_3Sn, $AuZn_3$, $AuCd_3$, $AuHg_3$, Cu_5Al_3, Au_3Sn, $MnZn_7$. There are no known exceptions to the 7:4 rule.

For these β, γ, ϵ "electron compounds" it is clear that the pattern of atomic positions, and not the actual distribution of atoms, is the significant feature; for example, a CsCl structure would demand the composition CuSn for the body-centered lattice of the β phase, whereas this phase has the composition Cu_5Sn, with the two atoms distributed at random in these proportions. In γ-brass, the 52 atoms in Cu_5Zn_8 are arranged with copper in $8 + 12 = 32$ positions, whereas, in Cu_5Cd_8, copper occupies $8 + 8 = 16$ positions and the other 36 positions are occupied by 32 Cd + 4 Cu at random. The ratios $\frac{3}{2}(\frac{21}{14})$, $\frac{21}{13}$, $\frac{7}{4}(\frac{21}{12})$ determine not the chemical properties or chemical analogy but the structures, and hence these may be called electron compounds. Bradley[1] has suggested that these ratios form a monotonic sequence $(2n - 1)/n$: α 1/1, β 3/2, γ 5/3, ϵ 7/4, η 2/1. The γ phase would require the empirical formulas $CuZn_2$, Cu_2Al, and $Cu_{28}Sn_8(Cu_7Sn_2)$ which are included within the composition limits of these phases (for example, between Cu_5Zn_8 21/13 and Cu_4Zn_9 22/13). Jones in 1934 showed that these relationships, first established empirically, are well explained by the Brillouin-zone theory of metals. There may well be a continuous transition from pure electron compounds to ionic compounds. The system Ag-Mg is an intermediate, not with definite Mg^{2+} and Ag^- ions but with some tendency towards acquiring charges in the β phase.

Thus the γ alloys have the properties of brittleness, high electrical resistance, etc., expected for a metallic crystal with a nearly completely filled (calculated 93.5 per cent) Brillouin zone. Reference has already been made to electronic perturbations in a space which is at the same time momentum space for the electron and reciprocal-lattice space for the crystal; the perturbations occur when the momentum vector terminates on polyhedral Brillouin surfaces, described by assigning the crystallographic indices of the planes which by Bragg reflection of the electron produce the perturbation that concentrates the energy levels into Brillouin zones. By contrast the β alloys with the highly metallic character of malleability, good conduction, and normal magnetic properties have only 75 per cent filled Brillouin zones.

[1] *Nature*, **163**, 683 (1949).

f. Pauling valence rules in electron compounds. Pauling has raised strong objections to the assignment by Hume-Rothery of the 0 valence to the transition elements, in order to maintain the constant ratios. In 1938[1] he proposed an alternative explanation based on the interpretation of values of the saturation magnetic moment of ferromagnetic metals, as already explained earlier in this chapter, and considerations of interatomic distances in metals and intermetallic compounds. From K to V the number of bonding orbitals increases from 1 to 5, with no electrons in d orbitals. Beginning with Cr there are 9 orbitals, five $3d$, one $4s$, and three $4p$ per atom, hybridized and divided into three classes: (1) 5.78 stable bonding orbitals for Cr, Mn, Fe, Ni, the transition metals; (2) 2.44 nonbonding stable atomic orbitals; (3) 0.78 unstable orbitals not utilized except at and beyond subgroup IVb of the periodic table but called metallic orbitals. In 1948 Pauling and Ewing[2] extended the theory to β- and γ-brass and α- and β-manganese by use of the valences Cu 5.4, Zn 4.4, Ga 3.4, Sn 2.4, instead of the Hume-Rothery values of 1, 2, 3, 4, respectively. Thus the β alloys instead of 3/2 will still be constant in CuZn, $(5.4 + 4.4)/2 = 4.9$; Cu_3Ga, $(16.2 + 3.4)/4 = 4.9$; Cu_5Sn, $(27 + 2.4)/6 = 4.9$. The fractional valences are to be considered as averages of integral valences; special stability is associated with bond numbers which are simple fractions $\frac{1}{2}$, $\frac{1}{3}$, $\frac{2}{3}$, etc.

5. *Alloys with a σ Phase.* In many alloys, especially of transition metals with metals of the fifth, sixth, and seventh periodic groups, such as Fe-Cr, Fe-V, Co-Cr, Co-Ni-Cr, Mo-Mn, etc., there appears a technically important phase which has been designated the σ phase. This structure has been determined only recently by means of single crystals of Co-Cr.† With a composition corresponding approximately to Cr_8Co_7 the unit tetragonal cell $(P4/mnm)$ contains 16 Cr + 14 Co atoms. Whether or not these alloys are electron compounds with a constant ratio remains to be determined, but of unusual importance is the fact that the σ phase has very likely the same structure as that of β-uranium. This recalls the identical structures of μ alloys such as Ag_3Al and β-Mn.

6. *Laves Phases*[3] (*Strukturbericht Types C14, C15, and C36*). In the foregoing discussion of alloy structures it is clear that at least three factors affect the structure of an alloy, namely, the size factor, the electrochemical factor, and electron concentration. The interplay of these of course is responsible for the complexities of alloy structures. Occasionally one factor such as size will almost completely dominate in typically intermetallic phases. For example, in cases where the sizes of constituent atoms differ too greatly for solid solutions to be formed, com-

[1] *Phys. Rev.*, **54**, 899 (1938).

[2] *Revs. Mod. Phys.*, **20**, 112 (1948).

† Kasper, Decker, and Belanger, *J. Appl. Phys.*, **22**, 361 (1951).

[3] O. W. Liebiger, *Am. Fiat Rev. Ger. Sci.*, **31**, 33 (1950).

binations AB_2 and A_2B with a radius ratio of 1.22 still differ character-istically from classical stoichiometric compounds. Hume-Rothery phases occur if the radius ratio is less than 1.20 and the valence-electron concentration is between 1 and 2. *Laves* phases are formed whenever an atom with a strong tendency to a metallic bond collides with another atom whose second outermost shell is not closed and has a 20 per cent smaller radius to form high coordination structures. Examples are $MgCu_2$,[†] $MgZn_2$, $MgNi_2$, Au_2Bi, KBi_2, $CaLi_2$, $CaMg_2$, $SrMg_2$, $BaMg_2$, $LaMg_2$, $LaAl_2$, $CeNi_2$, $GdMn_2$, $TiMn_2$, $TiCo_2$, $ZrCr_2$, $NbMn_2$, $ThMn_2$; $CaCu_5$, $CaNi_5$, $CaZn_5$, $LaNi_5$, $LaCu_5$, $LaZn_5$, $CeNi_5$, $CeCo_5$, $GdNi_5$, $ThZn_9$, (Th, Zn)Zn_5 are closely related. The ternary alloys Al_6CuMg_4 and $Al_2Mg_3Zn_3$, rewritten as $Mg_{12}Al_{18}Cu_3$ and $Mg_{12}Al_8Zn_{12}$, represent a group-ing of 21 or 20 atoms around the largest Mg ions.

7. *Zintl Phases*[1] (*Types C1 and B1*). These are intermetallic com-pounds that crystallize in nonmetallic, typically saline lattices according to the usual valences. Zintl phases in alloy systems contain the largest amount of base metal and contain an element of the third to seventh sub-group, thus covering most of the $T-B_2$ and $A-B_2$ alloys. The following all crystallize with a C1 (CaF_2) structure and perhaps are most typical: Mg_2Si, Mg_2Ge, Mg_2Sn, Mg_2Pb, $PtSn_2$, Pt_2P, Sr_2P, $LiMgN$, $LiZnN$, $LiMgAs$, $LiMgSb$, $LiMgBi$, $AgMgAs$, $CuMgSr$, $CuMgBi$, $CuCdSb$, Li_3AlN_2, Li_3GaN_2, Ag_2Te, $NiSn_2$. Many of the phases with NaCl (B1) structure can be counted as Zintl phases, such as TiN, TiC, UP, VN, VC, ZrC, etc.

8. *Alloys* T-B2. With these systems in which the subgroup metal of Groups IV, V, and VI is large and easily polarized there is an increasing tendency toward discrete structures, each approximating to a definite chemical compound and capable of taking up in solid solution only a limited excess of either constituent but still giving evidence of metallic properties. The most important type of structure is that of nickel arsenide, in which six arsenic atoms are coordinated octahedrally around each nickel atom and six nickel atoms around each arsenic atom at the corners of a hexagonal prism. Examples are CuSn, AuSn, FeSn, NiSn, PtSn, PtPb, MnAs, NiAs, CrSb, MnSb, FeSb, CoSb, NiSb, PdSb, PtSb, NiBi, PtBi, FeS, CoS, CrSe, FeSe, CoSe, NiSe, CrTe, MnTe, FeTe, NiTe, PdTe, PtTe.

Compounds like FeS_2, pyrites, all show unmistakable homopolar bonds but retain persistence of metallic bonds. The pyrite structure is obtained for —S_2, —Se_2, —Te_2, —As_2, —Sb_2 compounds with the smallest highly polarizing transition-metal atoms, whereas the larger T-metal atoms form layer lattices of the MoS_2 type (Mo, W), or CdI_2 type (Zr, Sn, Pt, Pd).

9. *Alloys* A-B1. These structures tend to be ionic. LiZn, LiCd,

[†] R. L. Berry and G. V. Gaynor, *Acta. Cryst.*, **6**, 178 (1953).

[1] *Am. Fiat Rev. Ger. Sci.*, **31**, 11, 106 (1950).

LiGa, LiIn, NaIn are like NaTl, which is body-centered cubic but with two nearly equal ions alternately at corners and centers; LiHg, LiAl, LiTl, MgTl, CaTl, SrTl are like CsCl but are to be distinguished on account of definite stoichiometric constitution from the β phase of the alloys like brass that form electron compounds. For other compositions structures in this class may be very complex; for example, in Mg_3Al_2 the Al atoms are bound into diatomic molecules, held by ionized Mg^{2+}.

10. *Alloys* A-B2. These are even more definitely ionic so that NaCl and CaF_2 structures are common. Examples are (Mg, Ca, Ba, Sr, Pb)-(S, Se, Te); (Li, Na, Cu)$_2$(Se, Te); Mg_2(Ge, Sn, Pb).

11. *Alloys of* B *Subgroup Metals.* These finally become the most definite chemical compounds of all those with ZnS structures (homopolar) as described in Chap. 17. Examples are (zinc blende), (Be, Zn, Cd, Hg)(S, Se, Te); AlAs, GaAs, (Al, Ga, In)Sb; wurtzite, MgTe, ZnS, CdS, CdSi. Carbides, nitrites, and hydroxides form a special case, many with NaCl structure if the radius ratio is greater than 0.41, in which the small atoms occupy interstitial holes.

Interstitial Solid Structures. In addition to the substitutional solid solutions and compounds already discussed, a series of alloys are recognized in which certain light atoms with small radii (carbon, nitrogen, boron, hydrogen) are held in the interstices between metal atoms on a regular lattice.

a. Distinguishing Features. It is possible to distinguish between interstitial solid solutions from a combination of spacings and densities. For example, in a face-centered cubic metal of atomic weight X (absolute weight X/A, where A is Avogadro's number) dissolve a, atomic percentage of metal of atomic weight Y. The mass associated with the unit cell in each case is derived and divided by the volume V to give the density, which is compared with the experimental value:

$$\rho_{\text{interstitial}} = \frac{(4X/A) + (4a/(100a)(Y/A)}{V}$$

$$\rho_{\text{substitutional}} = \frac{(4X/A) + 4a[(Y - X)/100A]}{V}$$

b. Crystal Chemistry of Carbides. The most important is the iron-carbon system, of which the members possess metallic properties, indeterminate composition, and a sequence of phases and hence class as alloys. Classification is on the basis not of composition but of the metal lattice and the coordination number of the interstitial nonmetal atom. Thus, there are never more of these than are required to fill every vacancy of one geometric kind, but there may be a deficiency with only some of the equivalent positions occupied; Fe_4N, built on a structure of ideal composition FeN, is such a case. The crystal chemistry of the interstitial structures has been generalized by the Swedish investigator Hägg. Hägg's laws connect the interstitial structure by hydrides, borides, carbides, and nitrides with the radius ratio of the nonmetal to metal atom. If this ratio is below 0.59, the lattices of the metal atoms are simple (face-centered cubic, or hexagonal close-packed, coordination number 12); if above 0.59, complex structures of lower symmetry (orthorhombic) and stability arise. Thus for the close-packed cubic and hexagonal carbides of Ti, Zr, V, Nb, Ta, Mo, and W the radius ratios are below 0.59, while for the complex (orthorhombic) carbides of Cr, Mn, and Fe the ratios are above 0.59. The coordination number of nonmetal atoms in normal interstitial structures is either 6 or 4, depending on the type of position occupied. The carbides of metals which form alloy steels are listed in Table 19-2. As a result of these simple ideas, including variable composition arising from nonfilling of some interstitial lattice holes, such interstitial alloys are often called Hägg carbides, etc. Fe_2C and other important carbides in alloy steels are discussed in later sections of this chapter.

In the dicarbides, two paired carbon atoms appear in interstices, producing distortion from cubic symmetry. In La, Ce, Pr, Nd, U, and V dicarbides, the pairs are parallel to each other and to one edge of the original metal cube (tetragonal $c/a > 1$); in ThC_2, ZrC_2, and ZrH_2, the pairs are parallel to a cube face and with axes in two perpendicular directions (tetragonal $c/a < 1$).

Ubbelohde[1] has demonstrated that hydrogen and deuterium behave as metals in their alloys with palladium, in that they dissolve as alloys, dissociate partly into protons and electrons, and form two solid solutions each with the same structure in equilibrium.

UH_3 is a good example of the fact that in interstitial compounds covalent forces between metal and nonmetallic atoms may operate. This hydride is metallike and very hard and has a crystal structure not related to any forms of uranium metal. The hydrogen atoms link uranium atoms together by fractional bonds; U_I atoms form 12 such half bonds to hydrogen and hence have a valence of 6. U_{II} atoms form 4 half bonds to hydrogen and 2 of about 0.15 to U atoms. The calculated valence is 2.3, corresponding to resonance between bi- and trivalent states. Bonds of $\frac{1}{2}$ to $\frac{2}{3}$ order between metal and nonmetal account for interatomic distances in many monocarbides, mononitrides, and monoxides and for more complex structures of Fe_3C, FeSi, etc.

c. *Isomorphy and Intersolubility.* The carbides, nitrides, borides, hydrides, and some oxides are distinguished by isomorphy and intersolubility. The systems TiC-NbC, TiC-TaC, TaC-ZrC, TaC-HfC form continuous series of solid solutions. So also do TaC-TaN and TiC-TiN.

---

[1] *Proc. Roy. Soc. (London),* **159,** 295 (1937).

The latter has importance in titanium-bearing austenitic steels. A typical analysis shows two phases each with a NaCl type of structure as follows:

	a_0	Solid solutions
TiC, pure	4.325	
Ti(C, N)	4.3245	0.65% N in TiC
Ti(N, C)	4.2419	9.6% C in TiN
TiN, pure	4.2330	

The very hard, brilliantly colored single crystals often found in furnaces with melts of this steel have been called Ti "cyanonitride," but this is not a real compound.

   d. Tungsten Carbides. Of special significance are the structures of the tungsten carbides used practically in cutting tools. Both WC and W_2C are hexagonal, with the following scheme of repeat of close-packed atomic sheets:

$$WC: \quad W—C—W—C—W$$
$$W_2C: \quad W—W'—C—W—W'—C—$$

where W and W' are layers of W atoms rotated through 30 deg to achieve close packing. Exactly the same relationship is found in the two forms of graphite (α, hexagonal, with sheets of C atoms repeated every alternate layer; β, rhombohedral every third layer). The possibility of fault formation is thus easily possible, just as Edwards and Lipson found imperfections in stacking of planes in hexagonal cobalt. Actually in pure WC and W_2C with ideal layer lattices, as in graphite, there should be easy slip on planes parallel to the hexagonal base, and thus greatly reduced hardness. Hence the observed extraordinary hardness must arise from a small excess of W in WC or excess C in W_2C to introduce imperfections in stacking. Thus fault formation may correspond to simulation of diamond structures with puckered, interlocking planes within small regions of tungsten carbide lattice, just as found for β-graphite. Becker[1] has noted in these carbides that the carbon has the atomic volume of diamond, and he attributes their great hardness to this fact.[2]

   e. Borides. Great interest has been added to the problem of the structures of metal borides by the work of Kiessling in Hägg's laboratory.[3] Boron of 99 per cent purity was prepared for the first time by vapor-phase reduction of BBr_3 with hydrogen at 750°C. Except for boride phases

---

[1] K. Becker, *Z. Elektrochem.*, **34**, 640 (1928).

[2] *Metallkunde*, **20**, 487 (1928).

[3] R. Kiessling, *Acta Chem. Scand.*, **1**, 893 (1947), **3**, 90, 595, 603 (1948), **4**, 146, 209 (1950).

TABLE 19-2. DATA ON BINARY CARBIDES

Carbide	Formula	Melting point (approx.), °C	Density	Hardness	Crystal structure	Lattice dimensions, kX	Heat of formation kcal/mole at 20–25°C
Nickel.........	Ni$_3$C†	....	......	......	Orthorhombic, cementite type (hcp)	$a = 2.646$, $c/a = 1.636$ }	+9 approx.
Cobalt.........	Co$_3$C†	....	......	......	Orthorhombic, cementite type	$a = 4.52$, $b = 5.08$, $c = 6.73$	
Iron..........	Fe$_3$C	1650	7.67	840 Brinell	Orthorhombic	$a = 4.5144$, $b = 5.0787$, $c = 6.7297$	+2.5 approx.§
	Fe$_2$C	....	......	......	Orthorhombic	$a = 9.04$, $b = 15.66$, $c = 7.92$	
Manganese.....	Mn$_3$C	1520	......	......	Orthorhombic, cementite type	$a = 10.564$	−23 ± 2
	Mn$_{23}$C$_6$	....	......	......	Cubic (complex), as Cr$_{23}$C$_6$	$a = 13.87$	
	Mn$_7$C$_3$	....	......	......	Hexagonal (as Cr$_7$C$_3$)	$c = 4.53$	
Chromium.....	Cr$_{23}$C$_6$	1550	6.97	......	Cubic (complex)	$a = 10.638$	
	Cr$_7$C$_3$	1665	6.92	......	Hexagonal	$a = 13.98$, $c = 4.523$	
	Cr$_3$C$_2$	1890	6.68	......	Orthorhombic	$a = 2.821$, $b = 5.52$, $c = 11.46$	
Vanadium.....	V$_4$C$_3$ VC }	2830	5.36	9–10 Moh's scale	Cubic cp	$a = 4.30$ or $= 4.152$	
Titanium......	TiC	3140 ± 90	4.25	8–9	Cubic cp	$a = 4.3189$ or $= 4.3251$	−114 ± 2

TABLE 19-2. DATA ON BINARY CARBIDES (*Continued*)

Carbide	Formula	Melting point (approx.), °C	Density	Hardness	Crystal structure	Lattice dimensions, kX	Heat of formation kcal/mole at 20-25°C
Molybdenum...	Mo_2C	2687 ± 50	8.9	7-9	Hcp	a = 2.99, c/a = 1.58	
	MoC	2692 ± 50	8.58	7-8	Hcp	a = 4.88, c/a = 1.34	
Niobium...	NbC (Nb_4C_3)	3500 ± 125	7.82	......	Cubic cp	a = 4.4404	
Zirconium...	ZrC	3550	6.90	8-9	Cubic cp	a = 4.687	−45 ± 2
Tungsten...	α-W_2C‡	2857 ± 50	17.20	9-10	Hcp	a = 2.99, c/a = 1.575	
	WC	2867 ± 50	15.50	+9	Hcp	a = 2.894, c/a = 0.973	
Tantalum...	Ta_2C	.....	.....	......	Hcp	a = 3.091, c/a = 1.595	
	TaC	3875 ± 150	14.48	+9	Cubic cp	a = 4.445	
Hafnium...	HfC	3887 ± 150	12.20	......	Cubic cp (probably)		

† Unstable, but retainable; persistent in melt.
‡ Transformation α-W_2C → β-W_2C above 2400°C.
§ Variously reported between −20 and +8.

with double chains of boron atoms the radius of B is 0.87 A. Some of the important observations are as follows:

1. B is soluble in Th, α-Zr, Ta, α-Ti at elevated temperatures.

2. Borides (Ta, W, Mo, Mn, Fe, Co, Ni) with isolated B atoms (Me_2B) crystallize like $CaAl_2$ (C16), with sheets of tetrahedra of metal atoms and B atoms in the holes between these sheets; geometrically these are arranged in strings through the metal lattice, indicating some tendency for B—B bond formations.

3. These closely related MeB borides (Mn, Fe, Co, W, Mo, Ta, Cb, Cr) with FeB, MoB, and CrB as types possess zigzag chains of boron atoms, with each B atom at the center of six metal atoms on a trigonal prism. However, the number of boron atoms in the channels of the metal lattice varies, especially in cases where the homogeneity range extends on either side of the ideal 50 per cent.

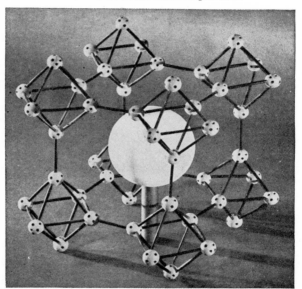

FIG. 291. Structure of framework of boron atoms in MB_6. (*Lafferty.*)

4. In borides of composition Me_3B_4 (Ta, Cb, Mn, Cr), the boron atoms form double chains, or fragments of hexagonal nets, in which B atoms are probably connected by double bonds since $2r_B$ is 1.50 instead of a normal 1.74 A.

5. The formation of hexagonal boron nets is found in MeB_2, of the AlB_2 (C32) type, and closely related M_2B_5 borides of W and Mo, the differences depending on the sequence of metal sheets and of plane or slightly puckered B nets.

6. Finally a considerably number of borides MeB_6 (and UB_{12}) with three-dimensional B frameworks are known. They are all isomorphous, and the metal atoms form a simple cubic lattice. The B atoms form octahedra, with the metal atoms in the interstices (Fig. 291). Each B atom has five B neighbors at a distance of 1.72 A, thus conforming with the $8 - n$ rule. These hexaborides have remarkable properties, recently discovered in a study of boride cathodes.[1] The valence electrons of the metal atoms are not accepted by the B_6 complex, thus giving rise to free electrons which impart a metallic character to these compounds. This, together with the strong

[1] J. M. Lafferty, *J. Appl. Phys.*, **22**, 299 (1951).

bonds between the B atoms in the framework, produces a series of compounds which have high electrical conductivities and high thermal and chemical stabilities. When this structure is heated to a sufficiently high temperature, the metal atoms at the surface evaporate away from the intact B framework but are replaced by diffusion of metal atoms from underlying cells. This process gives a mechanism for constantly

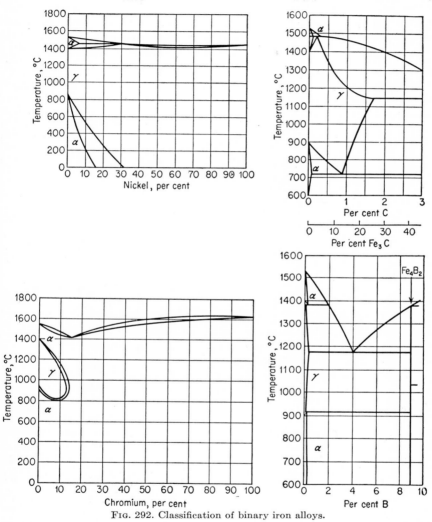

Fig. 292. Classification of binary iron alloys.

maintaining an active cathode surface in vacuum-tube applications. LaB_6 with highest thermal emission is especially useful for high current densities and voltages.

The Systematization of Binary Iron Alloys. From the viewpoint of crystal chemical generalizations the iron alloys form a unique series on account of the complications introduced by the polymorphic phases.

Sufficient x-ray data are now at hand so that some remarkable relationships have been observed by Wever.[1] All the many iron alloys may be classified under four types: (1) open γ field, illustrated by the iron-nickel system in Fig. 292; (2) closed γ field illustrated by iron-chromium; (3) expanded γ field (iron-carbon); (4) contracted γ field (iron-boron). Figure 293 shows a periodic arrangement of the atoms and the description of which type of binary alloy is formed. The open γ field for alloys with metals of Group VIII, the closed γ field in the center of the periodic table, and insolubility for elements of Groups I and II are clearly apparent. That these differences are due primarily to atomic dimensions is shown by Fig. 294. The elements with largest atomic radii are insoluble in iron,

	I		II		III		IV		V		VI		VII		VIII	
	a	b	a	b	a	b	a	b	a	b	a	b	a	b	a	b
I													1H			2He
II	3Li ▲		4Be ●			5B ○		6C □		7N □		8O		9F			10Ne
III	11Na ▲		12Mg ▲			13Al ●		14Si ●		15P ●		16S ○		17Cl			18A
IV	19K ▲		20Ca ▲		21Sc		22Ti ●		23V ●		24Cr ●		25Mn ■		26Fe ■ 27Co ■ 28Ni ■	
		29Cu □		30Zn □		31Ga		32Ge ●		33As ●		34Se		35Br			36Kr
V	37Rb ▲		38Sr ▲		39Yt		40Zr ○		41Cb ●		42Mo ●		43Ma		44Ru ■ 45Rh ■ 46Pd ■	
		47Ag ▲		48Cd ▲		49In		50Sn ●		51Sb ●		52Te		53I			54Xe
VI	55Cs ▲		56Ba ▲		58Ce ○		72Hf		73Ta ●		74W ●		75Re		76Os ■ 77Ir ■ 78Pt ■	
		79Au □		80Hg ▲		81Tl ▲		82Pb ▲		83Bi ▲		84Po		85–			86Rn
VII	87–		88Ra ▲		89Ac		90Th		91Pa		92U					

■ Open γ-field   □ Expanded γ-field   ▲ Insoluble
● Closed γ-field   ○ Contracted γ-field

FIG. 293. Periodic table showing effects of chemical elements in binary iron alloys.

and those with smallest radii are most soluble and are characterized by open or expanded γ field, whereas intermediate elements narrow the γ phase. Such generalizations are highly gratifying, and rapid progress may be expected in classifying similarly other systems of binary alloys. Important as examples may be cited the following: the identification of Fe_2W (hexagonal) and Fe_3W_2 (rhombohedral, 40 atoms per unit cell) and of the corresponding Fe_3Mo_2. The binary interstitial alloys of nitrogen with iron have great practical significance because of casehardening. The following phases have been identified: α (body-centered cubic); γ' (Fe_4N the principal constituent in casehardened steel), with the iron on a face-centered lattice, $a = 3.789$ A, and nitrogen at the cell center; ϵ (Fe_3N), hexagonal close-packed; ζ_1 (Fe_2N), orthorhombic, with which Fe_8C_3N is isomorphous.

[1] Ergebn. tech. Röntgenkunde, **2**, 240 (1931).

Steel (Fe-C *Alloys*). The most important possible application of x-ray analysis to the structure of alloys is, of course, to the series of iron-carbon alloys. There are several reasons for this, aside from the practical utility of steel. The equilibrium diagram is one of great complexity because of the great variety of forms involving the four allotropic forms of pure iron; hence, there has been among metallurgists for a great many years,

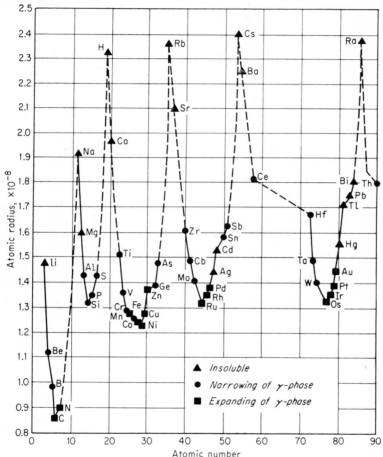

FIG. 294. Relation between atomic radius and formation of binary iron alloy.

the widest divergence of opinion concerning the actual constitution of many of the iron-carbon phases. The x-ray has been eagerly resorted to for a final answer to these moot problems; though it has already given many hopeful signs, the results are still insufficient to more than open the subject.

The facts established by x-ray analysis of steel may be briefly summarized as follows:

1. *Austenite,* formed by quenching Fe-C alloys from above the A_3 transformation point, has the structure of γ-iron (face-centered cubic). Carbon causes an enlargement of the lattice. Westgren and Phragmen found the dimensions of the unit cell to be 3.629 A for a saturated solution (1.7 per cent) quenched from 1100°C and 3.606 A for a specimen containing 0.9 per cent carbon quenched from 750°C. A specimen containing 12.1 per cent manganese and 1.34 per cent carbon had a parameter 3.624 A. As already explained, the carbon atoms are placed interstitially. The carbon may be atomically and irregularly dispersed, or the atoms may be more definitely arranged, in the sense that an atom of γ-iron may be replaced by a complex of an iron combined with one or more carbon atoms. In other words, austenite is a solid solution of carbon or Fe_3C (cementite) in γ-iron.

2. *Cementite.* The compound formed by iron and carbon, Fe_3C, is the prevalent carbide in plain carbon and low-alloy carbon steels and crystallizes in the orthorhombic system. The unit parallelepiped has the dimensions[1] 4.5144 by 5.0787 by 6.7297 A or the axial ratios 0.671 : 0.753 : 1. This compound is found in *pearlite* (the eutectoid mixture of α-iron and cementite formed by slow cooling of austentite from the transformation point), *troostite* (α-iron and cementite in colloidal dispersion), and *sorbite* and in the massive spheroidal condition. Meteoric cohenite has the same structure.

3. *Hägg carbide.* In 1934, Hägg[2] suggested the possibility of a metastable percarbide, Fe_2C, and this was experimentally confirmed by Jack,[3] who found by action of CO on iron nitrides below 500°C a range of compositions only from 30.5 to 32.1 atomic percentage of carbon. The structure is also orthorhombic, with the cell dimensions $a = 9.04$, $b = 15.66$, $c = 7.92$ kX, containing probably 4 $Fe_{20}C_9$ molecules. Actually the unit cells of Fe_3C and Fe_2C show a simple relationship:

$$a_{Fe_2C} \approx 2a_{Fe_3C}$$
$$b_{Fe_2C} \approx 3b_{Fe_3C}$$
$$c_{Fe_2C} \approx 1c_{Fe_3C} \text{ (slightly elongated)}$$

Thus 6 Fe_3C cells stacked together form a volume (924 kX³) similar to 1 of Fe_2C (934 kX³), the extra volume exactly providing for 8 more Fe and 12 more C atoms in the latter. The increased carbon content involves no major expansion or contraction from Fe_3C, and the transition takes place in the presence of excess carbons without major structural change. It is significant that above the melting point of Fe_3C (1550°C) the liquid solubility for carbon gradually increases from 25 to 33 atomic

[1] Latest values by Lipson and Petch, *J. Iron Steel Inst. (London),* **2**, 95 (1940).

[2] G. Hägg, *Z. Krist.,* **89**, 92 (1934).

[3] K. H. Jack, *Nature,* **158**, 60 (1946).

percentage at 2200°C, indicating the formation in the liquid of molecular aggregates first of Fe_3C and then of Fe_2C.

4. *Ferrite* has the body-centered cubic structure of pure α-iron. Carbon has a very limited solubility in it (0.06 per cent), since the diffraction lines for the numerous specimens have the same position as for pure electrolytic α-iron. A widening of the lines and the disappearance of the resolution of doublet lines may be taken as an indication of a slight increase (up to 0.3 per cent) in the lattice and local distortion to tetragonal symmetry, but nonuniformly since pure iron dimensions are still indicated. Williamson and Smallman have proved from an analysis of strain breadths of diffraction lines that at least 85 per cent of the interstitial carbon atoms occupy octahedral interstices (*i.e.*, halfway along the unit-cell edges with iron atoms at the corners and body center).[1]

5. *β-Iron*. There is no x-ray evidence of β-iron, since there is no structural discontinuity between α- and γ-iron.

6. *Martensite*. Martensite is formed and retained at room temperatures when the γ-α transformation is delayed by sufficiently rapid cooling until a temperature of 300°C is reached. The austenite $\rightarrow$ pearlite transformation at 200° requires hours; austenite $\rightarrow$ martensite at 100° is instantaneous. The cooling may be slower in the presence of retarding elements such as nickel and manganese. The simple facts were first established that martensite gives the spectrum of α-iron and that the diffraction lines are broad and diffuse.

More careful technique in the preparation of samples and in photographing diffraction spectra have served to clarify the problem. Fink and Campbell[2] found evidence in drastically quenched eutectoid and hypereutectoid steels of a body-centered tetragonal structure. This was not uniform with lower carbon contents, but with 1.5 per cent carbon the value of a was 2.85 A and of c, 3.02 A.U. (body-centered cubic α-iron, $a = 2.86$ A). It was found to be less stable at low temperatures than the γ-iron lattice and disappeared on tempering at 200°C, or even as low as 100°C into ferrite and cementite in the form of sorbite, coarser than pearlite. The martensitic tetragonal structure might represent an arrested stage in transformation from face-centered cubic (γ) to body-centered cubic iron (α). The axial ratio c/a increases with carbon content at constant heating and quenching conditions and with the temperature before quenching at constant carbon content. In a steel of eutectoid composition the ratio of carbon atoms to iron atoms is 1:24; thus in martensite of such a composition, one carbon atom belongs to a set of 12 α-iron unit cells, thus causing tetragonal distortion.

It may be concluded that martensite is a supersaturated solid solution of carbon in α-iron and that the intermediate tetragonal structure

[1] G. K. Williamson and R. E. Smallman, *Acta Cryst.*, **6**, 361 (1953).

[2] *Trans. Am. Soc. Steel Treating*, **9**, 717 (1926).

together with inherent complex strains accounts for hardness. The variable parameters, of course, could account for the very diffuse x-ray diffraction interferences as well as distortion or very small grain size.

Polycomponent Alloy Systems. The complications that are introduced immediately in passing from binary to ternary systems, not to mention more complex systems, are at once apparent. In the x-ray analysis of ternary alloys are involved three binary and the whole range of ternary systems represented by all points on the interior of a triangular diagram. It is not possible here to describe the methods by which a comparatively limited number of specimens and diffraction patterns suffice to establish the essential facts of the entire system, and the precautions necessary to assure equilibria. References in the literature may be found for about 75 ternary systems, mostly with Mg, Al, Fe, Cu, Zn, and Ag, more or less completely studied with x-rays, largely by the "stochastic" method.

An example of a fairly complete analysis from powder patterns is that of $Mg_6Si_7Cu_{16}$,† a cubic intermetallic compound with 116 atoms per unit cell. At (0,0,0) there is a group of 6 Mg atoms at the vertices of an octahedron, surrounded by 8 Cu atoms at the corners of a cube, in turn surrounded by 12 Si atoms at the vertices of a cuboctahedron (cuboctahedra are derived from cubes so that atoms in face centers are pushed out till all of these and the atoms at corners are equidistant from an atom at the body center); the Si atoms are shared with neighboring clusters. At $(\frac{1}{2},\frac{1}{2},\frac{1}{2})$ there is 1 Si atom surrounded by 8 Cu atoms at the corners of a cube. This structure is identical with that of the intermetallic compound Th_6Mn_{23}.‡

Of prime interest among ternary alloys are the permanent-magnet alloys discussed later in this chapter. Only five quaternary alloys have had anything like complete analysis thus far: Al-Bi-Pb-Sb, Zn-Mn-Cu-Ag, Al-Mg-Mn-Si, Al-Cu-Mg-Si, and Al-Fe-Mg-Si. The singular compound $Al_8Si_6Mg_3Fe$ is exceptional.

Alloy Steels. In ternary carbides formed by iron with the alloying metals indicated in Table 19-2 the following rules apply:

1. With the metals which form cubic carbides, iron forms no ternary carbides or solid solutions, for the available carbon is tied up by these metals.

2. With the metals which form hexagonal carbides, iron forms ternary carbides which themselves are cubic and have a limited solubility for iron (Fe_3W_3C-Fe_4W_2C, Fe_3Mo_3C-Fe_4Mo_2C).

3. With the transitional carbides such as those of Cr, no ternary carbides are formed, but the primary carbides of Fe and Cr are mutually soluble to a considerable extent.

4. With the orthorhombic carbides (Mn, Co, Ni), Fe forms its own carbide, cementite, which is isomorphous and completely intersoluble with Mn_3C, Co_3C, Ni_3C.

5. The structures of the three carbides $Cr_{23}C_6$ [or more generally (Cr, Fe, W,

† G. Bergman and J. L. T. Waugh, *Acta Cryst.*, **6**, 93 (1953).

‡ J. V. Florio, R. E. Rundle, and A. I. Snow, *Acta Cryst.*, **5**, 449 (1952).

Mo)$_{23}$C$_6$], Fe$_4$W$_2$C [or more generally Fe$_4$(W, Mo)$_2$C and Fe$_3$(W, Mo)$_3$C], and Fe$_3$C are of primary importance in the consideration of all ternary, quaternary, and higher alloy steels. There is an interesting structural relationship between the first two. The geometric arrangement of cuboctahedra and cubes in Cr$_{23}$C$_6$ gives way to plain octahedra and tetrahedra in Fe$_4$W$_2$C. There is no clear structural relationship to Fe$_3$C, but if eight unit cells of cementite are stacked together, the following data appear:

Carbide	Formula	Equivalent volume, kX³
Cementite	M$_{96}$C$_{32}$	1,234
Cr$_{23}$C$_6$	M$_{92}$C$_{21}$	1,204
Fe$_{21}$W$_2$C$_6$	M$_{92}$C$_{21}$	1,160
Fe$_4$W$_2$C	M$_{96}$C$_{16}$	1,346

Thus here are closely related "elementary bricks" upon which studies of carbides may be based.

6. In consideration of all available data it is possible to understand the structural relations among carbides, austenite, and ferrite:

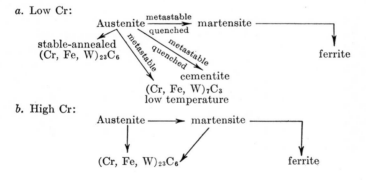

a. Low Cr:

b. High Cr:

Crystal Structure and Magnetism. The fact that α-iron is magnetic and β-iron nonmagnetic, though x-rays detect no structural discontinuity between these, seems to indicate that magnetic properties are not functions of the arrangement of atoms in space. However, Persson in Westgren's laboratory demonstrated that the magnetic Heusler alloys (copper-manganese-aluminum) always show the x-ray diffraction lines of the β phase. In this the basic lattice is body-centered cubic, upon which is superposed a face-centered cubic lattice of aluminum atoms with twice the dimensions of the basic lattice. Hence the unit cube contains 16 atoms, of which 12 are copper + manganese and 4 aluminum. The formula (Cu, Mn)$_3$Al is substantiated by the x-ray results. It is further essential that the concentration of manganese must be above a limiting value for magnetic properties to develop. In other words, the pattern for the β phase may appear for nonmagnetic specimens if manganese is insufficient.

Bradley and Taylor[1] in 1937 used x-ray patterns to characterize permanent magnets of iron, nickel, and aluminum. On the ternary

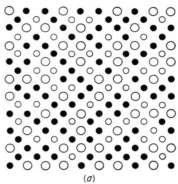

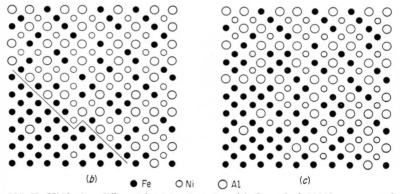

● Fe   ○ Ni   ○ Al

FIG. 295. Fe₂NiAl after different heat-treatments. (a) Quenched 1200°, one crystal; Fe atoms at random. (b) Slow-cooled, two crystals; Fe-rich crystal contracts in volume by 1 per cent. (c) Special heat-treatment for high coercivity, Fe atoms in "island"; no sharp boundary. (*Bradley and Taylor.*)

diagram established from the structural studies, the two-phase area $\beta + \beta_{2m}$ includes all compositions that are suitable for the manufacture of permanent magnets, with Fe₂NiAl typical. The maximum magnetic coercivity is obtained not by (1) quenching of Fe₂NiAl or by (2) slow cooling and separation into two phases but by (3) a special controlled cooling. In Fig. 295 are shown the atomic arrangements deduced directly from x-ray patterns for these three cases: (1) one lattice, nickel and aluminum atoms in definite positions and iron atoms at random;

[1] "Physics in Industry," p. 91, 1937.

(2) two lattices (double diffraction lines) for nearly pure iron atoms and for original lattice diminished in iron atoms; (3) one lattice but with non-uniform atomic distribution (indicated by characteristic line broadening). Here the iron atoms have begun to separate, forming only small aggregates without definite boundaries. These small islands of iron cannot break away to form separate crystals when the alloy is cooled at a definite rate. Being still forced to conform to the dimensions of the parent lattice, the iron atoms are held apart under a condition of immense strain—and therein lies the explanation of the remarkable properties of Fe_2NiAl as a permanent magnet. Since 1937 further progress has been made in developing permanent-magnet alloys, such as Alnico (Al 8%, Ni 14 to 15%, Co 24%, Cu 3%, Fe balance), both in massive and powder form.[1]

[1] For a complete review see Braileford, Oliver, Hadfield, and Polgreen, *JIEE*, **95**, 522 (1948).

CHAPTER 20

ORGANIC COMPOUNDS

The examination of the crystals of organic substances represents the newest phase of the still young science of x-ray crystal analysis. The hesitancy among experimenters until fairly recently to undertake complete crystalline and molecular structural analysis of organic compounds was in one sense surprising, inasmuch as the organic chemist long ago introduced the simplifying and logical conceptions of spatial arrangements of atoms which have been the strength of the science as compared with the wide varieties of apparently unrelated building plans with which inorganic chemists have been confronted. On the other hand, crystallographic examination has shown that the great majority of organic compounds crystallize in the very classes of low symmetry whose diffraction effects are the most difficult to interpret; and good crystals for analysis are usually difficult to obtain. The skill of Sir William Bragg prior to 1920 in combining x-ray data with other authentic information, to show that whole molecules, instead of atoms, are the units placed at the points of the lattice and held by relatively weak binding ties (van der Waals, or molecular, bonds), laid the foundation upon which the science of organic structures has been built. Today many laboratories throughout the world, with the powerful tools of interpretation, such as Fourier synthesis, which have been developed, are turning out an ever-increasing number of analyses of increasingly complex structures. The record of achievement, culminating in unique molecular analyses of penicillin, proteins, steroids, and many other compounds, both synthesized and from natural sources, is one of the most impressive and brilliant in the pages of science; theoretical and practical aspects of organic chemistry have received so great an impetus that the organic chemist accepts x-ray diffraction techniques as an indispensable research and control tool.

The Carbon Structures. The structure of the compounds of carbon must find ultimate prototypes in the structure of crystalline carbon. Of this there are two varieties: the diamond, crystallizing in the tetrahedral cubic system with each carbon very definitely at the center of four other equidistant carbons at the corners of a tetrahedron; and graphite, with a lower hexagonal symmetry.[1] "Puckered" six-carbon rings are easily

[1] A rhombohedral form of graphite may also be found, arising from a variation in the stacking of layers (see Chaps. 16 and 21).

identified in the diamond lattice (Fig. 296). After considerable controversy Bernal[1] succeeded in proving from x-ray data that the carbon atoms in graphite are flattened into a plane so that three of the carbon neighbors remain at somewhat smaller distance from the central atom than in the diamond tetrahedrons (1.42 A as against 1.54 A in diamond) and the fourth is at a greater distance (3.40 A) in the next layer. In other words, in graphite the atom has three strong bonds coplanar or very nearly so with itself and one weak bond at right angles to these bonds. This bond may be easily ruptured so that one layer will slide over another

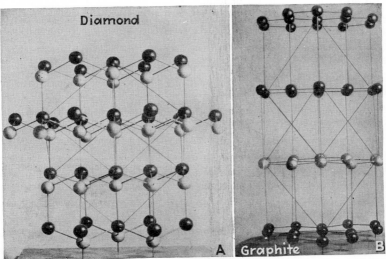

FIG. 296. Comparison of crystal models of diamond and graphite. (*Central Scientific Company.*)

to account for the lubricating properties of graphite. The peculiar lamellar structure also allows special types of reaction to occur as shown by Hofmann and Frenzel.[2] Graphite reacts with alkali metals to form stoichiometric compounds of the type C_8K and $C_{16}K$. X-ray diffraction data show no change in the distance between carbon atoms in the same layers, but the distance between layers increases from 3.38 A in graphite to 5.34 in C_8K. Treatment with mercury regenerates graphite. In graphitic acid this distance between layers is 6 A, which increases to 11 A by swelling with water. The fascinating subject of graphitic and carbon black structures is considered in detail in Chap. 21.

One of the most interesting questions in the whole science has been whether the carbon atoms in ring compounds, *e.g.*, aromatic series, lie in one plane, as in graphite and as the organic chemist has represented

[1] *Proc. Roy. Soc. (London)*, **106A**, 749 (1924).
[2] *Kolloid-Z.*, **58**, 8 (1932).

structures on paper, or are staggered, as in diamond and most probably in aliphatic (chain) compounds. A satisfactory answer to this question has been given; yet it cannot be maintained that the shape and dimensions of the benzene ring found for some compounds are necessarily the same in all aromatic compounds. A few of the important steps leading to the final conclusion will be outlined in a later section.

The X-ray Analysis of Organic Molecules. The general methods of interpretation of x-ray diffraction patterns of crystals outlined in Chap. 15 reach their highest point in the direct delineation of the structure of the organic molecule. The unit cell and the dimensions are evaluated without much difficulty. The intensities give a measure of the extent to which electrons are distributed in the structure. Since the crystal is a periodic structure built up by the repetition of identically arranged molecules in all directions, this periodic medium can be analyzed into a Fourier series of harmonic terms, the periods of which correspond to the spacings of all possible crystal planes, and best exemplified by the structural analysis of penicillin. On account of uncertainties introduced by lack of information on phase constants, assumptions and approximations and auxiliary data already described may be necessary, finally leading to a result that is an x-ray picture of the molecules. The complete expression of structure is given by a three-dimensional series whose terms correspond to all possible crystal planes. Such a series is difficult to evaluate numerically owing to the large number of terms; consequently in practice a two-dimensional series is usually employed, which represents a projection of the structure in a given direction. The coefficients in such a series correspond to the reflections from all the crystal planes that are parallel to the axis along which the projection is made. In such projections of a structure some atoms are often hidden behind others, but the complete structure can usually be worked out by piecing together the results of two or more projections along different crystal axes. The electron density is calculated by summing up the double series at many points taken close together on the projection, and the results are graphically represented by drawing contour lines to pass through points of equal electron density. And the result is the complete contour map of the molecule. The first contour line is usually dotted and represents a density of 1 electron/A^2 (fractional values are possible in the most recent analyses of high precision to give evidence of hydrogen atoms, long considered an impossibility). The remaining lines are drawn at unit intervals, so that peaks for usual organic molecules represent 6 or 7 electrons/A^2. This is the remarkably expressive method now applied for the delineation of the molecule, usually applicable to structures containing closed-ring systems where the possible configurations of the molecule are limited. Several examples of electron-density contour maps are illustrated in this chapter.

In the simple case of durene, 1,2,4,5-tetramethylbenzene (Fig. 309), the six carbon atoms forming the benzene ring and the four symmetrically attached methyl groups are easily apparent. Thus the structural formula of the organic chemist not only is verified but in a sense is registered by the organic molecule itself. It is recognized at once that sometimes the molecule is inclined at a considerable angle to the plane of projection, and thus the contour map is a foreshortened version of a molecule that may actually be perfectly planar, as determined by projections of other zones of reflection.

Molecular Dimensions. The x-ray results on these molecular structures involve quite directly interatomic distances, rather than atomic radii, since there is such a variation in unsymmetrical coordination. Experience has shown that the distance between two given atoms linked by a given type of bond is closely constant throughout all organic compounds. It is essential, therefore, to list these bond lengths, which, when combined with information on bond angles, permit construction of a molecular model. The true single bond between two atoms, for example, —C—C—, has one value, the double bond —C=C— another, the triple bond —C≡C— another. Thus the measurement of interatomic distances gives direct evidence of the type of binding even in very complex structures where chemical evidence is entirely inadequate. Intermediate bond lengths then represent resonance between two simple types—and we may calculate that a given bond may be, for example, 20 per cent double and 80 per cent single bond from an empirical curve calibrated by four fixed points: 1.54 A, pure single bond in diamond and aliphatic compounds; 1.34 A, pure double bond as in ethylene; 1.39 A in benzene (50 per cent double bond); and 1.42 A in graphite (33 per cent double bond).[1] Examples will be given during the discussion of specific structures. In Table 20-1 are listed the most accurately measured bond lengths in a wide variety of compounds. Certainly the accuracy of Fourier projections is now being pushed to the limit for the purpose of evaluating bond lengths and angles. Alternations of lengths in apparently symmetrical molecules seem to be the rule, rather than constant —C—C— bond lengths, for example.

Molecular Shape. Because of rotation around bonds and flexibility of structure it is not always possible from chemical evidence to predict the exact shape of molecules, whether flat or puckered or whether, in diphenyl, dibenzyl, etc., the aromatic nuclei are parallel or turned at an angle. Such features must be determined by detailed analysis of the distribution of neighboring molecules in the structure.

Intermolecular Binding. The third type of information concerning organic crystals, almost unique to the x-ray method and no less important than the information concerning interatomic binding within the molecule, is disclosure of the type of force responsible for molecular coherence in the

[1] L. Pauling and L. O. Brockway, *J. Am. Chem. Soc.,* **59,** 1223 (1937).

TABLE 20-1. BOND LENGTHS

Compound	Bond type	Length, A.U.
Diamond	C—C aliphatic (true single)	1.54
Paraffin chains	C—C aliphatic (true single)	1.54
Ethylene	C=C (true double)	1.34
Carbon suboxide	C=C	1.30
Acetylene	C≡C (true triple)	1.20
Tolane	C≡C	1.19
Graphite	C—C (33% C=C)	1.42
Benzene	C—C aromatic (50% C=C)	1.39
Naphthalene	C—C aromatic (average)	1.41
Anthracene	C—C aromatic (average)	1.41
Chrysene	C—C aromatic	1.41
Dibenzyl	C—C aliphatic	1.58
	C—C aromatic-aliphatic	1.47
	C—C aromatic	1.41
Benzoquinone	C—C ring	1.50
	C=C ring	1.32
Hexamethylbenzene	C—C aromatic	1.42
	C—C aromatic-aliphatic	1.48
Durene	C—C aromatic	1.41
	C—C aromatic-aliphatic	1.47
p-Diphenylbenzene	C—C aromatic	1.42
	C—C between rings	1.48
Diphenyl	C—C aromatic	1.42
	C—C between rings	1.48
Polyoxymethylene	C—O	1.49
Methyl ether	C—O	1.42
Benzoquinone	C=O	1.14
Urea	C=O	1.25
Oxalic acid dihydrate	C—O } resonance	{ 1.24
	C—OH	1.30
	O—O H bond	2.52
	O—O H bond	2.85
Resorcinol	C—OH	1.36
Pentaerythritol	C—OH	1.46
Urea	C—N	1.37
Thiourea	C—N	1.37
	C=S	1.64
Hexamethylenetetramine	C—N	1.42
Phthalocyanine	C—N } resonance	1.34
	C=N	
Hexachlorbenzene	C—Cl	1.86
Hexabrombenzene	C—Br	1.94
Iodoform	C—I	2.10
Di-iodocyclohexane	C—I	2.12
	N—O	1.38
Nitric oxide	N=O	1.15
p-Dinitrobenzene	N=O	1.20
Nitrogen	N≡N	1.06

crystal lattice. This may vary from strengths almost as great as homopolar bonds in hard, brittle high-melting compounds, to the weak residual, or van der Waals, force. For convenience molecular crystals may be classified as in Table 20-2, in terms both of molecular shape and of three types of intermolecular binding force increasing in strength in the order: (1) apolar, or residual; (2) polar linkage between molecules with local

TABLE 20-2. MOLECULAR SHAPE AND BINDING FORCE

Molecular shape	Type of intermolecular binding force		
	Apolar (residual)	Polar†	Ionic
Simple symmetrical molecules	Inert gases Diatomic gases Hydrides NH_3, CH_4, etc. Polyhalides CCl_4 Simple hydrocarbons Basic beryllium acetate	Urea, thiourea Hexamethylene-tetramine Pentaerythritol	Simple alkyl ammonium salts Oxalic acid† and oxalates Simple amino acids
Long molecules	Long-chain aliphatic hydrocarbons Cycloparaffins Plastic sulfur Rubber	Long-chain alcohols, ketones, esters	Fatty acids, soaps Long-chain alkyl ammonium salts Fibrous protein
Flat molecules	Rhombic sulfur Aromatic hydrocarbons Phthalocyanines Cyanuric triazide	Halogen, NO_2-, NH_2— derivatives of aromatic hydrocarbons Phenols, quinones Sugars Sterols	Aromatic acids and salts Aromatic bases and salts Methylene blue halides
Giant three-dimensional molecules	. . . .	. . . .	Globular proteins

† Includes structures, especially with OH groups, bonded by hydrogen bridges: pentaerythritol, oxalic acid dihydrate, resorcinol, sugars, etc.

dipoles packed so that adjacent dipoles neutralize each other (—OH, =NH, =O groups); (3) ionic (acids, bases, and salts).

The Results of Crystal Analysis of Organic Compounds. Some years ago all x-ray data on organic compounds could be considered in very little space, and in fact the "International Critical Tables," Volume I, listed only about 15 organic compounds for which space groups had been assigned. With the great improvements in technique and in methods of interpretation a very large number of organic compounds have now been analyzed for crystalline and molecular structures with results just as complete and convincing as the examples already cited. Ewald and Hermann more than a decade ago classified these into 64 main types, with many others still to be fitted into the scheme. Little would be gained in this book by presenting these experimental data, since even tabulation would be greatly extended and since they are to be found in full in the "Strukturbericht," in Wyckoff's compilation of "Crystal Structures,"[1] Volume III, Chapters XIII, Aliphatic Compounds, XIV, Derivatives of Benzene, and XV, Alicyclic and Heterocyclic Compounds, and currently in the *Acta Crystallographica*, official periodical of the International Union of Crystallography. Consequently only some conclusions of general interest to the chemist will be considered briefly.

1. *Inorganic Types with Organic Substituted Radicals.* The alkyl ammonium halides and chlorostannates are the chief representatives and have been classified into 10 types by Wyckoff in "Crystal Structures," Volume II. In almost every case a very clear relationship exists between the structure of the compound and the simpler compound in which a metal atom has been replaced by a radical. NH_3CH_3Cl was originally assigned a CsCl arrangement with one molecule per unit cell, but now it is known to have a tetragonal unit cell with two molecules, with half the $(CH_3NH_3)^+$ groups pointed upward and half downwards. Triethylammonium iodide is like wurtzite, ZnS, with the radical replacing zinc atoms; the length of the chain, of course, causes a large decrease in the axial ratio. Tetramethylammonium iodide is similarly related to phosphonium iodide (type B10), methylammonium iodide to rock salt, and methylammonium chloride to cesium chloride. A very curious result is that in the latter two cases the chains which replace one of the ions in the simple salts evidently appear to be linear rather than zigzag, in order to account for observed symmetry and spacings. The C—C separation is 1.26 A instead of 1.54 expected for an aliphatic chain. However, it is now established that this structure is due to free rotation of the carbon chain around its length, and the 1.26 spacing is the projection on the chain axis of the true inclined bond of length 1.54.

In general the rotational motion of the cations in most of these compounds is too complicated to permit any accurate description of atomic positions. For at lower temperatures where the rotation does not persist there is a polymorphic transition to a larger unit cell of lower symmetry, consistent with the usual zigzag chain. Several derivatives of hexachloroplatinates and hexachlorostannates, in which these ions are octahedrally coordinated, also have structures that might be predicted from the results on metal ion salts of these complex anions. The chief interest, of course, is in the effect on the symmetry of the ammonium group of substituting various combinations of alkyl groups.

2. *Metalloalkyl Compounds.* Wyckoff lists 12 types of these compounds which do not display well-defined groups. Examples are (1) alkyl chloromercury mercaptans, CH_3SHgCl; (2) diethyl mercaptan,

[1] Interscience Publishers, Inc., New York, 1953.

$Hg(SC_2H_5)_2$; (3) hydrated rare-earth ethyl sulfates; (4) dimethyl thallic bromide, $Th(CH_3)_2Br$; (5) trimethyl antimony halides, $SbBr_2(CH_3)_3$; (6) addition compounds of Cu_2Cl_2 such as $Cu\left(S{=}C{<}\genfrac{}{}{0pt}{}{CH_3}{NH_2}\right)_4 Cl$; (7) trialkyl phosphines and arsines of CuI and Ag; (8) $(CH_3)_3$ As.$PdBr_2$ dimers; (9) $P(CH_3)_3AuBr_3$; (10) $(C_3H_7)_2AuCN$ with 16 molecules per cell; (11) $(CH_3)_3PtCl$ and $Pt(CH_3)_4$ tetramers, cubic; (12) $Fe(CN.CH_3)_6$-$Cl_2.3H_2O$. There are interesting details of packing and coordination for all these compounds, which are discussed in Wyckoff's critical evaluation of x-ray data.

3. *Symmetrical Methane Derivatives.* The tetrahedral form of these compounds is the point of greatest interest. Methane crystallizes below 89°K in the face-centered cubic lattice of parallel CH_4 tetrahedra; tetramethylmethane has the diamond cubic structure, and tetraiodomethane is a simple cubic lattice of parallel tetrahedra. X-ray and electron diffraction researches have shown clearly the distortion of the tetrahedra that results when the hydrogen atoms are unsymmetrically replaced by halogens or other groups. Even carbon tetrabromide, which crystallizes in two modifications with a tetrahedral molecule for the lower temperature modification, loses symmetry at higher temperatures and forms a monoclinic lattice from bimolecules. In tetranitromethane, although cubic, one of the nitro groups evidently differs from the other three in space, and the formula is perhaps correctly written $O{=}N{-}O{-}C(NO_2)_3$.

Pentaerythritol, $C(CH_2OH)_4$, a tetragonal crystal, probably has the distinction of having been investigated more repeatedly than any other organic compound. It illustrates the case in which very slight differences in interpretation of x-ray and optical data lead to widely different molecular structures. In the early work it was concluded that the carbon atoms were all coplanar or formed a flat pyramid. Further work has demonstrated that it is impossible from the x-ray data to distinguish between symmetry classes $\bar{4}$ or 4 (tetrahedral). Researches on crystal growth and solution, etch figures, pyro- and piezoelectricity have given preponderance to the tetrahedral molecule and the space group $I\bar{4}$. Each OH group is attached to its CH_2 group by a bond that makes a nearly tetrahedral angle with the C—CH_2 link and is so directed that the four OH groups lie at the corners of a square. Four molecules are linked together by the hydrogen bonds of four OH groups in a square 2.69 A on a side. Besides pentaerythritol, the tetracetate and tetranitrate are also body-centered tetragonal with the same symmetry class, but they differ in the orientation of the center molecule with respect to the molecules at the corners of the unit cell. The compounds $C(C_6H_5)_4$, $Si(C_6H_5)_4$, $Ge(C_6H_5)_4$, $Sn(C_6H_5)_4$, and $Pb(C_6H_5)_4$ all have the same tetrahedral molecular structure and lattice as pentaerythritol tetranitrate. Tetramethyl orthothiocarbonate, $C(SCH_3)_4$, occurs in three modifications: the first is like pentaerythritol tetranitrate, the second is disordered to the extent of two orientations of CS_4 tetrahedra, and the third (cubic) has three-dimensional disorder of these units.

Tetraphenylmethane has considerable interest because of very low density and because the bond character is easily altered by substitution of active groups to form colored compounds such as crystal violet and malachite green. A recent analysis[1] shows a space group $P42_1c$, $a = 10.87$, $b = 7.23$ A, two molecules per unit cell, with bond lengths 1.47 A about the central carbon atoms and 1.37 in the six-membered rings, and the presence of much void space.

4. *Unsymmetrical Methane Derivatives without Chain Character.* Chief representatives of this class thus far studied are iodoform, urea and its derivatives, formic acid, and some formates. In iodoform the iodine atoms form a hexagonal packing of spheres. The carbon and hydrogen atoms enter octahedrally the holes in this lattice, so that the molecules CHI_3 form the unit. In triphenylmethyl chloride and bromide (hexagonal $H3$, six molecules per cell) the halogen atoms form rhombohedral packing, and the triphenylmethyl groups, like the tetraphenyl, are not planar.[2]

Formic acid, HCOOH, crystallized at $-50°C$[3] has an orthorhombic structure, *Pna*, with unit-cell dimensions $a = 10.23$, $b = 3.64$, $c = 5.34$ A. Infinite chains run through the crystal as the result of H bonds. The bond lengths are determined with high precision; $C—O = 1.26$ A, $C=O = 1.23$ A., $\angle O—C=O = 123$ deg, $O—H \cdot \cdot \cdot O = 2.58$ A. In urea, $OC(NH_2)_2$, the molecule consists of a central atom circumscribed by an almost equilateral triangle of one oxygen and two nitrogen atoms. By means of hydrogen bonds there are chains of the molecules parallel to the c axis or networks perpendicular. Unusual interest is attached to urea because of its simplicity and the extraordinary refinements in the crystallographic data. The space group, known correctly since the first analysis in 1923, is $P\bar{4}2_1m$, with $a = 5.661$, $c = 4.712$ A, and two molecules per cell. The interatomic distances are $C=O = 1.26$, $C—N = 1.34$ A, $\angle N—C—O = 121$ deg, hydrogen bond $N—H \cdot \cdot \cdot O = 2.99$ A, $N—H \cdot \cdot \cdot O' = 3.04$ A. With these values it may be calculated, with Pauling's equation, which relates bond length with double-bond character, that there are three resonance forms of urea:

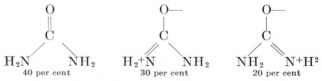

O	O—	O—
∥	│	│
C	C	C
H₂N NH₂	H₂⁺N NH₂	NH₂ N⁺H²
40 per cent	30 per cent	20 per cent

[1] N. T. Sumsion and D. McLachlan, Jr., *Acta Cryst.*, **3**, 217 (1950).

[2] Wang and Liu, *J. Am. Chem. Soc.*, **66**, 1113 (1944).

[3] F. Holtzberg, B. Post, and I. Fankuchen, *Acta Cryst.*, **6**, 127 (1953).

Therefore the urea molecule including H atoms must be planar, as shown by electron-density sections and disposition of H bonds. The remarkable "cagelike" complexes of urea with straight-chain hydrocarbons is discussed in a later section of this chapter. Thiourea is orthorhombic with four molecules per unit cell, instead of tetragonal with two molecules per cell for urea, and the carbon atoms are surrounded by the sulfur and two nitrogen atoms in the form of a flat pyramid. The nitrogen atoms are equivalent, so that the correct formula in the solid state is

A related compound acetoxime, $(CH_3)_2C$=NOH, has also been analyzed by Fourier methods. It has the hexagonal space group $C6_3/m$, $a = 10.61$, $c = 7.02$ A, $Z = 6$. The crystal is built from sheets of planar trimers with intermolecular hydrogen bonds of length 2.78 A.†

5. *Short Aliphatic Chains with Symmetry about a Central C—C Linkage.* Numerous compounds of this type have been investigated, of chief interest being ethane and its derivatives and oxalic, maleic and fumaric, and tartaric acids and their derivatives. Ethane, C_2H_6, and diborane, B_2H_6, crystallize alike with hexagonal cell. The dimensions for the former are $a = 4.46$, $c = 8.19$ A, distance C—C in the same molecule 1.55 A, C—C in different molecules 3.5 A, distance molecule center to center 4.46 A. Solid ethylene C_2H_4 at $-175°C$ has an orthorhombic structure, *Pnnm*, $a = 4.57$, $b = 6.46$, $c = 4.14$ A; C=C separation 1.33 A. Of the derivatives, $C_2H_4I_2$ and the isomorphous $C_2H_2I_2$ are most completely known with space group *Bmab* (orthorhombic) but actually monoclinic; C_2Cl_6, C_2Br_6, $C_2H_4Br_2$ (two modifications), C_2H_5F, $C_2Cl_3Br_3$, and $C_2H_4(CH_3)_2$ (two modifications) are isomorphous orthorhombic, space group *Pnma*; $C_2(CH_3)_4Br_2$ and $C_2Br_4(CH_3)_2$ have isomorphous tetragonal structures; $C_2(CH_3)_5OH$ is orthorhombic with eight molecules per unit cell. Further work is required to understand exactly the distortions of carbon tetrahedra caused by substituent groups and the temperature conditions of stability of polymorphic forms. 1,2-Dichloroethane recently studied has unusual interest because of evidence of molecular rotation around the Cl—Cl axis. This has been confirmed by structural analysis by Fourier methods by Milberg and Lipscomb.[1] The monoclinic $P2_1/c$ crystals with unit-cell dimensions $a = 5.04$, $b = 5.56$, $c = 8.00$ A, $\beta = 109.5$ deg are built from two molecules per unit cell in extended configuration with a Cl—Cl distance of 4.24 A and a center of symmetry. The CH_2 groups show free rotation, or complete orientation disorder, around the Cl—Cl axis.

† Bierlein and Lingafelter, *Acta Cryst.*, **4**, 450 (1951).
[1] *Acta Cryst.*, **4**, 369 (1950).

Of special interest to analytical chemists is the structure of the very useful dimethylglyoxime,

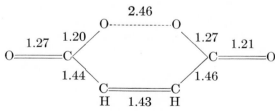

a highly selective reagent for nickel and palladium. The crystal unit cell containing one molecule is triclinic $P\bar{1}$, with $a = 6.10$, $b = 6.30$, $c = 4.48$ A, $\alpha = 122°31'$, $\beta = 90°6'$, $\gamma = 79°1'$. The crystal is built of chains of planar, centrosymmetric molecules joined by a network of H bonds. The central C—C bond has the abnormally short length of 1.44 A.

Representative of a series of trisulfides is the case of diiododiethyltrisulfide,[1] for which three configurations are conceivable: $R—S—\overset{\displaystyle S}{\underset{\displaystyle |}{S}}—S$

(thiodisulfide), $R—\overset{\displaystyle S}{\underset{\displaystyle |}{\underset{\displaystyle S}{|}}}—R$ (dithiosulfone), and $R—S—S—S—R$. The

first is eliminated by the fact that the crystals have point symmetry 2 in the space group $P4_12_1$ with unit cell containing four molecules having the dimensions $a = 6.01$, $c = 27.4$ A. Fourier analysis proved unequivocally the straight-chain structure which is shown in the projection on (010) in Fig. 297.

Fumaric acid, *trans*-$(CHCOOH)_2$, is distinguished from its isomer maleic acid in showing six molecules per unit cell, an unusual case of association or polymerization. Maleic acid recently analyzed by Fourier methods presents the case of an *intra*molecular hydrogen bond (2.46 A) with the result that the molecule is essentially a nearly flat six-membered ring.

$$
\begin{array}{ccc}
 & \overset{2.46}{O\text{------------}O} & \\
O\overset{1.27}{=\!=\!=}C\overset{1.20}{\diagup}\quad\quad\quad\overset{1.27}{\diagdown}C\overset{1.21}{=\!=\!=}O & & \\
1.44\diagdown\quad\quad\quad\diagup 1.46 & & \\
C\overset{1.43}{=\!=\!=}C & & \\
H\quad\quad H & &
\end{array}
$$

The molecules are held in layers by hydrogen bonds of 2.75- and 2.98-A lengths and the layers only by van der Waals forces. This crystal is

[1] I. M. Dawson and J. M. Robertson, *J. Chem. Soc.*, 1948, p. 1256.   J. Donohue, *J. Am. Chem. Soc.*, **72**, 2704 (1950).

monoclinic, $P2_1/c$, $a = 7.47$, $b = 10.15$, $c = 7.65$ A, $\beta = 123.5$ deg, $Z = 4$.†

Outstanding among early work were Astbury's analyses of d-tartaric acid and dl-tartaric acid (racemic acid).[1] The power of both crystals and solutions of tartaric acid to rotate the plane of polarized light is to be found in a spiral arrangement of the atoms. In the crystal two such spirals exist, one connected with the four central carbon atoms of the molecule and the second resulting from the way in which the molecules are combined in the crystal unit. These two spirals are in opposite directions, so that the rotary power of the solid is determined by the difference. In solution, of course, the second spiral structure is absent,

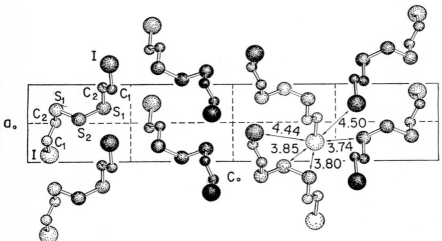

FIG. 297. Projection of structure of 2,2′-diiododiethyltrisulfide onto (010). (*Donohue.*)

and the rotary power depends only on the central carbon atoms. In racemic acid spirals are exactly balanced, so that there is internal compensation. While recent analyses have replaced these early data, Astbury was correct in his conclusion that racemic acid does not occur in the crystalline state as a double molecule of the two forms of tartaric acid. The hydrate crystallizes in the triclinic system with the unit cell containing one molecule of l-$C_4H_6O_6 \cdot d$-$C_4H_6O_6 \cdot 2H_2O$ of dimensions $a = 8.06$, $b = 9.60$, $c = 4.85$ A, $\alpha = 70°23'$, $\beta = 97°12'$, $\gamma = 112°28'$. The carbon chain is planar; each tartaric acid molecule forms hydrogen bonds to other tartaric acid molecules of both the same and opposite stereochemical configurations and the H_2O molecules. The structure is best shown by the diagram in Fig. 298 normal to the c axis, in which one hydrogen-bond-

† M. Shahat, *Acta Cryst.*, **5**, 763 (1952).
[1] *Proc. Roy. Soc. (London)*, **102**, 506, **104**, 219 (1923).

ing system forms columns of molecules parallel to the *c* axis and the other links the columns through the carboxyl groups to form sheets.[1]

6. *Short Aliphatic Chains without Symmetry around a Central* C—C *Linkage.* Examples of this classification are metaldehyde, aldehyde ammonia, acetamide, basic beryllium salts of fatty acids, and other metal salts, including acetylacetone compounds of trivalent metals. These last are isotrimorphic: α, monoclinic, β, rhombic, and γ, rhombic. The iron compound of the γ modification has 16 molecules per unit cell of the unusually large dimensions 13.68 by 15.74 by 33.0 A.

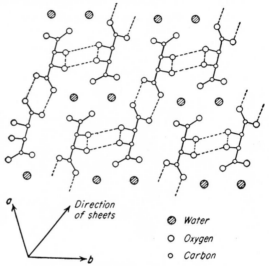

Direction
of sheets

⦸ *Water*

○ *Oxygen*

○ *Carbon*

FIG. 298. Racemic acid structure normal to *c* axis.

7. *Special Ring Compounds.* Hexamethylenetetramine, $C_6H_{12}N_4$, was probably the first organic compound to be subjected to a complete structure determination.[2] It is body-centered cubic with two molecules per unit cell. Each nitrogen atom is bound to three CH_2 groups, and each carbon atom to two nitrogen and two hydrogen atoms, forming so highly symmetrical a structure that dipole effects must be very slight. A comparison of x-ray data at low and room temperatures proves the presence of rotational thermal vibrations.[3] Latest data on bond angles and distances are C—N = 1.45 A; $\angle$C—N—C = 107°; $\angle$N—C—N = 113°30′. Exceptionally interesting are complexes of which the one with manganese chloride is an example. The crystals have the formula $MnCl_2.2(CH_2)_6.N_4.2H_2O$, the space group $P2_1nb$, unit-cell dimensions $a_1 = 11.80$, $a_2 = 2.20$, $a_3 = 7.21$ A. The molecule has a center of symmetry at the

[1] G. S. Parry, *Acta Cryst.,* **4,** 131 (1951).

[2] Dickson and Raymond, *J. Am. Chem. Soc.,* **45,** 22 (1923).

[3] P. A. Shaffer, Jr., *J. Am. Chem. Soc.,* **69,** 1557 (1947).

Mn atom which lies on the common threefold axis of the two hexamethyl-enetetramine molecules.[1] Crystals of the dihydrohalides of hexamethyl-enediamine have been analyzed by Patterson and Fourier synthesis (space group $P2_1/a$). The results indicate shortening and alternation in C—C bonds, a departure of the terminal N atoms from the plane of the chain, and hydrogen bonding between N and Cl.[†] The homologue decamethylenediamine recently studied seems to have a similar molecular arrangement. The crystals are orthorhombic $Pbca$, with cell dimensions $a = 7.25$, $b = 5.72$, $c = 29.4$ A, $Z = 4$.[‡]

A number of compounds of cyclic isomers of aliphatic type have been analyzed, with particular reference to the shape of the molecules. Examples are tetrachlorocyclohexane,[2] tetrabromocyclohexane,[3] tetra-phenyl cyclobutane,[4] dinapthylene cyclobutane,[5] octachlorocyclobutane, C_4Cl_8.[§] These compounds have nonplanar rings, and the cyclohexane derivatives have the famous "chair" configuration,

since the molecules are demonstrated to have a center of symmetry both for the orthorhombic chloro derivatives and the monoclinic bromo derivatives.

A ring compound of another type is that of diketene. Since its first synthesis in 1908 five molecular configurations have been proposed from chemical evidence.

$$\text{(I)} \quad CH_3COCH = C = O$$

$$\text{(II)} \quad \begin{array}{ccc} O = C & - & CH \\ | & & | \\ H_2C & - & C - OH \end{array}$$

$$\text{(III)} \quad \begin{array}{ccc} O = C & - & CH_2 \\ | & & | \\ H_2C & - & C = O \end{array}$$

$$\text{(IV)} \quad \begin{array}{ccc} CH_3 & - & C = CH \\ & & | \quad\quad | \\ & & O - C = O \end{array}$$

$$\text{(V)} \quad \begin{array}{ccc} CH_2 = C & - & CH_2 \\ | & & | \\ O & - & C = O \end{array}$$

[1] Tang and Sturdivant, *Acta Cryst.*, **5**, 74 (1952).
[†] Binnie and Robertson, *Acta Cryst.*, **2**, 116 (1949), **3**, 424 (1950).
[‡] McIntosh and Robertson, *Acta Cryst.*, **5**, 149 (1951).
[2] Hassel and Wang-Lund, *Acta Cryst.*, **2**, 309 (1949).
[3] Haak, de Vries, and MacGillavry, *Acta Cryst.*, **5**, 83 (1952).
[4] Dunitz, *Acta Cryst.*, **2**, 1 (1949).
[5] Dunitz and Weissman, *Acta Cryst.*, **2**, 62 (1949).
[§] Owen and Haard, *Acta Cryst.*, **4**, 172 (1951).

An x-ray analysis at temperatures below $-6.5°C$ has demonstrated conclusively that in the solid state the structure is that of configuration V, 3-buteno-β-lactone.[1] This is one of many successful solutions of difficult problems of organic chemical structures, the most famous of which is proof of the β-lactam linkage in penicillin described later in this chapter.

8. *Oxalic Acid.* The structure of oxalic acid dihydrate deserves special consideration as a typical case of successful x-ray analysis (Zachariasen, 1934; Robertson and Woodward, 1936). Figure 299 shows the projected Fourier contour map, the linking of molecules through H_2O, and the planar configuration of the $C_2H_2O_4$ molecule. Of the two oxygen atoms attached to each carbon atom one is at a distance of 1.24 A (type 1) and one at 1.30 A (type 2). This difference is too small to account for a clear distinction between $C{=}O$ and $C{-}OH$, and so it represents a partial resonance between the two bindings. The unexpected planar form is explained by the fact that rotation around the $C{-}C$ axis is restricted by conjugation of double bonds and the short spacing 1.43 instead of 1.54 A. Thus this bond has at least 30 per cent double-bond property. This explains why oxalic acid can be oxidized quantitatively with $KMnO_4$ to CO_2, whereas in other compounds a carboxylic acid is the usual end product. The linking of molecules by water is such that each H_2O molecule is bound to two oxygen atoms of the 1.30 spacing ($C{=}O$) and one oxygen atom of the 1.24 spacing ($C{-}OH$), from three different molecules. The $H_2O{-}O$ bond length of the first kind is 2.85 and of the second 2.52 A—the same value usually found to exist between oxygen atoms bound by a hydrogen bond. Thus oxygen atoms of type 1 are bound to only one H_2O as demanded by the hydrogen bond, while the oxygen atoms of type 2 are bound to two H_2O molecules by much weaker forces.

Similarly α and β forms of anhydrous oxalic acid (rhombic and monoclinic) have planar molecules held together by hydrogen bonds, as is also true for potassium and rubidium oxalates. In $(NH_4)_2C_2O_4.H_2O$ Hendricks and Jefferson found that the $C{-}C$ distance is 1.58 A and that, having no double-bond character, the two CO_2 groups in the molecule are no longer coplanar but inclined 28 deg to each other.

Amino Acids. As the fundamental building units of the giant molecules of proteins, it is obvious that the crystalline and molecular structures of the amino acids and the simpler peptides have primary importance. The structure of proteins, which constitutes the greatest of all challenges to the x-ray investigator, is discussed in the final chapter of this book. But some note may be taken here of the present information concerning the amino acids and related compounds. They are distinguished by: (1) A wide range of types: straight chain (norvaline,

[1] L. Katz and W. N. Lipscomb, *Acta Cryst.*, **5**, 313 (1952).

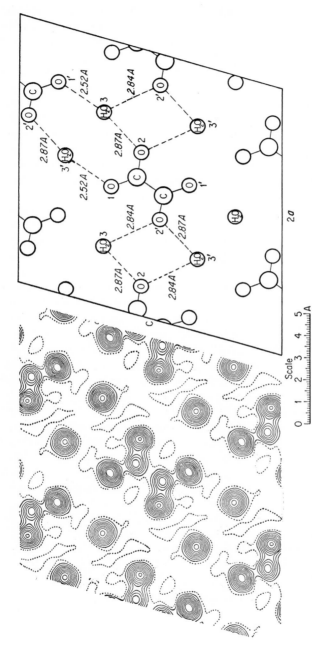

Fig. 299. Electron-density contour map for oxalic acid dihydrate; projection along *b* axis, covering two unit cells.

norleucine, methionine), monoclinic α, $P2_1/a$, β, $I2/a$, double-layer unit stacked along the c axis with the aliphatic chain nearly parallel to the axis; branched chain (valine, isoleucine, leucine), triclinic, $P1$ or $P\overline{1}$, double-layer unit stacking parallel to c with disorder; dicarboxylic (aspartic and glutamic acids and derivatives), monoclinic or orthorhombic (glutamic); ring and coordinated structures (proline, hydroxyproline, tryptophan, etc.). (2) The amino acid crystalline structures in general have extensive and characteristic systems of hydrogen bonding. (3) There is unmistakable evidence from hydrogen-bond distances and directions that amino acids are examples of "zwitter-ion" formation of $NH_3^+ + COO^-$. (4) The C—C bond distances are generally smaller than the normal 1.54 A. (5) The configurations are of primary interest in the architecture of protein chains since Pauling has predicted that proline and hydroxyproline, for example, must interfere with parallel arrangement of chains and force them to fold back on themselves.

Three laboratories engaged in research on protein structure have made major contributions on amino acids and dipeptides in their long-range programs. These are the Australian Commonwealth Scientific and Industrial Research Organization, from which results on 15 α-amino acids have been published;[1] the Chemistry Department of the California Institute of Technology, where analyses have been made on diketopiperazine[2] α-glycine,[3] dl-alanine,[4] β-glycylglycine,[5] N-acetylglycine,[6] l-threonine[7] (threo-α-amino-β-hydroxy-n-butyric acid), serine,[8] α-glycylglycine,[8] N,N'-diglycylcystine,[8] and hydroxyproline;[9] and the Cavendish Laboratory at Cambridge, where principal work is directed to the di- and tripeptides.[10] It was with the aid of data from these complete analyses that Corey was able to deduce the fundamental peptide configuration in proteins (Chap. 23). An example of exceedingly painstaking work with three-dimensional Fourier analysis is hydroxy-proline, studied both by Zussman[11] and by Donohue and Trueblood.[12] The crystals are orthorhombic, $P2_12_12_1$, with unit-cell dimensions $a = 5.00$, $b = 8.31$, $c = 14.20$ A, $Z = 4$. The molecule has the configuration

[1] B. Dawson and A. McL. Mathieson, *Acta Cryst.*, **4**, 475 (1951).

[2] R. B. Corey, *J. Am. Chem. Soc.*, **60**, 1598 (1938).

[3] G. A. Albrecht and R. B. Corey, *J. Am. Chem. Soc.*, **61**, 1087 (1939).

[4] H. A. Levy and R. B. Corey, *J. Am. Chem. Soc.*, **63**, 209 (1941).

[5] E. W. Hughes and W. J. Moore, *J. Am. Chem. Soc.*, **71**, 2618 (1949).

[6] G. B. Carpenter and J. Donohue, *J. Am. Chem. Soc.*, **72**, 2315 (1950).

[7] D. P. Shoemaker, J. Donohue, V. Schomaker, and R. B. Corey, *J. Am. Chem. Soc.*, **72**, 2328 (1950).

[8] In process of publication.

[9] J. Donohue and K. M. Trueblood, *Acta Cryst.*, **5**, 419 (1952).

[10] H. B. Dyer, *Acta Cryst.*, **4**, 42 (1951).

[11] J. Zussman, *Acta Cryst.*, **4**, 72, 493 (1951).

[12] Donohue and Trueblood, *loc. cit.*

$$\begin{array}{cc} H_2C & CHOH \\ \end{array}$$

HOOCHC $\diagdown$ CH$_2$

N
H

with a puckered pyrolidine ring, OH and COOH *trans*, extensive H bonds, and zwitter-ion form.

Long-chain Compounds. Out of the x-ray studies of the aliphatic series, from the early work by Müller and Shearer in Bragg's laboratory and by Trillat and Thibaud in De Broglie's laboratory, have come some of the most striking results of the science; these have been achieved in the face of such difficulties as the inability to use the simpler compounds (which are liquid) or to obtain single crystals of the higher members of the series, thus necessitating the use of the powder method except in a few cases. On this account there are still relatively very few complete analyses by Fourier synthesis of single crystals.

The great simplifying phenomena discovered in the study of the higher paraffin hydrocarbons, acids, esters, salts or soaps, ketones, etc., were that the unit cells into which the molecules, long pictured by chemists as chains, are packed have one side which is very much longer than the others and that this side grows in a uniformly constant manner as the number of carbon atoms increases. This dimension must, therefore, correspond to the length of the molecule. The other two dimensions remain nearly constant throughout the series; hence, they must correspond to the essentially constant cross section of a chain of carbon atoms.

For the usual diffraction experiments in which single crystals are not obtainable, a small flake of the substance is flattened on a glass or metal backing or melted or poured on a flat surface and placed on an oscillating-type spectrograph. On the film is obtained a single strong line repeated through many orders, corresponding to the long dimension and varying with the number of carbon atoms, and lines corresponding to the smaller side spacings. The x-rays measure the perpendicular distance between successive identical planes in the crystal; since the principal spacing increases a constant amount for each addition of a CH_2 group, the conclusion is that the molecules are parallel and either perpendicular (in which case the interplanar spacing measures the actual molecule length) or inclined at a constant angle to these reflecting planes. Bragg uses the picturesque analogy of a carpet as a layer, the pile of the carpet as the molecules, and a stack of carpets as the crystal.

This oriented film in a sense, therefore, acts like a single crystal which is oscillated in an x-ray beam so that reflections from a set of planes are registered by the Bragg method in accordance with $n\lambda = 2d \sin \theta$. The simultaneous appearance of the side spacings proves the powder nature of the specimen. Hence the oriented film consists of many crystal grains oriented exactly alike with respect to one axis but at random *around* this axis.

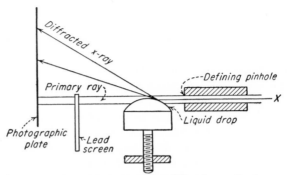

FIG. 300. The tangent-drop diffraction method.

Another technique which has been employed with great success by Trillat and by the author is the use of a curved surface upon which the molecules of a film may orient. Inasmuch as the x-ray beam may strike this spherical surface tangentially at a whole series of angles, one position will be correct for reflection from the long spacings of the film. Hence

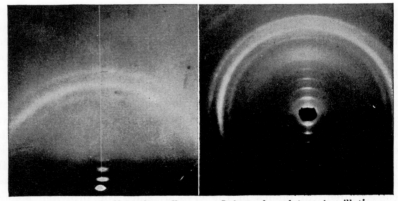

FIG. 301. Patterns for thin films of paraffin wax. *Left*, on glass plate and oscillation spectrograph; *right*, on mercury drop. The short lines or arcs at small angles are interferences in various orders for molecular length, while the long Debye-Scherrer rings correspond to molecular cross section.

oscillation of the specimen is obviously unnecessary. This method is illustrated in Fig. 300. Typical patterns for the same paraffin wax sample, by the methods, respectively, of oscillating a film on a flat plate and of orienting a film on a mercury drop, are illustrated in Fig. 301. Orientation of film on water, metals, molten liquids, etc., will be considered in a later paragraph.

Paraffin Hydrocarbons. In order fully to understand the results obtained from films of the hydrocarbons, a complete structure determination obviously was necessary, and, of course, this required a single crystal that could be analyzed by the rotation method. Müller[1] succeeded in obtaining a single crystal of $C_{29}H_{60}$ and in making rotation photographs, one showing 0, 0, 60 and higher reflections. The crystal is orthorhombic with the space group *Pnma*; the unit cell containing four molecules has the dimensions $a = 7.45$, $b = 4.97$, $c = 77.2$ A. It is evident, therefore, that two molecules with the planes mutually inclined in two different directions so as to produce close packing end to end are placed along the c axis, since a spacing d_1 of 38.6 A is observed by the powder (thin-film) method together with $d_2 = 4.13$, $d_3 = 3.72$, $d_4 = 2.98$, $d_5 = 2.48$, and $d_6 = 2.35$. These all correspond to the planar indices in the single-crystal analysis, respectively, of 002, 110, 200, 210, 020, and 120. The analysis further shows that the CH_2 groups of the chain molecule lie equally spaced on two parallel rows, the lines between successive centers thus forming a zigzag with an angle somewhat less than 92 deg (slightly distorted tetrahedral angle). The distance between two consecutive scattering centers on either row of the crystal molecule, that is, $(CH_2)_0$—$(CH_2)_2$, is 2.537 A, or the increment per CH_2 to the total length is 1.27 A. A gap of 3.09 A exists between the ends of two consecutive molecules in the crystal. The compound triacontane, $C_{30}H_{62}$, is isomorphous with the orthorhombic form of $C_{29}H_{60}$ and has the unit-cell dimensions $a = 7.452$, $b = 4.965$, and $c = 81.60$ A.†

Crystals of $C_{35}H_{72}$ gave unit-cell dimensions of $a = 7.43$, $b = 4.97$, $c = 46.2$ A (single-chain length).[2] Because of great intensity of the thirty-sixth and thirty-seventh orders, the vertical component of distance between neighboring carbon atoms must be 1.27 A as Müller found. Similarly $C_{36}H_{74}$ has unit-cell dimensions $a = 7.44$, $b = 4.96$, $c = 47.61$ A. In general it seems to be true that all paraffin hydrocarbons with $n = 16$ or more carbon atoms have a tetramolecular unit cell with dimensions expressed approximately by $a = 7.45$, $b = 4.96$, $c = 2.54n + 4.0$ A (the 4.0 A representing space between ends of molecules.) However, there is no satisfactory explanation as to why the C_{29} and C_{30} compounds have two molecules along the c axis, while the C_{35} and C_{36} analogues have only one.

An electron diffraction examination of $C_{30}H_{62}$ indicates a second monoclinic modification with $a = 5.58$, $b = 7.48$, $c = 39.90$ A, $\beta = 61°54'$, closely similar to one of the fatty acid modifications.[3]

The low-temperature modification of $C_{18}H_{38}$ is triclinic with $a = 4.28$,

[1] *Proc. Roy. Soc. (London)*, **A120**, 437 (1928).

† R. Kohlhaas and K. H. Soremba, *Z. Krist.*, **A100**, 47 (1938).

[2] *Z. Krist.*, **67**, 583 (1928).

[3] P. A. Thiessen and T. Schoon, *Z. physik. Chem.*, **B36**, 216 (1937).

$b = 4.82, c = 23.07$ A, $\alpha = 91°6', \beta = 92°4', \gamma = 107°18'$, thus indicating still a third form.[1]

Of principal interest in these studies is the significance of the zigzag chain in explaining the well-known alternations in properties for substances containing odd and even numbers of carbon atoms. An analysis of the most complete structures available on the isomorphous forms of $C_{29}H_{60}$, where n is odd, and $C_{30}H_{62}$, where n is even, gives an indication of the difference in relative positions of the symmetry planes with respect to the molecules. In the C_{29} hydrocarbon and presumably all others with n odd, the central (fifteenth) C atom lies in this plane and has the coordinates $\pm (u, v, \frac{1}{4}; u + \frac{1}{2}, \frac{1}{2} - v, \frac{1}{4})$. For $C_{30}H_{62}$ and others with n even, the reflecting plane lies midway between molecules, and hence all C atoms (as well as all except the fifteenth C atom in $C_{29}H_{60}$) are in general positions $\pm (xyz, x + \frac{1}{2}, \frac{1}{2} - y, \frac{1}{2} - z; \bar{x}, \bar{y}, z + \frac{1}{2}; \frac{1}{2} - x, y + \frac{1}{2}, \bar{z})$, where $x = 0.056$, $y = 0.046$.

In order to test the effect of even and odd hydrocarbons, Müller investigated[2] a number of normal paraffins ranging from C_5H_{12} to $C_{30}H_{62}$ at liquid-air, room, and nearly melting temperatures. The higher members of the paraffin series crystallize in the normal form as found for $C_{29}H_{30}$, irrespective of whether the carbon content is an even or odd number. Thus for these *long* chains the effects of the end groups are not sufficient to differentiate the two series as predicted. Differences in the behavior of even and odd members begin to appear, however, when the carbon content decreases. $C_{22}H_{46}$, $C_{20}H_{42}$, and $C_{18}H_{38}$ exist in two alternative structures, the normal one near the melting point and another structure at lower temperatures. The change from the normal form into another one also occurs in the series of odd members between $C_{11}H_{24}$ and C_9H_{20}. Paraffins tend to become hexagonal at the melting points; in the range C_{21} to C_{29} this state is reached, whereas others melt before becoming hexagonal. This is the result of close packing of freely rotating cylindrical molecules, and the crystal becomes optically uniaxial.[3] In spite of this complication, the fact is demonstrated that these chains have a constant increment in length of 1.25 A per carbon atom and that the x-ray pattern is a powerful method of identifying any member of a homologous series and of determining molecular weight. Hengstenberg's values of 46.2 A for $C_{35}H_{72}$ and 78.2 A for $C_{60}H_{122}$ are consistent.

Cycloparaffins, $C_{12}H_{24}$ to $C_{30}H_{60}$, were studied by Müller in 1933 and found to have the same zigzag form and interatomic distances as the chain paraffins. Cyclohexane forms a regular puckered ring, but the higher members of the series form a double chain, bridged at each end by a small ring of one to three carbon atoms. Halogenated derivatives of cyclo-

[1] A. Müller and K. Lonsdale, *Acta Cryst.*, **1**, 129 (1948).

[2] *Proc. Roy. Soc. (London)*, **A127**, 417 (1930).

[3] Müller, *Proc. Roy. Soc. (London)*, **138**, 514 (1932).

hexane proving the "chair" form of the ring and cyclobutane have been discussed on page 597.

X-ray diffraction results with ordinary paraffin waxes are of unusual interest. In spite of the fact that these waxes may contain as many as 18 or 20 different hydrocarbons, a single diffraction spacing corresponding to molecular length is obtained, together with the usual side spacings. Clark[1] first made x-ray measurements on a series of commercial waxes of varying melting points with these results:

Wax melting point, °F	d_1	Number of C atoms indicated
135	39.42	29.0
130	38.58	28.5
125	35.22	26.0
120	34.38	25.0

Clark and Smith[2] next studied series of samples from carefully fractionated paraffin waxes derived from mid-continent petroleum. In 16 fractions only five spacings were observed, corresponding to the values for pure hydrocarbons with 29, 31, 34, 38, and 42 carbon atoms by interpolation on the straight-line plot of d_1 against n. $C_{38}H_{78}$ and $C_{42}H_{86}$ were recognized as constituents of paraffin wax for the first time. Polymorphism was shown, exactly as for pure hydrocarbons, at least for waxes in the range from C_{25} to C_{35}. Each wax had a transition temperature below which crystallized plates and above which needles hollow at the core (as if thin sheets were rolled up) were produced. The transition did not occur for 160 to 165° waxes melting at 83.6°, whereas n-dotriacontane, $C_{32}H_{66}$, melting at 69.3°, showed the transition at 63.7°.

Microcrystalline Waxes. In addition to the normal straight-chain hydrocarbon paraffin waxes, petroleum also contains a type of wax which settles out in storage tanks and is characterized by extremely small crystals. These so-called microcrystalline waxes have many valuable commercial uses. By means of repeated fractional extractions with ethylene dichloride, and then a separation of each of these fractions into a number of others by isopropyl alcohol, a series of samples was obtained which represented very narrow cuts in composition. These were subjected to x-ray analysis by Clark and Burton,[3] following evaluation of molecular weights by a microebullioscopic technique. The wax films gave on long exposure usually only one order for the long spacing corresponding to molecular length, and this length was always shorter than

[1] *Science,* **66,** 136 (1929).

[2] *Ind. Eng. Chem.,* **23,** 697 (1931).

[3] R. L. Burton, Ph.D. thesis, University of Illinois, 1946; presented before the International Union of Crystallography, 1948.

the value for the normal hydrocarbon with the same number of carbon atoms. By proper allowance for tilt it was thus possible to determine the number of carbon atoms which would have to be attached in side chains of the isoparaffins in the microcrystalline wax fractions. These side chains varied in length from one to four carbon atoms; the isopropyl alcohol fractionation also separated chains attached to phenyl groups. The side spacings, which are nearly constant for all aliphatic compounds, were larger, indicating a looser lateral packing, as would be expected for molecules with side-chain protuberances. A typical example from a large mass of data is as follows: fraction number 8 from ethylene dichloride, separation temperature 100°; yield 7.81 per cent; solid point 155°, melting point 157.5; molecular weight 562; indicated formula $C_{48}H_{82}$; calculated length as paraffin 54.3 A, observed 51.2; average side-chain length 2.5. This fraction was then fractionated into eight fractions and a residue with isopropyl alcohol, with the following results: (1) formula indicated by molecular weight $C_{36}H_{74}$, paraffin length 49.6 A, observed length the same (hence a paraffin fraction); (2) $C_{40}H_{82}$, 54.3, 51.4 (same as original, side-chain length 2.5); (3) $C_{41}H_{84}$, 55.6, 52.08, side chain 3; (4) $C_{42}H_{86}$, 56.8, 53.0, side chain 3; (5) $C_{43}H_{88}$, 58.1, 54.3, side chain 3; (6) about $C_{43.5}H_{89}$ (mixture), 58.7, 54.9, side chain 3; (7) $C_{44}H_{90}$, 59.4, 55.4, side-chain average 3.2; (8) $C_{44}H_{90}$, 59.4, 54.3, side chain 4; residue $C_{40}H_{81}(C_6H_5)$—no x-ray long spacing. In connection with this study of isoparaffins considerable light was shed by the analysis of a series of pure fatty acids with side chains, described in the next section.

Urea Complexes with Straight-chain Hydrocarbons. Following World War II an American commission in Germany obtained information on the 1940 discovery by Bergen of crystalline complexes or adducts of urea with normal hydrocarbons and other straight-chain molecules. Since 1950 a number of investigations, largely in petroleum-refinery laboratories, have been concerned with the practical use of urea adducts for separation of normal hydrocarbons from isoparaffins, aromatics, etc., and with the structure of the unexpectedly stable complex.[1] Powder patterns proved that complexes of urea with *n*-hydrocarbons of length C_8 to C_{50} all had a similar structure which was different from urea. The culmination of structural analysis was the excellent single-crystal study by Smith in the Shell Laboratories[2] of the *n*-hexadecane, $C_{16}H_{34}$, and 1,10-dibromodecane–urea complexes. The structure is hexagonal, $C6_12$, with unit-cell dimensions $a = 8.230$ and $c = 11.005$ A and six molecules of urea per cell. This cagelike channel structure held by hydrogen bonds

[1] O. Redlich, C. M. Gable, A. K. Dunlap, and R. W. Miller, *J. Am. Chem. Soc.*, **72**, 4153 (1950). A. E. Smith, *J. Chem. Phys.*, **18**, 150 (1950). W. J. Zimmerschied, R. A. Dinerstein, A. W. Weitkamp, and R. F. Marschner, *Ind. Eng. Chem.*, **42**, 1300 (1952).

[2] A. E. Smith, *Acta Cryst.*, **5**, 224 (1952).

is most easily seen in Fig. 302 along the c axis to which the hydrocarbon chains are parallel. This channel formed by urea molecules will just accommodate the planar zigzag hydrocarbon molecule. The urea-hydrocarbon complexes resemble the clathrate compounds (page 527) in that the presence of the long-chain molecule induces the urea to take a configuration different from that of the normal tetragonal urea structure. Unlike the clathrate complexes of quinol the urea-hydrocarbon complexes do not have any simple molecular composition, except possibly chains of effective length equal to a multiple of the urea repeat distance (11.01 A). Smith shows that the length of the chain can be calculated

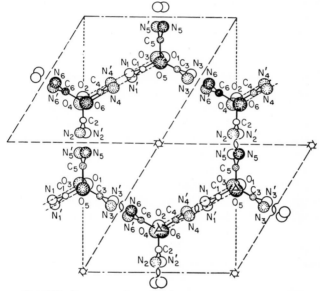

Fig. 302. Structure of urea-hydrocarbon complex. (*Smith.*)

from the equation $l = 1.256(n - 1) + 4.0$ A, where n is the number of carbon atoms. This holds exactly only for n odd since for n even the maximum length is slightly inclined to the axis passing through alternate carbon atoms. The urea-hydrocarbon ratio, therefore, is given by $0.6848(n - 1) + 2.181$, derived from $c = 11.01$ A, the number of urea molecules per cell (six), and the above length of a n-hydrocarbon molecule. This type of urea complex differs entirely from other types of complex with urea—H_2O_2, oxalic acid, 2,6-dimethyl pyridine, dioxane, and dihalogenated short-chain hydrocarbons. With urea solutions added in small increments Clark and Dehm[1] have fractionated paraffin wax into nearly pure hydrocarbons, the longest chains forming adducts first. Similarly, microcrystalline waxes were completely separated into normal

[1] Unpublished Ph.D. thesis of R. L. Dehm, 1954.

paraffins (about 50 per cent) and isoparaffins. Thiourea also forms adducts with long-chain compounds, but with a larger canal than that of the urea complex. Therefore, compounds which fail to react with urea may form adducts with $SC(NH_2)_2$ while straight-chain molecules have too small a cross section to form stable complexes unless anchored by a branched chain or cyclic group.[1]

Aliphatic Acids. The principal spacings vary from 6.66 A for crystallized acetic acid, $C_2H_4O_2$ (Saville), to 82.0 A for one modification of lacceroic acid, $C_{32}H_{64}O_2$ (Thibaud, powder method). The layers in any one acid have double the spacing displayed by the paraffin with the same number of carbon atoms; hence they are two molecules thick, with COOH groups together at the ends of two oppositely turned molecules. Until the remarkable photographs of Prins and Coster, showing as many as 34 orders for palmitic acid, it was believed that the odd orders were generally more intense than the even. These new results prove that this is true to about the ninth order, at which point even and odd intensities become equal; beyond this the even orders become more intense, reaching a maximum at the sixteenth. The thirty-fourth-order spectral line is much stronger than any of the adjacent lines, indicating a distinct periodic phenomenon in the fact that the spacing for one molecule (35.6 A) is 34 times the increment for a CH_2 group. The precision measurements of Trillat prove that the large lattice spacings (and hence the lengths of the molecules) for the fatty acids vary in proportion to the number of carbon atoms, but group the acids into two series, one for those containing an even number, the other for those containing an odd number of carbon atoms.

In addition the researches of Piper, Malken, and Austin,[2] Thibaud,[3] deBoer,[4] and others have demonstrated that there is a definite polymorphism of the higher fatty acids, each acid from palmitic, C_{16}, up, whether containing even or odd carbon atoms, having two forms. One form is obtained by melting the acid and forming a thin layer, the other by evaporating a solution. These are called, respectively, the C, or α, and the B, or β, forms. An A, or γ, form with still larger principal spacing appears very rarely. A graphical representation of the variation of the spacings corresponding to molecular length with the number of carbon atoms thus requires at least four curves: odd acids B and C, and even acids B and C. The best data are plotted in Fig. 303. The increase of the chain's length per carbon atom is, respectively, 1.327 and 1.146 A for the B and C forms of the odd acids and 1.21 and 1.10 A for the even acids. The polymorphic transitions occur at definite temperatures and are

[1] E. V. Truter, *Research*, **6**, 320 (1953); H. V. Von Lenne, *Acta Cryst.*, **7**, 1 (1954).

[2] *J. Chem. Soc.*, **129**, 2310 (1926).

[3] *Compt. rend.*, **184**, 24, 96 (1927), **190**, 945 (1930); *Nature*, **119**, 852 (1927).

[4] *Nature*, **119**, 50, 635 (1927).

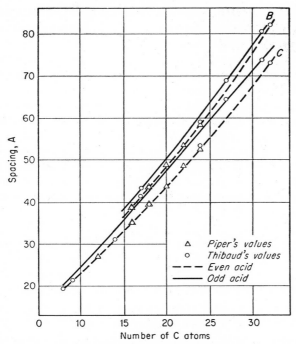

Fig. 303. Graph of normal aliphatic acids, showing effect of even and odd numbers of carbon atoms and of B and C modifications.

accompanied by a change not only in spacing but also in refractive index. The different forms are evidently related to the different tilts of the molecules with respect to the diffracting planes. Some representative data are shown in Table 20-3.

Complete analyses of single crystals have been made on stearic acid and

Table 20-3. Forms of Aliphatic Acids

Acid	B Spacing	C Spacing	Transition temperature
$C_{11}H_{22}O_2$	30.1	25.4	17 (deBoer)
$C_{13}H_{26}O_2$	35.1, 31.5	29.8	32
$C_{15}H_{30}O_2$	39.7, 35.9	34.4	44
$C_{17}H_{34}O_2$	40.2	38.7	54
$C_{12}H_{24}O_2$	30.6	27.4	10 (Thibaud)
$C_{14}H_{28}O_2$	35.0	31.2	25
$C_{16}H_{32}O_2$	39.3	35.6	40
$C_{18}H_{36}O_2$	43.95	39.9	55
$C_{16} + C_{18}$ acids	41.6	37.6	$40 < T < 55$
$C_{27}H_{54}O_2$	69.0	64.0	82.5

derivatives by Müller[1] and on lauric acid by Brill and Moyer,[2] and more recently with Fourier projections by Vand, Morley, and Lomer,[3] and partial analyses on several others.

Both the C_{12} and C_{18} acids are monoclinic, with four molecules per unit cell and with double molecules lying with their long direction almost parallel to the c axis. The zigzag aliphatic acid chain can be represented essentially as an elliptical rod with a ratio of axes of 0.64 as represented in Fig. 304. Latest data on single-crystal lauric acid are typical: form C, or α, space group $P2_1/a$; $a = 9.524$, $b = 4.915$, $c = 35.39$ A; $\beta = 129°13'$; angle of tilt $54°12'$; average distance between alternate C atoms 2.521 A (shorter than in soaps); molecules joined in pairs by H bridges 2.56 A in length between the double-bonded O of the upper molecule and the single-bonded O of the lower molecule, and vice versa.

FIG. 304. Form of zigzag carbon chain and cross section.

Very recently fatty acids with side chains have aroused unusual chemical and physiological interest because they occur in bile acids and in lipoids of tubercle bacilli. They are produced by oxidation of branched-chain hydrocarbons in the microcrystalline waxes discussed in the preceding section. It would be of course of great value to establish the x-ray diffraction criteria for the positions of side chains from pure synthesized acids of known configuration. Such a series was prepared by Prof. J. Cason of the University of California and kindly supplied to the author: 2-, 3-, 4-, 15-, 16-, and 17-methyloctadecanoic, 6-, 10-, and 14-methyltetracosanoic, 14- and 15-ethylhexadecanoic, and 15-ethylheptadecanoic acids. The powdered acids were pressed on sheet mica and oscillated at a grazing angle to the x-ray beams. The values for long spacings are below those for normal acids except for 2-methyloctadecanoic and 6-methyltetracosanoic acids. The isomers with the side chain equally distant from either end of the chain have closely similar long spacings: for example, 2- and 17-methyloctadecanoic 37.4 and 37.1 A; 3- and 16-methyl isomers 26.7 and 28.3 A; 4- and 15-methyl isomers 36.1 and 37.3 A. Single-crystal analyses have been completed on three of these acids in spite of crystalline imperfection in the flakelets so great that only the precession method could be used.[4] These data are assembled in Table 20-4.

[1] *Proc. Roy. Soc. (London)*, **114**, 542 (1927).
[2] *Z. Krist.*, **67**, 570 (1928).
[3] *Acta Cryst.*, **4**, 324 (1951).
[4] G. L. Clark and Cecilia Chu, *Acta Cryst.*, **4**, 470 (1951).

17-Methyloctadecanoic acid is an extraordinary case; it is triclinic but has four molecules per unit cell. Its probable space group is $P\bar{1}$, which requires two asymmetric units; thus a group of two molecules must constitute the asymmetric unit of structure. These two molecules are connected by a pseudo glide plane perpendicular to the a axis, whose presence is strongly suggested by the existence of an almost perfect halving of the $0kl$ planes when k is odd. 17-Methyloctadecanoic acid has a positive optic sign. This indicates that the chains are not crossed; therefore the chain is not tilted toward the pseudo glide plane, the bc plane. Moreover, the $h00$ reflections are weak, indicating that the plane of the chain must possess a pitch relationship to the bc plane.

TABLE 20-4. CRYSTALLOGRAPHIC PROPERTIES, FATTY ACIDS WITH SIDE CHAINS

Compound	a, A	b, A	c, A	α	β	γ	V, A^3	ρ_{exp}	ρ_{x-ray}	n	Space group	Optic sign
14-Ethylhexadecanoic acid.	5.58	6.79	27.96	93°15′	111°30′	100°14′	960.6	0.989	0.982	2	$P\bar{1}$	−
16-Methyloctadecanoic acid.	5.43	6.91	28.00	91°16′	94°16′	104°56′	1,011.3	0.988	0.979	2	$P\bar{1}$	−
17-Methyloctadecanoic acid.	5.64	9.66	37.10	90°24′	91°38′	102°33′	1,972.7	0.995	1.004	4	$P\bar{1}$	+

In earlier work on iso-fatty acids long spacings were measured,[1] indicating an increment of 1.776 A in a series, and more recently a fairly complete Fourier analyses of isopalmitic acid was reported.[2] This acid is triclinic, $P\bar{1}$, with unit-cell dimensions $a = 5.09$, $b = 5.68$, $c = 48.1$ A, $\alpha = 140$ deg, $\beta = 111.1$ deg, $\gamma = 72.7$ deg; tilt of chain axis and (001) 44 deg (greater than is true for any straight-chain acid, because of larger volume required for terminal branched group). The considerably longer c dimensions than for the acids in Table 20-4 is noteworthy.

Other Acids. Oleic, with one double bond, linolic with two, and linolenic with three when in thin layers on polished lead, demonstrate according to Trillat how chemical change may be followed by x-ray patterns. New lines appear as oxygen is absorbed at the double bonds. When the latter two become hard and dry, the x-ray spectra disappear as in the case with linseed oil. Two triple-bond acids have been quite intensively studied and seem to be isomorphous with one form of the saturated acids: stearolic, $CH_3(CH_2)C\equiv C(CH_2)_7COOH$, $a = 9.551$, $b = 4.686$, $c = 49.15$ A, $\beta = 53°4′$; behenolic, $CH_3(CH_2)_7C\equiv C(CH_2)_7-COOH$, $a = 9.551$, $b = 4.686$, $c = 59.10$ A, $\beta = 53°30′$.

[1] S. F. Velrick, *J. Am. Chem. Soc.*, **64**, 2317 (1947). K. E. Arosenius, G. Stallberg, E. Stenhagen, and B. Tagstrom-Eketorp, *Arkiv. Kemi. Mineral. Geol.*, **A25** (19), 1 (1948).

[2] E. Stenhagen, V. Vand, and A. Sim., *Acta Cryst.*, **5**, 695 (1952).

Patterson[1] studied a series of phenyl normal saturated fatty acids. Though benzoic acid is a purely aromatic acid, from ε-phenyl-caproic acid ($n = 5$) onward, the side chain tends to predominate and the substances tend to be like the aliphatic acids. The lower acids thus represent the stage in which the properties go over from aromatic to aliphatic, and these variations are quite complicated.

The diacids (succinic, adipic, pimelic, suberic, azelaic, etc.) diffract x-rays in the predicted manner from oriented films. Since there are two COOH groups in each molecule, the layers are only one molecule thick; the spacing of a C_8 diacid, for example, multiplied by 4, gives the observed spacing of the C_{16} fatty acid (with two molecules per layer).

An alternation is observed in the films between chains with even and odd numbers of carbon atoms. Caspari[2] prepared single crystals and found the effect greatly pronounced in complete-structure analyses. In Table 20-5 the data are assembled for the unit-cell dimension of the monoclinic unit cell (c) corresponding to molecular length, the number of molecules per cell (Z), and for comparison the principal spacings obtained by Henderson from films of the acids.

TABLE 20-5. SPACINGS OF DICARBOXYLIC ACIDS

Acid	Number of C atoms	c	Z	d (film)
Glutaric..................	5	17.40	4	
Adipic...................	6	10.02	2	6.90
Pimelic..................	7	22.12	4	7.65
Suberic..................	8	12.56	2	9.05
Azelaic..................	9	27.14	4	9.56
Sebacic..................	10	15.02	2	11.20
Brassylic................	13	37.95	4	13.3
Hexadecanedicarboxylic.....	18	25.10	2	

Part of the discrepancy between single-crystal and film data may be due to polymorphism, which has been observed for such diacids as malonic, succinic, and glutaric by Latour.[3] However, these acids substantiate the theory of Müller as to the effect of even and odd chains on properties. Recently it has been established in careful projections of electron densities for single crystals that for the acids with an even number of carbon atoms there is a slight shortening of C—C bonds below the normal value of 1.54 A, whereas the length is normal in pimelic and glutaric acids with odd numbers. Alternations in C—C bond lengths are shown in the following diagram of the centrosymmetric nearly planar adipic acid:

[1] *Phil. Mag.*, **3**, 1252 (1927).
[2] *J. Chem. Soc.*, 1928, p. 3235.
[3] *Compt. rend.*, **193**, 180 (1931).

Alcohols and Amines. Like the acids the primary alcohols are characterized by an association of molecules in pairs to form double layers, by virtue of the active OH groups. Polymorphism also depends on varying tilts of the molecules to the base of the cell.[1] Rotation of the carbon chain is found for $C_{12}H_{25}OH$, which has hexagonal structure at 24 deg and monoclinic at 16 deg. The change is irreversible as the temperature is raised on account of a change in molecular tilt as well as rotation. From the limited data available the amines crystallize in the same way as alcohols. Clark and Hudgens[2] have reported results on the normal temperature modifications of the dodecyl-, tridecyl-, tetradecyl-, hexadecyl-, and *n*-methyldodecylammonium chlorides. Dodecylammonium, tetradecylammonium, and hexadecylammonium chlorides are monoclinic, space group $P2_1$, $Z = 2$. Tridecylammonium chloride is orthorhombic, space group $C2ca$ or $Cmca$, with $Z = 8$. Cell dimensions of these compounds are:

	a, A	b, A	c, A	β
$C_{12}H_{25}NH_3Cl$	5.66	7.18	17.73	92°30′
$C_{14}H_{29}NH_3Cl$	5.67	7.20	20.13	95°52′
$C_{16}H_{33}NH_3Cl$	5.71	7.24	22.56	98°21′
$C_{13}H_{27}NH_3Cl$	7.57	7.61	56.49	90

n-methyldodecylammonium chloride is triclinic, space group $P\bar{1}$, with $Z = 2$. Cell dimensions are $a = 4.98$ A, $b = 5.29$ A, $c = 29.92$ A; $\alpha = 90°52′$, $\beta = 91°52′$, $\gamma = 90°45′$.

Esters. Ordinarily there is a normal decrease in intensity; the layers are one molecule thick; this is true except for acetates, $CH_3COO(CH_2)_n$-CH_3, with much greater spacings, suggesting doubling from the active double-bonded oxygen atom, while methyl esters, $CH_3(CH_2)_nCOOCH_3$, are normal; the increase per carbon atom is 1.22 A.

Soaps. The layers are one molecule thick, and the spacing is independent of the metal for any one acid. By the ingenious method depending upon the fact that the fatty acids on a lead support will form the lead

[1] Wilson and Ott, *J. Chem. Phys.*, **2**, 231 (1934).
[2] *Science*, **112**, 309 (1950).

soaps, Trillat has obtained the spectra for a series from the acetate, C_2, $d = 12.6$ A to the lacceroate, C_{32}, $d = 92.0$ A, the largest lattice spacing thus far measured. The increment per carbon atom is 1.3 A.

For a whole series of potassium salts, Piper[1] observed two different types with different lattice spacings, one for freshly prepared specimens and one for the same specimen after standing exposed in air which proved to be the acid salt. The acid salt molecules evidently are perpendicular to the diffracting layer and the neutral salt chains at an angle of 54°54'. Recent Fourier analyses have been made of potassium caprate and strontium laurate by Vand and associates.[2] Form A of the former has the monoclinic space group $P2_1/a$, with four molecules per unit cell. All molecules are parallel to (100), and the structure is layered along a. Within each layer the chain axes are parallel and tilted about 30 deg from (110). As viewed along a, chains from alternate layers are crossed at an angle of about 60 deg. The characteristic diffuseness of (11l) and (33l) reflections is accounted for by disorder in crossing of chains from layer to layer. The distance between alternate carbon atoms in chains is 2.598 A (2.610 in strontium laurate, 2.521 in lauric acid). Evidently this varies from compound to compound depending on lateral compressive forces within crystals. A whole series of silver salts of fatty acids also have been prepared and their structures analyzed.[3] They are all triclinic, $P1$, and the chains are tilted in a plane perpendicular to the a axis, similar to the triclinic form of $C_{18}H_{38}$.

Unquestionably the most comprehensive study of soaps was that of Buerger, which disclosed an amazing complexity even in commercial soaps, arising from polymorphism and varying degrees of hydration. Single-crystal analyses by the precession camera were made on neutral and acid sodium palmitates, P, and stearates, St:

	α-hemihydrate Monoclinic Aa or $A2/a$		1:1 acid soap Monoclinic $P2_1/a$		1:1 acid soap Triclinic
	NaP.$\frac{1}{2}$H$_2$O	NaSt.$\frac{1}{2}$H$_2$O	Hp.NaP	HSt.NaSt	HSt.NaSt
a	9.13 A	9.16 A	9.97 A	9.97 A	9.98 A
b	8.01 A	8.00 A	7.38 A	7.38 A	11.46 A
c	91.85 A	103.96 A	45.7 A	50.7 A	50.2 A
α					90.75°
β	94°	93.25°	93°	92.75°	90°
γ					94°
Z	16	16	4	4	6
ρ_{calcd}	1.13	1.10	1.05	1.15	1.02

[1] *J. Chem. Soc.*, 1929, p. 234.

[2] *Acta Cryst.*, **2**, 214 (1949); *Nature*, **163**, 285 (1949).

[3] V. Vand, A. Arthur, and R. K. Campbell, *Acta Cryst.*, **2**, 398 (1949).

However, the greatest contribution has been a phase study of soap by powder diffraction methods, introducing the concept of phase maps. It became early apparent that equilibrium could be obtained in a soap system involving water content and temperature as variables only by violent working. But since lowering the temperature is not attended by a shift in relative quantities of phases in the collection in equilibrium at elevated temperatures, it is possible to quench a sample and examine at least the *descendent* phases of the original ones in equilibrium at the elevated temperatures. If no transformations take place in quenching, the descendent phases are the same as the original. The phase map is derived from a phase diagram by replacing the original equilibrium phases at all points by their descendent phases and thus depicting the room-temperature

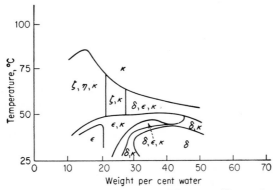

Fig. 305. Phase map of commercial soap. (*Buerger.*)

phase compositions of soaps produced under variations of water content and temperature. It was early shown that an α-phase molecule contains $\frac{1}{2}H_2O$; β, $\frac{1}{4}H_2O$; and γ is anhydrous. Subsequently Buerger identified seven phases in the phase maps of neutral sodium soaps with water, designated κ, ζ, μ, ϵ, δ, α, η. Thus all commercial soaps may be characterized uniquely by their phase maps indicating the presence or absence of these various phases. The extreme complexity of a commercial soap is illustrated in Fig. 305.

Ketones. In general for $CH_3(CH_2)_mCO(CH_2)_nCH_3$, the layers are one molecule thick; but for ketones with the CO group separated from the end only by a methyl group, double spacings occur, indicating activity of the $COCH_3$ group comparable with COOH for acids. The compound methyl heptadecyl ketone has double the spacing of the isomeric propyl pentadecyl ketone. The intensities of the normal diketones (oxygen in the middle of the chain) are strong in the odd orders and weak in the even, exactly as with acids, except that one molecule of a ketone acts like two molecules of the acid. If the oxygen atom is one-third along the chain, the third, sixth, ninth, etc., orders disappear. The increase in spacing per carbon atom is 1.3 A. A very complete x-ray and thermodynamic study of ketones by Oldham and Ubbelohde[1] shows that, although the crystal structure is closely similar to that of the corresponding paraffins and independent of the position of the CO group (except methyl ketones), the freezing points depend on this position, being higher when the dipole is near one end of the chain or in the middle. This suggests that the activation energy of melting is supplied by torsional oscillations of the carbon chains.

Hydrazones of Ketones and Aldehydes. In the discussion on page 440 of identification of crystalline solids by powder diffraction patterns mention was made of the 2,4-dinitrophenylhydrazones of ketones and aldehydes, data for 28 of which have been published by Clark, Kaye, and Parks.[2] Single-crystal data also were obtained for a number of these well-crystallized colored derivatives of 2,4-dinitrophenylhydrazine, $(NO_2)_2C_6H_3.NHNH_2$, which reacts with the carbonyl $C{=}O$ group of ketones and aldehydes. These resulting hydrazones are distinguished by prevalent polymorphism. The crystallographic data for a number of derivatives are summarized in Table 20-6; for rapid identification from powder patterns the powder data for the three strongest and the innermost (largest spacing) lines are listed in Table 20-7.

Conclusions and Applications. The following conclusions and practical applications from the x-ray analysis of long-chain compounds may be drawn:

1. *Molecular Form.* The molecules are confirmed as the long chains known to the chemists. The substances are truly crystalline, since the side spacings are observed, although some of the soaps are obtainable in the mesomorphic smectic state (see Chap. 21). The increments in spacing, per CH_2 group added, are on the average either 1.05 or 1.27 A. In diamond an addition of a carbon atom to the zigzag chain lying in one plane increases the length 1.26 A. Hence, for paraffins, ketones, etc., the increment is the same as in diamond, and the molecules may be considered as perpendicular to the layers; for acids, etc., with smaller increments, molecules tilted at about 30 deg may be the explanation. Weight to this explanation is given by the fact that measurements on single crystals of stearic acid show an angle of 30.3 deg between the *c* axis and the normal to the *c* plane in the unit monoclinic prism. Newest work indicates added complexities in the nonconstancy of C—C bond lengths normally 1.54 A. Branched-chain compounds are demonstrated by x-ray work on hydrocarbons and acids, and especially where the branch is next to the end of the chain a characteristic doubling occurs. Hydrogen

[1] *Trans. Faraday Soc.*, **35**, 328 (1939).

[2] G. L. Clark, W. I. Kaye, and T. D. Parks, *Ind. Eng. Chem., Anal. Ed.*, **18**, 310 (1946).

TABLE 20-6. CRYSTALLOGRAPHIC DATA OF 2,4-DINITROPHENYLHYDRAZONES

Compound	Color	Habit	Solvent	Mp, °C	System	a_0	b_0	c_0	Axial angle, deg	Density	n	Space group
Formaldehyde..........	Yellow	Tabular (010)	Isobutanol	166	Triclinic	10.00	10.41	4.23	$\alpha = 94$ $\beta = 95$ $\gamma = 87$	1.592	2	$P\bar{1}$
Acetaldehyde I	Yellow	Tabular (001)	n-Propanol	166	Tetragonal	7.15	7.15	18.69	......	1.541	4	$P4_2/n$
Acetaldehyde II......	Orange	Acicular*	n-Propanol	165	Orthorhombic	5.06	10.6	17.3	......	1.51	4	$P2_12_12$
Propionaldehyde I.....	Red	Acicular*	Xylene	150	Orthorhombic	5.34	11.44	17.35	......		4	$C22_12$
Propionaldehyde II....	Orange	Acicular	Ethanol	148	Orthorhombic	4.90	17.9	54.0	......			
n-Butyraldehyde I.....	Yellow	Acicular*	Methanol	123	Orthorhombic	7.0	25.0	25.8	......	1.3		
n-Butyraldehyde II....	Orange	Acicular*	Methanol	122	Orthorhombic	7.55	......	25.3	......	1.3		
n-Butyraldehyde III...	Amber	Tabular	Methanol	122	Orthorhombic							
Crotonaldehyde........	Red	Acicular*	Benzene	190	Orthorhombic	4.63	13.05	18.30	......	1.43	4	$P2_12_12$
Furfuraldehyde I......	Red (deep)	Prisms	Acetone	223	Monoclinic	7.63	13.23	13.07	$\beta = 99$	......	4	$P2/m$
Furfuraldehyde II.....	Red (light)	Pyramids	Acetone	218	Monoclinic	?	?	28.3				
Furfuraldehyde III....	Yellow	Acicular*	Ethylene dichloride	199	Monoclinic	3.63	11.7	7.7	$\beta = 95$	......	1	$P2/m$
Dimethyl ketone I.....	Yellow	Tabular	Ethanol	126	Triclinic	7.12	8.04	9.91	$\alpha = 66$ $\beta = 86$ $\gamma = 102$	1.42	2	$P\bar{1}$
Dimethyl ketone II....	Yellow	Acicular	Ethyl ether	114	Orthorhombic	5.22	11.0	22.6	......	1.4	4	$P2_12_12$

* Elongation parallel to a axis.

617

Compound	I	II	III	IV*
2,4-Dinitrophenylhydrazine (DPH) and Its Aldehyde Derivatives in Order of Decreasing Intensity				
2,4-DPH..............	3.50 (1.0)	3.15 (0.6)	5.81 (0.6)	8.9 (0.5)
2,4-DPH—HCl........	3.18 (1.0)	3.54 (0.8)	2.68 (0.5)	8.0 (0.2)
2,4-DPH—HCl decomposed in vacuum.....	3.11	3.91	4.51	7.0
Formaldehyde, yellow..	3.08 (1.0)	3.62 (0.97)	3.47 (0.88)	10.3 (0.86)
Acetaldehyde I, yellow..	3.21 (1.0)	9.35 (0.70)	4.65 (0.37)	9.35 (0.70)
Acetaldehyde II, orange	9.2 (1.0)	3.20 (0.92)	6.8 (0.38)	9.2 (1.0)
Propionaldehyde I, red..	9.6 (1.0)	3.24 (0.70)	4.30 (0.39)	9.6 (1.0)
Propionaldehyde II, orange..............	11.0 (1.0)	3.30 (0.8)	4.75 (0.3)	11.0 (1.0)
n-Butyraldehyde I, yellow................	14.0 (1.0)	3.77 (0.32)	3.21 (0.31)	14.0 (1.0)
n-Butyraldehyde II, orange..............	11.7 (1.0)	3.50 (0.38)	3.48 (0.29)	13.7 (0.16)
n-Butyraldehyde III, amber..............	12.6 (1.0)	3.28 (0.83)	4.33 (0.26)	12.6 (1.0)
Crotonaldehyde, red....	3.22 (1.0)	3.26 (1.0)	10.9 (1.0)	10.9 (1.0)
Furfuraldehyde I, red-black..............	3.17 (1.0)	3.20 (0.76)	4.20 (0.58)	13.7 (0.4)
Furfuraldehyde II, red..	3.24 (1.0)	5.68 (0.3)	5.36 (0.19)	11.7 (0.03)
Furfuraldehyde III, yellow................	3.26 (1.0)	6.17 (0.5)	7.7 (0.34)	11.7 (0.29)
Ketone–2,4-Dinitrophenylhydrazones				
Dimethyl I, yellow.....	3.27 (1.0)	5.70 (0.62)	9.30 (0.54)	9.30 (0.54)
Dimethyl II, yellow needles..............	9.45 (1.0)	11.15 (0.44)	3.03 (0.20)	11.15 (0.54)
Ethyl methyl, orange...	12.45 (1.0)	3.25 (0.71)	7.10 (0.54)	12.45 (1.0)
n-Propyl methyl, yellow-orange..............	3.61 (1.0)	12.50 (0.78)	10.64 (0.66)	12.50 (1.0)
n-Butyl methyl, orange.	12.80 (1.0)	7.75 (0.72)	3.47 (0.56)	12.80 (1.0)
n-Amyl methyl, yellow-orange..............	13.20 (1.0)	3.47 (0.70)	7.48 (0.48)	13.20 (1.0)
Isobutyl methyl, red-orange..............	13.70 (1.0)	7.60 (0.78)	3.48 (0.42)	13.70 (1.0)
Diethyl, red-orange.....	12.60 (1.0)	7.10 (0.76)	3.54 (0.37)	12.6 (1.0)
Di-n-propyl, yellow....	14.9 (1.0)	3.44 (0.56)	7.80 (0.30)	14.9 (1.0)
Diisopropyl, red-orange.	13.7 (1.0)	6.90 (0.78)	3.40 (0.62)	13.7 (1.0)
Diisobutyl, orange.....	11.20 (1.0)	3.72 (0.63)	4.45 (0.42)	11.2 (1.0)
Pinacalone, yellow.....	14.0 (1.0)	3.16 (0.52)	7.42 (0.50)	14.0 (1.0)
Cyclopentanone, orange.	11.1 (1.0)	3.23 (0.58)	5.80 (0.32)	11.1 (1.0)
Benzyl methyl, beet red	3.31 (1.0)	10.5 (0.82)	6.15 (0.78)	10.5 (0.82)
p-Cl-acetophenone, scarlet..................	3.30 (1.0)	6.10 (0.60)	5.35 (0.42)	12.3 (0.32)
Benzophenone, red-orange..............	18.2 (1.0)	4.37 (0.80)	8.89 (0.75)	18.2 (1.0)

* Innermost line.

bonding occurs widely in crystals, as it does over the whole field of organic compounds.

2. *Polymorphism.* The parallel arrangement of molecules and the tilt may be determined by preparation and working of the samples. Particularly with lower members of the series, depending on whether flakes are pressed on flat surfaces or the substance is melted and solidified in a film, different spacings are obtained. Polymorphism is very common, though previously unsuspected, in many series of compounds. Transitions occur at definite temperatures, at least for compounds with chains shorter than 38 carbon atoms.

3. *Molecular Weight.* The simple x-ray photographs may be used to determine molecular weights by interpolation of the observed spacing on the straight line relating number of carbon atoms to the interplanar spacing. Pure hydrocarbons will give results that fall on the curve, whereas mixtures will not; isomers are clearly differentiated as they fall on different curves. This matter is complicated for normal saturated acids with four or more curves necessary.

4. *Isomerism.* The position of ketonic oxygen atoms is accurately determinable in any compound from data on the intensities because of its greater scattering power for x-rays and the resultant effect upon the intensities of various orders. Cyclic and branched-chain isomers are generally detected by x-ray diffraction; but only fragmentary work thus far has been done.

5. *Structural Formula.* Alternative possible formulas may be tested; for example, the ketones may be

or $C_nH_{2n+1}.COC_mH_{2m+1}$, the length of the first being $n + 1$ or $m + 1$ and of the second $n + m + 1$ carbon atoms; the second is proved correct.

6. *Chemical Analysis.* Natural materials such as paraffin wax, glyceryl margarate, hydrogenated soybean oil, spermaceti, Chinese wax, ceresin, and lecithin all give lines and may be analyzed. Especially brilliant has been the identification by Chibnall and associates of ketones in complex natural waxes. Mixtures pressed together give lines for all constituents but, when melted together, may give lines for only one constituent which may actually be present in only a minor quantity, as found in paraffin wax. Solid solution over very wide ranges in mixtures of fatty acids has been demonstrated by Slagle and Ott.[1] Binary mixtures often follow Vegard's law in the linear relation of spacing and composition.

7. *Chemical Reactions.* These long-chain compounds are the best for

[1] *J. Am. Chem. Soc.,* **55,** 4404 (1933).

following the course of chemical reactions. Small quantities of the acids melted on metals show superposed spectra of the acid and the soap formed by interaction with the metal base; the latter spectra are intense with lead, tin, and antimony; less intense with iron, copper, and bismuth; faint with nickel, zinc, and molybdenum; and absent with aluminum, palladium, platinum, and gold. The absorption of oxygen at the double bonds of lead oleate, formed by painting a film of oleic acid on lead, may be followed perfectly by the gradual appearance of new spectrum lines and the disappearance of the oleate lines.

8. *Spectroscopy of Soft X-rays.* The large spacings characteristic of these stratified organic compounds made possible the spectroscopic measurement of long wavelengths and the bridging of the gap between ultraviolet and x-rays. Ruled gratings are used now more commonly for these researches.

9. *Films and Molecular Orientation at Surfaces and Interfaces.* Finally, the theory of orientation of molecules at surfaces and interfaces, long well known as the result of surface-energy studies of Hardy, Harkins, Langmuir, N. K. Adam, and others, could be subjected to the most rigorous direct experimental test by the methods discovered for the study of these long-chain organic compounds. In general, the x-ray study of the structure of thin films and surface and interfacial layers has fully substantiated the conception of definite molecular orientations, such as fatty acid molecules at the surface of water standing upright, with the polar carboxyl group turned into the water. Obviously, monomolecular films cannot serve as diffraction gratings, but the results obtained with layers only a few molecules thick fully substantiate the picture. A wide variety of experiments has been conducted to show orientation. The results obtained from very thin films on mercury drops have been noted already. Trillat[1] in a second paper reports a whole series of ingenious investigations on the surface structure of entirely solidified drops of fatty acids, diacids, paraffins, and triglycerides, of films of these substances obtained by cooling the surface of a liquid drop, the remainder being molten, and of films obtained by cooling in contact with heated water. An x-ray beam defined by a horizontal slit strikes tangentially upon the surface in each case. The appearance on the diffraction photograph of the interferences in several orders corresponding to the molecular lengths at once proves that the chains must be preferentially oriented at interfaces between solid or liquid substance and air and between water and air. Figure 306 shows a series of patterns for paraffin that was made in the author's laboratory by J. N. Mrgudich. Especially interesting is the center one, made as follows: The paraffin is melted in a small cup by means of a carefully controlled current through a resistance wire in contact with the cup. A blast of air is directed on the surface so as to form a

[1] *Ann. phys.*, **15**, 455 (1931).

transparent film on the molten drop. The pattern shows a liquid halo and in addition sharp interferences for the oriented film. The orientation theories are thus entirely substantiated.

10. *Blodgett-Langmuir Built-up Films.* This technique developed by Blodgett and Langmuir for building up films from unimolecular layers or monolayers of long-chain compounds, proteins, etc., spread on aqueous solutions has proved so successful and valuable that it is generally familiar to chemists, biologists, and x-ray analysts. A layer of stearic acid, for example, is spread one molecule deep on a water surface (best containing calcium or barium ions). A glass or metal plate is then lowered through this surface layer; as it is removed, a monolayer of the acid adheres to the base, with carboxyl groups turned in, and on the next

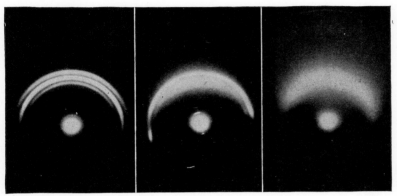

Fig. 306. Diffraction patterns for drops of paraffin wax. *Left,* surface of solidified drop; *center,* surface of molten drop with invisible film cooled by jet of air (molecular orientation indicated by short, sharp arcs near center); *right,* surface of liquid drop.

trip down another layer adheres, with carboxyl groups turned out. This alternating type is called the Y type. In this way a film of any known number of unimolecular layers is built up. Clark and Leppla[1] made the first x-ray structural studies of such films, obtaining patterns for films of calcium and lead stearate and stearic acid varying in thickness from 3 layers up to 300. Figure 307 illustrates the remarkable patterns obtained for 3, 7, and 50 layers. The measured spacings corresponded with those from melted films or powders (stearic acid 39.7, calcium stearate 49.4, lead stearate 49.6 A). The first direct test was made from the measurements of the theoretical equations for evaluating particle size in the colloidal range from line breadth (see Chap. 21). A large number of papers have appeared describing types of layers, especially Y, or alternating, and X, in which layers are deposited from alkaline water containing calcium or strontium ions only on the down trip; the effects of pH and temperature; surface potentials; optical measurements; thickness and refractive

[1] *J. Am. Chem. Soc.,* **57,** 330 (1935), **58,** 2199 (1936).

indices; chemical reactions on the underside of films; formation of skeleton films (mixed barium stearate and stearic acid with stearic acid dissolved out by benzene); adsorption by monolayers of dissolved salts, overturning of layers; and hydrolysis of esters as a function of orientation. References are given in the footnote below[1] to some of the principal contributions, not including the application of the method to the study of proteins, sterols, chlorophyll, pepsin, etc., which will be considered in Chap. 23.

11. *Solubilization and Emulsion Polymerization.* Two very important consequences of orientation of long-chain compounds are the solubilization of hydrocarbons and other oils in aqueous soap solutions, proved by x-ray diffraction measurements, and the development of new polymers by means of emulsions. These processes are discussed, respectively, in Chaps. 21 and 23.

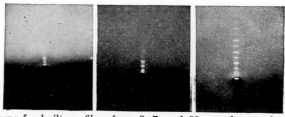

Fig. 307. Patterns for built-up films from 3, 7, and 50 monolayers of calcium stearate.

12. *Lubricating Films.* Lubricating films of the "boundary" type are quite thin, and under such conditions it would be expected that a high degree of preferred orientation of paraffin hydrocarbon or soap molecules must prevail. If these molecules were anchored at one end on each of two metal-bearing surfaces, then one metal surface would not rub on another with resultant damage and seizure but slippage would take place between the CH_3 ends of the molecules of the two oriented lubricant layers. X-ray analyses of lubricating films of oils and greases have fully confirmed this film structure. However, since the usual straight-chain paraffin hydrocarbons have no polar properties, the orienting tendency is comparatively weak. Some years ago Wells and Southcombe discovered that the addition of a small amount of fatty acid reduced the static coefficient of friction and increased the oiliness of a mineral oil to a marked degree. These polar molecules should be preferentially adsorbed at the

[1] Work at General Electric Research Laboratory (Blodgett, Langmuir, Schaefer), *J. Am. Chem. Soc.*, **56**, 495 (1934), **57**, 1007 (1935), **59**, 1762, 2400 (1937), **60**, 1140, 1513 (1938); *J. Franklin Inst.*, **218**, 153 (1934); *Phys. Rev.*, **51**, 964 (1937); *Science*, **87**, 493 (1938). Porter and Wyman, *J. Am. Chem. Soc.*, **60**, 1083 (1938). Holley and Bernstein, *Phys. Rev.*, **52**, 525 (1937), **53**, 534 (1938). Schulman and associates (Cambridge), *Phys. Rev.*, **53**, 909 (1938); *Nature*, **139**, 625 (1937); *Trans. Faraday Soc.*, **34**, 748, 1337 (1938); *Proc. Roy. Soc.* (*London*), **161**, 115 (1937), **163**, 170 (1937).

metal film interface, form double layers considerably more strongly anchored to the metal surface, and indeed improve the orientation of the hydrocarbon molecules. This also has been experimentally proved. Trillat showed that when metal ball bearings are immersed in an oil blended with polar addition agent the surface tension of the liquid changes gradually to that of the pure hydrocarbon oil and oriented layers of the acid are attached to the metal surface. The most comprehensive pioneer x-ray studies of lubricants were made by Clark, Sterrett, and Lincoln.[1] The x-ray evidence of the effects of methyl dichlorostearate used as an addition agent led to the concept of "oil plating." The additional lateral effects of the chlorine atoms on the hydrocarbon chain result in doubling the molecules in each adsorbed layer, while the unchlorinated ester forms only single molecular layers. In fact a reaction with the metal surface and polymerization of the substance results in an adherent *solid* film which resists rupture or abrasion. Acids, esters, and a variety of chlorinated derivatives of aliphatic and aromatic compounds (the last-named having molecules lying flat on the metal surface) have been subjected to careful study and the x-ray results correlated with measurements of cross-sectional areas of molecules in monolayers under different compressions on the hydrophil balance. Even in viscous lubrication with thick fluid films the effects on molecular regimentation are measured from the liquid diffraction patterns (see Chap. 21). A unique x-ray method of evaluating lubricants in terms of the protection of metal surfaces consists in the use of a fibered metal pin. The degree of preferred orientation of the metal crystals (see Chap. 22) is determined from the x-ray pattern. A metal collar is then rotated around this rod, so that wear will be at right angles to the fiber direction and thus tend to destroy the original arrangement as determined from another pattern at the same position on the pin. Quantitative measurement with the microphotometer before and after wear determines the degree of protection afforded by the lubricant between the surface of the pin and the collar. It is evident that the x-ray diffraction method has made a noteworthy contribution to the very practical problem of lubrication, based upon fundamental structural studies of long-chain carbon compounds. This includes an evaluation of the mechanism of modern heavy-duty additives, many of which are complex molecules derived from reactions of phosphorus pentasulfide. The evidence seems to be that very thin films of metal phosphides and sulfides form on bearing surfaces which are highly protective and serve in a sense as solid lubricants by virtue of layered structures, just as graphite and molybdenum disulfide colloidally dispersed in oils form effective solid lubricating films. In the newest work in the author's laboratory at

---

[1] *Ind. Eng. Chem.*, **28**, 1318, 1322, 1326 (1936); Chemical and Physical Forces in Lubrication, "The Science of Petroleum," p. 2566, Oxford University Press, New York, 1938.

least three phosphides have been identified in the film formed on metal surfaces from the oil additives.

13. *The Breakdown of High-voltage Cables.*   Cables for transmitting high-voltage electric currents are constructed from a paper tape insulation impregnated with pure insulating oil.   Occasionally these may fail and cause serious difficulties.   Clark and Mrgudich[1] found that such a failure is associated with the formation of one or more crystalline waxes polymerized in corona discharge, which have been identified by x-ray patterns and of which the distribution from core to sheath has been measured. Since cable wax can be detected in very small amounts, x-ray research has led to specifications for insulating oil and cable design that have greatly diminished failures.

The Structure of the Benzene Ring and Aromatic Compounds.   1. *Bragg Analysis of Naphthalene and Anthracene.*   The first selections some years ago for complete crystal analysis were naphthalene and anthracene, since solid benzene cannot be easily prepared.   Bragg found for the dimensions of the unit prisms of these monoclinic crystals, each containing two molecules, the following: naphthalene, $a = 8.34$, $b = 6.05$, $c = 8.69$, $\beta = 122°49'$; anthracene, $a = 8.7$, $b = 6.1$, $c = 11.6$, $\beta = 124°24'$.   The a and b axes are very nearly the same, but the c axis is considerably longer for anthracene than for naphthalene.   This difference in the c axis suggested the difference in the length of the two molecules, since anthracene is represented as three contiguous benzene rings and naphthalene as two. Bragg then assumed that the closed rings of six carbon atoms, which were definitely known to exist in diamond, were carried over essentially unchanged into benzene, naphthalene, and anthracene.   The difference in length between the two, 3 A, was exactly accounted for by the extra ring in anthracene.   The constancy of the cross sections of the two cells results from the fact that it is determined not by the length but by the breadth and thickness of a single ring and, hence, is a measure of the space necessary for side-by-side linking of the two molecules in each unit cell.   Furthermore, the theoretical length of the naphthalene molecule, 6.65 A, agrees with the length of the c axis, 8.69 A, if allowance of 1A is made for a hydrogen atom at each end.   Further consideration showed that the two molecules in the unit cell were arranged so that one is the mirror image of the other.   In the monoclinic prismatic class, there must exist a plane of symmetry, a twofold axis perpendicular to the plane, and, hence, a center of symmetry.   If the molecules lack symmetry, then there must be four of them in the cell, one obtained by rotation of another around 180 deg and the two from the first pair by reflection in the plane of symmetry.   Hence, the molecules must have a center of symmetry, since only two are found.   The cleavage of these crystals is easily accounted for as coming only in the direction where hydrogen atoms from *different*

[1] *Elec. Eng.*, **52**, 101 (1933).

adjacent molecules touch; in all other directions the strong forces due to the carbon atoms are involved.

Since this pioneer work, which really laid the foundations for the study of molecular structure from crystal-structure data, naphthalene and anthracene have been the subject of ever more critical and precise x-ray investigation, culminating in the complete Fourier analysis and the data summarized on page 628, which prove flat rings with variable bond lengths.

2. *The Structure of Hexamethylbenzene.* The classical research by Mrs. Lonsdale[1] on hexamethylbenzene was the first complete structure determination of an aromatic compound. Even though the rigorous Fourier method was not yet available, she demonstrated from x-ray diffraction data that in this compound the benzene nucleus is flat and that the carbon atoms in the methyl group also lie in this same plane. The choice of compound was particularly fortunate, since only one molecule per unit triclinic cell is found and the intensity data may be very directly interpreted. The direct x-ray information on axial lengths and angles is as follows: $a = 9.010$, $b = 8.926$, $c = 5.344$A; $\alpha = 44°27'$.

The facts that a and b are nearly equal and that the angle between them is nearly $2\pi/3$ immediately suggested hexagonal structure. The factors in the (001) zone should repeat themselves closely throughout the series of planes (100) → (010), (010) → (1$\bar{1}$0), ($\bar{1}$10) → ($\bar{1}$00). This was tested by a comparison of structure factors which were calculated from the observed intensities by the formula

$$F \ \alpha \ \sqrt{I} \div \left(\sum fe^{-M} \sqrt{\frac{0.15 + \cos^2 2\Theta}{\sin \Theta}} \right)$$

where $0.15 + \cos^2 2\Theta$ is the measure of the polarization factor for Mo $K\alpha$-radiation, f is the scattering power of the atoms, and e^{-M} is the temperature factor. Two sets of calculations were made corresponding to f values for diamond (Ponte) and graphite (Bernal), respectively. These proved conclusively the hexagonal arrangement and the graphite arrangement; there was a marked similarity in the intensities of various orders from the (001) cleavage plane and those from the corresponding cleavage plane of graphite. The structure factor was also larger than for any other plane in the crystal and almost independent of the order of reflections, proving that the carbon atoms lay in or near the (001) planes. The factors for planes (340), (4$\bar{7}$0), and ($\bar{7}$30) also were very large, and these gave a further clue, since these were small spacing planes and therefore any deviation of the atoms from these planes would cause a more rapid falling off of structure factor than would a similar movement away from a plane of larger spacing. In other words, the carbon atoms must lie at or near the intersections of these planes. There are 36 such intersections

[1] *Proc. Roy. Soc. (London)*, **A123**, 494 (1929).

and only 12 carbon atoms.   Since, however, there is a hexagonal arrangement in the (001) zone, the problem was greatly simplified.   Mrs. Lonsdale calculated structure factors for the first six orders of the (100) plane for each possibility, and the true arrangement at once was derived.

The immediate deductions are as follows:

1. The molecule exists in the crystal as a separate entity.
2. The benzene carbon atoms are arranged in ring formation.
3. The ring is hexagonal or pseudohexagonal in shape.   In order to answer the question as to the sizes of the atoms in the rings and the dimensions of the ring itself and whether or not the ring is plane, variations of three kinds are made from the positions of the atoms established: (1) a variation of atomic dimensions, (2) a variation in directions along which atoms lie (ring rotation), and (3) shifting of atoms perpendicular to the (001) plane, or a puckering of the benzene ring.   The effect of each kind of variation upon the structure factors was then determined and compared with experimental results, with the following further deductions.

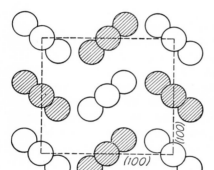

FIG. 308. The structure of benzene, C_6H_6. The shaded molecules are displaced vertically relative to the others through one-half of the height of the unit cell.

4. Distance between the nuclear carbon atoms 1.42 ± 0.03 A.   Length of the side chain   1.54 ± 0.12   A   (diamond).   The aromatic nucleus is therefore exactly like graphite in dimensions.

5. Only the plane ring gives anything like agreement with observations, again as in graphite.

6. The side-chain carbon atoms are attached radially to their respective nuclear atoms and lie in the plane of the ring.

7. Three of the valences of aromatic carbon are coplanar certainly, but no direct information is afforded concerning the fourth except that it must be so disposed as to give the ring as a whole a center of symmetry. This condition eliminates the Kekule static model with three double bonds.

3. *Further Information Concerning the Benzene Nucleus.*   After the analysis of hexamethylbenzene, renewed interest was taken in the question of the shape of the benzene nucleus.   The fact that in $C_6(CH_3)_6$ it corresponds so closely in structure to the graphite type of ring indicates that very little deformation can have taken place.

In 1932 Cox determined the structure of benzene itself and found the ring to have the same planar hexagonal form with the same interatomic distance of 1.42 A.   However, the accepted benzene value is now 1.39 A.[†] The mutual arrangement of molecules in the orthorhombic unit cell is shown in Fig. 308.   They are disposed with their planes parallel to the *b* axis, perpendicular to the plane of the figure but inclined in the other

† L. Pauling and L. O. Brockway, *J. Chem. Phys.*, **2**, 867 (1934).

directions nearly at right angles. The structure is quite loose-knit. The point of chief interest is the light that this molecular structure throws on the chemical valences. A static model of alternate double and single bonds is excluded by the symmetrical form; the constant interatomic distance 1.39 A intermediate between the aliphatic single bond 1.54 and the double bond 1.34 suggests resonance between the two types and between the two Kekule formulas

with the Dewar configurations

making a small contribution. With these x-ray results, heats of dissociation and other thermodynamic data are in full accord. This means, then, a 50 per cent double-bond character, on the average, for each C—C bond, while for graphite with an extended sheet structure represented by

as one of several resonating structures, there is only 33 per cent double-bond character on the average, and thus the longer 1.42-A carbon-to-carbon distance.

4. *Typical Aromatic Compounds Completely Analyzed.*[1] A whole series of benzene derivatives has now been subjected to complete x-ray analysis by the Fourier method. All these results confirm the structure of the benzene ring, in addition to the establishment of interesting details of each compound. Briefly summarized some of the results are as follows:

[1] For the most complete account see J. M. Robertson, "Organic Crystals and Molecules," Cornell University Press, Ithaca, N.Y., 1953.

Naphthalene

1.369 1.426 1.424 1.362

1.404   1.393

Anthracene

1.365 1.428 1.393 1.398 1.418 1.375

1.408   1.436

Plane hexagons; long axis of molecules nearly parallel to c axis, and planes mutually inclined in two directions, similar to many structures with weak residual forces packing molecules together. Structures, completely redetermined in 1949–1950, in which H-atom positions are indicated on electron-density maps by bulges in 0.5 electron contours, from triple Fourier series, indicating nonidentity of bond lengths, culminating in further refinements by finite-series corrections in 1952.

$$P2_1/a \quad a = 8.235 \pm 0.005 \text{ A}$$

Naphthalene:
$b = 6.003 \pm 0.010$
$c = 8.658 \pm 0.010$
$\beta = 122°55' \pm 5'$

Anthracene:
$a = 8.561 \pm 0.010$
$b = 6.036 \pm 0.010$
$c = 11.163 \pm 0.010$
$\beta = 124°41'$

Robertson, *Proc. Roy. Soc. (London)*, **140**, 79, **142**, 674 (1933). Robinson, *Proc. Roy. Soc. (London)*, **142**, 422 (1933), **147**, 467 (1934). Abrahams, Robertson, and White, *Acta Cryst.*, **2**, 233, 238 (1949) for naphthalene. Mathieson, Robertson, and Sinclair, *Acta Cryst.*, **3**, 245, 251 (1950) for anthracene. Ahmed and Cruickshank, *Acta Cryst.*, **5**, 852 (1952) for refinement.

Pyrene   1.39   1.39
          1.39   1.39
          1.46   1.42

       1.35   1.42

Planar molecules.
Dhar and Guhr, *Z. Krist.*, **91**, 123 (1935). Robertson, *Acta Cryst.*, **1**, 101 (1948).

Chrysene, $C_{18}H_{12}$

1.41

1,2,5,6-Dibenzanthracene (5 rings)
Coronene (7 rings)

Plane regular hexagons similarly packed in monoclinic cells; dibenzanthracene also has orthorhombic form.
Nature, **132**, 750 (1933). Iball, *Proc. Roy. Soc. (London)*, **146**, 140 (1934). Krishnan and Banerjee. *Z. Krist.*, **91**, 173 (1935). Robertson, *Acta Cryst.*, **1**, 101 (1948).

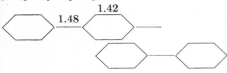

Diphenyl

p-Diphenylbenzene

p-Diphenyl diphenyl

2, 3, or 4 rings in same plane; distance between rings 1.48, shorter than single bond 1.54, showing effect of conjugation; all monoclinic and act like chains.

	a	b	c	β, deg
2	8.22	5.69	9.5	94.8
3	8.08	5.00	13.59	91.9
4	8.05	5.55	17.81	95.8

Pickett, *Proc. Roy. Soc. (London)*, **142**, 333 (1933); *J. Am. Chem. Soc.*, **58**, 2299 (1936).

o-Diphenylbenzene

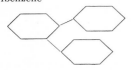

Because of close approach phenyl groups turned 50 deg out of plane of parent nucleus.
Clews and Lonsdale, *Proc. Roy. Soc. (London)*, **161**, 493 (1937).

1,3,5-Triphenylbenzene

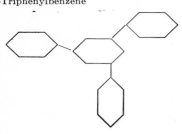

More nearly planar, but packed in layers; three substituent phenyl groups turned 25 deg from plane of parent nucleus.
Orelkin and Lonsdale, *Proc. Roy. Soc. (London)*, **144**, 630 (1934).

Durene
1,2,4,5-Tetramethylbenzene

117°
123°   1.54
      1.42

Planar, methyl groups displaced away from each other toward unsubstituted positions. Contour projection, Fig. 309. Robertson, *Proc. Roy. Soc. (London)*, **141**, 594, **142**, 659 (1933).

Dibenzyl, $C_6H_5.CH_2.CH_2.C_6H_5$

1.41   1.58
      1.47   109°

Nonplanar molecule, with two benzene rings parallel but not coincident, at 90 ± 13 deg to plane of central CH_2 groups linked by purely aliphatic bond at tetrahedral angle.

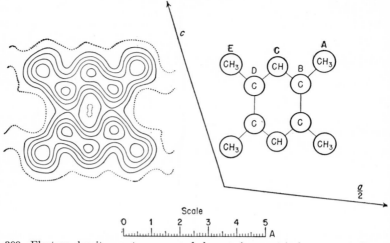

Scale

0   1   2   3   4   5
|..|..|..|..|..|..|..|..|..|..|..| A

FIG. 309. Electron-density contour map of durene (symmetrical tetramethylbenzene); projection along b axis, and corresponding formula. (*Robertson.*)

Stilbene, $C_6H_5.CH:CH.C_6H_5$

Planar molecule because of no rotation around double bond; 1.45 distance shorter than 1.54 indicates resonance between

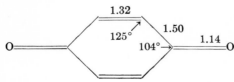

and

Tolane, $C_6H_5.C:C.C_6H_5$

Robertson and Woodward, *Proc. Roy. Soc. (London)*, **154**, 187 (1936), **162**, 568 (1937).
Planar, linear molecule; triple-bond length 1.19, single-bond length 1.40—unusual contraction in conjugation.

Benzoquinone, $C_6H_4O_2$

Distorted ring arising when resonance excluded—lengthening of bonds next to $C=O$ to 1.50 and shortening others to 1.32.
Robertson, *Proc. Roy. Soc. (London)*, **150**, 106 (1935).

p-Dinitrobenzene

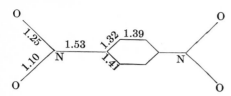

Distorted molecule, two oxygen atoms of NO_2 not equivalent; each oxygen atom associated with three CH groups of adjacent molecules in structure of high density.
James, King, and Horrocks, *Proc. Roy. Soc.* (*London*), **153**, 225 (1935). Refinement, Abrahams, *Acta Cryst.*, **3**, 194 (1950). NO_2 at angle of 9.5 deg to ring.

Resorcinol (*m*-dihydroxybenzene)

OH

1.36

1.39

OH

Molecules in spiral arrays about two-fold axis, OH groups of successive pairs approaching to 2.7 A, indicating hydrogen bond. Structure quite open, density 1.28; at 74 deg hydrogen bonds "melt" to form β-resorcinol, density 1.33, with more compact grouping (like hydrocarbons). Orthorhombic, *Pna*.

	a	b	c
α	10.53	9.53	5.66
β	7.91	12.57	5.50

Robertson, *Proc. Roy. Soc.* (*London*), **157**, 79 (1936). Robertson and Ubbelohde, *Proc. Roy. Soc.* (*London*), **167**, 122, 136 (1938).

trans-Azobenzene, $C_6H_5.N:N.C_6H_5$

1.39

1.41

1.23

N

N

121°

Monoclinic, isomorphous with dibenzyl; C—N distance indicates conjugation with N=N. Two independent molecules are present, one flat and in other N=N bond inclined 15 deg to rings lying in planes 0.32 A apart, causing small changes in dimensions.
DeLange, Robertson, and Woodward, *Proc. Roy. Soc.* (*London*), **171**, 398 (1939).

cis-Azobenzene

N=N

1.45

3.1

Orthorhombic, dyad axis of symmetry, benzene rings rotated 50 deg from planar positions.
Robertson, *J. Chem. Soc.*, 1939, p. 232.

Cyanuric triazide

N N

1.26 1.11

1.38

114°

113° 120°

1.38 1.31

127° C

113° 1.30

1.39

N N

N

N

C C

N N N

N

N

N

Threefold symmetrical planar ring of alternate carbon and nitrogen atoms, alternately 1.38 and 1.31 A apart (no resonance); azide groups linear, N=N 1.26, N≡N 1.11. Unstable and explosive character indicated by structure.
Knaggs, *Proc. Roy. Soc.* (*London*), **150**, 576 (1935).

Diketopiperazine

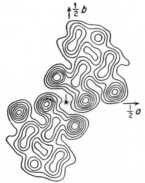

A fundamental unit in protein structure. Nearly flat hexagonal ring with center of symmetry; interatomic distances shown. Molecules held together with hydrogen bonds to form long parallel chains (NH of one molecule to oxygen of next).
Corey, *J. Am. Chem Soc.*, **60**, 1598 (1938).

Salicylic acid

Dimeric, H-bond formation between OH and adjacent O of same molecule (5 resonance forms) (Fig. 312).
Cochran, *Acta Cryst.*, **4**, 376 (1951), **6**, 260 (1953).

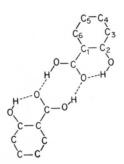

Electron densiy projected on (001)

Pauling's predicted molecular structure

FIG. 310. Electron-density map and predicted structure for salicylic acid.   (*Cochran.*)

5. *The Structure of the Phthalocyanines.* An outstanding example of complete structure analysis of an organic compound is that of phthalocyanine, a complex blue dye, and its metallic derivatives, which contain 32 carbon and 8 nitrogen atoms. The electron-density map and the idealized formula are illustrated in Fig. 311. The map, photographed directly from the fluorescent screen of X-RAC, is reproduced in Fig. 258 (page 458). The results are noteworthy, not only because of the complexity of the compound, but because the molecular configuration was derived by direct evaluation of the phase constant, because here was available an isomorphous series of crystalline compounds with a replaceable metal atom on a symmetry element, the center. Robertson of the Davy-Faraday Laboratory of the Royal Institution,[1] the author of this work, demonstrated the unique procedure made possible by this series in the following way: Each x-ray reflection is the resultant of the contributions scattered by all the electrons in the unit of structure, and the main problem in every case is to determine the unknown phase constant of this resultant wave. On page 456 it was shown that if the structure has a

[1] Now at the University of Glasgow.

center of symmetry the sine terms in the Fourier equation drop out and the only remaining uncertainty is concerned with the sign of the structure factor coefficient, *i.e.*, whether the wave has a peak or trough at the center of symmetry. Now if one of the scattering particles in the structure is situated exactly at the center, its contribution to the resultant wave will always be a maximum and will correspond to a small wave with a peak at the center of symmetry. Thus a metal atom at the center of symmetry gives a contribution to the resultant reflection that is always a peak, at least for all planes down to those with spacings small compared with the

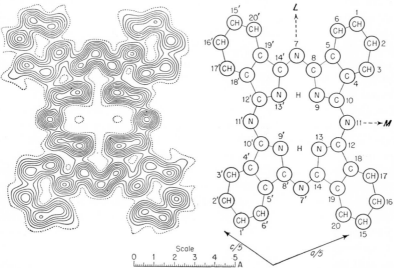

Fig. 311. Electron-density projection along the *b* axis, showing one complete phthalocyanine molecule. The plane of the molecule is steeply inclined to the plane of the projection, the *M* direction making an angle of 46 deg with the *b* axis, and the *L* direction 2.3 deg. Each contour line represents a density increment of 1 electron per A2, the one-electron line being dotted. (*Robertson.*)

size of the atom. The contribution from all the rest of the molecule may correspond either to a peak or to a trough at the symmetry center, and this question must be decided. In phthalocyanine itself there is no atom at the center of the molecule, but isomorphous derivatives may have a Be, Mn, Fe, Co, Ni, Cu, Pt, etc., atom at this point. The intensity of the x-ray reflection from a given plane in the free compound and in the metal derivative is noted. If the intensity is greater for the latter and *increases in a series* with the atomic number and atomic-structure factor of the central metal atom (*i.e.*, platinum is greater than copper), then it is established that the reflection from the free compound must correspond to a wave with a peak at the symmetry center which has been increased in amplitude by the single peak due to the metal atom. Thus the phase constant is 0, or has a positive sign. If the intensity is less, then the original wave has a trough at the center partly filled up by the metal contribution and the phase constant is π, or negative. Thus there is not the slightest uncertainty as to the sign, the Fourier synthesis is carried out directly, and all atoms in the complex molecule except hydrogen are located easily in the projection. Two coordinates X and Z ($h0l$ projection) are located; and Y is found from another projection, although the structure is so regular it is easy to estimate the Y coordinates.

It is at once observed that the inner system of 16 carbon and nitrogen atoms forms a very regular arrangement with a constant interatomic distance of 1.34 A. This must represent an equivalence between all C—N bonds and hence a single-double bond resonance, as must also be true for the four equivalent benzene rings and the eight C—C bonds 1.49 A in length linking them to the inner system. The whole molecule is a continuously conjugated system. However, the nitrogen atoms are separated by two distances 2.76 and 2.65, the latter made possible by *internal hydrogen bonds*.

The great importance of this structure is further indicated by the fact that a very similar nucleus with the four outer nitrogen atoms replaced by CH is the basis of the porphyrines—including chlorophyll, hemin, and other important animal and plant coloring agents.

6. *Pyrimidines and Purines.* Just as amino acids are the building units of proteins, pyrimidine, a six-membered heterocyclic ring, is of primary importance in the constitution of nucleic acids (Chap. 23), which are phosphoric esters of glucosides composed of unique sugars and pyrimidine and purine bases. It is not surprising, therefore, that extensive work, principally at Cambridge, has been done on the structure of these bases and their derivatives. The first analysis was made on a pair of isomorphous methylchloro and dichloro derivatives, whose formulas indicating resonance between two Kekule structures, may be represented as

The rings are found to be planar with C—C and C—N bonds in the ring having 50 per cent double-bond character. The crystals are monoclinic, $P2_1/a$; of considerable interest for the compound containing the methyl group is the discovery that CH_3 and Cl are distributed at random throughout the structure in two chemically but not crystallographically equivalent positions in the molecules. The structure is held together by van der Waals forces between Cl atoms of adjacent molecules and by a system of H bonds.[1] The first purine investigated was adenine hydrochloride,[2] where adenine has the structure

This also is planar, with a structure consistent with that of pyrimidine. Several subsequent papers have been concerned with other representative compounds and to an unusual degree with fixing of the positions of hydrogen atoms. Evidence is obtained that in H bonding the H is covalently bound to one atom but the proton interacts electrostatically with the unshared electron pair on the other.[3] Results have also been published on 4,6-dimethyl-2-hydroxypyrimidine[4] and 2-metanilamido-5-Br-pyrimidine (an active antimalarial).[5]

7. *The Structure of Penicillin and Other Antibiotics.* The remarkable contribution of x-ray diffraction analysis to the solution of the problems of the structure of the penicillin molecule is generally so well known that a detailed description is not required. A very full account of the work on this first great antibiotic, carried on under great pressure during World War II, is given in "The Chemistry of Penicillin," Princeton University Press, 1949, in Chap. XI, by D. Crowfoot, C. W. Bunn, B. W. Rogers-Lowe, and A. Turner-Jones (at Oxford University and the Research Laboratories of Imperial Chemical Industries, Ltd.) and in Chap. XII by G. L. Clark, W. I. Kaye, K. J. Pipenberg, and N. C. Schieltz (at the University of Illinois and the Northern Regional Research Laboratory, Peoria, Ill.). The dramatic history of the discovery of Sir Alexander Fleming and the subsequent attempts to determine the molecular structure as a necessary step prior to synthesis is given in Chap. XI. With every device of organic chemical degradation and synthesis and infrared and other instrumental types of analysis, the problem of structure finally resolved itself into two alternatives (discounting tricyclic possibilities).

[1] C. J. B. Clews and W. Cochran, *Acta Cryst.*, **1**, 4 (1948).

[2] J. M. Broomhead, *Acta Cryst.*, **1**, 324 (1948).

[3] III, C. J. B. Clews and W. Cochran, *Acta Cryst.*, **2**, 46 (1949); IV, Guanine Hydrochloride, J. M. Broomhead, *Acta Cryst.*, **4**, 92 (1951); V, Electron Distribution in Adenine Hydrochloride, W. Cochran, *Acta Cryst.*, **4**, 81 (1951).

[4] G. J. Pitt, *Acta Cryst.*, **1**, 168 (1948).

[5] J. Singer and I. Fankuchen, *Acta Cryst.*, **5**, 99 (1952).

These were

Thiazolidine oxazolone:

$$R.C \overset{N}{\diagup} \overset{}{\diagdown} \quad CH \!\!-\!\! CH \quad \overset{S}{\diagup} \overset{}{\diagdown} \quad C(CH_3)_2$$

$$O \!\!-\!\!\!-\!\!\!-\!\! CO \quad NH \!\!-\!\!\!-\!\!\!-\!\! CH.COOH$$

Thiazolidine β-lactam:

$$R.CO.NH.CH \!\!-\!\! CH \quad \overset{S}{\diagup} \overset{}{\diagdown} \quad C(CH_3)_2$$

$$CO \!\!-\!\! NH \!\!-\!\!\!-\!\!\!-\!\! CH.COOH$$

where R in the three principal types of penicillin is benzyl, C_6H_5—CH_2, 2-pentenyl, $CH_3.CH_2.CH\!\!=\!\!CH.CH_2$—, and n-amyl and n-heptyl groups. Intensive x-ray analysis of single crystals at Oxford and Illinois resulted in space groups and unit-cell dimensions, some of these data being recorded in Table 20-8. Then began the masterly work at Oxford, first on

TABLE 20-8. CRYSTALLOGRAPHIC DATA FOR PENICILLINS

	a	b	c	β, deg.	Space group	Z
Sodium 2-pentenylpenicillinate† . . .	37.08	6.0	18.4	106	C2	8
Sodium benzylpenicillinate	8.48	6.33	15.63	94.2	P2₁	2
Potassium benzylpenicillinate‡.	9.36	6.37	30.35	. . . . . .	P2₁2₁2₁	4
Rubidium benzylpenicillinate.	9.45	6.44	30.2	. . . . . .	P2₁2₁2₁	4
Methyl benzylpenicillinate	40.92	7.75	17.27	. . . . . .	?	12

† Four modifications were found, a trihydrate, a monohydrate, and a high- and low-temperature anhydrous, identified in powder patterns by Schieltz ("The Chemistry of Penicillin," Chap. XII). Data here are for trihydrate.

‡ Measurements have been further refined by G. J. Pitt, *Acta Cryst.*, **5**, 770 (1952).

two-dimensional Fourier projections using all helpful devices such as the fly's eye camera of Bunn, which seemed to show the square four-membered β-lactam ring; but in order to avoid any misinterpretation because of overlapping atoms in the projections, the three-dimensional Fourier analysis was undertaken with potassium benzylpenicillinate. It was the crowning achievement in 1947, and to this day, of unique, conclusive, accurate analysis; and the three-dimensional model in Fig. 312 shows without question the β-lactam structure as the correct one, together with every detail of the entire molecular configuration.

Powder diffraction data from patterns such as those in Fig. 253 for three varieties of sodium pentenylpenicillinate for a large number of derivatives, and degradation products such as penillic acid, are tabulated in Chap. XII of "The Chemistry of Penicillin." From these the observation is made that there are many minor differences in patterns, arising from variations in packing of these complex molecules.

More recently x-ray analyses have been begun on some of the newer antibiotics, but no complete molecular configurations have been established. Among these analyses is that for chloromycetin, or chloroamphenicol, $C_{11}H_{12}N_2O_5Cl_2$, which has been shown to be d-threo-2-dichloroacetamido-1-p-nitrophenyl-1,3-propanediol, which is orthorhombic, space group $C222_1$, $a = 17.6$, $b = 7.35$, $c = 22.3$ A, $Z = 8$. Aureomycin, which as the hydrochloride is probably $C_{23}H_{28}N_2O_8Cl_2$, is orthorhombic, $P2_12_12_1$, $a = 11.22$, $b = 12.89$, $c = 15.35$ A, $Z = 1$.†

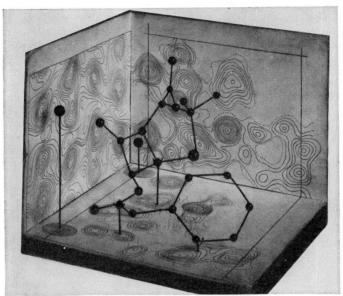

FIG. 312. Three-dimensional Fourier projection of penicillin molecule. (*Endeavour, Imperial Chemical Industries, Ltd., by permission.*)

8. The Structure of Strychnine. As another example of extraordinarily able structural analyses of very complex natural and synthetic molecules may be cited the structure of strychnine. Two independent investigations have been in agreement on the essential details of the molecule $C_{21}H_{22}N_2O_2$, as the bromide dihydrate[1] and the sulfate pentahydrate.[2] This seven-ringed molecule is shown in Fig. 313; rings II to VII form a compact three-dimensional structure from which I, a planar benzene ring, protrudes. The crystallographic data are as follows:

	a	b	c	β	Z	Space group
Bromide...........	7.64	7.70	33.20	. . . . . .	4	$P2_12_12_1$
Sulfate............	35.85	7.56	7.84	$107°20'$	4	$C2$

† J. D. Dunitz and J. E. Leonard, *J. Am. Chem. Soc.,* **72,** 4276 (1950).

[1] Robertson and Beevers, *Acta Cryst.,* **4,** 270 (1951).

[2] Bokhoven, Schoone, and Bijvoet, *Acta Cryst.,* **4,** 275 (1951).

9. *Sugars.* The principal early x-ray research on sugars was carried on by Hengstenberg and Mark,[1] Sponsler and Dore,[2] Marwick,[3] Astbury and Marwick,[4] and especially Cox.[5] Essential data are tabulated in Table 20-9.

TABLE 20-9. X-RAY DATA ON CARBOHYDRATES

| Carbohydrate | System | Dimensions of unit cell | | | | Density |
		a	b	c	β, deg	
Natural cellulose........	Monoclinic	8.3	10.3	7.9	84	1.52
Cellulose hydrate........	Monoclinic	8.14	10.3	9.14	62	1.56
Cellobiose..............	Monoclinic	5.0	13.2	11.1	90	1.556
Sucrose................	Monoclinic	11.0	8.7	7.65	103.5	1.588
Mannose...............	Orthorhombic	7.62	18.18	5.67	.....	1.501
Glucose (α-d)...........	Orthorhombic	10.40	14.89	4.99	.....	1.544
Fructose (d)...........	Orthorhombic	8.06	10.06	9.12	.....	1.598
Sorbose................	Orthorhombic	6.12	18.24	6.43	.....	1.654

Astbury and Marwick have pointed out that the small variation in density of these saccharoses suggests an approximate close packing of some molecular unit, and by further calculation of cross-sectional areas it

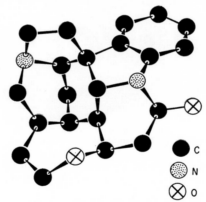

FIG. 313. Structure of 7-ringed molecule of strychnine.   (*Robertson and Beevers.*)

becomes apparent at once that the dimensions of this unit—the sugar ring and its side chain—impress themselves in the various unit cells. For mannose as an example, the ring may be drawn

[1] *Z. Krist.*, **72**, 301 (1929).
[2] *J. Am. Chem. Soc.*, **73**, 1639 (1931).
[3] *Proc. Roy. Soc.* (*London*), **A131**, 621 (1931).
[4] *Nature*, **127**, 12 (1931).
[5] *J. Chem. Soc.*, **1935**, 978, 1495.

The molecular dimensions so deduced are 7.27, 5.64, and 2 × 4.58. Thus probably the sugar ring takes about 4.5 A in thickness, or normal to the ring, about 5.5 A across the ring horizontally, and 7.5 A across the ring vertically in the direction of the side chain CH_2OH. All data were thought to be consistent with a flat form of pyranose and furanose rings, rather than with strainless forms with tetrahedral bond angles.

Of these sugars only two, α-glucose and sucrose, have been subjected to complete Fourier analysis, besides three compounds containing a sugar residue.   α-Glucose crystallizes in the orthorhombic system, space group $P2_12_12_1$, with $a = 10.36$, $b = 14.84$, $c = 4.97$ A, $Z = 4$, in good agreement with the 1930–1931 investigations.   The pyranose ring (five carbon atoms, one oxygen atom) is in the so-called Sachse-Moore transform, and there is a *cis*-glycol grouping on carbon atoms 1 and 2, as shown at the

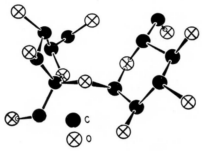

FIG. 314. Structure of sucrose molecule: pyranose ring, *right;* furanose ring, *left*.   [*McDonald and Beevers, Acta Cryst.*, **5**, 654 (1952).]

right in the perspective drawing (for sucrose) in Fig. 314.   The high density and hardness of the crystals indicate bonds stronger than van der Waals forces between molecules.   A complete system of strong hydrogen bonds involving the five available H atoms per molecule, and varying in length from 2.70 to 2.86 A, is found.   A layer structure is clearly seen in the *a*-axis projection, with the layers held together by H-bond formation between O_2 and O_3 and the different layers linked by the remaining H bonds.   The intermolecular bonding is equally strong in all directions, in agreement with the absence of any marked anisotropy in physical properties of the crystal.   There are similarities in the structure of sucrose.[1] The packing of molecules is governed by H-bond formation between OH groups mainly of the furanose residue (four carbon atoms and one oxygen atom in the ring), while the contacts between glucose residues are much weaker than in α-glucose because of a less extended H-bond system, resulting in marked cleavage.

In the author's laboratory x-ray analysis has been used to advantage in a number of investigations involving difficult sugar problems.   In most cases single crystals were not available so that powder patterns had to be

[1] C. A. Beevers, T. R. R. McDonald, J. H. Robertson, and F. Hern, *Acta Cryst.*, **5,** 689 (1952).

utilized, but the complexes of d-glucose and d-mannose with benzo-thiazoline (2-aminobenzenethiol) are in process of complete analysis. The d-mannose benzothiazolene has the configuration

These aldose compounds and the silver and uranyl (UO_2^{2+}) derivatives are light- and x-ray-sensitive and are under investigation as high-energy radiation dosimeters. They are unstable in water solution, yielding bis-(2-aminophenyl) disulfide.[1]

Another x-ray analysis which settled a controversy existing from 1897 was that of the chemical nature of glutose, a nonfermentable reducing substance in molasses or obtained from fructose or glucose by treatment with weak alkali or from heated fructose solutions. Because of the success of Clark, Kaye, and Parks in identifying carbonyl derivatives as the 2,4-dinitrophenylhydrazones (page 616) the same technique was applied to this problem. Standard x-ray powder patterns were made of the phenylosazones (the reaction products of the compounds and phenyl-hydrazone) of galactose, glucose, methylglyoxal, diacetyl, acetoin, levulinic acid, and hydroxymethylfurfuraldehyde and the 3,5-dinitro-benzoylhydrazones, diphenylacetylhydrazones, and 2,4-dinitrophenyl-hydrazones of the same compounds. With these the corresponding derivatives of the glutose could be compared to show that glutosazone is an impure glucosazone; acetal or methylglyoxal, or both, and acetoin are also in the nonfermentable residue. These compounds polymerize readily to give more than one amorphous product through aldol and acyloin condensations, one of these having the composition $C_{40}H_{40}O_{11}N_2$.[†]

Another subject in which there has been much confusion is the composi-tion of fructose and glucose anhydrides, newly prepared with anhydrous hydrofluoric acid or by prolonged boiling. For fructose so treated, x-ray analysis has demonstrated two diheterolevulosans [(I) di-d-fructopyran-ose dianhydride, (II) d-fructopyranose-d-fructofuranose dianhydride], each of which has two polymorphic forms, as is also true of the hexa-methyldiheterolevulosans, which in some cases can be converted from the metastable to the stable form. Here was an example of very successful combination of paper chromatography and diffraction analysis.[2] Still

[1] L. Sattler, F. W. Zerban, G. L. Clark, and C. C. Chu, Reaction of 2-Aminobenzene-thiol with Aldoses and with Hydroxymethylfurfural, *J. Am. Chem. Soc.*, **73**, 5908 (1951).

[†] G. L. Clark, Hung Kao, L. Sattler, and F. W. Zerban, *Ind. Eng. Chem.*, **41**, 530 (1949).

[2] L. Sattler, F. W. Zerban, G. L. Clark, Chia-Chen Chu, N. Albon, D. Gross, and H. C. S. de Whalley, *Ind. Eng. Chem.*, **44**, 1127 (1952).

another controversial matter was settled by the proof of the presence of *d*-allulose in heated fructose solutions from the x-ray pattern of its osazone.[1]

10. *Carcinogenic Compounds, Sterols, Hormones, Vitamins.* Reference has already been made to compounds of the type of 1,2,5,6-dibenzanthracene, one of the well-known carcinogenic hydrocarbons.

A significant contribution already has been made by x-ray diffraction methods to the knowledge of the chemical nature of these biologically important compounds, which are so complex that configuration and chemical composition are often unknown. Complete analyses in the sense of those accomplished for the phthalocyanines are not possible as yet, but the x-ray results do suggest the probable molecular arrangement. Crowfoot and Bernal performed a great service in their pioneer efforts. In 1932 the interpretation of studies on ergosterol, calciferol, and other compounds related to vitamin D led to the correction of previously accepted sterol carbon skeletons to the structure

It is not possible here to consider these complex materials, but reference may be made to original papers,[2] largely of Crowfoot and Bernal, with relatively few additions since 1937 because of inability to prepare single crystals. By the heavy atom method, two complete steroid analyses have been made: cholesteryl iodide,[3] and calciferyl-4-iodo-5-nitrobenzoate, $C_{35}H_{46}NO_4I$.[†]

11. *Highly Polymerized Natural and Synthetic Compounds.* The structures of a great range of compounds with giant molecules, synthetic polymers, cellulose, rubber, proteins are considered in Chap. 23.

[1] G. L. Clark, J. O. Gardner, L. Sattler, and F. W. Zerban, *Sugar,* **47** (5) (1952).

[2] General summary, *Chem. Weekblad,* **34** (January, 1937); *Nature,* **129**, 277 (1932); *Chem. Ind.,* **51**, 259 (1932), **54**, 701 (1935); *J. Chem. Soc.,* **1935**, 93; *Z. Krist.,* **93**, 464 (1936); *Trans. Faraday Soc.,* **29**, 1032 (1933); *Trans. Roy. Soc. (London),* **A239**, 135 (1940).

[3] C. H. Carlisle and D. Crowfoot, *Proc. Roy. Soc. (London),* **A184**, 64 (1945).

[†] D. Crowfoot and J. D. Dunitz, *Nature,* **162**, 608 (1948).

CHAPTER 21

THE STRUCTURE OF GLASSES, LIQUIDS, AND OTHER COLLOIDAL AND AMORPHOUS MATERIALS

X-ray Diffraction by Crystalline and Amorphous Substances. It is now evident that crystals act as three-dimensional diffraction gratings for x-rays by virtue of the arrangement of the lattice units (atoms, ions, molecules, or groups of these) on sets of equidistant parallel planes. It follows that a truly amorphous substance would be expected merely to scatter x-rays in all directions and produce a general fogging of the photographic plate without evidence of diffraction interference maxima, whereas any kind of arrangement of ultimate units, even though very imperfect, should produce a diffraction pattern characterized by interference maxima. Even a single diffuse broad diffraction ring would seem to indicate at least an elementary tendency toward organization. One of the most remarkable facts revealed by x-ray science is the extreme rarity of the truly amorphous state. Repeatedly it has been found that a specimen which by all ordinary methods of examination appears to be amorphous produces unmistakable evidence of an organized ultimate structure under the searching scrutiny of radiation with wavelengths only 1/10,000 as long as ordinary light, by means of which microscopic examination is made. Even liquids produce diffraction halos indicative of transient arrangement of molecules governed by distances of nearest approach in their thermal agitation or by some type of characteristic distribution of neighbors around any given atom. And recently results on diffraction halos from gases have given evidence of the true structure of atoms in the sense of the distribution of diffuse wavelike negative electricity according to Heisenberg and Compton, instead of sharply corpuscular electrons moving in orbits as depicted by the Bohr theory.

Diffraction by Colloids. A single crystal subjected to analysis by the pinhole method produces a Laue diffraction pattern characterized by a symmetrical array of spots, lying on a series of ellipses. As the size decreases and more individuals lie in the path of the beam, this symmetrical pattern gives way to a random "peppering" of spots. As the size decreases and the number increases still further, these small spots begin to assemble on a series of concentric rings. Finally the spots become so small and numerous that they merge into uniformly intense concentric rings, the so-called "powder" pattern. The maximum range of grain diameter over which these sharp rings are registered is 10^{-3} to 10^{-5} cm. It is clearly evident that a sharp interference effect can take place only with a certain minimum number of parallel diffracting planes in each particle. As this number falls below the minimum, in other words, as the particle size decreases below about 10^{-5} cm, it follows that interference is less perfect and that the diffraction rings (or lines by the Hull-Debye-Scherrer method) will become broader in proportion to decreasing size until in the neighborhood of 10^{-8} cm atomic dimensions are reached. Conceivably these "halos" might merge, and the pattern would then be classed as amorphous. A measurement of line breadth in the colloidal range will therefore allow calculation of particle size. The question arises of how small a particle can be and still produce a diffraction pattern upon which maxima may be detected. Levi in his study of metallic catalysts reports that particles only about five times as large as the unit crystal cell (in other words, 10 or 15 parallel planes) will produce resolved diffraction maxima, even though these are very diffuse.

Now it must be noted that diffuse diffraction maxima must be the consequence of any crystal grating which is imperfect in the sense of having too few parallel planes or of having these planes, ordinarily sufficient in number, distorted, bent, or imperfectly aligned. In other words, it is conceivable that an assemblage of fairly large colloidal particles might yield very diffuse patterns simply because molecules which may themselves be very large are not oriented in regular fashion. This condition is observed in the colloidal gels and is particularly interesting in the light of the prediction that simple mechanical stretching might tend to pull these diffracting units into parallel position and thus permit them to act as a diffraction grating.

The Measurement of the Size of Submicroscopic (Colloidal) Crystals. 1. *Theory and Equations.* Since the x-ray method of evaluating particle size was first applied to submicroscopic or colloidal particles from 10^{-6} to 10^{-8} cm, this range will be considered here first.

Debye and Scherrer were the first to derive an equation connecting particle size with an experimental measurement of the breadth of interferences at points of half-maximum intensities and applicable for the case of a parallel x-ray beam and a sample of negligible absorbing power, as follows:

$$B'_{\text{Scherrer}} = \frac{B}{R} = 2\sqrt{\frac{\ln 2}{\pi}}\frac{\lambda}{L}\frac{1}{\cos (\chi/2)} + b' \quad \text{or} \quad \beta(= B' - b') = \frac{K\lambda}{L}\cos \Theta$$

where B' is the measured breadth in radians of a diffraction interference at points of half maximum intensity (B is this breadth and R the camera radius in millimeters), λ is the wavelength, L is the edge length in angstroms of the crystal considered as cube, χ is the angle of diffraction, or

$\chi/2 = \Theta$, and b' is the natural minimum breadth in radians of the Debye: Scherrer diffraction line, which is a constant depending upon the particular apparatus and size and absorption of the specimen. Scherrer first determined b' by plotting measured values of B for various interferences against $1/\cos(\chi/2)$ for a sample of colloidal gold. The straight line drawn through the points was then extrapolated to cut the ordinate axis, which was the value of b in millimeters, and $b/R = b'$, where R is the radius of the camera in millimeters. This equation served for several years though comparatively little work was done on critical experimental tests. Selyakov, by a considerably more straightforward proof, derived the equation

$$B'_{\text{Selyakov}} = \frac{2\sqrt{3\ln 2}}{\pi} \frac{\lambda}{L} \cdot \frac{1}{\cos(\chi/2)} + b'$$

which differs from the Scherrer equation by less than 2 per cent. W. L. Bragg by remarkably simple reasoning and calculation utilizing the conception simply of n planes of thickness d arrived at the equation

$$B'_{\text{Bragg}} = 0.89 \frac{\lambda}{L} \frac{1}{\cos(\chi/2)} + b'$$

Expressed in the same form,

$$B'_{\text{Scherrer}} = 0.94 \frac{\lambda}{L} \frac{1}{\cos(\chi/2)} + b'$$

All these equations can be expressed in the form

$$\beta = \frac{K\lambda}{L} \cos\Theta$$

where K is the constant of the order of unity. Thus the particle size is calculated simply from $L = \lambda/(\beta \cos\Theta)$. It is obvious that for spherical or equiaxed crystals L will be constant for all reflections, while in other cases the variation of L with hkl (specified by $\cos\Theta$) will permit evaluation of crystal shape.

According to Warren,[1] however, the correction of broadening to the true value due to particle size alone, $\beta = B' - b'$, is incorrect and should be represented by $\beta = \sqrt{B'^2 - b'^2}$. In cases of very broad lines, of course, b' is negligible in comparison with B'. A large number of papers have been published on theoretical corrections, culminating in the development by Stokes of a Fourier method giving the true diffraction profile of a line corrected for all forms of instrumental broadening.[2] Similarly the theoretical calculation of K, which in all cases is near the

[1] *J. Am. Ceram. Soc.*, **21**, 49 (1938).
[2] *Proc. Phys. Soc. (London)*, **61**, 382 (1948).

value of 1, has been attempted several times.[1] Stokes and Wilson[2] showed that for a general reflection hkl from a crystal of any shape the simple equation $\beta = \lambda/L \cos \Theta$ will hold if L is defined as the volume average of the thickness of the crystal measured perpendicular to the reflecting planes, or $L = V^{-1}\int T(hkl)\ dV$.

In 1926, Laue deduced from vector analysis a new equation which in its most general form is free from the limitations of the cubic system and permits size evaluation in different directions and thus the *shape* of a particle. In the simplest rigorous form this equation is

$$\eta = 0.0885 \left[B' \cos \frac{\chi}{2} - \frac{1}{B'} \left(\pi \frac{r}{R} \right)^2 \cos^3 \frac{\chi}{2} \right]$$

where η is a pure number, B' is the measured width of the diffraction maximum at points of half-maximum intensity, in *radians* (actually Laue uses the ratio of total area under the peak to the maximum value of intensity, which for triangular peaks only is equivalent to B'), r is the radius of the cylindrical specimen, R is the radius of the camera and film, and χ is the diffraction angle. The quantity η is related to the size and shape of the particle by the equation

$$\eta = \frac{\lambda}{4\pi} \sqrt{\sum \left(\frac{b_i G}{m_i} \right)^2} \qquad G = \frac{\Sigma h_i b_i}{|\Sigma h_i b_i|}$$

where b_i is the ground vector of the reciprocal lattice, h_i are the indices of the reflecting planes, and m_i are numbers that express how many times the elementary cell measurement is repeated in the direction i; or

$$\eta = \frac{\lambda}{4\pi a} \sqrt{\frac{(h/m_h)^2 + (k/m_k)^2 + (l/m_l)^2}{h^2 + k^2 + l^2}}$$

for cubic crystals with the unit-cell constant a. This equation reduces to $\eta = \lambda/4\lambda m a_i$ for cubic crystals, where ma_i is the extension (or size L) of the crystal particle in the direction a_i, or the magnitude to be calculated with all the other factors known or experimentally measurable. For samples of negligible radius, the Laue expression reduces to the form of the Scherrer equation but with the coefficient 1.46 (Laue's original value 0.90 is in error) instead of 0.94. The necessary conditions for the Laue equation are for a divergent x-ray beam, for absorption in the crystal powder which is negligibly small, for completely random orientation, for particles of the same form and size, for undistorted lattices, and for known crystal structures. Patterson extended the theory to the case where the particles have different sizes and showed that the sizes must

[1] G. W. Brindley, *Discussions Faraday Soc.*, No. 11, p. 75 (1951).
[2] *Proc. Phys. Soc. (London)*, **56**, 174 (1944).

have a Maxwellian distribution, while Mark favored a symmetrical distribution of the Gauss type. Without information concerning the distribution function, the average particle size cannot be determined.

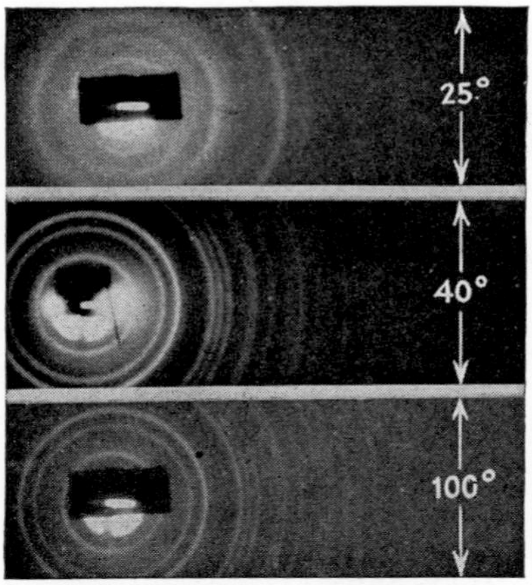

FIG. 315. Diffraction patterns for cadmium hydroxide, showing change in line breadths as a function of the temperature of precipitation.

Brill[1] extended the theory to the case of substances opaque to x-rays and derived corrections for absorption and for the overlapping of the α-doublet interferences.

2. *Examples of X-ray Determination of Submicroscopic Grain Size.* In Fig. 315 patterns for cadmium hydroxide precipitated at 25, 40, and 100° show clearly that, the lower the temperature, the smaller the particle size and the broader the interferences. Standard patterns for colloidal gold and silver sols indicate the following grain sizes: A, silver sol, 21×10^{-7} cm; B, gold sol, 13×10^{-7} cm; C, gold sol, 2×10^{-7} cm.

Brill compared the Scherrer and Laue equations for several samples of iron as follows:

Sample	Scherrer	Laue
Fe from Fe_3O_4...............	2.3×10^{-6}	2×10^{-6}
Heated 10 hr at 1000°..........	4.2×10^{-6}	∞
Fe from carbonyl:		
I (300°).....................	7.7×10^{-7}	1×10^{-6}
II.........................	6×10^{-7}	9×10^{-7}
III........................	1.0×10^{-6}	1.1×10^{-6}
IV.........................	1.2×10^{-6}	1.0×10^{-6}
(1000°).....................	3×10^{-6}	∞
Electrolytic iron..............	2.3×10^{-6}	2.3×10^{-6}

There is thus general agreement except for large sizes, where the Scherrer equation fails. It is adapted only for small particles in the range and for nonabsorbing substances.

The particle size of martensite has been determined several times, Westgren finding 10^{-7}, Wever 10^{-6}, and Selyakov 2×10^{-6} cm. Clark and Brugmann in studying the structure of case-hardened steel, which is martensite and troostite very largely, estimated a particle size of 10^{-7}.

One of the most important and interesting applications is that of

[1] *Z. Krist.*, **72**, 398 (1929), **74**, 147 (1930), **95**, 455 (1938).

particle size of metal catalysts.   Clark, Asbury, and Wick[1] were the first to make a study of particle size as related to the activity of finely divided catalysts.   They measured photometrically the line breadths of diffraction spectra from a number of nickel catalysts with identical crystal-lattice type and dimensions, prepared in various ways and differing widely in catalytic activity in hydrogenation and dehydrogenation processes.   Most of these catalysts consisted of particles larger than 10^{-6} cm so that the Scherrer equation did not apply.   In general, increase in activity and decrease in particle size did not run parallel as might be expected.   There is a more definite relationship for platinized-asbestos catalysts used in the contact sulfuric acid process.   Levi[2] made several measurements of particle size of the platinum family of metals from the photometered x-ray diffraction spectra, with the result that granules of platinum were 12 to 29 times as large on the side as the unit crystal cell, palladium 13 to 29, rhodium 6, iridium 4, ruthenium 7 to 8, osmium 6 (latter two hexagonal).

Some of the most interesting particle-size measurements have been made on such nonmetallic substances as carbon black, pigments, colloidal suspensions, rubber, and cellulose.   The question is raised of where the discontinuity between crystalline and amorphous states appears and whether or not there is any evidence of amorphous metal at grain boundaries, etc.   It is reasonable to suppose that diffraction lines may become so broad that they will coalesce and produce the effect of general fogging of the film, as an amorphous material would be expected to act.   From the evidence of carbon black an amorphous state may show transition to crystalline as judged by changes in physical or chemical properties, while the x-ray pattern is unchanged at first, simply because the crystalline planes are still too few and too distorted to allow sharp interference.   It must be realized that temperature oscillations of atoms in a lattice and also distortion both have the effect upon diffraction lines of broadening them, just as small grain size does.   These factors must be known, therefore, before adequate interpretation is possible.

3. *The Shape of Colloidal Particles.*   An important extension of this method is in the determination of the shape of colloidal particles.   If all points for all interferences lie smoothly on the same $\eta(R/r)$ curve, in other words, if the same value of L is calculated from the broadening of all interferences on the pattern, then a regular shape, *e.g.*, cubic, is immediately indicated.   In studies of colloidal nickel prepared electrolytically in the presence of varying sulfur contents Brill found that the B/r values for the (200) plane interferences were all too high.   The cause of the discrepancy could be determined by assuming various particle shapes and comparing the breadths for (200) interferences with the

[1] *J. Am. Chem. Soc.*, **47**, 2661 (1925).

[2] *Atti accad. naz. Lincei*, **3**(6), 91 (1926).

standard constant (111) interference breadths in the equation for the
cubic system noted under the discussion of the Laue equations.   Perfect
agreement is obtained when calculations are made for a particle built on
the octahedral planes and greatly elongated perpendicular to these planes.
For the nickel with 5.8 per cent sulfur the following results are obtained
by assigning the values $m_h = m_k = 9$ and $m_l = 27$, or the edge lengths
actually 45 and 165 A:

Indices	Half-value breadth found	Calculated
111	0.66	0.64
200	0.96	0.92
220	1.07	1.10

For the preparation with smallest particle size only the (111) interference
appears, simply because only these planes are present in sufficient
number in the tenuous elongated particle to produce visible diffraction
effects.   The importance of the shape factor in carbon blacks is discussed
in a later section.

4. *Broadening of X-ray Reflections Due to Strain.*   It has already been
indicated that diffraction lines are broadened by any departure of a
crystalline structure from strict regularity.   Crystal-size broadening,
just discussed, may be included in this general statement if the boundary
of a crystal is regarded as a discontinuity in its regularity.   As analyzed
in detail by Brindley,[1] strain broadening arises as follows: (1) if the strain
ϵ is uniform in a crystal but varies from crystal to crystal in a powder,
then $\beta \propto \tan \Theta$ and is independent of λ; (2) if the distortion in a crystal
is nonuniform so that ϵ varies with the direction hkl, then $\beta_s \propto \epsilon_{hkl} \tan \Theta$.
Hence strain broadening may be distinguished from crystal-size broaden-
ing by the variation of β with sec Θ or tan Θ, and by the variation of β for
a particular reflection hkl with λ.   This type of broadening has been
intensively investigated with respect to cold-worked metals and is further
discussed in the next chapter.   The determination from line broadening
of the interstitial positions of carbon atoms in ferrite is discussed on
page 579.

5. *Broadening of X-ray Reflections Due to Lattice Mistakes.*   This effect
appears in many types of colloidal layer structures such as clays, carbon
blacks, etc.   The profile of lines as observed on microphotometer curves
for films or on Geiger spectrometer curves is symmetrical for the case of
broadening due to crystal size; but for broadening due to lattice mistakes
the profile may be decidedly asymmetric, as demonstrated theoretically

[1] *Loc. cit.*

and experimentally by Laue,[1] Warren,[2] Wilson,[3] and Brindley and Nering.[4]   If in layer lattices such as graphitic carbons the displacements of layers are so frequent that the structure may be treated as a random stacking of two-dimensional lattices, the line profiles are characterized by a sharp low-angle side and a gradually sloping high-angle side.   For such a case, assuming a fairly constant structure factor F, Warren derived the equation, similar to the original Scherrer expression except for the value of the constant K, $\beta = 1.84\lambda/L \cos \Theta$.   In addition the peaks of these two-dimensional interferences are displaced from the positions of the normal, symmetrical lines by $\Delta(\sin \Theta) = 0.16\lambda/L$.   Thus for randomly stacked graphitic layers in carbon blacks, L_c, the particle size in the c direction, is calculated from the width of the symmetrical 0002 peak by the usual three-dimensional equation $L_c = 0.89\lambda/\beta \cos \Theta$, and L_a, the particle size in the a direction in the plane of the layers, is calculated from the width of the 10 (100 for graphite) peak by the two-dimensional formula.   The ratio L_a/L_c is, of course, the shape factor, presented in a succeeding section on the carbons.   Further complications are introduced for clay minerals arising from interstratification of layers of different kinds of thicknesses and scattering factors.[5]

6. *Experimental Tests of Particle-size Equations.*   It is evident that a direct test of the validity of theories involved in the Scherrer, Bragg, Laue, and Brill equations depends upon specimens in which grain sizes may be evaluated accurately by an entirely independent method.   In a few cases known optical microscopic values were checked by the x-ray method, though there was always the uncertainty whether the microscopic particle is really a single crystal or an aggregate.   The Blodgett-Langmuir technique of building up a film from a known number of layers of a long-chain compound of known molecular length (page 621) provides the means of making a rigorous test through the known thickness of films. Clark and Leppla[6] made the test for the first time with layers of calcium stearate, with the results in Table 21-1, comparing breadth measurements observed with those calculated from the simple form of the Laue equation.   Considering the difficulties the agreement is very satisfactory except for the thinnest films, for which it was demonstrated that distortion plays a considerable role.

With the advent of improved electron-microscope techniques it has been possible in some cases to compare the colloidal particle size measured

[1] *Z. Krist.*, **52**, 127 (1932).

[2] *Phys. Rev.*, **79**, 693 (1941).

[3] *Acta Cryst.*, **2**, 245 (1949).

[4] *Nature*, **161**, 774 (1948).

[5] Hendricks and Teller, *J. Chem. Phys.*, **10**, 147 (1942).   Brindley, "X-ray Identification and Crystal Structures of Clay Minerals," Chap. XI, Mineralogical Society, London, 1951.

[6] *J. Am. Chem. Soc.*, **58**, 2199 (1936).

TABLE 21-1

Number of layers	Breadth	
	Observed	Calculated
3	0.25	0.186
4	0.22	0.139
5	0.13	0.112
6	0.13	0.093
7	0.07	0.080
8	0.06	0.070
9	0.06	0.002
10	0.04	0.056
17	0.03	0.035
20	0.03	0.028
25	0.02	0.022
30	0.02	0.019
35	0.02	0.016

on electron micrographs with that calculated from x-ray diffraction line broadening. Figure 316 shows such a comparison for MgO samples, prepared by heating $MgCO_3$ at temperatures of 400 to 1000°C. The agreement is indeed gratifying.[1]

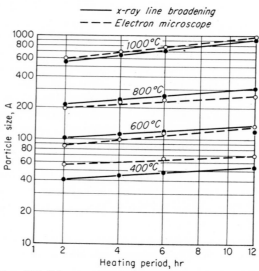

Fig. 316. Particle size of MgO by x-rays and electron microscope. (*Birks and Friedman.*)

7. *Particle Size and Shape in Carbon Blacks.* One of the greatest challenges to x-ray investigation of extremely finely divided materials arises for carbon blacks, all of which yield halo patterns strongly suggestive of colloidal graphite particles. Radial-distribution calculations (see page

[1] L. S. Birks and H. Friedman, *J. Appl. Phys.*, **17**, 687 (1946).

661) indicate single graphite layers, but uncertainty still remains as to how these layers are combined in larger units. The possibility of particle-size measurement by the Scherrer or Laue equations is therefore at least reasonable and not precluded by newer interpretations. Clark and Rhodes[1] made the most comprehensive and critical study prior to newer theoretical developments of the structure of a series of commercial blacks used in rubber compounding. Independent patterns were made under conditions conforming to the Scherrer and to the Laue equations, in both cases for nonabsorbing materials, the first being extended to the unenclosed wedge-shaped sample used so successfully in cylindrical cameras. For the Laue method the samples of necessity were made into cylinders for which the value of the radius r could be accurately measured.

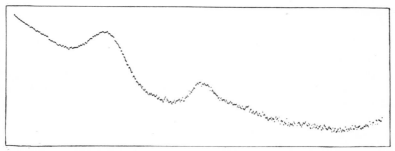

Fig. 317. Typical microphotometer curve of pattern of carbon black: *left*, 0002 peak; *right*, 10 (two-dimensional) peak.

Microphotometer curves were made under extraordinarily carefully controlled conditions, and from these were obtained the breadths at points of half maximum intensity for the two broad interferences corresponding to the 002 (basal plane) and 100 (prism) interferences of graphite. A typical curve is shown in Fig. 317. The results are briefly summarized as follows:

1. Excellent checks in particle size were obtained by the Scherrer and Laue methods.

2. The particle size of 18 rubber carbon blacks is of the order of 20 A for both interferences (at right angles in the hexagonal prisms, assuming graphite structure), and thus the particle shape is essentially equiaxed, though a tendency to flake formation ($L_{002} < L_{100}$) is indicated and is reflected in other physical properties.

3. The origin of the black, whether high-temperature or low-temperature channel, is clearly indicated by the particle sizes, which are larger the higher the temperature.

4. The sizes are identical in the black, in the rubber mix (the 100 interference only can be measured since 002 is obscured by the rubber halo), or in the black after extraction of rubber from the mix.

5. The x-ray method and the microscopic method of measuring particle size on the same sample gave values of entirely different orders of magnitude:

[1] *Ind. Eng. Chem., Anal. Ed.*, **12**, 243 (1940).

Sample	Microscopic size, μ	X-ray diffraction size, A		Particles per aggregate
		Altitude	Base diameter	
1	0.045	15.4	21.6	3.2×10^3
2	0.064	15.9	18.9	9.2×10^3
3 (thermal)	0.160	21.0	24.7	6.4×10^4
4	0.025	14.4	16.4	8.1×10^2
5 (thermal)	1.120	18.6	25.3	2.4×10^7

One explanation is that the x-ray method measures only primary particles with the maximum line breadth corresponding to the smallest particles in an undoubtedly heterogeneous mixture of many sizes, whereas the microscopic measures only the aggregate. In any case, though the material is nonuniform in particle size and distortion may exist in particles in which the single layers are twisted with respect to each other, like cards in a deck, the results on a typically mesomorphic material are of interest and importance.

Following this initial investigation, the theories of two-dimensional interferences particularly applicable to graphitic layer structures were developed by Warren and others, as discussed on page 649. At the request of the War Production Board 66 carbon black samples were subjected to a critical and quantitative diffraction study for the purpose of classifying blacks especially for rubber reinforcement.[1] The measurements were c, the spacing between the flat hexagonal basal planes, a, which indirectly measures the C—C bond distance within a plane from the two-dimensional 10 interference, the two crystallite dimensions L_c and L_a in the corresponding directions derived from the breadths of the diffraction interferences, and the shape factor L_a/L_c (the larger the ratio, the flatter the crystallite). All carbon blacks are characterized by unit-cell c values larger than that of pure graphite, 6.695 A, over a range up to 7.4 A. Thus when the fixed orientation of graphitic planes with respect to each other is lost in random stacking, the distance between the planes is greater. There is not so marked a variation in a, though the tendency is toward slightly smaller values than the 2.410-A values in graphite, indicating slightly more double-bond character. For all graphite samples the primary particle size is too large to be measured by L_c and L_a, whereas for gas and oil carbon blacks L_c usually lies between 12 and 17 A, which means three to five graphitic layers for the crystallite, and L_a between 15 and 30 A. The shape factor L_a/L_c seemed to be most readily correlated with ease of processing in rubber, for the larger the value of L_a/L_c and the flatter the primary crystallite flake, the more

[1] G. L. Clark, A. C. Eckert, Jr., and R. L. Burton, *Ind. Eng. Chem.*, **41**, 201 (1949).

easily processed.   This indication was fully confirmed in a later study[1] on new improved carbons, where the factor varied from 3.4 to 1.   When data were obtained on abrasion resistance of tires compounded with these carbons, it was found that there was a remarkable correlation, since the black with the maximum value of L_a/L_c (the largest ever found) had by far the best reinforcing properties in rubber, especially cold synthetic polymer, and the others with decreasing shape factors had decreasing abrasion-resistance values.   Acetylene black, with a value about 1.0, also had poorest reinforcement qualities, but it is interesting to note that, for other uses such as in dry cells, this carbon has by all odds the best properties.   In general high L_a/L_c values are also accompanied by high c values.   In electron micrographs the sizes of measured, apparently homogeneous single carbon black particles are 150 to 300 A ordinarily, but with no correlation between sizes and rubber reinforcement measured by abrasion resistance.   Thus the x-ray technique selects a *primary* crystallite only one-tenth to one-twentieth as large as the unit particle in electron micrographs, which must be a tight aggregate of the colloidal flakelike crystallites.   Optical microscopic sizes in turn represent still larger aggregates of the electron micrograph units.

An entire volume might be written on the extraordinary properties of graphite and the lower mesomorphic states of disordered stacking of graphitic planes, for there is no other material analogous except for the behavior of clay minerals in some instances.   In the author's experience with hundreds of samples of graphite, natural and synthetic, graphitic carbons from coal, cokes, etc., graphitic acids, carbon blacks graphitizable and nongraphitizable, no two have ever given identical x-ray patterns in every detail.   Some of the details of these complications in the light of the most recent work by Rosalind Franklin,[2] G. E. Bacon,[3] and Clark and associates are briefly summarized.

a. There is still some controversy over the structure of graphite itself. Generally accepted has been the original Bernal structure of plane hexagons with uniform side lengths of 1.42 A and the symmetry hexagonal holohedral.   However, Lukesh[4] maintains on the basis of precession patterns of single crystals showing twinning and satellite reflections that

---

[1] G. L. Clark and J. Fuchs, report to Rubber Reserve.

[2] On the Structure of Carbon, *J. Chem. Phys.*, **47**, 573 (1950); The Interpretation of Diffuse X-ray Diagnosis of Carbon, *Acta Cryst.*, **3**, 107 (1950).   The Structure of Graphitic Carbons, *ibid.*, **4**, 253 (1951).

[3] Unit Cell Dimensions of Graphite, *Acta Cryst.*, **3**, 137 (1950); The Interlayer Spacing of Graphite, *ibid.*, **4**, 558 (1951); The *a* Dimension of Graphite, *ibid.*, **4**, 561 (1951); The Reduction of the Crystalline Perfection of Graphite by Grinding, *ibid.*, **5**, 392 (1952); The Powder Diffraction Intensities of Graphite for X-rays and Neutrons, *ibid.*, **5**, 492 (1952).

[4] T. J. Lukesh, *Phys. Rev.*, **80**, 226 (1950).

the symmetry can be no higher than twofold and that the regular hexagons of C atoms must be distorted to unequal bond lengths and angles.

Three-dimensionally, crystalline graphite itself varies in the combination of hexagonal and rhombohedral stacking of the layers. Figure 318a for Madagascar graphite shows the richness of the pattern. The lines from left to right are easily identified [by hexagonal indices with rhombohedral stacking indicated by (R)] as follows: 0002, $10\bar{1}0$, $10\bar{1}\frac{2}{3}$(R), $10\bar{1}1$, $10\bar{1}\frac{4}{3}$(R), $10\bar{1}2$, 0004, $10\bar{1}\ \frac{8}{3}$(R), $10\bar{1}3$, $10\bar{1}\frac{10}{3}$(R), $10\bar{1}4$, $11\bar{2}0$, $11\bar{2}2$, $10\bar{1}5$, 0006, $20\bar{2}0$, $20\bar{2}\frac{2}{3}$(R), $20\bar{2}1$, $20\bar{2}\frac{4}{3}$(R), $20\bar{2}2$, $11\bar{2}4$, $20\bar{2}3$, ?, 0008, $20\bar{2}5$, $11\bar{2}6$, $12\bar{3}0$, $12\bar{3}\frac{2}{3}$(R), $12\bar{2}1$, $12\bar{3}\frac{4}{3}$(R), $12\bar{3}2$. With this is to be compared pattern (b) for electric-furnace graphite in which the rhombohedral lines are missing and which is considerably less perfect crystallographically. Bacon shows that in such graphites the hkil lines broaden with increase in l, except for 000l, which remains sharp. The c layers are stacked

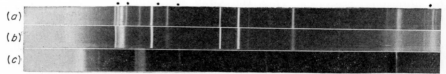

Fig. 318. Powder patterns of graphite. (a) Madagascar graphite, showing hexagonal and rhombohedral (dotted) lines (Cu-$K\alpha$ radiation); (b) electric-furnace graphite (Cu-$K\alpha$ radiation); (c) ground electric-furnace graphite for Aquadag (Co-$K\alpha$ radiation).

regularly for thickness t and with random twist but parallelism through distance H; t may be evaluated from $10\bar{1}3$, $11\bar{2}2$, $11\bar{2}4$, $11\bar{2}6$, by plotting $\beta \cos \Theta$ against $\sin \alpha$, where $\beta = (\lambda \sin \alpha)/(t \cos \Theta)$ and α is the inclination of the normal of the hkil planes; H is derived from 0004, 0006, 0008, and has a value of the order of 7t. Figure 318c represents electric-furnace graphite ground for preparation of Aquadag (colloidally dispersed lubricating graphite), with further decrease in perfection noted in some broadened lines and the disappearance of others. The decrease in H, over-all height of parallel stacks of layers, measured from the 0004 line is from 400 to 100 A in 70 hr of grinding; L_a measured from $11\bar{2}0$ decreases markedly; and p, the probability of layer displacement measured from $11\bar{2}2$, increases. In the author's laboratory the grinding deterioration noted several years ago from patterns has been correlated with loss of unctuosity and lubricating ability. It has not been possible, however, to degrade mechanically graphite to a nongraphitic carbon with diffuse two-dimensional hk interferences.

b. Carbons showing pure two-dimensional (hk) bands containing no true graphitic structure are classed as nongraphitic carbons. Franklin by means of Fourier's integral analysis deduced for a carbon black prepared by pyrolysis of polyvinylidene chloride at 1000° that 65 per cent is in the form of highly perfect and planar graphite layers of mean diameter 16 A and 35 per cent is in a much less organized state, giving only a gaslike contribution to x-ray scattering. About 55 per cent of the graphitic layers are grouped in pairs of parallel layers with an interlayer spacing of 3.7 A, and 45 per cent show no mutual orientation. The mean interparticle distance from low-angle scattering (see below) is 26 A.

c. The ability of nongraphitic carbons to form the ordered structure of crystalline graphite by high-temperature heating varies greatly. Clark, Eckart, and Burton found evidence of change in this direction at temperatures as low as 1100°C, but generally temperatures above 3000°C are required. Some of the blacks are nongraphitizable even at these temperatures. In most cases deformation of the asymmetric *hk* bands set in above 1700°C, and *hkl* ($l \neq 0$) reflections began to appear; thus it is possible to prepare a whole series of these intermediate structures classed as *graphitic carbons*. In these, graphitic layers are grouped in parallel packets within which there is a random distribution of oriented and disoriented layers. Franklin contends that there exist in graphitizing carbons two distinct and well-defined values of *c*, the interlayer spacing, 3.44 A characteristic of nongraphitic structure, and 3.354 A for true graphite. Intermediate values for partially graphitic carbons are merely mean values depending upon the proportion of the two states, and the fact that there is not superposition of *hkl* and *hk* bands, or a resolved 002 peak, means an intimately mixed single phase of randomly distributed oriented and disoriented layers. For the nongraphitizable carbons, as already noted, the interlayer spacing may be as high as 3.7 (0002), or 7.4 (0001). It is evident that a large fund of information has been obtained from x-ray patterns on carbons, ranging from the highly crystalline natural graphitic single crystals to the amorphous carbon blacks with two diffuse interferences corresponding to 0002 and 10; but much remains to be done on statistical interpretation of data from large numbers of samples—for it may be restated that no two samples of solid carbon give identical patterns in terms of number, intensities, breadths, and shapes of reflections.

8. *Particle-size Measurement from Small-angle Scattering.* Many colloidal materials, regardless of whether they may be classed as crystalline or amorphous, produce diffraction patterns with scattering at small angles unresolved from the undeviated primary x-ray beam, in addition to the halos corresponding to crystal planes. An extensive study of the theory and application has been made by Guinier.[1]

Treated similarly to scattering by gases, that is, dilute systems with separated particles of the same size and shape, the fundamental formula is derived as follows:

$$\frac{I}{I_e} = Mn^2 e^{(-4\pi^2/3\lambda^2)R^2\epsilon^2}$$

[1] *Ann. phys.*, **12**, 161 (1939).

where I is the intensity; I_e the intensity scattered by an electron at a small angle; M the number of particles; n the total number of electrons in a particle; R the "ray of gyration," or size function related to volume as $V = \frac{4}{3}\pi(\sqrt{\frac{5}{3}})^3 R^3$; and ϵ the diffraction angle. A curve drawn of $\log I$ as a function of ϵ^2, extrapolated to zero angle, gives $\log Mn^2I_e$. For a spherical particle the equation reduces to $I/I_e = N^2 e^{(-4\pi^2/5\lambda^2)R^2\epsilon^2}$. The scattering from a definite system of particles is closely approximated by a normal or Gaussian error curve. For elongated or flake-like particles, also, suitable graphical methods are employed. The following results were obtained for R: ovalbumin, 20.3 A; rubber, 35 A; colloidal silver, 64 A; Raney nickel catalyst, 23 A; graphite, diameter 400 A; cellulose, cylinders of diameter 30 A.

Since the original thesis investigation by Guinier a large number of papers have been published on techniques, interpretations, and applications. Best results are obtained with the monochromatizing, focusing type of camera with curved crystals, described in Chap. 14, or with the Geiger spectrometer, which has the advantage of direct recording without subsequent photometering. In the author's laboratory considerable success has been obtained by scanning the low-angle region with a small cadmium sulfide crystal which is self-amplifying. Yudowich in a series of excellent papers[1] has been most active in extending theory and applications. He found that, for extremely uniform samples of simple globular shape, a series of secondary intensity maxima, concentric about the center of the pattern, are observed. The positions of these maxima determine most accurately the size of spherical patterns and have been extensively studied for gold sols and the polystyrene latex sample of such exceptional uniformity that it is used for electron-microscope calibration. Complications arise for compact systems, for which the scattering becomes resolved into a halo, with a minimum of intensity (instead of maximum) at the lowest angle; and errors of various types have been recognized and attempts made to correct for them, especially for nonuniformity of particle size and shape. The linearity of the gyration-radius graph is of course the simplest indication of particle-size uniformity. This method of analysis has been applied to catalysts, alumina (as a function of temperature), carbon black, silica gels (solid glass does not produce low angle scattering), coal and coke, oil-water emulsions, argon and nitrogen near their critical points, hemoglobin, albumin and other proteins, soap solutions, evaporated metallic films, clays, latex, bacteria, metal sols, viruses, nickel oxide, and others. Under certain conditions silver-aluminum alloys produce low-angle scattering as a broad halo resolved from the undeviated x-ray beam. Guinier interprets this as due to segregated silver nuclei surrounded by a matrix volume deficient in silver atoms. This low-angle cutoff was also observed by the author for cellulose and is

[1] *Anal. Chem.*, **25** (May, 1953).

illustrated in Chap. 23. These scattering effects are to be clearly distinguished from true crystal diffraction interferences appearing at small angles for long spacings such as are noted in collagen. As an example of usefulness chrysotiles (asbestos), which gave the same wide-angle patterns, can be differentiated by low-angle scattering, which by use of very fine slits could be resolved into lines, thus probably indicating for these condensed systems diffraction from repeating structural units. In such a case the Bragg spacings can be computed for the diameter of fibrils: Canadian chrysotile 195; harsh variety, United States A, 250, soft variety 226; Italian 218 A.[†] Similarly from low-angle scattering calculations with the Bragg equation the spacings of concentrated bovine albumin solutions are 84.0 A (33%), 76.0 (39%), 72.5 (44%), 66.5 (50%), 65.5 (51.4%).[1]

Much can be done on soils and soil conditioners, foods, greases, ink and paint pigments, cements, polymers, and all biological materials beyond the reach of the microscope.[2]

Diffraction by Glasses, Liquids, and Other Amorphous Substances. We have just seen that the crystals may be subdivided into colloidal particles so small that the powder diffraction interferences become broad and diffuse, though they still represent the characteristic spacings of the crystalline lattice. There are substances that cannot be classified as crystalline colloids which also yield patterns of a few broad "halos." These include all glasses, of which vitreous silica is the simplest example, liquids, and a number of so-called "amorphous" solids, of which carbon blacks, already discussed, are actually an example. Since crystalline silica and silicates have been considered already in Chap. 18, it is logical to consider first the structure of a glass.

The Structure of Glass. Diffraction patterns of glass specimens are made by the usual pinhole method with registration on a flat film. Figure 319 illustrates the pattern obtained with the glass formed from molten silica. It is very advantageous on account of the diffuse nature of the pattern to use a strictly monochromatic beam of x-rays reflected from a crystal, such as pentaerythritol, and a vacuum camera by means of which troublesome background fogging is eliminated. To illustrate the general method of interpretation, the simple case of vitreous SiO_2 will be selected from the work of Warren. The two halos, calculated by means of Bragg's law for crystal reflection, correspond to spacings of 4.32 and 1.30 A. The two principal theories of interpretation are: (1) The glass is composed of colloidal crystallites of such minute size that the crystal

[†] I. Fankuchen and M. Schneider, *J. Am. Chem. Soc.*, **66**, 500 (1944).

[1] D. P. Riley and G. Oster, *Discussions Faraday Soc.*, No. 11, p. 107 (1951).

[2] K. L. Yudowich, *J. Appl. Phys.*, **20**, 1232 (1949), **21**, 174 (1949), **22**, 214 (1951); *Anal. Chem.*, **25** (1953). References to the entire literature on the subject are in these papers.

interferences are greatly broadened.   (2) The glass is a random network, and x-rays are scattered in this noncrystalline medium.

1. *Crystallite interpretation.*

a. Favorable data.   (1) Vitreous silica held at 1500° for several hours devitrifies to cristobalite, for which the strong crystalline (111) reflection (Fig. 319) corresponds roughly in angular position to that of the principal glass halo.   (2) Cristobalite is the stable crystalline form of SiO_2 in the temperature range through which the vitreous silica solidified.   (3) Randall, Rooksby, and Cooper evaluated the particle size upon the assumption of colloidal crystallites as 15 A, which seems not unreasonable.

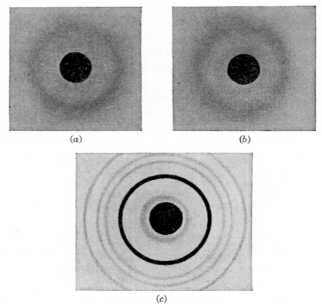

(a)   (b)

(c)

Fig. 319. Diffraction patterns for glasses and crystalline silica.   (a) Vitreous silica, $d = 4.32$ A; (b) pyrex glass, $d = 4.26$; (c) β-cristobalite, $d = 4.11$.

b. Unfavorable data.   (1) There is actually a discrepancy of 6 per cent in the spacing of the principal halo, 4.32 A, and that of the cristobalite crystal interference, 4.05 A.   (2) There is no sharp melting point of glass, whereas crystals, even of minute size, would be expected to have a definite value.   (3) As glass is annealed, there are no gradual increase in crystal-particle size, as is true for all cases of truly crystalline material, and no sharpening of the diffraction bands; instead, the broad peak of vitreous silica goes over abruptly into the sharp displaced ring of cristobalite.   (4) The origin and previous history of the sample have no effect on the pattern of the vitreous state, whereas they should exert an effect in the case of the crystallites.   (5) Cristobalite undergoes a marked volume change between 200 and 300°, whereas vitreous silica has no such change.

(6) Precision measurements by Warren[1] prove that the crystal-particle size calculated from the breadths of the halos at points of half maximum intensity is about 7.7 A.   Since the edge of the unit cell of low-temperature cristobalite is 7.0 A, it is necessary to postulate crystals comprising only a single unit cell in order to explain the observed peak width.   This has no real significance since the very essence of the crystalline state is regular repetition of the unit cell.   (7) The bonding in glass is continuous, rather than a structure in which there are small crystals with a break between them.   This is proved by the complete absence of x-ray scattering at small angles on glass patterns, whereas for silica gel there is very strong scattering at small angles, due to the existence of discrete particles (10 to 100 A), with breaks and voids between them.   Thus even if a cristobalite crystal is assumed to exist as a center, the scheme of bonding out from this center cannot follow a crystal pattern, for otherwise entirely different widths would be found.   Hence x-ray analysis proves that the major part of the material certainly cannot be in the form of cristobalite crystals of sufficient size to have this term mean anything.

2. *Random-network interpretation.*   The alternative theory of interpretation from a purely descriptive point of view, which we shall see has quantitative mathematical support, retains without change in glass the familiar plan of coordination of four oxygen atoms tetrahedrally around each silicon atom as definitely established in the various crystal forms of SiO_2.   Glass is a form of matter in which the coordination plan is exactly the same as in the crystalline phase but which cooled too rapidly from a viscous melt to permit the orderly construction of any regularly repeating structure; glass, therefore, is a liquid of very high viscosity in which atoms are so tightly bound together in an irregular network that there is no opportunity for the breaking and reforming into crystals.   The bonding is continuous even though in a random network.   Such a network, as proposed by Zachariasen, is illustrated in Fig. 320.   The absence of a sharp melting point and the temperature range of softening are to be explained by the varying energy required to break down each mesh of different size and arrangement.   The tendency of silica to form a glass resides in the tendency to form the SiO_4 coordinated group even in the melt and in the bonding of each oxygen between two silicon atoms.   Such linkages stiffen the liquid to a high viscosity so that there is not sufficient mobility to permit crystallization on cooling.   And yet the bonding is such that there is still enough flexibility so that the random network is about as stable as the crystalline arrangement and so continues to exist; devitrification occurs only at elevated temperatures over considerable time.

Theoretical Calculation of Glass Diffraction Pattern.   If the assumptions of oxygen coordination of silicon and the linking of these tetrahedra in a

[1] *J. Appl. Phys.*, **8**, 645 (1937).

random network in glass are sound, they may be subjected to mathematical test such that the pattern of halos may be theoretically deduced. The method of calculating the intensity of x-ray scattering on an amorphous solid is based upon the method originated by Zernicke and Prins[1]

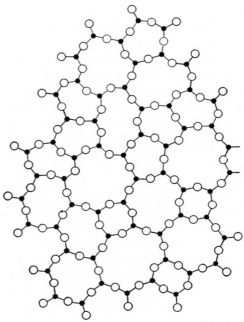

FIG. 320. Random network of SiO_4 tetrahedra (shown as triangles) in glass. (*Zachariasen.*)

for liquids and adapted by Warren.[2] The intensity of scattering I, from an array of atoms taking all possible orientations in space, is given by

$$I = \sum_m \sum_n f_m f_n (\sin s r_{mn})/s r_{mn},$$ where $s = (4\pi \sin \Theta)/\lambda$, f is the atomic scattering factor, and r_{mn} is the distance from atom m to n. For SiO_2,

$$I = N\left(f_{Si} \sum_n f_n \frac{\sin s r_{Si-n}}{s r_{Si-n}} + 2f_O \sum_n f_n \frac{\sin s r_{O-n}}{s r_{O-n}}\right)$$

when N is the effective number of SiO_2 molecules in the sample.

The next step is tabulation of the number of neighbors and their distances about any one atom. For vitreous silica this distribution is as follows:

[1] *Z. Physik*, **41**, 184 (1927).

[2] *Z. Krist.*, **86**, 349 (1933); *Phys. Rev.*, **45**, 657 (1934); *J. Am. Ceram. Soc.*, **21**, 49 (1938).

1 Si surrounded by		2 O, each surrounded by	
1 Si	$r = 0$	1 O	$r = 0$
4 O	$r = 1.60$	2 Si	$r = 1.60$
4 Si	$r = 3.20$	$6 \times \frac{1}{2} = 30$	$r = 2.62$
$12 \times \frac{1}{2} = 60$	$r = 4.00$	6 SiO_2	$r = 4.00$
12 SiO_2	$r = 5.20$		

Continuous distribution beyond $R_2 = 4.55$

Continuous distribution beyond $R_1 = 6.05$

This means that out to 5.20 A from each silicon atom the number of neighbors and distances is definite regardless of the orientation of the tetrahedral groups, whereas, beyond this, distances in a random network are indefinite and a continuous distribution of scattering matter is then assumed, equivalent to $-\frac{4}{3} R^3 \rho f \phi (sR)$, where ρ is the SiO_2 density and

$$\phi(x) = \frac{3}{x^2} \frac{\sin x}{x - \cos x}$$

Then

$$\frac{I_{\text{unmodified}}}{N} = f_{\text{Si}} \left[f_{\text{Si}} + 4f_{\text{O}} \frac{\sin 1.60s}{1.60s} + 4f_{\text{Si}} \frac{\sin 3.20s}{3.20s} + 6f_{\text{O}} \frac{\sin 4.00s}{4.00s} \right.$$
$$+ 12f_{\text{av}} \frac{\sin 5.20s}{5.20s} - 17f_{\text{av}} \phi(6.05s) \Bigg] + 2f_{\text{O}} \left[f_{\text{O}} + 2f_{\text{Si}} \frac{\sin 1.60s}{1.60s} \right.$$
$$+ 3f_{\text{O}} \frac{\sin 2.62s}{2.62s} + 6f \frac{\sin 4.00s}{4.00s} - 8f\phi(4.55s) \Bigg]$$
$$I_{\text{modified}} = N(I_{\text{Si}} + 2I_{\text{O}})$$

where $I = Z - \sum_1^Z (f_n)^2$, where Z is the atomic number.

Now values of $I_{\text{unmodified}} + I_{\text{modified}}$ expressed as electron units per SiO_2 molecule are plotted as a function of $(\sin \Theta)/\lambda [s = (4\pi \sin \Theta)/\lambda]$. This gives an intensity curve (Fig. 321a) that *corresponds exactly* with the experimental curve from the microphotometer record of the diffraction pattern. Thus a theoretical pattern is deduced which correctly places the halos (not a continuous fog) and yet assumes no crystalline arrangement whatever beyond about 5 A from any given atom. However, a still more direct method utilizes the experimental-intensity curve to calculate distances and number of neighbors at each distance. A radial-distribution function is introduced such that $4\pi r^2 \rho(r)\, dr$ is the number of atoms between distances r and $r + dr$, and a Fourier analysis is carried out.[1] For SiO_2 with two kinds of atoms

$$\sum K_m 4\pi r^2 \rho(r) = \sum K_m 4\pi r^2 \rho_0 + \frac{2r}{\pi} \int_0^\infty si(s) \sin rs\, ds$$

[1] Warren, Krutter, and Morningstar, *J. Am. Ceram. Soc.*, **19**, 202 (1936).

where Σ is the summation over molecular composition; K_m is the effective number of electrons in atom m and is equal to f_m/f_e, where f_m is the atomic structure factor and $f_e = \Sigma f_m/\Sigma Z_m$ or average f per electron;

$$i(s) = \frac{(I_{eum} - \Sigma f_m^2)}{f_e^2}$$

where I_{eum} is the experimental intensity of unmodified scattering in electron units per molecule; and ρ_0 is the average number of electrons per unit volume. The quantity $si(s)$ is obtained from the experimental-scattering curve, which is put on an absolute basis in electron units per SiO_2 by

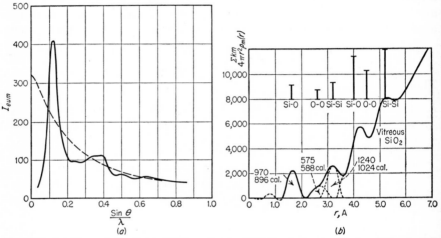

Fig. 321. (a) X-ray intensity curve for vitreous SiO_2 in electron units per SiO_2; *dashed line*, independent scattering per SiO_2. (b) Radial-distribution curve for vitreous SiO_2. (*Warren.*)

consideration of the fact that at large values of sin Θ it must approach the theoretical curve for independent scattering by the atoms. The integration is carried out for different values of r, and the values $\Sigma K_m 4\pi r^2 \rho_m$ plotted against r give the radial-distribution curve of vitreous silica. This really gives two superposed curves, one for distribution about silicon and one for that about oxygen, as in Fig. 321b. The area under the peaks allows calculation of the number of neighbors at the particular distance. The first peak at 1.62 A is to be compared with 1.60 for Si—O distance in crystalline silicates. If there are n oxygen atoms around each silicon atom and $n/2$ silicon atoms around each oxygen atom and if the values $K_{Si} = 16$ and $K_O = 7$ are taken, the area under the peak will be

$$A = \underbrace{\frac{1 \times 16 \times n \times 7.0}{}}_{\text{Si—O}} + \underbrace{\frac{2 \times 7.0 \times \frac{n}{2} \times 16}{}}_{\text{O—Si}}$$

If the measured value of A is introduced, $n = 4$. Similarly the next peak will be due to O—O (2.62), Si—Si (3.20), Si—O (4.00) and O—O (4.5) unresolved at 4.2, Si—Si (5.2), and then a smoothing out for continuous distribution.

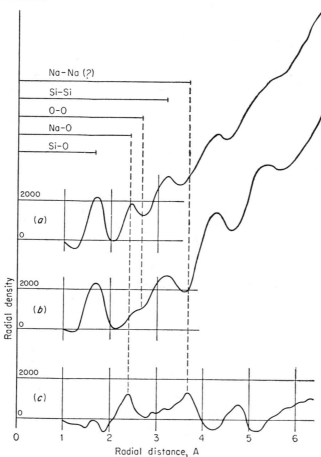

Fig. 322. Radial-distribution curve for sodium in a soda glass by subtraction of 2 curves. (*Lukesh.*)   (*a*) Curve of 19.5 per cent Na_2O–80.5 per cent SiO_2 glass; (*b*) curve of SiO_2 glass; (*c*) differential curve by subtraction of (*b*) from (*a*).

The x-ray results on silica glass are completely and quantitatively explained by a random network in which each silicon atom is tetrahedrally surrounded by four oxygen atoms, each oxygen atom bonded to two silicon atoms, the two bonds being roughly diametrically opposite, and by a random orientation of the tetrahedra around the Si—O—Si bond.

In two-component glasses such as soda-silica the question arises as to what information can be obtained concerning the distribution of the sodium atoms. It is obvious that if the radial-distribution curve for SiO_2 glass is subtracted from the curve for the soda-silica glass, presupposing an essentially constant distribution of silicon and oxygen atoms in both, a differential curve could be obtained whose peaks are due to radial distribution of scattering matter around sodium.[1] Figure 322 shows the two glass curves, and the differential curve with peaks at 2.4, 3.65, 4.75, and 6.3 A. The first indicates the Na—O distance, the second the Na—Na distance, the third a second Na—O or Na—Na distance, etc. In this same way Na_2O–boric oxide, glasses with peaks at 3.4 and 4.5 A, and K_2O–boric acid with a sharp peak at 3.3 A gave some indication of distribution. The area under peaks assigned to metal-to-metal separation increases regularly with increasing metal content.

Every other substance in the glassy state may be treated in analogous fashion. GeO_2 and BeF_2 glasses afford an excellent check on SiO_2. For soda-silica glass, part of the oxygen atoms are shared between two silicon atoms, and others are bonded to only one silicon. The double-bonded oxygen atoms build up the continuous framework, in the holes of which the sodium atoms are located at random, with no evidence of compound formation.[2] A complete Fourier radial distribution analysis has been made for soda–boric oxide glass.[3] In the random network the boron atoms are bonded either to three oxygen atoms in triangles or four tetrahedrally, and the sodium atoms are distributed at random in holes in the boron-oxygen network. Anomalous properties are due to the ability of the boron atom to change to tetrahedral coordination when Na_2O is present to supply the necessary oxygen.

It follows that the tendency of any substance to form large groups of polyhedra will make crystallization difficult and glass formation likely. As examples may be cited, the familiar oxides (acid anhydrides) with non-ionic character, Be_2O_3, SiO_2, P_2O_3, P_2O_5, GeO_2, As_2O_3, As_2O_5, similarly BeF_2 (BeO is ionic and forms no glass), H_3PO_4, $K_2Mg(CO_3)_2$, metallic selenium (chain fragments retained in melts), a large group of organic substances whose melts contain large and irregular molecules, or polymerized groups linked by rather strong forces that retard crystallization.[4]

The Structure of Amorphous Solids. By exactly the same radial-distribution methods as are employed for glass, it is possible to reproduce theoretically the halo patterns for a whole series of materials that are commonly described as amorphous and thus to account for their structures in terms of the immediate neighbors around any atom. The most

[1] J. S. Lukesh, *Proc. Natl. Acad. Sci.*, **28**, 277 (1942).

[2] Warren and Loring, *J. Am. Ceram. Soc.*, **17**, 249 (1934), **18**, 269 (1935), **21**, 259 (1938).

[3] Biscoe and Warren, *J. Am. Ceram. Soc.*, **21**, 287 (1938).

[4] Hägg, *J. Chem. Phys.*, **3**, 42, (1935).

familiar examples are the extremely fine powders of the carbon blacks, amorphous forms of elementary phosphorus and several metals, unstretched rubber, etc.

It is interesting to apply the methods already found so successful for the glass random networks to carbon blacks, already discussed in terms of particle sizes and shapes. From the experimental-intensity curve the distribution curve $4\pi r^2 \rho(r)$ is derived by a purely mechanical, straightforward method (harmonic analyzer) as already indicated. Four peaks are found as follows:

Carbon black		Single graphite layer (crystal)		
Distance, A	Approximate number of atoms from peak areas	Distance, A	Average distance	Number of atoms
1.5	3	1.42	...	3
2.7	10 ± 1	2.46 ⎫ 2.84 ⎭	2.6	6 ⎫ 3 ⎭ 9
4.05	12	3.75 ⎫ 4.25 ⎭	4.0	6 ⎫ 6 ⎭ 12
5.15	12	4.92 ⎫ 5.11 ⎭	5.0	6 ⎫ 6 ⎭ 12

Allowing for errors and overlapping of peaks it is at once evident that the distribution is that of single graphite layers (Fig. 323), which, therefore, must exist in carbon blacks. If other layers have a definite position and orientation with respect to a first layer, then graphite is indicated; if they are at random, then at least the carbon black can be considered to be two-dimensionally crystalline, or *mesomorphic*. From the data a distinction cannot be made. A characteristic feature of carbon black patterns is very intense scattering at small angles caused by the difference between grain density and average density from loose packing of extremely small grains. Hence the

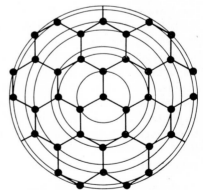

FIG. 323. Atomic arrangement in a single layer of graphite, with equidistant neighbors shown lying on circles.

blacks seem to be a heterogeneous mixture of particles ranging from single graphite layers up to graphite crystals several layers thick.[1] Coals,

[1] Warren, *J. Chem. Phys.*, **2**, 551 (1934).

vitrains, durains, charcoals, etc., have been studied, in similar fashion, at least in respect to the graphite halos and small-angle scattering.

Amorphous red, amorphous black, and *liquid* yellow varieties of phosphorus give remarkably similar patterns and distribution results with three nearest neighbors. In the liquid, P_4 molecules probably exist, but in the high-melting amorphous solids complications are probably introduced by a puckered network as in crystalline black phosphorus.[1]

	Peak 1	Peak 2	Peak 3
Amorphous red, 50°.............	2.29	3.48	
Amorphous black, 20°..........	2.27	3.34	
Liquid yellow, 48°..............	2.25	3.90	5.90
Liquid yellow, 226°.............	2.25	3.90	6.10

In recent years very intensive and quantitative analyses especially at Stuttgart have been made on a considerable number of amorphous metallic elements. The interest of course is in a comparison of the atomic distribution with that in the crystalline and liquid states in the further effort to evaluate the metallic bond. Very complete results have been reported for germanium,[2] arsenic,[3] and selenium,[4] and observations principally by electron diffraction on thin amorphous surface films, some prepared by polishing, for 13 other elements and 9 alloys.[5] As an example the results on selenium may be cited. For amorphous samples prepared by condensation from vapor, chemical precipitation, and sudden cooling of melts, the atomic distances and numbers were determined by the radial distribution method. Three peaks with average d values of 3.30, 1.76, and 1.12 A are found, and the radial-distribution curve leads directly to the conclusion that the chains of Se atoms existing in the crystals also persist with essentially the same structure and position in the amorphous state, but with considerably greater distance between chains. The chains are distributed statistically at random in the direction of the chain axes, and there is only one form of the amorphous state in contrast with other elements; also with heating the crystalline structure develops without apparent intermediate structures. Arsenic chains behave similarly; the 3 + 3 + 6 atoms in the first three coordinating spheres in crystalline arsenic are replaced by 3 + 0 + 9 atoms in the cor-

[1] Hultgren, Gingrich, and Warren, *J. Chem. Phys.*, **3**, 351 (1935). Thomas and Gingrich, *J. Chem. Phys.*, **6**, 659 (1938).

[2] O. Fürst, R. E. Glocker, and H. Richter, *Z. Naturforsch.*, **4a**, 540 (1949), **6a**, 38 (1951).

[3] S. Geiling and H. Richter, *Acta Cryst.*, **2**, 305 (1949). H. Richter and E. Breitling, *Z. Naturforsch.*, **6a**, 721 (1951).

[4] H. Richter, W. Kulcke, and H. Specht, *Z. Naturforsch.*, **7a**, 511 (1952).

[5] H. Richter, *Physik. Z.*, **44**, 406, 456 (1943).

responding spheres of the amorphous phase. It has been possible to compare crystalline, amorphous, and liquid germanium with respect to atomic distribution. The d spacings for amorphous Ge are 3.30, 1.83, 1.18 and 0.97 A, and for liquid Ge 2.52, 1.92, and 1.28 A. From radial-distribution curves and the crystalline structure the following atomic distances and coordination numbers are deduced:

	Coordination sphere					
	I		II		III	
	Atomic distance	Number of atoms	Atomic distance	Number of atoms	Atomic distance	Number of atoms
Crystalline.....	2.43	4	3.97	12	4.66	12
Amorphous.....	2.36	4	3.93	12	4.84	6.6
Liquid.........	2.70	8	4.14			

There are higher coordination spheres at 5.96 and 7.54 A for amorphous and 5.75 and 8.00 A for liquid states, corresponding with 5.62-, 6.11-, 6.56-, 7.30-, 7.95-, and 8.30-A distances in germanium crystals. The linking of tetrahedra in fixed positions in the crystals is replaced by the same arrangement but with random turning of the tetrahedra around the link.

The classical work of Hendus[1] has provided the best data for a considerable number of liquid metals, analyzed from the halo x-ray patterns in the same manner. Typical data on the number and distance of neighbors of a given atom in crystal lattice and in the melt are briefly summarized in Table 21-2. There is no case here in which the coordination number of the liquid melt is the same as in the crystal, though gold (also aluminum and argon) with 11 and 12, respectively, is closest. In most cases there is a lower coordination number for the liquid phase, but for gallium, germanium, lithium, and tin it is higher than for the crystal. Sodium and potassium have 8 for both liquid and solid at nearly the same distances (Gingrich).

Gingrich and associates[2] have published data for liquid He, Li, N_2, O_2, Na, Al, P, S, Cl, A (in liquid, vapor, and critical regions), K, Zn, Ga, Se, Rb, Cd, In, Sn, Cs, Hg, Tl, Pb, and Bi.

Unstretched rubber gives a typical "amorphous" pattern of broad halos. Again by the same Fourier distribution method it is found that each carbon atom has two carbon neighbors at 1.52 A, about 3.4 at 2.68 A, and others in its own chain or in adjacent chains at 4.0 and 5.0 A.

[1] H. Hendus, Z. Naturforsch., 2a, 505 (1947).
[2] N. S. Gingrich, Phys. Rev., 62, 261 (1942); Revs. Mod. Phys., 15, 90 (1943).

This is in excellent agreement with the concept of a structure of long-chain molecules, whose exact configuration in unstretched rubber, however, cannot be deduced.[1]

TABLE 21-2. DISTANCE AND NUMBER OF NEIGHBORS OF AN ATOM IN CRYSTALLINE AND LIQUID METALS

	Crystal lattice		Melt	
	Distance	Number	Distance	Number
1. Lead..............	3.49	12	3.40	8
			4.37	4
2. Thallium..........	3.45	12	3.30	8
			4.22	4
3. Indium.............	3.24	4	3.17	8
	3.37	8	3.88	4
4. Gold..............	2.88	12	2.56	11
5. Tin................	3.02	4	3.20	11
	3.15	2		
	3.76	4		
6. Gallium...........	2.43	1	2.77	11
	2.71–2.79	6		
7. Bismuth...........	3.09	3	3.32	7–8
	3.46	3		
8. Germanium.........	2.43	4	2.70	8

Synthetic Resins. All the numerous and familiar commercial plastics or synthetic resins such as bakelite yield halo patterns, and their structures may be represented by the distribution method exactly as in the case of unstretched rubber. These plastics probably having three-dimensional random networks are to be distinguished from the crystalline linear polymers with remarkably rich patterns. No complete analyses have been carried through as yet; from a qualitative point of view, the patterns are often sufficiently distinctive to permit identification of the variety of resin, as indicated in Table 21-3.

Diffraction by Liquids. *Older Concepts.* It has been known definitely since 1916 that liquids through which x-rays are passed produce diffraction patterns characterized by one or more halos or interference rings, usually somewhat diffuse. A large number of papers dealing with this subject theoretically or experimentally have appeared. It is not possible here to present the historical development, but only to give the status of experimental results as they now stand. An excellent survey of researches up to 1928 is given in a paper by Drucker.[2]

The preponderance of opinion up to 1933 was that the diffraction effects with liquids indicate orderly spatial arrangements of molecules,

[1] Simard and Warren, *J. Am. Chem. Soc.*, **58,** 507 (1936).
[2] *Physik. Z.*, **29,** 273 (1928).

The phenomenon is understood qualitatively in the same sense that crystal diffraction is understood.   Interference effects might be due to periodicities within the atom (electron distribution), within the molecule (atomic distribution), or between molecules.   The first must be true for monatomic substances, which were investigated by Debye and Scherrer in 1916.   Certain halos for other compounds may be due to atomic distribution, but certainly the third cause is predominating in complex molecules, since the chief diffraction maxima are accounted for by a periodicity in the distribution of molecules.   This would be particularly true for asymmetrical molecules.   In liquids these would have a certain distance of nearest approach side by side or end to end.   This concept of orderly arrangement in groups was called by Stewart[1] "cybotaxis."   If true, therefore, the Bragg law $n\lambda = 2d \sin \Theta$ could be applied to liquid diffraction interferences just as truly as to crystalline solids.

TABLE 21-3. SPACINGS IN PLASTICS

	d_1, A	d_2, A	d_3, A
Phenol formaldehyde...............	3.5	4.6	
o-Cresol formaldehyde...............	3.5	5.0	
m-Cresol formadelhyde..............	3.6	5.0	
p-Cresol formaldehyde..............	3.5	4.6	
Xylenol formaldehyde, liquid........	4.1	5.5	17.5
Xylenol formaldehyde, soft..........	4.2	5.5	14.7
Xylenol formaldehyde, infusible......	4.2	5.9	15.4
Xylenol formaldehyde, fusible........	4.2	6.2	12.65
Cumarone-indene..................	2.2	5.2	9.4
Stearic-glycerol phthalate...........	....	4.55	9.32
Half-acid ester....................	4.05, 4.80	6.3	14.0
Resin from rosin...................	2.25	5.51	
Glycerol-sulfur....................	....	4.8	9.32

The Modern Interpretation.   It was inevitable that a more quantitative and formal interpretation of liquid diffraction should replace such mechanical pictures as cybotaxis, a theory which was based on a concept that no catastrophic change occurred on melting and that temporary groupings of molecules over small elements of time and space are probable, thus assuming a transient structure closely similar to that of the solid.   The basis for this rigorous treatment was given by Debye in 1915 for the intensity of scattering by a noncrystalline liquid and by Zernicke and Prins in 1927 for the Fourier analysis of radial distribution.   Today it is unnecessary to postulate any kind of crystalline arrangement, however transient, in a liquid.   The diffraction patterns, exactly like those of glasses and amorphous solids, may be theoretically reproduced upon the basis of an arrangement of immediate neighbors around any atom and

[1] *Revs. Mod. Phys.*, **2**, 116 (1930).

of a completely random distribution beyond a distance of the order of 5 A. Liquid sodium gives a radial-density curve $4\pi r^2\rho(r)$ with a peak at 4.0 and another at 2.0 A. In the analogy of Warren[1] we may interpret the curve in terms of a box full of ball bearings continuously shaken. About the center of any one ball bearing we shall never expect to find another closer than the diameter of the balls. At about this distance we shall expect to find the centers of several balls, since at any instant there will be a number of balls in approximate contact with the one under consideration. At a somewhat larger distance the number of balls must drop a little since the immediate neighbors described will prevent others from coming into the immediate vicinity of the first ball.

Such is the structure of any liquid—a structure arrived at by the average distribution of neighboring atoms around any one atom. Liquid hydrocarbons have precisely the same treatment as rubber. Peaks represent the distances to the next neighbors, then the next, etc., including neighbors in the next molecule as well as in the same one.

Although there is great similarity between glass and liquid scattering and both are treated alike, there is one important difference: in all glasses the dip following the first peak comes down to the axis, whereas in liquids there is poor resolution in that the dip does not come more than halfway down. The explanation is that in a liquid a molecule does not have permanent neighbors, for some of these are free to move in or out of positions of approximate contact.

The deductions on the structure of water are interesting. The area under the first peak at distance 2.9 to 3.0 A indicates something less than four molecules. The tendency of the water molecule toward tetrahedral coordination, so definite in ice, persists, although on the average less than four neighbors are so bonded. This deficiency is indicated by Raman spectra and explains the latent heat of fusion as a bond breaking. Water has a greater density than ice in spite of a somewhat greater distance from a molecule to the first neighbors. Ice has an extraordinarily open structure (Fig. 324); when it melts, the second, third neighbors, etc., can fill in between the wide spacings in the solid framework.[2]

"Structure" persists for liquids above their critical temperatures, as might also be expected from the radial-distribution interpretation.[3]

Hydrogen peroxide has peaks on its radial-density curve at 3.0 A (12 neighbors) and at 4.25 (6 neighbors); this is precisely a type of face-centered cubic packing of OH groups, which are 0.1 A greater in radius than in water. The correct dipole movement is calculated from such a model.[4]

[1] Farasov and Warren, *J. Chem. Phys.*, **4**, 236 (1936). Trimble and Gingrich, *Phys. Rev.*, **53**, 278 (1938).

[2] Warren, *J. Appl. Phys.*, **8**, 645 (1937).

[3] Barnes, *Chem. Rev.*, **23**, 29 (1938).

[4] Randall, *Proc. Roy. Soc.* (*London*), **159**, 83 (1937).

Liquid Crystals and Mesomorphic States.   The ability has long been recognized of certain long-chain compounds, such as p-azoxyanisol, to form liquid crystals, easily recognized by characteristic anisotropic optical properties.   In 1922 Friedel proposed in a classical paper the classification of certain states intermediate between isotropic liquid and crystal as

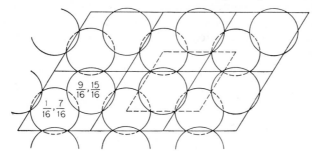

FIG. 324. The structure of ice, H_2O.

mesomorphic states (Fig. 325).   The process on cooling from the transparent liquid is as follows:

Liquid—random distribution of molecules
————Discontinuity (definite temperature)
Mesomorphic states:
    Nematic (from νημα, "thread")—long molecules; oriented in same direction, but not in layers
    ————Discontinuity (definite temperature)
    Smectic (from σμεγμα, "soap")—long molecules; oriented in same direction and in equidistant layers corresponding to length, but random laterally
    ————Discontinuity (definite temperature)
Crystal—3-dimensional orientation

Undoubtedly transition phenomena must occur in all cases of solidification of a molten substance, but only in the case of certain organic molecules is the temperature range of each state sufficiently extended to permit detection.   From the x-ray diffraction point of view it would be predicted that the nematic "liquid crystal" should give a pattern similar to that of the liquid and that the smectic "liquid crystal" should give a sharp interference in several orders corresponding only to the arrangement of oriented long molecules in equidistant layers.   The crystal, in addition, should give interferences for lateral arrangement.   In general, the prediction has been confirmed.   Comparison of details of liquid-crystal patterns (intensity, sharpness, and shape of peaks) with those of the isotropic liquid lead to the conclusion that "swarms" of long molecules exist in the liquid crystal of the order of 10^6 molecules with axes parallel and with mobility of the molecules within the swarm much less than they possess in the liquid state.[1]

[1] Stewart, *J. Chem. Phys.*, **4**, 231 (1936).   Ornstein and Kast, *Trans. Faraday Soc.*, **29**, 931 (1935).

In a magnetic field the directed orientation is indicated on the diffraction rings by localized intensity maxima (fiber pattern). The pattern is markedly sharper in passing from the nematic to the smectic phase in the magnetic field as observed by Hermann and Krummacher. These workers have also proved that, when a melt of a substance which displays mesomorphic phases solidifies in a magnetic field, the crystalline powder is fibered in a direction parallel to the field; the intensity maxima for the pattern correspond in position to those for the liquid crystals in the magnetic field.

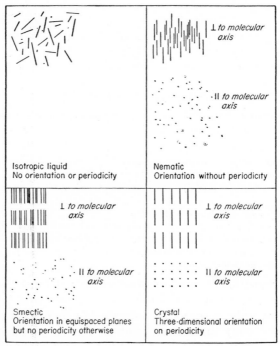

Isotropic liquid
No orientation or periodicity

⊥ *to molecular axis*

∥ *to molecular axis*

Nematic
Orientation without periodicity

⊥ *to molecular axis*

∥ *to molecular axis*

Smectic
Orientation in equispaced planes but no periodicity otherwise

⊥ *to molecular axis*

∥ *to molecular axis*

Crystal
Three-dimensional orientation on periodicity

FIG. 325. Molecular arrangements in liquid, mesomorphic, and crystalline states.

Solutions. Very little quantitative interpretation has been given as yet to x-ray diffraction patterns of solutions in comparison with electron diffraction analysis of molecular structure in gases. For a pure liquid, of course, intermolecular scattering obscures the molecular patterns. The scattering in dilute aqueous solutions does not differ markedly from that of pure water, but two effects are noticeable: (1) a change in sharpness of halos; (2) the appearance of marked scattering at small angles, close to the central undiffracted beam on flat film patterns. Prins[1] found that the principal water halo is markedly sharpened when alkali hydroxides are dissolved, as a result of orientation of the water molecules

[1] *J. Chem. Phys.*, **3**, 77 (1935).

by the dissolved ions.   Solutes also seem to have characteristic effects on changes in sharpness with changes in temperature, *i.e.*, the temperature coefficient of arrangements and number of neighbors around a central molecule.   Data on the apparent volume of alkali halides in water solutions are in harmony with the following interpretations: (1) In addition to hydration of Li^+ and Na^+ the ions affect the semiorderly structure of water at distances larger than the atomic radii, the general effect on water being to increase its density or decrease its volume.   (2) This structural effect is responsible for variation with concentration of the apparent volume occupied by a pair of ions.   (3) The structural effect, though characteristic of the halide, depends more on the alkali than on the halogen.   The concepts of superstructures (page 560) and of order-disorder (page 561), well known for alloys, have also been applied to solutions.[1]   In other words, ions are participants with water in one common or shared structure, different from that of either constituent, but not homogeneous.[2]   Phenomena somewhat akin are found in nonaqueous systems.   To illustrate with a single example, Clark, Sterrett, and Lincoln[3] found that the presence of a polar compound, such as methyl dichlorostearate in liquid paraffin hydrocarbons in lubricating oils, produced a marked orienting or regimenting effect in that liquid interference maxima are much sharper and remain so at elevated temperatures, at which usual halos become so diffuse that resolution practically disappears.   The importance of this "structure" especially in thick films for viscous lubrication is at once apparent.

In spite of limited success with dilute solutions there is still the far more favorable case for analysis of solute molecular structure, namely, the diffraction pattern obtained by passing a beam of monochromatic x-rays through a concentrated solution of a strongly scattering solute in a weakly scattering solvent.   Such a pattern consists of a series of diffuse concentric rings, the spacings and relative intensities of which depend primarily on the structure of the solute molecules; in other words, the scattering function is closely approximated by that of a gas of the solute molecules.   Only a few cases are on record.   As examples may be cited the determination of Br—Br distance in CBr_4 dissolved in benzene,[4] and the I—I distances in *p-p'*-diiododiphenylmethane and *p-p'*-diiododiphenyl ether;[5] the proof of persistence of $[Mo_6Cl_8]^{4+}$ groups, known to be present in crystals, in solutions in ethyl alcohol of so-called molybdenum chloroacid,[6] by techniques developed in Norway by Finbak;[7] and

[1] Stewart, *Trans. Faraday Soc.*, **33**, 238 (1937).

[2] Meyer, *Phys. Rev.*, **38**, 1038 (1931).

[3] *Ind. Eng. Chem.*, **28**, 1318, 1322, 1326 (1938).

[4] E. Rumpf, *Ann. Physik*, [5]**9**, 704 (1931).

[5] O. Kratley and W. Worthman, *Monatsch.*, **76**, 263 (1947).

[6] C. Brosset, *Arkiv Kemi.*, **1**, 353 (1949).

[7] C. Finbak, *Ark. Det. Norske. Vid. Akad. Oslo, Mat. Nat. Kl.*, (3) (1943).

especially the analysis at Pasadena of structures of groups $PtBr_6^{2-}$, $PtCl_6^{2-}$, $Nb_6Cl_{12}^{2+}$, $Ta_6Br_{12}^{2+}$, and $Ta_6Cl_{12}^{2+}$.† Figure 326 from this work shows for H_2PtBr_6 the visually estimated intensity curve from the film, the radial-distribution integral, and calculated-intensity curves for various values of a coefficient in the temperature factor of the shortest Br—Br term. Two pronounced maxima are observed on the radial-distribution

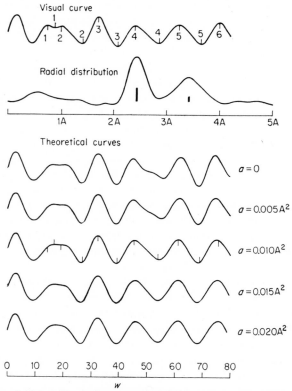

FIG. 326. Bromoplatinic acid solution scattering data. a = coefficient in the temperature factor of the shortest Br . . . Br term. (*Vaughn, Sturdevant and Pauling.*)

curve, at 2.43 and 3.41 A. Since $3.41/2.43 = \sqrt{2}$ a regular octahedral model is indicated with the Pt—Br distance equal to 2.43 A, compared with 2.45 A, the sum of the radii. The equations used, similar in form to those used for glass on page 661, were as follows:

1. Radial-distribution integral (calculated by a punched-card method):

$$rD(r) = \sum_{w=1}^{80} I^0(w)e^{-aw^2} \sin 0.03rw$$

† P. N. Vaughn, J. H. Sturdevant, and L. Pauling, *J. Am. Chem. Soc.*, **72**, 5477 (1950).

where $I^0(w)$ is the visual intensity function, a is chosen so that

$$e^{-a(80)^2} = 0.1$$

and $w = (70/4\pi)s = (70/\lambda) \sin \Theta = \frac{7}{4}q$ (a variable used in electron diffraction investigations).

2. Calculation of theoretical-intensity curve:

$$I(w) = \sum_i \sum_j \left[\sum_{R=-N}^{N} \frac{A_{ij}}{2 \sqrt{\pi a_{ij}}} e^{-\frac{(k \Delta r)^2}{4a_{ij}}} \sin \frac{4\pi w}{70} (r_{ij} + k \Delta r) \right.$$

$$+ \sum_l \sum_m A_{lm} \sin \frac{4\pi w}{70} r_{lm}$$

where A_{ij} is the amplitude, the exponential term is the temperature factor, the second summation terms with temperature factor unity, N chosen to make negligibly small the factor $\dfrac{A_{ij}}{2 \sqrt{\pi a_{ij}}} e^{-\frac{[(N+1)\Delta r)]^2}{4a_{ij}}}$.

The same octahedral configuration is found for $PtCl_6^{2-}$ ions and for the halogenated compounds of Nb and Ta the data are consistent with M_6X_{12} groups with M at the corners of an octahedron and halogen atoms on radial perpendicular bisectors of the edges of the octahedron. The shortest interatomic distances are as follows:

	M—M, A	M—X, A	X . . . X, A
$Nb_6Cl_{14}.7H_2O$	2.85	2.41	3.37
$Ta_6Br_{14}.7H_2O$	2.92	2.62	3.64
$Ta_6Cl_{14}.7H_2O$	2.88	2.44	3.41
$Mo_6Cl_8(OH)_4.14H_2O$	2.63	2.56	
(Brosset)			

The M—M distances are consistent with Pauling's theory of intermetallic distances.

Colloidal Solutions. Micelles and Solubilization. The molecular weight of dextrin calculated by Krishnamurti from the extent of "amorphous" scattering by means of the Bragg formula $n\lambda = 2d \sin \Theta$ was 600, and that of gelatin 3000, which are not improbable values. The solution of sodium oleate produced a ring due to the presence of big groups, or micelles, of sodium oleate in the solution. The extent of the gaseous scattering gave the dimension for the sodium oleate molecule, agreeing with that calculated from molecular weight and density. An excess of scattering directly adjoining the central spot was due to big groups of ionic micelles described by McBain. Aqueous solutions of starch, tannic acid, and gum arabic showed a further scattering at small angles to the primary beam, due to the dissolved molecules or micelles. The molecular weights calculated from the extents of the coronas were 6200, 3134, and 2810, respectively. Thus, a starch molecule contains about 10 dextrin molecules united together, and a tannin micelle contains 10 simple molecules of the formula $C_{14}H_{10}O_9$. The greater importance of these studies is at once apparent when it is considered that extremely valuable information should be obtained from biological fluids including blood, filtrable virus, etc.

Reference has been made already on page 527 to the structures of sols of the hydrous oxides and oxide hydrates, which x-ray analysis has shown to be far simpler than is usually assumed and fully consistent with results on the gels. Particularly significant are x-ray results on streaming sols, i.e., colloidal suspensions forced through fine capillaries under pressure.[1]

A 1.4 per cent colloidal solution, or sol, of vanadium pentoxide or a 3 per cent sol of mercury sulfosalicylate produces remarkably clear diffraction patterns indicative of a marked fiber structure, caused by the preferred orientation in streaming of rod-shaped colloidal particles, already observed in polarized light. The same sols at rest in the same capillary tubes produce only faint Debye-Scherrer rings for random arrangement. The spacings for these sols are not the same as for the dry powders of V_2O_5 or the mercury salt, a difference proving hydration; thus the 3.28-A spacing for the sol, completely missing for the powder, is due actually to an oriented water hull on each colloidal particle. The elongated shape of the particles is further indicated by the fact that planes parallel to the long axis and through the smallest dimension of the crystals produce very weak interferences as compared with planes normal to the axis.

A resolved long spacing of 48 A is found in streaming solutions of sodium oleate, corresponding to the length of two oleate molecules perpendicular to the diffracting planes. This distinguishes the colloidal micelle from the solid crystals of sodium oleate, in which the layer spacing is 41 A and the molecules are inclined at an angle of 60 deg to the planes. With decreasing concentration of the soap solution the flakelike micelles become thinner down to a limit of a bimolecular layer of oleate molecules, which is actually the structure of the thinnest black areas in soap-bubble films.

A considerable amount of work has been done on soap micelles particularly in correlating x-ray data with other measurements such as osmotic pressures, electrolyte properties, viscosities, light scattering, etc. An excellent recent summary of a complex subject is given by Philippoff.[2] For these dispersed soap micelles three diffraction bands are observed, two for long spacings designated M and I bands, and the "short-spacing"

[1] Hess and Gundermann, *Ber.*, **70**, 1800 (1937).

[2] Size and Shape Factor in Colloidal Systems, *Discussions Faraday Soc.*, No. **11**, p. 96 (1951).

band.   Data are consistent with a micelle model consisting of a double layer of soap molecules, the plane ends being hydrophilic, the sides hydrophobic.   The short spacing is determined by the lateral distance between the chains, which remains nearly constant for normal aliphatic chains, which have a cross-sectional packing area of about 30 A; the M band by the micelle itself; and the I band by the repeating structure of several

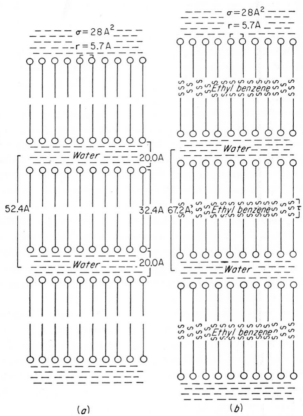

(a)   (b)

Fig. 327. Cross section of soap micelles in 15 per cent aqueous potassium laurate, showing solubilization.   (a) Without additive oil; (b) saturated with ethyl benzene.   [(W. D. Harkins, R. W. Mattoon, and M. L. Corwin, J. Colloid Sci., **1,** 105 (1946).]

micelles with their ends parallel to each other and with water between them.   The most remarkable feature of the micelle is the ability of the aqueous soap solution to *solubilize* nonpolar oils, and x-ray diffraction analysis has made the clearest contribution to an understanding of the phenomenon.   Figure 327 illustrates diagrammatically that for a 15 per cent aqueous potassium laurate a long-spacing M band of 52.4 A increases to 67.2 A when ethyl benzene is added.   Water is held in layers about 20 A thick in the soap solution between the polar end groups of the oriented soap molecules, and the nonpolar oil in layers within a double layer of molecules between the nonpolar ends of the chains. This is an extension of the long-known process measured by surface and interfacial energies of *similia similibus dissolvuntur* ("like dissolves like"). It is often true that solubilization greatly improves the x-ray pattern. This process is involved in emulsion polymerization of synthetic rubbers, the most effective means of commercial production since the polymer molecule upon formation is too large to be solubilized. This will be further considered in the final chapter on polymers.

With all the spectacular effects observed for soap micelles there is no adequate theory of micelle formation. This is independent of the size of the charge of the micelle-forming ion. Micelles are partially ionized; they form with non-ionizing detergents in water, and with ionizing detergents in hydrocarbons (Aerosol OT) showing that a charge is not essential to the process. Evidently micelles are larger and better organized with ionic detergents in H_2O; for example, in 30 per cent potassium laurate solutions the micelles consist on the average of 63 molecules.[1] A straight-chain compound is not necessary for micelle formation; for sodium desoxycholate with a single ionizing group on a sterol skeleton, arylalkyl sulfonates with a complicated hydrocarbon part of the molecule, polyethylene oxide derivatives, such as Tween, a polyethylene oxide sorbitan (sorbitol–hexahydroxy alcohol) monopalmitate with three hydrophilic chains, and many other compounds all form micelles. Mixed micelles form readily from detergents of widely differing chain lengths. The one common feature is the segregation of the hydrophilic and hydrophobic parts of a molecule.

In the *Discussions of the Faraday Society*, The Size and Shape Factor in Colloidal Systems (No. 11, 1951), several papers deal with x-ray investigations, especially on macromolecular systems such as proteins and cellulose. These will be mentioned in the final chapter on polymers, but attention is directed here to the papers by Riley and Oster on Some Theoretical and Experimental Studies of X-ray and Light Scattering by Colloidal and Macromolecular Systems; by Schulman, Matalon, and Cohen on X-ray and Optical Properties of Spherical and Cylindrical Aggregates in Long Chain Hydrocarbon Polyethylene Oxide Systems; and by Fournet on The Influence of the Size and Shape of Particles in the Interpretation of X-ray Diffuse Diagrams.

The principle of changing colloidal particle size as a function of concentration has been used effectively by Clark and Southard[2] for measuring capillary-pore diameters in cellulose fibers. The oxazine dye, Nile blue sulfate, in aqueous solution, has a varying molecular association as a function of concentration, indicated by potentiometric and spectrophotometric measures and proved by x-ray diffraction patterns. Solu-

---

[1] D. E. Andersen and G. B. Carpenter, *J. Am. Chem. Soc.*, **75**, 850 (1953).
[2] *Physics*, **5**, 95 (1934).

tions of the order of one-millionth molar approach obedience to the laws of dilute solutions; in moderate concentrations of the order of $5 \times 10^{-4} M$ the dye molecules associate to micellar structures, and in concentrated solutions the association proceeds to the stage of a colloidal suspension. The principal spacing varies as follows:

Concentration	d, A
0.0884	13.00 (solid powder 13.00)
0.00884	11.19
0.000884	10.26
0.0000884	8.14
0.00000884	7.10

Between the third and fourth of these solutions, absorption in the capillary pores of cotton fibers increases markedly.

The Determination of the Quantity of Amorphous Phase.   It has long been recognized that many materials, especially natural polymers such as cellulose, rubber, and proteins, consist of both ordered crystalline and disordered or amorphous phases.   Even an inorganic substance such as the PbO_2 in charged positive storage-battery plates, "amorphous" metals, and silicates seem to consist of an intimate mixture of crystalline and amorphous phase.   It is obvious that many physical and chemical properties such as density, tensile strength, absorbing capacity, and chemical reactivity may well depend upon the presence and amount of disordered phases.   Thus any reliable method which could be used to determine the ratio of crystalline to amorphous phase in any sample would be of great fundamental and practical value.   As described in the last chapter in those regions in cellulose films in which there is a close-packed crystalline array resulting from regular parallel arrangement of chains, the reactive OH groups are held in fixed positions and are relatively inaccessible; thus treatments which involve swelling chemical reactions as in producing viscose and fiber disintegration must encounter considerably greater resistance in crystalline than in amorphous regions. Hence a number of methods have been tried to evaluate crystallinity: thallous ethylate,[1] rate of periodate oxidation,[2] oxidative hydrolysis to CO_2,[†] rate of exchange of cellulose with heavy water,[3] absorption of Nile blue sulfate,[4] sorption of water vapor, and x-ray diffraction.[5]

There are many objections to the chemical methods although some fairly good results have differentiated cotton, linters, rayons, etc.   The

[1] Assaf, Haas, and Purvis, *J. Am. Chem. Soc.*, **66**, 59 (1934).

[2] Goldfinger, Siggia, and Mark, *Ind. Eng. Chem.*, **35**, 1083 (1943).

[†] Nickerson, Conrad, and Scroggie, *Ind. Eng. Chem.*, **34**, 85 (1942), **37**, 592 (1945).

[3] Frilette, Hanle, and Mark, *J. Am. Chem. Soc.*, **70**, 1107 (1948).

[4] Clark and Southard, *loc. cit.*

[5] Bunn and Alcock, *Trans. Faraday Soc.*, **35**, 482 (1939), **41**, 317 (1945).   Hermans and Weidinger, *J. Appl. Phys.*, **19**, 491 (1948).   Mathews, Peiser, and Richards, *Acta Cryst.*, **2**, 85 (1949).   Trillat, Barlezat, and Delalande, *J. Chem. Phys.*, **47**, 877 (1950).

appearance of the characteristic diffraction pattern of cellulose is an indication only of the crystalline or organized portions of the sample, since a varying percentage of amorphous phase would merely (1) affect the intensity under constant conditions of the crystal pattern, causing this to be weaker the higher the percentage of amorphous material, and (2) affect the general scattering or fogging on the film, increasing with increasing proportion of amorphous phase. Under properly controlled conditions and calibration the x-ray technique is potentially the most reliable. As an example may be cited results on synthetic polyethylene as a function of temperature. The pattern consists primarily of an amorphous halo at 4.5 A and crystalline interferences at 4.1 A (110 planes) and 3.7 A (200). Thus $\dfrac{W_A}{W_C} = \dfrac{I_{\text{amorphous}}}{I_{110} + I_{200}}$. The intensity values derived from the area under the microphotometered peaks are corrected, as outlined in Chap. 15, by a factor

$$f_C^2 \frac{1 + \cos^2 2\Theta}{\sin^2 \Theta \cos \Theta} e^{-2D} A \cos^3 2\Theta$$

where the first term is the atomic-structure factor for carbon, as a function of $(\sin \Theta)/\lambda$, the second is the angle factor, the third is the temperature factor, A is the absorption, and the last term corrects from flat to circular film. It is interesting to see what the total corrections amount to for polyethylene as calculated by Trillat, and the percentages of amorphous phase derived from the corrected intensity data:

	Temperature, °C						
	20	40	60	80	95	105	115
12°24′ halo..........	0.707	0.706	0.705	0.704	0.7035	0.7025	0.7015
13°36′(110) line......	1	1	1	1	1	1	1
15°10′(200) line......	1.578	1.583	1.586	1.590	1.595	1.597	1.6000
$W_A/(W_A + W_C)$, %.	26.9	28.5	39.8	44.3	58.0	63.0	76.7

Clark and Terford have determined the phase constitution of a long series of paper pulps with closely similar preferred orientations in fibers but widely different tensile strengths and absorption capacities. The technique was simplified by registering on each film a standard nickel-foil pattern by reference to which corrections could be easily made. There was a spread of 30 per cent in amorphous content, correlating better with performance of the pulps in papermaking than any other structural factor. Similarly Clark and Terford found for positive storage-battery plates a variation of 6 to 26 per cent amorphous phase in PbO_2, increasing linearly with decreasing H_2SO_4 concentration and from center to surface of the plates.

CHAPTER 22

THE TEXTURE OF METALS

The Scope of X-ray Diffraction Information. In the subject matter thus far developed in Chaps. 13 to 21, particular application of fundamental principles has been made to the analysis of crystalline constitution, or ultimate structure. It has been shown that such analyses of solids may involve the use of single crystals or of specimens composed of many fine grains, usually in random orientation. The various experimental methods employing either single crystals or aggregates have been outlined in Chap. 14. It has also been indicated that numerous other types of information besides ultimate crystalline structure may be obtained from the interpretation of the x-ray diffraction patterns. It is at once apparent that a whole series of specimens may give identically the same known crystal pattern characteristic of body-centered cubic α-iron, and yet from the standpoint of *practical behavior* these specimens may vary enormously. If, then, x-rays told us only that all the specimens were α-iron, they would perform a notable service but fall far short of the greatest usefulness. Fortunately, by means of these rays it is possible to make fundamental and subtle distinctions between the specimens, which all have the same unit crystal cell, far beyond the powers of any other testing agency, and thus scientifically to account for actual behavior in service and to further rational establishment of manufacturing processes that will ensure a desirable combination of properties in terms of a desirable structure. It is this information concerning grain size, internal strain, fabrication, heat-treatment, etc., which is the newest contribution of x-ray science and at the same time the most important from the actual industrial point of view. In this chapter consideration will be given to the fundamental interpretation of x-ray patterns in terms of some of these properties, followed by actual examples and achievements of the x-ray method in the metallurgical industry. In view of the recent publication of the second edition of "Structure of Metals" by C. S. Barrett,[1] in which extended treatment is given to this whole subject, it will suffice to give in this chapter only a brief summary in the hope that the reader will refer to this extended work for details.

[1] McGraw-Hill Book Company, Inc., New York, 1952.

Grain Size.   1. *X-ray Evidence of Grain Size.*   In Figs. 194*a* and 208 are shown the x-ray diffraction patterns for two extremes of grain size of α-iron, respectively, a single crystal grain and a random aggregate of very small grains.   The former is distinguished by a symmetrical array of Laue spots, the latter by a series of concentric, continuous Debye-Scherrer rings.   Both patterns are definitely characteristic of crystalline α-iron, and, in addition, each characterizes a particular condition of grain size.   Of course, there may be every possible gradation in grain size between the extremes and also extending to smaller grain sizes in the colloidal range than those represented by Fig. 208.   In general, it may be stated that specimens with grains larger than 10^{-3} cm in diameter produce a fairly uniform peppering of diffraction spots which grow larger and fewer in number as the grain size increases or the number of grains in the path of an x-ray beam of constant cross section decreases.   In the region of 10^{-3} cm these spots begin to lie on Debye-Scherrer rings as in Fig. 249 if the $K\alpha$ doublet of the radiation is present so as to exceed all other rays in intensity (*i.e.*, approaching monochromatic rays).   As the size still further decreases, the spots lying on rings decrease in size and increase in number until individual spots can no longer be distinguished and the diffraction rings appear of continuously uniform intensity and have maximum sharpness.   There is a range of particle sizes between 10^{-3} and 10^{-6} cm as limits which produce these sharp rings and which, therefore, cannot be accurately distinguished.   As the grain still further decreases in size below 10^{-6} cm into the colloidal range, the interference effects become less perfect as the number of parallel reflecting planes falls below a certain value.   This manifests itself as a *broadening* of the diffraction rings, so that a measurement of breadth leads directly to an evaluation of grain sizes of colloidal dimensions, as discussed in the preceding chapter.

2. *Particle-size Measurement in the Microscopic Range.*   A method of evaluating grain size to supplement and check microscopic measurement of grains of the order of 10^{-3} to 10^{-2} cm in diameter has long been needed, particularly if some information can be obtained about grains below the surface of a polished specimen.   X-ray patterns are now filling this requirement.   It has been demonstrated already that with grain sizes of 10^{-3} cm or larger the diffraction interferences are no longer uniform and continuous circles or lines.   These interferences show individual spots, and as the size increases, the Debye-Scherrer rings disappear and a uniform "peppering" appears.   The size of the spots depends upon the divergence of the primary x-ray beam, the size and shape of the focal spot on the target of the x-ray tube, and the extent of the crystal in the plane of the reflecting face.   Consequently, the size of the interference spot on the photographic film from a grain increases with increasing grain size as long as the cross section of the crystal perpendicular to the ray to be reflected is smaller than the cross section of the impinging bundle of

rays. Mark and Boss showed a linear relationship between the size of interference spots for particles between 10 and 100 μ (10^{-3} to 10^{-2} cm) and the grain size measured microscopically. The slope of the straight lines depends upon the experimental conditions and apparatus; but, once

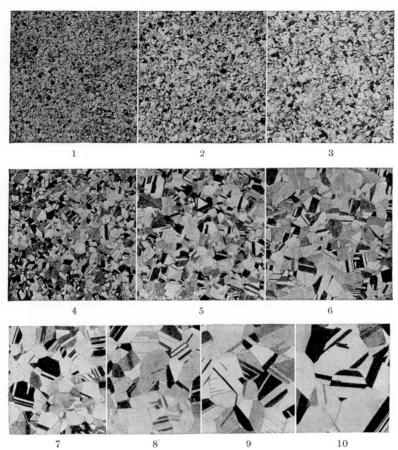

Fig. 328a. Grain-size standards (ASTM) for the estimation of the diameter of average grain of annealed materials, particularly nonferrous alloys such as brass, bronze, and nickel-silver. $\times$ 75. Average grain diameter as follows:

1. 0.010 mm.	5. 0.045 mm.	8. 0.120 mm.
2. 0.015 mm.	6. 0.065 mm.	9. 0.150 mm.
3. 0.025 mm.	7. 0.090 mm.	10. 0.200 mm.
4. 0.035 mm.		

known, grain sizes may be directly read off for any specimen from a measurement of the interference spots.

Clark and Zimmer greatly extended these results, using the brass samples from which standard ASTM grain-size photomicrographs were prepared (Fig. 328a). The corresponding standard x-ray patterns photographed in most carefully constructed cylindrical cameras are shown in Fig. 328b.   When the microscopic measurements are plotted against the lengths of the x-ray diffraction images, the straight-line plot of Fig. 328c is obtained.   The results with two other series of brass samples, steel, carborundum, silica, etc., all lie on this same curve, so that it undoubtedly represents a universal relationship.   It is essential, however, that the

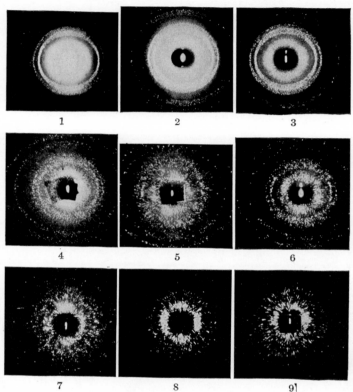

Fig. 328b. Standard x-ray diffraction patterns for increasing grain size in the microscopic range (cf. Fig. 328a).

1. 0.009 mm.	4. 0.033 mm.	7. 0.065 mm.
2. 0.012 mm.	5. 0.037 mm.	8. 0.085 mm.
3. 0.020 mm.	6. 0.045 mm.	9. 0.095 mm.

annealed metal sample shall not show residual preferred orientation or fibering.   It is essential that the grains should have uniform size, since otherwise the x-ray measurement will give the average only of the largest particles, the small particles producing no individual sharp interferences. The effect of size distribution is very clearly demonstrated in Fig. 329a. Two specimens of silica with the same average particle size as prepared and measured by Drinker and Hatch at the Harvard School of Public Health were subjected to x-ray analysis by Aborn and Davidson.   The

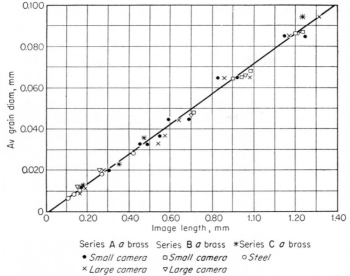

Series A *a* brass Series B *a* brass *Series C *a* brass
• *Small camera* □*Small camera* ○*Steel*
× *Large camera* ▽*Large camera*

FIG. 328c. Graphical correlation between image lengths of x-ray diffraction interferences and average grain diameters in microscopic range. (*Clark and Zimmer.*)

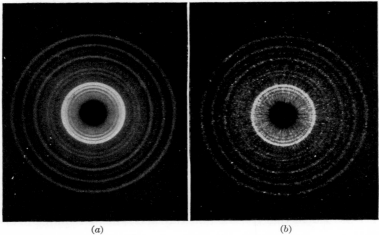

(a)   (b)

FIG. 329a. Diffraction patterns for two samples of silica with the same average particle size but differing widely in the distribution of sizes. (a) Average size 4.4 microns, distribution (standard deviation) 1.341; (b) 4.5 microns and 2.166, respectively.

difference is remarkable. In (a) the deviation from the average was very small, whereas in (b) it was large. Without a knowledge of the fact that the average particle sizes were the same, and of the distribution, the mistake would be made of assigning a considerably larger particle size to (b) in which the large grains producing individual interferences are balanced by grains too small to produce distinguishable spots. Micro-

photometric curves are reproduced in Fig. 329*b* for grain sizes of 4.4 *μ*,
standard deviation 1.34; and 36 *μ*, standard deviation 1.28. These
were made by turning the film around an axis so that one of the diffraction
circles was continuously registered. Obviously there are no equations
comparable with those for colloidal particles for calculating particle size
of large grains from a measured quantity such as diffraction interference
breadth. Hence the microphotometric curves were measured, including
number of peaks per unit length, average height of peaks, area per peak,
and the total area under peaks per unit length. When for specimens with
nearly the same size distribution the last-named quantities are plotted on

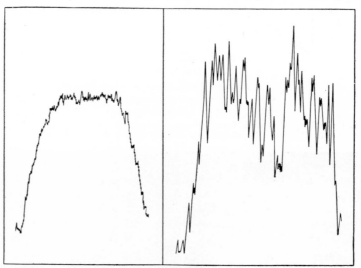

Fɪɢ. 329*b*. Microphotometric curves for diffraction rings of silica samples. *Left*, average
size 4.4 microns; *right*, average size 36.0 microns.

log paper against average particle size, the points lie on a straight line.
For specimens with widely different distribution but the same average
size, the points do not lie on this line. This work on silica is of great
importance in laying the foundation for further work on metal grain
sizes. It is evident that considerable care and skill are required in deducing accurately grain size for the region in question. For samples with
sufficiently small size so that spots tend to overlap it is possible to use
microbeams of x-rays to reduce the volume of irradiated material to such
an extent that individual spots appear on rings. Hirsch and Keller[1]
successfully used beams 35 *μ* in diameter to measure from back-reflection
patterns particle volumes and the changes on cold-working aluminum.

3. *Examples of Measurement of Size of Microscopic Particles.* It is
needless to point out the very great importance of grain size in terms of

[1] *Acta Cryst.*, **5**, 162 (1952).

practical behavior of commercial materials. Practically all annealing operations following mechanical work involve grain growth. Magnetic permeability and hysteresis loss in electric steels are certainly dependent upon grain size. The life of electrical contact points is a function of optimum grain size. Even the enameling of steel, corrosion, electrodeposition, and numerous other phenomena depend upon grain size. The control of grain size in metallurgical products is one of the great achievements of the science. Another typical application has been reached on the re-use of plaster of paris molds. These deteriorate very rapidly on re-use, the tensile strength becoming much less on each successive recalcination. X-ray photographs show that the gypsum particles grow larger as strength decreases. The addition of $\frac{1}{4}$ per cent Al_2O_3 increases strength by decreasing grain size. A basic patent on bright nickel, formed by electrodeposition, and of great commercial importance not only in nickel plating but also in undercoating for bright chrome plating, specifies a grain size less than 0.0001 mm. The x-ray method of grain-size evaluation has been used repeatedly in developing processes and in tests for infringement.

Orientation of Grains. Many research and practical problems arise in which a knowledge of orientation of crystal planes in a single metal crystal or of single grains in an aggregate is highly desirable. It has been demonstrated in Chap. 15 that the x-ray goniometer is a powerful method of ascertaining orientation. Single metal crystals are made frequently by cooling a melt in a quartz tube by extremely slow and careful cooling, as first devised by Professor Bridgman. Obviously, no planar faces are developed, and recourse must be had to goniometric establishment of orientation of planes with respect to one direction or another before physical data may be properly interpreted. There are frequent references to x-ray goniometry of this kind in the literature, especially with respect to the presence or absence of twinning. Again, a strip or sheet of metal may be polycrystalline and yet have certain properties dependent upon just how the individual grains (of course, large) are oriented with respect to the surface. This is especially true of electric or magnetic properties, which may differ widely for two specimens, say, of silicon steel, with the same apparent grain size and general structure. In this case the Laue method of crystal analysis may be employed. Standard Laue photographs for body-centered and face-centered cubic and hexagonal close-packed metals in every possible and known orientation, with respect to the x-ray beams, are to be found in the literature. All that is necessary, therefore, is to compare a Laue pattern for a grain in a sheet, to the surface of which the x-ray beam is perpendicular, with the standard patterns in order to establish easily the orientation of the lattice planes of the grain in question with respect to the surface.

Sir William Bragg indicated another field in which knowledge of orientation is of practical importance. The wearing properties of jewel bearings for watch movements depend upon how they are cut from original sapphires. Figure 330 shows Laue patterns for two such bearings with different crystallographic orientations and different resistance to wear.

Internal Strain. Many metal structures fail because of gross defects which may be detected readily by radiographic examination. But many metal objects may appear radiographically perfectly sound and still fail. The cause here is far more deep-seated and is concerned with residual internal strain or lattice-plane distortion. Strain in transparent objects

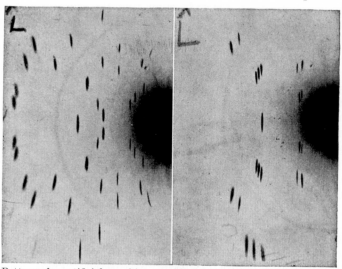

Fig. 330. Patterns for artificial sapphires used in jewel pivots of watch movements, with same structure but different orientations and different wearing properties. (*Sir William Bragg.*)

is readily ascertained by interference colors when examined in polarized light. In this manner glass apparatus is tested. Dirigible models of transparent celluloid have been studied under all conditions of stress. But for opaque objects such as metals the method is precluded. The use of gage marks for detecting strain in metals is well known. For example, the diameter of a cylinder of metal is very carefully measured. Successive layers from the inside of the cylinder are then removed on a lathe and the changes in the outside diameter with the relief of strain observed. There are many modifications of this technique that have been widely employed, but there are serious objections and limitations. In the first place, the dimensional changes may be too small to measure accurately. Again, the direction of the strain may be such as to be missed entirely by the gage-mark method. In all of metallurgy there has been no problem that has so urgently required an adequate method. To the detection and even quantitative estimation of internal strain x-ray diffraction science has made a great contribution, although the application still requires much fundamental research and standardization.

X-ray Evidence of the Effect of Stresses and of Residual Strain in Specimens. Depending on the texture of any material, single crystalline or aggregate, and the type and extent of stress or deforming force applied to this specimen above and below the elastic limit, x-ray diffraction patterns provide a number of manifestations of change. These will be enumerated first and then further consideration given to some of the more important.

1. *Radial Streaks, or "Asterism," on Laue Patterns for Bent or Distorted Single Crystals and on Large-grained Aggregates.* Figure 331 shows what happens to the Laue diffraction pattern of a single crystal (gypsum) when

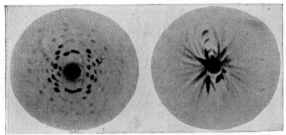

Fig. 331. Laue patterns of a normal and of a bent crystal of gypsum, illustrating asterism These are the first patterns ever made. (*Czochralski.*)

it is bent. The spots are elongated to radial streaks, or "asterism striations" (polychromatic radiation), caused by the reflection of different wavelengths by one set of distorted planes in which lattice orientation has been changed by elastic or plastic deformation. Any pattern, even for a polycrystalline material, that shows these radial streaks is an indication of internal strain. The crystal planes are distorted so that reflection takes place as though cylindrical mirrors had replaced plane mirrors. A strain pattern can be synthesized by loading successively a strip of iron while the exposure is made. Even under the elastic limit there is clear evidence of strain; at higher loads slipping on planes occurs and rupture accompanied by fibering of the metal in many cases. Figure 332 shows the strained condition of a block of cast steel which has been rapidly chilled.

2. *Shift in Positions of Spots.* Within the elastic limit and before deformation of Laue spots begins, the application of small stresses may cause rearrangement of spots by rotation of grains with approximate reversible recovery of original positions, although permanent change may accompany greater stresses. In this work double exposures on the same film though from identically the same position for unstressed and stressed conditions show the doubling of spots.

3. *Peripheral Widening of Spots.* For specimens with a range of grain sizes for which the Debye-Scherrer rings are made up of distinct sharp spots, a very sensitive and accurate method of evaluating distortion is the effect of stress in causing these spots to elongate or blur, and even to fuse together. For this method the back-reflection method has been employed usually so that large specimens may be utilized and high-angle diffraction rings registered. In fatigue studies of metals Gough and Wood derived a formula by which the change in orientation of a reflecting plane may be calculated from the elongation of spots in the peripheral direction. Barrett[1] devised a camera in which specimen and film oscillate together. A band instead of a narrow ring is registered, consisting of a series of rings, laid side by side, each being registered from a slightly different position of the specimen. This greatly enhances the chances of observing blurring and elongation of spots in one or more directions. Figure 333 represents the effect of cold work below the endurance limit for a commercial 2S-O aluminum specimen placed in the Moore rotating-beam fatigue machine. The pattern on the left is for the unstressed specimen; the pattern at the right is for the same specimen after it had withstood 505 million cycles without breaking. Spots have become blurred or elongated in one or more directions, as evidence of cold work *without damage* below the endurance limit. This result is one of many which have led Barrett to conclude that damage is not registered on the x-ray patterns and hence that fatigue failure cannot be safely predicted from evidences only of cold work, which may be actually beneficial. In 1954 no conditions have been found for which x-ray test or any other nondestructive test has proved to be a reliable prediction of fatigue failure.

FIG. 332. Pattern for chilled cast steel, showing internal strain.

Turning to a practical case of fatigue of a different type, from a study covering two years devoted to structural changes in duralumin airplane propellers, typical patterns are selected in Fig. 334 for the alloy in initial condition, after 900 hr use on a plane, and after 1,400 hr. After detailed study on all parts of a blade, the surface area near the hub, which seems to be a focus of component stresses, is located, and a reflection pattern made at different times. The increase in grain size and evidences of dis-

[1] *Metals & Alloys,* **8,** 13 (1937); "Structure of Metals," 2d ed., p. 440. McGraw-Hill Book Company, Inc., New York, 1952.

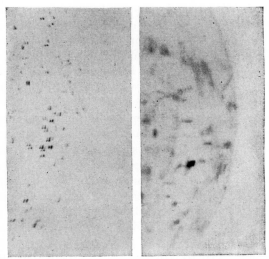

Fig. 333. Patterns by Barrett technique (oscillation of specimen and film, spreading out narrow area into band) for commercial aluminum [Fe *Kα*-radiation; (400) reflection]. *Left*, unstressed; *right*, after fatigue stressing without failure, withstanding 505 million cycles, with structural change due to cold work in safe range of stress. (*Courtesy of Charles S. Barrett.*)

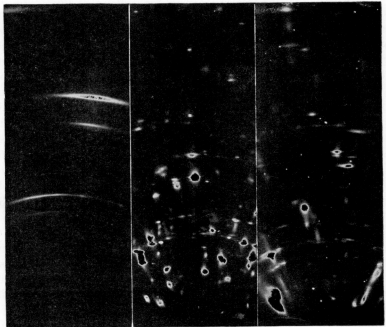

Fig. 334. Patterns for aluminum-alloy airplane propellers. *Left*, unused propeller; *center*, propeller used on airplane after 900 hr flying; *right*, the same after 1,400 hr. Grain growth and distortion with increasing use are indicated.

tortion by vibrational stresses in this age-hardening alloy are self-evident, and failure seems an inevitable result. Improvements in propeller design and in the composition and properties of the alloy within the past few years have greatly reduced such profound and dangerous changes.

In general, there is no difference in the mechanism of deformation of grains whether the deformation is brought about by fatigue stressing in the safe or in the unsafe range or by static loading, such as straight tension. This deformation results from a rotation of parts of a grain with respect to each other about one or more axes. Spot blurring on deformation occurs when a mild-steel bar is stretched until so-called Lüders' lines appear, which are strain bands inclined at 45 deg to the bar axis and made visible by the flaking off of oxide scale. The average plastic extension within the region is about 1.5 per cent. X-ray patterns show a concentration of deformation and pronounced blurring directly on these lines compared with regions between. The technique and theory of measurement of shapes of spots to evaluate radial and tangential broadening are quantitatively developed by Hirsch.[1] The broadening diminishes with time after deformation by rolling.

4. *Fragmentation of Grains.* One of the necessary consequences of stress is a fragmentation of large grains, easily apparent on a series of patterns with increasing stress. This is especially true for rolling deformation. A certain size is evidently required before rotation and slip can proceed. Clark and Beckwith found a periodicity in fragmentation at about each 3.3 per cent reduction, leading finally to preferred orientation of grains. Figure 340 shows how fragmentation proceeds from distinct spots to a nearly smooth series of powder lines. Hirsch and Kellar prove by their microbeam back-reflection technique that when aluminum is cold-rolled the original grains break up into smaller particles, a limiting size of 2 μ being reached after 10 per cent reductions. With this decrease in size there is an increase in misorientation for the original sharp spots spread into areas. If γ is the angle subtended by the arc at the center of the ring and β is the maximum angle between normals of the reflecting planes of two particles in the grain, $\sin \frac{1}{2}\beta = \cos \Theta \sin \frac{1}{2}\gamma$. The total range of misorientations in the original grain runs from 4 deg for 1.3 per cent reduction to 16 deg for 57 per cent reduction.

5. *Displacement of Debye-Scherrer Interferences.* In the case of a homogeneous elastic deformation applied to specially prepared specimens so that over many crystals there is a uniform displacement of atoms out of their normal positions in the lattice, the direction of the x-ray interferences is changed and the lines are shifted in position while remaining essentially unchanged in sharpness. The amount of displacement is proportional to the elastic stress. For this work where utmost precision is

[1] *Acta Cryst.*, **5**, 16 (1952).

required to detect the very small changes, the back-reflection method must be used. For an iron or steel specimen under stress, gold foil is closely attached to the surface or gold paint spread on it so that the gold interferences may serve as a standard of calibration.

Back-reflection interferences and x-ray wavelengths are chosen for planes as nearly as possible parallel to the surface, as follows:

Radiation	Specimen	Planes	θ
Co $K\alpha$	Fe or steel	310	80°37.5′
Cu $K\alpha$	Al	511	81°
Co $K\alpha$	Cu	400	81°46.5′
Co $K\alpha$	Brass, 68% Cu	400	75°30′ below the elastic limit
Ni $K\alpha$	Brass, cartridge	331	79°
Fe $K\alpha$	Mg	405	83°

A few of the fundamental equations for stress measurement by x-rays are as follows:

1. Strain $\epsilon = \dfrac{\Delta l}{l}$, where Δl is the change in length of a line in a stressed body having original length l.

2. Hooke's law $\epsilon = \dfrac{\sigma \text{ (stress)}}{E \text{ (Young's modulus) } (21{,}000 \text{ kg/mm}^2 \text{ for iron)}}$

3. Apply tension σ_x in X direction to isotropic body, then

$$-\epsilon_y = -\epsilon_z = \nu\epsilon_x = \nu\frac{\sigma_x}{E}$$

where $-$ signs denote contraction and ν is Poisson's ratio (0.28 for iron).

4. Sum of principal stresses in plane of a surface

$$\sigma_1 + \sigma_2 = \frac{-E}{\nu}\frac{d_\perp - d_0}{d_0}$$

where d_0 is the unstressed value of the atomic planes lying parallel to the surface and $d_\perp$ is the value after stress (both measured with high precision from back-reflection patterns).

5. σ_ϕ (in any direction) $= \dfrac{d_\psi - d_\perp}{d_\perp}\dfrac{E}{1 + \nu}\dfrac{1}{\sin^2 \psi}$, where d_ψ is the spacing in direction ψ, requiring two x-ray exposures, one perpendicular to the surface, and one inclined in the plane of the normal and the component σ_ϕ. These techniques and others are discussed in detail in Barrett's "Structure of Metals," second edition Chap. 14.

The change in lattice constant a with that in the radius of the Debye-Scherrer ring r is given by the equation

$$\frac{da}{dr} = \frac{a}{2A} \cot \theta \cos^2 2\theta$$

where A is the distance from specimen to film. Extensive measurements have been made by Dehlinger and Glocker,[1] by whom the theory and equations have been developed. From line shifts, measurement can be made of the total or directional stresses, as follows: With $2r = 50.0$ mm, for a gold diffraction ring as standard, a $\frac{1}{10}$-mm. shift of the line of the stressed material means the following changes in lattice constants and stress:

Metal	Radiation	Change in lattice constant, A	Change in single stress, kg/mm²	Stress sum, kg/mm²
Al....................	Cu	0.000461	0.94	2.41
Duralumin.............	Cu	0.000426	0.91	2.30
Fe....................	Co	0.000349	3.04	9.18
Cu....................	Co	0.000397	1.60	4.04
α-Brass..............	Co	0.000603	1.47	4.21

6. Broadening of Debye-Scherrer Interferences. Under the more usual conditions in which lattice stresses are not so uniformly applied as in bending so that different parts of the volume through which x-rays pass have different changes in lattice constants, the line is broadened rather than displaced. This effect is, therefore, the same as that which resides in diffraction by colloidal crystals. A consequent effect is the fusion of $K\alpha$-doublet lines into an unresolved broad interference. This effect and the experimental differentiation between size and strain broadening were discussed in the preceding chapter.

7. Increase in Background Fogging. Strained specimens tend to scatter x-rays to a greater degree than normal lattices. If less than half the atoms in a stressed specimen are displaced from normal positions, the interference line will not broaden but the scattering increases at the expense of interference intensity. This has the same effect as scattering by amorphous material, as discussed in Chap. 21.

8. Decrease in Intensities of Interferences. A more nearly quantitative method of measuring internal strain is concerned with the diminution in intensity of lines, particularly at large angles (high orders). Hengstenberg[2] made an investigation of KCl crystals, with the interesting results shown in Fig. 335 for intensity changes for 6 00, 8 00, and 10 00 reflec-

---

[1] Glocker, "Materialprüfung mit Röntgenstrahlen," 2d ed., p. 304, Springer-Verlag, OHG, Berlin, 1936. The most productive work on stress analysis has continued at Stuttgart with the following papers in 1950–1952: A. Schaal, Z. Metallkunde, **41**, 293 (1950), **42**, 271 (1951); R. Glocker, Z. Metallkunde, **42**, 122 (1951); Z. angew. Phys., **3**, 212 (1951); R. Glocker and E. Mačherauch, Z. Metallkunde, **43**, 313 (1952); G. Frohnmeyer, Z. Naturforsch., **6a**, 319 (1951); G. Frohnmeyer and E. G. Hofmann, Z. Metallkunde, **43**, 151 (1952).

[2] "Fortschritte der Röntgenforschung," p. 139, 1931.

tions. Such relationships have been observed qualitatively also for cold-worked and annealed metals, the ratio I_{200}/I_{400}, for example, being much greater for the cold-worked specimens.

9. *Fibering.* A final consequence of a unidirectional stress of sufficient magnitude is to align favorably sized grains in a preferred orientation or fiber structure (Fig. 255). The interpretation of such patterns is considered in the next section.

The Meaning of Strain. The exact mechanism involved in strain and the whole process of plastic deformation of metals is still not well understood though the development of the theory of dislocations has been a

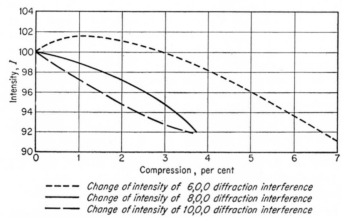

FIG. 335. Changes in intensity of high-order reflections with deforming force. (*Hengstenberg.*)

powerful aid. It is to be distinguished clearly from the effect of a uniform deforming force which produces slipping on lattice planes. Hengstenberg has calculated for the condition of strain that, for a certain degree of deformation of 4 per cent change in length of an edge parallel to the direction of compression, 3 per cent of the atoms are displaced from their normal positions to a maximum of one-eighth the distance between atoms. Strain must represent a condition of localized failure on the glide planes. In contrast to this irregularly distributed strain, plastic deforming forces on the surfaces of whole glide blocks do not change the lattice constants. The high-order lines remain perfectly sharp, so that the $K\alpha$ doublet is perfectly resolved. Consequently, whole blocks of the crystal at least 600 A in dimensions must slip relative to each other, since deviations of the lattice constant of only 0.5 per cent or the formation of glide blocks smaller than 600 A would cause inevitably an increase in breadth of the diffraction lines.

Lattice distortion can be produced not only by mechanical deformation but also by the introduction of foreign atoms which form solid solutions.

These effects may be expressed quantitatively by the intensity changes, as has been done by Hengstenberg. The intensity of a mixed crystal reflection according to Laue is

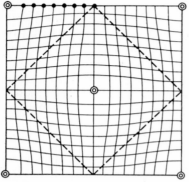

• *Atoms of dissolving substance*
◎ *Atoms of dissolved substance*

FIG. 336. Distortion of lattice by introduction of foreign atoms.

$$\Psi^2 \sim (p_1\Psi_1 + p_2\Psi_2)^2$$

(pure crystal $\Psi^2 \sim \Psi_1^2$), where p is the atomic per cent of each component and Ψ is the scattering power of the atoms, which is proportional to the atomic number at reflection angle 0. This expression has been experimentally verified for silver-gold alloys. The fact that all the diffraction interferences varied in intensity in the same way as compared with pure silver proved conclusively that gold atoms of about the same size as silver atoms had negligible distorting effect in the silver lattice.

An opposite effect is characteristic of mixed crystals with lattice distortion, such as duralumin.   The intensity data are as follows:

Quenched: $(p_1\Psi_1 + p_2\Psi_2)^2 = (0.02 \times 20 + 0.98 \times 13)^2 = 177.7$
  (copper 2 atomic per cent)
Tempered: $(p_1\Psi_1)^2 \qquad = (0.949 \times 13)^2 = 161.0$
  (CuAl$_2$ separated)

The 111 and 200 reflections for the quenched duralumin are actually more intense in the proportion above, but with increasing diffraction angle the ratio diminishes, and for (420) reflections the intensity is 10 per cent smaller. The explanation is to be found in lattice distortion, as exemplified in Fig. 336, caused by the presence of copper atoms in the aluminum lattice.

The Mechanism of Plastic Deformation. The properties of metals that permit plastic deformation under the stresses of shearing, drawing, rolling, forging, compression, torsion, etc., are the basis of all commercial processes of fabrication. It is of the greatest importance, therefore, to have some knowledge of the mechanism by which deformation and extension take place. Plastic deformation in a crystal occurs by the movement of the lamellae over one another. The displacement takes place along a specific crystallographic plane, called a slip plane, and in a definite crystallographic direction, called the slip direction. A detailed knowledge of the mechanism is necessary for an understanding of plastic flow, and subsequent strain hardening, cold work, and preferred orientations. From *electron microscope measurements on single crystals of aluminum,* the region in which displacement occurs is not over 50 A in thickness, and the neighboring slip lines appear to be separated by a distance of about 200 A in highly strained material. Apparently in most cases the blocks about 200 A in width are displaced more or less rigidly relative to the slip planes without undergoing internal plastic flow.[1]

The shearing stress required to produce plastic strain increases with increasing strain. This phenomenon of work hardening or cold-working implies that the strain produced by plastic flow decreases the ease with which further flow may be achieved. The work of Averbach and Warren on line breadths and shapes has proved that the principal effect of cold work is to reduce the size of the coherent domain to much smaller dimensions, but still large compared with atomic dimensions. All experiments are consistent with the association of the mechanism of plastic flow with one or more types of imperfection in the lattice which permit inelastic displacement at highly localized regions for stresses far lower than would be the case if the strain occurred homogeneously. It is necessary that at least one of the imperfections which plays a role in plastic flow can move from one region of the crystal to another, inducing strain within regions which were initially perfect. The fact that the size of coherent domains can be reduced at least by a factor of 10 during plastic flow proves that the imperfection is able to move through distances of the order of magnitude of the initial dimensions of the mosaic blocks of which, with few exceptions, real crystals consist. This imperfection moves through the lattice as a phase pattern of displacement somewhat in the manner in which a sound wave passes through a medium. The requirements are that it must produce slip; it must be able to move for stresses which are very small compared with those needed to produce an elastic strain near unity, and yet the ease of motion must be strongly affected by the presence of minor impurities; it must by its presence decrease the size of the coherent domain of a mosaic block; in brief, it must account for the observed properties of plastic flow of single crystals.[2] Such is the background of the *theory of dislocations* discussed in a subsequent section of this chapter.

The single crystal subjected to the tensile test is obviously the most direct method of evaluating fundamentally the processes involved in elastic behavior, plastic yielding, deformation, and rupture. The results on the far more common polycrystalline metals differ in that the test on these materials is the summation of the behavior of individual grains and grain boundaries such that the specimen reacts as an isotropic material and the deformation is governed by the applied stress system, which

[1] The most complete coverage of the topic of plastic deformation of crystalline solids is the symposium held at the Mellon Institute, May, 1950, Navexos—P—834, published by the U.S. Department of Commerce, Office of Technical Services.

[2] From F. Seitz, The Theory of Plastic Flow in Single Crystals, the first paper of the symposium held at the Mellon Institute, May, 1950, Navexos—P—834, p. 1, published by the U.S. Department of Commerce, Office of Technical Services.

results in inhomogeneous strain that varies from grain to grain, and from point to point within a grain, and which is considerably more difficult to deal with satisfactorily. A complete analysis of the behavior of a poly-crystalline aggregate in terms of the single crystal would involve an understanding of the mutual effects of neighboring crystals, since effects seem to occur near the boundaries which cannot be foreseen from the behavior of single crystals.[1] It is obvious that further refinements in microdiffraction techniques are required for a better understanding of these effects. The single crystal, however, behaves anisotropically, or

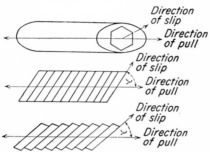

FIG. 337. Mechanism of deformation of zinc.

entirely differently in one direction from how it behaves in another. Instead of a conical necking and fracture it may neck down to a chisel edge or fracture on a cleavage plane. The lattice geometry rather than the stress is the determining factor. There is the further differ-ence that the single crystal is weaker and under the proper con-ditions far more ductile than the fine-grained aggregate.

The mechanism of plastic deformation is probably most easily exem-plified by the hexagonal close-packed metals such as zinc, cadmium, and magnesium, of which very extensive studies have been made by numerous investigators. In these metals there is only one densest packed plane, the basal plane (0001), so that a crystal may be represented as a pack of cards. It is a general rule that with greatest precision the parallel densest packed planes support slip and the densest packed direction is the direction of slip. Hence, for hexagonal closed-packed metals, (0001) are the slip planes and [2110] the slip direction. Therefore, when the basal planes in zinc are at an angle to the wire axis, a tensile pull stretches the wire by slip along these planes, which tilt still more toward the long axis during extension, as shown in Fig. 337. This causes the wire to stretch out into a thin ribbon, or band, with elliptical cross section. As soon as the angle of these planes reaches 70 to 80 deg, the crystal usually fails by cleavage on the basal or one of the three prismatic planes. If the basal planes are parallel or perpendicular to the axis of the wire and the direction of tensile pull, no slip can occur and the specimen fails by brittle cleavage. Thus plastic deformation can occur only when the basal planes start out a few degrees from parallel or perpendicular position, the latter being best for display of great ductility and elongation. The slip ellipses on the zinc crystal are distinct, and the changing angle of tilt

[1] B. Chalmers, Navexos—P—834, p. 193, U.S. Department of Commerce, Office of Technical Services.

during deformation may be followed optically, but best of all by x-ray patterns. Slip along the (0001) planes is restricted to one of the three diagonal axes such as [1010], and with these three assuming any position in the slip plane the one selected will be that which most closely coincides with the direction of maximum resolved shear or the major axis of the elliptical section. The basal planes tend to rotate about the hexagonal axis so that the slip direction may come into coincidence with the direction of maximum shear, with the result that the cross section widens and becomes eccentric. At the ends of the specimen held in grips this behavior disappears; it is also clear that at a transition zone between grip ends in initial condition and the plastically extended center section the basal planes must be bent through a very considerable angle.

In this whole process, complete correlations have been made with the stress-strain diagrams, for as soon as slip begins, the resistance to further slip increases. After the crystal wire has elongated to a thin elliptical ribbon during primary elongation, it may deform locally in a new place by marked constriction of the ribbon in the direction of the major axis. This results in formation of a fine "after-elongation" cylindrical thread, representing extension of several hundred per cent and a fiftyfold strengthening. Matthewson and Phillips proved that twinning about a pyramidal plane (1012) brings the basal planes into position for slip again.

In face-centered cubic metals, the (111) planes are most densely packed, and upon these slip occurs, the direction being [10$\bar{1}$]. There are four equivalent sets, each with 3 directions along which slip can take place, or 12 directions of slip in all. This starts on one set first, causing rotation of the lattice in order to line up slip planes and directions with the crystal axis or the direction of pull. But this brings another set of the (111) planes into position for slip, with the result that the crystal necks down locally to a chisel-edge fracture.

The body-centered cubic metals such as tungsten, molybdenum, and chromium have low ductility, as might be predicted from their structural geometry. The (110) planes and [111] direction are most densely packed, but the usual predictions on slip are not fulfilled for the plane of slip since this may be (112) or some other plane. Iron is a general exception in this group, but in spite of extensive study the mechanism of deformation is not well understood. This important metal is characterized by curved or wavy slip bands which render identification of the slip planes exceedingly difficult. Thus (110), (112), and (123) singly or in pairs have been reported, with probably best evidence for the last-named.

The foregoing descriptions apply to the gross features of deformation and fabrication of metals, many of which are visible. Barrett in Chap. XV of the second edition of "Structure of Metals" summarizes the very large body of information for single crystals on slip lines, critical resolved shear stress (that at which a crystal will begin to flow at an appreciable rate and below which *creep* occurs), and strain hardening; and for poly-crystalline metals the effect of grain boundaries and grain size on plastic flow and various aspects of strain hardening and the phenomena of creep, twinning, fracture. Attendant upon these are certain microchanges detected usually only by the x-ray pattern as a distortion, the evidences of which (primarily asterism on Laue patterns) have been considered on page 689. By following the changes of individual spots of a Laue pattern it is found that slip in one direction produces a greater change in the lattice in that direction than in other directions. As in bending a mica plate, the metal lattice becomes bent about an axis that lies in the slip plane and at right angles to the direction of slip. Actually the lattice

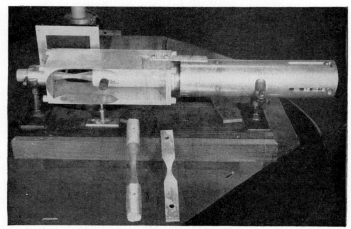

Fig. 338. Tensile apparatus in position on x-ray diffraction unit. (*Clark, Pish, and Seabury.*)

is acting in "blocks" or "fragments," based upon many observations of *"terraced" surfaces* after deformation; but these are curved, the thickness and degree of curvature being consistent with any observed change in spacings for interferences on patterns. This is Polanyi's concept of "flexural slip" (*Biegeleitung*), which in its main features still gives the best explanation of the x-ray evidences of distortion. Thus, though there is a remarkable preservation of crystalline structure even in most severe deformations, there is a modification such that motions along slip planes must occur in approximately whole numbers of unit lattice distances and such that the planes are no longer "smooth." From this has arisen in its various aspects the dislocation theory, which is described in the next section to account for strengthening and hardening of metals during cold-working.

Changes in x-ray diffraction patterns of aluminum crystals subjected to tensile deformation are typical. Figure 338 is a photograph of a cali-

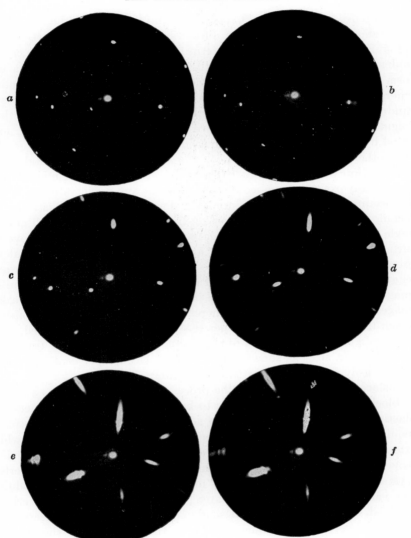

FIG. 339. Patterns for single aluminum crystal under increasing stress in apparatus shown in Fig. 338.

Pattern	Stress, psi	Elongation, per cent
a	0	0
b	3,000	0.8
c	6,000	2.67
d	9,000	7.5
e	12,000	25.0
f	After fracture	—

brated tensile apparatus, of Clark, Pish, and Seabury, for heavier specimens shown in position on the diffraction unit for back-reflection patterns; Fig. 339 shows selected patterns for the behavior of a single crystal
under increasing loads; Fig. 340, the characteristic behavior for a uniform polycrystalline sample. Fragmentation as indicated by the gradual
emergence of smooth Debye-Scherrer rings from a pattern of spots at
random with increasing stress is particularly striking. Rotation of these
fragments with still greater stress results in preferred orientation, indicated by localized intensity maxima on the rings.

Another technique for indicating the changes in metal crystals upon
deformation was proposed in 1945 by Barrett as a kind of microscopy.[1]
From many examples applied to single crystals and polycrystalline metals
one example is selected. Figure 341a diagrammatically illustrates the
technique, which consists in directing the x-ray beam at a small grazing
angle on the surface of the specimen, while the film is arranged above the
surface, as shown, so as to register any beams reflected by grains at the
proper Bragg angle with respect to the incident beams of given wavelength. For an entirely unstrained material there will appear magnified
images of these grains (the greatly inclined reflections produce streaked
images) as in Fig. 341b for commercial aluminum strip electropolished.
When the strip is elongated 20 per cent and again electropolished, these
uniform grain images break up into an intricate array of fragments
(0.005 mm in size) as shown in Fig. 341c. Even 1 per cent elongation
shows easily apparent distortion of the internal structure.

Dislocation Theory. While the process of slip in crystals as a gliding
of blocks over one another seems to be a simple visible phenomenon of
plastic flow, actually it is far from adequate to account for the stresses
required for flow and for the effects such as strain hardening which
attend plastic deformation. The amount of shear stress required to
move by elastic displacement one plane of atoms over another in a perfect
crystal can be easily calculated by multiplying shear by shear modulus.
The value is 10^3 to 10^4 times greater than the actually observed critical
resolved sheer stress for slip in single crystals. This great discrepancy
between theory and experiment has been the challenge for the development of adequate theories. The early theories based upon stress concentrations at loci of submicroscopic cracks and lattice flaws proved to be
inadequate to explain many experimental observations, and these were
replaced by the theory of dislocations, starting from very simple pictures
and expanding into a complex ramification of correlations of flow and
other characteristics of metals. It has proved to be fruitful to such an
extent that it is generally accepted as an explanation of the low yield
strength of metals.

[1] C. S. Barrett, *AIME Tech. Publs.* 1865; *Metals Technol.*, April, 1945.

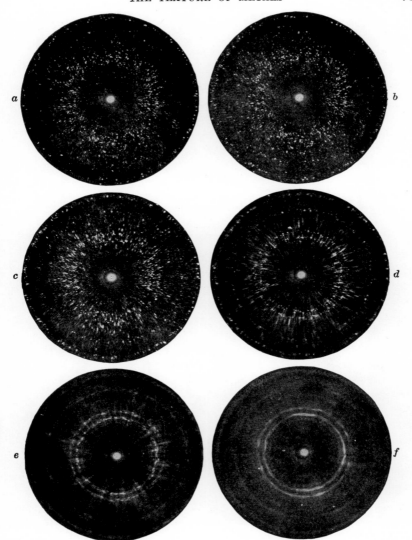

Fig. 340. Patterns for aluminum-sheet specimen with uniform small grains subjected to increasing tensile stress.

Pattern	Stress, psi	Elongation, per cent
a	0	0
b	3,000	0.5
c	6,000	1.0
d	9,000	3.2
e	12,000	10.0
f	After fracture	—

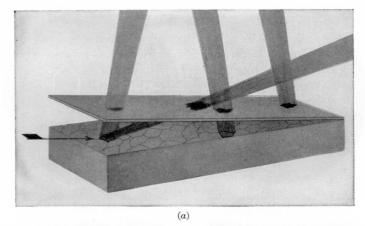

(a)

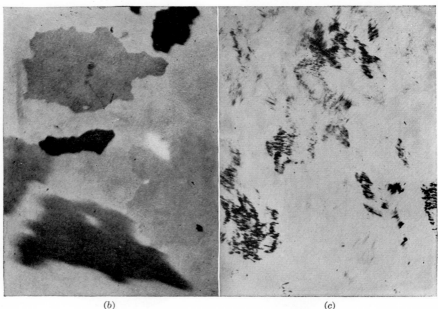

(b)   (c)

FIG. 341. (a) Barrett diffraction microscope technique for enlarging grain images. (b) Patterns by Barrett technique of polycrystalline aluminum before application of tensile stress, showing enlarged unstrained grains. (c) Patterns by Barrett technique of polycrystalline aluminum after elongation, showing sensitive detection of strain.

First of all an understanding of the elastic limit is gained by reference to the stress-strain curve for pure copper, in Fig. 342, for example. For carefully annealed copper single crystals, which at first are so soft that they bend by their own weight, a very small force causes a yield or permanent deformation. On the curve there is first a reversible, nearly vertical elastic range OA, which means that when the stress below A is removed, the specimen returns completely to its original dimensions and x-ray patterns are indistinguishable from that of the original unstressed crystal. At A, the elastic limit is reached, and beyond this point as stress is increased the metal begins to yield, reversibility is lost, and a permanent deformation is found if the stress is removed. The specimen becomes stronger the greater the deformation—in other words, greater and greater stress is needed to produce further equal increments in strain measured by per cent extension. Thus at point B if the stress is removed there is a much longer elastic range BO', and the properties of the metal in this state are represented by a curve beginning with O'. Finally fracture occurs at C. X-ray patterns at O' indicate blurred spots instead of the sharp spots at O. As a rough beginning picture it may be assumed that

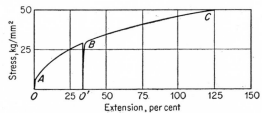

FIG. 342. Stress-strain curve for pure copper.

the initial perfect crystal is broken up into a mosaic of blocks slightly displaced with respect to each other (a condition proved and quantitatively measured in the 1952 papers of Hirsch[1]).

In the words of Sir Lawrence Bragg,[2] who has contributed so greatly to the theory of the metallic state and to clear exposition of this by means of familiar pictures:

In the initial annealed state, there are large regions of highly perfect crystalline structure in the metal. When slip occurs, it runs for long distances, the parameter we have called t being large, and the yield point is low. But this very act of yielding creates dislocations, which form new interfaces where differently orientated mosaic fragments meet. It is like a large ice floe, smooth and perfect when first formed, which under the action of winds and currents acquires ridges of fragments running across it in all directions which break it up into a mosaic such as we see in polar photographs. The parameter t diminishes and the crystal becomes stronger. At the same time the interfaces are centers of highly localized strain, in which the energy of cold-work resides. As deformation proceeds, the mosaic elements yield one after another with a "scrunch" along a plane of slip where the atoms move on one each time. The largest elements are the weakest and yield first. The process cannot be carried on beyond a certain limit, because of the recrystallizing power of the metal. However much cold-work is put into the metal, a limiting amount only can be retained. This corresponds to the crystal structure being broken into fragments of limiting small size, fitting as unconformably to each other as is possible geometrically. When this

[1] *Acta Cryst.*, **5**, 16, 162, 172 (1952).

[2] W. L. Bragg, Some Problems of the Metallic State, *Trans. North East Coast Inst. Engrs. & Shipbuilders*, **62** (Nov. 2, 1945); *Proc. Cambridge Phil. Soc.*, **45**, 125 (1949).

limit is reached, the elastic limit of the metal is determined approximately by an expression ns/t, where n is the rigidity modulus, s the distance between neighboring atoms, and t the average range over which each event of gliding can run.

The idea of "dislocation," mentioned above, was first presented in detail by G. I. Taylor,[1] with contributions also by Orowan[2] and Polanyi.[3] Taylor considered slip to take place by the movement of a line dislocation across a slip plane. A dislocation is a place where there is an excess or defect of one atom in each row above the plane in which it occurs, as compared with those below this plane. By compression, for example, an extra atom might be pushed into a row above the line of demarcation. If the dislocation starts at one side of a crystal and runs across to the other, the final result will be a shear in either the positive or the negative direction of one part of the crystal by one interatomic distance relative to the other part. If a single dislocation occurs in an otherwise perfect crystal subject to no constraints, a vanishingly small force will cause it to run in one direction or the other. The presence of other dislocations or faults in the structure, however, sets up strains which act as barriers to the run of a dislocation, and an external stress is necessary to enable the dislocation to move through them, so that a definite elastic limit is attained. By means of the line broadening in cold-worked metals Bragg was able to calculate limiting shear strain and thus ultimate shear strengths, from $T > \mu s/t$ $[1.46 \log_{10}(t/s) + 0.6]$, where μ is the modulus of rigidity, which are in reasonable agreement with experiment. By the microbeam technique already referred to, Hirsch[4] was able to calculate for cold-worked aluminum 10^{10} dislocations per square centimeter in the boundaries between particles after proof that the particles are distorted (by elastic bending) as well as fragmented to a limiting size to account for line broadening rather than merely by size. The number of dislocations is calculated on the basis that the boundary between two particles may be considered as a row, or wall, of edge dislocations. If s is the unit of slip (the interplanar distance), h the spacing of dislocations, and α the angle between neighboring particles, $\alpha = s/h$; if $\alpha = 2$ deg and $s = 2.3 \times 10^{-8}$ (the 110 spacing of aluminum), then

$$h = 0.5 \times 10^{-6} \text{ cm}$$

if t = particle size, the number of dislocations per boundary is t/h, or the density of dislocations in the boundaries is $(t/h)(1/t^2) = 1/ht$; and since $t = 2 \times 10^{-4}$, this density is 10^{+10} dislocations per square centimeter, with very few excess dislocations inside the particle.

Since the original "Taylor," or "edge," dislocation, which extends

[1] G. I. Taylor, *Proc. Roy. Soc. (London)*, **A145**, 362 (1934).

[2] E. Orowan, *Z. Physik*, **89**, 634 (1934).

[3] M. Polanyi, *Z. Physik*, **89**, 660 (1934).

[4] P. B. Hirsch, *Acta Cryst.*, **5**, 172 (1952).

perpendicular to the displacement, there have been several additions to the theory, such as "Burger's," or screw, dislocations when the displacement is parallel to the line of dislocation, "Shockey," or partial, dislocations, "Frank," or sessile, dislocations, which do not move in response to applied stress, and many other variations. For example, emerging from a surface of the crystal, an edge dislocation leaves a step that is one interatomic distance high. Since visible slip lines are thousands of times larger than this, a mechanism is necessary for sending a succession of dislocations after one another across the slip plane and many theories have been proposed, as they have been for strain hardening, age-hardening, segregation at dislocations, models of grain boundaries and subboundaries, and the relationship between dislocations and lattice vacancies or interstitial atoms. As Barrett has indicated, two edge dislocations of opposite sign on the same slip plane coming together will destroy each other, leaving a perfect crystal, whereas if they approach on adjacent slip planes and overlap, an extra row of interstitial atoms will be left, or if they combine when separated by a gap, a row of vacant lattice sites will be left. The theory of dislocations is still so decidedly in the formative stage that future developments must be awaited for an adequate explanation of many unanswered questions concerning deformation of metals.

However, in an exposition without a single mathematical equation, Slater describes and interprets the damage to metals by high-energy radiations, a matter of vital importance in atomic-energy developments, as involving dislocations inhibiting shearing deformation, and therefore having an effect similar to cold work. It is an experimental fact that materials such as aluminum which anneal at room temperature show practically no observable effects of radiation, whereas copper, which does not anneal, shows hardening under irradiation comparable with the maximum change induced by cold work. Similarly the ordered (super-lattice) alloy Cu_3Au is disordered and the Be-Cu alloy is hardened by precipitation upon irradiation.[1]

That dislocations play an essential role in crystal growth also is demonstrated by Verma.[2] Formerly growth of a crystal from solution was conceived to take place in layers. First, a nucleus forms on a flat, presumably perfect, crystal face and then completion of the layer is achieved by lateral growth on the nucleus. One nucleus would be required for each layer deposited, so the ease of nucleation would be the rate-controlling process. However, the observed rates of growth from solution or vapor do not agree with these assumptions, for if a nucleus of critical size must form before each layer can be deposited, growth rates must be prohibitively small. With a screw dislocation pres-

[1] J. C. Slater, The Effects of Radiation in Materials, *J. Appl. Phys.*, **22**, 237 (1951).
[2] A. R. Verma, "Crystal Growth and Dislocations," Academic Press, Inc., New York, 1954.

ent in the lattice, it is no longer necessary to nucleate each layer, for now there is always a wedge-shaped step in the surface which persists as growth proceeds. This step provides a place of easy attachment for depositing atoms and growth consists of a rotation of the wedge step about its apex at the center of the screw dislocation. Since all parts of the step grow at the same linear rate and one end is fixed, the step develops into a spiral ramp which is microscopically observable as a growth spiral.

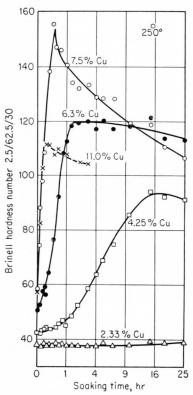

FIG. 343. Curves showing age-hardening of copper-silver alloys.

Age-hardening. Several alloy systems, notably Al-Cu-Si (duralumin), Au-Cu (intermediate state of AuCu), Ag-Cu, Cu-Be, Cu-Fe, low-carbon (armco) iron, etc., are characterized by hardening with time after a heat-treatment. Figure 343 shows the variation of hardness with time of mixed crystals of silver and copper as measured by Agnew, Hanan, and Sachs.[1] The alloy was quenched from 770°C and then held at a temperature of 250°C. This age-hardening has great technical significance, since an alloy may be fabricated while in easily worked condition and then the product subsequently hardened with aging. Difficulties are, of course, encountered even at room temperatures; for example, if steel sheets are not used for a considerable period after manufacture, they will form far less easily. The phenomenon of age-hardening therefore has been subjected to numerous investigations. If gold-copper mixed crystals containing about 50 atomic per cent gold with entirely random distribution of atoms above 425° are cooled, an intermediate state can be observed from x-ray patterns. The unit cell has the tetragonal form (AuCu) of the final equilibrium state, but in a part of the lattice the copper and gold atoms have definite arrangement and in the remainder are completely random. This inhomogeneous irregularity is to be distinguished from the true homogeneous substitutional solid-solution type. The intermediate state is characterized by great hardness. By long heating under 428° the much softer, entirely definitely arranged tetrag-

[1] Z. Physik, **66**, 350 (1930).

onal state is reached. Mild steel hardening may be due to Fe_4N, FeO, Fe_3C, AlN (in the presence of a trace of aluminum). Diffraction lines for $CuAl_2$ have been observed after long heat-treatment of duralumin. The theory of hardness has been based on the conception of separation of very small colloidal particles which tend to key slip on planes. However, newer x-ray researches seem to demonstrate that at the point of greatest hardness no new lattice is necessarily observed. There may be a slight broadening of x-ray lines, such as might be produced in very slight deformation, but no change in lattice dimension of the old lattice is observed, as ought to be expected from concentration changes, due to separation of a new phase. Upon the basis of magnetic measurements

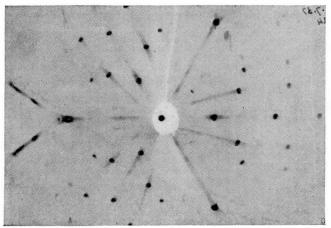

FIG. 344. Laue pattern showing definite effects (satellite streaks) of age-hardening of aluminum alloy. (*Preston.*)

on copper-iron specimens Tammann presented the hypothesis that, before the separation of a new phase, some kind of grouping within the coherent old lattice of the chemically different atoms occurs which in an unknown manner causes increase in hardness. This agrees with the actual observation of inhomogeneous atomic distribution in the intermediate state of AuCu and with the more recent observations on duralumin at maximum hardness by Preston.[1] The interpretation of diffuse and distorted interferences on x-ray patterns is given in Chap. 15.

In this x-ray investigation with single crystals of Al-Cu-alloy compared with pure aluminum, age-hardening is accompanied, before the slightest evidence of $CuAl_2$ precipitation, by the appearance of satellite streaks resolved into spots diverging to larger angles from each Laue spot (see Fig. 344). These effects are theoretically reproduced by a simple model of a pair of crossed gratings in two dimensions, which leads to the conclusion that age-hardening is associated with the segregation of

[1] *Proc. Royal Soc. (London)*, **167**, 526 (1938).

copper atoms on the 100 planes of the crystal, the quantity still being insufficient to precipitate $CuAl_2$ as a separate phase. Figures 228 and 229 also indicate "Preston" spots due to thermal effects on lattices.

THE X-RAY ANALYSIS OF FIBER DIAGRAMS AS RELATED TO THE FABRICATION OF METALS AND ALLOYS

1. Fiber Diagrams. It is now a familiar fact that metal powders or random aggregates yield pinhole diffraction patterns on flat photographic films consisting of concentric uniformly intense rings. Whenever a piece of drawn wire or thin rolled foil is used as a specimen, perpendicular to the primary beam, the diffraction rings are very intense in localized intensity maxima as though more crystal grains are contributing reflection effects in certain directions, whereas in other positions few, if any, crystal grains are available for reflection and there is little or no blackening on the film. Thus the rings observed for random arrangement of grains become series of symmetrical segments in the case of directed or preferred orientation. This type of pattern for worked metals, generally designated a fiber diagram, has been illustrated in Fig. 255 for aluminum wire and Fig. 345 for aluminum sheet.

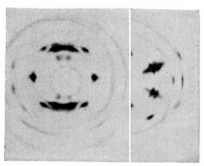

FIG. 345. Diffraction patterns for cold-rolled aluminum foil, showing fibering or preferred orientation. *Left*, x-ray beam perpendicular to rolling direction; *right*, beam parallel to rolling direction.

Drawn wires and rolled sheets represent different types of preferred orientation. In wires the same pattern is obtained with any orientation as long as the x-ray beam passes perpendicular to the wire axis, whereas in rolled sheets different-appearing fiber patterns are obtained with the beam perpendicular or parallel to the rolling plane.

These are fiber structures in the same sense as cellulose, stretched rubber, or asbestos fiber. None of these materials is a single crystal; all are built up of many crystal grains, but these are arranged so that a definite crystallographic axis is parallel to the axis of the fiber. In an aluminum wire that has not been annealed after drawing, the x-ray pattern demonstrates that the body diagonals, or [111] direction, in all the grains, each of which is a single crystal built up from unit face-centered cubes, lie parallel to the wire axis. Evidently, therefore, this common orientation has been induced in the process of mechanical working; the particular position is evidently that which will present maximum resistance to further deformation. It will be noted that no other limitation has been put on preferred orientation in an aluminum wire, for example, than that the

[111] direction is parallel to the wire axis, or direction of drawing. Hence any grain may be turned anywhere through 360 deg around a body diagonal as an axis and still fulfill conditions, and thus the outer form of grains in the wire may appear perfectly irregular with any kind of face in the surface. Herein lies the difference in the orientation of grains in a rolled sheet or foil, for in this case a definite crystallographic direction lies parallel to the direction of rolling *and*, *also*, a definite crystallographic plane in all the crystal grains lies parallel to the plane of rolling. For example, in strongly rolled iron or steel a *face* diagonal [110] direction lies parallel to the direction of rolling, and a cube face parallel to the plane of rolling. On account of this added limitation in rolled structure, which does not apply in drawn wires or complete fiber structure, this is called limited fiber structure.

In the foregoing discussion ideal cases of exact arrangements have been implied. In practice these cases are never realized, since the orientations are never perfect, though the greater the deforming force, the more nearly do the grain positions approach the ideal. As will become apparent, it is possible to determine from the x-ray patterns the departures from limiting ideal orientations.

As previously explained, the Laue or monochromatic pinhole method is almost exclusively used in the study of worked metals, since it affords a pattern 360 deg in azimuth. It is necessary only to mount a wire or sheet specimen over the outer pinhole so that the beam will pass perpendicular to the wire axis or rolling direction. The pattern is registered on a flat photographic film.

2. The Interpretation of Complete Fiber Patterns (Drawn Wires). Of first concern is the pattern of the Debye-Scherrer rings which defines the particular metal. All the lattice planes with the same lattice spacing d reflect rays on the same diffraction ring, which is continuous in the case of random orientation or segmented into spots or arcs for fibered materials. It is possible to determine the planar indices for each ring, as described in Chap. 15.

Next to be found are the positions of the intensity maxima upon the rings. One of the sets of parallel reflecting planes may be imagined rotated 360 deg around an axis perpendicular to the primary x-ray beam. In the course of this rotation it will pass four times through the proper angle for reflection in accordance with Bragg's law and produce upon a photographic plate placed behind the specimen a four-point pattern which is symmetrical with respect to a vertical line on the plate parallel to the rotation or fiber axis and also with respect to a horizontal line. In other words, these maxima are, for example, at the clock hour-hand positions of 1:30, 4:30, 7:30, and 10:30 (see Fig. 346). If this particular reflecting plane in a special case is parallel to the axis of rotation (or fiber axis), then only two spots are produced on the ring on the horizontal line (three and nine o'clock). No reflection occurs, of course, if this plane is exactly perpendicular to the rotation axis. Two spots occur on the vertical line (twelve and six o'clock) if the angle of the reflecting plane with respect to the rotation (fiber) axis is equal to the angle of incidence of the x-ray beam. It is at once clear, therefore, that the positions of intensity maxima on a given ring on the photographic plate may be measured and used directly to deduce the positions of lattice planes in the wire in a very simple manner. If α is the angle between the normal to the set of reflecting planes and the rotation (fiber) axis and δ is the angle measured on

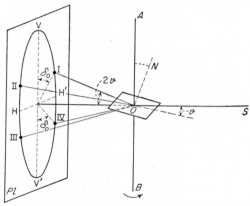

Fig. 346. Analysis of the ideal four-point fiber diagram, with x-ray beam perpendicular to the fiber axis. SO, x-ray beam; AB, fiber axis.

the film between a radius drawn through a particular intensity maximum and the vertical line VV' (which is known to be parallel to the rotation or fiber axis), then

$$\cos \delta = \frac{\cos \alpha}{\cos \Theta}$$

where Θ is the angle of incidence. At small reflection angles, such as are true for the most important diffraction circles for metals, $\cos \Theta$ is approximately 1. Hence $\delta = \alpha$. Thus a simple angle measurement on the film is also the value for the angle between the normal to a set of reflecting planes and the fiber axis.

In any cubic lattice the angle between the fiber axis with indices uvw and a lattice plane hkl is given by

$$\cos \alpha = \frac{uh + vk + lw}{\sqrt{u^2 + v^2 + w^2} \sqrt{h^2 + k^2 + l^2}}$$

In aluminum wire the [111] direction is the fiber axis. The innermost ring registers the reflection from all the octahedral planes (111), ($\bar{1}$11), ($1\bar{1}$1), ($\bar{1}\bar{1}$1) and the other four parallel to these. Hence α, and consequently δ, on the film will be 0 deg for (111), which means that the (111) planes are perpendicular to the fiber axis [111] (as by definition) and cannot reflect. For the others α = 71 deg = δ (see Fig. 347).

Further data for aluminum wire calculated in this way are presented in Table 22-1.

Since there is agreement between the calculated positions and those found experimentally for drawn aluminum (Fig. 255), the assumption of the [111] fiber axis is correct and the wire structure may be represented as shown in Fig. 348, with the unit crystal cubes oriented with cube diagonals parallel to the wire axis, but at random around these diagonals as axes.

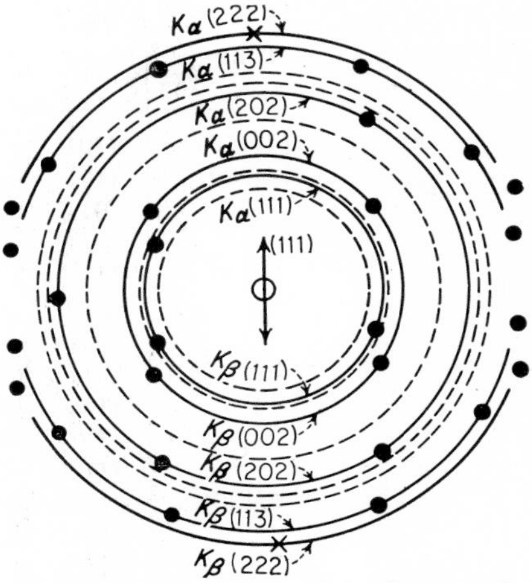

For body-centered cubic wires like iron the assumption may be

Fig. 347. Theoretical fiber diagram for aluminum wire with [111] parallel to wire axis.

made that the [110] direction is parallel to the wire axis, and this is then tested as in Table 22-2.

As a matter of fact, the intensity maxima lying on the Debye-Scherrer rings are not sharp spots but are really arcs of 10 deg in cases of extreme cold work or more (Fig. 349). This means, of course, that all the crystal

TABLE 22-1. ANALYSIS OF FIBER PATTERN OF ALUMINUM WIRE
(FACE-CENTERED CUBIC)

Ring number	Planes	Number cooperating	α, deg
⎰1(111) ⎱5(222)	(1̄11) (11̄1) (111̄)	6	71
⎰2(200) ⎱6(400)	(100) (010) (001)	6	55
3(220)	(110) (101) (011)	6	35
	(1̄10) (1̄01) (01̄1)	6	90
4(113)	113, etc.	6	30
	1̄13, etc.	12	59
	113̄, etc.	6	80

TABLE 22-2. ANALYSIS OF FIBER PATTERN OF IRON WIRE
(BODY-CENTERED CUBIC)

Ring	Planes	Number cooperating	α, deg
$\begin{cases} 1(110) \\ 4(220) \end{cases}$	(101) (10$\bar{1}$) (011) (01$\bar{1}$)	8	60
2(200)	(100) (010)	4	45
	(001)	2	90
3(112)	(211), (121), etc.	8	30
	(112), (11$\bar{2}$), etc.	4	55
	(2$\bar{1}$1), ($\bar{1}$21), etc.	8	73
	(1$\bar{1}$2), ($\bar{1}$12), etc.	4	90
5(130)	(130), (310), etc.	4	27
	(301), (031), etc.	4	48
	($\bar{1}$30), (3$\bar{1}$0), etc.	4	63
	(103), (013), etc.	12	77
6(222)	(111), (11$\bar{1}$)	4	35
	(1$\bar{1}$1), ($\bar{1}$11)	4	90

grains are not perfectly oriented and that there is a "scattering" in a cone around an average or ideal position which is the wire axis itself. The scattering angle or apex of this cone is obviously half the arc length of the intensity maxima. Every possible gradation of preferred orientation may be practically observed in metal specimens from sharp spots to continuous rings for random arrangement. The arc lengths of the maxima are, therefore, a measure of the amount of cold work and

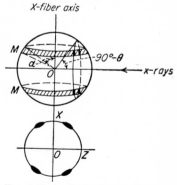

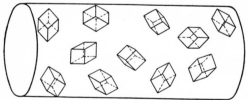

FIG. 348. Diagram showing unit crystal cubes in aluminum wire with cube diagonals parallel to wire axis, but oriented at random around this axis.

FIG. 349. Analysis of true fiber diagram. Compare with ideal four-point diagram in Fig. 346.

preferred orientation or fibering in a given specimen, either directly produced or residual after heat-treatment.

In many cases of examination of fabricated metals it may be impossible or undesirable to orient the specimen with the fiber axis perpendicular to the primary x-ray beam. If, then, the specimen is placed at an oblique angle, a pattern is obtained with exactly the same Debye-Scherrer rings as before but the four-point diagram is changed when two of the points move apart on a ring and the other two together, still retaining symmetry with respect to vertical and horizontal lines on the film. Instead of one angle δ to be measured for the four spots, there are now two angles δ and δ' evaluated by

$$\cos \delta = \frac{\cos \alpha - \cos \beta \sin \Theta}{\sin \beta \cos \Theta}$$

and

$$\cos \delta' = \frac{\cos \alpha - \cos (180° - \beta) \sin \Theta}{\sin (180° - \beta) \cos \Theta}$$

where α is the same as before, β is the angle between the fiber axis and the direction of the primary beam, and Θ is the angle of incidence (Fig. 350).

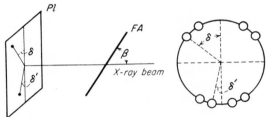

FIG. 350. Effect upon diffraction pattern of tilting fiber axis (FA) at angle β to x-ray beam.

For evaluation of the indices of the fiber axis in a drawn metal, two or three methods are available:

1. Trial-and-failure method by assuming indices, calculating the intensity maxima to be expected on the various rings, as illustrated above for aluminum and iron, and comparing with experimental film.

2. Use of patterns for obliquely oriented fiber axis with a series of values for the angle β. If the crystal-lattice plane perpendicular to the fiber axis (Polanyi's diatropic planes) reflect a beam of wavelength λ incident at the angle Θ, then, when $\beta = 90$ deg $- \Theta$, an intensity maximum will appear at the twelve o'clock position on one of the Debye-Scherrer rings due to (hkl) planes. For cubic crystals the evaluation of the (hkl) indices for the ring upon which the intensity maximum appears gives at once $[hkl]$ the fiber axis, since the normal to these planes is the same as the axis.

3. Sometimes only two or three intensity maxima are necessary to evaluate the fiber axis. Glocker and Kaupp[1] give the example of electrodeposited copper with maxima on the (111) and (200) [or (100), second-order] rings. Since

$$\cos \alpha = \frac{uh + vk + lw}{\sqrt{u^2 + v^2 + w^2} \sqrt{h^2 + k^2 + l^2}}$$

where $[uvw]$ is the fiber axis and (hkl) a set of planes, then for the (111) and (100) planes, respectively,

[1] *Z. Physik*, **24**, 121 (1924).

$$\cos \alpha_1 = \frac{u + v + w}{\sqrt{3}\ \sqrt{u^2 + v^2 + w^2}}$$

$$\cos \alpha_2 = \frac{u}{\sqrt{u^2 + v^2 + w^2}}$$

Intensity maxima appear on both rings at 90 deg; hence $\delta_1 = \alpha_1 = \delta_2 = \alpha_2$; furthermore, substituting the values of $\cos \alpha_1$ and $\cos \alpha_2$, $0 = u + v + w$ and $0 = u$, or $v = -w$. The fiber axis is therefore $[0\bar{1}1]$.

X-ray patterns taken with the beam parallel to the fiber axis are characterized by uniform Debye-Scherrer rings indicative of random orientation.

3. Multiple-fiber Structures in Drawn Wires. Sometimes more than one preferred orientation is observed as a multiple fiber structure. This is true of face-centered cubic metals in which both [111] and [100] directions serve as fiber axes. As indicated in Table 22-3, the distribution of grain orientations between these two varies depending on the metal. The

TABLE 22-3. MULTIPLE-FIBER STRUCTURES IN DRAWN WIRES

Metal wire	Per cent crystals with		Half length of interferences on (200) ring	
	[100]	[111]	[100]	[111]
	Parallel to direction of drawing			
Aluminum........	0	100	. . . .	3°30′
Copper..........	40	60	7°	3°
Gold............	50	50	8°30′	4°30′
Silver..........	75	25	7°30′	3°

presence of a double-fiber structure with varying proportions of each and variations in scattering around a fixed position have great practical significance in differentiating drawing, annealing, and physical properties of aluminum, copper, gold, and silver.

4. The Zonal Structures of Hard-drawn Wires. An interesting structural phenomenon in hard-drawn wires is found in patterns. A beam of monochromatic x-rays is reflected from the surface of a cold-drawn copper wire about 0.5 mm in diameter. The pattern shows a nearly random arrangement of grains in spite of the prediction concerning fibering. The wire is then etched down in successive steps and an x-ray examination made. The structure of the innermost core of the wire is characterized by extreme fibering. Hence, wires drawn through dies have distinctly zonal structures, with the grains becoming more perfectly oriented the nearer to the wire axis considered as a line at the exact center. In other words, in the passage through the die the flow of metal exactly in the direction of drawing occurs only in the middle of the wire, whereas in the walls the metal is flowing inward as well as along the length of the wire and the crystal grains are thus disposed at an angle to the core.

This condition of a central linear zone and a conical mantle, of course, is of primary importance in affecting the texture of the wire and in the proper interpretation of diffraction patterns. Not only does the sharpness of fibering shown by the shorter interference maxima increase as layers are removed, but there is also evidence of unsymmetrical interferences. From these the inclination of the fiber axis [111] to the copper wire axis in different zones is determined as follows:

Distance of layer from center, mm	Inclination angle, deg
1.75 (outer skin)	<2
1.6	9
1.3	6
0.9	4
0.4	0

This indicates that, in the outermost skin of the wire, the effect of the die has been to keep the grains which are oriented nearly parallel to the direction of drawing, but slightly below this the conical flow is evident. The texture of a hard-drawn wire, therefore, may be represented in Fig. 351.

The core zone of a wire has the highest tensile strength in keeping with its parallel preferred orientation. This anisotropic or zonal structure is an inherent property, and improve-

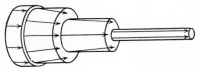

FIG. 351. Zonal texture of hard-drawn wires.

ment in the superficial zones is not gained by increasing the amount of cold work.

5. Summary of X-ray Results on Deformation Structures of Drawn Wires. All body-centered cubic metals when drawn are characterized by a [110] direction parallel to the direction of drawing; all face-centered cubic metals have a [111] direction in the wire axis, with a second orientation of [100], the proportion of crystal grains in the various metals varying as explained above. An exception in the case of copper wire recrystallized at 1000°C has been noted. Only the core of these wires and perhaps the outermost skin approximate these orientations, since in the mantle zones the fiber axis is inclined to the wire axis. In answering the question why a particular crystallographic direction becomes parallel to the direction of deformation it may be noted that the most thickly populated atomic planes in the body-centered cubic lattice are the (111) planes, with the (100) planes next most densely populated. It is a general drawing phenomenon, therefore, that the most densely populated planes take up positions perpendicular to the wire axis and that these orientations are such as to present maximum resistance to further deformation.

6. Interpretation of Fiber Patterns for Rolled Sheets (Limited Fiber Structure). It is possible for cold-rolled sheet metal to produce a diffraction pattern indicating nearly random orientation of grains, as in Fig. 352a. The structure of the sheet could then be diagrammatically

Fig. 352a. Pinhole pattern for rolled sheet metal (high-carbon steel) with nearly random grains.

drawn as in Fig. 352b. But in general, as explained above, crystal grains in a rolled sheet not only take up positions with a certain crystallographic direction parallel to the direction of rolling but are further limited by having certain crystallographic planes parallel to the plane of rolling and to the transverse direction. Thus the diffraction pattern for rolled sheet steel in Fig. 353a indicates clearly the structure of the sheet with pre-

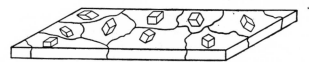

Fig. 352b. Texture of sheet metal with randomly oriented grains.

ferred orientation of grains as pictured in Fig. 353b. The diffraction patterns allow the evaluation of the indices of these three characteristic directions (*i.e.*, rolling direction, the normal to the rolling plane, and the transverse direction lying in the rolling plane at right angles to the rolling direction) and also with remarkable accuracy the departure, or scattering, from the theoretically ideal orientation as is always observed in practical cases. The rolling direction may be readily ascertained by the methods outlined above for drawn wires, although all the diffraction interferences will not be present on account of the further limitation in rolling. For the determination of the crystallographic indices of the transverse direction and the normal to the plane of rolling, a further step must be taken. A single metal crystal is considered to rotate through 360 deg

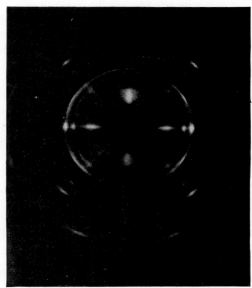

FIG. 353a. Pinhole pattern for usual type of rolled sheet metal with preferred orientation of grains.

around the known fiber axis, and the reflection angle 2Θ of the x-ray beam, impinging at right angles to the axis of rotation, on the different lattice planes of the crystal is plotted as a function of the angle of rotation. The result is a series of rotation curves which are extremely useful in interpreting results on rolled sheets or foils.

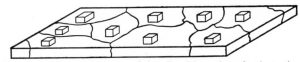

FIG. 353b. Texture of rolled sheet metal (steel) with preferred orientations of grains.

7. Detailed Analysis of Pattern for Rolled Steel. On page 713 and in Table 22-2 it was demonstrated that for iron wires (body-centered cubic) the [110] direction is parallel to the wire or drawing axis. It may be assumed that the rolling direction in iron sheets is also [110], and this assumption is tested by the positions of intensity maxima on the Debye-Scherrer rings in Fig. 353a. Since this orientation takes care of all the spots appearing on the diffraction pattern but calls for spots that do not appear, it is evident that the assumption of a [110] axis is correct but that there is a further limitation of orientation in a rolled sheet.

The other condition of a cube face lying parallel to the surface of a sheet that is usually given will be taken as the zero position, and angular rotation about the face diagonal fiber axis necessary to cause the appearance of various spots will be calculated. Then, by the presence or absence of certain spots, the degree of perfection of the fulfillment of this condition can be determined on each film. If this orientation were perfect, only a very few spots would appear on any ring and the ring itself would be missing.

The calculation of this angle of lateral rocking to one side and the other about the zero position necessary to cause the appearance of each spot is very involved in most cases, and a complete solution of this problem of a cubic lattice rotating about a [110] axis has been worked into the series of rotation curves. These curves were used in investigating how great an angle of rotation of the cube about the [110] fiber axis from the zero position of the (100) face in the sheet is necessary in order that a diffraction spot may occur by having fulfilled the law specifying the angle of diffraction (Table 22-4).

TABLE 22-4. ANGLES OF ROTATION AROUND [110] IN IRON TO
PERMIT REFLECTIONS

Necessary angle of rotation	Ring	Radiation	Azimuth, deg
4	110	White	90
9	112	$K\alpha$	73
10	110	$K\alpha$	90
18	112	$K\alpha$	30
18	110	$K\alpha$	60
20	100	$K\alpha$	45
22	110	White	60
45	112	$K\alpha$	90
70	112	$K\alpha$	55

It will be seen that in the special case of any planes containing the x-ray beam the necessary angle of rotation about any axis perpendicular to the beam will directly equal the angle Θ given in the diffraction equation.

The presence of spots on the two (110) rings at the twelve and six o'clock positions can be explained only by another type of imperfection in orientation. This is a *tipping* of planes, which in a perfect orientation would contain the x-ray beam and be perpendicular to the fiber axis, about an axis perpendicular to both the beam and the fiber axis. This is actually an *inclination of the fiber axis to the surface of the sheet*, and its calculation falls in the special case mentioned in the last paragraph. The angles of rotation necessary for the appearance of the various spots on the several rings arranged in the order of their appearance with increasing rotation were found to be as shown in Table 22–4.

The angle of inclination of the fiber axis to the sheet necessary to cause the appearance of spots at the six and twelve o'clock positions on the

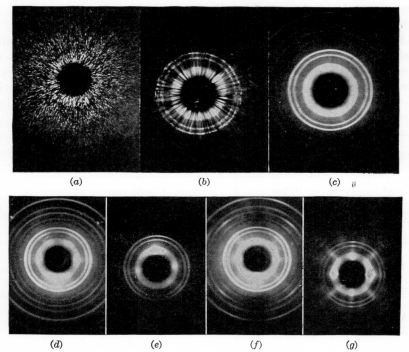

FIG. 354. Changes in structure with steps in rolling of low-carbon sheet steel. (a) Hot-rolled strip; (b) 1 pass, 7 per cent reduction; (c) 9 passes, 47 per cent reduction; (d) 14 passes, 71 per cent reduction; (e) 19 passes, 85.5 per cent reduction; (f) 21 passes, 90 per cent reduction; (g) 30 passes, 97 per cent reduction.

rings will be calculated. These reflections can originate only from (110) planes, and the inclination is directly equal to the angle of incidence given by the Bragg equation for this set of planes.

Ring	Radiation	Wavelength, A	Inclination angle
(110)	Mo $K\alpha$	0.710	10°18′
(110)	White	0.336	4°45′

Inclination of the fiber axis to the surface of the sheet in both directions with respect to the direction of the last pass will have the effect of causing the spots to extend over a wider angle on the circles and will cause spots to appear at slightly smaller rotation angles than those calculated to be necessary. If more grains are inclined in one direction than in the other, which in general seems to be the case, the intensity maxima will be displaced in one direction of azimuth and there arises a possibility of the appearance of spots on one side of the equator for which there are no corresponding spots on the other side. All these details of texture are most elegantly described graphically by pole figures, which are considered in section 10.

8. The Stages of Reduction and the Effects of Variables in Commercial Cold-rolling of Sheet Metals. *a. Structural Changes with Successive Reductions.* The change in x-ray patterns with successive reductions is best reported by Fig. 354a to g for low-carbon steel, selected from a series of 84 samples. Here the x-ray beam passed perpendicular to the rolling direction and to the surface of the sheet.

Figure	Pass	Gage, in.	Percentage reduction	Pattern
354a	0	0.158 (hot-rolled strip)	0	Large random grains
354b	1	0.1475	7	Fragmentation below 35μ and appearance of rings
354c	9	0.084	47	Nearly complete fragmentation, random
354d	14	0.046	71	Appearance of six-point fiber pattern characteristic of drawing
354e	19	0.023	85.5	Passing from six- to four-point pattern
354f	21	0.0165	90	Typical rolling pattern
354g	30	0.005	97	Perfected orientation

From a whole series of steel samples the following average results were obtained:

Appearance of	Per cent reduction
Continuous rings (fragmentation)...........	27
Sharp rings..............................	38
Six-point fiber pattern....................	54
Four-point fiber pattern...................	76

Such values, of course, are greatly dependent on type of mills, chemical composition, thickness, grain size, and orientation in the original material.

These results confirm those of Tammann, who found that in rolling two clearly defined changes in crystal orientation can be distinguished: (1) that in which the force due to rotation of the rolls acts as a stretching force (six-point x-ray pattern); (2) that in which the action of the rolls is similar to that of simple compression and exerts the greatest influence on the final orientation in cases of large reductions.

b. Effect of Carbon Content. Most of the previous work on preferred orientation in cold-rolled sheets has been carried out on pure metals. In steels the pearlite is hard and more brittle than ferrite and concentrates at the junctions of the ferrite grains, with the result that when pearlitic steel is cold-rolled gliding takes place only in the ferrite. During the rolling process the pearlite is dispersed, while the soft ductile ferrite forms a plastic bond that is not oriented, so as to form a straight fiber structure, but is curved around the pearlite particles. The x-ray pattern, therefore, gives the appearance of random arrangement for high-carbon steels (Fig. 352).

c. Effect of Rolling Variables. (1) The roll diameter has less effect on final structure than the total percentage reduction. The smaller the rolls, the greater is the angular divergence of the grains laterally in the rolling plane from the ideal preferred direction, while large rolls tend to produce more divergence normal to the rolling plane. Numerous other small differences may also be quantitatively ascertained, particularly for early and intermediate stages of reduction.

(2) With small rolls the same structure is obtained at speeds from 70 to 800 ft/min, and with unidirectional or reversed passes through the rolls.

(3) Various combinations of tension and compression of the sheets have been studied in detail, both experimentally and with vector theory. Fiber structures are ultimately obtained, but the appearance of the four-point pattern characteristic of compression can be greatly delayed by application of tension.

(4) Interesting results are obtained by rolling metals in all directions (random), at 90 deg (very perfect fibering), 60 deg (six-point instead of four-point patterns), etc.

(5) The intensity of fiber maxima decreases with increase in temperature at which rolling occurs. At 700°F the normal (001) [110] texture for low-carbon steel changes to (110) [001], and at intermediate temperatures the texture simulates that of random orientation.[1]

d. An X-ray Method of Determining the Amount of Cold Rolling to Which a Sheet Has Been Subjected. By the usual method of taking x-ray diffraction patterns of cold-rolled sheets, the x-ray beam passes perpendicular to both the rolling direction and the plane of rolling. Preferred orientation may appear only after 60 to 70 per cent reduction, depending on the type of mill and original material variables. If the beam is made to pass through the material perpendicular to the rolling direction and *parallel* to the rolling plane (edge on of the sheet), evidence of preferred orientation is obtained after 15 to 30 per cent reduction, depending upon the above-mentioned variables. This orientation gives a six-

[1] N. P. Goss, *Am. Soc. Metals Preprint*, October, 1952.

point fiber pattern similar to that for cold-drawn wires. Instead of the pattern changing to a fourfold pattern upon further reduction as is the case when the beam is normal to the rolling plane, the type of pattern remains the same. However, as the percentage reduction increases, the

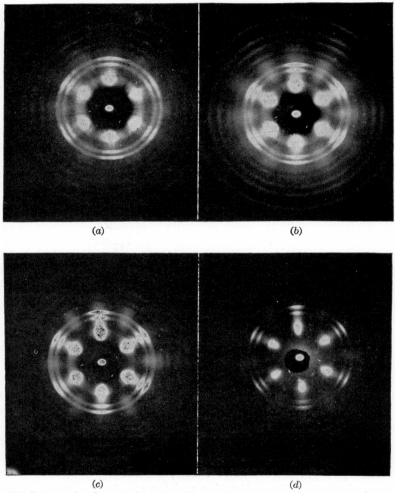

(a)   (b)

(c)   (d)

Fig. 355. Patterns for sheet steel, made with x-ray beam perpendicular to rolling direction and parallel to rolling plane, from which amount of cold work may be calculated. Percentage reduction: (a) 16; (b) 36.5; (c) 53; (d) 85.

intensity maxima become sharper, as illustrated in Fig. 355 for 16, 36.5, 53, and 85 per cent reduction. If the percentage reduction is plotted against the sine of the angle of arc formed by the intensity maxima on the broad inner band of the pattern, a straight line is obtained. For a large number of specimens this relationship has been found accurate within a maximum of 10 per cent.

In certain cases it has been possible even to determine very small amounts of cold work, such as roller leveling after annealing, by careful examination of the x-ray patterns (elongation and spreading of spots). This is particularly well shown with a microbeam; for example in a cold-rolled aluminum sheet with original grain size of 20 μ, a rolling reduction of only 1.3 per cent reduces the grain size to 4.3 μ.

9. Deformation Structures of Magnesium Alloys. The growing industrial importance of magnesium and its alloys also lends particular interest to the mechanism of its deformation. Figures 356a to f show diffraction patterns and theoretically calculated diagrams, respectively, for forged and extruded Dowmetal (nearly pure magnesium alloy). The analysis of the patterns proves that the forged magnesium alloy possesses a fiber axis parallel to the [001] direction, whereas the extruded alloy shows a [210] fiber axis in the direction of extrusion at low temperatures and a [110] direction at high temperatures, a curious change in glide direction with temperature. Schmid, working with single crystals, found translation on the basal planes with the diagonal axis of the first kind as glide direction. Above 225 deg translation on the pyramid faces occurs with the same glide direction. In many important respects, therefore, magnesium differs in behavior from zinc and cadmium.

10. Pole Figures. The generally accepted method of graphical expression of orientation of crystallites in fibered materials, and the statistical deviation around the ideal preferred positions, is the pole figure for the normals of the reflecting planes. Several diffraction patterns are made for a specimen with the primary x-ray beam at various angles to directions of drawing, rolling, etc., and to planes in sheet specimens. For each important set of lattice planes the position of planes is represented by a stereographic projection (page 346). The pole sphere and method of projection upon a plane are shown in Fig. 357a. For rolled sheets, for example, the plane of rolling is chosen as the plane of projection. From 15 patterns the projections in Fig. 357b for rolled α-brass were determined by von Göler and Sachs. These three pole figures give the positions of the normals to (100), (111), and (110) planes with respect to the direction of rolling. The crosshatched areas represent the greatest densities of positions of the normals, and the corresponding crystallite positions are predominant. Around these regions lines enclose wider areas corresponding to more widely scattered orientations. Thus the distribution of crystallites may be described as a scattering around an ideal orientation with a (110) plane parallel to the plane of rolling, a rolling direction [112], and a cross direction [111]. These ideal orientations are projected as dots on the figures. The correctness of interpretation is shown by the following: The point (c) in the center of Fig.

Fig. 356a. Pattern for forged Dowmetal (magnesium alloy).

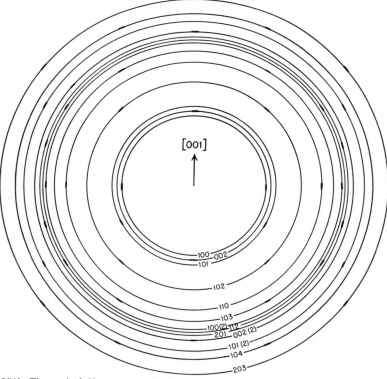

Fig. 356b. Theoretical fiber pattern for [001] parallel to fiber axis, hexagonal system, with which the actual pattern in Fig. 356a agrees.

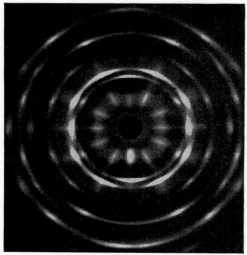

FIG. 356c. Pattern for Dowmetal extruded at ordinary temperatures.

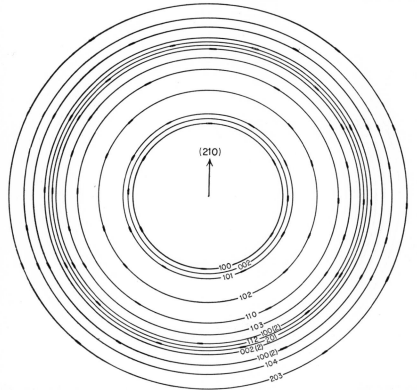

FIG. 356d. Theoretical fiber pattern for [210] parallel to fiber axis, hexagonal system, with which the actual pattern in Fig. 356c agrees.

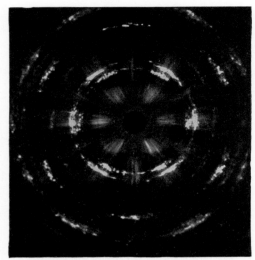

FIG. 356e. Pattern for Dowmetal extruded at high temperatures.   Note, in comparison with Fig. 356c, the effect of changing preferred orientation and greatly increasing grain size.

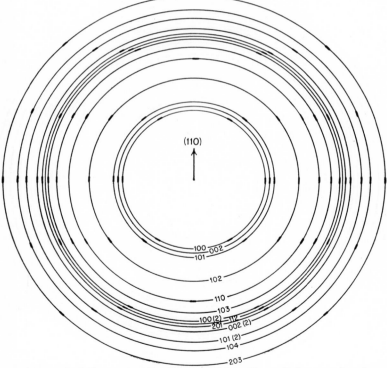

FIG. 356f. Theoretical fiber pattern for [110] parallel to fiber axis, hexagonal system, with which the pattern in Fig. 356e agrees.

357*b* means the normals that definitely identify the (110) rolling plane; the points (*b*) where the equator in Fig. 357*b* cut the circle indicate normals to (111) planes or the [111] direction. And so the rolling direction must be [112]. It is necessary only to project the ideal position for the arrangement on the (100), (111), and (110) planes and compare with this the pole figure from the diffraction patterns. Perhaps a second or third orientation will be required to account for all the observed interferences. The whole graphical projection is simplified by the fact that there is mirror symmetry about the vertical *W.R.* and horizontal *Q.R.* lines, and hence a quarter of the projection suffices to complete the entire figure. Thus

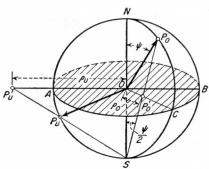

Fig. 357*a*. Derivation of pole figure by stereographic projection. P_o and P_u are two face poles; with the eye at S (south pole) the projection of P_o on the shaded equatorial plane is P_o'; that of P_u in the lower hemisphere is on the extended line at P_u'.

the pole figure as a terse representation of all orientations has superseded all other methods of interpretation of fiber patterns. As a formal means

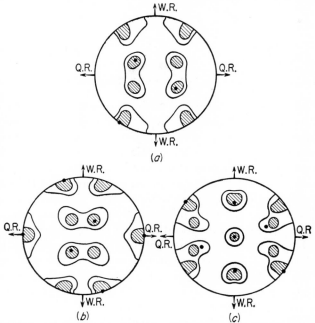

Fig. 357*b*. Pole figures for rolled brass; *W.R.*, rolling direction; *Q.R.*, cross direction. (*a*) (100) plane; (*b*) (111) plane; (*c*) (110) plane, which is parallel to the plane of rolling. (*von Göler and Sachs.*)

of comparison of cellulose and other natural-material-fiber orientations it is commonly applied. The accuracy increases with the number of patterns at different angles. In the example cited for rolled α-brass, the areas of most common normal distribution are correct within 5 deg.

Since the process of determining intensities for a large number of patterns required for the pole figure is a laborious one, a marked experimental advance was made by adapting the Geiger-counter diffractometer to the problem. This requires a special type of sample mount, or goniometer, by means of which the specimen of rolled sheet, for example, may be oriented. In 1948 Decker, Asp, and Harker[1] proposed such an arrangement whereby a pole figure could be constructed in 2 hr. The specimen holder was arranged so that a vertical shaft could be rotated

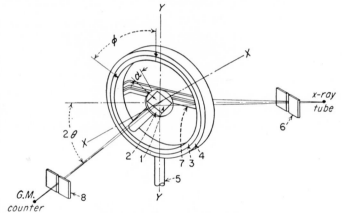

Fig. 358. Specimen holder for pole figures with Geiger spectrometer. (*Beck et al.*)

around its axis and the angle read off on the base. Mounted in a circular groove on top of the shaft was a vertical ring which could be turned in the groove, thus giving rotation about the axis of the ring over an angle which could be read off on a scale with the specimen mounted at the center of the ring so that the x-ray beam was transmitted through the specimen. In 1949 Schultz proposed a similar use of the Geiger spectrometer but with the x-ray beam reflected from the surface. The essential features of the specimen holder are illustrated in Fig. 358. The specimen (1) is placed on a rotatable table (2) by means of which rotation through an angle α is possible; rotation positions of rings (3) and (4) are through angle ϕ. Aperture slit (6), main slit (7), and detector slit (8) define the incident and reflected beams. On the Geiger counter the reflected x-ray intensity can be measured as a function of α and ϕ. These intensities, which represent a relative measure of the density of reflecting poles, are indicated in the resulting pole figure in the form of contour

[1] B. F. Decker, E. T. Asp, and D. Harker, *J. Appl. Phys.*, **19**, 388 (1948).

lines. The pole figure thereby gives the approximate relative pole density as a function of angles α and ϕ. In utilizing the Schultz method at the Argonne National Laboratory it was found that the useful ϕ-angle range is limited by defocusing effects. Therefore a series of improvements was made, including a removable gig which fits into the inner ring to permit rapid and accurate alignment of the specimen. Two different scanning devices allow the primary beam to cover successively a large

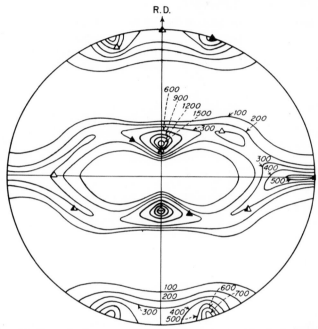

Fig. 359. Quantitative pole figure on (111) for 95 per cent cold-rolled aluminum. (*Beck et al.*) Open triangle: position of (111) poles for orientation (123) [1$\bar{2}$1]; solid triangles: position of (110)[$\bar{1}$12] orientation, previously proposed; half-filled triangles: position of (112)[11$\bar{1}$] orientation, previously proposed.

number of grains in the specimen surface. Finally an entirely automatic instrument was devised.[1]

By these improved pole-figure techniques have been made the most accurate evaluations thus far possible of rolling textures of face-centered cubic metals and the corresponding annealing textures. Previously for such metals the (110) [$\bar{1}$12] and (112) [11$\bar{1}$] orientations had been assigned (where the first symbol is the plane of rolling, and the second the direc-

[1] W. P. Chernock and P. A. Beck, Analysis of Certain Errors in the X-ray Reflection Method for the Quantitative Determination of Prefered Orientations, *J. Appl. Phys.* **23,** 341 (1952); Improvements in the X-ray Reflection Method for the Quantitative Determination of Preferred Orientations, in press. W. P. Chernock, M. H. Mueller, H. R. Fish, and P. A. Beck, An Automatic X-ray Reflection Specimen Holder for the Quantitative Determination of Preferred Orientation, in press.

tion of rolling), but these new quantitative pole figures show that the inside texture of Al and Cu may be described by four equivalent ideal orientations near (123) [1$\bar{2}$1]. With reversed passes through the rolls, copper remains the same, and aluminum has a (100) [011] texture. Figure 359 illustrates the (111) pole figure for the inside texture of 95 per cent rolled 2S aluminum strip. The formerly ascribed orientations are indicated on the figure. The annealing texture is described in the section of this chapter on annealing.

11. Summary of Deformation Textures of Metals.

Deformation and metal	Lattice type	Directions and planes parallel to force	
1. Drawing:			
Ag, Al, Au, Cu, Ni, Pd..........	Fcc	I [111] II[100] } distribution	
α-Fe, Mo, W	Bcc	[110]	
Mg, Zr	Hexagonal	[210]	
Zn	Hexagonal	(0001), inclined 70° from wire axis	
2. Compression:			
Al, Cu	Fcc	[110]	
α-Fe	Bcc	{ [111] { [100] (weak)	
Mg	Hexagonal	[0001]	
3. Rolling: (requires pole figures)			
			Rolling plane
Ag, α-brass, tin-bronze	Fcc	[$\bar{1}$12]	(110)
Pt	Fcc	I[$\bar{1}$12] II[100]	I(110) II(001)
Al, Au, Cu, Ni	Fcc	I[$\bar{1}$12] } or II[11$\bar{1}$] } [1$\bar{2}$1]	I(110) } or II(112) } (123)
Mo, Ta, W	Bcc	[110]	(001)
α-Fe	Bcc	I[110] II[110] III[112]	I(001) II(112) III(111) weak
Cd, Mg, Zr, Zn	Hexagonal	[100]	(0001) modified by twinning

12. Preferred Orientations, in Electrodeposited Metal Sheets.

In the preceding sections the production of a directed crystal orientation by means of mechanical work has been considered in detail. The question naturally arises of whether or not crystals may actually *grow* in such a way as to have a common crystallographic direction parallel to the axis of growth. Experiment proves that electrodeposited metal films show a fiber structure similar to that of drawn metals and that the grains grow out parallel to the streamlines of the current or perpendicular to the surface of the electrode. The interpretation of the fiber patterns leading to an evaluation of the indices of the fiber axes proceeds exactly as outlined for wires. Of course, the fiber axis is parallel to the cross section or thinnest dimension of the deposited sheet. If, then, an x-ray beam impinged at right angles upon the surface of such a sheet, it would pass parallel to the fiber axis. As demonstrated for wires, the pattern is usually indicative of random orientation, since the crystal units may be oriented anywhere through 360 deg around the fiber axis. It is necessary, therefore, to have films thick enough to pass the beam perpendicular to the fiber axis or to use the method of inclining the fiber axis at an oblique angle β to the primary beam. Bozorth[1] has published curves for graphical analysis of patterns so obtained with the formula

$$\cos \delta = \frac{\cos \alpha - \cos \beta \sin \Theta}{\sin \beta \cos \Theta}$$

Figure 360 shows theoretical patterns for bright nickel deposits at $\beta = 82$ deg all of which have been found, depending on variables of

100 110 111 210 211

FIG. 360. Theoretical patterns for bright-nickel electrodeposited films with various assumed crystallographic directions parallel to the fibering direction; $\beta = 82$ deg; D (distance from specimen to plate), 1.5 cm.

deposition. Many excellent papers have been published on detailed studies involving effects of electrolytes, current density, temperature, concentration, stirring, orientation as a function of thickness, effect of base electrode metal, recrystallization, presence of small amounts of addition agents, pH, electrode potential, etc.

Two recent investigations from the author's laboratory are illustrative of a very large number throughout the world on the fundamental and practical aspects of plating, which has ever increasing commercial importance. Clark, Pish, and Weeg[2] studied the bonding and structural variations of commercial electroplating 2 to 55×10^{-6} in. thick by means of reflection of x-ray beams from the sample tilted at 50 deg with the apparatus shown in Fig. 361, with which all specimens could be placed in exactly the same position. All dimensions and collimators were designed for focusing and maximum intensity so that patterns could be photographed in 5 min or less. Some of these are illustrated in Fig. 362 for a zinc base metal, C4, the same with copper flash coat, C3, and with thicker copper plating, C18; for a tin-plate base, D4, with copper flat coat, D3, and thicker copper plating, D18; and for a copper base, F3, with nickel plating, F18. It is evident that, in spite of the penetration of x-rays, the sensitivity for detecting thin layers is almost as great as that

[1] *Phys. Rev.*, **26**, 310 (1925).

[2] G. L. Clark, G. Pish, and L. E. Weeg, *J. Appl. Phys.* **15**, 193 (1944).

of electron diffraction.   Some of the conclusions of this work are briefly summarized.

In some systems the characteristic structure of the deposited metal is observed in the first plating only 0.000002 in. thick; in others the deposited metal simulates the lattice and interplanar spacings of the base metal before subsequently assuming normal structure.   Under the conditions of deposition employed, deposited platings upon base material with random orientation follow the random structure throughout the entire thickness.   On the other hand, coatings deposited on fibered base metals were also fibered in the initial plating.   Subsequent to the initial plating additional steps no longer show the orientation.

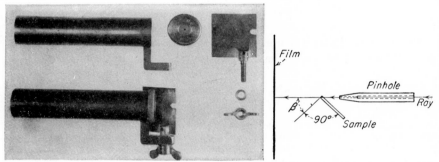

Fɪɢ. 361. Specimen holder and diagram of arrangement for making patterns of electro-deposited films.

From optical-reflectance measurements it is found that the substrate metal affects the deposited metal very markedly in the initial stages of the deposition process.   This effect then diminishes in characteristic fusion as the thickness of the film increased.

Three types of bonding of electroplates on substrate metals were demonstrated in the various combinations studied:

1. Mechanical, in which the deposited metal forms its own characteristic lattice from the beginning and clings to the faults and irregularities of the base-metal surface, which may appear at only high microscopic magnifications or in electron micrographs; the first atoms undoubtedly come within range of strong fields of force of the base-metal atoms in these minute faults, which increase the effective total surface of the interface.

2. Solid solutions, in which the first deposited atoms enter the lattice of the substrate metal, the resulting solid solution forming a transition layer between normal base metal and normal electroplated metal, which appears as a separate phase beyond a limiting thickness.

3. Pseudobasal isomorphism, in which through a few transitional atomic layers the deposited metal forms a crystalline arrangement which simulates and extends the type and dimensions of the base metal, though this may be entirely foreign to the depositing metal, until in thickening films it reverts to its normal structure.

Under best conditions bonds of great strength of all three types are possible and are commonly observed in commercial practice.

In a second investigation[1] utilizing the same apparatus and also a Geiger-counter diffractometer a study was made of a large number of nickel electrodeposits prepared under a wide variety of conditions, especially baths, additives, concentrations, pH and current densities (usually 4.3 amp/dm²) for the purpose of trying to correlate orientation,

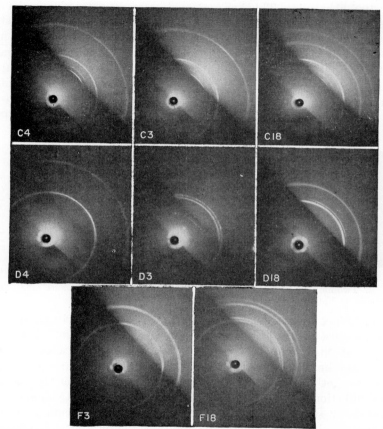

Fig. 362. Patterns of electrodeposited metals: C4, base metal zinc; C3, with Cu flash coating; C18, with thicker Cu coating; D4, tin-plate base; D3, with copper flash coat; D18, with thicker Cu coating; F3, copper base; F18, with nickel plating.

grain size, and brightness. Under prescribed conditions matte, semi-bright, and bright deposits could be produced. The following orientations were found. [100] (predominant), [110], [100] + [110], [112], [120] [120] + [110], and random; but no correlation was found between brightness and type or degree of orientation in the large number of panels examined, though it would be expected that the presentation of common crystallographic faces in the surface by the grains would determine

[1] G. L. Clark and S. H. Simonsen. *J. Electrochem. Soc.*, **98**, 110 (1951).

reflecting power. Nor was there any apparent difference in grain size between matte, semibright, and bright deposits. This lack of correlation was verified by electron micrographs.

One important contribution was an explanation of an anomalous meridional (12 o'clock) intensity maximum on the (200) ring of deposits having a [100] fiber axis. This has appeared on many patterns in published papers but has been disregarded because all other maxima are consistent only with [100]; nor does it appear on patterns of cold-drawn nickel having a [100] axis. The presence of twinning on the (111) plane, illustrated by the model in Fig. 363, also confirmed in electron micrographs, explains the anomalous maximum. The angle between the (100) plane and the (111) twinning plane is 54°44′, so that the angle between the (100) plane of the parent crystal and the (100) plane of the twin is

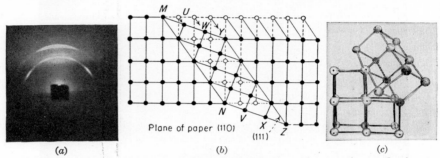

| (a) | (b) | (c) |

FIG. 363. Twinning in nickel electroplates: (a) Pattern with anomalous reflection on meridian for [100] fiber axis; (b and c) 2- and 3-dimensional models of twinning.

109°28′. Since the fiber axis is normal (90 deg) to the (100) plane of the parent, it must be at 19°28′ to the (100) plane of the twin. When this angle is substituted for α, δ for the (200) ring is 5°16′ when $\beta = 45°$. The two maxima, one on each side of the projected fiber axis on the pattern, fuse together to form the meridional spot. Only when the fiber axis is [100] direction is the orientation favorable to promote twinning.

Rooksby in studies of the structure and texture of speculum (tin-copper)[1] and tin-nickel electrodeposits[2] identifies the intermetallic phases as Cu_3Sn and Ni_3Sn_2 and also associates brightness with definite and pronounced preferred orientations, contrary to the findings of Smith, Keeler, and Read[3] and Clark and Simonsen[4] that preferred orientations of crystallites of nickel are not a prerequisite for a bright finish.

13. Deposition of a Metal from Solution by Displacement. Metallic silver deposited from a solution of silver nitrate by introducing a small piece of copper has a fibrous structure with the axis [110] which makes

[1] *J. Electrodepositor's Tech. Soc.*, **26** (1950).

[2] *Ibid.*, **27** (5) (1951).

[3] *Plating*, **36**, 355 (1949).

[4] *Loc. cit.*

an angle of 30 deg with the direction of growth. The microcrystals show a rotation around this axis with an angle of ± 11 deg. As the (111) planes of the silver crystals lie parallel to the flat surfaces of the deposited metal, the direction of growth of the deposited silver lies nearly parallel to the [112] axis.[1] Other examples have been reported.

14. Properties of Mirrors and Sputtered Films. Very thin films of metals have been frequently studied. Foils of platinum, nickel, and copper 7 to 18 μ thick produced by cathodic sputtering and thermal evaporation show a structure. The support upon which the film is deposited and the presence of gas have a profound effect upon the crystal arrangement.

15. Growth Texture of Castings. Superficial observation alone discloses the regularity of grain orientations and directions of growth in castings. In both body-centered and face-centered cubic metals the orientation is such that (100) planes lie parallel to the long axis of the crystal grain. In white tin (110), in the hexagonal close-packed metals (magnesium, zinc, cadmium) $(10\bar{1}0)$, with (0001) perpendicular, and in bismuth (111), planes lie parallel to this direction. It is obvious that these preferred arrangements in commercial metal castings are of great significance in determining the possibility of machining operations and the tensile strength. For example, a zinc casting with radially arranged dendritic crystal grains has a modulus of elasticity of 800 kg/mm² and a coefficient of expansion of 38×10^{-6}; if the crystallization is controlled so that the orientation is parallel to the long dimension of the casting, the modulus of elasticity is 12,000 kg/mm² and the coefficient of expansion is 14×10^{-6}. On the other hand, with the basal planes (cleavage) parallel to the long axis of the crystallites, profound splitting may ensue during rolling of the billet. It is possible therefore by means of x-ray analysis of structures of specimens cut in a certain way from castings prepared by a given technique to ascertain what crystallographic directions correspond to the dimensions of the unit. Other details are discussed by Barrett.[2]

THE X-RAY ANALYSIS AND CONTROL OF HEAT-TREATMENT AND RECRYSTALLIZATION OF COLD-WORKED METALS

1. The Province of Heat-treatment. When metals are worked by rolling or drawing, they become fibered. In other words, aggregates in which the crystal grains have random orientation assume in the process of mechanical deformation a structure in which the grains assume a definite orientation with respect to a common direction—that of rolling or

---

[1] Tsuboi, *Mem. Coll. Sci., Kyoto Imp. Univ.*, **11**, 271 (1928).

[2] "Structure of Metals," 2d ed., p. 670. McGraw-Hill Book Company, Inc., New York, 1952.

drawing. The analysis of the mechanism from x-ray patterns is given earlier in this chapter. These sheets or wires are now characterized by strongly directional properties, and it is the province of heat-treatment in general to cause a recrystallization of the grains while retaining the form of the sheet or wire, so that a random nondirectional orientation is again obtained as is absolutely required, for example, in forming steels. Again internal strains introduced by rapid chilling in castings, etc., are relieved by heat-treatment. The x-ray method finds powerful practical use in discovering just how completely the fiber structure or the internal strain has been removed. In its sensitiveness as such a control method it far transcends the microscopic or other physical tests.

It is the purpose of the present discussion to consider in a quantitative manner the mechanism of recrystallization during heat-treatment of single relatively pure metals, principally aluminum, silver, and copper. The information that has been derived from x-ray researches on these metals is astonishing in its scope.

2. Heat-treatment of Cold-rolled Foils. There are three possible effects of heat-treatment of cold-rolled foils: (1) The directed orientation of grains is completely lost, and the new grains are in random arrangement from the outset of recrystallization. (2) Between the states of fiber structure and final random arrangement there is an intermediate step consisting of a directed arrangement different from that produced in rolling, which goes over into the random type of temperatures in the neighborhood of the melting point. (3) The new recrystallization or intermediate directed orientation persists to the melting point.

a. Recrystallization of Aluminum Sheet. At all degrees of rolling, even up to 98 per cent reduction, aluminum recrystallizes with a random orientation of grains. Heating for 15 min at 265°C does not destroy the fiber pattern of the rolled sheet, but at 275°C, or above, this is lost. The pattern consists now of concentric rings with a spotted appearance indicative of a random arrangement of larger grains. This is the type of structure that might be generally expected, and for all the metals with degrees of rolling below 90 per cent reduction, including silver and copper, this is observed. Aluminum thus represents the first of the possible effects of heat-treatment. However, when pure aluminum is annealed for 5 min at the lowered temperature, giving recovery from the hardness increase due to cold-rolling, it is found by the new highly quantitative pole-figure method to have a crystallization texture below the surface consisting of the four retained components of the rolling texture near (123) [1$\bar{2}$1] (see page 732) and also a cubic texture component. Local reorientation corresponds to 40 deg rotation around a [111] axis.[1]

b. The Recrystallization of Silver. Glocker was the first to observe

[1] P. A. Beck and H. Hu, *J. Metals*, January, 1952.

that with strongly rolled silver (97 per cent) the recrystallization did not take place with chaotic arrangement of grains, but with a new crystallographic orientation with the (113) planes in the plane of rolling instead of the (110) planes as in the original rolled structure. This structure is maintained even after 10 days or more of heating at 300°C, but at higher temperatures (rapidly at 850 to 900°C) the random orientation results, together with a considerable increase in grain size. These facts illustrate the very important fact that long annealing at low temperatures does not necessarily produce the same effect as annealing for a short time at high temperatures, in spite of common belief and practice in metallurgical circles.

The very curious fact also was found that if the silver is reduced only partially in one rolling operation, is heated at 700°C, and is again rolled down to final thickness, then the properties are distinctly different from those of the silver reduced in one rolling only. In the former case the x-ray patterns indicated that the sheet begins to recrystallize at room temperature. Consequently annealing produces abnormally large grains and loss of tensile strength, and the metal is characterized by mixed, very large and very small grains, and is difficult to handle practically.

c. *Impurities Change Recrystallization Temperature.* The effects of small amounts of impurities on the recrystallization temperature of silver may be determined far more accurately from the x-ray patterns than from microscopic analysis.

It is clear that copper and aluminum raise the temperature, whereas all other elements, particularly iron, lower it. Five hundredths of 1 per cent of iron is sufficient to lower the temperature of recrystallization of silver to room temperature. Ancient as is the metallurgy of silver, this fact has been discovered only recently by means of x-rays. It is safe to conclude that silver, except of the highest purity, always has contained at least this trace of iron. Why then has not recrystallization served to ruin, practically speaking, cold-rolled silver articles? The answer is that copper also is universally present and in amounts of 0.1 per cent or less completely compensates for the powerful effect of 0.05 per cent iron. In the same way aluminum compensates for gold, which also lowers the recrystallization temperature of silver. It is interesting to note, however, that the temperature of 150°C for pure silver does not hold for the very purest silver (considerably less than 0.0005 per cent iron and 0.00002 per cent lead) possible to prepare. Very pure silver recrystallizes at room temperature. Copper has little effect on grain size and on the appearance of the intermediate-directed orientations of silver; iron, nickel, and especially lead increase grain size, and zinc decreases it. The recrystallization positions of grain are not so perfectly directed in the presence of the metals. Thus, for the first time is it possible to have a quantitative idea of the metallurgical importance of very small amounts of impurities.

In every case addition of larger amounts has little or no effect as compared with the introduction of the first traces.

d. The Recrystallization of Iron. Both α-brass (face-centered cubic) and iron (body-centered cubic) behave somewhat similarly to silver when rolled and annealed. For iron rolled to a reduction in gage of 97 per cent and heated above 600° there is an orientation so that the [350] direction is parallel to the rolling plane, while the cold-rolled metal is characterized by a [110] direction. Of particular interest are the new recrystallization orientation and the fact that random orientation is obtained only after heating above the upper critical point. Silver, brass, and iron, therefore, represent the second of the three recrystallization mechanisms.

e. The Recrystallization of Copper. When strongly rolled pure copper (99 per cent) is annealed, a new phenomenon is observed. The recrystallization structure shows a new orientation of grains with the cube faces parallel to the rolling plane (100) [001]. In contrast, the annealing texture of brass consists of four components of (225) [73̄4] type. Copper of ordinary purity, after complete reduction by cold-rolling, tends to recrystallize with a chaotic arrangement of grains; but if a first reduction of 50 per cent is made with hot rolls at 600°C, followed by cold-rolling, the cubic recrystallization arrangement is so nearly perfect that the x-ray diffraction pattern indicates practically a single crystal. The further remarkable fact is that this structure persists clear to the melting point. Not only does copper differ from silver (dependent, of course, on the method of rolling) in an entirely different recrystallization orientation, but also in the fact that this never goes over to the random structure. It follows, therefore, that such a sheet has greatly different properties from one in which the grains are in disordered arrangement.

The effects of impurities as ascertained from x-ray patterns are as follows: Tin, silver, lead, manganese, phosphorus, cadmium, antimony, and sulfur raise the recrystallization of electrolytic copper (205° unmolten, 250° molten); arsenic, nickel, gold, and silicon have little or no effect; and zinc, bismuth, iron, and aluminum lower this temperature.

f. The Recrystallization of Wires. The drawing of metals into wires represents also a fibering of the grains, but with a different mechanism which is somewhat simpler, as previously explained. For all face-centered cubic metals (silver, copper, aluminum, gold, lead, etc.) a [111] direction, or cube-body diagonal, is parallel to the wire axis with every possible orientation of the cubes (360 deg) around the diagonal; for body-centered cubic metals (α-iron, molybdenum, tungsten, etc.) a [110] or cube-face diagonal is parallel to this axis. In general, there are no intermediate new orientations of grains during recrystallization by heat-treatment. Instead, the sharply localized intensity maxima in the diffraction patterns for the wires gradually become more indistinct with increasing temperature. The last traces of fibering are remarkably persistent, and an entirely random arrangement is attained only after anneal-ing near the melting point. The change in tensile strength with change in texture on annealing is as follows:

$$Kg/mm^2$$

Original.............. 24.4
150°, $\frac{1}{2}$ hr........... 18.7
200°, $\frac{1}{2}$ hr........... 14.3
$\left.\begin{array}{l} 250° \\ 350° \\ 550° \end{array}\right\} \frac{1}{2}$ hr........... 11.0

3. Annealing of Cast Steel. Figure 364 shows the structures of cast steel as cast with large internal strain, of the steel annealed according to commercial practice, and of the same steel with an ideal structure obtained by the selection of correct temperature and time of heat-treat-ment through the agency of x-ray diffraction patterns. A short x-ray investigation proved beyond question to a manufacturer of castings who had been annealing large steel pieces for 6 hr at a somewhat indefinite temperature that the correct temperature of annealing could be deter-mined within $\pm 10°$ and that under these conditions a greatly improved structure could be obtained not in 6 hr but in $\frac{1}{2}$ hr. The economic value of such a single discovery is at once evident in speeding pro-duction twelvefold without additional expense. Such examples in this general field of heat-treatment for the removal of strains and directional properties might be multiplied many times.

4. Magnetic Properties as a Function of the Structure of Silicon Elec-tric Steels. The first series of pinhole diffraction patterns were made in the author's laboratory in 1924 for silicon-steel strips with varying mag-netic hysteresis loss. The magnetic loss could be calculated empirically from the number and size of diffraction spots on a given area of the vari-ous patterns—the fewer and larger the grains, the lower the loss.

More important from the standpoint of magnetic properties than grain size is grain perfection, *i.e.*, freedom from all strain. The x-ray pattern is the only guide to establishment of the correct rolling and heat-treat-ment that will ensure grain perfection. Figure 365a shows the pattern of supposedly highest quality silicon steel commercially produced, while Fig. 365b shows the result of a remarkably simple technique, derived, with the help of x-ray control, from the same raw material. The mag-netic properties of the latter, as well as the ductility, are markedly supe-rior; and scientific control of production is easily possible by regulation of the silicon content, percentage cold reduction without intermediate anneal, time and temperature of annealing, extent of a further pinch pass, and final heat-treatment. Pioneer correlations of magnetic prop-erties of silicon steels with residual distortion measurable on x-ray pat-terns were made by Clark and Beckwith (derivation of distortion moduli

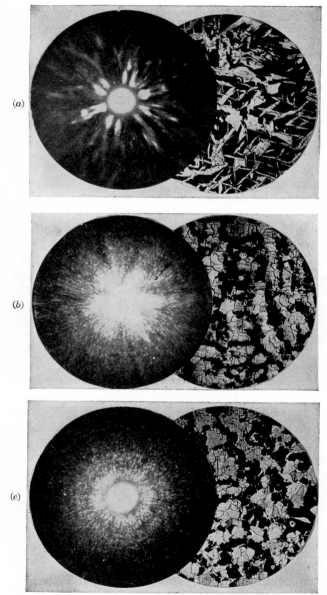

FIG. 364. Diffraction and microscopic studies of annealing of cast steel. (a) Original
structure, as cast, showing internal strain; (b) commercial anneal, showing incomplete
removal of detrimental structure; (c) ideal annealed structure of same steel.

from elongation of Laue spots)[1] and by Dunn and Clark (simultaneous magnetic measurements and x-ray patterns on mechanically deformed rings from sheet silicon steel).[2]

As the bending strains increase, the permeability decreases. At light loads the deformation is elastic; after release the permeability is restored, and the displacement of Laue spots also is reversible.

After greater bending strain, there is only partial recovery to the initial state. Similarly the Laue spots are permanently displaced and distorted, with as much as 75.2 per cent drop in magnetic induction. The changes in the shape of Laue spots agree at all stages with bending of strained crystals about axes lying in the original plane of the sheet.

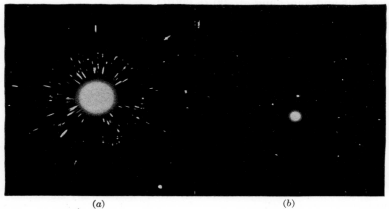

(a)   (b)

FIG. 365. Comparison of grain perfection in silicon electric steel. (a) Supposedly superior grade as now produced commercially, showing imperfect grains; (b) specimen free from strain, produced by simple technique.

These studies have led to the commercial production of electric steel of superior quality. They illustrate convincingly the value of correlation of structures with fundamental physical, mechanical, and even chemical properties.

5. Structure of Welds. Figure 366 shows the comparison of a weld of the same steel made by the ordinary arc method and by the hydrogen-atmosphere method. The former is characterized by very small, highly distorted grains (radial striations) and the latter by much larger, random unstrained grains with the requisite strength and ductility. This is a case of self-annealing.

6. Forming Steels. One of the great contributions has been to define specifications in terms of structure for forming steels, especially since unstrained and random properties are essential. Patterns and photomicrographs for supposedly four grades of forming steel, soft, quarter

[1] Z. Krist., **90**, 392 (1935).
[2] Phys. Rev., **52**, 1170 (1934).

hard, half hard, and hard, demonstrate that there are only two grades essentially. Satisfactory and unsatisfactory forming steels are easily differentiated by the patterns in Fig. 367. The latter retains a residual preferred orientation of grains introduced in the original rolling; hence the annealing has been entirely inadequate, and failure in the forming operation can be predicted definitely from such a pattern.

7. Forming Copper. Hard-rolled copper has a pronounced fiber structure most accurately described as (123) [1$\bar{2}$1]. A preferred orientation is found in the annealed sheet which forms ears on cupping, whereas that which forms without ears has random orientation. The formation of ears in drawn copper is avoided by the limitation of rolling reduction to 65 per cent and annealing at 500 to 600°C.

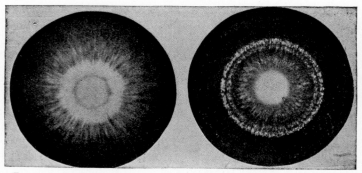

FIG. 366. Patterns showing comparison of steel welds. *Left*, ordinary arc method; *right*, hydrogen-atmosphere method.

In general, all sheet metals that fail in forming operations show evidences, by the sensitive diffraction method, of residual fibering which the annealing treatment has not removed or of a new crystallization orientation such as is commonly found for copper (page 740).

8. The Relation between Reduction, Temperature of Annealing, and Structure. Relationship between these three variables can best be shown by a three-dimensional diagram such as is represented in Fig. 368, which shows readily how research on a given metal can lead to a scientific method of heat-treatment rather than to an entirely empirical one. In this figure, the variable that may be determined from x-ray data in this case is grain size, though any other property might also serve. It proves that the final annealed structure of a sheet which has been cold-rolled to 90 per cent reduction without intermediate anneals must be different from that of the sheet which has been rolled down in steps with intermediate anneals. Each of these in effect places the specimen back at 0 per cent reduction. The diagram shows also that if very large grains are desired, following a complete cold reduction, the specimen is annealed, giving the size characteristic for the reduction at the right of the dia-

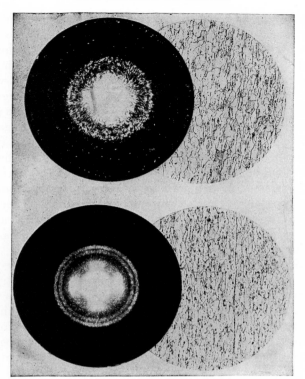

FIG. 367. Diffraction patterns and photomicrographs for satisfactory (*above*) and unsatisfactory (*below*) forming steels. Note residual rolling structure in the latter.

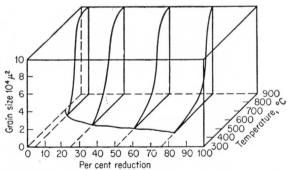

FIG. 368. Three-dimensional diagram illustrating scientific control of recrystallization of cold-worked metals.

gram, then given a pinch pass or very small cold reduction so that the conditions on the left of the diagram are realized, and then again heat-treated.

9. The Heat-treatment of Watch Springs. The manufacture of mainsprings for watches that have satisfactory properties and will withstand

breakage presents an extraordinarily difficult control problem. The
springs are annealed in baskets in electric furnaces, but even springs
from the same basket differ markedly, for some have "slow-motion"
action, some "fast-motion," and some are satisfactory. The first type
seems to be associated with metal that is too soft, the second with brittle
metal that breaks easily. X-ray patterns show convincingly the differences: the soft spring has been annealed until grains have grown to a
point where they register spots on the Debye-Scherrer rings; the hard
spring is incompletely annealed, and the preferred orientation of the
original rolled-steel strip persists; the satisfactory spring lies between
these two extremes, with smooth continuous rings of uniform intensity
indicative of removal of preferred orientation, but maintenance of fine
grains—possible only within an extremely narrow range. Several hundred new and untested springs were classified by single x-ray patterns
into the three groups, and subsequent behavior in watches was accurately predicted.

10. Control of Improvement of Metal Textures. X-ray diffraction
analysis has performed one of its greatest services to industry by diagnosis of causes of failures or deficiencies of metals and alloys which usually reside in one or more aspects of texture, as described in this chapter.
Usually, then, the cure or an improvement follows by alteration and control of composition and processing such as casting, quenching, and particularly annealing. Hundreds of cases of this kind might be cited,
but one from the author's laboratory must suffice to indicate these
possibilities.

A problem intensively investigated during World War II concerned
aluminum-alloy airplane motor-head castings. Since these motors powered the airplanes of American aviators in the war, it was vitally necessary to achieve the most dependable structure possible. Initially many
of the castings disclosed gross imperfections such as fine cracks called
"cold shuts," resulting from imperfect junction of metal flowing around
cores in molds. These would enlarge and cause failure under conditions
of motor vibration. By x-ray radiography and microradiography these
defects could be detected, and modifications in casting technique largely
eliminated them. But the castings, even when free from gross defects,
still failed in physical tests and sometimes tragically in operation. The
x-ray back-reflection technique was then used extensively to investigate
the texture of every part of the casting, thin and thick sections, with
every type of quenching of the casting. Figure 217 on page 381, used
to illustrate the back-reflection method, shows two of the castings in position on an x-ray diffraction unit. The patterns from different parts of
the same casting, even from contiguous areas, were almost shockingly
different, as shown in a typical series in Fig. 369a, ranging from continuous uniform rings for random fine grains to very large distorted grains

appearing as only two or three spots on the film. While any single texture may not have been unsafe with residual strain or under added stress, it is self-evident that the heterogeneity of texture might cause failure. With the x-ray pattern as a guide the processing was revised step by step to the final heat-treating and cooling. Figure 369b, which reproduces

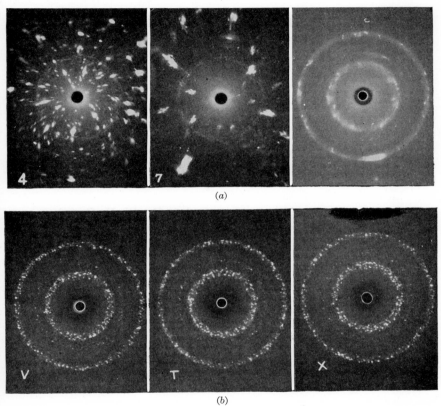

(a)

(b)

Fig. 369. Back-reflection patterns on three areas of airplane motor-head castings. (a) Unsatisfactory original casting; (b) satisfactory casting produced by foundry practice controlled by x-ray patterns.

patterns after this revision exactly in the same positions as in Fig. 369a for an unsatisfactory casting, is an eloquent proof of improvement. And with these improved castings the horsepower of the motor was doubled. There has never been any report of subsequent failure of motors arising from defective castings. Here then was a triumph of gross-structure radiographic and fine-structure diffraction diagnosis.

CHAPTER 23

POLYMERS—SYNTHETIC AND NATURAL MATERIALS WITH GIANT MOLECULES

The Importance of Polymers. Upon this fascinating and immeasurably important subject it would be far easier to write an entire book than a single chapter. For, if this is the chemical age, it is primarily the polymer hour of synthetic resins, plastics, chloroprene, nylon, and countless commercial products produced by man in his attempt to follow the pattern of nature in the building by living processes of cellulose, rubber, chitin, proteins, or the living cell.

No better tribute could be paid to the late Dr. W. H. Carothers, outstanding authority in the chemistry of polymerization, than to quote his sincere appraisal[1] of the peculiar significance of polymers in the world of today:

The most important peculiarity of high polymers is that they alone among organic materials manifest to a significant degree such mechanical properties as strength, elasticity, toughness, pliability, and hardness. Weight for weight cellulose and silk are stronger than steel; rubber exhibits a combined strength and elastic extensibility that is not even remotely approached by anything in the inorganic world; while diamond is harder than any other material. The practical uses of high polymers depend almost entirely on these mechanical properties: our clothing and furniture, and much of our shelter are made of such materials. The names cellulose, wool, rubber, and silk suggest at once the great importance of the non-chemical uses of natural high polymers.

Probably the bulk of the organic matter in living beings is made up of high polymers. The necessity of this lies in the fact that living organisms must have physical form and coherence, and polymers are the only organic materials capable of supplying these properties. The variability of living matter also requires a high degree of structural complexity, and the possibilities of high polymers in this connection are indicated by Fischer's well-known calculation that 20 different amino acids may form 2.3×10^{18} different polypeptides of 20 units. Another pertinent fact is that the physical properties of high polymers are profoundly affected by their physical history: the melting points of certain polyesters can be reduced several degrees by the mere application of stress, and their strength in the direction of stress is, at the same time, increased manyfold. Finally, reactions of polymerization also appear to be uniquely adapted to the chemistry of vital growth, because they are the only reactions that are capable of indefinite structural propagation in space.

[1] *Trans. Faraday Soc.*, **32**, 39 (1936).

To the still incomplete knowledge of the structures and building plan of these manifold materials with giant molecules, x-ray diffraction methods have made, are making, and will continue to make an indispensable and brilliant contribution, supplementing, and perhaps even surpassing, the results of chemical synthesis and analysis, microscopic examination, measurements of viscosity, fractionation and molecular-weight evaluation in the ultracentrifuge, and all other tests applied to colloidal materials.

Definition of Polymerization. Polymers are built up into what may be termed giant molecules or macromolecules from one or more monomers, or simple compounds of low molecular weight which are united by true primary homopolar valences.

Conventionally, it has been assumed that polymerization consists in self-addition and is limited to unsaturated compounds and that a monomer and its polymer or polymers have identical compositions. Today the connotation of the term polymerization is far broader. It implies an interatomic or intermolecular combination that is functionally capable of proceeding indefinitely, thus leading to molecules of infinite size. It is not limited to the organic compounds of carbon but also comprises a wide range of inorganic compounds capable of forming extended chains, sheets, lamellae, or three-dimensional networks.

Polymers need not have a composition identical with the parent monomer. Polymerization may proceed as addition and condensation; it may involve participating molecules that are not alike (copolymers), thus to form products like the well-established substitute for natural silk, nylon; and it may apply to unsaturated compounds, cyclic compounds, or polyfunctional compounds; in general, any compound x-R-y may polymerize when x and y are capable of mutual reaction (Carothers).

Complications in the Study of Polymers. The study of polymers has certain complications not involved in the study of simple, "chemically pure" substances composed of identical molecules.

1. Almost without exception the products obtained by synthesis or naturally occurring high polymers are mixtures of molecules differing in molecular weight. No two samples of starch or cellulose or many other polymers are identical. Thus these mixtures are themselves the object of investigation, and rarely the fractionated or "purified" materials. Analytical and molecular-weight data must be used with caution; for two molecules may associate by means of residual valences into larger units called micelles, or supermolecules, whose weight is indicated by osmotic data. Only at infinite dilution by extrapolation can an average molecular weight be evaluated which for cellulose has the same significance as the molecular weight of a paraffin wax or petroleum. Thus a measured physical property such as viscosity depending on molecular weight may be preferred to characterize a polymer.

2. Interest is centered almost entirely in the solid state of the polymers in which they are used, while compounds of low molecular weight are generally investigated in the liquid or dissolved state. Morphology is the prime concern in three steps of organization, the spatial arrangement of atoms in molecules, the arrangement of molecules in crystallites, and the arrangement of crystallites in the macroscopic solid as fibers, lamellae, or three-dimensional networks. Reactions of the solid, called topochemical, must be studied by any means in order to have any basis of understanding, for example, of biochemical aspects of vital processes, and yet the polymer chemist must make use of fundamental information on bonds, structures, thermodynamic behavior, and reactions of low-molecular-weight substances. This point of view has been thus far more successfully applied to inorganic than to organic polymers, though there are many current efforts to make statistical calculations on models and then apply the results to polymer molecules. However, as will appear in the x-ray study of polymer structures, it is almost essential to make use of macroscopic models with empirically adapted bond lengths, angles, etc., derived from single-crystal data on pure organic compounds.

Classification of Polymers. Macromolecular substances are classified in several ways: (1) inorganic or organic; (2) according to natural or synthetic origin, an older distinction now largely replaced by classification according to chemical composition; (3) according to the probable mechanism of formation; (4) according to configuration, depending upon whether linear chains, two-dimensional nets, stacked into laminated solids, or three-dimensional networks are formed; (5) primarily for organic linear polymers, according to macromolecular length (usually average), which determines many properties such as elasticity; (6) according to crystalline (ordered) or amorphous (disordered) arrangement in the solid state; (7) according to the effects of deformation such as stretching upon ordering or crystallization and preferred orientation or fibering.

Inorganic Polymers. Chapters 16, 17, 18, and 21, which review the structures of elements, inorganic compounds, silicates, and glasses, actually are concerned with polymers in many instances. For wherever chains or sheets or networks extend without interruption throughout a crystal and are as long or as extended as this crystal, however large, the definition of a polymer is obeyed, even though the familiar connotation is giant molecules built from small ones. Thus a diamond crystal is a giant three-dimensional "crystal" molecule of carbon atoms in continuous tetrahedral array; a graphite crystal is a giant molecule built from sheets of carbon atoms as large as the boundaries of a flake and stacked in a number as large as the thickness. But it is only recently that inorganic substances have been included in the list of high polymers when certain properties of organic polymers such as fiber formation and rubberlike elasticity were found. The late K. H. Meyer in the most complete and authoritative book on high polymers[1] lists the following:

I. Inorganic chain polymers
    1. Polymerized (elastic) S, —S—S—S—S— (Fig. 370a). Monoclinic, $P2_1/m$; seven S atoms disposed in two-turn spiral probable repeating unit[2]
    2. Polymerized Se
    3. Polyphosphonitryl chloride (inorganic rubber), —PCl$_2$=N—PCl$_2$=N— (Fig. 370b); also fluoride

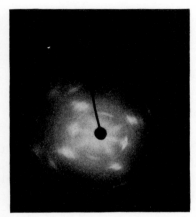

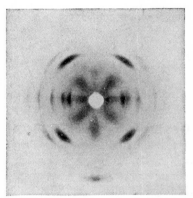

FIG. 370a. Pattern for sulfur fibers, made by spinning product of reaction of sodium thiosulfate and nitric acid.

FIG. 370b. Fiber pattern of polyphosphornitrylchloride. (*Meyer, Lotmar, and Parkow.*)

    4. Polysilene, —SiH$_2$—SiH$_2$—SiH$_2$—
    5. Polygermanene, —GeH$_2$—GeH$_2$—GeH$_2$—
    6. Silicon disulfide,
$$-\underset{\underset{S}{\diagdown}}{\overset{\overset{S}{\diagup}}{Si}}\quad\underset{\underset{S}{\diagdown}}{\overset{\overset{S}{\diagup}}{Si}}\quad Si-$$

    7. Alkyl Si oxides and all silicones,
$$O-\underset{\underset{R}{|}}{\overset{\overset{R}{|}}{Si}}-O-\underset{\underset{R}{|}}{\overset{\overset{R}{|}}{Si}}-O-$$

    8. SO$_3$, asbestoslike,
$$-\underset{\underset{O}{|}}{\overset{\overset{O}{|}}{S}}-O-\underset{\underset{O}{|}}{\overset{\overset{O}{|}}{S}}-\overset{\overset{O}{|}}{S}-$$

    9. Sulfur monoxide, —S—O—S—O—
    10. SeO$_2$
    11. Sb$_2$O$_3$ in valentinite,
$$\begin{array}{ccc}-Sb-O-Sb-O-Sb-\\ |\qquad\quad|\qquad\quad|\\ O\qquad\quad O\qquad\quad O\\ |\qquad\quad|\qquad\quad|\\ -Sb-O-Sb-O-Sb-\end{array}$$

[1] Natural and Synthetic High Polymers, Vol. IV, High Polymers Series, 2d ed., Interscience Publishers, Inc., New York, 1950.
[2] L. Pauling, *Proc. Natl. Acad. Sci.*, **35**, 495 (1948).

12. Silicates, pyroxene and amphibole, chrysotile asbestos (Chap. 18[1])

13. Polyphosphoric acids,

$$-\overset{\displaystyle O}{\underset{\displaystyle OH}{\overset{\displaystyle \|}{P}}}-O-\overset{\displaystyle O}{\underset{\displaystyle OH}{\overset{\displaystyle \|}{P}}}-O-\overset{\displaystyle O}{\underset{\displaystyle OH}{\overset{\displaystyle \|}{P}}}-$$

14. Polyborates,

$$O-\overset{}{\underset{\displaystyle O^-}{B}}-O-\overset{}{\underset{\displaystyle O^-}{B}}-O-$$

II. Inorganic net polymers
    15. Graphite and derivatives ⎫
    16. Boron nitride   ⎬ best solid lubricants
    17. MoS_2 ⎭
    18. Black P and PN
    19. $CaSi_2$ and siloxene, $Si_6O_3H_6$
    20. Talcs, clays, mica (Chap. 18)
III. Three-dimensional primary-valence lattices
    21. Diamond, silicon, boron
    22. SiO_2 and related oxides (B, Ti, Ge)
    23. Silicates, feldspars, ultramarine, zeolites
    24. Glasses

General Classification of Organic Polymers. To the linear chain group belong protein fibers, rubber, cellulose and its esters and ethers, many synthetic materials, such as the five most important commercial fibers in the United States—nylon, Orlon, Dacron, Dynell, and Acrilan— polyvinyl alcohol, chloride, acetate, etc., and thiokol (organic polysulfide). These are generally crystalline solids producing fiber diffraction patterns. The chain configurations of eight linear polymers are illustrated in Fig. 371. The three-dimensional networks, such as hard rubber, most synthetic resins like bakelite (phenol formaldehyde), vinyl resins (safety glass), hydroxy dicarboxylic resins (glyptal), methyl methacrylate (Lucite), linoxyn, etc., yield amorphous patterns usually like felted fibers, the interpretation of which has been considered in Chap. 20. The linear polymers are further classified according to length, which in turn determines important properties. Staudinger (1953 Nobel Prize winner) distinguishes the following:

1. Hemicolloids. Molecular weight up to 10,000 with chain lengths of 50 to 250 A; powdery, dissolving without swelling in solution of low viscosity.
2. Mesocolloids. Molecular length 250 to 2500 A; intermediate properties.
3. Eucolloids. Threadlike molecules over 2500 A in length up to 1 μ or more; characteristic for familiar natural fibers, some elastic, dissolving with swelling to solutions of high viscosity. It is only this type that may be spun into textile fibers.

It is generally true that a given material, especially of natural origin, is a mixture of many molecular lengths, which may be determined by ultracentrifuge analysis. A complete theory and calculation of molecular-size distribution in linear condensation polymers, based on the work of Carothers and coordinated with ultracentrifuge results, have been

---

[1] Also S. B. Hendricks, *J. Wash. Acad. Sci.*, **34**, 241 (1944).

derived by Flory[1] and subsequently by many others.   Molecular-weight analysis of mixtures by sedimentation equilibrium, is given by Lansing and Kraemer[2] and in a long series of papers by Wyckoff, applied especially to viruses, to which reference will be made in a later paragraph. In Table 23-1 are compiled by Mark general relationships between

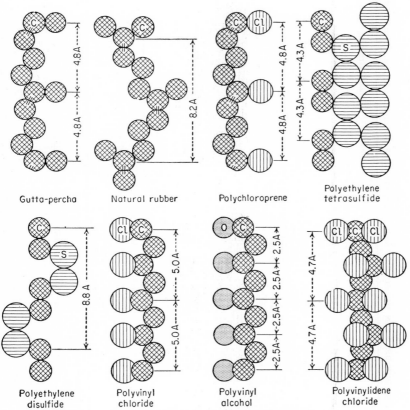

Gutta-percha   Natural rubber   Polychloroprene   Polyethylene tetrasulfide

Polyethylene disulfide   Polyvinyl chloride   Polyvinyl alcohol   Polyvinylidene chloride

Fig. 371. Chain configurations of various linear polymers.

structures of high polymers (chemical nature of monomer, chain length, chain flexibility, and netting number or cross linkages) and properties (heat, oil, and water resistance, impact and abrasive strength, and reversible elasticity).

Table 23-2 gives average data experimentally accumulated by Staudinger[3] for comparison of fibers of native and regenerated cellulose, natural and regenerated protein, and purely synthetic polymers.   Carothers and

[1] J. Am. Chem. Soc., **58**, 1877 (1936).

[2] J. Am. Chem. Soc., **57**, 1369 (1935).

[3] Über makromolekulare Verbindungen CCXXVI, Melliand Textilber., vol. 9, 1939.

TABLE 23-1. RELATIONSHIP BETWEEN STRUCTURE AND PROPERTIES OF HIGH-MOLECULAR POLYMERS (MARK)

	Heat resistance		Oil resistance		Water resistance		Impact strength		Abrasive strength		Reversible elasticity	
	Dec.	Inc.	Dec.	Inc.	Dec.	Inc.	Dec.	Inc.	Dec.	Inc.	Dec.	Inc.
a	x	x	By CH₃, OCH₃, and fatty groups	By OH groups and O-bridges	By OH, NH₂, OCH₃, HSO₃, COOH groups	By CH₃, C₆H₅, and fatty groups	x	x	By CH₃ or fatty groups	By OH groups	x	x
b	By short chains	By long chains	x	x	x	x	When chains are short	By long chains	By short chains	By long chains	By short chains	By long chains
c	xx	xx	By very flexible chains	When chains are not too flexible	When chains are very flexible	By rigid chains	x	x	x	x	By rigid chains	Very much by flexible chains
d	Low netting index	Very much by high netting index	By low netting index	Very much by high netting index	When netting index is very low	By high netting index	By low netting index	Very much by high netting index	By low netting index	Very much by high netting index	Very much by high netting index	By low netting index

a = chemical nature of the monomeric molecule.
b = length of the chains.
c = flexibility of the chains (e.g., cellulose, very low; polyvinyl alcohol, medium; polybutadiene, very high).
d = netting number or cross linkages (e.g., cellulose, rubber, 0; polystyrene, low, 3 to 5; polybutadiene, medium, 5 to 10; hard rubber, Buna, high, 10 to 20; bakelite, very high, 50).
x = little effect.
xx = no effect.

TABLE 23-2. AVERAGE STRENGTH AND DEGREE OF POLYMERIZATION
OF FIBERS

Fiber	Degree of polymerization (DP)	Number of chain members	Titer, deniers	Tensile strength, g/denier, dry	Breaking elongation, dry	Bending strength
Cellulose:						
Egyptian cotton.........	3,000	15,000	1.85	3.6	13.1	16,000
Ramie.................	3,000	15,000	4.1	6.7	4.1	3,500
Viscose rayon...........	290	1,450	1.4	2.35	16.0	150
Cuprammonium rayon....	560	2,800	3.9	1.97	26.0	175
Nitrorayon.............	170	850	6.5	1.75	17.5	50
Protein:						
Silk....................	....	.....	1.25	5.8	21.5	3,000
Wool...................	....	.....	5.5	1.5	41.4	40,000
Lanital (casein)...........	....	.....	3.3	0.9	84.2	70
Synthetic:						
PC, polyvinylchloride.....	2,000	4,000	4.1	1.4	24.0	1,200
Nylon.................	....	900 (molecular weight 12,500)	3.2	4.25	16.2	40,000

Hill[1] were the first to prove experimentally that a useful degree of strength and pliability in artificial fibers from synthetic linear-condensation superpolymers requires a molecular weight of at least 12,000 and a molecular length not less than 1,000 A. The macrocrystalline lattice is pictured in Fig. 372.

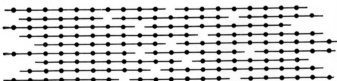

FIG. 372. Lattice from polymer molecules of unequal length.

Relation between Natural and Synthetic Polymers. It is a singular fact that many types of synthetic polymer can be made, but no naturally occurring polymerization has been exactly duplicated in the laboratory. Polyacetals, polyamides, and polyprenes have been synthesized in large numbers, but not the polyacetal cellulose, the polyamide proteins, or the polyprene rubber, though, in the last case, polyprenes like chloroprene have been made which equal natural rubber in strength and elastic extensibility and surpass it in some respects. The α-amino acids or esters can be polymerized in vitro to a cyclic dimer (diketopiperazine), whereas in the living organisms the polyamide is always linear, probably because of control of orientation by adsorption at interfaces. Nevertheless, the same basic principles of structure prevail, and it is reasonable to expect that some of the natural environmental conditions of reaction

[1] *J. Am. Chem. Soc.*, **54**, 1579 (1932).

may be artificially approached. Another fundamental difference lies in the fact that in natural fibers the molecules grow in length and into fibrils, possibly through an intermediate state of particles, or micelles, as a biological process. For synthetic fibers the macromolecules are first formed by polymerization by one of four methods: (1) Bulk—without diluting medium; applicable only for polymers which will melt without decomposition. (2) Solution—monomer soluble, polymer insoluble such as acrylonitrile. (3) Bead-droplet suspension, in water. (4) Emulsion—solubilizing monomer in soap micelles (see page 676), the most important, especially for synthetic elastomers; this material is then spun into artificial fibers from viscous solutions, or melts. Textile fibers, sheets, etc., are also manufactured in similar fashion from natural materials dispersed in solution: dispersed cellulose regenerated as rayon fibers and cellophane sheets; artificial wool fibers (lanital) from casein dispersions; etc.

Examples and Mechanisms of Polymerizations. 1. *Polymeric hydrocarbons.* *a.* Polymethylenes, $—CH_2—CH_2—CH_2—CH_2—$, and polyethylenes are representatives of polymeric paraffin chains. The crystalline structures are those described for the paraffin hydrocarbons in Chap. 20; Bunn found the same unit-cell dimensions for a chain of 3,000 CH_2 groups.

b. Polyisobutylenes. These form helical chains from branched paraffins in the presence of $TiCl_4$, BF_3, or $AlCl_3$ below 0°C, to form

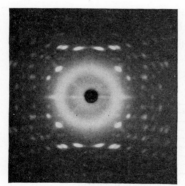

Fig. 373. Fiber pattern of stretched polyisobutylene. (*Fuller and Baker.*)

The high polymers are distinctly rubberlike, yielding in stretched form sharp fiber patterns (Fig. 373) indicating an orthorhombic cell with dimensions $a = 6.94$, $b = 18.63$ (fiber axis), $c = 11.96$ A.

c. Isoprene, butadiene, etc., which are the basic units of natural and synthetic rubber, are described in a later section.

2. *Polymeric Ethers.* A very familiar polymerization frequently studied as a structural model with x-rays is that of formaldehyde to form the polyoxymethylenes and derivatives. The possible mechanisms are

(1) $xCH_2O \rightarrow (CH_2O)_x$, dry, pure.

(2) $CH_2{=}O + H_2O \rightarrow HO—CH_2—OH$; $HOCH_2OH + CH_2{=}O \rightarrow HO—CH_2—O—CH_2—OH$; or $xCH_2O + H_2O \rightarrow HO—(CH_2—O)_x—H$.

(3) $HOCH_2O$ $\boxed{H + HO}$ CH_2O $\boxed{H + HO}$ CH_2OH (condensation, presence of acid) $\rightarrow HOCH_2OCH_2OCH_2OH$.

A half-dozen varieties of polyoxymethylenes, with various end groups (α, β, —OH; γ, —OCH_3; δ, diacetate; etc.) and with molecular weights up to 100,000, have been analyzed by x-rays. Ott[1] has claimed direct diffraction measurement of chain lengths (c axis) of 45 A for δ-polyoxymethylene (24 formaldehyde groups); 113.4 A for γ-polymer (60 CH_2O groups); 60 A for paraformaldehyde (32 CH_2O groups). But Sauter[2] has denied the existence of "inner" interferences, the identity period being 17.3 A. There is still some uncertainty which of the following forms the chains have, although the simple zigzag chain formulas appear more probable:

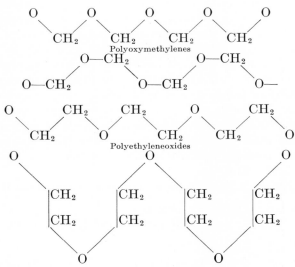

Other examples are polymeric glycol formals, polytetramethyleneoxide, polydecamethyleneoxide.

3. *Polyesters*. *a*. From glycols (dibasic alcohols) and dicarboxylic acids. These are formed as follows:

$$HO(CH_2)_xOH + HOOC(CH_2)_yCOOH \rightarrow$$
$$HO(CH_2)_xO—[OC(CH_2)_yCO—O(CH_2)_xO]_z—OC(CH_2)_yCOOH$$

where $x = 2$ to 16, $y = 2$ to 16, $z = 10$ to 200.

There are many examples of these polymers, ranging from those formed by succinic acid and glycol, through the polyethylene esters such as succinate, adipate, and sebacate, all of which are crystalline and are analyzed by *x-rays*, to polyethylene terephthalate (Terylene in Great Britain,

[1] *Z. physik. Chem.*, **B9**, 378 (1930).
[2] *Z. physik. Chem.*, **B18**, 417 (1932), **B21**, 186, 161 (1933), **B37**, 403 (1937).

Dacron in the United States)[1] from esterifying terephthalic acid and glycol to form

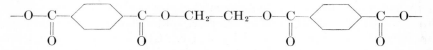

This polymer of outstanding qualities used for bristles, textile fibers, etc., like nylon, crystallizes with a triclinic ($P\bar{1}$) cell containing repeating unit dimensions $a = 5.5$, $b = 10.9$ (fiber axis), $c = 4.1$ A, $\alpha = 107°$, $\beta = 92°$, $\gamma = 112°$[2].

b. From tri- and polybasic alcohols and dicarboxylic acids. Of these the net polymer from glycerol and phthalic acid is a well-known example. These are the commercially important alkyd resins, glyptals, etc., most of which do not give crystalline patterns, but a halo "amorphous" type as noted in Chap. 21. In triglycerides containing unsaturated fatty acids, bridges may be formed to neighboring molecules at the double bonds, by oxidation, for example, with the resultant amorphous three-dimensional network of dried linseed oil, the liquid paint vehicle. Factice, familiar for its use in erasers, is formed by the reaction of S_2Cl_2 on castor oil.

In the same way polymers have been described of glycerol with tricarboxylic phosphoric acid, both synthetic and the important natural nucleic acids considered in the last section of this book, and also with boric, silicic, and sulfuric acids.

c. From hydroxy acids. There are numerous examples of the reaction:

$$HO(CH_2)_xCOOH + HO(CH_2)_xCOOH \rightarrow$$
$$HO(CH_2)_xCO—[O(CH_2)_xCO]_z—O(CH_2)_xCOOH$$

where $x = 1$ to 11, $z = 10$ to 200.

Ricinoleic acid, $CH_3(CH_2)_5CH(OH)CH_2CH:CH(CH_2)_7COOH$, has long been known to form polyesters of high molecular weight.

d. Epoxy polymers. These have become recently very important commercially and are represented by the Epon resins of the Shell Oil Company. The epoxy group

$$\begin{array}{ccc} C & & C \\ | & & | \\ —C & & C— \\ & \diagdown\!\!\diagup & \\ & O & \end{array}$$

can add carboxylic acids, $RCOOH$, alcohols, ROH, and amines, RNH_2; and with two epoxy groups in a molecule, chain and space polymers with

[1] C. S. Fuller and W. O. Baker, *Chem. Revs.*, **26**, 143 (1940); *J. Chem. Educ.*, **20**, 1 (1943).

[2] W. T. Astbury and C. J. Brown, *Nature*, **158**, 871 (1946).

polyvalent acids, alcohols, and amines form excellent lacquers and adhesives. These are usually not sufficiently ordered to give crystalline patterns.

4. *Polyamides.* *a.* From amino carboxylic acids.

$$NH_2(CH_2)_xCOOH + NH_2(CH_2)_xCOOH \rightarrow$$
$$NH_2(CH_2)_xCO—[NH(CH_2)_xCO]_z—NH(CH_2)_xCOOH$$

where $x = 6$ to 23, $z = 20$ to 200.

This type of polymer, known since 1899, was formed by heating ε-aminocaproic acid and was later studied by Carothers. The polyamide from ω-aminocaproic acid has the unit-cell dimensions $a = 9.66$ A, $b = 8.32$, $c = 17.0$. With this is to be compared natural silk, —NH—R—CO—NH—R'—CO—NH—R—CO—NH—R'—CO—.

b. From diamines and dicarboxylic acids.

$$NH_2(CH_2)_xNH_2 + HOOC(CH_2)_yCOOH \rightarrow$$
$$NH_2(CH_2)_xNH—[OC(CH_2)_yCO—NH(CH_2)_xNH]_z—OC(CH_2)_yCOOH$$

where $x = 1$ to 18, $y = 2$ to 18, $z = 20$ to 100.

The most famous representative of this class is *nylon*, manufactured by du Pont as a substitute for natural silk fibers. It is produced from the mutual reaction and polymerization of adipic acid (for type 6.16) or sebacic acid (type 6.10) and hexamethylenediamine.

$$HOOC(CH_2)_4COOH + H_2N(CH_2)_6NH_2 \rightarrow HOOC(CH_2)_4CO—$$
$$[NH(CH_2)_6NH—CO(CH_2)_4CO]_x - NH(CH_2)_6NH_2$$

Benzene, C_6H_6, is the starting commercial material, and the successive steps are phenol, C_6H_5OH, $\rightarrow$ cyclohexanone, $C_6H_{10}O$, $\longrightarrow$ adipic acid $\rightarrow$ adipamide $\rightarrow$ adiponitrile $\rightarrow$ hexamethylenediamine. The condensation of adipic acid and hexamethylenediamine is carried out by dissolving both in a high-boiling solvent, such as cresol or xylenol, and heating them at 200°C until the requisite viscosity and degree of polymerization are reached. The polyamide is, of course, a mixture of chains of different lengths and of polymer homologues, but its valuable properties seem to arise from the unusual regularity of the molecules, which permits the well-crystallized structure. Because of low solubility and high stability of the polymer, nylon fibers are spun, not from viscous solution, but from the melt at 270 to 280°C, under conditions of tension such that the solidifying filament is extended three- to fivefold. This promotes the unusual degree of preferred orientation, as shown by the x-ray pattern in Fig. 374 and displayed in the physical and mechanical properties that are shown in tables in comparison with those of natural fibers.

By ingenious interpretation of fiber patterns based on earlier work by Brill,[1] Ecochard,[2] arrived at the following triclinic-unit-cell data:

[1] R. Brill, *Z. physik. Chem.*, **53**, 61 (1943).
[2] F. Ecochard, *J. Chem. Phys.*, **43**, 113 (1946).

$$a = 5.00 \text{ A} \qquad \alpha = 81°11'$$
$$b = 4.17 \qquad \beta = 76°23'$$
$$c = 17.3 \text{ (fiber axis)} \qquad \gamma = 63°8'$$

Bunn and Garner[1] found evidence on x-ray patterns of two crystalline phases in nylon: α, appearing after a fiber is dipped in a phenol-water solution and then heated in boiling water for 2 hr; and β, in which the second chain is displaced upward 3.55 A with respect to the first, and then the third downward to the level of the first. In the α form each layer is displaced 3.5 A to each other in the same direction. The lattice dimensions were assigned as follows:

α

$$a = 4.9 \text{ A} \quad \alpha = 38.5°$$
$$b = 5.4 \qquad \beta = 77°$$
$$c = 17.2 \qquad \gamma = 66.3°$$

β

$$a = 4.9 \text{ A} \quad \alpha = 90°$$
$$b = 8.0 \qquad \beta = 77°$$
$$c = 17.2 \qquad \gamma = 67°$$

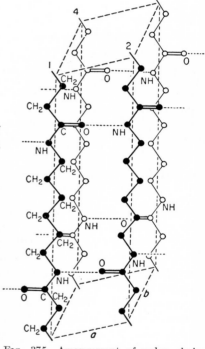

Figure 375 shows the arrangement of the nylon chains in the triclinic unit

FIG. 374. Diffraction pattern of nylon fibers (x-ray beam perpendicular to fiber axis).

FIG. 375. Arrangement of nylon chains in unit cell of nylon, α-form. (*Bunn and Garner.*)

cell, with hydrogen bonding, CO $\cdots$ NH, indicated by dotted lines.

The uses of nylon in the manufacture of stockings and clothing of all types and toothbrush bristles (Exton) are familiar to everyone. It is interesting to note that nylon has a comparatively low molecular weight and degree of polymerization—far lower than might be predicted for the properties that it has. Staudinger has shown that the strength of fibers

[1] C. W. Bunn and E. V. Garner, *Proc. Roy. Soc. (London)*, **A189**, 39 (1947).

does not increase in proportion to the degree of polymerization as measured by viscosities of comparable solutions; a "eutectic region" is reached at a polymerization degree (the number of monomer groups in a chain) of 700 to 800, at which tensile-strength curves flatten out to nearly constant value even though viscosities increase rapidly. Use can be made generally of this observation in avoiding the great difficulties in handling fluids of very high viscosity.

The structure of massive nylon. This polyamide is generally more familiar in the form of the fibers spun from the melt; these give fairly sharp fiber patterns indicative of a considerable degree of crystallinity. Less is known about nylon in massive form, even though it has growing

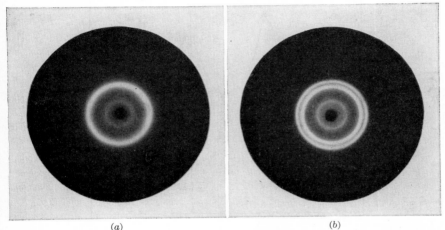

(a)   (b)

Fig. 376. Polyhexamethylene sebacamide: (a) unoriented; (b) after annealing at 200°C. (*Fuller and Baker.*)

commercial use as a typical plastic for tubes, gears, sheets, bearings, etc. The work of Fuller, Baker, and Pope[1] is applicable, however. The degree of polycrystallinity and the perfection of the lattice are dependent upon the rate of cooling; in annealing completely quenched specimens the crystalline-lattice arrangement is improved with increasing annealing temperature; but it never reaches the perfection of crystallinity obtained by slow cooling at the same temperature from the molten state. The quenching of all copolyamides causes extensive lateral disorder of the chains, including groups in the dipole layers. Annealing at a sufficiently high temperature below the melting point causes rotation of segments in the solid state, resulting in an ordered crystalline form and a definite hardening of all samples. This is shown for polyhexamethylene sebacamide in Fig. 376.

[1] C. S. Fuller, W. O. Baker, and N. R. Pope, *J. Am. Chem. Soc.*, **62**, 3275 (1940); C. S. Fuller, *Ind. Eng. Chem.*, **30**, 472 (1938); W. O. Baker and C. S. Fuller, *J. Am. Chem. Soc.*, **64**, 2396 (1942).

With the information as a background Clark, Mueller, and Stott[1] utilized familiar metallurgical techniques to study massive nylon, ranging in size from 0.011-in. strip to 3-in. rod. The purpose was to find a method of detecting stresses in large masses of nylon inasmuch as difficulties such as fracturing, warping, and nonuniform hardness of gears and bearings were being encountered. This gives two principal rings, an inner 100 reflection corresponding to a spacing of about 4.40 A and an outer combined 010 and 110 reflection for a 3.7- to 3.9-A spacing (Fig.

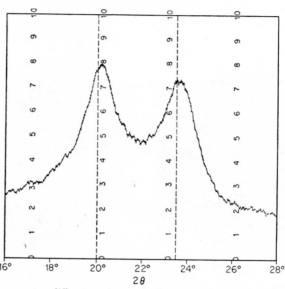

Fig. 377. Geiger-counter diffractometer peaks for two principal rings of massive nylon which change in angular separation, depending on size of specimen or temperature of annealing.

377). The angular separation $\Delta 2\theta$ of these two peaks on a Geiger spectrometer chart is smallest for the thinnest, most rapidly cooled strip and increases with the size of the specimen (with lower cooling rate from the melt) and with temperature of annealing as shown in Fig. 378a; the Knoop (and also Rockwell) hardness plotted in the same way (Fig. 378b) increases with temperature exactly as the $\Delta 2\theta$ values. Also the $\Delta 2\theta$ depends upon the annealing medium being greatest for water, smaller for oil and silicone fluid, and lowest for air. In all these cases the outer 010–110 ring does most of the shifting in position but through a continuous range from 3.92 A for the least massive to 3.76 A for the most massive or for annealed specimens. The 100 ring moves slightly in the opposite sense from about 4.33 A for quenched to 4.40 for annealed states. Thus a gradual movement of the chains in relation to each other must

[1] G. L. Clark, M. H. Mueller, and L. L. Stott, *Ind. Eng. Chem.*, **42**, 831 (1950).

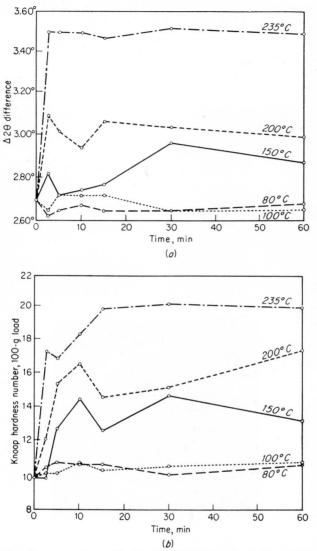

FIG. 378. (a) Angular separation Δ 2θ of two peaks for massive nylon as function of temperature and time of heating. (b) Knoop hardness values of massive nylon as function of temperature and time of heating, showing close correlation with Δ 2θ in (a).

be possible, along with a permissible variation in the dimensions of Bunn's unit cell, rather than the postulated change from β to α form. Parallel microscopic studies showed, as might be found for quenched and annealed metals, wide variation in apparent grain size in the massive nylon pieces from very fine in the thin strip (Fig. 379a) to very large grains appearing to be single crystals in the center of large rods (Fig.

379b). In Fig. 379 appear photomicrographs of fine and coarse textures and an x-ray pattern (Fig. 379c) taken through one of the large grains. The continuous rings prove that this is not a single crystal but a spherulitic aggregate.

Undoubtedly similar phenomena might be found in other plastics, most of which, unfortunately, are not as crystalline as nylon and therefore not

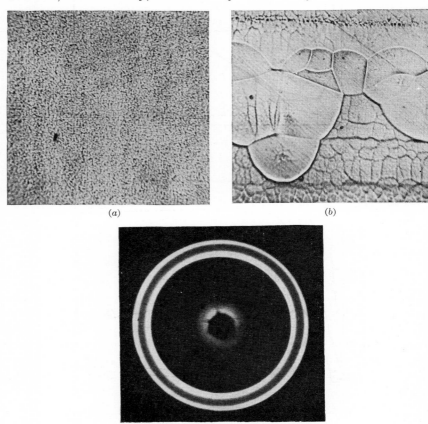

(a) (b)

(c)

FIG. 379. (a) Fine "grain" structure in 0.028 strip of massive nylon (100✕). (b) Large "grain" structure at center of 3-in. rod of massive nylon (100✕). (c) Pattern made through large "grain," showing it to be spherulitic aggregate.

so well adapted to the amazingly sensitive detection of changing structure and control of properties by x-ray patterns.

5. *Polyurethans*, from isocyanates and bivalent alcohols, are similar to polyamides and may be drawn out into fibers.

6. *Formaldehyde Condensation Polymers.* (a) With urea (aminoplasts), —CH$_2$—NH—CO—NH—CH$_2$—NH—CO—,   crystalline   unbranched chain polymer; some water-soluble adhesives. (b) With phenols (pheno-

plasts), bakelite, three-dimensional network, amorphous because of statistical linkage of ortho and para positions. (*c*) With aniline (anilinoplasts), resinlike polymers for thermoplastic molding.

7. *Polyvinyl Derivatives.* Vinyl polymerizations (including not only vinyl alcohol derivatives, but all polymerizations involving olefinic double bonds) are chain reactions in which the chain is propagated through successive addition of monomer molecules to a free radical.

$$-(CH_2-CHR_x)-CH_2-CHR \xrightarrow{+CH_2=CHR}$$

$$-(CH_2-CHR)_{x+1}-CH_2-CHR- \xrightarrow{etc.}$$

These processes have been extensively studied from the standpoint of kinetics, heats of reaction, and mechanisms of chain initiation, propagation, transfer, and termination. Thus initiation may be the result of thermal energy.

$$CHX=CH_2 + CHX=CH_2 + e \rightarrow -CHX-CH_2-CHX-CH_2-$$

Or it may result catalytically by impurities or on walls, thus lowering activation energy.[1]

$$CHX=CH_2 + O_2 \rightarrow -CHX-CH_2-O-O-$$

Or it may be brought about photochemically.

$$CHX=CH_2 + h\nu \rightarrow -CHX-CH_2- \text{ or } CHX=CH_{2\text{activated}}$$

Principles of distribution and probability, steric factors, and side reactions govern termination of their growth. In the last case, multimembered rings (Ruzicka and associates) may form by bending of two ends of a chain together (x-ray identification, page 604); or a hydrogen atom may wander along the chain and saturate one end (such isomerization reactions have been experimentally verified); or stabilizers such as hydroquinone in polymerizing styrenes may by side reactions with the free valences at chain ends terminate the chain.

Most vinyl polymers have a "head-to-tail" structure, as proved by Marvel[2] and associates. Familiar examples are

a. Polyvinylalcohol,

$$-CH_2-CHOH-CH_2-CHOH-CH_2-CHOH-$$

The diffraction pattern of the polymer as a fiber is illustrated in Fig. 380. Numerous derivatives with various substituent side groups have been synthesized and are used for safety-glass plastics, etc. These substituent groups seem to be attached along the chains at random, with the result

[1] Flory, *J. Am. Chem. Soc.*, **59**, 241 (1937).

[2] *J. Am. Chem. Soc.*, **60**, 1045, 280 (1938); **61**, 3241 (1939).

that the x-ray patterns are no longer indicative of sharply oriented macromolecules.

b. Polyvinylchloride, —CH₂—CHCl—CH₂—CHCl—CH₂— (PC fibers and sheets, common in Europe; Koroseal); for waterproofing, lacquer, filter cloth, chemical-resistant tubes, shoe soles, etc. Crystallizes on stretching, but prevented by addition of small amount of vinyl acetate.

c. Polyvinylidene chloride, —CCl₂—CH₂—CCl₂—CH₂—CCl₂—, from asymmetrical dichloroethylene (for coatings, fabrics, bristles; Saran); amorphous, but crystallizes on drawing.

d. Polychlorotrifluoroethylene, —CClF—CF₂—CClF—CF₂—CClF—, Fluorothene of Union Carbide and Carbon Corporation; for compression injection or extrusion into tubes, rods, and containers.

FIG. 380. Fiber pattern of polyvinyl alcohol.

e. Polytetrafluoroethylene, —CF₂—CF₂—CF₂—CF₂—CF₂—, Teflon of du Pont; extremely resistant to chemicals and heat and remarkable electric properties.

f. Polyvinylacetate, —CH₂—CH(OCOCH₃)—CH₂—CH(OCOCH₃)—CH₂—, from acetylene and acetic acid in presence of catalyst; head-to-tail formula; but cross-linked since even on stretching twentyfold no crystal-fiber pattern is obtained, while on hydrolysis polyvinyl alcohol easily crystallizes on stretching. Copolymers with polyvinyl chloride well known, also do not crystallize; Vinylite of Union Carbide and Carbon Corporation, and Vinyarn fibers; used for lagging, sleeves, packing, windows, etc.

g. Polyolefin aldehydes, from acrolein, CH₂=CH—CHO, and polyalkyl vinyl ketones,

$$CH—CH_2—CH—CH_2—CH$$
$$| \qquad\quad | \qquad\quad |$$
$$CO \qquad CO \qquad CO$$
$$| \qquad\quad | \qquad\quad |$$
$$R \qquad\quad R \qquad\quad R$$

(head to tail); for varnishes (noncrystalline).

h. Polyacrylic acid and derivatives (from CH₂=CHCOOH), —CH₂—CH(COOH)—CH₂—CH(COOH)—CH₂—CH(COOH)—; also chloride, amide, nitrile, and anhydride; all indicate irregular structure of head to tail and head to head with no crystal-fiber pattern on stretching. Most important α-methylacrylic acid (methacrylic) and its esters; vitreous (amorphous), transparent to ultraviolet light, Plexiglass; artificial leather surface, injection molding powder as Plexigum, Lucite, Diakon,

Perspex safety glass in airplanes and motorcars; acrylonitrile, spun into fibers from solution in dimethyl formamide, as Orlon (fiber patterns) (du Pont), Dynell, and Acrilan (Chemstrand); copolymer with butadiene gives elastomer, Buna N, or Perbunan.

i. Polystyrene, $-CH_2-CH(C_6H_5)-CH_2-CH(C_6H_5)-CH_2-$, from styrene, $C_6H_5CH=CH_2$(vinylbenzene); always amorphous though a chain polymer, unbranched at low temperatures and branched at high temperatures; with molecular weight 200,000 to 300,000 softens at 100 to 180°C and becomes elastic; useful for electrical properties, especially ultra-high-frequency uses, because hydrophobic; Lustron (Monsanto), Styron (Dow), etc., for radio cabinets, refrigerators, flashlights, kitchen utensils, foam; copolymer with butadiene, Buna S, GR—S.

8. *Polymeric Sulfides and Sulfones.* Sulfur often plays an important role in polymerizations. In fact, elastic sulfur itself consists of long-chain molecules in contrast with the S_8 rings in orthorhombic sulfur. A sulfur fiber, made from the reaction of sodium thiosulfate and nitric acid, produced the remarkably rich pattern in Fig. 370*a* already noted. Thiokol, a linear polymer of commercial value, is formed by the reaction of dichlorethylene and Na_2S_4 with splitting out of NaCl.

The polysulfones, extensively studied by Marvel[1] and associates at the University of Illinois, are formed by the reactions of olefin and acetylene derivatives with SO_2. The general reaction is a combination in the ratio 1:1, but vinyl chloride and bromide are unique in that two olefin units combine with one SO_2 unit in the presence of peracetic acid as catalyst to give the polysulfone, $-[SO_2CHClCH_2CHClCH_2]_x-$. Acetylene itself does not react, but $RC\equiv CH$ combines with SO_2 to give polymers

$$\begin{bmatrix} & R & H & & R & H & \\ -&C&=&C&-SO_2-&C&=&C&-SO_2- \end{bmatrix}_x \quad \text{or} \quad \begin{bmatrix} & R & H & & H & R & \\ -&C&=&C&-SO_2-&C&=&C&-SO_2- \end{bmatrix}_x$$

or both. These can be drawn into fibers that yield remarkably clear x-ray patterns, exemplified by Fig. 381 for pentyne polysulfone, and changing progressively in spacings with change in the R group.

[1] *Ibid.,* **60**, 2622 (1938), **61**, 2709, 2710 (1939).

Synthetic Rubber. Although natural rubber has not been synthesized, there have been produced a number of related "synthetic" rubbers, many of which possess the characteristic elastic properties. It is possible to distinguish by x-ray patterns of stretched samples every one of these products from natural rubber; for, as a matter of fact, only a few of the synthetic samples give any crystal pattern at all on stretching. If any polymer is ever synthesized which produces a pattern identical with that of natural rubber, to be discussed in a later paragraph, then it is safe to identify that polymer as truly synthesized rubber. The best-known examples of "synthetic" rubber derived from single monomers are

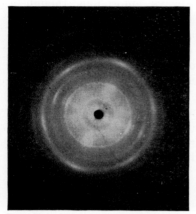

Fig. 381. Fiber pattern of pentyne polysulfone. (*Synthesized by Marvel and associates.*)

1. From butadiene, $-CH_2-CH=CH-CH_2-CH_2-CH=CH-CH_2-$ (Buna). This is done by mass polymerization with sodium as a catalyst or by emulsion polymerization.

2. From isoprene (probably the monomer of natural rubber in strictly uniform combination, but always in mixed 1,2 and 1,4 combination in synthetic products),

$$-CH_2-CH=C(CH_3)-CH_2-CH_2-CH=C(CH_3)-CH_2-$$

3. From β-chlorobutadiene,

$-CH_2-CH=CCl-CH_2-CH_2-CH=CCl-CH_2-$ chloroprene,

duprene

4. From dimethylbutadiene,

$-CH_2-C(CH_3)=C(CH_3)-CH_2-CH_2-C(CH_3)=C(CH_3)-CH_2-$

methyl rubber

In addition to these polymers from single monomers there is a variety of copolymers, including, until after World War II, the most important of all general-purpose synthetic rubbers, GR—S, the butadiene-styrene copolymers.[1]

In Chap. 20 solubilization of oils by aqueous soap solutions is diagrammatically represented and attention called to the fact that polymerization is most effectively accomplished in these emulsions. In the soap micelle, the monomer is dissolved, and here is the principal locus of polymerization. It is initiated when free radicals generated by the "initiator" are captured by the solubilized monomer. The polymer-monomer

[1] R. L. Bebb, E. L. Carr, and L. B. Wakefield, *Ind. Eng. Chem.*, **44**, 724 (1952).

particle grows too large to be held in the micelle and enters the aqueous phase, where polymer growth continues, the monomer largely disappears, and the remainder is removed by stripping. The end product then is a latex. A typical formula for GR—S is of interest:

	Parts		*Parts*
Water	180	Styrene	25.0
Soap flakes	5.0	Butadiene	75
$K_2S_2O_8$	0.3	Hydroquinone (stopping agent)	0.1
Dodecyl mercaptan	0.5	Phenyl-β-naphthylamine (antioxidant)	1.25

The initiation couple, $K_2S_2O_8$ + dodecyl mercaptan, act with the monomer M as follows:

$$K_2S_2O_8 + RSH \rightarrow KHSO_4 + RS^{\cdot} \quad \text{(free radical)}$$
$$RS^{\cdot} + M \rightarrow RSM^{\cdot} \quad \text{(initiation)}$$
$$RSM^{\cdot} + nM \rightarrow RS(M_{n+1})^{\cdot} \quad \text{(propagation)}$$
$$RS(M_{n+1})^{\cdot} + RSH \rightarrow RS(M_{n+1})H + RS^{\cdot} \quad \text{(termination and chain transfer)}$$

Hydroquinone is the most satisfying stopping agent in that it destroys $K_2S_2O_8$.

The copolymer chains are decidedly heterogeneous; butadiene is present predominantly as 1,4 units and 22 per cent as units 1,2; 20 per cent of the 1,4 units are in cis configuration.

The most recent contribution has been "cold" rubber, in which polymerizations take place at temperatures from 5 to $-40°C$, with greatly improved test properties, particularly for tire treads, such as abrasion, flex life, tear, and tensile strength. Cold rubber crystallizes more easily, proving that it has greater regularity in molecular structure, lowering of chain branching, and narrower range of molecular weights. This required low-temperature redox activators, of which three are developed and others are in process: diazothioethers, hydroperoxide–complexed iron type, and polyamines. The second has been most thoroughly investigated: cumene hydroperoxide, for example, reduced by ferrous ion forms a free radical which initiates polymerization; ferric ion must be sequestered by potassium pyrophosphate since if introduced into the polymer it catalyzes degradation. In the latest developments the time of polymerization has been reduced to as low as 12 min from a matter of hours.

The other most important copolymer is that of butadiene-acrylonitrile developed in Germany and remarkable for its oil resistance. The Perbunan (Standard Oil Company of New Jersey) and Buna N (German) products are similar.

The relationship between molecular structure and physical properties of natural or synthetic rubber is a matter of intensive investigation. An able résumé of this subject has been given by Gehman,[1] a distinguished authority:

Definite features of molecular structure are required for a material that exhibits rubberlike elasticity. These involve both geometrical characteristics of the molecules and favorable intermolecular forces. The molecules must be long-chain or thread-like molecules which owing to thermal agitation, assume random configuration. Theory also requires chemical bonds or cross linkages at intervals along the chains, so that they are connected at these points and form a network structure. The intermolecular forces or forces between neighboring molecules or groups of atoms are variously designated as secondary valence forces, van der Waals forces, or cohesive forces. They must be sufficiently weak to permit configurational changes of the molecules and deformation of the network structure by relatively low stresses and yet strong enough to provide adequate tensile strength. The retractive force of rubber arises from the tendency of the chain molecules to resume their random configurations when these are altered by stretching.

Thus there is a wide range of structural features of synthetic rubbers regarded as necessary for rubberlike elasticity; and a wide range of monomers could meet these requirements. There is a continuous gradation from viscous polymeric liquids to elastomers and from elastomers to fibers and hard plastics. The intermolecular forces in these plastics may be weakened by plasticizers or by raising the temperature to the point of elastomer characteristics without changing the structure of the long-chain molecules. Gehman discusses in detail the effect of the chemical nature of the monomer, the effect of molecular-weight distribution and of cross linking, inherently and by vulcanization, and the effect of arrangement of units in chain molecules. X-ray diffraction analysis has contributed largely to the last-named question whenever there is sufficient crystallinity. Briefly some of the possibilities are:

1. Head-to-tail arrangement, in polyisoprene,

$$\underset{\displaystyle |}{\overset{\displaystyle CH_2}{}} \qquad \underset{\displaystyle |}{\overset{\displaystyle CH_2}{}}$$

$$-CH_2-CH\!\!=\!\!C-CH_2-CH_2-CH\!\!=\!\!C-CH_2-$$

(predominant in natural rubber, polyisoprene, polychloroprene, over head-to-head).

2. Units in polyisoprene chains,

1,4	1,2	3,4

$$\underset{\displaystyle }{\overset{\displaystyle CH_3}{|}}$$

1,4: $-CH_2-C\!\!=\!\!CH-CH_2-$

1,2: $-CH_2-\overset{\displaystyle CH_2}{\underset{\displaystyle CH}{|}}-$ with $CH \!\!=\!\! CH_2$ below

3,4: $-CH_2-CH$ with $C-CH_3$ and $C\!\!=\!\!CH_2$ below

(20 per cent 1,2 in emulsion polybutadiene and its copolymer).

[1] S. D. Gehman, *Ind. Eng. Chem.*, **44**, 730 (1952).

3. Alternation of comonomer units in GR—S,

$$\underset{\displaystyle |}{\text{C}_6\text{H}_5}$$

—CH$_2$—CH=CH—CH$_2$—CH$_2$—CH—CH$_2$—CH=CH—CH$_2$—

(evidently random distribution, accounting for low crystallinity).

4. Units of cis and trans structure,

Natural rubber, *cis*, neoprene, *trans*, both good elastomers and crystallizable on stretching; mixture detrimental to properties connected with crystallization. Cold rubber has as a feature of its more regular molecular structure almost entirely a trans configuration.

5. Chain branching, which in the absence of other effects accounts for differences in polymer properties.

Natural Rubber. The long-known chemical facts concerning rubber derived from the latex of the *Hevea* tree are: (1) the elementary formula is $(C_5H_8)_n$, each group containing a double bond; (2) the molecules consist of long carbon chains, to which the name polyprenes was given by Weber in 1902. There was no evidence of the size of the molecule or the presence of cis or trans configuration. Molecular weights of the fraction soluble in benzene finally indicated values of 300,000 to 500,000, greatly decreased by mastication. When unstretched natural rubber is examined by x-rays, it produces a blurred ring, the halo that is typical of the amorphous or liquid state. Its behavior when stretched was first reported by Katz[1] who observed interference spots at 80 per cent elongation. Their intensity increased with increasing elongation, and at 400 per cent a definite fiber diagram was observed. Consequently, rubber when extended was considered to be crystalline, and the Joule effect to result from an actual formation of crystals (Fig. 382a).

The behavior of stretched rubber between 80 and 1,000 per cent elongations was investigated by Hauser and Mark,[2] who made a more accurate study of the positions and intensities of the interferences. The positions of the interferences were found to be independent of the degree of stretching, but their intensities increased proportionally with it. The position of the amorphous ring remained unchanged during extension, but its intensity decreased with continued elongation. Therefore, an amorphous or liquid phase in unstretched rubber was supposed to be changed to a crystalline phase when it was stretched. The positions of the interferences, which depend on the dimensions of the unit cell, did

[1] *Kolloid-Z.*, **36**, 300, **37**, 19 (1925).
[2] *Kolloidchem. Beih.*, **22**, 63 (1926).

not change with continued stretch, and consequently a definite space-lattice was indicated.   Other evidence showed that new crystalline units were constantly produced during elongation and that the major axis of the crystalline phase was oriented parallel to the direction of stretch. The interferences in stretched rubber disappeared at 60°C.   If rubber was milled or swollen by solvents before stretching, the interference spots did not appear at ordinary room temperatures.

Three-dimensional, or "higher," orientation in rubber can be produced in sheet specimens[1] in which the width decreases less than the thickness on stretching.   With this additional information a paper by Lotmar and

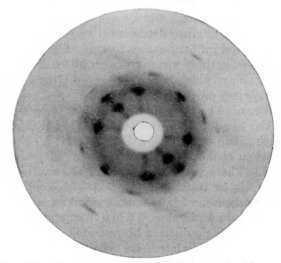

Fig. 382a. The crystal-fiber pattern of stretched rubber.

Meyer[2] reported accurate measurements of the structure of crystallized rubber.   The unit cell was derived by the graphical method of Sauter, is monoclinic and has the following axes:

$$a = 8.54 \pm 0.05 \text{ A}$$
$$b = 8.20 \pm 0.05 \text{ A (fiber axis)}$$
$$c = 12.65 \pm 0.05 \text{ A}$$
$$\beta = 83° \ 21'$$

Volume of unit cell $= 880 \text{ A}^3$ approximately

They report 7.6 molecules per unit cell, and this value is based on the highest value of density (0.965) reported in the literature.   Eight molecules are assumed to be present.   By an elimination of possible space

[1] Mark and von Susich, *Kolloid-Z.*, **46**, 11 (1900); *Z. physik. Chem.*, **4**, 431 (1929). Clews and Schossberger, *Proc. Roy. Soc. (London)*, **164**, 491 (1938).   Gehman and Field, *J. Appl. Phys.*, **10**, 564 (1939).

[2] *Monatch.*, **69**, 115 (1936).

groups, there remains the probable one $P2_1/c$, and the chains are presumed to have the symmetry of a twofold screw axis.   The crystallite is said to be a molecular racemate of right and left spiral molecules.   Very similar results had been obtained by the author in 1930.[1]

Sauter[2] in Staudinger's laboratory disagreed with the assignment of indices to interferences in the patterns of Lotmar and Meyer, as was

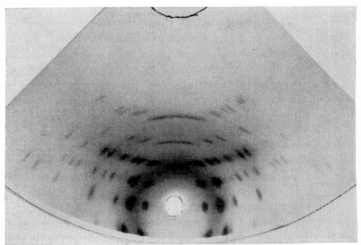

FIG. 382b. Pattern for stretched rubber on conical film by Sauter technique, permitting rapid indexing of interferences.

also the case with cellulose.   Sauter assigned the following values for the rubber unit cell:

$$a = 8.91 \text{ A}$$
$$b = 8.20 \text{ A (fiber axis)}$$
$$c = 12.60 \text{ A}$$
$$\beta = 90° \text{ (orthorhombic)}$$

A pattern made on Sauter's conical camera is reproduced in Fig. 382b.

In 1940 van der Wyk and Misch[3] with Weissenberg and oscillatory patterns of highly stretched specimens found that some reflections are doubled on the equator, first and second layer lines, indicating that the rubber crystallites must take up two preferred orientations, related by a 180-deg rotation.   Hence the orthorhombic-cell dimensions must be

$$a = 8.97 \text{ A}$$
$$b = 8.20 \text{ A}$$
$$c = 25.2 \text{ A}$$
$$Z = 16 \text{ isoprene units}$$

[1] G. L. Clark, *Ind. Eng. Chem.*, **31**, 1307 (1930).
[2] *Z. physik. Chem.*, **B36**, 405, 427 (1937).
[3] A. J. A. van der Wyk and L. Misch, *J. Chem. Phys.*, **8**, 127 (1942).

Extinction data still pointed to a smaller cell, but this is possible only if there are two unit cells in rubber simultaneously, one monoclinic and one triclinic, a very unusual condition which could be proved only by isolating two modifications such as gutta-percha has.   A still later analysis by Bunn[1] led to a monoclinic cell, with $a = 12.46$, $b = 8.20$, and $c = 8.89$ A, $\beta = 92$ deg, $Z = 4$, with adjacent C_5H_8 units different in configurations and each characterized by a marked bending of methyl groups out of the $—CH_2—C{=}C—CH_2—$ planes.   But there are objections to this on the basis of density agreement and disregard of interferences.   In any case the fiber-axis length of 8.20 A does not permit the isoprene residues in the chain to be in fully stretched configuration, which would require 9.15 A. Therefore some type of spiral rotation of the chain is necessary, and, on the basis of the analysis by van der Wyk and Misch, four different forms of chains may thus be present in stretched rubber.   In 1954, Nyburg,[2] with improved x-ray patterns of stretched rubber made at liquid-air temperature by single-crystal techniques, showed that stereochemical anomalies in proposed structures can be removed by assuming a statistical crystal structure wherein a given molecule or its mirror image in $y = \frac{1}{8}$ is equally likely.   On this basis the structure factor agreement is markedly improved over that for Bunn's structure.

Crystal interferences in frozen, unstretched smoked sheet were found by Hauser and Rosbaud,[3] Barnes,[4] and Clark.[5]   They were indicated by Debye-Scherrer rings.   Later von Susich constructed a melting curve from the behavior of patterns of frozen rubber at different temperatures. With unstretched rubber the powder pattern disappeared completely at approximately 35°C and with stretched rubber at about 90°C.   Above 90°C the pattern was that of an amorphous material.   Indices were assigned to four rings in the frozen-rubber pattern, but no spacings or calculations were mentioned.

The general conclusion from all these experiments and many others not specifically mentioned is that rubber consists of long chains of isoprene units.   In the stretched state these molecules are extended and oriented in parallel fashion and thus produce crystal-fiber patterns.   In the nonextended state rubber behaves as a liquid, and its diffraction pattern is that of a liquid (Chap. 21).   But the question remains whether the molecules themselves are folded or like springs in the unstretched state so that the extensibility of rubber is the result of the extensibility of these springs or whether they are fully extended and extensibility results from the bending and flexing of a tangled aggregate of chains.

[1] C. W. Bunn, *Proc. Roy. Soc. (London)*, **A180**, 40 (1942).
[2] S. C. Nyburg, *Acta Cryst.*, **7**, 385 (1954).
[3] *Kautschuk*, **3**, 17 (1927).
[4] *Can. J. Research*, **15**, 156 (1937).
[5] *J. Research Natl. Bur. Standards*, **19**, 479 (1937), **22**, 105 (1939).

Another related question is whether the molecules act separately or in bundles (crystallites).

One of the earliest concepts was a tangled snarl of long threadlike molecules in ordinary liquid rubber which can be pulled into parallel alignment. This has been subjected with some success to thermodynamic and mechanical analysis. There are numerous modifications of kinked chains in random orientation from thermal agitation, although an explanation of long-range elasticity of rubber is lacking.

The most extensive theory of structure proposed after the advent of the x-ray data was that of a two-phase system. Gel rubber forms a three-dimensional network soaked with liquid sol rubber of lower molecular weight. These micelles, or crystallites, of bundles of chains then preexist in unstretched rubber, but swelling and distortion destroy the possibility of crystal interferences until extension squeezes out the sol phase. That rubber can be fractionated into a gristly ether-insoluble gel phase and an easily extensible ether-soluble sol phase cannot be denied. It is also established that the gel phase which gradually develops on storage of fresh latex contains oxygen; only 0.01 per cent of oxygen, corresponding to 2 atoms of oxygen per chain of 20,000 carbon atoms, suffices to bring about cross linking.

The observation by Clark, Warren, and Smith[1] that pure sol rubber prepared at the National Bureau of Standards and protected against oxidation by extraordinary precautions fails to produce a fiber pattern even at 1,000 per cent elongation, whereas gel rubber and total rubber indicate crystalline organization at less than 200 per cent elongation, seems a significant point in favor of the two-phase concept.

If crystallites, or micelles, exist in rubber, then it should be possible to ascertain something about the size and shape from the measurement of the breadth of the x-ray crystal interferences. It is well known that these interferences broaden as particle size decreases in the colloidal range and that Scherrer, Laue, Brill, and others have provided the necessary fundamental formulas which are theoretically sound and have been verified by direct experiment. By this means Hauser and Mark[2] first determined that the length of the lattice in the fiber axis and thus the average length of crystallites was 300 to 600 A and that the breadth and thickness were as high as 500 A, in contrast with the narrower bundles (50 A) in cellulose; thus they correspond to 80,000 to 150,000 isoprene units in a crystallite. The breadths do not change (sharpen) with increasing elongation and intensity, which proves that particles do not enlarge but that new crystallites are formed with increasing extension.

Vulcanized Rubber. 1. Crystalline sulfur or additional new crystalline compounds formed by the vulcanizing agent and rubber in ade-

[1] *Science*, **79**, 433 (1934).
[2] *Loc. cit.*

quately cured stock are not indicated on diffraction patterns by the appearance of new rings or spots. Even in hard rubber with high sulfur content this is true. The only diffraction effects not due to rubber itself are due to excess crystalline vulcanizing agent or to crystalline fibers.

2. Vulcanized rubber unstretched produces an amorphous halo and, when sufficiently stretched, a crystal-fiber pattern. Three-dimensional, or higher, orientation can also be attained by proper stretching conditions (Gehman and Field).

3. The positions of halos and of crystal interferences are identically the same for crepe or smoked sheets and for vulcanized rubber. Hundreds of measurements with the aid of the best microphotometers have detected no shift in positions, alterations in relative intensities, missing or additional interferences. This simply means that vulcanization produces no measurable changes in intermolecular spacings or lattice arrangement of polymerized isoprene molecules. There is no evidence of solid solution, compound formation, separate crystalline phase (if the mix is heated sufficiently to remove crystalline sulfur), or any other structural changes in terms of the unit crystal cell.

4. The crystal-fiber pattern appears only after a considerably greater elongation after vulcanization than is required for crude rubber. For the latter the crystal pattern appears at 80 per cent extension and increases in intensity with further extension. Crude rubber that has been subjected to mastication must be stretched above 80 per cent (depending on the extent of the treatment). Vulcanized rubber (about 5 per cent of sulfur) must be stretched to 225 to 250 per cent elongation. Thus there is considerably greater resistance in vulcanized rubber to the parallel arrangement of molecules or crystallites, but once formed the crystal pattern indicates a lattice structure identical with that of stretched crude rubber. In the ebonite, or hard-rubber, state the pattern is obviously that of a nonparallel arrangement of molecular chains and crystallites in keeping with the very high viscosity and non-elasticity. A mix of rubber with 30 per cent sulfur and 1 per cent accelerator must be heated at least 1 hr at 132°C before all evidences of excess crystalline sulfur are removed.

5. Definite hysteresis effects are observed for vulcanized rubber. When a specimen is stretched rapidly to 250 per cent, crystal interferences appear at once which are much more intense than the patterns for a specimen stretched 250 per cent very slowly.[1] When the former is allowed to retract slowly, the crystal interferences remain visible down to 130 per cent. Furthermore, photometric analysis proves that the amorphous halo which is perfectly uniform for unstretched samples shows differential intensity of the equator compared with the poles for elongations of 100 per cent. This indicates that, even before reaching the

[1] Iguchi and Schossberger, *Kautschuk*, **12**, 193 (1936).

critical elongations, rubber molecules bearing sulfur are being directed toward a parallel arrangement within the amorphous, mesomorphic, or liquid crystal state. In 1940, Clark, Kabler, Blaker, and Ball[1] presented complete crystallization hysteresis loops determined from diffraction patterns made at various stages of elongation and retraction of rubber specimens. These loops were quantitatively correlated with stress-strain hysteresis loops and with the important practical property of resilience.

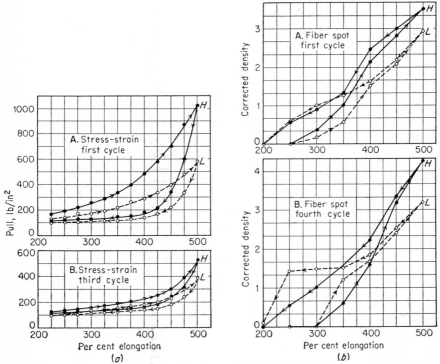

Fig. 383a, b. Hysteresis in stretched rubber: (a) stress-strain; (b) x-ray crystallization. H, high modulus, high resilience; L, low modulus, low resilience.

In Fig. 383a and b are compared the stress-strain and crystallization hysteresis loops for samples H with high modulus and high resilience and L with lower values. The data are obtained by quantitative evaluation of intensities of an equatorial spot on the pattern, calibrated with a diffraction ring of nickel foil on the same film. In subsequent work Clark and LeTourneau found the crystallization hysteresis loop to be by far the most sensitive indication of every variable in a rubber sample. For example, Fig. 383c shows the effect of sulfur content in the same rubber stock (A, 1%; B, 2%; C, 3%; D, 8% S).

[1] G. L. Clark, M. Kabler, E. Blaker, and J. M. Ball, *Ind. Eng. Chem.*, **32**, 1474 (1940).

6. Rubber vulcanized in the stretched state loses completely its crystal-fiber structure, thus proving the disorganizing effect of the vulcanizing agent.[1]

7. Experiments on vulcanized sol and gel rubber in the author's laboratory seem highly significant. Pure sol rubber does not tend to form crystal fibers even at 1,000 per cent elongation, as though the material were a fluid or the molecules too short to maintain a preferred orientation in the fiber once formed. Total rubber behaves normally in that greater elongations are required; vulcanized gel is quite similar to the untreated gel on the elongation required; but vulcanized sol rubber crystallizes and forms fibers at about 200 per cent, far below the value for the unvulcanized phase and nearly the same as the vulcanized gel. This seems to indicate that the primary action of the vulcanizing agent is to solidify and strengthen the sol phase in which the gel phase may be dispersed. Under the same experimental conditions the vulcanized-sol interferences are appreciably broader than those of vulcanized gel at the same elongation, which can mean that the degree of polymerization and the number of molecules in the crystallite are still below the values for the gel.

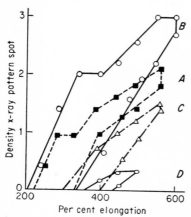

FIG. 383c. Crystallization hysteresis loops determined from fiber patterns as a function of sulfur content of rubber.

Thus the mechanism of vulcanization still remains an open question, largely because the presence of sulfur is not directly indicated by x-ray methods. Preponderance of evidence and of opinion favors chemical combination by one of the possibilities represented in Fig. 384 by Hauser.[2]

Reactions Involving Accelerators. An interesting side light on rubber processing and structure is the x-ray study reactions between accelerators and accelerator activators in rubber stocks at curing temperatures.[3] For example, it is established by x-ray powder patterns that the accelerator tetramethylthiuram disulfide (methyl Tuads) reacts with the activator zinc oxide to form zinc dimethyldithiocarbamate.

$$(CH_2)_2NC\!-\!S\!-\!S\!-\!CN(CH_3)_2 \xrightarrow{ZnO} (CH_3)_2NC\!-\!S\!-\!Zn\!-\!S\!-\!CN(CH_3)_2$$
$$\underset{S}{\|} \qquad\qquad \underset{S}{\|} \qquad\qquad\qquad\quad \underset{S}{\|} \qquad\qquad\qquad \underset{S}{\|}$$

[1] Hauser, *India Rubber World*, **101**, 1 (1939).

[2] *Ind. Eng. Chem.*, **30**, 1291 (1938).

[3] G. L. Clark, R. L. LeTourneau, and J. M. Ball, *Ind. Eng. Chem.*, **35**, 198 (1943).

Upon stretching the rubber matrix this compound becomes highly oriented, indicating a strong bond between rubber crystallites and grains of accelerator salt. Reinforcing pigments such as extremely fine whiting, $CaCO_3$, and ZnO also orient on stretching, as shown by the x-ray patterns, whereas coarse nonreinforcing fillers and pigments do not.

Gutta-percha, Balata, and Chicle. There has been considerable disagreement concerning the structures of gutta-percha and balata, which are, like rubber, polymers of isoprene. The discrepancies were finally explained in the work of Hopff and von Susich[1] and of Stillwell and

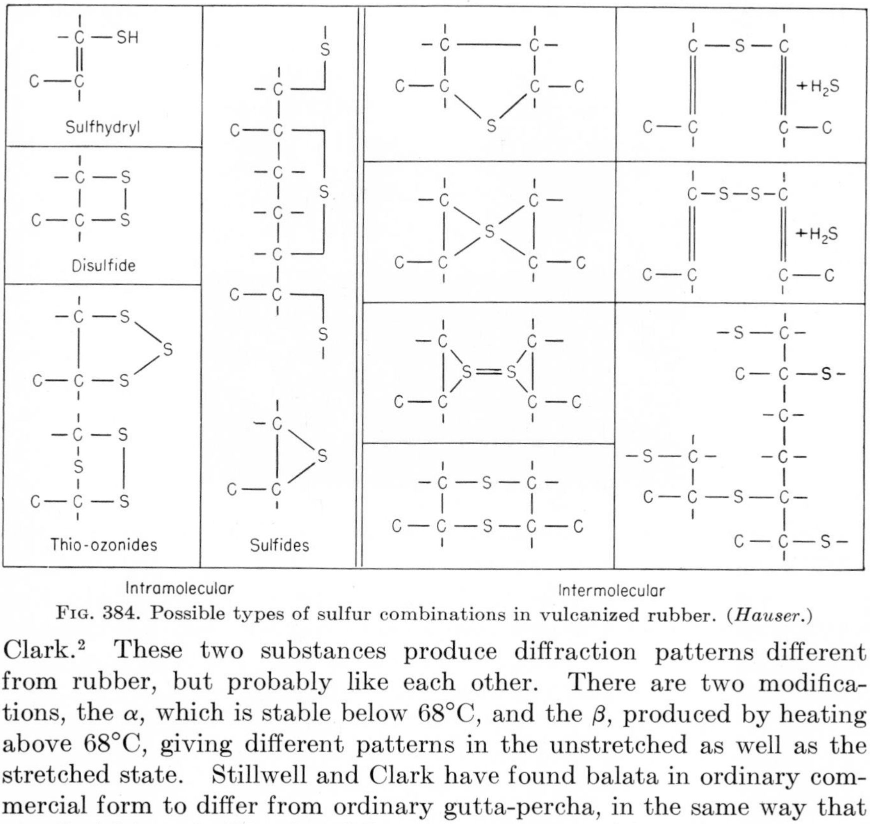

Intramolecular   Intermolecular

FIG. 384. Possible types of sulfur combinations in vulcanized rubber. (*Hauser.*)

Clark.[2] These two substances produce diffraction patterns different from rubber, but probably like each other. There are two modifications, the α, which is stable below 68°C, and the β, produced by heating above 68°C, giving different patterns in the unstretched as well as the stretched state. Stillwell and Clark have found balata in ordinary commercial form to differ from ordinary gutta-percha, in the same way that von Susich's α modification differs from β-gutta-percha (Fig. 385).

Chicle was studied by Stillwell and Clark. The hydrocarbon constituent here is identical with gutta-percha. The resins, calcium oxalate, and other substances constitute the remainder of this product.

Rubber, gutta-percha, balata, and chicle all are built from hydrocarbon chains of the same constitution. The difference comes in a cis con-

[1] *Kautschuk*, **11**, 234 (1930).

[2] *Ind. Eng. Chem.*, **23**, 706 (1931); *Kautschuk*, **5**, 86 (1931).

figuration for rubber where the identity period is 8.2 A and a trans form in the gutta-percha, or zigzag chains with an identity period of 8.7 A (α form).

For the α-gutta there is an identity period of 8.70 A, and the unit cell is probably monoclinic with 16 isoprene residues or 8 chains. An arrangement of the isoprene units in one plane, assuming normal bond lengths and angles to correspond with a twofold screw axis, leads exactly to the value 8.7 A.

For β-gutta, which will give sharp patterns in stretched condition, Fuller determined the orthorhombic unit cell to have the dimensions

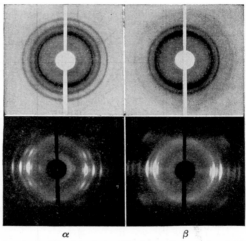

α   β

Fɪɢ. 385. Patterns for unstretched and stretched α-gutta-percha (*left*) and β-gutta-percha (*right*).

$a = 11.9$, $b = 4.8$, $c = 7.85$ A with four isoprene groups. Hence the identity found along the fiber axis is less than half that of α-gutta as follows:

α   β

$$CH_3 \qquad\qquad CH_3$$

$$-CH_3$$

Plane of reflection—plane of paper   No plane or center of symmetry

Furthermore a planar configuration analogous to that of the α form would require a value of 5.05 A. Hence, there must be a rotation of the chain around two of the C—C linkages to account for the dimensions, with the result that there is a greater difference between the two forms of gutta than that between two forms of rubber.   Bunn[1] proposed chain distortions similar to those in rubber already mentioned.   But Jeffrey[2] showed that x-ray intensities calculated for a β-gutta-percha structure involving no distortions gave as good qualitative agreement with experimental values as did the structure proposed by Bunn.

Cellulose. *Composition.* Polymers of dehydrated glucose residue represented by the formula $(C_6H_{10}O_5)_x$; 1,4 glucosidal linkage through oxygen bridge; cellobiose the repeating unit along macromolecular chains (Fig. 386).

Occurrence. The principal framework of plants as fibers of the commercially important wood, cotton, jute, sisal, hemp, ramie (Fig. 387), flax; sheets in the single-celled *Valonia;* in the green

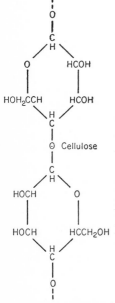

Fig.   386.   Structural formula of repeating cellobiose unit in cellulose.

Fig. 387. Fiber pattern of ramie, a natural source of cellulose.

alga *Halicystis,* in membranes formed by the action on glucose, fructose, sucrose, glycerin, etc., of *Acetobacteri xylinus,* and in the marine animal tunicin.   Cellulose dispersed in viscose and cuprammonium solutions regenerated as rayons.

Polymorphic Forms. At least three: Cellulose I, native, the usual form from all natural sources except in *Halicystis;* cellulose II, mercerized or hydrate, the native form in *Halicystis*[3] and formed from cellulose I by treatment with alkali solutions of requisite strength followed by complete washing out of alkali.   Cellulose II transformed to cellulose I or

[1] *Loc. cit.*

[2] G. A. Jeffrey, *Trans. Faraday Soc.,* **40,** 517 (1944).

[3] Sisson, *Science,* **87,** 350 (1938).

cellulose T (Kubo, Hess) by heating in glycerin at 250°C. Cellulose III by slow removal of ammonia from cellulose I or II swollen in liquid NH_3; reverted to cellulose I or II[1]; believed by Legrand to have α and β forms which react differently with water.[2]

Crystal Structures. For native cellulose (I) several structures based on x-ray diffraction data have been proposed since the first crystal model in 1926 of Sponsler and Dore. The now generally accepted structure is that of Meyer and Misch,[3] confirmed in a rigorous test by Gross and Clark:[4]

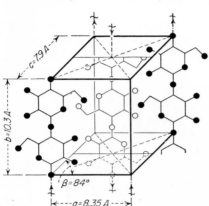

FIG. 388. The crystal unit cell of cellulose.

Monoclinic, space group $P2_1$,

$$a = 8.35 \text{ A}$$
$$b = 10.3 \text{ A (fiber axis)}$$
$$c = 7.95 \text{ A}$$
$$\beta = 84°$$
$$Z(C_6H_{10}O_5 \text{ groups per cell}) = 4$$

Figure 388 shows the disposition in the unit cell of cellobiose units along the macromolecules and the fact that the β-glucose residues are pointing alternately in opposite directions. There is extensive hydrogen bonding between OH groups of neighboring chains, which of course determines many properties. Without considering the details of alternative interpretations by Sauter and Sponsler, Gross and Clark calculated the nine patterns for highly oriented cellulose preparations to be expected for each of the Meyer and the Sauter structures, for the three experimental techniques, transmission, rotation, and goniometer (equatorial layer line), each in three directions (Fig. 389). Then, with stretched, highly oriented specimens of bacterial cellulose, *Valonia*, and tunicin, nine patterns were made and compared with those theoretically deduced—with complete substantiation of the Meyer structure.

Unit-cell data for the other polymorphic forms of cellulose are as shown in Table 23-3. Patterns for cellulose II and III appear in Figs. 390a and b.

The greater monoclinic angle and more open structure easily account for the ease in dyeing and processing the mercerized form of cellulose.

Orientations in Cellulose Fibers and Sheets. With the cellulose chain and unit cell common to all materials, each natural fiber or membrane

[1] Clark and Parker, *J. Phys. Chem.*, **41**, 777 (1937).

[2] C. L. Legrand, *J. Polymer Sci.*, **7**, 333 (1951).

[3] *Helv. Chim. Acta*, **20**, 232 (1937).

[4] *Z. Krist.*, **99**, 357 (1938).

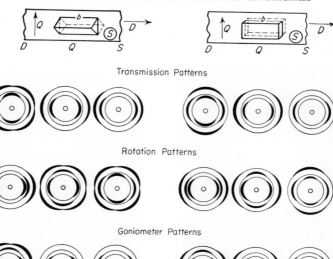

FIG. 389. Theoretical diffraction patterns for alternative interpretations of cellulose structure. *Left*, Meyer-Mark patterns; *right*, Sauter patterns. *D* is the direction of stretching; *Q*, the direction perpendicular to *D* and lying in the surface of the membrane; *S*, the direction normal to the surface of the membrane. Transmission patterns are made with the beam passing through the sample parallel to the direction indicated by the column heading. Rotation and goniometer patterns are obtained by rotating the sample about an axis parallel to the direction indicated by the column heading. (*Gross and Clark.*)

is distinguished by a typical diffraction pattern and a typical orientation of macromolecules or crystallites. Orientation is characterized by type and degree; this has been extensively studied in a series of papers by Sisson and Clark and by Sisson.[1] The x-ray method for quantitative

TABLE 23-3. UNIT-CELL DATA FOR POLYMORPHIC FORMS OF CELLULOSE

Unit-cell dimensions	Cellulose II (mercerized or hydrate)	Cellulose III	Cellulose T
a	8.14 A	7.48 A	8.11 A
b	10.3 A	10.3 A	10.3 A
c	9.14 A	8.61 A	7.9 A
β	62°	58°	90°
	(Fig. 390a)	(Fig. 390b)	

comparison of crystallite orientation in cellulose fibers is based on the assumption that the distribution around the pencil of x-rays is proportional to the distribution of intensity around the (002) diffraction ring.

[1] *Ind. Eng. Chem., Anal. Ed.*, **5**, 296 (1933); *Ind. Eng. Chem.*, **27**, 51 (1935); *J. Phys. Chem.*, **40**, 343 (1935); *Contrib. Boyce Thompson Inst.*, **9**, 239 (1938).

In cotton, for example, submicroscopic crystalline structure revealed by x-rays usually runs parallel to visible configuration such as fibrils (Fig. 391). Intensity measurements are made with a microdensitometer

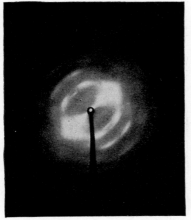

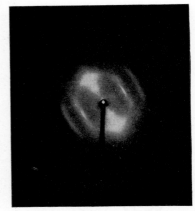

Fig. 390a. Fiber pattern of mercerized (hydrate or II) cellulose.

Fig. 390b. Fiber pattern of cellulose III.

equipped with a rotating stage. Curves are thus constructed, the value at each point representing the relative percentage of the total crystallites over a 5-deg angular range. The orientation of the cellulose structural units varies widely in different fibers and in the same fiber. The influence upon physical and chemical properties has been established with

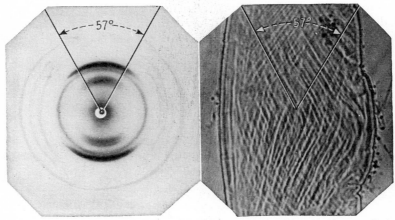

Fig. 391. Diffraction pattern and photomicrograph of cotton fiber, showing correlation of fibril spiral angle. (*Courtesy of W. A. Sisson.*)

reference to degree of mercerization, tensile strength, classification (the x-ray method is now used by the United States government), elasticity and dyeing properties of cotton; the swelling elasticity, tensile strength, dyeing properties, resistance to enzymatic decomposition, gloss, creasing resistance, refractive index of rayons; and the density, tensile strength,

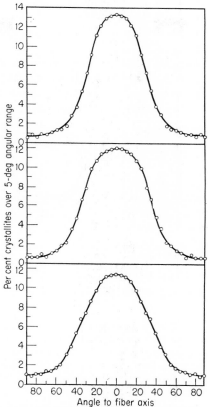

FIG. 392. Curves illustrating microphotometric method of comparison of chain or crystallite orientation in fibers from x-ray patterns. *Top*, Egyptian cotton; *center*, Eastern cotton; *bottom*, irrigated cotton.

expansion, and shrinkage of wood. The general method can be illustrated by three varieties of cotton, as in Fig. 392, and the methods for expressing differences in orientations are illustrated in the following table:

	Irrigated	Eastern	Egyptian
Tensile strength of cord, kg/mm².	17.6	18.3	20.0
Height of mode, mm.	11.4	12.0	13.35
Percentage of orientation.	45.06	49.94	52.86
Cosine summation factor.	85.38	87.79	88.58
Median.	17.83°	16.41°	14.38°
Mean.	27.27°	25.51°	24.10°
Standard deviation.	32.40°	29.30°	28.40°

Thus, the last six types of measurement from the curves run parallel with the practical property of tensile strength. Cotton fibers younger than 25 days show random orientation of cellulose chains. For these very young fibers, even 5 days old, crystalline cellulose is present, though the patterns may be obscured by effects due to waxes which may be removed by extraction.

X-ray data prove that in cellulose fibers the b axes of the crystallites (*i.e.*, the direction of the chains) approach an orientation in the cell wall either parallel to or at some spiral angle to the fiber axis. The types of preferred orientation, always assuming deviation from ideal 100 per cent

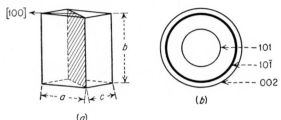

(a)

FIG. 393. (a) The cellulose unit cell with the (101) plane shaded; (b) the three principal diffraction rings appearing on patterns.

arrangement, are described by Sisson, specifically for fibers made from bacterial cellulose membranes but generally applicable, as follows:

1. Random.
2. Uniplanar; b axes parallel to a plane but at random otherwise.
3. Selective uniplanar (ring fiber); b axes parallel to but otherwise at random in a plane; (101) planes have a selective orientation parallel to plane.
4. Uniaxial; b axes parallel to fiber axis but planes at random.
5. Selective uniaxial; b axes parallel to fiber axes and (101) planes parallel to plane containing fiber axis.

The designation of the three principal interferences for cellulose, and the position of (101) planes, are given in Fig. 393. There are illustrated in Figs. 394a to e the sample orientation and directions A,B,C; the pole figures (Chap. 22) with dotted areas representing projection of b axes, and crosshatched the [101] directions; and the patterns for the three inner interferences (101), (10$\bar{1}$), (200) from the center out.

By such methods the structures of many fibers and of sheets both natural and deformed have been determined, largely by Sisson; for example, in spiral native fibers there is a nonselective orientation, adequately proved by the synthesis of theoretical patterns. Especial attention has been directed to *Valonia* in order to discover the mechanism of cell-wall deposition.[1] It has layers in which cellulose chains in any one layer are inclined to those of preceding and subsequent layers at an angle

[1] Astbury, Marwick, and Bernal, *Proc. Roy. Soc.* (*London*), **109**, 443 (1932). Preston and Astbury, *Proc. Roy. Soc.* (*London*), **122**, 76 (1937).

of about 80 deg; the chains of one set form a system of meridians in the roughly spherical cell wall, and those of the other set a spiral closing down on two "poles" (apex and base).   The (101) plane of spacing

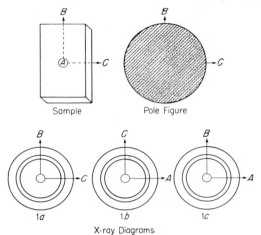

FIG. 394a. Random orientation in cellulose specimens.

6.1 A is approximately parallel to the cell wall.   It is a general rule that in any sample elongated in one direction the b axes are oriented parallel to that direction, and if the sample is constricted in one direction, the (101) planes are oriented normal to that direction.   Both elongation and

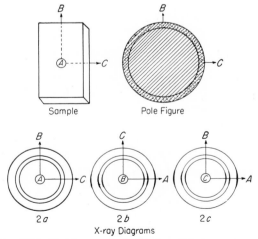

FIG. 394b. Uniplanar orientation in cellulose specimens.

shrinkage are involved in coagulated cellulose (rayons and cellophane): random, swollen state or shrinkage along three axes; uniaxial, by shrinkage along two axes or by elongation on one axis and shrinkage along two axes; uniplanar, by shrinkage on one axis or elongation on two axes and shrinkage on one axis; biaxial, shrinkage on one and elongation on one. In cellophane, shrinkage occurs perpendicular to the sheet and gives a

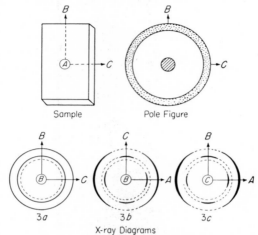

Fig. 394c. Selective uniplanar orientation in cellulose specimens.

pattern for selective uniplanar orientation. Shrinkage is actually more important than stretching elongation in establishing the structure of rayons. Viscose, if spun without tension, has a selective orientation with reference to the fiber surface, rather than the previously considered,

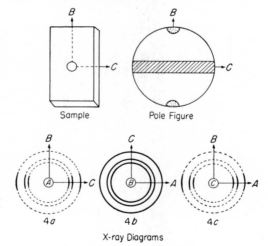

Fig. 394d. Uniaxial orientation in cellulose specimens.

highly oriented "skin." The control of the degree of orientation, guided by x-ray patterns, has resulted in vast improvement in the tensile strength, dry and wet, and in other properties of present-day rayon.

Figure 395 compares the patterns of old and new products, showing the greatly increased degree of fibering in the latter.

Orientation in wood is of great significance since it determines the properties of strength, splitting, swelling, shrinkage, etc. Wood is really

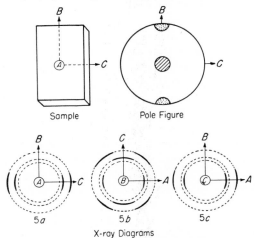

Sample   Pole Figure

5*a*   5*b*   5*c*

X-ray Diagrams

Fɪɢ. 394*e*. Selective uniaxial orientation in cellulose specimens.

two interpenetrating systems of cellulose fibers and of incrustants such as lignin. The crystallites, or chains, of cellulose may be parallel to the fiber axis (producing the usual fiber pattern with intensity maximum on the equator) or at a constant slope to the axis and parallel to each other

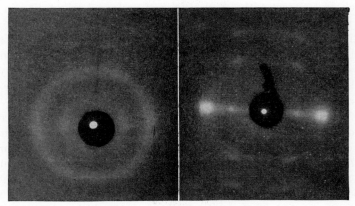

Fɪɢ. 395. Patterns for old (*left*) and new (*right*) varieties of rayon, showing great increase in degree of preferred orientation in latter, introduced by tension during coagulation.

(producing a four-point pattern); or they may deviate considerably from either position, usually the latter. The orientation depends on the species of wood, the season of growth (summerwood is denser and more perfectly oriented than springwood), and the position of growth. Compression wood on the leaning side of trunks or underside of branches is more perfectly oriented. Ritter and Stillwell have shown that the orientation is random for 1 ft or more from a growing tip and that complex transition structures occur at junctions with parent branches.

The correlation has been established that woods with cellulose chains parallel to the fiber axis split easily, have high tensile strength, and undergo little longitudinal shrinkage.

Clark has demonstrated that the degree of preferred orientation in kraft paper pulps can be correlated with the origin of the wood and the properties of the finished kraft paper.   On page 679 in the discussion of the determination of percentage amorphous constituent, the results of the study of pulps for such products as Kleenex were mentioned and a spread of 30 per cent noted.   Preston, Herman, and Weidinger[1] have similarly examined a number of celluloses of biological interest and find *Valonia* 70 per cent, crystalline; bamboo 50 to 60 per cent; bacterial cellulose 40 per cent; ramie and cotton 69 per cent; and rayon 39 per cent. Since 1940 a large number of papers have been devoted to orientations in cell walls, lamellae, etc., of a wide range of botanical specimens. Space does not permit a summary of these results, largely of R. D. Preston, H. J. Woods, and associates at the University of Leeds.   Meyer in his book[2] (pages 310ff) summarizes the complex fund of information on textures.

The orientation of wood fibers in violins is significant in terms of tone. Spruce in the tops is definitely fibered; instruments with the best tone quality show almost complete lack of orientation in the wood used for the back, in contrast with a high degree of preferred orientation in instruments with a harsh tone quality and weak response.[3]

Particles, Micelles, and Fringes. The structure of cellulose as considered thus far has related primarily to the primary-valence molecular chains of the polymer cellulose.   The question then very naturally arises as to the next step in organization in the series culminating in the visible fiber or sheet.   Five theories will be considered:

1. *Macromolecular Theory.* As illustrated in Fig. 372 the cellulose fibril, or filament, is a lattice of macromolecules with no intermediate stages of aggregation; probably best applicable to synthetic polymers.

2. *Micellar Theory.* A parallel bundle of cellulose chains undoubtedly would possess crystalline properties.   The size of such a bundle would be expected to be within the colloidal range and constitute the micelle (a familiar term introduced initially by von Nägeli in 1858), or crystallite.   This concept, the earliest to explain x-ray results on cellulose intro-

[1] *J. Exptl. Botany,* **1,** 344 (1950).

[2] K. H. Meyer, "Natural and Synthetic High Polymers," 2d ed., vol. 4, Interscience Publishers, Inc., New York, 1950.

[3] Lark-Horowitz and Caldwell, *Nature,* **134,** 23 (1934).

duced by the botanist Seifriz and by Meyer and Mark, is illustrated in
Fig. 396a.   Utilizing the Laue equation for particle-size evaluation from
the breadths of interferences, Hengstenberg and Mark[1] determined that
the micelle, or crystallite, should be greater than 600 A long and 55 A

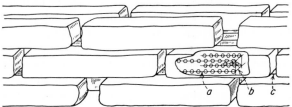

Fig. 396a. The micellar, or crystallite, model of cellulose fiber structure. (*Seifriz-Meyer-Mark.*)   a, Primary-valence chains; b, secondary-valence forces holding chains in bundle; c, tertiary forces (and cementing material) between micelles.

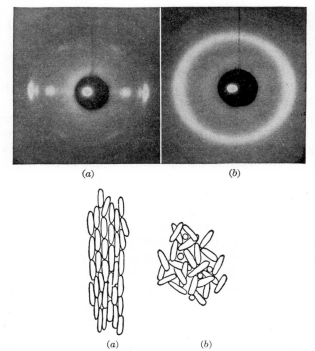

(a)   (b)

(a)   (b)

Fig. 396b. Effect of arrangement of micelles on diffraction patterns of cellulose.   (a) Fiber (improved rayon); (b) cellophane sheet.

thick—in other words, should consist of a bundle of chains each with
about 100 dehydrated glucose residues.   Primary-valence forces hold the
glucose residues in the form of a chain; secondary-valence forces (perhaps hydrogen bonds) hold the chains alongside each other; and tertiary

[1] Hengstenberg and Mark, *Z. Krist.*, **69**, 271 (1928).

forces or amorphous cementing material between micelles hold them together in a fiber. This structure accounts for a number of the properties of cellulose fibers, particularly the tensile strength conditioned by the pulling apart of the "bricks" rather than by the very high strength residing in the primary-valence bond. Swelling is also explained, for many fibers and sheets can swell in suitable liquids and still produce an unchanged diffraction pattern (intermicellar swelling), while other reagents cause a change in spacings because of penetration between the chains themselves, thus affecting the unit cell (intramicellar swelling). Cellulose is considered to be dispersed in solution in the form of micelles by solution of the intermicellar material; if the treatment is drastic, the micelles may be broken into fragments, even into single chains which may be greatly shortened, thus lowering viscosity and molecular weight. The disarrangement of micelles into a brush heap is easily distinguished in the x-ray pattern (Fig. 396b).

3. *Particle Theory.* In 1933 Farr and Eckerson announced the isolation of uniform ellipsoidal cellulose particles 1.5 μ long and 1.1 μ in cross section. The existence and significance of these microscopic particles have been the subject of considerable controversy, particularly from the standpoint of observed smaller dimensions in certain growth lamellae and the nonappearance in electron micrographs. Work at Leeds in 1950–1951 claims the isolation of particles 500 to 2,500 A in length, 50 A thick, and 150 to 200 A wide which will form into transparent, brittle films that give cellulose patterns with 101 and 10$\bar{1}$ reflections as rings, but 101 planes are oriented parallel to the plane of the film. Some of these micelles have been isolated from jute, which is heavily incrusted with lignin, as well as from ramie and cotton.[1]

4. *Net and Fringe Structure.* This theory is in a sense a compromise, but it is one that has found wide acceptance. As a result of the work of Mark, Kratky, and Frey-Wysfling especially, the "brick" structure representing regular termination of cellulose chains is discarded in favor of an essentially continuous network of longer chains. Over occasional areas these chains may be nearly parallel to form ordered regions corresponding to crystallites, or micelles, which therefore are not discontinuous "bricks" but are bound together with the same long cellulose chains in disorder (Fig. 397).

Various chemical and physical methods, namely, the determination of end groups, osmotic measurements, studies with the ultracentrifuge, viscosities, and x-ray investigations have in all cases pointed to the conclusion that the principal valence chains in native cellulose reach a degree of polymerization of at least 2,000. If the chains are assumed to be stiff, they would have a length of 1.5 μ and a diameter of about 7 A. If they are considered to be wound into a ball, the diameter would be about

[1] Mukherjee, Sikonski, and Woods, *Nature,* **167,** 821 (1951).

100 A.   It has been well established experimentally that every technical treatment of native cellulose causes a certain amount of degradation. Several investigators agree that in the precipitated material of technical threads and films, consisting of cellulose, the degree of polymerization lies between 150 and 500.[1]

It may now be asked at what length the chain will coincide with the linear dimensions of the micelle.   The measurements on the length of

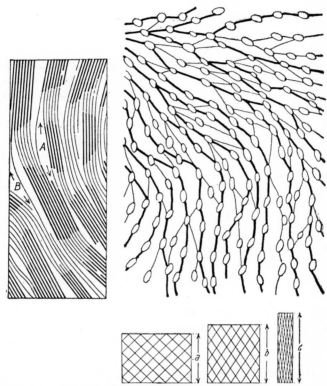

Fig. 397. Fringe and network structure of cellulose, showing ordered regions of parallel molecules and disordered regions corresponding to flexible joints; and the mechanism of extension of a network.   (*Mark, Kratky, and Frey-Wyssling.*)

the crystallized regions in cellulose have been deduced by Hengstenberg and Mark[2] from the widths of interferences on x-ray diffraction patterns. For the samples of cellulose under stress, the average length was found to be larger than 600 A.

More recently Kratky and Mark[3] applied the method of Frey-Wyssling to elucidate this problem further.   In this method small metal crystals,

[1] Kraemer, *Ind. Eng. Chem.*, **30**, 1200 (1938).

[2] *Op. cit.*

[3] *Protoplasma*, **25**, 261 (1936), **26**, 75 (1936), **27**, 372, 563 (1937).

usually gold, are deposited inside cellulose fibers, which are then subjected to x-ray diffraction analysis. These patterns are distinguished by the evidence of blackening of the photographic film at very small angles in the neighborhood of the primary beam. The marked intensity of scattered radiation at very small angles close to the primary beam indicates that something like a lattice with very large spacings is built up in the process of distribution of the heavy metal particles in the cellulose fiber. From this intensity distribution, it is possible to derive approximately the dimensions of the micelle in the material under stress. These measurements give values for the crystallized regions of 700 to 1,000 A in length, on the average, and 50 to 70 A as the diameters. As mentioned above, a definite drop in tensile strength is observed if the degree of polymerization falls below about 200. A single glucose residue has a length of about 5 A so that a degree of polymerization of 200 means a chain length of about 1,000 A. A comparison of this value with the average length of the micelle proves at once that the decrease in tensile strength takes place when the average length of the cellulose chains equals the average length of the crystallized regions. When the chains are five times longer (polymerization degree 1,000), then the chain ends have a greater probability of being concealed inside the micelles and, consequently, the tensile strength approaches the maximum value as measured by Meyer and Lotmar.

It may now be concluded that the crystallized portions of the structure are the reinforcing backbone of the structure, while the unordered regions may be regarded as the weak spots. If a film is soaked with water, the x-ray evidence shows that there is no change in the crystallized regions and that the water penetrates only the amorphous material which is built up by the fringes of the micelles. If chain ends occur, as they frequently do, in these swollen areas, then tensile strength will be a very sensitive function of swelling. The wet strength of cellulose fibers depends, therefore, to a large degree upon the average length of the chains; for the longer the chains are, the larger the amount of crystallized material and the smaller the chance of chain ends occurring in the unordered network of the fringes.

From this point of view, instead of distinguishing between intermicellar and intramicellar swelling, it is better to speak of entrance of water into the fringes or into the crystallized regions or micelles themselves.[1]

This conception of cellulose structure indicates that the *physical properties*, tenacity, elasticity, etc., are functionally related to the amount of crystalline material, whereas the *reactivity* of the fiber, swelling, drying, ease of chemical reactions, etc., is to be associated with the amorphous parts. The relative frequency and the length of the micelles depend

---

[1] Hermanns, *Kolloid-Z.*, **81**, 143, 300 (1937), **82**, 58, 83, 71 (1938).

upon the average chain length; hence, this in turn determines in large measure both physical and chemical properties.

The question now arises of what molecular changes accompany a macroscopic deformation of a film or filament. In commercial practice a cellulose material is formed in a swollen state. The water between the chains in the fringe areas gives to these regions between the stiffer crystallized micelles the role of joints which impart to the whole system a certain amount of flexibility. Thus, it is justifiable to visualize a swollen fiber as a flexible network in which the crystallized regions represent the stiff links and the fringe ranges, the bendable joints (Fig. 397).

The total behavior of the system is influenced by the following:

1. The relative amounts of crystallized and amorphous fractions.
2. The ratio between the average length of the main valence chains and the average length of the crystallized regions.
3. The flexibility of the fringe and its sensitivity to swelling and chemical reactions.

5. *Microfibril-Micellar Strand Theory.* Since the advent of the net and fringe structure, just discussed, several intensive investigations of cellulose texture have been made with the electron microscope, with results which are not adequately explained by any of the foregoing theories. Frey-Wyssling[1] in 1954 proposed a structure consistent with x-ray and electron-microscope data. The macrofiber is composed of microfibrils having diameters of 150 to 250 A which can be detected with the electron microscope. Further degradation of the microfibril by ultrasonics, hydrolysis, or oxidation results in *elementary fibrils* or *micellar strands* having dimensions of the order of 70 to 90 A by 30 A, and thus are flat filaments which aggregate laterally with each other. This crystalline core is flattened parallel to the (101) lattice planes as a result of the faster growth of (101) which is hydrophilic, as opposed to the slower-growing (10$\bar{1}$) plane. The crystalline core of the microfibrils is embedded in a *paracrystalline* (not completely amorphous) cellulose phase, in which the lack of order of the chain molecules is caused by the escaping water released during the polymerization of glucose and crystallization of the resulting cellulose chain molecules. Since the tendency toward aggregation in the (101) plane is greater than in the direction perpendicular to it, it follows that water may be occluded between the (101) planes. Thus the microfibrils are laminated and split easily parallel to the (101) plane, while the elementary fibrils or micellar strands adhere laterally to each other. By this means it is possible to account for the failure to observe amorphous cellulose as such in electron micrographs of fibers such as cotton, and yet provide for a matrix of disordered chains as indicated on x-ray patterns. The micellar strand dimensions

[1] *Science,* **119,** 80 (1954).

are consistent with the data by the Frey-Wyssling technique described in the preceding net-fringe theory.

Diffraction of X-rays at Very Small Angles by Celluloses and Rayons. From the author's laboratory more than 20 years ago were reported the measurements of very large spacings for a number of natural materials. These include 171 A in living nerve,[1] 440 A in collagen, 48 A for radially oriented natural wax in intestinal-wall collagen,[2] 81 A in keratin, 58 A in gel rubber, and 75 A in chitosan.[3] Since that time, of course, many similar measurements have been made and correlated with electron-microscope observations.

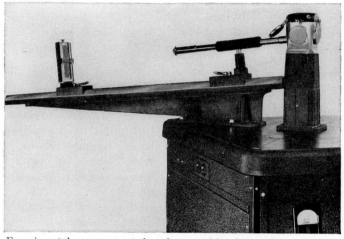

Fig. 398. Experimental arrangement for photographing low-angle scattering and long-spacing interferences.

By extending the experimental technique to its fullest possibilities using finely collimated x-ray beams of monochromatized radiation and increased distances from specimen to film (10 to 30 cm) as shown in Fig. 398, attempts have been made to resolve interferences at very small angles corresponding to very large spacings in cellulose and its derivatives. In most of these cases there is a definite but somewhat diffuse scattering at very small angles. Equatorial maxima run out from this halo like small arrowheads; but in spite of ingenuity in obtaining the very sharpest possible patterns it has been impossible to resolve these equatorial streaks into a series of individual spots. This is a case of true Guinier low-angle scattering (page 655), in which the inner edge is resolved from the primary undeviated x-ray beam. There are, however, some very interesting characteristics of this phenomenon.[4]

[1] *Radiology,* **25,** 131 (1935).
[2] *Radiology,* **27,** 339 (1936).
[3] *J. Am. Chem. Soc.,* **57,** 1509 (1935); *J. Phys. Chem.,* **40,** 863 (1935).
[4] Clark and Parker, *Science,* **85,** 203 (1937).

Figure 399a is a diagrammatic representation of the innermost part of a diffraction pattern for native ramie. A continuous streak runs along the equator from the central spot of the pattern, which is widest at the smallest angles and tapers gradually to a nearly constant width of blackening on the film. The greatest intensity seems to be reached at a spacing of about 40 A followed by a rapidly diminishing intensity down to about 20 A. The obvious explanation of this pattern seems to be that a whole range of lateral spacings between macromolecules, crystallites, or micelles occurs; or this may be the width of the micellar strands in the latest Frey-Wyssling theory of cellulose structure discussed in the preceding section. The greater this spacing is, *i.e.*, the smaller the angle,

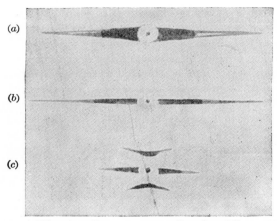

Fig. 399. Diagrams of diffraction effects at very small angles of fiber pattern. (a) Native ramie; (b) mercerized ramie dried under tension; (c) regenerated cellulose rayons (nitro, cuprammonium, viscose).

the less perfect is the longitudinal arrangement along the length of the chains in the crystallites so that the resulting diffraction effect is increasingly more diffuse or wider.

In Fig. 399b is represented the innermost part of the pattern of mercerized cellulose dried under tension so that the greatest preferred orientation can be gained. The same equatorial streak can be observed as with the original native ramie, but now it is very sharp and uniform in width until it merges with the trace of the undiffracted beam. The marked effect, therefore, of pulling the chains more nearly parallel to each other is directly indicated.

Figure 399c represents an entirely new finding for rayon. With the most careful technique involving very small pinholes, careful blocking of the primary beam, vacuum camera, and similar details, we find for all regenerated cellulose rayons, including nitro, cuprammonium, and viscose, the production of a very sharp equatorial streak and very definitely a first layer line on either side from which can be measured a fiber identity period of 154 A.   Acetate rayons do not give this pattern, but only a fairly diffuse general scattering around the central spot.   The progression in regularity of structure from native ramie to mercerized ramie when dried under tension and then to commercial rayons seems to be clearly indicated by these curious unresolved diffraction maxima at very small angles.

Topochemical Reactions of Cellulose as Revealed by X-rays.   Mercerization of cellulose is the first example of a topochemical reaction, *i.e.*, the conversion of one crystal form into another in a fiber without destroying or indeed even seriously affecting the fiber in over-all structure or strength.   Now almost all reactions of cellulose are topochemical in the same way.   This, of course, is exactly what should be expected for crystal particles that are embedded in a usually less resistant matrix.

A large amount of work has been done on *changes* in structure of cellulose—a familiar process in chemistry for a system concerning which for a given steady state there is a limited amount of information.   Nitration and acetylation, important commercial processes, are topochemical reactions in that the original fibrous form of cellulose may be retained without disintegration during esterification.   Another point of interest shown by x-ray patterns is the irreversibility of some reactions.   When an attempt is made to determine the point of equilibrium in chemical treatment of a fiber by an approach from both sides (building up and decomposing or concentrating and diluting a reagent in contact with cellulose), a very considerable hysteresis effect is shown.   Starting with cellulose and hydrazine, the former will be in equilibrium up to 38 per cent solutions of hydrazine and will still show only the cellulose pattern.   In decomposition of the cellulose-hydrazine complex, the interferences show the structure of the complex from 63 to 20 per cent solutions.   Hess has shown that mercerized cellulose gives the pattern of soda cellulose III in NaOH solutions under 11 per cent; soda cellulose I, 12 to 26 per cent; and soda cellulose II, above 28 per cent.   In dilution experiments the last pattern appears down to 2.16 per cent solutions.   These and similar experiments have thrown considerable light on the mechanism of these crystallite heterogeneous reactions.   In the building up of a cellulose compound the molecules of the reagent must pass into the interior of the crystallite, or micelle, *through* layers of the solid reaction product, whereas in dissociation by dilutions of the outer reagent the transport from the interior of the crystallite of the dissociated molecules corresponding to the original reagent must take place through layers of the solid disintegration product.   This micellar heterogeneous reaction is illustrated in Fig. 400.   The surface layers are too thin to allow registration on diffraction patterns.   Although mono- and diesters should be expected as intermediate products, they usually are not identified by x-ray patterns.

The chemical action on the three hydroxyl groups of cellulose to a final triester is entirely completed in a given layer before the reagent reaches the next molecular layer. Intermediate products would appear then only at interfaces, and on geometric grounds evidence on diffraction patterns could not be expected. On the other hand, if the ratio of speed of diffusion of the reagent into the cellulose particle to the speed of reaction is high, then intermediate products might be formed in second, third, fourth, etc., molecular layers before reaction is completed in the first layer. Distinctive patterns have been obtained for the hemimethylate of cellulose and dinitrocellulose. In some cases, especially for substituted products lower than triderivatives, very diffuse patterns are

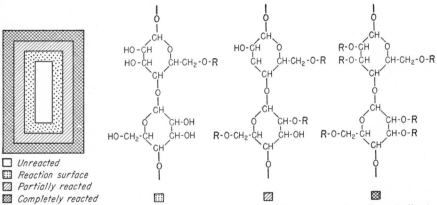

FIG. 400. Diagram of heterogeneous micellar reaction. The cross section of a micelle, in which the reaction has progressed to a greater degree on the outside layers, and the probable degree of reaction of the cellulose chain in the different layers are illustrated.

obtained. Hess has shown that one reaction product may be separated from another (for example hemimethylate from trimethyl cellulose) by extraction, so that both fractions then give characteristic sharp patterns. Stretched films of "amorphous" nitrate or acetate may yield evidence of fibering, called pseudocrystalline; actually a proportion of randomly oriented crystallites, undetected before stretching, are brought into more easily detected parallel orientation.

In all cases of topochemical addition reactions of cellulose the fiber will thicken but not lengthen, from which the conclusion may be drawn that the reagent penetrates between chains. This is a logical consequence of the disposition of reactive OH groups along the chains. As a result the identity period along the film axis is $n \times 5.15$ A for a wide variety of cellulose derivatives; these may therefore be grouped into families with 10.3 A ($n = 2$), 15.4 A ($n = 3$), 25.6 A ($n = 5$), with the single exception of d-camphor nitrocellulose with a period of 38.3 A, as follows:

I. 10.3 A	II. 15.4 A	III. 25.6 A	IV. 38.3 A
Cellulose derivative with:			
Ammonia I	Ammonia II	Nitro I	d-Camphor nitro I
Methylamine	Soda II	Acetone nitro I, II	
Other primary amines	Copper alkali II	Camphor nitro III,	
Hydrazine I, II	HClO₄ II	IV	
Ethylenediamine I, II	Ethyl oxalate	Cyclonexanone	
Tetralkylammonium	p-Methylcyclohexa-	nitro	
hydroxide	none nitrocellulose	Methyl cyclohexa-	
Lithium		none	
Soda I, III		Nitro II	
Potash		Fenchone nitro	
Copper alkali I			
Nitric acid (Knecht)			
Perchloric acid I			
LiSCN			
Acetate I, II			
Propionyl			
Methyl			
m-Xylol			

The increased multiplicity of the fiber-axis identity period of course comes from a distortion of the chains with increasing amount of substituent, and an increasingly more profound change in the lattice in moving from family I to II to III. In I the successive glucose residues make an angle of 180 deg with each other, while in II the angle is 120 deg; III is confined to trinitrocelluloses and their addition compounds with ketones.

Polymorphism of Cellulose Derivatives. The x-ray method is making possible the identification of a growing list of polymorphic compounds (usually dimorphic) as indicated in the preceding tabulation. The formation in the fibrous state depends on the choice of conditions of temperature, concentration of reacting compounds, etc.; once formed a given modification in fibrous form cannot in general be converted into another form. For example, fibrous acetylcellulose I is formed under 35°C, acetylcellulose II above 50°C, and a mixed diffuse pattern for the product at 35 to 50°C. These facts may be considered a proof that even in solution the particles are present in colloidal dispersion and that reactions are of the heterogeneous type mentioned above. The dimorphism may be of a type of certain keto-enol tautomeric relations for organic compounds which depend on the nature of the solvent for the equilibrium point. Dimorphism has been found not only for cellulose (when native cellulose goes over to so-called cellulose hydrate through a series of intermediate compounds) but for the HClO₄ compound, copper-alkali cellulose, acetone nitrocellulose, a complex with a solvent or swelling agent, acetylcellulose and many others. A whole series of new compounds has been made possible from the complexes with solvents (ketones especially). Thus, xylol will not combine with nitrocellulose directly but will displace acetone in acetone nitrocellulose or will react in the presence of acetone acting as a catalyst. All these identifications have been made possible by the x-ray diffraction method. In general one form is related to native cellulose, the other to mercerized cellulose. There are four forms of so-called soda cellulose. With 11 to 18 per cent NaOH cellulose gives form I (with $6H_2O$ water of crystallization); above 22 per cent form II, anhydrous, is identified. Form I when dehydrated does not give II, but another form III. Form III, as previously stated, is produced when mercerized cellulose is treated with less than 11 per cent solution of NaOH.

The compound 1NaOH/2 glucose has been classed as pseudostoichiometric since only the micellar-surface hydroxyl groups (about 50 per cent) are first affected. Many other reactions are considered in a thorough summary by Sisson[1] and later by Meyer[2] of the x-ray diffraction behavior of cellulose derivatives.

The Swelling of Cellulose. The great contributions of x-ray diffraction to classification of swelling phenomena already have been mentioned. Four types of swelling have been described:

1. Intermicellar. No change in x-ray pattern as cellulose + water.

2. Intramicellar. The interferences shift in position, a fact indicating a change in spacing with penetration of the agent into the lattice. Ammonia produces a great swelling and increase in the (101) spacing from 6.1 A in native cellulose to 10.3. Quaternary ammonium hydroxides with still larger molecules increase this spacing as high as 16.7 A, the b (fiber-axis) spacing remaining always constant at 10.3 A. Swelling of intercrystalline material is responsible for marked increase in fiber diameter.[3]

3. Permutoid. A complex formation that completely changes the pattern as inulin or agar + water. This might easily be classed as a special case of (2).

4. Osmotic. The swelling agent diffuses through a skin or membrane into the interior, giving an essentially amorphous pattern, as for some proteins such as nerve fibers and copper-alkali cellulose, and Brownian motion of the semifluid interior.

Some interesting special cases of swelling are the formation of the Knecht compound with nitric acid (oxonium combination on the oxygen bridge); and reaction with LiSCN. In swelling in $LiSCN/H_2O = \frac{5}{1}$, an identity period is obtained that is 10 times the 5.1-A length of a $C_5H_{10}O_5$ group. This means either short molecules or some peculiar regulatory principle in the addition of groups to the long cellulose chains which gives a repeating identity along the fiber.

[1] *Ind. Eng. Chem.*, **30**, 530 (1938).

[2] Meyer, *loc. cit.*, pp. 344ff.

[3] Clark and Parker, *J. Phys. Chem.*, **41**, 777 (1937). Sisson and Saner, *J. Phys. Chem.*, **43**, 687 (1939).

Starch. The monosaccharide is stored by plants in the form of granules of the familiar polysaccharide starch, which upon hydrolysis yields glucose. Starch gives crystalline powder diffraction patterns presumably as $(C_2H_{10}O_5.H_2O)_n$ since about 10 per cent of water is present; when this water is removed, the starch becomes amorphous. Native starches give one of three types of powder diffraction pattern called A, B, and C, though C is probably a combination of A and B. All efforts to orient molecules from unfractionated starch by pressure or by drawing out fibers have been unsuccessful; consequently it has not been possible as yet to derive a reliable interpretation of structure. Starch is a rather low condensation product of α-glucose-forming rings, whereas cellulose is formed linearly from β-glucose.

On precipitation by alcohol from water all starches give a V pattern, varying from very diffuse interferences to a sharper pattern for starch paste after drying. Samples of starch from various organs of the same plant species may show different types of the C or B pattern; a solution of starch gives instead of V the B pattern on evaporation at 20°C, A at 60°C, and C at intermediate temperatures. The spacings, intensities, and types of starch giving each pattern are as follows:

A	B	C
5.79m	15.77s	11.6w
5.02s	8.34vw	7.05m
4.42m	6.25m	4.5m
3.76s	5.79m	
3.40w	5.15s	
2.62vw	4.52m	
2.33vw	4.04m	
2.07vw	3.69m	
1.90vw	3.38w	
	2.87w	
	2.58vw	
	2.33vw	

Intensities: *s*, strong; *m*, medium; *w*, weak; *vw*; very weak

The types of starch giving each pattern are:

A, wheat, maize, rice, rye, millet, Ipomoea tjalappa (tropical morning-glory), *Arum escul.*

B, potato, *Canna indica*, *Canna edulis*, fritillaria, *Curcuma angustifolia*, *Musa paradisiaca* (type of banana), *Dioscoroea alata*, *Arracacia escul.*, *Jatropha manihot*, *Araucaria brasil*, xuxu (Brazilian cucumber), edible chestnut.

C, Sago, maranta, cassava, pea, bean, lentil, sweet potato, *Arenga pinnata*, *Colocasia escul.*, *Manihot utiliss.*, *Arum maculatum.*

Starch is by no means as homogeneous as cellulose, for it contains two differently constituted polysaccharides, amylose and amylopectin. Most starches contain about 20 per cent of amylose, which consists of long straight chains of α-glucose residues in 1,4 linkage (like maltose); these chains vary in length from molecular weights of 10,000 to 400,000. It is this constituent which forms the blue coloration with iodine, by means of which it may be quantitatively estimated. The other constituent of whole starch, amylopectin, consists of a mixture of branched chain molecules, with 1,4 and 1,6 linkages present. Separation is made best by heating defatted starch with water and butanol at 109° under pressure. On cooling an amylose-butanol complex separates, and the amylopectin remaining in solution is precipitated with alcohol. It is not surprising that amylose can be stretched and caused to produce sharp fiber patterns. Some interpretations of molecular configuration and unit cells have been published, but according to Meyer x-ray evidence up to the present time has neither revealed the size of the unit cell nor given any information about the form of the molecules. However, there is evidence that the chain of glucose residues is considerably more "kinked" on a trigonal screw axis than the cellulose, with an angle of 33 to 35 deg between the glucose rings and the fiber axis, allowing room for water molecules between the chains. Meyer's conclusion concerning the ultimate structure of the starch granule consisting of concentric layers is as follows: The layers contain crystalline micelles arranged perpendicular to the plane of the layer. The crystalline regions consist of starch chains or portions of such, and the crystallites are united by amorphous chains. It is probable that the crystallites differ in size, i.e., that there are small crystallites destroyed by warm water and larger crystallites which occur principally in the outermost layer and are responsible for the integrity of the shells on swelling. This system of crystallites united by molecular threads is built up from the giant branched molecules of amylopectin. At room temperature the outer layer does not permit amylose to escape into solution, while a damaged starch grain swells in the injured region and liberates amylose. Probably part of the amylose is stored in pure form in the interior of the grain, while the remainder is distributed in the amylopectin and there is embedded in mixed crystals.

Other Polysaccharides. Hemicelluloses, xylan and other pentosans, mannan and other hexosans, inulin, agar, glycogen, lichenin, pectin, etc., have all been subjected to diffraction study, but in the absence of single-crystal or good fiber patterns no molecular interpretations have been possible as yet. Humidity and swelling have a marked effect. Pectin forms films on drying with a marked selective orientation, indicating crystallites in the form of thin tablets 22 A thick.

Lignin. This complex substance, which plays so important a role in wood structure, gives in all cases a very diffuse pattern of two or three halos, similar to that of resins. A very careful study of 36 samples of lignin and derivatives by Harris, Parker, Sherrard, and Clark[1] proved

[1] *Biodynamica*, **31** (January, 1938).

that the spacing corresponding to the inner halo varies with the material from 6.5 to 12 A for methylated methanol maple lignin. The substances that separate out from the living cells to become membranes, coverings, skeletons, etc., form a graded series that extends from some simple inorganic salts to bodies that approximate in complexity that of living matter itself. Among these substances lignin possesses two distinguishing characters, which to a certain extent it has in common with living matter: It is apparently amorphous and highly cross-linked and

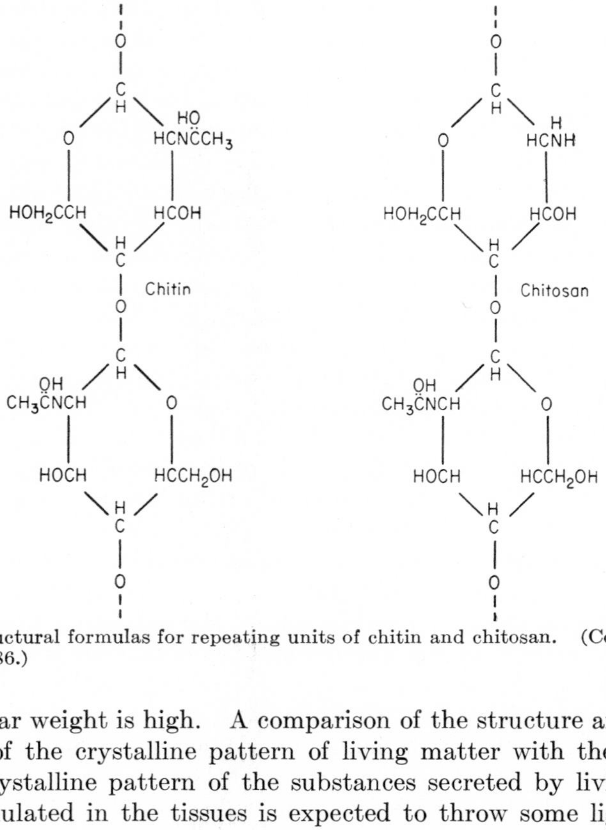

FIG. 401. Structural formulas for repeating units of chitin and chitosan. (Compare cellulose in Fig. 386.)

its molecular weight is high. A comparison of the structure and of what is known of the crystalline pattern of living matter with the structure and the crystalline pattern of the substances secreted by living matter and accumulated in the tissues is expected to throw some light on the dynamics of that fundamental vital process that is so little known, the protoplasmic secretion.

Chitin. Chitin is the compound that makes up most of the organic part of the skeletons of Arthropoda. In the animal kingdom, to which it is limited with very few exceptions, it occurs only in the invertebrates. In addition to forming the exoskeletons of insects, Crustacea, etc., it is the major constituent of the lenses of the eyes, the tendons, and the linings of the respiratory, excretory, and digestive systems. In recent work on soft anthropodal (blowfly larvae) cuticle there is x-ray evidence of alternating layers of protein and chitin (45 and 55 per cent).[1]

Chitin is remarkably similar to cellulose in the formation of long carbohydrate chains except that it contains nitrogen, thus moving a step toward the familiar proteins of the vertebrate world. Figure 401 shows the formula of the acetylglucosamine residue, which is to be compared with cellulose in Fig. 386.

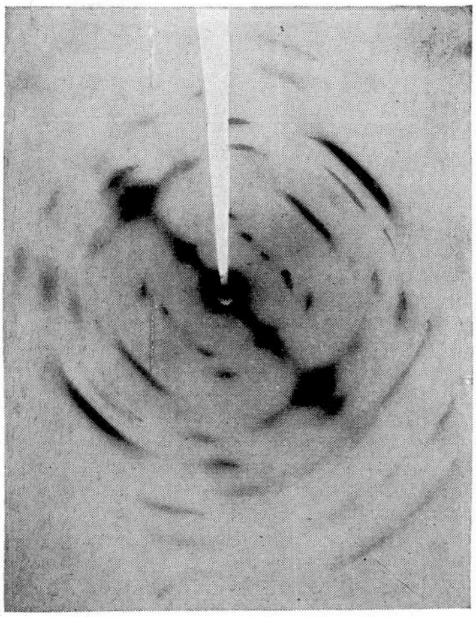

Chitin produces very rich fiber diffraction patterns (Fig. 402) from which is deduced the crystal structure.[2] This is probably orthorhombic with the unit-cell dimensions (Fig. 403)

$$a = 9.25 \text{ A}$$
$$b = 10.46 \text{ A}$$
$$c = 19.25 \text{ A}$$

FIG. 402. Fiber pattern for chitin, comprising the mandibular tendon of lobster.

As laid down in sheets the only orientation is that the b axes are parallel to the surface. Hydrogen bonding occurs between half of the CO.NH groups of adjacent amino acetyl side chains to form linked piles of chitin

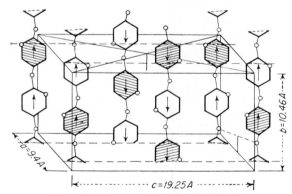

FIG. 403. The crystal unit cell of chitin.

chains within the crystalline regions; the other half is bonded CO · · · NO (cellulose OH · · · OH).[3] At a temperature of 200°C chitin forms

---

[1] G. Frankel and K. M. Randall, *Proc. Roy. Soc. (London)*, **B134**, 111 (1947); A. G. Richards, *Ann. Entomol. Soc. Amer.*, **40**, 227 (1947).

[2] Clark and Smith, *J. Phys. Chem.*, **40**, 863 (1936). Meyer and Mark, *Ber. deut. chem. Ges.*, **61**, 1936 (1928). Meyer and Pankow, *Helv. Chim. Acta*, **18**, 589 (1935).

[3] S. E. Darmon and K. M. Rudall, *Discussions Faraday Soc.*, 1950, No. 9, p. 251.

a definite addition compound with lithium thiocyanate, while at lower temperatures intramicellar swelling occurs. Various fractions of chitin nitrate have different average lengths of the carbohydrate chain. Chitin nitrate is orthorhombic with

$$a = \quad 9.2 \text{ A} \qquad b = 10.3 \text{ A} \qquad c = 23.0 \text{ A}$$

A whole series of compounds is formed with sodium hydroxide, but it is difficult to isolate pure compounds and to obtain sharp patterns because of hydrolysis.

Chitosan is the compound formed by hydrolysis of half the acetyl groups in chitin. When formed from a sheet it undergoes a change to

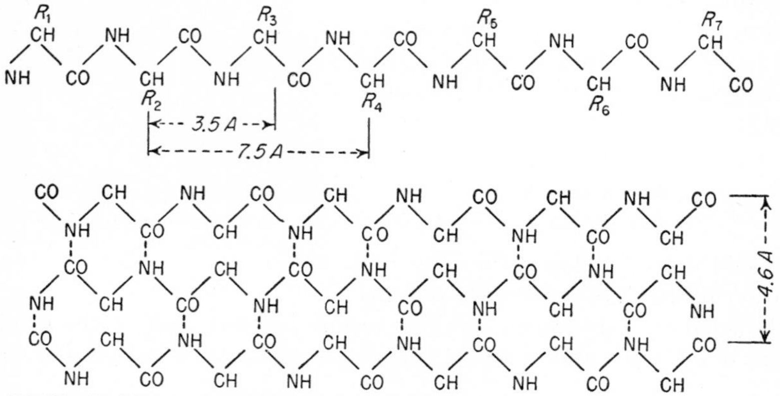

Fig. 404. The backbone polypeptide chain in proteins (*above*) and the cross linking of chains.

a more restricted orientation such that the 002 planes become parallel to the surface of the sheet. The unit cell of chitosan (monoclinic) has the dimensions

$$a = 8.9 \text{ A} \qquad b = 10.25 \text{ A} \qquad c = 17.0 \text{ A} \qquad \beta = 88°$$

Like chitin, chitosan forms a long series of interesting addition compounds with distinctive patterns. While chitin gives a continuous series of long equatorial spacings like cellulose, chitosan produces resolved maxima in several orders corresponding to a definite lateral spacing between molecular chains or crystallites of 75 A. This spacing increases markedly upon swelling in dilute alkali.

Proteins. Since the beginning of this century and as a result of the work of Emil Fischer and others, proteins have been considered to be long chains formed from repeated condensations of α-amino acids

$$(NH_2 - CH - COOH)$$
$$\mid$$
$$R$$

to a configuration of the type represented in Fig. 404. The structures of many of the amino acids and their simplest combinations into di- and tripeptides have been noted on page 598.   Ten years of intensive and critical analysis of crystal structures of such acids and their combinations led Corey and Donohue[1] to the dimensions of the fully extended polypeptide chain, the basic common unit in all proteins.   Figure 405 shows this chain with its interatomic distances and bond angles.   This reliable information enabled the development of the Pauling-Corey structural models for proteins, discussed in a later section.

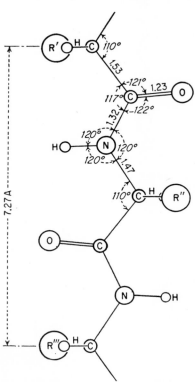

Thus a more or less common backbone is characteristic of all protein molecules (at least in fibers).   Proteins are classified as fibrous (crystalline) and nonfibrous, globular, or corpuscular (not obviously crystalline, although many have been crystallized and subjected to detailed analysis). They differ in R groups; and they exist naturally in specific folded or spiral configurations.   The four principal states of the polypeptide chains in fibrous proteins, illustrated in Fig. 406, were proposed by Astbury and generally accepted for many years.

Silk Fibroin.   Silk fibroin, a natural crystal fiber, is distinguished by stability and simplicity since it yields on hydrolysis principally glycine and alanine.   Thus its R groups are almost entirely hydrogen and CH_3.   The x-ray pattern (Fig. 407) is fully con-

FIG. 405. Dimensions of the fully extended polypeptide chain.   (*Corey.*)

sistent with the foregoing concept of a fully extended polypeptide chain.   The unit monoclinic cell for silk from *Bombyx mori* has the dimensions

$$a = 9.65 \text{ A}$$
$$b = 6.95 \text{ (2 amino acid residues of 3.5 A)}$$
$$c = 10.4 \text{ A}$$
$$\beta = 62.4°$$

The chains are united laterally by hydrogen bonds between CO— and NH— into grids, which are associated by weaker van der Waals forces. Stretching has no effect on the pattern: hence, the crystallites, being

[1] K. B. Corey and J. Donohue, *J. Am. Chem. Soc.*, 1950, p. 72.

already stretched to the fullest extent, merely slide over one another. Slight variations are observed for silk fibroin from different sources.

Keratin (Mammalian Hair). To Astbury is due the present extensive knowledge of keratin, or the protein of hair, wool, horn, etc. This pro-

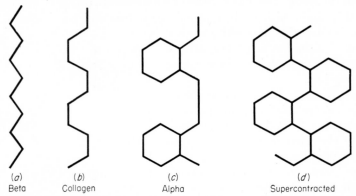

(a)	(b)	(c)	(d)
Beta	Collagen	Alpha	Supercontracted

FIG. 406. The four principal configurations of molecular chains by which all proteins may be classified. (*Astbury.*)

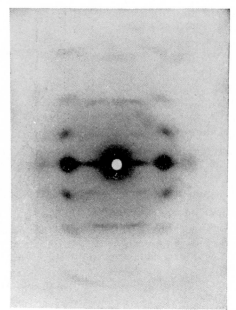

FIG. 407.   Fiber pattern of the protein fibroin constituting natural silk.

tein consists of at least 18 amino acids of which the sulfur-containing cystine is very important, with a repeating unit consisting of about 300 ammo acid residues. For the resistance and insolubility of hair must reside in —S—S— bridges between molecular chains (a self-vulcan-

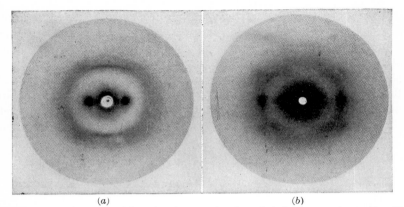

FIG. 408a. Fiber patterns of keratin, the protein of wool, hair, horn, spines, etc. (*Left*) α-form, unstretched; (*right*) β-form, stretched.

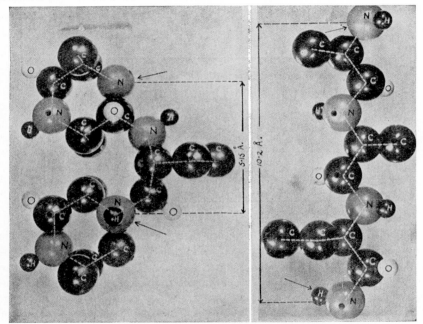

FIG. 408b. Molecular models for α- and β-keratin, deduced by Astbury from patterns in Fig. 408a.

ization). The hair and wool fibers are decidedly nonhomogeneous since there are three cellular layers (cuticle, cortex, and medulla) of which the spindle-shaped cells of the cortex predominate. Among other constituents are water-soluble compounds probably arising from the nuclei of the original cells. When stretched, these fibers produce patterns of β-keratin similar to silk fibroin; but, in the normal unstretched state, a completely different pattern for α-keratin (Fig. 408) indicates some regularly folded condition of the backbone of the molecule from which it may be pulled out straight in the presence of moisture and to which it returns upon release of tension. Thus the molecular configurations of the normal and stretched hair in Fig. 409 were proposed by Astbury to account for the x-ray interferences on the fiber patterns.

The β-keratin then forms a grid, built up by interactions and combinations between the R groups of neighboring main chains. The crystal particle consists of a series of parallel grids. The dimensions roughly are

Angstroms

Amino acid residue along main chain.......... 3.5
Side-chain spacing........................... 10.0
Spacing between grids........................ 4.5

Since β-keratin is the prototype of proteins with fully extended chains, it is useful to tabulate the details of the fiber pattern in Table 23-4.

TABLE 23-4. MEASUREMENTS OF FIBER PATTERN OF β-KERATIN

	Plane	Spacing	Intensity
Equator...............	001	9.7	*s*
	200	4.65	*vs*
	400	2.4	*w*
1-layer line...........	111	4.7	*m*
	210	3.75	*s*
	410	2.2	*w*
2-layer line...........	020	3.33	*s*
	220	2.7	*w*
3-layer line...........	030	2.2	*w*
	230	2.0	*w*

Thus the orthorhombic unit cell has the dimensions $a = 9.3$, $b = 6.66$, $c = 9.7$ A. This form may be permanently set when the hair or wool is steamed in the stretched state, simply because cross linkages are hydrolyzed and reformed in a configuration that will prevent return to the folded α state. The pattern is characterized by a smearing along the layer lines exactly as observed by the author years ago for asbestos (Fig. 254), indicating an irregular breakdown confined only to the direction of the side chains. Lateral pressure selectively orients the side-chain spacing perpendicular and the backbone spacing parallel to the plane of flattening, so that the β-keratin crystallites seem to be ribbon-shaped, longest in the direction of the main chains and thinnest in the direction of the side chains, which means that there are comparatively few main chains per grid but many grids piled on top of one another.

The natural unstretched form of the protein common to hair, wool, spines, nails, horn, etc., has α-keratin as the prototype with main chains folded so that the grids are buckled. The orthorhombic cell has the dimensions $a = 27$, $b = 10.3$, $c = 9.8$ A.   Half the length of the b axis corresponds to the folded length in the direction of the fiber axis of three amino acid residues; 9.8 A is again the side-chain spacing.   Keratin can be treated by steam or alkali in the extended state so that upon release the fibers exhibit supercontraction to a length shorter than normal. Thus the α folding is further elaborated to about one-third the length of β-keratin as indicated on the patterns.

Feather keratin produces the richest protein pattern known, but it is based fundamentally on the simple α and β structures with patterns greatly elaborated and actually approaching some of the crystallized proteins.   Most of the quill has polypeptide chains parallel to the length with a thin outer layer in which they run at right angles to this, thus accounting for the remarkable strength.   The periodicity along the fiber axis may be as high as 304 A, while the length of the amino acid residue is only 3.08 instead of 3.33 A as in β-keratin, but the quill may be pulled out to the latter value.   Such is the protective covering of birds and reptiles, as contrasted with the mammalian keratin; and the identity of the constitution and structure of feathers, beaks, claws, tortoise shell, and reptilian scales is remarkable and irrefutable evidence of the common ancestry of birds and reptiles.

Muscle.   All the observations on diffraction patterns, structure, behavior on stretching, and supercontraction in keratin have now been duplicated by Astbury for the principal protein in muscle, namely, myosin.   The photograph of washed and dried muscle, and indeed of living muscle, if the presence of water is taken into account, is remarkably like that of α-keratin; that of stretched myosin is also like that of β-keratin.   Hence, myosin possesses folded chains in the condition at rest, which are further folded upon supercontraction.

Lotmar and Picker assign the monoclinic $(P2_1)$ unit cell dimensions $a = 11.20$ A, $b = 5.65$ A, $c = 9.85$ A, $\beta = 73°30'$.   Two polypeptide chains with a spiral twist traverse the cell parallel to the b axis.   In living muscle the chains are in rubberlike condition in the resting state; under tension the chains are fully stretched, and the fraction possessing a lattice is increased, as shown by the x-ray pattern.   On contraction the muscle shows only an amorphous pattern, thus proving that the parallel stretched primary-valence chains of the resting fibrils lose their parallelism during contraction.   Since keratin possesses a much higher sulfur content from its cystine constituent, the side linkages between neighboring chains may be through the —S—S— groups, so that a hair may be considered as a "vulcanized" muscle fiber with reduced elastic sensitivity and increased resistance to chemical attack.[1]   Fibrin and

[1] Clark and Buhrke have proved that radioactive sulfur in the diet of sheep appears in the wool fibers and causes hysteresis in load-elongation curves, indicating the formation of disulfide bridges between molecules.

fibrinogen, the proteins from blood, also behave similarly; so Astbury has classed all proteins into two groups, the keratin-myosin-fibrin-fibrinogen group, and the collagen group, differing in the manner in which the chains are extended.

Similarly, fibrous proteins of the epidermis (skin of a cow's nose), fibrin, and even denatured "globular" proteins demonstrate in their diffraction patterns a very close relationship with the β-keratin (extended), α-keratin (folded), and supercontracted types under appropriate conditions.

Collagen.[1] The principal constituent of vertebrate tendons and tissues is the protein collagen, which, upon hydrolysis, yields gelatin. Surgical catgut ligatures are collagen fibrils from the intestinal walls of sheep. An extended x-ray study of catgut in the author's laboratory led to greatly improved processing of the ligatures with respect to uniformity

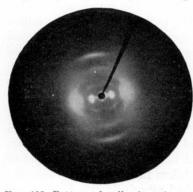

FIG. 409. Pattern of well-oriented catgut ligature.

and enhanced tensile strength. This was achieved largely through improved preferred orientation of protein crystallites under combined swelling and tension,[2] as shown in Fig. 409.

Collagen and gelatin, being made up of 15 or more amino acids of widely different functional groups and molecular weights, have previously not given patterns with sufficient orientation and number of interferences to lend themselves readily to analysis. Long-chain molecules are rather easily oriented by tension but lack sufficient organization of amino acid residues to produce a well-defined lattice. A sizeable proportion of bulky proline residues must be a feature of the structure and this imposes stereochemical restrictions on the polypeptide configuration. The existence of a halo, which shows indication of partial orientation, superimposed upon a faintly sharp interference pattern indicates a "pseudocrystalline" structure. On the pattern appear inner equatorial arcs for a spacing of 10.4 to 17.0 A, depending on the amount of water held by the protein and measuring the distance between main chains, or the length of cross linkages; a spacing of 4.5 to 6.1 A corresponding to the thickness of the grid; and a fiber-axis identity period of 9.75 A, or three times an amino acid residue length of 3.25 A. Another spacing of 2.84 A, thought by Astbury to be a contracted residue length, might be

[1] See "Nature and Structure of Collagen," edited by J. T. Randall, Academic Press Inc., New York, 1953.

[2] Clark and Ziegler, The X-ray in the Study of the Catgut Ligature, *Surgery, Gynecology and Obstetrics*, **58**, 578 (1936). Clark, Flege, and Ziegler, Surgical Ligatures, *Ind. Eng. Chem.*, **26**, 440 (1936).

due to planes that are not perpendicular to the fiber axis. Both collagen and stretched gelatin ribbons give essentially this same type of ordinary pattern (Fig. 410). These data were long assumed to be consistent with a sheet structure made up of parallel chains about 4.5 A apart, hydrogen-bonded together in layers with the 10.4-A spacing. The calculated density of this arrangement is too low unless bound water is assumed in the dry state. On improved patterns with stretched collagen fibers the main meridional arc is at a spacing of 3.1 A; a former 4.0 A meridional arc is split into two spots off the meridians and lie on a layer line at a vertical spacing of 4.4 A. The 9.5-A meridional arc has disappeared and sharp spots at 45 deg to the vertical lie on a layer line of 10.5 A vertical spacing. So the fiber axis spacings, according to Randall, are consistent with either a 31-A period with third, seventh, and tenth orders strong, or a 21-A period with strong second, fifth, and seventh orders. This interpretation is much more clearly suggestive of a helical arrangement of chains, as proposed by Pauling and Corey and discussed in the next section.

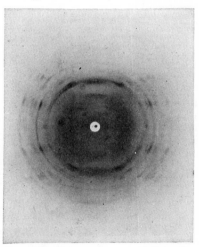

FIG. 410. Pattern from rattail tendon collagen.

Clark, Parker, Schaad, and Warren[1] first reported the existence of a spacing along the fiber axis in collagen of 432 A or twice this value (Fig. 411a) (one of the longest ever directly measured up to that time) which is completely missing in gelatin. This gives a remarkable clue to the organization of collagen in contrast with gelatin. This spacing indicates a regularly repeating residue along the chains or an over-all length of the molecules themselves. The spacing 432 A decreases to 408 A for chromicized gut without further evidence of interaction of the chromicizing solution with collagen. With these and other data Astbury in his Procter lecture[2] gave the most complete picture of the collagen molecular chain built up from a multiple of 72 amino acid residues in the configuration shown in Fig. 406.

One of the early contributions of electron microscopy was the verification of the existence in collagen films of a long spacing of the order of several hundred angstroms. In later work Bear made the greatest contribution to the study of these long spacings. It should be clearly noted that the diffraction effects at very small angles are not those of diffuse

[1] *J. Am. Chem. Soc.*, **57**, 1509 (1935).

[2] *Nature*, **145**, 421 (1940).

low-angle scattering from essentially amorphous materials, but very sharp arcs appearing in many orders.   Bear devised special cameras with

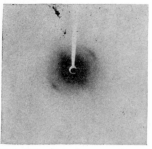

high resolving power and magnification to register these sharp short lines while retaining maximum camera speed.   The geometric dimensioning of these cameras for photographic registration is a masterpiece of theoretical and practical design, when it is realized that spacings between 100 and 1000 A represent Bragg angles of 0.5 deg to 3 minutes or diffraction angles of resolution from the undeviated primary beam twice these val-

FIG. 411a. Interferences at very small angles (long spacings) for collagen. The meridional interferences (*diagonal, upper left to lower right*) represent several orders of the spacing 432 or 864 A.

ues.[1]   Typical patterns for collagen from kangaroo-tail tendons are shown in Fig. 411b. For at least some samples of collagen according to Bear the long spacing is 642 A.[†]   In observing his patterns Bear noticed in several types, singly and in groups, variations in the lengths of the short arcs of the different orders of reflection, especially upon drying of specimens.[2]   By means of the reciprocal lattice it is demonstrated that this

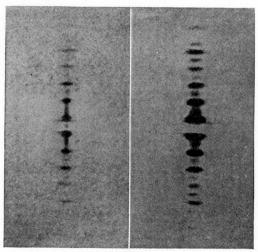

FIG. 411b. Long-spacing interferences in several orders of kangaroo-tail tendon (collagen), with special cameras.   (*Bear.*)

phenomenon is a clue to deficiencies in order of large size in fibrous systems.   Figure 412 illustrates three cases of arrangement with the corresponding patterns of the long-spacing lines in several orders.

[1] O. E. A. Bolduan and R. S. Bear, *J. Appl. Phys.*, **20**, 983 (1949).
[†] R. S. Bear, *J. Am. Chem. Soc.*, **64**, 727 (1942), **66**, 1293 (1944).
[2] R. S. Bear and O. E. A. Bolduan, *Acta Cryst.*, **3**, 230 (1950).

Collagen seems to form addition compounds with NaOH. This reaction is reversible since the original collagen pattern is regained after treatment of the alkali addition compound in a buffered solution at the isoelectric point pH 4.78. Addition compounds with entirely different structures and patterns are formed with KOH, LiOH, RbOH, and CsOH. Astbury believed that these changed patterns are due to the alkalies, entrapped as oriented crystals in the collagen.

The peculiar behavior of the 48-A equatorial interferences appearing on intestinal-wall but not tendon collagen patterns on treatment of the fibers with hot water, alkali solution, salts, and various organic solvents led to the discovery by Clark and Schaad of a waxlike substance whose molecules are radially oriented on collagen fibrils in these wall tissues and serve both as a lubricant and as a protection against enzyme digestion of the collagen. Analysis indicates an empirical formula of $C_{14}H_{28}O_2$ or a multiple and that the compound may be related to cholesterol derivatives rather than an ordinary ester. It is evident that this substance, which is completely absent in tendon, is synthesized or adapted by the body for this very specific purpose. The power of the x-ray diffraction method in biological research is clearly indicated by this example.

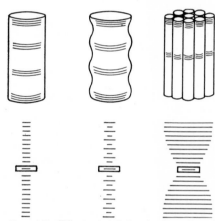

FIG. 412. Effect of deficiencies in order of large size in fibrous systems upon lengths and patterns of long-spacing arcs. (*Bear.*)

Collagen fibers contract in hot water above definite temperatures to as much as three-quarters of the original length. In this state they display long-range elasticity like that of keratin and myosin and diffraction halos corresponding to side-chain and backbone spacings. Elastin from the ligamentum nuchae (the very elastic neck ligament) is actually collagen in this supercontracted form.

The Pauling-Corey Models of Protein Structure. With the solid background of a decade of intensive structural analysis of amino acids, the simple synthetic peptides formed by linkage of two or three amino acids, and some of the simplest of the proteins, and with the fundamental characteristics of the extended polypeptide chain established, as shown in Fig. 405, Pauling and Corey in 1950 in a preliminary note[1] and then in eight almost simultaneous papers in 1951 startled the scientific world with new, logical, and apparently convincing interpretations of proteins

[1] L. Pauling and R. B. Corey, *J. Am. Chem. Soc.*, **72**, 5349 (1950),

of all principal types.[1]   An adequate description of these structures is
obviously impossible, and for the arguments defending each interpretation the original papers must be consulted.   A remarkable, well-illus-
trated summary of the 1954 aspect of these ideas will be found in the
Scientific American.[2]   Briefly, the principal concepts are as follows:

1. The protein chains constructed of successive units of equivalent amino acid
residues can have only a helical configuration.

2. Because of resonance of the double bond between C—O and C—N positions, the
residue

$$\begin{array}{ccc}
H & & C \\
 & \diagdown & \\
 & N\text{—}C & \\
 & \diagup & \diagdown \\
C & & O
\end{array}$$

must be planar (proved in all amides); C—N distance, 1.32 A, corresponds to 50 per
cent double-bond character.

3. Each nitrogen atom forms a hydrogen bond with an oxygen atom of another
residue (in the same chain) with the N—O distance 2.79 A approximately.   In one
structure each carbonyl and imino group is attached to the complementary group in
the third amide group removed from it in the chain, and in the other each is bonded
to the fifth amide group.

4. Two structures only satisfy all conditions with a rotational angle of 97.2 deg,
and hence 3.60 amino acid residues per turn in the helix; the second with an angle of
70.1 deg has 5.13 residues per turn.   The translation along the helical axis in the first
is 1.50 A, and for the second, 0.99 A; the values for one complete turn are 5.44 and
5.03 A, respectively; or the first helix, or α-helix, means 18 residues in 5 turns, and
the second helix, or γ-helix, 41 residues in 8 turns.[3]   While others have proposed
helical models, they have all involved an integral number of bonds per turn.

5. The α-helix is represented by the structures of α-keratin, α-myosin, and similar
proteins, by hemoglobin and other globular proteins, and by synthetic polypeptides.

6. The x-ray reflections of poly-γ-methyl-*l*-glutamate can be accounted for on the
basis of an 18-residue five-turn helix, and the corresponding benzyl ester as an 11-resi-
due three-turn helix.   The first has a sixfold screw axis of symmetry, since the
helical molecules arrange themselves side by side in hexagonal packing, and a unit
cell with dimensions $a = 11.96$, $c = 27.5$ A.

7. While there are close similarities between the x-ray patterns of horsehair (α-kera-
tin) and the synthetic polypeptide just described with α-helixes in hexagonal packing,
the former have strong vertical reflections which result from the presence of molecules
with the configuration of the α-helix which are twisted about one another.   The best

---

[1] The Structure of Proteins: Two Hydrogen-bonded Helical Configurations of the
Polypeptide Chain, *Proc. Natl. Acad. Sci.*, **37**, 205 (1951); Atomic Coordinates and
Structure Factors for Two Helical Configurations of Polypeptide Chains, *ibid.*, **37**,
235 (1951); The Structure of Synthetic Polypeptides, *ibid.*, **37**, 241 (1951); The
Pleated Sheet, A New Layer Configuration of Polypeptide Chains, *ibid.*, **37**, 251
(1951); The Structure of Feather Rachis Keratin, *ibid.*, **37**, 256 (1951); The Structure
of Hair, Muscle and Related Proteins, *ibid.*, **37**, 261 (1951); The Structure of Fibrous
Proteins of the Collagen-Gelatin Group, *ibid.*, **37**, 272 (1951); The Polypeptide-chain
Configuration in Hemoglobin and Other Globular Patterns, *ibid.*, **37**, 282 (1951).

[2] Vol. 191, No. 1, p. 51 (July, 1954).

[3] The existence of the γ-helix has been questioned by Pauling and Corey in later
work.

evidence indicates seven-strand cables, each about 30 A in diameter, which are made up of six compound α-helices twisted about a central α-helix. These seven-strand cables are arranged in hexagonal packing, and the interstices between them are occupied by additional α-helices. Validity is given to this configuration by electron micrographs of bacterium flagella, a larger structure described as three-strand ropes, each strand of which is a seven-strand cable built of seven-strand cables of α-helices.

8. Silk fibroin, stretched hair and muscle, and other polypeptide chains extended to about 3.6 A per residue have been assigned heretofore a structure such that chains form lateral hydrogen bonds with adjacent chains which have an opposite orientation. This is replaced now by the pleated sheet in which the plane formed by the two chain bonds of the α-carbon atom is perpendicular to the plane of the sheet and the successive residues are similarly oriented.

9. Feather keratin, with a very complex pattern supposed to indicate a structure with dimensions 9.5 by 34 by 94.6 A, has a residue length of 3.07 A, shorter than that of the extended polypeptide chain 3.6 A, silk fibroin 3.5 A, and β-keratin 3.3 A. This structure consists of three layers of protein, each about 11 A thick, one of these being a pleated sheet and the other two α-helices. All structure factors are in agreement with this arrangement. The fiber-axis length per pleat in the pleated sheet is 6.30 A, and 15 of these (30 amino acid residues) give the observed long spacing 94.6 A; the α-helix along this length consists of a 62-residue 17-turn helix with 3.65 residues per turn.

10. Muscular contraction is a mechanism arising logically by the conversion of the pleated sheet of β-keratin in extended muscle into a double row of α-helices; super-contraction probably produces the γ-helix with 5.1 residues per turn.

11. In collagen it may be predicted that the length of the amide group in cis configuration is 2.83 A, whereas an observed fiber-axis spacing is 2.86 A. The molecule of collagen and gelatin, essentially cylindrical in shape, consists of three polypeptide chains, required by the presence of two polypeptide chains with cis and one with trans

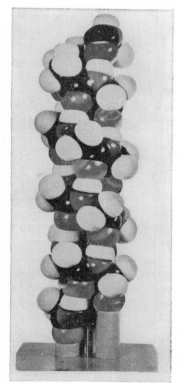

Fig. 413. Pauling-Corey model of three intertwined protein α-helixes, which is the structural basis for α-keratin.

configuration. These are coiled into a helix with a common axis, the three chains being related by a threefold axis of symmetry. This is consistent with x-ray data (10.9- and 5.42-A equatorial reflections), with chemical composition, and with the extensibility over only a limited range. The hexagonal unit has the dimensions $a = 12.5$ A and $c = 25.74$ A, the fiber-axis length of a residue. This originally proposed structure is now being revised.

12. Hemoglobin is similar to α-keratin, supporting the 3.6 residue helical configuration, spaced 11 A apart in agreement with Perutz's assignment of about 10.5 A and with integrated vector density, in a Patterson section, and agreement between calculated and observed radial-distribution functions.

TABLE 23-5. X-RAY DATA OF PROTEIN CRYSTALS*

	Wet or dry	Space group	Unit cell					No. of moles	Best value for mol. wt. × 10⁻³	
			a	b	c	β	Volume $A \times 10^{-3}$		In soln.	In crystal
Ribonuclease I	W	$P2_1$	30.8	38.5	53.5	107°	60	2	13–15	
Ribonuclease II	D	$P2_12_12_1$	28.7	29.3	45.2	100°	37.4	2	. . . . .	13.7
	D		36.6	40.5	52.3	. . . .	77.3	4		
Insulin	W	$R3$	49.4	. . . .	. . . .	114°16′	68	3	$n \times 12$	12
	D		44.4	. . . .	. . . .	114°28′	50	. . .		. . . . .
Metmyoglobin: horse	W	$P2_1$	57.3	30.8	57.0	112°	93	2	17	(17)
	D		51.5	28.0	37.0	98°	53.3			
whale	D	$P2_12_12_1$	97.4	39.8	42.5	. . . .	165	4?	. . . . .	(17)?
γ-Chymotrypsin	W	$P4_22_1$	69.5	. . . .	97.5	. . . .	471	8	27 }	30.1
	D		63.0	. . . .	74.5	. . . .	298	8	41 }	
Chymotrypsin	W	$P2_1$	49.6	67.8	66.5	102°	219	2		
Lysozyme	D	$P4_12_1$	71.1	. . . .	31.3	. . . .	158	8	. . . . .	14
Pepsin	W	$C6_12$	67.9	. . . .	292	. . . .	1,160	12	35.5–39.2	(50)
	D		60.5	. . . .	268	. . . .	848			
Lactoglobulin I (tabular)	W	$P2_12_12_1$	67.5	67.5	154	. . . .	702	8	36	(40)
	D		60	63	110	. . . .	416			

	W/D	Space group								
Lactoglobulin II (needles)	W	$P4_22_1$	67.5	67.5	133.5	......	608	8	36	(40)
	D		56	56	130	......	408			
Met-, oxy-, and carboxyhemoglobin:										
horse, I	W	$C2$	109	63.2	54.4	111°	349	2	66.7	33.4
	D		102	51.4	47	130°	189			
horse, II	W	$P2_12_12_1$	122	82.4	63.7	......	640	4	66.7	66.7
	D		95	72	61	......	416			
hamster	W	$P2_12_12_1$	123	88	60	......	......	4	66.7	
horse, III	W	$P2$	64.5	101	104	102°	662	4	66.7	133.4
Reduced hemoglobin, horse	W	$C3_12$	56.1	......	354	......	965	6	66.7	66.7
	D		47.4	......	308	......	600			
Methemoglobin:										
sheep adult	W	$C2$	164	70	66	94.5°	755	4	68	(68)
sheep fetus, I	W	$B22_12$	112	108	56	......	677	4	68	(34)
	D		78	99	54	......	417			
sheep fetus, II	W	$P2_1$	55	83	64	102°	286	2	68	(68)
	D		48	71	58	101°	194			
human, I	W	$P2_12_12_1$	85.2	77.0	86.0	......	564	4	68	(68)
	D		70.4	73.3	77.0	......	393			
human, II	D	$P2_12_12_1?$	50	55	123	......	338	4	68	(68)
	W		62.5	83.2	52.2	98.0°	......			
human, III	W	$P4_12_1$	47.4	......	174.0	......	391	...	68	(68)
	D		53.7	......	193.5	......	55.2	4		
Reduced hemoglobin, human	W	$P2_1$	66	98	110	98°	700	4	68	(136)

Table 23-5. X-ray Data of Protein Crystals* (Continued)

	Wet or dry	Space group	Unit cell					No. of moles	Best value for mol. wt. × 10⁻³	
			a	b	c	β	Volume A × 10⁻³		In soln.	In crystal
Serum albumin, horse	W D	H (hexagonal)	96.7 74.5	....	145 130	....	1,170 610	6	70–73	(82.8)
Tobacco seed globulin	D	F (cubic)	123	......	......	......	1,860	4	(300)	(322)
Excelsin	D	R3	85.5	......	......	60.5°	445	1	294	(100)?
Ferritin	W	F (cubic)	186	......	......	......	6,220	8?	650	......
Apoferritin	W	F (cubic)	186	......	......	......	6,220	8?	500	......
Bushy stunt virus	W D	I (cubic)	386 314	......	......	......	57,600 31,000	2	7,600–10,600	(13,000)
Tobacco necrosis virus, derivative	W	P1 (triclinic)	179	219	243	$\alpha = 87.5°$ $\beta = 97.5°$ $\gamma = 97.5°$	9,200	1	1,850	(1,600)
	D	P1 (triclinic)	157	154	147	$\alpha = 100°$ $\beta = 110°$ $\gamma = 120°$	......	......	......	......
Turnip mosaic virus	W D	F (cubic)	706 528	......	......	......	35,100 14,700	8	......	......

820

* Compiled largely by Perutz, in Meyer, "Natural and Synthetic High Polymers," 2d ed., vol. 4, Interscience Publishers, Inc., New York, 1950.

Globular Crystalline Proteins.   The obvious limit of the idea of folding and twisting protein chains is to be found in the so-called globular proteins such as egg albumin, hemoglobin, edestin, etc.   These substances may actually be crystallized in a sense far different from the fibers just discussed.   It would appear that they are built in a very delicately balanced fashion of somewhat spherical units which have been shown so brilliantly in the work of Svedberg with the ultracentrifuge to have molecular weights of 35,000 or a multiple.   X-ray work by Bernal and Crowfoot[1] as early as 1934 on pepsin and insulin crystals (Table 23-5) definitely confirmed this contention and gave the first clue to the unit cells of proteins.   Clark and Shenk[2] made an extensive study of crystallized and denatured egg albumin.   In the usual case the patterns for these proteins consist essentially of two halos corresponding to the two principal distances between main chains, 10 and 4.5 A.   By boiling and other methods of denaturation, the pattern resembles even more strongly that of *powdered* or *disoriented β-keratin*, showing that a highly specific and delicately balanced configuration in the original globular protein is broken down.   By stretching, Astbury succeeded in orienting denatured albumins and globulins so that fiber patterns are produced. Thus denaturation actually liberates polypeptide chains from crystalline proteins and permits their conversion into visible fibers which, on stretching, are found to be structurally analogous to stretched wool and unstretched silk.

However, the chief interest lies in the single-crystal analyses, which are summarized to date in Table 23-5.   When the protein crystals are wet, spacings down to 2.4 A may be measured, but only larger spacings are found for dried preparations (13 A in dried hemoglobin).   It is clear that the crystallized proteins contain considerable quantities of water of crystallization, and when they lose water, they shrink with alterations in patterns.   Perutz in his outstanding work with hemoglobin found a cell weight of 133,400 for horse hemoglobin, of which 52 per cent is water, leaving 63,300 for the protein.   Each of the two molecules contains four Fe atoms and in a flattened cylinder of diameter 57 A and height 34 A. The molecules form layers with water like graphitic acid.   In more recent papers[3] Bragg and Perutz have deduced the external form of the hemoglobin molecule by observation of the effects of substituting salt solution for water,[4] with the following results:

---

[1] *Nature* **133,** 794 (1934), **135,** 591 (1935), **141,** 521 (1938), **144,** 1011 (1939); *Proc. Roy. Soc. (London),* **A164,** 580 (1938), **B127,** 36 (1939).

[2] *Radiology,* **28,** 144 (1937).

[3] W. L. Bragg and M. A. Perutz, *Acta Cryst.,* **5,** 136, 277, 323 (1952).

[4] Some modifications in data are suggested by H. E. Huxley and J. C. Kendrew, *Acta Cryst.,* **6,** 76 (1953), who brought hemoglobin into equilibrium with water vapor pressures over $CaCl_2$ solutions.

Angstroms

Met-, oxy-, and carboxyhemoglobin of horse, I . . . . 50 × 50 × 75
Reduced hemoglobin of man . . . . 50 × 50 × 75
Reduced hemoglobin of horse . . . . 56 × 56 × 72
Met-, oxy-, and carboxyhemoglobin of man, III . . . . 54 × 54 × 69

If the protein molecules are in hexagonal packing with an interchain distance of 10.5 A, then Fourier projections are interpreted to show that in the hemoglobin molecule the chains seen in end-on projection are arranged in layers.   There are three inner layers containing 4-5-4 chains, respectively, and the outer layers contain only 2 or 3 chains.

The values of $F(0kl)$ for hexagonal array are only one-third of what would be expected if the chains were straight and parallel throughout the molecule.   This molecule consists of two halves joined along a plane which cuts across the chain direction.   This implies that the chains cannot continue in a straight line for more than 31 A without being forced to turn a corner.   This lack of alignment of the two halves, nonuniformity in side-chain distribution, and wandering of the chains from strict parallelism could account for the low $F(0kl)$ values.

The color constituent of hemoglobin, hemin, chlorohemin, potassium oxyhemin, and other derivatives are all identical from all sources.   Patterns are illustrated in Figs 414a and 414b.

Nucleic Acids and the Chromosomes.   Two kinds of structure pertaining to the very source of life are the chromosomes and the viruses, both of which have the power of reproducing themselves and an organization based on association of proteins and nucleic acids.   These are made up of nucleotides, which are double rings, one of purine or pyrimidine base and the other a sugar with phosphoric acid attached.   Actually the long unbranched chains are built up of four different nucleotides, each nucleotide being the phosphoric ester of a nucleoside, and each nucleoside the desoxypentose derivative of an aminopurine (adinene and guanine) or aminopyromidine (cytosine and thymine).   In the chromosomes is thymonucleic acid, located in the dark bands and rising and falling corresponding to the cycle of cell division.   The description of the structural features is given partly in the words of the experimenter himself, Prof. W. T. Astbury:[1]

Sodium thymonucleate is a fibrous material with an x-ray pattern showing a repeating spacing of 3.34 A along the fiber axis.   The properties indicate long rodlike particles of molecular weight up to a million.   Hence they are columns of flat nucleotides 3.34 A apart, or a pile of 2,000 plates.   The unusually high density is consistent with this interpretation of close packing of the nucleotides.   The spacing 3.34 A is the same as that between successive side chains in a fully extended polypeptide.   The logical conclusion is a matching of intramolecular patterns which nature has adapted to the processes of chromosome division.   During mitosis and meiosis the chromosomes pass

[1] *Science Prog.*, **133** (1939); *Symposia Soc. Exptl. Biol.*, No. 1, p. 66 (1947).

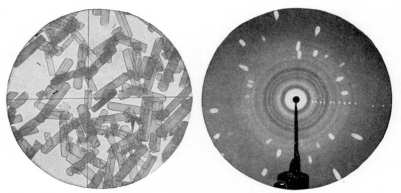

Fig. 414a. Photomicrograph and x-ray pattern for crystalline oxyhemoglobin from rat blood.

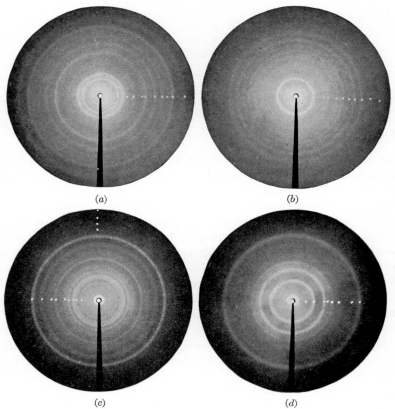

(a)   (b)

(c)   (d)

Fig. 414b. Patterns for color constituent of hemoglobin.   (a) Formic acid extracted hemin; (b) acetic acid extracted hemin; (c) chlorohemin; (d) potassium oxyhemin.

through a cycle of length changes, and the moment of full extension must be decided by this critical period between the nucleotides. To test these possibilities further Astbury has combined clupein, a simple polypeptide from sperm, with thymonucleic acid through the reaction of basic arginine sidechains with the phosphoric acid groups down the side of the acid column. This fibrous material (Fig. 415) resembles very closely the protein–nucleic acid compounds in the chromosomes, which seems strong evidence that the polypeptide chains must run along the length of the chromosomes. Since the genes form a linear sequence along the length of the chromosomes, here is an experimental beginning to contribute to the science of genetics. The proteins are the

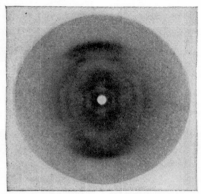

FIG. 415. The pattern of clupein thymonucleate. (*Astbury.*)

most important molecules in life: it may be that the patterns of life are only the patterns along polypeptide chains. The nucleotide is also directly indicated as the subunit within the giant molecules of viruses. This then is the building stone of the simplest "living" thing.

The structural changes which occur in sodium thymonucleate (or the sodium salt of desoxyribose nucleic acid) fibers when water content is varied show that the phosphate groups are exposed and accessible to water. The hydrogen-bond-forming $=CO$ and $—NH_2$ groups, which lie at the opposite end of the nucleotides from the phosphate groups, are inaccessible to water. The hydrogen bonds link neighboring chains through these groups to form stable aggregates or molecules which survive as a micelle in aqueous solution. This explains the ready availability of phosphate groups for interaction with proteins, which take the plane of water in the nucleoproteins. By means of the sharp fiber diagrams it has been possible to calculate the cylindrically symmetrical Patterson function and from this the unit cell of sodium thymonucleate as C-face-centered monoclinic, space group $C2$, $a = 22.0$, $b = 39.8$, $c = 21.8$ A, $\beta = 96.5$ deg. The number of nucleotides per unit cell is on the order of 50.†

† R. E. Franklin and R. G. Gosling, *Acta Cryst.*, **6**, 673, 678 (1953).

APPENDIX

Number	Schoenfliess	1935 International Tables	1952 International Tables
Triclinic			
1	C_1^1	$P1$	$P1$
2	C_i^1	$P\bar{1}$	$P\bar{1}$
Monoclinic			
3	C_2^1	$P2$	$P2$
4	C_2^2	$P2_1$	$P2_1$
5	C_2^3	$C2$	$B2$
6	C_s^1	Pm	Pm
7	C_s^2	Pc	Pb
8	C_s^3	Cm	Bm
9	C_s^4	Cc	Bb
10	C_{2h}^1	$P2/m$	$P2/m$
11	C_{2h}^2	$P2_1/m$	$P2_1/m$
12	C_{2h}^3	$C2/m$	$B2/m$
13	C_{2h}^4	$P2/c$	$P2/b$
14	C_{2h}^5	$P2_1/c$	$P2_1/b$
15	C_{2h}^6	$C2/c$	$B2/b$
Orthorhombic			
16	D_2^1	$P222$	$P222$
17	D_2^2	$P222_1$	$P222_1$
18	D_2^3	$P2_12_12$	$P2_12_12$
19	D_2^4	$P2_12_12$	$P2_12_12_1$
20	D_2^5	$C222_1$	$C222_1$
21	D_2^6	$C222$	$C222$
22	D_2^7	$F222$	$F222$
23	D_2^8	$I222$	$I222$
24	D_2^9	$I2_12_12_1$	$I2_12_12_1$
25	C_{2v}^1	Pmm	$Pmm2$
26	C_{2v}^2	Pmc	$Pmc2_1$
27	C_{2v}^3	Pcc	$Pcc2$
28	C_{2v}^4	Pma	$Pma2$
29	C_{2v}^5	Pca	$Pca2_1$
30	C_{2v}^6	Pnc	$Pnc2$

Number	Schoenfliess	1935 International Tables	1952 International Tables
31	C_{2v}^{7}	Pmn	$Pmn2_1$
32	C_{2v}^{8}	Pba	$Pba2$
33	C_{2v}^{9}	Pna	$Pna2_1$
34	C_{2v}^{10}	Pnn	$Pnn2$
35	C_{2v}^{11}	Cmm	$Cmm2$
36	C_{2v}^{12}	Cmc	$Cmc2_1$
37	C_{2v}^{13}	Ccc	$Ccc2$
38	C_{2v}^{14}	Amm	$Amm2$
39	C_{2v}^{15}	Abm	$Abm2$
40	C_{2v}^{16}	Ama	$Ama2$
41	C_{2v}^{17}	Aba	$Aba2$
42	C_{2v}^{18}	Fmm	$Fmm2$
43	C_{2v}^{19}	Fdd	$Fdd2$
44	C_{2v}^{20}	Imm	$Imm2$
45	C_{2v}^{21}	Iba	$Iba2$
46	C_{2v}^{22}	Ima	$Ima2$
47	D_{2h}^{1}	$Pmmm$	$Pmmm$
48	D_{2h}^{2}	$Pnnn$	$Pnnn$
49	D_{2h}^{3}	$Pccm$	$Pccm$
50	D_{2h}^{4}	$Pban$	$Pban$
51	D_{2h}^{5}	$Pmma$	$Pmma$
52	D_{2h}^{6}	$Pnna$	$Pnna$
53	D_{2h}^{7}	$Pmna$	$Pmna$
54	D_{2h}^{8}	$Pcca$	$Pcca$
55	D_{2h}^{9}	$Pbam$	$Pbam$
56	D_{2h}^{10}	$Pccn$	$Pccn$
57	D_{2h}^{11}	$Pbcm$	$Pbcm$
58	D_{2h}^{12}	$Pnnm$	$Pnnm$
59	D_{2h}^{13}	$Pmmn$	$Pmmn$
60	D_{2h}^{14}	$Pbcn$	$Pbcn$
61	D_{2h}^{15}	$Pbca$	$Pbca$
62	D_{2h}^{16}	$Pnma$	$Pnma$
63	D_{2h}^{17}	$Cmcm$	$Cmcm$
64	D_{2h}^{18}	$Cmca$	$Cmca$
65	D_{2h}^{19}	$Cmmm$	$Cmmm$
66	D_{2h}^{20}	$Cccm$	$Cccm$
67	D_{2h}^{21}	$Cmma$	$Cmma$
68	D_{2h}^{22}	$Ccca$	$Ccca$
69	D_{2h}^{23}	$Fmmm$	$Fmmm$
70	D_{2h}^{24}	$Fddd$	$Fddd$
71	D_{2h}^{25}	$Immm$	$Immm$
72	D_{2h}^{26}	$Ibam$	$Ibam$
73	D_{2h}^{27}	$Ibca$	$Ibca$
74	D_{2h}^{28}	$Imma$	$Imma$
Tetragonal			
75	C_{4}^{1}	$P4$	$P4$

SPACE-GROUP SYMBOLS (*Continued*)

Number	Schoenfliess	1935 International Tables	1952 International Tables
76	C_4^2	$P4_1$	$P4_1$
77	C_4^3	$P4_2$	$P4_2$
78	C_4^4	$P4_3$	$P4_3$
79	C_4^5	$I4$	$I4$
80	C_4^6	$I4_1$	$I4_1$
81	S_4^1	$P\bar{4}$	$P\bar{4}$
82	S_4^2	$I\bar{4}$	$I\bar{4}$
83	C_{4h}^1	$P4/m$	$P4/m$
84	C_{4h}^2	$P4_2/m$	$P4_2/m$
85	C_{4h}^3	$P4/n$	$P4/n$
86	C_{4h}^4	$P4_2/n$	$P4_2/n$
87	C_{4h}^5	$I4/m$	$I4/m$
88	C_{4h}^6	$I4_1/a$	$I4_1/a$
89	D_4^1	$P42$	$P422$
90	D_4^2	$P42_1$	$P42_12$
91	D_4^3	$P4_12$	$P4_122$
92	D_4^4	$P4_12_1$	$P4_12_12$
93	D_4^5	$P4_22$	$P4_222$
94	D_4^6	$P4_22_1$	$P4_22_12$
95	D_4^7	$P4_32$	$P4_322$
96	D_4^8	$P3_32_1$	$P4_32_12$
97	D_4^9	$I42$	$I422$
98	D_4^{10}	$I4_12$	$I4_122$
99	C_{4v}^1	$P4mm$	$P4mm$
100	C_{4v}^2	$P4bm$	$P4bm$
101	C_{4v}^3	$P4cm$	$P4_2cm$
102	C_{4v}^4	$P4nm$	$P4_2nm$
103	C_{4v}^5	$P4cc$	$P4cc$
104	C_{4v}^6	$P4nc$	$P4nc$
105	C_{4v}^7	$P4mc$	$P4_2mc$
106	C_{4v}^8	$P4bc$	$P4_2bc$
107	C_{4v}^9	$I4mm$	$I4mm$
108	C_{4v}^{10}	$I4cm$	$I4cm$
109	C_{4v}^{11}	$I4md$	$I4_1md$
110	C_{4v}^{12}	$I4cd$	$I4_1cd$
111	D_{2d}^1	$P\bar{4}2m$	$P\bar{4}2m$
112	D_{2d}^2	$P\bar{4}2c$	$P\bar{4}2c$
113	D_{2d}^3	$P\bar{4}2_1m$	$P\bar{4}2_1m$
114	D_{2d}^4	$P\bar{4}2_1c$	$P\bar{4}2_1c$
115	D_{2d}^5	$C\bar{4}2m$	$P\bar{4}m2$
116	D_{2d}^6	$C\bar{4}2c$	$P\bar{4}c2$
117	D_{2d}^7	$C\bar{4}2b$	$P\bar{4}b2$
118	D_{2d}^8	$C\bar{4}2n$	$P\bar{4}n2$
119	D_{2d}^9	$F\bar{4}2m$	$I\bar{4}m2$
120	D_{2d}^{10}	$F\bar{4}2c$	$I\bar{4}c2$
121	D_{2d}^{11}	$I\bar{4}2m$	$I\bar{4}2m$
122	D_{2d}^{12}	$I\bar{4}2d$	$I\bar{4}2d$

SPACE-GROUP SYMBOLS (*Continued*)

Number	Schoenfliess	1935 International Tables	1952 International Tables
123	D_{4h}^1	$P4/mmm$	$P4/mmm$
124	D_{4h}^2	$P//mcc$	$P4/mcc$
125	D_{4h}^3	$P4/nbm$	$P4/nbm$
126	D_{4h}^4	$P4/nnc$	$P4/ncc$
127	D_{4h}^5	$P4/mbm$	$P4/mbm$
128	D_{4h}^6	$P4/mnc$	$P4/mnc$
129	D_{4h}^7	$P4/nmm$	$P4/nmm$
130	D_{4h}^8	$P4/ncc$	$P4/ncc$
131	D_{4h}^9	$P4/mmc$	$P4_2/mmc$
132	D_{4h}^{10}	$P4/mcm$	$P4_2/mcm$
133	D_{4h}^{11}	$P4/nbc$	$P4_2/nbc$
134	D_{4h}^{12}	$P4/nnm$	$P4_2/nnm$
135	D_{4h}^{13}	$P4/mbc$	$P4_2/mbc$
136	D_{4h}^{14}	$P4/mnm$	$P4_2/mnm$
137	D_{4h}^{15}	$P4/nmc$	$P4_2/nmc$
138	D_{4h}^{16}	$P4/ncm$	$P4_2/ncm$
139	D_{4h}^{17}	$I4/mmm$	$I4/mmm$
140	D_{4h}^{18}	$I4/mcm$	$I4/mcm$
141	D_{4h}^{19}	$I4/amd$	$I4_1/amd$
142	D_{4h}^{20}	$I4/acd$	$I4_1/acd$

Rhombohedral (*trigonal*)

Number	Schoenfliess	1935 International Tables	1952 International Tables
143	C_3^1	$C3$	$P3$
144	C_3^2	$C3_1$	$P3_1$
145	C_3^3	$C3_2$	$P3_2$
146	C_3^4	$R3$	$R3$
147	C_{3i}^1	$C\bar{3}$	$P\bar{3}$
148	C_{3i}^2	$R\bar{3}$	$R\bar{3}$
149	D_3^1	$H32$	$P312$
150	D_3^2	$C32$	$P321$
151	D_3^3	$H3_12$	$P3_112$
152	D_3^4	$C3_12$	$P3_121$
153	D_3^5	$H3_22$	$P3_212$
154	D_3^6	$C3_22$	$P3_221$
155	D_3^7	$R32$	$R32$
156	C_{3v}^1	$C3m$	$P3m1$
157	C_{3v}^2	$H3m$	$P31m$
158	C_{3v}^3	$C3c$	$P3c1$
159	C_{3v}^4	$H3c$	$P31c$
160	C_{3v}^5	$R3m$	$R3m$
161	C_{3v}^6	$R3c$	$R3c$
162	D_{3d}	$H\bar{3}m$	$P\bar{3}1m$
163	D_{3d}^2	$H\bar{3}c$	$P\bar{3}1c$
164	D_{3d}^3	$C\bar{3}m$	$P\bar{3}m1$
165	D_{3d}^4	$C\bar{3}c$	$P\bar{3}c1$
166	D_{3d}^5	$R\bar{3}m$	$R\bar{3}m$
167	D_{3d}^6	$R\bar{3}c$	$R\bar{3}c$

SPACE-GROUP SYMBOLS (*Continued*)

Number	Schoenfliess	1935 International Tables	1952 International Tables
Hexagonal			
168	C_6^1	$C6$	$P6$
169	C_6^2	$C6_1$	$P6_1$
170	C_6^3	$C6_5$	$P6_5$
171	C_6^4	$C6_2$	$P6_2$
172	C_6^5	$C6_4$	$P6_4$
173	C_6^6	$C6_3$	$P6_3$
174	C_{3h}^1	$C\bar{6}$	$P\bar{6}$
175	C_{6h}^1	$C6/m$	$P6/m$
176	C_{6h}^2	$C6_3/m$	$P6_3/m$
177	D_6^1	$C62$	$P622$
178	D_6^2	$C6_12$	$P6_122$
179	D_6^3	$C6_52$	$P6_522$
180	D_6^4	$C6_22$	$P6_222$
181	D_6^5	$C6_42$	$P6_422$
182	D_6^6	$C6_32$	$P6_322$
183	C_{6v}^1	$C6mm$	$P6mm$
184	C_{6v}^2	$C6cc$	$P6cc$
185	C_{6v}^3	$C6cm$	$P6_3cm$
186	C_{6v}^4	$C6mc$	$P6_3mc$
187	D_{3h}^1	$C\bar{6}m2$	$P\bar{6}m2$
188	D_{3h}^2	$C\bar{6}c2$	$P\bar{6}c2$
189	D_{3h}^3	$H\bar{6}m2$	$P\bar{6}2m$
190	D_{3h}^4	$H\bar{6}c2$	$P\bar{6}2c$
191	D_{6h}^1	$C6/mmm$	$P6/mmm$
192	D_{6h}^2	$C6/mcc$	$P6/mcc$
193	D_{6h}^3	$C6/mcm$	$P6_3mcm$
194	D_{6h}^4	$C6/mmc$	$P6_3/mmc$
Cubic			
195	T^1	$P23$	$P23$
196	T^2	$F23$	$F23$
197	T^3	$I23$	$I23$
198	T^4	$P2_13$	$P2_13$
199	T^5	$I2_13$	$I2_13$
200	T_h^1	$Pm3$	$Pm3$
201	T_h^2	$Pn3$	$Pn3$
202	T_h^3	$Fm3$	$Fm3$
203	T_h^4	$Fd3$	$Fd3$
204	T_h^5	$Im3$	$Im3$
205	T_h^6	$Pa3$	$Pa3$
206	T_h^7	$Ia3$	$Ia3$
207	O^1	$P43$	$P432$
208	O^2	$P4_23$	$P4_232$
209	O^3	$F43$	$F432$
210	O^4	$F4_13$	$F4_132$
211	O^5	$I43$	$I432$

Space-group Symbols (*Continued*)

Number	Schoenfliess	1935 International Tables	1952 International Tables
212	O^6	$P4_33$	$P4_332$
213	O^7	$P4_13$	$P4_132$
214	O^8	$I4_13$	$I4_132$
215	T_d^1	$P\overline{4}3m$	$P\overline{4}3m$
216	T_d^2	$F\overline{4}3m$	$F\overline{4}3m$
217	T_d^3	$I\overline{4}3m$	$I\overline{4}3m$
218	T_d^4	$P\overline{4}3n$	$P\overline{4}3n$
219	T_d^5	$F\overline{4}3c$	$F\overline{4}3c$
220	T_d^6	$I\overline{4}3d$	$I\overline{4}3d$
221	O_h^1	$Pm3m$	$Pm3m$
222	O_h^2	$Pn3n$	$Pn3n$
223	O_h^3	$Pm3n$	$Pm3n$
224	O_h^4	$Pn3m$	$Pn3m$
225	O_h^5	$Fm3m$	$Fm3m$
226	O_h^6	$Fm3c$	$Fm3c$
227	O_h^7	$Fd3m$	$Fd3m$
228	O_h^8	$Fd3c$	$Fd3c$
229	O_h^9	$Im3m$	$Im3m$
230	O_h^{10}	$Ia3d$	$Ia3d$

INDEX